November 14–18, 2011
Alicante, Spain

Association for
Computing Machinery

Advancing Computing as a Science & Profession

ICMI'11

Proceedings of the 2011 ACM International Conference on
Multimodal Interaction

Sponsored by:

ACM SIGCHI

Supported by:

MIPRCV, Universidad Politecnica de Valencia, Universitat d' Alacant, Pascal2, LSI, IUII, AERFAI, Telefonica, AT&T, DSICC, Microsoft Research, ETSIFN, Gobierno de Espana, Siren Project, NSF

Association for
Computing Machinery

Advancing Computing as a Science & Profession

The Association for Computing Machinery
2 Penn Plaza, Suite 701
New York, New York 10121-0701

ISBN: 978-1-4503-0641-6 (Digital)

ISBN: 978-1-4503-0640-9 (Print)

Additional copies may be ordered prepaid from:

ACM Order Department
PO Box 30777
New York, NY 10087-0777, USA

Phone: 1-800-342-6626 (USA and Canada)
+1-212-626-0500 (Global)
Fax: +1-212-944-1318
E-mail: acmhelp@acm.org
Hours of Operation: 8:30 am – 4:30 pm ET

Printed in the USA

ICMI 2011 Chairs' Welcome

Welcome to Alicante and to the International Conference on Multimodal Interaction, ICMI 2011. ICMI is the premier international forum for multidisciplinary research on multimodal human-human and human-computer interaction, interfaces, and system development. It is the fusion of the International Conference on Multimodal Interfaces and the Workshop on Machine Learning for Multimodal Interaction which, for the last two years, held a combined event under the name ICMI-MLMI. Starting in this thirteenth edition the combined conference uses the new, shorter name.

This year we had the largest number of submissions ever achieved in ICMI/MLMI: 127 papers, 4 Special Session proposals, 10 Demonstration papers and 6 Workshop proposals. From the 4 Special Session proposals 2 were selected, including 7 papers. Out of the 120 regular papers submitted, 47 were accepted for oral or poster presentation, bringing the conference acceptance rate to 39%. This rate was higher for the Demonstration papers, from which 7 were accepted. In addition, the program includes three invited Keynote talks. Finally, from the 6 post-conference workshop proposals, 4 were selected, centered on hot specific topics of multi-modal interaction.

The review process was organized using the PCS submission and review system, which ICMI has used in the past. Aiming at improving the quality of the finally accepted papers, for the first time, this year the review process included a rebuttal step. The process was assisted by 15 Area Chairs (ACs) who helped the Program Chairs in defining the Program Committee. The papers were allocated to ACs in areas of their expertise according to the indications of the submitters, and then checked for conflicts. The Program Chairs distributed the papers to members of program committee and volunteer reviewers for comments. Once reviews were submitted, the ACs provided meta-reviews for all papers which were sent to the authors for rebuttal consideration. After hearing the authors' arguments, the scores of the papers were then collected and tabulated. All reviews and papers were then again checked by the Program Chairs, and papers with highly varying scores received an additional round of reviews. All papers and their reviews were finally discussed by the Program Chairs on a two-day remote meeting in order to decide on the list of accepted submissions.

The program was formed by grouping papers into main topics of interest for this year's conference. Following the trend in previous ICMI-MLMI events and many other academic meetings, to minimize paper consumption we decided to distribute the conference proceedings on USB Flash Drives. This year we have selected 5 top scoring papers as candidates for two awards: Outstanding Student Paper, and Outstanding Paper. An anonymous committee has been appointed by Program Chairs to select the two awarded papers. You will find the nominated papers in the conference program marked with special symbol. The final award decisions will be announced at the conference banquet.

As in previous events, ICMI-2011 has been organized with the support of ACM and SIGCHI. In addition, despite the financial crisis, many sponsors have given support to the event. A significant amount of funds has been provided by the Spanish "Ministerio de Ciencia e Innovación" (MICINN) and by several academic organizations of the Valencia Community: "Universitat Politècnica de València" (UPV), "Universidad de Alicante" (UA), the "Departamento de Sistemas Informáticos y Computación" (DSIC-UPV), the "Escola Tècnica Superior d'Enginyeria Informàtica" (ETSINF-UPV), the "Departamento de Lenguajes y Sistemas Informáticos" (LSI-UA) and the "Institut Universitari de Investigació Informatica" (IUII-UA). On the other hand, the US National Science Foundation (NSF) has generously provided us with travel and housing support for several students to help offset pressure on academic travel budgets. Two academic projects have also contributed to the conference organization: The Spanish "Multimodal Interaction in Pattern Recognition and Computer Vision" (MIPRCV) and the European "Social games for conflIct REsolution based on natural iNteraction" (SIREN). In addition, we thank the European network of excellence on "Pattern Analysis, Statistical Modeling, and Computational Learning" (PASCAL 2) for partially supporting travel expenses of keynote speakers and students and the "Asociación Española de Reconocimiento de Formas y Análisis de Imágenes" (AERFAI) for supporting ICMI-2011 registration expenses for its members. Even in these difficult times, important companies affirmed their support to the multimodal interaction and interface research community by providing ICMI with a reasonable level of financial support. These organizations deserve our warmest gratitude: Telefonica I+D, Microsoft Research and AT&T. Without the generous support of all these sponsors, this meeting would not have been possible.

The chairs would like to thank our colleagues on the conference organization committee for their tireless effort bringing this meeting together: Xavier Anguera, Jorge Calera, Fernando De-la-Torre, Li Deng, Antonio J. Gallego, Ida Hui, José M. Iñesta, Alejandro Jaimes, Helen Meng, Nuria Oliver, Jose Oncina, Kazuhiro Otsuka, Stefanie Tellex, Alejandro H. Toselli, Jordi Vitrià and, in particular, to the great work of our Local Organization Chair, Luisa Micó. We are also indebted to the Area Chairs: Tilman Becker, Trevor Darrell, Karrie Karahalios, Antonio Krueger, Anton Nijholt, Jean-Marc Odobez, Yiannis Patras, Catherine Pelachaud, Filiberto Pla, Alex Potamianos, Francis Quek, Adriana Tapus, Alessandro Vinciarelli, Jie Yang and Massimo Zancanaro. Finally our thanks are extended to all program committee members and volunteer reviewers who contributed their effort to the review process and made it easy to develop a high quality technical program.

Last, but not least, we would like to thank you: the authors and attendees. Thank you for your work and your time. We hope you find a meeting filled with new ideas, old colleagues and future collaborators!

Hervé Boulard
ICMI'11 General Chair
IDIAP, Switzerland

Thomas S. Huang
ICMI'11 General Chair
University of Illinois, USA

Enrique Vidal
MICMI'11 General Chair
Univ. Pol. de València, Spain

Daniel Gatica-Perez
ICMI'11 Program Chair
IDIAP, Switzerland

Louis-Philippe Morency
ICMI'11 Program Chair
Univ. Southern California, USA

Nicu Sebe
ICMI'11 Program Chair
University of Trento, Italy

Table of Contents

Oral Session 5: Virtual and Real Worlds

ICMI 2011 Organizing Committee

General Chairs: Hervé Bourlard *(Idiap Research Institute, Switzerland)*
Thomas S. Huang *(University of Illinois, USA)*
Enrique Vidal *(Universitat Politècnica València, Spain)*

Program Chairs: Daniel Gatica-Perez *(Idiap Research Institute, Switzerland)*
Louis-Philippe Morency *(Univ. Southern California, USA)*
Nicu Sebe *(University of Trento, Italy)*

Demo Chairs: Kazuhiro Otsuka *(NTT Communication Science Labs, Japan)*
Jordi Vitrià *(UB/CVC, Barcelona, Spain)*

Workshop Chairs: Fernando de la Torre *(Carnegie Mellon University, USA)*
Alejandro Jaimes *(Yahoo! Research, Barcelona, Spain)*

Publication Chair: Jose Oncina *(University of Alicante, Spain)*

Student & Doctoral Spotlight Chairs: Li Deng *(Microsoft Research and Univ. of Washington)*
Stefanie Tellex *(MIT CSAIL, USA)*

Sponsorship Chair: Nuria Oliver *(Telefónica I+D, Spain)*

Publicity Chair: Helen Mei-Ling Meng *(CUHK, Hong Kong)*

Local Organization Chair: Luisa Micó *(University of Alicante, Spain)*

Treasurer: Jorge Calera *(University of Alicante, Spain)*

Local Organizers: Xavier Anguera *(Telefónica I+D, Spain)*
Antonio Javier Gallego Sánchez *(University of Alicante, Spain)*
Ida Hui *(CUHK, Hong Kong)*
Jose Manuel Iñesta *(University of Alicante, Spain)*
Alejandro Toselli *(Universitat Politècnica València, Spain)*

Area Chairs: Tilman Becker *(DFKI)*
Trevor Darrell *(UC Berkeley / ICSI)*
Karrie Karahalios *(UIUC)*
Antonio Krueger *(DFKI / Saarland University)*
Anton Nijholt *(University of Twente)*
Jean-Marc Odobez *(Idiap Research Institute)*
Yiannis Patras *(Queen Mary University of London)*
Catherine Pelachaud *(CNRS / TELECOM ParisTech)*
Filiberto Pla *(University Jaume I)*
Alex Potamianos *(Technical University of Crete)*
Francis Quek *(Virginia Tech)*
Adriana Tapus *(ENSTA-ParisTech)*
Alessandro Vinciarelli *(University of Glasgow)*
Jie Yang *(CMU)*
Massimo Zancanaro *(FBK)*

Advisory Board: Samy Benjio *(Google)*
Hervé Bourlard *(IDIAP, Switzerland)*
Jean Carletta *(University of Edinburgh)*
James L. Crowley *(INRIA Grenoble Rhone Alpes, France)*
Trevor Darrell *(UCB/ICSI, USA)*
Sadaoki Furui *(Tokyo Institute of Technology, Japan)*
Yuri Ivanov *(MERL, USA)*
Kenji Mase *(University of Nagoya, Japan)*
Sharon Oviatt *(Incaa Designs, USA)*
Catherine Pelachaud *(CNRS, France)*
Fabio Pianesi *(FBK, Trento, Italy)*
Andrei Popescu Belis *(IDIAP, Switzerland)*
Alex Potamianos *(TUC,Greece)*
Steve Renals *(University of Edinburgh)*
Rainer Stiefelhagen *(KIT & Fraunhofer IITB, Germany)*
Matthew Turk *(UC Santa Barbara, USA)*
Wolfgang Wahlster *(DFKI, Germany)*
Jie Yang *(Carnegie Mellon Universiy, USA)*

ICMI 2011 Program Committee

Amir Aly
Lisa Anthony
Girouard Audrey
sileye ba
Joan-Isaac Biel
Lepri Bruno
Harry Bunt
Carlos Busso
prof nick campbell
Jorge Cardoso
Ginevra Castellano
Joyce Chai
Gokul Chittaranjan
Mario Christoudias
Henriette Cramer
Giuseppe Di Fabbrizio
Trinh Minh Tri do
Bruno Dumas
Patrick Ehlen
Ricci Elisa
Sibylle Enz
Bailly Gerard
Hatice Gunes
Joakim Gustafson
Hayrettin Gürkök
Norihiro Hagita
Nick Hawes
Hung Hayley
Dirk Heylen
Jeffrey Ho
Kotsia Irene
Dinesh Babu Jayagopi
Schoening Johannes
Michael Johnston
Kristiina Jokinen
Taemie Kim
Simon King
Sander Koelstra
Denis Lalanne
Luis Leiva
Katrin Lohan
Fabien Lotte
Saturnino Luz
Markus Löckelt
Mathew Magimai Doss
Poel Mannes
Cavazza Marc
Eskenazi Maxine
Chris Mccool
David McGookin
Peter W. McOwan
Helen Meng
Rohs Michael
Yukiko Nakano
Femke Nijboer
Yoshimasa Ohmoto
Daniel Olguin Olguin
Brdiczka Oliver
Nuria Oliver
Tim Paek
Hari Parthasarathi
Olivier Patrick
Fabio Pianesi
Andrei Popescu-Belis
Ronald Poppe
Benjamin Poppinga
Gerasimos Potamianos
Thierry Pun
Liu Qiong
Antoine Raux
Norbert Reithinger
Steve Renals
Laurel D. Riek
Amir Sadeghipour
Albert Ali Salah
Maha Salem
Dairazalia Sanchez Cortes
Yohichi Sato
Gianluca Schiavo
Bjoern Schuller
Candace Sidner
Paris Smaragdis
Erin Solovey
Dunne Stephen
Fairclough Stephen
Rainer Stiefelhagen
Yasuyuki Sumi
Dag Sverre Syrdal
Kazuya Takeda
Mariet Theune
Alejandro Héctor Toselli
Matthew Turk
Jan van Erp
Giovanna Varni
Radu-Daniel Vatavu
Gualtiero Volpe
Astrid von der Pütten
Michael Walters
Julie Rico Williamson
Hürst Wolfgang
Ming-Hsuan Yang
Chen Yu
Thorsten Zander
Liang-Guo Zhang

ICMI 2011 Sponsor & Supporters

Sponsor:

Supporters:

Still Looking at People

David A. Forsyth
University of Illinois,
Urbana, IL 61801
daf@illinois.edu

Abstract

There is a great need for programs that can describe what people are doing from video. Among other applications, such programs could be used to search for scenes in consumer video; in surveillance applications; to support the design of buildings and of public places; to screen humans for diseases; and to build enhanced human computer interfaces.

Building such programs is difficult, because it is hard to identify and track people in video sequences, because we have no canonical vocabulary for describing what people are doing, and because phenomena such as aspect and individual variation greatly affect the appearance of what people are doing. Recent work in kinematic tracking has produced methods that can report the kinematic configuration of the body automatically, and with moderate accuracy. There are good reasons to hope that recent advances in human body parsing could be adopted to improve accuracy. While it is possible to build methods that use kinematic tracks to reason about the 3D configuration of the body, and from this the activities, such methods remain relatively inaccurate. However, they have the attraction that one can build models that are generative, and that allow activities to be assembled from a set of distinct spatial and temporal components. The models themselves are learned from labelled motion capture data and are assembled in a way that makes it possible to learn very complex finite automata without estimating large numbers of parameters. The advantage of such a model is that one can search videos for examples of activities specified with a simple query language, without possessing any example of the activity sought. In this case, aspect is dealt with by explicit 3D reasoning.

An alternative approach is to model the whole problem as k-way classification into a set of known classes. This approach is much more accurate at present, but has the difficulty that we don't really know what the classes should be in general. This is because we do not know how to describe activities. Recent work in object recognition on describing unfamiliar objects suggests that activities might be described in terms of attributes --- properties that many activities share, that are easy to spot, and that are individually somewhat discriminative. Such a description would allow a useful response to an unfamiliar activity. I will sketch current progress on this agenda.

Categories & Subject Descriptors: I.4 Image Processing and Computer Vision

General Terms: Algorithms

Bio

David Forsyth spent three years on the faculty at the University of Iowa, ten years on the faculty at the University of California at Berkeley, and then moved to the University of Illinois. In 2006, he received an IEEE technical achievement award, and in 2009 he was named an IEEE Fellow.

ICMI'11, November 14–18, 2011, Alicante, Spain.
ACM 978-1-4503-0641-6/11/11.

Mining Multimodal Sequential Patterns: A Case Study on Affect Detection

Héctor P. Martínez
Center for Computer Games Research
IT University of Copenhagen
Rued Langgaards vej 7
2300, Denmark
hpma@itu.dk

Georgios N. Yannakakis
Center for Computer Games Research
IT University of Copenhagen
Rued Langgaards vej 7
2300, Denmark
yannakakis@itu.dk

ABSTRACT

Temporal data from multimodal interaction such as speech and bio-signals cannot be easily analysed without a preprocessing phase through which some key characteristics of the signals are extracted. Typically, standard statistical signal features such as average values are calculated prior to the analysis and, subsequently, are presented either to a multimodal fusion mechanism or a computational model of the interaction. This paper proposes a feature extraction methodology which is based on frequent sequence mining within and across multiple modalities of user input. The proposed method is applied for the fusion of physiological signals and gameplay information in a game survey dataset. The obtained sequences are analysed and used as predictors of user affect resulting in computational models of equal or higher accuracy compared to the models built on standard statistical features.

Categories and Subject Descriptors

H.1.2 [**Information Systems**]: User/Machine Systems—*Human factors*; I.2.1 [**Artificial Intelligence**]: Applications and Expert Systems—*Games*

General Terms

Algorithms, Experimentation, Human Factors

Keywords

sequence pattern mining, sequence classification, preference learning, heart rate variability, skin conductance, game events

1. INTRODUCTION

Most of the modalities available for the analysis and modeling of interaction with computers such as speech, gestures, physiology and key presses (among others) are temporal by nature. However, multimodal signal fusion and modeling methods require the transformation of those streams of data into a fixed-sized vector of scalar features that describe different characteristics of the signals; such features are given in a format suitable for empirical analysis and computational modeling. This process, namely *feature extraction*, generally involves a domain expert who chooses a set of statistical features (e.g. average values) based on the available data in an attempt to capture all the relevant qualitative characteristics of the signals.

This paper applies *frequent sequence mining* [1] techniques to automatically extract *sequential features* which capture a range of signal characteristics and potentially reveal important interaction factors hindered by traditional feature extraction. Sequential features can be used to analyse the temporal trends within and across modalities but also provide appropriate input vectors for classification or prediction models which are built in multimodal input spaces. Frequent sequence mining has been applied before to *sequence classification* in different tasks including protein classification and plan monitoring [4, 8]; however, this is the first time — to the best of the authors' knowledge — that has been applied to mine data streams across multiple user input modalities. With this approach, the different sources of information are combined before building a model (data-level fusion [14]) achieving deeper fusion than feature-level or decision-level fusion that facilitates a low level interpretation of the interrelation between modalities and its effect on the target user output. Even though there exist machine learning approaches that stream input data (e.g. Recurrent Neural Networks, Hidden Markov Models and Dynamic Bayesian Networks), the extraction of sequential features makes time-related information available for and generic across any other non-temporal based technique. Furthermore, the analysis of dynamic models is often far from trivial due to recurrent connections or complex state transitions.

We evaluate the proposed method in a game survey dataset that includes gameplay logs and physiological recordings of players. The Generalized Sequential Patterns (GSP) [18] sequence mining algorithm is utilized to find sequential patterns among the gameplay metrics and two physiological signals — skin conductance (SC) and blood volume pulse (BVP) — from the players. The sequences are analysed and compared to a set of statistical features as inputs to Artificial Neural Network (ANN) models trained to predict players' affective states reported as pairwise preferences. The results of this initial study show that sequential features yield models of affect that are equally or significantly more accurate

ICMI'11, November 14–18, 2011, Alicante, Spain.

than the models built on simple statistical features for all affective states examined.

2. RELATED WORK

This work applies sequence mining to fuse physiological signals and gameplay information to generate an input vector for the prediction of player emotional preferences. This section reviews earlier work on physiology and game-context fusion and studies in which sequential patterns have been used for prediction and classification tasks.

2.1 Fusion of Physiological Signals and Game Context Information

In the interaction between a user and a system, the user's inputs — both low level (e.g. moving the mouse) and high level (e.g. dragging an icon) — and their consequences on the system (e.g. cursor and icon moved) determine a key component of user experience. Fusing such information with other modalities can yield user experience models that are not only more accurate but also more informative since context is added to the model [20].

Within game-player interaction studies, McQuiggan et al. [13] created predictors of self-efficacy reports that rely on statistical features extracted from several heart rate and skin conductance signal intervals in conjunction with players' self-reports and information about the visited positions of the avatar and the cursor in a 3D learning environment. In that study, the sequential information from the bio-signals is transformed into a vector of features representing the average of the signals over different intervals. The gameplay data, in turn, is reduced to a set of spatio-temporal features such as the time spent on a task or a list of locations visited. On the same basis, Martinez et al. [12, 20] trained predictors of self-reported preferences in a 3D prey/predator game on statistical features derived from heart rate, skin conductance, blood volume pulse and different game events. In that study, the physiological statistical features (e.g. average, standard deviation and first and second absolute differences) are extracted from the full length of the game experience (i.e. 90 seconds) while the gameplay features consist of statistical information such as distance to enemies or pellets and performance measures such as the final score and the fraction of the map explored.

While there exist several studies in player experience research that use game context information and bio-signal information for the analysis and modeling of experience (e.g. [9, 10, 3] among others) none has fused the time-series data of these modalities by considering sequential patterns across modalities.

2.2 Sequence Classification using Frequent Patterns

Frequent sequential patterns are typically mined to detect interesting common trends in the data and discover association rules, correlations and other relationships [7] but they can be applied also to the classification and clustering of sequences.

Protein homology detection and classification is one of the most popular sequence mining tasks. In [2], a set of relevant subsequences (motifs) are predefined and each protein is represented as a vector of attributes; each attribute represents the number of occurrences of a motif in the represented protein (generally, each motif will either occur once or not occur).

In [4] a Naïve Bayes Classifier identifies the most probable family to which a protein belongs to using as inputs the number and average length of the frequent subsequences shared within each of the protein families.

One of the many differences between the task of classifying proteins and processing multimodal signals is the temporal nature of the signals: in a protein string every pair of consecutive elements has a distance of 1 unit while in a signal the time distance between two elements is derived by the sampling rate. This difference has an impact on the structure of sequences (e.g. in multiple time-series sequences two events might occur simultaneously), the matching conditions of sequential patterns and the procedure to match sequential patterns (e.g. in non-temporal sequences the number of gaps between elements can be constrained whereas in a temporal sequence the time between elements is constrained instead).

Lesh et al. [8] define an effective method to mine features for sequence classification. This method consists of mining all sequential frequent patterns and prune those that are either not distinctive of one of the target classes or correlated with a pattern already selected. This pruning stage is necessary since frequent mining can produce an enormous amount of features that cannot be efficiently handled by a classifier. In this paper, a similar approach to [8] is used but the set of frequent sequential patterns is reduced by automatic feature selection which searches for the combinations of sequences that are more relevant for predicting a target output (i.e. affective state in the case study presented).

3. FREQUENT SEQUENCE MINING

In this study we focus on the extraction of sequences that combine events across different user input modalities collected during the interaction with a system. We expect these sequences to be critical for the analysis of the interaction in terms of the interplay among different modalities of user input. We also anticipate that frequent sequences across multimodal signals can improve the detection accuracy of user affect over other approaches that involve the reduction of the signals through standard feature extraction. In this section we formalize the problem of mining frequent sequences and describe the algorithm applied to the case study.

Given a dataset in which each sample is a sequence of events, namely *data-sequence*, a sequential pattern defined as a subsequence of events is a *frequent sequence* if it occurs in the samples of the dataset regularly. In general, the events that form the sequences correspond to relevant changes on the observed signal or system and are associated with a time stamp (discrete moment on time when the event occurs) and an identification (type of event). An event could be for example an increase on heart rate, a key pressed or an action unit activation in a facial expression task [15].

More formally, a sequential pattern is an ordered list of *elements* — denoted as $\langle e_0 e_1 \ldots e_n \rangle$; e_i is the ith element of the sequence — each containing a non-empty (unordered) set of m simultaneous *events* — denoted as $(x_0, x_1, \ldots, x_m)$; x_i is an event. For example, an element could be two keys pressed simultaneously, several action units executed at the same time or an increase on heart rate (an element with only one event). A frequent sequence can be defined as a sequential pattern that is *supported* by, at least, a minimum

Algorithm 1 Generalized Sequential Patterns.

Input: a dataset of data-sequences, S_{min}, G_{max} and W_{max}
Output: the set of sequence patterns that are supported by more than S_{min} data-sequences.

procedure GSP(data, S_{min}, G_{max}, W_{max})
Count the number of data-sequences in which each different event is contained (support count).
Insert the events with a support count greater than S_{min} into the set of frequent 1-sequences (L_1).
k = 1
while L_k is not empty
  Generate the set of candidate $(k+1)$-sequences (C_{k+1}). See Algorithm 2 for more details.
  Determine the support count of the sequences contained in C_{k+1}.
  Create the set of frequent $(k+1)$-sequences (L_{k+1}) with the sequences in C_{k+1} that present a support count greater than S_{min}.
  k = k +1
return $L_1 \cup L_2 \cup \cdots \cup L_{k-1}$

Algorithm 2 Candidate generation in GSP.

Input: a set of $(k-1)$-sequences L_{k-1}.
Output: the set of candidate k-sequences C_k.

procedure generateCandidates(L_{k-1})
for each pair of sequences $s_x, s_y \in L_{k-1}$ with $s_x = \langle e_1^x e_2^x \dots e_n^x \rangle$ and $s_y = \langle e_1^y e_2^y \dots e_n^y \rangle$
  if the two sequences obtained by dropping the first event of s_x and the last event of s_y are identical
    if e_n^y has only one event $e_n^y = (y_1)$
      Generate the candidate sequence s_{xy} by inserting y_1 as last event of e_n^x: $s_{xy} = \langle e_1^x e_2^x \dots e_{n-1}^x (e_n^x, y_1) \rangle$
    else
      Generate the candidate sequence s_{xy} by replacing e_n^x with e_n^y: $s_{xy} = \langle e_1^x e_2^x \dots e_{n-1}^x e_n^y \rangle$.
    if all contiguous subsequences of s_{xy} are contained in L_{k-1}
      Insert s_{xy} into C_k.
return C_k

amount of data-sequences as determined by the *minimum support* (S_{min}) value. A data-sequence supports a sequential pattern if and only if it contains all the events present in the pattern in the same order. Note that this definition does not restrict that events in consecutive positions within the pattern must be strictly consecutive in the data-sequence. For example, the data-sequence $\langle x_0 x_1 x_2 x_3 x_4 x_5 \rangle$ supports the pattern $\langle e_0 e_5 \rangle$ with $e_0 = (x_0)$ and $e_5 = (x_5)$ if further constrains are not specified. The amount of data-sequences that support a sequential pattern is referred as the *support count*.

In this paper we extent the basic definition of frequent sequence with two of the generalizations proposed in [18] which are as follows:

- Sliding window: given an element e_i containing two or more simultaneous events $(x_0, x_1 ... x_m)$, a data-sequence contains e_i if and only if all events occur in the data-sequence within a given time window W_{max}. In other words, two or more events that occur in less than W_{max} may be considered to occur simultaneously.
- Time constrain: given two consecutive elements in a pattern, $e_i e_{i+1}$, a data-sequence may support the pattern only if both elements occur in the specified order and the time difference between their occurrences is lower than a specified time threshold, *maximum gap* (G_{max}).

3.1 GSP algorithm

The Generalized Sequential Patterns algorithm [18] is used for mining the frequent sequences in this study. GSP is a *candidate generation and test* algorithm which supports the constrains mentioned above. It first finds the frequent sequences with one single event, namely 1-sequences. That set of sequences is self-joined to generate all 2-sequence candidates for which we calculate their support count. Those sequences that are frequent (i.e. their support count is greater than a threshold value S_{min}) are self-joined to generate the set of 3-sequence candidates. The algorithm is iterational increasing the length of the sequences in each algorithmic step, until the next set of candidates is empty. The basic principle of the algorithm is that if a sequential pattern is frequent, then its *contiguous* subsequences are also frequent. Given two sequences s_x and s_y, s_y is a contiguous subsequence of s_x if either: 1) s_y is obtained by dropping the first or last event of s_x; or 2) s_y is obtained by dropping an event from an element of s_x with two or more events; or 3) there exists a sequence s_z such that s_z is a contiguous subsequence of s_x and s_y is a contiguous subsequence of s_z.

By self-joining a set of frequent sequences of length k, the algorithm obtains only the $(k+1)$-sequences whose contiguous subsequences are frequent, thereby, reducing the number of sequential patterns for which support counts have to be determined. The reader is referred to Algorithm 1 and Algorithm 2 for a more detailed presentation of the basic steps of the GSP algorithm.

4. USER EXPERIENCE MODELING

The dataset used in this paper contains sequences labeled with pairwise preferences of affect (see Section 5). Neuroevolutionary preference learning is applied to model those preferences relying on a subset of the available features selected automatically through Genetic Feature Selection. The two algorithms are briefly described in the following subsections.

4.1 Genetic Feature Selection

Feature selection (FS) is essential in scenarios where the available features do not have a clear relationship and, thus, impact to the prediction of a target output (i.e. it is not easy to decide *a priori* which features are useful and which are irrelevant for the prediction). Moreover the computational cost of testing all available feature sets is combinatorial and exhaustive search might not be computationally feasible in large feature sets. Under these conditions, FS is critical for finding an appropriate set of model input features that can yield highly accurate predictors [20].

Genetic feature selection (GFS) [12] is a global search FS algorithm guided by a genetic search. The fitness function is calculated as the average cross validation performance on unseen folds of classification data. The search starts by evaluating the fitness of several subsets with one feature; in subsequent iterations combinations of the fittest subsets from the previous iterations are evaluated. The algorithm stops after a fixed number of iterations or when highly fit feature subsets are found. More details about GSF can be found in [12].

4.2 Neuroevolutionary Preference Learning

We apply preference learning [5] to build affective models that predict users' self-reported emotional preferences based on the subsets of features selected by the GFS algorithm. In this study, the models are implemented as single layer perceptrons (SLPs) that are trained via neuroevolutionary preference learning (as in [19, 20]) to map the selected features to a predictor of the reported pairwise emotional preferences. The expressivity of SLPs allows us to analyse the impact of each one of the selected features to the reported affective preferences. For instance, when a feature with a corresponding high connection weight value increases from one game to another, the magnitude of the predicted preference is increased or decreased depending on the sign of the weight value. On the other hand, weight connections with low values have a small impact on the prediction of preferences.

Note that the pairwise preference relationship of the training data is known (e.g. game A is preferred to game B) but the value of the target output is not (i.e. the magnitude of the preference is unknown). Thus, any gradient-based optimization algorithm is inapplicable to the training problem since the error function under optimization is not differentiable.

5. DATA COLLECTION

The dataset used in this paper was gathered during an experimental game survey in which 36 participants played four pairs of different variants of the same video-game. The test-bed game named *Maze-Ball* is a 3D prey/predator game that features a ball inside a maze controlled by the arrow keys. The goal of the player is to maximize her score in 90 seconds by collecting the pellets scattered in the maze while avoiding the red enemies that wander around. The eight available variants of the game differ only on the virtual camera profile used which determines how the virtual world is presented on screen.

Blood volume pulse and skin conductance were recorded at 32Hz during the session; heart rate (HR) is inferred from the BVP signal every 5 seconds. Moreover, both gameplay information and user keystrokes are logged. The players filled in a 4-alternative forced choice questionnaire after completing a pair of variants reporting whether the first or the second game of the pair felt more anxious, challenging, exciting, frustrating, fun and relaxing, or whether both felt equally, or none of them did. The details of the Maze-Ball game design and the experimental protocol followed can be found in [20, 12].

5.1 Sequential Features

A data-sequence is created from the logs of each game, 224 in total, by concatenating all the events logged in temporal order. The following list describes the events we have chosen for this initial study:

- Performance Events
  - Player collects a pellet ($): 10 identical pellets are placed in different areas of the maze enforcing a difference of at least few seconds between two pellets. This event is picked as it is expected to have an impact on reported challenge and fun (among other reported user states).
  - Enemy hits the player (E): 14 enemies follow predefined paths guarding a pellet causing this event to occur very close in time with the $ events frequently. Enemy hits are selected as events since enemies are critical to player experience in a prey/predator game.
  - Countdown starts (t^{10}): when entering the last 10 seconds of the game the timer changes its color *rushing up* the player. This event occurs exactly once in each game, thus it does not provide sufficient information about the experience per se. However, sequences combining this event with physiological events or other gameplay events are expected to have a direct impact to reported anxiety and excitement.
- Navigation Events
  - Moving to a new area of the maze ($m^0, \ldots, m^7$): although there are not explicit boundaries between areas of the maze, 8 different sectors can be distinguished based on the different wall layout, placement of the pellets and movement of the enemies which, in turn, represent different degrees of difficulty. These events are expected to have a direct impact on the challenge reports.
  - Press an arrow key (▲, ▼, ◄, ►): pressing the right and left arrows make the ball turn if it is located in a corner; the down key forces the ball to turn 180° and the up arrow has no effect. Each single one of these events most likely holds a tiny piece of information about user experience; however, sequences combining many of these events may point to more complex navigation patterns with a potential impact on experience.
  - Inactivity for more than 1 second (*Stop*): the player avatar is moving forward at any time unless it hits a wall. In that case, the ball will only continue moving if the player turns. When the ball is stopped for 1 second, the event is logged. It could indicate that the player is planning a strategy or waiting for an enemy to move away from a pellet. Thus, this event is relevant for the identification of a player's behavioral patterns and, indirectly, for affect detection.
- Physiological Events
  - Difference between two inter-beat intervals (*RR intervals*) is greater than 50 ms (r^{+50}, r^{-50}): the heart beats are detected from the BVP signal and when two consecutive inter-beat intervals differ for more than 50 ms, an event is logged. The threshold of 50 ms is commonly used in affective and medical studies [6, 20] as an indicator of arousal which in turn is one of potential identifiers of the affective states examined.
  - SC increase/decrease ($s^{\Uparrow}, s^{\Downarrow}$): sudden changes in the SC signal are detected and logged as events.

They are normally detected in pairs: after $s^{\Uparrow}$ the SC will increase for a while and $s^{\Downarrow}$ will be logged when it starts decreasing. These SC signal events are picked because they suggest changes in sympathetic activity and, thereby, may relate to reported user experience.

This list of events is far from being inclusive of all relevant events available such as those derived from heart rate variability indexes. We consider the study of more sequential features out of the scope of this initial study which focuses on the efficacy of frequent sequence mining across modalities of user input for affect detection.

After the frequent sequences have been found in the full dataset, each data-sequence is transformed into a vector of sequential features. Each feature corresponds to the number of occurrences of a frequent sequence within the data-sequence that is been transformed. An alternative representation transforms each feature into a boolean value which is 0 when there are no occurrences of the associated sequential pattern in the data-sequence and 1 otherwise.

5.2 Statistical Features

A total of 42 statistical physiological features are extracted from the three physiological signals (BVP, SC and HR) including, for example, average and standard deviation of the three signals and heart rate variability measures such as standard deviation of the inter-beat time intervals. In addition, a total of 41 statistical gameplay features are extracted from the game metrics logged such as average and standard deviation of the distance to the closest pellet and enemy, and final score. For a full description of the statistical features extracted from both modalities of input, the reader is referred to [20, 11].

6. EXPERIMENTS

The first part of this section focuses on the process of mining and the analysis of multimodal frequent patterns obtained in the dataset examined. In the second part, sequence patterns are tested as inputs of computational models of affect.

6.1 Sequence Mining

In this section we first discuss the effects of the different GSP parameters in the task of mining sequences from multimodal datasets and later analyse the frequent sequences found in the Maze-Ball dataset.

6.1.1 Parameter Tuning

We set up the S_{min} to 100 sequences which forces a sequence pattern to occur in at least 44.64% of the samples (224 samples in total) to be considered frequent. We choose this high threshold because of the low *specificity* of the events that yields a high frequency of each event within the data-sequences. For example, consider the event of picking any of the ten available pellets ($) and ten different events associated to a specific pellet in the game $\{\$_0, \ldots, \$_9\}$. The support count for each $\$_x$ is expected to be lower than the support count of $ as different players will most likely pick different pellets. Consequently a lower minimum support would be required to consider sequence patterns containing the 10 specific $\$_x$ events frequent.

The W_{max} is chosen as a trade off between the frequency of the events within and across signals. On one hand, we require a low window to not consider simultaneous events that within the same signal are clearly not occurring at the same time (e.g. in a 90 second-long game, two gameplay events of more than a few seconds apart should not be processed as two simultaneous events). On the other hand, we need to allow a certain window to consider events from different asynchronous signals to occur at the same moment in time. For example, a variation on the RR signal is linked to the time interval between two heart beats; a gameplay event happening during this interval should be considered simultaneous to the RR variation even though the time stamps of both events are not identical. In all experiments reported in this paper W_{max} is 1 second.

The G_{max} parameter has a direct effect on the number of events that can be concatenated in a sequence and the support count of those sequences. Note that the definition of a sequence pattern does not require two consecutive events to occur immediately one after the other in the data-sequences. Consequently when G_{max} is much larger than the frequency of events in one modality, a high number of events can be skipped when matching a pattern with a data-sequence. For example, if we select a G_{max} of 5 seconds and we consider the sequence (▶)(▶), the number of data-sequences containing those two events in a 5 second interval is very high (arrow keys are pressed every 1-3 seconds) even though none of the players pressed the right arrow key twice in a row. This effect is enhanced by the fact that we are searching for sequences from different modalities. For instance, if we find the pattern (▶)($s^{\Uparrow}$)(▶) with a 5 second G_{max}, this sequence is supported by any data-sequence in which a player pressed the right key in a 5 second interval before and after his SC raised — independently of other keys being pressed before and after $s^{\Uparrow}$ or other events such as $ and E occurring. This has not only an effect on the informative value of the sequences but also increases greatly the number of frequent patterns (see Table 1). On the other hand, a large G_{max} may allow higher level sequences — i.e. sequences of high level events that do not occur very frequently — to emerge such as ($)($)($). Thus, when setting up this parameter, it is necessary to take into account the frequency of each event and the desired target sequences. In this initial study we decided to focus on the relationship between gameplay events and physiological responses and set up a G_{max} of 1.5 and 3 seconds which are both close to the frequency of the key presses (the most frequent event in the dataset). The two selected G_{max} values also approximate the physiological time responses to game events reported in several studies [16, 17].

6.1.2 Sequence Analysis

A large amount of frequent sequences were found in the dataset; specifically, looking at the 3 and 5 second G_{max} values (see Table 1) one may observe the exponential increase of frequent sequential patterns with regards to the number of events considered. The large amount of patterns is caused, in part, by the right and left key press events which are so frequent in the data-sequences that result in almost *wild card* events (i.e. between any two events is very likely that either the right or the left key are pressed).

The more restrictive G_{max} of 1.5 seconds did not produce any frequent sequence combining the sector events with

Table 1: Amount of frequent sequential patterns for different values of G_{max}.

# events	G_{max} 1.5	3	5
1	19	19	19
2	161	188	232
3	785	1650	2113
4	505	8387	18259
5	28	18985	118192
6	0	21704	545667
7	0	11251	NaN
8	0	1954	NaN
9	0	36	NaN

Table 2: Support counts of a subset of frequent sequences containing key board events.

Sequences	G_{max} 1.5	3
$(s^{\Uparrow})(s^{\Downarrow})$(►)(◄)(◄)(►)(►)(◄)(◄)	< 100	108
(◄)(►)(►)(►)(◄)(◄)(►)(►)(◄)	< 100	108
(◄)$(s^{\Uparrow})(s^{\Downarrow})(s^{\Uparrow})(s^{\Downarrow})$(►)(►)(◄)(◄)	< 100	101
(►)(◄)(◄)(►)(►)(◄)(◄)($)	< 100	104
(◄)(◄)(►)(►)(◄)(◄)($)(◄)	< 100	104
(◄)(◄)(►)(►)(◄)($)	< 100	149
(►)(◄)(m^7)(►)(►)(◄)	< 100	105
(◄)(◄)(►)(►)(◄)(E)	< 100	104
(◄)(►)(►)(E)(►)(◄)	< 100	102
(◄)$(s^{\Uparrow})(s^{\Downarrow})$(►)$(E)$(◄)	< 100	101
(◄)(◄)(►)(►)(◄)	115	202
(►)$(s^{\Uparrow})$(►)$(s^{\Downarrow})$(◄)	106	192
$(s^{\Uparrow})$(►)$(s^{\Downarrow})$(►)(◄)	101	187

the key presses making more difficult, if not impossible, to map a sequence of key presses to an area in the maze (e.g. (◄)(►)(►)(◄)(◄)). Even though specific paths can not be inferred from the key presses, some interesting results can be observed. For 1.5 and 3 second G_{max} values the sequences of maximum length found consist only of the events {◄, ►, $s^{\Uparrow}$, $s^{\Downarrow}$}; neither other gameplay events nor RR variations are included in the most frequent sequences (see Table 2). These sequences suggest that the combination of key press patterns in the Maze-Ball game and SC variation are frequent and should be considered in the analysis of player experience. Furthermore, in the longest sequences that combine key presses with the events {E, \$} (see Table 2), the latter always appear in the last position of the sequences suggesting that players follow similar strategies to approach pellets and enemies but more dissimilar behaviours are presented after picking a pellet or being hit by an enemy.

Table 3 shows some of the most frequent 2-sequences and 3-sequences that combine the main performance events, \$ and E, with physiological events. With the more restrictive value for G_{max} (1.5 second), all the frequent 3-sequences contain the subsequence ($s^{\Uparrow}$)($s^{\Downarrow}$) with the event \$ or E in any position, being the most frequent sequence in which the gameplay event occurs simultaneously with an increase of SC, followed by a decrease of SC. The 3 second G_{max} on the other hand, produced almost any combination of two physiological events with one of the gameplay events. This might indicate that the threshold is too large and does not capture a meaningful fusion of the modalities.

Table 3: Support counts of a subset of the most frequent sequences including physiological and performance events. Events enclosed in the same parentheses occur simultaneously (in any order within an interval of 1 second).

3-sequences	G_{max} 1.5	3	2-sequences	G_{max} 1.5	3
$(\$\ s^{\Uparrow})(s^{\Downarrow})$	141	168	$(\$\ s^{\Uparrow})$	184	184
$(E\ s^{\Uparrow})(s^{\Downarrow})$	131	163	$(\$\ r^{-50})$	178	178
$(s^{\Uparrow})(\$)(s^{\Downarrow})$	123	164	$(E\ s^{\Uparrow})$	175	175
$(s^{\Uparrow})(E)(s^{\Downarrow})$	116	164	$(E\ s^{\Downarrow})$	174	174
$(s^{\Uparrow})(s^{\Downarrow})(\$)$	112	181	$(E\ r^{+50})$	174	174
$(E)(s^{\Uparrow})(s^{\Downarrow})$	109	175	$(\$\ s^{\Downarrow})$	170	170
$(s^{\Uparrow})(s^{\Downarrow})(E)$	106	180	$(s^{\Uparrow})(\$)$	166	194
$(\$)(s^{\Uparrow})(s^{\Downarrow})$	105	186			
$(s^{\Uparrow})(\$\ s^{\Downarrow})$	105	158			
$(s^{\Uparrow}\ s^{\Downarrow})(\$)$	102	139			

The frequent 2-sequences correspond to all possible combinations of one of the gameplay events with one physiological event showing more occurrences when combined in the same element. Note that the count support indicates only the number of data-sequences in which the sequence pattern appears and not the number of occurrences within each data-sequence. Opposite to long sequences, these short patterns are expected to occur more than once in each sequence. Therefore, the number of occurrences of the patterns within each data-sequence is required for a full analysis of the physiological responses to game events. This study, however, is out of the scope of this paper and will be examined in future work.

It is worth mentioning that none of the other high level game play events occur frequently with the physiological responses. While this is not entirely surprising for the sector events — given that there is no visual or audio feedback when changing sectors in the maze — one would expect that the count down event would trigger a change on the player that would have been reflected on her physiology. However, such a relationship is not observed frequently via event sequences.

6.2 Preference Learning

For the preference learning experiments reported here we chose to use only the frequent sequences found using $G_{max} = 1.5$, $S_{min} = 100$ and $W_{max} = 1$ that did not contain the key board and *Stop* events. This last constrain reduces substantially the number of frequent patterns from 1498 to 140 in an effort to lower the dimensionality of space and the computational cost of training. Preliminary studies showed that using the full set of frequent patterns did not improve the prediction accuracy of the user preference models.

In this section we first test two approaches to transform the sequence patterns into feature vectors as those were mentioned in Section 5 and we then built and compare computational models of affect which are based on either sequential or statistical features, or both. In all tests GFS is applied to select the inputs of the computational models. The accuracy of the models is calculated as the average 3-fold cross-validation accuracy on predicting unseen pairwise preference data.

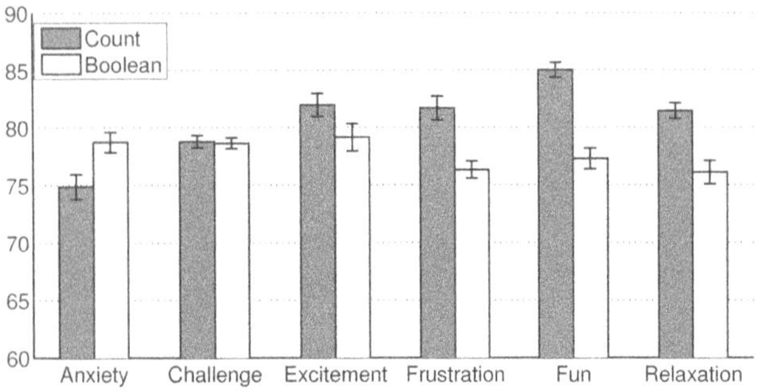

Figure 1: Average accuracy (3-fold cross-validation) and standard error of 10 runs of GFS in sequential multimodal features using the count of occurrences (count) or the existence to a data-sequence (boolean) as representation.

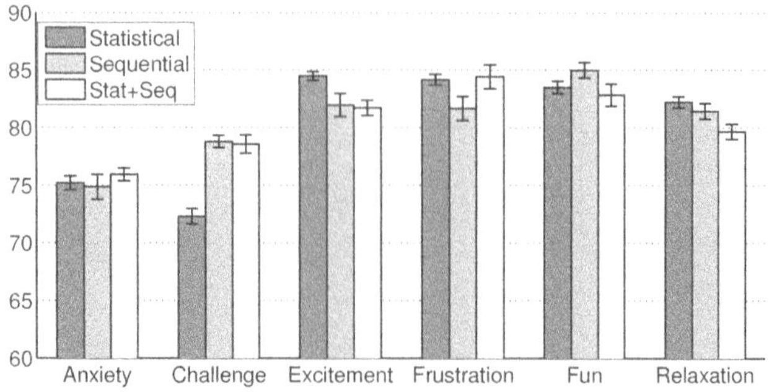

Figure 2: Average accuracy (3-fold cross validation) and standard error of 10 runs of GFS in statistical and sequential multimodal features.

6.2.1 *Sequences as User Preference Model Input*

Figure 1 shows the average accuracy of 10 user preference ANN models built on one of the two different representations of the frequent pattern: each frequent sequence is represented as its corresponding number of occurrences in each data-sequence (count) or alternatively represented as a boolean feature that is 0 when the frequent sequence does not occur in the data-sequence and 1 otherwise (boolean).

For the case study dataset examined, in which the frequent patterns are short and expected to occur a variant number of times across samples, the count representation is expected to yield higher accuracies since the boolean representation is far less informative. Results show that this hypothesis is valid for all affective states but anxiety. Apparently, the boolean representation provides sufficient information for predicting the reports of anxiety whereas it proves to be insufficient for the remaining of the user states examined.

6.2.2 *Comparison Between Sequential and Statistical Features*

Figure 2 depicts the average accuracies of ten ANN models built on subsets of features selected by GFS from a set of statistical features, a set of sequential features and a set combining both feature sets. Results show that the accuracies of models built on sequential patterns are comparable to models trained on statistical features and even significantly higher on fun — 1.48% higher accuracy ($p - value < 0.1$)— and challenge — 6.48% higher accuracy ($p - value < 0.01$) — showing that information about short intervals of the user experience across modalities is as valuable as information about the overall user experience for the prediction of affective self-reports.

Some of the information gathered by sequential patterns overlap with the information contained in statistical features (e.g. the final score of the player can be inferred from the 1-sequences ($) and ($E$)); however, most features are specific to one of the feature extraction approaches and provide complementary information about the multimodal interaction. Thus, it is surprising that models that can combine both sources of information cannot, in general, outperform models built on one of the sets of features only. Figure 2 shows that only in frustration and anxiety such models present a slightly higher average accuracy, which is not statistically significant in either dataset. This could indicate that in this particular dataset — as already reported in [20] — it might be impossible to find a subset that yields a higher performing predictor with a simple model such as a single layer perceptron. Additionally, the search space for automatic feature selection is increased substantially when joining the two sets of features, complicating the task of effectively finding the *optimal* subset of ANN inputs through genetic search. This is, in part, supported by the lower accuracy of the excitement, fun and relaxation models trained on both input sets than only trained on each one of them.

Table 4 depicts the best models trained for challenge and fun on sequential features. The challenge model combines sequences of physiological responses with only two gameplay sequences and no multimodal sequences. The sequence $(s^{\Downarrow})(s^{\Uparrow})$ associated with a negative weight suggests that repeated changes on SC — typically a decrease follows an increase — contribute to a lower challenge value. This relationship is consistent with results reported in [20] where higher SC variance is linked to lower challenge values. However, the effect on challenge is inverse when the sequence is preceded by a positive change in the RR intervals — $(r^{+50})(s^{\Downarrow})(s^{\Uparrow})$ — suggesting that sudden changes in sympathetic arousal indicated by both HR and SC variability lead to higher challenge values. A somewhat surprising result is that the predicted challenge is lower when pellets are picked and simultaneously an enemy hits the player. This could be a sign that some players do not try to get around the enemies to pick the pellets (which is a difficult and time consuming task) and instead prefer to pick a pellet as quickly as possible and run towards the next one even if an enemy is next to it. This further suggests that the negative reward scheme for enemies should to be increased for a more balanced game design.

Observing the best-performing ANN model of fun (see Table 4) it seems that the total number of pellets picked ($) has a positive impact on reported fun as well as when a sudden peak in SC is generated just before or just after picking a pellet — $(s^{\Uparrow})(s^{\Downarrow})(\$)$ and $(\$\ s^{\Uparrow})(s^{\Downarrow})$ — which could be related to a heightened arousal state when the player is about to pick a pellet. Sudden increases on the RR intervals length $(r^{+50}\ r^{+50})$ have also a positive impact on reported fun. On the other hand, enemy hits accompanied by a sudden decrease on SC ($E\ s^{\Downarrow}$), not surprisingly, seem to decrease the level of fun. Note, that a single event E would not necessarily have a negative effect on fun as it is a fundamental

Table 4: **Input features and corresponding connection weights for the highest performing ANN models for challenge and fun**

Challenge		Fun	
$(s^{\Uparrow}\ s^{\Downarrow})(r^{-50})$	5.00	$(\$)$	4.80
$(s^{\Uparrow}\ r^{+50})(r^{-50})(s^{\Downarrow})$	-5.00	$(r^{+50}\ r^{+50})$	4.69
$(s^{\Downarrow})(s^{\Uparrow})$	-4.82	$(E\ s^{\Downarrow})$	-4.56
$(\$\ E)$	-3.61	$(s^{\Downarrow}\ r^{-50})(r^{+50})$	-3.49
$(r^{-50})(s^{\Downarrow})$	-2.22	$(s^{\Uparrow})(s^{\Downarrow})(\$)$	3.06
$(r^{+50})(s^{\Downarrow})(s^{\Uparrow})$	2.21	$(\$\ s^{\Uparrow})(s^{\Downarrow})$	2.50
$(s^{\Downarrow}\ r^{+50}\ r^{-50})$	1.67	$(\$\ m^{6})$	-1.19
(r^{-50})	1.52	$(s^{\Uparrow})(r^{-50})(r^{+50})$	0.67
$(\$\ m^{6})$	-0.05	$(r^{+50})(r^{-50})(s^{\Downarrow})$	0.09
		$(s^{\Uparrow}\ r^{+50})(s^{\Downarrow}\ r^{-50})$	-0.18

part of the game; however, a decrease on SC might indicate a lowered level of the player's arousal as consequence of the game event.

7. CONCLUSIONS

In this paper we propose sequential pattern mining as a method to explore the relationship between asynchronous signals from different modalities for the discovery of frequent event sequences across modalities. We applied the GSP sequence pattern mining algorithm to a game dataset that includes physiological signals (blood volume pulse and skin conductance), context-based game metrics (e.g. key board presses) and self-reported affective preferences. This study served as a starting point to highlight the main advantages, limitations and practical considerations of this approach when applied to the analysis of multimodal interactions.

Additionally, as an alternative to standard statistical features, the frequent sequences mined are presented as inputs of affect detectors assisting the process of finding more accurate models of user affect and experience. The resulting affective models are analysed and compared against models trained on statistical features. The analysis of the affective models trained on the sequences found in the game dataset reveals relationships between sudden arousal level changes across physiological signals, critical game events and reported affect. Sequences outperform statistical features in two (fun and challenge) out of the six affective states examined in this study when used as inputs of affect detectors; the sequential features yield similar performances to standard statistical features in the other four affective states: anxiety, excitement, frustration and relaxation. Future work will aim to validate the proposed method in dissimilar datasets, including different modalities of user input, and explore a richer set of multimodal events for sequence mining.

8. REFERENCES

[1] R. Agrawal and R. Srikant. Mining sequential patterns. In *icde*, page 3. Published by the IEEE Computer Society, 1995.

[2] A. Ben-Hur and D. Brutlag. Remote homology detection: a motif based approach. *Bioinformatics*, 19(suppl 1):i26-i33, 2003.

[3] A. Drachen, L. Nacke, G. N. Yannakakis, and A. L. Pedersen. Correlation between heart rate, electrodermal activity and player experience in First-Person Shooter games. In *SIGGRAPH'10*, 2010.

[4] P. Ferreira and P. Azevedo. Protein sequence classification through relevant sequence mining and bayes classifiers. *Progress in AI*, pages 236–247, 2005.

[5] J. Fürnkranz and E. Hüllermeier. Preference learning. *Künstliche Intelligenz*, 19(1):60–61, 2005.

[6] J. Goldberger, S. Challapalli, R. Tung, M. Parker, and A. Kadish. Relationship of heart rate variability to parasympathetic effect. *Circulation*, 103(15):1977, 2001.

[7] J. Han and M. Kamber. *Data mining: concepts and techniques*. Morgan Kaufmann, 2006.

[8] N. Lesh, M. Zaki, and M. Ogihara. Mining features for sequence classification. In *Proc. of the fifth ACM SIGKDD Int. Conf. on Knowledge discovery and data mining*, pages 342–346. ACM, 1999.

[9] R. Mandryk, K. Inkpen, and T. Calvert. Using psychophysiological techniques to measure user experience with entertainment technologies. *Behaviour & Information Technology*, 25(2):141–158, 2006.

[10] R.L. Mandryk, and M.S Atkins. A fuzzy physiological approach for continuously modeling emotion during interaction with play technologies. *International Journal of Human-Computer Studies*, 65(4):329–347, 2007.

[11] H. P. Martinez, K. Hullett, and G. N. Yannakakis. Extending Neuro-evolution Preference Learning through Player Modeling. In *Proc. of 2010 IEEE CIG*, 2010.

[12] H. P. Martínez and G. N. Yannakakis. Genetic search feature selection for affective modeling: a case study on reported preferences. In *Proc. of the 3rd AFFINE workshop*, pages 15–20. ACM, 2010.

[13] S. Mcquiggan, B. Mott, and J. Lester. Modeling self-efficacy in intelligent tutoring systems: An inductive approach. *UMUAI*, 18(1):81–123, 2008.

[14] M. Pantic and L. Rothkrantz. Toward an affect-sensitive multimodal human-computer interaction. *Proceedings of the IEEE*, 91(9):1370–1390, 2003.

[15] M. Pantic, M. Valstar, R. Rademaker, and L. Maat. Web-based database for facial expression analysis. In *2005 IEEE International Conference on Multimedia and Expo*, page 5. IEEE, 2005.

[16] N. Ravaja, T. Saari, J. Laarni, K. Kallinen, M. Salminen, J. Holopainen, and A. Järvinen. The psychophysiology of video gaming: Phasic emotional responses to game events. In *Proc. of DiGRA'05*, 2005

[17] N. Ravaja, T. Saari, M. Salminen, J. Laarni, and K. Kallinen. Phasic emotional reactions to video game events: A psychophysiological investigation. *Media Psychology*, 8(4):343–367, 2006.

[18] R. Srikant and R. Agrawal. Mining sequential patterns: Generalizations and performance improvements. *Advances in Database Technology - EDBT'96*, pages 1–17, 1996.

[19] G. N. Yannakakis. Preference Learning for Affective Modeling. In *Proc. of ACII'09*, 2009.

[20] G. N. Yannakakis, H. P. Martínez, and A. Jhala. Towards affective camera control in games. *UMUAI*, 20:313–340, 2010.

Crowdsourced Data Collection of Facial Responses

Daniel McDuff
MIT Media Lab
Cambridge
02139, USA
djmcduff@media.mit.edu

Rana el Kaliouby *
MIT Media Lab
Cambridge
02139, USA
kaliouby@media.mit.edu

Rosalind Picard *
MIT Media Lab
Cambridge
02139, USA
picard@media.mit.edu

ABSTRACT

In the past, collecting data to train facial expression and affect recognition systems has been time consuming and often led to data that do not include spontaneous expressions. We present the first crowdsourced data collection of dynamic, natural and spontaneous facial responses as viewers watch media online. This system allowed a corpus of 3,268 videos to be collected in under two months.

We characterize the data in terms of viewer demographics, position, scale, pose and movement of the viewer within the frame, and illumination of the facial region. We compare statistics from this corpus to those from the CK+ and MMI databases and show that distributions of position, scale, pose, movement and luminance of the facial region are significantly different from those represented in these datasets.

We demonstrate that it is possible to efficiently collect massive amounts of ecologically valid responses, to known stimuli, from a diverse population using such a system. In addition facial feature points within the videos can be tracked for over 90% of the frames. These responses were collected without need for scheduling, payment or recruitment. Finally, we describe a subset of data (over 290 videos) that will be available for the research community.

Categories and Subject Descriptors

I.5.4 [**Image Processing and Computer Vision**]: Applications - Computer vision, Signal processing; I.5.5 [**Image Processing and Computer Vision**]: Interactive systems; J.4 [**Social and Behavioral Sciences**]: Psychology

General Terms

Design, Human Factors, Measurement, Performance

Keywords

Facial responses, non-verbal communication, crowdsourcing.

*Dr. Kaliouby and Dr. Picard also hold positions with Affectiva, Inc.

ICMI'11, November 14–18, 2011, Alicante, Spain.

Figure 1: A sample from the 3268 videos collected. There are significant variations in position, scale, pose, lighting and movement in the responses. These represent a subset of the public data.

1. INTRODUCTION

Computer-based machine learning and pattern analysis depends hugely on the number of training examples. To date much of the work automating the analysis of facial expressions and gestures has had to make do with limited datasets for training and testing. In addition these datasets often feature posed expressions and/or are collected in an artificial setting of a laboratory or studio. It has been shown in numerous studies that spontaneous expressions differ from those that are deliberate [19] and that they can communicate different information [27]. Further to this, it has been shown that in day-to-day life people exhibit complex and subtle affective states [1] such as worry and concentration [18].

There are cultural and gender difference in non-verbal responses [12, 8]. In designing systems that are able to detect non-verbal cues and affective states it is therefore necessary to collect data that reflects these nuances and contains a significant amount of examples across these different categories. Until now datasets have been limited to a relatively small number of examples. The populations from which these data are collected are often limited and do not reflect intra- and inter-person variability across different cultures, genders, ages and personalities.

This work was motivated by the desire to collect a large dataset of natural and spontaneous interactions. We present the first findings from an experiment to crowdsource data of facial responses over the internet. Until now it has not been clear what quality of data could be collected via crowdsourcing, what the natural limits on pose, lighting and image quality might be and how feature trackers would perform.

The main contribution of this paper is presenting the first-in-the-world crowdsourced facial expression corpus. We believe that this method of collecting and analyzing facial video can truly accelerate research in automated understanding of facial expressions and gestures. The method can also provide a mechanism to ask entirely new research questions, and to answer those questions with data that is ecologically valid. We present a massive dataset, collected via the internet in 54 days, containing 3,268 videos captured in natural environments whilst the viewers were presented with known stimuli, one of three commercials.

We compare the demographics, position, scale, pose, movement and lighting for these data collected with sets of videos from the CK+ [11] and the MMI [16] databases, datasets traditionally used for training and testing facial expression recognition systems. We contrast the dynamic ranges of the respective features across each of the datasets.

2. RELATED WORK

The internet provides the ability to crowd-source lots of useful information [17]. People are willing to engage and share visual images from their webcams [21] and these can be used for training automatic algorithms for learning. Inspired by these approaches, we capture videos of natural engagement with media online and show that this can be elicited without payment, providing motivation for the viewers by combining the experiment with popular and engaging media shown during recent Super Bowl television coverage. Joho et al. [9] show that facial activity can be used to identify personal highlights during video content; our work shows the potential for extending such algorithms to online content.

Public datasets truly help accelerate research in an area, not just because they provide a benchmark, or a common language, through which researchers can communicate and compare their different algorithms in an objective manner, but also because compiling such a corpus is tedious work - requiring a lot of effort which many researchers may not have the resources to do. In the area of facial expression analysis, the Cohn-Kanade database, in its extended form named CK+, played a key role in advancing the state of the art in this area. The CK+ database, contains 593 recordings of posed and non-posed sequences. The sequences are recorded under controlled conditions of light and head motion, and range between 9-60 frames per sequence. Each sequence represents a single facial expression that starts with a neutral frame and ends with a peak facial action. Transitions between expressions are not included. Several systems use the CK, or CK+, databases for training and/or testing. Since it was first published, a number of papers have been published that were trained and/or tested on this data set including: Bartlett et al. [3], Cohen et al. [5], Cohn et al. [6], Littlewort et al. [10] and Michel & El Kaliouby [15]. Since then, a few other databases have emerged, including: MMI [16], SEMAINE [14], RU-FACS [2], SAL [7]. A survey of databases and affect recognition systems can be found in [25]. However, there is a need for mechanisms to quickly and efficiently collect numerous examples of natural and spontaneous responses. Lab-based studies pose numerous challenges including recruitment, scheduling and payment. Efforts have

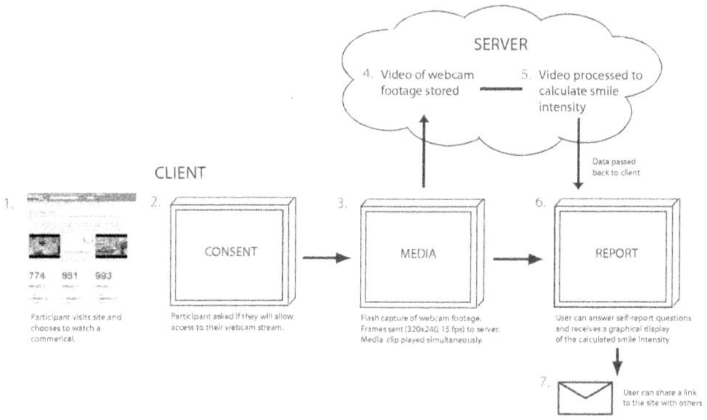

Figure 2: Overview of what the user experience was like and Affectiva's (www.affectiva.com) web-based framework that was used to crowdsource the facial videos. From the viewer's perspective, all that is needed is a browser with Flash support and a webcam. The video from the webcam is streamed in real-time to a server where automated facial expression analysis is performed, and the results are rendered back to the browser for display. All the video processing was done on the server side.

been made to collect significant amounts of spontaneous facial responses; however, the logistics of a laboratory based study typically limits the number of participants to under 100, e.g. 42 in [13]. By using the internet we can make data collection efficient, asynchronous and less resource intensive, and get at least an order of magnitude more participants.

3. CROWDSOURCING PLATFORM

Figure 2 shows the web-based framework that was used to crowdsource the facial videos and provides an overview of the user experience. The website was promoted on Forbes.com for the first day that it was live. Visitors may have found it via this route, a search engine or a shared link. Visitors to the website opt-in to watch short videos while their facial expressions are being recorded and analyzed. Immediately following each video, visitors get to see where they smiled and with what intensity. They can compare their "smile track" to the aggregate smile track. On the client-side, all that is needed is a browser with Flash support and a webcam. The video from the webcam is streamed in real-time at 15 frames a second at a resolution of 320x240 to a server where automated facial expression analysis is performed, and the results are rendered back to the browser for display. There is no need to download or install anything on the client side, making it very simple for people to participate. Furthermore, it is straightforward to easily set up and customize "experiments" to enable new research questions to be posed. For this experiment, we chose three successful Super Bowl commercials: 1. Doritos ("House sitting", 30 s), 2. Google ("Parisian Love", 53 s) and 3. Volkswagen ("The Force", 62 s). All three ads were somewhat amusing and were designed to elicit smile or laughter responses. Results showed that significant smiles were present in 71%, 65% and 80% of the responses to the respective ads.

On selecting a commercial to watch, visitors are asked to 1) grant access to their webcam for video recording and 2) to allow Affectiva and MIT to use the facial video for inter-

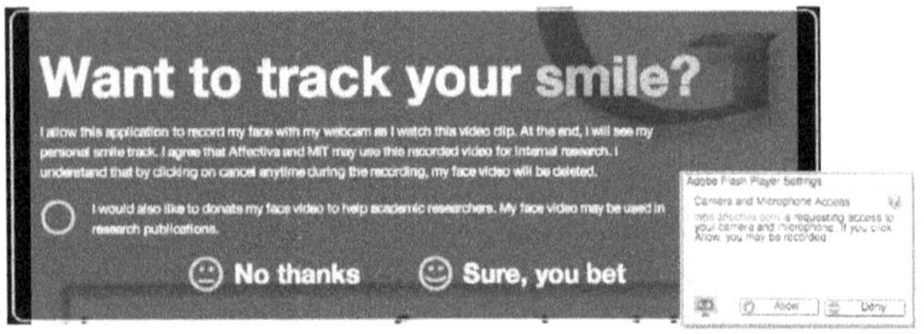

Figure 3: The consent forms that the viewers were presented with before watching the commercial and before the webcam stream began.

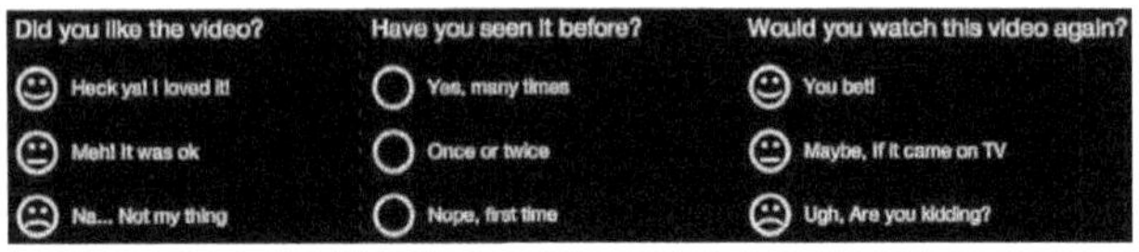

Figure 4: The self-report questions the viewers were presented with after watching the commercial.

nal research. Further consent for the data to be shared with the research community at large is also sought, and only videos with consent to be shared publically are shown in this paper. This data collection protocol was approved by the Massachusetts Institute of Technology Committee On the Use of Humans as Experimental Subjects (COUHES) prior to launching the site. A screenshot of the consent form is shown in Figure 3. If consent is granted, the commercial is played in the browser whilst simultaneously streaming the facial video to a server. In accordance with MIT COUHES, viewers could opt-out if they chose to at any point while watching the videos, in which case their facial video is immediately deleted from the server. If a viewer watches a video to the end, then his/her facial video data is stored along with the time at which the session was started, their IP address, the ID of the video they watched and responses (if any) to the self report questions. No other data is stored.

Following each commercial, the webcam is automatically stopped and a message clearly states that the "webcam has now been turned off". Viewers could then optionally answer three multiple choice questions: "Did you like the video?", "Have you seen it before?" and "Would you watch this video again?". A screenshot of the questions is shown in Figure 4. Finally, viewers were provided with a graphical representation of their smile intensity during the clip compared to other viewers who watched the same video; viewers were also given the option to tweet their result page or email it to a friend. All in all, it took under 5 seconds to turn around the facial analysis results once the video was completed so viewers perceived the results as instantaneous. Viewers were free to watch one, two or three videos and could watch a video as many times as they liked. In this paper we focus on the general characteristics of the collected videos (e.g., pose and lighting) and leave the analysis of the facial and self-report responses to future work.

4. THE DATASET

Using the framework described we collected 3,268 videos (2,615,800 frames) over a period of 54 days from 03/03/2011 to 04/25/2011. The application was promoted on the Forbes

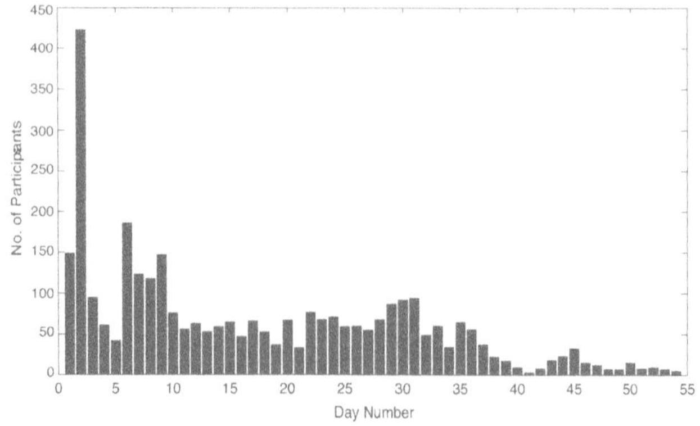

Figure 5: Histogram of the number of viewers that successfully completed the study on each of the 54 consecutive days (from 3/3/2011) that it was live.

Figure 6: Map showing the location of the 3268 viewers, based on their IP address. No viewers IP were located outside of the latitudes shown.

website - http://www.forbes.com/2011/02/28/detect-smile-webcam-affectiva-mit-media-lab.html. We refer to the data collected as the Forbes dataset. The number of visitors who clicked a video was 16,366. Of these 7,562 (46.2%) opted-in to allow webcam access. 5,268 (32.2%) completed the experiment. For the analysis here we disregard videos for which we were unable to identify a face within at least 90% of frames as they were significantly beyond the performance of the Nevenvision tracker; this left 3,268 videos (20.0%). Figure 5 shows the number of these videos that were completed on each of the 54 days. All videos were recorded with a resolution of 320x240 and a frame rate of 15 fps.

As this is the first experiment to collect this kind of data in the wild we compared these data to examples from other datasets collected in laboratories. We compare the statistics for these data collected with sets of videos from the CK+ and MMI databases, data traditionally used for training and testing facial expression and affect recognition systems.

For position, scale, pose, movement and illumination analysis we took all 722 videos from the MMI database that featured participants filmed with a frontal pose (14,360 frames) and all 593 videos from the CK+ dataset (10,708 frames).

5. CHARACTERIZING THE DATA

5.1 Demographics

The following section concerns statistics about the demographic profiles of the data. We compare these statistics of

Table 1: **Table showing the number of videos for each commercial broken down by continent and gender (no. of females shown in brackets).**

	No. of viewers (female)		
Continent	Doritos	Google	VW
Africa	14 (4)	14 (8)	18 (8)
Asia	74 (22)	68 (20)	88 (24)
Europe	226 (75)	228 (65)	222 (61)
North America	681 (245)	730 (273)	714 (260)
South America	42 (13)	43 (15)	43 (12)
Oceania	23 (6)	21 (5)	19 (5)
Total	695 (365)	718 (386)	735 (369)

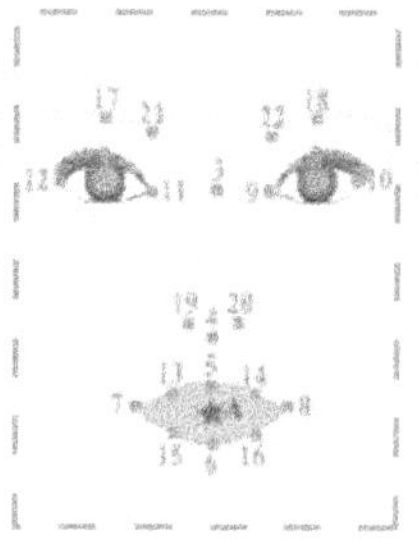

Figure 7: Location of the 22 feature points tracked by the Nevenvision tracker, the red line highlights the facial region used for evaluating illumination.

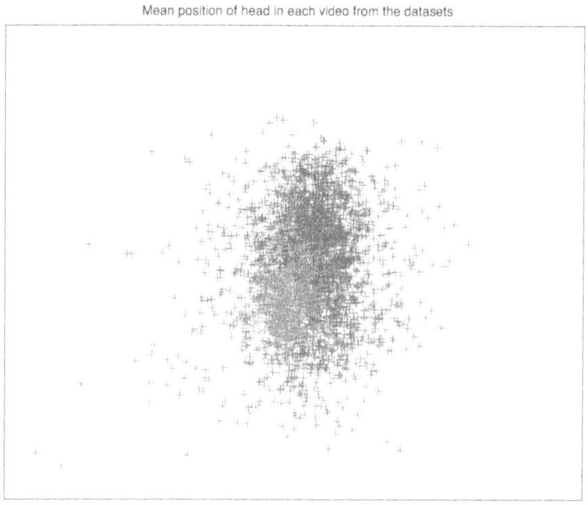

Figure 8: Scatter plot showing the mean location of the viewers' head within the frame for each video. The nose root was used as the location of the head. CK+ (red), MMI (green), Forbes (blue).

the viewers of the Forbes study with the participants from the CK+ and MMI datasets.

We use IP information to provide statistics on the locations of viewers by finding the latitude and longitude corresponding to each address. Statistics for gender were obtained by a labeler who watched the videos. IP addresses have been shown to be a reliable measure of location [20]. The IP address geo-location was performed using IPInfoDB [1]. We could not guarantee that the same viewer would watch all three of the commercials or that some may watch them more than once. As we do not have identifiable information from the viewers and we do not have the number of distinct viewers who took part, only a coarse calculation can be provided by the number of distinct IP addresses 1,495 (45.8%). This suggests that on average each location successfully completed the task for two viewings. Table 1 shows the number of viewers in each continent and in brackets the number of females. A majority of the viewers were located in North America and Europe. The geographic location of each of the viewers is shown on the map in Figure 6. Of the 3,268 videos 1,120 (34.3%) featured females as the main subject. The age of viewers was restricted to those over the age of 13 or with a parent or legal guardian's consent. In 924 (28.3%) of the videos the viewer was wearing glasses.

The CK+ dataset was obtained from a subset of data collected in America featuring 210 adults aged 18 to 50 years of age, 69% females, 81% Euro-American, 13% Afro-American, and 6% others. No participants wore glasses.

The MMI dataset initially consisted of data from 19 participants (44% female) aged between 19 to 62 from European, Asian, or South America ethnic background. It has since been extended [22] with data from 25 more participants (48% female) aged between 20 and 32 years from similar ethnic backgrounds. In 249 (34.5%) of the 722 frontal videos the participant was wearing glasses.

5.2 Position, Scale and Pose

The Nevenvision facial feature tracker[2] was used to automatically find 22 facial features within each frame of the videos. The locations of the points detected are shown in Figure 7. The following metrics need to be considered in the limitations of the facial feature tracker used. About three axes of pitch, yaw (turning) and roll (tilting), the limits are 32.6 (std=4.84), 33.4 (std=2.34) and 18.6 (std=3.75) degrees from the frontal position respectively (deviations reflect variability in performance in different lighting). We do not consider comparisons outside of these ranges.

The number of frames tracked for each of the datasets were as follows: Forbes 2,554,325 of 2,615,800 (97.7%), MMI 14,360 of 14,360 (100%) and CK+ 10,708 of 10,708 (100%)

Position within the frame was determined by position of feature point three, a fixed point at the nose root. We normalized these points to a relative position within a frame 320x240. Three Euler angles for the pose of the head, pitch, yaw and roll were calculated. The head scale within the frame was also calculated using the distance between the feature points; this can be approximated as an inverse measurement of the face from the camera.

Figure 8 shows a spatial representation of the mean location of the faces within the videos. We can see that there is significantly greater variance in the positions of the participants in the Forbes videos than those in both the MMI and CK+ sets. The means of these two distributions are similar and are close to the center of the frame. As we discarded any videos in which our tracker did not find a face for more than 90% of the frames it is possible that for some participants the webcam was pointed in the wrong direction and therefore they were not in the frame at all.

Figure 9 shows a histogram of the relative scales of the

[1]http://www.ipinfodb.com/ip_location_api.php
[2]Licensed from Google, Inc.

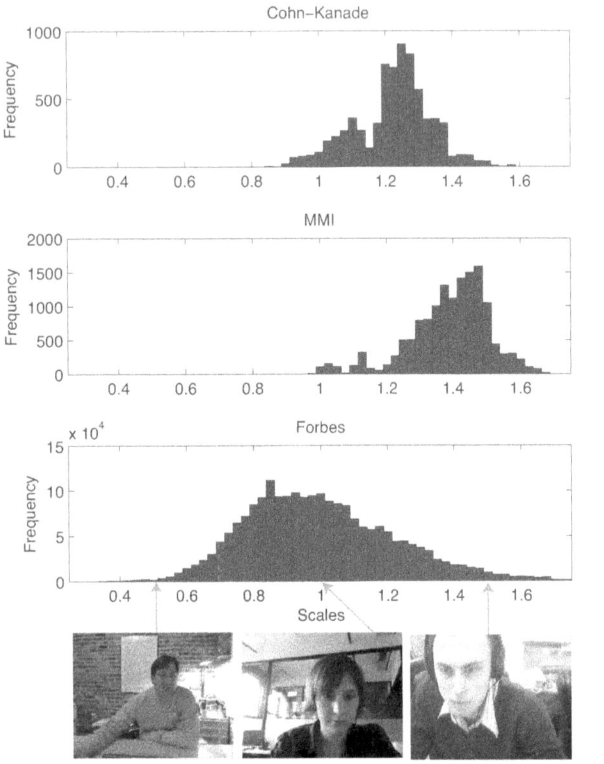

Figure 9: Histogram of head scales for the CK+ (top), MMI (center) and Forbes (bottom) datasets. The head scale was calculated for every frame in which a head was tracked. Examples of face scales of 0.5, 1 and 1.5 are shown below.

faces detected. Examples shown for scales of 0.5, 1 and 1.5. There is greater deviation in the scales for the Forbes set (std=0.256) than both the MMI (std=0.122) and CK+ (std=0.116) sets. The mean is significantly lower for the Forbes set (mean=0.987) versus the MMI (mean=1.39) and CK+ sets (mean=1.22), $p<0.05$. This suggests that in normal web interactions people sit further from the camera than represented in the lab and more significantly they fill less of the field of view of the camera. The average head scale was 19% smaller in the Forbes set relative to the scales in CK+.

Figure 10 shows a histogram of the pose angles (pitch, yaw and roll) for each of the detected faces, as calculated using the Nevenvision tracker. As with the position and scale distributions, the variance in the Forbes dataset is greater for all three angles compared to the other two sets. The overriding factor affecting the pose could be the position of the camera relative to the participant and not necessarily the participant's movement within each video. The greatest difference is in the case of head yaw, for which there is a standard deviation of 0.143 for the Forbes set and 0.0668 and 0.0579 for the MMI and CK+ sets.

5.3 Movement

Movement within the videos was evaluated by two methods. Firstly, sparse optical flow between frames was calculated using the Shi and Tomasi and the Pyramidal Lucas-Kanade [4] algorithms, to quantify the movement within the

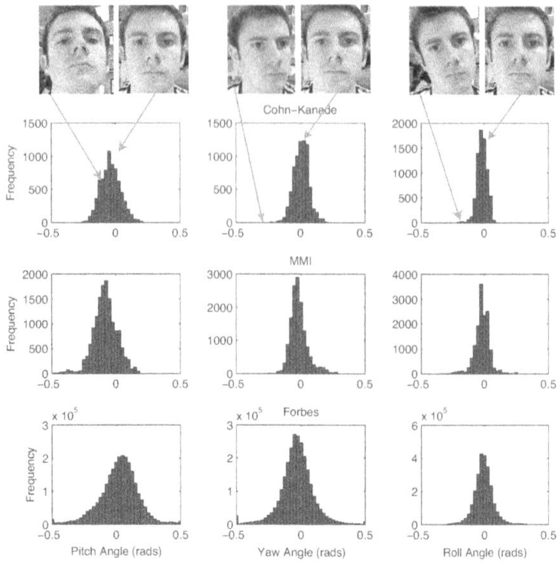

Figure 10: Histograms showing the pose angles of the heads in the CK+ (top), MMI (center) and Forbes (bottom) datasets. Examples of poses with pitch=-0.13 rads, yaw=-0.26 rads and roll=-0.19 rads are shown.

whole frame. Secondly, tracked motion of the head was used to compute the viewer head motion. The movement of the viewer within the frame was calculated as the absolute difference between the subsequent positions locations of the viewers head (nose root) for each second of the video.

Figure 11 shows the distribution of the magnitudes of the optical flow features across the frames for each dataset (bottom). Due to the extra head and body movement and the less intense expressions of the participants in the Forbes dataset the distributions are a lot less defined. Examples of the optical flow in videos for each of the datasets are also shown (top). Motion in specific regions of the face, in particular around the mouth and eyes, are identifiable for the examples from the CK+ and MMI datasets but not for the Forbes set as overall head motion dominates. This was typical for the data.

Figure 12 shows the mean movement trajectories for each of the stimuli. All three have the same form with considerably greater movement at the start of the clips. This is movement relative to the camera and therefore much of this movement could be due to viewers adjusting the direction of their webcam at the start and not their motion, this was observed in a number of the videos. The examples from the CK+ and MMI databases are relatively very short in duration and the participants move only slightly, therefore they do not reflect natural movement that could be expected.

5.4 Illumination

We calculated image quality metrics for the first tracked frame of each video. The metrics were calculated for the facial region within the image, using a box with corners defined by the rigid feature points 4, 10 and 12:

$$UL = [12.X - 0.2 * (10.X - 12.X), 12.Y + (12.Y - 4.Y)]$$
$$LR = [12.X + 0.2 * (10.X - 12.X), 4.Y - (12.Y - 4.Y)]$$

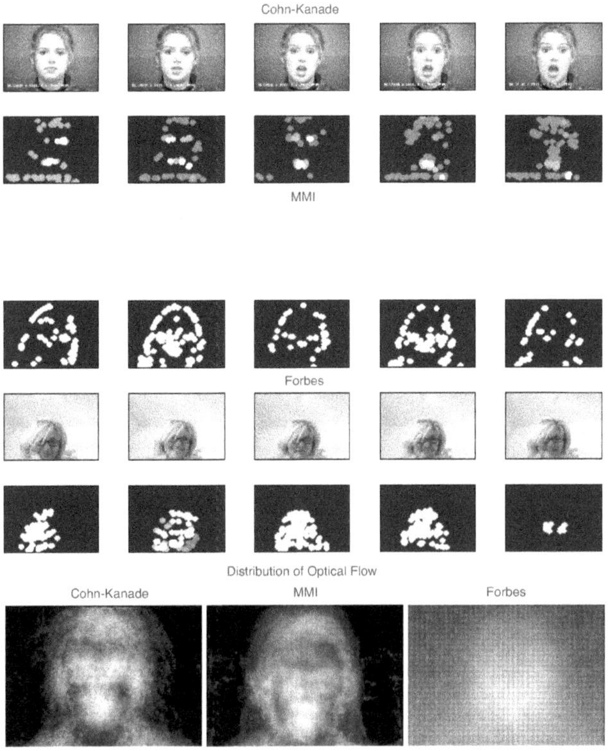

Figure 11: An example of the flow in one of the videos from each dataset (top) and the distribution of optical flow across the frames from the CK+, MMI and Forbes datasets (bottom).

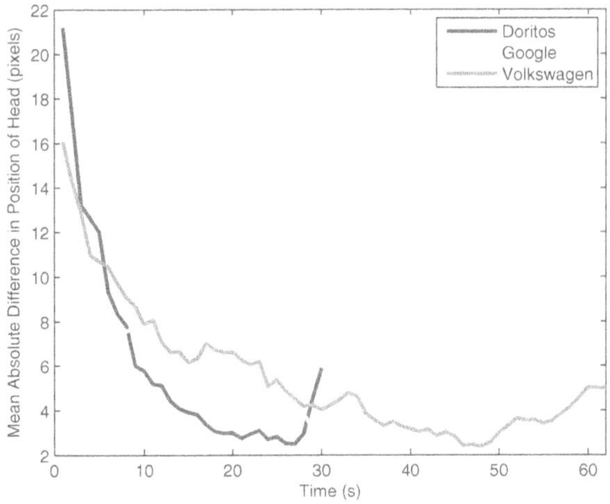

Figure 12: Mean absolute difference of the position of the viewer's heads (pixels) for each second during the videos. The data is divided into responses to each of the stimuli.

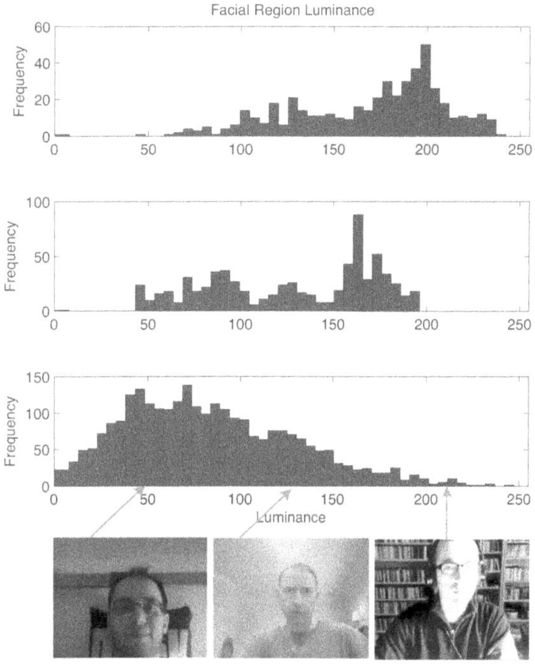

Figure 13: Histograms of the average luminance for the facial region for CK+ (top), MMI (center) and Forbes (bottom) datasets. Examples are shown for luminance values of 50, 125 and 216.

This region is also shown graphically in figure 7. Two illumination metrics were used. Since the CK+ set were grayscale images we evaluate only grayscale metrics.

Luminance was calculated as the average pixel intensity for the facial region. As this only indicates the brightness of the facial region we also compute the contrast of the region.

Figure 13 shows histograms of the mean luminance calculated for the facial region of the first tracked frame of each of the videos. There is a significant difference between the mean luminance in the videos from the Forbes database. The mean is significantly lower for the Forbes set (mean=84.3) versus the MMI (mean=128) and CK+ sets (mean=168), $p<0.05$. However, the deviation in the average luminance for the Forbes (std=45.2), MMI (std=44.0) and CK+ (std=41.1) sets were all similar.

Michelson contrast was calculated using the maximum and minimum pixel luminance values in the facial region. The formula for Michelson Contrast is shown in equation 1.

$$\text{Contrast} = \frac{L_{max} - L_{min}}{L_{max} + L_{min}} \quad (1)$$

Where L_{max} and L_{min} are the maximum and minimum values of the luminance within the facial region of the image under consideration.

Figure 14 shows histograms of the Michelson contrast calculated for the facial region of the first tracked frame in each of the videos. There is a marked difference between the contrast in the videos from the MMI database compared to those from the CK+ and Forbes databases. The contrast seems to be stronger on average for the Forbes set compared to the MMI set. Whether this means that the facial features will be more defined is not clear. However, it demonstrates

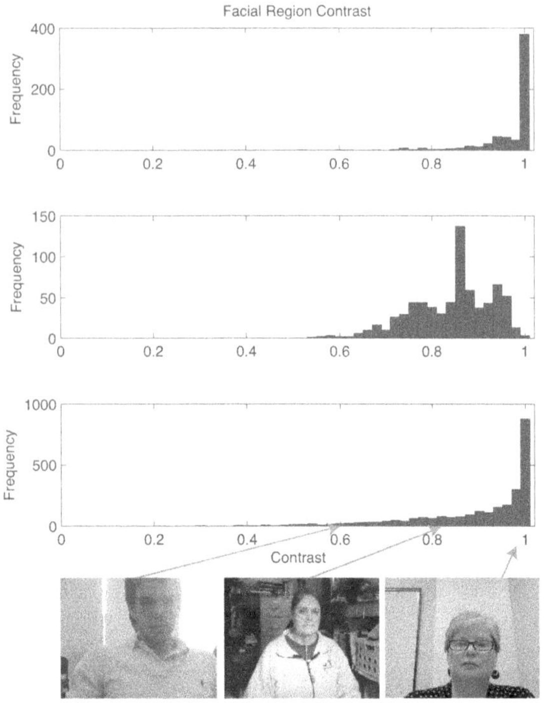

Figure 14: Histograms of the Michelson contrast for the facial region for CK+ (top), MMI (center) and Forbes (bottom) datasets. Examples are shown for luminance values of 0.60, 0.82 and 1.0.

that the current datasets do seem to cover realistic ranges of contrast even though they differ significantly in luminance.

6. CONCLUSIONS

We have presented results from the first crowdsourced collection of natural and spontaneous facial responses over the web. The framework allows very efficient collection of examples of natural and spontaneous responses from a large and varied population. We collected 5,268 videos, of which 3,268 were trackable in over 90% of the frames, over 54 days from locations across the world. These responses are aligned with stimuli that were simultaneously presented to the participants. The method did not require payment or recruitment or the viewers but rather used popular media to motivate opt-in participation. The method has the potential to allow new research questions to be asked in a scalable and ecologically valid way, including the exploration of cross-cultrual differences in emotion expression as well as nonverbal behavior in atypical populations.

We have shown that there are marked differences between the position, scale and pose of participants in these natural interactions compared to those in datasets traditionally used for training expression and affect recognition systems, the MMI and CK+ datasets. In particular we showed that position along the vertical axis of the frame, scale of the face within the field of view of the camera and yaw of the head had significantly different distributions to those in traditional lab-based datasets in which these degrees-of-freedom are often constrained. The results suggest that we need to include significantly more examples that accurately represent the full extent of these ranges in data used for training and testing systems that might be used in the wild. The average head scale was 19% smaller for the Forbes set compared to the other datasets. In addition we identify that there is much greater head and body movement in the data collected when compared to other data sets. Facial expressions occurred simultaneously with these movements and gestures which were often larger than the movements due to the facial expressions. Movement relative to the camera was greatest at the beginning and end of the clips.

Figure 15: Examples of some of the challenges involved in working with crowdsourced data: variable lighting, contrast, color, focus, position, pose, occlusions and number of viewers.

Similarly, we identified a statistically significant difference between the average luminance within the facial region between the Forbes dataset and the CK+ and MMI sets, although the variance of the luminance and the distributions of contrast were not significantly different.

Although, these data demonstrate that the dynamic range of viewer position, pose, movement and illumination are greater than those represented in existing datasets we have shown that we were able to collect thousands of trackable videos via the crowdsourcing platform. This presents a lot of promise for obtaining data for training future algorithms.

7. FUTURE WORK

Over 290 viewers opted to share their response videos with the research community and to allow them to be used in publications, we will make these available soon. We plan to add supplementary facial response labels to these videos.

The data present many challenges from a computer vision perspective in terms of dealing with extreme lighting conditions, occlusions and subtle facial expressions. Some challenging examples are shown in Figure 15.

One obstacle that remains in the collection of large datasets such as this is how to obtain groundtruth labels. If this is to be done by manual coding it could be very time consuming. However, by utilizing other crowdsourcing methods such as the service provided by Amazon's Mechanical Turk it could be feasible to label vast amounts of examples efficiently [23]. Although the labelers may not be "experts" there are several methods for calculating the reliability of such labels [24]. Methods of unsupervised learning for non-verbal data have also been demonstrated [26].

8. ACKNOWLEDGMENTS

Richard Sadowsky, Oliver Wilder-Smith and Affectiva provided generous support in providing access to the crowdsourcing platform. Brian Staats provided a great front end design for the site. Jon Bruner and Forbes kindly promoted the work on their site. This work was funded by the Media Lab Thing's Consortium and Procter and Gamble.

9. REFERENCES

[1] S. Baron-Cohen. *Mind reading: the interactive guide to emotions.* Jessica Kingsley Publishers, 2003.

[2] M. Bartlett, G. Littlewort, M. Frank, C. Lainscsek, I. Fasel, and J. Movellan. Automatic recognition of facial actions in spontaneous expressions. *Journal of Multimedia*, 1(6):22–35, 2006.

[3] M. S. Bartlett, G. Littlewort, I. Fasel, and J. R. Movellan. Real Time Face Detection and Facial Expression Recognition: Development and Applications to Human Computer Interaction. *Computer Vision and Pattern Recognition Workshop*, 5:53, 2003.

[4] J. Bouguet. Pyramidal implementation of the affine lucas kanade feature tracker description of the algorithm. Technical report, Intel Corporation, 2001.

[5] I. Cohen, N. Sebe, A. Garg, L. Chen, and T. Huang. Facial expression recognition from video sequences: temporal and static modeling. *Computer Vision and Image Understanding*, 91(1-2):160–187, 2003.

[6] J. Cohn, L. Reed, Z. Ambadar, J. Xiao, and T. Moriyama. Automatic analysis and recognition of brow actions and head motion in spontaneous facial behavior. In *Systems, Man and Cybernetics, 2004 IEEE International Conference on*, volume 1, pages 610–616. IEEE, 2004.

[7] E. Douglas-Cowie, R. Cowie, I. Sneddon, C. Cox, O. Lowry, M. Mcrorie, J. Martin, L. Devillers, S. Abrilian, A. Batliner, et al. The humaine database: Addressing the collection and annotation of naturalistic and induced emotional data. *Affective computing and intelligent interaction*, pages 488–500, 2007.

[8] J. Hall, J. Carter, and T. Horgan. 5. Gender differences in nonverbal communication of emotion. *Gender and emotion: Social psychological perspectives*, page 97, 2000.

[9] H. Joho, J. Staiano, N. Sebe, and J. Jose. Looking at the viewer: analysing facial activity to detect personal highlights of multimedia contents. *Multimedia Tools and Applications*, pages 1–19, 2011.

[10] G. Littlewort, M. Bartlett, I. Fasel, J. Chenu, and J. Movellan. Analysis of machine learning methods for real-time recognition of facial expressions from video. In *Proceedings of IEEE Conference on Computer Vision and Pattern Recognition*, 2004.

[11] P. Lucey, J. Cohn, T. Kanade, J. Saragih, Z. Ambadar, and I. Matthews. The Extended Cohn-Kanade Dataset (CK+): A complete dataset for action unit and emotion-specified expression. In *Computer Vision and Pattern Recognition Workshops (CVPRW), 2010 IEEE Computer Society Conference on*, pages 94–101. IEEE, 2010.

[12] D. Matsumoto. Cultural similarities and differences in display rules. *Motivation and Emotion*, 14(3):195–214, 1990.

[13] D. McDuff, R. El Kaliouby, K. Kassam, and R. Picard. Affect valence inference from facial action unit spectrograms. In *Computer Vision and Pattern Recognition Workshops (CVPRW), IEEE Computer Society Conference on*, pages 17–24. IEEE, 2010.

[14] G. Mckeown, M. Valstar, R. Cowie, and M. Pantic. The semaine corpus of emotionally coloured character interactions. In *Proceedings of IEEE Int'l Conf. Multimedia, Expo*, pages 1079–1084, July 2010.

[15] P. Michel and R. El Kaliouby. Real time facial expression recognition in video using support vector machines. In *Proceedings of the 5th international conference on Multimodal interfaces*, pages 258–264. ACM, 2003.

[16] M. Pantic, M. Valstar, R. Rademaker, and L. Maat. Web-based database for facial expression analysis. In *2005 IEEE International Conference on Multimedia and Expo*, page 5. IEEE, 2005.

[17] A. Quinn and B. Bederson. Human computation: a survey and taxonomy of a growing field. In *Proceedings of the 2011 annual conference on Human factors in computing systems*, pages 1403–1412. ACM, 2011.

[18] P. Rozin and A. Cohen. High frequency of facial expressions corresponding to confusion, concentration, and worry in an analysis of naturally occurring facial expressions of Americans. *Emotion*, 3(1):68, 2003.

[19] K. Schmidt, Z. Ambadar, J. Cohn, and L. Reed. Movement differences between deliberate and spontaneous facial expressions: Zygomaticus major action in smiling. *Journal of Nonverbal Behavior*, 30(1):37–52, 2006.

[20] D. Svantesson. Geo-location technologies and other means of placing borders on the 'borderless' internet. *J. Marshall J. Computer & Info. L.*, 23:101–845, 2004.

[21] G. Taylor, I. Spiro, C. Bregler, and R. Fergus. Learning Invariance through Imitation. In *Proceedings of IEEE Conference on Computer Vision and Pattern Recognition*, 2011.

[22] M. Valstar and M. Pantic. Induced disgust, happiness and surprise: an addition to the mmi facial expression database. In *Language Resources and Evaluation (LREC), Conference on*, 2010.

[23] C. Vondrick, D. Ramanan, and D. Patterson. Efficiently scaling up video annotation with crowdsourced marketplaces. *Computer Vision–ECCV 2010*, pages 610–623, 2010.

[24] P. Welinder and P. Perona. Online crowdsourcing: Rating annotators and obtaining cost-effective labels. In *Computer Vision and Pattern Recognition Workshops (CVPRW), IEEE Computer Society Conference on*, pages 25–32. IEEE, 2010.

[25] Z. Zeng, M. Pantic, G. Roisman, and T. Huang. A survey of affect recognition methods: Audio, visual, and spontaneous expressions. *Pattern Analysis and Machine Intelligence, IEEE Transactions on*, 31(1):39–58, 2009.

[26] F. Zhou, F. De la Torre, and J. Cohn. Unsupervised discovery of facial events. In *Proceedings of IEEE Conference on Computer Vision and Pattern Recognition*, 2010.

[27] M. Zuckerman, J. Hall, R. DeFrank, and R. Rosenthal. Encoding and decoding of spontaneous and posed facial expressions. *Journal of Personality and Social Psychology*, 34(5):966, 1976.

A Systematic Discussion of Fusion Techniques for Multi-Modal Affect Recognition Tasks

Florian Lingenfelser
Lab for Human Centered Multimedia
University of Augsburg
Universitätsstr. 6
Augsburg, Germany
lingenfelser@hcm-lab.de

Johannes Wagner
Lab for Human Centered Multimedia
University of Augsburg
Universitätsstr. 6
Augsburg, Germany
wagner@hcm-lab.de

Elisabeth André
Lab for Human Centered Multimedia
University of Augsburg
Universitätsstr. 6
Augsburg, Germany
andre@hcm-lab.de

ABSTRACT

Recently, automatic emotion recognition has been established as a major research topic in the area of human computer interaction (HCI). Since humans express emotions through various channels, a user's emotional state can naturally be perceived by combining emotional cues derived from all available modalities. Yet most effort has been put into single-channel emotion recognition, while only a few studies with focus on the fusion of multiple channels have been published. Even though most of these studies apply rather simple fusion strategies – such as the sum or product rule – some of the reported results show promising improvements compared to the single channels. Such results encourage investigations if there is further potential for enhancement if more sophisticated methods are incorporated. Therefore we apply a wide variety of possible fusion techniques such as feature fusion, decision level combination rules, meta-classification or hybrid-fusion. We carry out a systematic comparison of a total of 16 fusion methods on different corpora and compare results using a novel visualization technique. We find that multi-modal fusion is in almost any case at least on par with single channel classification, though homogeneous results within corpora point to interchangeability between concrete fusion schemes.

Categories and Subject Descriptors

I.5.1 [**Computing Methodologies**]: Pattern Recognition

General Terms

Algorithms

Keywords

Emotion Recognition, Multi-Modal Fusion

1. INTRODUCTION

In human interaction, social signals are generally expressed through multiple available modalities. Emotions in particular are illustrated by a combination of vocal behaviour, facial expressions, gestures and postures. One main goal of human computer interaction (HCI) is to make information about a users emotional state available to a machine via automatic emotion recognition and classification. A generic approach to this problem is to choose one type of signal, train the computer to extract and recognize preassigned features and cues from it, and finally associating made observations with predefined emotional classes. But as humans tend to base and refine their predictions on emotional states on more than one modality, a machine should do so too if possible.

This means fusing multi-modal observations at some point of the prediction-process. Generally said this effort can be done at different levels, mainly the feature level by merging cues from all modalities into one classification scheme, or at decision level by combining outputs of several classifiers (one can think of other levels of fusion and we will present some later on). If we however consider the great amount of meanwhile established and further possible ensemble based strategies, the question arises if there exist generally advisable ones or if the success of a strategy is based on the observed problem. The *No Free Lunch Theorem* [15] has proven for supervised machine learning that there is no universally applicable classification scheme for all given classification tasks. When observing all possible problems, solutions perform on an equal level on average. Studies like [3, 9, 8, 4] examine rather basic fusion strategies and sometimes try to give advise on which scheme dominates others. Results are not consistent throughout mentioned experiments, so suspicion that the *No Free Lunch Theorem* holds for combination rules as well as for the underlying classification methods seems reasonable.

In the field of emotion recognition fusion has been mainly applied to audio-visual data. Authors in [16] cite 18 studies dealing with audio-visual fusion. The authors distinguish between feature-, decision- and meta-level fusion, where the latter describes approaches, which use a 2nd-level classifier to combine predictions of the single channels. While none of the mentioned studies uses methods of all three kinds, it is also difficult to compare the results between the studies as they differ greatly in their methodology, as well as, the underlying databases. We will try to enrich the ongoing discussion with a comprehensive comparison of various established and novel fusion strategies, ranging from feature fusion and elaborated decision level combination rules to meta-level and hybrid-fusion. These will be applied to different corpora for emotion recognition in order to directly compare relative recognition-success on different classification-problems. Thus, on the one hand we investigate the general potential of multi-modal fusion compared to single channel emotion recognition and on the other hand give clear hints on benefits of certain fusion schemes or even their interchangeability for future studies. To our best knowledge this is the most comprehensive empirical fusion study applied on audio-visual emotion recognition.

2. APPLIED FUSION TECHNIQUES

When confronted with multi-modal fusion for audio-visual emotion recognition, a vast amount of eligible fusion strategies come into consideration. In the following, possible fusion techniques for combining available modalities are presented and discussed in detail. For the sake of clear arrangement, possible methods can be differentiated by the levels on which they are executed. Fusion at decision level can be further sub-divided into class-label combination strategies, algebraic combination rules and specialist selection methods.

2.1 Feature Level Fusion

A very straightforward way to fuse all observed channels is to merge all calculated features into a single and high dimensional feature set. One classifier is then trained for the task of classification. The accumulated features contain a bigger amount of information than a single modality. Thus, increased classification accuracy can theoretically be expected. The eventually occurring *Curse of Dimensionality* has to be accounted for on small datasets. If the available observations are not proportional to the amount of features covered by a sole classifier, the classification results become non-meaningful. As a second, it has to be mentioned that a growing feature vector may stress computational resources. However, appliance of feature selection techniques may relieve both problems.

2.2 Decision Level Fusion

Decision level fusion sums up combination rules[1] for the outputs of several classification models. Instead of using all available features for a sole classifier, the available feature set is divided into subgroups (e.g. one classifier per modality) and the partitions are used to form classifiers. The assembly of these classifiers is called an ensemble. The outcomes of these slim classifier models are taken into account for the final decision making process.

2.2.1 Class-Label Combination

Voting could be considered the most generic approach to decision level fusion, because it simply combines class labels gained from T classifiers by summing up decisions. The ensemble decision for an observed sample x is chosen to be the class ω_n which received the most votes (decisions) v_n. A definite decision is only guaranteed if an odd number of ensemble members handle a two-class problem (thus it is not capable of producing definite decisions in many practical applications and is therefore often replaced by the weighted variant).

$$v_n(x) = \sum_{t=1}^{T} d_{t,n}(x)$$

In Weighted Majority Voting each vote is associated with a pre-calculated weight (in our case weights are determined by evaluations of classifiers on training data) of the ensemble member. Ties are not likely to happen this way, which makes the weighted variant more suited for most classification problems.

Another way of combining the class labels generated by ensemble members is to construct a lookup-table. This method is introduced by [5] as Behavior Knowledge Space (BKS). During training the table counts combinations of labelling outputs together with the true class and occurrences of this composition. Test samples then are compared to that table and the true class for which the currently observed labelling combination was recorded most often gets chosen as ensemble decision.

2.2.2 Algebraic Combination Rules

Algebraic combiners for continuous outputs mathematically compute the ensemble decision from probabilities for each class over all classifiers. The Maximum Rule and Minimum Rule respectively choose the maximum or minimum support generated by T ensemble members. The ensemble decision for an observed sample x is chosen to be the class ω_n for which support $\mu_n(x)$ is largest.

$$\mu_n(x) = max, min_{t=1..T}\{s_{t,n}(x)\}$$

The Sum Rule simply sums up the support given to each class ω_n in order to generate total support μ_n for each class. By averaging the support ($\frac{1}{T}$ serves as normalization factor) given to each class ω_n we obtain the Mean Rule. When additionally adding classifier weights w_t, the Weighted Average method calculates total support μ_n for class n as:

$$\mu_n(x) = \frac{1}{T}\sum_{t=1}^{T} w_t s_{t,n}(x)$$

By multiplying the support given to each class ω_n, the Product Rule determines total support μ_n for class n as:

$$\mu_n(x) = \frac{1}{T}\prod_{t=1}^{T} s_{t,n}(x)$$

The following two combination rules make more extensive use of continuous outputs of ensemble classifiers. Given sample x, the decision profile $DP(x)$ for T ensemble members contains the probability distributions among N classes:

$$DP(x) = \begin{array}{c|c|c} s_{1,1}(x) & \dots & s_{1,N}(x) \\ \hline \dots & \dots & \dots \\ \hline s_{T,1}(x) & \dots & s_{T,N}(x) \end{array}$$

Decision template DT_n can then be defined for each class ω_n as respective decision profile during training, averaged by the cardinality of observed class. Given an unlabelled test-sample x, we first construct $DP(x)$ from ensemble members and then calculate similarity (as Squared Euclidean distance) S between $DP(x)$ and the decision template DT_n for

[1]For the explanation of reviewed algorithms the following annotations are used: The decision of ensemble member t for class n is denoted as $d_{t,n} \in \{0, 1\}$, with $t = 1..T$ and $n = 1..N$ and $d_{t,n} = 1$ if class ω_n is chosen, $d_{t,n} = 0$ otherwise. The support given to each class n (i.e. the calculated probability for the observed sample to belong to single classes) by classifier t is described as $s_{t,n} \in [1, 0]$.

each class ω_n. Finally the most similar class is chosen as ensemble decision.

Further utilisation of decision templates is based on on the Dempster-Shafer theory of evidence [12]. It can be applied to decision making by interpreting the classifiers outputs as a measure of evidence. Instead of similarities, proximities and resulting beliefs (evidence) is calculated. This represents the belief in one classifier correctly classifying observed instance into respective classes. Following Dempsters rule of combination, these beliefs can be multiplied throughout the ensemble in order to obtain the final decision.

2.2.3 *Specialist Selection*

In contrary to the fusion schemes described so far, the Cascading Specialists [6] method does not focus on merging outputs from all ensemble members, but on selecting specialists for each class and bringing them in a reasonable order. In a preparation step, experts for every class of the classification problem (based on evaluation of training data) are chosen. Next, classes are rank ordered, from worst classified class across all classifiers to the best one. The algorithm for classification works as follows: First class in the sequence is chosen and the corresponding expert is asked to classify the sample. If the output matches the currently observed class, this classification is chosen as ensemble decision. If not, the sample is passed on to the next weaker class and corresponding expert whilst repeating the strategy. Whenever the case occurs that none of the experts classifies its connected class, the classifier with the best overall performance on the training data is selected as final instance and is asked to label the sample. This strategy aims at a flattening effect among class accuracies that will – at best – improve overall classification performance.

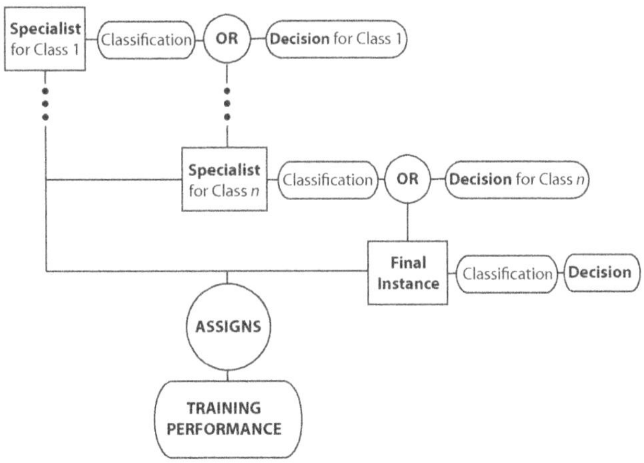

Figure 1: Cascading Specialists Scheme

2.3 Meta Level Fusion

In meta level fusion, the outputs of several ensemble classifiers are not fused by predefined combination rules. Instead their results are used as input for one or more meta classification models, that generate the final ensemble decision. This process is lent from meta-classification and conforming to notations used by Wolpert and Macready, ensemble classifiers correspond to level-0 base classifiers, the meta classifiers fusing their results equate to level-1 meta generalisers.

In Stacked Generalisation – as proposed by [13] – a level-1 classifier tries to learn the probability distribution among level-0 ensemble classifiers together with the true class that lead to this combination. When asked to classify an unknown sample x, the method first collects probability estimates of all ensemble members that consecutively form the basis for the level-1 classifier's final prediction.

Another approach to meta-classification is Grading [11], where the goal of level-1 classifiers is to correct potentially false decisions of level-0 ensemble members. During training every base classifier is complemented by a meta classifier with same training data but a graded label – a boolean value stating correct or incorrect prediction of the ensemble classifier. At classification time our implementation fuses ensemble predictions as every member adds the probability of correctness (generated by it's grading classifier) to the final support of the class it predicted. As usual, the class with highest support is chosen as final ensemble decision.

2.4 Hybrid Fusion

In this study we use the term hybrid fusion to characterise fusion techniques that incorporate classifiers with merged features into used ensembles and therefore combine decision and feature level fusion. Of course this approach is applicable to most ensemble combination rules discussed so far, but we decided to develop a refined fusion scheme with two variants in order to explore the capabilities of hybrid fusion.

The One Versus Rest approach trains N classifiers on every available feature-set (excluding merged features), each specialised in recognising one of N classes. This breakdown on several two-class classification problems is done by relabelling. Additionally the ensemble is completed by one multi-class classification model trained on the merged feature set.

Given test-sample x, variant one multiplies probabilities gained from classifiers trained on recognising class n with the associated probability generated by the multi-class classification model. This is done for classes $1..N$ and the class with the highest accumulated support gets chosen as ensemble decision. Variant two chooses among the two-class classification models the most promising one for every class. The specialist's probability is then summed with the respective probability from the multi-class classification model.

3. AFFECTIVE CORPORA

To draw a comparison of the presented fusion techniques we use two different corpora - the DaFEx and CALLAS corpus. These corpora have been chosen as they both contain audio-visual recordings of Italians. They differ, however, in the number of expressed emotional states and their level of naturalness. In the past most studies dealing with the recognition of emotions were based on recordings from professional actors. Lately, we can observe an increasing trend towards more natural data sets. It turned out that findings derived from acted data must not necessarily be transferred to spontaneous emotions [14]. Using corpora of both kinds allows us to investigate to what extent the choice of the fusion technique depends also on the naturalness of the observed data.

The DaFEx corpus [1] contains recordings of 8 professional Italian actors (4 male and 4 female) expressing 6 basic emotions and neutral. It was initially constructed as a benchmark for the evaluation of facial expressivity of Embodied

Conversional Agents, but is well suited for the evaluation of emotion recognition systems, too (see e. g. [10]). It consists of 1008 short videos clips, where each clip corresponds to one the basic emotions happiness, surprise, fear, sadness, anger and disgust, or neutral. The facial expressions are available at 3 intensity levels (low, medium and high), but for our purpose are combined to a single class. Finally, we select only those samples, where the actors were also uttering a sentence, resulting in 84 samples per subject equally distributed among the 7 classes.

The CALLAS expressivity corpus [2] was constructed within the European Integrated Project CALLAS. Designed for examination of cultural differences it was actually recorded in three countries, Germany, Italy and Greece. In contrast to the DaFEx corpus participants in the CALLAS corpus have no special acting abilities and were asked to perform expressions in the three broad categories positive, neutral and negative. For this study we only consider the Italian subcorpus consisting of 1539 samples of 13 persons (7 female and 6 male) equally distributed among the three classes. Specific emotions were elicited by a mood induction technique. For this study samples were consequently labelled corresponding to the state of the stimuli sentences.

4. METHODOLOGY OF EXPERIMENTS

Extraction of descriptive features is a necessary step to convert the raw signals into the compact form required for classification. From the audio channel we extract acoustic features related to the paralinguistic message of speech, i. e. "how" something is said. MFCCs and spectral features as well as prosodic features from pitch, energy, duration, voicing and voice quality total to the amount of 1316 features calculated by EmoVoice[2]. For video analysis we use SHORE, a library for facial emotion detection developed by Fraunhofer IIS[3] [7]. For each face detected, SHORE is able to extract a set of features including amongst others the position of the face, the eyes, nose and mouth, as well as information whether the eyes or the mouth are open or closed. Collected for each frame, these values build a series of 24 short-term features. Together with the calculation of 11 long-term measurements, we obtain a facial feature set with 264 entries.

Both resulting feature sets are then reduced by correlation based feature selection followed by a sequential forward search – a simple but popular wrapper approach that uses a classifier to determine significant features. This and all other classification tasks within this study is done via Naive Bayes. This classification model is a probabilistic classifier based on the Bayes' theorem, which makes the (unrealistic) assumption that the presence (or absence) of a particular feature of a class is unrelated to the presence (or absence) of any other feature. Hence, the probability for the occurrence of a certain category given a set of observations can be estimated as the product of the individual attributes. We chose this rather simple classification scheme due to its successful application in earlier emotion recognition tasks [14] and its fast computation, which allows us to run our experiments in a reasonable amount of time. After feature selection 35 audio and 40 video features remained for the DaFEx corpus, while on the CALLAS corpus 64 audio and 45 video features were chosen.

For evaluation of made experiments we agreed on a realistic, user independent approach: Leave-One-Person-Out. We consecutively draw samples belonging to one subject out of the available corpus. Remaining samples are used for training of classification models which then are tested against the isolated samples. The procedure is repeated until every person was once evaluated.

The described analysis was implemented and run with the Social Signal Interpretation (SSI) framework. SSI offers tools to record, analyse and recognize human behaviour in real-time, such as gestures, mimics, head nods, and emotional speech. In particularly it supports the machine learning pipeline in its full length and suits the fusion of multimodal information at different stages including early and late fusion. SSI is written in C++ and source code is available under LGPL[4].

5. RESULTS

Results for DaFEx and CALLAS corpora are summarised in Table 1. For the DaFEx data we observe an improvement of up to 7% and 10% compared to classification results on the audio and video channel. Here, BKS and One Versus Rest turn out to give the best performance closely followed by Feature Fusion, Mean Rule, Sum Rule, Weighted Average, Product Rule, Grading and One Versus Rest-Specialists. All in all, remarkable are results established across all fusion levels on the acted affective corpus.

In case of the more natural CALLAS corpus no improvement is achieved compared to the audio channel. However, on the video channel an enhancement of up to 8% is observed. Except for Grading and Min Rule results of all other fusion strategies lie within 3%.

Across corpora, simple fusion techniques like Feature Fusion as well as Mean, Sum and Product Rule perform on a very stable basis. More elaborate strategies seem to be more reliant on the structure of observed data. For example, the Cascading Specialist method generates the desired flattening effect among classes on the CALLAS corpus and therefore lists among the best fusion approaches. In contrary, needed specialist selection seems to be harder on the DaFEx corpus and it ranges among worst combination rules. Sophisticated ensemble strategies bare the potential to outperform more simple ones, but success is not guaranteed. Differences in accuracy tend to be rather small among all considered fusion techniques.

6. DISCUSSION

In Figure 2 recognition results are visualized per sample, as we compare the prediction for each sample with its real label. If the sample was correctly classified, it is marked with a white square, otherwise with a black one. Each column represents one sample of the data set and each row stands for the used classification method. The first row, for instance, visualizes classification results obtained for the single audio channel. We can for example infer from the DaFEx pattern on top of Figure 2 that the first two samples were correctly classified by audio, video and most fusion schemes, while sample three and four were obviously misclassified.

[2]http://hcm-lab.de/EmoVoice.html

[3]http://www.iis.fraunhofer.de/en/bf/bv/ks/gpe/demo/

[4]http://hcm-lab.de/ssi.html

	DaFEx								CALLAS			
	anger	disgust	fear	happiness	neutral	sad	surprise	**average**	positive	neutral	negative	**average**
Single Modalities												
Audio	0.39	0.32	0.43	0.21	0.86	0.67	0.25	**0.45**	0.59	0.64	0.61	**0.61**
Video	0.57	0.34	0.11	0.82	0.72	0.59	0.22	**0.48**	0.60	0.50	0.48	**0.53**
Feature Level Fusion												
FeatureFusion	0.54	0.36	0.36	0.79	0.77	0.70	0.26	**0.54**	0.57	0.59	0.62	**0.59**
Decision Level Fusion												
WeightedMajorityVoting	0.57	0.34	0.11	0.82	0.72	0.59	0.22	**0.48**	0.59	0.64	0.61	**0.61**
BKS	0.53	0.45	0.30	0.84	0.85	0.51	0.35	**0.55**	0.62	0.62	0.56	**0.60**
MaxRule	0.48	0.31	0.22	0.80	0.84	0.69	0.16	**0.50**	0.62	0.55	0.64	**0.60**
MinRule	0.44	0.39	0.41	0.44	0.73	0.59	0.39	**0.48**	0.56	0.61	0.55	**0.57**
MeanRule	0.52	0.38	0.36	0.79	0.78	0.71	0.26	**0.54**	0.59	0.58	0.59	**0.59**
SumRule	0.52	0.38	0.36	0.79	0.78	0.71	0.26	**0.54**	0.59	0.58	0.59	**0.59**
WeightedAverage	0.58	0.41	0.28	0.83	0.77	0.66	0.23	**0.54**	0.61	0.58	0.58	**0.59**
ProductRule	0.50	0.39	0.38	0.79	0.77	0.70	0.27	**0.54**	0.59	0.58	0.59	**0.59**
DecisionTemplate	0.51	0.41	0.30	0.67	0.81	0.61	0.22	**0.50**	0.57	0.60	0.59	**0.59**
DempsterShafer	0.48	0.41	0.31	0.67	0.81	0.59	0.25	**0.50**	0.56	0.62	0.59	**0.59**
CascadingSpecialists	0.35	0.38	0.44	0.53	0.90	0.66	0.27	**0.50**	0.60	0.63	0.61	**0.61**
Meta Level Fusion												
StackedGeneralisation	0.53	0.40	0.39	0.72	0.74	0.61	0.28	**0.52**	0.59	0.57	0.64	**0.60**
Grading	0.60	0.44	0.18	0.80	0.89	0.64	0.23	**0.54**	0.67	0.50	0.49	**0.55**
Hybrid Fusion												
OneVersusRest	0.53	0.34	0.36	0.83	0.79	0.71	0.25	**0.55**	0.59	0.59	0.60	**0.59**
OneVersusRest-Specialists	0.59	0.31	0.40	0.82	0.76	0.70	0.21	**0.54**	0.60	0.58	0.63	**0.60**

Table 1: Recognition results for DaFEx and CALLAS corpora

A clear characteristic shown by this visualisation on both corpora is the behaviour of fusion schemes in relation to single modalities. Depending on the outcomes of audio and video, there is a clear trend of forming white and black vertical columns within the picture: If both modalities classify correctly, most fusion approaches do so too; if both channels misinterpret the sample, most fusion strategies fail. Especially algebraic combiners like the sum or product rule amplify consistent (correct or incorrect) ensemble decisions because of their inherent combination rules. An exception to this trend is shown by some decision level approaches (BKS, decision template and dempster shafer) and the meta-learners of stacked generalisation and grading: These approaches are meant to learn the behaviour of available modalities. The logical connection between observed ensemble members' decisions and the actual true-class enables the phenomenon of "error learning" and therefore the potential of generating correct predictions though both modalities classify incorrect. This is visualized by white break-ups in black columns caused by consistent miss-classification of audio and video. Figure 2 unfortunately show that this desirable "error-learning" is also the reason for these ensemble methods to predict wrong classes even though both modalities chose the correct one – an undesirable characteristic that is not likely to be manifested by more simple fusion schemes.

Both modalities perform on an equal level in the DaFEx corpus (with a slightly better video channel), the more realistic CALLAS corpus clearly shows better results on prosodic observations and therefore the audio channel outperforms the facial modality (though former studies like [17] have shown a rather contrary behaviour). These results may be caused by the appliance of mood-inducing sentences for CALLAS sample generation: As the DaFEx corpus features professional actors, vocal and facial expressions are be expressed on an equally convincing level, while the unexperienced CALLAS probands focus strongly on expressing the given sentences verbally. Sample-wise recognition outcomes for the two modalities are therefore clearly more consistent on the DaFEx corpus than on CALLAS data. Some fusion strategies seem to benefit from consistency of modalities, leading to improved fusion results compared to the single channel-classifiers on the DaFEx corpus. But then again do recognition accuracies on the CALLAS corpus show the potential of combination rules to handle disagreeing modalities in away so that at least comparable results to the best channel can be received. However, it is difficult to recognize from the graphs in Figure 2, what exactly causes a potential gain in recognition accuracy for combination rules compared to the two single channels. To carve out those samples, which are misclassified in one of the single channels, but correctly recognized after fusion, we have included Figure 3.

Figure 3 compare sample-wise the results obtained from the superior modality with the results for the fusion techniques. For each corpus, the topmost row again shows sample-wise classification results for respective best modality. Within the following block we mark for each fusion strategy those samples with a white square, which receive a false recognition on the observed channel, but a correct one if fused with a further modality. The numbers behind listed methods gives the amount of relative improvement. Within the lower block, samples which are correctly predicted from the video channel, but misclassified after fusion with the audio channel are marked black. The numbers behind the method now illustrates the amount of impairment. For example did Feature Fusion correct 13% of the misses in the video channel on the DaFEx corpus. On the other hand it failed in 7% of the cases in which the facial modality did classify correctly. This leads to an overall improvement of 6% compared to the video channel.

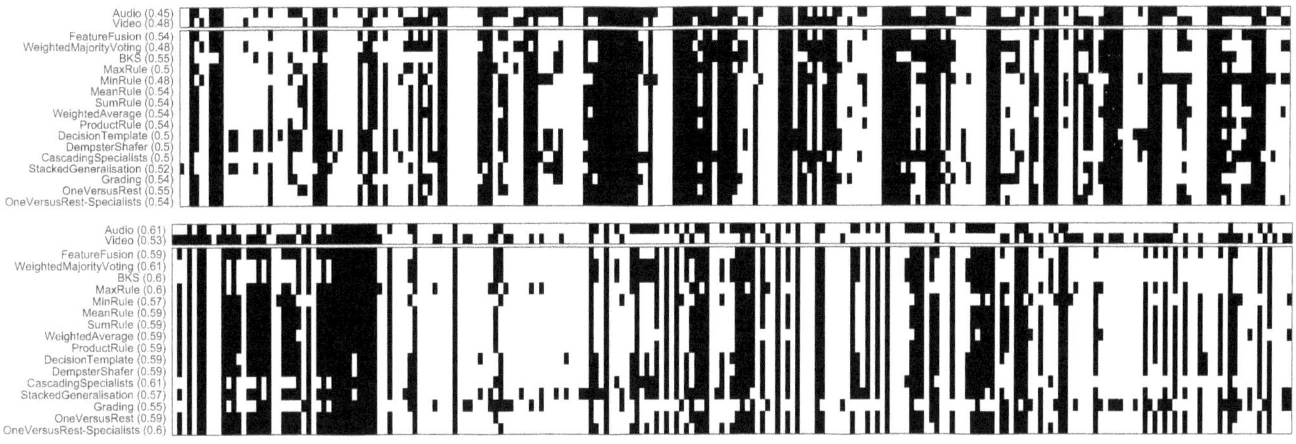

Figure 2: Visualization of predictions for excerpts of the DaFEx and CALLAS samples

Again, a clear trend to vertical columns in the patterns is obvious. This means that gains and losses of different fusion schemes are – most generally spoken – produced on the same samples. Outlying improvements achieved by elaborate ensemble combination techniques like the mentioned "error learning" are subsequently lost by outlying misclassification, caused by just this technique. The same regularities become apparent if we compare the amount of improvement with the amount of impairment between the different fusion methods. Obviously does a high amount of positive correction on miss-classified samples come along with a high number of errors on samples that were already correctly classified. For instance, on DaFEx we improve correct classification on 16% of the samples with stacked generalisation, but at the same time also lose a correct prediction in 11%, while for the weighted average rule a smaller improvement of 10% is accompanied by a lesser impairment of 5% (note that these numbers describe absolute, sample-wise values and do not directly transfer into class-wise recognition rates presented in Table 5). The difference between both values is more or less the same for all tested methods. On the CALLAS corpus rates for improvement are mostly smaller than generated impairments (as the audio channel clearly performs better than the facial modality), resulting at best in equal recognition results for some ensemble approaches as for the single modality classification with vocal features.

Made observations imply to a certain degree an interchangeability of presented fusion schemes. Sample-wise investigations show a common recognition-behaviour and gains in some specialised areas are paid for in others. Fusion techniques, on the other hand, have the potential to outperform single-channel classification on multi-modal datasets. Results are either considerably improved (DaFEx) or at least in line with the dominating modality (CALLAS). This characteristic is especially desirable, whenever the best modality is not known in advance. But is there a generally advisable fusion scheme? Performance of different strategies lie within a close range, sophisticated methods do not necessarily outperform simple combination rules. Without prior knowledge, appliance of feature fusion simple algebraic combiners seems reasonable, as they perform stable across different datasets despite simple mechanisms.

7. CONCLUSION

In this study we performed a comprehensive comparison of fusion techniques for multi-modal affect recognition tasks. Experiments were run on two Italian emotion corpora featuring vocal and facial modalities: The acted DaFex corpus and the more natural CALLAS expressivity corpus. Implemented fusion rules included feature, decision, meta and hybrid level strategies and results were discussed using novel visualisations. We found interesting, common characteristics among ensemble methods as well as uncommon effects like "error learning". Though a certain degree of interchangeability between tested fusion approaches can be suspected – and therefore no fusion scheme can be advised in general – are most approaches capable of enhancing single channel classification or are at least on par with the superior modality, if inconsistency of observed modalities prevent further improvements. Inconsistencies of fusion schemes performances across corpora make no strategy advisable in general, the applied fusion method should be chosen based on the underlying classification problem.

8. ACKNOWLEDGMENTS

The presented work is funded by the EU under research grant CALLAS (IST-34800) and CEEDS (FP7-ICT-2009-5).

9. REFERENCES

[1] A. Battocchi, F. Pianesi, and D. Goren-Bar. Dafex: Database of facial expressions. In M. T. Maybury, O. Stock, and W. Wahlster, editors, *INTETAIN*, volume 3814 of *Lecture Notes in Computer Science*, pages 303–306. Springer, 2005.

[2] G. Caridakis, J. Wagner, A. Raouzaiou, Z. Curto, E. André, and K. Karpouzis. A multimodal corpus for gesture expressivity analysis. Multimodal Corpora: Advances in Capturing, Coding and Analyzing Multimodality, LREC, Malta, 2010.

[3] R. Duin and D. Tax. Experiments with classifier combining rules. In *Lecture Notes in Computer Science*, volume 1857, pages 16–29. Springer, 2000.

[4] G. Fumera and F. Roli. A theoretical and experimental analysis of linear combiners for multiple classifier

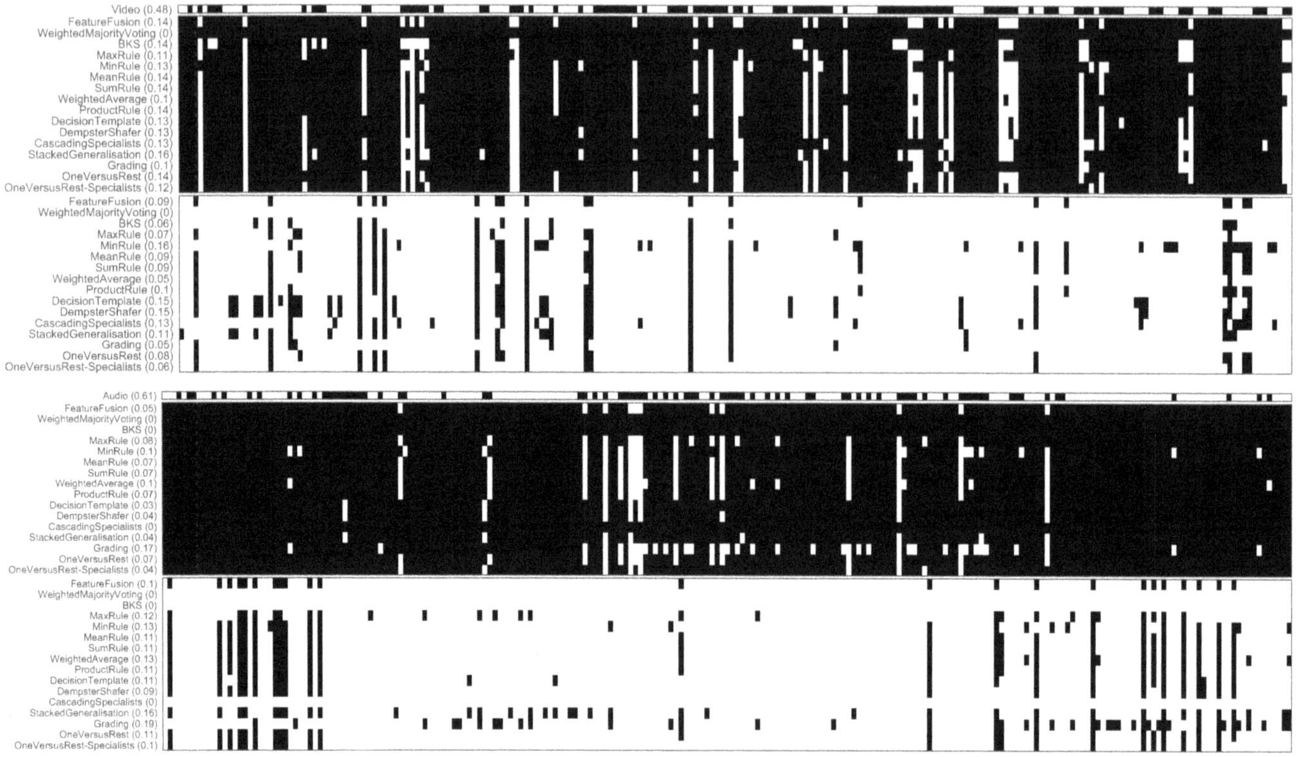

Figure 3: Visualization of recognition improvements and impairs of the DaFEx and CALLAS samples

systems. *IEEE Transactions on Pattern Analysis and Machine Intelligence*, 27(6):942–956, 2005.

[5] Y. S. Huang and C. Y. Suen. Behavior-knowledge space method for combination of multiple classifiers. *Proc. of IEEE Computer Vision and Pattern Rcog.*, 20:347–352, 1993.

[6] J. Kim and F. Lingenfelser. Ensemble approaches to parametric decision fusion for bimodal emotion recognition. In *Int. Conf. on Bio-inspired Systems and Signal Processing (Biosignals 2010)*, 2010.

[7] C. Küblbeck and A. Ernst. Face detection and tracking in video sequences using the modifiedcensus transformation. *Image Vision Comput.*, 24:564–572, June 2006.

[8] L. I. Kuncheva. Switching between selection and fusion in combining classifiers: An experiment. *IEEE Transactions on Systems, Man, and Cybernetics, Part B: Cybernetics*, 32(2):146–156, 2002.

[9] L. I. Kuncheva. A theoretical study on six classifier fusion strategies. *IEEE Transactions on Pattern Analysis and Machine Intelligence*, 24(2):281–286, 2002.

[10] A. Rabie, B. Wrede, T. Vogt, and M. Hanheide. Evaluation and discussion of multi-modal emotion recognition. In *Proceedings of the 2009 Second International Conference on Computer and Electrical Engineering - Volume 01*, ICCEE '09, pages 598–602, Washington, DC, USA, 2009. IEEE Computer Society.

[11] A. K. Seewald and J. Fuernkranz. An evaluation of grading classifiers. In *Advances in In Intelligent Data Analysis, 4th International Conference, IDA 2001, Proceedings*, volume 10, pages 271–289. Springer, 2001.

[12] G. Shafer. *A Mathematical Theory of Evidence*. NJ: Princeton Univ. Press, Princeton, 1976.

[13] K. M. Ting and I. H. Witten. Issues in stacked generalization. *Journal of Artificial Intelligence Research*, 10:115–124, 1999.

[14] T. Vogt and E. André. Comparing feature sets for acted and spontaneous speech in view of automatic emotion recognition. In *IEEE International Conference on Multimedia & Expo (ICME 2005)*, 2005.

[15] D. H. Wolpert and W. G. Macready. No free lunch theorems for optimization. *IEEE Transactions on Evolutionary Computation*, 1(1):67–82, 1996.

[16] Z. Zeng, M. Pantic, G. I. Roisman, and T. S. Huang. A survey of affect recognition methods: Audio, visual, and spontaneous expressions. *IEEE transactions on pattern analysis and machine intelligence*, 31(1):39–58, January 2009.

[17] Z. Zeng, J. Tu, M. Liu, T. Zhang, N. Rizzolo, Z. Zhang, T. S. Huang, D. Roth, and S. Levinson. Bimodal hci-related affect recognition. In *Proceedings of the 6th international conference on Multimodal interfaces*, pages 137–143, 2004.

Adaptive Facial Expression Recognition Using Inter-modal Top-down Context

Ravi Kiran Sarvadevabhatla
Honda Research Institute USA
425 National Ave, Suite 100
Mountain View 94043, USA
RSarvadevabhatla@hra.com

Mitchel Benovoy
Neural Prosthetics Lab
Department of Electrical and Computer Engineering
McGill University
Montreal H3A 2A7, Canada
benovoym@mcgill.ca

Sam Musallam
Neural Prosthetics Lab
Department of Electrical and Computer Engineering
McGill University
Montreal H3A 2A7, Canada
sam.musallam@mcgill.ca

Victor Ng-Thow-Hing
Honda Research Institute USA
425 National Ave, Suite 100
Mountain View 94043, USA
vngthowhing@hra.com

ABSTRACT

The role of context in recognizing a person's affect is being increasingly studied. In particular, context arising from the presence of multi-modal information such as faces, speech and head pose has been used in recent studies to recognize facial expressions. In most approaches, the modalities are independently considered and the effect of one modality on the other, which we call inter-modal influence (e.g. speech or head pose modifying the facial appearance) is not modeled. In this paper, we describe a system that utilizes context from the presence of such inter-modal influences to recognize facial expressions. To do so, we use 2-D contextual masks which are activated within the facial expression recognition pipeline depending on the prevailing context. We also describe a framework called the Context Engine. The Context Engine offers a scalable mechanism for extending the current system to address additional modes of context that may arise during human-machine interactions. Results on standard data sets demonstrate the utility of modeling inter-modal contextual effects in recognizing facial expressions.

Categories and Subject Descriptors

I.5.4 [**Pattern Recognition**]: Applications—*Computer Vision,Signal Processing*

General Terms

Algorithms, Design, Experimentation

Keywords

facial expression recognition, multi-modal, context, mask, human-computer interaction

1. INTRODUCTION

With growing prevalence of mobile devices and natural user interfaces, there is a need for applications that monitor and help understand the user's affective state (such as anger, sadness, happiness, etc.). Such user-aware applications provide a better scope for adapting and shaping the overall interaction experience into an engaging and enjoyable one. Among the methods to understand the affective state, facial expression recognition has been the dominant choice. Depending on the application domain, many varieties of facial appearances are encountered. For example, faces can occupy a relatively high percentage of screen area for mobile device applications while in human-robot interaction, they may be smaller due to the distance of the person from the cameras on the robot. There are numerous other factors such as lighting and changing head pose that need to be addressed while determining facial expressions.

In general, facial expressions are influenced by the overall context which typically operates in a top-down fashion [3][5]. In real-life situations, there are many categories of context that determine affect such as physical,sensory,multi-modal, cultural and temporal. For example, multi-modal context attempts to capture factors arising from the presence of multiple affect modalities such as speech, body posture and gesture and combinations thereof. Temporal context captures factors emerging from the knowledge of what has happened within a neighborhood of time of affect expression. This could be a sequence of events or incidents which informs the affect interpretation.

Among these categories, we are particularly interested in multi-modal and temporal contexts. This is in light of observations from recent results that context established from multi-modal and temporal information can lead to increased robustness and accuracy beyond considering just a single (usually visual) modality [18][29][23][36]. In the majority of these cases, though, the modalities are considered to be independent sources of information and the effect of one modality on the other, which we call *inter-modal influence*, is not modeled. In fact, if we examine the basic frameworks for many of the existing multi-modal methods, we see that they consist of directly analyzing multi-modal features which in turn are used to train a classifier [18][29][23]. However, certain contexts (e.g. obscuring part of the face with hands, speaking while expressing surprise) may render some or all of the features unreliable. Therefore, it would be certainly beneficial to determine the temporal and spatial reliability of features from a particular modality as the affect unfolds and utilize the information therein to recognize it. As we show in this paper, exploiting even rudimentary knowledge from the inter-modal influence such as type of modality and its onset and duration can provide additional information which can help remove outliers and improve accuracy for facial expression recognition.

1.1 Contributions

In this work, we describe a facial expression recognition system which can utilize context arising from the presence of inter-modal information (speech or head pose available along with facial appearance) to determine affect. We adopt a simple but effective strategy based on the modal context: 2-D *contextual masks* are dynamically applied to facial feature locations influenced by the current context and based on these features, classification is performed. Once the particular context ceases to be active, the corresponding mask ceases to be applied. A more detailed explanation can be found in Section 3 where we describe our system including details of the mask design and its application.

We demonstrate the effectiveness of this strategy in Section 4 with results on a standard multi-modal data-set. In addition, we also show the general effectiveness of our facial expression recognition pipeline over existing methods on a non-multi-modal dataset.

As a second contribution, we also describe the broader framework in which the facial expression recognition is performed. This framework, called the *Context Engine*(Section 3.1), offers a scalable mechanism to address various modes of context that arise during human-machine interaction.

It must be pointed out that each modality does offer additional information(e.g. pitch, prosody in speech signal) beyond merely its presence or absence at a given moment. While such information can certainly be utilized to improve the recognition performance [12][18], utilizing such additional information is not the focus of this work. However, our framework does not preclude such a possibility.

2. RELATED WORK

Researchers have examined the temporal evolution of multimodal features such as head nods [20], full head pose [24][16] and speech-based features [15][23] which can detect a potentially wider range of affective states and establish appropriate context. For a survey of multi-modal approaches, refer to [36].

The large variety of the methods for facial expression recognition is reflected in the feature extraction component of the pipeline. On one hand, here are facial feature point-based features such as Active Appearance Models (AAM) [14] and Facial Action Parameters (FAP) [32]. These methods can be used to monitor the shape of the face in fine detail but given the localized and small footprint of the points, they do not work well at all scales (e.g. when the face is situated at a distance from the camera). On the other hand, patch-based features such as Local Binary Patterns provide good facial expression discrimination while being fast to compute and offer reasonable scale invariance [30]. Since our aim is to have the system work in multiple scenarios (close-in faces as well as far away) while maintaining interactive responsiveness, we adopt the LBP features in our work(Section 3.2).

The notion of applying masks to facial features used in our work (see Section 3.4) is partly motivated by studies which have examined the saliency of facial regions for expression recognition [3]. Some of these studies have examined the saliency based on different emotional contexts. For example, [13] had viewers categorize facial expressions while being presented with only the top half or bottom half segments of the face. Their result indicated that some expressions (such as anger) were more recognizable from the top half whereas others (such as disgust) were better recognized from the bottom half. [28] use a data-driven approach, similar to ours, to arrive at precise masks which localize to specific sub-regions of the face.

3. SYSTEM OVERVIEW

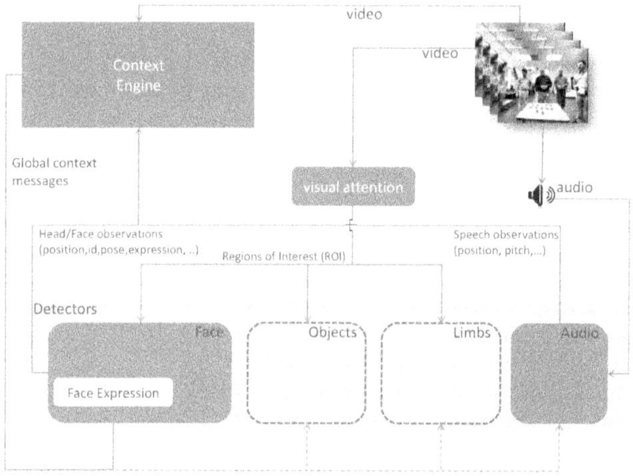

Figure 1: An overview of our system architecture. Labels alongside the lines connecting modules indicate the type of data that passes between them. Dotted lines indicate planned additions and solid boxes indicate currently deployed modules.

We now briefly describe some of the important components of our overall system. Low-level cues are collected from sensor modalities using the attention system and assigned semantic label(s) using specialized modality-specific **Detectors**(see Figure 1). The localized and specialized nature of low-level attentional processing provides speedup while minimizing false positives during the process of assigning semantics. The semantically-labeled cues produced by the **Detectors** form evidence streams. These are processed within the *Context Engine* to register the presence of higher-level entities such as people whose state information can be delivered to other modules via context messages.

Visual attention: This module implements a low-level human-like bottom-up visual attentional mechanism [27]. It acts as a filter on the video frames and produces the so-called Regions of Interest (ROIs) – designated areas of the image which are deemed salient according to certain criteria [19]. In the process of generating ROIs, relevant feature maps are generated from incoming video frames. Since our domain of interest involves human interactions, we compute feature maps which extract skin regions. The generated ROIs are processed by select modules among the set of **Detectors**(E.g.face or limb detectors).

Detectors: The outputs from the visual attention (the ROIs mentioned above) as well as raw sensory streams (such as audio data from microphones) are independent of semantic information. Such outputs are processed by detectors which assign semantics. The video-based ROIs are semantically labeled as faces, limbs, object observations and for auditory data the semantic labeling results in speech observations. Such observations are collected as evidence streams which in turn are used to establish the state of cognitively higher-level entities within the *Context Engine*(see Section 3.1). We now briefly describe the detector modules used in our system.

Audio module: This module operates on the raw audio signal obtained from a microphone array. After processing, we obtain information about presence of speech (if any) and angular direction of speech utterances relative to the position of the microphone array. This information forms the speech observations that are processed within the *Context Engine*.

Face module: This module processes ROIs from visual attention as input and produces facial feature information when a face is present within the ROI. This information includes position of the face, location of facial attributes such as mouth corners, eyes as well as head pose (yaw, pitch and roll). Detected faces are examined for presence of facial expressions as well. Details of the facial expression recognition are described in Section 3.2.

3.1 Context Engine

The purpose of the *Context Engine* is to provide a framework to transform incoming observations from **Detectors** to multiple levels of state inference about the physical environment as well as to provide contextual feedback to external components of the system. The Panoramic Attention Layer (see Figure 2) serves as the central container for organizing the different elements of the machine's sensory field and perception. In our system, the major elements are comprised of *detectors*, *track managers* and *entities*. To help establish the material below, we will refer to two types of observations, *audio* and *faces* which are produced by the **Detector** modules.

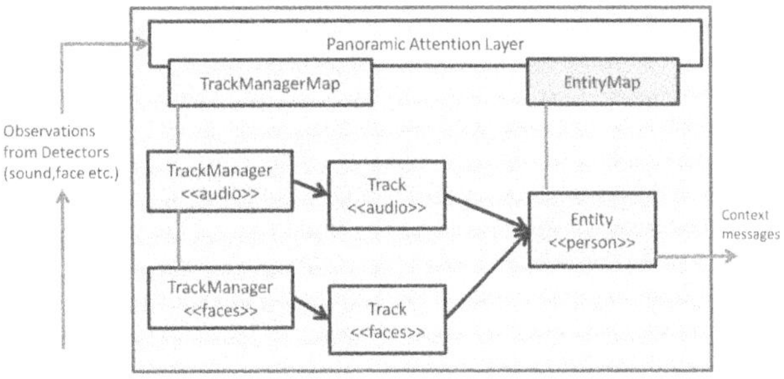

Figure 2: The *Context Engine*: Observations from Detectors(such as *audio*, *face*) are used to infer the state of entities (such as *person*), a part of which forms the context messages (indicated in red) sent out to modules of interest.

Track Managers: Observations are semantically-labeled outputs from **Detectors**. Observations are routed into one or more *Track Managers* depending on their modality type, where they are used to generate *tracks*. For audio observations, tracks correspond to spatio-temporally evolving 3-D clusters with each cluster corresponding to a sound source. For faces (of which multiple instances can be present in the environment), tracks are maintained with multi-hypothesis tracking using Kalman Filters and global nearest-neighbor clustering[4][7]. Also, *Track Managers* can run in parallel and can process observations at different rates.

Entities: Once observations have been assigned to tracks, these can be recruited to form *entities* such as a `person`. In a sense, tracks are evidence streams that help reason about the state of entities within the environment. For example, in our implementation, reasoning about a `person` entity involves evidence from a multi-modal combination of sound and face tracks. In addition, the state inference outputs of the entities can be in turn passed onto other entity types to make higher level inferences. Once the presence of an entity is established, its state information[1] is collected into a *context message* and sent to modules which make use of such contextual information in a top-down manner (the red arrows in Figures 1 and 2 indicate the flow of *context messages*). In our case, the context messages contain information about the onset and duration of a speaking person as well as his/her head pose which are utilized within the facial expression recognition framework as described in the next section.

Together, the *Context Engine*, consisting of the Panoramic Attention Layer and related *tracks* and *entities*, allows multimodal information to be processed and analyzed to obtain multiple state inferences at different levels of detail. These inferences can then be used to create contextual messages which in turn trigger appropriate system behaviors.

3.2 Facial Expression Recognition

The pipeline for facial recognition processing can be seen in Figure 3. To begin with, a face detector searches the incoming Regions of Interest from visual attention module for faces[26].

Normalization: Once the face is located, the 2D locations of the left and right pupils are estimated since these are usually the easiest and most reliably identifiable features in a face. Using pupil locations, the in-plane rotation angle θ of the face is estimated and the face is rotated accordingly, aligning the eyes at $\theta = 0^o$ (see Figure 5). The face is then warped to set the inter-eye distance to 55 pixels and resized to 110×150 pixels, omitting the top and bottom of the head in order to reduce the influence of hairstyle and clothing on classification.

For appearance-based methods, it is important to correct and normalize the photometric characteristics of both the training and testing faces since different lighting conditions can severely change the look of facial expressions relative to the training data(where lighting is usually designed to illuminate the face uniformly). To correct for both specularities and shadows, we use homomorphic filtering [22], which efficiently models local illumination patterns and then eliminates them from the facial image. As Figure 5(b) shows,

[1]E.g. For a `person` entity, state information could consist of identity, whether the person is talking, his or her position within the scene, etc.

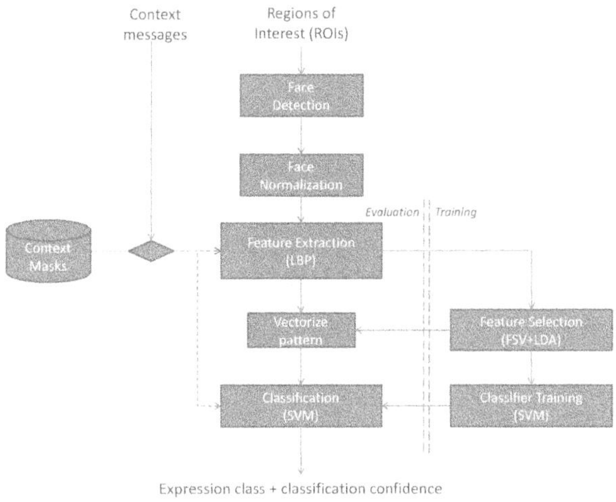

Figure 3: The pipeline for facial expression recognition. When a context message is received, the context-specific, stored Context Mask is retrieved and applied as long as the context is active. The dotted red arrows indicate portions of recognition pipeline where the Context Mask is used. The portion shaded in yellow in this figure corresponds to the solid yellow box labeled Face Expression in Figure 1.

the uneven lighting on the person's face is corrected while important structural details are preserved by homomorphic filtering.

Feature Extraction: We use Local Binary Patterns(LBP) as features[30]. To extract these features, the normalized face image is first divided into sub-regions. The feature extraction consists of sequentially comparing each pixel in a sub-region to its spatial neighbors in a circular, clockwise fashion. The sweep of each pixel's neighbors produces a 8-bit binary code which is then converted to decimal(Figure 4). A histogram of the LBP code occurrences is computed over each sub-region. Finally, each sub-region's histogram is concatenated, forming the face's feature vector. We used a 6×7 sub-regional grid for the face resulting in a $42 \times 2^8 = 10752$ sized feature for each face. These grids can be viewed in Figure 6(a).

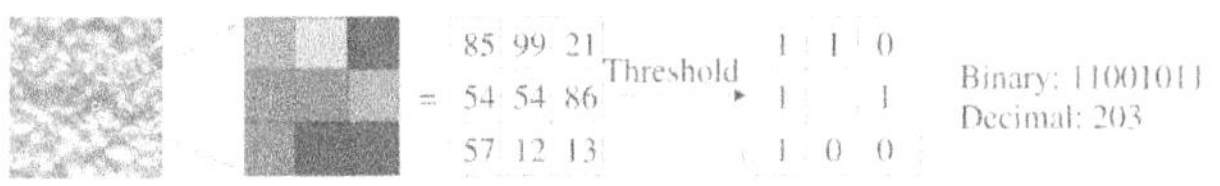

Figure 4: An illustration from [1] showing how LBP codes are computed.

Feature selection and dimensionality reduction: The relatively large feature vector formed by the LBP operation on the face's sub-regions is likely to contain redundant, noisy, or irrelevant features for recognizing facial expressions. Therefore, we select informative features by using the concave minimization (FSV) framework[8]. This method is effective at identifying features that contribute to good generalization performance, while maintaining a significantly smaller set compared to other methods. Through iterative testing, the optimal number of features obtained with the FSV approach results in a reduced feature vector (of length 768). In addition, we also perform Linear Discriminant Analysis (LDA) [6] on the LBP feature set which result in $c - 1$ features, where $c = 7$ is the number of expression categories(anger, disgust, fear, happy, sad, surprise, neutral). The final feature vector (of length 774) is a concatenation of FSV and LDA features.

Classification: To perform classification, we train a set of binary Support Vector Machine classifiers with a one-versus-rest decision strategy to perform multi-class classification [10]. The SVMs were trained with a RBF kernel for which the parameters were determined concurrently using an iterative grid selection technique. The SVM module outputs the identity of the recognized expression, along with an associated classification confidence value.

3.3 Temporal Context

Our framework contains two mechanisms to establish temporal context. Firstly, the Face *Track Manager* (see Figure 2) utilizes multi-hypothesis tracking which ensures that the association between faces and people in the dynamic environment is maintained temporally. Concurrently, the Sound *TrackManager* provides location and utterance-related estimates of people present. This information is packaged into the context message, thus ensuring that the mask application in face **Detector** module is performed to the correct person(s) speaking among the group present.

The second mechanism to establish temporal context acts on the stream of facial expressions associated with a particular face track. A moving window mode filter (with window size of 5) is applied on the stream to obtain a smoothed estimate of the person's facial expression.

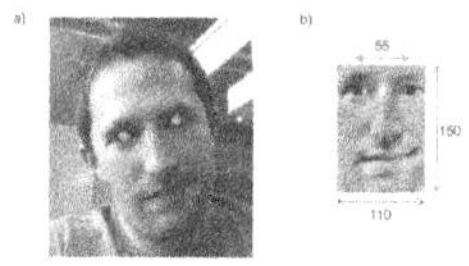

Figure 5: Face registration and normalization: a) Detected face and eyes, b) Geometrically and photometrically normalized face.

3.4 Localized face masking using context messages

In the course of normal operation, the facial expression recognition proceeds as described previously in Section 3.2. However, facial expressions can occur concurrently with activities that alter the appearance of facial features. Such alterations consequently propagate through the facial expression pipeline. For example, a talking subject's face exhibits typical structural deformations around the mouth area causing misrecognized facial expressions. Therefore, it becomes important to recognize the presence of such context inducing activities and adapt the recognition pipeline to the presence of such activities. To accomplish this, we use *context masks*.

The presence of context inducing activities such as talking is initially conveyed to *Detector* modules and in particular, to the Face module as a context message(see Figure 2). The reception of this message causes a specific, spatial 2-D context mask to be applied during the feature extraction stage. In addition, it also causes a mask-specific classifier to be used further down the pipeline(see Figure 3). Effectively, the mask ensures that facial recognition estimation is performed using only those facial features that are not affected by the activity (talking in this case). Once the context ceases to be active (e.g. person stops talking), the mask application is stopped and recognition is performed as before using the entire complement of facial features. The construction of these masks for the activities of speaking and head motion is described next.

Speech mask: In order to create the mask, we used the following data-driven procedure: The spatial distribution of the salient, emotion-relevant LBP features for each of the seven expressions (anger, disgust, fear, happy, sad, surprise, neutral) using the feature selection procedure explained above was performed on Cohn-Kanade database [21], producing the saliency maps shown in Figure 6(a). Since the Cohn-Kanade database does not contain any audio information associated with the expression sequences, we adopted the following method: video sequences of 15 subjects were recorded uttering the sentence – "Quarters, dimes, nickels and bills"– while keeping a neutral facial expression and tone. Using the sequences of these speaking subjects, an average deformation map corresponding to the areas of the face active during speech, called the Speech Deformation Map, was constructed. For this, successive frame differencing was performed on the frames of the video. The resulting difference images contain pixels active from one frame to its next. The number of such pixels were summed for each LBP grid cell and averaged and after thresholding to remove noise, the binary Speech Deformation Map was obtained(second image in Figure 6(b)). This Speech Deformation Map was then subtracted from the union of the binary emotion saliency maps to obtain the final, binary *Speech context mask*. When the context of *speaking* is active, only the non-masked portions of the face (corresponding to the white cells in the Speech context mask of Figure 6(b)) are utilized for recognizing expressions.

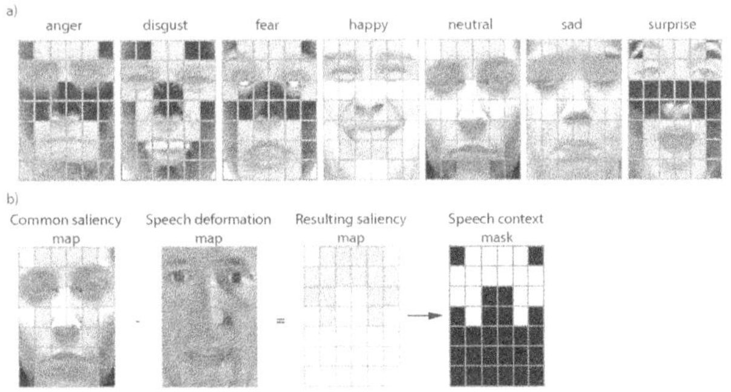

Figure 6: a) Saliency maps showing the distribution of salient regions for the seven expression categories, b) Speech context mask construction.

Head pitch mask: Due to the limited availability of public databases that contain both parametrized head rotation and varying facial expressions, we created our own database of 30 subjects emoting the seven expressions while pitching their head in an up-down motion. Each subject performed the pitching task 10 times for the pitch values of $+45°$ and $-45°$. We then created saliency maps for each expression and head rotation using the same method outlined previously for the speech mask. The union of the saliency maps across the seven emotions and subsequent head pitch context maps for both rotations are shown in Figure 7.

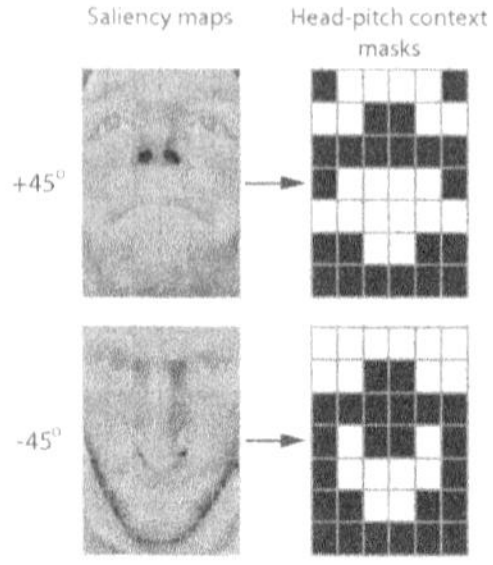

Figure 7: Saliency maps and head pitch context masks for $\pm 45^o$ rotations.

4. EVALUATION

The performance of the system was evaluated on two public databases, namely the Cohn-Kanade (CK) [21] and the Interactive Emotional Dyadic Motion Capture (IEMOCAP) [11]. For both databases, we compared the performance of the computer-based system to a manual annotation performed by a group of 30 human evaluators. For each condition, the mean recognition rate (MRR) and confusion matrix(rows representing classification results and columns representing ground truth labels) are presented. For the rest of the section, unmasked refers to using the full set of facial features while masked refers to using only those features made available by the speech or head pose mask during the training and evaluation phases. We now describe the setup for the experiments and the results below.

4.1 Results on CK database

As a long standing benchmark for static-image facial expression recognition and given its large subject and sample size, the CK database was used to validate the system's processing pipeline and serve as a baseline performance measure to compare with other methods. We selected 90 subjects[2] from the database emoting one to six expressions in sequences consisting of the subject starting with a neutral expression and ending with the maximum intensity of the target expression. From these sequences, we used only the first (neutral) and last (maximum intensity) frame for training and evaluation.

For the unmasked condition, the MRR of the computer system is 97.6% (with a standard deviation(s.d.) of 3.5%). See Table 1 for the comparitive performance of other methods. In addition, even though the database does not contain speech, we compared the performance of the computer-based system versus the human observers on masked samples to quantify the effect of the loss of visual information. For the CK tests, we performed a 10-fold cross-validation on both masked and unmasked samples independently. For the unmasked condition, the human observer performance was lower compared to the computer-based system with a MRR of 90.1% (s.d. 5.3%). A similar trend was noticed when the

[2]The CK database contains 100 subjects, however our selection criterion was that each subject had to produce all of the basic expressions (6 + neutral) to be included, which corresponds to 90 subjects.

mask was applied. For the masked condition, the computer-based system's performance was 83.6% (s.d. 10.4%), while the human observer performance was 72.4% (s.d. 9.3%). The expressions that are affected the most by the masking for both the computer-based system and human observers are fear and sadness (Tables 2 and 3). Indeed, these two emotions induce less skin deformation than the others and ostensibly contain more useful information in the mouth region[28].

Method	MRR (%)
Fiducial face feature tracking [33]	75.8
Eigenspace decomposition [25]	77.5
Hough forest on whole sequences [17]	87.1
Non-rigid deformation estimation [9]	89.1
Optical flow on whole sequences [35]	90.9
Boosted-LBP + SVM [31]	91.4
Facial animation patterns + HMM [2]	93.6
LBP+FSV+LDA+SVM (our method)	**97.6**

Table 1: Mean recognition rate using Cohn-Kanade database. Comparison of our method to other methods.

In these static tests, the human observers performed worse than the computer-based system for both conditions. However, the loss of accuracy is considerably larger when the humans are presented with the masked faces. Evidently, for the human observers, the information contained in the mouth region is important for accurate expression recognition. The computer-based system has the advantage of re-learning the salient features while training on masked samples, which gives it superior recognition performance.

Expression	Anger	Disgust	Fear	Happy	Sad	Surprise	Neutral
Anger	100 (74)	6 (4)	0 (0)	0 (0)	0 (2)	0 (0)	0 (0)
Disgust	0 (11)	91 (87)	0 (0)	0 (0)	0 (17)	0 (0)	0 (0)
Fear	0 (0)	0 (4)	95 (70)	0 (0)	0 (0)	0 (2)	0 (4)
Happy	0 (0)	0 (0)	0 (0)	100 (94)	0 (0)	0 (0)	0 (2)
Sad	0 (0)	3 (0)	3 (4)	0 (0)	97 (75)	0 (0)	0 (2)
Surprise	0 (9)	0 (3)	0 (3)	0 (1)	0 (0)	100 (96)	0 (0)
Neutral	0 (6)	0 (2)	2 (23)	0 (5)	3 (6)	0 (2)	100 (89)

Table 2: Confusion matrix(in %) for computer-based method on Cohn-Kanade database using unmasked and masked(in brackets) modes.

Expression	Anger	Disgust	Fear	Happy	Sad	Surprise	Neutral
Anger	89 (84)	8 (10)	1 (0)	0 (0)	0 (1)	1 (0)	0 (0)
Disgust	4 (6)	88 (76)	1 (0)	0 (0)	8 (0)	0 (0)	0 (9)
Fear	2 (0)	2 (11)	84 (64)	0 (0)	0 (12)	0 (6)	6 (0)
Happy	3 (0)	0 (0)	0 (3)	98 (75)	0 (0)	2 (11)	0 (15)
Sad	0 (4)	2 (0)	4 (9)	0 (2)	88 (57)	0 (0)	7 (5)
Surprise	0 (0)	0 (0)	0 (0)	2 (2)	0 (0)	97 (80)	0 (0)
Neutral	2 (6)	0 (3)	10 (24)	0 (21)	4 (30)	0 (3)	87 (71)

Table 3: Confusion matrix(in %) for human observers on Cohn-Kanade database using unmasked and masked(in brackets) modes.

4.2 Results on IEMOCAP database

The IEMOCAP database consists of multi-modal and multi-speaker video sequences of actors performing scripted and improvised sessions constructed to elicit facial expressions. We tested the effect of applying the speech context mask to the faces of the IEMOCAP database when speaking was detected. To evaluate the IEMOCAP database, we trained the computer system with the entire CK database. However, as the computer-based system did not use any voice information, the IEMOCAP sequences were muted when presented to the human observers for consistency.

The computer-based system's unmasked performance of 39.7% (s.d. 11.6%) was considerably lower than the human observers' 76.4% (s.d. 7.6%). Compared to CK, this database contains speech which changes the usual appearance of the expression and therefore, the classifier's output is unreliable when the subjects' mouths move. The human observers performed well even though the sequences were muted. It is reasonable to assume that human observers were capable of picking up emotion-related visual cues "betwen the words" uttered by the subjects. For the masked condition, the computer-based system's performance increased substantially to 65.0% (s.d. 8.4%) compared to the unmasked case. Clearly, the speech context mask is beneficial as it removes the visually noisy (non-emotion relevant) mouth movements.

As was the case with the CK database, the human observers performed worser when the mask was applied, resulting in a MRR of 69.3% (s.d. 7.9%). The drop in performance here is noticeably less than with the static CK database as the humans have the advantage of observing the low-level spatio-temporal evolution of the skin deformation, thus integrating much more information to decide on the facial expression. On this note, it is important to point out that the computer-based system does not integrate as much temporal information. Indeed, the temporal mode filter operates only on the high-level raw classification scores.

For both the computer-based system and humans observers, across all conditions, fear was the hardest expression to recognize, while surprise, a full-face expression, was the easiest for the computer-based system (see Tables 4 and 5). For the human observers, happy was the best identified expression in the unmasked condition and neutral had the highest score using the masked faces.

Expression	Anger	Disgust	Fear	Happy	Sad	Surprise	Neutral
Anger	27 (57)	24 (6)	6 (5)	11 (7)	4 (12)	5 (0)	7 (4)
Disgust	11 (7)	36 (68)	0 (0)	12 (0)	10 (0)	8 (7)	2 (6)
Fear	12 (0)	11 (0)	25 (59)	4 (3)	5 (0)	7 (0)	7 (5)
Happy	15 (14)	2 (0)	32 (5)	40 (78)	6 (0)	14 (9)	3 (12)
Sad	0 (6)	0 (0)	6 (11)	3 (0)	42 (56)	7 (0)	12 (0)
Surprise	23 (0)	26 (23)	0 (0)	25 (0)	16 (0)	55 (73)	16 (9)
Neutral	12 (16)	1 (3)	31 (20)	5 (12)	17 (32)	4 (11)	53 (64)

Table 4: Confusion matrix(in %) for computer-based method on IEMOCAP database using unmasked and masked(in brackets) modes.

Expression	Anger	Disgust	Fear	Happy	Sad	Surprise	Neutral
Anger	79 (60)	4 (1)	5 (6)	0 (6)	0 (0)	2 (0)	0 (7)
Disgust	2 (0)	77 (72)	1 (0)	2 (9)	1 (0)	0 (0)	0 (0)
Fear	3 (20)	5 (1)	65 (65)	0 (0)	4 (18)	15 (21)	1 (0)
Happy	3 (0)	0 (1)	0 (11)	86 (66)	5 (0)	4 (3)	6 (5)
Sad	0 (7)	0 (24)	11 (10)	0 (12)	69 (70)	4 (3)	9 (0)
Surprise	5 (13)	14 (1)	0 (6)	4 (7)	0 (6)	75 (67)	0 (3)
Neutral	8 (0)	0 (0)	18 (2)	8 (0)	21 (6)	0 (6)	84 (85)

Table 5: Confusion matrix(in %) for human observers on IEMOCAP database using unmasked and masked(in brackets) modes.

A similar trend persists when the head pitch context mask is evaluated (Table 6). The unmasked mode results in a MRR of 78.6% (s.d. 4.0%), while the masked mode performs better at 86.4% (s.d. 5.1%). For the human observers, it is easier to recognize the emotion on the unmasked faces as seen in Table 7. They are indeed more accurate than the computer, with a MRR of 89.7% (s.d. 7.3%). This score, however, drops considerably to 73.9% (s.d. 9.4%) when the mask is applied. The drop is likely due to the loss of visual information for the humans. The gains present for the computer-based system in the masked mode is the result of re-learning the salient feature points, as was the case above.

Expression	Anger	Disgust	Fear	Happy	Sad	Surprise	Neutral
Anger	84 (84)	5 (3)	0 (2)	5 (4)	0 (5)	5 (2)	0 (0)
Disgust	6 (5)	81 (89)	2 (7)	0 (1)	0 (3)	0 (4)	0 (0)
Fear	2 (2)	0 (4)	83 (82)	0 (5)	4 (3)	9 (0)	5 (5)
Happy	3 (6)	4 (0)	7 (2)	76 (88)	6 (0)	6 (0)	5 (3)
Sad	1 (0)	6 (3)	1 (2)	9 (2)	75 (79)	3 (0)	14 (3)
Surprise	4 (3)	4 (1)	0 (5)	0 (0)	0 (0)	77 (94)	2 (0)
Neutral	0 (0)	0 (0)	7 (0)	10 (0)	15 (10)	0 (0)	74 (89)

Table 6: Confusion matrix(in %) for computer-based method on head-pitch database using unmasked and masked(in brackets) modes.

Expression	Anger	Disgust	Fear	Happy	Sad	Surprise	Neutral
Anger	95 (86)	2 (7)	0 (3)	0 (4)	0 (1)	0 (2)	0 (5)
Disgust	4 (6)	93 (79)	1 (4)	0 (3)	5 (8)	2 (4)	0 (0)
Fear	0 (1)	0 (0)	80 (67)	0 (8)	9 (9)	6 (8)	4 (15)
Happy	0 (0)	0 (2)	0 (3)	98 (78)	3 (3)	0 (4)	1 (9)
Sad	1 (0)	0 (7)	13 (6)	1 (2)	79 (65)	0 (1)	4 (10)
Surprise	0 (7)	2 (5)	0 (0)	0 (0)	0 (0)	92 (81)	0 (0)
Neutral	0 (0)	3 (0)	6 (17)	1 (5)	4 (14)	0 (0)	91 (61)

Table 7: Confusion matrix(in %) for human observers on head-pitch database using unmasked and masked(in brackets) modes.

5. DISCUSSION AND FUTURE WORK

In this paper, we have shown how to utilize context arising from the presence of inter-modal information (speech or head pose) to determine affect. Our facial expression recognition pipeline achieves good accuracy on the Cohn-Kanade dataset with a mean recognition rate of 97.6%. We build upon this baseline performance by utilizing inter-modal contextual information(speech and head pose) from the *Context Engine* framework to robustly recognize facial expressions in the multi-modal IEMOCAP database.

In the facial recognition pipeline, homomorphic normalization can be thought of addressing the lighting context to an extent. This, combined with the scale invariance and the suitability of LBP features, ensures that we obtain good baseline performance. Another reason for this performance is the fact that our FSV feature selection does locally optimal feature selection while LDA features operate across classes in a global scale, thereby resulting in a feature vector which captures local as well as global information in a sparse fashion. Moreover, since the mask encodes context-driven features, it ensures that only the most relevant features are utilized while attempting to recognize facial expressions in the presence of multi-modal contextual information. Thus, we can avoid mistakenly using all features including the noisy and unreliable ones on one extreme or discard all features on the other extreme.

The *Context Engine* framework is appealing from a design standpoint as well since it abstracts away the details of context generators and helps avoid the dissonant design that results when inter-modal messages are communicated directly to Detectors. In addition, such a design offers mediation mechanisms which can be utilized in frameworks which seek to combine multiple modalities.

In our current implementation, handling a new context requires re-training a new classifier with the appropriate binary mask. One drawback of this approach is that when we seek to handle combinations of contexts (e.g. person talking with head tilted downwards while emoting happiness), it results in a combinatorial increase in the number of classifiers to train. A more scalable alternative would be to have a classification mechanism which can handle weighted features[34]. In this scheme, the weights could indicate feature component reliability as expressed by concurrence of simultaneously active contexts. Alternatively, if each pose context mask is designed to capture local feature variations(e.g. by clustering head poses observed during typical interactions), the number of masks which arise can be greatly reduced.

In this work, the evaluation was performed using publicly available databases. It would be interesting to evaluate using videos "in the wild" such as from TV shows, movie clips and interviews. We expect this to be considerably harder since it requires a greater detail of context than what we currently use. As a step towards utilizing stronger contextual cues, the semantics of recognized speech(e.g. words indicating happiness or anger) can be utilized – existing literature already points to the gains by doing so[18]. It would also enable a more natural comparison between computed-based systems and human observers wherein the full audio information is made available as opposed to specification of onset and end of speech. Adding the ability to handle other commonly known context-inducing cues such as prosody, full 3D head pose and gesture also remain ideas to explore in future.

6. ACKNOWLEDGMENTS

We thank Rishi Rajalingham and Caitlin Wharin for their invaluable advice and help with the testing of the software. We would also like to thank Shrikanth Narayanan for permitting us to evaluate using the IEMOCAP database.

7. REFERENCES

[1] T. Ahonen, A. Hadid, and M. Pietikainen. Face description with local binary patterns: Application to face recognition. IEEE Trans. Pattern Anal. Mach. Intell., 28, December 2006.

[2] P. S. Aleksic and A. K. Katsaggelos. Automatic facial expression recognition using facial animation parameters and multi-stream hmms. In Information Forensics and Security, IEEE Transactions on Volume 1, Issue 1, March 2006 Page(s):3, 2005.

[3] H. Aviezer, R. Hassin, S. Bentin, and Y. Trope. Putting facial expressions back in context. First impressions., pages 255–288, 2008.

[4] Y. Bar-Shalom and T. Fortmann. Tracking and data association. 1988.

[5] L. F. F. Barrett and E. A. Kensinger. Context is routinely encoded during emotion perception. Psychological science : a journal of the American Psychological Society, 21(4):595–599, 2010.

[6] P. N. Belhumeur, J. P. Hespanha, and D. J. Kriegman. Eigenfaces vs. fisherfaces: Recognition using class specific linear projection. In IEEE Pattern Analysis and Machine Intelligence, volume 19, 1997.

[7] G. Bradksi. Computer vision face tracking as a component of a perceptual user interface. IEEE

Workshop on Applications of Computer Vision, pages 214–219, 1998.
[8] P. Bradley and O. L. Mangasarian. Feature selection via concave minimization and support vector machines. In Machine Learning Proceedings of the Fifteenth International Conference(ICML ï£¡98, pages 82–90. Morgan Kaufmann, 1998.
[9] J. Buenaposada, E. Muï£¡oz, and L. Baumela. Recognising facial expressions in video sequences. Pattern Analysis and Applications, 11:101–116, 2008.
[10] C. J. Burges. A tutorial on support vector machines for pattern recognition. Data Mining and Knowledge Discovery, 2:121–167, 1998.
[11] C. Busso, M. Bulut, C. Lee, A. Kazemzadeh, E. Mower, S. Kim, J. Chang, S. Lee, and S. Narayanan. Iemocap: Interactive emotional dyadic motion capture database. Journal of Language Resources and Evaluation, 42(4).
[12] C. Busso, Z. Deng, S. Yildirim, M. Bulut, C. M. Lee, A. Kazemzadeh, S. Lee, U. Neumann, and S. Narayanan. Analysis of emotion recognition using facial expressions, speech and multimodal information. In Sixth International Conference on Multimodal Interfaces ICMI 2004, pages 205–211. ACM Press, 2004.
[13] A. J. Calder, A. W. Young, J. Keane, and M. Dean. Configural information in facial expression perception. Journal of Experimental Psychology: Human Perception and Performance, 26(2):527 – 551, 2000.
[14] T. Cootes, G. Edwards, and C.Taylor. Active apperance models. PAMI, 23(6):681–685, 2001.
[15] D. Datcu and L. J. M. Rothkrantz. Semantic audio-visual data fusion for automatic emotion recognition. Proc. of EUROMEDIA, 2008.
[16] F. Dornaika and F. Davoine. Simultaneous facial action tracking and expression recognition in the presence of head motion. International Journal of Computer Vision, 76:257–281, 2008.
[17] G. Fanelli, A. Yao, P. L. Noel, J. Gall, and L. V. Gool. Hough forest-based facial expression recognition from video sequences. In Workshop on Sign, Gesture and Activity (SGA'10), 2010.
[18] G.Castellano, L.Kessous, and G.Caridakis. Emotion recognition through multiple modalities: Face, body gesture, speech. In C. Peter and R. Beale, editors, Affect and Emotion in Human-Computer Interaction, volume 4868 of Lecture Notes in Computer Science, pages 92–103. Springer Berlin, 2008.
[19] L. Itti, C. Koch, and E. Neibur. A model of saliency-based visual attention for rapid scene analysis. IEEE Transactions on Pattern Analysis and Machine Intelligence., 28:1254–1259, 1998.
[20] R. E. Kaliouby and P. Robinson. Real-time inference of complex mental states from facial expressions and head gestures. In Intl. Conf. Computer Vision and Pattern Recognition, page 154, 2004.
[21] T. Kanade, J. F. Cohn, and Y. Tian. Comprehensive database for facial expression analysis. Fourth IEEE International Conference on Automatic Face and Gesture Recognition, pages 46–53, 2000.
[22] V. K. Madisetti and D. B. Williams. The Digital Signal Processing Handbook. CRC Press, Boca Raton, Florida, 1999.
[23] W. Martin, M. Angeliki, E. Florian, B. S., and S. S. Narayanan. Context-sensitive multimodal emotion recognition from speech and facial expression using bidirectional lstm modeling. In INTERSPEECH, pages 2362–2365, 2010.
[24] S. Moore and R. Bowden. The effect of pose on facial expression recognition. In Proc. British Machine Vision Conference, 2009.
[25] G. R. S. Murthy and R.S.Jadon. Effectiveness of eigenspaces for facial expressions recognition. In International Journal of Computer Theory and Engineering, volume 1, pages 638–642, 2009.
[26] M. C. Nechyba and H. Schneiderman. Pittpatt face detection and tracking for the clear 2006 evaluation. In LNCS 4122: Multimodal Technologies for Perception of Humans, First International Evaluation Workshop on Classification of Events, Activities and Relationships, pages 161–170. Springer, 2007.
[27] R. K. Sarvadevabhatla and V. Ng-Thow-Hing. Panoramic attention for humanoid robots. In Proceedings of the 9th IEEE-RAS International Conference on Humanoid Robots, pages 215 – 222, December 2009.
[28] P. G. Schyns, L. S. Petro, and M. L. Smith. Transmission of facial expressions of emotion co-evolved with their efficient decoding in the brain: Behavioral and brain evidence. PLoS ONE, 4(5), 05 2009.
[29] N. Sebe, I. Cohen, and T. Huang. Multimodal emotion recognition. In Handbook of Pattern Recognition and Computer Vision. World Scientific, 2005.
[30] C. Shan, S. Gong, and P. W. McOwan. Facial expression recognition based on local binary patterns: A comprehensive study. Image and Vision Computing, 27(6):803 – 816, 2009.
[31] C. Shan, S. Gong, and P. W. McOwan. Facial expression recognition based on local binary patterns: A comprehensive study. Image and Vision Computing, 27(6):803 – 816, 2009.
[32] I. Spiros, C. George, K. Kostas, and K. Stefanos. Robust feature detection for facial expression recognition. J. Image Video Process., 2007:5–5, August 2007.
[33] R. Tripathi and R. Aravind. Recognizing facial expression using particle filter based feature points tracker. In PReMI, pages 584–591, 2007.
[34] X. Wang and Q. He. Enhancing generalization capability of svm classifiers with feature weight adjustment. Lecture Notes in Computer Science, 3213:1037–1043, 2004.
[35] M. B. Yeasin and R. B. Sharma. Recognition of facial expressions and measurement of levels of interest from video. In IEEE Transactions on Multimedia, volume 8, pages 500–508, 2006.
[36] Z. Zeng, M. Pantic, and T. S. Huang. Emotion recognition based on multimodal information. In J. Tao and T. Tan, editors, Affective Information Processing, pages 241–265. Springer London, 2009.

Brain-Computer Interaction: Can Multimodality Help?

Anton Nijholt
University of Twente
Faculty EEMCS, PO Box 217
7500 AE Enschede, the Netherlands
31 53 4893740
anijholt@cs.utwente.nl

Brendan Z. Allison
Graz University of Technology
IKD, Krenngasse 37
8010 Graz, Austria
43 316 873 5305
allison@tugraz.at

Robert J.K. Jacob
Tufts University
CS department, 161 College Avenue
Medford, Mass. 02155 U.S.A.
1-617-627-2225
jacobs@cs.tufts.edu

ABSTRACT
This paper is a short introduction to a special ICMI session on brain-computer interaction. During this paper, we first discuss problems, solutions, and a five-year view for brain-computer interaction. We then talk further about unique issues with multimodal and hybrid brain-computer interfaces, which could help address many current challenges. This paper presents some potentially controversial views, which will hopefully inspire discussion about the different views on brain-computer interfacing, how to embed brain-computer interfacing in a multimodal and multi-party context, and, more generally, how to look at brain-computer interfacing from an ambient intelligence point of view.

Categories and Subject Descriptors
H. Information Systems, H.5 INFORMATION INTERFACES AND PRESENTATION (I.7), H.5.2 User Interfaces (D.2.2, H.1.2, I.3.6). Subjects: Input devices and strategies (e.g., mouse, touchscreen); Evaluation/methodology.

General Terms
Algorithms, Measurement, Performance, Design, Reliability, Experimentation, Human Factors.

Keywords
Brain-computer interaction, hybrid BCIs, multimodal interaction, bandwidth.

1. INTRODUCTION
In the last years, there has been considerable enthusiasm about Brain-Computer Interface (or Brain-Computer Interaction) (BCI) research, BCI technology and applications and BCI commercialization. New applications have proven successful, simple BCI games have been sold to over a million healthy users, media attention is growing, and the word "revolutionary" has been used many times (e.g. [1]) Clearly, such excitement can – and often should – elicit criticism and cynicism about previous 'hypes' and promises in the past. For example, there was once tremendous enthusiasm for scientific progress in neurofeedback, cold fusion, or Artificial Intelligence (AI), which led to a backlash when these fields did not deliver on unrealistically high expectations.

This paper is an introduction to a special ICMI session on BCI. During this paper, we first discuss problems, solutions, and a five-year view for BCIs. We then talk further about unique issues with multimodal and hybrid BCIs, which could help address many current challenges. This paper presents some potentially controversial views, which will hopefully inspire discussion about the different views on brain-computer interfacing (BCI), how to embed brain-computer interfacing in a multimodal and multi-party context, and, more generally, how to look at BCI from an ambient intelligence point of view.

2. PROBLEMS AND CHALLENGES
This section briefly overviews the top ten problems that impede wider BCI adoption. The top seven are problems with BCIs themselves, whereas the last three are more general challenges for the BCI community.

Reliability: Once ready, BCIs should be usable in any environment, any time of day or night, with minimal preparation, maintenance, discomfort, embarrassment, inconvenience, and cleaning. In real world settings, particularly with patients, BCIs may be unreliable because of fatigue, changes in the user's brain within or across days, background activity that produces electrical noise, or activity the user cannot control that produces noise, such as fasciculations, spasms, or other movements.

Proficiency: There has not been any BCI approach that works for all users. That is, for any given BCI approach (P300, SSVEP, ERD), at least a few percent of users cannot attain any control whatsoever [2], [3].

Bandwidth: BCIs have attained ITRs above 60 bits per minute, and more recently 100 [4], [5], [6]. However, this remains far slower than other communication means, and reflects laboratory performance with elite subjects. Many real world BCIs still allow about 10-25 bits per minute, which is unchanged in almost 10 years [7].

Convenience: An assistive device or other communication tool should be available on-demand. Most BCIs instead require at least 20 minutes of preparation before each usage, and the hair and cap must be washed after each session. It should only function when needed, supporting asynchronous operation and a standby mode.

Support: Very few people can use BCIs. A typical end user today needs help to identify, buy, setup, configure, maintain, repair and upgrade the BCI [8], [9].

ICMI'11, November 14–18, 2011, Alicante, Spain.

Training: Some BCIs require weeks or months of training. BCI training can be boring and repetitive, with no clear progress during early training [10].

Utility: Most BCIs can do only one thing, such as spell. An ideal BCI can allow users to easily choose any application desired with minimal delay or hassle [11].

Image: People are less likely to buy a device if they do not know about it or think it is ineffective, dangerous, nerdy, over-hyped, or ugly. BCIs are usually portrayed inaccurately and negatively in the popular media, which may lead to unreasonable fears or concerns [1].

Standards: The BCI community needs numerous standardized elements, including standard file formats, data interchange protocols, ethical procedures, media reporting guidelines, bit rate reporting guidelines, and terminological clarifications [3].

Infrastructure: The community needs improved resources that could lower the barriers to entry and development, such as better software tools that are freely available, improved documentation and help, downloadable (anonymous) data and processing tools, and a central repository of IP, articles, and other information.

3. SOLUTIONS AND TRENDS

The ten problems described above are generally recognized by BCI researchers. There are many research trends that could help address these problems.

Reliability: Improved sensors (including practical electrodes), high impedance amplifiers, and noise reduction software can help make BCIs work in more environments. Wireless BCIs are becoming more common. There also needs to be more attention to numerous aspects of clinical validation and integrating BCI hardware and software with existing devices.

Proficiency: Improved signal processing can reduce but not eliminate "BCI illiteracy". Switching to an alternate input signal is an increasingly popular research direction [3], [9], [12].

Bandwidth: Improved signal processing, new stimuli and tasks, and improved interfaces and environments will continue to increase bandwidth [13]. Hybrid BCIs can provide an additional control signal, increased accuracy, and/or reduce selection time. Shared control, context awareness, and error correction improve effective bandwidth.

Convenience: Practical electrodes could considerably reduce the time needed to mount the cap, and washing the hair or electrodes is no longer necessary [14], [15], [16]. Improved electrodes might be better integrated with head mounted devices or clothing, and wireless transmission also improves convenience. Invasive BCIs are always available.

Support: Numerous research efforts, largely funded by the EC, are focusing on developing free tools to reduce the need for expert help. Practical electrodes require considerable less support, since the user could don the sensor system without any help, and cleaning is not needed.

Training: This is an area of substantial progress. The BCI approach that requires such extensive training is no longer used. Numerous groups reduce training time, not only through improved signal processing, but also immersive environments and an effective reward structure. If BCIs gain attention for functional rehabilitation, training time for them will emerge as a new challenge.

Utility: Ongoing research is identifying new BCI applications, and producing tools to help people switch between them [11].

Image: As more companies and groups solve the technical problems associated with robust high quality signal capture, focus will move to design and ergonomics, with greater focus on design-centered approaches. We need to produce and/or encourage professional, fair, and positive media about BCIs, such as interviews, documentaries, and news programs. Media guidelines could help, although they cannot be enforced. Public demonstrations at expositions or other events can help inform and engage the public.

Standards and infrastructure: Developing the backbone of a more integrated BCI community. requires intensive and often polemic interactions among key stakeholders. One recommendation is a "BCI Society" or steering board that consists of highly respected established researchers and thus has the authority to propose and develop various standards, guidelines, tools, and resources.

4. FIVE YEAR VIEW

We expect the following changes over the next five years.

Reliability and Proficiency: The underlying problem of "BCI illiteracy" will probably not be solved. That is, in five or even ten years, it is unlikely that a specific BCI approach will be proven to work for 99.9% of users. However, it will become easier to find the right BCI for each user, and switch between BCIs or other systems, which will considerably improve reliability and reduce illiteracy.

Bandwidth: The 100 bit per minute barrier was just broken [6], and (especially with invasive systems) there is hope for BCIs with much higher bandwidth or vocabulary. However, these developments will have little impact on home users within five years. Bandwidth will see modest to good progress within five years, due more to existing trends like identifying the right BCI and parameters for each user.

Convenience: BCIs will become considerably more convenient. In particular, driven largely by corporate funds, new headwear will be developed that can provide information about brain activity less obtrusively than modern headwear. Practical electrodes that are better integrated with head-mounted devices will become prevalent. However, BCIs will remain far from transparent devices.

Support: We have mixed anticipations. On the bright side, there will be substantial improvements in various tools to help reduce demand for experts. These will include introductory materials, online and printed documents and manuals, troubleshooting and problem solving guides, tele-monitoring tools. But, these will only reduce the demand for expert help. In five years, many end users without technical backgrounds who want a BCI will still need some help, excluding most simple games.

Training: Two trends will continue. First, BCI flexibility will improve, making it easier to choose a BCI that requires no training. Second, due to improved signal processing and experimentation, BCIs that do require training will require less training.

Utility: This is an area of considerable uncertainty. It will be easier to switch between BCI applications and adapt to new applications. However, it is too early to say whether BCIs for functional improvement will gain traction, which would greatly increase utility

Image: We are very concerned about how people will view BCIs in five years. There is no "check" on inaccurate and negative portrayals in science fiction and news media. Also, there is considerable risk that the "bubble will burst" – that is, that the unrealistic expectations that many people have will not be fulfilled and lead to a backlash against BCIs akin to the neurofeedback backlash.

Standards: We anticipate modest progress in the next five years. At least, numerous technical standards will be established, including reporting guidelines. Ethical guidelines will probably also proceed well. We think the disagreement over the exact definition of a BCI will only grow, and cannot be stopped with any reasonable amount of funding. We are helping form a BCI Society.

Infrastructure: We also anticipate modest progress. Many software tools will improve, and improved online support will advise people on the best systems and walk people through setup and troubleshooting. Infrastructure development depends heavily on outside funding.

5. MULTIMODAL AND/OR HYBRID BCIs

BCI means measuring and interpreting brain activity. Activity in various regions of the brain allows different interpretations of this activity because of different functions of brain regions. Hence, we can, for example, distinguish brain activity related to different kinds of movements (measured in the motor cortex) from brain activity related to visual, auditory or haptic perception, or activity that tells us about a more global mental or affective state of the user.

This has been the traditional view on BCI in medical, rehabilitation and research environments. Research focused on brain research and BCI applications of this brain research. Or research focused on patients with a particular disability and how knowledge of brain activity could overcome this disability. This is a quite different approach from multimodal research in human computer interaction, where information that can be obtained from a particular modality is just one of the many sources that can be obtained from the 'user', his or her context, the domain application and the 'history' of the user (background, interests, preferences, previous interactions, etc.). HCI researchers look at BCI as embedding information obtained from measuring brain activity as just one added modality to modalities that receive much attention at this moment (such as speech recognition, gesture recognition, facial expression recognition, affect recognition, physiological measurements, etc.) and to more direct traditional mouse, keyboard, touch pad and joy-stick input modalities.

Today, most BCIs are "simple" systems that only rely on one type of input. The BCI community has started looking at hybrid BCIs, where initially the interest remained at looking at brain activity, but activity that can be detected from different regions and functions of the brain and using different BCI modalities. This is a research shift made possible because of increasing knowledge of brain functions and how to exploit the associated activity, and also because of a growing interest BCI research for applications not necessarily related to the medical domain.

From this point of view hybrid BCIs can combine a device that relies on brain signals with another tool to send information. The additional tool might be another BCI, a device based on other physiological signals, or a conventional input such as a keyboard or joystick. There are many different types of multimodal signal combinations, and many ways that hybrid BCIs could capitalize on different indicators of users' mental states. Hybrid BCIs have already shown promise in improving reliability, proficiency, bandwidth, convenience, and utility [12], [17], [18], [19]. The typical point of view is how can we intelligently design BCIs so that any additional signals provide useful information for the particular application?

From the HCI and multimodal interaction point of view it is rather the other way around. From the HCI point of view BCI is an area that is rather unexploited [20]. Clearly, measuring EEG activity has already been considered to be useful for investigating new interface designs. How can we measure workload and design interfaces that require less mental workload? But presently, from a multimodal interaction point of view, the main question, assuming interesting applications, is how information available from measuring brain activity (and that is what BCI is about) can be embedded with information on other human activity that can be detected, measured, and interpreted [21]. EEG or other methods of measuring brain activity can be combined with other methods of detecting human activity. For example, sensors might collect physiological information that can help identify the mental state of the user. Other intelligent sensors (using cameras and microphones) can look at human activity and try to interpret, predict and anticipate human activities, decisions and preferences. Other sensors could know about each user's position relative to other people or objects, and provide information about other users, such as whether they are in the same physical location or somewhere else. Rather than having BCI as starting point and giving BCI priority above other modalities, in multimodal BCI research we look at embedding information from the BCI modality in a multimodal, artificial intelligence, social intelligence, and computer science context.

Brain activity, skin conductivity and heart rate variations provide us with information of the cognitive state of a human performing individual, interaction and collaboration activities (interacting with the environment, other humans, virtual humans, social robots), but so does information collected from cameras, microphones, and other sensors. These other sensors provide us with other information about the mood and emotional state of the user and in particular, when available, from keyboard, mouse and speech recognition, more explicit information about what the user wants the computer (virtual human, social robot, environment) to do.

Information obtained from brain activity must be fused with information obtained from other modalities while collecting information about the user, to be used in a pro-active and reactive way, and while interacting with a user. From a human-computer interaction point of view, brain activity could be used in much the same way as other sources of information. Hence, similar challenges arise. How can brain-based information enhance human-computer interaction? What information is available, how can it be correlated with the user's actions and desires, and how can the system act on this information, both in real-time and non-real-time? How can brain-based information best be fused with other information about the user in a smart and supportive environment using multimodal and multi-party context information?

There are several problems when we want to consider embedding the brain activity modality in a multimodal and multi-party context, or, more generally, an ambient intelligence context.

However, does looking at and including this brain activity recognition modality really differ from including a speech recognition, a gesture recognition, or an emotion recognition modality in getting a complete view of the user's need of support?

We should mention that decades of research have passed before we saw applications of speech recognition and identification, facial expression recognition or human behaviour and activity classification. However, none of the technologies that resulted from this research can be considered as reliable or robust. Speech recognition can be looked at as an example. Distinguishing between 'yes' and 'no' was already an achievement in the early years. And, probably, being able to make binary decisions, opened the way to speculate about all kinds of applications where interaction choices and decision making could be expressed as a series of binary decisions. Currently, the possibilities of speech recognition technology allow domain-dependent applications where not only hundreds of words can be recognized, but we can also recognize these words in their linguistic context, allowing us to assign meaning to sequences of words, that is, to sentences, using linguistic knowledge. This knowledge makes it possible to design useful applications in rather controlled contexts. In this case, 'controlled' means that the user operates in a context in which it is 'unnatural' to behave outside of the domain of the particular application.

Similar observations can be made when looking at recognizing, interpreting, and using information obtained from facial expressions. Or, information that can be obtained from nonverbal features of speech signals or whatever signals that can be detected and measured using physiological sensors, cameras, microphones, pressure sensors, proximity sensors, et cetera. From a multimodal point of view there is no reason to look at BCI in a different way than at these other modalities.

6. A ROADMAP FOR FUTURE BCI RESEARCH

From the previous sections, it should be clear that BCI research is increasing. And, it should also be clear that there is considerable interest for applications for users without physical disabilities [22]. Practical electrodes and increasing commercial interest could make previously impractical technologies much more feasible for everyday field use. On the other hand, many possible directions might initially seem clever but would provide little or no benefit over simpler interfaces. Here, we briefly discuss some possible directions for BCI applications that might have been impractical only a few years ago.

First, passively recorded information might become much more common in future BCI systems. This refers to information that is recorded without any active effort from the user, such as changes that occur when a user becomes tired or frustrated. "Affective" BCI systems could adapt interfaces and interaction possibilities in many ways according to user state changes.

Second, multimodal and hybrid BCIs could help address many current problems with BCI systems, notably reliability, performance, and usability. Eventually, most complete BCI systems will be hybrid BCIs, meaning that users can effect control via whichever mental tasks and associated brain signals are easiest and most effective for them. This may not occur within five years, but will eventually be the norm.

Third, BCIs might be used not just for communication, control, and monitoring, but also for neuromodulation. That is, people might use BCIs because they want to produce changes in their brains, particularly chronic changes that reduce or eliminate an unwanted condition. For example, BCIs might help people with autism or stroke by producing long-term changes that counteract unwanted effects of these conditions [23], [24], [25]. Of course, a portable home system that could treat major disorders could dwarf other BCI applications, particularly if these disorders remain resistant to other forms of treatment. However, this direction requires substantial clinical validation before mainstream use, which is unlikely within five years.

Of course, technical progress is only one facet of developing and successfully launching a new product. More generally, a future roadmap of BCI research should take into account marketability of current and future BCI applications by looking at emerging markets and commercial opportunities. The future Brain/Neuronal Computer Interaction project (fBNCI; http://future-bnci.org/ aims to develop such a roadmap by drawing on the expertise of BCI researchers, as well as many other stakeholder groups, including companies, end users, patient organizations, policy makers, and the general public. In the context of this project BCI researchers were surveyed on the marketability of BCIs at the 4th International BCI Meeting, which took place at the Asilomar conference centre in June 2010 [26], and a BCI expert meeting was organized in Graz in September 2010 where various short- and long-term scenarios for BCI research and applications were designed and elaborated.

These workshops, and other events and discussions, have underscored the complexities inherent in analyzing future directions. As noted, different user groups, and different types of applications, are emerging, and often cannot be lumped together within a single coherent analysis. For example, the most commonly sold BCI system today is a very simple game that allows very limited control, with questionable reliability, that costs less than $100. For such BCIs, users probably would not be inclined to pay substantially more. Consider another example: an EEG system that can be used in the home, or even on an outpatient basis, that can substantially alleviate the motor problems resulting from stroke. Users might easily pay tens of thousands of dollars for such a system.

7. ACKNOWLEDGEMENTS

The authors gratefully acknowledge the support of the European Future BNCI project (Project number ICT-248320; http://future-bnci.org/) and of the BrainGain Smart Mix Program of the Netherlands Ministry of Economic Affairs and the Netherlands Ministry of Education, Culture and Science.

8. REFERENCES

[1] Allison, B.Z. 2010. Toward ubiquitous BCIs. In: *Brain-computer interfaces: Revolutionizing Human-Computer Interaction*. Graimann, B., Allison, B.Z., and Pfurtscheller, G. (Eds.), Springer Verlag, Berlin Heidelberg, 357-387.

[2] Kübler A, Müller, K-R. 2007. Toward brain-computer interfacing. In: *An Introduction to Brain-Computer Interfacing*. MIT Press, Boston, 1–25.

[3] Allison, B.Z. and Neuper, C. 2010. Could anyone use a BCI? In: *Brain-Computer* Interfaces: *Applying our Minds to Human-Computer Interaction*, Tan, D.S. and Nijholt, A. (Eds.) Human-Computer Interaction Series, Springer Verlag, London, 35-54.

[4] Gao, X., Xu, D., Cheng, M., and Gao, S. 2003. A BCI-based environmental controller for the motion disabled. *IEEE Transactions on Neural Systems and Rehabilitation Engineering* 11, 137–140.

[5] Bin, G.Y., Gao, X.R., Wang, Y.J., Hong, B, Gao, S.K. 2009. VEP-based brain-computer interfaces: time, frequency, and code modulations. *IEEE Comput Intell Mag* 4, 4, 22–26. DOI= http://dx.doi.org/ 10.1109/MCI.2009.934562.

[6] Brunner, P, Ritaccio, A.L., Emrich, J.F., Bischof, H., and Schalk, G. 2011. Rapid communication with a "P300" matrix speller using electrocorticographic signals (ECoG). *Frontiers in Neuroscience* 5, 5. DOI= http://dx.doi.org/10.3389/fnins.2011.00005

[7] Wolpaw, J. R., Birbaumer, N., McFarland, D. J., Pfurtscheller, G., Vaughan, T. M. 2002. Brain-computer interfaces for communication and control. *Clin. Neurophysiol.* 113, 767–791. DOI= http://dx.doi.org/10.1016/S1388-2457(02)00057-3.

[8] Allison, B.Z. (2009). The I of BCIs: Next generation interfaces for brain – computer interface systems that adapt to individual users. In: *Human-Computer Interaction: Novel Interaction Methods and Techniques*, Jacko, J. (Ed.), Springer-Verlag, Berlin Heidelberg, 558 - 568.

[9] Millan J. del R., et al. 2010. Combining brain–computer interfaces and assistive technologies: state-of-the-art and challenges *Front. Neuroscience* 4 161.

[10] Birbaumer, N., Cohen, L.G. 2007. Brain-computer interfaces: communication and restoration of movement in paralysis. *J. Physiol.* 579, 621–636.

[11] Navarro, N.A., Ceccaroni, L., Velickovski, F., Torrellas, S., Miralles, F., Allison, B.Z., Scherer, R., and Faller, J. 2011. Context-Awareness as an Enhancement of Brain-Computer Interfaces. *International Workshop on Ambient Assisted Living*, Malaga, Spain.

[12] Brunner, C., Allison, B.Z., Altstätter, C. and Neuper, C. A comparison of three brain-computer interfaces based on event-related desynchronization, steady state visual evoked potentials, or a hybrid approach using both signals. *Journal of Neural Engineering* 8:025010, 2011.

[13] Jin, J., Allison, B.Z., Sellers. E.W., Brunner, C., Horki, P., Wang, X., and Neuper, C. 2011. Optimized stimulus presentation patterns for an event-related potential EEG-based brain-computer interface. *Medical and Biological Engineering and Computing* 49, 2, 181-191.

[14] Popescu, F, Fazli, S, Badower, Y, Blankertz, B, Müller KR. 2007. Single trial classification of motor imagination using 6 dry EEG electrodes. *PLoS One* 2, 7 (July 25, 2007) e637.

[15] Lin, C.T., Liao, L.D., Liu, Y.H., Wang, I.J., Lin, B.S., Chang, J.Y. 2011. Novel dry polymer foam electrodes for long-term EEG measurement. *IEEE Trans Biomed Eng.* 58, 5 (May 2011), 1200-1207. Epub 2010 Dec 30.

[16] Luo, A, Sullivan, T.J. 2010. A user-friendly SSVEP-based brain-computer interface using a time-domain classifier. *J Neural Eng.* 7, 2 (April 2010), 26010. Epub 2010 Mar 23.

[17] Su, Y., Qi, Y., Luo, J.-X., Wu, B., Yang, F., Li, Y., Zhuang, Y.-T., Zheng, X.-X., and Chen, W.-D. 2011. A hybrid brain-computer interface control strategy in a virtual environment. *Journal of Zhejiang University – Science C*, 12, 351–361.

[18] Pfurtscheller, G., Allison, B.Z., Brunner, C., Bauernfeind, G., Solis-Escalante, T., Scherer, R., Zander, T.O., Müller-Putz, G., Neuper, C., and Birbaumer, N. 2010. The hybrid BCI. *Frontiers in Neuroscience* 4, 30.

[19] Leeb, R., Sagha, H., Chavarriaga, R., and Millán, J. del R. 2011. A hybrid brain-computer interface based on the fusion of electroencephalographic and electromyographic activities. *Journal of Neural Engineering* 8, 2, 025011.

[20] Laar, B. van de, Gürkök, H., Plass-Oude Bos, D., Nijboer, F., Nijholt, A. 2011. Perspectives on User Experience Evaluation of Brain Computer Interfaces. In *Proceedings Universal Access in Human-Computer Interaction, Part II, 14th International Conference on Human-Computer Interaction (HCII 2011)* (Orlando, USA, July 9-14), C. Stephanidis (Ed.), Lecture Notes in Computer Science 6766, Springer, Heidelberg, 600-609. DOI=http://dx.doi.org/10.1007/978-3-642-21663-3_65.

[21] Gürkök, H., and Nijholt, A. 201. Brain-computer interfaces for multimodal interaction: a survey and principles. *International Journal of Human-Computer Interaction,* preprint. DOI= http://dx.doi.org/10.1080/10447318.2011.582022.

[22] Nijholt, A. Towards Multimodal, Multi-Party, and Social Brain-Computer Interfacing. In *Proceedings 4th International ICST Conference on Intelligent Technologies for Interactive Entertainment (INTETAIN 2011)* (Genoa, Italy, May 25-27, 2011), Lecture Notes of the Institute for Computer Sciences, Social-Informatics and Telecommunications Engineering (LNICST), Springer-Verlag, Berlin, to appear.

[23] Pineda, J.A., Brang, D., Hecht, E., Edwards, L., Carey, S., Bacon, M., Futagaki, C., Suk, D., Tom, J., Birnbaum, C., Rork, A. 2008. Positive behavioral and electrophysiological changes following neurofeedback training in children with autism. Research in Autism Spectrum Disorders 2, 3 (July-September 2008), 557–581. DOI= http://dx.doi.org/10.1016/j.rasd.2007.12.003

[24] Kouijzer, M.E.J., van Schie, H.T., de Moor, J.M.H., Gerrits, B.J.L., Buitelaar, J.K. 2010. Neurofeedback treatment in autism. Preliminary findings in behavioral, cognitive, and neurophysiological functioning. Research in Autism Spectrum Disorders 4, 3, 386-399. DOI= http://dx.doi.org/10.1016/j.rasd.2009.10.007.

[25] Birbaumer, N., Sauseng, P. 2010. BCIs in neurorehabilitation. In: Brain-Computer Interfaces: Non-invasive and Invasive Approaches. Graimann, B., Allison, B.Z., Pfurtscheller, G. (Eds.) Springer-Verlag, Heidelberg.

[26] Nijboer, F., Allison, B.Z., Dunne, S., Plass-Oude Bos, D., Haselager, P., and Nijholt, A. 2011. A preliminary survey on marketability of Brain-Computer Interfaces for various target populations. In *Proceedings 5th International Brain-Computer Interface Conference 2011* (Graz, Austria, September 22-25, 2011), IKD, Graz, to appear. DOI= http://doi.acm.org/10.1145/332040.332491.

Modality Switching and Performance in a Thought and Speech Controlled Computer Game

Hayrettin Gürkök
Human Media Interaction
University of Twente
Enschede, the Netherlands
h.gurkok@utwente.nl

Gido Hakvoort
Human Media Interaction
University of Twente
Enschede, the Netherlands
gido.hakvoort@gmail.com

Mannes Poel
Human Media Interaction
University of Twente
Enschede, the Netherlands
m.poel@utwente.nl

ABSTRACT

Providing multiple modalities to users is known to improve the overall performance of an interface. Weakness of one modality can be overcome by the strength of another one. Moreover, with respect to their abilities, users can choose between the modalities to use the one that is the best for them. In this paper we explored whether this holds for direct control of a computer game which can be played using a brain-computer interface (BCI) and an automatic speech recogniser (ASR). Participants played the games in unimodal mode (i.e. ASR-only and BCI-only) and multimodal mode where they could switch between the two modalities. The majority of the participants switched modality during the multimodal game but for the most of the time they stayed in ASR control. Therefore multimodality did not provide a significant performance improvement over unimodal control in our particular setup. We also investigated the factors which influence modality switching. We found that performance and peformance-related factors were prominently effective in modality switching.

Categories and Subject Descriptors

B.4.2 [**Input/Output Devices**]: Channels and controllers; H.5.2 [**User Interfaces**]: Input devices and strategies

General Terms

Experimentation, Human Factors, Performance

Keywords

Brain-computer interface, automatic speech recogniser, multimodal interaction, hybrid BCI, SSVEP, games

1. INTRODUCTION

Traditional human-computer interaction (HCI) modalities, mouse and keyboard, have long served as a reliable means of input. Despite their reliability, they restrict user's expressive capabilities and therefore the information transferred from the user to the computer. As a response to this problem, modern HCI uses natural human input such as speech and gestures [10]. Moreover, through brain-computer interfaces (BCIs), even brain activity can directly be provided as input to computers [18].

In real-world settings, every input recognition technology has its weaknesses. For instance, automatic speech recogniser (ASR) is affected by factors such as speaker accent and background noise [6]. Similarly, BCI is prone to artefacts due to bodily movements and electromagnetic interference. In addition, due to BCI illiteracy, it cannot be used by some people at all [15]. Thus, even after training a recogniser and/or the user, it might not be possible to achieve a perfect communication between the user and the computer. In this case, offering multiple modalities for input (i.e. multimodality) can be helpful. If multiple modalities are available for use, then people can switch to the modality they believe is most accurate and efficient for conveying particular content. In this way they can improve their own and also the system's overall accuracy [16]. Based on this fact, the first goal of this study is to verify that offering users multiple modalities in a computer game would improve their overall performance.

Besides performance, there might be other reasons for switching modality. For example in entertainment computing the primary goal of users is not to optimise the task performance. While playing a game, users (i.e. players) might still have tasks to complete but their actual purpose in playing the game is enjoyment. The feeling of enjoyment, which is often explained as flow, occurs when the player is exposed to a challenge that matches their skills [3]. In accordance with the flow phenomenon, the player may get bored using the mouse and the keyboard, which offer no challenge to them, but enjoy tackling the shortcomings of a non-traditional modality, such as BCI [14]. Therefore, in multimodal games, players might switch modality not only for improved performance, but for improved enjoyment. Knowing users' modality switching reasons is important for offering them the correct modalities for particular tasks and situations. Based on this motivation, our second goal is to investigate the factors influencing users' modality switching behaviour and preference on certain modalities in a computer game.

In this paper we will consider a realistic game (i.e. an uncontrolled experimental setup) in which players make selections (i.e. direct control) using one of the two available modalities; a steady-state visually evoked potential (SSVEP)

based BCI and an ASR. BCI and ASR are both imperfect but natural input modalities. Moreover, they are suitable candidates for multimodal control in gaming applications, considering the assumption that the majority of the primary game controllers already occupy the players' hands. We will investigate whether users switch modality during the game and, if so, what factors influence their switching behaviour. To explore the switching factors, we will rely on interviews with the players and game logs. We will consider possible factors beyond, but not excluding, performance such as task load, usability, engagement, curiosity and fatigue.

The rest of the paper is organised as follows. In section 2, we introduce BCIs based on the SSVEP and report research related to our study. Then, in section 3, we describe our method and tools. Section 4 describes our experiment details and analysis results. In section 5 we discuss these results and in section 6 we conclude by re-stressing the important results.

2. BACKGROUND

2.1 BCIs Based on SSVEP

BCIs can infer a user's mental/emotional state or intention by interpreting brain activity. First, brain activity is acquired and quantified as a signal, which is mostly done through the use of an electroencephalograph (EEG). EEG measures electrical brain activity via electrodes in contact with the scalp. Then, the signal is processed and analysed in guidance of neuromechanisms. Neuromechanisms signify certain changes in the signal with respect to an event. The event can be a voluntary action such as moving a hand or looking at something as well as an involuntary reaction to a stimulus or an error.

SSVEP is a stimulus dependent, widely used neuromechanism. When a person attends to a visual stimulus repeating with a certain frequency, the amplitude of the signal measured from the visual brain area is enhanced at the frequency of the stimulation. This enhancement is known as the SSVEP [7]. SSVEP is frequently used for selection tasks. By presenting multiple stimuli with distinct repetition frequencies, it is possible to detect which of the stimuli a person was paying attention to. So if each of these stimuli is associated with a choice, then it is possible to detect the person's selection. The strength of the SSVEP is dependent on the stimulation properties. These include flicker frequency, size, colour and shape of the stimulus [1].

2.2 Multimodal Interaction and BCI Games

Most of the applications controlled by BCI are unimodal. This is the case mainly due to the sensitivity of brain activity measurement devices to bodily movements, even to blinking. Nevertheless there are some multimodal BCI applications developed recently [4]. Multimodal BCI games are encountered rarely in the literature but are becoming common with the advances in portable consumer BCI hardware. Finding Star [9] is such a game in which the players control the entities in the game world with emotional signals from the BCI and use the keyboard and mouse to defeat monsters and solve puzzles in the world. In the game NeuroWander [20] the players control an avatar using the keyboard and mouse while their emotional and attentional states are used in fulfilling various quests. In the Bacteria Hunt game [12] the player uses the keyboard to move an amobea at the same time trying to relax to slow down the bacteria they have to catch. In none of the aforementioned games performance or user experience factors were contrasted between multimodal and unimodal control.

Here, we find it useful to mention the concept of hybrid BCI (hBCI) which is used more regularly by the BCI community. An hBCI is defined as a system which *"can either use two different brain signals (e.g. electrical and hemodynamic signals), one brain signal (e.g. EEG) associated with two mental strategies (motor imagery and spatial visual attention), or one brain signal and another input."* [17]. Especially the last phrase of this definition (i.e. combining brain signals with other modalities) matches the multimodality phenomenon as it is employed by the HCI community. Although the definition does not impose any restrictions, so far, the motivation to build hBCIs has been limited to improve the performance of assistive technologies. This trend of practice neglects combining BCI with other modalities for non-performance purposes, such as improving user experience which is a crucial matter of concern in HCI research. The game we use in our study does not violate the definition of hBCIs but with respect to the research we conduct, we consider our game to be a multimodal system rather than an hBCI.

3. METHOD

3.1 Rationale

In this study we used a realistic game, thus an uncontrolled experimental platform, in order not to affect the game flow. We first let the users play unimodal games, in which only ASR or BCI is an available modality, so that they became aware of the performances of the modalities. Then we asked them to play the multimodal game where both modalities were available for use. To evaluate performance in each of the three games we analysed the objective data obtained through game logs. To investigate modality switching reasons of the players we opted for subjective analysis. This was mainly because BCI is a private input modality, preventing us from obtaining ground truth for user actions. For example when a user switches from BCI to ASR we have no objective cue to speculate on what has changed or went wrong. There are a number of subjective analysis methods such as think-aloud, retrospective think-aloud, questionnaires and interviewing [11]. We refrained from think-aloud since we did not want to force users to talk in order to sustain the natural interaction. Moreover, speaking could induce artefacts to the EEG data. We did not prefer retrospective think-aloud either because it lacks the game context which can deeply influence the user experience. Questionnaires are also not very suitable because they can not provide detailed information about specific events occurred during the game. Therefore we decided to do a semi-structured interview at the end of the experiment. We asked the users directly the reasons for switching or staying at a particular modality. Then we elaborated by some predefined potential factors which might have influenced their preferences.

3.2 The Game: Mind the Sheep!

Mind the Sheep! (see Figure 1) is a multimodal computer game where the player needs to herd a flock of sheep across a field by commanding a group of dogs. The game world

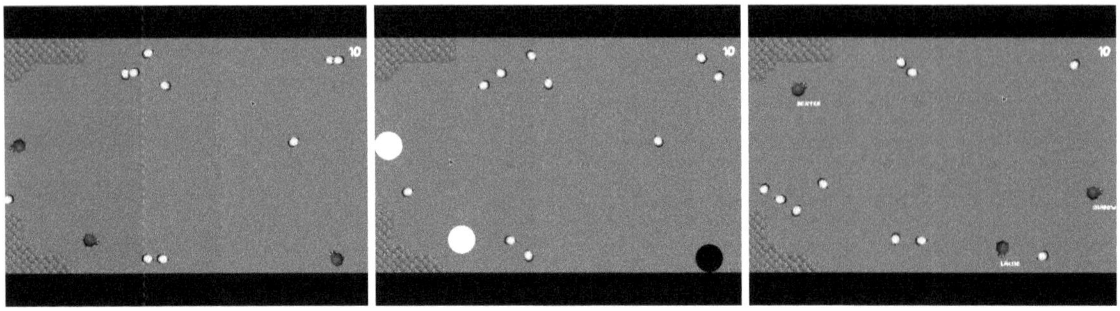

(a) (b) (c)

Figure 1: Screenshots from the game. In (a) and (b) BCI game with stimulation off and on respectively. In (c) ASR game.

contains three dogs, ten sheep, a pen and some obstacles. The aim is to pen all the sheep as quickly as possible.

To command a dog, the player positions the cursor at the point to which the dog is supposed to move. The player holds the mouse button pressed to provide the command to select the dog. Meanwhile, the game displays cues specific to the active modality (ASR or BCI). When ASR is the active modality, names appear under the dog images and the player pronounces the name of the dog they want to select. When BCI is the active modality, dog images are replaced by circles flickering at different frequencies and the player concentrates on the circle replacing the dog they want to select (so as to obtain an SSVEP). The stimulation persists and, depending on the active modality, EEG or acoustic data is accumulated as long as the mouse button is held. When the user releases the mouse button, the signal is analysed and a dog is selected based on this analysis. The selected dog immediately moves to the location where the cursor was located at the time of mouse button release. When configured, it is possible to switch between the modalities by pressing the Ctrl key on the keyboard.

3.2.1 Balancing ASR and BCI Recognition Performances

Ensuring the equivalence of the ASR and the BCI in terms of recognition performance was a concern, as this could highly affect the game experience. We did not want to artificially deteriorate the performance of modalities by introducing noise or random errors but we did try to equalise the performances by tuning game parameters. We conducted two pilot studies to standardise the recognition performances of the ASR and the BCI.

Seven non-native English speakers participated in the first pilot study in which we collected data to compare ASR performance among different sets of dog names (trios formed by candidate names Hector, Victor, Dexter, Pluto, Shadow and Lassie). To record speech, we placed the microphone behind the participant because when the microphone was in the front, the ASR performance was so high that it could not be matched by the BCI. The participants pronouced each name five times. For each name trio we computed the average recall of the recognition carried out by the ASR as described in section 3.2.3.

In the second pilot study another 7 people participated. This time we collected data to evaluate BCI performance with respect to different sets of frequencies (trios formed by candidate frequencies 6 Hz, 6.67 Hz, 7.5 Hz, 8.57 Hz, 10 Hz, 12 Hz, 15 Hz). The setup and procedure for this pilot study is described elsewhere in detail [5]. Just as in the first pilot study, for each frequency trio we computed the average recall of the recognition performed by the BCI as described in section 3.2.2.

We sorted the name trio-frequency trio pairs with respect to their similarity in average recall, which was assessed by Wilcoxon rank-sum tests (higher p-values indicated more similarity). Among the most similar name trio-frequency trio pairs, the pair with the highest average recall was selected. In this way, we decided to use Dexter, Lassie and Shadow (yielding an average recall of 83%) as dog names and 7.5 Hz, 10 Hz and 12 Hz (yielding an average recall of 84%) as flicker frequencies. This pair yielded a p-value of 0.97. We set the flicker diameter length to 3 cm. Literature also confirms that flicker frequencies between 5-12 Hz can evoke strong SSVEP and size of 3 cm can provide an optimal comfort-performance combination [1].

3.2.2 BCI Details

In our study, EEG signals were acquired and recorded by the five BioSemi Active-electrodes placed in contact with the scalp at locations PO3, O1, Oz, O2 and PO4 according to the international 10-20 system [8]. The continuous signals were digitised at a sampling rate of 512 Hz using BioSemi ActiveTwo system. No further processing was carried out in the hardware. In the game software, the digitised EEG data was re-referenced to linked-ears and processed using canonical correlation analysis (CCA) [2] including the three harmonics of each flicker frequency (i.e. fundamental frequency, second and third harmonics). The dog with the frequency that yielded the maximum correlation in CCA was selected by the game.

3.2.3 ASR Details

Speech was acquired by a microphone located to the right, behind the participants as described in section 3.2.1. Acquired acoustic data was recorded, processed and analysed using the CMU Sphinx speech recognition toolkit [19]. All the parameters were left as default except for the following: `absoluteBeamWidth=-1`, `wordInsertionProbability=1E-36`, `relativeBeamWidth=1E-80` and `languageWeight=8`. The Wall Street Journal model supplied within the Sphinx toolkit was used for the dictionary and the acoustic model. Word level unigrams representing the three dog names were used to form the language model. Then, Sphinx constructed a search graph using the acoustic model, the dictionary and the language model. The signal processing pipeline consisted of pre-emphasiser, raised cosine windower, discrete Fourier transform, mel frequency filter bank, discrete cosine transform, cepstral mean normalization and feature extraction. Decoding was performed by a frame synchronous Viterbi search on the constructed search graph using the extracted features. The dog with the name matching the result of the decoding was selected by the game. If there was no result at the end of decoding (e.g. in case of silence), no action was taken.

3.3 Interview

We prepared a semi-structured interview to be conducted at the end of the experiment to learn about users' reasons to switch or stay at a particular modality. The interviews were conducted by the first author of the paper. He read the questions one by one, as they were written on the paper in front of him. The interview was videotaped for post-experiment analysis. The interview began with the question "Did you switch modality during the last game?" and followed by "Why?" or "Why not?" depending on user's answer to the first question. This way, without cueing the user, we identified the factors affecting their preference. Then we asked specifically about possible factors which might have influenced their preference: "Was [factor] a reason for switching from or staying at one modality?" The factors were usability, engagement, task load, performance, tiredness and curiosity. If the answer was just a Yes/No, then we asked "Can you explain?". Finally we repeated our first question as: "Are there any other reasons for switching from or staying at one modality?" in order to extract possible additional reasons that might have been triggered during the interview.

4. EXPERIMENT

4.1 Participants

Twenty people (3 female) participated in the experiment. They had an average age of 24.9 ($\sigma = 2.87$), ranging from 19 to 29 years, and normal or corrected vision. None of them were native English speakers. Eight of them had previous experience with BCIs and fourteen of them with ASRs. Six of them indicated that they played games more than five hours per week. Informed consent was obtained from all participants and they were paid according to the regulations of our institution.

4.2 Procedure

Participants sat on a comfortable chair approximately 60 cm away from a 20″ screen with a resolution of 1280 × 960. They played Mind the Sheep! once with BCI and once with ASR in counterbalanced order to diminish the effect of familiarity with the game. Then they played the multimodal game. They played each game until all the sheep were penned or the play time reached 10 minutes. Games ran on full screen. In the ASR game, BCI control was not available and brain signals were not analysed while in the BCI game, ASR was not available and speech was not recognised. During neither the ASR nor the BCI game could the participants switch between modalities. During the multimodal game both ASR and BCI controls were available, one active at a time. The starting modality was selected randomly. The players could switch between the modalities at any time by pressing the Ctrl key. During all games, each key press and mouse click was time-stamped and logged. The game world layout was different in each game but comparable in difficulty.

4.3 Analysis

We grouped the participants according to their modality switching motivations based on the interview answers. We defined two groups: active switchers and non-switchers. Non-switchers were those who did not switch modality at all and those who switched only at the beginning of the game to decide on which modality to use. These people continuously used a single modality until the end of the game and penned the sheep using one modality. The rest of the participants were active switchers. They reported switching modality during the game after some errors or knowing that certain selections were easier using a particular modality.

To investigate whether using multiple modalities improved performance, for each of the three games played by active switchers, we calculated the number of selections (i.e. number of times the mouse button was released) and game duration as indicators of performance. We expect that the performance of active switchers in the multimodal game would be higher than that in both unimodal games. We calculated the same statistics for the multimodal game played by non-switchers as well as for the preferred and non-preferred unimodal games. For example if a non-switcher stayed at the BCI modality during the multimodal game, then their preferred unimodal game would be the one that they had played using the BCI and their non-preferred unimodal game would be the one that they had played using the ASR. We expect that in the multimodal game non-switchers would achieve a performance better than that in their non-preferred unimodal game and comparable to that in their preferred unimodal game.

To study the modality switching motivations of the participants, we extracted from the interviews the factors for switching or staying at a modality. We combined these with the pre-determined factors which we explicitly asked during the interview. We computed the total number of participants reporting each factor.

Although we computed and report the means in analysis results, we opted for non-parametric statistical testing for assessing the significance of all differences since we neither can assume nor could prove normally distributed samples. Thus, the significance of differences mentioned throughout the paper were assessed by the Wilcoxon signed-rank test ($p < 0.05$). Moreover, the Bonferroni correction was applied during the analyses reported in subsection 4.4 ($p < 0.017$). Unless otherwise stated, reader should assume non-significant difference.

4.4 Results

4.4.1 Performance Analysis

Of the 20 participants, 6 were identified as non-switchers and 14 as active switchers. The box plots in Figure 2 demonstrate scores belonging to the two performance indicators for the unimodal (i.e. ASR and BCI) and multimodal games played by active switchers. The number of selections were not different in BCI ($\mu = 72.64$, $\sigma = 35.48$), ASR ($\mu = 75.00$, $\sigma = 36.94$) and multimodal ($\mu = 73.93$, $\sigma = 46.61$)

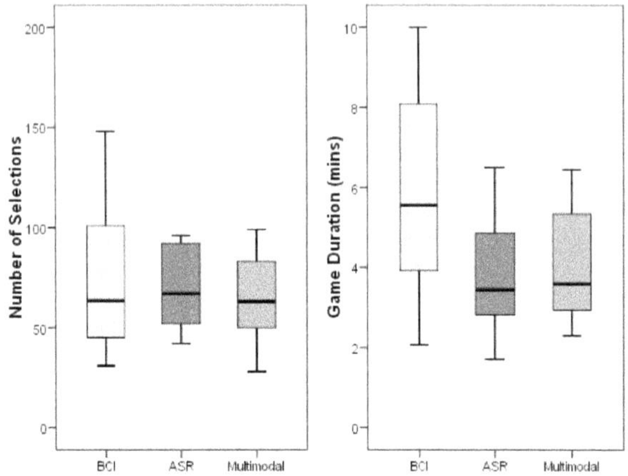

Figure 2: Performance indicators for the BCI, ASR and multimodal games played by active switchers: Average number of selections (left) and average game duration (right).

games. The duration (in minutes) was longer for the BCI game ($\mu = 5.92$, $\sigma = 2.45$) compared to ASR ($\mu = 4.11$, $\sigma = 2.11$) and multimodal ($\mu = 4.60$, $\sigma = 2.54$) games. The difference between the BCI game duration and ASR game duration was significant.

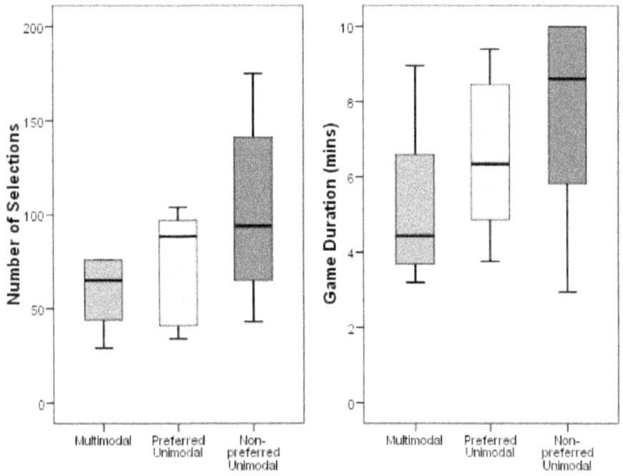

Figure 3: Performance indicators for the multimodal, preferred unimodal and non-preferred unimodal games played by non-switchers: Average number of selections (left) and average game duration (right).

Figure 3 illustrates the performance related scores across non-switchers for the multimodal game they played as well as for the their preferred and non-preferred unimodal games. During the multimodal game 4 people stayed at BCI control while 2 people preferred ASR control. The number of selections during the multimodal game ($\mu = 72.00$, $\sigma = 43.31$) was less than that during the preferred unimodal game ($\mu = 75.50$, $\sigma = 30.16$) which in turn was less than that during the non-preferred unimodal game ($\mu = 102.00$, $\sigma = 48.74$). The same relationship can be observed for the duration (in minutes) of multimodal ($\mu = 5.21$, $\sigma = 2.17$), preferred unimodal ($\mu = 6.53$, $\sigma = 2.18$) and non-preferred unimodal ($\mu = 7.66$, $\sigma = 2.88$) games. None of the differences were significant.

4.4.2 Modality Switching Analysis

Figure 4 shows the number of people reporting a factor as affecting their modality switching or preference. No factors different than those we had set before the experiment were identified during the interviews. Twenty people indicated that performance was a factor affecting their choices. This factor was followed by usability (14 people), curiosity (12), engagement (7), task load (6) and fatigue (5).

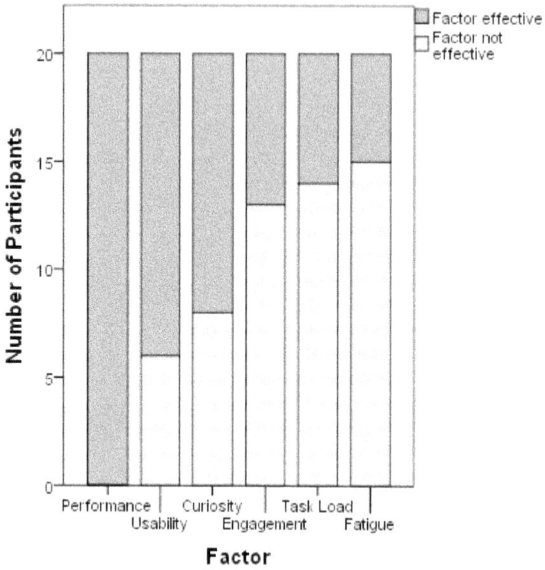

Figure 4: Per factor, number of participants reporting whether it was effective or not in modality switching or preference.

5. DISCUSSION

5.1 Performance Results

Log analysis results did not confirm our expectation that active switchers' performance in the multimodal game would be higher than that in both unimodal games. We found that the number of selections during active switchers' multimodal and unimodal games were comparable. Also the duration of the multimodal game was not significantly different than that of either unimodal game although the unimodal BCI game lasted significantly longer than the unimodal ASR game.

We performed some additional analyses to explain our findings. Firstly, we were interested in why the unimodal BCI game lasted significantly longer than the unimodal ASR game although the number of selections were not different. We thought this could be related to the difference in average selection times between the two modalities. Figure 5(a) shows the average selection duration in the unimodal games. Indeed, during the unimodal BCI game selections lasted significantly longer than the unimodal ASR game. In this case, while making a selection during the unimodal BCI game, the game state would change more than it would in the unimodal ASR game. This might necessitate recreating a strategy after some selections in the unimodal BCI game thus increase the game completion time.

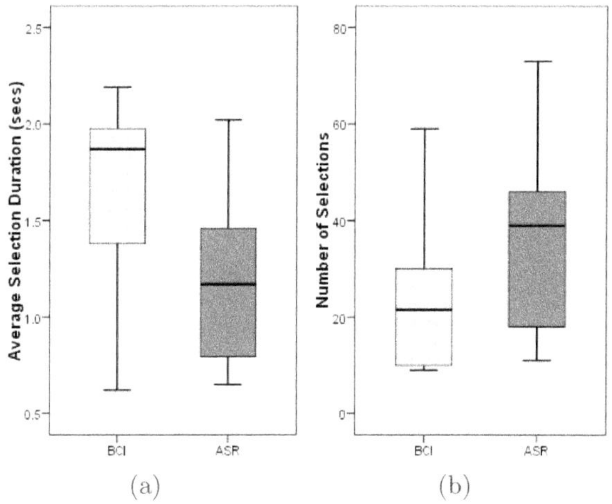

Figure 5: (a) Average selection duration during unimodal games, (b) Number of selections made by active switchers per modality during the multimodal game.

Secondly, we were interested in why the unimodal ASR and multimodal games lasted in very similar times. We hypothesised that during the multimodal game players used ASR more frequently than BCI. To investigate this we extracted the number of selections per modality during the multimodal game. As Figure 5(b) displays, during the multimodal game more number of selections were performed using ASR than that using BCI, although the difference is not significant. Nevertheless, interview results provided some clues supporting our hypothesis. Of the 14 active switchers, 7 indicated that they could not command the dog "Dexter" so switched to BCI when they wanted to control this particular dog. If we assume that they used BCI to control one dog and ASR to control the remaining two, then they would be in ASR mode more frequently than the BCI mode. This can explain why the game durations were comparable in the unimodal ASR and multimodal games.

For non-switchers, our expectations were partly verified by log analysis results. The multimodal game required comparable number of selections and time to complete as with the preferred unimodal game. Also as expected, the multimodal game lasted shorter than the non-preferred unimodal game and took less number of selections. However the differences were not significant probably due to the small sample size. The latter finding might be due to the learning effect as the multimodal game was always played after the unimodal games. It is possible that players gained experience with their preferred modality during the corresponding unimodal game and performed better during the multimodal game using their preferred modality exclusively.

5.2 Modality Switching Results

The participants unanimously indicated that performance was *the* factor in their modality preference. They changed modality when their commands were not understood by the game or they did not change at all knowing that otherwise their commands would not be understood. Log analysis results which we provided in the previous subsection confirmed that non-switchers were able to achieve a better performance in multimodal game but active switchers could improve their performance in the multimodal game only in comparison to the BCI game. Fourteen people reported usability as an influencing factor, which is a concept tightly coupled with the accuracy of an interface [13]. Twelve people (out of 14 active switchers, as this factor only applies to them) indicated that curiosity was a reason to switch modality. However they explained that the curiosity originated when their commands were interpreted incorrectly so that they wanted to see whether the other modality would recognise the command correctly. So this item was tightly coupled to performance as well. Engagement was not a major factor in modality choice. The shortcomings of BCI did not seem to introduce a challenge and improve engagement in this particular game context. Task load and fatigue were also not reported as major factors. Participants were not disturbed by the stimulation while using BCI and they were not tired of putting in effort to use the modalities.

6. CONCLUSIONS

In this paper, we investigated whether providing multiple modalities to players would improve their direct control performance. In an experiment we let 20 participants play two unimodal games, once using a BCI and once using an ASR. Then they played a multimodal game where they could switch between BCI and ASR control whenever they wanted. From the game logs we extracted the number of selections made and game durations for the unimodal and multimodal games as objective indicators of performance. The analysis results showed that 14 participants actively switched modality during the multimodal game while 6 preferred to use a single modality. Active switchers made comparable amount of selections in unimodal and multimodal games. Though non-significantly, their multimodal games lasted shorter than their unimodal BCI game. We found that this difference occurred because during the multimodal game active switchers used ASR control more frequently than BCI control. This suggests that active switchers tended to play using ASR but switched to BCI when ASR did not respond correctly in some particular situations. Non-switchers made comparable number of selections during the unimodal and multimodal games and also finished each game in similar amount of time. Consequently, we cannot conclude that multimodality improved direct control performance in our experimental conditions. We suggest that for direct control BCI is not a preferred alternative to more reliable modalities, such as ASR.

We also investigated what factors, including but not limited to performance, affect players' modality switching or preferences. In a post-hoc interview with participants, we asked them about the reasons to switch or prefer a particular modality. They unanimously indicated that improving the performance was their utmost aim. We also found that usability, a concept highly correlated to the performance of an interface, was a major factor. Curiosity, about the performance of the other modality, was a factor in cases when a modality did not work as expected. The other factors namely engagement, task load and fatigue were not reported as major modality choice factors. It appeared to be that even the non-performance related factors were influenced by the accuracy of the interface. This suggests that before evaluating the non-performance related aspects of an imperfect interface used for direct control of an application, a high accuracy should be guaranteed and that this holds for entertainment applications as well.

Our findings are not necessarily against using BCIs in games. Instead of direct control which leads players to strive for the best performance, BCIs can be used to control less vital dynamics of the game. For example, through passive BCIs [21] a player's state of relaxedness can continuously be monitored and used as an auxiliary controller which tunes the look of a game or other game parameters. So passive BCIs might relax the requirements on performance and timeliness of BCI recognition. We also argue that our findings do not oppose using SSVEP-based BCIs for direct control in games. The game used in our study relied on an SSVEP-based BCI to make selections, which is the most common practice with these BCIs. For example the SSVEP, obtained using a single stimulus (rather than 3 stimuli as we used in our game), can be used to determine a player's concentration level and mapped to actions or a decision mechanism in the game. This might assign a more intuitive function to an SSVEP-based BCI and make it easier for the player to use.

7. ACKNOWLEDGMENTS

The authors gratefully acknowledge the support of the BrainGain Smart Mix Programme of the Netherlands Ministry of Economic Affairs and the Netherlands Ministry of Education, Culture and Science. They would also like to thank L.E. Packwood for her help in improving the language of the article.

8. REFERENCES

[1] J. Bieger and G. G. Molina. Light stimulation properties to influence brain activity: A brain-computer interface application. Technical Report TN-2010-00315, Philips Research, Eindhoven, The Netherlands, 2010.

[2] G. Bin, X. Gao, Z. Yan, B. Hong, and S. Gao. An online multi-channel SSVEP-based brain-computer interface using a canonical correlation analysis method. *Journal of Neural Engineering*, 6(4):046002, 2009.

[3] M. Csikszentmihalyi, S. Abuhamdeh, and J. Nakamura. Flow. In *Handbook of Competence and Motivation*, pages 598–608. The Guilford Press, New York, NY, USA, 2005.

[4] H. Gürkök and A. Nijholt. Brain-computer interfaces for multimodal interaction: a survey and principles. *International Journal of Human-Computer Interaction*, 2011. To appear.

[5] G. Hakvoort, B. Reuderink, and M. Obbink. Comparison of PSDA and CCA detection methods in a SSVEP-based BCI-system. Technical Report TR-CTIT-11-03, Centre for Telematics and Information Technology, University of Twente, Enschede, The Netherlands, 2011.

[6] J.-P. Haton. Automatic speech recognition: A review. In *Enterprise Information Systems V*, pages 6–11. Springer, Dordrecht, The Netherlands, 2005.

[7] C. S. Herrmann. Human EEG responses to 1–100 Hz flicker: resonance phenomena in visual cortex and their potential correlation to cognitive phenomena. *Experimental Brain Research*, 137(3–4):346–353, 2001.

[8] H. H. Jasper. Report of the committee on methods of clinical examination in electroencephalography: 1957. *Electroencephalography and Clinical Neurophysiology*, 10(2):370–375, 1958.

[9] M. Ko, K. Bae, G. Oh, and T. Ryu. A study on new gameplay based on brain-computer interface. In *Proceedings of the DiGRA 2009*. Brunel University, London, UK, 2009.

[10] P. Kortum. *HCI Beyond the GUI*. Morgan Kaufmann, San Francisco, CA, USA, 2008.

[11] R. L. Mandryk, K. M. Inkpen, and T. W. Calvert. Using psychophysiological techniques to measure user experience with entertainment technologies. *Behaviour & Information Technology*, 25(2):141–158, 2006.

[12] C. Mühl, H. Gürkök, D. Plass-Oude Bos, M. E. Thurlings, L. Scherffig, M. Duvinage, A. A. Elbakyan, S. Kang, M. Poel, and D. Heylen. Bacteria Hunt: Evaluating multi-paradigm BCI interaction. *Journal on Multimodal User Interfaces*, 4(1):11–25, 2010.

[13] J. Nielsen. *Usability Engineering*. Morgan Kaufmann, San Francisco, CA, USA, 1993.

[14] A. Nijholt, B. Reuderink, and D. Oude Bos. Turning shortcomings into challenges: Brain-computer interfaces for games. In *Intelligent Technologies for Interactive Entertainment*, pages 153–168. Springer-Verlag, Berlin/Heidelberg, Germany, 2009.

[15] A. Nijholt, D. Tan, G. Pfurtscheller, C. Brunner, J. del R. Millán, B. Allison, B. Graimann, F. Popescu, B. Blankertz, and K.-R. Müller. Brain-computer interfacing for intelligent systems. *IEEE Intelligent Systems*, 23:72–79, 2008.

[16] S. Oviatt. Taming recognition errors with a multimodal interface. *Communications of the ACM*, 43:45–51, 2000.

[17] G. Pfurtscheller, B. Z. Allison, C. Brunner, G. Bauernfeind, T. Solis-Escalante, R. Scherer, T. O. Zander, G. Mueller-Putz, C. Neuper, and N. Birbaumer. The hybrid BCI. *Frontiers in Neuroprosthetics*, 4:30, 2010.

[18] D. Tan and A. Nijholt, editors. *Brain-Computer Interfaces: Applying our Minds to Human-Computer Interaction*. Springer-Verlag, London, UK, 2010.

[19] W. Walker, P. Lamere, P. Kwok, B. Raj, R. Singh, E. Gouvea, P. Wolf, and J. Woelfel. Sphinx-4: A flexible open source framework for speech recognition. Technical Report SMLI TR-2004-139, Sun Microsystems Inc., Menlo Park, CA, USA, 2004.

[20] M.-S. Yoh, J. Kwon, and S. Kim. NeuroWander: a BCI game in the form of interactive fairy tale. In *Proceedings of the Ubicomp '10*, pages 389–390, New York, NY, USA, 2010. ACM.

[21] T. O. Zander and C. Kothe. Towards passive brain-computer interfaces: applying brain-computer interface technology to human-machine systems in general. *Journal of Neural Engineering*, 8(2):025005, 2011.

An Approach towards Human-Robot-Human Interaction Using a Hybrid Brain-Computer Interface

Nils Hachmeister, Hannes Riechmann
CITEC, Bielefeld University
Universitätsstraße 21-23
33615 Bielefeld, Germany
{nhachmei,hriechma}@cit-ec.uni-bielefeld.de

Helge Ritter
CITEC & CorLab, Bielefeld University
Universitätsstraße 21-23
33615 Bielefeld, Germany
helge@cit-ec.uni-bielefeld.de

Andrea Finke
CITEC & CorLab, Bielefeld University
Universitätsstraße 21-23
33615 Bielefeld, Germany
afinke@cit-ec.uni-bielefeld.de

ABSTRACT

We propose the concept of a brain-computer interface interaction system that allows patients to virtually use nonverbal interaction affordances, in particular gestures and facial expressions, by means of a humanoid robot. Here, we present a pilot study on controlling such a robot via a hybrid BCI. The results indicate that users can intuitively address interaction partners by looking in their direction and employ gestures and facial expressions in every-day interaction situations.

Categories and Subject Descriptors

K.4.2 [**Computers and Society**]: Social Issues—*Assistive technologies for persons with disabilities*; H.5.2 [**Information Interfaces and Presentation**]: User Interfaces—*Input devices and strategies*; I.2.9 [**Artificial Intelligence**]: Robotics—*Operator interfaces*

General Terms

Experimentation, Human Factors

1. INTRODUCTION

One major application for brain-computer interfaces (BCIs) is to open a communication channel for totally locked-in patients. We propose a BCI-based interaction system, which is inspired by a statement in a study from Kübler et al. [5] about BCI spelling systems:

"*Patient 002 [...] was able to use the Language Support Program [...] and liked to use the program. Unfortunately, none of his family or friends were interested in communicating with him. After several weeks [...] he terminated further use.*"

Why could friends and family be disinterested in BCI-based communication with a severely disabled relative? In our opinion, communication via BCI spellers has two major drawbacks: (i.) It is slow. (ii.) It lacks several affordances provided by face-to-face communication (in particular gestures and facial expressions). Social interaction is more than pure spelling and, hence, entirely lacking these affordances while being co-present, makes interaction feel unnatural and unintuitive. A severely disabled patient should be able to accompany words with facial expressions and gestures, allowing for a much more natural way of interaction. We present a concept that is intended to implement these requirements: A humanoid robot serves patients as a mediator for social interaction, enabling them to make use of said affordances. We present a pilot study towards such an interaction mediator showing its technical feasibility. Therefore we constructed and tested a prototype system employing a hybrid BCI.

Various studies have demonstrated that language is the major channel needed for interaction [9]. For joint cognitive task solving, adding a visual to a text-only communication channel in order to provide affordances such as gestures and facial expressions, has been shown to have little impact on the interaction [3]. However, for social tasks and negotiation, adding these affordances to a text-only communication has been shown to alter interaction content and success [9]. Additionally, text-only communication is considered impersonal and the users have low social presence [4]. Interaction with a relative constitutes a social task which is, for locked-in patients using a BCI speller, limited to text-only communication. All other affordances are not available for these patients.

We aim to transfer a patient's social presence to a robot. A similar transfer was tested by Paulos et al. [7], who proposed a robotic system called Personal Roving Presence (PRoP). They enabled users to operate a robot via a Java applet, established two-way video and audio channels and equipped their robot with a pointing device. In contrast to our publication, Paulos et al. focused on technical solutions to realize telepresence for healthy users. That is, they focused on robot design employing an ordinary graphical user interface, while we used an existing robotic solution and focused on interface design.

There are several studies about controlling a humanoid robot via BCI. Controlling a humanoid this way can be tricky due to the high latency, unavoidable classification errors, and low transfer rate. This means that we need reliable, fault-tolerant, semi-autonomous robot behaviour, which can be controlled with few, simple commands. In Bell et al. [1],

ICMI'11, November 14–18, 2011, Alicante, Spain.

Figure 1: *Left* - iCub crawling, Figure from www.robotcup.org *Right* - iCub displaying different facial expressions. Figure adapted from [2].

a humanoid robot had to pick one out of several objects and transport it to one out of several potential target locations. The user simply selected object and target location via two separated P300 trials and the robot autonomously executed these high-level commands. In contrast to this publication, the scope of their study was to demonstrate that a humanoid can be controlled via a BCI. Aspects which are central to this publication, such as human interaction and affordances of such interaction, were not considered.

The BCI system we used is a so called hybrid BCI system as proposed by Riechmann et al. [8]. It employs multiple brain activity patterns (BAPs): P300 triggered by an odd-ball paradigm[1] and ERD evoked by motor imagery (MI)[2]. Although both BAPs can be measured with the same physical device they still constitute different modes of communication: (i.) From the user's perspective, as the two BAPs require different mental activities on the part of the user. (ii.) From a signal processing perspective, as the two BAPs are very distinct in nature and the recorded data, therefore, has to be filtered, processed, and classified in different ways. (iii.) From the control logic's perspective, as the two BAPs are used to control disjunct aspects of the robot's behaviour. In particular, P300 is used to control discrete aspects (e.g. to choose one out of several objects to grasp), while ERD is used to control continuous aspects (e.g. the speed at which the robot moves forward). These two different BAPs should allow for intuitive control over the robot. However, whether users can maintain the degreed of mental control necessary in a real robotic scenario, is yet to be determined.

2. METHODS

In the following, we will describe the robot and the BCI system we used. Subsequently, we will discuss the scenario and the experimental setup we developed.

2.1 iCub Humanoid Robot

We chose the iCub humanoid robot as the robotic platform for our system. It was developed as an *"open platform for research in embodied cognition"* [6]. This open approach and the ongoing development of the project will facilitate the progress of an interaction mediator system. The iCub has 53 degrees of freedom, is 104 cm tall and has roughly the physical capabilities of a three-and-a half year old child. It can mimic different facial expressions, some of which are depicted in Figure 1. Mouth and eyebrows are emulated using LEDs, the eyelids are moved mechanically. Nose and ears are stationary. While there is currently no software to make the iCub stand or walk, it is already capable to gesture, point, reach and grasp. Thereby, it provides all features needed for an interaction mediator.

[1]Positive cortical potential 300 ms after the target stimulus.
[2]Decrease of μ- and $\beta-$ band power in the motor cortex.

2.2 Asynchronous Hybrid BCI

We used the hybrid BCI system presented in [8]. Two BAPs, ERD and P300, were detected independently on the same EEG data stream. As an addition to the existing hybrid BCI system, we propose a P300-based start/stop function, which can be triggered asynchronously by users. Therefore, the P300 stimulus presentation is running continually. Even parallel use of the start/stop function and an ERD classification can be realised. For example, when adjusting the movement speed of the robot via MI the user has to be able to terminate the speed adjustment when the desired velocity is reached. When the start/stop function is running parallel and asynchronously to the speed adjustment, this can be done at any time. In order to trigger the start/stop function users have to concentrate on a specific target-symbol out of n symbols used for the P300 stimulus presentation. Otherwise, they have to ignore the presentation. Therefore, whether or not the user concentrated on the P300 stimulus presentation has to be automatically detected by the system. This is done by comparing the highest classification score of all symbols in a given trial with a threshold. The start/stop function is triggered if and only if the threshold is reached and the corresponding symbol is the target-symbol. Otherwise, the stimulus presentation is continued.

To implement the start/stop function two minor modifications of the system were implemented: (i.) The classification results for both BAPs were forwarded to the control software of the robot instead of choosing one of them. (ii.) The classification of both BAPs was done asynchronously, i.e. P300 trials and ERD trials did not start at the same time. As one ERD trial is much shorter than one P300 trial, several ERD trials can be completed during one P300 trial.

2.3 Scenario

We chose an every-day interaction situation to test our system: A couple of people are sitting on chairs, chatting. The patient participates in this interaction via an interaction mediator. It allows the patient to naturally address individual interaction partners by looking in their direction and make use of non-verbal communication by performing gestures and putting on facial expressions. We designed an experimental scenario to evaluate if the proposed system is suitable in such a situation: The participant had to make the robot look in the direction of a target object representing a point of interest (e.g. an interaction partner) and trigger the display of an emotional response (a combination of facial expression and gesture). The target object is placed in the direction of the robot's sagittal axis. The robotic control system cycles through three different phases (see Figure 2). These phases are enumerated 1-3 and the transitions between these phases are enumerated a-c.

1. **Random Swaying:** The robot is not controlled by the participant and just sways its torso randomly. The BCI system is active the whole time to enable the participant to take control, i.e the start/stop function is running.

   (a) The participant triggers the start/stop function. The robot turns its torso to an orientation 50° to the right of its sagittal axis and the participant is granted control of the robot's orientation.

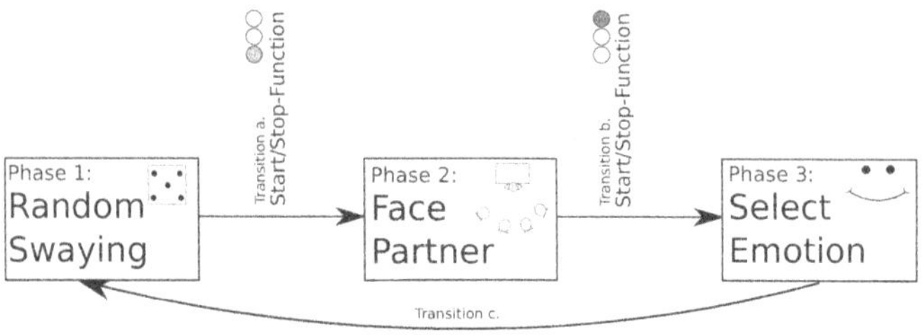

Figure 2: Phases cycled during the experiment.

2. **Face Partner:** The robot turns its torso left or right, controlled by the participant by imagining movements of the left or right hand. Approximately every five seconds a new MI trial begins. After the end of the trial the robot turns its torso up to 10° to the left or right depending on the classification confidence. The robot's camera images are projected onto a screen in front of the participant. This allows the participant to judge if the robot faces the target object. The start/stop function is running parallel.

   (b) When the desired orientation is reached the participant triggers the start/stop function.

3. **Select Emotion:** The participant selects one out of a set of predefined displays of emotional responses via a P300 trial. Available combinations are: neutral, greet (raising the hand + smiling), handshake (stretching out hand + looking shy), angry (looking angry) and jumping jack (taking the jumping jack pose + looking cunning). The robot executes the selected command.

   (c) The system returns to phase 1.

One central criterion for the evaluation of the scenario will be the successful passing of the second phase. During this phase multiple BAPs have to be employed by the participant, which might lead to problems with regard to the classification or the degree of mental control required from the user.

The scenario covers the basic building blocks for an interaction mediator. It is possible to address interaction partners and to perform gestures and facial expressions to transport the emotional response of the user.

2.4 Experimental Setup

During our experiment, the healthy participant sat in front of two screens, one showing the P300 stimulus presentation and the other showing the images from the robot's cameras. For this experiment a simulation of the iCub was used[3]. Prior to the experiments, the participant was instructed about the procedure of the scenario verbally. Additionally, she received an instruction sheet.

Data was acquired using a gUSBamp (Guger Technologies) amplifier. 16 channels were equipped with Ag/AgCl electrodes placed at Fz, Cz, Pz, Oz, F3, F4, C3, C4, C5, C6, CP3, CP4, P3, P4, PO7, PO8 according to the extended international 10-20 system. This configuration was designed to cover the motor cortex bilaterally and the areas in which P300 is most prominent (in particular parietal and central cortex). A ground and a common reference electrode were placed on the mastoids (A1 and A2). Electrode impedances were kept below 5 $k\Omega$. The amplifier sampled the EEG data at 256 Hz, performed high-pass filtering at 0.1 Hz and notch filtering at $48 - 52$ Hz. For the P300 stimulus presentation (for the start/stop function as well as for the selection of emotional responses) five symbols were used. One trial consisted of ten subtrials, during which, in random order, each symbol flashed once. The inter-stimulus interval (ISI) was set to 150 ms. For each P300 stimulus, a data segment of 800 ms starting at the beginning of the stimulus was generated. For each ERD trial, ten overlapping data segments of 4000 ms were generated, with an inter-segment interval of 100 ms. The first and the last 300 ms of each segment were discarded, in order to remove possible motor and filter artefacts. The classification results of all segments of one trial were averaged and scaled into the interval $[-10, 10]$ resulting in the angle by which the robot turned its torso.

The system was tested with the designed scenario. The participant had completed three MI training sessions of about thirty minutes on different days before the actual experiment. On the day of the experiment a P300 training data set containing fifty trials was recorded and, subsequently, a shortened MI training was conducted until ERD classification accuracy was stable. Then, the participant performed one experimental session where the three phases were repeated five times.

3. RESULTS AND DISCUSSION

For brain-robot control, measuring classification accuracy would require information about the participants' intentions. Because an analysis of the (original) system's classification accuracy can be found in [8], we decided not to gather this information. Therefore, we define alternative criteria to evaluate system performance: i) Did the implemented start/stop function allow for smooth transition between the phases? ii) Did the system recognize the selected gestures/facial expressions correctly? iii) How precisely could the participant gear the robot's torso towards the target object?

The start/stop function can only be assessed qualitatively, as we do not know precisely at which time the participant wanted to trigger the function. However, except for the first iteration, the participant reported that, when she intended to activate the start/stop function, it was triggered after the completion of the next full P300 trial. Hence, this function allows to control phase transitions smoothly.

The selection of emotional responses (phase 3) can be measured quantitatively, because the participant was told which combination of gesture/facial expression to choose for each iteration. The system correctly recognised the target response in every iteration.

The participant had to turn the robot's torso via MI towards a target object (phase 2). It was up to the participant to judge, depending on the robot's camera view, at which point this was accomplished. When the participant reached an angle which she found satisfactory, she had to turn her attention to the P300 start/stop function running parallel in order to switch to phase 2. The right (orange) bars in Figure 3 show the final distances from the target orientation per iteration of the scenario. During the first iteration the participant was unable to trigger the start/stop function properly and the robot turned to the left boundary of the

[3]Additionally, a video with a slightly adapted scenario employing the real iCub is available online: see also `http://www.youtube.com/watch?v=L2DUGOKA35c`.

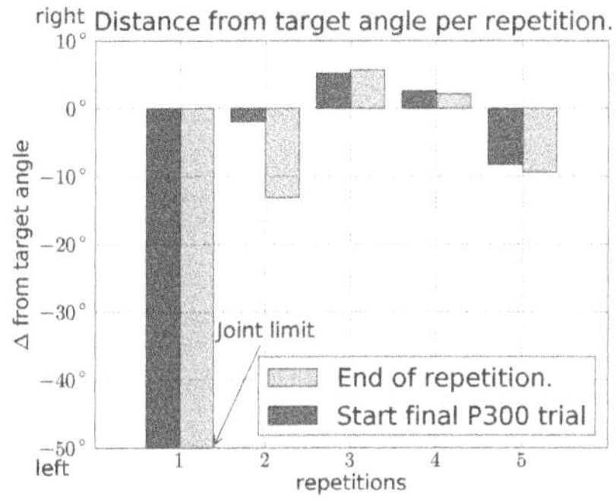

Figure 3: Deviation from target angle.

joint in the process. In the following iterations the participant achieved reasonable (max. 13.1°) up to good (min. 2.1°) distances from the target orientation.

We assumed that during the P300 trial which finally triggered the start/stop function, the participant had concentrated on the stimulus presentation and had not performed any MI. However, the robot might turn away from the desired orientation, due to misclassification and the high degree of mental control required from the participant. Hence, we considered the orientation at the beginning of the final P300 trial as well (left (blue) bars in Figure 3). During the second iteration, the robot, indeed, turned away from the desired orientation (from an error in the orientation of 2° at the beginning of the final P300 trial to 13.1° at the end of the trial). For the following iterations, this effect almost vanished. Orientations at the beginning and the end of the final P300 trial were almost identical. These results raise the question whether suppressing ERDs during the use of the P300 start/stop function can be learned by users.

In an informal interview after the experiment the participant reported to be satisfied with the system. In particular, she found it was well usable and not extraordinarily exhausting. She did not consciously use a mental strategy to achieve the observed ERD suppression.

4. CONCLUSION

We demonstrated that our system can be used for everyday interaction situations and is a good starting point for further development of an interaction mediator. While the scenario presented here is limited, it demonstrates that the system provides the main building blocks for a more elaborate interaction mediator enabling more complex and flexible interaction situations. It allows to smoothly control the robot without the use of any neuro-muscular channels, addressing discrete as well as continuous aspects of the robot's behaviour in a natural way. With respect to the studied scenario, it allows to address individual persons within a group in an intuitive way and to perform gestures and facial expressions towards this person. Furthermore, the user can share the robot's view. However, each use of the system requires some preparation effort. Additionally, due to the limited speed of current BCIs, interaction is still rather slow.

The promising results of this pilot study encourage us to further pursue the idea of an interaction mediator. Among other aspects, we plan to examine the experience of the partners in interaction with such a mediator.

5. ACKNOWLEDGEMENTS

The study was partially funded by the German Research Council (DFG), EXC 277.
Andrea Finke gratefully acknowledges the financial support from Honda Research Institute Europe.
We thank Hendrik Koesling for his constructive comments.

6. REFERENCES

[1] C.J. Bell, P. Shenoy, R. Chalodhorn, and R.P.N. Rao. Control of a humanoid robot by a noninvasive brain–computer interface in humans. *Journal of Neural Engineering*, 5(2):214–220, 2008.

[2] A. Bernardino, R. Nunes, L. Vargas, R. Beira, M. Lopes, and J. Santos-Victor. Facial expressions: Design and integration. Technical report, Universidade Técnica de Lisboa, Instituto Superior Técnico (IST), March 2007.

[3] A. Chapanis, R.N. Parrish, R.B. Ochsman, and G.D. Weeks. Studies in interactive communication: II. The effects of four communication modes on the linguistic performance of teams during cooperative problem solving. *Human Factors: The Journal of the Human Factors and Ergonomics Society*, 19(2):101–126, 1977.

[4] S.R. Hiltz, K. Johnson, and M. Turoff. Experiments in group decision making communication process and outcome in face-to-face versus computerized conferences. *Human Communication Research*, 13(2):225–252, 1986.

[5] A. Kübler, B. Kotchoubey, J. Kaiser, J. Perelmouter, J. Wolpaw, and N. Birbaumer. Brain-computer interface: Unlocking the locked-in. *Psychological Bulletin*, 127(3):358–375, 2001.

[6] G. Metta, G. Sandini, D. Vernon, L. Natale, and F. Nori. The iCub humanoid robot: an open platform for research in embodied cognition. In *Proceedings of the 8th Workshop on Performance Metrics for Intelligent Systems*, PerMIS '08, pages 50–56, New York, NY, USA, 2008. ACM.

[7] E. Paulos and J. Canny. PRoP: personal roving presence. In *Proceedings of the SIGCHI conference on Human factors in computing systems*, pages 296–303. ACM Press/Addison-Wesley Publishing Co., 1998.

[8] H. Riechmann, N. Hachmeister, H. Ritter, and A. Finke. Asynchronous, parallel on-line classification of P300 and ERD for an efficient hybrid BCI. In *Proceedings of the 5th International IEEE EMBS Conference on Neural Engineering*, in press.

[9] S. Whittaker. Theories and methods in mediated communication. *The handbook of discourse processes*, pages 243–286, 2003.

Towards Multimodal Error Responses: A Passive BCI for the detection of Auditory Errors

Thorsten O. Zander*
Max Planck Institute for Intelligent Systems & Team PhyPA, TU Berlin
72076 Tübingen Germany
tzander@gmail.com

Marius David Klippel†
Team PhyPA, TU Berlin
10587 Berlin Germany
marius.klippel@googlemail.com

Reinhold Scherer‡
Institute for Knowledge Discovery, Graz University of Technolgy
8010 Graz Austria
reinhold.scherer@tugraz.at

ABSTRACT

The study presented here introduces a Passive BCI detecting responses of the subjects brain on the perception of correct and erroneous auditory signals. 10 experts in music theory who actively play an instrument listened to cadences, sequences of chords, that could have an unexpected, erroneous ending. In consistence with previous studies from the neurosciences we evoked an event-related potential, mainly consisting of an early right anterior negativity reflecting syntactic error processing followed by a stronger negativity in erroneous trials at 500 ms, induced by semantic processing. We could identify single trials of these processes with a standardized, crossvalidated offline classification scheme, resulting in an accuracy of 75.7%. The here presented system is a further step towards a multimodal, BCI-based Human-Computer Interaction, also inclduing auditory feedback channels.

Categories and Subject Descriptors

H.1.2 [**Information Systems**]: Models and Principles—*User/Machine Systems, Human information processing*

General Terms

HUMAN FACTORS

Keywords

Passive Brain-Computer Interfaces, Electroencephalogram, Machine Learning, Auditory modality, Automated adaptation

*

†

‡

1. INTRODUCTION

Multimodality gets more and more important for contemporary Brain-Computer Interface (BCI) research. With the introduction of *hybrid BCIs* [1] the fusion of BCI input channels with other modalities has been defined. First studies, e.g. [2], have shown the high potential arising from this extension of the initial definition of BCI. Until now most of the BCI systems rely on displaying information to the user via the visual domain. This information might also be displayed through vibro-tactile interfaces [3, 4] as well as through auditory interfaces [5, 6]. Hence, it might be valuable to investigate how much of the knowledge about BCIs based on the visual domain can be transferred to other modalities. One interesting and relevant approach is the detection of error responses of the brain and it's utilization for setting up an automated correction system based on a Passive BCI [7, 8, 9, 10, 11]. A first step for investigating error responses with a Passive BCI from the tactile domain has been done in [4]. Here, we are going to discuss a similar approach for the auditory domain.

Passive BCIs provide a valuable input channel for Human-Computer Interaction, like discussed in [7]. It can be used to access information about latent changes in user state, like changes in cognitive/mental workload, for adapting the system. It also can be used to reveal internal reactions or interpretations of the user following the perception of specific events, that can be fed back to the technical system for enhancing the interaction. The above mentioned responses on error detection is one example for the detection of such *cognitive events.* From a general perspective, cognitive events can deliver valuable information in multimodal systems, as they potentially can be related to specific input and output streams in different modalities. This assumption can be concluded from experiences made in the visual domain and theoretical knowledge from the neurosciences. The study presented in the following parts of this paper goes one step towards the usage of Passive BCI technology for multimodal systems by investigating the detectability of auditory error responses.

Recent studies from the neurosciences have shown how the brain reacts on perceiving mistakes in syntax or semantic of speech [12], as well in that of music [13]. Both result in an Event-Related Potential (ERP) of similar morphology, which is not surprising as there is evidence for a functional

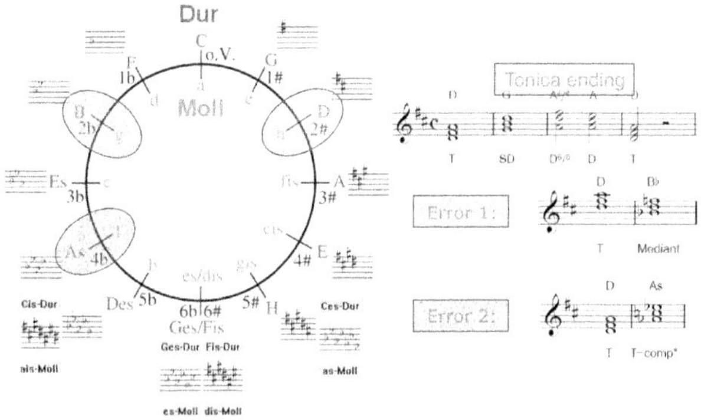

Figure 1: (Cadence endings) This figure shows the three types of endings for the cadences: D-major (Tonica), As-major (Subdominant), Bb-major (Dominant). Left: The circle of fifths. Right: Chords on staves. Deviant endings (marked orange and red) occurred with a chance of 15% while standards had a probability of 70%.

similarity of both types of auditory communication along the evolving of the human species in time [13]. Here, we are going to show results of a study that transferred an approach introduced by Stefan Koelsch in 2005 [13] for investigating auditory error responses with magneto-encephalography (MEG) to a BCI system based on electro-encephalography (EEG).

The presented experimental paradigm is based on sequences of chords, namely cadences. In cadences a chord will be determined by some degree by its predecessors. With processing the cadence further, this dependency grows stronger, such that the expectancy of an auditor for a specific last chord is very high. A violation of this expectancy initiates an error processing in the human brain, leading to the potentials mentioned above.

2. EXPERIMENTAL SETUP

We invited 10 subjects with strong background in music theory who actively play a classical instrument to our experiments. They were equipped with 32 channels of Brain Products ActiCap system, distributed in a standard way along the international 10/20 system. Impedances were kept below 20 $k\Omega$ for each electrode and data was recorded with a sampling frequency of 1000 Hz. Additionally, they were equipped with a standard, fully closed headset of Sennheiser. An experimenter instructed each subject before the starting of the recordings about the purpose of the experiment, it's duration and the planned course of events. Subjects sat in a sound insulation cabin during the experiments, for ensuring no distraction from environmental noise. During the experiment there was no feedback provided and no action required except for concentrated listening. Subjects were positioned in a comfortable chair and asked to either stare at one point or keep their eyes closed during the experiment. The experiment's auditory stimulus was a a standard classical cadence consistent of three kinds of different endings. The harmonic structure was: Tonica, Subdominant, Dominant (6-5 | 4-3), concluded by a variable ending. This ending was in 70% the Tonica, in 15% the large lower mediant and in the 15% a harmonically totally unrelated chord, the Tonica of the complementary key, from half way around the circle of fifth. Since the trials were played in D-major, the absolute chords were the following: D-major, G-major, A(6|4)-major, A(5|3)-major and the variable ending, which was one of D-major, As-major, Bb-major. We chose two kind of endings to avoid overfitting of subjects and classifier to one deviant (figure 1).

Each trials consisted of a sequence of 6 chords. Time between chords was equidistantly 1 second, an pause of 2 seconds was following each sequence, summing up to a total trial length of 8 seconds. Each subject listened to 270 trials. 190 trials were 'standard' trials with tonica ending while each 'deviant' class consisted of 40 trials. The presentation of the trials was distributed randomly through standard and the deviant classes. In total the presentation of the stimulus took 36 minutes.

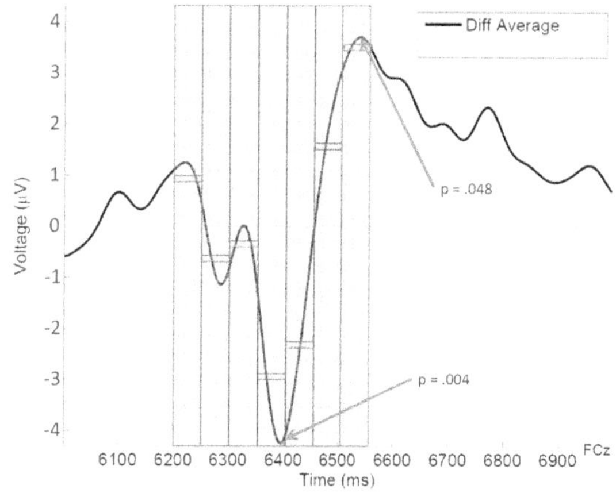

Figure 2: (Difference plot) This figure shows the grandaverage of the differences between correct and erroneous trials. Grey marked areas indicate the time windows used for feature extraction. Orange bars in these time windows reflect estimates of the feature values for this channel (FCz). Significance of the differences was checked with a t-test at averages of 50ms around the peaks across subjects. The error negativity was highly significantly different from the standards, while the error positivity was significantly different.

3. CLASSIFICATION SCHEME

For investigating how well a Passive BCI would perform in detecting the perception of erroneous cadences we set up an offline classification scheme. A classifier is trained and tested via crossvalidation on the data that has been recorded for a single subject. Features extracted from standard trials are discriminated against those from deviant trials.

We adopted the pattern matching method described in [14] for feature extraction in combination with a linear discrim-

Subject No.	Classification error
01	13.2
02	11.4
03	26.0
04	33.9
05	32.1
06	22.0
07	23.4
08	32.7
Average	**24.3**

Table 1: (Classification errors) This table shows the of the regularized classifier estimated for each subject with a 10x(5,10)-crossvalidation (10 times repeated, 5 folded nested, 10 folded outer)

inant analyses (LDA) regularized with shrinkage [14] for classification. This classification scheme showed best performance for detection of ERPs as can be seen in [15]. The procedure of feature extraction can be described in a few steps. The data recorded was bandpassfiltered with a fast Fourier transform between 0.5 and 15 Hz and downsampled to 200 Hz. The highpass filter eliminates slow shifts in the data, making baseline corrections obsolete for further analyses and plots. Then epochs of 1 second length were extracted after the marker indicating that the last chord of a cadence was initiated. Features were extracted for seven sequential time windows of 50 ms length, starting at 200 ms relative to the marker, by averaging the EEG within each window. This results in a $7 * 32 = 224$ dimensional feature space. We equalized the number of trials for each of the two extracted classes (standard and deviants) to 80 trials (number of trials in the smaller class) to avoid class specific overfitting of the LDA. The LDA was trained for each subject with a 10x(5,10)-crossvalidation (10 times repeated, 5 folded nested, 10 folded outer), and regularized with shrinkage [14, 16] for dealing with the bad dimensionality ratio between features and trials.

4. CLASSIFICATION RESULTS

Data of two subjects was discarded because of technical problems with the recordings. The average, crossvalidated classification accuracy across subjects is 75.4%, with equally distributed errors between the classes. It can be seen as an estimator for the performance of the Passive BCI system in an online appication. The real application performance is likely to be a bit worse as the preliminary for crossvalidation of independent noise structures between trials is not fulfilled in trialbased EEG experiments. Nevertheless, recent studies showed that the difference between offline and online results ususally is not too big. Hence, and because there is no other standardized method for estimating classification accuracies in offline studies in the field of BCI reserch, we decided for taking crossvalidation as measure for our estimation here. See table 1 for details on individual error rates.

5. DISCUSSION AND CONCLUSION

We found evidence that ERPs related to processing of syntactic and semantic errors can be detected by a Passive BCI. The accuracy of this detection is a little bit below that reported in studies from the visual domain. Further analyses of the experimental series could bring more insight into the underlying reasons. Nevertheless, it still is good enough for application in online scenarios. These results open up the research of Passive BCIs for multimodal systems with auditory information channels. In combination with the results on visual and tactile error responses this outcome shows potentially that an automated error correction in the major modalities is indeed possible relying on EEG data. The focus on errors in cadences obviously limits the bandwidth of possible applications resulting from this study. It rather can be seen as a first step towards investigating what potential lies in the approach of passive BCIs. Further studies will investigate what other types of auditory signals can be analyzed online with an automated error correction based on Passive BCI. Also comparisons of Passive BCIs for different modalities should be done in single experiments. If errors in different modalities can be discriminated from each other, the resulting system could also be used to detect the level of attention the user puts into a single modality. We hope that these results will be beneficial for the development of new multimodal BCI-systems, also utilizing the auditory domain. Furthermore, this Passive BCI gives to some degree insight into internal interpretation of the subject. It allows us to see whether he or she accepts the presented cadence ending or not. This might be especially interesting for ongoing neuroscientific studies investigating cultural differences in music perception. In further studies we will focus on the development of new classification schemes that could improve the accuracy of the detection, as well as the evaluation whether this approach can be extended to other auditory signals, not embedded so strongly in music theory.

6. REFERENCES

[1] G. Pfurtscheller, B.Z. Allison, C. Brunner, G. Bauernfeind, T. Solis-Escalante, R. Scherer, T.O. Zander, G. Mueller-Putz, C. Neuper, and N. Birbaumer. The hybrid bci. *Frontiers in Neuroprosthetics*, 2010.

[2] T. O. Zander, M. Gaertner, C. Kothe, and R. Vilimek. Combining eye gaze input with a brain–computer interface for touchless human–computer interaction. *International Journal of Human-Computer Interaction*, 27(1):38–51, 2011.

[3] F. Aloise, I. Lasorsa, F. Schettini, A. Brouwer, D. Mattia, F. Babiloni, S. Salinari, M. Marciani, and F. Cincotti. Multimodal stimulation for a P300-based BCI. *International Journal of Bioelectromagnetism*, 9(3):128–130, 2007.

[4] Moritz Lehne, Klas Ihme, Anne-Marie Brouwer, Jan van Erp, and Thorsten Oliver Zander. Error-Related EEG Patterns during Tactile Human-Machine Interaction. In IEEE Computer Society Press, editor, *Proceedings of ACII 2009*, Los Alamitos, CA, 2009.

[5] F. Nijboer, A. Furdea, I. Gunst, J. Mellinger, D.J. McFarland, N. Birbaumer, and A. Kuebler. An auditory brain-computer interface (BCI). *Journal of neuroscience methods*, 167, 1:43–50, 2008.

[6] M. Schreuder, B. Blankertz, and M.PL Tangermann. A new auditory multi-class brain-computer interface paradigm: spatial hearing as an informative cue. *PLoS ONE*, 5(4), 2010.

[7] T.O. Zander and C. Kothe. Towards passive brain–computer interfaces: applying brain–computer

interface technology to human–machine systems in general. *Journal of Neural Engineering*, 8:025005, 2011.

[8] T.O. Zander, C. Kothe, S. Welke, and M. Roetting. Enhancing human-machine systems with secondary input from passive brain-computer interfaces. In *Proceedings of the 4th International BCI Workshop & Training Course. Graz University of Technology Publishing House, Graz*, 2008.

[9] T.O. Zander, C. Kothe, S. Jatzev, and M. Gaertner. Enhancing human–computer interaction with input from active and passive brain–computer interfaces. In D. Tan and A. Nijholt, editors, *The Human in Brain–Computer Interfaces and the Brain in Human–Computer Interaction*, pages 24–29. Springer, 2010.

[10] PW Ferrez and J. del R Millan. Error-related eeg potentials generated during simulated brain-computer interaction. *IEEE Trans Biomed Eng.*, 55(3):923–9, 2008.

[11] B. Blankertz, G. Dornhege, C. Schafer, R. Krepki, J. Kohlmorgen, K.R. Mueller, V. Kunzmann, F. Losch, and G. Curio. Boosting bit rates and error detection for the classification of fast-paced motor commands based on single-trial EEG analysis. *IEEE Transactions on Neural Systems and Rehabilitation Engineering*, 11(2):127–131, 2003.

[12] A.D. Friederici, E. Pfeifer, and A. Hahne. Event-related brain potentials during natural speech processing: Effects of semantic, morphological and syntactic violations. *Cognitive Brain Research*, 1(3):183–192, 1993.

[13] S. Koelsch. Neural substrates of processing syntax and semantics in music. *Current opinion in neurobiology*, 15(2):207–212, 2005.

[14] B. Blankertz, S. Lemm, M. Treder, S. Haufe, and K.R. Mueller. Single-trial analysis and classification of ERP components-a tutorial. *NeuroImage*, 2010.

[15] T.O. Zander, K. Ihme, M. Gaertner, and M. Roetting. A public data hub for benchmarking common brain–computer interface algorithms. *Journal of Neural Engineering*, 8:025021, 2011.

[16] J. Schaefer and K. Strimmer. A shrinkage approach to large-scale covariance matrix estimation and implications for functional genomics. *Statistical applications in genetics and molecular biology*, 4(1):32, 2005.

Pseudo-Haptics: From the Theoretical Foundations to Practical System Design Guidelines

Andreas Pusch
IIHM – UJF-Grenoble 1 – LIG
110 av. de la Chimie – BP 53
38041 Grenoble Cedex 9, France
andreas.pusch@imag.fr

Anatole Lécuyer
BUNRAKU – INRIA Rennes
Campus Universitaire de Beaulieu
35042 Rennes Cedex, France
anatole.lecuyer@inria.fr

ABSTRACT
Pseudo-haptics, a form of haptic illusion exploiting the brain's capabilities and limitations, has been studied for about a decade. Various interaction techniques making use of it emerged in different fields. However, important questions remain unanswered concerning the nature and the fundamentals of pseudo-haptics, the problems frequently encountered, and sophisticated means supporting the development of new systems and applications. We provide the theoretical background needed to understand the key mechanisms involved in the perception of / interaction with pseudo-haptic phenomena. We synthesise a framework resting on two theories of human perception, cognition and action: The Interacting Cognitive Subsystems model by Barnard et al. and the Bayesian multimodal cue integration framework by Ernst et al. Based on this synthesis and in order to test its utility, we discuss a recent pseudo-haptics example. Finally, we derive system design recommendations meant to facilitate the advancement in the field of pseudo-haptics for user interface researchers and practitioners.

ACM Classification Keywords
H.1.2 [Models and Principles]: User/Machine Systems---Human Factors, Human Information Processing; H.5.2 [Information Interfaces and Presentation]: User Interfaces---Haptic I/O, Theory and Methods

General Terms
Design, Human Factors, Theory

Authors' Keywords
Pseudo-haptics, human perception and action, human information processing, foundations framework, system design guidelines

1. INTRODUCTION
Haptic feedback, no matter whether passive or active, whether tactile or force-returning, whether realistic or simple, has gained much importance for a holistic / compelling user experience in various fields of human-computer interaction (HCI). Ever new intriguing approaches occur on the scientific and commercial "markets", often stimulated by multidisciplinary efforts. Thus it is not surprising to see haptics hardware, software and multimodal interaction concepts rapidly evolving.

ICMI'11, November 14–18, 2011, Alicante, Spain.

About ten years ago, user interface researchers experimented with an alternative means – pseudo-haptics [1] – to reduce system and device complexity while still providing a rich haptic sensation. As it will be addressed in this paper, pseudo-haptics correpsonds to a haptic percept that is different from what the real haptic sensory supply would suggest by "playing" with the multimodal – mainly the visual – feedback of a system. In [1], an interactive virtual piston is displayed on a computer screen. By pressing a SpaceBall support device with the thumb, the user can make the piston move according to both the actual force applied and the simulated spring stiffness. Varying degrees of visual compression of the virtual piston lead to different levels of perceived stiffness.

Since then, a number of haptic properties have successfully been implemented (e.g., [2, 3, 4]) and even brought to a productive state (e.g., [5, 6]). However, the perceptual mechanisms behind pseudo-haptics remain largely unclear. And so do the reasons why there was often a considerable user population unaffected, why reported impressions were sometimes unexpected or "strange", and why there was mostly a large user-dependent variability in the induced sensations. In [7], some of these open questions have already been discussed in more depth and first guidelines for the design of pseudo-haptics systems have been proposed.

Our intention is to extent this state of research on pseudo-haptics. We want to move forward both on the theoretical foundations side as well as regarding a more complete and generic set of system design recommendations. The overall objectives are thus first, to prepare the ground for a better understanding of the phenomenon, second, to demonstrate how existing systems can be assessed and possibly improved in order to approach the quality of robust contingent effects, and third, to facilitate the development of future reliable pseudo-haptics-enabled interaction techniques.

2. PREVIOUS WORK
Here, we are going to review the related work with respect to the main goals of this paper. For a detailed presentation of the human perception and action models we will base our foundations synthesis on, refer to the "Theoretical Foundations" section.

2.1 Classification of "Pseudo-Haptics"
Systems or interaction techniques labelled "pseudo-haptics" globally fall into two distinct domains. On the one hand, there are approaches that attempt to stimulate a unified percept of a specific haptic environmental property in the sense that the user actually "feels" it (e.g., [1, 2, 4]). Perceiving the weight or stiffness of an object would be practical examples. This kind of sensation can be regarded as the result of an automatic lower level processing of multisensory information blended or merged with what is already known about the world and with the user's intentions [8, 9, 10, 11]. The user is ideally not able to escape from the induced sensation which usually differs from the "real" percept and thus qualifies pseudo-haptics as a type of haptic illusion [7]. Most of the existing techniques, including the original work of Lécuyer [1], can be attributed to this domain.

On the other hand, there is a group of approaches mostly relying on the cognitive interpretation of a visuo-haptic simulation (e.g., referred to as "optically simulated haptic feedback", [12, 13]). Visually presented haptic effects like mouse cursor drifts meant to reflect a surface slope have effectively to be "understood" by the user in order to relate these observations to the simulated phenomena. Although the meaning of the visual feedback is tightly linked to the haptic property, it is not necessarily the case that the user "feels" it in the way he would sense the weight of an object. The final percept or mental representation of the phenomenon is thus more the result of a "strategic decision-making process" [7] and requires explicit learning. However, exceptions are possible. Even if unintended, it is not completely unlikely to produce conditions under which the interaction between the contributing multimodal cues becomes qualitatively appropriate to trigger some weaker form of the above-mentioned illusion. We will discuss these conditions later on.

Please note that, in the remainder of in this paper, emphasis will be put on the illusion and not on the cognitive interpretation aspect of pseudo-haptics. We will therefore use the term pseudo-haptics only within this context – unless otherwise stated.

2.2 Towards Explaining the Principles

Throughout the past decade, various works in the field of pseudo-haptics have, from very different points of view, provided first insights on how and why the presented techniques may have worked. Lécuyer collected various key arguments and claimed [7]: "Pseudo-haptic feedback corresponds to the perception of a haptic property that differs from the physical environment, by combining visual and haptic information and proposing a new coherent representation of the environment." The following four "key assertions" have been extracted:

1. Involvement of one or more visuo-haptic sensory conflicts.
2. Dominance of vision over touch when perceiving spatial environmental properties.
3. Correspondence to a new and coherent visuo-haptic representation of the environment.
4. Possibility of creating haptic illusions altering the perception of a given haptic property.

Pusch stated that, in a pseudo-haptics setup like HEMP (i.e., Hand-displacEMent-based Pseudo-haptics) [4], "the visually presented phenomenon should theoretically be capable of returning some kind of force. Appropriate haptic information related to this phenomenon has then to be provided as a carrier stimulus to the user. [...] Finally, if well-defined actions can successfully be coupled with a plausible visual feedback, then the user's central nervous system (CNS) may adapt to the new, the artificial multisensory supply – and the illusion occurs." [14]

Paljic et al. argued that users were able to discriminate different levels of torque because of a "perceived mechanical work" cue that might have triggered the observed illusion effect [2].

In a study designed to identify a "boundary of illusion" for a spring stiffness setup, Lécuyer et al. found that "more visual deformation is necessary to compensate large haptic differences" [15]. The fundamentals likely to underly this observation have recently been studied in a number of psychophysical experiments and will be discussed further down. It has also been remarked that "this boundary varies greatly depending on the subjects and their strategy of sensory integration". But it remained unclear as to what might cause such a strong variability in the perception of the existing pseudo-haptic phenomena, and how to handle it.

We will discuss all these findings, assumptions and observations in the light of a comprehensive framework of human perception and action that aims at clarifying the interplay of all perceptual key processes and modalities contributing to a pseudo-haptic sensation. We further hope to answer some of the important open questions.

2.3 Existing Design Recommendations

Developments in this domain seem largely to be characterised by an exploratory research approach. Such explorations can take fairly long and it is often rather hard to predict what the outcome will be. Several authors provided detailed rationales (e.g., [14]), but yet without bringing them to a set of more generic design recommendations for a larger variety of systems.

The first attempt towards such specific guidelines has been made by Lécuyer who suggested to follow these steps while keeping the application context in mind [7]:

1. Identification of a law that controls a haptic property.
2. Association of this law with related spatial parameters.
3. Setting up a visuo-haptic sensory conflict focussing on one or more of these parameters.
4. Modification of the visual feedback of the respective parameter(s).

Although these steps provide a good starting point, there is still much space left for interpretations. Moreover, even if certain facets of reality are frequently "mimicked" (to varying degrees of realism), the entire aspects of how the haptic property to be simulated is normally perceived by the user and what the role of prior knowledge might be remain unclear. A discussion of potential perceptual and ergonomics side effects and limitation of playing with multisensory conflicts would be important as well, since this is the (still relatively fragile) practical means of pseudo-haptics. So, for approaching more compelling and reliable designs in the future that convey nearly robust contingent effects, we think that considering as many of these pain points as possible would be an indispensable requirement.

3. THEORETICAL FOUNDATIONS

There are different models of human perception, cognition and action, all representing excellent resources for the explanation of a number, if not most of the perceptual and cognitive processes likely to underly pseudo-haptics. But rather than testing all of them for their applicability to our questioning, we decided to synthesise a compact "practitioners framework" based on two successful, popular concepts that we believe are rich enough: The Interacting Cognitive Subsystems (ICS) model by Barnard et al. [8, 9] and the Bayesian multimodal cue integration (BMI) framework by Ernst et al. [16, 10, 11]. We think these two models are complementary: While ICS provides the "big picture", BMI sheds additional light on some very specific details.

Both concepts will each be briefly presented before we highlight those principles that are the most important to a profound understanding of pseudo-haptics. We will also elaborate on what else these models can teach us and where, for the targeted more complete explanation of pseudo-haptics, we need to consult additional material.

3.1 Interaction Cognitive Subsystems

The ICS model represents a high level "macro theory" of human perception and cognition. It covers the processing chain which transforms multimodal sensory raw data into progressively more abstract mental representations that permit to understand and to interact with the environment. It also addresses realtime information blending, storage and access. ICS may hence model various central aspects of pseudo-haptics.

Model structure. ICS consists of nine equally organised interacting subsystems each of which receiving one or more (data) representations generated by other subsystems as input. The incoming data is stored (or used to refine stored information) and processed (i.e., blended and transformed) according to the respective subsystem's purpose. The following subsystems (also: "Levels") were identified:

I. Sensory subsystems: Encoding of raw inputs and basic structuring => **1.** Acoustic level, **2.** Visual level, **3.** Body state level (i.e., proprioception, touch, taste, smell)

II. Perceptual subsystems: Basic interpretation and grouping of information => **4.** Morphonolexical level (i.e., abstract structures of sounds, incl. language), **5.** Object level

III. Central subsystems: High level cognitive interpretation and interrelation of information => **6.** Propositional level (i.e., factual representation), **7.** Implicational level (i.e., meanings, emotions)

IV. Effector subsystems: "Feedback channels" used for interaction with the environment => **8.** Articulatory level (i.e., speech and related gestures), **9.** Limb level (i.e., motor actions)

Internal main processes. All subsystems form a common network within which information is simultaneously processed. Any data arriving at a level can either in part, if certain patterns match, or completely be replaced by representations already learned and stored in memory. In case of multiple inputs, a process called information blending takes place. Blending has a direct influence on a subsystem's output, but it requires that the representations to be blended are of a consistent / coherent structure with respect to the psychological subject (i.e., object attended to), its predicate (i.e., other objects at the same level of perceptual scene decomposition) and its constituent structure (i.e., objects making up the subject). By adding reciprocal feedback loops between the morphonolexical and propositional levels, the object and propositional levels as well as between the propositional and implicational levels, the crucial role of prior knowledge during information processing is reinforced. An interactive mode of operation can be maintained, even if inputs are qualitatively or quantitatively limited.

ICS and pseudo-haptics. Doubtlessly, ICS can help a lot in explaining different key principles of pseudo-haptics. Suppose the user had the intention (i.e., an implicational representation of his goal) to manipulate an object. He performs all required (motor) actions and his perceptual "entry subsystems" continuously receive sensory raw data. These inputs, typically from the visual and the body state subsystems, is structured, related to each other and then interpreted or "sensed" to form a mental representation of any experienced (real / virtual / mixed) haptic environmental property. Regarding the contribution of vision, this means, transforming retinal stimuli into actual object representations. If an object is recognised, associated information can be revived and retrieved from memory (e.g., this texture felt rough, this material was solid, this is my hand). This way, it is possible to organise further interaction and to anticipate the feedback that will then be blended with and compared to the multisensory inputs. At body state level, relevant sensory raw data usually originates from touch and / or proprioception. Once this information has passed low level structuring, implicational blending can directly merge a given sensation with what has visually been identified – and what one associates with the observation. For this, the representations have to be sufficiently consistent (e.g., this feature or sensation is related to this type of object or action, these events occurred "spatio-temporally aligned"). Blending weights vary according to the context-dependent degree of perceptual reliance and faithfulness of the estimates within each of the concerned sensory modalities [10]. Pseudo-haptics, as it has been explored to date, relies on that vision is largely favoured over haptics.

Incomplete or inappropriate inputs can be the result of poor multimodal displays (e.g., only few, vague cues), ambiguities in the system response (e.g., contradictory multisensory supply) or too weak relationships between the representations to be blended (e.g., too large system lags or visuo-haptic conflicts, too less meaningful connexions between the inputs). In most of these cases, ICS' internal feedback loops can, at least to some extent, compensate for sensory or perceptual gaps. This strategy again highlights the importance of prior knowledge. However, the more gaps or uncertainties are to be handled the more likely is a "subjectively coloured" final sensation that is prone to instabilities for the user and among a group of users each having his own individual background. Practically, the user may not perceive or feel, if anything at all, what has originally been designed. Or he perceives something rather unexpected, unrelated as his brain is forced to compute a "solution" to whatever the current state of perception is. In the end, if all this becomes too confusing, the user might just refuse using the system.

To our knowledge, pseudo-haptics simulations have barely exploited the auditory modality (see, e.g., [17]), although a direct link to implicational blending would strongly suggest to do so (e.g., accompanying real or synthetic sounds). Even if not used for immediate blending, sounds would help establish or support mental representations / propositional descriptions, also of non-acoustic environmental properties. These representations would then be available for the later blending. In the same vein, one could turn the "risk" of relying on or requiring too much prior knowledge into a benefit. Why not deliberately preparing the ground for a stable blending by "early seeding" of the right information? We are going to elaborate more on this somewhat controversial concept in the "Deliberate 'User Priming'" section.

Main "limitations". Apart from the many good points of ICS like its holistic view, the handling of multimodal interdependencies, representation transformations and the role of memory at various stages of the model, there are a couple of things it cannot answer in full breadth. One of the most important open questions is related to low(er) level modality blending and its prerequisites. How have representations undergoing blending spatio-temporally to be configured? In fact, this is essential first, for a deeper understanding of modality blending in general and second, to deriving more sophisticated design recommendations for pseudo-haptics systems. What also needs to be addressed in more detail is the aspect of disambiguation. If our brain is confronted with ambiguous multisensory data, it attempts to resolve it by recalling related information from memory in order for the final percept to settle. How can this process be supported? Are there alternative strategies? It seems the modelling of intention, motivation and thus goal-directed actions may be made more explicit. We hope to close some of these "gaps" in the course of the next two sections.

3.2 Bayesian Multimodal Cue Integration

This second model of human perception which we will base our synthesis framework on is primarily dedicated to multisensory information blending. It is thus more a "micro" than a "macro theory", although it also proposes a broader perception-action loop concept incorporating a Bayesian inference approach at perceptual level and a gain / loss function approach at both decision making and action planning level.

From mandatory Maximum-Likelihood-Integration ... BMI evolved from the special case Maximum-Likelihood-Estimate (MLE) integration model [16] which, in a way, is still included in BMI. MLE states that redundant multisensory information (e.g., from vision and touch) about an environmental property (e.g., the size of an object) is integrated by summing up the contributing sensory estimates' weighted averages. The resulting percept is statistically optimal in that it has a smaller variance than each of the individual estimates alone. Weights represent the reliability of a given sensory supply and typically depend on modality specifics (e.g., receptor noise level, feedback stability => signal variance). However, it has been found that the mandatory fusion within this one-dimensional approach does not apply to a number of observations made in different experiments [11]. Subjects did not seem to completely fuse the between- or within-modality data as predicted by MLE. It has been argued that the brain retains access to lower level sensory information in order for it to detect possible mismatches (i.e., sensory or perceptual conflicts) and, within certain limits, to perform compensatory mappings between the senses. This flexibility of our sensorimotor / perceptual system is key to a fast adaptation to sudden changes in the environment or the current configuration of the own body.

... to a Bayesian view on human perception and action. In continuation of their previous work, Ernst et al. have proposed a Bayesian view on multimodal cue integration [10, 11]. They introduced Bayesian Decision Theory (BDT) in order to model the following two consecutive steps: First, at perceptual level, multisensory interaction and second, at decision / action level, the effects of intention and task goal on a generalised "perception-action loop". BMI also accounts for uncertainties about the world, the environment and the multisensory feedback. Regarding Bayes' Rule, prior knowledge (here: The "coupling prior") is represented by the prior probability distribution, the "sensory evidence" at a given moment by the likelihood function and the resulting most likely percept by the posterior (i.e., $p(W|I) \propto p(I|W) \times p(W)$). The main estimates (e.g., from vision and touch), if spatio-temporally corresponding (i.e., likely to originate from the same environmental property – see further down), are characterised by their specific reliabilities (i.e., inverse signal variance).

Relative reliabilities of multiple estimates define the direction of the bias induced by the coupling prior (e.g., tending towards vision or visual dominance, resp.). This prior is responsible for the integration process and thus for modality mapping, and gains influence with an increased variance in the likelihood (i.e., a more uncertain sensory supply). It further determines the "strength of coupling", for instance, by means of a (simplified!) Gaussian distribution along the identity line / concordance diagonal. Along this line, multisensory feedback agrees on the object property or sensation in question. However, the prior could also become "sharply tuned" and take the form of a delta function leading to a pure MLE integration, so, mandatory fusion. The likelihood of correspondence can be reinforced by co-occurrence of supporting multimodal attributes, similar to the formerly described "sensory combination" process [10]. Another goal of this process, beside (spatial) information alignment between non-redundant cues (i.e., determining the transformations needed), is to collect as much information as possible, no matter through which modality, in order to resolve perceptually ambiguous situations and therefore interrelate different estimates. Each multimodal attribute makes up one dimension of a "hyper-dimensional multimodal space" that can affect the coupling prior. It might hence become narrower or steeper in the same way as it would become more flat or spread for stronger discrepancies and contradictory cues (see also [18]). A completely flat prior illustrates signal independence which does not mean that, at cognitive level, a correspondence cannot be established. But then active feedback interpretation would take place – as it seems to be the case for "visually simulated haptic feedback". The coupling prior's shape may further depend on the user's perceptual preferences, capabilities and experiences.

There is not much known about when it becomes obvious to the user that there is something "odd" in the multimodal feedback (e.g., a too large visuo-haptic conflict), simply because oddity detection depends on a number of variables. In this context, Hospedales et al. [19] proposed a Bayesian ideal observer which includes a "causal structure inference" approach to model oddity detection. They found evidence that the brain might perform a probabilistic hypothesis selection and switching during multimodal cue combination, in particular under uncertain cue correspondence (in brief: Is the incoming multisensory data from the same source / environmental property or not? If so, compute a unified percept like it has been described in BMI.). What has indirectly been shown is that the task goal can influence the multisensory integration process (here: Identification of a potentially "odd probe" characterised by conflicting multisensory feedback). Ernst et al. already considered this by including a BDT-like decision making process based on goal-dependent gain / loss functions [10, 11] – although in a much less formal way. However, even if the user recognised the conflict (i.e., is aware of the oddity), an optimal solution, under the given constraints, would nevertheless be generated – sometimes resulting in objectively "illogical" yet unified percepts. Specially when relying on (weaker) illusions like pseudo-haptics to date, a poor multimodal display or simulation, and therefore a lack of belief in the observation, can quickly become an issue and strongly perturb both perception and action. After all, a pseudo-haptic property could still deliver a certain "sensation", if a minimum coupling between the contributing multimodal cues is retained. In this light, it can be expected that some of the existing mouse-style pseudo-haptics techniques may indeed induce a (weaker) "feeling" or sensation and thus not always rely on a pure cognitive interpretation of visually observed haptic effects (see also 2.1).

BMI and pseudo-haptics. We are convinced that BMI is highly useful to describe the heart of the low(er) level information blending underlying pseudo-haptics. Its multisensory interaction processes can further be related to the blending mechanisms at Level II of ICS (i.e., perceptual subsystems). In addition to this, BMI provides various references to ICS and either confirms or complements it this way (e.g., concerning the overall multimodal structure and processing sequence, the impact of intention on perception and action, the role of prior knowledge, the information transformation processes). What we learned in particular is first, how the human brain produces "operational percepts" from multimodal cues, second, how these cues have to be configured and third, how perceptual stability can be achieved and supported. The Bayesian approach permits to account for sensory, perceptual and environmental uncertainties as well as it permits a very flexible cue integration scheme with the coupling prior as multisensory interaction modulator. Pseudo-haptics can therefore be seen as another applied example of BMI – enriched and framed by ICS. In the next section, we will develop our (simplified) synthesised foundations view.

3.3 Foundations Synthesis Framework

The synthesis (see also Fig. 1) is meant to provide an "operational picture" of the underlying processes to both HCI researchers and practitioners. Its simplicity and reduction to the most important components of two fairly complex frameworks will later help us establish a set of more generic and easily applicable system design guidelines.

Multimodal "raw data" processing and transformations. The user experience starts with observing the current environment, including the own body, "the self". Multimodal "raw data" from vision, audition and the body state (e.g., proprioception and touch), reflecting the basic feedback from the environment, will then be processed in several steps. Each cue's input is structured and transformed into higher-level information representations (e.g., for object identification and scene understanding). During this process, missing or incomplete data can be replaced, complemented or refined by information retrieved from memory (i.e., prior knowledge or previous experiences). Learning corresponds to the information transfer back to memory.

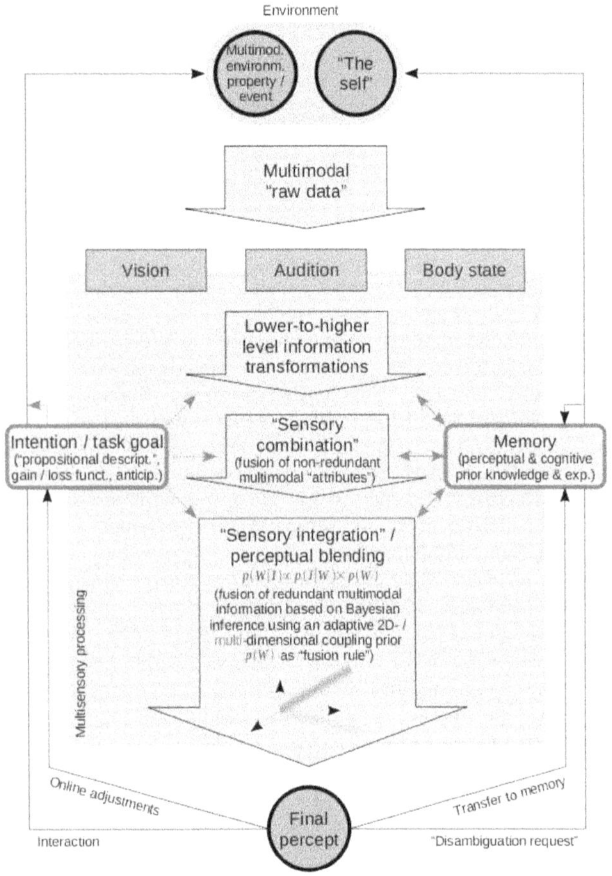

Figure 1. Foundations synthesis framework based on ICS and BMI. In brief: Observation of the environment, lower level information structuring and interpretation, fusion of non-redundant and redundant information, production of the final percept, interaction. Embedded graph: 3D coupling prior (i.e., nb. of dimensions => contrib. single- or multimodal cues).

Sensory combination and integration. At this level, a first fusion takes place, given all non-redundant multimodal "attributes" appeared at a sufficient level of temporal coherence: "Sensory combination". The brain attempts to spatially align them in order to obtain coherent coordinates for the final "sensory integration" step. This, together with the attempt to resolve potential ambiguities by requesting additional information about other attributes, serves adapting the ultimate integration rule: The "coupling prior". This prior models, in the Bayesian sense, individual knowledge and can more or less be tuned (i.e., "strength of coupling / fusion"), depending on the conditions at a moment. A completely flat prior (i.e., signal independence) means that the cues are insufficiently related to each other to result in an unified percept. A simultaneous multi-cue fusion might further be represented by a multi-dimensional coupling prior with each dimension signifying one of the contributing single- or multimodal cues.

Intention / task goal and interaction. The "intention / task goal" has another strong influence on multisensory processing. It directs attention and therefore emphasises certain modalities and attributes. Through the generation of motor plans needed to execute movements [20], it is indirectly also responsible for how an environmental state is evaluated with respect to previous observations and the own actions (i.e., certain sensory feedback patterns predicted by the internal model of action [21]). Resulting mismatches may lead to online adjustments of either (motor) actions or the current (sub)objective. Further, through another Bayesian component at decision making level, final action execution is optimised. Performance costs are computed based on gain / loss functions. More practically: With some goal or mental model of a scene in mind, the user consciously and subconsciously anticipates changes or things to happen in the observed environment and does then react accordingly. The more space for interpretations is left to the user due to an insufficient or bad multimodal display, the more subjectively coloured (i.e., biased expectations and assessments) will be the final percept – and actual motor performance or interaction. This is a risk and an opportunity at the same time as mentioned in earlier, since deliberate priming can indeed pave the way to "guiding experiences" (for more, see 5.2).

Final percept. In the context of perceptual illusions, Berthoz has suggested that the brain provides the best suitable hypothesis to a given multisensory supply [22]. This agrees to the Bayesian concept discussed so far. The brain computes the most likely percept from the following three major entries: Incoming multimodal data, the user's memory and experience, and the task to be performed. An illusory percept is thus the result of a (yet) successful multisensory integration (i.e., no confusing or "flipping" sensations) – even if there are discordant multimodal cues or biased interpretations. Pseudo-haptics can, without any restrictions, be seen in the same light. When seeing that the weights or degrees of reliability can vary a lot among different modalities or cues within one modality, it is not surprising that a number of intriguing pseudo-haptics techniques have already been found to effectively fool the user's perception. To be more explicit on this, we will review a recent contribution to the domain in the next section. This includes the discussion of the problems encountered, important open questions and improvement potentials with respect to the synthesis framework.

4. EXAMPLE DISCUSSION

Only few systems have been proposed to date which use neither passive nor active support devices to produce pseudo-haptic feedback. One of them, called Hand-displacEMent-based Pseudo-haptics (HEMP), makes the user feel a virtual force field [4]. Distantly related phenomena were observed in psychophysical and neuromotor experiments like the flexible / rubber arm illusion [23] or the visual touch illusion [24]. However, the sensations subjects had in the latter two cases occurred incidentally. Whereas HEMP was designed to induce an "active" force field illusion – to our knowledge, the first time pseudo-haptics became "active".

Due to HEMP's intriguing properties, we have chosen to discuss it here in detail. We will test both applicability and utility of our synthesis framework, further discuss problems and open questions raised by the original work, and highlight improvement potentials wherever appropriate. The discussion follows our model's global structure:

1. **Environment.** The user is presented with a stereoscopic Augmented Reality / Virtuality environment using a video see-through head-mounted display (HMD). The scene consists of a virtual stream tube object which is cut open on top and has some animated particles (or: "Force field" lines) rotating through it. The user's hand is embedded as co-located, spatially displaceable live video data. Varying force field levels lead to an (adaptive) lateral visual shift of the user's hand once it has been exposed to the virtual flow. The displacement increases progressively up to a force-level-dependent distance and velocity, then fades out within

another specific distance within the capturing space of the HMD's built-in stereo cameras (see also [4, 14]). Flow animation parameters do not change.

2. **Multimodal raw data processing.** After lower level visual information processing, the virtual scene, the own hand and their observable dynamics are (expected to be) recognised. Video feedback of the hand is meant to convey both a visually faithful look [25, 26, 27] and a plausible motion feedback [28]. This may contribute to a more convincing user experience in the form of a more tuned, sharper coupling prior. At body state level, two main information sources are at focus: First, proprioceptive hand position feedback and second, activity in the principal horizontal arm flexor and extensor muscles [29]. However, there are more "arm motion cues" available, for instance: Skin deformation, tendon and muscle length variations all over the articular structure involved and tactile feedback of sleeves sliding over the arm surface. Acoustic feedback has not been used.
3. **Sensory combination.** Two steps are important at visual level. First, with stereo vision and the embedded live video of the own hand, the user is likely to experience the space in front him, viewed through the HMD, as kind of an integral peripersonal environment. The small field-of-view of the HMD might impair this experience whereas the employed mixing approach might support it due to a correct occlusion handling. On the contrary, the planar hand texture carrier objects and unrealistic cutting edges on intersections with virtual object might sometimes perturb this picture. Second, the visual virtual force field creates a certain expectation with respect to the effects to occur on exposure. Despite the artificial virtual stream tube and the very simple particle flow feedback, the design of the interactive region provides some useful hints on what this simulation is likely to do. At visual-haptic level, the initial hand co-location feeds the mental representation of a coherent interactive space. To maintain or regain this sensation of coherence, visual hand offsets can be reduced in order to return to co-location. As concerns body state, the proprioceptive hand or arm motion, position and muscle contraction cues are fused – which, due to their partially contradictory nature in HEMP, can indeed "soften" the final coupling prior. What might hide this conflict to some extent is that hand shifts are performed slowly (see also [30]). Another strategy of HEMP is to trigger an automatic motor reaction at the moment the user's hand enters the virtual flow: A compensatory postural adjustment after hand or arm have visually started to drift. Either the arm flexor or extensor group will be activated and produce the main haptic carrier stimulus to be modulated by the visual feedback. No other controlled haptic or tactile cues are provided.
4. **Sensory integration.** The coupling prior will now be used to merge all spatially aligned, redundant multimodal data so as to converge to a unified and stable final percept. What is this "redundant information" in HEMP? We think, the complex psychological subject or key cue is the strength / pushing effect of the force field in the direction of the rotating particles. Its constituent structure comprises the perceived states of real and virtual hand / arm motion and position as well as the actual muscle work for movement execution. It has been argued by Pusch that, as long as the visual feedback remains plausible to the user, related motor activity might be integrated with it and therefore lead to the modified, illusory force percept [14]. However, one difficulty we see in this design is that it relies on only one single haptic carrier stimulus which, at the same time, contradicts most of the other available body state cues. When resisting with the hand against a force exerting phenomenon, one would anticipate a feeling of pressure around the contact region. Being aware of this issue, the author proposed to add disambiguation cues like physical air streams for tactile and / or auditory feedback, or simple vibro-tactile stimuli at hand level. The coupling prior could effectively become "sharper" this way. There is another problem related to the visual quality of the video hand embedding approach. The feeling of presence could be negatively affected leading to "doubts" about the simulation. Smaller weights may be assigned to the visual feedback, thus directly affecting sensory integration. More realistic hand-scene intersections as well as sophisticated visual interactions between the hand and the force field particles could perhaps limit these undesirable effects.

   To compute the final percept, the contributing cues will be merged by taking their specific weights (i.e., reliabilities and noise levels with respect to the user's sensibility and prior knowledge) into account. "Perceptual gaps" or "confusing uncertainties" can be cleared up by retrieving related information from memory or by requesting disambiguation attempts. The percept of the visually constant virtual flow is subject to an ongoing modulation by accelerated, decelerated or steady hand shifts. To leave exploitable traces in memory for evoking the illusion, the following events have been accentuated: The intense dynamics around the reaction peak and the perceived terminal visual-haptic hand offset.
5. **Interaction.** With an operational final percept computed, the user is now able to interact with the environment. According to his goals (e.g.: Force field strength comparison) and the multimodal experience, he will focus his attention, weigh up "optimal" (in the sense of BDT) actions to take, anticipate consequences of his actions, plan and perform movements and so forth. In short, the continuous perception-action loop as described by Ernst et al. [10, 11] is closed. What should be recalled is the dynamic character of the simulation in terms of highly variable hand displacements. Independent of the precautions taken to deliver a clear idea of the system's purpose, it does not always behave in the same way as the amounts of possible hand shifts vary over time. The feedback could thus diverge from the anticipated or expected one and so leave the user confused.

Summary. In the context of the mechanisms enabling HEMP, we could demonstrate applicability and usefulness of our synthesis framework. It seems to turn out that the original HEMP concept carries a considerable risk to confront the user with too many adverse multisensory conflicts. To avoid some of them or, at least, to minimise the chance of detection and therefore reduce the inherent fragility, one could add disambiguating cues like simple tactile stimuli or dynamic visual flow effects. Better hand-scene intersections and a strategic "user priming" (see below) would also improve sensation / illusion effectiveness and stability.

5. DESIGN RECOMMENDATIONS

Two aspects are important for the evolution and the diffusion of pseudo-haptics: First, to understand how and why this type of illusion works and second, to transfer this theoretical knowledge to practical design recommendations. Enabling and facilitating the development and implementation of new systems is what we focus on in this section. We start from the list of guidelines given by Lécuyer [7] and extend it as needed. Beyond that, we will introduce our concept of a deliberate "user priming".

5.1 Main Guidelines

Conceiving a system that offers at the same time a simple to set up, stable over a large number of users and relatively rich haptic illusion is a challenge. The more important it is to have more sophisticated means at hand for user interface researchers and practitioners to safe their development resources and, at best, to avoid pursuing "dead ends". The guidelines catalogue presented here has been worked out based on our synthesis framework and the above discussions. It is "generic" in that it is not restricted to a particular type of haptic property. We do not claim the guidelines would be applicable to every phenomenon that could possibly be simulated using pseudo-haptics. However, we are confident that all existing approaches can easily be replicated. We are also able to highlight potential design issues as shown in Section 4.

The following steps we propose to take (*italic:* Taken from [7]):

1. **Observation of the user, while he is interacting with or experiencing a real haptic property close to the one to be simulated by pseudo-haptic feedback** (i.e., analysis of the environment, the phenomenon's attributes and constituent structure, the sensations induced, the tasks and [inter-]actions performed, and the user's body parts involved).
2. ***Identification of a law that controls a haptic property*** (i.e., a law matching our prior knowledge of the physical world; remark: There might be multiple laws for different facets of the same haptic property. Laws should therefore be ordered by relevance of their contribution to the final percept.).
3. ***Association of this law with related spatial parameters*** (i.e., identification of spatial components of the haptic property; remarks: There may also be "non-spatial" parameters useful for replication and simulation, e.g., tactile or acoustic ones. Physical correctness seems not essential, but helpful, since it best matches common prior knowledge.).
4. **For each parameter, testing its suitability for simulation with respect to perceptual and technical constraints** (i.e., priority for the contribution to the multimodal experience of the haptic property, best requiring only small magnitudes of conflicts to be combined and integrated, avoiding [too] many and [too] strong conflicts; further, efficiently to implement and comfortable to use from an ergonomics point of view).
5. ***Setting up a visuo-haptic sensory conflict focussing on one or more of these parameters*** (i.e., modelling multimodal feedback and interaction; remark: Sensory and perceptual conflicts can occur at different levels of processing as well as within and between the concerned modalities, or better: Between the cues belonging to the simulated phenomenon.).
6. **For all other characteristics of the haptic property not being controlled, envisaging easy-to-add complementary stimuli** (i.e., enriching the environment in order to reduce spreading effects on the coupling prior by feeding sensory combination and disambiguation).
7. ***Modification of the visual feedback of the respective parameter(s)*** (i.e., actual runtime simulation linked into the perception-action loop; Remarks: This has to be extended to multimodal feedback. It is also at this step where conflict intensity has to be tuned to convey a stable and reliable final sensation. Usability should be optimised, too. Outcomes of step 4 may help reduce experimentation costs.).
8. **Harmonising prior knowledge by means of deliberate "user priming"** (for details, see next section) – best before the first contact of the user with the system.

5.2 Deliberate "User Priming"

It is well known that perception (and thus action) can be biased multifariously, for instance, by task instructions, by the way how things are told or by other "hints" – whether provided on purpose or not (e.g., [31]). This fully agrees to the models and frameworks discussed earlier in this paper. From a scientific perspective, such a "user priming" would, in most cases, be found to contaminate the results of controlled experiments. So, researchers typically try to minimise the risk of producing skewed data by avoiding the above-mentioned factors. Without any doubt, this practice is an indispensable requirement of rigorous scientific working.

However, it can sometimes lead to unnecessarily artificial or restricted scenarios which barely apply to the complex reality of HCI. On the other hand, experimental environments and protocols often implicitly provide information related to a system's or a study's goals (e.g., by scene or user interface layout, tasks design, questionnaires) and so "prime" even "naive subjects" right from the beginning. We think that, in this vein, a deliberate seeding of the right information at the right time is a promising strategy with regard to (haptic) illusions and pseudo-haptics.

That is, the user has to be introduced to the simulation, the context of the application, to how things should be done, and what kind of output / feedback can be expected – and why. Once this "story" is clearer (i.e., new prior knowledge has been established), weaker parts of the system's multisensory feedback might be compensated for by the user's "vivid imagination". Pusch et al. did this (though probably not on purpose) by asking the subjects to determine those trials of a comparison pair in which they found it harder to hold the hand at the indicated position (author's note: Within a virtual force field) [4]. The implied sensation may thus have been the resistance against something of varying intensity. Together with the visible force field cues, the CNS had enough information available to come up with a (more or less) stable flow or stream illusion and so permit subject to take a decision.

More generally speaking: A future user is made develop his own mental model, suggested by the designer, of what he will see, feel or hear and then perceive the environment accordingly. This form of "user tuning" might be of interest to many other HCI domains.

6. CONCLUSION AND FUTURE WORK

Our first objective was to discuss and clarify the foundations of pseudo-haptics by building on two prominent models of human perception, cognition and action: First, the Interacting Cognitive Subsystems model by Barnard et al. [8, 9] and second, the Bayesian multimodal cue integration framework by Ernst et al. [16, 10, 11]. From these two complementary theories, we have synthesised our simplified foundations framework, nevertheless meant to provide a comprehensive picture of the key processes underlying (certainly not only) pseudo-haptics. We also wanted to offer an elaborate means for the assessment of existing techniques or those to be developed. Given the validity of ICS and BMI, we expect our framework to be valid, too. Except for one extension: The multidimensional coupling prior. Though its existence seems likely (see also: Trimodal interaction [32]), multidimensionality has not been experimentally shown yet and is therefore not part of the original BMI. Future studies on this topic may help gain the required insights. Independent of this particularity, we could demonstrate applicability and utility of our foundations synthesis by discussing the HEMP force field application by Pusch et al. [4]. During this review, we could isolate a number of design issues and propose ways to overcome them. In order to test that the suggested modifications effectively improve the respective system, it would be necessary to conduct another experiment focussing on changes in the final sensation (e.g., by measuring variations in presence and appropriate biosignals, see also [29]). We assume that the analysis process can easily be applied to other examples of pseudo-haptics systems with a similar outcome.

The second objective of our work was to bring pseudo-haptics to a larger audience of scientists and practitioners by introducing generic, but still practical system design recommendations. The proposed set of guidelines has been developed as an extension of [7] and draws from the discussions and analyses in this paper. As with other guidelines assembled to support creative work, ours need to stand the test of time, too. We already have a couple of concepts on the desk which we would like to implement and study in near future. After all, we hope that we can encourage people to explore and exploit pseudo-haptics much more efficiently.

7. ACKNOWLEDGMENTS

Andreas Pusch has been supported by the FUI Minalogic project NOMAD.

8. REFERENCES

[1] Lécuyer, A., Coquillart, S., Kheddar, A., Richard, P., and Coiffet, P., "Pseudo-Haptic Feedback: Can Isometric Input Devices Simulate Force Feedback?", In Proc. of IEEE Virtual Reality, 2000.

[2] Paljic, A., Burkhardt, J.-M., and Coquillart, S., "Evaluation of Pseudo-Haptic Feedback for Simulating Torque: A Comparison Between Isometric and Elastic Input Devices", In Proc. of HAPTICS, 2004.

[3] Dominjon, L., Lécuyer, A., Burkhardt, J.-M., Richard, P., and Richir, S, "Influence of Control / Display Ratio on Perception of Mass of Manipulated Objects in Virtual Environments", In Proc. of IEEE VR, 2005.

[4] Pusch, A., Martin, O., and Coquillart, S, "HEMP – Hand-Displacement-Based Pseudo-Haptics: A Study of a Force Field Application", In Proc. of IEEE 3DUI, 2008.

[5] Crison, F., Lécuyer, A., Savary, A., Mellet-D'Huart, D., Burkhardt, J.-M., and Dautin, J, "The Use of Haptic and Pseudo-Haptic Feedback for the Technical Training of Milling", In Proc. of EuroHaptics, 2004.

[6] Bibin, L., Lécuyer, A., Delbos, A., Burkhardt, J.-M., and Bonnet, M., "SAILOR: A 3D Simulator for Loco-Regional Anaesthesia Based on Desktop Virtual Reality and Pseudo-Haptic Feedback", In Proc. of ACM VRST, 2008.

[7] Lécuyer, A., "Simulating Haptic Feedback Using Vision: A Survey of Research and Applications of Pseudo-Haptic Feedback", In Presence: Teleoperators and Virtual Environments, 18 (1), pp. 39 – 53, 2009.

[8] Barnard, P. J., "Interacting Cognitive Subsystems: A Psycholinguistic Approach to Short-Term Memory", In Progress in the psychology of language, 2, pp. 197 – 258, 1985.

[9] Barnard, P. J., and Teasdale, J. D., "Interacting Cognitive Subsystems: A Systematic Approach to Cognitive-Affective Interaction and Change", In Cognition and Emotion, 5 (1), pp. 1 – 39, 1991.

[10] Ernst, M. O., and Bülthoff, H. H., "Merging the Senses into a Robust Percept", In Trends in Cognitive Sciences, 8 (4), pp. 162 – 169, 2004.

[11] Ernst, M. O., "A Bayesian View on Multimodal Cue Integration", In Human Body Perception From The Inside Out, pp. 105 – 131, 2006.

[12] van Mensvoort, K., Hermes, D. J., and van Montfort, M., "Usability of Optically Simulated Haptic Feedback", In Internat. J. of Human-Computer Studies, 66 (6), pp. 438 - 451, 2008.

[13] Lécuyer, A., Burkhardt, J.-M., and Tan, C. H., "A Study of the Modification of the Speed and Size of the Cursor for Simulating Pseudo-Haptic Bumps and Holes", In ACM TAP, 5 (3), 2008.

[14] Pusch, A., "Visuo-Proprioceptive Conflicts of the Hand for 3D User Interaction in Augmented Reality", Ph.D. thesis, 2008.

[15] Lécuyer, A., Burkhardt, J.-M., Coquillart, S., and Coiffet P., "'Boundary of Illusion': An Experiment of Sensory Integration with a Pseudo-Haptic System", In Proc. of IEEE VR, 2001.

[16] Ernst, M. O., and Banks, M. S., "Humans Integrate Visual and Haptic Information in a Statistically Optimal Fashion", In Nature, 415, pp. 429 – 433, 2002.

[17] Rocchesso, D., "Acoustic Cues for 3-D Shape Information", In Proc. of ICAD, 2001.

[18] Gepshtein, S., Burge, J., Banks, M. S, and Ernst, M. O., "The Combination of Vision and Touch Depends on Spatial Proximity", In Journal of Vision, 5 (11), pp. 1013 – 1023, 2005.

[19] Hospedales, T., and Vijayakumar, S., "Multisensory Oddity Detection as Bayesian Inference", In PLoS ONE, 4 (1), 2009.

[20] Wise, S. P., and Shadmehr, R., "Motor Control", In Encyclopedia of the Human Brain, 3, pp. 137 – 157, 2002.

[21] Wolpert, D. M., Ghahramani, Z., and Jordan, M. I., "An Internal Model for Sensorimotor Integration", In Science, 269 (5232), pp. 1880 – 1882, 1995.

[22] Berthoz, A., "Le Sens du Mouvement", Odile Jacob (ed.), 1997.

[23] Gauthier, G. M., Vercher, J.-L., Mussa Ivaldi, F, and Marchetti, E, "Oculo-Manual Tracking of Visual Targets: Control Learning, Coordination Control and Coordination Model", In Experimental Brain Research, 73 (1), pp. 127 – 137, 1988.

[24] Biocca, F., Kim, J., and Choi, Y., "Visual Touch in Virtual Environments: An Exploratory Study of Presence, Multimodal Interfaces, and Cross-Modal Sensory Illusions", In Presence: Teleoperators and Virtual Environments, 10 (3), pp. 247 – 265, 2001.

[25] Perani, D., Fazio, F., Borghese, N. A., Tettamanti, M., Ferrari, S., Decety, J., and Gilardi, M. C., "Different Brain Correlates for Watching Real and Virtual Hand Actions", In Neuroimage, 14 (3), 2001.

[26] Blakemore, S.-J. , and Frith, C. D., "Self-Awareness and Action", In Current Opinion in Neurobiology, 13 (2), pp. 219 – 224, 2003.

[27] Lok, B., Naik, S., Whitton, M. C., and Brooks, Jr., F. P., "Effects of Handling Real Objects and Avatar Fidelity on Cognitive Task Performance in Virtual Environments", In Proc. of IEEE VR, 2003.

[28] Vercher, J.-L., "Perception and Synthesis of Biologically Plausible Motion: From Human Physiology to Virtual Reality.", In Lect. Notes in Computer Science, 3881, pp. 1 – 12, 2006.

[29] Pusch, A., Martin, O., and Coquillart, S, "HEMP – Hand-Displacement-Based Pseudo-Haptics: A Study of a Force Field Application and a Behavioural Analysis", In Internat. J. of Human-Computer Studies, 67 (3), 2009.

[30] Burns, E., Razzaque, S., Panter, A. T., Whitton, M. C., McCallus, M. R., and Brooks, Jr., F. P., "The Hand is Slower than the Eye: A Quantitative Exploration of Visual Dominance Over Proprioception", In Proc. of IEEE VR, 2005.

[31] Slater, M., "How Colorful Was Your Day? Why Questionnaires Cannot Assess Presence in Virtual Environments", In Presence: Teleoperators and Virtual Environments, 13 (4), pp. 484 – 493, 2004.

[32] Wozny, D. R., Beierholm, U. R., and Ladan Shams, "Human Trimodal Perception Follows Optimal Statistical Inference", In J. of Vision, 8 (3), pp. 1 – 11, 2008.

6th Senses for Everyone! The Value of Multimodal Feedback in Handheld Navigation Aids

Martin Pielot, Benjamin Poppinga, Wilko Heuten
OFFIS Institute for Information Technology
Oldenburg, Germany
pielot,poppinga,heuten@offis.de

Susanne Boll
University of Oldenburg
Oldenburg, Germany
boll@informatik.uni-oldenburg.de

ABSTRACT

One of the bottlenecks in today's pedestrian navigation system is to communicate the navigation instructions in an efficient but non-distracting way. Previous work has suggested tactile feedback as solution, but it is not yet clear how it should be integrated into handheld navigation systems to improve efficiency and reduce distraction. In this paper we investigate augmenting and replacing a state of the art pedestrian navigation system with tactile navigation instructions. In a field study in a lively city centre 21 participants had to reach given destinations by the means of tactile, visual or multimodal navigation instructions. In the tactile and multimodal conditions, the handheld device created vibration patterns indicating the direction of the next waypoint. Like a sixth sense it constantly gave the user an idea of how the route continues. The results provide evidence that combining both modalities leads to more efficient navigation performance while using tactile feedback only reduces the user's distraction.

Categories and Subject Descriptors

H.5.2 [**User Interfaces**]: Haptic I/O

General Terms

Human Factors, Experimentation

Keywords

Tactile & Haptic UIs, Multi-modal interfaces, User Studies

1. INTRODUCTION

With more and more powerful handheld devices sold, location-based services and navigation systems have become common applications on our mobile phone. In particular, navigation aids, such as Google Maps, can be found on virtually any Smartphone. These aids allow us to find our way in unfamiliar environments and places we never visited before.

Figure 1: Being distracted is a serious issue when interacting with handheld devices on the move, e.g. when employing them as navigation aids.

Typical applications locate users on a map and allow calculating route. In addition, some recent navigation systems, such as Google Maps Navigation, also provide turn-by-turn instructions by text, visual cues, or speech.

An important problem is the distraction caused by the audio-visual information presentation of such systems, as illustrated in Figure 1. According to a study by Madden and Rainie [9] one in six adults report to have physically bumped into another person because they were distracted using their phone. Ear plugs free the eyes but may lead to the "iPod Zombie Trance"[1], which refers to the loss of situational awareness from listening to audio content. According to the Sydney Morning Herald, authorities in Australia are speculating that this might be a contributing factor to the still increasing pedestrian fatalities. Safety considerations aside; looking at a display or having to listen to spoken instructions might simply be undesirable, e.g. when having a lively discussion with a companion. Therefore, interaction techniques are needed that support pedestrian navigation to not distract travellers from their primary tasks.

Recently a number of research groups have investigated different ways of enhancing Smartphone-based navigation systems with vibro-tactile feedback [8, 10, 14, 15, 21]. One emerging metaphor is the *sixth sense*, which Froehlich et al.

[1]`http://www.smh.com.au/digital-life/mp3s/pedestrian-death-rise-blamed-on-ipods-20100905-14w4d.html`, Sydney Mordning Herald, last visited September 21, 2011.

[3] define as "multimodal feedback to alert users of changes and opportunities in the dynamic environment." For example, Lin et al. [8] used encoded turning instructions, such as "turn right now" in vibration patterns. In our previous work [14] we proposed a *Tactile Compass* that encodes compass directions in vibration patterns. For both approaches it was shown that they can effectively guide a pedestrian to a given destination. However, it is not yet clear if and how these techniques can be used in combination with today's pedestrian navigation systems. Shall they be used to replace or complement existing visualisations? Will they be beneficial in terms of navigation performance and distraction?

To answer these questions we conducted a field study. We experimentally compared visual, tactile, and multimodal navigation instructions with a handheld pedestrian navigation system. Data from 21 participants and 63 routes were collected. The results provide evidence that the distraction could be reduced by providing tactile feedback only. The efficiency could be improved by providing multimodal feedback. These findings may help designers to tailor navigation systems and similar location-based systems towards efficiency or distraction.

2. RELATED WORK

Tscheligi and Sefelin [19] argue that considering the context of use appropriately is one of the main prerequisites for the success of pedestrian navigation systems. A well-known issue is that the interaction with the mobile device only happens in short bursts [11] and thus can be highly distractive. Thus, pedestrians might lose their situation awareness, which may be dangerous when walking through a lively, traffic-heavy area [9].

To accommodate the pedestrian's context of use, many researchers have investigated the use of tactile information presentation. Tan and Pentland [18] proposed a 3x3 array of tactile actuators worn on the back for conveying navigation information. By e.g. having a series of pulses moving from the left to the right of the display could be used to indicate "turn right" or "right-hand side". Tactile belts are a different form of tactile displays that have proven successful to support (pedestrian) navigation. An early example by Tsukada and Yasumura [20] is the ActiveBelt, which is equipped with eight vibro-tactile actuators. It allows creating tactile stimuli around the wearer's torso to "point" into a horizontal direction. By pointing into the direction the user has to go, such tactile belts can guide pedestrians along a route. This form of waypoint navigation has found to be effective and beneficial for the user's distraction [2, 12].

Disadvantages of these early devices are that they are custom-made hardware devices, which might not always be available when the user is travelling. User might also just not want to carry such a device if navigation support is not required too often. Therefore, researchers have investigated whether navigation support can also be provided with the most ubiquitous tactile display: the vibration alarm of mobile phones. There are two predominant solutions, which Frohlich et al [3] refer to as the *magic wand* and *sixth sense*.

The *magic wand* metaphor, as illustrated in Figure 2, follows the idea that a user points at a distant object with a handheld device to learn about its presence or access information about it. Technically this is possible as nowadays smartphones are equipped with a digital compass. Recent implementations provide feedback when the user roughly points into the correct direction of a relevant geographic location, such as the travel destination [10, 15, 21]. Thus, by actively scanning the environment the user can stay aware of the general direction of her or his travel destination. It has been shown that this technique is very intuitive and allows users to effectively reach a given destination [10, 15, 21]. However, the intuitiveness is traded with the drawback that the device has to be held in the hand and actively needs to be pointed at the object, which has been found undesirable by some users [15].

Figure 2: Magic Wand metaphor: user learns about location of an object by pointing at it with a mobile device.

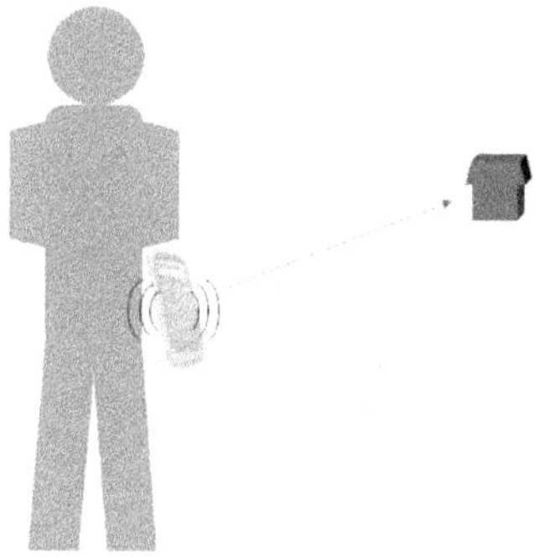

Figure 3: Sixth Sense metaphor: location of an object is encoded in e.g. vibration patterns.

The *sixth sense* metaphor, as illustrated in Figure 3, describes solutions that use multimodal feedback to alert the user about changes in the environment. This has been applied by issuing turning instructions in vibration patterns [8] as well as cueing the direction in which the user has to go in vibration patterns [14, 10]. Both approaches have proven to be effective in user studies. The advantage of the sixth sense approach versus the magic wand approach is that users are not required to do pointing gestures to acquire the presented information.

While previous work has provided evidence that tactile belts can reduce the navigator's distraction, it is not yet clear whether this benefit can also be found for these novel handheld-based interaction techniques. Also, previous work has compared tactile and visual navigation systems but did not investigate the multimodal combination of both. Thus, it is not clear what effects multimodal cueing of directions will have on the navigation performance and the user distraction, and if/how it therefore should be employed.

3. FIELD EXPERIMENT

To study these novel handheld-based interaction techniques [8, 10, 14, 15, 21] in multimodal usage we conducted a field experiment. 21 participants were asked to navigate through a crowded urban environment. In three conditions, they were equipped with either a handheld-based tactile navigation system, or a state-of-the-art pedestrian navigation system, and the combination of both. We wanted to investigate whether the handheld-based tactile feedback shows the same positive effects on the user's distraction as tactile belts do [2, 12]. Also, we wanted to investigate whether users can integrate the tactile and the visual cues in a way that is beneficial for the navigation performance.

3.1 Evaluation Environment

The study was conducted in the summer of 2010. It took place in the pedestrian zone of *Oldenburg, Germany*, a European city with about 150,000 inhabitants. The winding layout of the streets makes it difficult to stay oriented, even for locals. During shopping hours the city centre becomes very crowded, so a lot of attention is required to evade other people and obstacles. We defined two training routes and three evaluation routes (see Fig. 4). Each route covered about 450 meters. All routes started and ended in calm, less frequented areas and led through the central, most crowded area.

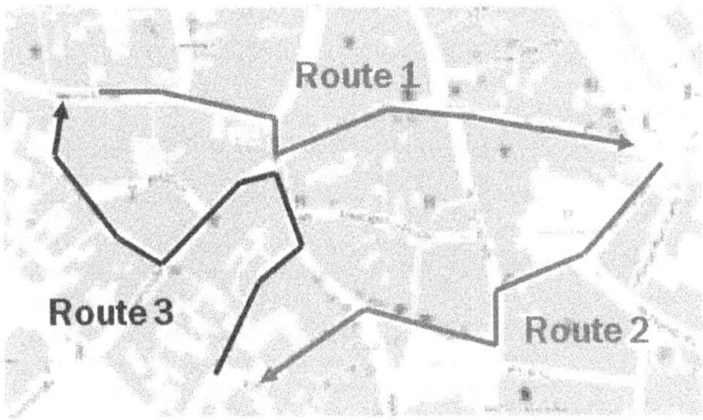

Figure 4: The three evaluation routes covering the city centre of *Oldenburg, Germany* (the two test routes are not shown). Map by OpenStreetMap.org

3.2 Visual Navigation System

As baseline for the experiment we used a self-built navigation system similar to Google Maps. We did our own implementation to provide OpenStreetMap data which - unlike Google Maps - has all pedestrian paths available. Otherwise, the application provides all the relevant functionality available in Google Maps: the user's position and orientation is indicated by an icon drawn onto the map. The map can be set to automatically rotate and align itself with the environment, so the "up" direction on the screen corresponds to the device's orientation. The route is highlighted on the map. Additionally an arrow icon in the bottom left corner of the screen visually indicates into which direction to go. In pilot studies we learned that many users feel embarrassed and distracted by speech output, especially in lively areas. Therefore, only visual feedback was provided.

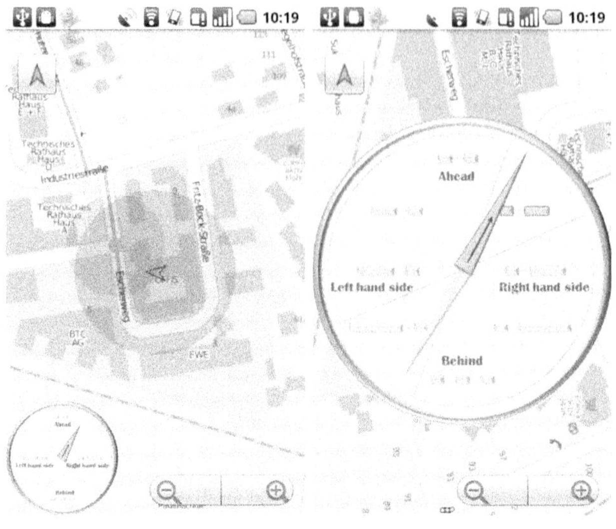

Figure 5: Screenshot of the visual navigation system used in the study. The user location and the route are shown on a map. The icon in the lower left provides a visual cue where to go. It also visualises the vibration patterns associated with each direction (see grey bars in enlarged version).

3.3 Tactile Navigation System

For the tactile navigation system we combined previously proposed instances of the magic wand and the sixth sense metaphor.

As instance of the magic wand metaphor we used the pointing design proposed by [15, 21, 10], which allows the used to scan for a geographical entity by pointing gestures. When the device e.g. points at the next waypoint, this waypoint is considered being "ahead".

As instance of the sixth sense metaphor we used the Tactile Compass proposed in [14], which provides directional information in vibration patterns. When the user e.g. walks towards the next waypoint, two short pulses indicates "ahead" (see Fig. 5 for all eight vibration patterns). The Tactile Compass has found to be an effective navigation aid [10, 14] without requiring any active gestures, which may be tiresome during extended usage [15].

Technically the tactile information presentation techniques are applied as waypoint navigation techniques [2, 12]. Therefore, routes are divided into sets of waypoints. The system constantly conveys the direction of the waypoint that has to be reached next. Once this waypoint has been reached the system switches to the subsequent waypoint. The user is thus dragged along the route until reaching the destination. In our particular implementation we also allowed the user to skip waypoints when e.g. going cross country, finding a shortcut, or simply taking a wrong turn.

The success of waypoint navigation also depends on how close the user needs to get to a waypoint until the system switches to the subsequent waypoint. Switching too late causes the user to reach the decision point without knowing where to go. Switching to the next waypoint too early can result into direction information that may be hard to interpret, since e.g. the system points at a building. In a series of pilot studies we optimised the switching time to provide the new directional information in the most suitable moment. One of the tweaks we used was to switch to the next waypoint earlier, the faster the user walked and the less accurate the GPS signal was.

3.4 Participants

21 participants (10 female, 11 male) took part in the study. Their age ranged from 18 to 41 with an average of 26.6 years (SD 6.68). Prior to the study we assessed the participants' familiarity with (pedestrian) navigation systems and their sense of direction. The sense of direction was assessed by the Santa Barbara Sense of Direction Scale (SBSOD) [5]. In a possible range from 1 (low) to 100 (high) the participants scored 54.72 (SD 15.37) in average. The participants judged their familiarity to be average with car navigation systems (3.05, SD 1.02 / 1=low - 5=high) and below average with pedestrian navigation systems (1.95, SD 1.16 / 1=low - 5=high). Although no personally identifiable information was collected all participants signed an informed consent. All participants received a gift to compensate their participation in the study.

3.5 Design

The navigation system configuration served as independent variable with three levels: *visual*, *tactile*, and *combined*. In the *visual* condition the participants only used the visual feedback of the navigation system. In the *tactile* condition the screen was blinded so only the tactile feedback could be used. In the *combined* condition, both, the tactile feedback and the visual feedback were available.

The experiment followed a within-subjects design, so every participant contributed to all three conditions. The order was counter-balanced to cancel out sequence effects. The following dependent measures were taken to assess the navigation performance, the cognitive workload, and the level of distraction:

Navigation Performance.

Inspired by previous field studies (e.g. [7, 16, 12]) navigation performance was measured in terms of completion time, number of navigation errors, number of orientation phases, and number of orientation losses. *Completion time* was defined as the time the participants travelled from start to end of each route. A *navigation error* was counted when a pedestrian took a wrong turn and entered the wrong street for more than 5 meters. *Disorientation events* were defined as situations where the participants stopped for more than 10 seconds or stopped and expressed their disorientation verbally. An *orientation phase* was counted when the participant stopped shortly (less than 10 s) to re-orient themselves.

Cognitive & Mental Workload.

The cognitive workload was measured by subjective and objective measures. As subjective measures we issued the widely accepted Nasa TLX [4] questionnaire. As objective workload measure we monitored the participants' walking speed, as Brewster et al. [1] suggested that people walk slower when the cognitive workload increases while interacting with a handheld device. The walking speed was extracted from the GPS signal.

Distraction.

The distraction was quantified by measuring how much participants interacted with the mobile device and how well they could pay attention to the environment. To assess how well the participants paid attention to the environment we asked the participants to count the number of cafes, hair dressers, and pharmacies and name the sum of all of these shops at the end of the route. Since the experimenters were aware of all of these shops they could calculate the ratio of how many shops have been detected. Interacting with the device was divided into two groups: looking at the map and using the pointing gestures. The participants were considered *looking at the map* when the device was held in an angle that allowed that participant to look at the display. The participant was considered *pointing* when the device was held nearly parallel to the ground. Since in the *combined* condition the user could also be looking at the map when pointing and vice versa, such situations were contributing to both dependent measures at the same time. How the device was held was logged automatically by the device, so these measures could be taken without having to use a video camera.

3.6 Procedure

Informed consents, demographic questionnaires, and additional information were sent out to the potential participants prior to the study. Only those participants who signed the consent forms were invited to the study.

Training sessions allowed the participants to get used to the navigation system. A dedicated application was developed to train the tactile feedback. It allowed the participants to explore and learn the different patterns. To complete the learning phase, 16 random patterns had to be recognized. Response time and recognition errors were logged for later analysis.

Afterwards the participants could train the use of the application on two test routes. The first route was done with visual and tactile feedback, the second with tactile feedback only. During both routes we trained the participants to use the pointing gesture or to look at the device' screen only when needed and otherwise keep the device in a position where the arm was relaxed.

When the actual evaluation started we explained the participants that they had to count cafes, hair dressers, and pharmacies they pass by on their route. The navigation time started to be recorded when the route was selected on the mobile device. The experimenter followed the participant in some distance and took notes about navigation errors, orientation losses, and orientation phases. The experimenter also watched out for the number of shops to be counted when participants left the correct route due to a navigation error. When arriving at the last waypoint of the route the completion time was automatically taken. The participants filled out the Nasa TLX for the past condition and then switched to the next condition.

After having completed all three routes we conducted an open post-hoc interview with the participants. The goal was to learn about any of the participants' impressions and suggestions. Our strategy was to not ask any question unless the interview went stuck but encourage the participants to express their thoughts freely. The whole procedure took about 90 minutes for each participant.

4. RESULTS

All participants succeeded to reach the destination in all three conditions. In the following we present the quantitative and qualitative findings.

4.1 Quantitative Results

This section presents the quantitative results of the dependent variables. The diagrams show mean value and standard deviation per condition. Statistical significance was analyzed using ANOVA and Tukey post-hoc tests.

Navigation Performance.

Figure 6 shows the results related to the navigation performance. No significant effects could be found on the *completion time* ($F(2) = 2.93, p = .06$) and the number of *orientation losses* ($F(2) = 0.47, p = .63$). There was a significant effect on the number of *navigation errors* ($F(2) = 3.65, p < .05$). In the *combined* condition participants took less wrong turns than in the *visual* or the *tactile* condition (both $p < .05$). Further, there was a significant effect on the number of *orientation phases* ($F(2) = 4.93, p < .01$). In the *tactile* condition the participants made more short stops than in the *visual* condition ($p < .01$). In summary, participants stopped more often to reorient when using the tactile feedback only. The multimodal combination of visual and tactile led to less navigation errors.

We also found several noteworthy correlations: participants with better knowledge about the city had a higher walking speed in the visual condition ($r = .47$). More previous experience with navigation systems lead to lower completion times ($r = -.37$) and fewer orientation phases ($r = -.47$) in the tactile condition. In the visual condition participants with more previous experience looked at the device less often ($r = -.34$). Participants who completed the training faster performed better in terms of completion time ($r = .44, .53, .67$), navigation errors ($r = .55, .69, .42$), disorientation events ($r = .50, .60, .11$), and orientation phases ($r = .46, .50, .59$) (for conditions visual, tactile, combined).

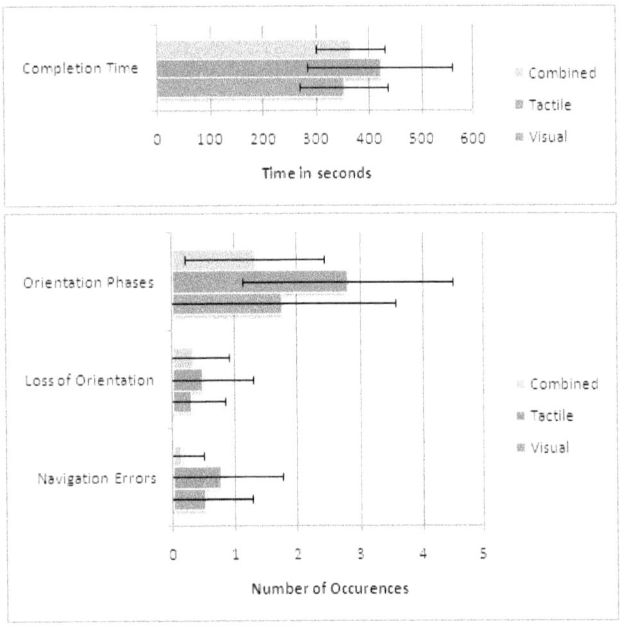

Figure 6: Navigation performance measures.

Cognitive Workload.

Figure 7 shows the results related to the cognitive workload. There was a significant effect on the participants' walking speed ($F(2) = 5.01, p < .01$). Participants walked faster in the *visual* condition than in the *tactile* condition ($p < .01$) or in the *combined* condition ($p < .05$). Thus, the objective cognitive workload was higher when the tactile feedback was present. However, the subjective judgement of the cognitive workload via the NasaTLX showed no significant differences between the conditions ($F(2) = 1.04, p = .36$).

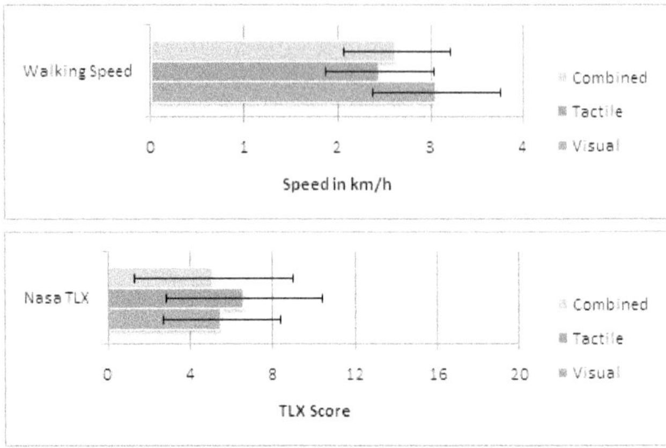

Figure 7: Cognitive workload measures.

Distraction.

Figure 8 shows the results related to the distraction. There was no significant effect on the number of shops found ($F(2) = .94, p < .40$). But, there was a significant effect on the amount of interaction ($F(2) = 3.41, p < .05$). The interaction was significantly lower in the *tactile* and in the *combined* condition than in the *visual* condition (both $p < .05$). Considering only the time spent *looking at the map* in the conditions where the map was available, the participants in the *visual* condition looked significantly less often at the map compared to the *combined* condition ($p < .05$). In the two conditions where the tactile feedback was present, the participants used the pointing gesture significantly less often in the *combined* condition than in the *tactile* condition ($p < .01$). In summary, the visual feedback reduced the amount of pointing interaction and the tactile feedback had a positive effect on the amount of distractive interaction.

4.2 Comments and Observations

In the beginning of the experiment, many participants were questioning whether the tactile feedback only was sufficiently easy to use. During the study, however, none of the participants failed interpreting the tactile cues. One participant nicely summarized this by stating: *when reading the information sheets I never thought these vibration patterns would work. But in retrospect, it was much more intuitive than I expected.*

4.2.1 Navigation Strategies

Visual Condition.

In the *visual* condition the predominant strategy was "read 'n' run": the participants studied the map, memorized the upcoming route segment, and then passed the memorized part as quickly as possible without looking at the map. Participants using this strategy were walking faster than in any other situations we observed. Since the study took place in summer, sunlight reflections were one of the major issues in

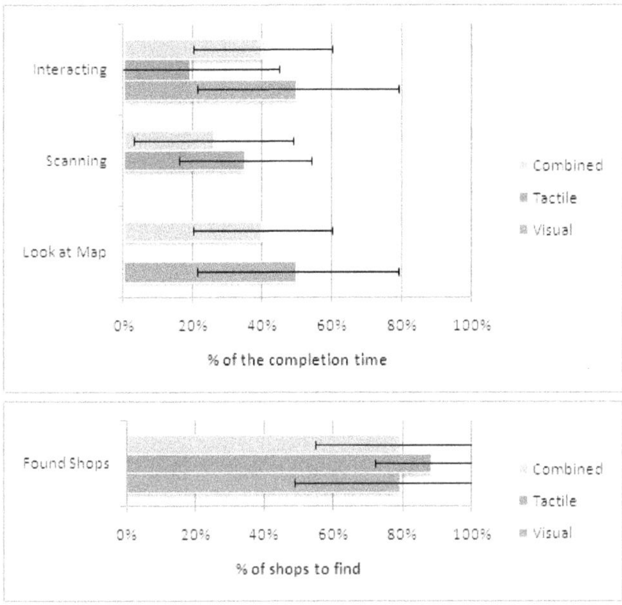

Figure 8: Distraction-related measures.

reading the map. Three participants reported to have major trouble with reading the display (see Fig. 9).

Figure 9: Participant struggling to read the display due to sunlight reflections (left). Participant scanning for the next waypoint (right).

Tactile Condition.

As suggested, the participants used the pointing gestures only when there was a specific need for more accurate information, such as when the GPS signal strength declined or when the participants wanted to reorient themselves at a crossing. Usually the participants pointed the device forward into their walking direction. They tried to learn the direction of the next waypoint from the pattern rather than actively pointing the device in different directions to find the "ahead" pattern by pointing into different direction. Thus, the pointing interaction studied in [10, 15, 21] has rarely be observed. Although there was no technical need, there was a tendency that the participants stopped when doing pointing gestures.

In the post-hoc interview many participants stated that they found the tactile feedback surprisingly more easy to be used than they had expected. The lack of an overview was named five times as notable drawback. Four participants stated that they were missing the map to understand how the route proceeded beyond the next waypoint. However, regarding the *tactile* condition six participants expressed that they were not missing the map at all.

Combined Condition.

The combination of tactile and visual feedback was named most often as the preferred condition. The participants enjoyed to have the map to get an overview and at the same time receive constant confirmation by the tactile cues. Many participants focused on one source of information primarily and used the other as support. Eight participants reported to have relied on the map and used the tactile feedback to be reminded of an upcoming turn. Seven participants reported to have primarily used the tactile feedback and used the map only when being uncertain. Unlike the *visual* condition, the "read 'n' run" strategy was hardly observed in this condition.

4.2.2 Cognitive Workload and Distraction

Many participants stated that they were constantly monitoring the tactile feedback. Three participants explicitly mentioned that processing the constant feedback was mentally demanding. On the other hand, four participants appreciated the continuous feedback. They felt that people having bad sense of direction would greatly benefit from the constant confirmation.

With respect to the distraction, participants appreciated that the tactile feedback made it unnecessary to look at a display. Nine participants positively mentioned the private and eyes-free usage, in particular when the display is hard to read due to sunlight reflections.

4.2.3 Tactile Compass Design

In order to identify areas of improvement we also collected feedback on the design of the tactile feedback. In the dedicated training session the participants recognized 78.19% (SD 14.61) of the presented patterns correctly Roughly 80% of the errors was a confusion of neighbouring directions, e.g. left was chosen instead of left-behind. In the post-hoc interviews we identified two reoccurring issues:

The first issue was the number of directions to present. Our design cued eight directions in vibration patterns. However, seven participants stated that they mentally ignored the intermediate directions and therefore navigated by ahead, behind, left-hand side and right-hand side only. Additionally, five participants reported to have difficulties to discriminate the *ahead* and the two adjacent directions (ahead/right - ahead/left). Three participants explicitly suggested reducing the number of directions to four.

The second issue was the constant presence of the tactile feedback. It was explicitly appreciated by four participants who felt to have a bad sense of direction. However, the bigger share of the participants pointed out that their attention was drawn too much by the constantly repeated vibration patterns. Some said that they could not stop listening for changes in the vibration signals. During the study we observed many cases, where the participants appeared to concentrate a lot on the tactile patterns (see e.g. Fig. 9). Suggestions for improvement were to play the tactile patterns only on the user's request or only in situations where it is necessary, e.g. when approaching a turn or when leaving the route.

5. DISCUSSION

All participants were able to reach the given destinations with the visual, the tactile, and the multimodal, combined feedback. The multimodal feedback improved the navigation performance by reducing the number of navigation errors. The tactile feedback only led to less distractive interaction with the handheld device. The presence of the tactile feedback in the *tactile* and the *combined* condition led to slower walking speeds, which we believe may be a sign for an increased cognitive workload.

Navigation Performance.

The results support previous work showing that cueing directions is possible with a single actuator [10, 12, 15, 21] and can form effective navigation aids. Although no statistically significant differences could be observed, there was a tendency towards a decreased navigation performance in the *tactile* condition. We did not find this surprising given the fact that most participants had previous experience with visual navigation systems while the tactile system was completely new to them. The time needed to get to the destination increased by 15% for the *tactile* condition, which may still be acceptable if reducing distraction is preferred over efficiency. Although we included two training routes, the question remains whether the performance would converge over time as the user gains more experience in using the tactile compass.

The combination of both modalities, in contrast, could improve the navigation performance in terms of navigation errors. Similar findings have been made with body centric cues provided by tactile waist belts. In two studies [17, 13] it was shown that cueing the location of the destination can improve the navigation performance. However, there are two notable advancements: (1) the work presented here is based on abstract patterns and pointing gestures, not body centric cues. The latter are presumably easier to interpret. (2) in the reported studies the tactile displays were used in combination with maps. Here we provided turn-by-turn instructions, which are presumably more powerful. Thus, we could show that navigation performance can still be increased, even if the tactile cues are less intuitive and the visual cues are more intuitive.

Cognitive Workload.

The results indicate that the tactile feedback induced cognitive workload. The walking speed was significantly higher in the *visual* condition which according to Brewster et al. [1] is a sign of less cognitive workload. Many participants who reported that they have been constantly feeling for vibration patterns confirmed this. Notably, this happened in the *tactile* and in the *combined* condition, although in the *combined* condition the participants could have used the system as in the *visual* condition by just ignoring the tactile feedback.

We are surprised that we did not observe an equivalent of the cocktail party effect, where people selectively listen to a single speaker while ignoring all other conversations and background noise. Our results indicate that even in the *combined* condition, where interpreting the tactile patterns was not necessary at all, the participants tried to interpret them. One explanation might be found in the work by Ho et al. [6] who found that the sense of touch can be used to attract and direct the human's attention. The tactile cues could have attracted the users' attention even in situations where it was unnecessary. Future design iterations could address this issue by simplifying the tactile icons further (e.g. by reducing the number of directions) and providing information only when necessary. On the good side, these findings indicate that tactile cues are well perceived on the move and do not suffer from external interferences. So, tactile cues would be particularly effective in drawing the user's attention if required.

Distraction.

The tactile feedback had a positive effect on the distraction. Complementing the visual system with tactile feedback helped reducing the time spent interacting with the device significantly. Compared to the *visual* condition the participants looked less often at the map. Compared to the *tactile* condition the participants used the pointing gesture less often. Taking the overall time spent scanning & looking on the map into account, the participants were interacting most when having visual feedback only. These findings show that the reduction of the user's distraction shown for tactile belts [2, 13, 12] also applies to the sixth sense and the magic wand metaphors for handheld devices.

However, although the participants found most shops in the *tactile* condition, no significant effect was found on the detection rate. This can be explained by the fact that the detection rates were generally high (between 77 % and 88 %). We therefore cannot confirm the findings by Elliott et al. [2] where soldiers could spot most "targets" with a tactile navigation system. However, Elliott et al. compared their tactile navigation system with a head-mounted display and an alphanumeric handheld GPS coordinate representation. Both baseline systems presumably require more effort to interpret the navigation information compared to the navigation system used in our study. Thus, the findings by Elliott et al. might be confirmed when the tactile feedback is employed with improvements with respect to the cognitive workload and more training.

Limitations of the study.

Some participants were not completely unfamiliar with the city centre. This could account for the "read'n'run" strategy we observed in the *visual* condition and thus have favoured the conditions with the visual feedback. In completely unfamiliar environments the tactile feedback might therefore have performed better in comparison. In particular, this shows that maps are distracting even though users already have some understanding of their content. In terms of ecological validity we do not see the results threatened, as it is not uncommon to use navigation systems in somewhat familiar environments.

6. CONCLUSIONS

The main contribution of this paper is the first field study reporting from an experimental investigation of visual, tactile, and multimodal (visual *and* tactile) feedback for providing turning instructions in a pedestrian navigation system on handheld devices. The study provides evidence that the tactile feedback reduces the user's distraction while the multimodal feedback improves the navigation performance. Further, it suggests taking into account to reduce the amount of tactile feedback to not increase the cognitive load unnecessarily.

These findings will allow tailoring navigation systems towards the context of use, i.e. whether navigation performance or reduced distraction is required. The findings may also be applied to applications beyond navigation systems, as cueing directional information is a core feature of many location-based services. The results suggest that providing tactile feedback will improve the user's situation awareness and therefore be beneficial for the safety of use.

Future works needs to address the challenge of reducing the cognitive workload. Solutions we proposed, such as reducing the complexity of the directional information and reducing the amount of feedback should be subject of further studies. Further, all studies on tactile feedback in navigation systems studied time-limited usage only. Longitudinal studies are in order to investigate how tactile feedback performs, once the participants get acquainted to it.

7. ACKNOWLEDGMENTS

The authors are grateful to the European Commission which co-funds the IP HaptiMap (FP7-ICT-224675). We like to thank our colleagues for sharing their ideas with us.

8. REFERENCES

[1] S. Brewster, J. Lumsden, M. Bell, M. Hall, and S. Tasker. Multimodal 'eyes-free' interaction techniques for wearable devices. In *CHI '03*, 2003.

[2] L. R. Elliott, J. van Erp, E. S. Redden, and M. Duistermaat. Field-based validation of a tactile navigation device. *IEEE Transactions on Haptics*, 99, 2010.

[3] P. Fröhlich, A. Oulasvirta, M. Baldauf, and A. Nurminen. On the move, wirelessly connected to the world. *Commun. ACM*, 54:132–138, January 2011.

[4] S. Hart and L. Staveland. *Human Mental Workload*, chapter Development of NASA-TLX (Task Load Index): Results of empirical and theoretical research. Amsterdam: North Holland, 1988.

[5] M. Hegarty, A. E. Richardson, D. R. Montello, K. Lovelace, and I. Subbiah. Development of a self-report measure of environmental spatial ability. *Intelligence*, 30:425–447, 2002.

[6] C. Ho, H. Z. Tan, and C. Spence. Using spatial vibrotactile cues to direct visual attention in driving scenes. *Transportation Research Part F: Psychology and Behaviour*, 8:397–412, 2005.

[7] T. Ishikawa, H. Fujiwara, O. Imai, and A. Okabe. Wayfinding with a gps-based mobile navigation system: A comparison with maps and direct experience. *Journal of Environmental Psychology*, 28(1):74–82, 2008.

[8] M.-W. Lin, Y.-M. Cheng, W. Yu, and F. E. Sandnes. Investigation into the feasibility of using tactons to provide navigation cues in pedestrian situations. In *OZCHI '08*, 2008.

[9] M. Madden and L. Rainie. Adults and cell phone distractions. Technical report, Pew Research Center, 2010.

[10] C. Magnusson, K. Rassmus-Groehn, and D. Szymczak. The influence of angle size in navigation applications using pointing gestures. In *HAID '10*, 2010.

[11] A. Oulasvirta, S. Tamminen, V. Roto, and J. Kuorelahti. Interaction in 4-second bursts: the fragmented nature of attentional resources in mobile hci. In *CHI '05*, 2005.

[12] M. Pielot and S. Boll. Tactile Wayfinder: comparison of tactile waypoint navigation with commercial pedestrian navigation systems. In *Pervasive '10*, 2010.

[13] M. Pielot, N. Henze, and S. Boll. Supporting paper map-based navigation with tactile cues. In *MobileHCI '09*, 2009.

[14] M. Pielot, B. Poppinga, J. Schang, W. Heuten, and S. Boll. A tactile compass for eyes-free pedestrian navigation. In *INTERACT '11: 13th IFIP TC13 Conference on Human-Computer Interaction*, 2011.

[15] S. Robinson, M. Jones, P. Eslambolchilar, R. Murray-Smith, and M. Lindborg. "I Did It My Way": Moving away from the tyranny of turn-by-turn pedestrian navigation. In *MobileHCI '10*, 2010.

[16] E. Rukzio, M. Müller, and R. Hardy. Design, implementation and evaluation of a novel public display for pedestrian navigation: the rotating compass. In *CHI '09*, 2009.

[17] N. J. J. M. Smets, G. M. te Brake, M. A. Neerincx, and J. Lindenberg. Effects of mobile map orientation and tactile feedback on navigation speed and situation awareness. In *MobileHCI '08*, 2008.

[18] H. Z. Tan and A. Pentland. Tactual displays for wearable computing. In *ISWC '97*, 1997.

[19] M. Tscheligi and R. Sefelin. Mobile navigation support for pedestrians: can it work and does it pay off? *Interactions*, 13:31–33, 2006.

[20] Tsukada and Yasumura. Activebelt: Belt-type wearable tactile display for directional navigation. In *UbiComp '04*, 2004.

[21] J. Williamson, S. Robinson, C. Stewart, R. Murray-Smith, M. Jones, and S. Brewster. Social gravity: a virtual elastic tether for casual, privacy-preserving pedestrian rendezvous. In *CHI '10*, 2010.

Adding Haptic Feedback to Touch Screens at the Right Time

Yi Yang[1,2], Yuru Zhang[1], Zhu Hou[1], Betty Lemaire-Semail[2]

[1]State Key Laboratory of Virtual Reality Technology and Systems, Beihang University
37 Xueyuan Road, 100191 Beijing, China
{eyang, houzhu_buaa} @me.buaa.edu.cn
yuru@.buaa.edu.cn

[2]L2EP-IRCICA
University Lille 1, 50, Avenue Halley,
Parc Scientifique de la Haute Borne,
59650 Villeneuve d'Ascq, France
betty.semail@polytech-lille.fr

ABSTRACT
The lack of haptics on touch screens often causes errors and user frustration. However, adding haptic feedback to touch screens in order to address this problem needs to be effected at an appropriate stage. In this paper we present two experiments to explore when best to add haptic feedback during the user's interaction. We separate the interaction process into three stages: Locating, Navigation and Interaction. We compare two points in the Navigation stage in order to establish the optimal time for adding haptic feedback at that stage. We also compare applying haptic feedback at the Navigation stage and the Interaction stage to establish the latest point at which haptic feedback can be added. Combining previous research with our own, we find that the optimal time for applying haptic feedback to the target GUI at the Navigation stage is when the user reaches his destination and that haptic feedback improves user's performance only if it is added before the Interaction stage. These results should alert designers to the need to take into consideration timing when adding haptic feedback to touch screens.

Categories and Subject Descriptors
H5.2 [**Information interfaces and presentation**]: User Interfaces – *graphical user interfaces, haptic I/O, input devices and strategies.*

General Terms
Design, experimentation, performance.

Keywords
Haptic feedback, force feedback, touch screen, timing.

1. INTRODUCTION
Touch screens have become more and more attractive user-interface in our daily lives. However, a significant disadvantage of touch screens is their lack of haptic feedback [1, 2]. Users' attention to visual and audio feedback is weakened if there is no haptic feeling associated with real controls such as buttons, switches, and knobs [3]. Moreover, users' performance also deteriorates since users cannot rely on haptic cues to accomplish even the most basic interaction tasks. For example, a range of errors occurs, such as wrong letters, slips and double taps when tapping on a soft keyboard on a PDA [4].

The direct and effective way to solve the problem of lacking haptic feedback is to add artificially rendered haptic feedback when the user operates on the screen. However, a question arises immediately. How should haptic feedback be added so that it will improve users' performance? Previous research has produced mixed results, showing that sometimes adding haptic feedback was successful and sometimes not (see reviews in section 2). How can we account for these results? We suppose a significant issue in adding haptics is the timing. Regardless of guiding strategies [5], the magnitude of the feedback [5] and even unsatisfactory manufacturing of the prototype [6], an important reason for failures to improve users' performance by adding haptics to touch screens was because the haptic feedback was not added at an appropriate time.

We separate the process of a single interaction between the user and a GUI into three stages, as presented in Figure 1: Locating, Navigation and Interaction. We investigate *when* to apply haptic feedback to touch screen GUIs through two experiments. The first experiment compares adding the same haptic feedback at the edge and the center of a GUI respectively. This experiment answers the question of whether haptic feedback should be added earlier or later in the Navigation stage. The second experiment compares adding haptic feedback at the Navigation stage and the Interaction stage to prove that haptic feedback can only improve users' performance before an interaction is implemented.

In the following sections, we introduce the three stages in the interaction process and review the literature about adding haptic feedback at these stages. We then describe the force feedback touch screen that we use and present the two experiments. Finally, we discuss about when to add haptic feedback to touch screens.

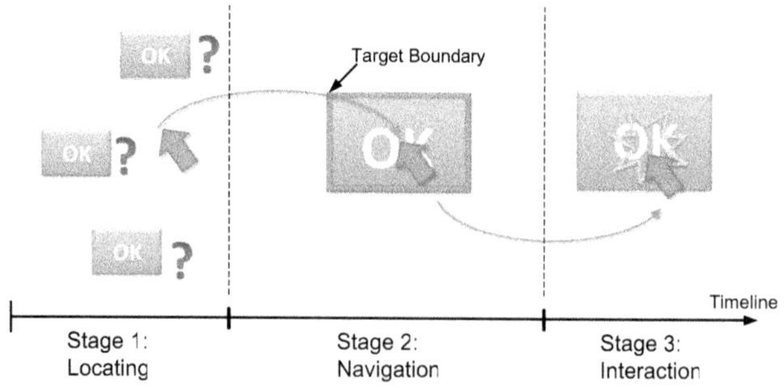

Figure 1. Three stages in a single interaction process.

ICMI'11, November 14-18, 2011, Alicante, Spain.

2. ADDING HAPTIC FEEDBACK TO TOUCH SCREENS

Little research has been undertaken to determine when to add haptic feeback to touch screens. In order to investigate the effect of timing on adding haptic feedback to touch screens, we intentionally separate the interaction process into three stages and categorize previous research into these stages. We find that previous research has yielded different results depending on at which of the three stages haptic feedback has been applied.

Stage 1: Locating. A user may wish to interact with a GUI for a particular purpose such as editing a document or viewing a picture. Or he may be reacting to a reminder such as a message pop-up. In either case, he needs to locate a particular GUI at first. *At this stage, Haptic feedback can be added to help the user to locate the GUI on touch screens.*

The haptic enhanced progress bar is a typical example of this. Different patterns caused by the change of frequency [7-9], magnitude [9] and rhythms [8] of vibrations were applied to indicate the state or the speed of an ongoing program. Experimental results showed that, with haptic feedback, participants responded faster to the completion of the program and thus completed the task faster. In these examples, haptic feedback reminded the user to react to a particular event – the end of a program. The event was mapped with a particular GUI. The user reacted to the haptic feedback by interacting with the GUI, such as by clicking directly on the "Done" button [9]. Therefore haptic feedback eliminated the time that the user had to spend on locating the GUI. This effect is similar to that of a twinkling icon which reminds the user of an instant message.

Stage 2: Navigation. After the target GUI is located, the user needs to move the input interface (mouse, pen or his finger) towards to the GUI, cross its boundary and finally reach the inside of the target. *Adding haptic feedback at this stage to assist the user to reach the target is useful.*

Steering tasks are commonly used to evaluate users' performance when they move the input interface towards to the target GUI. Sun et al. [10] investigated multi-model "error feedback" in a circular steering task on a tablet PC. They attached a vibration motor at the end of a stylus to generate vibration whenever the user moved out of a circular tunnel. Compared with visual and audio feedback, users performed most accurately with haptic feedback. However, there was no significant difference between the feedbacks on movement time since the tactile feedback only indicated errors rather than helping the user move in the quickest way. Although not implementing the steering task on touch screens, Dennerlein et al. [11] used a force feedback mouse to apply a force field in the haptic tunnel to pull the cursor to the center of the tunnel. This effect increased movement speed in a liner steering task by 52 %. Campbell et al. [12] compared users' performance in different feedback conditions with a tactilely enhanced Trackpoint. They created lots of haptic bumps in a circular tunnel so that the user was able to follow the bumps to keep moving along the centre of the tunnel. This effect resulted in a significant faster task completion speed compared with visual only feedback. However, the prerequisite of these effects was that the target was known by the computer [9]. This condition is rare and so haptic feedback is seldom practical. The alternative method is to apply haptic feedbacks to GUIs when the user makes contact with them.

Boundaries are the first items that a user encounters when reaching a GUI. Adding haptic feedback to simulate boundaries of buttons [13], icons or keys [14] is a way of introducing physical properties to GUIs. This technique enables the user to feel the edges of GUIs as if he is touching mechanical buttons or keys. The tangible edges remind the user that he is encountering an icon or a button so that he can slow down or stop moving if the icon or button is the target, thus avoiding errors like sliding over the target [15]. Poupyrev et al. [16] used a piezoelectric-actuated display-glass system to evaluate users' performance in a reciprocal dragging task with a stylus. Tactile vibration at the boundary improved user performance in the drawing (dragging) task by a statistically significant amount. Similar users' performance improvement was also found in a text entry task with haptic enhanced key boundaries on a PDA [14] and 22% faster task completion in a liner list selection task with haptic enhanced list item boundaries on a handhold device [17]. In addition, shorter final positioning times were also found when tactile feedback was added at the target boundary in a routine target selection task with a tactilely enhanced mouse [18].

However there is little research comparing adding the same haptic feedback at different times. For example, will adding the same haptic feedback at the boundary (earlier) be better than at the center (later) of the target? It is worth making a comparison to answer this question and find the optimal time to add haptic feedback at this stage.

Stage 3: Interaction. This stage is after the user reaches the target GUI. At this stage, interactions like clicking a button and releasing the dragging file are implemented. *If haptic feedback is added after an interaction is implemented, then it has little effect on the user's performance.* For example, adding haptic feedback to simulate the button-click feeling has been proved to have no effect on improving task completion speed and error rate in number entering tests [9, 19] and Fitts' tapping experiment [16, 20]. However, this result also varied according to the coupling type of the input device and the display surface. Forlines et al. [20] found that tactile button-click feeling improved the indirect input condition (by 11.9%) but had no effect on the direct input condition in the Fitts' pointing experiment. However, in the crossing experiment, tactile feedback after a crossing provided almost no benefit in the indirect input condition but led to about 11% faster selection times in the direct input condition.

Summary. We can identify a pattern in the literature we reviewed, showing that users' performance was improved mostly by adding haptic feedback before Stage 3. This fact indicates that there may be a time limit within which haptic feedback is effective. In addition, we hypothesize that there exists an optimal time in each stage for adding haptic feedback. However, there is little research into the timing of adding haptic feedback to touch screens. Our contribution explores how the effect of the *timing* of adding haptic feedback to touch screens on users' performance and offers guidelines accordingly.

3. FORCE FEEDBACK TOUCH SCREEN PROTOTYPE

The force feedback touch screen prototype consists of three parts: a 17 inch LCD monitor, an off-the-shelf infrared (IR) touch screen and a FingViewer-I force feedback device. The prototype is presented in Figure 2.

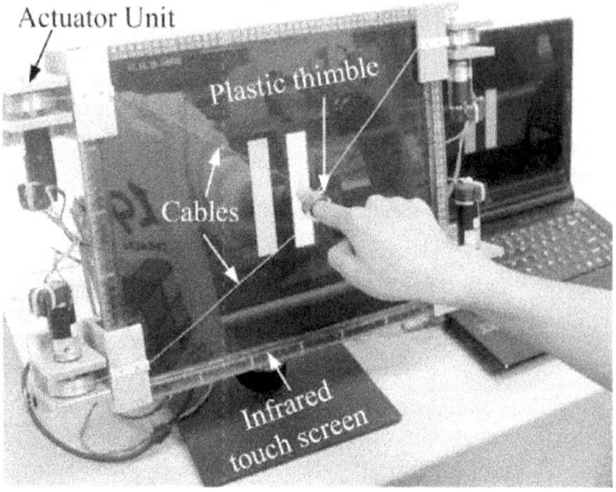

Figure 2. The prototype of the force feedback touch screen

The FingViewer-I force feedback device is a planar cable-driven haptic device. It is used because of its transparent workspace. It comprises four identical actuator units (Figure 2). Each actuator unit includes a pulley, a DC motor and an optical encoder. The pulley and the encoder are fixed to the draft of the motor. One end of the cable is wound on the pulley. The other end is connected to a plastic thimble. The rotation of the pulley is tracked by the encoder to deduce changes in the length of the cable. Then the position of the thimble (i.e. the index finger) is obtained through calculating the lengths of the cables, i.e. the forward kinematics of the mechanism. The force feedback is realized by controlling cable tensions. When the user moves the thimble and contacts any virtual object, the motors will tense the cables so that cable tensions will increase in order to resist the user's finger and prevent it from penetrating the virtual object. In this way, the user perceives the force feedback. The FingViewer-I force feedback device can realize 3 Degree-Of-Freedom (DOF) force feedback on a plane (two translation and one rotation), but we only use the two translational force feedbacks in the experiments. The principle of the planar 3 DOF force feedback device can be found in [21].

The IR touch screen is fixed on the frame of the LCD monitor by the four actuator units. The resolution of the IR touch screen is only about 2 mm, which is not sufficient. But its scanning frequency is around 50 to 60 Hz, which is sufficient to detect tapping on the screen. So we use the force feedback device to track the finger position and the IR touch screen to detect tapping on the screen. The position resolution of the force feedback device is 0.1 mm. In the experiments, the LCD monitor is connected with a Lenovo F40M laptop running C++ and OpenGL codes. The resolution of the monitor was set as 1024 × 768 pixels for presentation of the targets. The frequencies of the visual and haptic renderings were 50 Hz and 1000 Hz respectively.

4. EXPERIMENT ONE: ADDING HAPTICS AT STAGE 2 - EARLY OR LATE?

4.1 Participants

12 participants (3 females and 8 males) between the ages of 20 and 29 were recruited from the laboratory pool. All participants were right-handed. They all had some experience of handling force feedback devices and touch screens but had never operated the force feedback touch screen before. The participants volunteered to participate in the study and were not paid.

4.2 Task and Stimuli

This experiment was designed according to the Task #3 (Dragging Task) described in the ISO 9241 standard, part 9 [22], which is based on Fitts' experimental paradigm. In the experiment, participants were required to drag an object and drop it in the destination target. Two rectangular stripes were located on the screen (Figure 2). Participants pressed on the starting stripe and maintained continuous contact with the screen to drag the "object". However, there was no moving object on the display to show the movement of dragging since the finger and the dragging object were collocated. Participants relied on their fingers' positions to decide if they had reached the target. They could release the object by moving their fingers off the target strip.

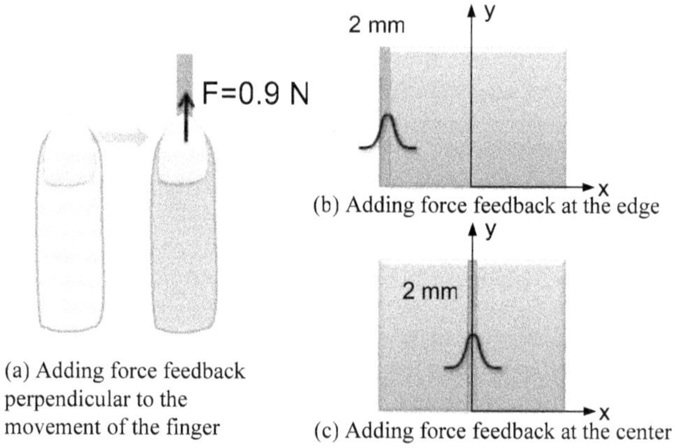

Figure 3. Force feedbacks in Experiment 1.

There were three feedback conditions – visual-only feedback (*V*), force feedback at the edge of the stripe (*FE*) and force feedback at the center of the stripe (*FC*). In all of these conditions, the target stripe was displayed in green and the start stripe in grey. The opposite target turned green only upon the successful drop on the target stripe. The force feedback was a constant force perpendicular to the dragging direction. The feedback operated when the finger was in the feedback area with a width of 2 mm. If this area was too narrow, the participant passed by without even feeling it. The magnitude of the force feedback was 0.9 N, which felt like a bump on the screen (Figure 3). The force feedback was added at the edge or the center of the target stripe. Before the experiment, the only instructions to the participants were to complete the task as quickly and accurately as possible.

4.3 Design

The experiment was a 3 × 3 × 3 repeated-measures within-subjects design. The independent variables and levels were as follows:

Feedback conditions: *V*, *FE*, *FC*

Target Amplitude (A): 40, 80, 160 mm

Target Width (W): 5, 10, 20 mm

The target amplitude and width were selected according to [16]. But the 2 mm target width was replaced by 5 mm since the force feedback area was 2 mm wide at least. Moreover, our input interface was the participant's index finger instead of a stylus. According to the ISO standard [22], the recommended size of the touch-sensitive area should be at least equal to the breadth of the index finger distal joint for the ninety-fifth percentile male. The 2 mm width target was too narrow for touch screen operation.

The participants were randomly divided into three groups. The order of presentation of the three feedback conditions was counterbalanced using a Latin-squares design between each group. Each participant implemented 2 blocks of trials for each of the feedback conditions. Within each block, participants performed 4 repetitions for each of the 9 A-W combinations, which were presented in random order. Prior to each new feedback condition, participants were given a practice block. Breaks were allowed between blocks and between changes of feedback conditions. But participants had to complete all feedback conditions in one sitting. The entire experiment lasted approximately 30 minutes per participant.

To measure and compare the performance of the three feedback conditions, three dependent variables were used: task completion time (ms), error rate (%), throughput (bit/sec). Error rate was the percentage of out-of-target drop. Throughput was calculated with the "effective index of difficulty" as recommended in ISO 9241-9 [22]. In addition, the position where a participant dropped the object was recorded. This variable was defined as offset (mm).

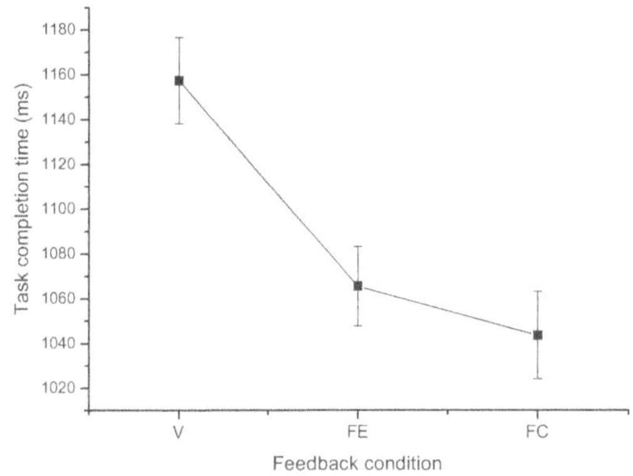

Figure 4. Mean task completion time in the dragging task, by feedback condition.

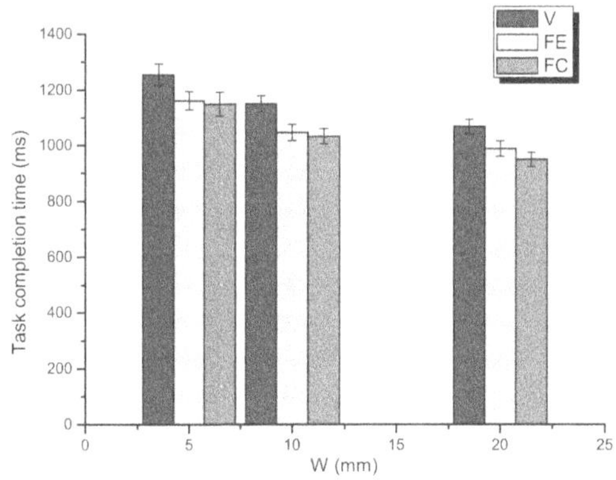

Figure 5. Mean task completion time in the dragging task, by feedback condition and target width.

4.4 Results

4.4.1 Task completion time.

The mean task completion times for the visual-only feedback (*V*), force feedback at the edge (*FE*) and force feedback at the center (*FC*) conditions were 1157 ms, 1066 ms, and 1044 ms respectively (Figure 4). The feedback condition had a significant effect on task completion time ($F_{2,22} = 79.3$, $p < .0001$). The post-hoc Tukey test showed that participants in the *FE* and *FC* conditions completed the task with increased speeds of 7.9% and 9.8% respectively ($p < .0001$). Although the mean task completion time in the *FC* condition was less than that in the *FE* condition, the effect was not statistically significant ($p = .058$). Figure 5 presents the task completion times in the three feedback conditions versus target widths. In general, visual-only feedback (*V*) resulted in the longest task completion time. The mean task completion time in the *FC* condition was shorter than that in the *FE* condition. The differences between the *FE* and *FC* conditions in small target widths (W = 5 mm, 10 mm) were not significant. However, in large target widths (W = 20 mm), participants in the *FC* condition completed the task faster than in the *FE* condition. This effect was statistically significant ($p < .01$).

4.4.2 Error rate

The error rates overall were much higher for the *FC* (mean = 24.4%) and the *FE* (mean = 22.8%) conditions than for the visual-only condition (mean = 12.7%). The effect was statistically significant ($F_{2,22} = 29.8$, $p < .0001$). However the difference between the *FC* condition and the *FE* condition were not significant. The high error rate will be discussed in the following discussion section.

4.4.3 Throughput

The throughput is the counterpart of the "Index of performance" as defined by Fitts. The measure of throughput took into consideration not only the speed of the performance but also accuracy. In this experiment, the effect of feedback conditions on throughput was not significant ($F_{2,22} = 2.60$, $p > .05$), though the mean throughput of the visual-only condition (mean = 1.92 bit/sec) was greater than those of the *FC* (mean = 1.83 bit/sec) and the *FE* condition (mean = 1.80 bit/sec).

4.4.4 Offset

The offset indicates the distribution of locations where participants dropped the dragging object in the experiment. The feedback conditions had a significant effect on offset ($F_{2,22} = 3.75$, $p < .05$). The offset in the visual-only feedback condition (mean = 0.81 mm) was smaller than in the *FE* conditions (mean = 1.15 mm). This effect was statistically significant ($p < .05$). However, there was no statistically significant difference between either the *FC* (mean = 1.05 mm) and *FE* conditions or the *FC* and visual-only conditions.

4.5 Discussion

In this experiment, the same haptic feedback was applied to two successive locations (edge and center) on the target. The task completion speed was increased by adding haptic feedback. This result proved that adding haptic feedback can improve users' efficiency in Stage 2. The result can be explained by the fact that participants were assured by the haptic feedback that they had reached the target so that they released the dragging object (lifted their fingers from the screen) quickly without any hesitation. In the visual-only condition, however, participants had to aim at the target carefully in order to find a "safe" place which guaranteed that the object could be released accurately on the target. This took a longer task completion time.

It may be noted that we did not inform participants about what the haptic feedback stood for, where the feedback was applied and how to react to the feedback. We intended to explore the natural reaction of participants. There was no doubt that participants handled the haptic feedback as soon as they perceived such a signal. Nevertheless, how a participant reacted to this signal depended on her/his intention. In this experiment, the only instruction to participants was that they should complete the task as quickly and accurately as possible. As a consequence, not releasing the object until reaching the center of the target was far preferable to releasing the object as soon as encountering the edge of the target. This pattern was proved by the fact that the mean offsets were positive in all feedback conditions. This result indicated that participants were intent to lift their fingers after they reached the center of the target. Thus we were able to explain why adding haptic feedback at the center was better than adding it at the edge. When a participant encountered the haptic feedback at the edge, he had to handle this signal. However, finding that the location where he perceived the signal was not his target (i.e. the center of the target stripe), he would ignore the signal and keep moving until he reached the center. In this process, the movement of the participant was interrupted by the "bump" created by the force feedback. As a result, the time to complete the task was delayed. By contrast, when haptic feedback was applied at the center of the target, the participant did not slow down until he reached the center. Meanwhile, the participant's intention to stop at the center was enhanced by the haptic feedback. Therefore the participant lifted his finger as soon as he perceived the haptic feedback at the center, thus resulting in a faster task completion. This explanation was supported by the result that the decrease in task completion time in large targets (W = 20 mm) was statistically significant ($p < .01$). In small targets (W = 5 mm, 10 mm), the decrease was not significant due to the narrow spacing between the edge and center.

The overall error rate in the experiment was high, especially when haptic feedback was added. For the visual-only condition, high error rates were also found in other touch interaction research [20, 23]. In general, the errors were a result of selecting small targets. In our experiment, force feedback was applied as a pulse which pulled the finger upward during its lateral movement (Figure 3.(a)). Participants had to balance this force as soon as they perceived it so that they could keep moving horizontally. After the force feedback disappeared, however, participants could not release the force which balanced the force feedback and stop moving their fingers immediately. So they usually lifted their fingers when sliding off the target stripe, especially when the targets were narrow. This effect not only caused errors but also great standard deviation (SD_x) which significantly decreased the throughputs. Therefore a properly designed haptic feedback effect is very important even when the haptic feedback is added at the right time.

In summary, this experiment has proved that adding haptic feedback at Stage 2 is effective in improving users' efficiency. Adding haptic feedback at the center of the GUI is slightly better than adding the same feedback at the edge. The haptic effect needs to be improved so that it can act in accordance with the user's intention.

5. EXPERIMENT TWO: ADDING HAPTIC FEEDBACK AT STAGE 2 AND 3 - EARLY OR NEVER.

5.1 Participants

12 participants (2 females and 10 males) between the ages of 24 and 29 were recruited from the laboratory pool. All participants were right-handed. They all had some experience of handling force feedback devices and touch screens but had never operated the force feedback touch screen before. The participants were volunteers and were not paid. Nine of them participated in Experiment 1.

5.2 Task and Stimuli

This experiment was designed according to the Task #1 (Tapping Task) described in the ISO 9241 standard, part 9 [22], which is an imitation of original Fitts' reciprocal tapping task. The general task was similar to that of Experiment 1. Participants proceeded to tap alternately between the two stripes as quickly and accurately as possible.

There were three feedback conditions – visual-only feedback (*V*), force feedback before the participant tapped on the target (*FB*) and force feedback after a successful tap on the target (*FA*). In all three feedback conditions, the target stripe was displayed in green and the start stripe in grey. The opposite target would turn green only upon a successful tap on the target stripe.

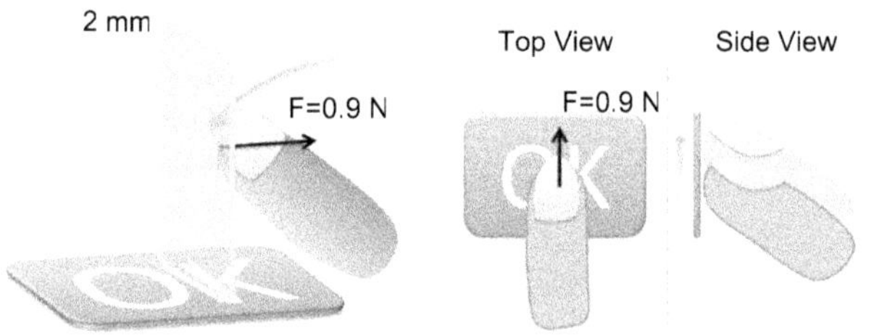

(a) Adding force feedback in Stage 2. The haptic wall helps the finger to stop at the center.

(b) Adding force feedback in Stage 2. The haptic button-click feeling is realized by moving the finger longitudinally slightly.

Figure 6. Force feedbacks in Experiment 2.

The magnitude of the force feedback was 0.9 N in this experiment. According to the experience obtained in Experiment 1, we added the force feedback at the center of the target with a width of 2 mm in the *FB* condition. Moreover, the force feedback was designed to be resistant to the finger when it moved inside the feedback space. It felt like a wall that helped participants to stop at the center of the target (Figure 6.(a)). It may be noted that the feedback was applied before the participant tapped on the target. When the participant tapped on the screen, there was no force feedback.

In the *FA* condition, force feedback was added after participants tapped successfully on the target. A button-click feeling was simulated by adding a pulse of force which pulled the participant's finger to move slightly longitudinally (Figure 6.(b)). Similar simulations have been developed by tactile feedback, such as the Touchsense system [24] and an ultrasonic vibration device [25]. The button-click feeling felt like a "crisp click" and was recognized by the participants. Before the experiment, participants were instructed to complete the task as quickly and accurately as possible. However, they were not instructed about how to respond to the force feedbacks.

The design of the experiment was identical to that of Experiment 1 except that participants completed three blocks in each feedback condition instead of two as in Experiment 1.

5.3 Results

5.3.1 Task completion time

There was a significant effect of feedback conditions on target completion time ($F_{2,22}$ = 12.9, $p < .0001$). The mean task completion times in the visual-only condition, the *FA* condition and the *FB* condition were 618 ms, 613 ms, and 592 ms respectively. The post-hoc Tukey test was applied to compare differences between feedback conditions. There was no significant difference between the *FA* condition and the visual-only condition ($p > .1$).

However the *FB* condition led to a decrease in task completion time by comparison with the visual-only condition and the *FA* condition (Figure 7). This effect was statistically significant ($p < .0001$).

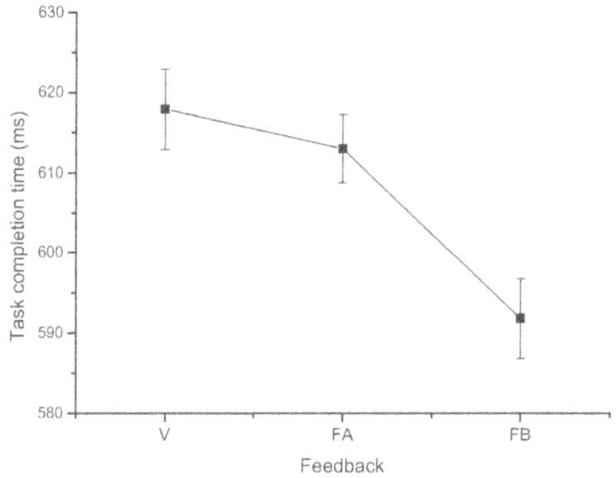

Figure 7. Mean task completion time in the tapping task, by feedback condition.

5.3.2 Error rate

The error rate in the visual-only condition (mean = 13.2%) had no significant difference ($p > .1$) compared with the *FA* condition (mean = 12.0%). The *FB* condition (mean = 6.6%), however, dramatically eliminated 50% of errors caused in the visual-only condition and 45% errors caused in the *FA* condition. The effect of feedback conditions on error rate was statistically significant ($F_{2,22} = 19.3, p < .0001$).

5.3.3 Throughput

The *FB* condition also yielded the highest throughput. The overall mean throughput for the *FB* condition was 4.64 bit/sec, which was 27.5% higher than the 3.64 bit/sec observed for the *FA* condition and 31.1% higher than the 3.54 bit/sec observed for the visual-only condition. Although there was a significant effect of feedback conditions on throughput ($F_{2,22} = 19.1$, $p < .0001$), the difference between the visual-only condition and the *FA* condition was not significant ($p > .1$).

5.4 Discussion

In general, participants in the *FB* condition outperformed those in other feedback conditions. Haptic feedback in the *FB* condition worked in two ways. In the one, haptic feedback assured the participants that they had reached the target so that they were able to press on the target without spending time aiming at its center. This effect was identical to that in Experiment 1. In the other, haptic feedback prevented participants from moving their fingers over the target. The force feedback in the *FB* condition worked as a wall that fingers were "bounced off" as soon as they encountered the resistance. Then participants pressed on the target very close to the "wall" which was located at the center of the target. As a result, the error rate decreased significantly. By contrast, adding haptic feedback in the *FA* condition had no effect on users' performance compared with the visual-only feedback. This result is understandable. Because the haptic feedback worked after the interaction, it could not affect the user's conduct at any stage of the interaction process. As far as users' performance is concerned, it is more fruitful to add haptic feedback at Stage 2 rather than at Stage 3.

6. GENERAL DISCUSSION

6.1 When to Apply Haptic Feedback to Touch Screens

As noted in the introduction, we divided the process of interaction with GUIs into three stages. The two experiments we conducted were to investigate when the right times were for adding haptic feedback on touch screens. The first experiment compared adding haptic feedback at two points within Stage 2. The second experiment compared adding haptic feedback between Stage 2 and Stage 3. However we did not present any experiment related to Stage 1 due to the existence of studies at that stage. Here we bring together previous research with our own discussion of when to apply haptic feedback to touch screens at the three stages. Results are depicted in a schematic diagram in Figure 8.

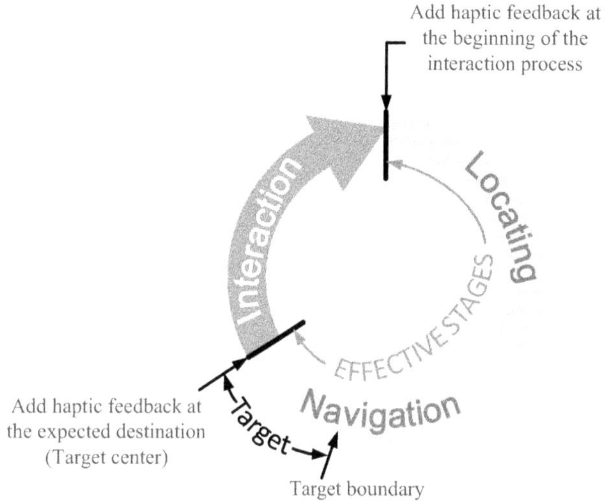

Figure 8. Times to add haptic feedback to touch screens in the interaction process. The end of the arrow is connected to its start to represent successive interaction processes.

Stage 1: Locating. The earlier the better.

Haptic feedback is useful at this stage since it helps the user locate the GUI. In this case, haptic feedback functions as a reminder to the user that he needs to react to a coming event, such as a new email, an instant message or the completion of a program. As soon as the haptic feedback alerts the user, he interacts with the particular GUI which was mapped with the event. In this way, haptics eliminates the time that the user has to spend locating the GUI. This effect is similar to that of a twinkling icon which reminds the user of an instant message. The earlier the reminder appears, the sooner the user will react to the event. So *we suggest adding haptic feedback at the beginning of the interaction process* (Figure 8).

The haptic feedback in Stage 1 is particularly useful in mobile devices, since the screen space is too limited to display all the information at the same time. In addition, in mobile environments, users have to concentrate on walking and navigation and thus have no time to check their mobile devices. Previous research [7-9] has reported that haptic enhanced progress bars on mobile devices have improved users' response time and are generally preferred. This evidence proves that adding haptic feedback at Stage 1 can improve users' performance.

Stage 2: Navigation. The later the better.

Adding haptic feedback can also improve users' performance at this stage. During the navigation towards the target, haptics helps the user to move his input interfaces in the quickest way and reach at his targets accurately. For instance, haptic tunnels that connected the target and the original position of the input interface prevented the user deviating from the tunnel and helped participants to reach the target in the quickest way. This effect decreased the movement time [11, 12] and error rate [10] in steering tasks. In our experiments, adding haptic feedback at the edge and center of the target increased the task completion speed by 7.9% and 9.8% respectively. In Experiment 2, the haptic wall at the center of the target not only reduced the task completion time but also eliminated 50% of errors caused in the visual-only condition.

The results of Experiment 1 proved that adding haptics feedback at Stage 2 can improve users' efficiency. Moreover, the results also demonstrated that adding haptic feedback at the center was slightly better than at the edge of the target. Haptic feedback's effect of reducing the task completion time was more noticeable on the 20 mm width target than on smaller ones. In fact, it should be noted that the edge and center represent the beginning and the expected destination of users' movements in the target. Therefore the results of Experiment 1 should be interpreted as: adding haptic feedback at the *expected destination* was better than adding haptic feedback at the start of the target. In the experiment, the users' expected destination coincided with the center of the stripe since the target widths were smaller than or similar to the user's index finger. In larger targets, however, the expected destination may vary and the effect of haptic feedback may also be weakened.

In Experiment 1, we did not compare adding haptic feedback outside the target and inside the target. There were two reasons for this. First, adding haptic feedback outside the target such as the haptic tunnel [10-12] requires the computer to be aware of the particular target in advance. This situation seldom occurs. By contrast, it is more practical to add haptic after the user contacts the targets (i.e. GUIs). Secondly, following the idea of adding haptic feedback inside the target, we compare the effect of adding identical haptic feedback but at different times in order to find the *optimal* time to apply haptic feedback on the target. So, "adding haptic feedback the later the better in Stage 2" does not mean adding feedback inside the target is better than adding it outside the target. It means that adding it at the user's expected destination is more practical than adding it ahead of the target; it is also better than adding it at the start of the target. Therefore *we recommend adding haptic feedback at the user's expected destination on the target* (Figure 8).

Stage 3: Interaction. Never!

Haptic feedback will not improve users' performance after an interaction. There was no effect after we added button-click feedback to normal buttons in the tapping experiment (Experiment 2). Similar results have also been reported in number entering tests [9, 19] and Fitts' tapping experiment [16, 20] on touch screens. By contrast, adding the haptic wall before the participant tapped on the target improved participants' performance by reducing both the task completion time and the error rate. Thus we can conclude that *haptic feedback should be added before the interaction, or it will have no effect* (Figure 8, Effective stages).

The above conclusion is deduced for a single interaction process. However, in real Human-Computer environments, more than one interaction happens successively. The end of one interaction may become the start of the next. Therefore haptic feedback after the first interaction may become a reminder of the start of the next (Figure 8). In this case, we should attribute the improvement from adding haptic feedback to Stage 1 rather than to Stage 3. For example, in our tapping experiment, participants operated directly on the screen so that they were able to see exactly where they tapping. Visual feedback dominated the task to locate the target. Haptic feedback thus had no effect. By contrast, in Forlines et al.'s experiment [20], when visual feedback was unable to remind users about the location of the target (e.g. losing the system pointer and the hand or pen's occlusion of the target), haptic feedback was helpful in "providing a confirmation of the selection without the need for visual attention" [20]. Such a confirmation prompted participants to complete the next task (e.g. to interact with the alterative stripe) and thus improved users' performance.

6.2 Feedback Effect vs. Feedback Time

Besides the time, the effect of haptic feedback also plays a significant role in affecting users' performance. Adding haptic feedback at the right time does not mean adding any feedback will be successful. For example, the haptic well [15] (or tunnel [11]) which trapped the user in it to avoid slipping off from GUIs led to frustration when users overcame the force of the wall in order to exit the tunnel intentionally, and thus cause delay in completing the task [15] even when they acted in Stage 2. In our experiments, the haptic bump in Experiment 1 only reminded participants that they needed to stop. By contrast, the haptic wall in Experiment 2 helped participants to stop at their destination. As a result, the haptic wall outperformed the haptic bump by not only increasing the speed but also reducing the error rate. The above examples prove that the haptic effect should support rather than oppose the intent of the user [5]. Then adding the proper haptic feedback at the right time will further enhance users' performance.

7. CONCLUSION AND FUTURE WORK

We present two experiments to explore when to add haptic feedback during the user's interaction. The first experiment compared adding the same haptic feedback at the edge and the center of the target respectively. The haptic feedback at the edge and the center of the target improved the task completion speed by 7.9% and 9.8% respectively. Haptic feedback at the center slightly outperformed that at the edge. This effect was more noticeable for 20 mm wide targets than for smaller targets. The second experiment compared adding haptic feedback before and after an interaction. Results showed that adding haptic feedback before the interaction increased the task completion speed and eliminated 50% of errors. Haptic feedback after the interaction, however, had no such effect. In combination with previous research, we conclude that the optimal time to apply haptic feedback to the target GUI is when the user reaches his expected destination. A haptic feedback is useful only if it is added before an interaction.

The present research is based on two most basic and frequently-used interaction techniques – tapping and dragging. We will continue to investigate the optimal time to add haptic feedback in more complex and realistic tasks on touch screens.

8. REFERENCES

[1] Levin, M. and Woo, A. 2009. Tactile-feedback solutions for an enhanced user experience. *Information Display, 25* (10). 18-21.

[2] Banter, B. 2010. Touch screens and touch surfaces are enriched by haptic force-feedback. *Information Display, 26* (3). 26-30.

[3] Buxton, W., Hill, R. and Rowley, P. 1985. Issues and techniques in touch-sensitive tablet input. In *SIGGRAPH Comput. Graph. 19* (3). 215-224.

[4] Brewster, S., Chohan, F. and Brown, L.2007. Tactile feedback for mobile interactions. In *Proceedings of the SIGCHI Conference on Human Factors in Computing Systems* (San Jose, CA, United states, April 28–May 3, 2007), CHI '07. ACM, New York, NY, 159-162.

[5] Alison, I.O., Adams, A., Brewster, S. and Gray, P. 2002. Guidelines for the Design of Haptic Widgets. In *Proceedings of British HCI 2002*. British Computer Society, 195-212.

[6] Yatani, K. and Truong, K.N.2009. SemFeel: a user interface with semantic tactile feedback for mobile touch-screen devices. In *Proceedings of the 22nd annual ACM symposium on User interface software and technology* (Victoria, British Columbia, Canada October 4–7, 2009). UIST '09. ACM, New York, NY, 111-120.

[7] Brewster, S.A. and King, A. 2005. The design and evaluation of a vibrotactile progress bar. *In Proceedings of World Haptics 2005*. 499-500.

[8] Hoggan, E., Anwar, S. and Brewster, S.A. 2007. Mobile multi-actuator tactile displays. *In Proceedings of the 2nd international conference on Haptic and audio interaction design* (Seoul, South Korea, 2007), Springer-Verlag, 22-33.

[9] Leung, R., MacLean, K., Bertelsen, M.B. and Saubhasik, M. 2007. Evaluation of haptically augmented touchscreen gui elements under cognitive load. In *Proceedings of the 9th international conference on Multimodal interfaces* (Nagoya, Aichi, Japan, November 12–15, 2007), ICMI'07, ACM, New York, NY, 374-381.

[10] Sun, M., Ren, X. and Cao, X. 2011. Effects of Multimodal Error Feedback on Human Performance in Steering Tasks. *Information and Media Technologies, 6* (1). 193-201.

[11] Dennerlein, J.T., Martin, D.B. and Hasser, C. 2000. Force-feedback improves performance for steering and combined steering-targeting tasks. In *Proceedings of the SIGCHI conference on Human factors in computing systems* (The Hague, The Netherlands, April 01 - 06, 2000). CHI '00. ACM, New York, NY, 423-429.

[12] Campbell, C.S., Zhai, S., May, K.W. and Maglio, P.P. 1999. What You Feel Must Be What You See: Adding Tactile Feedback to the Trackpoint. In *Proceedings of 7th IFIP Conference on Human Computer Interaction*. INTERACT'99, IOS Press, 383-390.

[13] Pakkanen, T., Raisamo, R., Raisamo, J., Salminen, K. and Surakka, V. 2010. Comparison of three designs for haptic button edges on touchscreens. In *Proceedings of Haptics Symposium 2010*, IEEE, 219-225.

[14] Hoggan, E., Brewster, S.A. and Johnston, J. 2008. Investigating the effectiveness of tactile feedback for mobile touchscreens. In *Proceedings of the SIGCHI Conference on Human Factors in Computing Systems* (Florence, Italy, April 5–10, 2008). CHI '08. ACM, New York, NY, 1573-1582.

[15] Oakley, I., McGee, M.R., Brewster, S. and Gray, P. 2000. Putting the feel in "look and feel". In *Proceedings of the SIGCHI Conference on Human Factors in Computing Systems* (The Hague, The Netherlands, April 01 - 06, 2000). CHI '00. ACM, New York, NY, 415-422.

[16] Poupyrev, I., Okabe, M. and Maruyama, S. 2004. Haptic feedback for pen computing: directions and strategies. *In CHI '04 extended abstracts on Human factors in computing systems* (Vienna, Austria, April 24–29, 2004), ACM, New York, NY, 1309-1312.

[17] Poupyrev, I., Maruyama, S. and Rekimoto, J. 2002. Ambient touch: designing tactile interfaces for handheld devices. In *Proceedings of the 15th Annual ACM Symposium on User Interface Software and Technology* (Paris, France, October 27-30, 2002). UIST '03. ACM, New York, NY, 51-60.

[18] Akamatsu, M., Mackenzie, I.S. and Hasbroucq, T.1995.A comparison of tactile, auditory, and visual feedback in a pointing task using a mouse-type device. *Ergonomics, 38* (4). 816-827.

[19] Koskinen, E., Kaaresoja, T. and Laitinen, P. 2008. Feel-good touch: finding the most pleasant tactile feedback for a mobile touch screen button. In *Proceedings of the 10th international conference on Multimodal interfaces* (Chania, Crete, Greece, October 20–22, 2008), ICMI'08, ACM, New York, 297-304.

[20] Forlines, C. and Balakrishnan, R. 2008. Evaluating tactile feedback and direct vs. indirect stylus input in pointing and crossing selection tasks. In *Proceedings of the SIGCHI Conference on Human Factors in Computing Systems* (Florence, Italy, April 5–10, 2008). CHI '08. ACM, New York, NY, 1563-1572.

[21] Gosselin, C., Poulin, R. and Laurendeau, D.2008. A planar parallel 3-dof cable-driven haptic interface. In *Proceedings of the the12nd World Multi-Conference on Systemics, Cybernetics and Informatics* (Orlando, Florida, USA, 2008) WM-SCI '08. 266-271.

[22] ISO. Ergonomic requirements for office work with visual display terminals (VDTs), Part 9: Requirements for non-keyboard input devices. 2000.

[23] Farzan, S., I. Scott, M. and Stacey, D.S.2009. Evaluation of Mouse and Touch Input for a Tabletop Display Using Fitts' Reciprocal Tapping Task. In *Proceedings of the Human Factors and Ergonomics Society Annual Meeting*. 839-843.

[24] Touchsense Tactile Feedback Overview, Immersion Corporation.

[25] Tashiro, K., Shiokawa, Y., Aono, T. and Maeno, T. 2009. A Virtual Button with Tactile Feedback Using Ultrasonic Vibration. *Virtual and Mixed Reality*, LNCS 5622, 385–393.

Robust User Context Analysis for Multimodal Interfaces

Prasenjit Dey
Hewlett-Packard Laboratories
24, Salarpuria Arena, Hosur Road,
Adugodi, Bangalore-560030, India
prasenjit.dey@hp.com

Muthuselvam Selvaraj
Hewlett-Packard Globalsoft Limited
Olympia Technology Park, Plot # 1
Guindy, Chennai-600032, India
muthuselvam.selvaraj@hp.com

Bowon Lee
Hewlett-Packard Laboratories
1501, Page Mill Road, Palo Alto
CA-94304-1100, USA
bowon.lee@hp.com

ABSTRACT
Multimodal Interfaces that enable natural means of interaction using multiple modalities such as touch, hand gestures, speech, and facial expressions represent a paradigm shift in human-computer interfaces. Their aim is to allow rich and intuitive multimodal interaction similar to human-to-human communication and interaction. From the multimodal system's perspective, apart from the various input modalities themselves, user context information such as states of *attention* and *activity*, and *identities* of interacting users can help greatly in improving the interaction experience. For example, when sensors such as cameras (webcams, depth sensors etc.) and microphones are always on and continuously capturing signals in their environment, user context information is very useful to distinguish genuine system-directed activity from ambient speech and gesture activity in the surroundings, and distinguish the "active user" from among a set of users. Information about user identity may be used to personalize the system's interface and behavior – e.g. the look of the GUI, modality recognition profiles, and information layout - to suit the specific user. In this paper, we present a set of algorithms and an architecture that performs audiovisual analysis of user context using sensors such as cameras and microphone arrays, and integrates components for lip activity and audio direction detection (speech activity), face detection and tracking (attention), and face recognition (identity). The proposed architecture allows the component data flows to be managed and fused with low latency, low memory footprint, and low CPU load, since such a system is typically required to run continuously in the background and report events of *attention*, *activity*, and *identity*, in real-time, to consuming applications.

Categories and Subject Descriptors
H.5.2 [**Information Interfaces and Presentation**]: User interfaces; H.1.2 [**User/Machine Systems**]: Human information processing, human factors; I.4.8 [**Scene Analysis**]: Motion.

General Terms
Algorithms, Human Factors

Keywords
User context, multimodal systems, speech, human-computer-interaction.

ICMI'11, November 14–18, 2011, Alicante, Spain.

1. INTRODUCTION
Multimodal Interfaces (MMI) employ multiple natural input modalities such as touch, hand gestures, and speech for human-computer interaction and offer advantages of higher task efficiency, lower error rates and higher user satisfaction, compared to unimodal ones [1]. Such interfaces are becoming feasible for a spectrum of interaction scenarios ranging from personal devices to immersive environments, owing to the ubiquity of sensors such as microphones and cameras, and the presence of sufficient processing power for interpreting various types of user input. While personal devices such as tablets and notebooks are largely used by one user at a time, immersive environments often have multiple co-present users.

In order to realize effective multimodal interfaces, it is important not only to reliably interpret explicit user input, but also to interpret implicit information about the user context, such as the *attention*, *activity*, and *identity* of the interacting user(s).

Attention relates to knowing whether a given user is paying attention to the system, and if yes, understanding the object of user's attention. Although attention is a state of the mind of a user in response to his or her surroundings, it manifests itself in several observable cues such as head pose, gaze, pointing towards an object etc., which can be used to infer the state and object of user attention with some degree of confidence. In a *co-present multi-user* interaction scenario, where may co-located users are interacting at the same time, a user's attention may be on the system, but the user may not interact with the system and may be a passive observer while another user actively interacts with the system. In such situations the system needs to clearly distinguish the state of (passive) attention from that of *activity*.

Such contextual information can be used for various purposes in a multimodal system. For example, when modality sensors such as cameras and microphones are always on and continuously capturing signals in the environment, information about attention and activity levels of the user(s) towards the system can help distinguish genuine system-directed commands from ambient speech or gesture activity in the surroundings that can interfere with the designed application behavior. In a co-present multiple-user scenario, such information can also help distinguish the active user from among a set of interacting users. User attention information may also be useful to turn application features on and off, modify the GUI, or wake-up/sleep compute-intensive modalities as required.

The identity of the user can be used to automatically personalize application behavior, load personalized modality recognizer profiles, fetch profile-specific information, etc.

In a multiple user interaction scenario, fusion of *attention*, *activity* and *identity* information can be used to enable interactions like "load my photos", where based on the active user information, one can determine who spoke the command among the multiple users, and the identity information can be used to resolve the word "my".

Multimodal cues such as speech, hand gestures, pointing, and lip movement can be used to determine the user's level of system-directed activity. Determination of users' attention can also inform the system regarding which users to keep a watch on for activity.

Attention and activity of a user are difficult to determine based solely on a single modality, and often require fusion of multiple cues from different modality-recognizers from different sensors. The use of multiple modalities also helps improve robustness when interpretations from any single given modality are unreliable [1].

However, for such user context information to be useful for real-time interaction, all context events should not only be extracted reliably but also be available to the multimodal application with very low latency. If the user context events are received at the client application with a delay perceptible to the interacting user, the very purpose of using user context data to improve interaction experience can be lost, and this may frustrate and confuse the user. CPU and memory consumption of such context analysis should also be very low so that it does not interfere with the performance of the active applications themselves, and the analysis may need to be run on different platforms (mobile, desktop).

The key contributions of this paper are as follows:

Lip Activity Detection: We present a robust and lightweight algorithm for lip activity detection to distinguish genuine speech activity from spurious speech activity, with low latency.

Genuine Speech Detection: We use spatial and temporal fusion of lip activity and audio direction to determine genuine speech activity. This is useful in rejecting spurious speech (background conversations, TV sound etc.) in single user interactions, and in co-present multiuser interactions, it can be used to attribute speech activity to a particular user.

Architecture: We propose an architecture that manages different audio-visual recognizers, sensors (camera, microphone array), and their data flows in a time bound manner, and enables *fusion* of these data streams to generate attention, activity, and identity events. The architecture has been designed to meet the requirements of low latency, low memory, and low CPU load, since such a system may be required to run continuously in the background generating real-time events for interactive applications.

The paper is organized as follows. We review some of the related work on user context analysis in Section 2. We describe the proposed architecture and the algorithms in Section 3. Results from experimental evaluation of the system are presented in Section 4. We conclude the paper with a summary of contributions and next steps.

2. RELATED WORK

Most prior work related to user context analysis has been in the area of identifying attention and activity of users in meeting rooms [2,3] and detection of active speaker in kiosks [4]. In meeting room scenarios, the detection of active speaker is used to steer a camera towards the active speaker and/or enhance the speech capture by beamforming using the microphone array towards the direction of the active speaker. A service has been developed by Fraunhofer IIS [5] for facial data analysis (face detection, demography, expression etc.). However, it does not take into account directional audio information to determine genuine speech activity, which is essential in systems using the speech modality.

For fusion of multimodal cues, various techniques have been used. Several works use higher level (decision level) fusion of information to find an active speaker [6, 7]. The work of Kapralos et al. [6] detects faces using color histogram to identify locations of skin pixels and uses sound source localization to confirm the co-presence of a face and a sound source. The use of sound source localization to capture camera images in a specific direction and detect a face is described in [7]. A PTZ (Pan-Tilt-Zoom) camera is then used to zoom into the face of the active speaker. In [8], audio as well as video features are put in a common pool of features, and instead of separate classifiers for audio and video features, a boosting algorithm is used to select the best features and the best weak classifier at each step. The fusion of the classifiers is achieved through a weighted sum of the classifiers and a thresholding mechanism.

Lin et al. [9] use a SVM based meta-classifier to fuse results of the classifiers for individual modalities (speech, face) to associate the speech of a user with the face. The general techniques of classifier combination [10, 11] can be used to fuse decisions of individual components e.g., audio localization, face detection, lip movement, etc. to determine the attention and activity level of the users.

Though [4] looks at the problem of active speaker detection for command and control in kiosks, it uses the fusion of 3D head pose and audio direction to determine the active speaker. The visual cue of head pose is useful for determining the active speaker but in the absence of lip activity detection, background speech audio from the direction of the face can result in the user being wrongly identified as an active speaker.

3. PROPOSED APPROACH

In this section, we describe our approach to user context analysis. Central to our approach is a system architecture that manages the modality recognizers, sensors, and their data flow, and provides a mechanism for fusion of information from different modalities. The architecture enables generation of *user context events* about *attention*, *speech activity*, and *identity* of the users in front of the system. The key design goals for this architecture are:

- Low latency
- Low CPU load
- Low memory footprint

This is to ensure that the user context events are available to end-user applications in a timely manner without adversely impacting the normal functioning of foreground applications that the user is interacting with. For ease of use by applications, we have

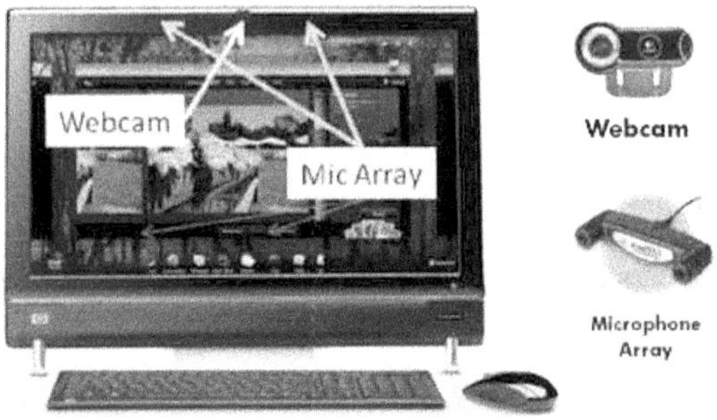

Figure 1. System setup and sensor requirements.

implemented the architecture and integrated the modality recognizers into a service which enables registered client applications to receive various types of user context events. We refer to our complete system as the **User Context Service (UCS).**

3.1 System Setup

A typical system configuration for deploying UCS is as shown in Figure 1. The configuration includes a built-in webcam and a microphone array with two or more microphones. When these sensors are not built into the system, external sensors such as Andrea Superbeam microphone array [12] may be used.

3.2 UCS Architecture

Figure 2 shows the architecture of UCS and the individual modality recognizer components. The vision-based components which are *Lip Activity Detector (LAD)* and *Face Detector (FD),* and the audio component which is the *Sound Source Localizer (SSL)* run in different threads. The *Face Recognition (FR)* engine runs only when a new face appears in the scene, at which point a new thread is spawned to run FR and then closed. This is described in more detail in subsequent sections. The *Gesture Activity Detector (GAD)* and *Audio Clean-up* (noise suppression) components shown in the figure are currently not integrated.

The results from all the modality recognizers are sent to the *UC Data Manager,* where the *UC Data Fusion Engine* fuses the LAD, SSL and FD results, according to the rules described earlier, to determine genuine speech activity. The *Client Session Manager* keeps track of event subscription information for various client applications. Once the user context events are available, the *UC Data Dispatcher* sends them to different clients based on the subscription information from *Client Session Manager.* The *UC Service UI* provides a user interface invoked via the system tray icon( ) that supports the ability to select sensors such as cameras and microphones from those available to the system, manage FR profiles, show feedback window etc. This is described in more detail in Section 3.6. Client applications need to integrate the *UC Client API* which communicates with the UCS on behalf of the client application. This provides an interface for the client to register for receiving the specific user context events of interest. UCS is implemented in C++. A C# and a Java implementation of UC Client API are available.

3.2.1 UCS and UC Client Interaction

A typical interaction between an application and UCS is as follows:

1. Application registers itself with UCS with a list of interested context events.
2. UCS creates a unique session for the client with session state set to active and stores the list of interested context events. When a user interacts with the system, the individual UC Data Recognizer detects and reports context data to the UCS.
3. UCS takes a list of active clients and according to the individual client's interest, the UC data stream is created and sent over client connection.
4. The UC Client API in a client receives the UC data stream from the service and creates the necessary user context events and notifies the application.
5. The UC event handlers in the application receive the events and execute the application logic to respond to the user.

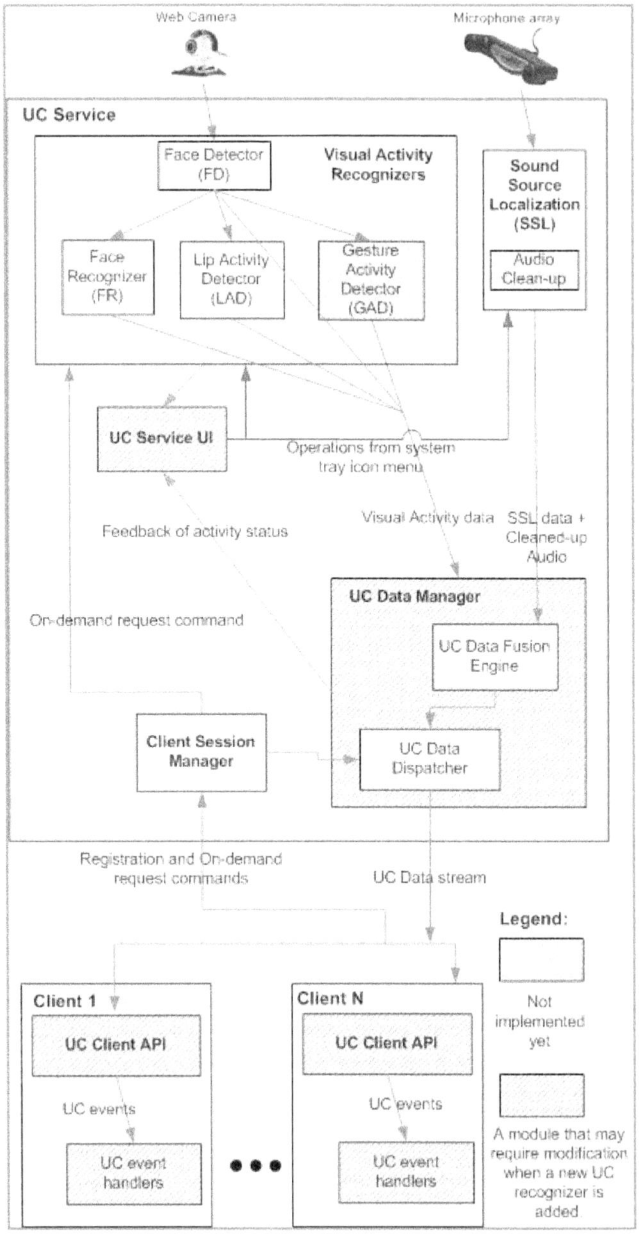

Figure 2. UCS architecture diagram.

The sequence diagram in Figure 3 explains the interactions that happen between client application, UC Client API in the client application, and the Client Session Manager in the UCS for context events registration and show how context events are notified to the client application. Client registers with UC Client API with a list of interested user context events.

When the UCS sends context data to the clients, following sequence of events happen. UC Data Manager detects messages from context data recognizers; the individual context messages are passed through applicable 'Combined Context Data Interpreters' for any possible combined context events (e.g. Speech activity detected by combining co-occurring LAD and SSL events) and then passed to UC Data Dispatcher. The UC data Dispatcher gets the active clients list and dispatches the context event data stream as per their interest. The UC Client API in each client receives the context data stream and creates the individual context events and notifies to the client application.

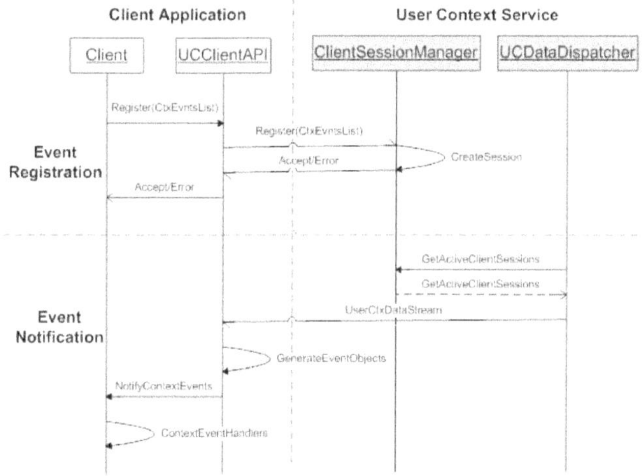

Figure 3. Sequence diagram for context event registration.

The different user context events, along with the different audio/visual modality recognizer components that make them possible, are described below.

3.3 Attention

The event for user *attention* uses frontal face detection (FD) as a proxy for attention. We use the OpenCV library for face detection. The key challenge was to reduce CPU load. We perform face detection on every 50th frame of the video and use a mean-shift tracker to track for the rest of the time. This is as illustrated in Figure 4. This helps in bringing down the CPU load considerably compared to when the FD is performed on every frame. The choice of frame interval to perform FD can be configured by the user in a configuration file (described in Section 3.6.2) based on the application requirement. If the application has very less user movement and change, the frame interval for FD can be increased and vice-versa. The event also returns multiple user face locations and their boundaries. More details about the event data are provided in Section 3.6.1.

3.4 Speech Activity (SA)

The speech activity of the user is determined by using the *visual cue from lip activity* and looking for the presence of a co-occurring *directional audio cue* from the direction of the user whose lips are moving. The presence of only lip activity from a particular direction indicates non-speech lip movement (lip biting, chewing, etc.); the presence of only audio and no lip activity indicates ambient speech or noise in the surroundings.

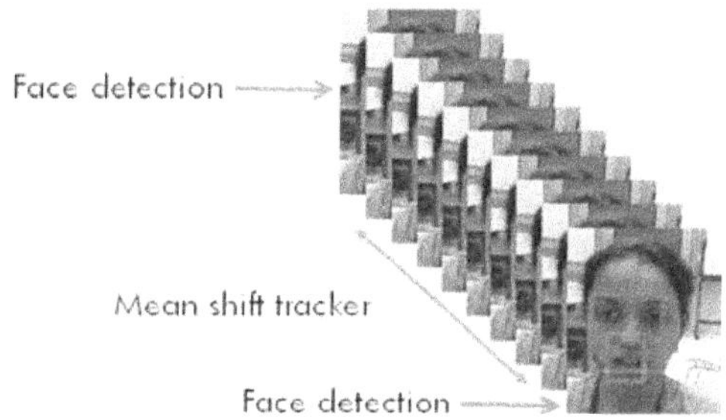

Figure 4. Face tracking and CPU optimization in FD module.

3.4.1 Lip Activity Detector (LAD)

We propose a robust lip activity detection (LAD) algorithm that uses a detected frontal face to localize the lip region of the user and look for bi-directional and vertical (along Y-axis) optical flow in that region for capturing genuine lip movements. During genuine lip movements, we observe that the vertical components of optical flow along both the positive and negative vertical axis are large and almost equal in magnitude. Moreover, the number of features in this region having a vertical component of optical flow along the positive axis is almost equal to the number of features with negative optical flow. We use a combination of these metrics to determine lip activity. A more detailed analysis to determine lip activity could be done, however it was required to be lightweight for real-time interactions without compromising the robustness.

In order to detect lip activity, based on the face geometry, a coarse localization of the lip region within the detected face region is carried out. We deliberately do not attempt fine localization of the lip region in order not to miss the actual lip region due to differences in face geometry, inaccuracies in the face detection, or sudden head movements. As shown in Figure 5, the coarse localization is in broad terms, the center of the lower half of the face region reported by the face detector, extended downwards to ensure inclusion of the entire lip region.

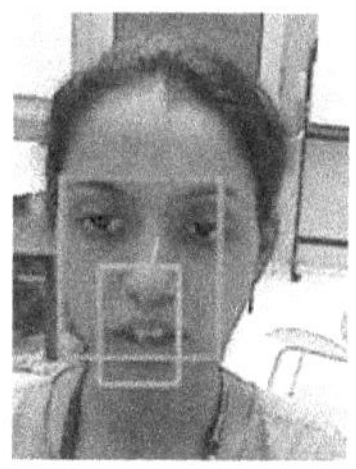

Figure 5. Localization of the lip region from the result of the face detector

We then detect lip activity by computing optical flow in the lip region. A 3-level pyramidal Lucas-Kanade optical flow method is used on VGA image for the computation of optical flow. We use a combination of both, the *magnitude* and the *direction* of the optical flow vectors in this region as a measure of lip activity. Since lip movements are primarily along the vertical axis (Y), the total optical flow is estimated by adding up only the vertical components of the optical flow vectors, as shown in Figure 6.

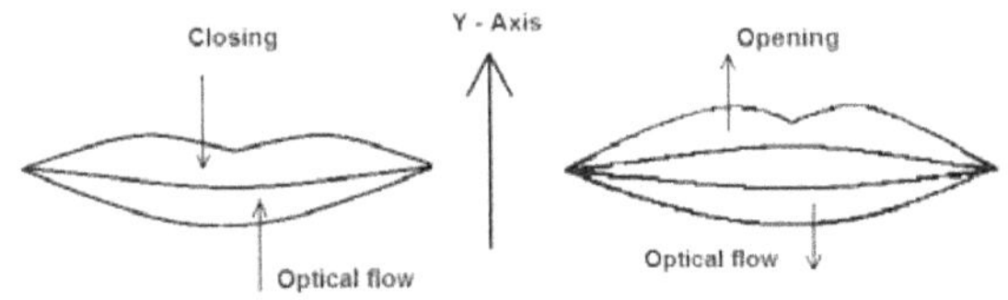

Figure 6. Optical flow for lip activity.

The algorithm [13] is as shown in Figure 7. It is robust for noise conditions due to head movements and works with ordinary webcam images. Based on the location of the face and hence the lip activity in the image frame, the user is assigned a coarse spatial location (left, left-center, center, right-center, right). The LAD has been tested on a dataset of about 44000 frames of video for 5 users, and resulted in a detection accuracy of about 93%.

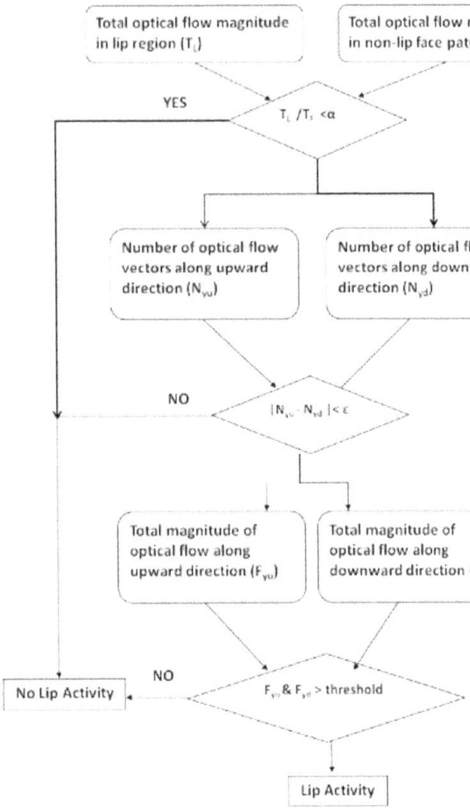

Figure 7. Lip Activity Detection algorithm.

3.4.2 *Sound Source Localization (SSL)*

For determining audio direction, which we call SSL, we use a microphone array (with at least two microphones) to continuously monitor the input audio stream to determine audio activity. Audio activity is detected using Microsoft SAPI *silence detection* (SD) which has a very low response time. Low latency silence detection is important because the result of silence detection is used to determine the boundary of audio activity within which the SSL audio direction is measured. The total time taken for SD and SSL was optimized to be very low so that the result is available to the client application with no perceptible delay to the interacting user. Once an audio segment is detected, the SSL estimates time delay between the microphones using a generalized cross correlation method with the Phase Transform (PHAT) frequency weighting [14], as shown in Figure 8. Based upon the time-delay information, it localizes the audio input to one of the three regions (left, center and right). The resolution of localization can be improved if more than 2 microphone elements are used in the array.

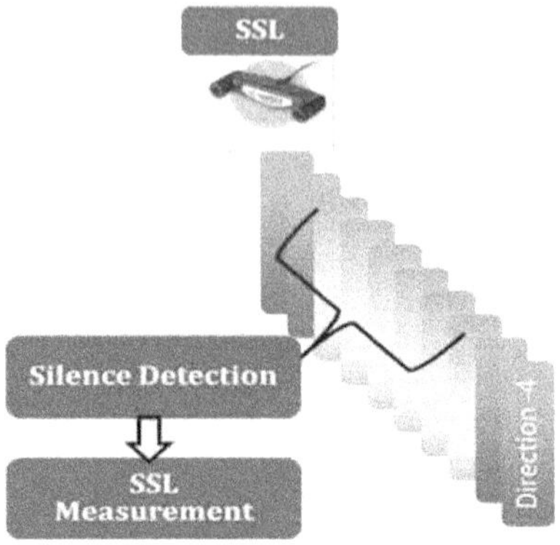

Figure 8. SSL measurement and silence detection.

3.4.3 *Fusion of LAD and SSL for Speech Activity*

Once the locations are available from SSL and LAD, an *evidence fusion engine* fuses these results to determine whether the audio was genuine-speech directed at the system. The fusion is valid if the LAD and SSL results fuse both *spatially* as well as *temporally*. We propose a rule based fusion engine with soft decision boundaries. The fusion happens in the *UC Data Fusion Engine* as shown in the UCS architecture.

Spatial Fusion: Currently the directions output from LAD and SSL are of LEFT, CENTER and RIGHT. This is based on the number of users that can be accommodated in the camera's field of view when the users are at a distance of 2-3ft from the camera. If the direction from LAD and SSL are the same, the output of the fusion engine is a successful spatial fusion. However, to have softer decision boundaries, we have decisions from LAD which are LEFT-CENTER and RIGHT-CENTER. This is based on whether the user face center, which has lip activity, is detected at the boundary region of LEFT and CENTER, or RIGHT and CENTER. The rules for spatial fusion are as shown in Table 1. The LEFT-CENTER and RIGHT-CENTER locations in LAD allows for more robust fusion where otherwise the user may be at the boundaries and a strict demarcation may cause the fusion to fail.

Table 1. Rules for spatial fusion.

LAD	SSL	Spatial Fusion
LEFT	LEFT	SUCCESS
LEFT	CENTER/RIGHT	FAIL
LEFT-CENTER	LEFT/CENTER	SUCCESS
LEFT-CENTER	RIGHT	FAIL
CENTER	CENTER	SUCCESS
CENTER	LEFT/RIGHT	FAIL
RIGHT	RIGHT	SUCCESS
RIGHT	CENTER/LEFT	FAIL
RIGHT-CENTER	RIGHT/CENTER	SUCCESS
RIGHT-CENTER	LEFT	FAIL

Temporal Fusion: The results from SSL and LAD must also have a successful temporal fusion which makes sure that the information from these different modalities came from the same event time window. The recognizers for LAD and SSL work at different data rates mainly due to the fact that the camera for LAD and the microphone array for SSL have different refresh rates. In our system, the LAD produces an output every 76 ms and the SSL every 85 ms. The differences in frame processing rates lead to challenges in temporal fusion because the frame boundaries of the different recognizers may not match exactly. This is shown in Figure 9.

A sliding window based approach is used for temporal fusion. Once the silence detector detects the boundary of audio activity, a 100 ms tolerance band is added before and after the silence detection, and this is taken as the actual temporal fusion boundary. This helps ensure that important data from a recognizer is not missed due to lack of synchronization of the data rates, and this also makes the fusion robust to any missing data.

Once both the temporal and spatial fusions are successful, a successful fusion of LAD and SSL is declared and hence a genuine Speech Activity (SA) event from that particular direction is generated. The fusion rule is as shown in Figure 10.

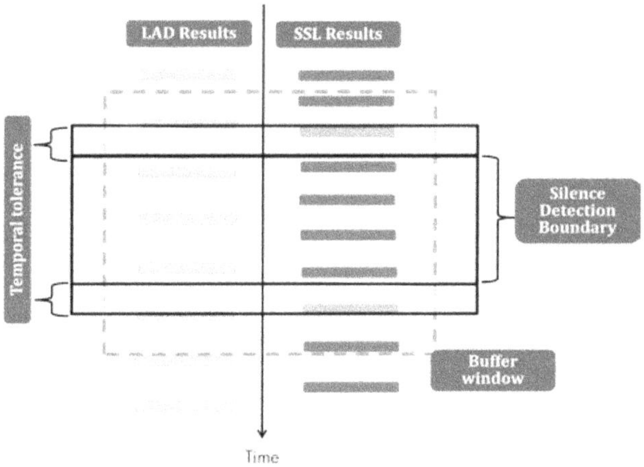

Figure 9. Temporal fusion of SSL and LAD.

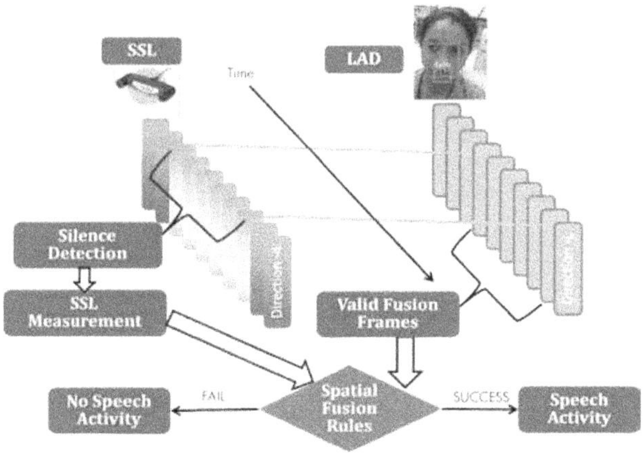

Figure 10. Speech Activity fusion rule.

3.5 Identity

For identity we use our own face recognition (FR) engine. The FR engine has a training mode where it takes 6 snapshots of the user and computes a feature vector. The feature vector is stored and then compared with the test image feature vector during the recognition phase. UCS can recognize multiple users in camera view, who have been previously added in the system, in real-time. The FR engine produces a confidence value between 0 and 1 for the face recognition result which can be used to reduce false positives depending on the application. The configuration file, described in Section 3.6.2, allows for setting of FR result rejection threshold based on confidence values, which ensures that low confidence results are not sent by the UCS to the application at all. Since FR is a very CPU intensive task, one of the key challenges in the design of UCS was to reduce FR computation when the UCS is running continuously in the background. The other challenge was to reduce the response time of the result of recognition on video frames.

To reduce the CPU load for FR, we do not run the FR engine on every captured camera frame. Instead, we do a book-keeping of the faces in the scene based on face detector and face tracker output. If the face tracker information suggests that a face has left the scene or a new face has appeared in the scene, the FR engine is run for the subsequent few frames to get the new face recognition results. Subsequently the face tracker keeps a repository of the users in the scene again. This brings down the sustained CPU load significantly. The CPU load goes up momentarily whenever there is a change of users in the scene, and then comes down again. If the scene is very dynamic where users are rapidly moving in and out, the FR engine runs at the same frequency as the FD because that is when the presence or absence of a user is detected. If the scene is more static the FR may run only once in the beginning of the session and then go to sleep.

For the response-time, lot of optimization was done on the data structure. This optimization helped to get the FR result response time at the client application to a maximum of 600 ms.

There is also a provision in the API for the application to request FR results *on-demand* and receive a response. This is to support application scenarios wherein the face recognition needs to be performed on request (e.g., authentication via a login button on the user interface) rather than continuously. This also helps to run the FR engine at a minimum level.

3.6 Other UCS Options

The system tray icon (◉) menu allows the user to control various options of the UCS. It supports the ability to select sensors such as cameras and microphone arrays from those available to the system. It manages FR profiles and allows the user to register new users, delete/update existing users for face recognition. One can bring up a feedback window which displays the activity status in the form of FD, LAD, FR results superimposed on the camera feed. It also displays the direction (LEFT, CENTER, RIGHT) of audio, lip activity and speech activity results from fusion. If the lip activity direction is LEFT-CENTER or RIGHT-CENTER then the activity is displayed in both CENTER and LEFT/RIGHT location respectively. The system tray menu also allows switching on/off various recognizers in UCS through Modality Configuration option.

3.6.1 UC Client API

The events reported from UCS to UC Client API are as follows. Each event packet is marked with a time stamp to enable the user to make a decision on an event that arrived too late due to system delays.

Activity Type	Description
ATTENTION	Frontal face detection result. Contains all detected faces; also contains the identity information (in FRData) apart from face location information.
SPEECH ACT.	Speech Activity detection is formed by a successful fusion of LAD and SSL.
LIPACTIVITY	The result of LAD recognizer.
AUDIO ACT.	The result of SSL recognizer.

3.6.2 Configuration File

A configuration file "UCS.cfg" is provided to help configure various parameters of the UCS. A part of the file is shown in Figure 11. The user can configure the FR threshold, minimum face detection size, microphone array separation etc.

```
EVENT_REPORTING_RATE = 700

#Logging Level possible values are DEBUG, INFO,
WARNING and ERROR
LOG_LEVEL = INFO

### Camera capture settings ###
FRAME_WIDTH = 640 # units in pixels
FRAME_HEIGHT = 480 # units in pixels

#Minimum Face Size (Width x height in pixels)
detectable
FACE_MIN_SIZE = 1000

#Face location shift thereshold in pixels; Value
in pixels unit
FACE_LOCATION_SHIFTTHRESHOLD = 30

#Face Recognition Threshold; Range: 0 - 1
FR_Threshold = 0.5

#Keep displaying lip activity for 'N' more Frames
duration after lipactivity completed
Keep_Activity_Display_For = 10

SSL_SamplingRate = 48000 #Array Microphone audio
device sampling rate in Hz

SSL_MIC_Spacing = 0.15 # Inter-microphone spacing
in meter

### Range of delay score to divide audio source
```

Figure 11. UCS Configuration file.

4. RESULTS

UCS is currently supported on any Windows system that has a (internal or external) webcam and a microphone array. We have a fully functional implementation for Windows Vista and Windows 7 platforms. UCS is implemented in C++. A C# and a Java implementation of UC Client API are available. UCS can presently detect attention, genuine speech activity, and identity for multiple users, and can be used at a distance from 2-6 ft by changing configuration parameters.

Significant effort has been invested to reduce the response time of the events. Speech activity detection takes less than 100 ms, and face recognition events are available within 600 ms following the first appearance of the user. The memory footprint of UCS is about 140MB. UCS runs with about 15% CPU load on a standard laptop, which goes up to 50% whenever FR engine runs (when there is a change of user in the scene). CPU load is about 3-4% on a workstation desktop, going up to 35% whenever the FR engine runs.

4.1 Lip Activity Detection

In order to evaluate the effectiveness and robustness of the lip activity detection algorithm, it was tested on a dataset of 50 video recordings of users performing specific tasks for about 30 seconds each. They were recorded at 30 frames per second and 640X480 pixel resolution, representing about 1500 seconds or 44309 frames of data. The video sequences are from 5 different individuals, sitting at a distance of up to 3 feet in front of the camera.

The videos were annotated manually with an annotation tool written in MATLAB. The videos were annotated to indicate frame-wise segments for each of the following events

a) SILENCE
b) LIP ACTIVITY
c) FORWARD BACKWARD MOTION OF HEAD
d) SIDEWAY MOTION OF HEAD
e) VERTICAL MOTION OF HEAD

The events (a), (c), (d) and (e) are negative events and (b) is the positive event.

The detection of lip activity *anywhere in the segment* where the speech utterance happened is enough to indicate the speech activity event by a user in front of the system. When combined with speech audio activity on the microphone, one can reasonably conclude the presence of genuine speech activity. When no lip activity is present at all in a speech segment even though speech audio was detected at the microphone, it is a good indicator of the speech being spurious and not from a user who is actively using the system. Thus for our application, presence of at least one lip activity event in a speech segment is a true positive event. A false negative event would thus be one in which there was genuine lip activity during a speech segment which was not detected by the algorithm. Therefore

$$FNR = \frac{number\ of\ speech\ segments\ with\ missed\ LAD}{total\ number\ of\ speech\ segments}$$

$$FPR = \frac{number\ of\ false\ LAD}{number\ of\ non-speech\ frames}$$

where *FNR=False Negative Rate* and *FPR = False Positive Rate*.

Our test videos consist of a total of 727 segments, of which 271 were *speech segments*, consisting of 14112 frames and the remaining 456 were *non-speech segments*, consisting of 30197 frames. The non-speech segments included segments corresponding to silence, forward backward motion, sideway motion and vertical motion in the plane of the camera. We evaluated the true and false positive rates of the algorithm for various thresholds on intensity of optical flow (as described in the algorithm) and the resulting ROC curve is as shown in Figure 12. The overall accuracy of the algorithm was found to be 93%. For more details please refer [13].

4.2 UCS Enabled Experiences

We are extensively testing UCS, and have shared it with a small community of developers (e.g. university collaborators) to use and test. We have used the user context events from UCS to implement various multimodal interaction experiences, especially for scenarios involving multiple co-present users such as photo and video sharing. Some of the features enabled by UCS include:

Who-said-what: The Speech Activity event used to determine who among the multiple users uttered the command so that based on the *Identity* (from face recognition) of the active user, the command can be carried out appropriately. For example if one of the users said "load my photos", the photos of that specific user can be loaded.

Attention aware interface: Based on the Attention event, the interface can choose not to react or wake up until the user attention is on the interface. For instance, a slide show can be automatically paused when user attention is lost, and resumed when attention is detected.

User Metadata: UCS events may be used to extract metadata about the users in the context of media consumption scenarios, so that such metadata may be used for improved organization and navigation of the media collection.

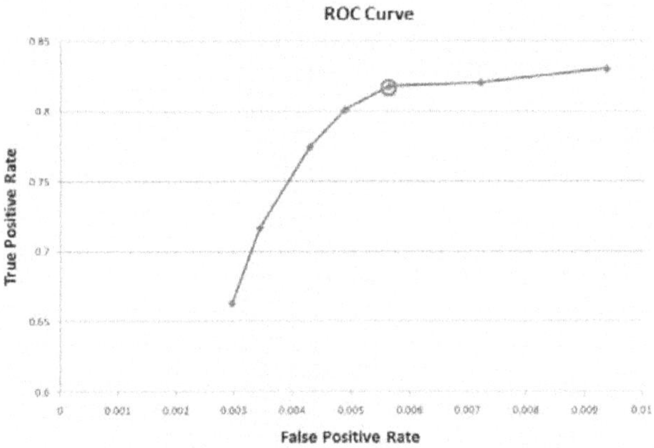

Figure 12. ROC curve for lip activity detection.

5. SUMMARY AND NEXT STEPS

We presented an architecture and a set of algorithms for user context analysis. Key design characteristics of the architecture are low latency, low memory and CPU consumption. The architecture manages different sensors and recognizers for real-time interactions. The proposed rule-based fusion framework allows for robust fusion of lip activity and audio direction to determine genuine system-directed speech activity, and generates low latency user context events for consumption by registered client applications. The LAD algorithm is lightweight and robust, and thus well suited for real-time interactions. The user attributes of *attention*, *activity*, and *identity*, and the implicit multimodal cues that are used to determine these user attributes, were also discussed. The creation of a service for the implemented architecture and the components provides an API, and various configurable options to the application developers to rapidly leverage user context events for use in their application.

For attention information we are currently using frontal face detection. Unfortunately this does not allow us to capture "partial attention" wherein the user may have his head half-turned. As a next step we would like to have an estimate of the head pose to determine the level of "partial attention" of the user. We are planning to analyze the whole body of the user using depth information from a depth camera to understand the context of the user (posture, engagement, and presence). Migrating some of the tasks like face tracking and optical flow computation to the GPU to further reduce the CPU load would also be among the next steps. The resolution of SSL is not as dense as the FD resolution due to the limited audio sampling rate. We are investigating ways to get higher SSL resolution given the same sampling rate. We are also working on a more robust evidence fusion which is resistant to sensor data variations and time-constrained, missing, and inaccurate data from various recognizer components. We plan to make the LAD robust to illumination variation, where we will use the infrared information of the image, and fuse it with RGB image to get an illumination compensated image for analysis.

6. REFERENCES

[1] Oviatt, S.L. Multimodal interfaces, Handbook of Human-Computer Interaction (revised edition), (ed. by J. Jacko & A. Sears), Lawrence Erlbaum Assoc: New Jersey, 2006..

[2] AMI Project, "State-of-the-art overview - Recognition of Attentional Cues in Meetings", http://www.amiproject.org.

[3] AMI Project, "State-of-the-art overview - Localization and Tracking of Multiple Interlocutors with Multiple Sensors", http://www.amiproject.org , January 2007.

[4] Siracusa, M., et. al. "A multimodal approach for determining speaker location and focus", ICMI,03, Vancouver, Canada, Nov. 05 - 07, 2003. ACM, New York, NY, 77-80.

[5] Fraunhofer SHORE, http://www.iis.fraunhofer.de/en/bf/bv/ks/gpe/demo

[6] Kapralos, B., Jenkin, M., and Milios, E., "Audio-visual localization of multiple speakers in a video teleconferencing setting", *IJIST*, Vol. 13(1):95-105, 2003.

[7] Yoshimi, B., and Pingali, G., "A multimodal speaker detection and tracking system for teleconferencing," in Proc. ACM Conf. Multimedia, 2002.

[8] Zhang, C. et al., "Boosting-Based Multimodal Speaker Detection for Distributed Meeting Videos", IEEE Trans. on Multimedia (10), No. 8, Dec. 2008, pp. 1541-1552.

[9] Lin et al., "Meta-classification: Combining Multimodal Classifiers", O.R. Zaïane et al. (Eds.): *Mining Multimedia and Complex Data, LNAI 2797*, pp. 217–231, 2003.

[10] Kittler, J. et al., "On Combining Classifiers", *IEEE Trans. Pattern Anal. Mach. Intell.* 20, 3 (Mar. 1998), 226-239.

[11] Tax, D. M. J., et. al., "Combining multiple classifiers by averaging or by multiplying?", *PR* 33(9): 1475-148, 2000.

[12] Andrea Microphone Array, http://www.andreaelectronics.com/buy/microphones.htm

[13] Dabholkar, J., Dey, P.,"Robust Lip Activity Detection using Bi-Directional Optical Flow", Hewlett-Packard Labs Tech Report HPL-2010-87.

[14] Knapp, C. H., and Carter, G. C.,"The generalized correlation method for estimation of time-delay", IEEE Trans. Acoust., Speech and Audio Proc., vol ASSP-24, (4), 320-327, 1976.

The Picture Says It All! Multimodal Interactions and Interaction Metadata

Ramadevi Vennelakanti, Prasenjit Dey, Ankit Shekhawat, Phanindra Pisupati
Hewlett-Packard Labs
24 Salarpuria Arena
Hosur Main Road, Adugodi
Bangalore 560030
INDIA
{rama.vennelakanti, prasenjit.dey, ankit.shekhawat} @hp.com

ABSTRACT

People share photographs with family and friends! This inclination to share photographs lends itself to many occasions of co-present sharing resulting in interesting interactions, discussions, and experiences among those present. These interactions, are rich in information about the context and the content of the photograph and if extracted can be used to associate metadata with the photograph. However these are rarely captured and so, are lost at the end of the co-present photo sharing session.

Most current work on extracting implicit metadata focuses on *Content* metadata - analyzing the content in a photograph and *Object* metadata that is automatically generated and consists of data like GPS location, date and time etc. We address the capture of another interesting type of implicit metadata, called the "*Interaction* metadata", from the users multimodal interactions with the media (here photographs) during co-present sharing.

These interactions in the context of photographs contain rich information: who saw it, who said what, what was pointed at when they said it, who did they see it with for how long, how many times and so on; which if captured and analyzed can create interesting memories about the photograph. These will over time, help build stories around photographs, aid storytelling, serendipitous discovery and efficient retrieval among other experiences. Interaction metadata can also help organize photographs better by providing mechanisms for filtering based on, who viewed, most viewed, etc. Interaction metadata provides a hereto under explored implicit metadata type created from interactions with media.

We designed and built a system prototype to capture and create interaction metadata. In this paper we describe the prototype and present the findings of a study we carried out to evaluate this prototype. The contribution of our work to the domain of multimodal interactions are: a method of identifying relevant speech portions in a free flowing conversation and the use of natural human interactions in the context of media to create *Interaction Metadata,* a novel type of implicit metadata.

ICMI'11, November 14–18, 2011, Alicante, Spain.

Categories and Subject Descriptors

H.5.2 [User Interfaces]: User interface management systems; Voice I/O; Natural language; D.2.2 [Software Engineering]: Design Tools and Techniques - user interfaces

General Terms

Algorithms, Design, Human Factors.

Keywords

Photo sharing, interaction metadata, tagging, multimodal interactions

1. INTRODUCTION

Explicit tagging of photographs is considered a tedious process and is rarely or diligently done. With the growing size of personal media collections, there have been efforts towards making tagging automated to aid efficient retrieval. Current efforts have been towards extracting implicit *content metadata* [16, 14] by analyzing photographs. Content metadata includes information about the content in the photograph – for example - who is in it, is it an outdoor or indoor location, what was the occasion, etc. Another kind of implicit metadata called the *object metadata* [7] is also extracted and includes information from the camera – for example - GPS location, time and date, photo type, etc.

Photographs are often the context of a lot of rich social interactions; people get together for co-present photo sharing during which many conversations take place. These conversations, in the context of the photographs, are rich in information about the photographs. They contain and reveal relevant information such as – who or what is in the photograph, where was it taken, who took it, when was it taken, is it liked or not, who likes it and who doesn't, what about the photograph is particularly interesting and so on. Other information that these interactions contain are who saw it and with whom, for how long, when etc. However, most of this information about the interactions is lost at the end of the session, unless users explicitly tag the photographs with this information. If captured implicitly, interaction metadata can later be used to enhance the photo viewing experience such as aiding storytelling, serendipitous discovery, organizing, filtering based on viewership, popularity etc.

In this paper we present our approach towards extracting relevant information from these interactions to create *interaction metadata.* We describe a prototype and present the findings of a study we carried out to evaluate our prototype and identify issues that need to be addressed to make it more robust.

The paper is organized as follows. In Section 2 we review some of the Related Work on implicit tagging. In Section 3 the Motivation for the work is described, in Section 4 we describe the Prototype and the sample interactions. Results from a pilot study using the prototype, and some initial conclusions are presented in Section 5. Section 6 is the Discussion and Section 7 has the Summary.

2. RELATED WORK

In this section we discuss related literature, with the focus on efforts around photo metadata.

There is potential in social theatre that takes place around photographs [10, 12]. Narrations around photographs are a commonplace occurrence during family social events, and are used to strengthen social bonds with family and friends. So much so, that, photographs have been used as a social lubricant in anthropology [5], therapy [6] and language development [3]. When showing photographs to a friend or relative, people talk freely about the contents, situations, moods and personal likings about the photograph [1, 4, 11]. There is a body of work around semi-automatic data mining around these conversations [2].

With advent of digital cameras and camera phones people are taking more photographs than ever [23], as a result, personal photo collections have exploded sizably. Retrieving the right photograph from these enormous collections becomes an obvious problem. [13].However the task of tagging and indexing these huge collections of photographs is daunting, and rarely done. [1, 21, 22]. People also do not see the usefulness of annotating and indexing photographs when they are adding new images to the collection [9]. The real need only surfaces when they already have a massive un-indexed photo collection and then, the task of annotating the whole collection is no longer appealing. There have been efforts in the area of making it easier for the user to tag photographs. There is work on using speech input rather than typing the content information [1, 17].

There is a major body of work towards making this content retrieval automatic. There are some computer vision algorithms that can decipher the content of the photograph and try to infer the occasion [15, 14, 19]. For example presence of a bride in a photograph could infer that it's a photograph from a wedding. These methods are still unreliable and are very expensive problems to solve. GPS data has also been used to extrapolate context [18], for example a photograph taken next to a tourist landmark could help label the photograph. In automatic annotation system there has been work on exploiting group discussions, Instant Messaging (IM), and online comment system to extract tags [20] while some systems capture text associated with photographs in an email or a text document [16]. These systems can give accurate annotation. However these conversations happen too far between and do not have content [9] and spatial richness required to create rich metadata.

Fleck's [9] work which is the closest to our work, is in this under explored domain and has demonstrated that we can acquire data like which photographs the users like to talk about, who is in the picture, what is the picture about. Fleck [9], in her work has discussed the challenge that the discussion at many times may drift away from the photograph and can be erroneously attributed to the photograph; however she was not able to weed out those conversations. She explores scenarios of a system that observes groups of people naturally generate a semantically rich multimodal discourse as they discuss and present photos to friends and families. Fleck's initial investigation identified challenges and potentials that surround extracting semantically indexed tags from free flowing unobstructed conversations.

More specifically Fleck points out – identifying the start and end of a conversation, explicitly having to turn on and off the audio capture, associating the audio with the right photo, capturing audio that is only directed at the photo, transcribing accurately the speech, among others. These are the very issues we address with segmenting speech from silence to silence when gesture-speech co-occurs and key words are spotted. While our work is similar to Fleck's work what differentiates it from Fleck's work are the following:

- We do not transcribe the speech, as speech in the context of photographs is bound to contain a number or proper nouns and speech recognition engines do not perform well on proper nouns
- All our querying is based on user data as available for the user context captured by our system prototype
- We are able to compute popularity of a photograph based on the frequency of views and the duration of view

We are interested in

- Who are the people viewing the photograph
- Who said what
- What region of the photograph were they pointing at when they said it
- How many times was a photograph viewed and by whom
- How long did each view last
- Segmenting out relevant speech portions to record using key word spotting, silence detection and gesture-speech co-occurrence in real time
- Storing speech as audio tags, thus preserving comments in the voice of the speaker, and adding another element of personalization to the memory

There are certainly more challenges while mining free flowing conversations as compared to explicitly authored conversations. Because photographs are often shown to close friends and family, they may not explicitly identify familiar objects and people [4, 6, 11]. Synchronizing audio with photographs is often achieved (e.g. [1, 10]) by cutting the audio recording at the point when a new photograph is selected, this may lead to awkward cut-offs. It also noted that users would not consistently annotate all their pictures.

In our work on multimodal interaction metadata, interactions with a photograph are viewed as interplay between the photograph, the photographer, the subject and the audience. This encompasses not only solitary reflections on the photograph but also involves three way interactions between participants around the photograph involving recollection, reminiscing and storytelling.

3. INTERACTION METADATA

3.1 Motivation

Our interest in multimodal interactions has had us exploring the space on various dimensions. One was a study (internal, unpublished) around interactions with media and media devices. We observed and studied users as they interacted with media and media devices singly or in a co-present manner. This gave us some interesting insights regarding gesture-speech patterns that occur during multiuser co-present photo sharing.

These are summed up below:

i) Interactions and conversations around photographs are rich in information about the photograph – who/what is in it, where was it taken, if it is liked or not and by whom etc.

ii) Gesture–speech co-occurs in a pattern

   a. People point out and speak about things of interest in a photograph, to the person/s they are sharing it with.
   b. Speech that co-occurs with a 'pointing' gesture specifically contains information about the photograph, and regions that are pointed at are of particular interest.
   c. Speech in this gesture-speech co-occurrence contains key words like 'who', 'what', 'this' 'that', 'where' etc.
   d. Speech that follows these gesture-speech co-occurrences (mostly as response to queries) also reports specific information about the photograph in context- names of people and places, occasions, etc. (Table 1).

We believe these multimodal interactions, if captured and extracted intelligently will aid in the creation of implicit metadata for the photograph in context. This type of metadata is what we call 'interaction metadata' and is the motivation for our work presented in this paper.

Table 1. Gesture-Speech co-occurrence and possible metadata

Speech	Gesture	Speech	Possible Tags
Who is that?	Pointing	That is Ron	Ron
Where is this?	Pointing	This is in Agra / Taj Mahal	Taj Mahal / Agra
What is that?	Pointing	This is the Taj Mahal	Taj Mahal

3.2 Interaction Metadata

We refer to metadata generated / created out of multimodal interactions people have with media like photographs as *Interaction Metadata.* Interaction metadata comprises of data regarding interactions with the photograph – who viewed it / with whom, who said what, who pointed at what while speaking, how long was an how many times each photograph viewed from logging information on the users interacting with the photograph. It also generates content metadata - who is in it, where is it etc, as extracted from conversations around the photograph.

In particular, photographs may be tagged with the identities of the users interacting with the media, as well as the contents of the photograph itself. The capture of interaction metadata, we believe, will enable new ways of searching and categorizing media collections. For example:

- "photographs seen by me and John yesterday"
- "photographs not yet seen by John "
- "photographs most viewed by me over the past year "

4. PROTOTYPE

Based on this understanding of multimodal interaction patterns we designed and built a system prototype to capture interaction metadata. The system was designed to identify key and relevant speech portions that accompany a pointing gesture on specific regions of the photograph along with user context data to create and present interaction metadata for these photographs, in the form of identified regions of interest (ROI), audio (speech) tags associated with each ROI and user context information (number of users interacting, their identities and the active user).

The prototype works with *touch*, visual *hand gesture* and *wiimote* supported distance interaction. We built our own photo application to enable and demonstrate interaction metadata for multiple users. We use a variety of recognizers and sensors to capture multiple interaction modalities as described below.

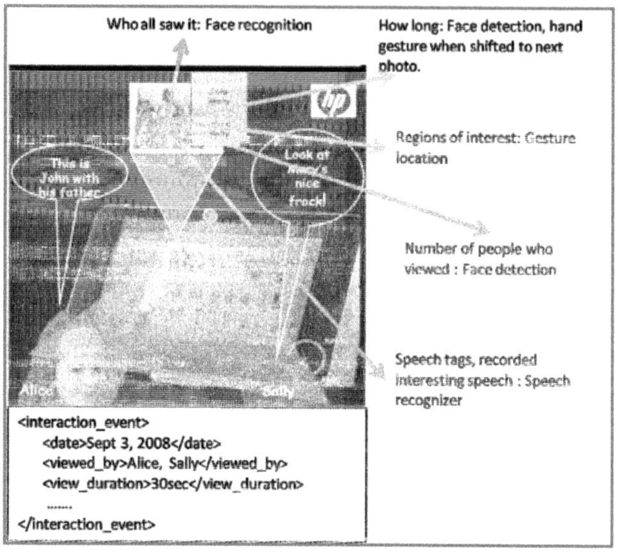

Figure 1 Metadata Realized for a Photograph

The prototype does the following (described in more detail, later):

- Identifies the presence of users, the number of users and their identities - Face Detection and Recognition
- Identifies and recognizes visual hand gestures directed at the system – Hand Gesture Recognizer
- Identifies silences and key words in the speech to segment speech - Speech Recognizer
- Identifies the co-occurrence of gesture and speech – Fusion Engine
- Records speech from silence to silence when key words are spotted and speech co-occurs with a pointing gesture. – Speech Recognizer
- Identifies and records the ROI that is being pointed at – Hand Gesture Recognizer

4.1 Facial Analysis Data

We use our own facial analysis software called the User Context Service (UCS) [8] for facial data analysis. It provides an API for multi-user face detection, face recognition, and active speaker identification. This service requires a webcam and a microphone array to function. We use face detection to know how many users are present in front of the system viewing the photograph. The face recognition module recognizes a registered user. When there are multiple users in front of the system, the speech activity detection (fusion of lip movement and audio direction) provides information about which particular user uttered the speech.

4.2 Hand Gesture and Pose Recognition

To recognize hand gestures for photo manipulation, and hand poses to know when a person is pointing, we use our own visual hand gesture recognizer. The gesture recognizer uses data from a

Kinect depth camera. With this API we capture metadata about regions pointed at and swipe gestures (indicating a transition to the next photograph). The gesture recognizer provides information about the gesture being made (pointing, encircling, swipe, etc.) and the coordinates of the regions of the photograph being gestured at (referred to as region of interest - ROI). The 'swipe' gesture informs the application the move to the next photograph and provides information about the duration of view.

4.3 Speech Segmentation

We use Microsoft's SAPI to detect silence so as to segment speech for creating recorded-speech tags. In our prototype we maintain a speech recorded speech buffer of 10 seconds and when a pointing gesture co-occurs with the key words 'this/ that' the buffer is segmented from silence to silence and the audio stored.

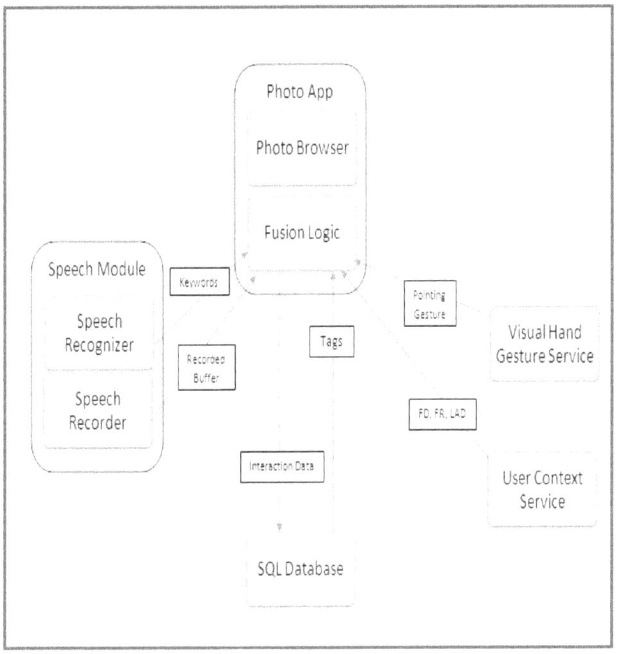

Figure 2 System Architecture

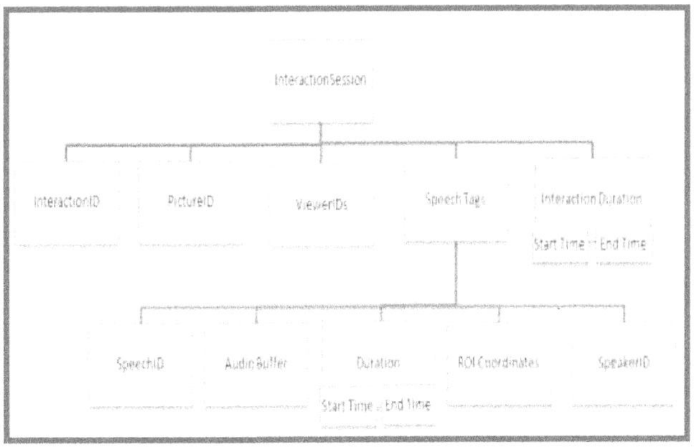

Figure 3 Interaction Metadata Structure

4.4 Keyword Spotting

We also use Microsoft's SAPI Speech recognizer for keyword spotting. It uses the microphone array to capture speech. Once the speech is segmented from one silence to the next as described earlier, the SAPI engine is used to record speech and spot keywords "this/that" in the recorded speech.

4.5 Gesture and Speech Fusion

The co-occurrence of gesture and speech is validated by a temporal fusion logic which bounds the ROI coordinates (from among the regions gestured at) which are temporally aligned to the speech segment obtained from silence detection.

In the current implementation we capture a variety of interaction metadata as shown in Figure 1. For each photograph, the metadata is stored in a database and accumulated over multiple interactions. The architecture of the prototype is as shown in Figure 2. The Photo Application contains a Photo Browser and a Fusion Logic that combines multimodal interaction data. The Speech Module comprises a Speech Recognition Engine and a Speech Recorder component. This module returns the recorded audio buffer as well

Figure 4 Application UI

as the keywords spotted in that buffer. The Photo Application uses the Hand Gesture Recognition API to capture pointing gestures, and the Facial Analysis API to recognize users and capture lip activity. Another module handles the saving and retrieving of tags from a SQL Database.

For every interaction session with the Photo Browser, the Fusion Logic; analyses the pointing gesture data from the VHG Service to identify the ROI, looks at the audio data from the Speech Module to understand what is said and saves the relevant audio buffer and uses Face Identity and Lip Activity results to determine the identity of the active speaker. Subsequently, the Fusion Logic gathers this multimodal interaction data and sends it to the SQL database. The structure of interaction data is shown in Figure 3.

The interaction data and the speech tag data are stored in a MySQL Database. At the end of each interaction session (each view of a photograph), the following data is stored: - unique ID of interaction session, unique ID of photograph, duration of viewing for that photograph, IDs of users who viewed the photograph and the list of speech tags that was generated during that interaction session. Each speech tag contains a unique ID, a link to the audio record on the hard disk, duration of speech, ROI (the coordinates and the size of the region) and the ID of the speaker.

A screen shot of the current application's user interface (UI) is shown in Figure 4. The metadata is displayed on the canvas around the photograph - who saw the photograph, duration of view, date and time of tag. Recorded speech tags are shown as clickable play buttons and can be played by to hear the speech comments, and the corresponding ROI is shown outlined in red.

5. THE STUDY

With our prototype, we conducted a small study among seven pairs of users to study the interaction metadata created, the relevance of the metadata to the photograph and to identify issues if any with the speech tags and the regions of interest identified towards making the prototype and the experience more robust.

Figure 5 The Study Setup

5.1 Participants

The participants, seven pairs of friends who knew each other well, from our office premises were invited to participate in the study in lieu of a small compensation. They came from different departments – sales, marketing, finance and support. They all took and shared digital photos through file share, social networking sites or photo sharing sites.

Figure 6 Views on the Participant and Observer Monitors

5.2 The Set up:

The prototype was set up in a test room. Participants were seated on a couch at a distance of four feet from the system for distance interaction (Figure 5). For this study we used the *wiimote* version, where the users used *wiimotes* to point at and interact with photographs. To ensure some discipline in the way the system responded, the owner of the photographs had the *wiimote* that could control interactions (go to the next photo) while pointing was allowed for both users. The interactions were recorded with the prototype (Figure 6). Each of the participants (Participant A and Participant B) was asked to bring with them a set of 10 digital photographs of varied variety (people, places, occasions, etc.) that they wanted to show their friend. These photographs were loaded on to our photo browser application.

5.3 The Task

The tasks the participants were required to perform, was to share their photographs with each other and have a conversation about them. Participant A first shared his/her set of photographs (Session 1). Prior to the start of Session 2 (where participant B shared his/ her set of photographs), participants were instructed to have a more structured conversation: use complete sentences, speak one at a time. Task A has been referred to as 'free flow' and Task B as 'structured' in the rest of the paper.

Figure 7 Tag Validation

5.4 Validation

Validation of the metadata created by the system was carried out at two stages. In Stage 1, participants reviewed system tags in a playback mode for correctness of speech & ROI. Invalid Tags, were corrected on the hardcopy of the photo (provided to them) by indicating the correct ROI & writing the speech tag in long hand. In Stage 2, annotators analysed & classified tags on various parameters identified by the researchers to enable statistical analysis & identify issues associated at a more technical level for system refinement.

After the sharing sessions were completed the participants were asked to validate the tags created by the system for both ROI and speech. Printouts of the photographs were provided, and the participants made any corrections to the system created metadata by marking out the correct ROI on the printout and writing the relevant speech in long hand for each of the tags created by the system (Figure 7). They validated for:

- Placement of ROI and relevance: is the marked region of interest of the right size and is it positioned correctly?
- Recorded speech (relevance and completeness): is the recorded speech portion relevant and complete?

These tags were further classified and clustered for statistical analysis and meaningful action at a more technical level, prior to the data analysis. In this paper the only data from participants is the validity and invalidity of a tag and reasons for their invalidity.

The rest of the data is based on the further classification parameters identified by the researcher.

5.5 Data Structure and Analysis

The data was annotated by two independent annotators, on the following parameters identified by the researches:

1. Validity of complete tag (audio and region of interest)
    1.1 Placement of region of interest: Correct/ Displaced/ Too big/ Too small/ Wrong photograph, etc.
    1.2 Correctness of audio tag: Correct /Audio too long-short/ Noisy-garbage/ Question/Not relevant.
2. Type of tag was also classified as:
    2.1 Name of a person /Name of an object /Relationship with a person /Description of a person or an object /Description of the event the photograph was taken at /Description of the situation /Description of the location /Mood of persons in the photograph /Name of the group /Comment on quality of the photograph /Not relevant

To ensure inter rater reliability a set of two data files was annotated independently by two annotators based on the above parameters. Then, line by line annotations were compared and the differences identified (Cohen's K=0.827, Pr[a]=0.935, Pr[e]=0.623). The identified differences were then reviewed by the two annotators and a researcher to arrive at a consensus and revise parameters, where required. Post this another sample set of two data files was annotated independently and the results compared. The differences were within acceptable levels (Cohen's K = 0.893, Pr[a]=0.956, Pr[e]=0.589). The complete data set was then annotated.

For this paper, relevant data has been consolidated for presentation. However the detail in the data allows us to address specific issues for the next version of the prototype. In this paper the terms 'metadata' and 'tags have been used interchangeably.

5.6 Analysis and Findings

In this section we present the findings and insights from the data analysis of the study we carried out with our prototype.

Seven pairs of participants tagged 140 photographs in all. Of the 140 photographs, 133 were people photographs and the rest were of objects and locations. Of the 133 people photographs, 58 were photographs of a group (more than three people) and the rest were photographs of single person, two people or three people.

5.6.1 Overall

In all, 311 tags were generated by the system. Of these 51% (183) were accepted as valid (ROI and speech present and relevant) by the participants and 49% (128) were declared invalid (Invalid ROI and / or speech). Of the valid tags, an almost equal number 49% and 51% were generated during free flowing speech and structured speech respectively.

The main reasons associated with speech for invalidating a tag by the participants are:

- Speech not relevant to the context of the photo: 45%
- Noise (cough, a cell phone ring, etc.,) associated as speech: 38%
- Speech not related to that specific photograph: 15%

The main reasons associated with ROI for invalidating a tag by the participants are:

- ROI attributed to a specific location on the photograph instead of the whole photograph: 53%
- ROI displaced: 41%
- Size of the ROI

Let us look at insights form further classification of the metadata in more detail, below.

5.6.2 Tags

Further classification shows that of the 183 valid tags 13% had both the ROI and the speech correctly identified, while the others had an issue with the ROI, the speech or both (Figure 8).

68% of the tags were descriptive- describing the event or the happening around the photograph and 28% were identifiers – identifying people, places or objects in the photograph.

Group photographs generated more descriptive tags while single person photographs generated identifier tags (Figure 9).

Figure 8 Tag Validity

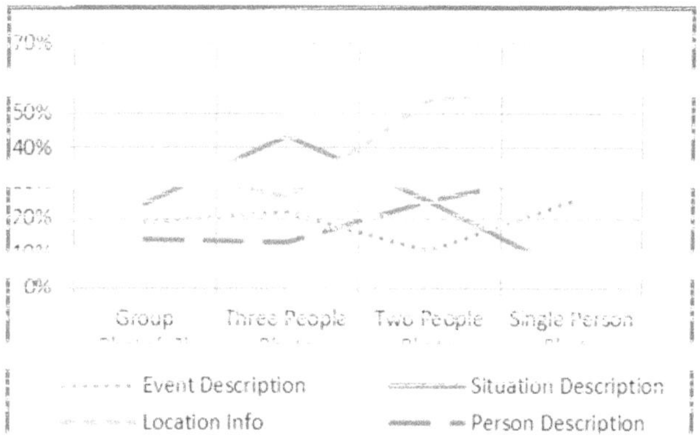

Figure 9 Types of Tags by Photograph Type

5.6.3 Speech Tags

Even among 183 valid tags 23% of the tags had an issue with the speech. These issues can further be classified as (Figure 10):

- Multiple sentences being clubbed into one tag: 46%
- Incomplete speech: 33%
- Merged tags due to incorrect sentence segmentation: 21%

The content of the speech tags can further be categorized as (Figure 11):

- Descriptive tags: 68%

- Tags identifying persons, objects, relationships, etc.: 28%
- Others: 4%

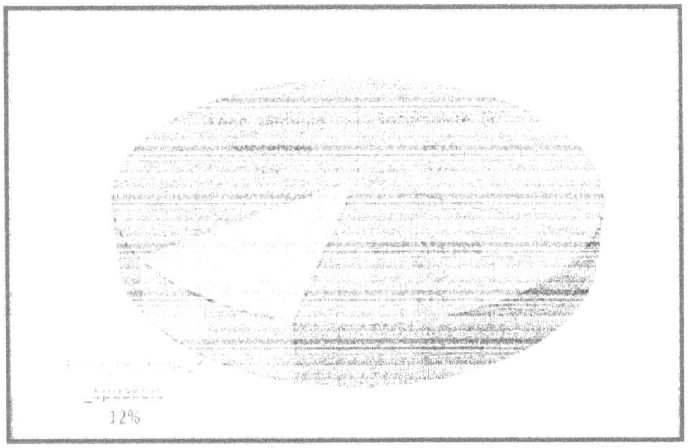

Figure 10 Speech Tag Issues

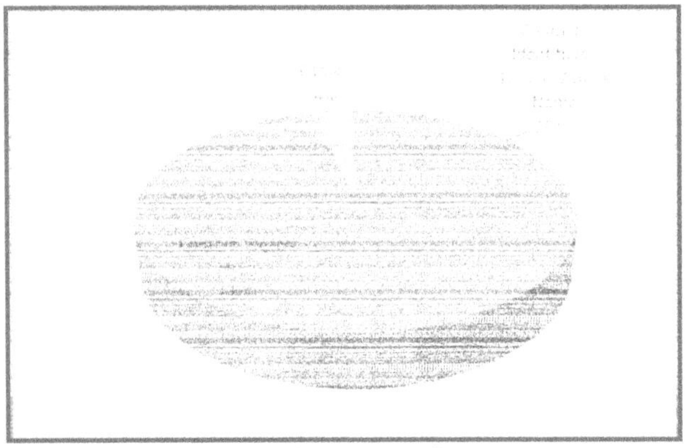

Figure 11 Speech Tag Content

5.6.4 ROI

The two main issues with ROI were:

- ROI association 53%
- ROI placement 41%

ROI associated with descriptive tags were the ROI that the participants wanted associated with the whole photographs rather than a specific location on the photograph.

Participants had varied opinions on where the ROI should be indicated on a photograph. In a small group photo (2-3 people) the ROI was preferred to be indicated around the face of the person where as in photographs with fewer people the participants were accommodative of the ROI being placed anywhere on the person's torso. In the case of large group photographs participants were accepting of the ROI spanning across multiple people.

6. DISCUSSION

We have with our prototype and experiment demonstrated that it is possible to create interaction metadata captured from the natural multimodal interactions people have in the context of media, here photographs. Interaction metadata is a hereto underexplored type of implicit metadata. It captures details regarding the users and their interactions with the photograph to create interaction metadata. While the captured interactions are also used to create content metadata, the interaction metadata that pertains to the users and their interaction in the scenario are of special interest.

This information can also be used to create interesting interaction experiences

- It can be used to determine if this is a personal photograph or one that is often shared with guests
- Retrieve photographs based on who has interacted or not interacted with them by enabling queries like – "show me photographs that John has seen or not seen
- It can be used to retrieve photos based on the ROI - "show photographs of the
- This information on the users and their identities, along with the frequency and duration of viewing, can be used to compute the popularity of a photograph among various groups of users.

The captured interaction metadata is also used to construct interesting queries as shown in Table 2.

Table 2: Metadata query structure

Query	Realized as
Photographs of John I saw yesterday	date=yesterday, viewed by=me, subjects=John
Recent photographs of London, Susie found interesting	Date_taken = within last month, GPS_Location = London, Viewed_by=Susie, Activity >60%
Photographs NOT seen by me and Sally yet	Viewed by does not contain Sally or me
Videos most viewed by me over the past year	Aggregate of view duration over past year > threshold

The insights into speech tags and ROI also provide interesting challenges to deal with:

- Associating speech and ROI to the whole image or the album when made in the context of a specific photographs based on the content of the speech – descriptive vs. identifier
- Placement of the ROI especially for people images

During the course of the evaluation we observed the following clusters of system errors that need to be addressed to make the prototype more robust.

Silence Detection: One of the key features of our system is to segment (silence-to-silence) and record only relevant sentences containing certain keywords. However, in noisy environments the notion of "silence" is disturbed. Entire segments of conversations are recorded in the buffer. Overlapping conversations also result in un-segmented recordings which result in information that are not relevant to the indicated ROIs.

Keyword Spotting: The keyword spotting indicates the importance of a sentence which is then segmented. Due to various pronunciations and similar sounding words, the keyword spotting errors resulted in segmentation of sentences that are not relevant to the ROI.

Multimodal Fusion: Based on the spotted keyword, the silence detection boundary, and the points from ROI, a temporal fusion is performed to know which speech segment corresponds to which ROI. Sometimes due to natural patterns of user gestures preceding speech and vice-versa, the temporal fusion fails resulting in wrong association of ROIs and speech segments.

Apart from this the other key elements that need to be addressed

Querying: Currently we allow only structured queries in the query box filled with specific information. In the future we plan to allow more natural language queries. Querying based on ROI and people will provide interesting interaction experiences.

Placement of the ROI: The placement of the ROI and its presentation is important. While the ROI may be the persons face, placing it over the face ends up occluding the face

Metadata Association: Metadata generated in the context of one photograph may apply to the whole album; we need to address how this is to be dealt with. One simple way would be to make metadata editable at least on a few parameters.

Visualization of the metadata: Given that interaction metadata will be captured and stored over time, the visualization of the metadata itself becomes important.

7. SUMMARY

Our work on creating implicit interaction metadata from user's multimodal interactions around photographs enables and aids storytelling, serendipitous discovery and efficient discovery, and is different from the current approaches.

Our approach of detecting co-occurrence of speech & a pointing gesture with the presence of keywords to generate interaction metadata allows for implicit tagging of images and other media.

The application and relevance of this work extends to beyond personal photo collections. Medical images can be tagged in a similar manner. Consumer reactions to a new idea in a marketing scenario, say a concept car, can be collected in a similar manner.

8. REFERENCES

[1] Balabanovi, M., Chu, L.L., and Wolff, G.J. 2000. Storytelling with digital photographs. In *Proceedings of the SIGCHI conference on Human factors in computing systems* (CHI '00). ACM, New York, NY, USA, 564-571.

[2] Barthelmess, P., Kaiser, E., and McGee, D.R. 2007. Toward content-aware multimodal tagging of personal photo collections. In *Proceedings of the 9th international conference on Multimodal interfaces* (ICMI '07). ACM, New York, NY, USA, 122-125.

[3] Berman, R. A. and Slobin, D. I. *Relating Events in Narrative*. Lawrence Erlbaum, 1994.

[4] Chalfen, R. *Snapshot Versions of Life*. Popular Press, Bowling Green Ohio, 1987.

[5] Collier, J. Jr. and Collier M. *Visual Anthropology: Photography as a Research Method*, University of New Mexico Press, Albuquerque, 1986.

[6] Cronin, O. Psychology and Photographic Theory. In *Jon Prosser Image-based Research*. RoutledgeFalmer, London and Philadelphia, 1998.

[7] Davis, M., King, S., Good, N., and Sarvas, R. 2004. From context to content: leveraging context to infer media metadata. In *Proceedings of the 12th annual ACM international conference on Multimedia* (MULTIMEDIA '04). ACM, New York, NY, USA, 188-195.

[8] Dey, P., Selvaraj, M., Lee, B., 2011. Robust User Context Analysis for Multimodal Interfaces. Accepted. International Conference on Multimodal Interfaces (ICMI 2011), 14-16th Nov 2011, Alicante Spain.

[9] Fleck, M. *Eavesdropping on storytelling*. Technical Report, HPL-2004-44, HP Laboratories Palo Alto, 2004.

[10]Frohlich, D., Adams, G., and Tallyn, E. 2000. Augmenting Photographs with Audio. Personal Ubiquitous Computing (January 2000), 205-208.

[11]Frohlich, D., Kuchinsky A., Pering, C., Don, A., and Ariss, S. 2002. Requirements for photoware. In *Proceedings of the 2002 ACM conference on Computer supported cooperative work* (CSCW '02). ACM, New York, NY, USA, 166-175.

[12]Frohlich, D.M. 2004. *Audiophotography: Bringing Photos to Life with Sounds* (The Computer Supported Cooperative Work Series). Springer-Verlag New York, Inc., Secaucus, NJ, USA.

[13]Kustanowitz, J. and Shneiderman, B. *Annotation for personal digital photo libraries: Lowering barriers while raising incentives.* Technical Report HCIL-2004-18, Univ. of Maryland, January 2005.

[14]Lemstrom, K., Korte, J., Kuusi, P., Kyheroinen, P., Paivakumpu, P. PICSearch – A Platform for Image Content-based Searching Algorithm. In *The Sixth Int. Conf. in Central Europe on Computer Graphics and Visualization*, Plzen, 1998.

[15]Lenat, D. 1998 The dimensions of context-space, Technical report, CYCorp www.cyc.com

[16]Lieberman, H., Rozenweig, E., and Singh, P. 2001. *Aria: An Agent for Annotating and Retrieving Images*. IEEE Computer 34, 7 (July 2001), 57-62.

[17]Mills, T.J., Pye, D., Sinclair, D., and Wood, K.R. *Shoebox: A digital photo management system.* Technical Report Technical Report 2000.10, AT&T Research, 2000.

[18]Naaman, M., Paepcke, A., Garda-Molina, H. From *Where to What: Metadata Sharing for Digital Photographs with Geographic Coordinates*, Stanford Database Group technical report 2003-37.

[19]Piamsa-nga, P., Alexandridis, N.A., Blankenship, G.C., Jr., Subramanya, S.R. 1999. In-picture search algorithm for content-based image retrieval. In *International Conference on Image Processing*. (ICIP '99).

[20]Qian, Y. and Feijs, L.M.G. Exploring the potentials of combining photo annotating tasks with instant messaging fun. In *MUM '04: Proceedings of the 3rd international conference on Mobile and ubiquitous multimedia*, pages 11–17, New York, NY, USA, 2004. ACM Press.

[21]Rodden, K. and Wood, K.R. 2003. How do people manage their digital photographs? In *Proceedings of the SIGCHI conference on Human factors in computing systems* (CHI '03). ACM, New York, NY, USA, 409-416.

[22]Schiano, D., Chen, C.P. and Isaacs, E. *How Teens Take, View, Share, and Store Photos*, CSCW 2002.

[23]Worthington P. *Kiosks and print services for consumer digital photography.* Future Image Market Analysis, 2004

Mudra: A Unified Multimodal Interaction Framework

Lode Hoste, Bruno Dumas and Beat Signer
Web & Information Systems Engineering Lab
Vrije Universiteit Brussel
Pleinlaan 2, 1050 Brussels, Belgium
{lhoste,bdumas,bsigner}@vub.ac.be

ABSTRACT

In recent years, multimodal interfaces have gained momentum as an alternative to traditional WIMP interaction styles. Existing multimodal fusion engines and frameworks range from low-level data stream-oriented approaches to high-level semantic inference-based solutions. However, there is a lack of multimodal interaction engines offering native fusion support across different levels of abstractions to fully exploit the power of multimodal interactions. We present Mudra, a unified multimodal interaction framework supporting the integrated processing of low-level data streams as well as high-level semantic inferences. Our solution is based on a central fact base in combination with a declarative rule-based language to derive new facts at different abstraction levels. Our innovative architecture for multimodal interaction encourages the use of software engineering principles such as modularisation and composition to support a growing set of input modalities as well as to enable the integration of existing or novel multimodal fusion engines.

Keywords

multimodal interaction, multimodal fusion, rule language, declarative programming

Categories and Subject Descriptors

D.2.11 [**Software Engineering**]: Software Architectures; H.5.2 [**Information Interfaces and Presentation**]: User Interfaces

General Terms

Algorithms, Languages

1. INTRODUCTION

Multimodal interaction and interfaces have become a major research topic over the last two decades, representing a new class of user-machine interfaces that are different from standard WIMP interfaces. As stated by Oviatt [13], multimodal interfaces have the added capability to process multiple user input modes not only in a parallel manner, but also by taking temporal and semantic combinations between different input modes into account. These interfaces tend to emphasise the use of richer and more natural ways of communication, including speech or gesture, and more generally address all five senses. Hence, the objective of multimodal interfaces is twofold: first, to support and accommodate a user's perceptual and communicative capabilities; and second, to embed computational power in the real world, by offering more natural ways of human-computer interaction [5].

However, the process of recovering the user intent through multiple different input sources and their potential combination, known as "multimodal input fusion", presents a number of challenges to be overcome before multimodal interfaces can be experienced to their fullest. First, the processing has to happen in real time, demanding for architectures to efficiently manage parallel input streams as well as to perform the recognition and fusion in the presence of temporal constraints. Second, the type of data to be managed by a multimodal system may originate from a variety of different sources. For example, a multi-touch surface might deliver multiple streams of pointer positions along with identifiers for different fingers, hands or even different users. On the other hand, a speech recogniser may deliver a list of potential text results in combination with the corresponding recognition probabilities. Being able to fuse user input from such different channels is one of the strengths of multimodal interfaces, but in practice only a few tools have been able to fully support data-agnostic input. In effect, most multimodal interaction tools either focus on extracting semantic interpretations out of the input data or offer low-level management of input data streams. Semantic-level tools are typically high-level frameworks that consume semantic events from multiple modalities to achieve a more intuitive and improved human-computer interaction. In these approaches, fusion is done on sets of individual high-level interpretations mostly coming from different recognisers. The second family of tools and frameworks focus strongly on dataflow paradigms to process raw data at the data level. These approaches typically declare the flow of primitive events by chaining multiple *boxes* serving as a filter or via event-specific fusion of multiple sources. The consequence is that we have, on the one hand, semantic tools which struggle with low-level and high frequency data and, on the other hand, frameworks to manage low-level input data streams which have to resort to ad hoc and case by case implementations for higher-level information fusion.

Sharma et al. [17] identified three different levels of fusion of input data: *data-level fusion*, *feature-level fusion* and *decision-level fusion*. These fusion levels are seen as distinct entities, working at completely different stages. On the other hand, fusion as a whole is supposed to be able to take into account data from any of these three levels, be it x/y coordinates from a pointer or semantic information

ICMI'11, November 14–18, 2011, Alicante, Spain.

coming from speech. In this paper, we address this conflict between seemingly irreconcilable fusion levels and data-agnostic input. A first open issue is the correlation between the events processed by dataflow approaches with a high throughput and low-throughput high-level events produced by semantic inference-based fusion. A second issue is how to retain access to low-level information when dealing with interpreted high-level information. For example, a gesture can be described by a set of x/y coordinates, by a sequence of atomic time-stamped vectors or by a semantic interpretation denoting that the user has drawn an upward-pointing arrow. Only a few tools keep track of the three different information levels and consider that users might express either deictic pointing information, manipulative movements or iconic gestures. Finally, in order to achieve multimodal fusion, some specific metadata has to be extracted regardless of the level of fusion. For instance, for raw-level data provided by a simple deictic pointing gesture that is freely performed and captured by a 3D camera, the start and end time of the gesture is required in order to resolve temporal relationships with other modalities.

To accommodate this missing link between low-level and high-level events, we developed a unified multimodal fusion engine capable of reasoning over both primitive and high-level information based on time window constructs. We encourage the use of modularisation and composition to build reusable and easily understandable building blocks for multimodal fusion. These software principles are emphasised by Lalanne et al. [11] stating that the *"engineering aspects of fusion engines must be further studied, including the genericity (i.e., engine independent of the combined modalities), software tools for the fine-tuning of fusion by the designer or by the end-users as well as tools for rapidly simulating and configuring fusion engines to a particular application by the designer or by the end-users."*

We start by discussing related work in Section 2 and investigate how existing approaches address the correlation between low-level and high-level events. In Section 3, we present the architecture of our multimodal interaction framework, called Mudra, and introduce the features that enable Mudra to deal with data-level, feature-level as well as decision-level fusion while retaining temporary fusion information. We further introduce the declarative rule-based language forming part of the Mudra core. A discussion and comparison of our unified multimodal interaction framework with existing multimodal engines as well as potential future directions are provided in Section 4. Concluding remarks are given in Section 5.

2. BACKGROUND

The fusion of multimodal input data can take place at different levels of abstraction. In this section, we first present these different levels together with some classical use cases. We then discuss existing solutions for the fusion of multimodal input at these abstraction levels and identify some of their limitations.

2.1 Multimodal Fusion Levels

As mentioned earlier, Sharma et al. [17] distinguish three levels of abstraction to characterise multimodal input data fusion: data-level fusion, feature-level fusion and decision-level fusion.

- *Data-level fusion* focuses on the fusion of identical or tightly linked types of multimodal data. The classical illustration of data-level fusion is the fusion of two video streams coming from two cameras filming the same scene at different angles in order to extract the depth map of the scene. Data-level fusion rarely deals with the semantics of the data but tries to enrich or correlate data that is potentially going to be processed by higher-level fusion processes. As data-level fusion works on the raw data, it has access to the detailed information but is also highly sensitive to noise or failures. Data-level fusion frequently entails some initial processing of raw data including noise filtering or very basic recognition.

- *Feature-level fusion* is one step higher in abstraction than data-level fusion. Typically, data has already been processed by filters and fusion is applied on features extracted from the data rather than on the raw data itself. Feature-level fusion of modalities typically applies to closely coupled modalities with possibly different representations. A classical example is speech and lip movement integration [14], where data comes from a microphone that is recording speech as well as from a camera filming the lip movements. The two data streams are synchronised and in this case the goal of the data fusion is to improve speech recognition by combining information from the two different modalities. Feature-level fusion is less sensitive to noise or failures than data-level fusion and conveys a moderate level of information detail. Typical feature-level fusion algorithms include statistical analysis tools such as Hidden Markov Models (HMM), Neural Networks (NN) or Dynamic Time Warping (DTW).

- *Decision-level fusion* is centered around deriving interpretations based on semantic information. It is the most versatile kind of multimodal fusion, as it can correlate information coming from loosely coupled modalities, such as speech and gestures. Decision-level fusion includes the merging of high-level information obtained by data- and feature-level fusion as well as the modelling of human-computer dialogues. Additionally, partial semantic information originating from the feature level can yield to mutual disambiguation [12]. Decision-level fusion is assumed to be highly resistant to noise and failures as it relies on the quality of previous processing steps. Therefore, the information that is available for decision-level fusion algorithms may be incomplete or distorted. Typical classes of decision-level fusion algorithms are meaning frames, unification-based or symbolic-statistical fusion algorithms.

Note that a single modality can be processed on all three fusion levels. For example, speech can be processed at the signal (data) level, phonemes (features) level or utterances (decision) level. In the case of speech, the higher fusion levels might use results from lower-level fusion. Surprisingly, existing multimodal interaction frameworks often excel at one specific fusion level but encounter major difficulties at other levels. We argue that the reason for these limitations lies on the architecture level and in particular how the initial data from different modalities is handled.

2.2 Data Stream-Oriented Architecture

One approach to build multimodal interaction architectures is to assume a continuous stream of information coming from different modalities and to process them via a number of chained filters. This is typically done to efficiently process streams of high frequency data and to perform fusion on the data and/or feature level. Representatives of this strategy are OpenInterface [16] and Squidy [10], employing a data stream-oriented architecture to process raw data sources and fuse multiple sources on an event-per-event basis.

Although these data stream approaches advocate the use of *composition boxes*, they do not provide a fundamental solution to define temporal relations between multiple input sources. All incoming events are handled one by one and the programmer manually needs to take care of the intermediate results. This leads to a difficult management of complex semantic interpretations. Data stream-oriented architectures show their limits when high-throughput information such as accelerometer data (i.e. more than 25 events per second) should be linked with low-throughput semantic-level information such as speech (i.e. less than one event per second). When confronted with the fusion of information coming from different abstraction levels, these architectures tend to rely on a case-by-case approach, thereby losing their genericity. Furthermore, the decision-level fusion of semantic information between multiple modalities requires classes of algorithms, such as meaning frames, which address temporal relationships and therefore need some kind of intermediate storage (e.g. *registers*). These algorithms are not in line with the stream-oriented architecture and developers have to rely on ad hoc solutions.

2.3 Semantic Inference-Based Approach

A second type of architecture for multimodal interaction focuses on supporting fusion of high-level information on the decision level. These approaches offer constructs to specify sets of required information before an action is triggered. Information gathered from the different input modalities is assumed to be classified correctly. Furthermore, these approaches work best with relatively low frequency data and highly abstracted modalities.

Four classes of fusion algorithms are used to perform decision-level fusion:

- Meaning frame-based fusion [19] uses data structures called frames for the representation of semantic-level data coming from various sources or modalities. In these structures, objects are represented as attribute/value pairs.
- Unification-based fusion [9] is based on recursively merging attribute/value structures to infer a high-level interpretation of user input.
- Finite state machine-based approaches [8] model the flow of input and output through a number *states*, resulting in a better integration with strongly temporal modalities such as speech.
- Symbolic/statistical fusion, such as the Member-Team-Committee (MTC) algorithm used in Quickset [21] or the probabilistic approach of Chai et al. [2], is an evolution of standard symbolic unification-based approaches, which adds statistical processing techniques to the fusion techniques described above. These *hybrid fusion techniques* have been demonstrated to achieve robust and reliable results.

The presented approaches work well for the fusion of semantic-level events. However, when confronted with lower level data, such as streams of 2D/3D coordinates or data coming from accelerometers, semantic inference-based approaches encounter difficulties in managing the high frequency of input data. In order to show their potential, these approaches assume that the different modalities have already been processed and that we are dealing with semantic-level information.

However, even when confronted with semantic-level data, several issues can arise with existing approaches. First, they have to fully rely on the results of the modality-level recognisers without having the possibility to exploit the raw information at all. This can lead to problems in interpretation, for example with continuous gestures (e.g. pointing) in thin air.

Second, as decision-level fusion engines assume that the creation of semantic events happens at a lower level, they have no or only limited control over the refresh rate of these continuous gestures. The typical solution for this scenario is to create a single pointing event at the time the hand was steady. Unfortunately, this considerably slows down the interaction and introduces some usability issues. Another approach is to match the pointing gesture for every time step on the discrete time axis; for example once per second. However, this conflicts with the occupied meaning frame slot and demands for ad hoc solutions.

A third issue that arises when employing meaning frames or similar fusion algorithms is related to the previously discussed problem. Suppose that a user aborts and restarts their interaction with the computer by reissuing their commands. Already recognised information from the first attempt, such as a "hello" speech utterance, are already occupying the corresponding slot in the meaning frame. A second triggering of "hello" will either be refused and possibly result in a misclassification due to an unexpected time span when matched with a newer pointing gesture, or it will overwrite the existing one which introduces problems for partially overlapping fusion since meaningful scenarios might be dropped.

Finite state machine-based approaches such as [8], typically lack the constructs to express advanced temporal conditions. The reason is that a finite state machine (FSM) enforces the input of events in predefined steps (i.e. event x triggers a transition from state a to b). When fusing concurrent input, all possible combinations need to be manually expressed.

The two major benefits are the flexible semantic and temporal relations between edges and the inherent support for probabilistic input. However, the manual construction of complex graphs becomes extremely difficult to cope with as the number of cases to be taken into account is growing. When such systems have to be trained, the obvious problem of collecting training sets arises and once again increases with the number of considered cases. Additionally, these approaches require a strict segmentation of the interaction. This implies a clear specification of the start and stop conditions before the matching occurs. Hence, supporting overlapping matches introduces some serious issues and also has an impact on the support for multiple users and the possible collaborative interaction between them.

2.4 Irreconcilable Approaches?

Finally, other issues, such as multi-user support, are currently problematic in both data stream-oriented and semantic inference-based approaches. For instance, at the raw data level, potentially available user information is frequently lost as data is treated at the same level as other pieces of data and requires some ad hoc implementations. When employing meaning frame-based fusion or any other decision-level fusion, slots can be occupied by any user. However, this means that events from one participant can be undesirably composed with events from another user. Note that a major additional effort is required from the programmer to support multi-user scenarios, since every meaning frame has to be manually duplicated with a constant constraint on the `user` attribute, resulting in an increased fusion description complexity.

In conclusion, data stream-oriented architectures are very efficient when handling data streams and semantic inference-based approaches process semantic-level information with ease. However, none of the presented approaches is efficient in handling both high frequency data streams at a low abstraction level and low frequency semantic pieces of information at a high abstraction level. Not to mention the possibility to use data-level, feature-level and decision-level information of the very same data stream at the same time. In the next section, we present our unified multimodal interaction architecture called Mudra, which reconciles the presented approaches by supporting fusion across the different abstraction levels.

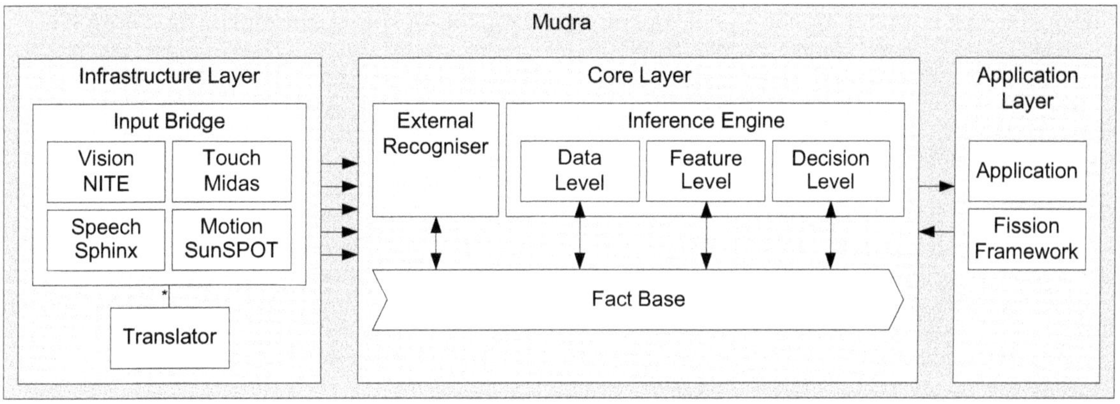

Figure 1: Mudra architecture

3. MUDRA

In order to build a fusion engine that is able to process information on the data, feature and decision level in real-time, we believe that a novel software architecture is needed. We present Mudra, our multimodal fusion framework which aims to extract meaningful information from raw data, fuse multiple feature streams and infer semantic interpretation from high-level events.

The overall architecture of the Mudra framework is shown in Figure 1. At the infrastructure level, we support the incorporation of any arbitrary input modalities. Mudra currently supports multiple modalities including skeleton tracking via Microsoft's Xbox Kinect in combination with the NITE[1] package, cross-device multi-touch information via TUIO and Midas [15], voice recognition via CMU Sphinx[2] and accelerometer data via SunSPOTs[3]. These bindings are implemented in the infrastructure layer. On arrival, event information from these modalities is converted into a uniform representation, called facts, and timestamped by the translator. A fact is specified by a type (e.g. speech) and a list of attribute/value pairs, called slots (e.g. `word` or `confidence`). For example, when a user says "put", the fact shown in Listing 1 is inserted into a fact base. Facts can address data coming from any level of abstraction or even results from fusion processing. A fact base is a managed collection of facts, similar to a traditional database.

Listing 1: "Put" event via Speech

```
1 (Speech (word "put") (confidence 0.81)
2         (user "Lode") (on 1305735400985))
```

However, instead of activating queries on demand, we use continuous rules to express conditions to which the interaction has to adhere. A production rule consists of a number of prerequisites (before the $\Rightarrow$) and one or more actions that are executed whenever the rule is triggered. Such a prerequisite can either be a fact match or a test function. A match is similar to an open slot in meaning frames but with the possibility to add additional constraints and boolean features, which leads to more flexible expressions. Test functions are user defined and typically reason over time, space or other constraints (e.g. `tSequence` or `tParallel` for sequential and parallel temporal constraints). Finally, when all prerequisites are met, an action (after the $\Rightarrow$) is triggered. Typical behaviour for an action is the assertion of a new, more meaningful fact in the fact base while bundling relevant information.

[1]NITE and OpenNI: `http://www.openni.org`
[2]CMU Sphinx: `http://cmusphinx.sourceforge.net`
[3]Sun SunSPOT: `http://www.sunspotworld.com`

The encapsulation of data enables the modularisation and composition while modelling complex interactions. This is inherently supported by our approach and allows developers to easily encode multimodal interaction. These constructs form the basis of our solution and allow developers to match the complete range from low-level to high-level events. The inference engine is based on CLIPS[4] (C Language Integrated Production System), which is an expert system tool developed by the Technology Branch of the NASA Lyndon B. Johnson Space Center. We have substantially extended this tool with an extensive infrastructure layer, the support for continuous evaluation, the inclusion of machine learning-based recognisers (e.g. DTW and HMM) and a network-based communication bus to the application layer. The application layer provides flexible handlers for end-user applications or fission frameworks, with the possibility to feed application-level entities back to the core layer.

3.1 Unified Multimodal Fusion

3.1.1 Data-Level processing

Data-level processing is primarily used for two purposes in the Mudra framework: noise filtering and recognition. Kalman filtering [20] typically allows for easier recognition of gestures in accelerometer data. This processing is achieved at the infrastructure layer since filtering is tightly coupled with specific modalities. Employing rules at the data level has already been shown to be effective for the recognition of complex multi-touch gestures [15]. The use of production rules to encode gestures based on vision data-level input has also been exploited by Sowa et al. [18] who used the following declarative encoding for a pointing gesture: *"If the index finger is stretched, and if all other fingers are rolled (pointing hand- shape) and if the hand simultaneously is far away from the body, then we have a pointing gesture"*. A similar approach is used in Mudra in the form of production rules to deal with the correlation of information at the data level.

3.1.2 Feature-Level processing

To improve recognition rates, fusion at the feature level can be used to disambiguate certain cases where a single modality falls short. For example, in multi-touch technology, every finger gets assigned a unique identifier. However this does not provide information whether these fingers originate from the same hand or from different users. The fusion of existing techniques, for example shadow images [6] or the use of small amounts of electrical current to identify individual users [4], is possible at the feature level.

[4]CLIPS: `http://clipsrules.sourceforge.net`

It is important to stress that we do not enforce a strict dataflow from the data level to the feature level. This has the advantage that data-level recognisers can benefit from information provided at the feature level. If existing feature-level techniques are incorporated in the framework, the data-level processing of multi-touch gestures can, for example, immediately profit from their results.

3.1.3 Decision-Level processing

At the decision level, the advanced modelling of multimodal fusion can be described in a very flexible manner, as developers have access to events ranging from low to high level. External data-level, feature-level or decision-level fusion algorithms can also be applied to any facts available in the fact base. The underlying complexity is hidden from developers, as illustrated in Listing 2 showing our implementation of Bolt's famous *"put that there"* example [1].

Listing 2: Bolt's "Put that there"

```
1  (defrule bolt
2      (declare (global-slot-constraint (user ?user)))
3      ?put <- (Voice (word "put") {> confidence 0.7})
4      ?that <- (Voice (word "that"))
5      ?thatp <- (Point)
6      (test (tParallel ?that ?thatp))
7      ?there <- (Voice (word "there"))
8      ?therep <- (Point)
9      (test (tParallel ?there ?therep))
10     (test (tSequence ?put ?that ?there))
11  =>
12     (assert (BoltInteraction)))
```

In this fusion example, we assume some high-level events. For example, line 3 and 4 show a pattern match on a voice fact containing a "put" (see Listing 1) and a "that" string at the `word` slot. Resulting fact matches are bound to variables, denoted by a question mark (i.e. `?put` and `?that`). Line 5 specifies a point event, which could be issued by a touch interaction or a hand pose. The point fact also contains a modality type slot, but if the developer does not constrain the attribute information to a single or multiple modalities, the rule will trigger for all cases. This example illustrates the abstraction level of our declarative rules, where the underlying complexity of the point event is hidden by one or multiple rules or external recognisers.

Different temporal operators, such as `tParallel` (line 6) or `tSequence` (line 10), are user defined rather than being fixed and limited to engine-level constructs. Developers can introduce their own operators at any time. It is important to note that the voice events generated by recognisers in the infrastructure layer are merged with point events extracted by data-level processing. Although pointing is a continuous interaction which generates multiple events per second, our system is able to fuse both inputs. Fusion algorithms at different fusion levels may find patterns in the fact base. In the future we plan to further exploit this feature by dynamically analysing speech in fusion-aware speech grammars.

3.2 Fundamental Features of Mudra

Attribute Constraints Additional constraints can be enforced by developers before a matched fact type is bound to a variable. A first constraint is realised by assigning a constant value on an attribute. This is shown on line 3 of Listing 2 by stating the string `"put"` for the `word` slot. A boolean OR operator supports alternative constant values in the case that this is required.

A second interesting constraint is available via inline function calls (denoted by curly braces), which is outlined on line 3. This construct not only supports boolean operators such as AND, OR and NOT, but it can also be used to specify value ranges (e.g. for sliders) or to call user-defined functions. In Listing 2, we applied an inline function call to enforce a minimal probability for the correctness of the recognised word.

A third type of attribute constraint is to use variable bindings. In production rules, a variable can only be bound once. Thus, if a single variable is used at multiple locations, it indicates that all these instances should contain the same value. This is very flexible as developers are not enforced to provide a constant value. Typically, this feature is applied in a multi-user context, where all matched events should be produced by a user without referring to a particular username. In Listing 2, we applied this mechanism via a macro (`global-slot-constraint`) which spans over all fact matches that contain user information.

Negation of Events A powerful feature is the use of negation to denote that an event should not happen during the defined scenario. This construct can also be used to define priorities between different modalities, for instance to express that pointing should be active as long as there is no voice input. The rich expressiveness of the negation feature is very handy when describing certain types of multimodal interactions.

Local Integration of Probability Probability information originating from external recognisers (e.g. speech recognition) can be integrated as attribute values. Due to the advanced attribute constraint mechanism, a threshold can be set locally and is not required to be system wide. It is very interesting to exploit this feature to reduce false positives as one can enforce a higher threshold for key components of the fusion. For instance, line 3 in Listing 2 requires a recognition probability higher than 0.7 for the speech recognition of "put", which is higher than the default threshold of 0.5. When extending the system with additional but similar fusion rules like "clone that there", the possibility to refine these probabilities on a per-event basis is a clear advantage.

Overlapping Matches Support for overlapping matches is an important benefit of our approach and enables to bridge the gap between low-level and high-level fusion. New events that overlap with partial matches are not thrown away but create new, additional partial matches. The mechanism relates to an automated replication strategy of meaning frames whenever a register is occupied. Developers do not have to decide between skipping new events or overwriting existing partial matches. Overlapping matches are handled very efficiently by the Rete algorithm [7]. Since we inherently support the bookkeeping of partial matches, we provide an additional `delay` construct to control the frequency of the rule triggering. The delayed triggering is important for data-level processing since many low-level events correlate to similar conclusions and a reduction of events minimises the processing necessary by the inference engine. Note that the delay construct can be applied to define the refresh rate of continuous gestures (e.g. pointing). Decision-level fusion greatly benefits from this control mechanism in our unified multimodal framework.

Sliding Window The fact base only contains facts that have not yet outlived their time span. This time span parameter is necessary for performance and memory reasons. A time span is specified per fact type, which allows developers to keep high-level semantic events with a low throughput longer in the fact base than low-level events generated with a higher refresh rate. The result is a flexible time-windowing strategy where developers can choose between performance and accessibility of older data for fusion.

Multi-User Support Multi-user support is exploited by specifying conditions on attributes. Whenever any user information is available—either originating from hardware, extracted by a recogniser or fused from multiple modalities—it can be included as an attribute in a fact. As mentioned earlier, the use of a single variable binding in a rule can be used to enforce events generated by the same user. However, specifying this attribute for every conditional element introduces a lot of redundant program code resulting in more complex rules. We therefore introduced a new language construct to declare constraints on all matches whenever the specified attribute is present. This is illustrated on line 2 of Listing 2 which enforces all events to be issued by the same user. Due to the inherent support for overlapping matches, Listing 2 supports the concurrent interaction of multiple users in the multimodal "put that there" scenario.

Collaborative User Support To go one step further, we show how rules can be employed to support collaborative interaction. Hoccer[5] is an example of a simple collaborative scenario where users can share data by initiating a throw and catch gesture. The implementation of this scenario, which matches a throw and a catch fact, is shown by Listing 3. The rule declares that the throw and catch fact should originate from two different users (`nequal` test on line 4) and that the former should happen before the latter (temporal constraint on line 5). Finally, the spatial constraint on line 6 tests whether the throw was performed in the direction of the catch. Again, the recognition of multiple users concurrently throwing data at each other is completely handled by the inference engine without any additional programming effort.

Listing 3: Collaborative multimodal interaction

```
1  (defrule throwAndCatch
2      ?throw <- (Throw (user ?user1))
3      ?catch <- (Catch (user ?user2))
4      (test (nequal ?user1 ?user2))
5      (test (tSequence ?throw ?catch))
6      (test (sInDirectionOf ?throw ?catch))
7   =>
8      (assert (ThrowAndCatch
9          (user1 ?user1) (user2 ?user2)
10         (on:begin ?throw.on) (on:end ?catch.on)
11         (on ?catch.on))))
```

Compilation Rules are compiled to a Rete network to accommodate soft real-time performance. Rete is a very efficient mechanism that compiles multiple rules to a dataflow graph and stores intermediate results to speed up pattern finding problems. Note that the engine itself will take care of storing intermediate results, which usually puts an additional burden on application developers. It is also important to mention that the temporal and other constraints are handled at each node level. This means that we are open to incorporate more advanced approximation (e.g. based on data obtained by training) at runtime, without running into architectural or performance issues. This compilation step is provided by CLIPS and allows us to process an average of 9615 events per second with the two code samples (i.e. Listing 2 and Listing 3) active on an Intel Core i7 with 4GB of RAM. The data consisted of 80% Points, 10% Voice and 10% Throw/Catch facts with a successful fusion rate of 20%. The assumed data input in a realistic environment is around 25 (Point) +1 (Voice) +2 (Throw/Catch) events per second which implies that our engine definitely has no problems processing these scenarios in real-time. Figure 2 shows an example of the compiled Rete network for the rule defined in Listing 2. Note that the evaluation of depending matching is postponed whenever possible and the system only spends very little time for newly arriving event. However, this also implies that the ordering of the declared constraint in a rule can significantly influence the performance.

[5]Hoccer: `http://hoccer.com`

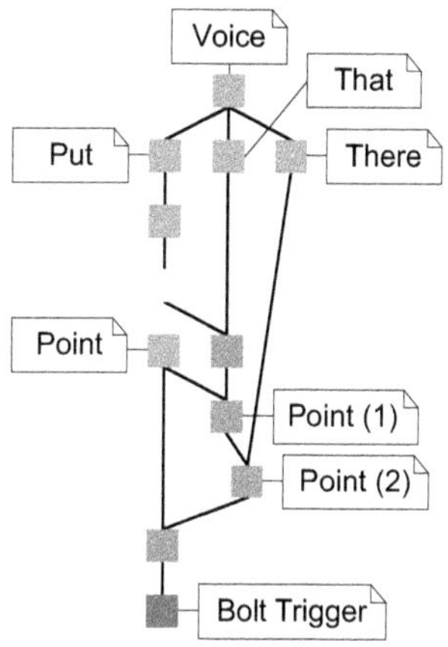

Figure 2: Compiled directed acyclic graph of Bolt's example

External Recognisers We also support the possibility to plug external recognisers into Mudra, along the fusion algorithms. Such external recognisers access data from the fact base and enrich it in turn. Recognition algorithms such as Dynamic Time Warping and Hidden Markov Models are examples of external recognisers. Flexible publish/subscribe handlers are provided for these recognisers. In future work, we would like to exploit this external recogniser feature even further via our concept of *smart activations*. As developers have access to low-level information in high-level fusion scenarios, it is easy to initiate additional low-level recognition techniques when desired. This initiation can embody computational intensive algorithms, which do not have to run continuously since their information is only interesting in certain scenarios. Typical applications are voice localisation using beam formation or the application of image processing for user identification.

3.3 Current Limitations

Our main focus is directed towards (1) finding meaningful patterns out of low- and high-level data, either via unimodal recognition or multimodal fusion, and (2) providing developers with high-level domain-specific language constructs to express advanced multimodal interaction with respect to the CARE properties [3]. Mudra supports a wide range of recognition techniques (DTW, HMM, production rules at the data-, feature- and decision-level), but it does not provide abstractions to set up a chain of raw data filters. We employ noise filtering for input data at the infrastructure layer (e.g. via a Kalman filter for accelerometer data), but we do not offer a complete infrastructure to chain stream boxes as for example offered by OpenInterface or Squidy. In case this is needed for future applications, it could be interesting to connect the output of these frameworks to our infrastructure layer.

A second limitation of our current implementation is the lack of advanced conflict resolution. A basic conflict resolution is offered via a numeric salience indication per rule, which allows developers to prioritise rules. However, since this construct only works when two rules trigger at the same time, we cannot always exploit this functionality. We also argue that a numeric salience value is insufficient to model all conflicting cases [15].

Dealing with probabilities at the attribute level permits a powerful control mechanism using high-level constructs. Although we frequently exploit this explicit mechanism, we lack constructs to automatically reason over the combination of multiple probabilities, as implemented by fuzzy logic approaches. It is an open question to see whether the increase of complexity at the performance and programming level is worth the extra effort.

Developers using our unified multimodal framework have to be aware of the ordering of their conditional elements. As mentioned earlier, the order of conditions can significantly influence the performance. An initial, automated reordering of conditions is provided by CLIPS; however it is limited to trivial situations. To improve the performance, we propose a simple guideline: position events with a higher throughput at a later position in the rule and put conditions as close as possible to the matches, allowing the engine to avoid unnecessary event processing.

4. DISCUSSION

In this section, we discuss how Mudra's unified fusion relates to other existing approaches. Frameworks positioned at the data level, such as OpenInterface, Squidy and other data stream-based approaches, rely on the linear chaining of processing components. Although these *boxes* encapsulate the implementation complexity, the internal implementation of such a box is far from trivial. Suppose that a high throughput (vision) and a low throughput (speech) input stream have to be fused. The composition of such a box, which handles all events one by one, requires a lot of bookkeeping. Key events have to be kept in local variables (state management) and all combinations of matches have to be manually exploited (pattern matching). This ad hoc composition of boxes is of course feasible but puts a burden on the application developer who is only interested in expressing a simple correlation. This issue is particularly present when other developers would like to extend the internals of the box (e.g. to support multiple or collaborative users).

Most feature-level processing tools rely on preprocessed data, such as noise filtering or multi-touch identification, before the fusion occurs. However, this means that data-level processing can typically not benefit from recognised features as existing architectures enrol a one way propagation of events as illustrated in Figure 3. In Mudra, we benefit from a single fact base with a garbage collector, from which recognisers can access all available information at any time. Via this structure, data-level recognisers can incorporate optional feature data. It is worth mentioning that dealing with "optional" data is fairly easy to accomplish via rules. For instance, one rule is responsible for reasoning over raw data and another rule augments this data whenever additional features are found in the fact base. Due to the continuous evaluation of the inference engine, the second rule will automatically be triggered as soon as the feature information becomes available.

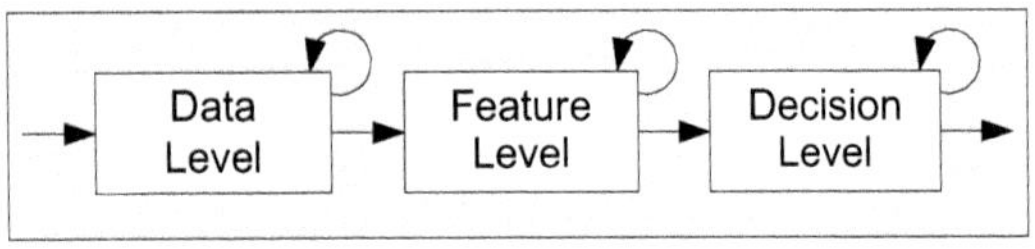

Figure 3: Traditional chaining of fusion

Decision-level multimodal fusion assumes the existence of high-level semantic data. This type of fusion is also known as *late fusion* where all high level information is gathered and correlated. Despite the introduced robustness, typical decision-level frameworks cannot recover from the loss of information which might occur at lower levels. A secondary limitation of these frameworks is the lack of support for overlapping matches. A commonly used implementation technique for high-level fusion is the incorporation of meaning frames. As already mentioned in Section 2.3, apparent issues arise when dealing with overlapping matches and continuous information. An important assumption of decision-level frameworks is the atomic compilation of meaningful events by data- and feature-level recognisers. However, for continuous gestures, such as pointing, it is hard to control the frequency. The continuous pointing in Bolt's "put that there" scenario is a simple example to stress this issue. The refresh rate of the pointing gesture is declared at the data-level processing. A high refresh rate introduces the problem of occupied slots in meaning frames, while a low refresh rate can lead to skipped decision-level integration since they are invalidated by the temporal constraints. It should be possible to circumvent these problems with an ad hoc solution, however, for more complex scenarios such as a multi-user environment, existing meaning-frame based solutions cannot be employed without inherent support for overlapping matches.

We argue that current frameworks are bound to their implementation approach, which means they can only offer well-defined abstractions either at the data-, feature- or decision-level. There is typically a one-way chaining from the lower to the higher level as shown in Figure 3. We have incorporated existing techniques in our unified approach and offer developers powerful language constructs to express their multimodal fusion requirements. One of the important benefits is that developers are freed from the manual bookkeeping of events. The declarative rules support the definition of multimodal fusion in terms of conditions on one or more primitive events via composite high-level rules. All recognisers build on top of each other, while they are still able to access low- or high-level information to improve their recognition rates. We also explicitly enforce every fact to be annotated with a timestamp for fine-grained garbage collection.

Our unified approach solves a number of important issues. However, there is still a lot of room for improvements and future research. For instance, we plan to evaluate the use of multiple recognisers on the same data. A combination of rules with multiple machine learning techniques that reason over the same data could significantly improve recognition rates.

Another issue that we are currently investigating is the incorporation of user feedback via supervised gesture learning. Since all low-level and high-level information is available in the fact base, rules could be used to manage user feedback intentions. Whenever such a rule is triggered, we could delegate the training process of gesture recognisers using knowledge of previous handling. Additionally, a batch learning approach can be used, in which the training of a gesture is only triggered with a threshold number of positive and negative examples.

Finally, we would like to include the smart activation of input modalities. For example, a low-level movement sensor could trigger the activation of a 3D camera, which in turn could activate the speech recognition module whenever a user is close to the microphone to improve speech recognition rates. The same *smart activation* constructs could also be used to control the propagation of information to machine learning techniques, as they are computationally too expensive for continuous evaluation.

5. CONCLUSION

Multimodal interfaces have become an important solution in the domain of post-WIMP interfaces. However, significant challenges still have to be overcome before multimodal interfaces can reveal their true potential. We addressed the challenge of managing multimodal input data coming from different levels of abstraction. Our investigation of related work shows that existing multimodal fusion approaches can be classified in two main categories: data stream-oriented solutions and semantic inference-based solutions. We further highlighted that there is a gap between these two categories and most approaches trying to bridge this gap introduce some ad hoc solutions to overcome the limitations imposed by initial implementation choices. The fact that most multimodal interaction tools have to introduce these ad hoc solutions at one point confirms that there is a need for a unified software architecture with fundamental support for fusion across low-level data streams and high-level semantic inferences.

We presented Mudra, a unified multimodal interaction framework for the processing of low-level data streams as well as high-level semantic inferences. Our approach is centered around a fact base that is populated with multimodal input from various devices and recognisers. Different recognition and multimodal fusion algorithms can access the fact base and enrich it with their own interpretations. A declarative rule-based language is used to derive low-level as well as high-level interpretations of information stored in the fact base. By presenting a number of low-level and high-level input processing examples, we have demonstrated that Mudra bridges the gap between data stream-oriented and semantic inference-based approaches and represents a promising direction for future unified multimodal interaction processing frameworks.

Acknowledgements

The work of Lode Hoste is funded by an IWT doctoral scholarship. Bruno Dumas is supported by MobiCraNT, a project forming part of the Strategic Platforms programme by the Brussels Institute for Research and Innovation (Innoviris).

6. REFERENCES

[1] R. A. Bolt. "Put-That-There": Voice and Gesture at the Graphics Interface. In *Proc. of SIGGRAPH 1980, 7th Annual Conference on Computer Graphics and Interactive Techniques*, pages 262–270, Seattle, USA, 1980.

[2] J. Chai, P. Hong, and M. Zhou. A Probabilistic Approach to Reference Resolution in Multimodal User Interfaces. In *Proc. of IUI 2004, 9th International Conference on Intelligent User Interfaces*, pages 70–77, Funchal, Madeira, Portugal, 2004.

[3] J. Coutaz, L. Nigay, D. Salber, A. Blandford, J. May, and R. Young. Four Easy Pieces for Assessing the Usability of Multimodal Interaction: The CARE Properties. In *Proc. of Interact 1995, International Conference on Human-Computer Interaction*, pages 115–120, Lillehammer, Norway, June 1995.

[4] P. Dietz and D. Leigh. DiamondTouch: A Multi-User Touch Technology. In *Proc. of UIST 2001, 14th Annual ACM Symposium on User Interface Software and Technology*, pages 219–226, Orlando, USA, 2001.

[5] B. Dumas, D. Lalanne, and S. Oviatt. Multimodal Interfaces: A Survey of Principles, Models and Frameworks. *Human Machine Interaction: Research Results of the MMI Program*, pages 3–26, March 2009.

[6] F. Echtler, M. Huber, and G. Klinker. Hand Tracking for Enhanced Gesture Recognition on Interactive Multi-Touch Surfaces. Technical Report TUM-I0721, Technische Universität München, Department of Computer Science, November 2007.

[7] C. L. Forgy. Rete: A Fast Algorithm for the Many Pattern/Many Object Pattern Match Problem. *Artificial Intelligence*, 19(1):17–37, 1982.

[8] M. Johnston and S. Bangalore. Finite-State Methods for Multimodal Parsing and Integration. In *Proc. of ESSLLI 2001, 13th European Summer School in Logic, Language and Information*, Helsinki, Finland, August 2001.

[9] M. Johnston, P. Cohen, D. McGee, S. Oviatt, J. Pittman, and I. Smith. Unification-Based Multimodal Integration. In *Proc. of ACL 1997, 35th Annual Meeting of the Association for Computational Linguistics*, pages 281–288, Madrid, Spain, July 1997.

[10] W. König, R. Rädle, and H. Reiterer. Squidy: A Zoomable Design Environment for Natural User Interfaces. In *Proc. of CHI 2009, ACM Conference on Human Factors in Computing Systems*, pages 4561–4566, Boston, USA, 2009.

[11] D. Lalanne, L. Nigay, P. Palanque, P. Robinson, J. Vanderdonckt, and J. Ladry. Fusion Engines for Multimodal Input: A Survey. In *Proc. of ICMI-MLMI 2009, International Conference on Multimodal Interfaces*, pages 153–160, Cambridge, Massachusetts, USA, September 2009.

[12] S. Oviatt. Advances in Robust Multimodal Interface Design. *IEEE Computer Graphics and Applications*, 23(5):62–68, September 2003.

[13] S. Oviatt. Multimodal Interfaces. In *The Human-Computer Interaction Handbook: Fundamentals, Evolving Technologies and Emerging Applications, Second Edition*, pages 286–304. Lawrence Erlbaum Associates, 2007.

[14] E. Petajan, B. Bischoff, D. Bodoff, and N. Brooke. An Improved Automatic Lipreading System to Enhance Speech Recognition. In *Proc. of CHI 1988, ACM Conference on Human Factors in Computing Systems*, pages 19–25, Washington, USA, June 1988.

[15] C. Scholliers, L. Hoste, B. Signer, and W. D. Meuter. Midas: A Declarative Multi-Touch Interaction Framework. In *Proc. of TEI 2011, 5th International Conference on Tangible, Embedded and Embodied Interaction*, pages 49–56, Funchal, Portugal, January 2011.

[16] M. Serrano, L. Nigay, J. Lawson, A. Ramsay, R. Murray-Smith, and S. Denef. The OpenInterface Framework: A Tool for Multimodal Interaction. In *Proc. of CHI 2008, ACM Conference on Human Factors in Computing Systems*, Florence, Italy, April 2008.

[17] R. Sharma, V. Pavlovic, and T. Huang. Toward Multimodal Human-Computer Interface. *Proceedings of the IEEE*, 86(5):853–869, 1998.

[18] T. Sowa, M. Fröhlich, and M. Latoschik. Temporal Symbolic Integration Applied to a Multimodal System Using Gestures and Speech. In *Proc. of GW 1999, International Gesture Workshop on Gesture-Based Communication in Human-Computer Interaction*, pages 291–302, Gif-sur-Yvette, France, March 1999.

[19] M. Vo and C. Wood. Building an Application Framework for Speech and Pen Input Integration in Multimodal Learning Interfaces. In *Proc. of ICASSP 1996, IEEE International Conference on Acoustics, Speech, and Signal Processing*, pages 3545–3548, Atlanta, USA, May 1996.

[20] G. Welch and G. Bishop. An Introduction to the Kalman Filter. Technical Report TR 95-041, Department of Computer Science, University of North Carolina at Chapel Hill, 2000.

[21] L. Wu, S. Oviatt, and P. Cohen. From Members to Teams to Committee - A Robust Approach to Gestural and Multimodal Recognition. *IEEE Transactions on Neural Networks*, 13(4):972–982, 2002.

Humans and Smart Environments: A Novel Multimodal Interaction Approach

Stefano Carrino
Univ. of Applied Sciences of Western Switzerland and Univ. of Fribourg, Switzerland
stefano.carrino@hefr.ch

Alexandre Péclat
Univ. of Applied Sciences of Western Switzerland in Fribourg, Switzerland
alexandre.peclat@hefr.ch

Elena Mugellini
Univ. of Applied Sciences of Western Switzerland in Fribourg, Switzerland
elena.mugellini@hefr.ch

Omar Abou Khaled
Univ. of Applied Sciences of Western Switzerland in Fribourg, Switzerland
omar.aboukhaled@hefr.ch

Rolf Ingold
University of Fribourg
Fribourg, Switzerland
rolf.ingold@unifr.ch

ABSTRACT
In this paper, we describe a multimodal approach for human-smart environment interaction. The input interaction is based on three modalities: deictic gestures, symbolic gestures and isolated-words. The deictic gesture is interpreted using the PTAMM (Parallel Tracking and Multiple Mapping) method exploiting a camera handheld or worn on the user arm. The PTAMM algorithm tracks in real-time the position and orientation of the hand in the environment. This information is used to point real or virtual objects, previously added to the environment, using the optical camera axis. Symbolic hand-gestures and isolated voice commands are recognized and used to interact with the pointed target. Haptic and acoustic feedbacks are provided to the user in order to improve the quality of the interaction. A complete prototype has been realized and a first usability evaluation, assessed with the help of 10 users has shown positive results.

Categories and Subject Descriptors
H.5.1 **[Multimedia Information Systems]**: Artificial, augmented, and virtual realities; H.5.2. **[User Interfaces]**: Graphical user interfaces, Input devices and strategies; I.3.6 **[Methodology and Techniques]**: Interaction techniques.

General Terms
Algorithms, Performance, Design, Experimentation, Human Factors.

Keywords
Ambient intelligence, multimodal interaction, gesture recognition, pointing, wearable and pervasive computing.

ICMI'11, November 14–18, 2011, Alicante, Spain.

1. INTRODUCTION
In natural human-human interaction people communicate through multiple modalities: voice, gestures, gaze, expressions are typical examples. However, human-computer communication is essentially characterized by interactions born in a desktop interaction model (mouse and keyboard). With the spreading of ubiquitous and wearable interaction paradigms (post-desktop models), novel interaction modalities allowing the machine to understand the natural language of human beings become of great interest. In the ambient intelligence (AmI) domain natural interfaces can be used to facilitate the communication among human and smart, augmented environments. Indeed, smart environments offer novel services, opportunities and interfaces (e.g. remotely control the devices in a room, the heating system, augmented reality elements, etc.). However, it could be complex for inexpert users to exploit these possibilities without convenient interaction modalities. Natural interactions and user-centered interface designs are active research areas addressing these challenges. Among different modalities, the gestures are a suitable way for a person to interact with the environment and the objects around him [1] [2]. In augmented reality applications, manipulative gestures [3] can be used to naturally interact with virtual objects and tools. On the other hand, deictic gestures [3] play an important role since they are intuitive and commonly used by humans to reference objects and devices by pointing at them. In contrast with other types of natural communication (e.g. voice or sign gestures), deictic gestures are not performed independently of the context. Indeed, the interaction actors are both the user and the environment, and both the pointing gesture and the referenced object have to be recognized. Moreover, the pointed object is actively involved in the interaction, therefore it should offer a communication channel to receive commands and transfer information.

Dealing with these issues, the major contribution of this paper is an approach for human-smart environment interaction, based on a multimodal and natural communication. This approach aims to facilitate the dialog among smart environments and their inhabitants through three modalities: deictic gestures, symbolic gestures (also described as iconic or stroke gestures) [4] and speech commands. To the best of our knowledge, we propose a novel pointing approach in HCI field, in which the camera is worn on the user arm itself, and a target is pointed whether it is in the projection of the optical axis of the camera. Once the object (real or virtual) is selected, symbolic gestures and voice commands can be provided to the system.

1.1 Target scenario

Natural interactions can be used in different contexts. However, working in dissimilar conditions means different requirements in terms of precision and responsiveness. For instances, gestures performed to control a robotic arm in medical area entails high responsiveness and accuracy; at the contrary, to point a light to turn it on, has surely less strict requirements.

In the context of AmI, the interaction with devices in a typical house (lights, heating system, television, etc.) could tolerate a rough accuracy (e.g. in the pointing interactions), however the system should be efficient enough to ensure real-time interactions and good performances in terms of usability and experience satisfaction.

The target scenario addresses a special case of interaction with an augmented, smart environment, in which a human can point at "smart entities" and start interacting with them through gestures and/or voice commands. Figure 1 describes a possible configuration of our system. In order to start the interaction with a device, the user will point at the target using a camera worn on the wrist of his dominant arm. An object is considered to be the target of the interaction if it is on the optical axis of the camera.

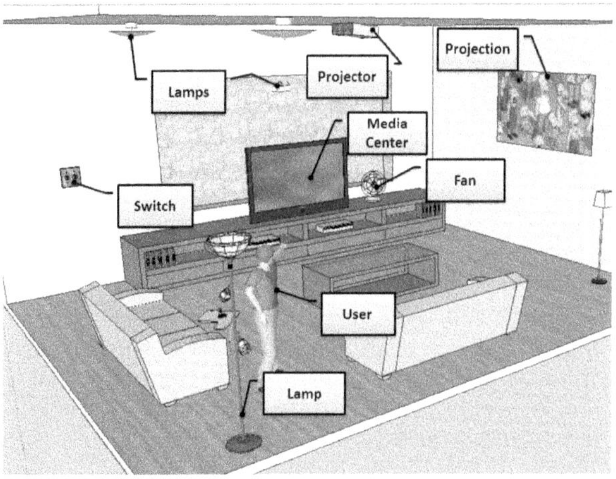

Figure 1. Possible environment configuration (smart living room). Tags highlight interactive entities present in the room

The multimodal system presented in this paper is composed by the three following input modules: a deictic gesture manager, a symbolic gesture recognizer and isolated-words speech recognizer. Regarding the output modalities, the system is designed to acknowledge and dialog with the inhabitants of the interactive space through acoustic and haptic signals. These components allow the user to interact with smart entities in the environment using a natural interaction approach as detailed in the following sections.

1.2 Paper Outline

This paper is organized as follow: section 2 presents related works in the field of HCI with special attention to the interaction among human and smart environments. Section 3 describes the context of this project and how this work is integrated and extends our previous work. Section 4 introduces the conceptual models of our approach. Section 5 shows the implementation issues related to the realization of a prototype. Section 6 describes an evaluation our system. Finally section 7 concludes the paper.

2. RELATED WORK

The study of multimodal, natural interaction paradigms combining voice and gestures has a long history starting in 1980 with A. Bolt and the "Put-That-There" system [5]. Deictic gestures are used jointly with isolated word commands allowing the user to point at a location on a large screen display in order to locate and move visual targets. Among the different communication modalities, the recognition and interpretation of deictic gestures is of great importance not only in AmI field but also for more general HCI applications (such as human-robot interaction). Moreover it is easier and more accurate to point an object than to give a verbal description of its location. Starting from this motivation Kahn et al. [6] demonstrate the use of pointing gestures to locate objects in a test environment. Their system operates on various feature maps (intensity, edge, motion, disparity, color). Whereas Jojic et al. [7] detect and estimate pointing gestures solely in dense disparity maps and depth information, since color-based approaches are sensitive to lighting changes and the clothing worn by the user. Also Nickel et al. [8] use color and disparity information to recognize and understand the pointing gesture. In [9], Cipolla et al. use the position and the shape of the hand, (e.g. the index finger) from different views in order to locate the pointing destination on a 2-dimensional workspace (detected through uncalibrated stereo vision with active contour).

Unlike these approaches, in which sensors are external to the user (they are placed in the environment or on a robot), we present a solution focused on a hand-hold or wrist-worn camera avoiding the expensive tasks of hand and head detection and tracking.

Our work uses the researches and results of Murray et al. about the localization, tracking and mapping (particularly to the results achieved in [10] and [11]). In [12] an interesting object recognition approach for augmented reality applications using PTAMM is presented. Differently from their work, our approach has special focus on natural and multimodal interactions; in addition we cover multiple aspects of the dialog between the environment and the user.

In relation to our previous work this project focus on the multimodal aspect of the interaction.

3. MULTIMODALITY AND CONTEXT

The approach proposed in this paper describes a main component of our human-smart environment dialog model, dealing with multimodality with a focus on the role of deictic gestures in human-smart environment interaction. Indeed, this approach is based on a novel technique enabling deictic gesture and user tracking in smart environments. This model has been conceived in order to enhance the interaction possibilities of human-beings through a hybrid approach in which pervasive and wearable computing paradigms, virtual and real worlds, optical and non-optical sensing technologies are combined in order to improve system expressivity, reliability and accuracy.

Our previous work [13] facilitates the fusion of information originated from different sensors. Data sensed from different devices (e.g. cameras, accelerometers, etc.) on the user or on the environment can be merged at three different levels (raw, features or decision). To reach this goal our model provides the infrastructure for coordinating sensors and modalities in a distributed manner exploiting a service oriented approach. A service can encompass any logical module (pointing, gesture recognition, accelerometers data acquisition, etc.) and can be loosely coupled with other modules present in an application through the service interface in order to easily design an application structure.

In this paper we extend the previous work focusing on multimodal interaction. This project takes into account a late fusion approach [14] in order to avoid strict time limitations (modalities can be analyzed separately), moreover the training requirements are smaller and the software development process is simpler [15]. Each modality is weighted with a default value. This value is then rescored and adjusted by parameters coming from the context.

Finally, our architecture includes the NAIF framework (presented by Perroud et Al. in [16]) that offers the possibility to create interface with *smart entities* present in the environment. It exploits a distributed, XML-based approach for the message exchange protocol, aiming to increase the system portability. In this context, we intend as "smart entities" real or virtual tools, devices and objects that have the following requirements: can communicate and are controlled by software interfaces.

4. HUMAN-SMART ENVIRONMENT MULTIMODAL INTERACTION: CONCEPT

This section describes the conceptual elements composing our approach. After a short introduction, it presents of the three input modalities (deictic gestures, symbolic gestures and voice commands) and the fusion mechanism, the feedback issues and shows how the environment is augmented. Finally the outline of the interaction protocol is illustrated.

A central element of our model is the presence of a camera (used for tracking the user and pointing the smart entities) on the user hand or arm. This choice allows us to realize a wearable approach in which the user can move from an environment to another. In addition, since the camera is on the user's arm the system could use vision information (e.g. optical flow [17]) to improve the recognition of the movements of the arm or augmenting the number of detectable gestures.

Figure 2 presents an overview of the global architecture in our system; it simply outlines the main modules and should be used as reference in the next sections.

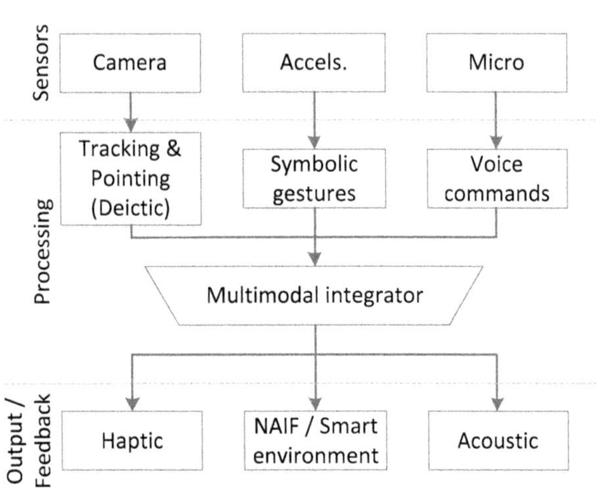

Figure 2. System architecture

The sensor layer manages all the technical aspects tied to management of the sensors devices (configuration, communication, drivers, API, etc.). In the processing layer three modalities (deictic gesture, symbolic gestures and voice commands) are managed and integrated together. Finally the feedback layer offers the outputs toward the user.

4.1 Deictic Gesture

Classical approaches dealing with deictic gesture recognition use cameras in the environment [6] [7] [8] or worn on the user shoulders [18] or head [19]. In these cases the pointing direction must be computed taking the relative position of the camera and the arm (and, sometimes, the head). This computation is challenging using a single camera, and can slow down the whole interaction system if multiple sensors are used. Our approach uses one single camera, worn on the arm of the user, and needs to track just the pose of the pointing hand. As aforementioned, an object is considered as pointed if it is crossed by the optical axis of the camera. However the deictic gesture will be taken into account only if the tracking and pointing module, that follows the user hand, is able to provide to the system the hand position and orientation in the 3D space.

In our concept the deictic modality has two main goals depending if the system is working in the configuration phase or in run-time phase (more details in section 5.2): firstly (at configuration time), the selection of the 3D point in which to depose a virtual object, in order to augment the environment; secondly (at run-time), the choice of the real or virtual object or device that will be the target of the interaction. Combining real and virtual entities we create an augmented interactive environment with novel possibilities of interaction (e.g. posing a "virtual trigger" on a physical light switch in order to enable the control of the illumination of a room by remote interaction). In the case that multiple targets lay in the same line of sight it is possible to switch among them using a symbolic gesture.

4.2 Symbolic Gesture Language

As second modality, the system offers users the possibility to interact through symbolic gestures. Our model defines a simple hand-gesture language composed by movements and rotations of one hand along the axes of the system.

Figure 3 represents some gestures that can be recognized in our system along an axis; the same pattern can be done long the three axes.

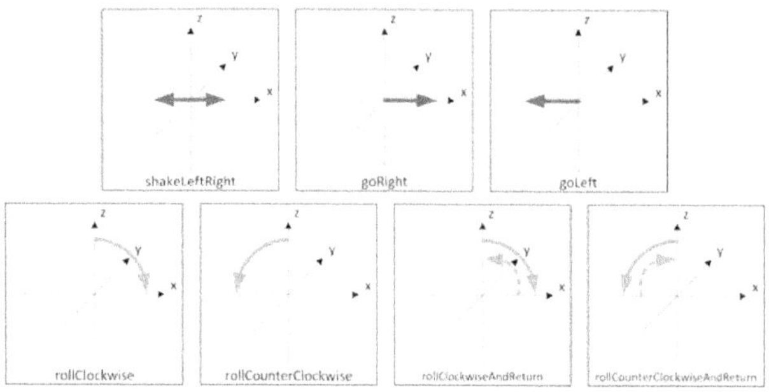

Figure 3. Symbolic gesture vocabulary

The interaction vocabulary is dynamically adapted by the system according to the pointed entity. For example, an interactive lamp is controlled with only three gestures (turn-on, turn-off and switch state) whereas a media center should need at least 7 commands for a rich interaction.

4.3 Speech Recognition

The third modality of interaction integrated in our model is based on isolated-words recognition. Voice inputs are captured by a microphone worn by the user. The vocabulary is composed by simple words reflecting the action executed on the object that, as in the case of symbolic gestures, are adapted according to the pointed target (typical examples are up, down, left, right, ok, etc.).

4.4 Multimodality Management

Deictic gestures, symbolic gestures and speech are modalities important to naturally interact with the smart entities and devices in the augmented interaction space. Deictic modality is considered by the system always activated. At the contrary voice and symbolic gestures can be performed only if an object has been pointed. The deictic modality is, thus, complementary to the two others modalities. On the other hand, the voice has an alternate functionality with regard to symbolic gestures, allowing the user to select the preferred communication channel and to freely switch between them. Indeed, voice and symbolic gestures are interaction channels designed for an alternate task (i.e. a task with temporal alternation of modalities, using coreference; as defined in the CASE model presented in [20]); in other words, gesture and voice modalities are equivalents from a usability point of view (CARE model [21]); hence, most of the commands performed with a gesture can be done also with the voice and it is up to the user to choose which modality to use.

As aforementioned the three modalities are finally merged using a late fusion approach [14]. In which features from the different channels are not mixed together and only the final results of the different modalities are used to select the final command.

4.5 Multimodal Feedback

In AmI context, the first sources of feedback are the entities present in the environment. In fact, if the user wants to turn a light on, the object itself will reveal if the command has been correctly interpreted. However additional feedbacks are important, for example to indicate if a gesture has been detected but misunderstood or if no input at all has been detected. With regard to the deictic modality, a feedback can assure that an object (the correct one) is pointed. Moreover if two targets are on the same line of sight the user can not exactly know which one is selected without an appropriate form of feedback.

Two different output modalities have been taken into account in our model: acoustic and haptic. If a command (gesture or voice) has been detected a short ambient sound is executed (without information about the kind of command recognized). Moreover, in the case that an object is pointed, a synthetic voice pronounces the name of the target; but, if the target is pointed again in the following few seconds, the information is not repeated. This technique reduces the number of redundant messages provided to the user. A user can also deactivate this feedback modality. The second modality, a vibration on the user arm performed by a haptic device, indicates that a new interactive target has entered the center of the camera field of view.

4.6 Augmenting the Environment: Map and Smart Entities

In order to have augmented interactions also the environment has to be augmented. In our model are present two kinds of elements: maps and smart entities.

A map is a 3D virtual reference system of a real room (or a part of it). The map and the real space are superimposed. This allows the system to merge real and virtual spaces locating an entity disregarding the space of origin (real or virtual). A smart entity is a tool, device or object (real or virtual) that can communicate and be controlled by software interfaces and have networking capabilities. More in detail, a smart entity is composed by a real or virtual element coupled with a virtual trigger. A virtual trigger is the interface of the smart entity. Placed in the map, triggers represent the activation points that the user has to point in order to start the interaction. Figure 4 shows an example in which a lamp is associated with two virtual triggers (colored cubes in the image on the right): one on the lamp itself and the other placed on a switch on the wall. It means that the user can interact with the lamp pointing at the lamp itself or pointing at the switch. Moreover multiple triggers can be associated with the same object, in order to have more activation points, or a trigger can be associated with multiple objects (one trigger to turn on all lamps in a room). The size of the virtual trigger can be chosen in order to facilitate the pointing task (e.g. matching the related real object). At the moment of the interaction the virtual trigger is invisible to the user; it is, hence, good practice to associate the triggers to real elements.

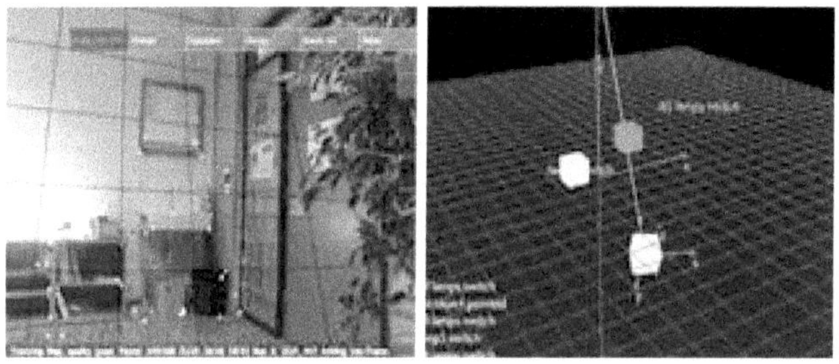

Figure 4. On the Left – Real environment with superposed AR information. On the right – White cube: camera. Yellow cube (not pointed): lamp. Red cube (pointed): switch.

4.7 Interaction Protocol

The diagram displayed in figure 5 schematizes the interaction protocol.

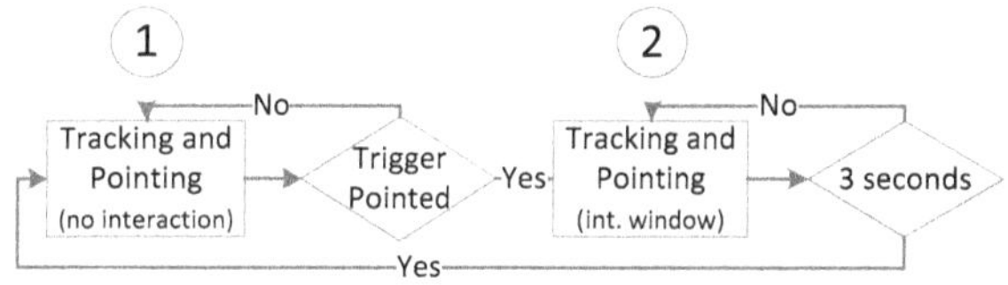

Figure 5. Schematization of the interaction protocol.

It is important to highlight that the tracking and pointing modules are always active and, in both states, the system will try to localize the user hand pose. Starting the description from the first state (on the left in figure 5), if the user dominant arm is directed toward a virtual trigger, that trigger is immediately considered as pointed by the system, and the user could start the interaction (passing in the second state). With this approach the deictic gesture does not need external inputs defining time boundaries (gesture segmentation). With the system in the second state (on the right in figure 5), the user can start interactions using gestures or voice commands. However, in order to avoid undesired interactions, the gestures commands are segmented by dynamics features (the pre-stroke conditions presented in section 5.3) and speech commands are reduced according to the pointed object (for a lamp only the words *on*, *off*, and *switch* will be possible inputs). The user has a limited temporal window of time (fixed at 3 seconds after preliminary experimentations) to provide a command to the system. The temporal window starts and is prolonged if a trigger is pointed. This allows users to interact with a target that is no more pointed making the system more robust against short losses of tracking. In addition, the user can provide a gestural input also with the hand performing the pointing (and affecting the pointing direction). When the interaction window is closed, the system comes back to the initial state (tracking and pointing with no other interactions allowed).

In order to interact with objects disposed in the environment the position of the user must be known by the system. However this information is actually needed only when the user has to select the target of the interaction or a spot in the room in which to depose a virtual trigger. Therefore the loss of the tracking during casual and fast movements will not influence the performance of the system, since not meaningful commands can be done at this time.

5. PROTOTYPE IMPLEMENTATION

This section describes the practical implementation of the presented approach and after an introduction on the set-up, the implementation of the tree input modalities is detailed. Finally, a description of the multimodal integration of these modalities concludes the section.

5.1 Set-ups

Two different set-ups for the input devices have been taken into account: the first using a handheld device, the second using a wearable (free hands) approach. Figure 6 shows the handheld device, composed by a Wii Remote Plus controller and a webcam with a microphone, fixed together.

Figure 6. Handheld device: a Wii Remote with a camera

Figure 7 schematize the wearable configuration. The user wears the webcam with microphone on his dominant arm and the Wii Remote on his non-dominant arm (tests have been done also with all the sensors embodied on the dominant arm of the user). In both configurations the elaboration is done by a computer situated on the user back.

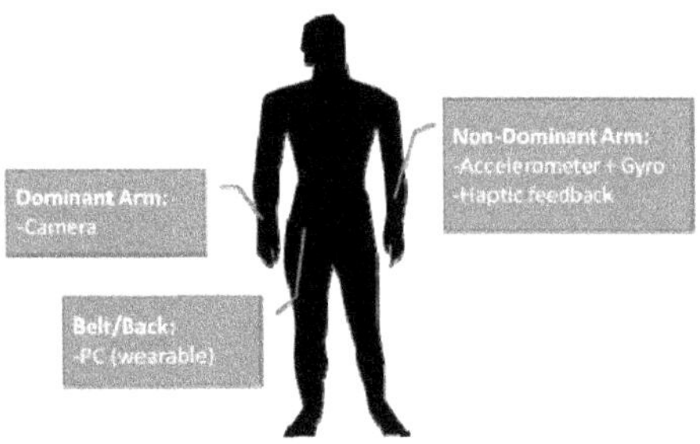

Figure 7. Wearable configuration

5.2 Deictic Gesture Implementation

In order to track the position and orientation of the user arm in the environment we adopted the Parallel Tracking and Multiple Mapping (PTAMM [12]) method. Similarly to several simultaneous localization and mapping (SLAM) algorithms PTAMM is used to build up or update a map of an unknown environment without the use of markers or a priori knowledge and to track the position of a camera in such environment, using observations (key frames) and features extraction and matching (FAST corner detection and epipolar search).

5.2.1 Augmenting the Environment

Augmenting the environment around the user is the first configuration phase needed to allow augmented interactions.

Using the PTAMM approach and the camera on the user hand (principally used for the pointing gesture) a map of the surrounding environment is created. Storing several key frames from different points of view, it is possible to save the map for a later use. Several maps can be combined in order to extend the area of interaction. Once the map is ready, the user will pose the virtual triggers in the 3D map. In order to place triggers at the desired location, the user must exploit information from the pointing module (the process is depicted in figure 8). Selecting the *"world edition mode"* the pointing service will be used to select a point in a 3D space by a triangulation algorithm. This process requires at least two rays virtually shot from the optical axis of the camera in order to calculate the object coordinates as the closer point to the different rays. (According empirical tests three rays are enough for an accurate selection).

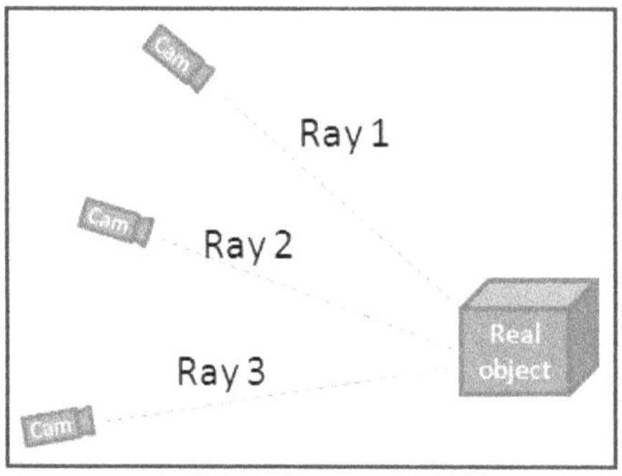

Figure 8. Object triangulation

Finally the user has to associate the virtual trigger to the real object interface (e.g. a media center), the multimodal commands (e.g. a sweep left-to-right gesture, the "ok" vocal input) and an action (e.g. play the music).

Once the creation of the map is completed and several smart entities have been deployed in the environment, the configuration phase is finished.

5.2.2 Using PTAMM for pointing

A map is a representation of a 3D world in which the PTAMM algorithm manages the position of the camera. The creation of a map itself is left to the PTAMM algorithm. When PTAMM creates a map, it defines it using its own 3D reference system. The point of origin, the scale used and the rotation of the system depend on the initialization of each map and are unknown to our system. Using multiple maps, PTAMM does not define a spatial relation between them. This can be exploited in several ways. For example, if a map is centered on an object with several easy-to-track points (as for example a media center composed of a large

LCD screen, a set of box and a rack) the map is linked only to the object, thus changes in the room configuration do not influence the virtual trigger posed on the object that will be associated to a map by the PTAMM algorithm.

The tracking system performances and consequently the pointing precision are strictly correlated to the map initialization. A map correctly initialized (several key frames taken from different points of view) will remain utilizable in environments with different light conditions and partial changes to the environment. Finally, at any time the users to improve a poorly initialized map adding new key frames.

5.2.3 Virtual Trigger's types

As aforementioned, virtual triggers are virtual interfaces. They allow real and virtual devices to be controlled by gestures and speech commands. Triggers are highly configurable according to the device to control, the associated multimodal commands, and the actions linked to these commands. However, in order to facilitate the deployment of these virtual elements, we have implemented six default types of triggers to use in our prototypes:

- *PPT-Trigger* opens a Powerpoint presentation and allows going in slideshow mode and navigating the slides.
- *PDF-Trigger* opens a PDF document and allows browsing the pages.
- *Winamp-Trigger* allows controlling a Winamp player.
- *Relay-Trigger* controls simple two states switches.
- *Projector-Trigger* deployed to control a projector.
- *MediaCenter-Trigger* allowing the control a Windows Media Center

Each trigger can perform one or more actions, on one or more devices (e.g. start an external process, such as a presentation software, activate a relay or turn on a fan and a lamp at the same time). In addition triggers can memorize their state and adapt their behavior depending on it; in this way the system could know the state of any entity at any time (e.g. the Relay-Trigger is on or off, the MediaCenter-Trigger is playing music, etc.). Figure 9 schematizes the set-up of our test environment. The tags highlight the interactive objects and the devices present in the room.

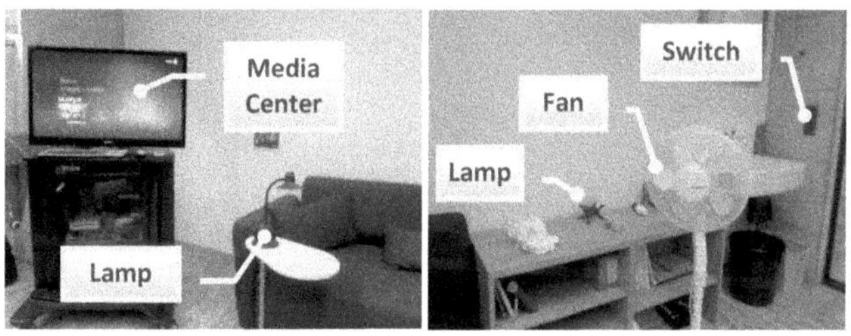

Figure 9. Environment set-up

5.3 Symbolic Gesture Recognition Implementation

Symbolic gestures performed by the users are recognized using inertial sensors (accelerometers and gyroscopes). These gestures follow the principle of "pre-stroke, stroke, post-stroke" or "preparation, stroke, retractation" presented in [22] and [23].

Each gesture has been modeled with a state machine composed of states in which a part of the gesture recognition algorithmic is hard coded in order to improve the system performances. Gestures have: a *pre-stroke* state that waits for stable inertial data in order to start the recognition process; one or more *stroke* states which model the recognition process; a *post-stroke* state that waits again for stability in the signals from the accelerometers and gyroscopes before validating the gesture. During the recognition, each stroke state is fed by inertial data and chooses between three transitions: stay in this state, go to next state or reset the state machine. The last case corresponds to a refusal and asserts that a gesture is not the one represented by the state machine. We choose hard coded gestures (despite of machine learning approaches) because of the simplicity of our lexicon of gestures and the shortness of our movement in terms of temporal duration. This approach is not as flexible as other techniques like Hidden Markov Models but having decomposed the logic into states allows us to reuse them to assemble other, more structured, gestures. Moreover, parameters like accelerometer thresholds or state duration can be tuned and customized for each user. After a first test, it was clear that some gestures are more difficult to be performed than others. This reduced to 11 the number of gestures we actually implemented in our applications (e.g. roll gestures are recognized only around the axis of the arm). Symbolic gestures have different thresholds according to the sensors configuration. In fact, with the hand-held device the user can perform small, more accurate and faster gestures. This is reflected also in the appearance of the gestures: small and fast with the hand-held device (above all wrist movements), larger and slower using the inertial sensors posed on the arm.

5.4 Speech Recognition Implementation

In the realization of our prototype we do not focus on the realization of a specific speech recognizer tool, since well performing solutions are available. We used the Microsoft Speech API to train a simple dictionary of 18 commands presented in the last column of table 1.

5.5 Speech Recognition Implementation

In the realization of our prototype we do not focus on the realization of a specific speech recognizer tool, since well performing solutions are available. We used the Microsoft Speech API to train a simple dictionary of 18 commands presented in the last column of table 1.

Table 1. Prototype Configuration

Trigger type	Actions	Gestures	Voice
Relay:	Turn On	goUp/roll	On
-Lamp	Turn Off	goD./rollInverse	Off
-Fan	Switch State	shakeUpDown	Switch
Media	Left	goLeft	Left
Center	Right	goRight	Right
	Up	goUp	Up
	Down	goDown	Down
	Ok	rollClockwise	Ok / Play
	Stop	-	Stop
	Back	shakeLeftRight	Back
	Mute	shakeUpDown	Mute
	VolumeUp	-	Volume up
	VolumeDown	-	Volume down
PDF	Previous pag.	goRight	Previous
	Next pag.	goLeft	Next
	Scroll Up	goUp	Up
	Scroll Down	goDown	Down

5.6 Multimodality

Virtual triggers have been designed to provide a default lexicon of interaction composed of symbolic gestures and isolated-words commands. However, triggers and multimodal inputs (gestures or speech) are loosely coupled by our framework and new kind of associations are easy to reconfigure using XML configuration files.

Table 1 shows the configuration used in our application scenario to link smart entities, actions and multimodal commands (all ordered by trigger type). For example, a lamp in our test environment can accept three inputs (being associated to a Relay-Trigger), and offers three actions (turn on, turn off, and switch state); user can interact with it using gestures (goUp/rollClockwise, goDown/rollCounterClockwise and ShakeUpDown) or pronouncing a voice commands ("On", "Off", "Switch").

6. SYSTEM EVALUATION

In order to demonstrate the usability of our system ten users (with different backgrounds, origins and gender) have been asked to interact with an augmented space (presented in figures 1 and 9). After a preliminary test session we chose to focus the evaluation just on the gestural modalities since they are more challenging for the user. Therefore users have to interact through deictic and symbolic gestures, using the lexicon presented above (table 1).

In the environment were arranged several interactive objects: two lamps, a fan and a media center. After a training phase of about 2 minutes, in which the users were introduced to the test environment and could try the gestures to realize, we asked them to follow two simple scenarios: firstly, to turn on and off the lamps and the fan in the preferred order; secondly, to navigate the media center menu and play a selected song, finishing the interaction coming back to the welcome menu. At the end of the interaction, users had to evaluate the experience through a System Usability Scale (SUS) [24] questionnaire rating the system features according to a 5-point Likert scale. The SUS questionnaire focused on effectiveness (can users achieve the objectives in the scenario), efficiency (how much effort is necessary in achieving those objectives) and experience satisfaction. The system obtained a SUS score of 78.8 globally assessing the system usability between good and excellent. The pointing gesture was indicated as intuitive and natural, the pointed object was always almost in the center of the field of view of the camera during the interaction (with the exception of a case in which the camera slightly moved from the mechanical fixation); the symbolic gestures lexicon were evaluated as intuitive, with a single user needing more training to correctly perform the goLeft and goRight gestures. The system achieved an efficiency of 95% (almost no superfluous actions have been done by the user to complete the scenarios) with 0.5 losses of the tracking per person during meaningful interactions. The response time of the system in order to interpret a command (gesture or voice) is of about 300 ms. Interacting with the different entities in the room this time was perceived as acceptable by the users.

A different set-up was used to evaluate the accuracy of the pointing system. Firstly, we evaluate the Fitts's law (as formulated in by MacKenzie [25]) linked to the task of aiming at and selecting real objects (we considered their projection on a sphere surrounding the user in order to calculate the virtual representation of the targets). We obtained an average Index of Performance of 1.336 bits/s, with significant differences between users (from 0.582 to 3.1 bits/s). Secondly, in order to evaluate the system capacity to distinguish between close targets, a configuration with different targets posed at different distances has been used. Results are shown in figure 10. Aiming at isolated target (D > 1m) from a distance of 4 meters there is an average error rate less of ~1%, the confusion between close objects start rising at D = 50cm the error rate start rising.

As result of this evaluation we plan as next step to use a PDA as sensing device and processing unit, making available novel interesting feedback modalities. In fact, on a screen it could be possible to display the pointed object, the related commands and how to perform them.

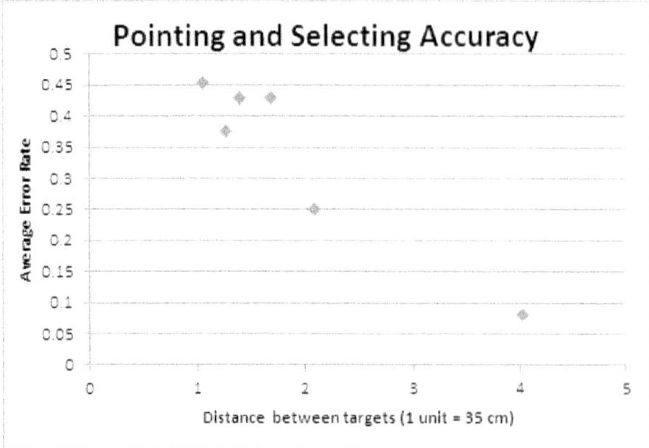

Figure 10. Error Rate aiming at targets from a distance of 4 meters

6.1 Limitations and Future Work

At the current state of development the process of map creation, virtual trigger positioning and the configuration protocol is still too complex for people without an appropriate knowledge of the system (and for this reason it not was included in the testing scenario). However a suitable multimodal interface would facilitate these activities (e.g. following the put-that-there approach: "depose *trigger_name* here").

Moreover, the lack of a rich feedback interface (e.g. visual) does not allow the system to efficiently communicate temporary errors in the tracking system (caused, in some cases, by fast movements of the user arm, or by a sequence of out-of-focus frames passed to the PTAMM algorithm); however, even if users (unaware of the logic behind the system) were indirectly conscious about some problems due to the lack of the vibration when an object was pointed, not indications were provided on how to "correct" their behavior. Therefore, in cases of tracking failures the haptic-acoustic feedback was perceived and judged as inadequate. This limitation brings to plan the future evolution of the system toward a richer interface making available a display on the arm of the user presenting the state of the system (in addition a visual feedback would be also useful to indicate the available commands to inexpert users improving the learnability of the system). Finally, improvements in the tracking module are also needed in order to increase the usability of the system. For example environments with large homogeneous texture are not suitable for the PTAMM (or more in general optical) tracking methods. A depth camera could be integrated to the system in order to augment the robustness of the system.

7. CONCLUSION

In this paper we presented a multimodal approach for human-smart environments interaction based on three input modalities (deictic gestures, symbolic gestures and isolated-words) with simple feedback provided to the user by haptic and acoustic modalities. Deictic gestures are interpreted using a camera hand-held or worn on an arm by the user. The projection of the optical axis of the camera is used to aim virtual triggers allowing the user to interact with real and virtual objects. The PTAMM method is used to track the position and orientation of the arm of the user in the environment.

11 symbolic gestures (accelerometer and gyroscopes) and 18 voice commands allow the user to interact with the smart entities present in the environment. A late fusion approach allows us to exploit these three modalities. A usability test, demonstrating the validity of our approach for what concern the effectiveness, the efficiency and the experience satisfaction, has been conducted.

As next step we plan to realize a richer user interface presenting visual feedback to the user. Moreover, we plan to realize a flexible multimodal fusion based on the context (gestures and voice commands are weighted according the environmental condition: for example a noisy ambient will penalize the voice recognition results).

8. REFERENCES

[1] D. J. Cook and S. K. Das, "How smart are our environments? An updated look at the state of the art," *Pervasive and Mobile Computing*, vol. 3, no. 2, pp. 53–73, 2007.

[2] R. a Bolt and E. Herranz, "Two-handed gesture in multi-modal natural dialog," *Proceedings of the 5th annual ACM symposium on User interface software and technology - UIST '92*, pp. 7-14, 1992.

[3] M. Karam, "A taxonomy of gestures in human computer interactions," pp. 1-45, 2005.

[4] S. Kopp, P. Tepper, and J. Cassell, "Towards integrated microplanning of language and iconic gesture for multimodal output," in *Proceedings of the 6th international conference on Multimodal interfaces*, 2004, pp. 97–104.

[5] R. A. Bolt, *"Put-that-there": Voice and gesture at the graphics interface*. New York, New York, USA: ACM Press, 1980, pp. 262-270.

[6] R. E. Kahn, M. J. Swain, P. N. Prokopowicz, and R. J. Firby, "Gesture recognition using the Perseus architecture," *Proceedings CVPR IEEE Computer Society Conference on Computer Vision and Pattern Recognition*, pp. 734-741, 1996.

[7] N. Jojic, B. Brumitt, B. Meyers, S. Harris, and T. Huang, *Detection and estimation of pointing gestures in dense disparity maps*. IEEE Comput. Soc, 2000, pp. 468-475.

[8] K. Nickel and R. Stiefelhagen, "Visual recognition of pointing gestures for human–robot interaction," *Image and Vision Computing*, vol. 25, no. 12, pp. 1875-1884, Dec. 2007.

[9] R. Cipolla, "Human-robot interface by pointing with uncalibrated stereo vision," *Image and Vision Computing*, vol. 14, no. 3, pp. 171-178, Apr. 1996.

[10] G. Klein and D. Murray, *Parallel Tracking and Mapping for Small AR Workspaces*. IEEE, 2007, pp. 1-10.

[11] R. Castle, G. Klein, and D. W. Murray, *Video-rate localization in multiple maps for wearable augmented reality*. IEEE, 2008, pp. 15-22.

[12] R. O. Castle and D. W. Murray, "Object recognition and localization while tracking and mapping," *2009 8th IEEE International Symposium on Mixed and Augmented Reality*, pp. 179-180, Oct. 2009.

[13] S. Carrino, E. Mugellini, O. Abou Khaled, and R. Ingold, "ARAMIS: Toward a Hybrid Approach for Human-Environment Interaction," in *Human-Computer Interaction. Towards Mobile and Intelligent Interaction Environments*, HCII 2011, pp. 165-174.

[14] A. Jaimes and N. Sebe, "Multimodal human–computer interaction: A survey," *Computer Vision and Image Understanding*, vol. 108, no. 1-2, pp. 116-134, Oct. 2007.

[15] M. Turk, "Multimodal human-computer interaction," in *Real-Time Vision for Human-Computer Interaction*, Real-Time., B. Kisačanin, V. Pavlović, and T. Huang, Eds. Springer, 2005, pp. 269-283.

[16] D. Perroud, F. Barras, S. Pierroz, E. Mugellini, and O. A. Khaled, "Framework for Development of a Smart Environment: Conception and Use of the NAIF Framework," in *2011 11th Annual International Conference on New Technologies of Distributed Systems*, 2011, pp. 1-7.

[17] B. K. P. Horn and B. G. Schunck, "Determining optical flow," *Artificial intelligence*, vol. 17, no. 1-3, pp. 185–203, 1981.

[18] T. De Campos, W. Mayol Cuevas, and D. Murray, *Directing the Attention of a Wearable Camera by Pointing Gestures*. IEEE, 2006, pp. 179-186.

[19] M. Bauer, G. Kortuem, and Z. Segall, "'Where are you pointing at?' A study of remote collaboration in a wearable videoconference system," *Digest of Papers. Third International Symposium on Wearable Computers*, IEEE Comput. Soc, pp. 151-158.

[20] L. Nigay and J. Coutaz, "A design space for multimodal systems: concurrent processing and data fusion," in *Proceedings of the INTERACT'93 and CHI'93 conference on Human factors in computing systems*, 1993, pp. 172–178.

[21] J. Coutaz, L. Nigay, D. Salber, A. Blandford, J. May, and R. Young, "Four easy pieces for assessing the usability of multimodal interaction: the CARE properties," in *Proceedings of INTERACT*, 1995, vol. 95, pp. 115–120.

[22] S. Mitra and T. Acharya, "Gesture Recognition: A Survey," *IEEE Transactions on Systems, Man and Cybernetics, Part C (Applications and Reviews)*, vol. 37, no. 3, pp. 311-324, May. 2007.

[23] F. K. H. Quek, "Unencumbered gestural interaction," *Multimedia, IEEE*, vol. 3, no. 4, pp. 36–47, 1996.

[24] J. Brooke, "SUS-A quick and dirty usability scale," *Usability evaluation in industry*, pp. 189–194, 1996.

[25] I.S. MacKenzie, W. Buxton "Extending Fitts' law to two-dimensional tasks," in *Proceedings of the SIGCHI conference on Human factors in computing systems - CHI'92*, pp.219-226

Exploiting Petri-net Structure for Activity Classification and user Instruction within an Industrial Setting

S. F. Worgan
School of Computing
University of Leeds
Leeds, LS2 9JT
S.Worgan@leeds.ac.uk

A. Behera
School of Computing
University of Leeds
Leeds, LS2 9JT
A.Behera@leeds.ac.uk

A. G. Cohn
School of Computing
University of Leeds
Leeds, LS2 9JT
A.G.Cohn@leeds.ac.uk

D. C. Hogg
School of Computing
University of Leeds
Leeds, LS2 9JT
D.C.Hogg@leeds.ac.uk

ABSTRACT

Live workflow monitoring and the resulting user interaction in industrial settings faces a number of challenges. A formal workflow may be unknown or implicit, data may be sparse and certain isolated actions may be undetectable given current visual feature extraction technology. This paper attempts to address these problems by inducing a structural workflow model from multiple expert demonstrations. When interacting with a naive user, this workflow is combined with spatial and temporal information, under a Bayesian framework, to give appropriate feedback and instruction. Structural information is captured by translating a Markov chain of actions into a simple place/transition petri-net. This novel petri-net structure maintains a continuous record of the current workbench configuration and allows multiple sub-sequences to be monitored without resorting to second order processes. This allows the user to switch between multiple sub-tasks, while still receiving informative feedback from the system. As this model captures the complete workflow, human inspection of safety critical processes and expert annotation of user instructions can be made. Activity classification and user instruction results show a significant on-line performance improvement when compared to the existing Hidden Markov Model or pLSA based state of the art. Further analysis reveals that the majority of our model's classification errors are caused by small de-synchronisation events rather than significant workflow deviations. We conclude with a discussion of the generalisability of the induced place/transition petri-net to other activity recognition tasks and summarise the developments of this model.

Categories and Subject Descriptors

I.2 [**Artificial Intelligence**]: Applications and expert systems, Knowledge representation formalisms and methods, Learning; I.5 [**Pattern Recognition**]: Models, Clustering, Applications

General Terms

Algorithms, Experimentation, Performance

Keywords

Petri-net, qualitative spatial relation, histogram of pairwise relation (HoPR), workflow modeling, Hidden Markov Model (HMM)

1. INTRODUCTION

Despite increasing automation in manufacturing, the adaptability and capabilities of human workers remains vital in industrial environments [26]. However further efficiencies can be identified as current experts train and supervise naive workers on an ad-hoc basis, tutoring by example and correction. We can improve upon this process through visual activity recognition and augmented reality instruction, enabling ambient multi-modal interaction between system and user. By deploying expert systems, training costs can be lowered and safety critical tasks can be continuously monitored. Before this potential can be realised however, we have to overcome a number of existing problems. Frequently, the maintenance or construction task under consideration will not be directed by a formal workflow model and the action sequence required to complete the task will be an implicit part of the experienced user's knowledge. To formalise this ad-hoc approach, we need to capture implicit expert knowledge as an explicit workflow process. Through accurate activity recognition we can then guide the user through the complete task sequence.

Historically, activity detection approaches have focused upon wearable sensor networks, operating over clearly distinguishable highly active gestures. The features of an established set of actions (walking, standing, jogging, hopping, climbing, etc..) coupled with wearable accelerometers have resulted in accurate classification results [17, 10, 12].

Current research employs a number of techniques ranging from Echo State Networks [21] to boosted-SVMs [12] to give a true positive rate between 60 and 90%. Building upon these techniques, a number of researchers have attempted to classify more challenging actions within an industrial setting [21, 13, 7, 14, 24] by supplementing accelerometer data with microphones [13], ultrasonic hand tracking [19] or marker based video tracking [7].

Within these industrial settings, existing Hidden Markov Model (HMM) [16] activity recognition systems [24, 14] perform well on offline sequential action recognition tasks but our own research suggests that when required to classify temporally incomplete or underspecified data, the resulting deterioration in performance can be marked. In order to exploit the constrained sequential nature of most workflows, these approaches [24, 14] train HMMs on large training sets (one for each atomic action) and then employ a Context Free Grammar (CFG) to determine their sequential likelihood. For example, the Gesture and Activity Recognition Toolkit builds directly upon the HTK recognition library [25] – hand-coding the workflow as a CFG and training each action on a separate HMM. In testing, the model constructs a Viterbi path [6] with fixed transition functions from one model to the next as determined by a stochastic or deterministic CFG. As stated by Ivanov, [11] "The grammar and parser provide longer range temporal constraints, disambiguate uncertain low-level detections, and allow the inclusion of a priori knowledge about the structure of temporal events in a given domain."

If a system is to continuously monitor and instruct a live user, offline classification accuracy must be maintained in an online setting. In the HMM/CFG approach, the detection accuracy is often dependent upon the final re-estimation of the Viterbi path, far too late for live activity recognition and user instruction. In addition to this, CFG structures are incapable of capturing certain real workflow features such as limited depth recursion and temporally independent subtasks, while hand crafted workflows can fail to capture expert behaviour [20].

Avoiding these problems, we will build upon the general approach of workflow mining [8] and induce a petri-net to capture the probable structure of the observed workflow. Unlike the workflow limitations of previous activity detection approaches [14], petri-net formalisms can capture advanced structural restrictions and can be easily translated into other – human readable – workflow formats. Formed from a graph of states, transitions, arcs and markers, petri-nets capture "an intuitive graphical representation of the processes being modelled" [4] while possessing strong mathematical foundations. Unlike other structural representations petri-nets can model both limited depth recursion and temporally independent subtasks. In general terms, a marker location in a current state represents the overall state of the system (*i.e.* the current state of the workbench). Markers can move from state to state across arcs and through transitions, with each marker recording the current state of an identified sub-sequence. Sub-sequence switching then becomes possible as each marker records the progress within each independent task.

A combination of probabilistic reasoning and petri-net structural constraints has previously been demonstrated in [2]. By exploiting a hand crafted petri-net to capture domain knowledge and combining it with uncertain observations, various activity classes can be differentiated. This paper takes a similar approach but will instead induce a petri-net workflow model to record the overall global state of the system. Due to the persistent marker values of a petri-net, users are free to switch between multiple activity streams in the course of completing a global task. This will provide a high degree of user task autonomy while maintaining a useful level of interaction with the system.

In the next section, this induced structure will be integrated with a naive Bayes model to address the identified HMM/CFG shortcomings. Specifically, this model:

1. Maintains 'on-line' classification accuracy from partial information – enabling the accurate instruction of a live user.
2. Exploits a marker based transition network to capture the structural properties of the workbench.
3. Provides structural classification constraints that can be translated into real workflows.
4. Successfully trains over relatively sparse annotated data sets.
5. Induces and exploit workflows from example activity sequences – capturing what is done not what 'should' be done.

We will then, in Section 3, assess our model's classification and user instruction accuracy before concluding in Section 4.

2. WORKFLOW INTERACTION

To monitor the naive user, we record the object configuration of the workbench and wrist positions of the user at any given time. To counter any residual noise or occlusion we first quantise these continuous observations as the latent states of a Hidden Markov Model [18]. Separately, we induce the structure of our place/transition petri-net from multiple annotated expert examples. Once induced, our naive Bayes activity recognition and user instruction model operates over the quantised workspace configuration. We will now describe each part in detail.

2.1 Feature Quantisation

A general workbench consists of a number of key objects $[o_1 \dots o_i \dots o_n]$. At each time step, the relation between pairs of objects o_i and o_j, with positions $\boldsymbol{x}_t^i$ and $\boldsymbol{x}_t^j$ at time t, is represented in a view-invariant fashion by a real valued vector composed of the separation and the first derivative of separation with respect to time i.e. $\boldsymbol{r}_t^{i,j} = (d_t^{i,j}, \dot{d}_t^{i,j}) \in \Re^2$, for $\forall i < j$ where $d_t^{i,j} = \|\boldsymbol{x}_t^i - \boldsymbol{x}_t^j\|$. For notational convenience, we vectorise the set of pair-wise relations $\{\boldsymbol{r}_t^{i,j}, i < j\}$ into $\{\boldsymbol{r}_t^m, 1 \leq m \leq M\}$, where $M = \frac{n*(n-1)}{2}$. These real vectors $\boldsymbol{r}_t^m$ are then quantised, q_t^m, as the latent states of a Gaussian Hidden Markov Model, χ, to minimise noise and capture the temporal dependencies. As shown by [18] this quantisation approach outperforms k-means clustering for visual activity classification. A complete workflow sequence of T time steps will have M parallel series of relational features i.e. $R = [\boldsymbol{r}_t^m]_{M \times T \times 2}$ and after discretisation it will be represented by corresponding HMM states $S_\chi = [q_t^m]_{M \times T}$. Where T captures the entire complete activity

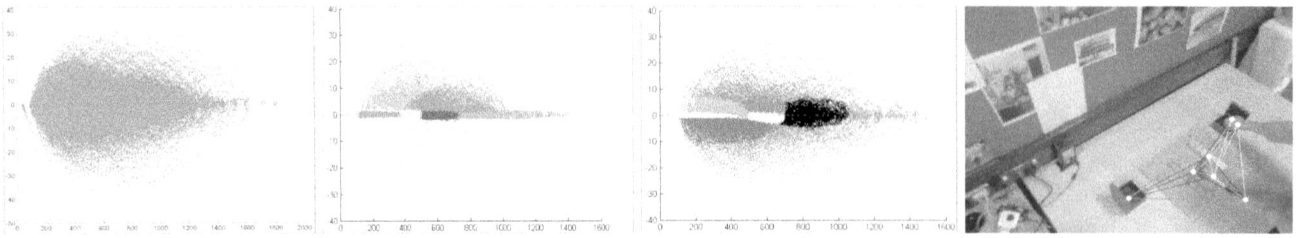

(a) 2-state HMM (b) 8-state HMM (c) 12-state HMM (d) Workbench configuration of pairwise relationships.

Figure 1: A partition of the recorded pairwise relationships with distance on the x-axis and the first derivative on the y-axis, formed from 2, 8 and 12 latent HMM states respectively. The complete configuration of relationships is shown on the right.

sequence, with each $t \in T$ recorded at 50Hz. Figure 1 shows the resulting partition of the pairwise relationships for a varying number of latent HMM states. The count of these quantised relationships then forms a Histogram of Pairwise Relationships (HoPR), $h_{q^t_m}$, at each timestep, where a set of relationships captures the current spatial configuration, this is then concatenated over a sliding window of size w, $\boldsymbol{h}_t = (h_{q^1_t - w}, \cdots, h_{q^M_t})$. The naive Bayes model, detailed in Section 2.3, then operates over these features.

2.2 Workflow structure induction

To form an explicit workflow from implicit expert knowledge we first train a Markov chain on multiple annotated, expert demonstrations of the complete task. The Markov chain ψ is defined as follows:

$$\psi = (A_\psi, P_\psi, \pi_\psi) \quad (1)$$

$$P_\psi = A_\psi \times A_\psi \quad (2)$$

where A_ψ is the set of possible action states, P_ψ the associated transition probabilities, and π_ψ the initial state probabilities. The Markov chain transition probabilities are then obtained from the frequencies of observed transitions in the annotated expert set.

With each state capturing a unique action, the trained Markov chain identifies the highly probable state transitions from one action to the next and the initial states identify the initial actions within the workflow. Typically, this trained first-order structure, extended to a Hidden Markov Model to account for uncertain observations, would be sufficient to identify the temporal relationships between actions. However, workflows typically consist of temporally independent subtasks and certain actions only become possible once local tasks have aligned to form a specific global configuration state. A HMM is incapable of capturing the global consequences of local actions as no global record of local changes can be made without an intractably large state-space or an equally intractable second-order formalisation of the model. Accordingly, in this paper, the trained HMM will be converted into a simple place/transition petri-net [15] enabling marker configurations to give the global state of the workbench after an observed sequence of locally enacted actions. This petri-net θ is defined as follows:

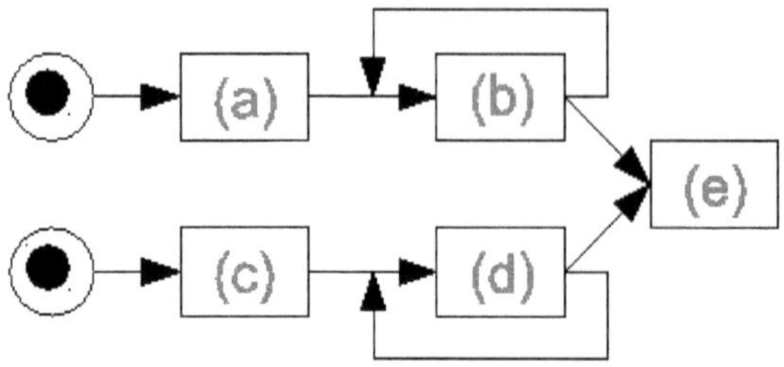

Figure 2: A simplified representation of an induced petri-net, showing parallel sequences and recursive processes.

$$\theta = f(\psi) = (S_\theta, T_\theta, W, M_0) \quad (3)$$

$$S_\theta = A_\psi \quad (4)$$

$$T_\theta = \{(a_i, a_j) : P_\psi(a_i, a_j) \geq r\} \quad (5)$$

$$W : (S_\theta \times T_\theta) \times (S_\theta \times T_\theta) \quad (6)$$

$$M_0 = \{a^j_\theta : \pi^j_\psi > 0\} \quad (7)$$

Forming a tuple $(S_\theta, T_\theta, W, M_0)$, the resulting petri-net consists of a set of places S_θ, transitions T_θ, initial marker values M_0, and a multiset of arcs, W joining places and transitions, Equation 3. Transitions, Equation 5, are simply formed by eliminating those that fall below a certain likelihood within the initial Markov chain. Each transition of the Markov chain, ψ, captures the fact that it is possible to transition from one action to the other. We then define each place $s_\theta \in S_\theta$ of the petri-net as an action potential for each $a_i \in A_\psi$ in the Markov chain. This action potential is tied to the unobserved state of the workbench as certain actions are only possible given certain configurations. Initially, each place is assigned to an action identified by the Markov chain, Equation 4, it is then the assignment of marker values and the inherent properties of the petri-net representation that converts transient actions into static configurations. The appropriate arcs, Equation 6, then results as a structural property of the petri-net, and all transition evaluation functions are set to true. The initial marker configuration is determined by the initial state probability of the Markov chain where all possible initial states are assigned a marker, as defined in Equation 7.

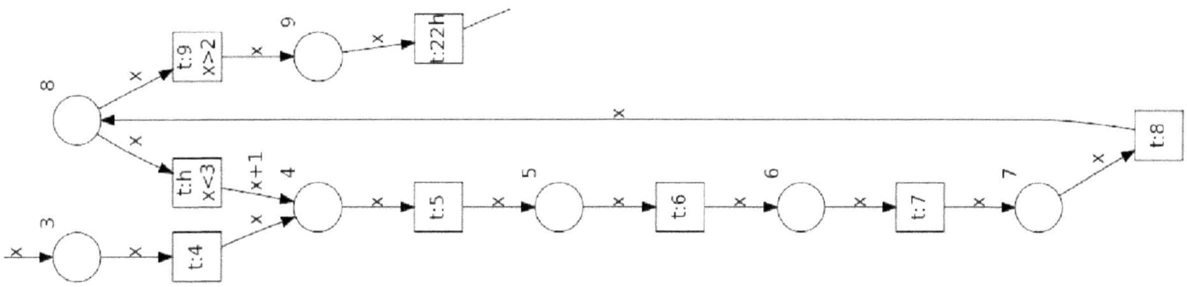

Figure 3: A detailed view of component (d) from Figure 2, by transitioning from a place/transition to a coloured petri-net we can limit the number of recursive transitions within the workflow.

A highly simplified representation of a typical induced petri-net is shown in Figure 2. Abstracting away from place or transition details, we can see that two independent tasks, on the same workbench, are each represented by an initial chain of events (components (a) and (c)) before entering a recursive action phase (components (b) and (d)) and then completing the overall task (component (e)). Due to the conversion of a petri-net representation and the introduction of marker states, the user is free to switch between these two tasks at will, as the markers record the local workbench configuration at the time of the switch. By comparison, two connected parallel HMMs would be unable to keep track of the previous local state whenever a switch occurred.

Figure 3 presents a more detailed view of component (b) in Figure 2 and demonstrates the transparency of this workflow representation. This transparency enables two kinds of expert annotation which can then be integrated into the live interaction system. Firstly, places can be annotated to provide a richer semantic representation; secondly, markers, arcs and transitions can be developed to capture more subtle structural constraints. For example, component (b) describes the hammering of a nail and the recursive relationship captures the hammering of multiple nails, by transitioning from a place/transition petri-net to a coloured petri-net we can enforce limited depth recursion as a structured constraint. By incrementing each marker as it transitions around the recursive loop and modifying the transition function to prevent markers over a certain value from further recursion we can ensure that the user hammers three *and only three* nails. Overall, this petri-net, whether coloured or place/transition, captures the structural constraints of the workflow and tracks workbench state changes in response to user actions.

As we do not directly observe this workbench the induced petri-net infers the current state by assuming that an observed transition from one action to another implies that the underlying state has changed. Under certain scenarios this assumption will not always hold true as switching from one asynchronous state to another may generate transitional actions. As these transitional actions represent apparent workflow violations they result in erroneous marker transitions within the petri-net model and are treated as insertion noise by the unified Naive Bayes model. This model accounts for such noise by combining the induced petri-net structural constraints with temporal and spatial observations to provide live user monitoring and instruction.

2.3 Naive Bayes Model Formation

We define a workflow instance e as a tuple (H_e, g), where $H_e = h_1 \cdots h_t$, representing a series of HoPR features, and g assigns an action to each HoPR window. Activity $a_i \in A$ occurs in e if there exists $h_j \in H_e$ with $g(h_j) = a_i$.

In total, three key components are trained on the observed data and combined into a naive Bayesian model, the first captures the temporally independent spatial HoPR features, h_t, by training a Support Vector Machine (SVM) equipped with a RBF kernel using a 1-vs-all methodology. This then returns a complete probability distribution over the candidate atomic actions at time t, $P(a_t^i|h_t, \Delta)$.

Accordingly, we define a set of Support Vector Machines (SVMs) Δ, where $|\Delta| = |A|$, and a function f_Δ assigning each $\delta_i \in \Delta$ to a corresponding action $a_i \in A$. Each SVM then solves a binary classification problem where for each δ_i, a set of input HoPR features is formed from all e drawn from the training set with a corresponding classification output set, Y_{δ_i}, such that $y_i \in 1, -1$, assigning 1 to all positive examples of the action and -1 otherwise. Each δ_i then attempts to solve the binary classification problem, employing the RBF kernel [5]. The resulting output for each action at time t, $P(a_t^i|h_t, \Delta)$ is then the probability of action a_t^i drawn from a complete probability distribution over the combined, normalised, beliefs of Δ.

The second model gives a rough measure of absolute temporal values (e.g. putting away tools typically occurs at the end of a workflow); accordingly a Gaussian, $\omega_i \in \Omega$, is trained for each recognised atomic action, $a_i \in A$. These Gaussians, Equation 8, are centered on the average absolute duration midpoints, $a_{\mu,i}$, for each action with their variance set equal to the average event duration variance, $a_{\sigma,i}$. At each time step, t, a normalised probability distribution is provided by the combination of Gaussian models, Ω, $P(a_t^i|t, \Omega)$.

$$\omega(a^i, t) = \frac{1}{\sqrt{2\pi a_{i,\sigma}^2}} e^{-\frac{(t-a_{i,\mu})^2}{2a_{i,\sigma}^2}} \tag{8}$$

$$P(a_t^i|t, \Omega) = \frac{\omega(a^i, t)}{\sum_{j=1}^{|A|} \omega(a^j, t)} \tag{9}$$

Finally, to capture the structural transitions of the induced workflow, a transition probability matrix is calculated according to the induced petri-net structure, as shown in Equation 10. This structure, which captures the believed global configuration of the workbench at a given time, represents a latent property of the system. We are faced with two uncertainties, the accuracy of the spatial/temporal observations and the validity of the marker transitions that we believe have taken place up to this point. Accordingly, we maintain a complete belief distribution over all states of the induced petri-net, this is drawn from the complete distribution formed by the previous timestep, S_{t-1} with $s^j_{t-1} \in S_{t-1}$.

$$P(a^i_t|\theta, S_{t-1}) = \sum_{j=1}^{|S^{t-1}|} P(s^i_t|s^j_{t-1}, d^{i,j}_\gamma)P(s^j_{t-1}) \tag{10}$$

When considering the likelihood of a current state, s^i_t, we generate a reachability graph, γ, [15] from each possible petri-net state in turn. These reachability graphs are bi-directional and capture the number of marker transitions required to reach the proposed state given the marker configuration and structural constraints of the network. The likelihood that all of these transitions have taken place since the previous set of observations is captured by a discrete Gaussian distance measure, $f_\gamma(d^{i,j}_\gamma)$, where $d^{i,j}_\gamma$ equals the minimum number of transitions between s^i_t and s^j_{t-1}, Equation 11. This discrete measure captures the high likelihood that the current workbench remains unchanged with a decreasing likelihood the greater the number of steps taken to reach the proposed petri-net state, s^i_t. By considering the probability of the previous state $P(s^j_{t-1})$ combined with the probability that the system has transitioned from that state to the current state $P(s^i_t|s^j_{t-1})$ we return (in Equation 10) the combined probability that the workbench has reached a state $P(s^i_t)$ that makes the proposed action possible $P(a^i_t) = P(s^i_t)$. In use, the complete set of transition probabilities, modified by the prior probability of the previous state, $P(a^j_{t-1})$, are considered as possible routes when calculating the transition likelihood.

$$f_\gamma(d^{i,j}_\gamma) = \frac{1}{\sqrt{2\pi^2}}\, e^{-\frac{(d^{i,j}_\gamma)^2}{2^2}} \tag{11}$$

$$P(s^i_t|s^j_t - 1, d^{i,j}_\gamma) = \frac{f_\gamma(d^{i,j}_\gamma)}{\sum_{i=1}^{|S|} f_\gamma(d^{i,j}_\gamma)} \tag{12}$$

All three of these models, spatial, temporal and structural are assumed to be independent, and are combined according to a naive Bayes formalisation (Equation 13). At each timestep the most likely action a_{MAP} is selected given this combined probability distribution.

$$a_{MAP} = \arg\max_{a_t} P(a_t|h_t, \Delta)P(a_t|t, \Omega)P(a_t|\theta, S_{t-1}) \tag{13}$$

In use, a_{MAP} and a^{t+1}_{MAP} are supplied to the user, in a similar manner to Equation 10, Equation 14 selects the next likely action given the current believed state of the petri-net.

$$a^{t+1}_{MAP} = \underset{a_{t+1}, a_{t+1} \neq a_t}{\text{argmax}} \quad P(a_{t+1}|\theta, S_t) \tag{14}$$

3. RESULTS

The complete set of workflow examples consists of two complex tasks performed eight times by two different people on the same workbench. The workbench itself consists of 7 objects, each of which is identified by a VICON marker [1], while the motion of the user is identified by two further markers – one on each wrist. This forms a complete set of 9 *key objects* $[o_1 \cdot o_i \cdot o_9]$. Formed from 22 atomic actions and totalling approximately 20 minutes of data, this small dataset represents a realistic amount of training data, given expected industry constraints. The task itself captures a basic construction activity, where one batten is affixed to an object by three screws and other is affixed by three nails. Each atomic action corresponds to semantically meaningful components of this task, e.g. place batten, hammer nail.

For all of the following results we have used a HoPR window length of 6 with 32 quantised states, petri-net transitions were induced with a threshold of $r = 0.005$, these parameter values where found through experimentation. Given this dataset the induced petri-net structure captures the entire workbench configuration and the assumed independence of the two tasks, within the data this assumption remains valid as no transitional actions, arbitrarily switching between the two tasks, occur.

We will assess this model according to its classification accuracy, prediction accuracy and robustness to occlusion for leave-one-out training and testing. Given 16 training sequences, with 2 people performing 8 complete workflows each, we will train on 15 and test on the remaining one. The following results are then averaged over all permutations of this division. When considering classification accuracy we will compare it to the current HMM based state of the art, a pLSA topic model and an unconstrained multi-class SVM.

The HMM based state of the art was developed according to the work of Lyons [25] resulting in a HMM-CFG based activity recognition model. To ensure a fair comparison, the Context Free Grammar (CFG) structure was translated directly from the induced petri-net model. Obviously, the task switching abilities could not be captured by the CFG and each sub-sequence, once started, had to be completed. A separate left-right 5-state HMM was then trained on each identified atomic action with online classification accuracy recorded as the current Viterbi path re-estimation at the given time. This approach has demonstrated accurate classification results in activities ranging from Tai-Chi (69.2% classification, [3]) to workshop construction tasks (66% recall, [23]).

The pLSA-topic model [9, 22], operated over the displacement of objects in the workspace with each k-means clustered value represented as a word, w, and each action identified as a topic, z. For each topic, z_i, we compute $P(w|z_i)$ and when testing an unknown sequence (document, d) identify $z^* = \text{argmax}_z P(z|d)$ according to the procedure described in [9]. For testing, the documents represent a sliding window of duration 0.25 second and is scanned over the workflow sequences with 50% overlap. We will also train a standard Support Vector Machine (SVM) model on the HoPR features to identify the benefits of the complete naive Bayes model (HoPR-NB).

3.1 Classification Accuracy

In testing the current state of the art, the HMM approach performed well for offline classification (77.2%) – given the final Viterbi path re-estimation. However, the task of live user instruction and interaction requires accurate real time online classification so that useful instructions can be given at the appropriate time and not simply after

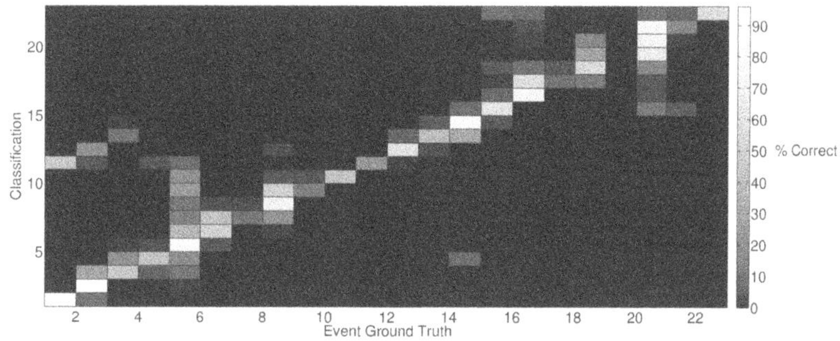

Figure 4: A confusion matrix for the HoPR-NB model.

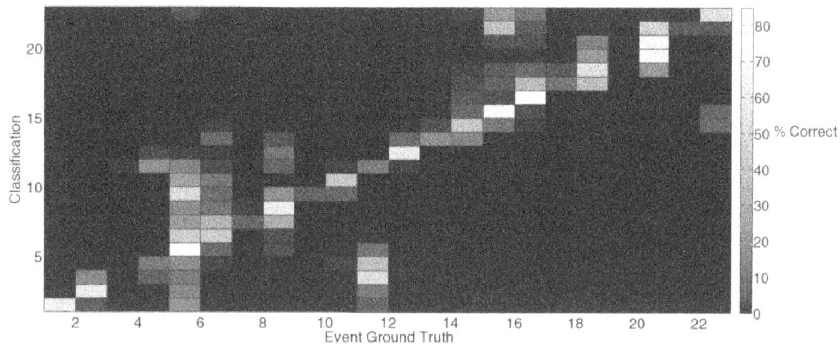

Figure 5: A confusion matrix for the HoPR-SVM model.

Model	Frame-wise accuracy %
Online-HMM:	12.2
pLSA:	36.8
HoPR-SVM:	62.5
HoPR-NB:	70.1

Table 1: Results showing a clear improvement in online performance for our model.

the event. As can be seen in Table 1, the current HMM state of the art deteriorates significantly when the complete workflow remains unknown. Further analysis reveals that the successful exploitation of the CFG requires knowledge of the end point of the sequence. Accordingly, the final re-estimation of the Viterbi path is significantly more accurate than all re-estimations up to that point. By comparison, HoPR-NB outperforms the current state of the art, the unconstrained SVM model (HoPR-SVM) and the alternative pLSA approach for leave-one-out classification accuracy. A significant amount of this improvement is clearly due to the multi-class SVMs operating over the HoPR features. However, results show that further gains can be made through the exploitation of the structural constraints found in the complete HoPR-NB model. We will now consider the nature of these improvements in greater detail.

3.2 Synchronisation Error

Further analysis of these classification results reveals, as shown in Figure 4, that due to the structural constraints of the petri-net the majority of classification errors occur at the transition points from one action to the next. This

Model	Safe%	Predictive%	Erroneous%
HoPR-NB:	11.6	56.3	32.1

Table 2: Results showing safe, predictive and erroneous workflow instructions.

compares favourably to the SVM errors, shown in Figure 5, where clearly nonsensical misclassification errors can be identified. The errors, identified in Figure 4, could be due to uncertainty over the annotation of the ground truth as the exact transition point from one action to the next is a matter of subjective judgement by the human annotators. Figure 4 also illustrates how errors are distributed for different actions, for example there is a wide spread of misclassification for action 5. The remaining errors, confusion between action 1 and action 11 for example, are due to an initial misidentification of the two sub-tasks with sub-task 1 capturing actions 1-10 and subtask 2 actions 11-21. In use, these synchronisation errors should not significantly degrade user experience as they typically result in a slight transition delay from one action to the next. This delay is significantly less intrusive than a clear misclassification.

3.3 Action Prediction Accuracy

The role of synchronisation errors can be further explored when we consider the action prediction accuracy results, Table 2. The majority of user action predictions remain accurate ('Predictive') while a number of predictions are incorrect but simply reinforce the users current state ('Safe'). These 'Safe' predictions are significantly less annoying than the remaining 'Erroneous' predictions, while the 'Predictive'

Occluded objects	HoPR-NB %
Screw driver	66.7
Wood piece:	66.9
Nail baton:	66.9
Hammer:	66.8
Nail box:	66.7
Screw baton:	66.8
Screw box:	66.6
Left wrist:	66.7
Right wrist:	67.1

Table 3: Performance for the HoPR-NB given the complete occlusion of one object.

output results in a successful interaction with the user. In safety critical systems a slight delay in instruction is preferable to a, potentially dangerous, erroneous instruction.

3.4 Occluded Objects

In our unmodified dataset some markers were naturally occluded for a total of 2.37% time steps. To further investigate the robustness of HoPR features to occlusion, we completely occluded each marker in turn for the duration of the workflow. The average performance of complete removal of an individual object in testing sequences for leave-one-out experiment is shown in Table 3.4. As shown by these results, our approach considers the spatio-temporal configurations (pair-wise relations) of objects positioned in 3D space and therefore, a workflow can be recovered even though one of the objects in the workspace is occluded.

4. DISCUSSION

Returning to our specific claims in Section 1, the combined temporal, spatial and structural information allows on-line classification accuracy to be maintained. The induced petri-net structure is human readable and can be edited or adjusted to suit other workflow representations. Live user instruction then consists of presenting the next available action given the current marker configuration. Our second claim is also fulfilled, as compared to the classification accuracy of the unconstrained SVMs, the decisions taken by the complete model result in a higher overall performance. Given only 20mins of training data our model is also robust to sparse training data (claim 4) as the combination of multiple sources of information in the naive Bayes model allows activity detection to take place in scenarios where the production of large training sets remains impractical. Finally, the induced transparent petri-net representation, claims 3 and 5, enable expert domain knowledge to be integrated into the classification and instructional accuracy of the system.

4.1 Future Work

In future work, the role of the petri-net workflow representation will be explored in greater detail. This workflow, and resulting stochastic model, can either be constructed by individuals with expert knowledge of the workflow under consideration or it can be induced from noisy unconstrained action classifications. In initial testing, induction from the results of the unconstrained SVM model proved accurate enough to enable subsequent accurate user instruction. This approach can then be adapted to any activity recognition task that can be formed from multiple independent subtasks. Further work will also have to consider how erroneous subtask transition actions can be accounted for by the petri-net workflow model.

4.2 Conclusion

This paper has considered the current HMM-CFG approach to continuous activity recognition: in previous work a high degree of off-line activity recognition accuracy could be maintained by combining the structural constraints of a CFG with the stochastic classification results of a set of HMMs. However, this approach faces difficulties when confronted with sparse training data, increasingly complex underlying workflow models and the requirement to provide on-line classification results. Accordingly, we have presented an alternative HoPR-NB approach that is capable of accurate on-line classification and can form complex workflow models from a limited set of observations. These workflow models exploit the state based petri-net formalism to maintain a global record of the current workbench configuration. This allows the system to keep track of the user as they switch between multiple independent independent subtasks. This represents an improvement over HMM or CFG approaches to structural knowledge as each is incapable of sustaining multiple simultaneous independent subtasks. Furthermore, as each component of the model is trained offline the combined naive Bayes approach can provide on-line activity classification and user instructions in real-time. Accurate continuous activity recognition is maintained over a wide range of expressive (hammering etc...) and discreet (button pressing, switch flicking) workshop activities, enabling informative live user direction and accurate safety critical monitoring of current workflow activity.

5. ACKNOWLEDGMENTS

The research in this paper is supported by EU under grant ICT-248290 via COGNITO (`www.ict-cognito.org`) project. We thank Dima Damen and Andrew Gee (Department of Computer Science, University of Bristol) for providing the Vicon dataset used in our experiments. We thank Elizabeth Carvalho (Center for Computer Graphics, Portugal) for supplying ground-truth for this dataset.

6. REFERENCES

[1] Vicon systems. `http://www.vicon.com`.

[2] M. Albanese, R. Chellappa, V. Moscato, A. Picariello, V. Subrahmanian, P. Turaga, and O. Udrea. A constrained probabilistic petri net framework for human activity detection in video. *IEEE Transaactions on Multimedia*, 10(8):1429–1443, 2008.

[3] M. Brand, N. Oliver, and A. Pentland. Coupled hidden Markov models for complex action recognition. In *CVPR*, pages 994–999, 1997.

[4] V. Bulitko. Machine learning for time interval Petri nets. *AI 2005: Advances in Artificial Intelligence*, pages 959–965, 2005.

[5] C.-C. Chang and C.-J. Lin. *LIBSVM: a library for support vector machines*, 2001. Software available at `http://www.csie.ntu.edu.tw/~cjlin/libsvm`.

[6] G. David Forney. The Viterbi Algorithm. *Proceedings of the IEEE*, 61(3):268–278, 1973.

[7] B. Hartmann, C. Schauer, and N. Link. Worker behavior interpretation for flexible production. In

World Academy of Science, Engineering and Technology, pages 494–502. CESSE, 2009.
[8] J. Herbst. Workflow mining with InWoLvE. *Computers in Industry*, 53(3):245–264, 2004.
[9] T. Hofmann. Probabilistic latent semantic analysis. In *Proceedings of Uncertainty in Artigicial Intelligence*, pages 22–29, 1999.
[10] T. Huynh and B. Schiele. Analyzing features for activity recognition. In *sOc-EUSAI '05*, New York, New York, USA, 2005. ACM Press.
[11] Y. A. Ivanov and A. F. Bobick. Recognition of visual activities and interactions by stochastic parsing. *IEEE Transactions on Pattern Analysis and Machine Intelligence*, 22(8):852–872, 2000.
[12] N. C. Krishnan and S. Panchanathan. Analysis of low resolution accelerometer data for continuous human activity recognition. In *ICASSP '08.*, pages 3337–3340. IEEE, 2008.
[13] P. Lukowicz, J. Ward, H. Junker, M. Stäger, G. Tröster, A. Atrash, and T. Starner. Recognizing workshop activity using body worn microphones and accelerometers. *Pervasive Computing*, pages 18–32, 2004.
[14] K. Lyons, H. Brashear, T. Westeyn, J. Kim, and T. Starner. GART: The gesture and activity recognition toolkit. In *Proc. of the 12th int. conf. on Human-computer interaction*, pages 718–727. Springer-Verlag, 2007.
[15] T. Murata. Petri nets: Properties, analysis and applications. *Proceedings of the IEEE*, 77(4):541–580, 1989.
[16] L. Rabiner and B. Juang. An introduction to hidden markov models. *ASSP Magazine, IEEE*, 3(1):4–16, 1986.
[17] N. Ravi, N. Dandekar, P. Mysore, and M. Littman. Activity recognition from accelerometer data. In *Proc. of the Nat. Conf. on AI*, volume 20. London; AAAI Press, 2005.
[18] M. Sridhar, A. G. Cohn, and D. C. Hogg. From video to RCC8: Exploiting a distance based semantics to stabilise the interpretation of mereotopological relations. In *COSIT*, 2011.
[19] T. Stiefmeier, G. Ogris, H. Junker, P. Lukowicz, and G. Troster. Combining Motion Sensors and Ultrasonic Hands Tracking for Continuous Activity Recognition in a Maintenance Scenario. *2006 10th IEEE International Symposium on Wearable Computers*, 1:97–104, Oct. 2006.
[20] W. M. P. van der Aalst, B. Vandongen, J. Herbst, L. Maruster, G. Schimm, and a. Weijters. Workflow mining: A survey of issues and approaches. *Data & Knowledge Engineering*, 47(2):237–267, Nov. 2003.
[21] G. Veres, H. Grabner, L. Middleton, and L. Van Gool. Automatic Workflow Monitoring in Industrial Environments. In *Asian Conference on Computer Vision*, pages 1–14, 2010.
[22] X. Wang, X. Ma, and W. E. L. Grimson. Unsupervised activity perception in crowded and complicated scenes using hierarchical bayesian models. *IEEE Trans. PAMI*, 31:539–555, 2009.
[23] J. a. Ward, P. Lukowicz, G. Tröster, and T. E. Starner. Activity recognition of assembly tasks using body-worn microphones and accelerometers. *IEEE transactions on pattern analysis and machine intelligence*, 28(10):1553–67, Oct. 2006.
[24] T. Westeyn, H. Brashear, A. Atrash, T. Starner, and A. Drive. Georgia Tech Gesture Toolkit : Supporting Experiments in Gesture Recognition. In *ICMI '03*, pages 85–92, 2003.
[25] S. Young. HTK: Hidden Markov Model Toolkit: Design and philosophy.
[26] D. Zuehlke. Smartfactory – from vision to reality in factory technologies. In *Proceedings of the 17th International Federation of Automatic Control*, pages 82–89, 1997.

JerkTilts: Using Accelerometers for Eight-Choice Selection on Mobile Devices

Mathias Baglioni
Télécom ParisTech - LTCI-CNRS – Alcatel Lucent Bell Labs
46 rue Barrault
75013 Paris, FRANCE
mathias.baglioni@telecom-paristech.fr

Eric Lecolinet
Télécom ParisTech - LTCI-CNRS
46 rue Barrault
75013 Paris, FRANCE
eric.lecolinet@telecom-paristech.fr

Yves Guiard
Télécom ParisTech - LTCI-CNRS
46 rue Barrault
75013 Paris, FRANCE
yves.guiard@telecom-paristech.fr

ABSTRACT
This paper introduces JerkTilts, quick back-and-forth gestures that combine device pitch and roll. JerkTilts may serve as gestural self-delimited shortcuts for activating commands. Because they only depend on device acceleration and rely on a parallel and independent input channel, these gestures do not interfere with finger activity on the touch screen. Our experimental data suggest that recognition rates in an eight-choice selection task are as high with JerkTilts as with thumb slides on the touch screen. We also report data confirming that JerkTilts can be combined successfully with simple touch-screen operation. Data from a field study suggest that inadvertent JerkTilts are unlikely to occur in real-life contexts. We describe three illustrative implementations of JerkTilts, which show how the technique helps to simplify and shorten the sequence of actions to reach frequently used commands.

Categories and Subject Descriptors
H5.2 [Information interfaces and presentation]: User Interfaces. - Input devices and strategies

General Terms
Design, Human Factors.

Keywords
Interaction techniques, mobile interaction, 3D motion gestures, self-delimited gestures, Marking menu, sensors.

1. INTRODUCTION
Suppose you want to quickly check on your smartphone whether a certain email is there, but you are wearing gloves or for some reason your fingers are greasy. Since the only thing the device can understand is a sequence of touches performed by a bare and reasonably clean fingertip, you are stuck for a moment. JerkTilts, the input technique we are introducing in this paper, would avoid you that frustration. In essence a JerkTilt is a quick, jerky to-and-fro rotation of the device, which works as a one-step gestural shortcut, making it possible to directly access a command from a small set of favorites with no reason to care about mode—because a JerkTilt is a self-delimiting gesture.

ICMI'11, November 14–18, 2011, Alicante, Spain.
Copyright 2011 ACM 978-1-4503-0641-6/11/11...$10.00.

A standard PC has both a keyboard, with some special modifying keys designed to be used in parallel, and at least one pointing device equipped with a number of state buttons. One severe shortcoming of commercially available smartphones, in comparison with PCs, is that they essentially rely on a single input channel: the touch screen. These devices can be carried away because they have been made small, but the inevitable cost is an impoverishment of their input equipment.

However, thanks to onboard technology (accelerometers and gyroscopes) for detecting self 3D-motion, smartphones can also make use of another input channel with no fewer than six degrees of freedom (three translations, three rotations) [18]. Unfortunately, tilts are often indistinguishable from everyday motions (e.g., walking) and often need a delimiter. In response to this difficulty a solution consists in using a specific motion gesture, such as DoubleFlip [21], which acts as a delimiter for other motion gestures. Our option is to merge the gestural command and its delimiters. The JerkTilts technique involves a set of *self-delimiting* gestures, which avoids the need for explicit delimiters. Because JerkTilts consist of abrupt back-and-forth movements whose kinematic signature is unique, inadvertent activations are very unlikely.

The JerkTilts technique rests on rotations of hand-held devices. Unlike a device translation, often impracticable in many public situations, a rotation of the device about itself requires minimal workspace. Also, provided that angular amplitudes are moderate, the screen of a rotating device may remain visible for users, enabling them, when necessary, to receive output information. Using tilts gestures has also the advantage to be performable one-handedly [23]. This is an important factor in the context of mobility since the second hand is often reserved for an alternate use (carrying a bag, holding the subway handrail, etc.). Finally, partitioning 360° into eight angular sectors is an easy matter for the human cognition, which has a familiar name for each sector (East, North-East, etc.). Eight-item angular selection has for instance been repeatedly proven to be reliable with hand gestures in the context of Marking menus [13].

The two experiments to be reported below investigated the workability for command or item selection of quick, jerky rotations of a smartphone. We will also report the data of an experiment that investigated the usability of JerkTilts in the context of everyday life, paying special attention to the problem of inadvertent command activation. In a final section we will present three applications that take advantage of JerkTilts. These implementations are illustrations of the fact that JerkTilts is fully compatible with standard applications and can enhance interaction on mobile devices by providing eyes-free and quick shortcuts commands.

2. RELATED WORK

3D-gesture interaction on mobile devices is possible thanks to sensors like accelerometers, which are low-cost micro electro-mechanical (MEM) systems. Accelerometers report the accelerations of the device they are embedded in, allowing the recording of translational motion. They can also be used to determine the absolute orientation of a motionless device. Indeed, by analyzing the projection of the constant gravity acceleration on the three axes, it is possible to determine pitch and roll orientations (Figure 1). However, accelerometers do not allow the determination of static yaw orientation [7].

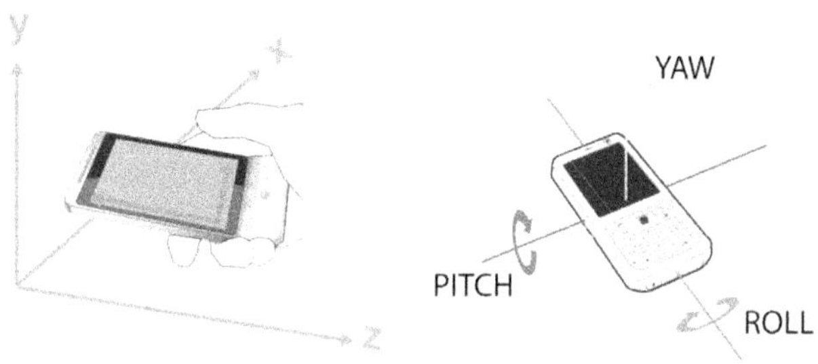

Figure 1. Left: the motion space of the device (in blue) and on the device screen (in red). Right: the three axes of rotation of the device, relative to its own coordinate system.

As argued by Kauppila [11], real-time recognition of complex gestures used to be difficult on mobile device due to shortage of computing power, but things are rapidly improving. Due to their earlier appearance on commercial products, to date accelerometers have been more widely used for interaction than alternative sensors. Smooth device tilts have been mainly considered so far [17]. The problem is that weak acceleration signals from slow gestures may be difficult to distinguish from background noise, this resulting in involuntary activations. In practice, smooth tilts can hardly be used for issuing commands in the absence of a discrete validation act because, for a typical user, handheld orientation is highly variable and essentially unpredictable. Combinations of button presses and gestures have been considered as a way to solve this problem in a number of studies, particularly to make it possible to identify the start and end of gestures [14][15][24]. The JerkTilts technique avoids these problems by relying on strong acceleration signals. The need for motion gesture delimiters hence vanishes, thus providing for self-delimiting commands.

Rahman et al. [17] evaluated the dexterity of users asked to tilt a device using just the wrist. These authors showed that up to 16 different angular sectors could be recognized by the system and provided guidelines for one-handed mobile tilting interaction. However the gestures considered in the Rahman et al. study were relatively slow tilts of the device, and they were dependent on visual control.

Oakley and Park [14] evaluated device tilting for activating commands in a Marking menu and reported that recognition rates were better with single-step rather than multiple-step selection. With TiltType [15], device tilts served for text entry on a wrist-watch-like device, a physical button working as a gestural-mode controller. The authors evaluated the incidence of inadvertent activation due to background noise in a traveling bus, offering solutions based on signal filtering. With TiltText [24] device tilts were also combined with a key press to allow text entry on a mobile phone. Examples of tilting the device for menu navigation or scrolling were offered in [6] and [18]. We must also mention TimeTilt [20] for navigation among applications: smooth tilts were used for novice-mode navigation where the user needs to look at the screen. The paper also reported using jerks along the longitudinal axis of the handheld to quickly reach the previous/next opened application with a backward/ forward jerk.

Previous work that considered dynamic tilts involves [3], [4], [21] et [22]. As already mentioned, DoubleFlip [21] is a specific motion gesture that acts as a delimiter for other motion gestures. [22] and [4] are dedicated to text entry, a different purpose than ours. More specifically [4] investigated four different input modalities, screen touch, device tilt, speech, and foot tap: if touch-screen interaction produced the highest throughput for text entry, the tilting technique was fastest for making a selection. Finally, four-directional gestures were used in [3] for interacting between mobile phones and distant displays but this short paper does not provide an evaluation nor a precise analysis of the gestures that were actually used.

Other research has been conducted on gestural interaction but much of it is irrelevant to mobile devices (for example Gestext [9]). New kinds of gestures have been proposed that are in fact inapplicable to a mobility context, like for example [19]. That is also true of commercial products. The Wii, the Wiimote, and the Kinect platform have familiarized game players with new ways of interacting with gestures. But these large amplitude gestures can hardly be performed out of the living room, as they will interfere with the physical as well as social environment. Small-amplitude rotations like those used in JerkTilts are more compatible with the social and physical constraints of the usual environment [2].

3. THE JERKTILTS TECHNIQUE: CONCEPT AND IMPLEMENTATION

The JerkTilts technique involves quick, short-extent tilting gestures that rely on various combinations of device roll and device pitch (Figure 2 presents each gesture relative to the rest position).

One important characteristic of a JerkTilt gesture is that it consists of one complete cycle of to-and-fro movement: the device is tilted in a certain direction and immediately brought back to its initial rest position thanks to the natural elasticity of the wrist. The return phase of such movements is quite automatic, the mechanical energy stored as elastic potential energy in the antagonist muscles of the forearm during the initial tilt being converted back into kinetic energy during the return to rest [10]. This helps understand why the spontaneous execution of this sort of movement takes remarkably little time and costs remarkably little effort.

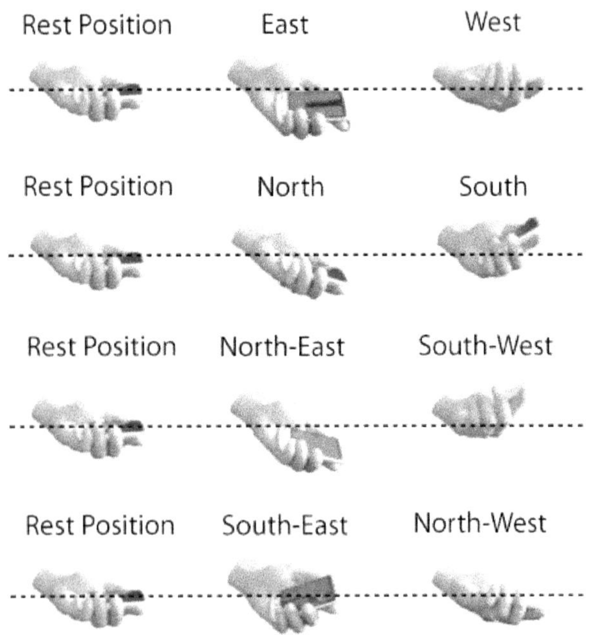

Figure 2. The eight quick back-and-forth tilting directions relative to rest position.

Eight different directions, obtained by various combinations of device roll and pitch, can be differentiated by users and discriminated by the system. JerkTilts are not exclusive of touch-screen interaction. They are respectful of the social context and require little 3D space. Perhaps most importantly, they can be performed eyes free.

We evaluated the gestural technique in three steps, detailed below. Experiment 1 asked about the discriminability of tilting directions, paying special attention to between-individual variability. No feedback was given to participants on recognition of the gesture by the system. Not only did we need to record the tilting movements that the participants would judge representative of the eight specified directions, but our recognizer (detailed below) required a pre-existing gestural database. Recognition could thus only be performed post hoc, based on a sufficient sample of gestures from participants. Thus the goal of Experiment 1 was both to evaluate to what extent users were able to realize the specified gestures in the absence of system feedback, and to build a learning base for our gesture recognizer.

We used a K-Nearest-Neighbors algorithm for automatic gesture recognition [12]. K was empirically fixed to 5, a value that turned out to be optimal—in fact, the KNN algorithm is pretty stable and the setting of K affects the results only to a marginal extent, provided that the K value is reasonably small relative to the number of data points representing each class in the database. A six-dimension vector, Euclidean distance serving to compute the distance between pairs of data points, characterized each gesture.

The six dimensions were based on the measurement of acceleration during a complete to-and-fro gestural cycle. As soon as the device left its neutral position with an acceleration of at least $4m/s^2$, we started to record accelerations. The dimensions of the vector were the following:

- Peak of acceleration on the X axis (positive or negative)
- Peak of acceleration on the Y axis (positive or negative)
- Mean of accelerations on the X axis
- Mean of accelerations on the Y axis
- Median of accelerations on the X axis
- Median of accelerations on the Y axis

These six dimensions, which were chosen empirically, provide a concise but efficient signature of a gesture. Using just the peak values proved insufficient. The median and the mean values during a gesture, which summarize the entire set of its acceleration values, turned out to be effective for improving recognition. While complementary dimensions may further improve recognition, they would also require more computation time, especially for computing distances (the KNN algorithm, at least in its standard version, compares the sample to be recognized to all the samples of the learning base). Our six dimensions signature hence seems to offer a reasonable compromise between computation speed and recognition accuracy.

Finally, in order to avoid wrong detections, the gesture had to be performed in a small enough amount of time. As JerkTilts are quick back-and-forth gestures, this means that the device must be turned back to its (approximate) initial position in less than 500ms. The gesture was otherwise ignored and had no effect.

Experiment 2, which focused on an eyes-free task, aimed at comparing the performance of device tilts vs. thumb motion on the touch screen (i.e., as in Marking menus [13], a technique that is notoriously efficient and served here as a baseline). Contrary to Experiment 1, here each gesture was followed by recognition feedback, as would happen in real life applications where the user normally knows if (s)he has successfully performed the desired command.

Another difference is that the recognition algorithm was then run in adaptive mode. A personal learning base was created for each user. This learning base initially contained all the gestures collected during Experiment 1, except a few outliers, which were manually removed. Then, each time the user performed a correct gesture, it would be added to its own personal learning base. This simple algorithm enabled the recognition system to adapt to the specific gestural repertoire of each user. Such an algorithm makes sense in the context of mobile interaction because smartphones are essentially personal devices—it does not prevent other people from using the device, but it improves performance for the device owner.

Two improvements were added to this adaptive algorithm. First, when recognition results seemed good enough we stopped adding new gestures to the learning base not to excessively raise the recognition computing time, which depends on the number of gestures in the learning base. Second, it appeared that South-East and North-East gestures are more difficult to perform and recognize than other gestures. The previous algorithm does not work well in this case: as "difficult gestures" tend to be poorly recognized (especially when the learning base has not been personalized yet), very few of them would be added to the personal learning base, so that the learning base would never adapt to this sort of gestures. This would result in an unbalanced database, containing a small percentage of difficult gesture samples. The adaptive algorithm would then decrease performance for these gestures instead of improving their recognition.

We used an heuristic approach to solve this problem: wrongly recognized samples of difficult gestures are added to the learning base if they are close enough to a sample of the expected gesture that is already in the database ("closeness" here corresponds to the number of votes of the KNN algorithm). In other words, we forced the algorithm to consider some wrong gestures as correct, which helped it to learn the user's more or less unique way of making difficult gestures.

We also developed a simple self-calibration mechanism that allowed users to perform the gesture from any arbitrarily chosen hand position. This mechanism just consisted in resetting the neutral point after a stationary episode of at least 200ms. Hence, users were asked neither to hold their device slanted at a specific angle nor to reposition it in Experiment 2 (this mechanism was not used in Experiment 1, aimed at collecting raw gestures).

Finally, in a third experiment, we asked about the inadvertent activation of the gestures. For this purpose we developed a logging system for evaluating whether accidental accelerations of the device could lead to false identifications of JerkTilt gestures.

4. EXPERIMENT 1: SMALL JERKY DEVICE ROTATIONS

We wished to get a first sense of the extent to which a set of eight different back-and-forth rotations of the handheld device induced by fast, short-amplitude hand movements mainly involving the wrist could be correctly performed by users. As explained above, no error feedback was given to participants, as the recognition algorithm could not be used at this stage. Another question we were interested in was whether users could perform back-and-forth rotations with the same accuracy with the thumb maintained in contact with the screen.

In this experiment the visual stimulus indicating the particular tilt that had to be produced appeared on the smartphone screen so that the participants permanently fixated the device. The participants were asked to start with the device slanted horizontally as the self-calibration mechanism was not used during this experiment. The purpose of this experiment was to see how users would naturally perform such gestures and to create a gesture database for the recognition algorithm used in Experiment 2.

4.1 Method

4.1.1 Equipment

We used an HTC Hero device running Android 2.1, with a 3.5', 320x480pixel touch screen. The software was developed in Java with the Google Android API. The participant were comfortably seated, handling the device in their right hand—all our participants were right-handed and all happened to manipulate the smartphone with that hand.

4.1.2 Task and conditions

Each trial consisted of the participant performing, in response to a visual stimulus (Figure 3), one of the eight possible tilts resulting from differing combinations of pitch and roll motion (for example, as in Figure 2, a counter-clockwise roll produced by wrist supination was labeled "West", and the same roll component combined with an upward or downward pitch produced a tilt that was labeled "N-W" or "S-W", respectively, etc.).

The participants were to perform the gestures either with or without the thumb in contact with the screen. The device had to be brought back to its horizontal orientation after each tilt, horizontality being signaled by a grey square appearing at screen center. The trial was validated by a terminal thumb tap (or a thumb release in the thumb-on condition), which triggered the presentation of the next stimulus.

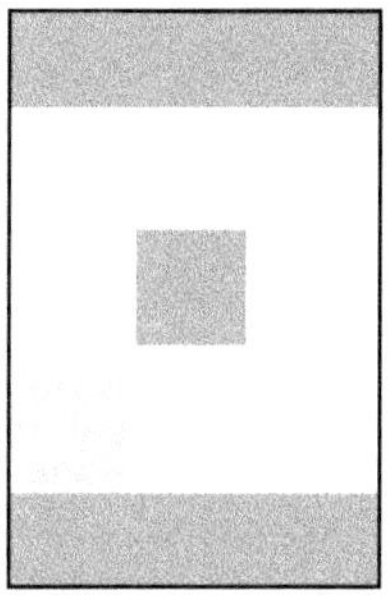

Figure 3. The stimulus is displayed as a green square. The central gray square appears when the device is horizontal..

4.1.3 Procedure

After some warm up terminated by the participant's decision that (s)he felt familiar enough with the task, four 32-trial blocks were run, each composed of four occurrences of each of the eight possible directions. Twelve adult volunteers (all right-handed, ten male) participated in a single 15-min session. We used a within-participant design, with 2 postural conditions x (8 gestural directions x 4 times a block) x 4 blocks = 256 individual movements per participant.

4.1.4 Recognition Algorithm

A K-nearest-neighbors algorithm [12] was used for automatic gesture classification after the experiment. The data of even-numbered blocks were reserved for algorithm training, the remaining blocks serving for recognition. Each individual data set was submitted to the algorithm twice, after training with the data of all but this particular participant (group training) and after training with the participant's own data (participant-specific training).

4.1.5 Results and Discussions

Recognition rates were fairly high, especially with the participant-specific training algorithm (Figure 4). The hand-posture factor (thumb on/off the screen) exerted no significant effect ($F_{1,11}<1$) neither did it interact with training type ($F_{1,11}<1$). This means that the thumb can safely be used as a mode controller to enrich the gestural input vocabulary.

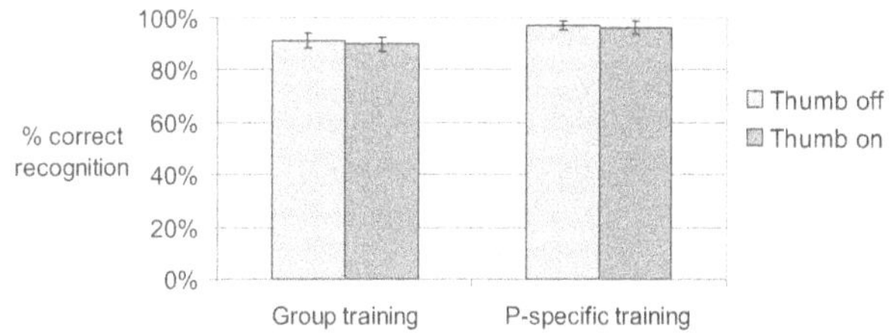

Figure 4. Offline recognition rate for group and participant-specific training with the thumb off/on the touchscreen. Error bars are confidence intervals based on between-participant standard deviations.

As expected, the recognition rates were consistently higher with participant-specific training ($F_{1,11}$=33.90, p<.0001), presumably a reflection of subtle individual idiosyncrasies in the making of gestures. This result confirms the improved efficiency of recognition algorithms that adapt themselves to the user. Another interesting result is that recognition rates remained just as high with the thumb in contact with the screen, a promising outcome, as will become apparent later in this paper.

5. EXPERIMENT 2: DEVICE TILTS VS. THUMB MARKING

This experiment exploited the database built in Experiment 1, with the participants now receiving immediate feedback after each gesture on how the tilt had been classified by the system. As explained in section 3 the recognition algorithm was run in adaptive mode, so that recognition accuracy would improve with practice. JerkTilts were however evaluated in a more realistic and more challenging setting than in Experiment 1. Participants had no indication of device orientation. Instead a self-calibration mechanism was triggered whenever the device, no matter its orientation, remained stationary for 200ms. Device rotations being now relative, the participants no longer had to start the gesture from the horizontal.

Another important difference was that all gestures had to be carried out eyes-free in Experiment 2. The system recognition feedback that followed each gesture was presented away from the smartphone, on a vertical screen facing the participant at usual viewing distance (about 50 cm) (Figure 5). The participants were actually not allowed to look at the mobile device during this experiment. This setting mimicked the case of users interacting with an application without looking at the device (typically a music player while walking or running).

Selection performance was evaluated with device tilts in comparison with Marking menus [13], that is to say thumb slides on the device touchscreen. Marking menus, which are notoriously efficient, are here used as a baseline. The rationale was to compare the efficiency of the two sorts of motion (3D motion vs. 2D on-screen motion) for making an eight-item radial selection.

Figure 5. Feedback delivered on an external screen after a selection classified by the system as correct (left) and incorrect (right). The arrow indicates the intended tilt direction.

5.1 Method

We used the same HTC Hero device as in Experiment 1, but now the output came from an external 22' screen (Figure 5) placed at a distance of about 50 cm. The stimulus was an arrow appearing over a square whose color varied. It was initially displayed in grey and turned green in response to a correct selection (Figure 5, left). Following an error the square would remain grey, the response recognized by the system being then shown as a red square (Figure 5, right), and the movement had to be made again. The smartphone and the participant's hand were out of sight.

5.1.1 Procedure

Twelve adults volunteers (all right-handed, one female) participated in a single 25min session. After some warm up, each participant ran ten 32-trial blocks with each technique, each block requiring four times each of the eight different movements in a random order. Participants held the device in their right hand, the preferred option for all.

Unsurprisingly, since we used an adaptive algorithm, data inspection revealed several blocks were needed for performance to stabilize. We thus decided to discard the first three trial blocks as warm up. Our within-participant design thus involved 2 techniques x (8 directions x 4 times per block) x 7 blocks = 448 gestures per participant overall.

5.1.2 Results and Discussions

Our dependent variables were recognition rate and total selection time (TT), the latter representing the sum of a reaction time (RT) and a movement time (MT). Below we will leave aside the negligible amount of time taken by the algorithm for input processing, which never exceeded 50ms.

Concerning performance accuracy, on average the recognition rates (Figure 6) were similar, 91.0% and 92.6%, for the JerkTilts and the thumb slides ($F_{1,11}$<1). The only significant effect for this dependent measure was movement direction ($F_{7,77}$=2.25, p<.04), an effect common to both technique (for the interaction, $F_{7,77}$=1.41, p>.2). The direction effect was consistent but quite small in the absolute, mean recognition rates revolving around a pretty acceptable 92%.

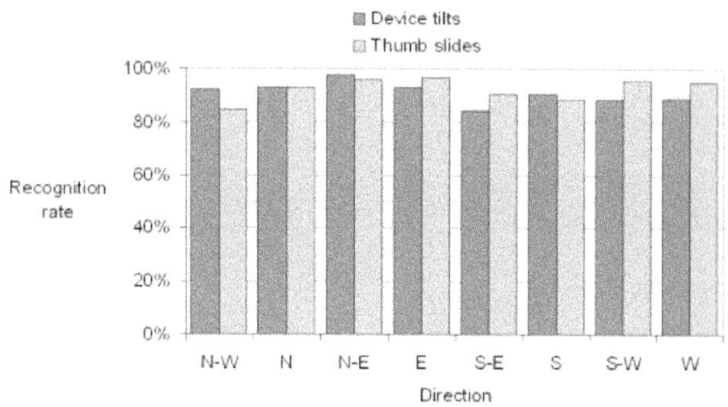

Figure 6. Mean recognition rate for the two techniques and the eight directions.

Concerning performance speed, it took participants on average 936ms and 707ms to prepare and perform a JerkTilt and a thumb slide respectively ($F_{1,11}$=8.19, p<.02), as illustrated in Figure 7. Mean MT was shorter with the tilts (177.2ms vs. 211.3ms) but not significantly so (p>.05). On RT the difference was in the opposite direction (694.8ms vs. 494.9ms) and it was significant ($F_{1,11}$=19.8,p<.001).

There was a significant technique x direction interaction on TT ($F_{7,77}$=2.44, p<.03) (Figure 7): unsurprisingly, the fastest directions were not exactly the same for the two kinds of gestures. For example, the South direction was somewhat favorable to the thumb and somewhat unfavorable to the tilts.

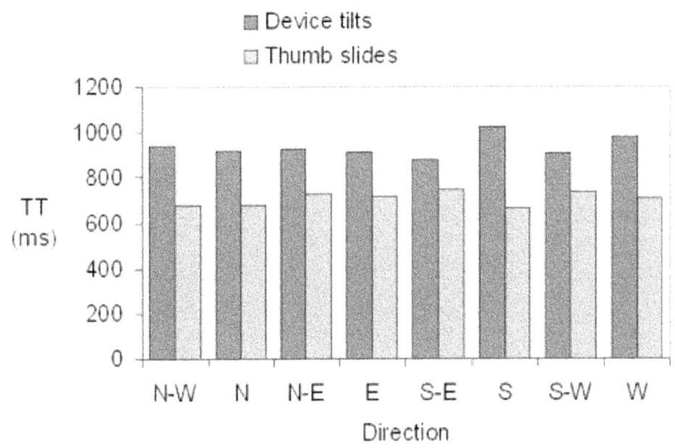

Figure 7. Mean total selection time for the two techniques and the eight directions.

A major advantage of JerkTilt gestures is that they do not interfere with finger activity on the touch screen, where slide gestures typically serve to scroll views or drag objects. This is obviously not the case for Marking menus which rely on the same input resource as standard interactions. Mouse-based interfaces provide interaction states [1] that allow solving this problem (e.g. by pressing a modifier key or the right mouse button). But passive touch screens used on smartphones do not provide this capability. Hence, an actual implementation of a Marking menu on a smartphone would require waiting for a delay or activating a software or hardware button first (the only other option being to forbid standard interactions). This is likely to make JerkTilts more convenient to use, and possibly faster, than Marking menus. However, JerkTilts were not designed to replace Marking menus: both techniques can cohabit, hence enriching the interaction capabilities, and they can even be combined, as proposed in the conclusion.

Marking menus were taken as a reference baseline in this study because of their well-known efficiency. However, it is interesting to notice that the Marking menus condition produced more errors than what was generally observed in previous studies. This result, which is consistent with those of [5], comes from the fact that the device was operated using only one hand (the thumb serving for interacting). Such an observation seems relevant as many users routinely operate the touch screen with the thumb of their holding hand.

In our experiment performance was eyes-free, which entails an error cost for both techniques. Such a condition might look harsh, but it is far from being unrealistic on a mobile device, especially for activating shortcuts (e.g. launching a given application or rapidly switching from one to another).

6. EXPERIMENT 3: REAL-WORLD LOGGING

We finally conducted an experiment with permanent logging of all accelerations of a mobile device to evaluate the workability of JerkTilts in the context of real-life mobility. Even if JerkTilts are performable we want them to be actually practicable without jeopardizing other input resources. Our main concern was the false positive, the misinterpretation of an involuntary acceleration as a JerkTilt.

We developed a logging system and recorded all acceleration signals from the device during twenty-four hours of normal use (but not when phone was in sleep mode). We sent e-mail to recruit volunteers, attaching the application package to install and instructions on a PDF document. Fourteen users accepted to apply for the experiment (12 using their own phone and 2 using our device, a HTC Hero). The application logged every acceleration of the device and after twenty-four hours of recording proposed to users to send the data files by FTP. To preserve anonymousness users were able if they wished to ask for the destruction of their data once analyzed.

Table 1. Mean false detection and awake time.

	Mean	95% confidence interval	
False Detections	0.7	0.02	1.4
Awake Time (min)	665	340	992

On average we found only 0.7 false detections a day per user, for an average awake time (i.e., with phone logging) of 665 minutes (Table 1, Figure 8). This result suggests that JerkTilts are suitable for everyday use. We were not surprised by this outcome, because, as already mentioned, a JerkTilt is by definition a jerky sort of gesture that generates quite conspicuous accelerations signals.

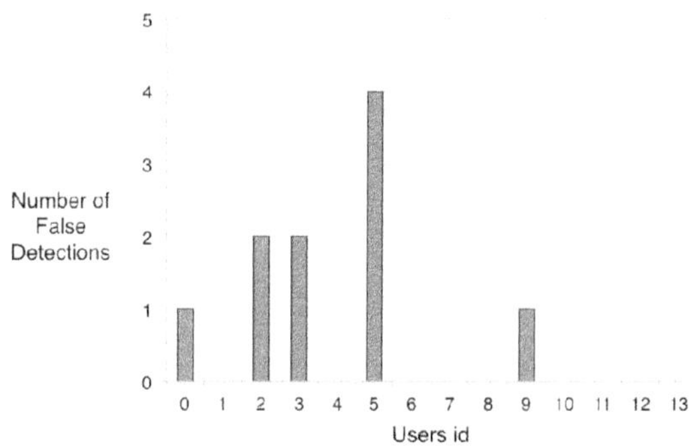

Figure 8. Number of false positives per participant over the 24h real-world logging period.

We plan to conduct a more extensive long-term study to confirm these results and to study how users perform in various real-world conditions, including public transportation, which impose constraints on attention and gesturing space.

7. SOME APPLICATIONS OF THE JERKTILTS CONCEPT

Various applications can benefit from JerkTilts. In general it is possible with 3D gestures to design gestural commands that do not interfere with standard on-screen interaction and do not require standard menu widgets. Moreover, recourse to gestures allows eyes-free commands to be triggered easily. The concept of proprioception itself encourages gestures for one-handed interaction, users being well aware of the spatial location and the posture of their hand, and hence of the location and orientation of the device they are holding. These gestures, we believe, enjoy a light cognitive load.

We have started to design and develop three sorts of exploitation of JerkTilts. One, JerkTilts Window, takes place at the *system* level and is conditional upon thumb contact to minimize the risk of false detections. The other two, JerkTilts Copy&Paste and JerkTilts Music Remote, take place at the *application* level

7.1 JerkTilts Window

JerkTilts Window is a technique for quickly switching between application windows on a mobile. We have developed two different versions, one for navigating within the set of currently opened applications, and the other for navigating among favorite applications. With these implementations one can easily switch applications, as suggested in Figure 9. One sensible option is to minimize the risk of false detections at the system level by making JerkTilts conditional on thumb contact on the touch screen.

Figure 9. An example of an implementation of JerkTilts for switching among applications.

This application reduces the actual sequence of action a user has to face on commercial mobile devices to switch to another application. In the state of the art, switching between application requires at least two actions: clicking a button (often with a delay or a double-click for instance) then selecting the correct application. To open a favorite application one typically needs to first return to the home screen and then select the application.

In the same vein, JerkTilts can be used to easily reach previously saved favorite bookmarks in a web browser application. Users will be in a better position to concentrate on and interact with the page they are looking at if access to their favorite web pages does not require navigation through a list of thumbnails or a classic menu interface.

7.2 JerkTilts Copy and Paste

We have implemented a version of JerkTilts that makes it possible to copy and paste an object between two different applications in a three-step sequence: (1) copy an object, (2) switch applications, and (3) paste the object. For example, one may copy an image from a web page to another application as shown in Figure 10. In comparison with the complex manipulations required on current smartphones, with delays and/or multiple pointing actions, this would significantly reduce user actions.

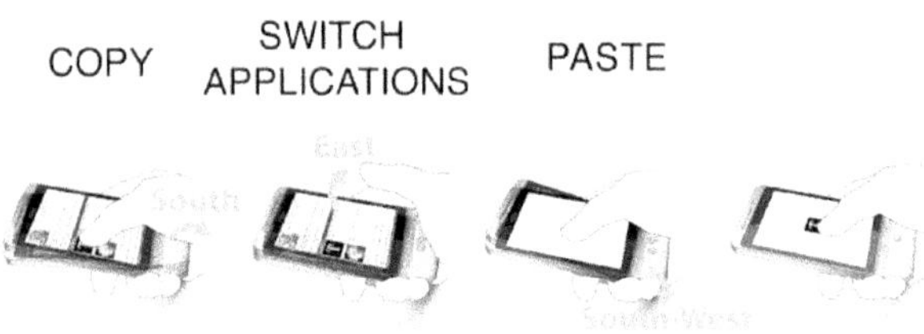

Figure 10. An example of a copy-and-paste operation between two different applications. A JerkTilt to the South copies whatever object is under the thumb; a JerkTilt to the East switches applications; a JerkTilt to the South-West pastes the object at the location designated by thumb contact.

7.3 JerkTilts Music Remote

We have developed two versions of the technique for controlling a music player eyes-free. One version makes it possible to control the player of a laptop, the smartphone playing the role of a remote control. In the other version JerkTilts serves to control music playing on the mobile device itself, with the advantage that the user can still control the music when the device is locked. In either version the gestures are mapped onto the commands as shown in Figure 11. The suggested layout of commands is consistent with the old conventional arrangement for sound players. The most frequently used commands correspond to the four cardinal directions because the gestures they require are easiest to make for users.

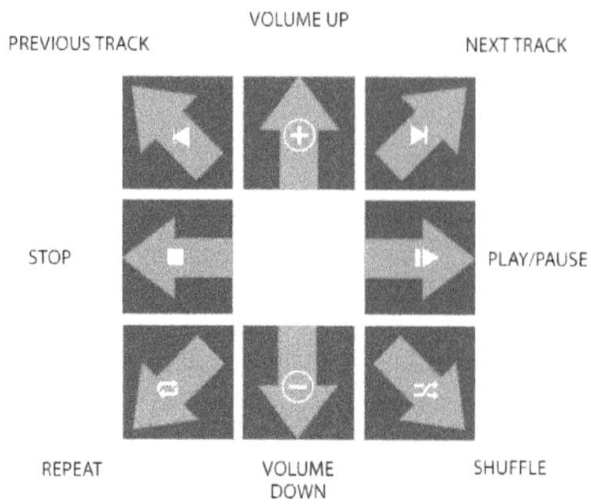

Figure 11. Association between gestures and music player commands.

The version we have developed to control the music player of a laptop relies on AppleScript and iTunes. This application could easily be adapted to video players.

8. CONCLUSIONS AND FUTURE WORK

JerkTilts are quick back-and-forth device tilts that can be performed eyes free, relying on fast open-loop control and leveraging the natural elasticity of the wrist. They actually do not require any resetting of device orientation and they need not start from a horizontal orientation. No mode-switching button presses are required with JerkTilts, these input gestures being self-delimiting. Therefore they do not interfere with common interaction techniques based on touch screen events and they can serve as gestural shortcuts in most application contexts (one obvious exception being games that involve 3D gestures). The JerkTilts technique requires little space because the motion consists of an essentially stationary rotation of the handheld device. The gestures are discrete, thanks to their short duration and amplitude, meaning that JerkTilts should be practicable is most social contexts. And because the technique relies on large amplitude acceleration signals, it is well immune to the risk of inadvertent false detections.

In this paper we reported some performance data illustrating the efficiency of JerkTilts in a laboratory selection task. Our participants were able to make eight-item selections as accurately with JerkTilts as with touch-screen slide movements using the thumb, and nearly as fast (not taking into account that the latter technique may in fact require an activation step). We also showed that JerkTilts can be as efficiently performed with the thumb either on or off the touch screen, meaning the thumb may be used in combination with JerkTilts.

We developed three applications that illustrate how the JerkTilt gestures can be exploited. By reducing the number of steps required to express highly-frequent commands, these applications alleviate some tricky interaction problems that have been a real concern so far for mobile users.

Designing efficient methods for the parallel exploitation of finger motion on touch screens (leveraging the opportunities offered by multi-touch technologies) and device motion in 3D space is quite an important challenge in HCI research [8]. In the future we plan to perform a long-term field study so as to extend our first data about false detections. We also envision using a gyroscope to and alternative recognition algorithms to enhance gesture recognition. We also want to go further in the exploitation of JerkTilts. Of special interest, we believe, are combinations of JerkTilts and on-screen marking thumb gestures, which leverage the complementary advantages of the two techniques. While JerkTilts allows quick activation of discrete commands, marking gestures can be very useful to control continuous values as shown in [16].

9. ACKNOWLEDGMENTS

This work was funded by Ubimedia, a joint research laboratory of Alcatel-Lucent Bell Labs and Institut Telecom. We thank Johann Daigremont, Patrick Legrand, Bruno Legat and Sylvain Malacria for valuable discussions. We thank anonymous reviewers for thoughtful criticisms and constructive suggestions.

10. REFERENCES

[1] Bragdon A., Nelson E., Li Y., Hinckley K. 2011. Experimental Analysis of Touch-Screen Gesture Designs in Mobile Environments. In Proc. CHI'11.

[2] Crossan A., Williamson J., Brewster S., Murray-Smith. R 2008. Wrist rotation for interaction in mobile contexts. In Proc. MobileHCI '08. ACM, 435-438.

[3] Dachselt, R., Buchholz, R. 2008. Natural Throw and Tilt Interaction between Mobile Phones and Distant Displays. In Proc. CHI '09 Extended Abstracts.

[4] Dearman, D., Karlson, A., Meyers, B., and Bederson, B. 2010. Multi-modal text entry and selection on a mobile device. In Proc GI'10.

[5] Francone, J., Bailly, G., Lecolinet, E., Mandran, N., and Nigay, L. 2010. Wavelet menus on handheld devices: stacking metaphor for novice mode and eyes-free selection for expert mode. In Proc. AVI'10. ACM.

[6] Harrison, B. L., Fishkin, K. P., Gujar, A., Mochon, C.,Want, R. 1998. Squeeze me, hold me, tilt me! An exploration of manipulative user interfaces. In Proc. CHI'98, ACM 17-24.

[7] Hinckley, K., Pierce, J., Sinclair, M., and Horvitz, E. 2000. Sensing techniques for mobile interaction. In Proc. UIST'00. ACM, 91-100.

[8] Hinckley K., Song H., 2011. Sensor Synaesthesia: Touch in Motion, and Motion in Touch. In Proc. CHI'11. ACM.

[9] Jones, E., Alexander, J., Andreou, A., Irani, P., and Subramanian, S. 2010. GesText: accelerometer-based gestural text-entry systems. In Proc. CHI '10. ACM. 2173-2182.

[10] Guiard, Y. 1993. On Fitts' and Hooke's laws : simple harmonic movement in upper-limb cyclical aiming. Acta Psychologica, 82, 139-159.

[11] Kauppila M. 2008. Filler Models for Accelerometer Based Continuous Gesture Recognition. Sc.Thesis, Dept. of Mathematical Sciences, University of Oulu, May 2008.

[12] KNN: http://en.wikipedia.org/wiki/K_nearest_neighbor_algorithm

[13] Kurtenbach, G. and Buxton, W. 1991. Issues in combining marking and direct manipulation techniques. In Proc UIST '91. ACM, 137-144.

[14] Oakley, I. and Park, J. 2007. A motion-based mark-ing menu system. In Proc. CHI'07. ACM, New York, NY, 2597-2602.

[15] Partridge, K., Chatterjee, S., Sazawal, V., Borriello, G., and Want, R. 2002. TiltType: accelerometer-supported text entry for very small devices. In Proc. UIST '02. ACM.

[16] Pook, S., Lecolinet, E., Vaysseix, G., and Barillot, E. 2000. Context and interaction in zoomable user interfaces. In Proc. AVI '00. ACM, 227-231.

[17] Rahman, M., Gustafson, S., Irani, P., and Subrama-nian, S. 2009. Tilt techniques: investigating the dex-terity of wrist-based input. In Proc. CHI'09. ACM, 1943-1952.

[18] Rekimoto, J. (1996). Tilting operations for small screen interfaces. In Proc. UIST '96. ACM, 167-168.

[19] Rehm, M., Nikolaus, B., and André, E. 2008. Wave like an Egyptian: accelerometer based gesture recognition for culture specific interactions. In Proc. BCS-HCI '08, Vol. 1. British Computer Society, 13-22.

[20] Roudaut A., Baglioni M. et Lecolinet E. 2009. TimeTilt: Using Sensor-Based Gestures to Travel Through Multiple Applications on a Mobile Device. In Proc. INTERACT'09. Springer-Verlag.

[21] Ruiz J., Li Y. 2011 DoubleFlip: A Motion Gesture Delimiter for Mobile Interaction. In Proc. CHI '11. ACM.

[22] Sazawal, V., Want, W., and Borriello, G. 2002. The Unigesture Approach. In Proc. Mobile HCI '02. Fabio Paternè (Ed.). Springer-Verlag, 256-270.

[23] Van Tonder, B., and Wesson, J. 2010. Is tilt interaction better than keypad interaction for mobile map-based applications?. In Proc. SAICSIT '10. ACM,, 322-331.

[24] Wigdor, D. and Balakrishnan, R. 2003. TiltText: using tilt for text input to mobile phones. In Proc. UIST'03. ACM, 81-90.

On Multimodal Interactive Machine Translation Using Speech Recognition

Vicent Alabau
Institut Tecnològic d'Informàtica, Universitat Politècnica de València
València, Spain
valabau@iti.upv.es

Luis Rodríguez-Ruiz
Departamento de Sistemas Informáticos, Universidad de Castilla-La Mancha
Albacete, Spain
Luis.RRuiz@uclm.es

Alberto Sanchis
Institut Tecnològic d'Informàtica, Universitat Politècnica de València
València, Spain
asanchis@iti.upv.es

Pascual Martínez-Gómez
Aizawa Laboratory
University of Tokyo
Tokyo, Japan
pasmargo@gmail.com

Francisco Casacuberta
Institut Tecnològic d'Informàtica, Universitat Politècnica de València
València, Spain
fcn@iti.upv.es

ABSTRACT

Interactive machine translation (IMT) is an increasingly popular paradigm for semi-automated machine translation, where a human expert is integrated into the core of an automatic machine translation system. The human expert interacts with the IMT system by partially correcting the errors of the system's output. Then, the system proposes a new solution. This process is repeated until the output meets the desired quality. In this scenario, the interaction is typically performed using the keyboard and the mouse. However, speech is also a very interesting input modality since the user does not need to abandon the keyboard to interact with it.

In this work, we present a new approach to perform speech interaction in a way that translation and speech inputs are tightly fused. This integration is performed early in the speech recognition step. Thus, the information from the translation models allows the speech recognition system to recover from errors that otherwise would be impossible to amend. In addition, this technique allows to use currently available speech recognition technology. The proposed system achieves an important boost in performance with respect to previous approaches.

Categories and Subject Descriptors

I.2.7 [**Natural Language Processing**]: Machine translation, Speech recognition and synthesis

General Terms

Design, Algorithms, Experimentation

Keywords

Interactive machine translation, Interactive pattern recognition, Multimodality, Automatic speech recognition

1. INTRODUCTION

Although the current state-of-the-art in machine translation (MT) has been greatly improved in the last ten years, MT systems are not able, so far, to provide the high quality results that are needed for industrial and business purposes. Owing to this fact, in these domains, a professional translator is required to ensure the quality standards demanded. However, the productivity that a completely manual process can offer is not always high enough and the task can take an excessive amount of time. This productivity can be increased by relying on an MT system so that the human translator only has to supervise the system results in order to correct the mistakes arisen in the process. Nevertheless, when the amount of errors is quite high, this approximation can be counterproductive and the fully manual approach might be preferable.

In the last years, however, this problem has been addressed by considering a new interactive paradigm. Interactive machine translation (IMT) [9, 3, 14] is focused on improving the cooperation between an MT system and a human translator. In this new proposal, unlike in *classical* MT, the system goal is not to produce translations in a completely automatic way, but rather to help the user build a perfect translation with the least possible effort. To this end, user and system are continuously collaborating to produce the final result. Two main benefits can be achieved from this interactive approach. First, users can save a significant amount of time since the system automatically provides part of the final text. Second, the MT system can take advantage of user responses to improve the quality of its own outcomes.

Because we are dealing with an interactive system, the way the user communicates with the application is really important to ensure a successful operation mode. Devices as keyboard or mouse are commonly used as input peripherals. Nevertheless, more natural modalities can also be adopted with the purpose of improving system ergonomics, eg. on-line handwriting or speech.

The problem to face with these alternative modalities is that they are not deterministic, ie. they need to be decoded by a specific system which may commit errors. Since the user would seldom use an error prone system, their utility is conditioned to high accuracy rates. Thus, one of the most important research problems in this area is how to take advantage of the information available in the translation process and in the alternative modality to improve the final accuracy, leading to an interesting and challenging fusion problem. The multimodal aspects of the interaction process, i.e. how keyboard, mouse and the alternative modalities could be used simultaneously, are typically left apart for future study. On the contrary, it is assumed that the user will prefer to use the alternative modality as long as the recognition accuracy is high enough. The user will fall back to the keyboard just in case of a decoding mistake.

In this context, several alternatives for the fusion problem have been explored. Interaction based on on-line handwriting was studied in [1, 2]. In these works, the user was expected to fix the first erroneous word with an electronic pen or writing on a touch-screen. The recognition probability of the on-line word was added as a feature in a log-lineal model with other language and translation features.

An interesting alternative modality is speech. Several techniques for dictating translations were explored in the nineties [4, 8], but this topic has received some attention recently [23]. However, the first study of a speech-enabled interactive system was [29]. In that work, several scenarios were proposed, where the user was expected to speak aloud parts of the current hypothesis and possibly one or more corrections. The technique consisted on rescoring the language model with the probabilities of word-based translation models [5], which are not aware of the context of the source and target sentence. Latter, several methods were proposed in [12] that took advantage of context information. Lattices from speech and translation were generated and combined in different ways including speech and translation lattice composition using finite-state automata toolkits and lattice rescoring with word-based translation models and posterior n-grams from m-best lists.

This paper is devoted to exploring new techniques for fusing the translation and speech inputs to provide a more reliable speech-enabled input interface that can lead to a real multimodal system. Especially, we focus on approaches that can be seamlessly integrated with current speech recognition technology. In particular, we propose a technique, based on the state-of-the-art in statistical translation models, which allows a context aware decoding. Compared to word-based translation models, this technique exhibits an important increase in recognition performance. In addition, a new way of integrating word-based translation models is analysed.

The remainder of this paper is organized as follows: Multimodal IMT is described in Section 2. Then, a general framework for including speech recognition into IMT is discussed in Section 3. Next, the proposed approach for fusing speech and translation models is presented in Section 4. Section 5 is devoted to the evaluation of the proposed models. Here, the results will be analysed and compared to previous approaches. Finally, conclusions and future work will be discussed in Section 6.

2. INTERACTIVE MACHINE TRANSLATION

A typical approach to IMT is shown in Fig. 1 to translate a source sentence $\boldsymbol{f}$ into a target sentence $\boldsymbol{e}$. The IMT process starts producing a full translation $\hat{\boldsymbol{e}}_s$ of the source sentence $\boldsymbol{f}$ based on conventional statistical MT techniques. Then, according to the source sentence, the user analyses $\hat{\boldsymbol{e}}_s$ in order to detect some possible translation errors. Typically, the user analyses $\hat{\boldsymbol{e}}_s$ from left to right and the first error found is replaced by some text κ to produce a *validated* error-free prefix $\boldsymbol{e}_p,\kappa$. This prefix is used by the IMT system in the next iteration to produce a new prediction $\hat{\boldsymbol{e}}_s$ so that the concatenation of $\boldsymbol{e}_p,\kappa$ and $\hat{\boldsymbol{e}}_s$ constitutes a whole translation of the source sentence. This process is repeated until a completely error-free translation of the source sentence is achieved.

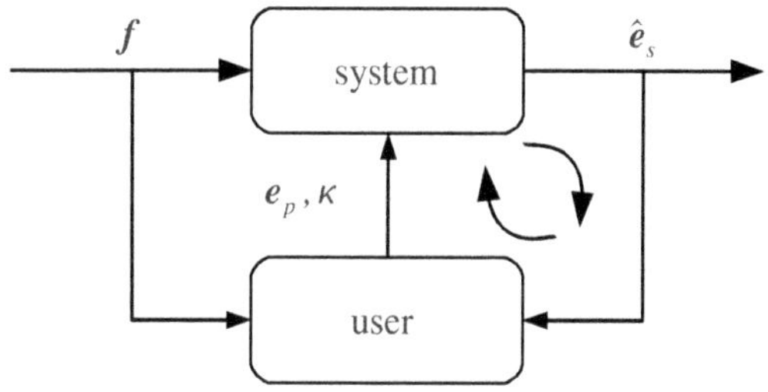

Figure 1: Diagram of a typical approach to IMT

The user feedback is aimed at validating a fragment of the suggestion (prefix selection, $\boldsymbol{e}_p$) as well as introducing a correction after this prefix (κ). This interaction is usually carried out by using keyboard and mouse actions, but more natural interaction modalities (i.e. speech) can also be considered. Speech can be employed to set the error-free prefix by uttering the final word or words in the prefix to be chosen. In fact, this is a very easy task since it is restricted to utter a fragment of the current IMT prediction. On the other hand, speech can be used to introduce the correction (κ) once the error-free prefix has been fixed.

An example of the multimodal IMT process using keyboard and speech is shown in Fig. 2. To distinguish when keyboard or speech is used, we will denote κ to represent a word (or sequence of words) introduced by using the keyboard, and t to represent a speech utterance to be decoded. As the example shows, the process starts with an empty prefix $\boldsymbol{e}_p$, so the system proposes in the first iteration a full translation $\hat{\boldsymbol{e}}_s$. This output would be the same of a conventional MT system. Then, the user selects the error-free prefix $\boldsymbol{e}_p$ and corrects the first translation error using the keyboard (i.e. *that* is replaced by *is*). In the second iteration, the system proposes a new suffix $\hat{\boldsymbol{e}}_s$ based on the user feedback. The user amends *to* by uttering the word *in* and the system reacts by predicting a new suffix $\hat{\boldsymbol{e}}_s$. Since this suffix is fully correct the process ends. Note that multimodal IMT approach has allowed to obtain the correct translation with only two user corrections, whereas more effort would have been required if the conventional approach, based on fully automatic MT and human post-editing had been applied.

3. SPEECH-ENABLED IMT

Formally, IMT can be defined as the problem of finding the optimal suffix $\hat{\boldsymbol{e}}_s$ given the user feedback $(\boldsymbol{e}_p, \boldsymbol{d})$ and the

SOURCE ($\boldsymbol{f}$):		si alguna función no se encuentra disponible en su red
TARGET ($\boldsymbol{e}$):		if any feature is not available in your network
ITER-0	($\boldsymbol{e}_p$)	
	($\hat{\boldsymbol{e}}_s$)	if any feature that is provided by the network is not available
ITER-1	($\boldsymbol{e}_p$)	*if any feature*
	(κ)	**is**
	($\hat{\boldsymbol{e}}_s$)	not available to be provided by your network
ITER-2	($\boldsymbol{e}_p$)	*not available*
	($\boldsymbol{t}$)	
	($\hat{\boldsymbol{d}}$)	**in**
	($\hat{\boldsymbol{e}}_s$)	your network
FINAL	($\boldsymbol{e}_p \equiv \boldsymbol{e}$)	if any feature is not available in your network

Figure 2: Example of a multimodal IMT session for translating a Spanish sentence $\boldsymbol{f}$ from the Xerox corpus into an English sentence $\boldsymbol{e}$.

source $\boldsymbol{f}$:

$$\hat{\boldsymbol{e}}_s = \operatorname*{argmax}_{\boldsymbol{e}_s} Pr(\boldsymbol{e}_s|\boldsymbol{e}_p, \boldsymbol{d}, \boldsymbol{f}) \quad (1)$$

where $\boldsymbol{d}$ is a word (or sequence of words) introduced by typing some keystrokes (κ) or by means of a speech utterance ($\boldsymbol{t}$). Note that when the IMT process starts, no user feedback is available in this step and, therefore, the system behaves like a conventional MT system.

Obtaining $\boldsymbol{d}$ from speech decoding is not as trivial as in the case of keyboard input (where $\boldsymbol{d}$ is univocally represented by the sequence of key-strokes κ). Although an integrated decoding of Eq. (1) could be possible, it would require specific decoding algorithms. However, an important goal of this paper was to find solutions compatible with existing speech technologies. For this reason, to enable speech multimodality in IMT, the optimal suffix $\hat{\boldsymbol{e}}_s$ is can obtained in two steps:

1. First, a decoding $\hat{\boldsymbol{d}}$ of the speech $\boldsymbol{t}$ is obtained:
2. Then, based on Eq. (1), $\hat{\boldsymbol{d}}$ is used to obtain the optimal suffix $\hat{\boldsymbol{e}}_s$:

$$\hat{\boldsymbol{e}}_s \approx \operatorname*{argmax}_{\boldsymbol{e}_s} Pr(\boldsymbol{e}_s|\boldsymbol{e}_p, \hat{\boldsymbol{d}}, \boldsymbol{f}) \quad (2)$$

A first approximation, referred as DEC in [29], is based on the use of a conventional automatic speech recognition (ASR) system to obtain $\hat{\boldsymbol{d}}$ as:

$$\hat{\boldsymbol{d}} = \operatorname*{argmax}_{\boldsymbol{d}} Pr(\boldsymbol{d}|\boldsymbol{t}) = \operatorname*{argmax}_{\boldsymbol{d}} Pr(\boldsymbol{t}|\boldsymbol{d}) Pr(\boldsymbol{d}) \quad (3)$$

where $Pr(\boldsymbol{t}|\boldsymbol{d})$ represents the *acoustic model*, which is a representation of the probability distribution for the constituent speech elements (usually phonemes or phoneme sequences) in the input utterance. $Pr(\boldsymbol{d})$ denotes the *language model* (LM), which deals with the probability of $\boldsymbol{d}$ being a sequence of words in a specific language.

The approach just described regards the ASR as a completely independent module (black-box) and, therefore, it could be adopted to build a speech input interface for any kind of interactive system. However, in IMT, we can benefit from the environment provided by the interactive system itself to introduce speech recognition in such a way that the speech decoding accuracy can be improved. It is reasonable to assume that the user will utter something that is both a suitable continuation to the current selected prefix and a fragment of a correct translation for the source sentence. This fact can be profitably used to actually improve the ASR performance.

With this purpose, in [29] it was proposed a new alternative (DEC-PREF) to introduce the prefix as a LM constrain in Eq. (3):

$$\hat{\boldsymbol{d}} = \operatorname*{argmax}_{\boldsymbol{d}} Pr(\boldsymbol{t}|\boldsymbol{d}) Pr(\boldsymbol{d}|\boldsymbol{e}_p) \quad (4)$$

Here, the LM is conditioned to the current prefix. Consequently, the search space in the ASR decoding can be constrained to those hypotheses that are suitable continuations of $\boldsymbol{e}_p$.

Similarly, the source sentence can be introduced into the LM in Eq. (3) as a constraint:

$$\hat{\boldsymbol{d}} = \operatorname*{argmax}_{\boldsymbol{d}} Pr(\boldsymbol{t}|\boldsymbol{d}) Pr(\boldsymbol{d}|\boldsymbol{f}) \quad (5)$$

Now, this constraint favours decodings of $\hat{\boldsymbol{d}}$ whose words result from translations of $\boldsymbol{f}$. In this case, the information on the target sentence context is not taken into account.

Clearly, a more interesting and challenging approach is to consider dependencies on both $\boldsymbol{f}$ and $\boldsymbol{e}_p$:

$$\hat{\boldsymbol{d}} = \operatorname*{argmax}_{\boldsymbol{d}} Pr(\boldsymbol{t}|\boldsymbol{d}) Pr(\boldsymbol{d}|\boldsymbol{e}_p, \boldsymbol{f}) \quad (6)$$

The use of Eq. (6) has been addressed in previous works [29, 25, 12]. In [29] word-based translation models were used to rescore the ASR LM. Later, [25] rescored n-best list hypotheses from the ASR output with word-based models. However, in word-based models the word probabilities of the target sentence are independent from each other, and thus contextual information is not used. This is a known limitation, since translation models using contextual information as n-gram-based [7, 16] or phrase-based [19] models greatly outperform word-based models.

On the other hand, the techniques in [12] used a word lattice from an ASR system, as input to a series of combinations with word-based and phrase-based translation models. The problem of these approaches is that the best solution is limited by the quality of the ASR lattice. A way of measuring such quality is by the error rate of the sentence in the lattice closest to the reference, as it is a lower bound on the error rate. Rescoring the ASR lattice cannot recover from errors in the ASR stage. Hence, an early fusion of the translation models would allow to recover some of these errors otherwise impossible to amend.

4. SPEECH AND TRANSLATION FUSION

Typically, state-of-the-art ASR systems approach the language modelling with n-gram models [10]. Then, if the constraints can be encoded as an n-gram LM, the integration with ASR systems will become trivial. A simple way to do so is to transform word-based translation models into a n-gram-style LM to model Eq. (5). Word-based translation models assume independence of the words in the target sentence. Thus, the posterior probability of the translation model can be decomposed based on the naïve Bayes assumption, $Pr(\boldsymbol{d}|\boldsymbol{f}) \approx \prod_i p(d_i|\boldsymbol{f})$. Then, the probability of a target word being a translation of the source sentence can be computed as

$$p(d_i|\boldsymbol{f}) \quad = \quad \sum_{j=1}^{|\boldsymbol{f}|} p(j|\boldsymbol{f})p(d_i|\boldsymbol{f}, j) \tag{7}$$

where $p(j|\boldsymbol{f})$ is an alignment model which can be approximated by $\frac{1}{|\boldsymbol{f}|+1}$ and, $p(d_i|\boldsymbol{f}, j)$ is a dictionary which can be approximated by a statistical lexicon $l(d_i|f_j)$ as in IBM1 models [5]. Luckily, Eq. (7) can be easily encoded as a 1-gram language model.

On the other hand, to deal with the application of Eq. (6), we propose a new approach to overcome the problems of recent works briefly summarized in previous section. The proposed approach is based on the estimation of n-gram posterior probabilities over word lattices. As a result, a (smoothed) n-gram language model is obtained.

4.1 Lattice Posterior n-grams

For this approach, a subset of the search space should be obtained from the translation models as a word lattice [22, 28]. A word lattice L is a directed, acyclic, weighted graph with an initial node q_i and a final node q_f. The nodes correspond to discrete points in time in the case of a ASR system or different alignment coverage in IMT. Besides, they are conditioned on a specific state of the language model. A link l is defined as any edge between two nodes; each link has associated a starting node $s(l)$, an end node $e(l)$, a hypothesised word $w(l)$, and a likelihood $f(l)$; each link can be considered as a hypothesis $w(l)$ between the nodes $s(l)$ and $e(l)$ with likelihood $f(l)$.

To obtain a n-gram model from a word lattice, posterior probabilities for each node and link must be computed. These probabilities are based on the forward and backward probabilities of the nodes. The forward probability $\alpha(q)$ can be defined as the sum of the probability of all the prefix paths in the lattice reaching a node q from q_i. Correspondingly, the backward probability $\beta(q)$ can be defined as the probability of all the suffix paths in the lattice reaching q_f from q. These probabilities can be efficiently computed with the well-known *forward-backward* algorithm [30]. The posterior probability for a specific link l can be computed by summing up the posterior probabilities of all hypotheses of the word lattice containing it:

$$p(l \mid \boldsymbol{f}) = \frac{\alpha\left(s(l)\right) \cdot f(l)^{1/\eta} \cdot \beta\left(e(l)\right)}{\alpha(q_f)} \tag{8}$$

where η is the posterior scale and it is used to balance the scores of the competing links. High values of η make the word posterior probability smoother, while low values make it sharper. In practice, this scaling factor adjust the difference in probability between the first and runner up hypotheses. Similarly to Eq. (8), the posterior probability for a specific node q is

$$p(q \mid \boldsymbol{f}) = \frac{\alpha\left(q\right) \cdot \beta\left(q\right)}{\alpha(q_f)} \tag{9}$$

Then, the expected n-gram counts can be estimated efficiently as in [6]. For a given n-gram length (or order) N:

$$C^*(d_{i-N+1}^i \mid \boldsymbol{f}) = \sum_{l_1^N \in \mathcal{N}(d_{i-N+1}^i)} \frac{\prod_{n=1}^N p(l_n|\boldsymbol{f})}{\prod_{n=2}^N p(s(l_n)|\boldsymbol{f})} \tag{10}$$

where $\mathcal{N}(d_{i-N+1}^i)$ are all the sequences of concatenated links in L generating d_{i-N+1}^i. An example of how this expected counts are estimated is shown in Fig. 3.

Now, word posterior probabilities can be calculated after a proper normalisation:

$$p(d_i|d_{i-n+1}^{i-1}, \boldsymbol{f}) = \frac{C^*(d_{i-n+1}^i \mid \boldsymbol{f})}{C^*(d_{i-n+1}^{i-1} \mid \boldsymbol{f})} \tag{11}$$

The estimation in Eq. (11) presents the problem that many n-grams are not seen in the lattice. Then, they will have zero probability, and the ASR system will fail to recognise them. A common approach is to rely on simpler models to account for unseen events using back-off models [11]. As the estimated counts are not real counts (they vary from 0 to the number of times the n-gram occurs in a sentence), typical discount methods cannot be applied. However, absolute discount can be used [18], which consists in subtracting a constant ϵ from C^*. Although this is a simple discounting method, it has an interesting read. Word posterior probabilities have been extensively used for computing word-based confidence measures [30, 26]. They usually define a threshold over the word posterior probability to identify correctly recognised words. In the same sense, ϵ establishes a threshold over the expected counts. If a count C^* is bellow ϵ, then it is considered to have low confidence and discounted to zero.

Furthermore, only words present in the lattice are included into the model (which implies a high number of out-of-vocabulary words, since lattices only contain the words of the most likely hypotheses). The out-of-vocabulary (OOV) problem is solved again by backing-off to the word-based 1-gram, $p(d_i|\boldsymbol{f})$. In addition, for the remaining words in the vocabulary the model backs off to $p(d_i)$, which is a standard 1-gram.

Finally, the restriction of $\boldsymbol{e}_p$ can be added as in Eq. (4). The resulting language model (we will refer later to it as $n$gr-POST) can be defined as

$$p(\boldsymbol{d}|\boldsymbol{f}, \boldsymbol{e}_p) = \prod_i p(d_i|\boldsymbol{f}, \boldsymbol{e}_p, d_{i-n+1}^{i-1}) \tag{12}$$

A last approach to avoid poor estimations of $p(\boldsymbol{d}|\boldsymbol{f}, \boldsymbol{e}_p)$ is

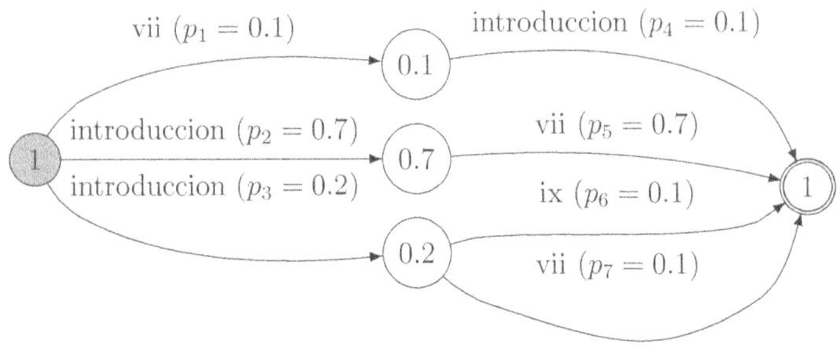

$$p(s(4)) = 0.1 \quad p(s(5)) = 0.7 \quad p(s(6)) = p(s(7)) = 0.2$$

$$\begin{aligned} C^*(\text{vii}) &= p_1 + p_5 + p_7 = 0.9 \\ C^*(\text{introduccion}) &= p_2 + p_3 + p_4 = 1 \\ C^*(\text{ix}) &= p_6 = 0.1 \end{aligned}$$

$$\begin{aligned} C^*(\text{vii introduccion}) &= \frac{p_1 \cdot p_4}{p(s(4))} = 0.1 \\ C^*(\text{introduccion ix}) &= \frac{p_1 \cdot p_4}{p(s(4))} = 0.1 \\ C^*(\text{introduccion vi}) &= \frac{p_2 \cdot p_5}{p(s(5))} + \frac{p_3 \cdot p_7}{p(s(7))} = 0.8 \end{aligned}$$

Figure 3: Example of computation of the expected counts. The number in the state is the posterior probability of that state. In the links, the word with the link posterior probability between parentheses. The sub-index represents the link identifier. To the right, the expected counts for all the 1-grams and 2-grams in the lattice.

a linear interpolation with DEC-PREF:

$$p_\gamma(\boldsymbol{d}|\boldsymbol{f}, \boldsymbol{e}_p) = \gamma p(\boldsymbol{d}|\boldsymbol{f}, \boldsymbol{e}_p) + (1-\gamma) p(\boldsymbol{d}|\boldsymbol{e}_p) \qquad (13)$$

5. EXPERIMENTAL FRAMEWORK

5.1 Corpora

We used three data sets in our experiments. The first one is the standard English-Spanish XEROX benchmark parallel text acquired as part of the TT2 project [27]. The training part of this corpus is used here mainly to estimate the translation model parameters needed in MT and IMT. The target (Spanish) part of this training set is further used to train most of the language models required in the speech decoding and speech-enabled IMT experiments.

Table 1: Features of the text English-Spanish translation Xerox Corpus (K$= \times 1,000$)

		English	Spanish
Training-set	Running words	572K	657K
	Vocabulary	26K	30K
Test-set	Running words	7.6K	9.4K
	Running characters	47K	59K
	Perplexity (3-gram)	103	61

The second data set is a relatively large speech corpus, containing phonetically balanced spoken sentences in Spanish[17] and it was employed to train the acoustic HMMs.

The last data set consists of utterances of fragments of target-language (Spanish) sentences, extracted from the test part of the original parallel TT2 corpus. These utterances are used as a test set to simulate real interactions of the IMT system with human translators. All the speech data was acquired using high quality microphones and 16 KHz sampling frequency. A summary of relevant features of these corpora is shown in Tables 1, 2 and 3.

Table 2: Features of the Spanish speech acoustic training corpus (K$= \times 1,000$)

Speakers	164
Running words (4 hours)	42K

Table 3: Spanish speech test utterances (from the XEROX-corpus)

Text	Original complete sentences	128
	Different sentence fragments uttered	485
	Average prefix length	4.5
	Running words	1,138
	Running characters	7,320
Speech	Number of speakers	10
	Number of utterances	5,337
	Running words	13,998

The set of test utterances described in Table 3 was obtained as follows. First a subset of 128 sentence pairs was selected from the text partition of the XEROX text corpus. For the target (Spanish) sentence of each of these pairs, several segmentations into prefixes and suffixes were randomly performed and, for each generated suffix, a set of prefixes was randomly derived. All the prefixes of suffixes generated in this way constitute the set of sentence fragments uttered by several speakers. In order to approach real IMT user interactions as much as possible, this generation process was performed in such a way that the lengths of the generated fragments were similar to the lengths of accepted parts of system suggestions observed in text-only experiments with a real IMT system applied to the original set of 128 sentence pairs (see next section for details).

Each of the utterances obtained in this way is the acoustic signal denoted by $\boldsymbol{t}$ in the previous sections.

5.2 Models

Speech models are HMM with three states, with left-to-right topology with loops and 128 Gaussians per state. Each speech model represents a phonetically context-independent unit (monophone). These models were estimated using the data of the Albayzin Spanish speech corpus [17] described in Section 5.1.

Lexical models consist of stochastic finite-state automata (SFS), representing all the possible concatenations of individual characters or phonemes to compose the word. Finally, Kneser-Ney back-off smoothed [13] 3-gram models were used as language models in all the experiments.

Finally, the MT and IMT are log-linear phrase-based models [19, 21], which constitute the state-of-the-art in MT.

IBM1 models [5] were adopted for word-based models, when applicable.

5.3 Evaluation metrics

Our system was assessed by means of *word error rate* (WER), which obtains the ratio between the number of edit operations (substitutions, deletions and insertions) necessary to transform the hypothesis into the reference, and the number of words in the reference. Similarly, *oracle* WER (OWER) is the best WER that can be obtained from the word lattice resulting from the decoding process. OWER was used to evaluate lattice quality.

In addition, in order to evaluate the complexity of the chosen corpus and different language modelling techniques, perplexity was employed [24]. Perplexity, measured for a text with respect to a language model, is a function of the likelihood of that text being produced by repeated application of the model.

5.4 Results

This section is devoted to analysing the experimental results of the methods proposed in Sections 3 and 4. The experiments were carried out in the following way. First, the publicly available toolkit for IMT, Thot[1] [21], was used to estimate the word-based and phrase-based models. With the word-based models, IBM1 LM were generated as in Eq.(7). In addition, the phrase-based models were used to generate the translation lattices for each source sentence in the test dataset. These lattices were used to estimate the n-gram posterior models ($n$gr-POST) in Eq. (12). For the models needing parameter adjustment, as posterior scale or ϵ in absolute discount, a range of parameter values were explored. However, only the most promising models, in terms of perplexity, were selected for the experiments. The analysis of this will be shown later in this section. Next, the parameters of the speech recogniser were estimated over a held-out development dataset for the 3-gram language model, to optimise WER. Finally, the baseline and selected models wer used to generate ASR word lattices with the publicly available iATROS[2] [15] speech recognition software. As iATROS is open source, it was modified to allow prefix decoding (as in DEC-PREF) and some extra parameters were added to seamlessly allow the decoding of fragments of sentences. The quality of the models was then assessed by the perplexity of the model, the WER of the hypothesis with maximum probability, and the OWER, i.e. the hypothesis in the lattice with minimum WER.

As a baseline, two scenarios, shown in Table 4, have been considered. The DEC system in Eq. (3), which uses an unconstrained language model, obtains a 26.7 of WER and a 12.0 of OWER. The DEC-PREF system in Eq. (4), which is conditioned on $\boldsymbol{e}_p$, obtains 23.1 and 10.4, respectively. Note that, not only the performance is better, but the quality of the lattices also improves. Both of them were based on a 3-gram LM.

Conversely, Table 5 shows the results for the models not depending on $\boldsymbol{e}_p$, that is, independent of the target language context. The IBM1 system proposed in this work is only conditioned on $\boldsymbol{f}$. Although perplexity results are better than the previous approaches (34 vs 57 of DEC-PREF and 163 of DEC), WER results are quite worse (29.9) and the lattice quality is bad. However, IBM1 has no contextual information, so it is more similar to a 1gr system. In fact, it is encoded as such. In this comparison, the IBM1 system outperforms the 1gr system. The last contestant of this category is 1gr-POST. This is actually the one with more information, since it has been obtained from a phrase-based model including various sources of information from the log-linear translation model. In fact, it shows the best performance of the three, outperforming the DEC and being close to the DEC-PREF system. When these systems are combined with a DEC-PREF (3gr) model to provide contextual information the results are comparable or better than the DEC-PREF model alone (with interpolation factor $\gamma = 0.6$ for IBM1 and $\gamma = 0.8$ for 1gr-POST). It is worthy of note the OWER results, that improve dramatically compared to non interpolated models. With respect to the DEC system, which would be the one used in [12], interpolated models improve the lattice quality at least a 27%. Hence, those lattice rescoring techniques would be able to improve its results if applied on our lattices.

[1]http://sourceforge.net/projects/thot/

[2]http://prhlt.iti.upv.es/w/iatros

Table 4: Perplexity, WER and oracle WER (OWER) for the baseline system.

model	Eq.	PPL	WER	OWER
DEC (3gr)	(3)	163	26.7	12.0
DEC-PREF (3gr)	(4)	57	23.1	10.4

Table 5: Perplexity, WER and oracle WER (OWER) for models independent from target language context (e_p) and respective linear interpolation models.

model	Eq.	PPL	WER	OWER
DEC (1gr)[a]	(3)	455	43.2	37.6
IBM1	(7)	34	29.9	26.2
1gr-POST	(12)	27	24.7	21.5
IBM1 + DEC-PREF	—	22	23.2	8.7
1gr-POST + DEC-PREF	(13)	28	22.4	8.5

[a]Note that DEC (1gr) and DEC-PREF (1gr) are the same models since both lack of dependency on $\boldsymbol{e}_p$ or $\boldsymbol{f}$

The posterior scale parameter in Eq. (8) is crucial in word posterior probability estimation [20]. Typically, this parameter must be adjusted to balance the probabilities of the competing hypotheses. Fig. 4 shows the results in perplexity of three $n$gr-POST systems when varying the posterior scale. Unexpectedly, the best posterior scale is found at 1. However, the explanation for this is rather simple. The word posterior probabilities have been used mainly on ASR lattices in the literature. Here, the acoustic score is not actually a probability but a density. Hence, the scores are very low and the posterior scale is needed to obtain sensible word posterior probabilities. On the contrary, translation models are based on counts, and thus, the lattices encode actual probabilities. Then, it is not necessary to scale the scores to balance the competing hypotheses.

The $n$gr-POST approach was tested for various orders of n-grams, from 1 to 5. The results for perplexity and WER are displayed on Fig. 5. Diamonds ($\diamond$) represent $n$gr-POST models while squares ($\square$) represent $n$gr-POST models inter-

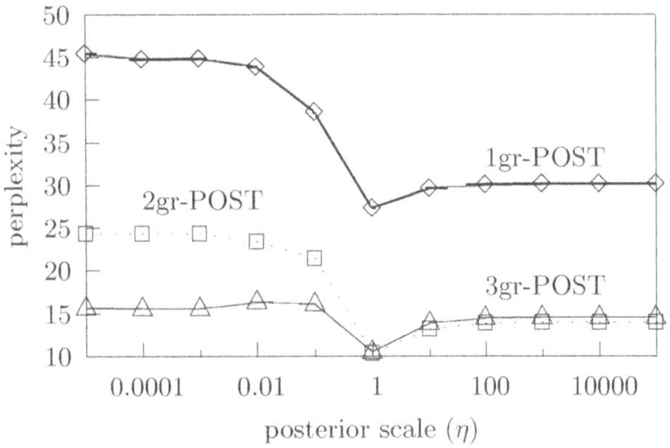

Figure 4: Perplexity for various posterior n-grams when varying the posterior scale.

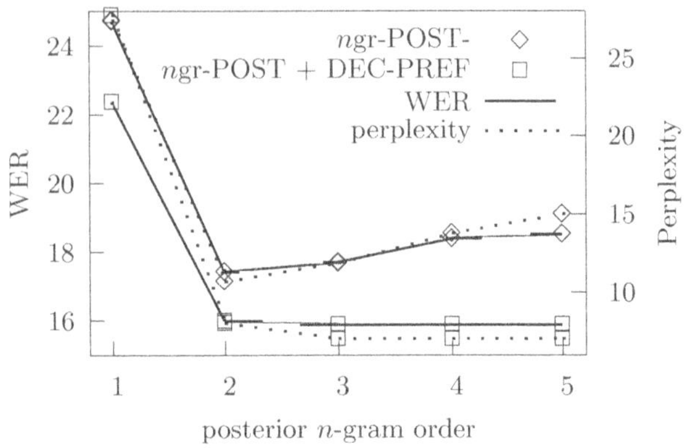

Figure 5: WER and perplexity (PPL) results for different orders of posterior n-grams.

polated with a DEC-PREF (3gr) model. First note that perplexity and WER results overlap. This has been made on purpose to show the clear correlation in perplexity and WER for this kind of models. A minimum is obtained at 2gr-POST. Then as the n-gram order increases, so does the error. This seems a symptom of model overfitting. However, all the systems outperform significantly the previous models for orders of 2 or more. Not surprisingly, these models have managed adequately the integration of the source sentence $\boldsymbol{f}$ and the target context $\boldsymbol{e}_p$. At last, when interpolating with DEC-PREF models a consistent improvement is shown. In addition, this smoothing is able to overcome the problems of overfitting and, now, the performance stabilises for higher order of n-grams.

Finally, Table 6 summarises the experiments conducted on this paper. Interpolation factors are $\gamma = 0.6$ for IBM1 and $\gamma = 0.8$ for 3gr-POST. As it can be observed, all proposed models outperform previous models in their respective categories. Besides, the generated lattices have also greater quality in terms of OWER improving in 44.2% relative with respect to *DEC* for the best model. This would allow lattice rescoring techniques to improve their results.

Table 6: Summary of perplexity, WER and oracle WER (OWER) for the different approaches. Baseline results in the first block. The second block for alternatives not using e_p. In the third block alternatives using e_p and $\boldsymbol{f}$.

model	Eq.	PPL	WER	OWER
DEC (3gr)	(3)	163	26.7	12.0
DEC-PREF (3gr)	(4)	57	23.1	10.4
DEC (1gr)	(3)	455	43.2	37.6
IBM1	(7)	34	29.9	26.2
1gr-POST	(12)	27	24.7	21.5
IBM1 + DEC-PREF	—	22	23.2	8.7
2gr-POST	(12)	11	17.7	8.9
3gr-POST + DEC-PREF	(13)	**7**	**15.9**	**6.7**

6. CONCLUSIONS

In this paper we have described two approaches to improve speech-enabled IMT systems. Both techniques can be encoded in the form of n-grams so they can be seamlessly integrated in state-of-the-art ASR software. The systems that do not take information from the context of the target sentences exhibit an increase in the recognition performance with respect to competing alternatives. Furthermore, we have shown that if the integration of all the sources of information is carried out early in the recognition process, the achieved WER improvements are remarkable. In addition, if this integration is performed in the ASR step, the generated lattices improve in quality so that techniques using ASR lattices can benefit from it.

However, as results are still far from perfect, the error rate may prevent the users from effectively using the speech modality. Thus, we should make an effort to reduce the WER to a point where speech-enabled IMT is usable. We could take advantage that the user is in front of the screen to capture face expressions and lip movement to perform audio-visual speech recognition.

Finally, the multimodal aspects of this problem should be studied, i.e. how the speech interface and keyboard and mouse can be used alternatively or simultaneously. Eventually, human evaluation should be carried out to assess the proposed scenarios in a real-like situation.

7. ACKNOWLEDGMENTS

Work supported by the Spanish MEC/MICINN under the MIPRCV "Consolider Ingenio 2010" program (CSD2007-00018), iTrans2 (TIN2009-14511) and MITTRAL (TIN2009-14633-C03-01) projects. Also supported by the Spanish MITyC under the erudito.com (TSI-020110-2009-439) project and by the Generalitat Valenciana under grant GV/2010/067, and by the UPV under grant UPV/2009/2851.

8. REFERENCES

[1] V. Alabau, D. Ortiz-Martínez, A. Sanchis, and F. Casacuberta. Multimodal interactive machine translation. In *Proceedings of the 2010 International Conference on Multimodal Interfaces (ICMI-MLMI'10)*, pages 46:1–4, Beijing, China, Nov. 2010.

[2] V. Alabau, A. Sanchis, and F. Casacuberta. Improving on-line handwritten recognition using translation models in multimodal interactive machine translation. In *Proceedings of the 49th Annual Meeting of the Association for Computational Linguistics: Human Language Technologies*, pages 389–394, Portland,

Oregon, USA, June 2011. Association for Computational Linguistics.

[3] S. Barrachina, O. Bender, F. Casacuberta, J. Civera, E. Cubel, S. Khadivi, A. L. Lagarda, H. Ney, J. Tomás, E. Vidal, and J. M. Vilar. Statistical approaches to computer-assisted translation. *Computational Linguistics*, 35(1):3–28, 2009.

[4] P. Brown, S. Chen, S. D. Pietra, V. D. Pietra, S. Kehler, and R. Mercer. Automatic speech recognition in machine aided translation. *Computer Speech and Language*, 8:177–187, 1994.

[5] P. F. Brown, S. A. D. Pietra, V. J. D. Pietra, and R. L. Mercer. The mathematics of machine translation. 19(2):263–311, 1993.

[6] W. Campbell and F. Richardson. Discriminative keyword selection using support vector machines. In J. Platt, D. Koller, Y. Singer, and S. Roweis, editors, *Advances in Neural Information Processing Systems 20*, pages 209–216. MIT Press, Cambridge, MA, 2008.

[7] F. Casacuberta, E. Vidal, and D. Picó. Inference of finite-state transducers from regular languages. *Pattern Recognition*, 38:1431–1443, 2005.

[8] M. Dymetman, J. Brousseau, G. Foster, P. Isabelle, Y. Normandin, and P. Plamondon. Towards an automatic dictation system for translators: the TransTalk project. In *Proceedings of International Conference on Spoken Language Processing (ICSLP94)*, pages 193–196, Yokohama, Japan, 1994.

[9] G. Foster, P. Isabelle, and P. Plamondon. Target-text mediated interactive machine translation. *Machine Translation*, 12:175–194, 1998.

[10] F. Jelinek. *Statistical Methods for Speech Recognition*. MIT Press, 1998.

[11] S. Katz. Estimation of probabilities from sparse data for the language model component of a speech recognizer. *Acoustics, Speech and Signal Processing, IEEE Transactions on*, 35(3):400 – 401, mar 1987.

[12] S. Khadivi and H. Ney. Integration of speech recognition and machine translation in computer-assisted translation. *Audio, Speech, and Language Processing, IEEE Transactions on*, 16(8):1551 –1564, nov. 2008.

[13] R. Kneser and H. Ney. Improved backing-off for m-gram language modeling. In *Proceedings of ICASSP 95*, volume 1, pages 181–184, Los Alamitos, CA, USA, 1995. IEEE Computer Society.

[14] P. Koehn and B. Haddow. Interactive assistance to human translators using statistical machine translation methods. In *Proceedings of MT Summit XII*, pages 73–80, Ottawa, Canada, 2009.

[15] M. Luján-Mares, V. Tamarit, V. Alabau, C. D. Martínez-Hinarejos, M. P. i Gadea, A. Sanchis, and A. H. Toselli. iATROS: A speech and handwritting recognition system. In *V Jornadas en Tecnologías del Habla (VJTH'2008)*, pages 75–78, Bilbao (Spain), Nov 2008.

[16] J. Mariño, R. Banchs, J. Crego, A. de Gispert, P. Lambert, J. Fonollosa, and M. Costa-jussà. N-gram-based machine translation. *Computational Linguistics*, 32(4):527–549, 2006.

[17] A. Moreno, D. Poch, A. Bonafonte, E. Lleida, J. Llisterri, J. B. Mariño, and C. Nadeu. Albayzin speech database: design of the phonetic corpus. In *Proceedings of EuroSpeech'93*, pages 175–178, Berlin, Germany, sep 1993.

[18] H. Ney, U. Essen, and R. Kneser. On the estimation of 'small' probabilities by leaving-one-out. *Pattern Analysis and Machine Intelligence, IEEE Transactions on*, 17(12):1202 –1212, dec 1995.

[19] F. J. Och and H. Ney. Discriminative training and maximum entropy models for statistical machine translation. In *Proceedings of the 40th ACL*, pages 295–302, Philadelphia, PA, July 2002.

[20] A. Ogawa, K. Takeda, and F. Itakura. Balancing acoustic and linguistic probabilites. In *Proceeding IEEE CASSP*, volume 1, pages 181–184, Seattle, WA, USAR, May 1998.

[21] D. Ortiz-Martínez, I. García-Varea, and F. Casacuberta. Thot: a toolkit to train phrase-based statistical translation models. In *Proceedings of the MT Summit X*, pages 141–148. 2005.

[22] S. Ortmanns, H. Ney, and X. Aubert. A word graph algorithm for large vocabulary continuous speech recognition. *Computer Speech and Language*, 11(1):43–72, Jan. 1997.

[23] A. Reddy and R. Rose. Integration of statistical models for dictation of document translations in a machine-aided human translation task. *Audio, Speech, and Language Processing, IEEE Transactions on*, 18(8):2015 –2027, nov. 2010.

[24] R. Rosenfeld. Two decades of statistical language modeling: Where do we go from here? In *Proceedings of the IEEE*, volume 88, pages 1270–1278, 2000.

[25] L. R. Ruiz. *Interactive Pattern Recognition Applied to Natural Language Processing*. Tesis doctoral en informática, Departamento de Sistemas Informáticos y Computación, Universidad Politécnica de Valencia, 2010.

[26] A. Sanchis, A. Juan, and E. Vidal. Improving utterance verification using a smoothed naive bayes model. In *IEEE International Conference on Acoustic, Speech and Signal Processing*, pages 592–595. IEEE Press, April 2003.

[27] SchulmbergerSema S.A., Celer Soluciones, Instituto Técnico de Informática, R.W.T.H. Aachen - Lehrstuhl für Informatik VI, R.A.L.I. Laboratory - University of Montreal, Société Gamma, and Xerox Research Centre Europe. X.R.C.: TT2. TransType2 - Computer assisted translation. Project technical annex, 2001.

[28] N. Ueffing, F. J. Och, and H. Ney. Generation of word graphs in statistical machine translation. In *Proceedings of the ACL-02 conference on Empirical methods in natural language processing - Volume 10*, EMNLP '02, pages 156–163, Stroudsburg, PA, USA, 2002. Association for Computational Linguistics.

[29] E. Vidal, F. Casacuberta, L. Rodríguez, J. Civera, and C. Martínez. Computer-assisted translation using speech recognition. *IEEE Transaction on Audio, Speech and Language Processing*, 14(3):941–951, 2006.

[30] F. Wessel, R. Schluter, K. Macherey, and H. Ney. Confidence measures for large vocabulary continuous speech recognition. *IEEE Trans. Speech and Audio Proc.*, 9(3), Mar 2001.

Multimodal Segmentation of Object Manipulation Sequences with Product Models

Alexandra Barchunova
Research Institute for Cognition and Robotics,
Bielefeld University, Germany
abarch@cor-lab.uni-bielefeld.de

Robert Haschke
Neuroinformatics Group, Bielefeld University
Bielefeld, Germany

Mathias Franzius
Honda Research Institute Europe
Offenbach am Main, Germany

Helge Ritter
Neuroinformatics Group, Bielefeld University
Bielefeld, Germany

ABSTRACT

In this paper we propose an approach for unsupervised segmentation of continuous object manipulation sequences into semantically differing subsequences. The proposed method estimates segment borders based on an integrated consideration of three modalities (tactile feedback, hand posture, audio) yielding robust and accurate results in a single pass. To this end, a Bayesian approach – originally applied by Fearnhead [4] to segment one-dimensional time series data – is extended to allow an integrated segmentation of multimodal sequences. We propose a joint product model which combines modality-specific likelihoods to model segments. Weight parameters control the influence of each modality within the joint model. We discuss the relevance of all modalities based on an evaluation of the temporal and structural correctness of segmentation results obtained from various weight combinations.

Categories and Subject Descriptors

G.3 [**Probability and Statistics**]: Probabilistic algorithms, Multivariate statistics; H.1.2 [**User/Machine Systems**]: Human information processing

General Terms

Algorithms, Experimentation, Human Factors

Keywords

Multimodal Segmentation, Manual Interaction

1. INTRODUCTION

A large part of human interaction with the environment consists of manual object manipulation operations. Identification of human actions is an important part of today's research in robotics and wearable computing. An approach to segmentation and identification of object manipulation operations from low-level data is essential for building autonomous interactive systems, e.g. in the domains of human-machine interaction, imitation learning and activity recognition.

Inspired by the fact, that humans employ different information sources – like hearing, proprioception, haptics and vision – we propose a multimodal approach for unsupervised segmentation and identification of uni- and bi-manual action primitives in continuous observation sequences. To this end we consider time series data consisting of (i) an audio signal recorded with a structure-borne microphone attached to the manipulated object, (ii) hand postures acquired from a pair of Immersion CyberGloves [2], and (iii) tactile sensor readings obtained from pressure sensors attached to all fingertips of the gloves. We recorded manipulation sequences in which a human demonstrator performs basic manipulations such as lifting, shaking, putting down, screwing and unscrewing the lid of a bottle, and pouring. Our method aims at *unsupervised* partitioning of this sequence of low-level sensor data into segments that correspond to the above mentioned high-level manipulation primitives.

The vast amount of research in the fields of action and activity recognition reflects the importance of the problem. In the domain of action recognition, Matsuo et al. focused on force feedback [7] while a combination of different sensors like CyberGlove, Vicon or magnetic markers and tactile sensors was used by Kawasaki et al. [5] and Li et al. [6]. In the domain of activity spotting, acceleration data, tactile sensors, audio and ultra-wide band tags have been successfully used in [8] and [9]. However, many approaches are restricted to a single sensory channel.

In principle, all unsupervised multimodal approaches face two challenges: identification of actions and sensor fusion in multimodal sequences. These problems are commonly addressed with a heuristic-based, action-specific approach [5, 11]. Its disadvantage is the dependence on domain-specific knowledge. Ogris et al. describe the method of incremental masking for activity spotting, that consists of employing N independent processes for spotting of N activities [8]. In this approach a method for fusing of the individual spotting streams to estimate the final segments is required.

In our procedure we employ an unsupervised Bayesian segmentation method to identify segments of homogeneous activity across the multiple modalities in a single pass. Thus,

ICMI'11, November 14–18, 2011, Alicante, Spain.

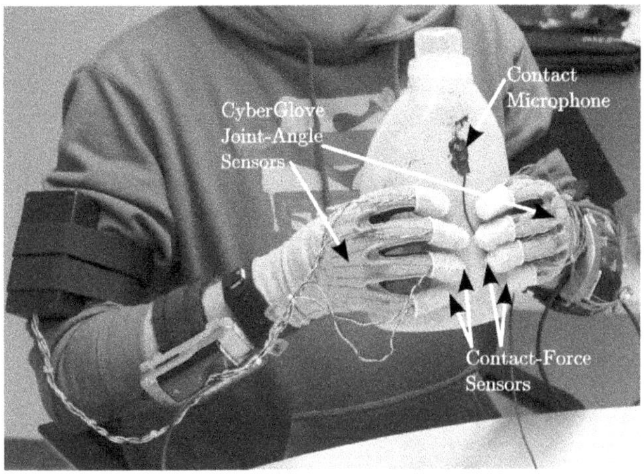

Figure 1: Experimental setup: a human demonstrator wearing contact and joint-angle sensors performs manipulation operations with a plastic bottle equipped with a structure-borne microphone.

the sensor fusion is conducted implicitly within the segmentation procedure and estimated segments span all modalities. Our approach does not require any specific knowledge about the number of segments or any domain-specific heuristics to describe each action primitive. Rather, the method splits the time series based on qualitative changes of more general models representing dynamical properties of subsequences. The resulting segments still constitute semantically relevant, high-level action primitives. Formally, the proposed approach is based on modelling the likelihood of a homogeneous subsequence as a product of modality-specific likelihoods, thus assuming statistical independence of all sensor modalities. The handling of all sensor information in a uniform probabilistic framework generates convincing segmentation results, which can smoothly compensate for local variations of single modalities. To demonstrate the feasibility of the method, we apply it to a set of manipulation sequences consisting of everyday tasks like grasping, pouring, and shaking.

The rest of the paper is organized as follows: Sec. 2 presents the scenario and the experimental setup. In Sec. 3 we describe the segmentation method and the models that constitute the main contributions of this paper. In Sec. 4.1 we specify the data and ground truth acquisition. We assess structural and temporal accuracy of the resulting segmentation in Sec. 4.2. In the final section 5 we summarize our results and give an outlook for future work.

2. EXPERIMENTAL SETUP

In our scenario, a human demonstrator performs sequences of simple uni- and bi-manual object manipulations with a gravel-filled plastic bottle[1], as can be seen in Fig. 1.

We use the following sensors to record multimodal time series of the performed action sequences (corresponding modality names used in formulas appear in parentheses):

- A structure-borne microphone attached to the bottle records an audio signal (`a`), which is focused on in-object generated sound, ignoring most environmental noise.
- 2×24 joint angles calculated from the measurements of two Immersion CyberGlove devices (`j`: both hands, `jl`: left hand, `jr`: right hand), describe the individual postures of both hands.
- 2×5 FSR pressure sensors attached to the fingertips of each CyberGlove (`t`: both hands, `tl`: left hand, `tr`: right hand) record the contact forces.

This collection of sensors yields a 29-dimensional (24 + 5) representation for each hand in addition to a scalar audio signal. The human demonstrator was told to perform a sequence of basic manipulation actions in the fixed order showed in the following enumeration. To obtain ground truth for later evaluation of computed segment borders, the aspired beginning or end of an action within a sequence was signalled to the human demonstrator via headphones as explained in Sec. 4.1. To achieve a rich variance of timing for individual subactions, the timing schedule of each trial was randomized by adding Gaussian noise to the nominal durations of all action primitives as specified in parentheses:

- pick up and hold the bottle with both hands (2 s + η)
- shake the bottle with both hands (.7 s + η)
- hold the bottle with both hands (.3 s + η)
- put down the bottle and pause (1 s + η)
- unscrew the cap with both hands (1.2 s + η)
- release cap and pause (1 s + η)
- grasp and lift the bottle with right hand (2 s + η)
- pour with right hand (1 s + η + 1 s + η)
- hold the bottle (.3 s + η)
- put down the bottle and pause (1 s + η)
- screw the cap with both hands (1.2 s + η)

The random variables $\eta \sim \mathcal{N}(0, .5\ s)$ denote the randomized timing of subsequences. The overall length of the time series of a trial accumulates to approximately 30 seconds.

3. SEGMENTATION METHOD

The recorded time series of multiple sensor modalities capture high-dimensional descriptions of action sequences. The focus of this paper is on unsupervised segmentation of this observation data based on all modalities. Our segmentation approach applies Fearnhead's method [4, 3] previously used for unsupervised detection of multiple change points in one-dimensional time series. In his work Fearnhead describes a deterministic method that maximizes the posterior distribution of the number and location of change points w.r.t given observations. The estimated change points are optimal in the sense that a combination of a prior distribution on segmentations and segment-wise likelihoods is maximized. For each of the resulting segments the likelihood is computed w.r.t. a single model chosen from a fixed set of models.

Xuan and Murphy apply Fearnhead's method to multidimensional time series using a single model that spans all dimensions [10]. This limits the applicability of their method to cases where the multidimensional time series originates from a single modality.

[1]The use of gravel instead of liquid is due to the necessity of a distinct audio signal and also safety concerns.

Our approach combines a preprocessing step with a set of simple, modality-specific models to come up with a uniform probabilistic description of all modalities as the basis for applying Fearnhead's algorithm (introduced in Sec. 3.1). In the preprocessing step the multidimensional data of each sensory channel is reduced to a compact scalar description capturing its temporal structure. Subsequently, two basic data models are employed, namely a constant model and a threshold model (see Sec. 3.2), to estimate the homogeneity of subsequences. These basic models are associated to individual modalities as explained in Sec. 3.3. A multiplicative combination yields a joint likelihood which describes the homogeneity of all sensor channels within a subsequence as detailed in Sec. 3.4.

3.1 Bayesian Segmentation

In general, Fearnheads' algorithm segments an arbitrary time series $y_{1:T}$ by determining a set of change points $1 < \tau_1 < \cdots < \tau_N < T$ at which qualitative changes occur in the data. Within the probabilistic framework of Fearnhead's algorithm, the optimal segmentation is obtained by maximizing the Bayesian posterior[2] $P(y_{1:T} \mid \tau_{1:N})P(\tau_{1:N})$ which consists of a likelihood term and a prior distribution over segmentations $P(\tau_{1:N})$. In a common choice of this prior, the probability $P(\tau_{1:N})$ is composed of probabilities of individual segment lengths which are computed according to the geometric distribution $P(l) = \lambda(1-\lambda)^{l-1}$. Consequently, the prior is characterized by a single parameter λ that is reciprocal to the expected segment length under a geometric distribution, i.e. $\lambda \propto 1/u$ where u is the expected length of subsequences. Once λ has been chosen, neither the number of change points N nor any information regarding their positions have to be specified in advance. Based on an empirical analysis we have chosen $\lambda = 5 \cdot 10^{-6}$.

The likelihood term represents the probability, that the observed time series originates from a set of given data models, which are fixed over the period of individual segments. To this end, a finite set of data models $\mathcal{M}$ is employed. Given a particular model $m \in \mathcal{M}$, the marginal likelihood $P(y_{s:t} \mid m)$ determines the probability, that the entire subsequence $y_{s:t}$ originates from this model. Prior probabilities $P(m)$ can be associated with all models to reflect their relative frequency. In this paper, we consider a set of four joint models with uniform prior probabilities. Each joint model is a product composed from five basic models, describing the homogeinity of a subsequence $y_{s:t}$ w.r.t. the individual sensor channels. In the following section we introduce the basic models which we later apply to individual modalities.

3.2 Basic Data Models

In order to locally represent scalar sensor data we employ two simple kinds of probabilistic models: a *threshold* model and a *constant* model.

The threshold model is a binary model designed to estimate whether the entire segment data lies below or above a given threshold γ. The marginal likelihoods associated to these models, denoted by $m_{<\gamma}$ and $m_{>\gamma}$ resp., indicate how well the time series segment $y_{s:t}$ fits the assumptions of being below or above the threshold. For $m_{<\gamma}$ we define the improper[3] marginal likelihood as follows:

$$P(y_{s:t} \mid m_{<\gamma}) = \prod_{k=s}^{t} p(y_k | m_{<\gamma}), \tag{1}$$

$$\text{where} \quad p(y_k \mid m_{<\gamma}) = \begin{cases} 1, & \text{if } y_k < \gamma \\ p_o & \text{otherwise} \end{cases} \tag{2}$$

where $p(y_k|m_{<\gamma})$ is the probability, that a single sample y_k fits the model assumption. The parameter p_0 is the probability of a simple data point y_k being an outlier w.r.t. the model. Denoting the segment length by $u = t - s$ and the number of not fitting samples by $n = |\{y_k > \gamma \mid s \le k < t\}|$, and ignoring the constant normalization factor, we can derive the following, more compact formulas for both models:

$$P(y_{s:t} \mid m_{<\gamma}) = {p_o}^n \quad \text{and} \quad P(y_{s:t} \mid m_{>\gamma}) = {p_o}^{u-n} \tag{3}$$

As can be seen from Eq. 3, the marginal likelihood becomes smaller, the more data points are on the wrong side of the threshold.

The constant model is employed to estimate how well a scalar segment can be described by a constant function. Again, we assume that individual samples y_k are i.i.d., now according to a Gaussian distribution:

$$y_k \sim \mathcal{N}(\mu, 1)\,,$$

where the mean μ is the unknown parameter of the constant model m_c. We assume a Gaussian prior distribution for μ as well, i.e. $\mu \sim \mathcal{N}(\eta, u)$, where we set $\eta = \langle y \rangle$. This choice of η yields the following simplified log marginal likelihood of $y_{s:t}$ for the constant model m_c [4] :

$$\begin{aligned}\log P(y_{s:t} \mid m_c) &= \log \int P(y_{s:t} \mid \mu, m_c) P(\mu \mid m_c) d\mu \\ &= -u\mathrm{Var}(y_{s:t}) + C\,.\end{aligned}$$

This result can be interpreted as follows: the empirical variance of an approximately constant segment gets close to zero, thus maximizing the log likelihood to be well fitted by a constant model – independent of the exact value level of μ. If the segment comprises two constant sub segments of different value levels, the variance will become much larger, indicating that such a segment cannot be well fitted by a single constant model, but would be better fitted by two constant models in separate segments.

3.3 Preprocessing and Model Selection

In the initial preprocessing step we align individual sensor data streams based on timestamps and obtain a single multimodal, 59-dimensional times series. Further preprocessing steps are modality-specific and facilitate subsequent likelihood calculations.

Audio signal. Often, actions are accompanied by a typical sound, whose structure and volume stays constant during the whole segment. Consider for example shaking an object or pouring water into a glass. Also segment boundaries are sometimes accompanied with a short, but strong change of the audio signal, e.g. placing or dropping an object.

Hence, we consider the local variance of the recorded audio signal, which is calculated with the sliding window method

[2]We suppress the constant normalization factor $P(y_{1:T})^{-1}$.

[3]For the sake of clarity, we neglect the constant normalization factor to yield a proper probability distribution.

[4]Except for the choice of η, this likelihood calculation is identical to the one proposed by Fearnhead [4] in Sec. 4.2.

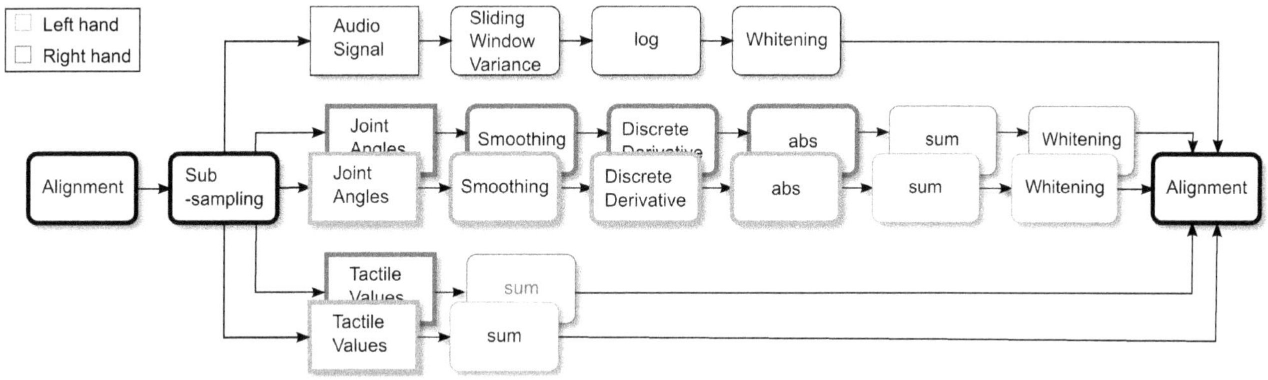

Figure 2: Schematic illustration of the preprocessing. Bold frame borders represents vector-valued data or operations.

(window length is $W = 20$ samples). The resulting time series is logarithmized and whitened for normalization. In order to separate segments of similar structure, i.e. approximately constant signal variance, we apply a *constant model* denoted by m_a to this preprocessed audio signal. In our previous work we have applied Auto Regressive (AR) models of the order one, two and three to model the raw audio signal [1]. The proposed, much simpler constant model yields comparable segmentation results (cf. Sec. 4.2), and facilitates the application in product models. Please note, that this approach tries to segment based on overall audio activity, but not based on audio content, which would require much more complex audio features.

Hand postures. Most action primitives are characterized by a homogeneous overall level of finger motion – e.g. consider the uniform joint motion when grasping or releasing an object. Hence we reduce the 24-dimensional joint-angle trajectories to a scalar time series representing the overall level of joint activity for each hand. All joint angle trajectories are smoothed and their discrete derivative is calculated to obtain joint velocities. To measure the overall joint activity, we accumulate the absolute values of all joint velocities and whiten the resulting trajectory for normalization. Again we apply *constant models* – denoted by m_{jl} and m_{jr} for the left and right hand resp. – in order to segment regions of sustained, fixed hand activity, independently of the exact velocity level.

Tactile sensors. The *threshold models* are applied to the accumulated tactile data to discriminate "object contact" from "no object contact" for each hand. The parameter γ specifies the threshold for recognizing hand-object contact. As the tactile feedback is susceptible to strong noise and larger variations within action primitives (e.g. during shaking), the constant model is not applicable anymore. We denote the "object contact"-models with capital-letter subscripts: m_L and m_R for the left and right hand respectively. The corresponding notations for the "no object contact"-models are m_l and m_r. Note, that the assignment of a contact or no-contact model automatically yields an identification of the contact status during the segment.

In summary, the described preprocessing reduces the multidimensional sensor readings to five aligned scalar, non-negative modality-specific sensor channels. A schematic illustration of all preprocessing steps is given in Fig. 2.

The following table summarizes the association of data models to sensor channels:

Sensor channel	Model	Notation
tactile sum left hand	threshold	m_L, m_l
tactile sum right hand	threshold	m_R, m_r
joint-angle activity left hand	constant	m_{jl}
joint-angle activity right hand	constant	m_{jr}
audio signal	constant	m_{a}

Table 1: Association of modalities to data models.

3.4 Sensor Fusion

To combine all sensor channels within a multimodal joint model, we combine the introduced individual likelihoods into a joint likelihood. Assuming statistical independence of all sensor channels, the individual modality-specific likelihoods are combined multiplicatively. Since two alternative models are available for both tactile modalities, the final set $\mathcal{M}$ of models applied in Fearnhead's algorithm comprises four joint models formed by the Cartesian product of channel-specific models, i.e. $\mathcal{M} = \{m_{lr}, m_{Lr}, m_{lR}, m_{LR}\}$. Each joint model contains two tactile threshold models and three constant models for audio and joint angles: "m_{lr}: no contact for both hands", "m_{Lr}: contact for left hand only", "m_{lR}: contact for right hand only", "m_{LR}: contact for both hands". Hence, the marginal log-likelihood of each joint model is computed as the weighted sum of five individual log-likelihoods, e.g.:

$$\begin{aligned}\log P(y_{s:t} \mid m_{lR}) = & w_t(\log P(y_{s:t} \mid m_l) + \log P(y_{s:t} \mid m_R)) + \\ & w_a \log P(y_{s:t} \mid m_{\mathrm{a}}) + \\ & w_j(\log P(y_{s:t} \mid m_{\mathrm{jl}}) + \log P(y_{s:t} \mid m_{\mathrm{jr}})),\end{aligned}$$

where w_a, w_t and w_j are the weights determining the influence of audio, tactile and joint-angle modality.

4. EXPERIMENTAL RESULTS

In this section we first describe the data pool and the acquisition of the ground truth. After that we illustrate in a few examples the influence of the weight parameters w_t, w_a, w_j on the timing quality and structure of estimated segmentations.

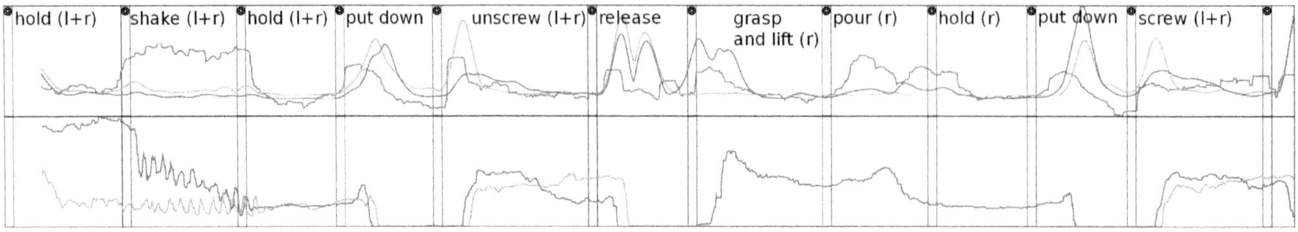

Figure 3: Annotated time series of a complete trial. Emissions of the main audio cues are drawn as black frames with an ❂ indicator. The upper part depicts the preprocessed joint-angles trajectories for the left (red) and right (blue) hand as well as the audio signal (brown). The lower part of the plot shows the cumulative tactile feedback for the left (red) and right (blue) hand.

4.1 Data Pool

We recorded 30 trials of the action sequence described in Sec. 2 with a single human demonstrator in one session. This corresponds to ca. 10^5 data points and $30 \times 11 = 330$ expected change points in total.

To avoid time-consuming hand-labelling of the recorded time series, we employ automatically generated audio cues provided to the human demonstrator in order to indicate the desired start or end times of primitive actions. We use the known timing of these cues as ground truth information about segment boundaries and rely on the human demonstrator to align their executed actions as closely to them as possible.

The audio cues (similar to dial tones) are provided via headphones to prevent their presence in the recorded audio modality. Each cue consists of a sequence of four beep sounds: the first three are preparatory and allow the human demonstrator to anticipate the fourth signal (*main cue*) which notifies the associated event (beginning or end of action execution) to the human demonstrator. We write $c^{\alpha}_{i,j}$, $j \in \{1, 2, 3, 4\}$ to denote the point in time at which the j-th signal of the i-th cue is emitted in trial α. We omit the superscript α if the trial is not important. Note, that the ground truth provided by the main audio cues is only an approximation to the actually observed segment boundaries, because the human demonstrator cannot exactly stick to the desired timing as illustrated in Fig. 4.

Fig. 3 shows an example of a preprocessed time series and the temporal structure of the main cues – indicated by a ❂ symbol. The upper part of the plot depicts the preprocessed joint-angle trajectories for the left and right hand as well as the audio signal. The lower part of the plot shows the cumulative tactile feedback for the left and the right hand. Note, that the beginning ("pick up") and end ("release") of the original time series is missing as a result from the preprocessing of joint-angle data.

A visual inspection of the time series plotted in Fig. 3 reveals a problem of our ground-truth acquisition method: Actions performed quickly after each other, e.g. the sequence of putting down and releasing an object, cannot be individually indicated by cues. Also, regimes of different levels of hand activity cannot explicitly marked by audio cues, provided to the demonstrator, without artificially slowing down and interfering with the natural execution of actions. Therefore, the cue schedule representing ground truth information only covers a subset of actual action primitives in the sequence. As an example, consider the peak of hand activity at the beginning of the *unscrewing* action. This peak – corresponding to the opening and closing motion during pre-grasping and grasping – is clearly separated from the subsequent, much smaller hand activity corresponding to the actual screwing motion. However, we do not have a cue signal separating these semantically different sub actions. Obviously this will impair the temporal accuracy statistics and could be resolved with an elaborate manual annotation of the time series, instead of using the automated labelling based on the provided audio cues.

4.2 Segmentation Quality

In this section we report on segmentation results for different combinations of sensor modalities determined by the weights w_t, w_a, w_j. Although we performed a detailed evaluation with different weight combinations in a regular lattice of size $5 \times 5 \times 5$, we focus here on the effect of individual modalities onto segmentation results. The quality of the segmentation is evaluated w.r.t. to structural and temporal correctness considering three measures: (i) the temporal deviation of the found and expected boundaries (temporal accuracy index), (ii) the number of not detected segment boundaries (missing segments index), and (iii) the number of estimated change points between expected segment boundaries (oversegmentation index). These measures are evaluated for each expected segment boundary individually to identify problems in recognizing specific boundaries.

To obtain quantitative results, the cue-based ground truth data is exploited as follows: For each main cue $c^{\alpha}_{i,4}$ within each trial α, the temporally closest generated change point is searched within the interval $I_{t,i} = [c_{i,3}, (c_{i,4} + c_{i+1,1})/2]$. This temporal window is defined by the audio cues of two adjacent segments. If such a change point can be identified within $I_{t,i}$, the temporal distance to the main cue $c_{i,4}$ serves as an indicator of the temporal accuracy of the segmentation. Otherwise the segment boundary is considered as missing. To assess the oversegmentation index, we count the number of identified change points between two adjacent cues, i.e. within the interval $I_{o,i} = [c_{i,3}, c_{i+1,3}]$ as illustrated in Fig. 4. More than one change point will indicate oversegmentation.

The segmentation results discussed in the following paragraphs are illustrated by segmentation plots (Fig. 5 – 8) corresponding to four different weight parameter combinations. Each segmentation plot refers to the same typical trial, showing the time series and segmentation result in the same fashion like Fig. 3. Figures 9 – 11 present the quantitative measures introduced in the previous paragraph in individual bar plots. Results in these plots are averaged

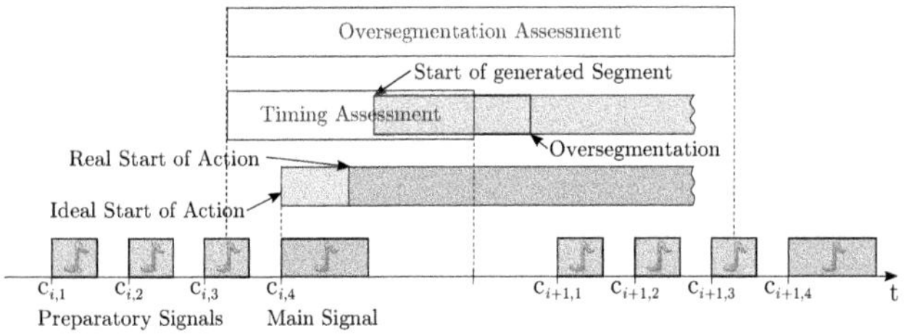

Figure 4: Temporal relations between cues, actions and generated segments. The execution of an action by the human demonstrator is expected to start (light green bar) at the beginning of the main cue signal $c_{i,4}$, but the actual beginning of the execution usually deviates (dark green bar). The autonomous evaluation looks for generated change points (dark yellow bar) corresponding to these expected segment boundaries in different intervals (light gray boxes).

over all 30 trials. Colors correspond to individual combinations of weight parameters. The plot in Fig. 9 shows the **timing deviation**. Smaller values indicate better temporal quality of the segmentation. Fig. 10 shows the **oversegmentation** statistics, indicating the number of change points between adjacent cues. Finally, Fig. 11 illustrates the **missing segments** statistics, showing the averaged number of not detected segments. This plot illustrates how well each particular segment boundary has been detected on average.

As explained in Sec. 3.3 we apply threshold models to the **tactile** data, in order to discriminate "contact" and "no contact" regions. Fig. 5 shows a segmentation example solely based on the tactile modality. The threshold models can robustly and accurately identify regions with and without object contact. Although the left and right hand do not synchronously grasp or release the object (consider the beginning and end of the non-contact regions 2, 4, and 6), the Bayesian approach only generates a single change point. Hence, employing the prior distribution of segment lengths, the approach can smoothly ignore such small and semantically irrelevant details. The *missing-segments* plot (Fig. 11 - red bars) shows that segment borders for actions like "put down", "start and stop pouring", "start and stop shaking" cannot be estimated from the tactile data, which is not surprising, because those actions mainly involve object motion which is captured by the audio channel. Accordingly, the "put down" cue is immediately followed by a peak in the audio signal generated by the object when placed on the table. The structural correctness (Fig. 10) for the segments associated to *contact*-regimes such as "pick up", "start, end screwing", is very high: The oversegmentation index equals one on average.

If we add **joint angles** as an additional modality considered for segmentation, grasping and releasing actions are additionally segmented by subdividing regions 2, 4, 6 of Fig. 5 into three regions each, as shown in Fig. 6. Those additional segments at the beginning and end of previous non-contact regions, indicate segments of strong *finger motion*. Again, there is no oversegmentation w.r.t. the considered modalities, due to the smoothing property of the Bayesian approach. However, the oversegmentation plot (Fig. 10 - green bars) indicates a doubling of the number of found change points for the corresponding cue signals, which is due to the missing end-signal for the release action in our ground truth data. Obviously, purely audio-related segment boundaries still are not found (cf. Fig. 11).

(w_t, w_a, w_j)	μ_t (σ_t)	μ_o (σ_o)	μ_m
(.3 0 0)	0.21 ± 0.03	0.64 ± 0.23	0.70
(.3 0 .3)	0.20 ± 0.02	1.28 ± 0.79	0.54
(.2 .2 0)	0.21 ± 0.01	1.10 ± 0.23	0.30
(.2 .3 .2)	0.21 ± 0.01	1.71 ± 0.65	0.18

Table 2: Summary of segmentation results for 4 different combinations of modalities. The mean values for temporal error (μ_t), oversegmentation (μ_o) and missing segments (μ_m) are obtained from averaging over all trials and all cues.

Fig. 7 illustrates segmentation results based on the combination of **audio** and **tactile** modalities. In this case, the generated segment structure almost perfectly reproduces the cue schedule, which is also reflected in the oversegmentation plot (Fig. 10 - blue bars). Again, the end of the "putting down" action is correctly recognized as an additional change point, which is missing in the ground truth data.

Considering **all three modalities** provides the most detailed segmentation results (Fig. 8). Including the joint angles, generates additional segment borders indicating the beginning and end of hand motions during grasping and releasing of the object, again resulting in an increase of the oversegmentation index, similar to the tactile-joint modality situation. Action primitives like "putting down", "releasing object" and "pausing" (Fig. 8, regions 4,5,6; 9,10; 14, 15 and 16) correspond in our evaluation to a single cue, i.e. to one search range $I_{i,o}$ for segment candidates. As a result the number of detected segment borders in the "no contact" regimes increases (see Fig. 10 - purple bars).

Table 2 summarizes the evaluation measures in the selected situations. Values of temporal error, oversegmentation and missing segments are averaged over all trials and all cues. They are denoted by $\mu_t(\sigma_t)$, $\mu_o(\sigma_o)$ and μ_m respectively. The table shows that the combination of all modalities yields only 18% of missing segments along with the temporal deviation of 0.21 seconds.

5. CONCLUSIONS AND OUTLOOK

In this paper we have introduced a multimodal, unsupervised approach to segmentation of continuous object manipulation sequences. Our procedure does not require any prior knowledge about the content of the sequences. A set of weight parameters allows to directly control the influence of individual modalities (joint angles, tactiles and audio) on segmentation results. Our segmentation results demonstrate the importance of the multi-modal approach to segmentation. Especially the tactile and audio channels are essential for successful recognition of the desired action primitives. The joint-angle modality capturing overall hand motion, provides a more fine-grained segmentation structure, which is not captured by our ground truth data, thus leading to oversegmentation. However, looking at the generated segment boundaries, they all are reasonable. The Bayesian approach can successfully fuse sensor information of all channels, without oversegmenting in regions of con-

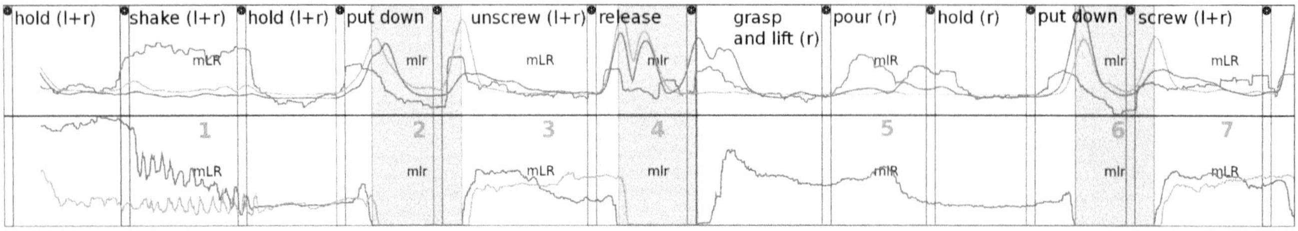

Figure 5: Segmentation of a trial based on tactile modality only, i.e. $(w_t, w_a, w_j) = (.3, 0, 0)$. Segments 1,3 and 7 are "contact" regions for both hands, region 5 is a "contact" regions for the right hand only. The tactile values of the "no contact" regions are approximately zero corresponding to "the object is not in the hand". Notice that although the left and right hands are not precisely synchronized during "grasp" or "release" (beginning and end of the regions 2, 4, 6) only a single change point is generated by the algorithm.

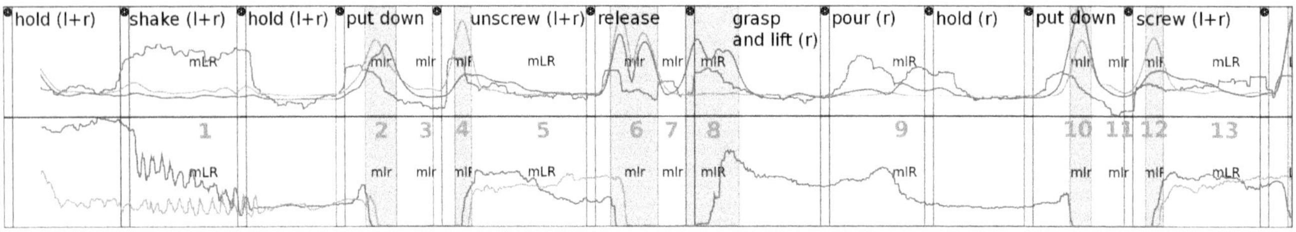

Figure 6: Segmentation of a trial with tactile *and* joint-angle modalities, i.e. $(w_t, w_a, w_j) = (.3, 0, .3)$, leads to a further subdivision of regions 2, 4, 6 of previous Fig. 5. Higher finger activity associated with grasping (regions 4, 8, 12) and releasing (regions 2, 6, 10) allow to recognize this fine-grained action sub structure. Note, that no ground truth information is available to assess the segmentation quality for those change points.

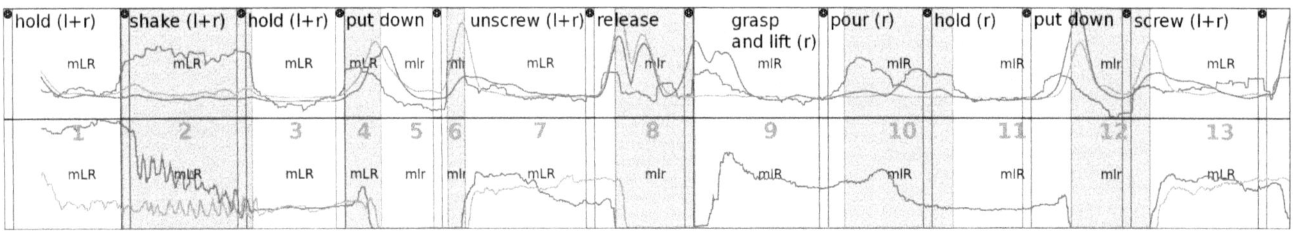

Figure 7: Segmentation of a trial based on tactile and audio modalities, i.e. $(w_t, w_a, w_j) = (.2, .2, 0)$. Similar to the previous plot, the sub sequence "put down" and "start unscrewing" is further subdivided into release and grasp based on the strong audio signal. However, in regions 8 and 12, the audio signal associated with grasping and releasing was not strong enough to trigger the creation of separate segments. Additionally to Figs. 5 and 6, the "shaking" and "pouring" sub sequences are correctly found based on the associated noise (regions 2 and 10).

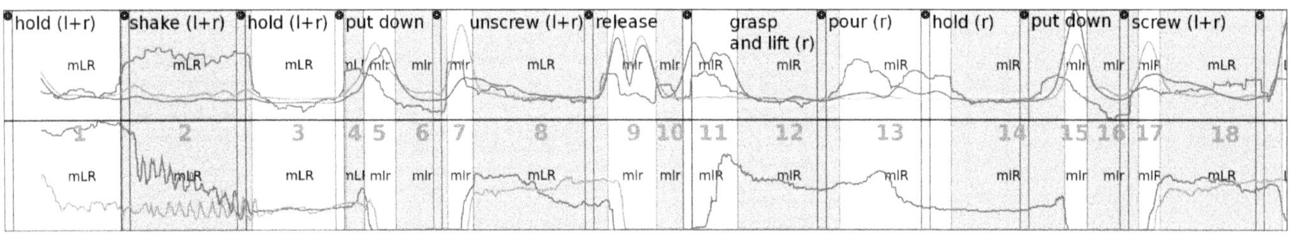

Figure 8: The segmentation based on all three modalities, i.e. $(w_t, w_a, w_j) = (.2, .3, .2)$, yields the most detailed action structure, correctly subdividing into semantically different sub sequences. The automatically generated, fragmentary ground truth information can only coarsely capture the underlying structure.

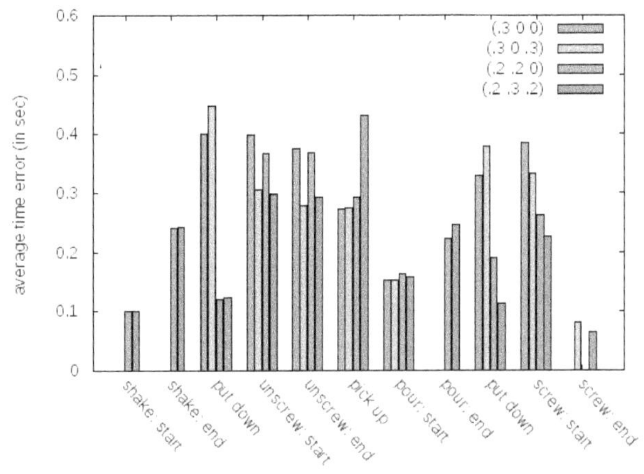

Figure 9: Temporal accuracy index; smaller deviation indicate better temporal quality of the segmentation.

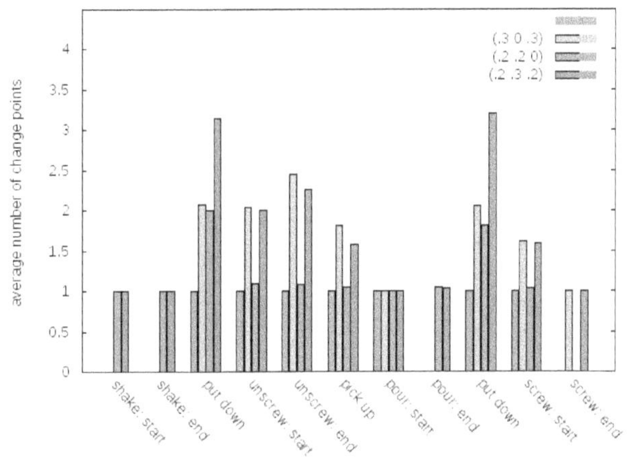

Figure 10: Oversegmention index; The value of the y-achsis indicates the number of change points between adjacent cues.

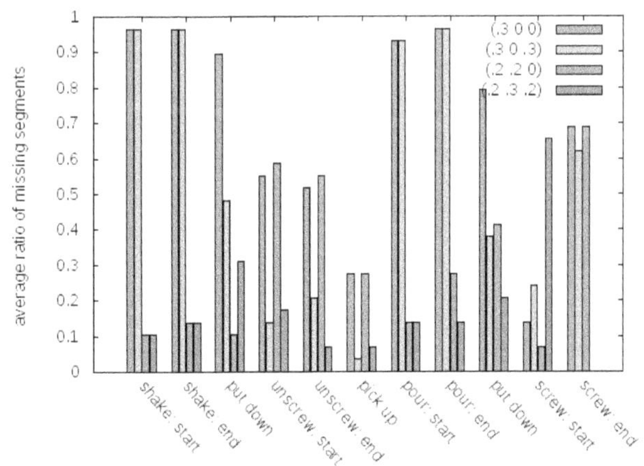

Figure 11: Missing segments index; Ratio of not detected segments to number of trials.

secutive, but unaligned changes of individual modalities. Rather, the approach can ignore those details and generate a common change point within such regions.

The experiments have showed that our procedure yields satisfactory results w.r.t. temporal and structural correctness of generated segmentations. For the weight combination $(w_t, w_a, w_j) = (.2, .3, .2)$ we have achieved an average timing error of 0.21 seconds and an average detection failure rate of 0.18. Our future work will focus on evaluating the approach on a larger dataset involving multiple human demonstrators, and considering manually annotated data to improve ground truth quality.

6. ACKNOWLEDGEMENTS

Alexandra Barchunova gratefully acknowledges the financial support from Honda Research Institute Europe for the project "Multimodal Recognition of Manual Interaction". We are very thankful to Jan Moringen for discussions and proofreading.

7. REFERENCES

[1] A. Barchunova, R. Haschke, U. Grossekathoefer, S. Wachsmuth, H. Janssen, and H. Ritter. Unsupervised segmentation of object manipulation operations from multimodal input. In B. Hammer and T. Villmann, editors, *New Challenges in Neural Computation*, Machine Learning Reports. 2011.

[2] Immersion CyberGlove II. http://www.cyberglovesystems.com/products/cyberglove-ii/overview.

[3] P. Fearnhead. Exact bayesian curve fitting and signal segmentation. *Signal Processing*, 53, 2005.

[4] P. Fearnhead. Exact and efficient Bayesian inference for multiple changepoint problems. *Statistics and Computing*, 2006.

[5] H. Kawasaki, K. Nakayama, and G. Parker. Teaching for multi-fingered robots based on motion intention in virtual reality. In *IECON*, 2000.

[6] C. Li, P. Kulkarni, and B. Prabhakaran. Motion Stream Segmentation and Recognition by Classification. In *ICASSP*. IEEE, 2006.

[7] K. Matsuo, K. Murakami, T. Hasegawa, K. Tahara, and K. Ryo. Segmentation method of human manipulation task based on measurement of force imposed by a human hand on a grasped object. In *IROS*. IEEE, 2009.

[8] G. Ogris, T. Stiefmeier, P. Lukowicz, and G. Troster. Using a complex multi-modal on-body sensor system for activity spotting. *Wearable Computers, IEEE International Symposium*, 2008.

[9] J. A. Ward, P. Lukowicz, G. Troster, and T. E. Starner. Activity recognition of assembly tasks using body-worn microphones and accelerometers. *TPAMI*, 2006.

[10] X. Xuan and K. Murphy. Modeling changing dependency structure in multivariate time series. In *ICML*. ACM, 2007.

[11] R. Zöllner, T. Asfour, and R. Dillmann. Programming by demonstration: Dual-arm manipulation tasks for humanoid robots. In *IROS*. IEEE, 2004.

Could a Dialog Save your Life? Analyzing the Effects of Speech Interaction Strategies while Driving

Akos Vetek, Saija Lemmelä
Nokia Research Center, Helsinki, Finland
P.O. Box 407
00045 Nokia Group

akos.vetek@nokia.com, saija.lemmela@nokia.com

ABSTRACT

We describe a controlled Wizard-of-Oz study using a medium-fidelity driving simulator investigating how a guided dialog strategy performs when compared to open dialog while driving, with respect to the cognitive loading these strategies impose on the driver. Through our analysis of driving performance logs, speech data, NASA-TLX questionnaires, and bio-signals (heart rate and EEG) we found the secondary speech task to have a measurable adverse effect on driving performance, and that guided dialog is less cognitively demanding in dual-task (driving plus speech interaction) conditions. The driving performance logs and heart rate variability information proved useful for identifying cognitively challenging situations while driving. These could provide important information to an in-car dialog management system that could take into account the driver's cognitive resources to provide safer speech-based interaction by adapting the dialog.

Categories and Subject Descriptors

H.1.2 [**User/Machine Systems**]: Human factors and Human information processing

General Terms

Measurement, Performance, Design, Experimentation, Human Factors, Languages

Keywords

In-vehicle interaction, dialog management, cognitive load, biosignals

1. INTRODUCTION

The number of in-vehicle entertainment and information systems has continually increased in the last decades. More recently, technologies like Terminal Mode promise seamless connectivity between a smart phone and the in-vehicle infotainment system providing access to all phone applications within the car [1].

At the same time, people spend significant amount of their time in a car. According to a 2001 national travel survey in the United States, 77% of adults commute to work alone using personal vehicles with an average commute time of 25.5 minutes one way [2], while the number of extreme car commuters who travel more than 90 minutes to work, one way, is estimated at 3.4 million, and is the fastest growing commuter group.

With current lifestyles and such advanced in-vehicle technology, it is inevitable that drivers will perform secondary tasks, or operate driver assistance and entertainment systems while driving. In general, some of the common secondary tasks performed in a driving environment includes: cell-phone dialing, navigation/destination interaction, e-mail processing, music retrieval and other generic command and control in-vehicle telematics systems [3]. These secondary tasks are a serious safety issue as well, as a substantial number of car accidents are results of driver distraction.

Since driving is an eyes- and hands-busy activity, it has been long recognized that traditional driver-vehicle interaction techniques are inadequate for safe and effective use of these increasingly complex in-car devices and the various services they provide access to. People have begun to investigate alternative methods, such as speech-based interaction in the car to allow the driver to stay focused on the road. Spoken dialog systems are often considered one of the most attractive features of in-car entertainment and information systems, since speech is the only wideband communication channel not thought to be significantly engaged during the driving process [2].

Although spoken dialog systems do afford users hands-free, eyes-free interaction, the benefits of leveraging speech can be forfeit if users are expending cognitive effort for the dialog interaction. Indeed, research has shown that the cognitive demands of dialog seem to play a more important role in distracting drivers than physically handling cell phones [4]. Furthermore [6] have found that when users encounter problems with in-car speech interfaces, they tend to drive more dangerously as they attempt to figure out, for instance, why their utterances are failing. Hence any approach to speech interactive systems in automobiles must avoid distracting drivers with errors and be highly usable while users are engaged in their primary task, driving.

Ideally, drivers should pay primary attention to driving, rather than any secondary tasks. If such secondary tasks or distractions lie within the limit of the amount of spare cognitive resources for the driver, he or she can still focus on driving. Therefore, the design of safe speech interactive systems for in-vehicle environments should take into account factors from the driver's cognitive capacity, driving skills, and their degree of proficiency for the cognitive load estimation. With knowledge of such factors, an effective driver behavior model with real-time driving information can be integrated into a smart vehicle support or control driver assistance system to manage driver distractions (e.g. suspend applications in a situation of heavy driving workload) [3].

In this paper we set out to investigate how different dialog strategies affect the cognitive load and driving performance of users, to aid the design of spoken dialog systems which can be capable of adapting itself to support a driver's cognitive capacity.

The rest of the paper is organized as follows. We first provide background information and review related work, followed by a description of the study we carried out. We then describe our findings and end with a discussion of the main findings and conclusions drawn.

2. BACKGROUND AND RELATED WORK

In this section we discuss about spoken dialog systems. We also introduce some existing work and theories on the cognitive requirements speech based systems set for drivers as well as present strategies to mitigate distractions. Finally, we present a set of approaches recently suggested for measuring the workload while driving.

2.1 Spoken dialog systems

Considerable progress has been made in recent years in the development of dialog systems [7]. Spoken dialog systems aim to enable users to interact with computer systems via natural and intelligent dialogs, as they would with human agents.

The dialog manager is the core component of the dialog system and as its name implies it is responsible for maintaining the dialog flow [7]. The dialog flow can take various forms. In this paper, we will concentrate on two types of dialog strategy to control the flow of the interaction. In the case of guided, or system-initiative, dialog the system is in control to guide the user through the dialog step-by-step via a series of voice prompts often accepting only a set of commands at a time. In the case of open dialog the user can respond freely using natural language. These systems typically rely on sophisticated Natural Language Understanding (NLU) as well [8]. These two types were chosen for our investigation as they represent the two extremes when it comes to dialogue strategies.

The choice of guided and open dialog strategies are also influenced by the limitations and capabilities of the underlying speech and language technologies. Guided dialogs make use of simple grammars that specify the available spoken commands the user can select from to respond to the system. These commands are typically listed in the system's voice prompts. For example, "Please, specify the time. Say morning, afternoon or evening". Open dialog strategies are used by systems that understand natural, conversational speech and thus the interaction with such systems closely mimics the normal human-to-human communication. For example, "When would you like to depart?" or "How may I help you?"

2.2 Distractions while driving

Previous research with cellular telephones suggests that speech-based interaction with an in-vehicle computer is likely to increase cognitive load on the driver and draw attention away from the roadway. This could undermine driver awareness of the roadway and delay driver response to roadway events. Increasing the complexity of the in-vehicle computer system could exacerbate these effects. Increasing the complexity of the driving environment might also increase the drivers' cognitive load, and the interaction between the two could further delay drivers' response to roadway events [9].

People have the ability to perform multiple concurrent activities, as long as there are enough cognitive resources available and there is no conflict in the resource demands from different tasks [10]. The core aspects of driving are "automated" and easily backgrounded as other tasks come to the fore [11]. However, multiple studies have shown the detrimental effects of cell phone conversations, texting, or interacting with music players on driving safety [12]. Drivers who engage in phone conversations while driving have been found to have slower braking reaction time [11], degraded steering performance [16], and to have accidents with higher likelihood [17] than drivers without phone conversations. The common solution of mandating that calls be made in a hands-free manner while driving, has not been found to improve safety [18]. A large body of findings suggests that it is not the motor action of holding the phone, but primarily the cognitive demands of dual-task scenarios that degrade performance on one or both tasks [4].

Findings from basic research on attention also confirm the potential for speech-based interaction to distract drivers. The multiple resource theory of attention suggests that speech-based interaction with an in-vehicle computer would be less detrimental to the manual control task of driving than a visual display, for instance [10]. Speech-based interaction should demand the resources associated with auditory perception, verbal working memory, and vocal response. Driving should demand the resources associated with visual perception, spatial working memory, and manual response. Because these resources are independent timesharing should be quite efficient. However, the attentional demands that speech-based interaction may place on common central processing resources might undermine timesharing and compromise driving safety. Other researchers suggest that central processing limits will predominate, and that a single channel, limited-capacity theory better reflects how speech-based interaction might undermine driving safety [19]. More important than the specific attentional resources may be the strategies of task management. Initial data suggests that drivers may not prioritize and manage their speech-based tasks effectively [20]. Specifically, studies have shown that a concurrent verbal task increased drivers' propensity to take risks, and that drivers did not compensate as verbal interactions slowed their reaction times [21]. These results suggest that drivers may not fully recognize the distractions of speech-based interaction and may fail to compensate for the distraction that these demands induce.

While a lot of research exists on the distraction and safety consequences of speech communication or standard concurrent verbal tasks while driving, the distraction and safety consequences of speech-based interfaces are not easily extrapolated from these studies. Some simple differences include the added cognitive load of interpreting a poor quality synthetic voice [22]. Recalling commands and remembering system syntax could also add a substantial demand not experienced in conversations. Similarly, the spatial demands of navigating a complex menu structure may introduce a cognitive load that may compete with the spatial demands of driving in a way that a conversation would not [23]. On the other hand, interaction with a speech-based system may be less distracting than conversations because drivers may have more flexibility to abort an interaction with an in-vehicle computer. In addition, unlike conversation with passengers, current in-vehicle computers are not able to modulate their interaction with the driver as a function of the driving situation.

2.3 Strategies to mitigate distractions

Findings that conversations with collocated passengers have less negative impact on driving compared to those with remote callers have led [24] to propose that in-vehicle spoken dialog systems include dialog management capabilities that also take the cognitive workload of the driver into consideration.

Other researchers have explored the abilities of people to interleave driving with other activities. Brumby et al. [26] studied how dialing a phone number can be interleaved with driving by chunking the dialog task to be accommodated within driving.

2.4 Measuring workload while driving

Over recent years car manufactures and research groups have suggested different techniques to measure driver distraction and workload, ranging from simple laboratory tests to high fidelity driving simulators. Various direct and indirect methods have been used and proposed to gauge the workload imposed on the driver, including driving performance measures (consisting of driver inputs to the vehicle or measures of how well the vehicle was driven along its intended path) [27], task performance measures, and even information from physiological sensors such as Galvanic Skin Response (GSR), Electrocardiogram (ECG) and Electroencephalogram (EEG) that can inform about driver stress and their cognitive and affective states. In the case of spoken interaction, various conversational and linguistic features of the interaction have been analyzed as well [25], [28].

3. STUDY

A spoken dialog system that is considerate of the cognitive workload of the driver, could in response to elevated workload level intervene and alter the interaction, for instance by pausing the dialog to let the driver concentrate on the driving task, or in less serious situations the dialog system could change its behavior by, for instance, reformulating its question to make the dialog task easier for the driver [25].

In order to explore the latter scenario, we set out to understand and compare the effects of two different dialog strategies (guided and open) on cognitive load while driving. While the open strategy might be considered more natural and is often seen as a better solution for speech user interfaces, their behavior is still far from the behavior of a human communication partner who can flexibly adapt the conversation to suit the current context, for instance, when changing lane in heavy traffic. On the other hand, guided dialog might support well a person who is already loaded by a primary task, for instance, by offering more specific memory cues. We conducted a controlled Wizard-of-Oz (WoZ) study using a medium-fidelity driving simulator to find out how the guided dialog strategy performs when compared to open dialog.

3.1 Setup

In Figure 1 the overall setup of the hardware in the experiment is shown. The setup was created to simulate a driving situation, complete with a steering wheel and pedals. A first person view of the road was presented on a large screen (47" LCD monitor). The participants sat comfortably about one and half meters away from the screen.

While driving the car simulator, participants conducted secondary tasks using a speech user interface emulated by a Wizard-of-Oz (WoZ) setup. During the task the state of the participants was measured by biosignal sensors and after each task the participants also reported their cognitive loading via the NASA-TLX [29] questionnaire. Each test sessions was video recorded. Detailed information about the driving performance was logged by the driving simulator, while the spoken interaction was recorded by the WoZ tool.

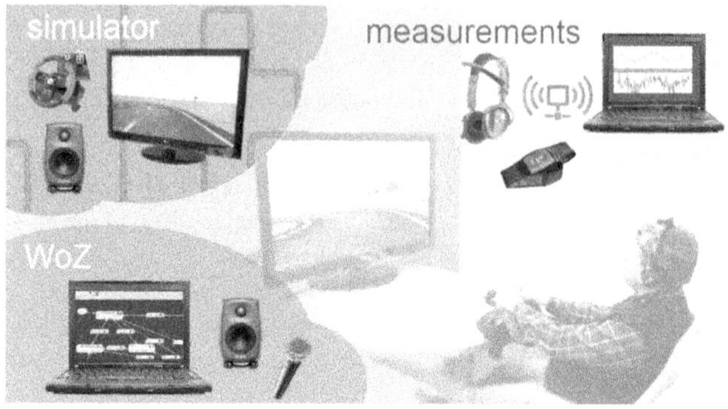

Figure 1. The overall test setup

3.1.1 Driving simulator

CARS [27] is an open source driving simulator tool with analysis capabilities that provide detailed information about driver performance. CARS consists of three main components: a map editor for creating the route according to specific requirements with different street elements, traffic signs, etc., the driving simulation tool and an analysis tool for calculating drivers' performance.

Two driving tracks (see Figure 2) were created for the study using the driving simulator's map editor. While the participants drove on these tracks their route and performance including their speed, braking behavior, lane keeping, steering wheel position etc., were recorded by the system for later analysis.

While the analysis tools of CARS can calculate a variety of statistics based on [30] and [31], for the driving performance in this study we limited our investigation to two measures: lane keeping (defined by standard deviation of the mean distance to the racing line) and average speed.

3.1.2 Wizard-of-Oz simulation

The effort it takes to build even simple speech systems make it difficult for interaction designers to iteratively design speech UIs. Wizard-of-Oz experiments, in which users are led to believe that they are interacting with an automated system, while all or part of the system is simulated by a human, enable designers to investigate different design options in an easy, flexible way. For this reason we used SUEDE [32], a freely available WoZ tool to prototype the speech user interfaces in our study. SUEDE offers a comprehensive computer supported WoZ toolset that also captures test data, allowing detailed examination of the interface after testing.

In the study the wizard controlled the system while sitting in the same room with the test participant. The wizard also acted as the moderator, introducing the tasks and instructing the participants during the course of the test session, making her presence in the room feel natural from the participant's viewpoint. The speech prompts were played out via a loudspeaker set close to the participant. Participants' commands were collected via an external microphone connected to the Wizard's laptop. The interaction between the system and the participant was recorded for further analysis by utilizing the tools offered by SUEDE.

3.1.3 Bio-signal measurements

In addition to audio, video and driving performance recordings during the experiment, we also measured the user with two bio-sensors: a heart rate belt, and an electroencephalography device to monitor brain activity.

We chose these sensing modalities, as previous studies exist that used them to infer cognitive workload. An electroencephalograph (EEG) measures electrical potentials related to brain activity and has been demonstrated to be sensitive to changes in cognitive effort [33]. Heart rate and heart rate variability have been used in psychophysiology to provide insight into attention, effort, arousal and other emotion-related processes [34].

A common concern with many physiological measures is their obtrusive nature and lack of comfort. Hence, we chose measurement devices that are relatively unobtrusive. For example, the NeuroSky MindSet EEG device we used, unlike most brain imaging systems, is simply a lightweight, cordless headset. Thus, even though the test users were extensively monitored, their user experience was rather natural. The measurement environment is illustrated in Figure 1.

3.2 Participants

Eight 25-44 years old drivers (5 male, 3 female) participated in the study. All the participants had normal hearing and normal or corrected to normal vision. Five participants had prior experience with speech user interfaces, like name-dialing on mobile phones or speech dictation software for MS Word. The remaining three users were complete speech user interface novices. Six participants were driving regularly. Four participants were also familiar with driving simulators.

3.3 Tasks

Each study consisted of eight test scenarios (see Table 1) during which the participants were driving, using a speech interface or driving and using speech interface simultaneously. These scenarios were conducted in a randomized order for each test session.

3.3.1 Driving task

As the primary tasks, users were asked to drive two courses we developed with easy driving and difficult driving conditions, while obeying all rules of the road, as they would in real driving and not in a video game. The course for the easy condition was made up of mainly long straight sections, while the difficult condition consisted of shorter straight sections followed by bends (see Figure 2). The difficult course was designed to fully engage the attention and cognitive resources of the drivers.

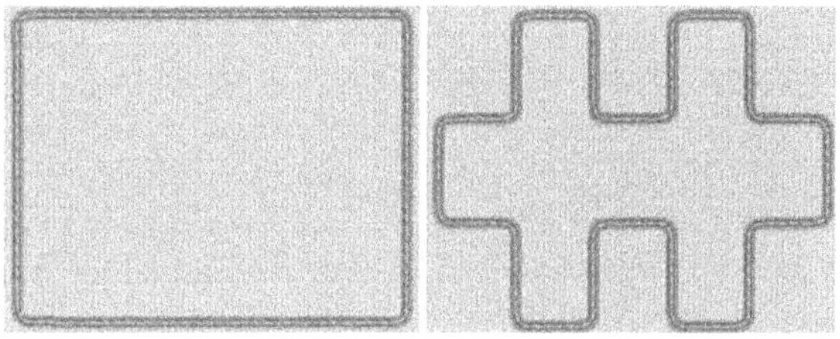

Figure 2. Driving tracks, easy and difficult

3.3.2 Speech task

The speech interfaces were created by utilizing guided and open dialog strategies. An overview of tasks categories and example speech tasks are presented in Table 1. Both guided and open speech interface tasks included hotel, restaurant, flight and ferry reservations as well e-mail and traffic information system management. Each test participant conducted either guided or open version of each of these tasks. The tasks were randomized among the test scenarios.

The speech tasks were designed so that the tasks and the dialogs could be easily compared. All tasks required similar amount and type of information exchange between the user and the system to be successfully completed. All the speech dialogs of the same dialog strategy (guided or open) had similar dialog structure with comparable amount of possible/available dialog steps.

During the study each participant used both open and guided dialogs in both driving conditions. The participants also conducted one open and one guided dialog alone without a concurrent driving task, as well as drove one round on each of the tracks without any secondary task.

Table 1. Task types randomized during test session

Task category	Task name	Task components		Speech task, Examples
		Driving task	Speech dialog	
Driving (D) only tasks	D/Easy	Easy	-	-
	D/Difficult	Difficult	-	-
Speech (S) only tasks	S/Guided	-	Guided	You are planning to fly from Helsinki to Manchester. You should reserve a flight for tomorrow at 1:35 pm. Your frequent flyer number is 1234.
	S/Open	-	Open	You are planning to take a ferry from Stockholm to Tallinn. You should reserve a ferry ticket for tomorrow morning at 6:10 am. Your StarClub membership number is 1234.
Combined tasks	D/Easy & S/Guided	Easy	Guided	You'll get announcements via your traffic announcement system. You notice that the announcement for the Second street is outdated. You should correct the information by dictating and sending a message for the system administrator.
	D/Easy & S/Open	Easy	Open	You'll get information about new arrived messages. Mary is proposing a dinner. Reply to this message to agree with her.
	D/Difficult & S/Guided	Difficult	Guided	You need a hotel room for tomorrow for one night, in the center of Budapest. You should reserve a room that is moderately priced and offers complimentary wireless internet.
	D/Difficult & S/Open	Difficult	Open	You would like to eat in a cheap Italian restaurant in Madrid. The restaurant should have a selection of vegetarian dishes. You should reserve a table for 2 at for tonight at 7 pm.

3.4 Procedure

Before the start of the experiment the participants signed a consent form, the measurement systems were fitted on them and the video recording was started. Then the participants familiarized themselves with the dialog systems and the simulator. The participants had a short introduction to guided and open dialogs. During this introduction, they also had a chance to try the two types of dialogs, which also served as an opportunity for them to familiarize themselves with the synthetized speech utilized in the study. The participants also practiced driving on the easy and difficult road courses. The study did not start until they felt that they were driving confidently enough.

When the participants had completed the practice session, they began the experimental scenarios. Each participant conducted eight tasks in a randomized order. Before each task, the speech dialog task was introduced to the participant. The participants were also given a cheat sheet from which they were able check the task details in case they forget them. The sheet was placed so that it was easily in sight but not obstructing the view of the display. In the combined driving and speech-dialog tasks, the participants first started driving and then indicated when they were ready to start the speech task. Participants were instructed to try to first solve problem situations caused by the speech task with the system's help and only after that ask help from the moderator.

After each task the participants filled in the NASA-TLX form. After all eight tasks were completed, the test concluded with a short semi-structured interview to collect interaction preferences and impressions as well as to check how the participants understood the system, and whether they found speech user interfaces useful and what aspects of the study they found challenging or easy.

4. FINDINGS

In this section we present the findings of the speech analysis, NASA-TLX questionnaires and interviews. We also discuss about the analysis of bio-signals and driving performance logs. Finally we present some ideas how the findings could be utilized when building a dialog management system for a car environment.

4.1 Speech interaction

During the study we collected 48 dialogs: 16 dialogs from speech only tasks, 16 dialogs conducted concurrently with easy driving condition and 16 dialogs conducted concurrently with the difficult driving condition. Dialog tasks lasted from 55 sec to 2 min 34 sec. Average length of a dialog task was 1 min 26 sec.

Open and guided dialogs significantly differed in the length of user and system turns, as well as in the count of turns per dialog. In the guided dialogs the average count of turns was higher (average 8.5 cf. 6.8 sec), system prompts were longer (average 7.6 cf. 6.2 sec), and user turns shorter (average 2.8 cf. 4.7 sec) than in open dialogs.

4.1.1 Speech analysis

According to previous studies summarized for example by [28] features of speech appear in several respects to be a promising source of information about a user's cognitive resource limitations. Various indicators like duration and number of silent and filled pauses, repetitions, sentence fragments and false starts are increasing under conditions of high cognitive load. Also self-corrections have been found in some studies to increase under high cognitive load, but the pattern is inconsistent.

For our analysis we identified and calculated utterances (user turns) containing pauses, filled pauses, self-corrections, repetitions, false starts, missing user inputs, help requests and mistakes in the dialog task. The self-corrections and mistakes (e.g. selecting the wrong option) were rare and occurred always in the same utterances with repetitions or pauses. Thus they did not affect our statistics.

When comparing the amount of utterances containing pauses, filled pauses, repetitions and false starts Kurskal-Wallis did not show any significant difference between the guided and open dialogs (see Figure 3). In driving situations open dialogs seemed though to be more challenging than guided dialogs. While driving, the participants skipped significantly more often their turn or asked for help during open dialogs than during guided dialogs ($p<0.03$). In the speech-only case the difference between guided and open dialogs was not significant.

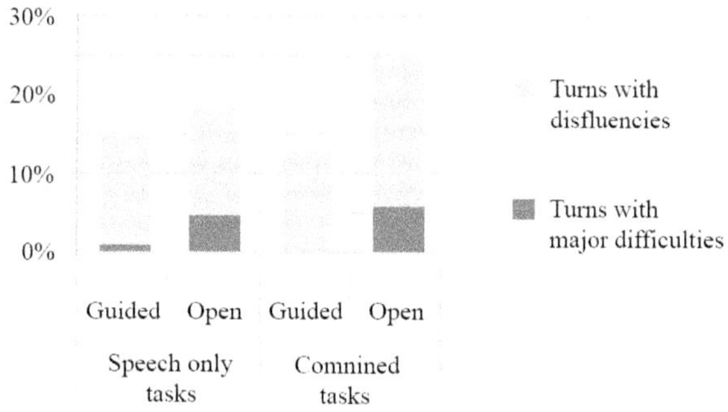

Figure 3. The percentages of dialog turns containing disfluencies (pauses, filled pauses, repetitions and false starts) and major difficulties (missing user input, help request)

While analyzing the dialogs we noticed that the most common place for hesitations, pauses, false-starts and repetitions was the first turn of an open dialog. During the guided dialogs the disfluencies were most typically pauses scattered around the dialog. See example dialogs below.

Example 1. Open dialog:

System (S): Welcome to the Flight reservation system. How may I help you?

User (U): *Umm... I would like to book tickets, flight tickets from Manchester to Hel. From Helsinki to Manchester.*

S: When would you like to fly from Helsinki to Manchester?

U: *Tomorrow ...*

Example 2. Guided dialog:

S: Welcome to the ferry reservation system! Where will you embark? Say the departure city name, or the harbor name.

U: *Stockholm*

S: Where would you like to travel to? Say the destination city name, or the harbor name.

U: *Tallinn*

S: When would you like to travel? Say the date.

U: ... *January... 3rd*

This could indicate that as a secondary task while driving, the open dialog strategy could require more mental resources than guided dialog.

4.2 Questionnaires and interview

Participants filled in the NASA-TLX questionnaire after each task. The NASA-TLX data were analyzed by combining the six scales, with each scale receiving an equal weight. The overall task loads with more detailed scores for different test conditions are presented in Figure 4. Kurskal-Wallis showed significant differences in the overall task loads of guided and open dialogs in speech-only tasks, in the task loads caused by difficult and easy driving tracks as well as in the task loads of the different task categories.

In the case of speech-only tasks the overall task load was significantly higher ($p<0.003$) for guided dialogs when compared to open dialogs. The effect could be seen especially in the frustration scale, which was significantly higher during guided dialog when compared to open dialog in the case of speech-only tasks ($p<0.04$). For combined tasks, where participants were driving and using speech interface at the same time, the clear differences between guided and open dialogs disappeared.

The tasks including driving on the difficult track showed significantly higher overall task load when compared to the easy track ($p<0.0001$). The participants also considered their performance being significantly better while conducting combined tasks on the easy track when compared to the difficult track ($p<0.02$).

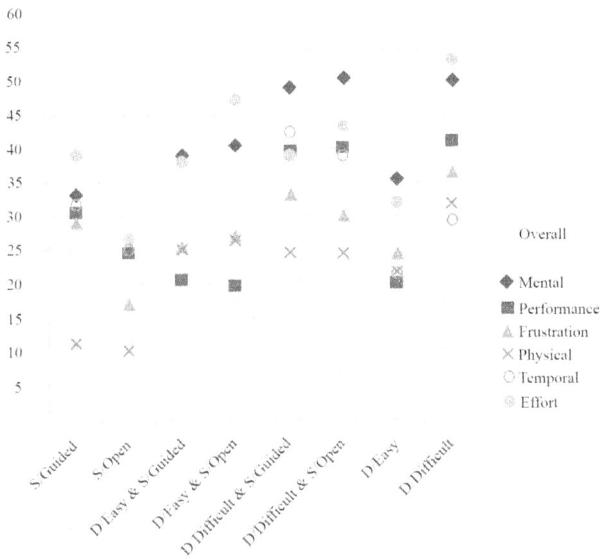

Figure 4. NASA-TLX score averages (max.value = 100)

The mental and physical loads scored significantly higher during combined tasks when compared to speech-only tasks ($p<0.02$, $p<0.04$, respectively). Also, driving only tasks were considered physically more loading than speech only tasks ($p<0.004$).

During the semi-structured interview, especially the speech user interface novices expressed their preference for guided dialog, which clearly gave them the command options from which to select. Some of the more experienced speech user interface users found guided dialog at times frustrating, thus they preferred the open strategy. Some participants found the driving task challenging, while for others it was relatively easy. This opinion was correlating more with the experience with car simulators than with the regularity of real driving. All in all, participants commented that the driving simulator served its purpose well. Participants also expressed that they would generally find a reliable speech user interface useful, especially while driving.

4.3 Bio-signal and driving performance

We further processed the captured raw bio-signals (EEG and heart rate information) and driving performance data and analyzed them to see whether they corroborated the previously discussed findings.

4.3.1 Heart rate variability and EEG analysis

The heart rate belt recorded RR intervals, the time elapsed between two consecutive R waves in the electrocardiogram (ECG) often used to estimate heart rate. From the RR interval captured by the heart rate monitor, we estimated the instantaneous heart rate, in two-second windows, and a measure of short-term heart rate variability: the root-mean-square of successive differences (rMSSD) [35], defined as the standard deviation of successive RR interval differences. For computing the rMSSD we used 12-heart-beat windows with a three beat overlap.

The EEG device measures single channel EEG from the FP1 location of the International 10-20 system [35]. The EEG signal, originally sampled at 512 Hz, was low-pass filtered to 0–50 Hz. We then computed average powers of 8 frequency bands corresponding to traditional classification of EEG frequencies (see Table 2) in two second windows. From these, we focused on alpha and theta bands as they have been shown to be predictive of memory and cognitive loads [36].

Table 2. EEG bands

Band	Range (Hz)
Delta	0.5-2.75
Theta	3.5-6.75
Alpha Low	7.5-9.2
Alpha High	10-11.75
Beta Low	13-16.75
Beta High	18-29.75
Gamma Low	31-39.75
Gamma Mid	41-49.75

Analysis of heart rate variability showed significant difference in workload between speech-only conditions and combinations of driving and speech conditions ($p<0.01$) with heart rate variability being higher (thus less loading) for speech-only tasks. When comparing the two dialog strategies in the speech-only conditions, we found marginally significant difference showing open dialog to be less loading.

We failed to find any significant differences between the tasks based on EEG data. Further investigation revealed large individual differences in participants' brain activity with respect to the selected features. Similar findings have been made by [33], where they found that users had signals that were inverted from the expected levels, while when averaged across large numbers, the data typically exhibited the previously reported trends. We assume that these characteristics are due mainly to individual differences and that with larger amount of data and sophisticated feature selection (to better account for individual differences) more reliable consequences could be drawn [33].

4.3.2 Car logs

For the driving performance in this study we limited our investigation to two measures: lane keeping (defined by standard deviation of the mean distance to the racing line) and average speed.

According to the driving performance measures secondary speech task has a significant effect on driving performance. The driving was significantly more erratic and slower in combined conditions when compared with driving only conditions using ANOVA (average speed: 42.251 vs. 28.846, $p<0.005$; lane keeping: 41.266 vs. 79.003, $p<0.005$). The driving speed was compromised to control the load, but the quality of driving still suffered.

5. Discussion

The analysis of the driving performance revealed that the secondary speech tasks have a significant adverse effect on driving performance. This tendency was not visible in the NASA-TLX scores. This could be due to the fact that drivers may not prioritise and manage their speech-based tasks effectively. Specifically, other studies [9] have also shown that a concurrent verbal task increased drivers' propensity to take risks, and that drivers did not compensate as verbal interactions slowed their reaction times. These results suggest that drivers may not fully recognize the distractions of speech-based interaction and may fail to compensate for the distraction that these demands induce. This points to the potential usefulness of intelligent dialog management systems based on driving behaviour information from a vehicle's on-board diagnostic and reporting subsystem to increase safety.

Relying only on external information sources, such as, for instance, traffic information based on GPS location, could be deceptive as well when it comes to optimally adjusting interaction strategies. According to research by [37] studying phone call patterns while driving, they found that phone calls were often initiated at traffic lights and in the middle of traffic jams. Thus situations that look busy at first glance might actually provide opportunity to safely interleave the driving and the secondary task (e.g. slow moving traffic or car queues on motorways). One way to identify suitable moments of interaction and the attentional needs of the situation could be to estimate the driver's cognitive state via, for instance, a heart rate monitor attached to the driver's seat, driving wheel or the devices drivers normally wear (e.g. headset) [38]. The proposed measurements can be easily performed in real-time and this can be provided as a data source to the dialog manager for adaptation decision making.

Open dialog was reported to be less loading and frustrating when performed as a speech-only task. This is reflected by the NASA-TLX results and this is also borne out by evidence from HRV, which yielded marginally significant results in this respect. In combined (driving plus speech) conditions this difference disappeared. At closer inspection, after analysing the disfluencies of the spoken interaction we found significantly more serious difficulties (asking for help, or skipping a turn) during open dialogs as opposed to guided dialogs in the combined condition. Thus our results suggest that while the open dialog seems to be preferable when the speech task is the only task, it not only does not seem to perform any better when the speech task is a secondary task, but the increased amount of missed turns and dialog related questions presented to the moderator is a reflection of increased cognitive load.

6. Conclusion

This paper investigated how the guided dialog strategy performs when compared to open dialog while driving, with respect to the cognitive loading these strategies may impose on the driver. We conducted a controlled Wizard-of-Oz (WoZ) study using a medium-fidelity driving simulator and measured the cognitive capacities of the study participants via the driving performance logs, speech analysis, NASA-TLX questionnaires, heart rate variability and EEG.

We found that the secondary speech task has an effect on driving performance, even though drivers might not notice it themselves.

Our results also show that that while the open dialog approach performs better in speech-only tasks compared to the guided dialog strategy, this performance lead disappears in the combined driving and speech conditions.

The driving performance logs from the simulator and heart rate variability information proved useful for identifying cognitively challenging situations while driving. These could provide important information to an in-car dialog management system that could take into account the driver's cognitive resources to provide safer speech-based interaction.

7. REFERENCES

[1] Terminal Mode, http://www.terminalmode.org

[2] Tashev, I., Seltzer, M., Ju, Y.-C., Wang, Y.-Y. and Acero A. 2009. Commute UX: Voice Enabled In-car Infotainment System, In *Mobile HCI '09: Workshop on Speech in Mobile and Pervasive Environments (SiMPE)* (Bonn, Germany, 15.9.2009).

[3] Angkititrakul, P., Kwak, D., Choi, S., Kim, J., PhucPhan, A., Sathyanarayana, A. and Hansen, J.H. L. 2007. Getting start with UTDrive: driver-behavior modeling and assessment of distraction for in-vehicle speech systems. In *Proc. of Interspeech-2007*, 1334-1337.

[4] Nunes, L.M. and Recarte, M.A. 2002. Cognitive demands of hands-free-phone conversation while driving. *Transportation Research Part F: Traffic Psychology and Behaviour*, 5, 2, 133-144.

[5] Strayer D. L. and Johnston,W. A. 2001. Driven to Distraction: Dual-Task Studies of Simulated Driving and Conversing on a Cellular Telephone. *Psychological Science* (Nov. 2001), 462-466.

[6] Kun, A., Paek, T. and Medenica, Z. 2007. The effect of speech interface accuracy on driving performance. In *Proceedings of Interspeech-2007*.

[7] Pittermann, J. 2005. Spoken Dialogue Technology: Toward the Conversational User Interface by Michael F. McTear. *Comput. Linguist.* 31, 3 (September 2005), 403-406.

[8] Gorin, A.L., Parker, B.A., Sachs, R.M. and Wilpon, J.G. 1996. How may I help you?. In *Proceedings of Third IEEE Workshop on Interactive Voice Technology for Telecommunications Applications* (30. 9-1.10.1996). 57-60.

[9] Lee, J.D., Caven, B., Haake, S. and Brown, T.L. 2001. Speech-based interaction with in-vehicle computers: The effect of speech-based e-mail on drivers' attention to the roadway. *Human Factors*, 43, 631-640.

[10] Wickens, C.D. 1984. Processing Resources and Attention. In *Parsuraman, R. and Davies, R. eds. Varieties of Attention*, Academic Press, New York.

[11] Levy, J. and Pashler, H. 2008. Task Prioritisation in Multitasking during Driving: Opportunity to Abort a

Concurrent Task Does not Insulate Braking Responses from Dual Task Slowing. *Applied Cogn. Psych.* 22, 4, 507-525.

[12] Iqbal, S. T., Horvitz, E., Ju, Y.-C. and Mathews, E. 2011. Hang on a sec!: effects of proactive mediation of phone conversations while driving. In *Proc. of the SIGCHI conference on Human factors in computing systems*. CHI '11. ACM, New York, NY, USA, 463-472.

[13] Briem, V. and Hedman, L. R. 1995. Behavioral effects of mobile telephone use during simulated driving. *Ergonomics*, 38, 2536-2562.

[14] Salvucci, D. D., Markley, D., Zuber, M. and Brumby, D. P. 1007. iPod distraction: effects of portable music-player use on driver performance. In *Proc. of the SIGCHI conference on Human factors in computing systems*. CHI'07, ACM, NY, 243-250.

[15] Alm, H. and Nilsson, L. 1995. The effects of a mobile telephone task on driver behavior in a car following situation. *Accident Analysis and Prevention*, 27, 5, 707-715.

[16] Brookhuis, K. A., De Vries, G. and De Waard, D. 1991. The effects of mobile telephoning on driving performance. *Accident Analysis and Prevention*, 23, 309-316.

[17] Redelmeier, D. A. and Tibshirani, R. J. 1997. Association between cellular-telephone calls and motor vehicle collisions. *N. Engl. Journal of Medicine*, 336, 7, 453-458.

[18] Imeier, D. A. and Tibshirani, R. J. Association between cellular-telephone calls and motor vehicle collisions. *N. Engl. Journal of Medicine*, 336, 7, 453-458.

[19] Goodman, M.J., Tijerina, L., Bents, F.D. and Wierwille, W.W. 1999. Using cellular telephones in vehicles: Safe or unsafe. *Transportation Human Factors*, 1, 1, 3-42.

[20] Tulga, M.K. and Sheridan, T.B. 1980. Dynamic decisions and work load in multitask supervisory control. *IEEE Trans. on Systems, Man, & Cybernetics*, 10, 5, 217-232.

[21] Horswill, M. S. and McKenna, F. P. 1999. The effect of interference on dynamic risk-taking judgments. *British Journal of Psychology*, 90, 2, 189-199.

[22] Smither, J.A.-A. 1993. Short term memory demands in processing synthetic speech by old and young adults. Behaviour & Information Technology, 12, 6, 330-335.

[23] Vicente, K. J. and Williges, R.C. 1988. Accommodating individual differences in searching a hierarchical file system. *Int. J. Man-Mach. Studies*, 29, 6, Academic Press. London.

[24] Chen, F., Jonsson, I.-M., Villing, J. and Larsson, S. 2010. Applications of Speech Technology in Vehicles. *In Fang Chen and Kriistina Jokinen, eds.: New Trends in Speech Based Interactive Systems.* Springer Verlag, Berlin, 195-219.

[25] Villing, J. 2009. Dialogue Behaviour under High Cognitive Load. *Proceedings of the SigDial 2009 Conference* (London, Great Britain 11-12 September 2009).

[26] Brumby, D.P., Salvucci, D.D. and Howes, A. 2009. Focus on driving: How cognitive constraints shape the adaptation of strategy while dialing while driving. In *Proc. of the SIGCHI conference on Human factors in computing systems*. CHI '09, ACM, New York, NY, USA, 1629-1638.

[27] Kern D., Müller M., Schneegaß S., Wolejko-Wolejszo L., Schmidt A. 2008. CARS – Configurable Automotive Research Simulator. In *Automotive User Interfaces and Interactive Applications – AUIIA '08. Workshop at Mensch und Computer*, Lübeck.

[28] Jameson, A., Kiefer, J., Müller, C., Großmann-Hutter, B., Wittig, F. and Rummer, R. 2009. Assessment of a User's Time Pressure and Cognitive Load on the Basis of Features of Speech. In *Resource-adaptive cognitive processes*. Berlin, Springer. 171-204.

[29] Hart S, and Staveland L. 1988. Development of NASA-TLX (Task Load Index): Results of empirical and theoretical research. In: *Hancock P, Meshkati N (eds). Human Mental Workload.* North Holland, Amsterdam. 139-183.

[30] Reed, M. and Green, P. 1999. Comparison of driving performance on-road and in a low-cost simulator using a concurrent telephone dialling task. *Ergonomics, 42,* 1015-1037.

[31] Green, P., Lin, B. and Bagian, T. 1993. Driver Workload as a Function of Road Geometry: A Pilot Experiment. Technical Report UMTRI-93-39, 55ff.

[32] Klemmer S.R., Sinha A.K., Chen J., Landay J.A., Aboobaker N. and Wang A. 2000. Suede: a Wizard of Oz prototyping tool for speech user interfaces. In *Proceedings of the 13th annual ACM symposium on User interface software and technology (UIST '00).* ACM, New York, USA, 1-10.

[33] Grimes D., Tan D.S., Hudson, S., Pradeep, S. and Rao, R. 2008. Feasibility and Pragmatics of Classifying Working Memory Load with an Electroencephalograph, *CHI 2008* In *Proc. of the SIGCHI Conference on Human Factors in Computing Systems*. CHI '08, ACM, New York, 835-844.

[34] Rowe, D.W., Sibert, J., and Irwin D. 1998. Heart rate variability: indicator of user state as an aid to human-computer interaction. In *Proc. of the SIGCHI conference on Human factors in computing systems*. CHI '98, ACM, NY.

[35] Sörnmo, L. and Laguna, P. 2005. Bioelectrical Signal Processing in Cardiac and Neurological Applications. *Elsevier Academic Press*, Burlington, MA, 2005.

[36] Gevins, A. and Smith M. E. 2003. Neurophysiological measures of cognitive workload during human–computer interaction. Theoretical Issues in Ergonomic Science, 4, 1, 113–131.

[37] Esbjörnsson, M., Juhlin, O. and Weilenmann, A. 2007. Drivers using mobile phones in traffic: An ethnographic study of interactional adaptation. *International Journal of Human-Computer Interaction*, 22, 1&2, 37-58.

[38] Sezgin, T.M., Davies, I. and Robinson, P. 2009. Multimodal inference for driver-vehicle interaction. In *Proceedings of the 2009 international conference on Multimodal interfaces. ICMI '09*. 193-198.

Decisions about Turns in Multiparty Conversation: From Perception to Action

Dan Bohus
Microsoft Research
One Microsoft Way
Redmond, WA, 98052
+(01) 425 706 5880
dbohus@microsoft.com

Eric Horvitz
Microsoft Research
One Microsoft Way
Redmond, WA, 98052
+(01) 425 706 2127
horvitz@microsoft.com

ABSTRACT
We present a decision-theoretic approach for guiding turn taking in a spoken dialog system operating in multiparty settings. The proposed methodology couples inferences about multiparty conversational dynamics with assessed costs of different outcomes, to guide turn-taking decisions. Beyond considering uncertainties about outcomes arising from evidential reasoning about the state of a conversation, we endow the system with awareness and methods for handling uncertainties stemming from computational delays in its own perception and production. We illustrate via sample cases how the proposed approach makes decisions, and we investigate the behaviors of the proposed methods via a retrospective analysis on logs collected in a multiparty interaction study.

Categories and Subject Descriptors
H.1.2 **[Models and Principles]**: User/Machine System – *Human Information Processing*; H.5.2 **[Information Interfaces and Presentation]** User Interfaces – *Natural Language*;

General Terms
Algorithms; Human Factors

Keywords
Multiparty turn taking; decision-theoretic approach; multiparty interaction; floor management; gaze; speech; spoken dialog; situated interaction; multimodal systems.

1. INTRODUCTION
The naturalness and usability of spoken dialog systems depends critically on the control of the *fine structure* of the timing of turns. Challenges in this realm include unexpected, long pauses after the completion of an utterance by a user, barge-ins by a system before a user has completed speaking, and floor conflicts resulting from confusion about turns. To date, most research on controlling turn taking has been undertaken in dyadic settings. Here, we consider the problem of turn taking in *multiparty settings*, where a spoken dialog system engages several people in a joint conversation.

ICMI'11, November 14–18, 2011, Alicante, Spain.
Copyright 2011 ACM 978-1-4503-0641-6/11/11...$10.00.

In multiparty interactions, beyond challenges with the detection of the end of the utterances of speakers, a system also must reason about the source and target of utterances, and, more generally, the state and dynamics of the floor. At any point, one participant may speak to another or to the system, or wait for a response from another participant or the system, or even openly reflect about one's own thoughts or plans before generating a contribution or while waiting for someone else to contribute. Given the multiparty and mixed-initiative nature of this process, a dialog system cannot assume that it can take the floor upon the detected end of another participant's turn, even if perfect end-of-turn predictions were available. Effective turn taking in multiparty dialog hinges on making accurate inferences about the multiparty conversational dynamics from streams of perceptual data, and on reasoning under uncertainty about various possible outcomes, their utilities, and tradeoffs between acting and waiting for additional information. In addition, given the time-critical nature of turn-taking decisions, a system should also take into account uncertainties arising from delays in its own perception and rendering pipelines.

We present a decision-theoretic approach for guiding turn taking in a spoken dialog system in multiparty settings. Our goal is to highlight opportunities and directions with moving from heuristics for turn taking to the use of principled decision policies guided by the computation of the expected utilities of different actions. We focus on decisions by a system to take the floor at different times after detecting the end of utterances of other participants in a multiparty dialog. We show how inferences about the conversational dynamics and the system's processing delays can be coupled with the assessed utilities of different outcomes to make floor control decisions under uncertainty. We explore the behaviors of the expected-utility policy and compare these with performance of heuristic procedures used in a previous version of the system. The comparative study is based on a retrospective analysis of logs captured by a spoken dialog system in multiparty settings.

We begin by reviewing related work. Then, we discuss a multiparty interaction user study, including lessons learned. Next, we formalize the turn-taking problem we shall focus on, and describe the approach. We showcase by example how the expected-utility methods guide actions, and we report results from a comparative analysis of the use of heuristics versus more principled inference and decision making.

2. RELATED WORK
Researchers in the psycholinguistics, sociolinguistics and conversational analysis communities have investigated various facets of

turn taking in human-human interaction. Sacks, Schegloff and Jefferson [11] proposed a basic model for the organization of turns in conversation, centered on the notions of *turn constructional units*, separated by *transition relevance places* which provide opportunities for speaker changes. Subsequent works have brought to the fore the important role played by gaze, gesture, and other non-verbal communication channels in regulating turn taking in interaction. For instance, Duncan [5] highlights the role of non-verbal signals in turn taking, and proposes that turn taking is mediated via a set of verbal and non-verbal cues. Wiemann and Knapp [22] survey a number of previous investigations and perform a quantitative analysis of turn-taking cues in dyadic conversations. Goodwin [7] also discusses various aspects of the relationship between turn taking and attention.

In contrast, most spoken dialog systems built to date operate in dyadic settings, and simply try to alternate turns with the user in a *"you speak then I speak"* manner. In this case, one of the key ingredients for making good turn-taking decisions is the ability to predict the end of the user's turns. A number of research efforts have addressed this problem. For instance, [1] describes a system that uses a semantic parser to classify incoming utterances as *closing* or *non-closing*. Machine learning techniques have also been used in conjunction with prosodic, syntactic, semantic, and/or higher-level dialog features to make predictions about end of turns [6, 12, 15, 18], or to optimize end-pointing thresholds [9].

Efforts with spoken dialog systems have also been directed towards developing, implementing and testing more comprehensive computational models and architectures for managing turn taking, in both dyadic [10, 19, 20] and multiparty settings [2, 4, 21]. With respect to turn-taking decisions, a number of more principled approaches have been proposed. As an example, [16] proposes a bidding approach to turn taking and investigates in simulations the use of reinforcement learning techniques for choosing appropriate turn bids, based on utterance importance. [8] proposes and evaluates via simulations a reinforcement learning approach whereby a system learns how to take turns online, by using a reward measure based on gaps and overlaps.

In more closely related work, [10] presents a turn-taking model for dyadic interactions based on a 6-state finite-state machine, and articulates a decision-theoretic approach for end-pointing user utterances and grabbing the floor. Uncertainties are considered about the turn-internal or turn-final nature of each detected pause. Under a specific set of cost functions motivated by turn-taking principles, the authors compute analytically the time at which the cost of waiting exceeds the cost of grabbing the floor and use it to perform end-pointing. Experiments in batch and with a live system indicate the approach improves the system's responsiveness.

3. BACKGROUND

We begin by outlining the computational model for multiparty turn taking that provides the basis for this work, and we review lessons learned from a multiparty interaction experiment with an initial, heuristic implementation of turn-taking policies [4].

3.1 Turn-Taking Model

In a multiparty turn-taking model that we described previously [2, 3], we consider turn taking as a mixed-initiative, collaborative process that emerges from coordinated floor actions produced by participants engaged in a conversation. The participant who is ratified to speak via this collaborative process is said to have the *conversational floor*. Participants continuously produce one of four *floor management actions*: the participant that currently has the floor produces either a *hold* action, indicating that they continue to hold the floor, or a *release* action, indicating that they are releasing the floor to someone else. The *release* action also specifies the set of participants the floor is being released to; an empty set allows for self-allocated next speaker selection [11]. Participants who currently do not have the floor produce either a *take* action, indicating that they want to take the floor, or a *null* action, indicating that they make no floor claims. Under this model, floor shifts emerge from the joint actions of the participants in the conversation. Specifically, the floor transitions from one participant to another when a *release* action is met with a corresponding *take* action.

The model subsumes components for sensing the conversational dynamics, for making floor control decisions, and for rendering these decisions into an appropriate set of coordinated behaviors. In short, the sensing component subsumes inference models that leverage audio-visual evidence to estimate the current speaker, the addressee roles for each participant with respect to the current utterance, as well as the floor state, actions and intentions for each engaged participant. The decision component uses the estimated state information as well as high-level dialog context to select the floor management actions to be performed by the system. The floor actions are communicated both to the dialog management layer, which generates the system's semantic contributions, and to a turn-taking behavioral control component that renders these actions into synchronized gaze, gesture and speech [2, 3].

3.2 Experiment and Lessons Learned

We implemented an initial version of the turn-taking model in a multimodal interactive dialog system that can play a *questions game* with groups of people [3, 4]. In the game, the system asks trivia questions (see Figure 1) and displays the list of possible answers on the screen. Users can discuss the question and provide answers. After a confirmation, the system provides an explanation if the answer is incorrect, and then moves on to the next question. We conducted a large-scale user study with this system [3, 4] and collected a total of 150 interactions: 90 with groups of two people interacting with the system and 60 with groups of three people interacting with the system. Sample interactions are available online [17].

The initial implementation of the turn-taking model was based on heuristics for sensing, decision making, and behavioral control, and is described and evaluated in detail in [3, 4]. On perception and inference, the current speaker and set of addressees for the current utterance were identified via handcrafted models that used sound source localization information from the microphone array in conjunction with information from a visual scene analysis (e.g. the location and estimated head-pose for each speaker), as well as some additional rules (e.g. non-understandings and utterances longer than three seconds were assumed to be addressed to others). At the end of each utterance, the system assumed that the floor was being released to the person or people that the utterance was addressed to. While this is not always true, we found it to be a good assumption for the questions game.

Turn-taking decisions were also based on a heuristic policy. When the system detected that the floor was being released to it, it generally took the floor immediately and generated a turn. In a limited number of cases, the system did not generate a verbal contribution, but instead tried to pass the floor to another participant via a non-verbal gesture: it turned the avatar's face towards the other participant and lifted the eyebrows [3]. When the system detected that the floor was not released to it at the end of an utterance, it waited for a predefined duration (in most cases 3.5 seconds), before trying to take the floor, giving someone else a

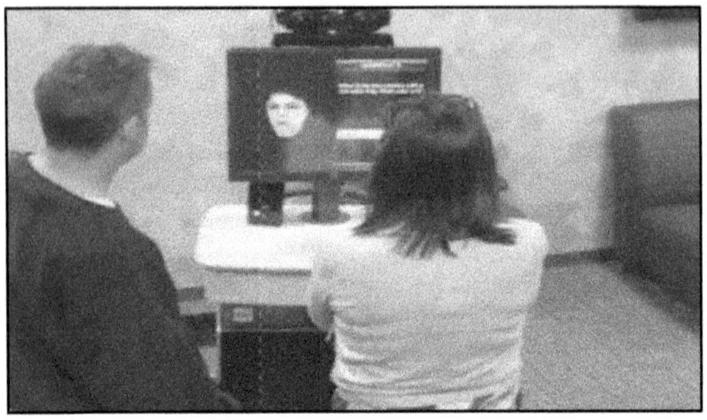

Figure 1. Questions game with two participants.

chance to take the floor. This duration was set to give participants a reasonable time for reflection about another participant's response or question. In a limited number of cases, where the system tried to quickly regain the floor after having been interrupted while posing a question, the waiting duration was set to 0.5 seconds. The system released the floor at the end of its own utterances, and also when interrupted while asking a question.

Following the experiment, the *addressees* of each utterance were tagged by a human annotator. This enabled us to assess the accuracy of the system's heuristic inference models. We found an overall error rate of 18% on detecting whether an utterance was addressed to the system or not, and therefore on identifying floor releases to the system, as described earlier.

For 9% of utterances, the system *incorrectly inferred that the floor was being released to it.* In the majority of these cases, the system took the floor and immediately issued a verbal contribution. As the floor was in fact not released to the system, this action often (42%) led to significant turn-taking problems, manifested as *floor transition battles* marked by *turn-initial overlaps*: a participant started talking at around the same time as the system did, and an undesirable overlap was created. The data shows that such turn-initial overlaps also occurred (albeit in lower proportion, 10%) when the system produced a verbal contribution after *correctly identifying* that the floor was being released to it. We believe these turn-initial overlaps are explained in part by the system's response delay. Due to technological limitations in the input (~700ms) and output (~150ms) processing pipelines the system's response arrives after a delay. This delay can be taken as a cue that the system does not intend to take the floor, provoking other participants to take initiative. Turn-initial overlaps are also caused by the mixed-initiative nature of turn taking, with participants vying for the floor and inserting their own contributions immediately after an answer directed to the system.

On another 9% of utterances, the system *failed to detect that the floor was being released to it.* In these cases the system waited for a specified duration (in most cases 3.5 seconds), after which, if no one generated another contribution, the system took the floor. In these cases the system can appear unresponsive and the participants often re-take the initiative prior to the system's timeout.

4. DECISION-THEORETIC APPROACH

The decision-theoretic approach we describe below provides a more principled solution for making turn-taking decisions and for dealing with some of the issues highlighted above. The approach allows the system to continuously deliberate about key uncertainties in the world and in its own processing delays, and resolve tradeoffs between waiting and taking the floor. It helps reduce the number of floor battles, and minimize gaps in the conversation.

We focus on the situation where the system does not have the floor and has to decide whether it should attempt to take the floor, or simply wait. We restrict the search to the subspace of turn-taking policies where: (1) the system may take the floor only if no one else is speaking, e.g. the system never interrupts a speaking participant, and (2) the system always takes the floor once a silence longer than a specified duration (δ_{MAX}) is observed. While we limit our focus to making take versus wait decisions, we believe similar methods can be applied to make decisions over richer sets of turn-taking strategies.

As delays with computational processing can influence time-critical turn-taking decisions, we need to build explicit machinery that takes them into account. We assume a stochastic input processing delay (ID) between the moment an utterance starts (or ends) and the moment that this event is detected by the system. Such processing delays are common with voice activity detectors, as they employ an audio buffer (and sometimes run a phone-loop or even leverage grammar) to segment spoken signals. Speech recognition may introduce additional delays. Similarly, we assume a stochastic output delay (OD) between the moment the system decides to speak and the moment speech is actually produced. We assume these delays can be observed retroactively by the system and can be probabilistically modeled from data.

4.1 Decision-Theoretic Representation

We consider that an instance of a decision problem is generated each time the endpoint of a participant's utterance is detected and the system does not already have the floor. We denote this moment by t_e', the time of origin for our analysis, i.e. $t_e' = t_0 = 0$. Given delays in the input processing pipeline, the actual time at which the detected speech segment ended can be determined to be $t_e < t_e'$ (see Figure 2(a)) We use the regular notation t_v to denote the *actual time* a particular event v happens, and the prime notation t_v' to denote the time when the system *detected* that event.

Starting at t_0, the system faces a sequential decision-making problem: at each time step between t_0 and $t_{MAX} = t_0 + \delta_{MAX}$, it must decide whether to take the floor, i.e. speak, or perform a null action, i.e. wait. Note that once the system decides to take the floor and does so, the problem instance is completed. A new problem instance will be generated after the next detected segment of user speech. Similarly, if another participant takes the floor while the system is waiting and the system observes the take, the floor transitions to that participant and the problem instance is again completed. Due to this special structure of the decision problem, the number of possible action sequences (plans) that the system can follow is linear rather than exponential in the length of the $[t_0, t_{MAX}]$ time interval. If we discretize this time interval, the alternative action sequences to consider have the form: *null, null, ... take.* Each action sequence can thus be described as $TakeAt(t_s')$, meaning *wait until a time* t_s' *and take the floor at that point.* We also note that, given output processing delays, the system will actually start producing speech at a later time, $t_s > t_s'$.

We can compute the expected cost for each action sequence. Initially, at t_0, we compute the optimal time for the system to take the floor as:

$$t^* = \underset{t_s' \in [t_0, t_{MAX}]}{\operatorname{argmin}} E_{P(O|\psi_0)}[Cost(O, TakeAt(t_s'))]$$

where $P(O|\psi_0)$ is the *probability of the final outcome* O of the system's plan, conditioned on the *evidence we have collected so far* up to t_0, denoted by ψ_0; we shall discuss the set of possible outcomes O shortly. If the cost-minimizing time is $t^* = t_0$, the system will perform a floor take right away, at t_0. If the cost-minimizing time is $t^* \neq t_0$, then the system waits at t_0. By the next time tick, t_1, additional evidence has accumulated: the new evidence set is ψ_1 and the system can re-compute the optimal point for taking the floor. Generally, if we have arrived by successive null actions, i.e. by waiting, to the current moment t_c (see Figure 2), we estimate the optimal point for taking the floor as:

$$t^* = \text{argmin}_{t'_s \in [t_c, t_{MAX}]} E_{P(O|\psi_c)}[Cost(O, TakeAt(t'_s))]$$

The proposed approach rests on two ingredients: a cost function, and a probabilistic model for tracking uncertainties in the world. The cost of the system's plan to $TakeAt(t'_s)$ depends ultimately on the final outcome of that plan, and on the conversational context. Depending on whether and when another participant starts speaking, three types of outcomes may stem from the system's decision to take the floor at some future time: the floor might transition to the system, the floor might transition to another participant, or a floor transition battle might arise. To define these outcome types more precisely, we denote by t_u the next moment at which a participant will start speaking again. Let t'_u ($t'_u > t_u$) denote the moment when the system detects this event. Finally, recall that the system starts speaking at time $t_s > t'_s$. The three potential outcome types can then be defined as follows:

1. *FloorTransitionToSystem:* $t_s + \epsilon < t_u$ (Fig. 2.b)
   The floor successfully transitions to the system if the system takes the floor and no one else claims the floor for up to some time ϵ after the system started speaking, i.e. $t_s + \epsilon < t_u$, i.e. no turn initial overlap occurs.
2. *FloorTransitionToOther*: $t'_u < t'_s$, (Fig. 2.c)
   The floor transitions to another participant if that participant starts speaking and the system detects that event before it starts its own attempt to take the floor, i.e. $t'_u < t'_s$. In this case, the system abandons its own plan to take the floor at t'_s.
3. *FloorTransitionBattle:*$(t'_u \geq t'_s) \wedge (t_u \leq t_s + \epsilon)$, (Fig. 2.d)
   A floor transition battle occurs if another participant starts talking around the same time as the system does, i.e. a turn-initial overlap occurs. First, the system must not have detected that the participant has started talking at the time it started its own take action, i.e. $t'_u \geq t'_s$ (otherwise the system would have let the floor transition to the participant). Second, the participant must have started talking no later than some ϵ after the system started talking, i.e. $t_u \leq t_s + \epsilon$ (otherwise the floor would have transitioned to the system).

The possible outcomes depend on the relationships among t_u, t_s, t'_u, t'_s. The cost of each outcome is also influenced by additional context. An important factor is the floor action produced by the floor holder at the end of the previous utterance: the cost of a system *take* will be different depending on whether the floor was released to the system or not. We model release actions via a binary variable fa. The magnitude of the timings involved in the floor transition also plays an important role. For instance, if the floor was released to the system, we expect that the cost increases with the amount of time the system waits until it takes the floor.

Having identified fa, t_u, t'_u, t_s, t'_s as the key world state variables that condition the possible outcomes and cost, we model uncertainty over these variables and compute the expected cost for the system's plan. Given the evidence ψ_c accumulated up to t_c, the system's plan to $TakeAt(t'_s)$ will therefore lead to an outcome $O = \langle FA, T_u, T'_u, T_s, t'_s \rangle$ with probability P_O (capital letters denote random variables and lowercase letters denote known quantities):

$$P_O = P(FA, T_u, T'_u, T_s | t'_s, \psi_c)$$

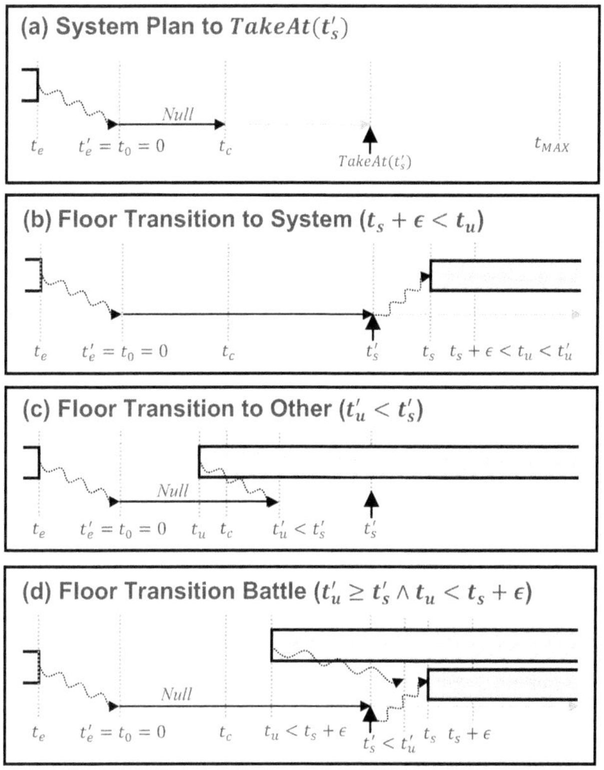

Figure 2. Illustrations of system plan to take the floor at time t'_s (a), and three possible outcomes (b,c,d).

Given a set of reasonable independence assumptions that we review below, we can factor P_O as follows:

$$P_O = P_{cd}(FA, T_u | \psi_c) P_{id}(T'_u | T_u, \psi_c) P_{od}(T_s | t'_s) \quad [1]$$

The first factor in the equation above, P_{cd}, represents uncertainty over the conversational dynamics in the world, including, in this case, the floor release action and the next moment a contribution will arrive from one of the participants. The second and third factors, P_{id} and P_{od}, further integrate the uncertainty about the system's input and output processing delays. We have made the assumptions that (1) given ψ_c, FA and T_u are independent of the time t'_s the system plans to take the floor, (2) T_u depends only on T'_u (and not FA), and (3) T_s depends only on t'_s. Below, we discuss each component factor from Equation 1 in more detail.

4.2 Modeling Conversational Dynamics

P_{cd} represents the joint distribution over the floor release action FA and the moment T_u when the next contribution will arrive from other participants, given the evidence ψ_c accumulated up to time t_c. We can factor P_{cd} as follows:

$$P_{cd}(FA, T_u | \psi_c) = P(FA | \psi_c) \cdot P(T_u | FA, \psi_c)$$

The first factor, $P(FA|\psi_c)$, represents the uncertainty over the floor release action. This model can be trained from labeled data, for instance using discriminative learning techniques. The second factor, $P(T_u|FA, \psi_c)$, models when the next contribution will arrive from one of the participants given the last floor action and additional evidence. We note that, since time t_c was reached without yet detecting that someone is speaking, the evidence ψ_c includes the time constraints that $T_u > t_e$, that $T'_u > t_c$, as well as additional evidence ϕ_c, e.g. audio-visual information, dialog context, etc. In this work we assume that given the floor release action FA, T_u only depends on the time constraints above, and is independent of the additional evidence ϕ_c, i.e.:

$$P(T_u|FA,\psi_c) = P(T_u|T_u > t_e, T_u' > t_c, FA)$$

If ID is a random variable that captures the input processing delay ($T_u' = T_u + ID$), this term can be computed by marginalizing over the delay, as follows:

$$P(T_u|FA,\psi_c) = \sum_d P(T_u, ID = d|T_u > t_e, T_u + ID > t_c, FA)$$

The term inside the sum can then be computed with Bayes' rule:

$$P(T_u, ID|T_u > t_e, T_u + ID > t_c, FA) \propto 1(T_u > t_e) \cdot 1(T_u + ID > t_c) \cdot P(T_u|FA) \cdot P(ID)$$

where $P(ID)$ models the input processing delay and $P(T_u|FA)$ models the prediction of when the next contribution will arrive from one of the participants, given the last floor release action. The other two terms integrate the time constraints.

The factorization described above is one approach to constructing a model of the conversational dynamics P_{cd}. Other alternatives can be envisioned. For instance, we are interested in directly learning the joint $P_{cd}(FA, T_u|\psi_c)$ from data, using structured discriminative learning techniques.

4.3 Modeling System Delays

To model the system's input processing delay $P_{id}(T_u'|T_u, \psi_c)$, we note that given T_u, T_u' depends on ψ_c only via the additional time constraint on $T_u' > t_c$:

$$P_{id}(T_u'|T_u, \psi_c) = P(T_u'|T_u, T_u' > t_c)$$

Given that $T_u' = T_u + ID$, we can write:

$$P_{id}(T_u' = t_u'|T_u = t_u, T_u' > t_c) = P(ID = t_u' - t_u|ID > t_c - t_u)$$

which yields via applying Bayesian reformulation:

$$P_{id}(T_u' = t_u'|T_u = t_u, T_u' > t_c) \propto 1(t_u' > t_c) \cdot P(ID = t_u' - t_u)$$

In effect, P_{id} can be directly computed from $P(ID)$.

The system output processing delay is captured via the distribution $P_{od}(T_s|t_s')$. If OD is a random variable that captures the output delay ($T_s = t_s' + OD$), we have:

$$P_{od}(T_s = t_s|t_s') = P(OD = t_s - t_s')$$

and therefore P_{od} can be directly computed from $P(OD)$.

4.4 Modeling Cost

We now turn our attention to utility of outcomes. As previously discussed, the cost for each outcome depends on several contextual factors including the last floor action, the timings involved, etc.

To further investigate the cost structure, we conducted a small-scale cost assessment experiment [4]. 9 human annotators were asked to review videos of 9 interactions from the user study. Each annotator reviewed 3 interactions and each interaction was reviewed by 3 annotators. The annotators were asked to identify turn-taking errors committed by the system in each interaction and to assess the cost of each of these errors on a scale from 0 ("no error") to 5 ("worst error"). The authors aligned each turn-taking error identified by the judges with one of the turn-taking decisions made by the system and its corresponding outcome.

Based on this data, we fit two cost models: one for the case where the floor was released to the system, and one for the case where it was not. The dependent variable in these models is the cost, as assessed by the human judges. The independent variables are the time elapsed until the transition occurs and the transition type. We assumed a sigmoid parameterization for extrapolating the assessments to time points of outcomes that were unavailable for assessment. The resulting fitted models, together with the points based on which they were constructed, are displayed in Figure 3.

In general, the fitted cost functions align with our intuitions about costs in turn taking. For the case when the floor was released to the system, cost increases with time, and a transition to other is more costly than a transition to the system (it was the system's responsibility to take the floor). There is no significant difference in the fitted functions between a transition to other and a floor battle; we found this result somewhat counterintuitive, as we had assumed floor conflicts would generally add to the cost. When the floor was not released to the system, the cost is zero if another participant takes the floor, regardless of the timing. If the system takes the floor right away with no turn-initial overlap, the cost is positive. If however no one else talks and the system takes the floor successfully after a delay the cost drops towards zero as the delay increases, which aligns with the intuition that it would be okay for the system to take the floor if no one else takes it after a while. Finally, floor transition battles are more severe in this case, especially if they happen right away; the floor was not released to the system and a system intervention that leads to an overlap is penalized significantly.

We note that this analysis suffers to some degree from biases and sparsity in the data. For instance, due to the system's runtime heuristic policy, floor transitions to the system and floor battles tend to happen either immediately after the detected end of an utterance or about 3.5 seconds later. Transitions at points in between, which would help to better estimate the influence of time on cost, are not available and therefore the fitted models general-

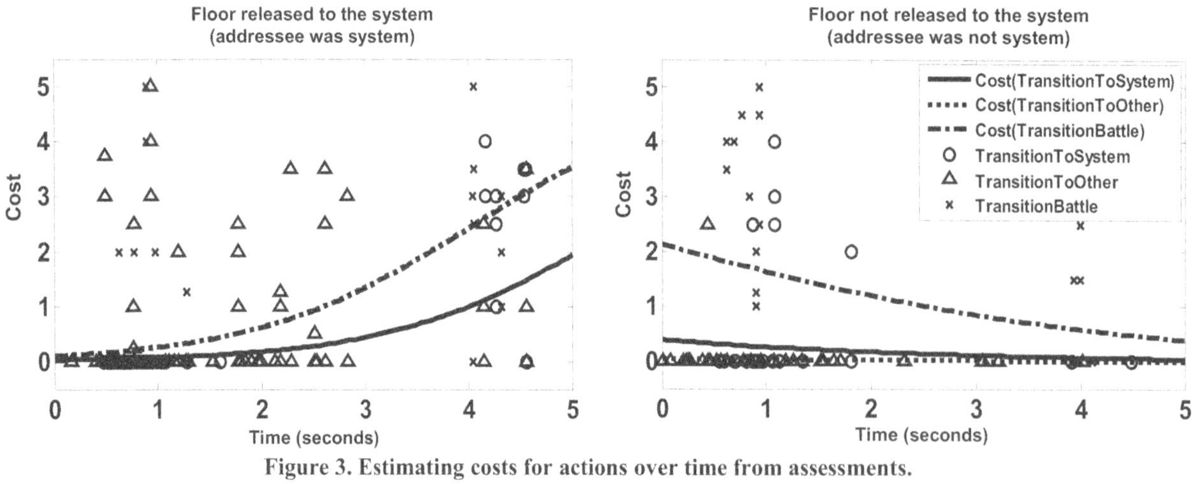

Figure 3. Estimating costs for actions over time from assessments.

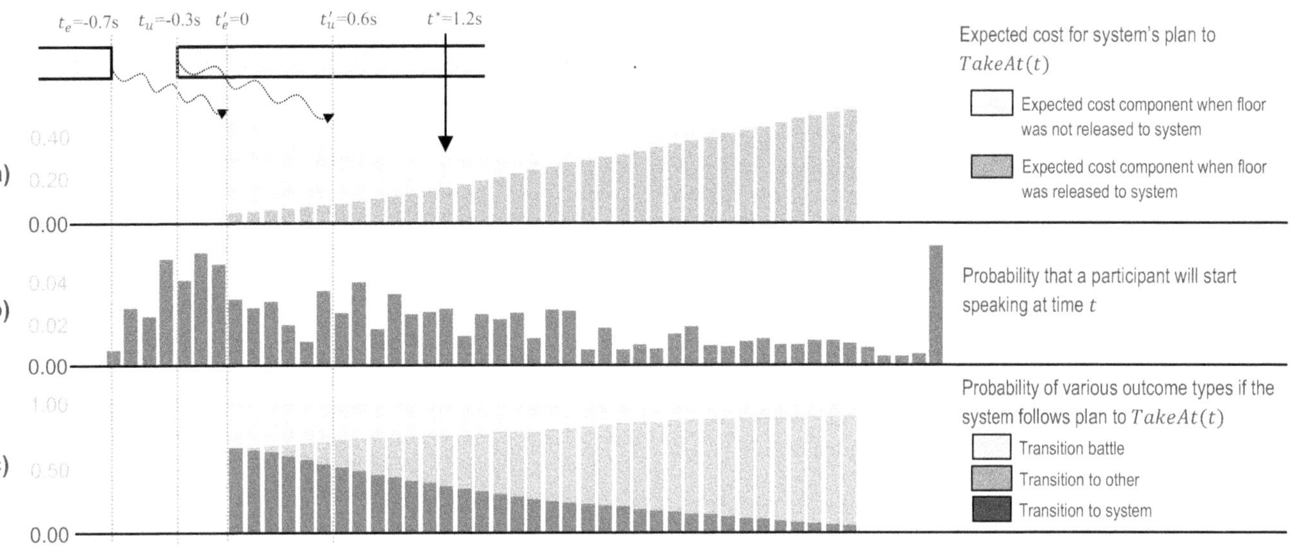

Figure 4. Decision-theoretic model avoiding floor conflict. (a) Expected cost for plan to $TakeAt(t)$, (b) probability distribution over time that the user will speak, and (c) inferred outcome-type probabilities for plan to $TakeAt(t)$.

ize from the available points and the sigmoid assumption. While we believe that this assumption is a reasonable first approximation (the costs are bound in the 0-5 interval and we assume monotonicity in the effect of time elapsed), data collected under a more exploratory policy would allow for fitting more accurate nonparametric models that make less assumptions about the overall structure of the cost function and effect of various outcomes.

We use the cost functions assessed above in the preliminary model assessment described in the next section. We note that the decision-theoretic approach can use any cost functions, either assessed through experimentation, or asserted by system engineers.

5. MODEL ASSESSMENT

We now illustrate with specific examples how the proposed model makes turn-taking decisions, and we investigate its behaviors based on a retrospective analysis of logs.

In the assessments described below, we assume t_{MAX}=3.5s. In addition, we used ϵ=0.3s, based on an analysis reported in [4]. The dataset was split into a train set containing 76 interactions and a test set containing 67 interactions. The distributions described below were learned or estimated from the training set, and the assessments were conducted on the test set.

We discretized the time axis into 100 millisecond intervals and modeled time as a multinomial variable over these intervals, with one last bin capturing times greater than t_{MAX}. $P(ID)$, $P(OD)$, and $P(T_u|FA)$ were therefore modeled as multinomial distributions and estimated from data. The latter distribution was estimated from cases where the system inferred that the floor was not released to it and decided to wait for 3.5 seconds or longer.

The model for inferring floor actions, $P(FA|\psi_c)$, was approximated by $P(FA|\psi_e)$, i.e. no incremental inference was performed for floor actions. This model was learned as a maximum entropy model from labeled data, based on a large set of multimodal features, including: *acoustic* features, e.g. average energy in the signal; *sound source localization* features, e.g. direction of the microphone array beam and its relative position to the actors; *spatial* features, e.g. location of actors; *visual focus of attention* features, e.g. for each actor a face detector reports whether a face is frontal, slightly turned left or right, or completely turned left or right; *understanding* features, e.g. whether the last utterance was a non-understanding, the confidence score, number of decoding alternates, etc.; *turn-taking* features, e.g. duration of current utterance, time since previous utterance, overlap with the system, etc.; *dialog* features, e.g. descriptors of the current dialog state. To account for structure in the temporally streaming signals (e.g. energy, beam location, visual focus-of-attention, etc.), we constructed features by computing relevant statistics of these streams in various windows relative to the current utterance. The trained model improves the accuracy of the floor action inferences significantly, attaining on test non-overlap utterances a classification error rate of 13% versus 20% error for the heuristic previously used by the system (described in Section 3.2.)

The first example we discuss, displayed in Figure 4, illustrates an instance from our collected data where the system made a poor decision to take the floor and entered into a floor battle. The system detected the end of a participant's utterance at time t'_e=0s (the actual end of the utterance was at t_e=-0.7s), and incorrectly inferred that the floor was being released to it. Based on its heuristic policy, the system took the floor and started speaking. However the participant's utterance was immediately followed by another utterance, which in fact begins at t_u=-0.3s, but is actually not detected by the system until t'_u=0.6s. The system therefore overlaps with the participant, inadvertently creating a floor conflict. The estimated cost for this outcome is 1.78.

The decision-theoretic policy would have avoided this conflict. The new floor action inference model is less confident that the floor was actually released to the system, i.e. $P(FA|\psi_0)$=0.6. At time t_0, the system computes the expected cost for the plans to take the floor at different time-points in the future, shown in Figure 4(a). Figure 4 also shows the inferred probability that a participant starts speaking at a time t, i.e. $P(T_u = t|\psi_0)$, and the probability of different outcome types if the system follows the plan to take the floor at a given time t. Since the time that minimizes the expected cost is t^*=1.2s, the system chooses to wait. After 100ms, at the next time tick, the system re-assesses the expected cost, but the minimizing cost is again found at 1.2s. On subsequent reassessments the optimal time shifts to t^*=1.5s, and the system keeps waiting, up until that time. The decision-theoretic system would have been able to detect the next utterance at t'_u=0.6, and would have avoided the floor conflict. The estimated cost would have been 0.04 (versus 1.78 incurred by the runtime model).

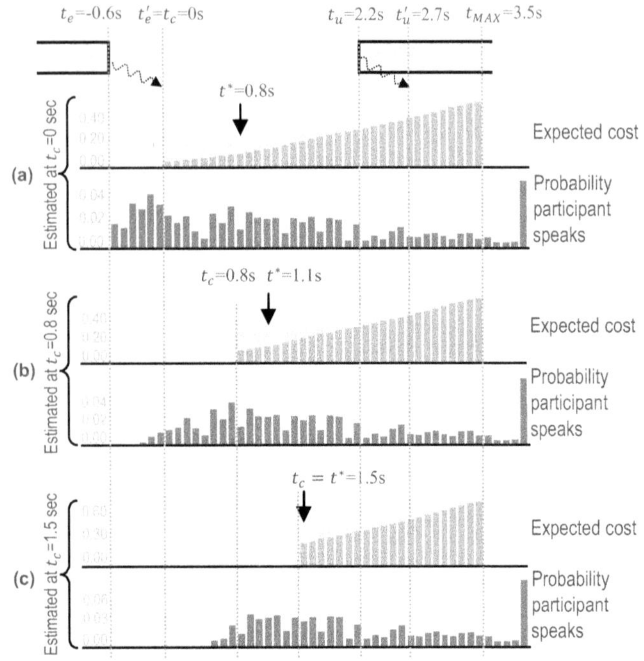

Figure 5. Decision-theoretic model avoiding undesirable gap.

The second example, shown in Figure 5, corresponds to a case where the floor was released to the system. At runtime the system inferred incorrectly that the floor was not released to it, and, according to its heuristic policy, decided to wait for 3.5 seconds prior to taking the floor. In this case, a participant intervened at t_u=2.2s, and the beginning of that utterance was detected by the system at t'_u=2.7s. The floor transitioned to the participant and the estimated cost for this outcome is 1.09.

With the new model, this situation could have also been averted. The learned predictive model infers that the probability that the floor was released to the system is $P(FA|\psi_e)$=0.76. The expected cost computation at time t_0 indicates that the optimal time to take the floor would be at t^*=0.8s. Hence the system would wait initially. As time goes by, the system re-computes the expected cost at each tick. For instance, consider the inferences at time t_c=0.8s as illustrated in Figure 5(b). At this point, the optimal time to take the floor has shifted in light of new evidence, and the expected cost computation indicates that the system should wait even longer, up until t^*=1.1s. Note that, because of time constraints (e.g. we haven't yet detected any participants' speech up to t_c=0.8s, i.e. T'_u>0.8s), the probability distribution over when a participant is expected to start speaking $P(T_u = t|\psi_8)$, has shifted accordingly. Once time t_c=1.5s is reached, the expected cost computation indicates that this is now the optimal time to take the floor, i.e. $t_c = t^*$ =1.5s, and the system does so. Under the new model the outcome would have been a transition to the system, with an estimated cost of 0.22 (versus 1.09 incurred by the runtime model).

The two illustrated cases highlight the abilities of the decision-theoretic model to integrate over inferred uncertainties to identify actions that minimize turn-initial overlaps and undesirable gaps in the conversation. Moving from our focus on methods to a comprehensive evaluation of the decision-theoretic variant of the system requires a second user study. While such an experiment remains for future work, we present a preliminary assessment for the proposed approach by investigating how some of the system's turn-taking decisions would have changed if the new model was used. As in the examples discussed above, we can revisit portions of the data observed at runtime and explore how the revised decisions compare to actions taken with the prior heuristic policy.

Table 1. Cost assessment for various decision models.

Model		Cost
Floor Release Inference	Policy	
Heuristic	Heuristic	0.43
Learned	Heuristic	0.29
Learned	Decision-theoretic	0.21

We cannot re-run in batch all situations observed in the original study as turn taking is an interactive process and outcomes hinge on user responses. However, sets of states are available for revisitation in a comparative analysis. Recall that three possible outcomes resulted from the system's floor decisions in the user study: transitions to others, transition battles, and transitions to the system. Because we know when the user intervened, in the first two situations we can actually revisit the data and assess *what would have happened had the system been using the new policy*. If the new policy leads the system to wait until after the point where the participant spoke at runtime, the new outcome would be a *transition to other*, and we can assess its cost. Similarly if the new policy decides to take the floor before the user did, we can also assess the new outcome—which will be *either a transition to the system or a floor transition battle*. In contrast, when the floor transitioned to the system during the user study (see Figure 2(b)), we can re-evaluate the situation only if the decision-theoretic model decides to take the floor at an earlier time than the original system did. If the new model decides to wait longer, we cannot know whether or not another participant would have intervened. Thus, in this comparative analysis, we focus only on the portion of the test set where we can fully assess the new policy, i.e. cases where in the collected data we had a transition to other, or a transition battle. We additionally remove cases where the run-time system employed special turn-taking strategies (one for rapidly re-acquiring the floor when the system was interrupted during the posing of a question, and the other where a non-verbal gesture was used to prompt for a response [3, 4]). The cases used in the assessment below account for 33% of all of the study data.

Running the heuristic policy that had been originally used on these cases instructs the system to take the floor immediately when the floor is released to it, or otherwise wait 3.5 seconds before trying to take the floor, giving someone else a chance to take it. As shown in Table 1, the mean cost associated with this heuristic policy is 0.43. In contrast, the decision-theoretic approach leads to outcomes with a mean cost of 0.21. An investigation of outcome details revealed that the largest reductions in cost were attained by *avoiding turn-initial overlaps* (i.e. avoiding floor conflicts), and *reducing response time* following floor releases to the system. The situations are represented by the cases discussed earlier and displayed in Figures 4 and 5. Although these findings are encouraging, we note that they address performance only on a specific subset of data as drawn from the prior user study. A comprehensive evaluation requires analysis of the performance of the revised system in a new user study.

As previously discussed, the decision-theoretic approach uses a learned model for predicting floor release actions $P(FA|\psi_e)$ that performs better than the original heuristic that had been used for inference. We also assessed the gains that can be attained by solely switching to this more accurate inference model, while keeping the same heuristic policy for actions: take the floor immediately if the floor is released to system or otherwise wait 3.5 seconds giving someone else a chance to take the floor. The resulting cost, shown in the third line of Table 1, is 0.29. This represents a significant reduction from the baseline, confirming the importance of accurate inferences. At the same time, the result is worse than when using the learned model *together with* the decision-theoretic policy for identifying ideal actions, which highlights the importance of reasoning about uncertainty, timings, and taking actions that minimize the expected costs of outcomes.

6. CONCLUSION

We presented a decision-theoretic approach for managing turn-taking actions in multiparty settings. The proposed methodology endows a dialog system with the ability to reason continuously about uncertainties in multiparty conversational dynamics, and about its own processing delays for perception and rendering. The model couples these uncertainties with assessments of potential outcomes and takes actions that minimize expected cost. While we focused on floor take versus wait decisions, similar machinery for inference and action can be harnessed for making decisions about when to release the floor.

Our main goal was to lay out key concepts with the time-dependent guidance of turn-taking actions in multiparty settings via computations of expected utility. As part of this effort, we have investigated the behavior of the proposed approach via a retrospective analysis of logs collected in a prior study. While new user studies are required for a comprehensive evaluation of the value of the approach, our preliminary comparative analysis highlights how the decision-theoretic methods can minimize turn-initial overlaps and reduce unnecessary gaps in the conversation.

We are interested in several directions for refining the performance of turn taking in multiparty settings. We believe that turn-taking decisions will benefit from further enhancements in the accuracy of inferences. As one direction in this realm, we are exploring the discriminative training of models for jointly and incrementally inferring the last floor action and start time of the next utterance as new evidence streams in. Inferential competencies can also be enhanced by developing means for better identifying the intentions and semantics associated with utterances. We are also interested in opportunities for extending the set of floor control actions available to a system. For example, we can add graded floor management strategies, such as a softer version of a floor take, where the system starts a contribution with a filler, e.g. *"So...* [pause] *What do you think?"*, constructing an opportunity to more gracefully back out of a potential floor conflict right after *"So..."*. We believe that taking a principled approach to turn taking in multiparty dialog systems will lead to more natural and flexible systems, with the ability to respond effectively to a wide range of dialog situations.

7. ACKNOWLEDGMENTS

We thank Isabelle Bouanna, Qin Cai, Ece Kamar, Zicheng Liu, Anne Loomis Thompson, and Cha Zhang for their contributions to this project.

8. REFERENCES

[1] Bell, L., Boye, J., and Gustafson, J., 2001. Real-time handling of fragmented utterances, In *Proceedings of NAACL-2001 workshop on Adaptation in Dialog Systems.*

[2] Bohus, D., and Horvitz, E., 2010. *Computational Models for Multiparty Turn Taking*, Microsoft Technical Report, MSR-TR-2010-115

[3] Bohus, D., and Horvitz, E., 2010. Facilitating Multiparty Dialog with Gaze, Gesture and Speech, In *Proceedings of ICMI'2010,* Beijing, China

[4] Bohus, D., and Horvitz, E., 2011. Multiparty Turn Taking in Situated Dialog: Study, Lessons, and Directions, In *Proceedings of SIGdial'2011*, Portland, OR.

[5] Duncan, S. 1972. *Some Signals and Rules for Taking Speaking Turns in Conversation*, Journal of Personality and Social Psychology 23, 283-292.

[6] Ferrer, L., Shriberg, E., and Stolcke, A. 2003. A Prosody-Based Approach to End-Of-Utterance Detection That Does Not Require Speech Recognition, In *Proceedings of ICASSP-2003*, 608-611, Hong Kong.

[7] Goodwin, C. 1980. *Restarts, pauses and the achievement of mutual gaze at turn-beginning*, Sociological Inquiry, 50(3-4), 272-302.

[8] Jonsdottir, G.R, Thorisson, K.R. and Nivel, E. 2008. Learning Smooth, Human-Like Turntaking in Realtime Dialogue, In *Proceedings of IVA-2008*, Tokyo, Japan.

[9] Raux, A. and Eskenazi, M., 2008. Optimizing end-pointing thresholds using dialogue features in a spoken dialogue system, In *Proceedings of SIGdial-2008*, Columbus, OH.

[10] Raux, A. and Eskenazi, M., 2009. A Finite-State Turn-Taking Model for Spoken Dialog Systems, In *Proceedings of HLT'09*, Boulder, CO.

[11] Sacks, H., Schegloff. E., and Jefferson, G. 1974. *A simplest systematics for the organization of turn-taking in conversation*, Language, 50, 696-735.

[12] Sato, R., and Higashinaka, R., 2002. Learning decision trees to determine turn-taking by spoken dialogue systems, In *Proceedings of ICSLP-2002*, 861-864, Denver, CO.

[13] Schegloff, E. 2000a. *Accounts of Conduct in Interaction: Interruption, Overlap and Turn-Taking,* The handbook of sociological theory, 287-321, New York: Plenum.

[14] Schegloff, E. 2000b. *Overlapping talk and the organization of turn-taking in conversation*, Language in Society, 29, 1-63.

[15] Schlangen, D., 2006. From reaction to prediction: Experiments with computational models of turn-taking, In *Proceedings of Interspeech 2006*, Panel on Prosody of Dialogue Acts and Turn-Taking, Pittsburgh, PA.

[16] Selfridge, E.O., and Heeman, P.A. 2010. Importance-Driven Turn-Bidding for Spoken Dialogue Systems, In *Proceedings of ACL-2010*, Uppsala, Sweden.

[17] Situated Interaction project web-page, 2011. http://research.microsoft.com/~dbohus/si.html

[18] Takeuchi, M., Kitaoka, N., Nakagawa, S. 2004. Timing detection for realtime dialog systems using prosodic and linguistic information, In *Proceedings of International Conference: Speech Prosody 2004*, 529-532.

[19] Thorisson, K.R. 2002. Natural Turn-Taking Needs No Manual: Computational Theory and Model, from Perceptions to Action, *Multimodality in Language and Speech Systems*, Kluwer Academic Publishers, 173-207.

[20] Traum, D., 1994. *A Computational Theory of Grounding in Natural Language Conversation*, TR-545, U. of Rochester.

[21] Traum, D., and Rickel, J., 2002. Embodied Agents for Multiparty Dialogue in Immersive Virtual World, In *Proceedings of AAMAS'02*, 766-773.

[22] Wiemann, J., and Knapp, M., 1975. *Turn-taking in conversation*, Journal of Communication, 25, 75-92.

Evaluation of User Gestures in Multi-touch Interaction: a Case Study in Pair-programming

Alessandro Soro[1,2]
asoro@crs4.it

Samuel A. Iacolina[2]
samueliacolina@gmail.com

Riccardo Scateni[2]
riccardo@unica.it

Selene Uras[1]
selene@crs4.it

(1) CRS4 - Center for Advanced Studies, Research and Development in Sardinia - Italy

(2) University of Cagliari, Dept. of Mathematics and Computer Science - Italy

ABSTRACT
Natural User Interfaces are often described as familiar, evocative and intuitive, predictable, based on common skills. Though unquestionable in principle, such definitions don't provide the designer with effective means to design a natural interface or evaluate a design choice vs another. Two main issues in particular are open: (i) how do we evaluate a natural interface, is there a way to measure 'naturalness'; (ii) do natural user interfaces provide a concrete advantage in terms of efficiency, with respect to more traditional interface paradigms? In this paper we discuss and compare observations of user behavior in the task of pair programming, performed at a traditional desktop versus a multi-touch table. We show how the adoption of a multi-touch user interface fosters a significant, observable and measurable, increase of nonverbal communication in general and of gestures in particular, that in turn appears related to the overall performance of the users in the task of algorithm understanding and debugging.

Categories and Subject Descriptors
H.1.2 [**MODELS AND PRINCIPLES**]: User/Machine Systems – *Human factors*.

General Terms
Human Factors, Verification.

Keywords
Evaluation Methods, Multi-User Interaction / Cooperation, Multi-touch, Pair Programming, Gesture.

1. INTRODUCTION
Multi-touch interaction has been a topic of research since the mid-eighties [7][10][11], but it's with the recent work of Han [5] than this interaction paradigm has become popular and multi-touch interaction is now so often taken as an example of natural interface.

However, applications based on this interaction paradigm are still in a phase of creative envisioning (see for example [21][19]) and little, if any, study exists on the real advantages of direct manipulation in traditional application fields; For example, Owen and colleagues [15] explores the advantage of bimanual input on a curve matching task; Patten and Ishii [16] presents a study that compares the strategies (and effectiveness) of spatial organization with tangible and traditional user interfaces.

These studies let foresee an advantage of direct manipulation, and by extension of multi-touch tables, over traditional desktop for very specific tasks that have in common a certain physicality, but don't settle the point on whether or not surface computing can replace the desktop in traditional work or learning scenarios.

A generally accepted, while hard to quantify, advantage of multi-touch tables and walls over desktops is their being inherently multiuser: people cooperate to the task at hand, sharing or negotiating the use of the device in a natural manner. Depending on the specific task it is easy to observe an increase of nonverbal communication (gestures, body postures, facial expressions, etc.) that, although not intuitive at all, are proven to have a positive impact on many cognitive processes (see below, related work).

Gestures in particular represent an easy to measure virtuous practice that in desktop computing appear limited almost exclusively to pointing with hand or finger, while observing users of multi-touch tables it often happens to see fluent, dual-handed metaphorical gestures.

This raises the questions we tried to answer. Is there any practical advantage (e.g., in terms of efficient problem solving) when using a natural interface? More precisely: is multi-touch better than the desktop for some traditional application? Moreover: can gesticulation be used as a suitable signal of natural interaction justifying the chain that more gestures provoke a more natural, and, thus, better interaction?

We opted to experiment with pair-programming [18]. It is a practice strongly recommended by agile methodologies and, thus, represents a realistic and not artificial test-bed both for desktop and multi-touch setting. Additionally, gesticulation, which we aim to observe, is more easily, though not exclusively, triggered during group-work.

We will be able to show how interacting in a multi-touch environment determines quantitative increase of nonverbal communication in general and, especially, of gestures, that in turn appears related to the overall performance of the users in the task of algorithm understanding and debugging.

The rest of the paper is organized as follows. Section 2 discusses in depth related work, with emphasis on gestures in human computer interaction and in related disciplines, such as psychology and anthropology. Section 3 describes the experimental setting.

Section 4 presents the results and discusses their implications. Finally, in section 5 conclusion and further work are presented.

2. RELATED WORK

Gesture in Human Computer Interaction has been variously addressed by computer scientists, initially as part of multi-modal user interfaces (following seminal work by Bolt, [1]), and more recently, as a dominant aspect of, to name a few themes, tangible interaction [6] kinetic interaction [2], emotions recognition [3].

However, research in gestural interaction so far has concentrated rather on sensing gestures, (e.g., Pavlovich and colleagues [17]; Wu and Huang [20]) than on defining what a gesture is and how to give meaning to gestures in interactive systems often tailoring this issue to the specific needs of applications (e.g., pen computing) or technologies (e.g., multi-touch displays). Additionally, gesture has been mostly regarded to as an alternative, rather than a companion, to other input devices, that allows a more *natural* form of interaction.

On the other hand, gestures and non-verbal communication, together with those human activities and social interactions which it is functional to, has been the subject of deeper investigation by anthropologists and psychologists.

Among the many movements that we perform with our body, gestures are, according to Kendon, intentional excursions that are meant to convey some message [8] and can be classified along a continuum that spans from gesticulation to sign languages, passing through speech linked gestures, emblems and pantomimes. McNeill underlines how such categories are in relation with the presence/absence of speech and linguistic properties; gesticulation is (almost) always accompanied by speech, emblems may or may not, while sign languages (almost) never are. Additionally gesticulation doesn't have any linguistic property, emblems have some linguistic properties, sign languages have full linguistic properties [13].

This cognitive role of gestures has an analogous in manipulations. Manipulations are actions performed on objects in order to change the state of the world. Their potential is being explored in the context of tangible interaction, and the role that manipulations play in human cognition has been explained by Kirsh and Maglio [9] in terms of epistemic and pragmatic action, the former being actions performed in order to improve cognition, where the latter are planned and performed to reach a specific goal.

The advantages of such behavior are that: (i) the complexity of the task is moved from the head of the user to the world, available strategies and possible solutions to a given problem appear at a glance; (ii) the (limited) resources of attention and memory are not wasted to concentrate on the strategy and can be used to explore alternative solutions; (iii) such exploration performed by means of manipulations on the world (or tools) are easier (i.e., they require less cognitive effort) and faster (i.e., they require less time) than it is to do the same mentally.

There is also strong evidence that epistemic action increases with skill [12]. This means that in HCI this is not a behavior of naïve computer users, but rather a powerful feature to leverage in interaction design. Tangible and multi-touch interaction, both build on this concept of providing direct manipulation of physical/graphical objects.

But interfaces don't define the interaction. Users' behavior is far more rich of what can be recognized and supported by the interface. In [4] Goldin-Meadow and co-workers show that gesturing lightens cognitive load while a person is thinking and explaining how she solved a math problem, resulting in an improved performance in a short term memory exercise. Similarly, Cook and co-workers [22] show how gesturing during a learning session helps children retain the knowledge gained.

Nonverbal communication in a group is also a positive behavior indicating healthy cooperation. Morrison and colleagues [14] show how the introduction of an electronic patient record in a hospital can disrupt some virtuous practices, partially voiding the benefits of the digital support.

3. EXPERIMENTAL SETTING

A convenience sample of 44 people participated to this study, age 20-35, all students of computer science or ICT professionals, thus quite literate in computer programming.

Working in pairs (see Figure 1), the testers were asked to review 7 snippets of C code (1 demo, and 6 exercises), each one containing a bug, and to point out the bug to an assistant. The review of the code snippets was performed through a very simple interface implemented with the identical look and feel both for the desktop and for the multi-touch environment.

Figure 1: Testers participating at the experiment on the Multi-touch Table (top) and at a traditional Desktop (bottom).

The appearance of the graphical interface is shown in Figure 2; it consists of

- a square text-area that shows one snippet of code at a time. The snippets of code are short enough to fit the visible area, so no scrolling is ever needed and no scrollbars are thus provided;

- a small control panel with a timer, and buttons to jump to the next/previous exercise

Multi-touch functionalities where enabled on the MT table and simulated with keyboard/mouse combinations on the desktop. However, in practice, testers seldom manipulated the interface, except for hitting the 'next' button.

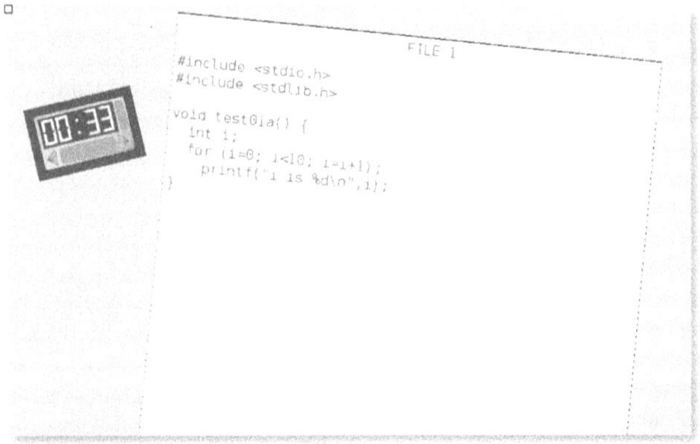

Figure 2: The Graphical User Interface of the program used for the tests, both at the Multi-touch and at the Desktop.

3.1 Pre-test briefing

Before the beginning of a test session the testers where briefed on the purpose and method of the research. We had great care to specify that the goal of the work was to evaluate the quality of the tool (Desktop vs Multi-touch) and not the ability of the users. The need of a video recording was justified by explaining our need to monitor 'collaboration and non-verbal communication' but without explicitly mentioning *gestures*, or their supposed connection with efficient problem solving. The testers where then encouraged to cooperate to the solution of the problems.

The testers were also informed that:

1. every snippet contains one (and only one) bug;
2. the bug is not in the syntax, but in the logic of the code;
3. comments (where provided) are not misleading;
4. bugs, although trivial to explain, where sometimes well concealed, and intended to be difficult to spot;
5. finally, although no time constraints were given, the testers were informed that the whole test required between 15 and 25 minutes on average. This was not intended to fix a goal for the performance, but to prepare the testers to the effort needed to complete the test.

Of course all participants were given written warranty of privacy and non-disclosure of videos and disaggregated data.

3.2 Test session

The 44 testers (spontaneously organized in 22 couples) were then asked to complete the experiment. 11 tests were run at the Desktop and 11 were run at the Multi-touch table, the assignment to one or the other setting was performed randomly. The F-test was used to verify if a significant difference exists between the two methods, multitouch and desktop. Note that the same 7 exercises were administered at the 2 settings.

Of the 7 snippets of C code, the first one was intended as a *demonstration* to get into confidence with the interface and clarify latest doubts; results are not taken into account in the following discussion.

For each one of the remaining 6 snippets, the testers had to perform the following:

1. examine the snippet for as much time as needed, discussing, if necessary, to decide what the bug was;
2. as soon as an agreement was reached on the exercise, press a pushbutton (that turns green) on the control panel;
3. testers could then point out the bug to an assistant, who annotated it in a block notes, without either confirming or refusing the answer;
4. by pressing a pushbutton on the control panel the testers could then proceed to the following exercise.

Note that in both settings:

- the interface didn't allow any editing of the C code; so the users were not able to correct the error;
- since the assistant did not comment on the proposed solution, the test actually measures the time spent before reaching an agreement, we did not measure the accuracy (i.e. if the testers positively solve the exercise or not) of the exercise; thus, wherever in the rest of the paper we talk of *solving* an exercise it should be clear that we mean *reaching an agreement on the solution*;
- the cases in which the testers were not able to reach an agreement (either on the correct or on a wrong answer), were also included; in a sense this results indicate the time spent before deciding that additional tools/information was needed to positively solve the exercise; of course such cases should better be taken into account in a deeper investigation (see later, Conclusion and Further work)
- the testers hit a button after reaching an agreement and another one to switch to next exercise, thus the time spent in reporting the bug to the assistant is known and has been expunged in the following discussion.

3.3 The 6 code snippets

The various exercises have been designed to be of increasing complexity and length (and in general took increasing time to solve). The exercise can be divided in 4 categories, and were administered in the same order in which they are described below:

Type 1: controversial exercises such as the one below are likely to cause debate between the testers.

```
void test2() {
  int i;
  for (i=0; i<10; i=i+1)
    if (i=2)
      printf("i is 2\n");
    else
      printf("i is not 2\n");
}
```

In the specific case the use of an assignment as argument of a truth evaluation, though not syntactically wrong, is typically deprecated. There are exceptions however, and the testers spent time discussing whether or not the use of such construct was acceptable in the context of the exercise.

Type 2: slips or careless errors are very common in everyday programming and are easily spotted since often result in meaningless or inconsistent code.

```
void test3() {
  int i;
  i = 0;
  while (i < 10);
    i = i + 1;
  printf("Finished. i = %d\n",i);
}
```

In this case the body of the `while` construct is actually an empty statement (because of the semicolon), resulting in an infinite loop.

Type 3: pattern matching error are those ones that require visual memory or recognition, and represent a class of errors almost unknown to modern programmers, thanks to the use of visual editors that provide syntax highlighting. Examples include misplaced parentheses due to a wrong indentation, and comments opened and not closed, such as the example below.

```
1 void test4() {
2   int i;
3   for (i=0; i<10; i=i+1)
4     /* check the value of i */
5     switch(i){
6       /* is i 0? */
7       case 0: printf("i is 0\n");
8               break;
9       /* is i 1?
10      case 1: printf("i is 1\n");
11              break;
12      /* now the default case */
13      default: printf("i is more than 1\n");
14   }
15 }
```

Most modern editors would help the programmer to find the error here: the comment in line 9 is not closed at the end of the line, and runs through to line 12, voiding in practice the body of the function. Without the help of syntax highlighting, the testers were forced to check the syntax of comments, which is trivial in practice, but not intuitive.

Type 4: algorithm understanding exercises are those ones for which the most effort were required. The bugs presented were in practice overrun of array indexes, such as in the example below.

```
void bubble_sort(int array[], int n) {
  int i, j;
  // sort array of length n
  for (i = (n - 1); i > 1; i++) {
    for (j = 0; j < i; j++) {
      if (array[j] > array[j + 1]) {
        // swap values
        int tmp = array[j];
        array[j] = array[j + 1];
        array[j + 1] = tmp;
      }
    }
  }
}
```

Here the outer `for` cycle will never end and causes an array overrun on the subsequent instructions. Testers were able to solve the exercise only after understanding (or recollecting from previous study) the basic logic of the algorithm.

3.4 Data collection

Data collected during or following the test are:

1. the time spent on each exercise;
2. the proposed solution, that may or may not be correct;
3. the video footage of the whole session.

These were used in the analysis described in the next section. Other data gathered, but not discussed in detail here are:

1. whether or not the testers were able to reach an agreement on the solution of the exercise;
2. subjective scores of the difficulty of each exercise.

This information, as we already noticed, will be subject to further investigation on the accuracy of the performance and on the subjective perceived difficulty of the exercises in the two settings.

3.4.1 Analysis of the video logs

To better understand the role of gestures in collaborative work we have analyzed the video logs of the test sessions in order to count the gestural events. As pointed out in Section 2 there is strong evidence that a fluent gesticulation has a positive influence, among others, on short term memory [4] and learning [22].

We claim that a similar behavior exists in solving complex tasks such as the one considered here, and that a system that allows (or encourages) a fluent gesticulation allows better performances.

The video collected were annotated using Anvil [23], a platform for multilayered annotation of video with gesture, posture, and discourse information.

3.5 Experimental Hypotheses

As mentioned earlier, our research questions are two:

1. Is there any practical advantage (e.g., in terms of efficient problem solving) when using a natural interface? More precisely: is multi-touch better than the desktop for some traditional application?
2. Can gesticulation be used as a suitable signal of natural interaction (i.e., the more gestures, the more natural, and the better interaction)?

Hence the null hypothesis relates to question 1.

H1. Participants will be no faster in solving an exercise containing a *controversial* bug, when using the Multi-touch table or the Desktop.

H2. Participants will be no faster in solving an exercise containing a careless error, when using the Multi-touch table or the Desktop.

H3. Participants will be no faster in solving an exercise requiring a *pattern matching*, when using the Multi-touch table or the Desktop

H4. Participants will be no faster in solving an exercise that require *algorithm understanding*, when using the Multi-touch table or the Desktop.

In order to positively answer question 2 we should first prove that the observed difference in fluency of gestures couldn't be otherwise explained:

H5. Participants will gesture with no more of less fluency (measured as gestural units/time) at the Desktop or at the Multi-touch table.

Further hypotheses, showing if fluency of gestures has any direct impact on efficient problem solving (i.e., couples with more fluent gesture actually perform better), or a deeper exploration in the nature of gestures involved in this specific task (e.g., what *pantomimes*, *icons, metaphors* were used in addition to *deictics* that helped the participants who scored the better results) are outside the scope of this paper.

4. RESULTS AND DISCUSSION

The experiments show that people perform significantly better at the multi-touch table (for the task examined) than at the desktop for some of the exercise, namely those ones involving cooperation, discussion, and, more generally, exchange of communicational information.

Do participants perform better when solving an exercise containing a *controversial* bug, when using the Multi-touch table than the Desktop? As shown in Figure 3 tester scored slightly better performances at the Multi-touch; the difference is significant, $F(10,10) = 4.72$. Hypothesis ***H1*** should then be rejected.

The analysis of results of exercise does not show any significant difference between the Desktop and the Multi-touch, F(10,10) = 1.46, n.s. Figure 4 shows means and standard errors for the results of the experiments.

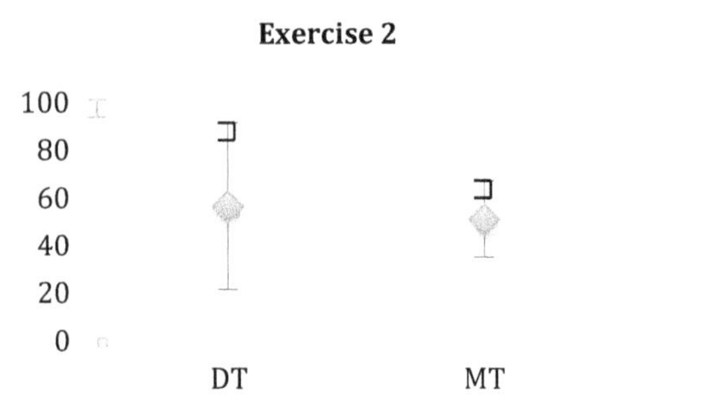

Figure 3: Time (in seconds) to solve exercise 2 (controversial) at the Desktop (DT) and at the Multi-touch (MT). Error bars indicate standard error.

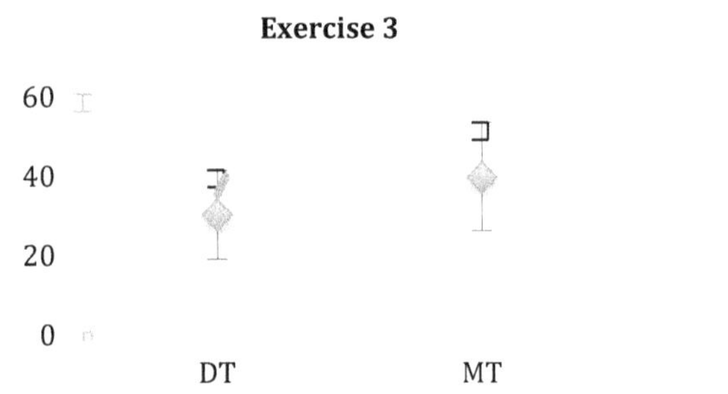

Figure 4: Time spent to solve exercise 3 (slip error).

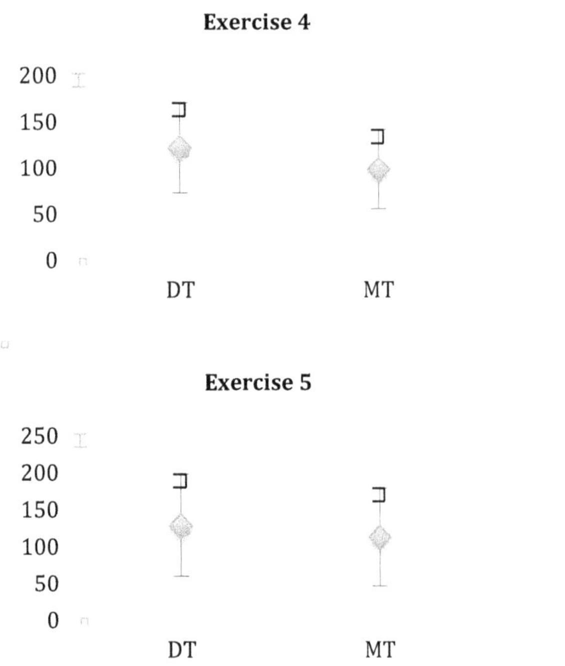

Figure 5: Time spent to solve exercise 4 and 5 (pattern matching exercise).

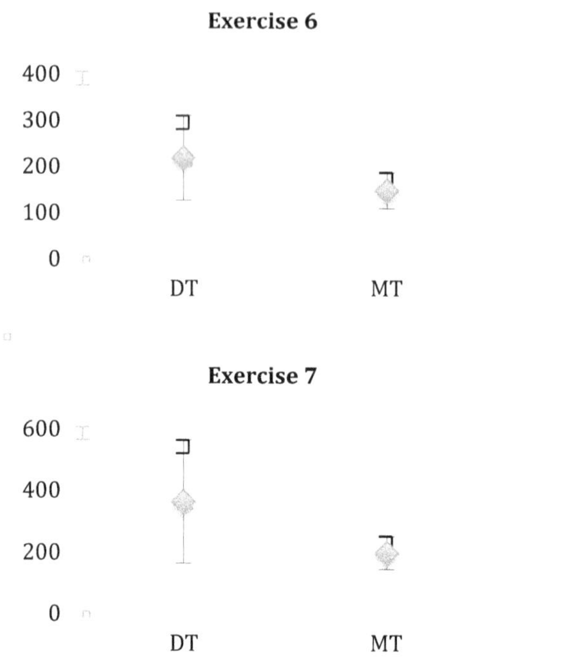

Figure 6: Time spent to solve exercise 6 and 7 (algorithm understanding).

Similarly, no significant difference was observed in the execution of exercises 4 and 5, both containing errors requiring a *pattern matching*: precisely: F(10,10) = 1.29, n.s. for exercise 4 and F(10,10) = 1.08 for exercise 5. Figure 5 shows the results.

Finally, exercise 6 and 7 required the most effort from the testers (as shown by the longer time to solve on average, Figure 6), and the Multi-touch setting allowed a tighter cooperation resulting in a significant better performance: F(10, 10) = 5.56 for exercise 6, F(10,10) = 13.50 for exercise 7.

The timing are summarized in Table 1.

Table 1: Time spent on average on each exercise. Desktop (left column) and Multi-touch (right column) performances are compared.

Exercise #	Avg. Time (Desktop)	Avg Time (Multi-touch)
2	55.18	49.91
3	29.64	39.18
4	119.27	95.82
5	125.64	109.36
6	213.55	143.09
7	356.55	190.80

4.1 Gesture Fluency

Our last test was aimed at showing if users show a difference behavior with respect to gesture fluency in the MT and DT settings. We observed proper gestures according to the related literature given in Section 2. In particular:

- Only movements of the hands were counted as gestures, thus excluding nodding and changes in body postures; specifically, *pointing with the mouse was not counted as gesturing*; in fact, mouse pointing is not a proper gesture and comparison to previous work is problematic. Additionally, we can't assume the visibility of the mouse gesture to the other user, i.e. there is no clear communicative intent (see later).

- Movements of the hands were counted as gestures when they had a clear communicative intent: folding the hands together is not a gesture; pointing, mimicking an action, and counting with fingers are all considered gestures;
- Gesture phrases were counted as their atomic components where possible; for instance, when a tester points a section of code, then another to show correlation, and finally makes sharp movements to show progress, even if these three movements are executed without any visible pause, were counted as 3 separate gestures.

We, thus, introduced for simplicity a measure of *gesture fluency*, as the number of gestural events per second of both testers, and, for each one of the 22 couples, we counted the gesture events of both testers. The gesture fluency of a couple is the total number of gestures performed divided by the total time spent solving the 7 exercises. Results are shown in figure 7.

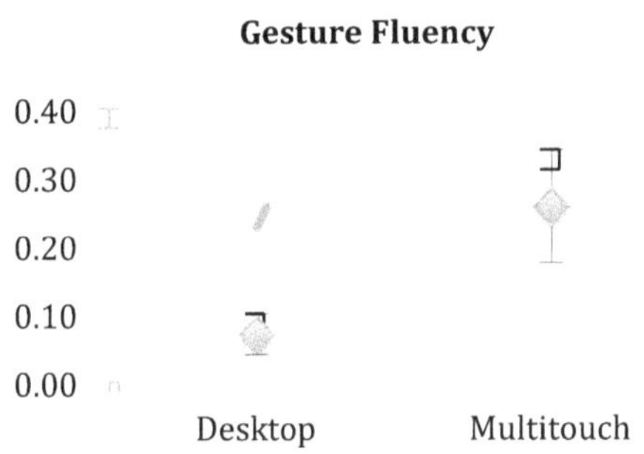

Figure 7: Measures of gesture fluency in the two interaction environments.

The experiment shows that participants use significantly more gestures when using the Multitouch than when interacting at the Desktop, $F(10,10)=7.70$; thus we can reject hypothesis **H5**.

4.2 Discussion

The results shown above indicate that while working at the multi-touch table people perform better than at a traditional desktop, and such improvement is associated to an increased gesticulation.

Some remarks are due here. Not all types of exercise seem to benefit from the adoption of a multi-touch system, in particular snippets containing *careless errors* (exercise 3) and *pattern matching* (exercises 4 and 5) were not significantly affected by the different setting. *Controversial* exercises (such as exercise 2) are better addressed at the multitouch, where a tighter cooperation is possible. This is hardly a surprise, since this sort of problems requires discussion and sometimes negotiation between the users.

The results obtained for exercises 6 and 7 (*algorithm understanding*) are perhaps less intuitive and their implications in the design of interactive applications deserve some attention.

On one hand this work gives a further confirmation of the already observed connection between gesturing and problem solving. In this case an improvement in the interactive systems did not involve improvements *in the interface*, but rather the design of a work-setting more suitable for cooperation, and fluent gesturing was taken as a metric for the cooperation itself.

On the other hand, one can notice that the exercises taking the most benefit from the multitouch setting were the more difficult among the 7 administered, and still were trivial with respect to the typical problems that programmers face in daily work. Our experiments suggest that multi-touch tables, encouraging cooperation, help people express their potential, thus resulting in a better performance. The registered difference in performances for code understanding and debugging time could make a significant difference in many practical cases. If confirmed, these results may help reconsidering the design of our offices and programming labs towards a more widespread adoption of tabletops, that today are mostly regarded as research prototypes and curiosities.

Some further empirical observations are worth mentioning here. Our metric of *gesture fluency* was suitable for the work at hand, but hides the real complexity of gesture phrases. If the gesture largely more exploited by all participants was *pointing* with one finger, others where frequently observed:

- Gestures indicating progress or continuity, both single and dual-handed, are executed moving the hand(s) on a circle or sharply from left to right; such gestures are not easily performed when sitting, and not surprisingly they are less frequently seen at the Desktop;
- Some gestures are performed primarily for communicating, they are a sort of *visible words*; as such they have to be performed in a well-defined and visible space; again, such space (close to the screen) is easier to reach at the Multitouch than it is at the Desktop;
- At the Multitouch *pointing* with the finger was sometimes used to negotiate the attention of the mate; testers often pointed at the same point on screen as to reinforce and confirm a gesture; this behavior was not observed at the Desktop;
- In one case a tester asked if she could use paper and a pencil, which was not possible, actually; several participants at the Multitouch setting were observed while mimicking the use of paper and pencil on the palm of the open hand.

5. CONCLUSION AND FUTURE WORK

We have shown how the adoption of a multi-touch user interface can lead to a significant, observable and measurable, increase of nonverbal communication in general and of gestures in particular, that in turn appears related to the overall performance of the users in the task of code understanding and debugging. Our results indicate that working at the multi-touch table people perform better than at a traditional desktop, and such improvement is associated to an increased gesticulation. Users at the multi-touch outperformed desktop user for specific classes of problem, and such gap corresponded to 4 as much gestural events, indicating an improved cooperation.

As noted throughout the work however, several questions remain open.

- We didn't observe the accuracy of the solutions proposed. For the scope of this research a problem was considered solved when an agreement on the proposed solution was reached; though in principle cooperation and discussion lead to accurate results, a precise measure of such accuracy is likely to expose new insights;
- The choice of gestures to observe was arbitrary, though shared in literature; for example, pointing with the mouse is a common behavior at the Desktop, whose impact should be evaluated;
- How strong an interrelation exists between gestures and efficiency/accuracy? Do couples that show more gesture fluency perform better?

- What new insights may come from a more detailed analysis of gestures; gesture fluency doesn't capture the richness of expression that emerges at the multitouch table, where dual-handed symbolic gestures are often used compared to bare single-handed deictic that form the majority of gestures at the Desktop.

In future work, we wish to further explore the relationships between natural interfaces (including, but not limited to multi-touch tables) and user efficiency in traditional tasks, with the aim of understanding the applicability of new interface paradigms to real workplace and learning environments. In particular, the relationship between gesture fluency and performance at the single exercise is likely to throw light on how people address the task considered (algorithm understanding and debugging).

Our ultimate goal is to identify new practices and guidelines for designers and practitioners, to help evaluate new natural interfaces, and testing design choices respect how they encourage or obstruct those virtuous practices such as gesturing and non-verbal communication.

6. ACKNOWLEDGEMENTS

Some of the C code snippets were adapted from fragments available online under GNU GPL or analogous licenses. Snippets 1-4 were adapted from [24].

7. REFERENCES

[1] Bolt R. A.: "Put-that-there": Voice and gesture at the graphics interface . In Proc. Of SIGGRAPH '80: the 7th annual conference on Computer graphics and interactive techniques

[2] Bruegger, P. and Hirsbrunner, B. Kinetic User Interface: Interaction through Motion for Pervasive Computing Systems, in Proc. of the 5th International on ConferenceUniversal Access in Human-Computer Interaction. UAHCI '09

[3] Castellano, G. and Kessous, L. and Caridakis, G. Emotion Recognition through Multiple Modalities: Face, Body Gesture, Speech. in: Affect and Emotion in Human-Computer Interaction: From Theory to Applications (2008)

[4] Goldin-Meadow, S., Nusbaum, H., Kelly, S.D., & Wagner, S. (2001). Explaining math: Gesturing lightens the load. Psychological Science, 12, 516–522.

[5] Han J. Y.: Low-cost multi-touch sensing through frustrated total internal reflection. In UIST '05: Proceedings of the 18th annual ACM symposium on User interface software and technology (New York, NY, USA, 2005), ACM, pp. 115–118

[6] Ishii, H., and Ullmer, B. Tangible bits: towards seamless interfaces between people, bits and atoms. In CHI '97: Proceedings of the SIGCHI conference on Human factors in computing systems, pages 234–241, New York, NY, USA, 1997. ACM.

[7] Kasday L. R., NJ P.: Touch position sensitive surface, 1981/12/23 1984. 3

[8] Kendon, A. 2004. Gesture: Visible Action as Utterance. Cambridge University Press

[9] Kirsh, D. and Maglio, P. On Distinguishing Epistemic from Pragmatic Action. Cognitive Science 18, 513-549 (1994)

[10] Krueger M. W., Gionfriddo T., Hinrichsen K.: Videoplace—an artificial reality. SIGCHI Bull. 16, 4 (1985), 35– 40. 3

[11] Lee S., Buxton W., Smith K. C.: A multi-touch three dimensional touch-sensitive tablet. SIGCHI Bull. 16, 4 (1985), 21–25. 3

[12] Maglio P. P., Kirsh D.: Epistemic action increases with skill. In In Proceedings of the Eighteenth Annual Conference of the Cognitive Science Society (1996), Erlbaum, pp. 391–396. 3

[13] McNeill, D. Hand and Mind: What Gestures Reveal About Thought. University of Chicago Press, Chicago. 1992.

[14] Morrison, C., Jones, M., Blackwell, A., Vuylsteke, A. (2008) Electronic patient record use during ward rounds: a qualitative study of interaction between medical staff, Critical Care 2008

[15] Owen, R. Gordon Kurtenbach, George Fitzmaurice, Thomas Baudel, and Bill Buxton. 2005. When it gets more difficult, use both hands: exploring bimanual curve manipulation. In Proceedings of Graphics Interface 2005 (GI '05). Canadian Human-Computer Communications Society, School of Computer Science, University of Waterloo, Waterloo, Ontario, Canada, 17-24.

[16] Patten, J and Ishii, H. 2000. A comparison of spatial organization strategies in graphical and tangible user interfaces. In Proceedings of DARE 2000 on Designing augmented reality environments (DARE '00). ACM, New York, NY, USA, 41-50.

[17] Pavlovic V. I., Sharma R., Huang T. S.: Visual interpretation of hand gestures for human-computer interaction: A review. IEEE Trans. Pattern Anal. Mach. Intell. 19, 7 (1997), 677–695.

[18] Williams, L. and Kessle, R. 2002. Pair Programming Illuminated. Addison-Wesley Longman Publishing Co., Inc., Boston, MA, USA.

[19] Wilson, A. D. and Hrvoje Benko. 2010. Combining multiple depth cameras and projectors for interactions on, above and between surfaces. In Proceedings of the 23nd annual ACM symposium on User interface software and technology (UIST '10). ACM, New York, NY, USA, 273-282.

[20] Wu Y., Huang T. S.: Vision-based gesture recognition: A review. In GW '99: Proceedings of the International Gesture Workshop on Gesture-Based Communication in Human-Computer Interaction (London, UK, 1999), Springer-Verlag, pp. 103–115.

[21] Zeleznik, R., Andrew Bragdon, Ferdi Adeputra, and Hsu-Sheng Ko. 2010. Hands-on math: a page-based multi-touch and pen desktop for technical work and problem solving. In Proceedings of the 23nd annual ACM symposium on User interface software and technology (UIST '10). ACM, New York, NY, USA, 17-26.

[22] Cook, S. W., Mitchell, Z., Goldin-Meadow, S. (2008). Gesturing makes learning last. Cognition, 106, 1047-1058.

[23] Kipp, M. (to appear) Multimedia Annotation, Querying and Analysis in ANVIL. In: M. Maybury (ed.) Multimedia Information Extraction, Chapter 19, IEEE Computer Society Press

[24] Love, T. ANSI C for Programmers on UNIX Systems. Cambridge University Engineering Department (available online: *ftp://svr-www.eng.cam.ac.uk/misc/love_**C**.ps.Z*)

Towards Multimodal Sentiment Analysis: Harvesting Opinions from the Web

Louis-Philippe Morency
Institute for Creative Technologies
University of Southern California
Los Angeles, CA 90094
morency@ict.usc.edu

Rada Mihalcea
University of North Texas
Denton, TX 76203
rada@cs.unt.edu

Payal Doshi
University of Southern California
Los Angeles, CA 90094
doshi@usc.edu

ABSTRACT

With more than 10,000 new videos posted online every day on social websites such as YouTube and Facebook, the internet is becoming an almost infinite source of information. One crucial challenge for the coming decade is to be able to harvest relevant information from this constant flow of multimodal data. This paper addresses the task of multimodal sentiment analysis, and conducts proof-of-concept experiments that demonstrate that a joint model that integrates visual, audio, and textual features can be effectively used to identify sentiment in Web videos. This paper makes three important contributions. First, it addresses for the first time the task of tri-modal sentiment analysis, and shows that it is a feasible task that can benefit from the joint exploitation of visual, audio and textual modalities. Second, it identifies a subset of audio-visual features relevant to sentiment analysis and present guidelines on how to integrate these features. Finally, it introduces a new dataset consisting of real online data, which will be useful for future research in this area.

Categories and Subject Descriptors

I.2.7 [**Artificial Intelligence**]: Natural Language Processing—*Discourse*

General Terms

Algorithms, Experimentation

Keywords

Multimodal signal processing, Subjectivity and sentiment analysis, Audio-visual integration, YouTube videos

1. INTRODUCTION

Subjectivity and sentiment analysis focuses on the automatic identification of private states, such as opinions, emotions, sentiments, evaluations, beliefs, and speculations in natural language. While subjectivity classification labels data as either subjective or objective, sentiment classification adds an additional level of granularity, by further classifying subjective data as either positive, negative or neutral.

Much of the work to date on subjectivity and sentiment analysis has focused on textual data, and a number of resources have been created including lexicons [28] or large annotated datasets [18, 29]. Given the accelerated growth of other media on the Web and elsewhere, which includes massive collections of videos (e.g., YouTube, Vimeo, VideoLectures), images (e.g., Flickr, Picasa, Facebook), audio (e.g., podcasts), the ability to address the identification of opinions and sentiment for diverse modalities is becoming increasingly important. With only one exception [20], we are not aware of any previous work that attempted to combine multiple modalities for the purpose of opinion and sentiment analysis. Moreover, although there is a significant amount of previous work on multi-modal emotion analysis, that work has not addressed specifically the polarity (or sentiment) of data, and has generally focused on visual and audio cues, and mainly ignored the knowledge that can be gathered from textual analysis.

In this paper, we address the task of multimodal sentiment analysis, and conduct proof-of-concept experiments that demonstrate that a joint model that integrates visual, audio, and textual features can be effectively used to identify sentiment in web data. Specifically, this paper makes three important contributions. First, we address for the first time the task of tri-modal sentiment analysis by integrating three different modalities: visual, audio and linguistic features, which are jointly used to determine the polarity of an input stream. This is unlike most of the work done on multimodal emotion analysis, which often addressed only one or two modalities at a time (e.g., visual and audio cues). Second, we present a qualitative and statistical analysis that identifies five multimodal features that are found helpful to differentiate between negative, neutral, and positive sentiments: polarized words, smile, gaze, pauses, and voice pitch. Finally, in our experiments we target and use real online data, which poses additional challenges with respect to the artificial datasets that have been typically used in the past in multimodal research. We introduce a new dataset consisting of video opinions, collected from the YouTube web site, which we analyse and annotate for sentiment. The results of our initial experiments show that the joint use of multiple modalities can improve significantly over classifiers that use only one modality at a time, thus demonstrating the potential of multimodal sentiment analysis.

The paper is organized as follows. We first review related work on sentiment and emotion analysis, followed by a description of the problem of multimodal sentiment analysis in Section 3. Section 4 introduces the new dataset that we use in the experiments, including a description of the data acquisition, transcription, and annotation. Section 5 describes our qualitative and statistical analysis of several audio-visual features relevant to sentiment analysis. Section 6 presents our multimodal sentiment classifier, our multimodal features, followed by experimental methodology and a discussion of the results.

2. PREVIOUS WORK

Our paper follows a novel approach of combining audio-visual and text features from videos for sentiment analysis. It evolved from thoughtful reading of many different methods followed previously for audio-visual emotion recognition or text based sentiment analysis. Each of these methods involves a different approach, dealing with either the extraction and processing of data, or with the machine learning algorithms used for the classification.

To date, a large number of text processing applications have already used techniques for automatic sentiment and subjectivity analysis, including automatic expressive text-to-speech synthesis [1], tracking sentiment timelines in on-line forums and news [3], and mining opinions from product reviews [14]. In many natural language processing tasks, subjectivity and sentiment classification has been used as a first phase filtering to generate more viable data. Research that benefited from this additional layering ranges from question answering [31], to conversation summarization [8] and text semantic analysis [27].

The techniques developed so far for sentiment analysis focus primarily on the processing of text, and consist of either rule-based classifiers that make use of sentiment lexicons, or data-driven methods that assume the availability of a large dataset annotated for polarity. For instance, one of the most frequently used lexicons is the subjectivity and sentiment lexicon provided with the OpinionFinder distribution [28], which contains 6,856 unique entries that are also associated with a polarity label, indicating whether the corresponding word or phrase is positive, negative, or neutral. Another lexicon that has been often used in polarity analysis is the General Inquirer [24], which is a dictionary of about 10,000 words grouped into about 180 categories that have been widely used for content analysis. Two of the largest categories in the General Inquirer are the valence classes, which form a lexicon of 1,915 positive words and 2,291 negative words. SentiWordNet [10] is a resource for opinion mining built on top of WordNet, which assigns each synset in WordNet with a score triplet (positive, negative, and objective), indicating the strength of each of these three properties for the words in the synset.

Another major line of work in sentiment and subjectivity analysis consists of data-driven methods based on annotated corpora. One of the most widely used datasets is the MPQA corpus [29], which is a collection of 535 English-language news articles from a variety of news sources manually annotated for opinions and other private states (i.e., beliefs, emotions, sentiments, speculations, etc.). The corpus was originally annotated at clause and phrase level, but sentence-level annotations associated with the dataset can also be derived via simple heuristics [28]. Another manually annotated corpus is the collection of newspaper headlines created and used during the Semeval task on "Affective Text" [25], which consists of 1000 test headlines and 200 development headlines, each of them annotated with the six Eckman emotions (anger, disgust, fear, joy, sadness, surprise) and their polarity orientation (positive, negative). Two other data sets, both of them covering the domain of movie reviews, are a polarity data set consisting of 1,000 positive and 1,000 negative reviews, and a subjectivity data set consisting of 5,000 subjective and 5,000 objective sentences. Both data sets have been introduced in [18], and have been used to train opinion mining classifiers.

Building upon these or other related resources, there is a growing body of work concerned with the automatic identification of sentiment in text, which often times addresses online text, such as reviews [18],news articles [3], or blogs [12]. While difficult problems such as cross-domain [5] or cross-language [16]portability have been addressed, not much has been done in terms of extending the applicability of sentiment analysis to other modalities, such as speech, gesture, or facial expressions. The only exception that we are aware of is the research reported in [20], where speech and text have been analyzed jointly for the purpose of opinion identification. This previous work, however, did not address other modalities such as visual cues, and did not address the problem of sentiment analysis.

Also related to our work is the research done on multimodal emotion analysis [7, 23, 32]. For instance, a novel algorithm is defined in [30], based on a combination of audio-visual features for emotion recognition. The features used by these novel algorithms are usually basic and low level like tracking points for collecting visual data. An engineering approach is then applied to this large set of data points, in order to extract the ones that would be useful for the actual analysis. To our knowledge, there is no previous work analyzing sentiments using all three modalities: textual, audio and video.

Further, most sentiment analysis datasets are created by the researchers in the scientific environment with accurate precision recording and reduced noises [6, 4, 11]. In real world data, however, there are many additional difficulties to overcome. The real world data is the one recorded by people on their own with household instruments like an inbuilt microphone system and an inbuilt web cam of a laptop. Such data would typically have a much greater amount of noise, and the algorithms that work well on scientifically recorded data might prove inefficient on the real world data.

3. MULTIMODAL SENTIMENT IN WEB VIDEOS

Sentiment analysis has recently become a new trend in social media, where it helps users (whether they are brands or consumers) to understand the opinions being expressed about events, products, people, locations, etc. Most of these opinions are given voluntarily and hence are considered to be honest feedback. With the advancement of technology and its increased use amongst masses, in addition to the large body of opinions expressed in textual format, there is a growing number of opinions that are available in video format. Thus, in addition to sentiment analysis for textual data, we also need means to analyze multimodal data, and thereby understand the large number of recorded videos where opinions are being expressed.

Consumers tend to record videos using their web cams or similar devices, to express their opinion on various topics. The main goal is to let other people know about their personal experiences regarding a particular event, product or entity, which they would like to share with others. These videos might include a discussion of the user opinions on a certain topic; a comparison of various brands or products; a discussion of the strengths and weaknesses of a specific product; etc. All these categories are equally helpful to understand the consumer needs and opinions.

These opinion videos are often openly available to all who need to know about a certain topic, through various open Web sources such as YouTube or Facebook. A person who needs to buy a product would first look at the reviews by people already using it. Similarly, someone who tries to determine the movie to watch on a Saturday night will first check the reviews available for that movie. Videos are known to have maximum impact on a person's views, and hence such video feedbacks or opinions have the potential to make a strong impact over the consumer market and are important for understanding the consumer expectations and needs.

The greatest advantage of analyzing video opinions as compared to text-only opinions is that additional cues can be used. In textual opinions, the only available source of information consists of the words in the opinion and the dependencies among them, which may sometime prove insufficient to convey the exact sentiment of the consumer. Instead, video opinions provide multimodal data in the form of vocal as well as visual responses. The vocal modulations in the recorded response help us determine the tone of the speaker whereas visual data can provide information regarding the emotional state of the speaker. Thus a combination of text and video data can help create a better analysis model.

The video data can be a good source for sentiment analysis or opinion mining but it also comes with many challenges that need to be addressed before using the freely available video opinions. The expressiveness of emotions varies from person to person. Some people express themselves more vocally while others more visually. A person with more vocal modulation will have most of the data that would be necessary for opinion mining stored in audio responses. On the other side, a person whose expressing herself more visually would have most of the data stored in facial expressions and non-verbal cues that need to be recognized. A generic model should be able to adapt itself based on each user and give a consistent result.

Thus, the main challenges consist of the noise that is often present in such online, multimodal data, as well as the differences in person-to-person communication patterns. Both these conditions result in difficulties that need to be addressed in order to effectively extract useful data from these sources.

Figure 1: Selected snapshots from our new video dataset.

4. YOUTUBE DATASET

As discussed in the previous section, the automatic analysis of sentiment and subjectivity from real-world videos is a challenging research problem. To properly address this new research direction, we created a dataset[1] from online social videos that encompasses the different facets of sentiment analysis:

- **Diversity:** Diversity comes in multiple dimensions when analyzing real-world interactions. People express sentiments in multiple ways, and some people will be more subtle than others. Also, the topics addressed in online social videos are extremely diverse (e.g., religion views, politic opinions, product reviews). Our dataset contains videos of people from different age and gender groups, expressing opinions on diverse topics.

- **Multimodal:** While an image is worth a thousand words, selecting the appropriate word (e.g., gorgeous, ridiculous) can get you a long way in expressing a sentiment. Through a mixture of facial expressions, body postures, intonations and choice of words, people are extremely efficient at expressing different sentiments. Our dataset contains multimodal videos where one person is speaking directly at the camera, expressing their opinion and/or stating facts.

- **Ambient noises:** A robust computational model of sentiment analysis needs to be able to handle the real-world variability and noises present in most video recordings. While the previous research on audio-visual emotion analysis used videos recorded in laboratory settings[4, 6, 11], our dataset contains videos recorded by users in their home, office or outdoor, using different web cameras and microphones.

Social media Web sites such as YouTube are the perfect place to acquire such an interesting dataset. In fact, more than 10,000 videos are added to YouTube every day. People from all around the world post videos online and these videos are freely available (given proper acknowledgment of publishing licenses). Also, social media Web sites contain the diversity, multi-modality and ambient noises characterizing real-world sentiment analysis.

The following section describes how we acquired our dataset and Sections 4.3 and 4.2 present our approaches to transcribe and annotate the videos. The details about the automatically extracted multimodal features are described later in the Experiment section (see Section 6.2).

[1]Please visit the following website for the video links, transcriptions and sentiment annotations: http://projects.ict.usc.edu/youtube/

4.1 Acquisition

We collected 47 videos from the social media web site YouTube. As mentioned earlier, an important characteristic of our dataset is its generalized nature. The dataset is created in such a way that it is not based on one particular topic. The videos were found using the following keywords: opinion, review, product review, best perfume, toothpaste, war, job, business, cosmetics review, camera review, baby product review, I hate, I like.

The final video set has 20 female and 27 male speakers randomly selected from youtube.com, with their age ranging approximately from 14-60 years. Although from different ethnic backgrounds (e.g., Caucasian, African-American, Hispanic, Asian), all speakers expressed themselves in English. The videos are converted to .mp4 format with a standard size of 360x480. The length of the videos varies from 2-5 minutes.

All videos are pre-processed to address the following issues: introductory titles and multiple topics. Many videos on YouTube contain an introductory sequence where a title is shown, sometime accompanied with a visual animation. As a simple way to address this issue, the first 30 seconds of each video is removed. In the future, this step could be optimized by automatically performing optical character recognition (OCR) on the videos [19].

The second issue is related to multiple topics. Videos posted on social networks can address more than one topic. For example, a person can start by talking about the new movie she recently saw and then switch to a new (or related) topic such as food served in movie theaters. To simply address this issue, all video sequences are normalized to be 30 seconds in length. We keep as future work to automatically segment topics based on transcriptions [2] or directly based on the audio-visual signals.

4.2 Transcriptions

All video clips are manually transcribed to extract spoken words as well as the start time of each spoken utterance. The Transcriber software was used to perform this task. The transcription is done using only the audio track of each video clip. In other words, the transcriptions are done without the visual information. Although not used in this paper, the word elongations and filler pauses are also transcribed. Each video contains 3-11 utterances with most videos having 5-6 utterances in the extracted 30 seconds. The utterance segmentation was based on long pauses which could easily be detected using tools such as Praat and OpenEAR [22].

Multimodal sentiment analysis using manual transcription is a precedent step to fully automatic sentiment classification. This paper is a proof-of-concept that tri-modal sentiment classification can be performed. Automatic speech recognition can also be used as input to our approach. In the recent years, many technologies have emerged to automatically transcribe voicemails (e.g., Google Voice) and videos (e.g., Adobe Translator). In fact, not all words need to be accurate since we are using a dictionary of polarized words and valence shifters, and thus only the words in the dictionary need to be properly recognized.

4.3 Sentiment Annotations

An important step in creating such a dataset is sentiment label annotation. Since our goal is to automatically find the sentiment expressed in the video clip, we decided to perform our annotation task at video sequence level. For each video, we want to assign one of these three labels: negative, neutral or positive. All 47 video clips are annotated by three annotators who were shown videos in three different random sequencing orders, so as to reduce the compound effect. It is important to note that we are not annotating the sentiment felt by the person watching the video. The annotation task is to associate a sentiment label that best summarizes the opinion expressed in the YouTube video.

To perform this annotation task, we built a web interfaces that shows one video clip at the time and the three label options. The annotators can replay the video as often as they want. Once they are ready, they select the sentiment label and go to the next video clip.

The pair-wise coder agreements are 89.4%, 82.9% and 63.8% respectively, with an average coder agreement of 78.7%. None of the videos had a complete disagreement where all three coders disagreed. Always two out of three annotators agreed. Based on this observation, we define our final ground truth labels using majority voting. Out of the 47 videos clips, 13 were labeled as positive, 22 as neutral, and 12 as negative.

5. SENTIMENT ANALYSIS EXPERIMENTS

The study of human verbal and nonverbal behaviors when interacting with social medias such as Skype and Youtube is an ongoing research topic. Much needs to be analyzed to completely understand the influence of these new technologies on human multimodal interactions. The goal of this paper is not only to create technology to automatically classify sentiments (as described in Section 6) but also to gain a better understanding of how nonverbal cues accompany positive and negative sentiments. This section presents a first step in this direction where we analyze the nonverbal behaviors co-occurring with negative, neutral and positive videos.

5.1 Qualitative Analysis

We started our analysis by observing qualitatively the videos of our corpus, searching for nonverbal cues that could be correlated with sentiments. In this first stage, we look for audio-visual cues that vary among people present in our 47 videos. We focus on facial motion and the basic prosodic cues (voice intensity and pitch).

Please note that a more engineering approach could have been used to perform this pre-filtering step. In fact, many researchers from the signal processing community approach this problem by simply trying all possible features under all possible representations [30]. While this is a valuable approach, these models often end up really large (containing multiple features) and are harder to interpret. In contrast, we decided to start with a more behavioral approach where we first studied the videos directly, searching for relevant nonverbal cues. Applying the engineering approach to our YouTube dataset will be a great future research direction but it is not necessary at this point.

From this qualitative pre-study, four audio-visual cues were identified as potential features: smile, gaze, pauses and voice pitch. In all four cases, we observed large variations which could possibly be correlated with sentiment expression. The details related to tri-modal feature extraction are described in Section 6.2. The following present the results of our statistical analysis.

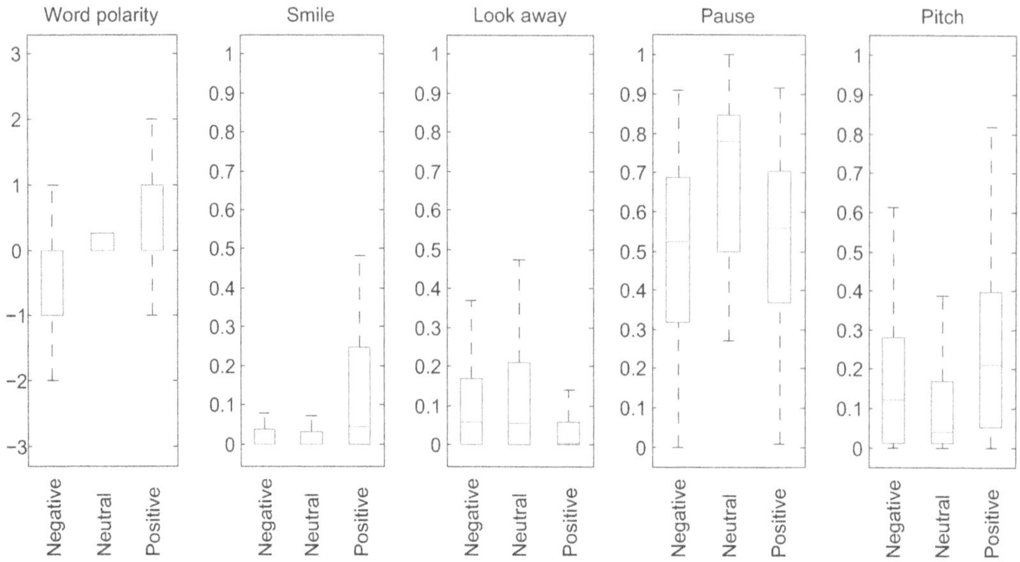

Figure 2: Average values of multimodal features when clustered per sentiment label. In all five graphs, the red line represents the median, the top blue line represents the 75th percentile and the bottom blue line represents the 25th percentile. Word polarity is a great way to differentiate sentiment but many utterances do not contain polarized words as shown by all three medians equal to zero. The visual features (smile and look away) are good ways to differentiate positive utterances from neutral or negative utterances. Audio features (pauses and pitch) are great ways to differentiate neutral utterances from positive or negative utterances.

5.2 Statistical Analysis

To confirm a correlation between the observed nonverbal cues and the sentiment expressed by the person, we perform a statistical analysis based on percentile ranking. This analysis will give us a better insight on which nonverbal and verbal cue is relevant to identify a specific sentiment (negative, neutral and positive). We will later use these results to learn a computational model and automatically classify sentiments in web videos.

Using the audio-visual features identified in the previous section (see details in Section 6.2), we perform percentile ranking per sentiment labels. In other words, we look at variation of each multimodal features for each sentiment label. The sentiment labels come from the annotations described in Section 4.3.

Figure 4.1 shows the results of the percentile ranking. In all five graphs, the red line represents the median, the top blue line represents the 75th percentile and the bottom blue line represents the 25th percentile. From these results, many interesting observations can be made:

- **Polarized words:** As shown in previous work on text-based sentiment analysis[15, 26], using a dictionary of positively or negatively polarized words, sentiment polarity can be effectively differentiated. One of the main issues with using only textual features is that most utterances do not contain polarized words. This is shown in Figure 4.1, where all three medians of Polarized Words are equal to zero.

- **Smile:** The fact that people smile when expressing positive sentiment does not come as a surprise. Smile has been shown to be correlated with happiness [9]. Smile is a good feature to differentiate positive utterances from neutral or negative utterances.

- **Look away:** People gaze patterns seem correlated with sentiment. We can see that people look away from the camera more often when expressing neutral or negative utterances. Another way to interpret this result is to see that people try to create mutual-gaze more often when expressing positive utterances. In this case, mutual-gaze is approximated by having the speaker looking at the camera. It was shown that people have more mutual gaze when they are creating rapport and engagement [13], which can be seen as more positive.

- **Pauses:** Our analysis show that people seem to pause less often when expressing polarized (negative or positive) utterances. Often these polarized utterances are spoken with more energy and faster pace. So we see more pauses with neutral utterances.

- **Pitch:** A similar pattern emerged with the voice pitch where polarized utterances are spoken with a wider range of variation in the pitch level. The neutral utterance are spoken at a more monotone level.

In summary, polarized words are great to differentiate sentiment although many utterances do not contain polarized words. The visual features are good ways to differentiate positive utterances from neutral or negative utterances. Audio features are great ways to differentiate neutral utterances from positive or negative utterances. By combining all three modalities we expect a better classification performance.

6. SENTIMENT CLASSIFICATION EXPERIMENTS

Our final goal is to be able to automatically classify an audio-visual clip into one of these three sentiment labels: positive, negative, or neutral. The experiment described in this section is based on the expertise and knowledge learned from the qualitative and statistical analysis described in the previous section. We know that textual, audio and visual features can be used to differentiate sentiment in spoken data. The remaining question is whether these modalities are complementary, and if so, can they help each other in the classification?

To test this hypothesis, we train a computational model of spoken sentiments and test it using our Youtube dataset. The following three sections describe our computational model, the feature extraction and the experimental methodology, while Section 6.4 presents and discusses our results.

6.1 Computational Model

Human communication is a dynamic process and explicitly modeling this dynamic has been shown to improve tasks such as gestures recognition [17] and speech recognition [21]. One probabilistic model which was shown to perform well in these situations is the HMM classifier. This model learns the hidden structure in the input signal by jointly learning the observation model (i.e., the relationship between the input features and the hidden variables) and the dynamic (or motion) model.

In our case, the dynamic is most prominent at the utterance level. We are thus learning HMMs that take as input tri-modal features summarizing each utterance. In other words, we model the YouTube video clip using a Markov chain where each element of the chain represents one spoken utterance (see Section 4.2 for details about the utterance segmentation). For each utterance, we compute tri-modal features (described in the following section) summarizing the audio-visual cues happening during this utterance. The observation and dynamic models of our tri-modal HMM learn the relative importance of each audio-visual cues as well as the dynamic between utterances. For example, people often insert one or two negative points during a positive opinion to show that they considered both the positive and the negative aspects of issue being discussed. We use a mixture of Gaussian as our observation model and two hyper parameters are automatically validated: the number of Gaussian mixtures and the number of hidden states.

6.2 Automatic Feature Extraction

Given an video clip with transcribed words (e.g., captions), we want to automatically extract multimodal features for sentiment analysis. Based on the literature and our own qualitative analysis, we define five important tri-modal features: polarized words, smile, look-away, pauses, and voice pitch. Following previous work on audio-visual emotion recognition [30, 7], we extract features at the utterance level so that we can represent local changes. Our multimodal sentiment classifier described in Section 6 will learn the hidden dynamic between utterances and output sentiment labels at the video level. The following three subsections describe how we automatically extract these multimodal features.

6.2.1 Text features

We generate textual features by automatically identifying linguistic cues of sentiment present in the text of the utterance. First, using two lexicons of words labeled as positive or negative, the presence of sentiment words in the text is identified, and a polarity score is calculated. The lexicons are compiled from a distribution of the MPQA dataset (Wiebe 2005), and consists of words loaded with positive (e.g., "good") or negative (e.g., "bad") sentiment. We assign each word in these lexicons with a predefined polarity value; for instance, a positive word could be assigned with a value of 1, and a negative word could be assigned with a value of -1. Other polarity values can also be used, and can lead to different accuracy figures in the automatic annotation of sentiment.

Next, we use a lexicon of valence shifters, which can change the polarity of a word (and correspondingly its polarity value) if a valence shifter is found within a certain distance. For instance, if the valence shifter "not" is found within two words from the positive word "good," the polarity of "good" is shifted from positive to negative, and its polarity value is changed from 1 to -1.

Given these lexicons, the polarity score of a text is calculated as the sum of the polarity values of the lexicon words found in the text, while also accounting for the valence shifters found in the text within close proximity of the lexicon words. The current system implementation defines "proximity" as words found within a distance of at most two words, but other window sizes can be used.

6.2.2 Visual features

The visual features are automatically extracted from the video sequences. Since only one person is present in each video clip and they are most of the time facing the camera, current technology for facial tracking can efficiently be applied to our dataset. We use a commercial software called OKAO Vision that detects at each frame the face, it extracts the facial features and extrapolates some basic facial expressions as well as eye gaze direction. The main facial expression being recognized is smile. This is a well-established technology that can be found in many digital cameras. For each frame, the vision software returns a smile intensity (0-100) and the gaze direction, using both horizontal and vertical angles expressed in degrees. The sampling rate is the same as the video framerate: 30Hz.

For each utterance in each video in our dataset, we define two series of summary features:

- **Smile duration:** Given the start and end time of an utterance, how many frames are identified as "smile." In our experiments, we use three different variants of this feature with different thresholds: 50 and 75.
- **Look-away duration:** Given the start time and end time of the utterance, in how many frames is the speaker looking at the camera. The horizontal and vertical angular thresholds were experimentally set to 10 degrees.

The visual features are normalized by the total number of frames during the utterance. Thus, if the person is smiling half the time, then the smile feature will be equal to 0.5 (or 50%).

6.2.3 *Audio features*

The audio features are automatically extracted from the audio track of each video clip. The audio features are extracted at the same framerate as the video features (30Hz) with a sliding window of 50ms. We used the open source software OpenEAR [22] to automatically compute the pitch and voice intensity. Speaker normalization is performed using z-standardization. The voice intensity was simply thresholded to identify samples with and without speech. The same threshold was used for all the experiments and all the speakers.

For each utterance in our dataset, we define two summary features:

- **Pause duration:** Given the start and end time of the utterance, how many audio samples are identified as silence. This audio feature is then normalized by the number of audio samples in this utterance. This feature can be interpreted as the percentage of the time where the speaker was silent.

- **Pitch:** Compute the standard deviation of the pitch level for the spoken utterance. This measure represents the variation of voice intonation during the same utterance.

These tri-modal features (polarized words, smile, gaze, pause and pitch) were used for both the statistical analysis described in the next section as well as the sentiment classification experiment described in Section 6.

6.3 Methodology

We perform leave-one-out testing where one video clip is kept for testing and all remaining 46 clips are used for training and validation. This process is repeated 47 times. All models described before are trained and tested using the same procedure. The optimal hyper-parameters (number of hidden states and number of mixtures) were automatically validated using the training error. The number of hidden states was validated with values 2, 3, 4, 5, 6 and 7 respectively. Four different number of Gaussian mixtures were tested for the HMM model: 1, 2, 3 and 4.

The performance is measured by using the F-measure, which is the weighted harmonic mean of precision and recall. Precision is the probability that predicted backchannels correspond to actual listener behavior. Recall is the probability that a backchannel produced by a listener in the test set was correctly predicted by the model. We use the same weight for both precision and recall, resulted in the so-called F1 measure. The same evaluation metric is applied to all the models. The training of all the HMMs models is done using the BNT Matlab toolbox from Kevin Murphy.[2]

6.4 Results

As stated earlier, the main goal of this experiment is to test if the multimodal features identified in Section 5 are able to work together to improve sentiment classification or if they are simply redundant features.

Table 1 shows the classification performances of four different models: text-only, visual-only, audio-only and tri-modal integration. These results show a significant improvement when all three sources of information are integrated,

	F1	Precision	Recall
Text only HMM	0.430	0.431	0.430
Visual only HMM	0.439	0.449	0.430
Audio only HMM	0.419	0.408	0.429
Tri-modal HMM	**0.553**	**0.543**	**0.564**

Table 1: Automatic sentiment classification performances of four different models: text-only, visual-only, audio-only and tri-modal integration.

and, importantly, these improvements are observed for both precision and recall. The tri-modal HMM is able to learn the hidden interaction between all three modalities and take advantage of their respective discriminative power.

7. DISCUSSION AND CONCLUSIONS

In this paper, we addressed the task of multimodal sentiment analysis, and explored the joint use of multiple modalities for the purpose of classifying the polarity of opinions in online videos. Through experiments performed on a newly introduced dataset, consisting of videos where people express their opinion about different topics, we showed that the integration of visual, audio, and textual features can improve significantly over the individual use of one modality at a time.

We believe this paper made three important contributions. First, we addressed for the first time the task of tri-modal sentiment analysis, and showed that it is a feasible task that can benefit from the joint exploitation of different modalities. Second, we identified five multimodal features helpful to differentiate negative, neutral and positive sentiments: polarized words, smile, gaze, pauses, and voice pitch. Finally, we introduced a new dataset consisting of real online data, which we hope it will be useful for future research in this area.

In future work, we plan to run experiments on a significantly larger scale, so that we can also address the problem of sentiment analysis at utterance level (rather than video level, as done in this paper). We would also like to explore other domains, such as movie reviews or even political debates, which may pose additional difficulties in terms of recognizing the visual and audio features.

Acknowledgments

The authors are grateful to the three annotators who helped with the sentiment annotations. This material is based in part upon work supported by the National Science Foundation IIS award #0917170 and by the U.S. Army Research, Development, and Engineering Command. Any opinions, findings, and conclusions or recommendations expressed in this material are those of the authors and do not reflect the views of the National Science Foundation or of the Government, and no official endorsement should be inferred.

8. REFERENCES

[1] C. Alm, D. Roth, and R. Sproat. Emotions from text: Machine learning for text-based emotion prediction. In *Proceedings of the Conference on Empirical Methods in Natural Language Processing*, pages 347–354, Vancouver, Canada, 2005.

[2]http://code.google.com/p/bnt/

[2] J. Arguello and C. Rose. Topic segmentation of dialogue. In *HLT-NAACL Workshop on Analyzing Conversations in Text and Speech*, 2009.
[3] K. Balog, G. Mishne, and M. de Rijke. Why are they excited? identifying and explaining spikes in blog mood levels. In *Proceedings of the 11th Meeting of the European Chapter of the As sociation for Computational Linguistics (EACL-2006)*, 2006.
[4] T. Banziger and K. R. Scherer. *Introducing the geneva multimodal emotion portrayal (gemep) corpus.* Oxford University Press, 2010.
[5] J. Blitzer, M. Dredze, and F. Pereira. Biographies, bollywood, boom-boxes and blenders: Domain adaptation for sentiment classification. In *Association for Computational Linguistics*, 2007.
[6] C. Busso, M. Bulut, C. Lee, A. Kazemzadeh, E. Mower, S. Kim, J. Chang, S. Lee, and S. Narayanan. Iemocap: Interactive emotional dyadic motion capture database. *Journal of Language Resources and Evaluation*, 42(4):335–359, December 2008.
[7] C. Busso and S. Narayanan. Interrelation between speech and facial gestures in emotional utterances: a single subject study. *IEEE Transactions on Audio, Speech and Language Processing*, 15(8):2331–2347, November 2007.
[8] G. Carenini, R. Ng, and X. Zhou. Summarizing emails with conversational cohesion and subjectivity. In *Proceedings of the Association for Computational Linguistics: Human Language Technologies (ACL-HLT 2008)*, Columbus, Ohio, 2008.
[9] P. Ekman. Facial expression of emotion. *American Psychologist*, 48:384–392, 1993.
[10] A. Esuli and F. Sebastiani. SentiWordNet: A publicly available lexical resource for opinion mining. In *LREC*, Genova, IT, 2006.
[11] G.McKeown, M. Valstar, R. Cowie, and M. Pantic. The semaine corpus of emotionally coloured character interactions. In *ICME*, pages 1079–1084, 2010.
[12] N. Godbole, M. Srinivasaiah, and S. Sekine. Large-scale sentiment analysis for news and blogs. In *International Conference on Weblogs and Social Media*, Denver, CO, 2007.
[13] J. A. Harrigan, T. E. Oxman, and R. Rosenthal. Rapport expressed through nonverbal behavior. *Journal of Nonverbal Behavior*, 9(2), 1985.
[14] M. Hu and B. Liu. Mining and summarizing customer reviews. In *SIGKDD*, Seattle, Washington, 2004.
[15] N. Kaji and M. Kitsuregawa. Building lexicon for sentiment analysis from massive collection of html documents. In *Proceedings of the Conference on Empirical Methods in Natural Language Processing*, Prague, Czech Republic, 2007.
[16] R. Mihalcea, C. Banea, and J. Wiebe. Learning multilingual subjective language via cross-lingual projections. In *ACL*, Prague, Czech Republic, 2007.
[17] L.-P. Morency, A. Quattoni, and T. Darrell. Latent-dynamic discriminative models for continuous gesture recognition. In *CVPR*, June 2007.
[18] B. Pang and L. Lee. A sentimental education: Sentiment analysis using subjectivity summarization based on minimum cuts. In *Proceedings of the 42nd Meeting of the Association for Computational Linguistics*, Barcelona, Spain, July 2004.
[19] T. Plotz and G. A. Fink. Markov models for offline handwriting recognition: a survey. *International Journal on Document Analysis and Recognition*, 12(4), 2009.
[20] S. Raaijmakers, K. Truong, and T. Wilson. Multimodal subjectivity analysis of multiparty conversation. In *Proceedings of the Conference on Empirical Methods in Natural Language Processing*, pages 466–474, Honolulu, Hawaii, 2008.
[21] L. Rabiner. A tutorial on hidden markov models and selected applications in speech recognition. *Proceedings of the IEEE*, 77(2), 1989.
[22] F. E. M. W. B. Schuller. Openear introducing the munich open-source emotion and affect recognition toolkit. In *ACII*, 2009.
[23] N. Sebe, I. Cohen, T. Gevers, and T. Huang. Emotion recognition based on joint visual and audio cues. In *ICPR*, 2006.
[24] P. Stone. *General Inquirer: Computer Approach to Content Analysis.* MIT Press, 1968.
[25] C. Strapparava and R. Mihalcea. Semeval-2007 task 14: Affective text. In *Proceedings of the 4th International Workshop on the Semantic Evaluations (SemEval 2007)*, Prague, Czech Republic, 2007.
[26] M. Taboada, J. Brooke, M. Tofiloski, K. Voli, and M. Stede. Lexicon-based methods for sentiment analysis. *Computational Linguistics*, 37(3), 2011.
[27] J. Wiebe and R. Mihalcea. Word sense and subjectivity. In *Proceedings of the Annual Meeting of the Association for Computational Linguistics*, Sydney, Australia, 2006.
[28] J. Wiebe and E. Riloff. Creating subjective and objective sentence classifiers from unannotated texts. In *CICLing-2005*, 2005.
[29] J. Wiebe, T. Wilson, and C. Cardie. Annotating expressions of opinions and emotions in language. *Language Resources and Evaluation*, 39(2-3):165–210, 2005.
[30] M. Wollmer, B. Schuller, F. Eyben, and G. Rigoll. Combining long short-term memory and dynamic bayesian networks for incremental emotion-sensitive artificial listening. *IEEE Journal of Selected Topics in Signal Processing*, 4(5), October 2010.
[31] H. Yu and V. Hatzivassiloglou. Towards answering opinion questions: Separating facts from opinions and identifying the polarity of opinion sentences. In *EMNLP*, pages 129–136, Sapporo, Japan, 2003.
[32] Z. Zhihong, M. P. G. Roisman, and T. Huang. A survey of affect recognition methods: Audio, visual, and spontaneous expressions. *PAMI*, 31(1), 2009.

The Impact of Unwanted Multimodal Notifications

David Warnock
warnock@dcs.gla.ac.uk

Marilyn McGee-Lennon
mcgeemr@dcs.gla.ac.uk

Stephen Brewster
stephen@dcs.gla.ac.uk

Glasgow Interactive Systems Group, School of Computing Science
University of Glasgow, Glasgow, G12 8QQ, UK

ABSTRACT

Multimodal interaction can be used to make home care technology more effective and appropriate, particularly for people with sensory impairments. Previous work has revealed how disruptive notifications in different modalities are to a home-based task, but has not investigated how disruptive unwanted notifications might be. An experiment was conducted which evaluated the disruptive effects of unwanted notifications when delivered in textual, pictographic, abstract visual, speech, earcon, auditory icon, tactile and olfactory modalities. It was found that for all the modalities tested, both wanted and unwanted notifications produced similar reductions in error rate and task success, independent of modality. The results demonstrate the need to control and limit the number of unwanted notifications delivered in the home and contribute to a large body of work advocating the inclusion of multiple interaction modalities.

Categories and Subject Descriptors

H.5.2 [**Information Systems Applications**]: User Interfaces—*interaction styles*

General Terms

Design, Experimentation, Human Factors

Keywords

Multimodal Interaction, Home Care, Reminders

1. INTRODUCTION

A home reminder system is a form of assistive technology designed to help people manage their lifestyle and environment by providing helpful notifications. Wang & Turner [29] argued that home care technology should be adaptable, personalised, customisable and dependable in order to be both effective and appropriate. Many researchers have argued that user acceptability is also a vital factor when developing technology for the home environment [18, 19, 24, 27, 30]. Rejection could lead to the user ignoring or disabling the system [18], limiting its ability to help its users achieve a higher quality of life.

Multimodal interaction can help home care technology to achieve both Wang & Turner's key properties and acceptability requirements by *(i)* providing interaction opportunities in user-preferred modalities, *(ii)* providing alternative modes of communications for various social and environmental contexts, *(iii)* allowing for the consideration of sensory impairment and *(iv)* providing flexibility in the face of changing requirements. A number of researchers have advocated the inclusion of multiple modalities to make such technology more effective and appropriate [1, 11, 16, 18, 19, 20, 31].

While both hardware and software exists for the inclusion of multiple interaction modalities, a lack of general guidelines and models for their use in commercialised systems has prevented their wide-spread adoption. Existing guidelines for multimodal interaction design need to be refined and validated, which will help give developers the knowledge and confidence to include a wider range of modalities in their technology. In the case of home care technology this could lead to significant improvements in the effectiveness and user acceptability of reminder systems.

The continued development of guidelines and models for multimodal interaction requires wide-scale evaluations of the individual properties of different modalities, both individually and compared with each other. In the case of home reminder systems, this involves examining the underlying properties of different multimodal notifications to determine which ones are more and less effective. Presented here is a study into the potential of unwanted notifications in various modalities to disrupt a home-based primary task. The results of this study will contribute towards the continued development of guidelines and models for multimodal notification design.

2. RELATED WORK

The primary users of home reminder systems are elderly persons and people with sensory or cognitive impairments. Providing multiple ways to interact can improve accessibility, which has prompted a number of researchers to call for the inclusion of multiple modalities in home care technology [11, 19, 25]. In addition, researchers have argued that dynamically switching between modalities when appropriate will also lead to increased user acceptability [1, 18, 30, 31]; for example, switching to a more private modality (e.g. tac-

ICMI'11, November 14–18, 2011, Alicante, Spain.

tile) when delivering sensitive information in a social context might be desirable.

It is well documented that interruptions can cause stress [10, 17], annoyance and anxiety [4], a higher chance of making a mistake [15] and increased speed [7, 9, 17]. Notification schedulers can be used to manage *when* and *how* notifications are delivered to minimise such negative effects. Deciding *when* to deliver notifications has received a great deal of attention in HCI research, mostly focussed around office and high-pressure environments. This usually involves a cost-benefit calculation based on the importance of the notification and how 'interruptible' the user is. Horovitz's attentive user interface paradigm [13] uses attentional focus to measure interruptibility. Monk, Boehm-Davis & Trafton [22] suggested that it was most important to consider the stage of the task; that interruption at the start or end was preferable to interruption mid-task. Iqbal & Bailey's OASIS [14] framework scheduled around *breakpoints*, naturally occurring mental pauses between units of work, such as when the user has finished writing an e-mail.

When developing notifications for the home context, user acceptability is a key factor. Unhappy or irritated users might sabotage or ignore the system [18], which could be dangerous if it is intended to deliver safety or care-based reminders. There have been numerous attempts at creating a model of when to deliver notifications in the home. Vastenburg, Keyson & Ridder [27] argued that user acceptance of a notification is dependent on the message urgency and the attentional focus of the user, but did not take into account user activity or social context, which other researchers have argued is very important in the home [18, 19, 24]. Nagel, Hudson & Abowd [24] found that people had different opinions on which activities could be acceptably interrupted. McGee-Lennon, Wolters & Brewster [19] reported that people expressed a strong desire for personalisation in home reminder technology.

When it comes to *how* to deliver a notification, there is a great deal of research into different ways to deliver information, but little on how this relates to notification acceptability. Vastenburg, Keyson & Ridder [27] found that the salience of the delivery method combined with the urgency of the notification had a strong relationship to acceptability in the home. McBryan & Gray [18] suggested a configurable model for changing the modality of a notification based around the user's current activity. McGee-Lennon, Wolters & Brewster [19] highlighted the importance of personal preference when examining modality, and found that interaction modality preference varied with the type of task being carried out. McGee-Lennon, Wolters & McBryan [20] examined 3 types of audio reminders and found that a person's preferences did not necessarily match the modalities they performed best with.

For the successful inclusion of multiple modalities in home reminder systems, models need to be created that allow developers to identify which modality is appropriate based on factors such as current user activity, user location, social context, user impairment, message urgency and user preference. This requires a good understanding of the relationships between the individual properties of a wide range of interaction modalities.

Warnock, McGee-Lennon & Brewster [31] carried out a study into the performance and disruptiveness of visual, audio, tactile and olfactory notifications and found that modality did not affect error or activity rates, but did provide different response accuracies and timings. In their experiment, all of the notifications required a response.

However, it is likely that a home reminder system will sometimes deliver notifications that the user will not want or need. Vastenburg, Keyson & Ridder [28] reported that people did not want to be interrupted for low-urgency information. A notification may be unwanted because the user is engaged in an important or demanding task and does not want to be distracted. The notification may not be valid due to a deviation from normal routines: e.g. a reminder to pick up keys before leaving the house may become irritating when the user only wishes to go into the garden. For other occupants of the home all the notifications may be unwanted. It is important to understand the effect that such unwanted notifications could have as an unwanted notification provides no benefit. The inherent differences between modalities may make some modalities harder to ignore or process than others, causing more disruption. This paper reports on an experiment to examine the effects of unwanted notifications in various interaction modalities on performance in a simple card matching game.

3. DESIGN & METHOD

An experiment was carried out to objectively evaluate how disruptive notifications in different modalities were. The experiment was a within-subjects design ($N = 18$) consisting of a primary task and a range of unimodal notifications which instructed the participant to carry out a brief secondary task.

The independent variables were:

1. The modality of the notification (text, pictogram, abstract visual, speech, earcon, auditory icon, tactile and olfactory modalities).
2. The percentage of notifications that were unwanted (100%, 66%, 33%).
3. The type of notification (wanted vs. unwanted).

The dependent variables were:

1. The error rate in the primary task (measured as superfluous views per click).
2. The activity rate in the primary task (measured as clicks per second).
3. The success rate in the primary task (measured as matches per game).
4. The pause time post-notification (measured in seconds).

The experiment was carried out with 18 participants (12 male and 6 female). The participants consisted of 17 people aged 18-30 and 1 person aged 31-45.

3.1 Primary Task

The task chosen was a simple card-matching game called 'Concentration' (also known as Memory or Pairs), as used by Warnock, McGee-Lennon & Brewster [31]. In concentration, pairs of cards are presented face-down to the player. The player can then turn over two cards per turn in an attempt to find the pairs and remove them from the game. Concentration is a simple leisure activity that might well be carried out at home, it is a well-known game with simple rules and it can quickly build a mental workload. The game was configured in the same way as by Warnock, McGee-Lennon & Brewster; the cards showed simple alphabet caricatures[1] and each game comprised 24 cards with a 60 second time limit.

[1]Speech Teach UK, `http://www.speechteach.co.uk`

Table 1: Modal Specification

Modality	Message: Heating	Lights	Telephone	Description
Text	"Heating"	"Lights"	"Phone"	A simple one-word message displayed in a large bold font above the game area on-screen.
Pictogram	IEC-60878 Thermometer	IEC-60878 Light	ISO-7001 Telephone	Taken from two international standards; IEC-60878 and ISO-7001.
Abstract Visual	Yellow Light	Green Light	Blue Light	Projector used to shine a coloured light against the wall.
Voice	Spoken "Heating"	Spoken "Lights"	Spoken "Phone"	Created using the same synthetic voice that was used by McGee-Lennon, Wolters & McBryan [20].
Earcon	Rollercoaster	Static Ride	Water Ride	The earcons varied in rhythm and instrument and were taken from McGookin & Brewster [21].
Auditory Icon	Gas Ignition	Light Switch Click (x2)	Phone Dialing Beeps	Auditory icons at 1 second each taken from an online sound effect archive.[2]
Tactile	multiSP	textMP	voiceLP	Tactons varied in rhythm and roughness, taken from an experiment by Brewster & Brown [5].
Olfactory	'Dark Chocolate'	'Riverside'	'Raspberry'	Smells were created by Dale Air and selected based on the findings of Brewster, McGookin & Miller [6].

3.2 Secondary Task

The secondary task in the experiment was to press a single, large red button when instructed to do so by a notification. This button was placed directly in front of the participant within easy reach, as shown in Figure 1. There were two different *notification functions* in the experiment, defined as follows:

The Target Notification

When the participant receives the target notification, they are to press the red button.

Distractor Notifications

When the participant receives a distractor notification, they are to attempt to ignore it entirely and continue focussing on the primary task.

Figure 1: The configuration of the experiment.

3.3 Notification Design

To evaluate the differences between notifications in different modalities, a wide range of unimodal notifications were designed for the experiment based on those used by Warnock, McGee-Lennon & Brewster [31]. These included common notification techniques such as text and speech along with less common notification modalities such as olfaction and abstract visual display. Eight unimodal notifications in total were developed for the experiment. The exact configuration of each notification is shown in Table 1.

The text and pictogram notifications were delivered directly into the game window to the top of the play area. No additional hardware was required for this. The abstract visual display was created with a short-throw projector positioned to project a coloured light against the wall adjacent to the participant. The projector was deliberately aligned so that the projection lay in the peripheral vision of the participant as shown in Figure 2a.

In all audio conditions notifications were delivered through a pair of Sennheiser HD 25-1 II closed-back headphones as shown in Figure 2b. These headphones helped to prevent background noise from causing interference.

Tactile notifications were delivered via an Engineering Acoustics Inc. C2 vibrotactile actuator[2] powered by a small amplifier. This was secured to the top of the wrist on the par-

[2]Engineering Acoustics, `http://www.eaiinfo.com`

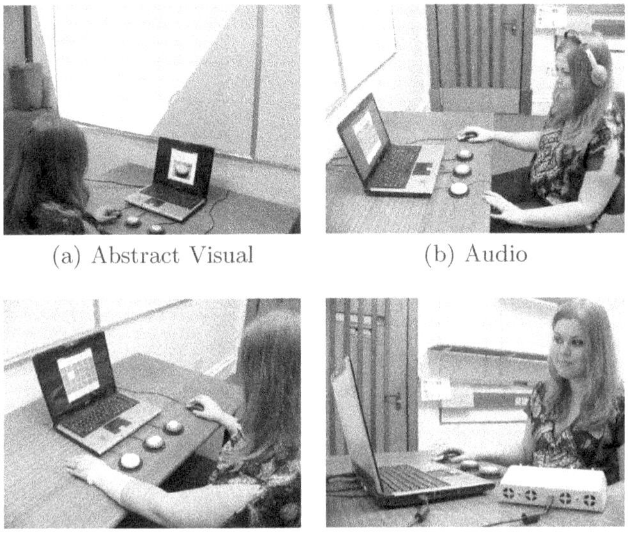

(a) Abstract Visual (b) Audio

(c) Tactile (d) Olfactory

Figure 2: Hardware configurations.

ticipant's non-dominant hand with a stretchable bandage, as shown in Figure 2c. The device had a very low latency and was able to create precise tactile messages.

Olfactory notifications were delivered using a Dale Air[3] Vortex Active smell device, which has the capacity for 4 different smells. Smells are stored on 1-inch disks, which are blown on by a fan to deliver the smell. Delivery times are much longer than other devices, so to ensure the smells were delivered in a reasonable amount of time, the smell device was placed directly in front of the participants as shown in Figure 2d.

3.4 Measurements

Other experiments into disruption have examined errors introduced into the primary task and changes in activity rate post-notification [1, 2, 16, 31]. Latorella [16] observed that activity rate and error rate disruptions have distinctly different properties. In order to measure the effects of a distraction, both error rate and activity rate should be measured.

Warnock, McGee-Lennon & Brewster [31] measured both error rate and activity rate in their card-matching game; activity rate was measured as *'turns per second'*, while error rate was measured as *'superfluous views per turn'*. A superfluous view occurs when the participant repeatedly views a card without successfully matching it, suggesting that their mental mapping of cards to locations has been damaged. This type of error more accurately reflects disruption than other error measures (such as failed match attempts) which could be disproportionately influenced by chance or participant playing speed. In this experiment, error rate is measured as *'superfluous views per click'*.

Higher error and activity rates might not necessarily mean a higher failure rate in the primary task. Success rate in the primary task is measuring by the number of matches made per game, representing a real-world measure of performance. As discussed in Section 3.1, there are 24 cards meaning this measure has a range of 0 to 12.

The pause time post-notification is measured as the longest event-to-event time in seconds between the start of notification delivery and the end of the notification response period. It is assumed that the longest gap at this point represents the time taken to process notifications when they arrive; for the *target notification* this includes the time taken to receive the notification, process it, stop the primary task, press the button, and resume. For the *distractor notifications* this represents the time taken to receive the notification, process it, and return to the primary task.

Measurements were taken over two ranges. Primary measurements are taken over the course of the whole game, while post-notification measurements are measured from notification delivery till the start of the next notification delivery (or the end of the game). Post-notification measurements are derived from the primary measurements but allow the removal of the unwanted data measured before the first notification, and also allow each notification to be examined individually. As described in Section 3.6, notification delivery times are randomised and split into 'delivery windows', meaning that measurements taken post-notification are not taken over a uniform time range; this is does not affect the quality of measurement as post-notification measures are expressed independent of time.

3.5 Hypotheses

In order to explore the impact of distractor notifications on the primary task, the following hypotheses were tested.

H1: Notification function will have an effect on the error rate in the primary task post-notification *(measured as superfluous views per click)* and there will be an interaction effect between notification function and modality.

Warnock, McGee-Lennon & Brewster [31] have shown that these modalities produced equivalent changes in error rate when all the notifications were useful, and suggested that it was the act of task-switching that primarily caused the disruption. However, Sanders & Baron [26] found that distractions could display similar properties to interruptions. It is hypothesised that an unwanted notification will lead to a lower error rate in the primary task post-notification as task-switching will not take place. In addition, Warnock, McGee-Lennon & Brewster [31] found differences in response time that suggested some modalities took longer to process than others. This could result in a different levels of error rate change based on the modality of the notification.

H2: Notification function will have an effect on the activity rate in the primary task post-notification *(measured as clicks per second)* and there will be an interaction effect between notification function and modality.

Warnock, McGee-Lennon & Brewster [31] found that modality affected activity rate, which was in line with other research that showed activity rate in a task increases when multitasking [15]. It is hypothesised that the activity rate will not differ with the notification function, as the participants will not know *a priori* if the notifications are distractors or not.

H3: The number of distractor notifications present will have an effect on the success rate in the primary task *(measured as number of matches)* and there will be an interaction effect between the number of distractors present and notification modality.

[3] Dale Air, `http://www.daleair.com`

[2] PacDV Sound Effects, `http://www.pacdv.com/sounds/`

While it is not expected that notification modality will affect success rate, it is anticipated that distractors will cause less disruption than target notifications, which should mean a higher success rate in games with a higher percentage of distractors. As H1 hypothesises that disruption will vary with notification modality and notification function, it follows that there is likely to also be an interaction effect between the number of distractors present and the modality.

H4: Both notification function and notification modality will have an effect on the pause time post-notification *(measured in seconds)* and there will be an interaction effect between notification function and modality.

Warnock, McGee-Lennon & Brewster [31] found that reaction times for olfactory and tactile notifications were much longer than for other notification types. Although it is hard to differentiate between the mental processing time and actual delivery time, the longer response time for tactile suggested that participants spent longer processing tactile signals. It is anticipated that the different notification modalities will produce different pause times, despite having similar payload delivery times (as discussed in Section 3.3). As target notifications require carrying out a secondary task, it is expected that the pause times for target notifications will be significantly longer, and that there will be an interaction effect between the notification modality and the notification function.

3.6 Procedure

At the beginning of each trial participants were given an information sheet and consent form, then asked to take a short demographic survey to collect gender and age information. Participants were also asked to self-assess their sensory ability on a 21-point Likert scale. Each participant then had the opportunity to practice the primary task (the card matching game described in Section 3.1).

The experiment itself consisted of 8 experimental conditions (one for each modality, as specified in Section 3.3) and a control condition (where no notifications were delivered). The conditions were delivered sequentially in a random order until all 9 conditions had been completed. Each experimental condition consisted of a training segment and 4 games. At the start of each condition a screen described the notification modality and the hardware was configured as required (see Sect. 3.3). Each participant was given the opportunity to make minor comfort adjustments (such as volume) before proceeding to the training segment.

Training began by introducing each of the 3 notifications in turn. One of the notifications was then randomly selected to be the 'target notification' that participants were to respond to. Participants pressed a button to reveal this notification and were asked to press the red button (as shown in Figure 1) in order to signal their understanding. Participants could re-deliver the target notification as many times as they liked before continuing. It was stressed to the participants that they should ignore all other notifications except the target notification. All 3 notifications were delivered again, with the participant expected to acknowledge the target and ignore the distractors to complete the training. Participants who failed this test returned to the previous screen and were asked to re-acknowledge the target notification and repeat the test. The participant then played four games of concentration, each with 3 notifications. Each of the 4 games had a specific configuration, as follows:

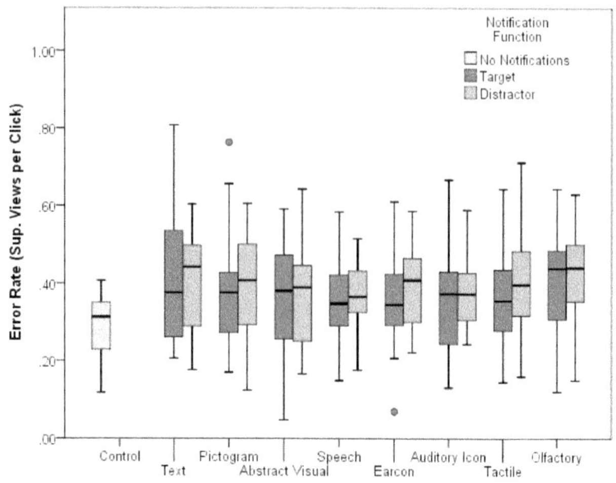

Figure 3: Graph showing the error rate in the primary task, grouped by modality and notification function.

- No target notifications, 3 distractor notifications.
- 1 target notification, 2 distractor notifications.
- 2 target notifications, 1 distractor notification.
- 3 notifications randomly determined to prevent participants deducing a pattern in notification delivery.

The 4 game configurations were played in a random order. Notifications in each game were delivered at random points with buffers between them to prevent overlap. A large buffer at the end of the game helped to ensure that quick participants could not finish before all the notifications had been delivered. At the end of each game participants were provided with the opportunity to rest before the next game started. Once all the conditions had been completed participants were paid and offered the opportunity to ask questions. The experiment required around 60 minutes per participant.

4. RESULTS

H1: Notification function will have an effect on the error rate in the primary task post-notification *(measured as superfluous views per click)* and there will be an interaction effect between notification function and modality.

A within-subjects two-way ANOVA found no main effect of notification modality on error rate in the primary task ($F(7,119)=1.20$, $p=0.31$), which agrees with earlier studies [31] as expected. Notification function was found to have a significant main effect on the error rate ($F(1,17)=7.36$, $p<0.05$). No interaction effect was found between the notification function and the notification modality ($F(7,119)=0.29$, $p=0.96$). These results appear to suggest that the distracting notifications actually cause a *larger* change in error rate than target notifications, which can be seen in Figure 3. This result will be discussed in Section 5.

H2: Notification function will have an effect on the activity rate in the primary task post-notification *(measured as clicks per second)* and there will be an interaction effect between notification function and modality.

A within-subjects two-way ANOVA found no main effect of modality on activity rate in the primary task

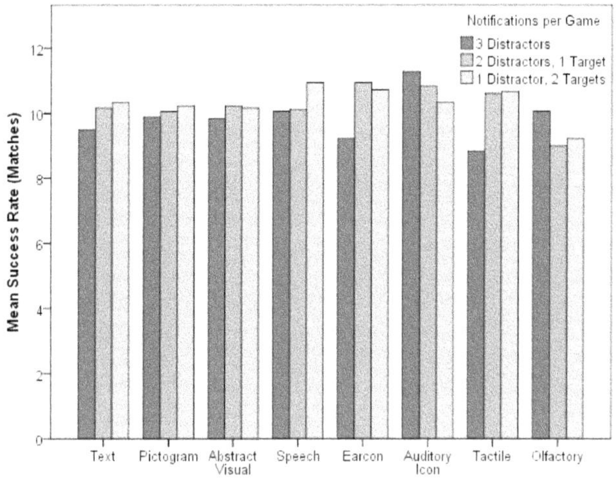

Figure 4: Graph showing the success rate in the primary task, grouped by modality and the number of notifications present.

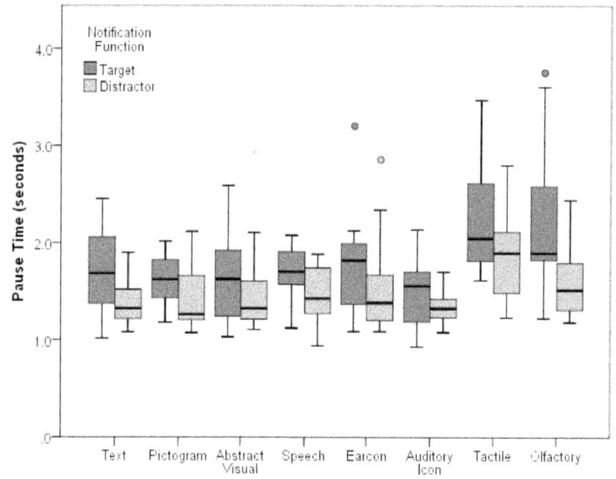

Figure 5: Graph showing the pause time post-notification, grouped by modality and notification function.

(F(7,119)=1.16, p=0.33) and no effect of notification purpose (F(1,17)=0.0, p=0.99). No interaction effects were found between the two factors (F(7,119)=1.251, p=0.28). This result does not support the hypothesis.

H3: The number of distractor notifications present will have an effect on the success rate in the primary task *(measured as number of matches)* and there will be an interaction effect between the number of distractors present and notification modality.

A within-subjects two-way ANOVA found a main effect of notification function (F(2,34)=4.84, p<0.05) on the success rate, but found no main effect of modality on success rate in the primary task (F(7,119)=1.29, p=0.26). No interaction effects were found between the two factors (F(14,238)=1.40, p=0.15). As shown in Figure 4, participants generally performed very well. However this graph also shows that the mean number of matches is lower in games with 100% notifications. This finding adds weight to the result of H1, which seems to show that distractor notifications produced higher error rate than target notifications. This will be discussed in Section 5. Post-Hoc pairwise comparisons with Bonferroni corrections found no significant differences between the conditions.

H4: Both notification function and notification modality will have an effect on the pause time post-notification *(measured in seconds)* and there will be an interaction effect between notification function and modality.

A within-subjects two-way ANOVA found a main effect of modality on the pause time post-notification (F(7,119)=14.53, p>0.001) and a main effect of notification function (F(1,17)=27.63, p<0.001). The interaction test did not satisfy Mauchly's test of sphercity ($X^2(27) = 61.51, p < 0.05$), so the results were corrected using the Greenhouse-Geisser correction ($\epsilon = 0.6$). The results found that an interaction effect existed between the notification function and the modality on the pause time post-notification (F(3.23,54.86)=2.93, p<0.05). Post-Hoc pairwise comparisons with Sidak corrections found significant differences between some of the conditions; similarly to the findings of Warnock, McGee-Lennon & Brewster [31], olfactory and tactile notifications seem to produce a significantly longer pause than the other modalities tested, as shown in Table 2. The mean difference in pause time between target and distractor notifications is surprising small at 0.29 seconds.

5. DISCUSSION

The primary finding of the experiment was that error rate in the primary task will increase irrespective of whether the notifications were wanted or not. This disagrees with the suggestion put forward by Warnock, McGee-Lennon & Brewster [31] that the disruptive effect comes primarily from stopping and restarting the task. Experimental conditions without target notifications did not require the users to carry out a secondary task yet produced a significantly higher error rate (F(1,)=11.1, p<0.001). In addition, there appears to be no link between error rate in the primary task and response accuracy, showing that even when the participants had difficulty interpreting the notifications, it did not result in a higher error rate; changes in error rate must come from another source.

One possibility is that error rate is not influenced by stopping and starting the task but as a result of increased mental demand caused by multi-tasking. Research has shown that a predictable interruption has a lower negative impact [8], but in this experiment participants did not know what

Table 2: Table showing the *p*-values from *post-hoc* pairwise comparisons between modality and pause time.

Modality	Olfactory	Tactile
Text	p<0.05	p<0.001
Pictogram	p<0.01	p<0.001
Abstract Visual	p<0.01	p<0.05
Speech	p=0.12	p<0.01
Earcon	p=0.06	p<0.01
Auditory Icon	p<0.001	p<0.001
Tactile	p=0.97	-
Olfactory	-	p=0.94

the next notification would be or when it would be delivered. This could leave participants constantly 'expecting' additional work; as shown by Bailey, Konstan & Carlis [4] notifications can increase anxiety and the task's perceived difficulty, which could explain the increased error rate. This can also explain why no differences were found in H2; participants mitigated the risk of a high workload by maintaining a high activity rate, which is in alignment with other research [7, 8, 10, 15, 17, 26].

Another possibility is that the participants cannot process notification while carrying out the primary task; so while *physical* task-switching does not take place, the *mental process* of stopping and restarting does. This is supported by research showing that very short interruptions (as short as .25 of a second) will introduce a negative effect [23].

Although the source of the primary task error rate increase is unclear, it is apparent that unnecessary notifications cannot easily be ignored and will produce negative effects. This highlights the importance of a good notification scheduler, able to manage and control notifications of all modalities so that low-priority notifications are not delivered disruptively and that important notifications are delivered in a timely manner in an appropriate modality. This is an active area of research which has already shown how effective a well-designed notification scheduler can be [3, 12, 28]. However, more research is needed to guide the design of multimodal notification systems for the home.

This experiment was carried out using a card-matching task, so at present it is unknown if these results will transfer across to other tasks such as walking. Our project partners are currently running experiments using other tasks including reading, walking and serial recall to clarify this. This experiment was also carried out with younger participants; older participants would be more representative of the home care user group. As such further experiments are currently taking place to investigate if age will affect the results of these experiments.

6. CONCLUSION & FUTURE WORK

The study presented here found that unwanted notifications are detrimental to error and success rates, however notification modality does not have an effect. Notification modality does not affect *any* of the primary task performance metrics except for longest pause, which suggests that some modalities (*i.e.* tactile and olfactory) took longer to process than others. The results showed that unwanted notifications have the potential to be more disruptive than notifications requiring a response, highlighting the need for effective notification scheduling systems. This knowledge will help to guide the development of such notification schedulers as well as contribute to the continued refinement of guidelines and models for the inclusion of multiple modalities.

Development of schedulers, models and guidelines depends on a knowledge of which modalities are appropriate when delivering different kinds of information. Vastenburg, Keyson & Ridder [28] have provided the foundation for this work by evaluating the relationship between message urgency and the salience of the delivery method. Further work is needed in this area in order to evaluate the relationship between modality, salience, message urgency and acceptability. Further experiments are currently taking place to investigate if these results transfer across different tasks and age groups.

In conclusion, the results of this study have provided much-needed groundwork exploring the properties of individual modalities. The findings show that modality would not affect the disruptive effects of both wanted and unwanted notifications, also suggesting that if unwanted notifications are not controlled they are likely to be highly disruptive in the home. This implies that home care developers are free to capitalise on differences in delivery speed, information capacity, message obfuscation and salience of delivery method between modalities to account for factors such as personal preference, sensory impairment, social context, message urgency and user activity. This study provided new knowledge about the role modality plays in delivering notifications, contributing to a large body of work that advocates the inclusion of multiple modalities with the aim of making technology both more effective and more appropriate.

7. ACKNOWLEDGMENTS

This research was funded by the EPSRC (grant number EP/G069387/1). We would like to thank the anonymous reviewers, experiment participants and Miss M. Vernigor for modelling the equipment.

8. REFERENCES

[1] ARROYO, E. AND SELKER, T. Self-adaptive multimodal-interruption interfaces. In *Int. Conf. on Intelligent User Interfaces* (2003), pp. 6–11.

[2] ARROYO, E., SELKER, T. AND STOUFFS, A. Interruptions as multimodal outputs: which are the less disruptive? In *Proceedings. 4th IEEE Int. Conf. on Multimodal Interfaces* (2002), IEEE Comput. Soc, pp. 479–482.

[3] ARROYO, E., SULLIVAN, S. AND SELKER, T. CarCoach: a polite and effective driving coach. In *Conf. on Human Factors in Computing Systems* (2006).

[4] BAILEY, B., KONSTAN, J. AND CARLIS, J. The effects of interruptions on task performance, annoyance, and anxiety in the user interface. In *Proc. of INTERACT* (2001), vol. 1, Citeseer, pp. 593–601.

[5] BREWSTER, S. AND BROWN, L. M. Tactons: structured tactile messages for non-visual information display. In *ACM Int. Conf. Proc. Series; Vol. 53* (Darlinghurst, Australia, 2004), pp. 15–23.

[6] BREWSTER, S., MCGOOKIN, D. AND MILLER, C. Olfoto: designing a smell-based interaction. In *Conf. on Human Factors in Computing Systems* (2006), ACM, pp. 653–662.

[7] BURMISTROV, I. AND LEONOVA, A. Do Interrupted Users Work Faster or Slower? The Micro-analysis of Computerized Text Editing Task. In *HCI: Theory and Practice (Part I) Proc. of HCI Int.* (2003), vol. 1, Citeseer, pp. 621–625.

[8] CARTON, A. M. AND AIELLO, J. R. Control and Anticipation of Social Interruptions: Reduced Stress and Improved Task Performance. *Journal of Applied Social Psychology 39*, 1 (Jan. 2009), pp. 169–185.

[9] CELLIER, J.-M. AND EYROLLE, H. Interference between switched tasks. *Ergonomics 35*, 1 (Jan. 1992), pp. 25–36.

[10] COHEN, S. Aftereffects of stress on human performance and social behavior: A review of research

and theory. *Psychological Bulletin 88*, 1 (1980), pp. 82–108.

[11] EMERY, V. K., EDWARDS, P. J., JACKO, J. A., MOLONEY, K. P., BARNARD, L., KONGNAKORN, T., SAINFORT, F. AND SCOTT, I. U. Toward achieving universal usability for older adults through multimodal feedback. *Proc. 2003 conf. on Universal usability - CUU '03* (2003), p. 46.

[12] HORVITZ, E., APACIBLE, J. AND SUBRAMANI, M. Balancing awareness and interruption: Investigation of notification deferral policies. *User Modeling 2005* (2005), pp. 433–437.

[13] HORVITZ, E., JACOBS, A. AND HOVEL, D. Attention-sensitive alerting. *Conf. on Uncertainty and Artificial Intelligence* (1999).

[14] IQBAL, S. T. AND BAILEY, B. P. Oasis. *ACM Trans. on Computer-Human Interaction 17*, 4 (Dec. 2010), pp. 1–28.

[15] KAPITSA, M. AND BLINNIKOVA, I. Task performance under influence of interruptions. In *Operator functional state: the assessment and prediction of human performance degradation in complex tasks* (Amsterdam, 2003), no. 02, Ios Pr Inc, pp. 323–329.

[16] LATORELLA, K. A. Effects of Modality on Interrupted Flight Deck Performance: Implications for Data Link. Tech. rep., NASA Langley, 1998.

[17] MARK, G., GUDITH, D. AND KLOCKE, U. The cost of interrupted work: more speed and stress. In *Proc. 26th SIGCHI conf. on Human factors in computing systems* (Florence, Italy, 2008), CHI '08, ACM, pp. 107–110.

[18] MCBRYAN, T., MCGEE-LENNON, M. R. AND GRAY, P. An integrated approach to supporting interaction evolution in home care systems. *PETRA 282* (2008).

[19] MCGEE-LENNON, M., WOLTERS, M. AND BREWSTER, S. User-Centred Multimodal Reminders for Assistive Living. In *ACM CHI* (Vancouver, CA, 2011).

[20] MCGEE-LENNON, M. R., WOLTERS, M. AND MCBRYAN, T. Audio Reminders in the Home Environment. In *Proc. 13th Int. Conf. on Auditory Display* (Montreal, Canada, 2007), pp. 437–444.

[21] MCGOOKIN, D. AND BREWSTER, S. Understanding concurrent earcons: Applying auditory scene analysis principles to concurrent earcon recognition. *ACM Trans. on Applied Perception 1*, 2 (2004), pp. 130–155.

[22] MONK, C., BOEHM-DAVIS, D. AND JG. The attentional costs of interrupting task performance at various stages. *Human Factors and Ergonomics Society Annual Meeting Proc.* (2002), pp. 1824–1828.

[23] MONK, C., BOEHM-DAVIS, D. AND TRAFTON, J. Very brief interruptions result in resumption cost. In *Proc. 26th Conf. of the Cognitive Science Society* (2004), CogSci 2004, Citeseer, p. 1606.

[24] NAGEL, K. S., HUDSON, J. M. AND ABOWD, G. D. Predictors of availability in home life context-mediated communication. *Proc. ACM conference on Computer supported cooperative work 6*, 3 (2004), p. 497.

[25] NAUMANN, A. B., WECHSUNG, I. AND HURTIENNE, J. Multimodal interaction: A suitable strategy for including older users? *Interacting with Computers 22*, 6 (Nov. 2010), pp. 465–474.

[26] SANDERS, G. S. AND BARON, R. S. The motivating effects of distraction on task performance. *Journal of Personality and Social Psychology 32*, 6 (1975), pp. 956–963.

[27] VASTENBURG, M. H., KEYSON, D. V. AND RIDDER, H. Considerate home notification systems: a field study of acceptability of notifications in the home. *Personal and Ubiquitous Computing 12*, 8 (June 2007), pp. 555–566.

[28] VASTENBURG, M. H., KEYSON, D. V. AND RIDDER, H. Considerate home notification systems: A user study of acceptability of notifications in a living-room laboratory. *Int. Journal of Human-Computer Studies 67*, 9 (Sept. 2009), pp. 814–826.

[29] WANG, F. AND TURNER, K. Towards personalised home care systems. *PETRA 282* (2008).

[30] WARNOCK, D. A Subjective Evaluation of Multimodal Notifications. In *Pervasive Health* (Dublin, Ireland, 2011).

[31] WARNOCK, D., MCGEE-LENNON, M. AND BREWSTER, S. The Role of Modality in Notification Performance. In *INTERACT 2011* (Portugal, 2011), pp. 572–588.

Freeform Pen-Input as Evidence of Cognitive Load and Expertise

Natalie Ruiz, Ronnie Taib and Fang Chen
NICTA
Level 5, 13 Garden Street
Eveleigh, NSW, Australia
+61 2 9376 2160
<firstname.lastname>@nicta.com.au

ABSTRACT

This paper presents a longitudinal study that explores the combined effect of cognitive load and expertise on the use of a scratchpad. Our results confirm that such cognitive support benefits users under high cognitive load through visual aid, perceptual motor use and helps to improve meaningful learning and successful problem solving. Indeed, we found significant changes in stroke frequency affected by cognitive load, which we believe are caused by the scratchpad essentially augmenting or extending working memory capacity. However, the discrepancy between stroke frequencies under low and high load is reduced with expertise. These results indicate that pen stroke frequency, which can be automated with electronic devices, could be used as an indicator of cognitive load, or conversely, of expertise level.

Categories and Subject Descriptors

H.1.2 [**User/Machine Systems**] – *Human information processing;* H.5.2 [User Interfaces] - Interaction Styles

General Terms

Measurement, Experimentation, Human Factors.

Keywords

Cognitive Load, Pen Input, Measurement and Assessment, Multimodal.

1. INTRODUCTION

While still ubiquitous on control centre desks and in other high-tech, high-demand environments, pen input remains a fairly unexplored behavioural feature to assess cognitive load. Cognitive load (CL) refers to the capacity and resources used in working memory while solving complex tasks and during learning where novel information and processing are required [1, 2].

However, CL is experienced differently across individuals and levels of expertise [3] making it difficult to measure. Four main methods are used in the literature: (a) physiological measures, such as galvanic skin response (GSR), and heart rate [4]; (b) subjective (self-report) measures, where users rank their experienced level of load [5]; (c) performance measures, which include dual-task, test scores and error rates [6]; and, (d) behavioural measures such as mouse speed, linguistic or dialogue patterns [7, 8].

Thus far, only behavioural measures promise real time, non intrusive load indicators, e.g. speech signals [9], linguistic or grammatical features [10], or changes in the quality of interactive digital pen input [11]. The latter modality is of main interest in this study, since it offers a way to implicitly capture changes in behaviour without affecting task completion. It has been suggested that pen-based interfaces can dramatically improve subjects' ability to express themselves over traditional interfaces because linguistic, alphanumeric and spatial representations bear little cognitive overhead. They can be said to be spontaneous since pen marks can be produced almost as quickly as they are envisaged [12]. In particular, pen input supports thought-organising activities such as counting, ordering, grouping, labelling and showing relationships, helping complex problem solving in high CL contexts [12].

More generally, informal note-taking activities augment working memory [13], by imitating the basic function of temporary memory storage in order to avoid information decay [14]. A scratchpad then becomes a substitute for low-level cognitive processes, such as active rehearsal of memory elements, freeing more working memory resources for higher order problem solving [15]. Note-taking itself is a type of visualisation strategy that can have a number of specific benefits in learning how to solve complex problems [13] such as planning and organisation [15]. The literature suggests that imagery and spatial representations in general, whether mental images or external drawings and symbols, give learners an opportunity to more easily generate, test and discard hypotheses as a problem solving strategy [15], and making salient previously unrecognised issues or solutions. This, in turn, facilitates the process of understanding [12] and ultimately, learning.

Moreover, writing and drawing can make effective use of people's perceptual motor system, further engaging working memory, for example by encouraging multimodal cueing or encoding, and perception-action coupling [16]. Such low-level perceptual and cognitive processes are closely intertwined in the human brain, as suggested by neurological evidence that perceptual regions of the brain are activated whether people actually move, or merely imagine movement [17]. In fact, generating spatial representations can precipitate understanding and problem solving, animating mental models and enlightening otherwise unrecognised semantic links between concepts, giving rise to novel and emergent solutions for problems.

Inspired by traffic incident management scenarios, this paper explores note taking as an indicator of CL, based on a longitudinal

ICMI'11, November 14–18, 2011, Alicante, Spain.

multimodal user study involving pen input. In particular, the usage frequency of an electronic 'scratchpad', was analysed, in light of varying levels of CL and increased expertise.

2. USER STUDY

In this study there are two independent variables: trial complexity, which induced varying levels of CL, and expertise. The dependent variable is the amount of strokes performed in the "scratchpad", a note-taking area at the bottom of a pen tablet monitor, imitating a paper scratch pad sitting in front of the subjects (see Figure 1).

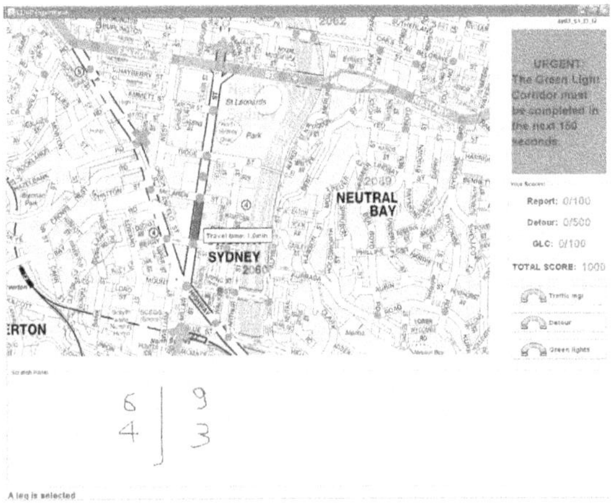

Figure 1: Map-based interface during a green light corridor task. The bottom of the screen is the scratchpad.

In terms of hypotheses, it was expected that:

- The subjects would use the scratchpad relatively more in high load trials than low load trials, since note-taking activities of any kind would help manage high CL;
- The subjects would use the scratchpad less overall as they became more expert, since they would be less dependent on external memory aid or visualisation techniques, and would become more accustomed to the tasks and system.

2.1 Tasks and Sessions

There were 20 different study trials set in the context of traffic management. Subjects used an interactive map-based interface, as shown in Fig. 1. In each trial, they performed the following three sub-tasks:

1) **Spoken report** of a traffic incident over the phone;
2) **Organisation of 'cheapest' Detour** between two given locations based on route segment distance cost and traffic flow values retrieved using interactive queries and calculated manually;
3) **Organisation of a Green Light Corridor**, by request and on the fly, between two given locations, by manually calculating and setting traffic light time parameters, based on estimated travel time and default green time, retrieved using interactive queries.

The collection of intuitive multimodal interaction data required a longitudinal study. In the first session the subjects were trained to use the system and were allowed to familiarise themselves with the application domain logic, modalities and functions. Each session thereafter, subjects completed a unique set of trials.

2.2 Cognitive Load Levels

The trial sets in each session were designed to impose three distinct levels of complexity and thus CL (low, medium and high). An increasing number of possible detours, legs in each detour and traffic lights in the corridor, as well as more complex values for the distance cost and flow of each route leg, travel time and default green time for the lights were all used to manipulate complexity in each trial (Table 1). In order to verify whether the appropriate level of CL was imposed, subjects were asked to indicate their perceived level of load on a 9-point semantic differential scale, at the end of each trial. In addition, performance measures were calculated at the end of the sessions, based on the number of correct answers for detour solutions, and green light times for the Green Light Corridor.

Table 1: CL contributors

CL level	Detours		Green light corridors		
	#	Legs	#	Complexity	Time pressure
Low (1)	2	3	4	Integers	130s
Medium (2)	4	6	6	Integers	140s
High (3)	6	8	8	Decimals	165s

2.3 Participants

For this study, 8 remunerated, native English-speaking participants (1 female and 7 males, aged 18-39) volunteered. The group comprised researchers, corporate/administrative staff and students. None were directly involved with the experimenters and all were naive to the aims of the study. Most subjects completed five 45 minute sessions within a week, with no more than 48 hours between sessions.

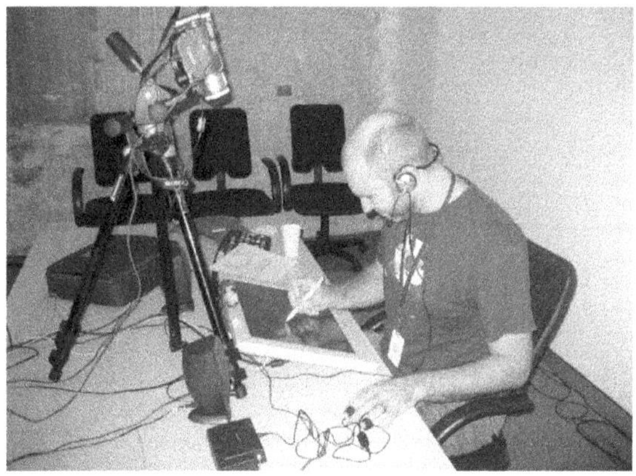

Figure 2: Physical set-up – Pen and speech interface

2.4 Pen and Speech Input

Circling gestures and a set of 3 predefined symbols were used to *interact* with the map locations and elements, on the map. Natural speech was combined with pen input to execute any of the queries with simple spoken commands, such as "What is the cost for this?" However, the free form pen markings analysed were used solely in the scratchpad area and did not trigger any specific functionality but served merely as a digital scrap paper. A participant using the set-up is shown in Fig. 2.

3. ANALYSIS AND RESULTS

3.1 Subjective Ratings

The mean subjective ratings (1: lowest CL, 9: highest CL) from each session are summarised in Table 2.

Table 2: Mean Subjective Ratings

Level	Low	Med	High
Ratings (of 9)	2.82	5.01	7.20
SD	0.49	0.45	0.65

A Friedman test was used, as the experimental design has one within-subjects independent variable (designed CL) with two or more levels, and a dependent non-parametric variable that is not interval, but is at least ordinal (subjective ratings). It is difficult to assume that subjects have the same internal interval scale between the points on a semantic differential scale, hence we cannot treat the responses as evenly spaced equal intervals across subjects. However, the ordinal information from the subjective ratings is very useful in determining relative ranks. The Friedman test also does not make the assumption of normality for the dependent variable.

Session by session results confirm that the level of reported CL matches the designed levels. Session 2's data shows significant differences between the reported subjective difficulty for trials in Session 2 (Friedman's $\chi^2(8, 2) = 9.750$, $p = 0.008$), with mean ranks of 1.38, 1.75 and 2.88 for Levels 1, 2 and 3 respectively, increasing as expected, though the greatest difference occurs between Level 2 and Level 3. In Session 3, a Friedman test also shows significant differences between the reported subjective ratings (Friedman's χ^2 (8, 2) = 15.548, $p < 0.001$), with mean relative ranks increasing: 1.00, 2.06 and 2.94 for Levels 1, 2 and 3 respectively. Similarly in Session 4, a Friedman's test again shows significant differences between the reported subjective trial difficulty (Friedman's χ^2 (8, 2) = 16.00, $p < 0.001$), with mean ranks of 1.00, 2.00 and 3.00 for Levels 1, 2, and 3. Finally, a Friedman test for Session 5 data shows significant differences between the reported subjective trial difficulty (Friedman's χ^2 (8, 2) = 16.00, $p < 0.001$), with mean ranks of 1.00, 2.00 and 3.00 for Levels 1, 2 and 3 respectively. The statistics suggest that the relative ratings correlate strongly with the increased levels of designed complexity in all sessions.

3.2 Frequency of Scratchpad Strokes

The number of pen strokes in the scratchpad was operationalised by counting individual pen down events above a minimum length to filter out noise (e.g. taps). A scratchpad stroke frequency was then obtained through normalisation over time spent on trial, in seconds. These automated counts were compared to manual counts of whole semantic entities (e.g. a whole diagram or complex symbol accounted for a single stroke), and while obviously not quantitatively matching, both sets exhibited very similar statistical features for stroke count and frequency. This allowed us to perform the rest of the analysis on automated counts for greater accuracy, with aim to deploy as a real-time index.

The summary averages for each level and session, are shown in Table 3, however, the complete set of data was used in the analysis.

Table 3: Frequency of scratchpad strokes (stroke/s)

Session	Low	Med	High
Session2	0.059	0.0974	0.114
Session3	0.078	0.0933	0.095
Session4	0.080	0.077	0.093
Session5	0.091	0.101	0.092
Average	0.077	0.092	0.099
SD	0.020	0.021	0.021

The values suggest that subjects spend relatively more time using the scratchpad when load increases. A two-way repeated measures ANOVA (3x4) was conducted on the factors of load and expertise (sessions), using the full set of automated frequencies. Mauchly's test of sphericity was not significant for the factor of load ($\chi 2(2) = 464$, $p = 0.793$), or for the factors of expertise($\chi 2(5) = 1.278$, $p = 0.938$) and load x expertise ($\chi 2(20) = 28.544$, $p = 0.199$). A two-way repeated-measures ANOVA shows there is a main effect of load ($F(2, 12) = 5.898$, $p = 0.016$), and an interaction effect of expertise and load ($F(6, 36) = 2.881$, $p = 0.021$), but no main effect of expertise ($F(3, 18) = 1.038$, $p = 0.399$).

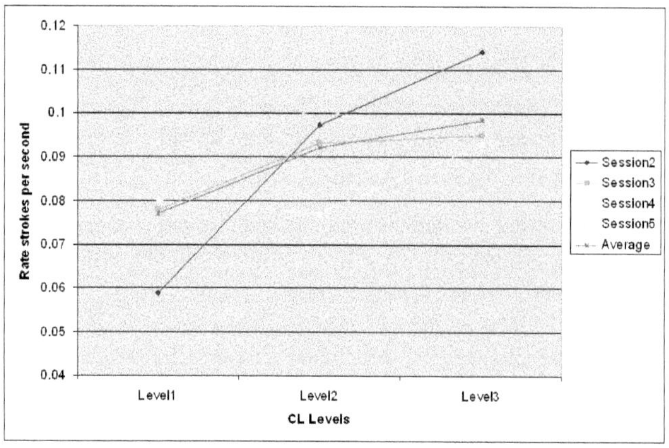

Figure 3: Frequency of Scratchpad Strokes by Load

Subsequent polynomial contrasts show a linear fit for the factor of load is significant to the 0.05 level, with a large effect size ($F(1, 6) = 10.144$, $p = 0.019$, $r = 0.79$), revealing a proportionate and uniform linear increase in the frequency of scratchpad strokes per second from low load (Level 1) to high load (Level 3), as seen in Fig. 4. No other linear, quadratic or cubic polynomial contrasts are significant in any of the other factors. Higher stroke frequencies in high trials indicate that the subject is more prolific in using the scratchpad, generating more strokes per second in high load trials. The interaction effect of expertise and load exists because as expertise increases, the frequency of scratchpad strokes increases in the low load trials (Level 1), while it decreases in the high load trials (Level 3), almost to the point where all levels converge.

This is illustrated in Figure 4, where distinct differences in frequency of scratchpad usage are evident in the most novice session (Session 2), from 0.06 strokes per second in Level 1, to 0.12 strokes per second in Level 3.

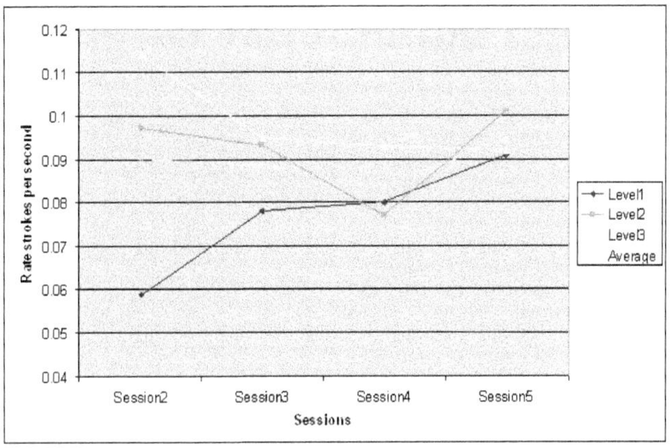

Figure 4: Frequency of scratchpad strokes by expertise

4. DISCUSSION AND CONCLUSION

The literature suggests that cognitive support tools such as a scratchpad can benefit users under high cognitive load (CL) through visual aid, perceptual motor use and improvements in meaningful learning and successful problem solving. This longitudinal study focussed on the combined effect of CL and expertise on the use of a scratchpad. Subjective ratings validated the alignment of trial complexity and CL. The trials and subtasks within them were standardized and well-controlled in terms of complexity. The subjects' use of the scratchpad was completely spontaneous and particular to each user in form, content and amount which ensures the fairness of our features. We found that the frequency of strokes can serve as an indicator of complexity and in turn an indirect measure of CL.

As expected, the results exhibit a main effect of CL on stroke frequency, because the scratchpad essentially augments or extends the working memory capacity. However, we found that the discrepancy between stroke frequencies under low and high loads reduces with expertise, both eventually converging. This suggests using a convergence of stroke frequency in spite of varying trial complexity to diagnose gains in expertise, Increased expertise indicates an improvement in schema representations in working memory and the fact that learning has taken place.

There are some limitations to this work. While more subjects would allow greater assurance in the patterns identified, this would only serve to make the effect more pronounced. Generalisability extends to applications where the scratchpad use is spontaneous, the domain content is made up of discrete "chunks" of information, the trials can be relatively ranked in terms of complexity, and most importantly, a baseline is used to compare the change in behavior. More studies need to be carried out in order to verify this, and further testing of generalisation potential in other domain areas is needed. On the other hand, a feature like stroke frequency can easily be extracted in real-time and unobtrusively using a tablet monitor or electronic pen, and practically used in educational/high demand domains to detect when expertise has been achieved and progression to the next level is recommended.

5. ACKNOWLEDGMENTS

NICTA is funded by the Australian Government as represented by the Department of Broadband, Communications and the Digital Economy and the Australian Research Council through the ICT Centre of Excellence program. The authors would also like to thank all participants who completed the study.

6. REFERENCES

[1] J. Sweller, J. vanMerrienboer, and F. Paas, "Cognitive architecture and instructional design," *Educational Psychology Review*, vol. 10, pp. 251-296, 1998.

[2] F. Paas, J. E. Tuovinen, H. Tabbers, and P. W. vanGerven, "Cognitive Load Measurement as a Means to Advance Cognitive Load Theory," *Educational Psychologist*, vol. 38, pp. 63-71, 2003.

[3] S. Kalyuga, P. Ayers, P. Chandler, and J. Sweller, "The expertise reversal effect," *Educational Psychologist*, vol. 38, pp. 23-31, 2003.

[4] A. F. Kramer, "Physiological metrics of mental workload: a review of recent progress," in *Multiple Task Performance*, D. L. Damos, Ed. London: Taylor & Francis, 1991, pp. 279-328.

[5] D. Gopher and R. Braune, "On the psychophysics of workload: Why bother with subjective measures?," *Human Factors*, vol. 26, pp. 519-532, 1984.

[6] C. D. Wickens, "The structure of attentional resources," in *Attention and Performance VIII*, R. Nickerson, Ed. Hillsdale, N.J.: Lawrence Erlbaum, 1980.

[7] C. S. Ikehara and M. E. Crosby, "Assessing Cognitive Load with Physiological Sensors," in *HICSS'05: 38th Annual Hawaii Int'l Conference on System Sciences* Hawaii, 2005, pp. 295a-295a.

[8] S. Oviatt, R. Coulston, and R. Lunsford, "When do we interact multimodally? Cognitive Load and Multimodal Communication Patterns"," in *ICMI 2004* Oregon: ACM, 2004, pp. 129-136.

[9] B. Yin, F. Chen, N. Ruiz, and E. Ambikairajah, "Speech-based Cognitive Load Monitoring System," in *IEEE Int'l Conference on Acoustic Speech and Signal Processing (ICASSP'08)* Las Vegas: IEEE, 2008, pp. 2041-2044.

[10] M. A. Khawaja, F. Chen, C. Owen, and G. Hickey, "Cognitive Load Measurement from User's Linguistic Speech Features for Adaptive Interaction Design," in *12th IFIP Int'l Conference on Human-Computer Interaction INTERACT'09* Uppsala, Sweden: ACM, 2009, pp. 485-489.

[11] N. Ruiz, R. Taib, Y. Shi, E. Choi, and F. Chen, "Using Pen Input Features as Indices of Cognitive Load," in *9th Int'l Conference on Multimodal Interfaces (ICMI'07)* Nagoya, Japan: ACM, 2007, pp. 315-318.

[12] S. Oviatt, "Designing Interfaces that stimulate ideational superfluency," in *INKE 2009: Research Foundations for Understanding Book and Reading in the Digital Age: Implementing New Knowledge Environments*. vol. 1, 2009.

[13] W. G. Lutters, "Identifying expertise markers in routine work artifacts: Exploring micronote taking behaviour. ," *Computers in Human Behavior*, vol. 20, pp. 185-199, 2004.

[14] J. R. Anderson, *Cognitive Psychology and Its Implications*. New York City, NY: Worth Publishing, 2000.

[15] S. P. Lajoie, *Computers as cognitive tools: No More Walls*. Hillsdale, NJ.: Lawrence Erlbaum, 2000.

[16] D. L. Schwartz and J. Heiser, "Spatial representations and imagery in learning," in *Handbook of the Learning Sciences*, K. Sawywe, Ed. Cambridge: Lawrence Elrbaum, 2006.

[17] S. M. Kosslyn, *Image and Brain: The resolution of the Imagery Debate*. Cambridge, MA.: MIT Press, 1994.

Acquisition of Dynamically Revealed Multimodal Targets

Teemu Ahmaniemi
Nokia Research Center
Itämerenkatu 11-13
00180, Helsinki, Finland
teemu.ahmaniemi(at)nokia.com

ABSTRACT
This study investigates movement time needed for exploring and selecting a target that is not seen in advance. An experiment where targets were presented with haptic, audio or visual feedback was conducted. The task of the participant was to search the targets with a hand held sensor-actuator device by horizontal scanning movements. The feedback appeared when the pointing was within the target boundaries. Range of distances to the target was varied between the experiment blocks. The results show that the modality did not have a significant effect on the total movement time but visual feedback yielded the shortest and haptic feedback the longest dwell time on target area. This was most probably caused by a visual priming effect and the slow haptic actuator rise time. The wider range of distances yielded longer movement times and within the widest range of distances the closest targets were explored longer than the targets in the middle. This was shown to be caused by the increased number of secondary submovements. The finding suggests that an alternative model to Fitts' law or linear prediction of target acquisition time should be developed taking into account the user's prior knowledge about target location.

Categories and Subject Descriptors
H.5.2 Information interfaces and presentation: User Interfaces: Auditory (non-speech) feedback, Haptic I/O

General Terms
Fitts' law, Augmented reality, Pointing, Multimodal interaction

1. INTRODUCTION
Fitts' law [1] provides a model for predicting the movement time needed for selecting targets with prior knowledge of their location. It presumes that if a target is further away, the movement is initiated with higher velocity than if it is closer. This explains the non-linear behavior of movement time as a function of distance.

$$MT=a+b\log(D/W) \qquad (1)$$

where D is distance to target, W is target width and a and b are constants. The logarithm term is often called index of difficulty (ID).

ICMI'11, November 14–18, 2011, Alicante, Spain.

However, in several computer human interaction scenarios, location of the target is not known in advance. For example, in mobile augmented reality interaction [2],[3] user does not see which objects in the real world are augmented with virtual content until they are pointed at e.g. with a mobile phone camera. Similarly, in peephole pointing interaction [4], the targets outside the peephole window cannot be seen. A user may have an approximate idea about where to look for but the exact location of the target is unknown. Cao et al. [5] studied the selection of targets in a peephole pointing concept. In their study, the first task of the participant was to seek a target into a peephole window. Although the target was not seen in advance, the movement time was predicted with an equation of the same form as the Fitts' law (eq. 1). The similar approach was used in the study by Rohs and Oulasvirta [6], where the targets were revealed by a mobile phone camera application that recognized objects on a paper map and overlaid additional information on the screen resembling a peephole interaction. Friedlander et al. [7] showed that in a non-visual target selection task a linear model provides better fit than Fitts' law.

$$MT=aD+b \qquad (2)$$

A similar linear model was proposed in a study by Andersen [8] investigating movement time in a simple scrolling task in desktop interaction.

Figure 1. Sensor-actuator device used in the experiment

Although the above studies yielded satisfactory results in terms of goodness of fit, they ignore a phenomenon that relates to the closest targets. In the data of Andersen [8], the closest target out of the six distances was not selected any faster than the next closest target. Also, the data in the study by Cao et al. [5] shows also a slight non-linear relation to index of difficulty (ID). With lower values of ID (shorter distance) the movement time did not increase as rapidly as it did with higher values. Furthermore, in the study of Rohs and Oulasvirta [6] movement times with lowest values of ID caused the highest variability. A similar pattern was found in the data of our previous studies [2]. We developed an experiment setup where invisible haptic targets were placed on a virtual circle around the user. The studies revealed rather good fit to Fitts' law but also hinted about the special role of the closest targets. The movement times of the previous studies (PE1 and PE2) are presented in Figure 2.

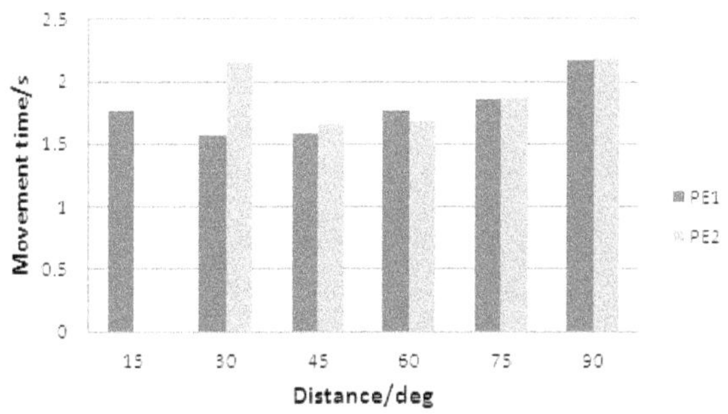

Figure 2. The movement times of the two previous experiments (PE1 & PE2). In both studies the closest targets were in a special role.

If the user does not know in advance where the target is, the interaction becomes exploratory and thus more careful. It cannot be ballistic since the movement cannot be planned that accurately in advance. The user either attempts to find the target by minimizing the risk of passing it (overshoot) with too high velocity or tries to speed up the process by increasing the velocity with the cost of passing the target. As brought out by Meyer et al [9], missing the target on a first part of the movement (primary submovement) is followed by a correcting movement (secondary submovement). In interaction with invisible targets the role of the secondary submovements plays presumably more important role than in interaction with visible targets. This assumption forms the motivation for the current investigation.

The study has three main research questions. Firstly, how does the movement time pattern change when the range of distances to the target is varied? This question refers to person's prior knowledge about the target. Secondly, can the behavior of the movement time be explained with number of secondary submovements? Thirdly, how does the modality visual, audio or haptic influence in movement time? In a study by Akamatsu et al. [10] mouse pointing was augmented with additional visual, haptic or auditory on-target feedback. In their study, haptic feedback yielded the fastest and visual feedback the slowest response when measured from the moment of entering the target to the selection. We could expect that the modalities have the same role in the current study.

2. MULTIMODAL POINTING EXPERIMENT

The experiment setup was related to an augmented reality scenario where targets could be explored with a mobile device by horizontal (rotational) hand or arm movements (see Figure 3.). While the previous experiment concentrated on haptic feedback, this time we included also visual and audio modalities in the setup. Since we wanted to investigate how the participants' uncertainty of the target distance influences the movement time, we created three different uniform distributions of target distances with common mean but different range. Furthermore, because in our previous study the effect of target width seemed obvious (wider target leads to shorter movement time), the target width was kept constant in the current experiment.

2.1 Experiment setup

The setup consisted of laptop PC, a monitor and a small keypad. The hand held sensor-actuator device (115x57x25mm, see Fig. 1) consisted of a tactile actuator (C2 tactor) and a motion sensor based on accelerometer, gyroscope and magnetometer (xsens MT9). Only horizontal, rotational movements were used in the experiment; the sensor provided the readings within the accuracy of 0.1° sampled at 100Hz. The device was connected to the PC by a cable. The rendering of the haptic, audio and visual cues was done with Pure Data synthesis software (http://puredata.info). The targets were 10° wide sectors within a virtual circle around the test participant (see Figure 3.). The haptic cue was a continuous vibration of 250Hz presented as long as the pointing stayed within the target boundaries. Similarly, the audio cue was a continuous sinusoidal sound of 400Hz presented through the headphones. The visual cue was a red circle that appeared on the monitor when pointing was on the target. The auditory interference of the tactile actuator was masked with 1 kHz low-pass filtered noise played through headphones.

The target distances (n=9) were arranged in three groups based on the range of uniform distribution. Mean of the distances in all groups was 40°, but the range (σ) was 16°, 32° or 64° in each group, respectively. Therefore e.g. in the group of distance range 16°, the nine distances were 32°, 34°, 36°, 38°, 40°, 42°, 44°, 46°, and 48°. Each distance was repeated four times in randomized order in an experiment block yielding 36 targets (trials) with various distances from each other. The targets appeared in turn on left and right of the previous target.

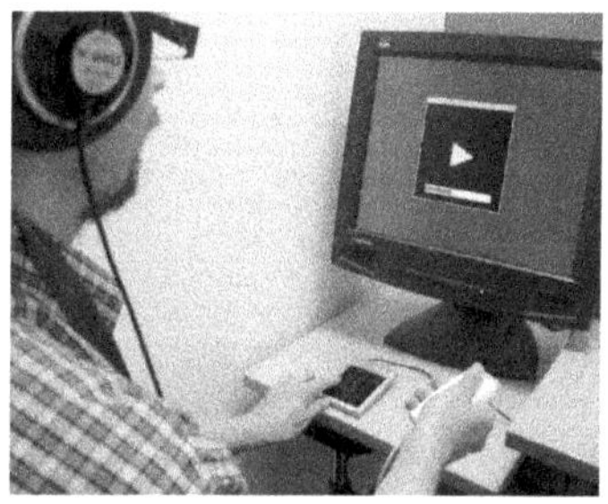

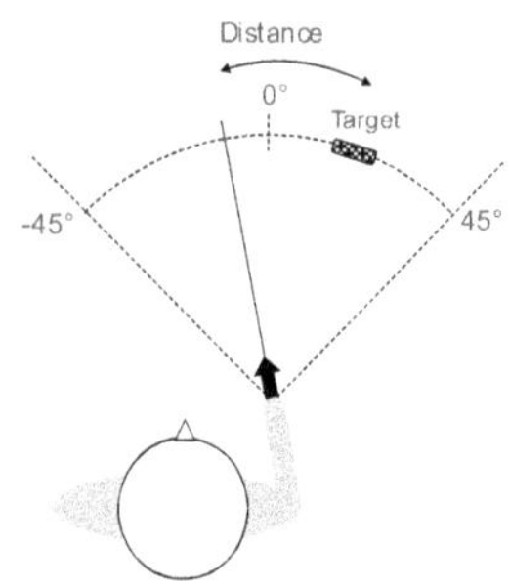

Figure 3. The experiment setup (left) and the rendering of the targets on a virtual circle (right).

The task of the participant was to find the target by horizontal rotational scanning and press a dedicated button on the keypad with the free hand when the pointing was on the target. Right after a successful selection, a green arrow on the screen indicated the direction of the next target. The arrow was visible only for 500ms. The test did not proceed until a target was found. 36 subjects (12 women, 24 men, mean age 35) participated the experiment. Each participant went through three blocks, one in each modality and distance group. All the modality/distance range combinations were counterbalanced yielding 36 different orders of blocks. The test took approximately 30 minutes and was compensated with a cinema voucher.

2.2 Results

The raw data of each experiment block was preprocessed to obtain movement times, average velocities and movement direction changes (number of secondary submovements) per each target. The processing and analysis was done using Matlab.

2.2.1 *Modality and Distance Range vs. Movement Time*

The movement times were analysed with two-way ANOVA (modality x 3, distance range x 3) Overall, the modality did not have main effect on the overall movement time (F=2.01, p=0.13). However, dwell time i.e. the time that the pointing spent on the target before the selection, was significantly affected by the modality (F=90, 11, p<0.01). In pair wise comparison, the visual modality yielded the shortest and haptic modality the longest dwell time. All differences between the modalities were significant. Distance range also had significant influence in movement time (F=77.55, p<0.01). A multiple comparison analysis reveals that all groups differed from each other significantly; the movement time increased along with the range of distribution, 1.65s, 1.75s and 2.05s with ranges 16°, 32° and 64°, respectively. Figure 4 presents the movement times with respect of modality and distance range. The dwell time is illustrated as the black area of each bar.

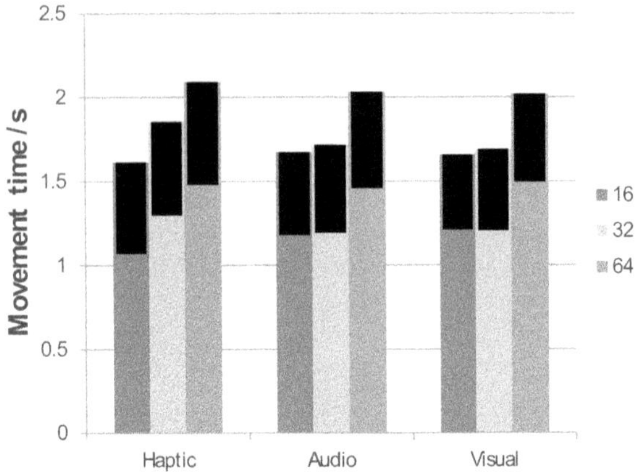

Figure 4. Movement times with respect of modality and distance range (16°/32°/64°). The black areas on top of each bar reflect the dwell time (on-target time) before the selection.

2.2.2 *Velocity and number of secondary submovements*

Neither modality nor the distance range had main effect on the movement velocity, p=0.3 and p=0.072, respectively. However, target distance itself had significant effect on velocity (F=7.99, p<0.01). The shorter distances yielded significantly slower velocities than longer distances, especially with wide distance range (Pearson correlation 0.85). On average, number of secondary submovements was 0.48 per each target. Range of distances had significant effect on the submovements (F=31.5, p<0.01). The widest range produced the highest number. Also, within the widest range (σ=64°), the shortest distance (8°) yielded much more submovements than the other distances on average (0.93 vs. 0.60). This is illustrated in Figure 5a. Furthermore, when dividing all the data items into ten groups of equal size based on velocity, the faster movements appeared to lead into more secondary submovements. This is illustrated in Figure 5b. Pearson correlation between the velocity and number of secondary submovements was 0.79.

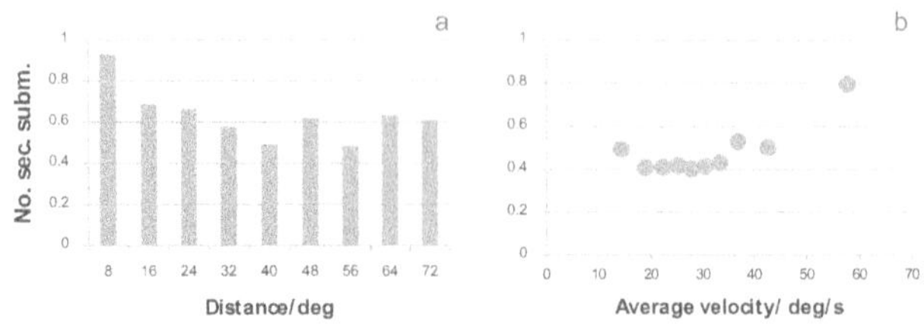

Figure 5. The average number of secondary submovemens within the widest (σ=64°) range of distances (a) and as a function of movement velocity divided into 10 groups (b).

2.2.3 *Effect of predictability*

Since the modality did not have significant effect on movement time, all the data was combined into one set. The movement times within each distance group with respect of distance is presented in Figure 6. Especially within the widest distance group, the movement time pattern approaches a 'J' –shape curve. And, as in our previous studies [2], the closest targets seem to lead into longer movement time than the next closest targets.

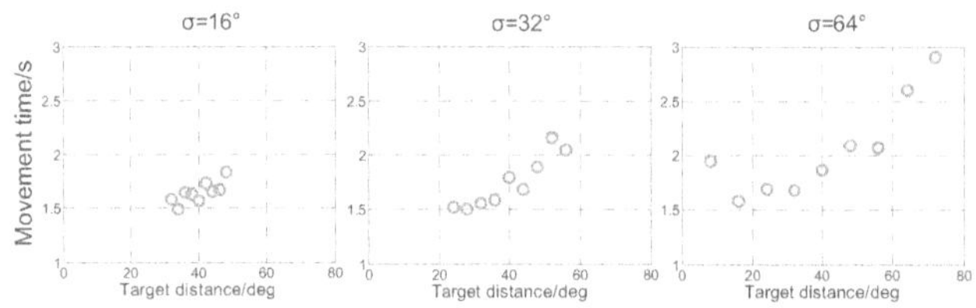

Figure 6. The average movement times of each distance range groups.

2.2.4 *System latency*

In order to explain the possible differences in the movement and selection times, we measured the overall system latency with a setup described in detail by Kaaresoja and Brewster [11]. The visual feedback on the monitor was captured with high-speed camera, tactile feedback with accelerometer attached on top of the device and auditory feedback by a microphone. The sensor-actuator device was placed on a table and the system was reset so that a target was 0.5° away from the pointing direction. Knocking the device into the target direction by an iron rod caused an impulse signal in the accelerometer and triggered the on-target cue (visual/audio/haptic). The time difference between the impulse and the onset of the on-target cue was measured. The latency with visual feedback was 93ms and with audio and haptic feedback 82ms.

3. DISCUSSION

In the presented study, modality did not have effect on the target selection time. This may have been caused by the clinical laboratory conditions that eliminated the possible difference between the modalities while the exploratory characteristics of the interaction dominated the movement time. Furthermore, effect of modality in dwell time was quite the opposite our expectations and the results of Akamatsu et al. [10]. The differences in system latencies across the modalities were negligible, only 0.5% of the average overall total movement time. Therefore, the latency does not explain the differences in dwell time. We propose three alternative explanations. Firstly, the haptic actuator used in the study had relatively long rise time i.e. it took approximately 30-40ms for it to reach its maximum amplitude. Thus, it is possible that the participants perceived the haptic targets slightly later than the other targets. Secondly, because the participants were looking at the monitor during the experiment in all experiment conditions, their attention may have been more focused on the visual stimuli. This visual priming could explain the shorter dwell time. Thirdly, the haptic feedback and the method for providing the response were not co-located as in the study by Akamatsu et al. [10]. The keypad was operated with other hand while the exploration was performed with the other one.

According to Figure 6, the 'J'-shape of the movement time pattern was more obvious with wider range of distances. The finding hints that neither Fitts' law (eq. 1.) nor the linear model (eq. 2.) predicts sufficiently the movement time when selecting targets without prior knowledge of their location. Hence, an alternative model should be developed. The model could be approached by investigating the movement patterns in our data more in detail. The 'J'-shape can be, to some extent, explained by analysing the movement velocity and number of secondary submovements. The average velocity of the movement increased along the target distance indicating that selecting the closest targets took proportionally longer time than selecting the further targets. In addition, the very closest targets led into more secondary submovements and thus yielded longer total movement times. Therefore, if the person does not know how far the target is, it has to be predicted. On the other hand, the prediction depends on the range and distribution of the previous targets (a priori). As seen in Figure 5, the participants made least number of secondary submovements in the middle most targets hinting that they were expecting to find the targets somewhere there. The closer and further targets were more unexpected. Now, together with the fact that the further targets lead into longer movement time, these findings could show the direction to an alternative model. However, more data points and variations in the distance distribution should be available. These are to be obtained in future studies.

4. CONCLUSIONS

We showed that in an acquisition task of dynamically revealed targets there is no significant difference in total movement time between visual, audio or haptic modality. The finding suggests that haptic modality can be as efficient as the other modalities in indicating the location of a target in e.g. augmented reality interaction. The benefits of the tactile feedback are e.g. tolerance to ambient noise of the environment and eyes free interaction. On the other hand, haptic feedback does not suit very well for describing the type or details of the target. Therefore, other modalities and modes of interaction are needed for satisfactory overall user experience. For example, haptic feedback could reveal the direction of relevant point of interest and if user still is interested in it, more information could be presented by speech or visually on device screen. Thus, haptic feedback could provide an answer to user's question: is there anything interesting in this direction?

We also showed that neither Fitts' law (eq. 1.) nor the linear model (eq. 2.) predict sufficiently the movement time when selecting targets without prior knowledge of their location. It is evident that there is need for an alternative model where the prior information about target location is taken into account. As mentioned, a further study with more emphasis on the distribution of the targets should be conducted. The current study showed that in such interaction, at least in laboratory conditions, all modalities, visual, audio and haptic are as efficient in presenting the target location.

5. ACKNOWLDGEMENTS

We would like to thank valuable work of Sointu Karjalainen and Sanna Eklund in Suuntaamo community in recruiting the participants and assisting in conducting the experiments.

6. REFERENCES

[1] P. M. Fitts, "The information capacity of the human motor system in controlling the amplitude of movement," *Journal of Experimental Psychology*, vol. 47, pp. 381-391, 1954.

[2] T. T. Ahmaniemi and V. T. Lantz, "Augmented reality target finding based on tactile cues," presented at the Proceedings of the 2009 international conference on Multimodal interfaces, Cambridge, Massachusetts, USA, 2009.

[3] A. Morrison, A. Oulasvirta, P. Peltonen, S. Lemmela, G. Jacucci, G. Reitmayr, J. Näsänen, and A. Juustila, "Like bees around the hive: a comparative study of a mobile augmented reality map," presented at the Proceedings of the 27th international conference on Human factors in computing systems, Boston, MA, USA, 2009.

[4] K.-P. Yee, "Peephole displays: pen interaction on spatially aware handheld computers," presented at the Proceedings of the SIGCHI conference on Human factors in computing systems, Ft. Lauderdale, Florida, USA, 2003.

[5] X. Cao, J. J. Li, and R. Balakrishnan, "Peephole pointing: modeling acquisition of dynamically revealed targets," presented at the Proceeding of the twenty-sixth annual SIGCHI conference on Human factors in computing systems, Florence, Italy, 2008.

[6] M. Rohs and A. Oulasvirta, "Target acquisition with camera phones when used as magic lenses," presented at the Proceeding of the twenty-sixth annual SIGCHI conference on Human factors in computing systems, Florence, Italy, 2008.

[7] N. Friedlander, K. Schlueter, and M. Mantei, "Bullseye! when Fitts' law doesn't fit," presented at the Proceedings of the SIGCHI conference on Human factors in computing systems, Los Angeles, California, United States, 1998.

[8] T. H. Andersen, "A simple movement time model for scrolling," presented at the CHI '05 extended abstracts on Human factors in computing systems, Portland, OR, USA, 2005.

[9] D. E. Meyer, R. A. Abrams, S. Kornblum, C. E. Wright, and J. E. K. Smith, "Optimality in human motor performance: Ideal control of rapid aimed movements," *Psychological Review*, vol. 95, pp. 340-370, 1988.

[10] M. Akamatsu, I. S. MacKenzie, and T. Hasbrouc, "A Comparison of Tactile, Auditory, And Visual Feedback in a Pointing Task Using a Mouse-Type Device," *Ergonomics*, vol. 38, pp. 816-827, 1995.

[11] T. Kaaresoja and S. Brewster, A., "Feedback is... Late: Measuring Multimodal Delays in Mobile Device Touchscreen Interaction," in *International Conference on Multimodal Interfaces*, Beijing, China, 2010.

Emotional Responses to Thermal Stimuli

Katri Salminen, Veikko Surakka, Jukka Raisamo, Jani Lylykangas, Johannes Pystynen, Roope Raisamo
Tampere Unit for Computer Human Interaction, School of Information Sciences, Kanslerinrinne 1, 33014 University of Tampere, Finland
{katri.salminen, veikko.surakka, jukka.raisamo, jani.lylykangas, johannes.pystynen, roope.raisamo}@cs.uta.fi

Kalle Mäkelä
Tampere University of Technology, Department of Electronics, P.O. Box 692, FI-33101 Tampere, Finland
kalle.makela@tut.fi

Teemu Ahmaniemi
Nokia Research Center, Itämerenkatu 11-13, 00180, Helsinki, Finland
teemu.ahmaniemi.nokia.com

ABSTRACT

The present aim was to study if thermal stimuli presented to the palm can affect emotional responses when measured with emotion related subjective rating scales and changes in skin conductance response (SCR). Two target temperatures, cold and warm, were created by either decreasing or increasing the temperature of the stimulus 4 °C in respect to the participants current hand temperature. Both cold and warm stimuli were presented by using two presentation methods, i.e., dynamic and pre-adjusted. The results showed that both the dynamic and pre-adjusted warm stimuli elevated the ratings of arousal and dominance. In addition, the pre-adjusted warm and cold stimuli elevated the SCR. The results suggest that especially pre-adjusted warm stimuli can be seen as effective in activating the autonomic nervous system and arousal and dominance dimensions of the affective rating space.

Categories and Subject Descriptors

H.5.2 [**User Interfaces**]: Haptic I/O, Input devices and strategies

General Terms: Human Factors

Keywords: Thermal stimuli, haptics, affective computing

1. INTRODUCTION

Sensing variations in temperature is frequently argued to be connected to emotions. Especially the experience of pleasantness is assumed to be affected by thermal stimulation so that warm temperatures are perceived as comfortable and pleasant [3] while cold temperatures are perceived as uncomfortable [5]. However, in the field of human-technology interaction (HTI) studies that map the relationship between thermal stimuli and emotions are rare although thermal stimulation could be seen as a novel and appealing way to convey information and evoke emotion-related experiences, for example, when communicating warm feelings related to affection. The present aim is to be among the first to take steps towards systematically mapping the emotion-related responses to thermal stimuli from HTI framework.

ICMI'11, November 14–18, 2011, Alicante, Spain.

Previous work on utilizing temperature variations in HTI has concentrated mostly on presenting thermal properties of object surface materials (e.g., wood or steel) [2]. The results have shown that different surface materials can be recognized relatively well based on their thermal properties even when presented via thermal actuators. To improve the thermal sensitivity, in most of the previous studies the participant's hands have been preheated to a predefined temperature (e.g., 33°C in [2]). However, in real use cases the temperature of the hand is dependent of the current body temperature and it fluctuates in response to the environmental conditions (e.g., room temperature). The current study was motivated by a scenario where a thermal actuator would be attached to a mobile phone to provide stimuli to the user's palm. In respect to this scenario, we chose not to preheat the participant's hand.

The scenario also affected the stimulus presentation methods. When the user is holding the mobile phone, for example, during a phone call the user can feel when the thermal stimulus warms up or cools down towards the desired target temperature. However, if the mobile phone is, for instance, on the table the stimulus may have already reached the target temperature before the user grabs the phone. Therefore, two stimulus presentation methods were used to achieve the target temperature. In the dynamic presentation method the target temperature was heated or cooled during stimulus presentation. In the pre-adjusted presentation method the target temperature was set before stimulus presentation. It is worth noting that when the user operates with the device the temperature of the thermal actuator is roughly the same as the user's hand. So, in both presentation methods the stimuli were cooled or heated to the target temperature in respect to the participant's current hand temperature.

Both the subjective ratings and physiological responses were collected to study if thermal stimuli can affect the human emotional system. The subjective ratings were measured with scales for pleasantness, approachability, arousal, and dominance. These scales are based on the dimensional theory of emotions which is widely used and validated in the field of emotion research [1]. In addition, the participants were asked to rate their subjective experience of the stimulus temperature. To track down emotion-related physiological reactions the participants' SCR were measured. Changes in the SCR are argued to be centrally connected with the level of emotional arousal. There is evidence that stimuli which have higher level of emotional arousal evoke responses that are faster and higher in magnitude than stimuli which have lower level of emotional arousal [7].

2. METHODS

2.1 Participants

Eight voluntary participants (four female and four male with a mean age of 25 years, range 18 - 36) took part in the study. All had normal sense of touch by their own report. Their mean hand temperature was 28.6°C (range 24.5 – 33.6°C). The experiment was approved by the ethical committee of the local hospital district.

2.2 Apparatus

The thermal stimuli were provided with a Peltier thermal actuator (see Figure 1). The actuator contained a Multicomp PF-031-10-25 (15mm x 15mm x 4.8mm) thermoelectric module attached to an aluminum heatsink with double-sided heat-conducting tape. The actuator also had an integrated Labfacility DM-310 PT1000 temperature sensor attached to the surface of the actuator to monitor the temperature of the actuator. The actuator was driven with a driver module that was hosted by an Atmel ATmega324P microcontroller to receive drive instructions via serial connection and convert the instructions into PWM signal to drive the actuator accordingly.

E-Prime 2.0 Professional application suite [5] was used to run the experiment and to collect the user input. Arduino prototyping platform with Atmel ATMega328P was used both to control the driver module via serial connection and to listen to another serial connection where E-Prime sent the id of the next stimulus. After receiving the stimulus id Arduino, first, queried the temperature of the hand placed over a Melexis MLX90614 IR temperature sensor. Second, Arduino used a simple proportional–integral–derivative (PID) control loop to adapt the Peltier temperature close to that of the hand to meet the starting condition. Third, Arduino used the PID control loop to meet the parameters defined by the current stimulus with the user's hand placed over the Peltier actuator. When running the control loop the driver module constantly sent temperature data from the actuator that was used to refine the driving instructions. All the temperature data received from the actuator as well as the initial hand and room temperature measurements were written to a log for later inspection. Nexus-10 platform and Biotrace+ software version 2010A was used to measure the SCR.

2.3 Design and stimuli

The experiment was a within-subject repeated measures design. Two target temperatures were created by decreasing or increasing the stimulus temperature 4 °C in respect to the participants current hand temperature. The stimuli were divided in two stimulus groups based on their presentation method (see Figure 2).

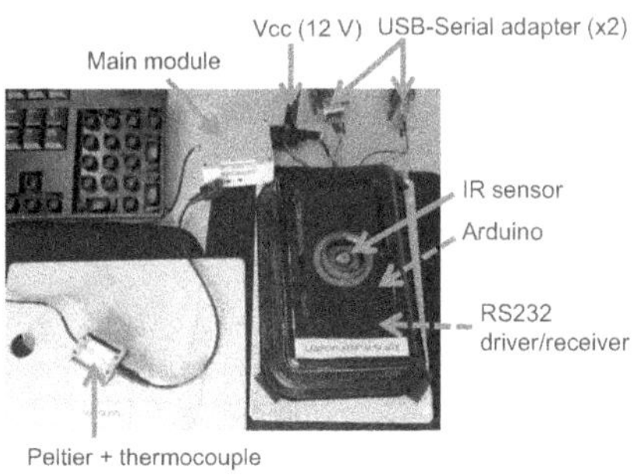

Figure 1. Apparatus used in the experiment.

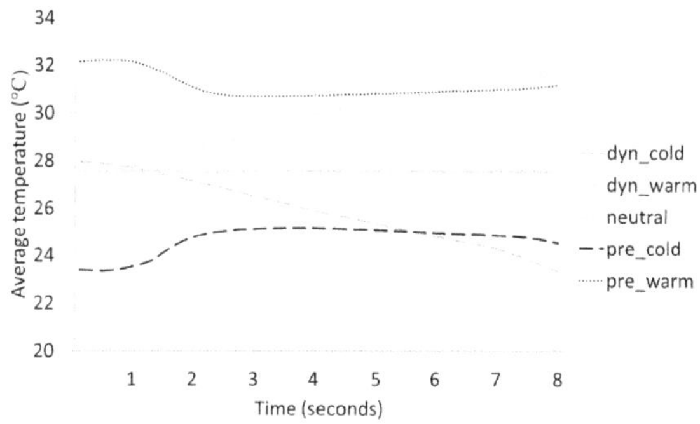

Figure 2. Average stimulus temperatures measured during the stimulus presentation. As the neutral stimulus was roughly the same in both stimulus groups, the temperatures measured during neutral stimulus presentation are merged in the figure. Dynamic stimuli are referred as dyn and pre-adjusted as pre.

In the dynamic presentation method the participants sensed the cooling or heating of the stimulus towards the target temperature (i.e., cold or warm dynamic stimulus). In the pre-adjusted presentation method the target temperature was kept as constant as possible during stimulus presentation (i.e., cold or warm pre-adjusted stimulus). However, after the contact with the skin the temperature of the pre-adjusted cold stimulus increased and the temperature of the pre-adjusted warm stimulus decreased in respect to the aimed target temperature (see Figure 2). To compare the possible effects of thermal variation to a neutral reference point, a stimulus where the temperature was kept at the participant's current hand temperature (i.e., neutral stimulus) was presented in both stimulus groups.

2.4 Procedure

The experiment was divided in two blocks. In the first block a stimulus presentation trial proceeded as follows. First, the participant put the dominant hand's palm on the IR sensor for 6000 ms to measure the current hand temperature. Then, the participant laid the palm on the Peltier actuator which presented a thermal stimulus for 8000 ms. After the stimulus presentation the participant was instructed to rate the immediate impression of the stimulus with four nine-point scales for pleasantness (varying from "the stimulus felt unpleasant" to "the stimulus felt pleasant"), approachability (varying from "the stimulus felt avoidable" to "the stimulus felt approachable"), arousal (varying from "I felt calm during stimulus presentation" to "I felt aroused during stimulus presentation") and dominance (varying from "I was in control during stimulus presentation" to "the stimulus was in control during presentation"). The mid-point of each scale represented a neutral experience (e.g., neither unpleasant nor pleasant). After the participant had rated the stimulus with all the four scales, a next trial was initialized. The second block proceeded similarly to the first block with the exception that the participants rated their experience of the stimulus temperature with a nine-point scale varying from cold to hot. The mid-point of the scale represented a neutral experience (e.g., neither cold nor warm).

The order of the stimulus groups and rating scales was counterbalanced. The stimulus presentation was fully randomized within a group. The total amount of stimulus presentation trials was 12. Conducting the experiment took approximately 30 minutes. During the experiment the SCR was measured from non-dominant hand's index finger and middle finger.

2.5 Data analysis

The subjective rating data was analyzed with the Wilcoxon signed-ranks test. The magnitude (i.e., the highest peak) and the rise time (i.e., the rate from the beginning of the response until the highest peak) of the SCR were analyzed with the repeated measures analysis of variance (ANOVA). The SCR reactions were calculated from the data collected in the first experimental block during 5000 ms time frame from the stimulus onset (i.e., 1000 to 6000 ms). One participant was excluded from the SCR analysis due to technical problems.

3. RESULTS

Figures 3 – 7 show the means and standard error of the means (S.E.M.s) of the ratings by presentation method and target temperature. Figure 8 shows the SCRs.

3.1 Subjective ratings

Either for the pleasantness or approachability ratings (see Figures 3 and 4) there were no statistically significant effects of the stimuli.

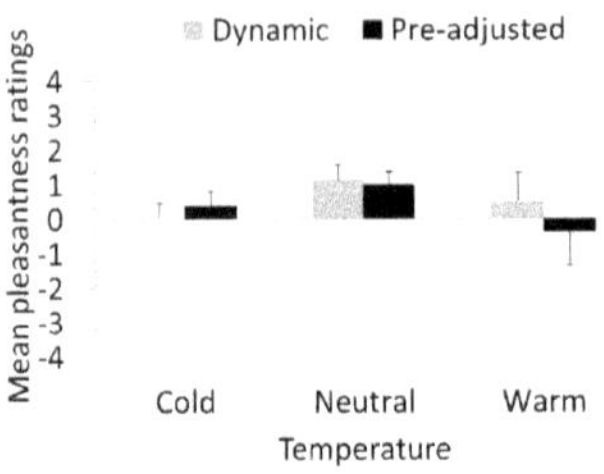

Figure 3. Mean pleasantness ratings.

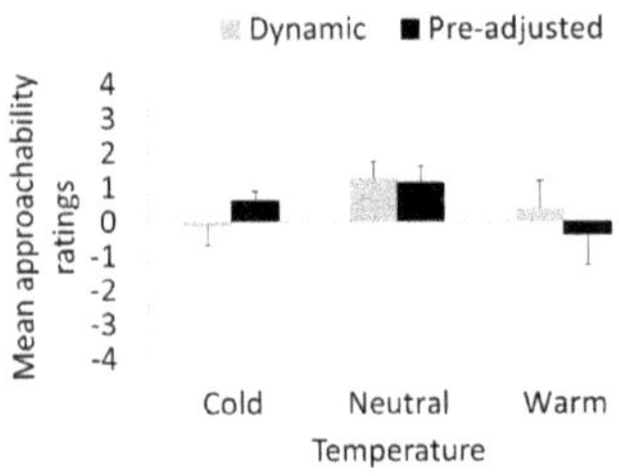

Figure 4. Mean approachability ratings.

The ratings of arousal (see Figure 5) showed that the dynamic and pre-adjusted warm stimuli were rated as significantly more arousing than the neutral stimuli, $Z = 2.56$, $p < 0.05$, and $Z = 2.03$, $p < 0.05$, respectively. Also, the pre-adjusted warm stimulus was rated as significantly more arousing than the pre-adjusted cold stimulus $Z = 2.05$, $p < 0.05$.

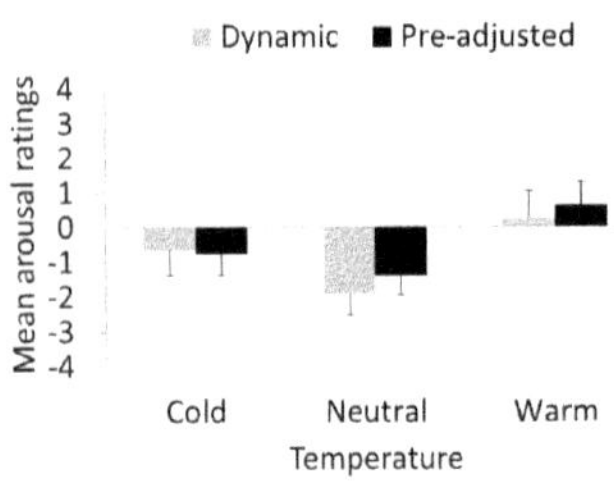

Figure 5. Mean arousal ratings.

The ratings of dominance (see Figure 6) showed that the participants rated the dynamic warm stimulus as more dominant than the neutral stimulus $Z = 2.21$, $p < 0.05$. The pre-adjusted warm stimulus was rated as more dominant than the pre-adjusted cold stimulus $Z = 2.21$, $p < 0.05$.

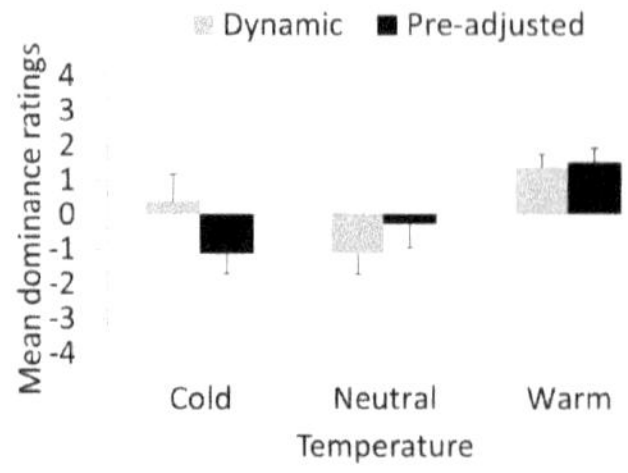

Figure 6. Mean dominance ratings.

The ratings of temperature (see Figure 7) showed that the dynamic warm stimulus was rated as warmer than the neutral stimulus $Z = 2.59$, $p < 0.01$ or the dynamic cold stimulus $Z = 2.56$, $p < 0.05$. Also, the pre-adjusted warm stimulus was rated as warmer than the neutral stimulus $Z = 2.46$, $p < 0.05$ or the pre-adjusted cold stimulus $Z = 2.56$, $p < 0.05$. Finally, the neutral stimulus was rated as warmer than the pre-adjusted $Z = 2.59$, $p < 0.01$ and dynamic $Z = 2.38$, $p < 0.05$ cold stimuli.

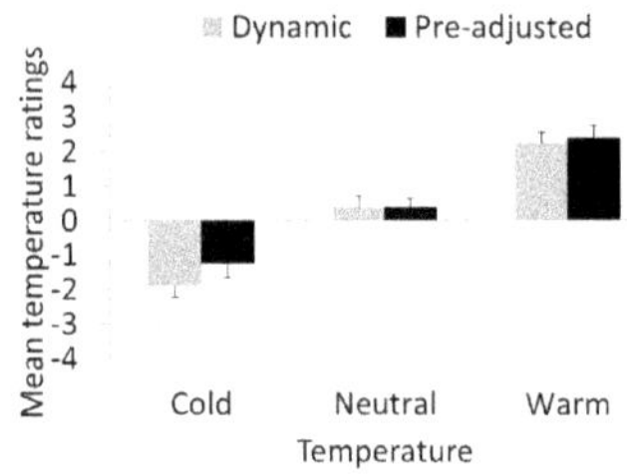

Figure 7. Mean temperature ratings.

3.2 Skin conductance responses

For the magnitude of the SCR (see Figure 8) a 3 × 2 (target temperature × presentation method) ANOVA showed no statistically significant effects of the stimuli. However, it can be seen from Figure 8 that in general the magnitude of the response was higher to the pre-adjusted warm stimulus than to other stimuli.

For the rise time of the SCR a 3 × 2 (target temperature × presentation method) ANOVA showed only a statistically significant interaction of the main effects of target temperature and presentation method $F = 4.1$, $p < 0.05$. The interaction was due to the fact that the response to the pre-adjusted warm stimulus was slower than the response to the dynamic warm stimulus. In contrast, the response to the dynamic cold stimulus was slower than the response to the pre-adjusted cold stimulus.

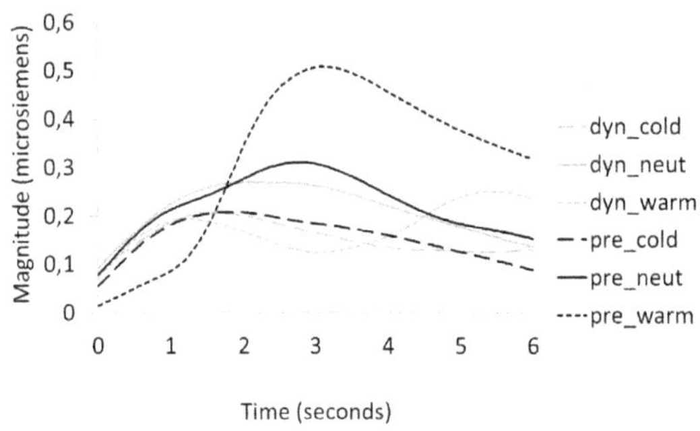

Figure 8. Average SCR during 0–6000 ms after stimulus onset.

4. DISCUSSION

Both the dynamic and pre-adjusted warm stimuli were rated as more arousing and dominating than the neutral or cold stimuli. Thus, temperatures warmer than the participant's hand were able to elevate the experienced level of arousal and dominance despite of the presentation method. However, ratings of pleasantness and approachability were not affected by the stimuli. This was surprising because previous literature [3], [5] suggested that the temperature of the stimulus would affect the subjective ratings so that the warm stimuli would be experienced as more pleasant than the neutral or cold stimuli.

In addition, the results of the subjective ratings showed that the participants rated the stimulus adequately in respect to the experienced temperature (i.e., cold as colder than neutral and warm stimuli and warm as warmer than neutral and cold stimuli). This result suggests that 4 °C changes in temperature are sufficient for creating distinguishable thermal stimuli, for example, for mobile contexts. This result is in line with a recent study [6] indicating that 3 °C changes in temperature can be detected relatively well when walking in an indoor office environment.

The physiological responses showed that both the magnitude and rate of the SCR were clearly affected by the stimulus presentation method. When the stimulus was warm the magnitude of the SCR was higher to the pre-adjusted than to the dynamic stimulus. When the stimulus was cold the rate of the SCR was faster to the pre-adjusted than to the dynamic stimulus. Therefore, it seems that the physiological level of arousal can be elevated more efficiently with pre-adjusted than dynamic stimuli.

The dimensional theory of emotions [1] suggests that the elevated level of arousal represents the activation of the motivational tendency related to approaching or avoiding the stimulation. In the current study warm stimuli activated this motivational system more efficiently than neutral or cold stimuli. Intuitively it seems that the reason behind this could be that high temperatures can burn the skin. Thus, elevated level of arousal may prepare the user to withdraw the hand off the actuator if the temperature rises too high. However, the direction of the motivation (i.e., approachability ratings) was not affected by the stimulus temperature suggesting that at least with 4 °C changes in temperature warm stimuli are not experienced as avoidable but as approachable or neutral (see Figure 4).

Then, the higher and faster SCR to the pre-adjusted than to the dynamic stimuli may be due to the adaptation to the stimulus temperature. When the presentation style is pre-adjusted the shift in the stimulus temperature in respect to the hand temperature is abrupt thus causing the reaction at the autonomic nervous system (ANS) level. However, when the presentation style is dynamic the ANS has time to adapt to the temperature change and therefore the rapid physiological response does not occur.

It should be noted that in the current study we had only 4 °C changes in stimulus temperature. Also, the pre-adjusted stimuli had some fluctuation in temperature during stimulus presentation due to the technical restrictions (see Figure 2). Next, we aim to use a wider set of stimulus temperatures and an updated stimulus control system to deepen the understanding of the relationship between thermal stimulation and emotions.

In summary, warm stimuli with both presentation methods were effective in activating the human emotional system by shifting the experienced level of arousal and dominance. In addition, the pre-adjusted warm stimulus elevated the level of SCR. From a theoretical point of view [1] the enhancement in the subjective level of arousal can be easily seen as means to elevate the level of attentive behavior. From application point of view the results suggest that warm stimuli especially when pre-adjusted can be used in mobile contexts to catch the user's attention during an ongoing task if, for example, the battery needs to be recharged or a calendar event alarms.

5. ACKNOWLEDGMENTS

This research was a part of Human Emotional Interaction project funded by the Finnish Funding Agency for Technology and Innovation, TEKES and steered by Nokia Research Center.

6. REFERENCES

[1] Bradley, M.M., and Lang, P.J. 1994. Measuring emotion: the self-assessment manikin and the semantic differential. Journal of Behavior Therapy and Experimental Psychiatry, 25, 49–59.

[2] Jones, L.A. and Ho, H. 2008. Warm or cool, large or small? The challenge of thermal displays. IEEE Transactions on Haptics, 1, 53-70.

[3] Kanosue K., Sadato N., Okada T., Yoada T., Nakai S., Yoshida K., Hosono T., Nagashima K., Yagishita T., Inoue O., Kobyashi K., and Yonekua Y. 2002. Brain activation during whole body cooling in humans studied with functional magnetic resonance imaging. Neuroscience Letters, 329, 157-160.

[4] Schneider, W., Eschman, A., and Zuccolotto, A. 2002. E-Prime User's Guide. Psychology Software Tools, Inc, Pittsburgh.

[5] Sung E.-J., Yoo S.-S., Yoon H.W., Han S., and Park, H.W. 2007. Brain activation related to affective dimension during thermal stimulation in humans: A functional magnetic resonance imaging study. International Journal of Neuroscience, 117, 1011-1027.

[6] Wilson, G., Halvey, M., Brewster, B., and Hughes, S. Some Like It Hot? Thermal Feedback for Mobile Devices. Procedings of CHI 2011, 2555-2564.

[7] Witvliet, C.V.O., and Vrana, S.R. 1995. Psychophysiological responses as indices of affective dimensions. Psychophysiology, 32, 436-443.

An Active Learning Scenario for Interactive Machine Translation

Jesús González-Rubio
Instituto Tecnológico de Informática
U. Politècnica de València
46021 Valencia, Spain
jegonzalez@iti.upv.es

Daniel Ortiz-Martínez
D. de Sistemas Informáticos y Computación
U. Politècnica de València
46021 Valencia, Spain
dortiz@dsic.upv.es

Francisco Casacuberta
D. de Sistemas Informáticos y Computación
U. Politècnica de València
46021 Valencia, Spain
fcn@dsic.upv.es

ABSTRACT

This paper provides the first experimental study of an active learning (AL) scenario for interactive machine translation (IMT). Unlike other IMT implementations where user feedback is used only to improve the predictions of the system, our IMT implementation takes advantage of user feedback to update the statistical models involved in the translation process. We introduce a sentence sampling strategy to select the sentences that are worth to be interactively translated, and a retraining method to update the statistical models with the user-validated translations. Both, the sampling strategy and the retraining process are designed to work in real-time to meet the severe time constraints inherent to the IMT framework. Experiments in a simulated setting showed that the use of AL dramatically reduces user effort required to obtain translations of a given quality.

Categories and Subject Descriptors

I.2.7 [**Natural Language Processing**]: Machine Translation;
I.5.5 [**Implementation**]: Interactive Systems

General Terms

Algorithm, Experimentation

Keywords

Active learning, Interactive machine translation

1. INTRODUCTION

In the *statistical machine translation* (SMT) framework, the translation process is modelled as a decision problem. For a given source sentence $\mathbf{f} \equiv f_1 \ldots f_j \ldots f_{|\mathbf{f}|}$, we seek for the target sentence $\mathbf{e} \equiv e_1 \ldots e_i \ldots e_{|\mathbf{e}|}$ that maximizes posterior probability:

$$\hat{\mathbf{e}} = \arg\max_{\mathbf{e}} Pr(\mathbf{e}|\mathbf{f}) \ . \quad (1)$$

Unfortunately, SMT systems are far from being perfect and their outputs usually require human post-editing in order to achieve high-quality translations. Within the IMT framework [9, 14, 2], a state-of-the-art SMT model and a human translator collaborate to obtain good translations with minimum human effort. For a given source sentence, the SMT model fully automatically generates an initial translation. The human user checks this translation, from left to right, correcting the first error. Then, the SMT model proposes a new extension taking the correct prefix $\mathbf{e}_p$ into account. These steps are repeated until the user accepts the translation. Figure 1 illustrates a typical IMT session. In the resulting decision rule, we maximize over all possible suffixes $\mathbf{e}_s$ that complete the correct prefix $\mathbf{e}_p$:

source ($\mathbf{f}$): Para ver la lista de recursos
desired translation ($\hat{\mathbf{e}}$): To view a listing of resources

inter.-0	$\mathbf{e}_p$	
	$\mathbf{e}_s$	*To view the resources list*
inter.-1	$\mathbf{e}_p$	To view
	k	[a]
	$\mathbf{e}_s$	*list of resources*
inter.-2	$\mathbf{e}_p$	To view a list
	k	[i]
	$\mathbf{e}_s$	*ng resources*
inter.-3	$\mathbf{e}_p$	To view a listing
	k	[o]
	$\mathbf{e}_s$	*f resources*
accept	$\mathbf{e}_p$	To view a listing of resources

Figure 1: IMT session to translate a Spanish sentence into English. The desired translation is the translation the real user have in mind. At interaction-0, the system suggests a translation ($\mathbf{e}_s$). At interaction-1, the user moves the mouse to accept the first eight characters "To view " and presses the [a] key (k), then the system suggests completing the sentence with "*list of resources*" (a new $\mathbf{e}_s$). Interactions 2 and 3 are similar. In the final interaction, the user accepts the current suggestion.

$$\hat{\mathbf{e}}_s = \arg\max_{\mathbf{e}_s} Pr(\mathbf{e}_s|\mathbf{f}, \mathbf{e}_p) \ . \quad (2)$$

The aim of the IMT framework is to obtain translations of maximum quality while minimizing the effort required from the human translator. However, most of the IMT implementations only made a partial usage of the information provided by the user. Corrected prefixes are used to improve the predictions of the IMT system, but the underlying SMT model remains constant, which implies that the user may have to correct the same error repeatedly [16, 12]. Ortiz-Martínez et al. [20] propose to overcome this problem by retraining the SMT model used by the IMT system with the user-validated translations. Such proposal requires the user to check all the sentences, but significantly reduces the required user-effort to generate error-free translations.

ICMI'11, November 14–18, 2011, Alicante, Spain.

A parallel line of research involves the study of alternative interaction protocols to make human-machine interaction more efficient. González-Rubio et al. [10] present an alternative IMT system where only those sentences whose initial automatic translation is not good enough are interactively translated. Since the user does not have to check all the sentences, the final translations may contain errors. Such system allows to achieve a balance between user effort and final translation error to adapt the system to suit the requirements of each particular task.

In this work, we propose to unify the ideas presented in [20] and [10] to develop an AL [7] scenario for IMT. In this AL scenario, the IMT system selects the source sentences that are worth to be interactively translated and uses their user-validated translations to retrain the SMT model. The potential improvements of our proposal are twofold. On the one hand, we minimize the user interactions with the system, thus reducing the required user effort. On the other hand, the SMT model is updated with user feedback, preventing the user from having to correct repeatedly the same errors.

Experiments in a simulated setting showed that our AL scenario for IMT almost halved the required user effort to obtain translations of a given quality.

2. ACTIVE LEARNING FOR IMT

Various works have studied the application of the AL scenario to SMT [11, 1, 4], but, to the best of our knowledge, there are no previous works on AL applied to IMT. These previous works on SMT follow the *pool-based AL* scenario [15]. Pool-based AL assumes the availability of a closed pool of source sentences from where sentences are queried in a greedy fashion according to an informativeness measure used to evaluate all the sentences in the pool. On the contrary, an IMT system processes the sentences sequentially, i.e. instead of a pool of sentences we work with a stream of them, hence, pool-based AL cannot be applied to IMT. The appropriate AL scenario for IMT is known as *sequential* or *stream-based AL* [7]. In the sequential AL scenario, each unlabeled instance is drawn one at a time from the data source, and the learner must decide individually for each sentence whether to request its label or not.

Algorithm 1 describes our proposed AL scenario for IMT. The algorithm receives as input an initial SMT model, M, and a stream of source sentences, $\mathcal{S}$, which is sampled one by one. For each source sentence, $\mathbf{f} \in \mathcal{S}$, the current SMT model generates an initial translation, $\hat{\mathbf{e}}$ (line 3). If this translation meets the desired quality criterion (line 4), we output it as our final translation. Otherwise, the user is required to interactively translate the source sentence (lines 5–10). The source sentence $\mathbf{f}$ and its user-validated translation, $\mathbf{e}$, are used to retrain the statistical model (line 11).

This AL scenario for IMT allows us to reduce the user effort in two ways. First, the user only has to supervise those sentences that do not meet the quality criterion, hence, the number of sentences being interactively translated is minimized while retaining a high translation quality. Second, for those interactively translated sentences, user feedback is used to improve the underlying SMT model. This way, the SMT model is able to learn new translations or to adapt its output to the translation preferences of the user.

Our proposed AL scenario for IMT has two main modules. On the one hand, we must define a quality criterion to detect the incorrect translations that need supervision from the user (line 4). On the other hand, we need to retrain the SMT model with the user-validated translations (line 11). It is worth of notice that, due to the interaction with the user, IMT systems must work in real-time. Therefore, we have to take into account this severe time constraint when designing these two modules.

```
   input : M (initial SMT model)
           S (stream of source sentences)
 1 begin
 2   foreach f ∈ S do
 3     ê=translate(f,M);
 4     if !enough_quality(f,ê) then
 5       e = ê;
 6       repeat
 7         e_p=correct_prefix(e);
 8         ê_s = argmax_{e_s} Pr(e_s|f,e_p);
 9         e = e_p ê_s;
10       until validate_translation(e) ;
11       M=retrain(f,e,M);
12       output(e);
13     else
14       output(ê)
15 end
```

Algorithm 1: Pseudo-code of our proposed AL scenario for IMT.

2.1 Sentence selection strategy

Following the ideas presented in [10], we use a sentence confidence measure as the quality criterion to classify the initial automatic translations. We estimate the reliability of a translation by combining the confidence scores of their individual words. The confidence score of a word e_i of the translation $\mathbf{e}$ generated from the source sentence $\mathbf{f}$ is computed as [23]:

$$\mathcal{C}_w(e_i, \mathbf{f}) = \max_{0 \leq j \leq |\mathbf{f}|} p(e_i|f_j) \ , \tag{3}$$

where $p(e_i|f_j)$ is the IBM model 1 [5] bilingual lexicon probability and f_0 is the empty source word. The confidence measure for the full translation $\mathbf{e}$ is computed as the ratio of its words classified as correct by the word confidence measure[1]:

$$\mathcal{C}(\mathbf{e}) = \frac{|\{e_i \mid \mathcal{C}_w(e_i, \mathbf{f}) > \tau_w\}|}{|\mathbf{e}|} \ . \tag{4}$$

Each translation is classified as either correct or incorrect depending on whether its confidence score exceeds or not a sentence classification threshold τ_s.

This sentence confidence measure can be computed very fast, thus meeting the severe time constraints of the IMT scenario, and, additionally, it obtains similar results [3, 24, 22] as other more complex confidence measures.

2.2 Retraining of the SMT model

To retrain the SMT model, we implement the online learning techniques proposed in [20]. In that work, a state-of-the-art log-linear model [19] and a set of techniques to incrementally train this model were defined. The log-linear model is composed of a set of feature functions governing different aspects of the translation process, including a language model, an inverse sentence–length model, inverse and direct translation models, a target phrase–length model, a source phrase–length model and a distortion model.

The incremental learning algorithms allows us to process each new training sample in constant time (i.e. the computational complexity of training a new sample does not depend on the number of previously seen training samples). To do that, a set of sufficient statistics is maintained for each feature function. If the estimation of the feature function does not require the use of the well-known expectation–maximization (EM) algorithm [8] (e.g. n-gram language models), then it is generally easy to incrementally extend

[1]A word e_i is classified as correct if its confidence score $\mathcal{C}_w(e_i, \mathbf{f})$ exceeds a word classification threshold τ_w.

corpus	use	sentences	words (Spa/Eng)
Europarl	train	731K	15M/15M
	dev	2K	60K/58K
News Commentary	test	51K	1490K/1220K

Table 1: Size of the Spanish–English corpora used in the experiments. K and M stand for thousands and millions of elements respectively.

the model given a new training sample. By contrast, if the EM algorithm is required (e.g. word alignment models), the estimation procedure has to be modified, since the conventional EM algorithm is designed for its use in batch learning scenarios. For those models, the incremental version of the EM algorithm [17] is applied. A detailed description of the update algorithm for each of the models in the log-linear combination is presented in [20].

3. EXPERIMENTS

We tested the proposed framework in a simulated AL setting. The training data comes from the Europarl corpus as distributed for the shared task in the NAACL 2006 workshop on statistical machine translation [13]. The weights of the different translation features were tuned by means of minimum error–rate training [18] executed on the Europarl development corpus. Once the SMT model was trained, we simulated the interactive translation of a set of sentences extracted from the News Commentary (NC) corpus [6]. The size of these corpora is shown in Table 1. We chose the NC corpus to carry out our experiments for two reasons. First, its size is large enough to test our AL techniques in the long term. Second, since it constitutes an out-of-domain test set, it allowed us to define a real-world difficult task for applying our techniques.

3.1 Assessment criteria

To estimate user effort, the target translations which a real user would have in mind are simulated by the given references. The first translation hypothesis for each given source sentence is compared with a single reference translation and the longest common character prefix (LCP) is obtained. The first non-matching character is replaced by the corresponding reference character and then a new system hypothesis is produced (see Figure 1). This process is iterated until a full match with the reference is obtained. Each computation of the LCP would correspond to the user looking for the next error and *moving the pointer* to the corresponding position of the translation hypothesis. Each character replacement, on the other hand, would correspond to a *keystroke* of the user. Bearing this in mind, we measure the user effort by means of the keystroke and mouse-action ratio (KSMR) [2]. This measure has been extensively used to report results in the IMT literature. KSMR is calculated as the number of keystrokes plus the number of mouse movements divided by the total number of reference characters. From a user point of view the two types of actions are different and require different types of effort [16]. In any case, as an approximation, KSMR assumes that both actions require a similar effort.

Additionally, since we allow the final translations to be different from the ones the user would have in mind, we also used the well-known BLEU score [21] to measure the quality of the final translations.

3.2 Results

In the experimentation, we studied the required user effort and the final translation quality obtained by our proposed IMT system with AL. To this end, we carried out a series of experiments ranging the value of the sentence classification threshold, τ_s, while the

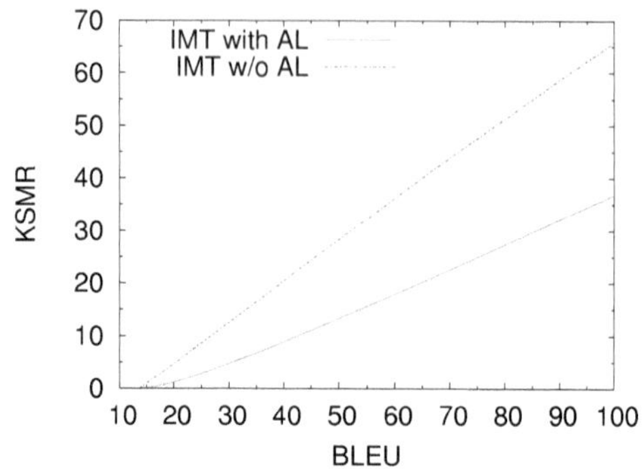

Figure 2: User effort (KSMR) required to translate the NC corpus with a given translation quality (BLEU) using the proposed AL scenario for IMT and the IMT system without AL.

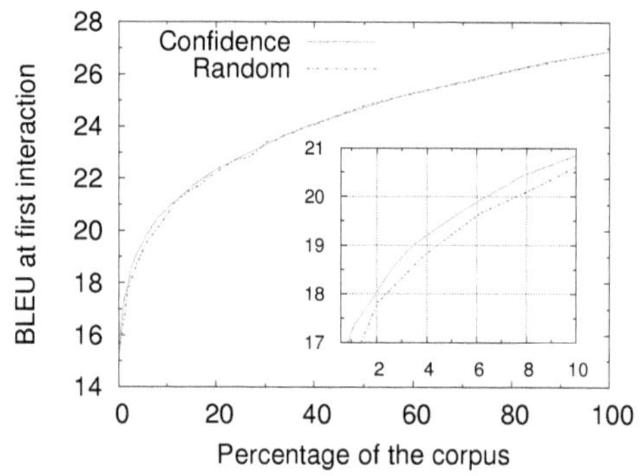

Figure 3: BLEU at first iteration of a function of the number of words used to retrain the model.

word classification threshold is fixed, $\tau_w = 0.4$. For each sentence threshold value, we calculated the effort that is required from the user in terms of KSMR and the quality of the final translation as measured by BLEU. We compared the results of our proposal with the results obtained by the IMT system without AL proposed in [10]. This system only differs from the one proposed here in its inability to incorporate new knowledge to the SMT model.

Figure 2 displays the user effort required to translate the full NC corpus with a given translation quality, for both the proposed AL scenario for IMT and the IMT system without AL. Results show a consistent reduction in user effort when applying AL to IMT. For a given translation quality, the application of AL allows to reduce to almost one half the effort required to translate the test corpus.

Additionally, we carried out experiments to study the performance of our confidence-based selection strategy (see section 2.1). To this end, we compare such selection strategy with a random selection strategy. Figure 3 shows the BLEU score of the initial automatic translations, i.e. the BLEU score calculated at the first interaction of the IMT process, for both strategies. BLEU score is represented as a function of the percentage of the corpus (measured in number of running words) used to retrain the SMT model.

According to Figure 3 BLEU results improved as new sentences were added to the model. Confidence-based selection strategy slightly outperformed the baseline (+0.4 BLEU points) when a small fraction of the corpus was used to retrain the model. For larger percentages of the corpus both selection strategies had similar performance. This is due to the fact that the larger the selected percentage of the corpus, the more similar the sets of sentences.

Finally, it should be noted that our IMT system is able to generate new suffixes and retrain new sentence pairs in tenths of a second. Thus, our proposed IMT system can be used in real time scenarios.

4. SUMMARY

We presented the first experimental study on AL applied to IMT. Unlike other IMT implementations where user feedback is used only for improving the predictions of the system, our IMT implementation takes advantage of user feedback to update the statistical models involved in the translation process. Specifically, we propose a technique to detect the source sentences that require user supervision and a technique to retrain the model with user-validated translations. Both techniques are designed to meet the severe time restrictions inherent to IMT.

Experiments in a simulated setting showed that our IMT system with AL reduces to almost one half the required user effort with respect to a system without AL. Additionally, our confidence-based selection strategy slightly outperformed the strong random sentence selection baseline. Finally, the response and retraining times of our IMT system allows us to use it in real-time scenarios.

As future work we plan to carry out further experiments involving human users.

Acknowledgements

Work supported by EC (FEDER/FSE) and Spanish MEC/MICINN under MIPRCV "Consolider Ingenio 2010" (CSD2007-00018) and iTrans2 (TIN2009-14511), by UPV under grant 20091027, by Spanish MITyC under erudito.com (TSI-020110-2009-439) and by Generalitat Valenciana under Prometeo/2009/014.

5. REFERENCES

[1] V. Ambati, S. Vogel, and J. Carbonell. Active learning and crowd-sourcing for machine translation. In *Proc. of the conference on International Language Resources and Evaluation*, pages 2169–2174, 2010.

[2] S. Barrachina, O. Bender, F. Casacuberta, J. Civera, E. Cubel, S. Khadivi, A. Lagarda, H. Ney, J. Tomás, E. Vidal, and J.-M. Vilar. Statistical approaches to computer-assisted translation. *Computational Linguistics*, 35:3–28, 2009.

[3] J. Blatz, E. Fitzgerald, G. Foster, S. Gandrabur, C. Goutte, A. Kulesza, A. Sanchis, and N. Ueffing. Confidence estimation for machine translation. In *Proc. of the international conference on Computational Linguistics*, pages 315–321, 2004.

[4] M. Bloodgood and C. Callison-Burch. Bucking the trend: large-scale cost-focused active learning for statistical machine translation. In *Proc. of the Association for Computational Linguistics*, pages 854–864, 2010.

[5] P. F. Brown, V. J. D. Pietra, S. A. D. Pietra, and R. L. Mercer. The mathematics of statistical machine translation: parameter estimation. *Computational Linguistics*, 19:263–311, 1993.

[6] C. Callison-Burch, C. Fordyce, P. Koehn, C. Monz, and J. Schroeder. (Meta-) evaluation of machine translation. In *Proc. of the Workshop on Statistical Machine Translation*, pages 136–158, 2007.

[7] D. Cohn, L. Atlas, and R. Ladner. Improving generalization with active learning. *Machine Learning*, 15:201–221, 1994.

[8] A. Dempster, N. Laird, and D. Rubin. Maximum likelihood from incomplete data via the EM algorithm. *Journal of the Royal Statistical Society.*, 39(1):1–38, 1977.

[9] G. Foster, P. Isabelle, and P. Plamondon. Target-text mediated interactive machine translation. *Machine Translation*, 12:175–194, 1998.

[10] J. González-Rubio, D. Ortiz-Martínez, and F. Casacuberta. Balancing user effort and translation error in interactive machine translation via confidence measures. In *Proc. of the Association for Computational Linguistics*, pages 173–177, 2010.

[11] G. Haffari, M. Roy, and A. Sarkar. Active learning for statistical phrase-based machine translation. In *Proc. of the North American Chapter of the Association for Computational Linguistics*, pages 415–423, 2009.

[12] P. Koehn and B. Haddow. Interactive assistance to human translators using statistical machine translation methods. In *Proc. of Machine Translation Summit XII*, 2009.

[13] P. Koehn and C. Monz. Manual and automatic evaluation of machine translation between european languages. In *Proc. of the Workshop on Statistical Machine Translation*, 2006.

[14] P. Langlais and G. Lapalme. Trans Type: development-evaluation cycles to boost translator's productivity. *Machine Translation*, 17:77–98, 2002.

[15] D. Lewis and W. Gale. A sequential algorithm for training text classifiers. In *Proc. of the ACM SIGIR conference on Research and development in information retrieval*, pages 3–12, 1994.

[16] E. Macklovitch. TransType2: the last word. In *Proc. of the conference on International Language Resources and Evaluation*, pages 167–17, 2006.

[17] R. Neal and G. Hinton. A view of the EM algorithm that justifies incremental, sparse, and other variants. *Learning in graphical models*, pages 355–368, 1999.

[18] F. Och. Minimum error rate training in statistical machine translation. In *Proc. of the Association for Computational Linguistics*, pages 160–167, 2003.

[19] F. Och and H. Ney. Discriminative training and maximum entropy models for statistical machine translation. In *Proc. of the Association for Computational Linguistics*, pages 295–302, 2002.

[20] D. Ortiz-Martínez, I. García-Varea, and F. Casacuberta. Online learning for interactive statistical machine translation. In *Proc. of the North American Chapter of the Association for Computational Linguistics*, pages 546–554, 2010.

[21] K. Papineni, S. Roukos, T. Ward, and W.-J. Zhu. BLEU: a method for automatic evaluation of machine translation. In *Proc. of the Association for Computational Linguistics*, pages 311–318, 2002.

[22] A. Sanchis, A. Juan, and E. Vidal. Estimation of confidence measures for machine translation. In *Proc. of the Machine Translation Summit XI*, pages 407–412, 2007.

[23] N. Ueffing and H. Ney. Application of word-level confidence measures in interactive statistical machine translation. In *Proc. of the European Association for Machine Translation conference*, pages 262–270, 2005.

[24] N. Ueffing and H. Ney. Word-level confidence estimation for machine translation. *Computational Linguistics*, 33:9–40, 2007.

Move, and I Will Tell You Who You Are: Detecting Deceptive Roles in Low-quality Data

Nimrod Raiman
University of Amsterdam
Amsterdam, Netherlands
Nimrod@Raiman.nl

Hayley Hung
University of Amsterdam
Amsterdam, Netherlands
H.Hung@uva.nl

Gwenn Englebienne
University of Amsterdam
Amsterdam, Netherlands
G.Englebienne@uva.nl

ABSTRACT

Motion, like speech, provides information about one's emotional state. This work introduces an automated non-verbal audio-visual approach for detecting deceptive roles in multi-party conversations using low resolution video. We show how using simple features extracted from motion and speech improves over speech-only for the detection of deceptive roles. Our results show that deceptive players were recognised with significantly higher precision when video features were used. We improve the classification performance with 22.6% compared to our baseline.

Categories and Subject Descriptors

H.3.1 [**Information Storage and Retrieval**]: *Content Analysis and Indexing Methods*

General Terms

Multimodal

Keywords

multi-party conversation, deception, human behavior

1. INTRODUCTION

Lies and deception are part of everyday life [1]. *"On average we each try to dupe others more then once a day"* Vrij [1, page 11]. Some lies, such as "I'm fine", can be seen as a social lubricant, while others are of course more harmful. *"Lying is such a central characteristic of life that better understanding of it is relevant to almost all human affairs" Ekman [2, page 23].* Despite the quantity and consequences of lies, people are very bad at recognizing them [2]. A possible explanation for this is the ostrich effect [1]: people do not always want to hear the truth.

In this paper we propose a method for detecting deceptive roles in multi–party conversations using audio and low–quality video data. Deception is defined by Vrij [1, page 15] as *"a successful or unsuccessful deliberate attempt, without forewarning, to create in another a belief which the communicator considers to be untrue".* This can be achieved by telling a lie or (partially) concealing the truth. A lie is a specific instance of deception in the form of an untruthful statement. This paper's goal is particularly challenging because a person in a deceptive role is not lying or deceiving all the time. Current approaches for detecting deception are based on either non–verbal audio or video cues. We extend both approaches by combining automatically extracted non–verbal audio and video cues for detecting deceptive roles. Our proposed models are tested on the werewolf corpus [3], a multi-party conversation dataset where players have either a deceptive role (wolf) or a non-deceptive role (villager) (sec.2). The wolves' goal is to deceive the villagers and make them believe they are one of them.

To our best knowledge very little research is done on automated audio-visual analysis of social interaction concerning deception detection [4] and no research has been done on automated detection of deception in multi-party conversations using low-quality video data. This paper introduces a fully automated method for detecting deception with audio and low-quality video data in multi-party conversations. Analysing the content of audio and video recordings of social interaction can be done using three different approaches: the verbal approach [4–6], where the content of a conversation is analysed; the non-verbal audio approach [4–12], where the focus is not on what is being said, but how it is said; and the non-verbal video approach [4, 8–11, 13, 14], where body motions, gestures and facial expressions are analysed.

There is a large range of video features that can help understand social interactions between people. Some are very subtle and detailed (e.g. eye blinking, barely noticeable lip-clenching, eyebrow movement, etc.) [2, 8]. Some are more obvious (e.g. head nod, head shake, arm folding, etc.) [8–11, 13, 14]. In this paper we focus on detecting deceptive roles in audio and low-quality video data by analysing gross body movements. Approaches that work for low video quality and are not based on facial expressions are more widely applicable because of two reasons: first, not all video recording systems (e.g. webcams, mobile phone cameras, surveillance cameras, etc.) have sufficient quality for extracting detailed features such as facial expressions; and second, because in real world situations faces are not always visible for the camera. The maximal size of the faces of the people in the dataset for example is 30 by 30 pixels. Extracting robust detailed facial expression from this is challenging. Also the lighting conditions are not ideal, in many cases the skin colour of the persons in the dataset is very similar to the background. Because of this, detecting skin in the video stream is not trivial.

In this paper we focus on non-verbal cues. Chittaranjan

Figure 1: Screenshot of the video recordings

and Hung [7] show that by using automatically extracted non-verbal audio features for detecting deceptive roles in recordings of a multi-party role playing game (RPG), their system's performance is significantly higher than the participants' in the game. Meservy et al. [13] explain an automated non-verbal video approach for inferring deception in dyadic conversations from a set of features extracted from head and hands movements in a video. Our hypothesis is that since both the voice and the body are a source of information on the current state of mind of a person [1, 2] and because audio and video features contain different information, looking at both will give a more complete picture of the social interactions and the current state of mind of a person.

2. DATA

The "Werewolf" dataset (made by Idiap[1]) used for training and testing the models in this paper is the same as used by Chittaranjan and Hung [7]. The dataset contains 3 hours of conversational data of 4 games played by 2 groups. The groups consisted of 10 and 8 different participants playing the RPG "are you a werewolf?". All participants in the game sat on a chair while they were alive in the game. On the video recordings the upper bodies are fully visible, but the legs are often occluded. A screen shot of the video data is shown in figure 1.

In the simplest setting of this game there is one mayor that leads the game, two of the players have the role of werewolves and the other players are villagers. The game has two phases, night and day. During the night phase the werewolves choose one player which they kill overnight and thus will not wake up in the morning. During the day phase all villagers that are alive and the werewolves in disguise discuss who they want to kill. The villagers try to find out who the werewolves are and it is the werewolves' task to deceive the group to avoid being killed and losing the game. This setting provides a good motivation for the players to lie and conceal their identity. During the game the participants identified with their role, resulting in real emotions. From the dataset only the day phases are used for training and testing the models.

The audio data were recorded using headset microphones, the video data with three frontal cameras. The layout of the recording room is shown in figure 2. The lighting conditions in the recording room were not ideal, the lighting is not equal throughout the room and in many cases the skin colour of the players is very similar to the background colour due to highlights.

3. CUE EXTRACTION

This paper proposes an automated approach for detecting deceptive roles using audio and visual cues in low-quality video data. Since this approach is developed for low-quality data, no attempt is made at detecting detailed features such as micro expressions. Instead, the focus is on gross body motion. Before one's behavior was analysed, speaking activity and motion features were extracted.

[1] http://www.idiap.ch/scientific-research/resources/wolf-corpus

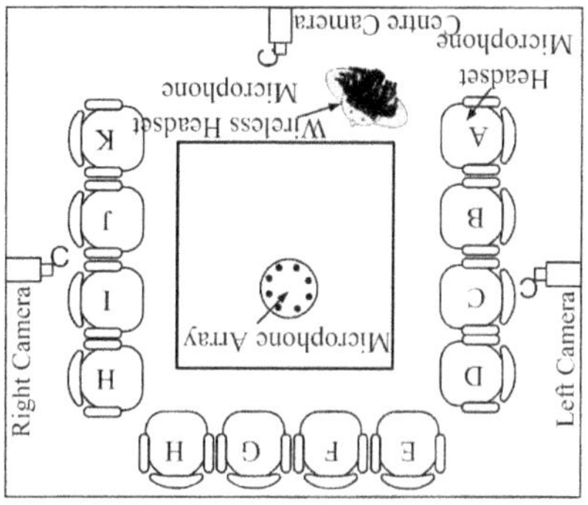

Figure 2: The layout of the recording room

3.1 Speaking activity

We used the method presented by Chittaranjan and Hung [7] to extract the speaker turn segmentation. Output of a voice activity detector (VAD) was synchronised to the corresponding frames of the video. A VAD classifies a segment as speech when the energy in that segment exceeds a certain threshold. The result was a binary vector for each player with ones for the frames where speech was measured and zeros for the frames where this person was silent.

3.2 Motion cues

Each individual's motion was extracted by first locating their body, using the frontal face Haar cascade classifier implementation from OpenCV. Once the faces were located and the number of individuals in the video were known the areas of their bodies was determined. The average width of the extracted body area was empirically set to 140 pixels symmetrically aligned around the face area and the height was set to 250 pixels. The body areas were resized according to their distance to the camera, measured by the size of the chair. Meservy et al. [13] explain in their approach that different areas of and around the body can be informative (e.g. to discriminate between an open and closed posture) concerning motion and location of the hands. Inspired by this approach the extracted area of the body from the video stream is divided in six regions, see figure 3. By analysing each region separately, different clues from the behavior can be captured. The head (**H**) region captures head motion (an increase in head motion can indicate one is being more alert). The region above the shoulders (**AS**) captures motion from self touching in the neck and head area (self touching can indicate anxiety). The left body region (**BL**) and the right body region (**BR**) capture motion involved with a more open posture. Finally the left (**BML**) and right (**BMR**) side of the body middle region capture motion involved with a more closed posture.

We used two different techniques to detect body motion: **Temporal difference.** This technique is based on subtracting consecutive frames. It is computationally cheaper but less accurate than full optical flow (described next). The result of subtracting frames from each other is assumed to be the motion between the two recorded frames. The outputs from this method were thresholded. Finally for each region the binary values are summed to give the visual activity (M_r).

$$M_r = \sum_{p \in P_r} f(p), \text{ where } f(p) = \begin{cases} 0 & \text{if } p \geq \theta \\ 1 & \text{if } p < \theta \end{cases},$$

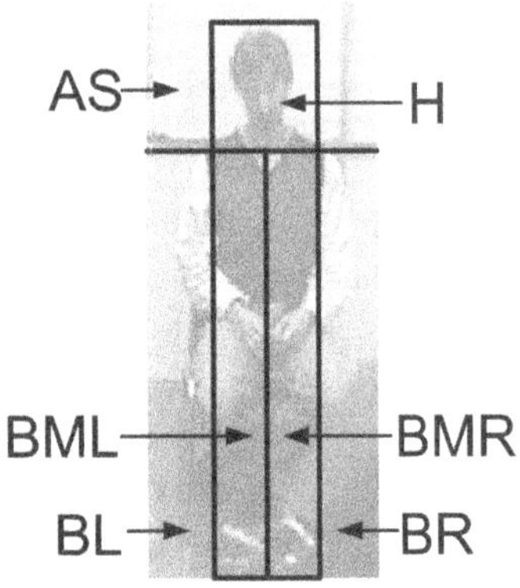

Figure 3: Six regions the body area is divided in

P_r is the set of pixels in region r and θ is the threshold parameter. θ was empirically set to remove noise from areas of uniform texture.

Optical flow. We used the method of Liu [15] to extract the optical flow. This technique allows us to achieve a more accurate mapping of motion between two consecutive frames. The outputs of this algorithm are two flow fields, in horizontal and vertical directions. These flow fields are transformed in two different features; the *motion magnitude* and the *orientation of the motion*. A histogram of the motion magnitudes and orientation is stored per region per frame.

4. DETECTING DECEPTIVE ROLES

People in a deceptive role talk and move differently from people who are not deceiving [1, 2, 7, 13]. In order to discriminate between deceivers and non-deceivers we apply supervised learning with two learning algorithms: RVM and SVM. Classification is done after each day phase of the game. First the z-scores of the features are calculated over all features of each player. We use z-scores in order to take out user–specific behavior (e.g. visual activity, size of body) by subtracting the mean from each measurement and dividing it by the standard deviation of its distribution. This enables us to compare features from different individuals. For each game day, for each feature, we obtain a large set of z-scores (one per frame). From these, we extract statistics (e.g. entropy, mode, median, range, skew and kurtosis) that are used to learn the models.

5. EXPERIMENTS

For all players in the game, the frames where they speak are processed separately from the frames where there was no voice activity measured through their microphones. This allows experiments to be done on motion while speaking and while not speaking.

Because each game has only two wolves and many more villagers, the number of datapoints (all day games for all players) for villagers and wolves is not balanced. To balance both datasets, random subsampling is applied to the villagers datapoints. This results in 36 data points for wolves and 36 data points for villagers. To obtain comparable results with [7] 18-fold cross-validation was done. To ensure a representative variation for the experiments this process is repeated 1000 times.

The purpose of our experiments is to evaluate how much information about deception can be extracted from gross body motion, and to identify whether different parts of the body provide different information. Our focus is not on the specifics of the classification algorithm, and we report results with two different classifiers so as to make comparison with earlier work possible. These classifiers are: the Relevance Vector Machine (RVM), which was also used in [7] and the Support Vector Machine (SVM), because it is considered one of the best off-the-shelf general-purpose classifiers.

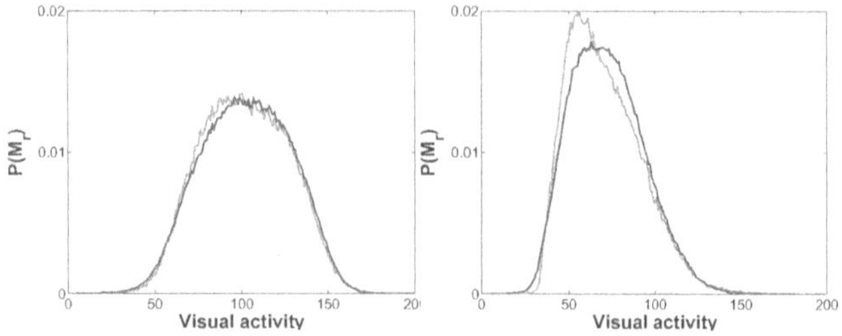

(a) H region (b) BML region

Figure 4: visual activity plots for regions H and BML. Red line shows wolves' and blue the villagers' distribution

Experiment 1: temporal difference. Features that are extracted from this data's distribution are entropy, mode, median, range, skew and kurtosis. This experiment is done on speech frames, non-speech frames and all frames.

Experiment 2: motion magnitude: For this experiment one histogram is calculated from all the motion magnitude histograms of all the frames of each player in a game day. The same features as in experiment 1 are extracted from these combined histograms.

Experiment 3: motion orientation: Similarly as in experiment 2, the motion orientation histograms for each region and player per game day are combined. The same features are extracted as mentioned in experiments 1 and 2

Experiment 4: combined video: In this experiments all features from the experiments 1, 2 and 3 are combined. PCA is applied on the features to reduce the dimensionality and get rid of non-informative features.

Experiment 5: combined audio video: For this experiment all video features from experiment 4 were used and fused with the audio features used by Chittaranjan and Hung [7]. PCA is applied on the features to reduce the dimensionality and get rid of non-informative features. Each of these experiments was carried out three times; first, for the features extracted from frames with speech; second, for features extracted from frames without speech; third, for features extracted from all frames.

6. RESULTS

Figure 4 a and b show normalized plots of the z-scores of the distribution of the temporal difference for the H and BML regions. The red lines represent the wolves' and blue lines represent the villagers' visual activity. Plots 4a and b clearly show that wolves move less then villagers. This phenomenon varies per region but occurs in all and is consistent with prior research [1, 2, 13]. Plots 4a and b also show BML region is more informative for deception detection than region H as the distribution of the wolves is clearly more skewed to lower visual activity values.

For all experiments the results are shown in tables 1 and 2. The best performing result of Chittaranjan and Hung [7] was used as baseline for our experiments. Their method's best performance, f-measure of 0.62, was obtained by fusing all the audio features.

Our best performing model is the one trained on all frames and all the video features fused (exp. 4). This model's f-

Table 1: Mean F-measures of liar (L) and non-liar (NL) classification using RVM.

Ex.	all frames		speech		non-speech	
	Reg.	L vs. NL	Reg.	L vs. NL	Reg.	L vs. NL
1	BML	0.62 ± 0.13	BML	0.61 ± 0.13	BML	0.62 ± 0.12
2	BML	0.66 ± 0.12	BML	0.67 ± 0.13	BML	0.66 ± 0.13
3	BL	0.60 ± 0.13	BL	0.61 ± 0.12	BL	0.60 ± 0.13
4	all	0.71 ± 0.18	all	0.66 ± 0.17	all	0.68 ± 0.18
5	all	0.72 ± 0.18	all	0.67 ± 0.17	all	0.70 ± 0.18

Table 2: Mean F-measures of liar (L) and non-liar (NL) classification using SVM.

Ex.	all frames		speech		non-speech	
	Reg.	L vs. NL	Reg.	L vs. NL	Reg.	L vs. NL
1	BML	0.62 ± 0.13	BR	0.60 ± 0.13	BML	0.62 ± 0.13
2	BML	0.69 ± 0.12	BML	0.68 ± 0.13	BML	0.71 ± 0.13
3	BL	0.61 ± 0.13	BML	0.65 ± 0.12	BL	0.61 ± 0.13
4	all	0.76 ± 0.17	all	0.66 ± 0.16	all	0.72 ± 0.18
5	all	0.75 ± 0.18	all	0.68 ± 0.17	all	0.73 ± 0.18

measure is 0.76, which is an improvement of 22.6% over the baseline. For all experiments the best performing regions are the body regions. From the body regions it seems that the area in the middle of the body (**BML** and **BMR**) is most informative for detecting deception in multi-party conversations. The **BML** and **BMR** regions' performance is almost identical.

From the models that are trained on either speech or non-speech frames, the model trained on non-speech frames and all the video features combined with the audio features, as used by Chittaranjan and Hung [7], (exp. 5) performs best with an average f-measure of 0.73. In the experiments where features are combined (exp. 4 and 5), models trained on non-speech frames always outperform models that are trained on speech frames. A possible explanation is that when people talk the focus is on them, therefore they try to control their body motion more. Another explanation is that only 12.16% of all frames are speech frames which might effect the quality of the model.

Out of all the uncombined video features (exp. 1, 2 and 3), regardless of speech activity, the motion magnitude of region **BML** performed the best. The average f-measure of this model is 0.69, which is an improvement of 11.3% over the baseline. This model's performance increased to 0.71 when it was trained on non-speech frames only. In the experiments with the uncombined features, the models learned on features from all frames never outperform the models that are trained on features extracted from speech or non-speech frames.

We performed a t-test to support our models' performance. The results from experiments 4 and 5 all outperform the baseline significantly at $\alpha = 0.05$. None of the models from experiments 1, 2 and 3 were significantly better than the baseline.

7. CONCLUSIONS

We successfully show that simple non-verbal video features, extracted automatically from low-quality video, can be used as indicators of deception in multi-party conversations. Our results also shows an increase in performance when classifiers trained on video features and on only speech frames. This is a promising result for audio-visual analysis of social interaction for detecting deception.

8. ACKNOWLEDGEMENTS

This research was supported in part by a Marie Curie Research Training Network fellowship in the project "AnaSID" (PIEF-GA-2009-255609) and by the SIA project 'Smart Systems for Smart Services'. We thank Gokul Chittaranjan for providing help and code for extracting audio features and the RVM.

References

[1] Aldert Vrij. *Detecting Lies and Deceit: Pitfalls and Opportunities, 2nd Edition.* Wiley, 2008. ISBN 978-0-470-51624-9.

[2] Paul Ekman. *Telling lies.* Norton, New York, New York, 2001. ISBN 0-393-32188-6.

[3] Hayley Hung and Gokul Chittaranjan. The idiap wolf corpus: exploring group behaviour in a competitive role-playing game. ACM MM, 2010.

[4] Matthew Jensen, Thomas Meservy, Judee Burgoon, and Jay Nunamaker. Automatic, multimodal evaluation of human interaction. *Group Decision and Negotiation*, 19: 367–389(23), July 2010.

[5] Sebastian Germesin and Theresa Wilson. Agreement detection in multiparty conversation. ICMI-MLMI, 2009.

[6] Julia Hirschberg, Stefan Benus, Jason M. Brenier, Frank Enos, Sarah Friedman, Sarah Gilman, Cynthia Gir, Martin Graciarena, Andreas Kathol, and Laura Michaelis. Distinguishing deceptive from non-deceptive speech. In *Interspeech*, 2005.

[7] Gokul Chittaranjan and Hayley Hung. Are you a werewolf? detecting deceptive roles and outcomes in a conversational role-playing game. In *ICASSP*, 2010.

[8] Konstantinos Bousmalis, Marc Mehu, and Maja Pantic. Spotting agreement and disagreement: A survey of nonverbal audiovisual cues and tools. ACII, 2009.

[9] Nick Campbell. An audio-visual approach to measuring discourse synchrony in multimodal conversation data. In *Interspeech*, pages 2159–2162. ISCA, 2009.

[10] Hayley Hung, Dinesh Jayagopi, Chuohao Yeo, Gerald Friedland, Sileye Ba, Jean-Marc Odobez, Kannan Ramchandran, Nikki Mirghafori, and Daniel Gatica-Perez. Using audio and video features to classify the most dominant person in a group meeting. ACM MM, 2007.

[11] Dinesh Babu Jayagopi, Hayley Hung, Chuohao Yeo, and Daniel Gatica-Perez. Modeling dominance in group conversations using nonverbal activity cues. *IEEE Trans. Audio, Speech and Lang. Proc.*, 17:501–513, March 2009.

[12] S Benus, F Enos, J Hirschberg, and E Shriberg. Pauses in deceptive speech. *Speech Prosody*, 18:2–5, 2006.

[13] Thomas O. Meservy, Matthew L. Jensen, John Kruse, Douglas P. Twitchell, Gabriel Tsechpenakis, Judee K. Burgoon, Dimitris N. Metaxas, and Jay F. Nunamaker Jr. Deception detection through automatic, unobtrusive analysis of nonverbal behavior. *IEEE Intelligent Systems*, 20:36–43, 2005.

[14] Thomas O. Meservy, Matthew L. Jensen, John Kruse, Judee K. Burgoon, and Jay F. Nunamaker. Automatic extraction of deceptive behavioral cues from video. In *ISI*, pages 198–208, 2005.

[15] Ce Liu. *Beyond Pixels: Exploring New Representations and Applications for Motion Analysis.* PhD thesis, Massachusetts Institute of Technology, May 2009.

Multimodal Person Independent Recognition of Workload Related Biosignal Patterns

Jan Jarvis, Felix Putze, Dominic Heger and Tanja Schultz
Cognitive Systems Lab, Karlsruhe Institute of Technology
Karlsruhe, Germany
jan.jarvis@student.kit.edu, felix.putze@kit.edu, dominic.heger@kit.edu, tanja.schultz@kit.edu

ABSTRACT

This paper presents an online multimodal person independent workload classification system using blood volume pressure, respiration measures, electrodermal activity and electroencephalography. For each modality a classifier based on linear discriminant analysis is trained. The classification results obtained on short data frames are fused using weighted majority voting. The system was trained and evaluated on a large training corpus of 152 participants, exposed to controlled and uncontrolled scenarios for inducing workload, including a driving task conducted in a realistic driving simulator. Using person dependent feature space normalization, we achieve a classification accuracy of up to 94% for discrimination of relaxed state vs. high workload.

Categories and Subject Descriptors: I.5.4 [Pattern Recognition]: Signal Processing;

General Terms: Human Factors, Design, Experimentation.

1. INTRODUCTION

In the context of human-machine interaction, real-time detection of user states becomes increasingly interesting. While modern dialog systems are making their way into real life applications the communication with the user remains to be independent of his inner state. This leads to unnatural and often time consuming communication behavior between users and their machines. We believe that empathic dialog systems that adapt their strategies to the user's inner state would greatly improve the human-machine-interaction. This is especially true for the task of car driving. Mental distraction has a negative impact on driving performance and therefore seriously affects safety in every day traffic (e.g. [9]). In-vehicle dialog systems designed to facilitate, support and entertain the user while driving could benefit from a greater insight in the driver's workload level by reacting appropriately to his inner state [5].

ICMI'11, November 14–18, 2011, Alicante, Spain.

Assessing human mental workload using biosignals has been subject to many studies in the past few years (e.g. [3], [5]). Although some of them prove to work well using user specific training data, yet the task of building a user independent system remains to be a challenge. We propose to use feature space adaptation to remedy this constraint.

Especially while driving, the inner state of humans can be subject to rapid changes. This imposes extra constraints on time resolution of workload detection for in-vehicle purpose. The time resolution of classification systems based on biosignals is usually governed by the frame size used. Therefore we investigate how far it is possible to reduce the frame size without affecting classification accuracy.

In contrast to workload detection in a controlled laboratory environment, biosignals recorded during car driving are subject to various external and internal artifacts. In this work both data from a controlled laboratory scenario and lesser controlled data recorded in a car driving scenario were used to evaluate the classification system.

2. RELATED WORK

Techniques for assessing biosignals in an in-vehicle environment are converging into real-world experimental settings. Lin et al. [10] present a steering wheel containing a set of sensors for measurement of various biosignals. The steering wheel captures the driver's pulse and breathing wave using a polivinylidene fluoride film, skin temperature using a simple temperature sensor, and gripping force using a piezoelectric element. The sensors are placed around the steering wheel, rendering the position of the driver's hands on the wheel irrelevant to continuous signal capturing.

Systems for assessing the driver's vigilance using cameras for cornea- or eyelid tracking have been subject to various studies. Bergasa et al. [2] developed a real-time system for monitoring driver vigilance. In this work six parameters are calculated from facial features: percentage of eye closure, eye closure duration, blink frequency, nodding frequency, face position and fixed gaze. The system was tested and evaluated in a real car condition at day and night. At night a classification accuracy near 100% was reported for detection of simulated fatigue. Bright lighting conditions and drivers wearing glasses caused difficulties.

Healey and Picard [3] developed a classifier to monitor the stress levels in daily life car driving tasks. They collected data from 24 real-life drives of at least fifty minute duration using the biosignals electromyography and skin conductance for classification. Linear discriminant analysis (LDA) was used for dimensionality reduction and a classifier using a linear decision function was able to discriminate the three classes with accuracies of 100% (low workload), 94.7% (medium workload), and 97.4% (high workload).

Heger et al. [5] conducted a study towards online workload recognition using EEG data only. In their study, they present an EEG based workload recognition system trained and evaluated on five participants exposed various workload inducing tasks. They reported classification accuracies of up to 91% using user dependent training and an average accuracy of 72% using a user independent approach.

3. DATA COLLECTION

The data used for this work was collected during an extensive biosignal collection study[1] at Karlsruhe Institute of Technology (KIT). In this study a total number of 152 participants were presented a variety of cognitive tests.

We distinguish two data collection scenarios:

Controlled: In this scenario the participant was presented a cognitive test following a switching paradigm: In each trial the subject was visually presented a number from the set $[1, \ldots, 4, 6, \ldots, 9]$ surrounded with a box (solid or dashed). Depending on the line style the subject had to decide whether the number was even or odd (solid outline) or if the number was greater or smaller than 5 (dashed outline).

Uncontrolled: In this scenario the participant was seated in realistic driving simulator based on a real car corpus and presented the following tasks: a plain driving task using the Lane Change Task (LCT) [8], the LCT with an additional visual task and finally the LCT with an additional auditive switch-back-2 task. This scenario will be referred to as the *uncontrolled* scenario, as the recorded biosignals are expected to contain an increased amount of artifacts e.g. caused by movement of the participant. Both data collection scenarios included at least one relaxing phase.

In the visual secondary task the participant was presented a screen containing a set of graphical symbols and asked to indicate the position of a specific one. The auditive secondary task was a switch-back-2 task. The participant listened to a series of pre-recorded numbers from the set $[1, \ldots, 9]$ and were asked to identify pairs of identical numbers in the series, placed exactly two places apart.

While working on the tasks a variety of biosignals was recorded: Peripheral blood volume pressure was measured using a photoplethysmograph (PPG) placed on the participant's left index finger and recorded at a sampling rate of 256 Hz. Electrodermal activity (EDA) was recorded at a rate of 256 Hz and measured by a skin conductivity sensor placed on the palm of the participant's left hand. EDA and PPG sensor were both placed in a glove transmitting the signals to the recording system via BlueTooth. Respiration (RESP) was measured using a respiration belt. The belt was placed below the participant's thorax and worn above all layers of clothing. The RESP signal was sampled at 512 Hz. An active EEG-cap (Brain Products' *ActiCap*) was used to measure brain activity. The EEG-cap contains 16 active electrodes placed at the following positions according to the international 10-20-positioning system: FP1, FP2, F3, F4, F7, F8, T3, T4, C3, Cz, C4, P3, Pz, O1 and O2 with reference to the left mastoid. EEG data was recorded at a sampling rate of 256 Hz. For data recording and stimulus presentation we used *BiosignalsStudio* [4].

[1]We owe special thanks to Janina Krell and Klaus Bös of KIT and Alexander Stahn of *Charité Berlin* for collaborating in participant recruitment and organization of the study.

id	ctrld	low task	high task
C0	yes	relax phase	switching task
U0	no	relax phase	switch back auditive 2 with additional driving task
U1	no	plain driving task	switch back auditive 2 with additional driving task
U2	no	plain driving task	visual search task with additional driving task

Table 1: Binary discrimination tasks, using data from controlled (ctrld) and uncontrolled data collection scenario.

We defined a subset of the first 75 sessions as *development set* on which we use session-wise cross-validation to train and evaluate the system during development. All other sessions are left untouched to form a test set for final evaluation. We deliberately dispense with manual inspection of raw data for detection of faulty sessions as we expect recording artifacts to be a common problem for real-world applications. All recorded sessions are used for system evaluation, regardless of recording errors like poorly placed or missing EEG electrodes. We believe that this approach yields a reliable estimate for classification accuracy in real-world applications. From these scenarios we define four binary classification tasks summarized in table 1. Here we also give the abbreviations used for reference in the following.

4. SYSTEM SETUP

Our classification system is implemented using Linear Discriminant Analysis (LDA) for classification. To retrieve a continuous measure of the user's workload, classification is performed on features extracted from moving data frames. The different natures of the biosignals used in this study require the usage of individual frame sizes. A careful analysis of the signal and consideration of feature stability lead us to choose: EEG: 2s, PPG: 6s, EDA: 4s and RESP: 10s. The features in each time step are aligned by the latest sample used for feature calculation. We chose a 0.25 second frame shift to gain a decision rate of 4 Hz. As the frequency of the user's workload level change is expected to be well lower than 4 Hz, a running majority vote filter of 2 second length is applied to the decision output of each classifier prior to fusion. For each modality an individual LDA classifier is trained and decision fusion is performed to gain a final classification result. The decisions of all classifiers are fused in every time step using weighted majority voting. The voting weights are set to a value between 0 and 1 depending on the classification accuracy during classifier training.

4.1 Preprocessing and Feature Extraction

The features derived from the PPG, EDA and Respiration signals were chosen as follows (for details see [11]):

PPG: mean heart rate (PPG_MHR), standard deviation of heart rate (PPG_STD) and band powers in the three bands 0-0.08 Hz, 0.08 - 0.15 Hz and 0.15-5 Hz (PPG_BPWR_1, ..., PPG_BPWR_3).

EDA: signal mean and standard deviation (EDA_MEAN, EDA_STD), number of startles, sum of startle amplitudes, sum of startle duration and estimated area under startles (EDA_STNO, EDA_STSUM, EDA_STDUR AND EDA_ST_AREA). *Startles* are sudden rises in the signal amplitude and are automatically detected inspecting the signals slope after removing the signals linear trend and applying a low pass filter with a cut off frequency of 1 Hz.

RESP: mean respiration rate and variance (RESP_MEAN, RESP_VAR), respiration depth (RESP_DPTH). Additionally: signal energies in the four bands 0-0.1 Hz, 0.1-0.2 Hz, 0.2-0.3 Hz and 0.3-0.4 Hz (RESP_BPWR_1, ..., RESP_BPWR_4).

Prior to EEG feature calculation, a preprocessing step based on Independent Component Analysis (ICA) is applied to remove eye movement artifacts from the raw signal. ICA is a blind source separation algorithm decomposing a set of (mixed) signals into a set of source signals [6]. The usage of ICA for the purpose of reducing eye movement artifacts in EEG signals was proposed by Jung et al. in [7]. As eye movement artifacts occur highly correlated in all electrodes near the frontal lobe, ICA is expected to return a decomposition containing these artifacts in one single component. Usually this component is identified manually. We propose an algorithm using the ICA components' energies for automatic eye movement component detection. The components are first filtered using a band-pass filter with cut off frequencies 1 - 6 Hz. Choosing the component with the highest energy leads to a robust estimate of the eye movement component. The filtered signal is obtained, by applying a high-pass filter with a cut off frequency of 20 Hz to the eye movement component and calculating the inverse ICA transform of the modified components.

Two feature extraction methods are applied to the preprocessed EEG signals:

EEG Bandbased: Signal energies in the classical frequency bands θ: 4-7 Hz, α: 8-12 Hz β: 12-30 Hz and γ: 30-40 Hz. To avoid leakage effects a hamming window is applied to the signal before calculation of Fast Fourier Transform. Additionally the spectrum is logarithmized to boost lower frequency coefficients. The band energies for all channels are concatenated yielding a 64 dimensional feature vector.

EEG Wavelet: The EEG wavelet feature extraction was implemented using Discrete Wavelet Transformation. We chose Daubechies' order 3 wavelets and the decomposition levels 2 to 5, to let the pseudo-frequencies roughly correspond to the classical bandpowers [1]. The signal power in each decomposition level and for each EEG channel is used as a feature, yielding a 64-dimensional feature vector, too.

4.2 Feature Space Normalization

We evaluate three different feature space normalization approaches to person independent workload classification. A naïve approach using no feature normalization (NO_NORM), which is not expected to perform very well as inter-individual signal properties are ignored. As a second approach we evaluate feature space normalization using a person-wise z-norm approach (mean subtraction and division by standard deviation) in every feature space dimension (TEST_NORM) on both training and test data. However, this is an approach not suited for many real-world applications, as data is used for normalization which is not in general available to an online recognizer (at a given time data not yet recorded would have to be used for calculation of mean and standard deviation). Therefore, we use a normalization scheme calculating mean and standard deviation for each feature and user, from a previously recorded data set not used in training or testing (EXT_NORM). This approach can be carried into real-world applications using bootstrapping from unlabeled data at the beginning of a session. However, it is important to note that mean and standard deviation estimates - and therefore the z-normalization result itself - are dependent on class distributions. For TEST_NORM, the class distribution has to be assumed to be equal in training and evaluation data. When using EXT_NORM the class distribution has to be assumed to be equal during the bootstrapping phase for each session. In our data set, this constraint is met rendering both normalization methods applicable.

5. EVALUATION

We used two different measures to assess the discriminative power for each feature presented in section 4.1 individually. As a straight forward approach we evaluate a linear classifier on a one-dimensional feature space for each feature and use the resulting f-scores as a measure of discriminative power (FDP). For an alternative measure - discriminative power by significance (SDP) - we calculate non-paired t-tests. For the t-tests, two samples are formed by the feature means from all sessions for the low and high workload class. The null-hypotheses is rejected for p-values lower than 1%.

To assess the impact of feature space normalization we compare the discriminative power measures applying the NO_NORM, TEST_NORM and EXT_NORM normalization methods obtained on the C0 classification task (table 2). Using no normalization yields a total number of 11 features with statistical significant feature means. In contrast, using the TEST_NORM normalization method, only one feature misses statistical significance, while EXT_NORM still leads to 16 significant features. These results are supported by the average FDP value for the normalization methods. While the NO_NORM method leads to an average of only 61%, an average of 67% is achieved using TEST_NORM. EXT_NORM yields an average FDP in between (65%). This suggests that classification using EXT_NORM is only slightly worse than using TEST_NORM and is a valuable alternative if TEST_NORM is not available, e.g. for online workload recognition systems.

	NO_NORM		TEST_NORM		EXT_NORM	
	FDP	SDP	FDP	SDP	FDP	SDP
PPG_MHR	60.61	0.001	74.65	0.000	74.86	0.000
PPG_STD	63.24	0.000	64.34	0.000	63.76	0.000
PPG_BP_1	52.69	0.022	54.55	0.000	54.52	0.000
PPG_BP_2	53.67	0.011	55.89	0.000	56.13	0.000
PPG_BP_3	65.66	0.000	72.04	0.000	70.15	0.000
EDA_MEAN	62.65	0.012	89.78	0.000	82.99	0.000
EDA_STD	65.50	0.002	69.76	0.000	66.93	0.001
EDA_STNO	49.98	0.000	56.45	0.000	55.30	0.000
EDA_STSUM	59.09	0.001	67.31	0.000	65.35	0.002
EDA_STDUR	53.65	0.006	53.49	0.000	53.56	0.001
EDA_STAREA	66.27	0.001	67.80	0.000	65.60	0.000
RESP_MEAN	71.76	0.000	74.10	0.000	74.25	0.000
RESP_DPTH	66.83	0.211	72.60	0.003	70.95	0.000
RESP_BPWR_1	51.96	0.383	53.77	0.000	46.16	0.169
RESP_BPWR_2	64.59	0.000	67.95	0.000	66.94	0.000
RESP_BPWR_3	63.99	0.000	64.43	0.000	65.01	0.000
RESP_BPWR_4	67.37	0.000	72.77	0.000	66.37	0.000
μ(FDP) NSF	61.15	11	66.57	17	64,64	16

Table 2: Discriminative power for single feature evaluation using cross-validation on C0 classification task and number of significant features (NSF).

As the feature space dimensions yielded by the EEG feature extractors are too large for a comparable evaluation, we dispense with a detailed analysis in this paper. Nevertheless it should be stated that our research revealed a similar im-

	EEG_B	EEG_W	PPG	EDA	RESP	DEC
C0	85.54	84.92	79.66	84.90	81.60	93.28
U0	72.14	49.66	81.27	71.70	72.25	83.29

Table 3: F-scores using session wise leave-one-out cross validation on the C0 and U0 classification tasks and f-scores of decision fusion (DEC) using EXT_NORM normalization.

	EEG_B	EEG_W	PPG	EDA	RESP	DEC
U1 (TN)	65.19	76.16	47.07	58.35	57.53	69.99
U1 (EN)	55.69	65.15	49.04	62.64	42.49	60.50
U2 (TN)	75.47	70.73	50.77	57.35	67.29	76.76
U2 (EN)	73.82	62.89	51.03	56.45	49.41	66.16

Table 4: F-scores obtained using session-wise cross validation on U1 and U2 classification tasks, using TEST_NORM (TN) and EXT_NORM (EN) normalization.

pact of normalization on the feature spaces yielded by both EEG feature extraction methods.

To determine the impact of the controlled vs. uncontrolled data collection scenario, we compare the classification accuracies yielded on the C0 and U0 classification task (table 3). While all single-modal classifiers yield decreased f-scores in the uncontrolled scenario the accuracy reduction is especially pronounced for the EEG classifiers. Visual inspection of EEG data in both data collection scenarios revealed a strong disturbance of the EEG signals recorded in the driving simulator (predominantly due to head movement and electromagnetic fields produced by various electrical devices). We account the reduction of EEG classification accuracy to these signal artifacts. Yet the accuracy obtained by decision fusion (83%) is only 10% absolute below the accuracy obtained in the controlled data collection environment.

The classification tasks U1 and U2 define low and high workload classes using two tasks of different difficulty (single-task vs. dual-task) instead of a relaxed state and a task. This is more difficult to differentiate from physiological parameters and thus recognition rates drop to 61% and 66% for EXT_NORM and respectively 70% and 77% for TEST_NORM. Still, we see that using decision fusion we achieve a respectable person-independent f-score. Interestingly, we also see an inversion of the performance for the single modalities, as EEG features are now contributing most to the overall result. This indicates that EEG is more suited for classification tasks with more subtle differences between conditions. As no modality was dominant across all conditions, this again underlines the importance of multimodal fusion.

The previous results were obtained using session-wise cross validation on the development set. In table 5 we present the recognition accuracies yielded by our classification system, trained on the development set and evaluated on the test set as described in section 3. Although the classification accuracies of the individual classifiers differ slightly, the accuracies obtained by decision fusion are not more than 4% absolute below the results obtained on the development set for all classification tasks. These results indicate that the system generalizes well across participants.

To validate the ground truth learned by the system, we analyzed the feature space distributions in table 2. This analysis revealed an increased sympathic nervous system activity during the high workload tasks thus indicating an excited psychological state. The discriminative powers in table 2 suggest, that low p-values correspond to high classification

	EEG_B	EEG_W	PPG	EDA	RESP	DEC
C0	76.16	76.04	73.40	84.75	81.24	90.66
U0	80.54	71.74	86.41	67.83	81.66	93.58
U1	64.35	65.31	49.15	57.51	43.65	64.48
U2	75.93	62.82	43.59	49.96	45.17	62.40

Table 5: F-scores obtained on test set for all classification tasks using the EXT_NORM normalization method.

accuracies. From this we conclude, that the classification systems learned to discriminate classes by employing features that are actually related to human mental workload. Additionally, we validated that the participants' subjective mental workload in the evaluation tasks actually matched the expected level of workload using the well known NASA-TLX questionnaire.

In this paper we prove that feature space adaption is effective for the task of building a person independent workload recognition system. Yet, using an approach comparable to the TEST_NORM normalization method, leads to over estimated accuracies for online-recognition systems. Using the EXT_NORM normalization method we obtained accuracies of 91% (controlled) and 94% (uncontrolled data collection scenario) for the task of discrimination between relaxed states and high mental workload states.

6. REFERENCES

[1] H. Adeli, Z. Zhou, and N. Dadmehr. Analysis of EEG records in an epileptic patient using wavelet transform. *Journal of Neuroscience Methods*, 123(1):69–87, 2003.

[2] L. Bergasa, J. Nuevo, M. Sotelo, R. Barea, and M. Lopez. Real-time system for monitoring driver vigilance. *Intelligent Transportation Systems, IEEE Transactions on*, 7(1):63–77, 2006.

[3] J. Healey and R. Picard. Detecting stress during real-world driving tasks using physiological sensors. *Intelligent Transportation Systems, IEEE Transactions on*, 6(2):156–166, 2005.

[4] D. Heger, F. Putze, C. Amma, M. Wand, I. Plotkin, T. Wielatt, and T. Schultz. Biosignalsstudio: a flexible framework for biosignal capturing and processing. *KI 2010: Advances in Artificial Intelligence*, 2010.

[5] D. Heger, F. Putze, and T. Schultz. Online workload recognition from eeg data during cognitive tests and human-machine interaction. *KI 2010: Advances in Artificial Intelligence*, pages 410–417, 2010.

[6] A. Hyvärinen and E. Oja. Independent component analysis: algorithms and applications. *Neural networks*, 13(4-5):411–430, 2000.

[7] T. Jung, S. Makeig, C. Humphries, T. Lee, M. McKeown, V. Iragui, and T. Sejnowski. Removing electroencephalographic artifacts by blind source separation. *Psychophysiology*, 37(2):163–178, 2000.

[8] F. Kuhn. Methode zur Bewertung der Fahrerablenkung durch Fahrerinformations-Systeme. *World Usability Day*, 2005.

[9] T. Lansdown, N. Brook-Carter, and T. Kersloot. Distraction from multiple in-vehicle secondary tasks: vehicle performance and mental workload implications. *Ergonomics*, 47(1):91–104, 2004.

[10] Y. Lin, H. Leng, G. Yang, and H. Cai. An intelligent noninvasive sensor for driver pulse wave measurement. *Sensors Journal, IEEE*, 7(5):790–799, 2007.

[11] F. Putze, J.-P. Jarvis, and T. Schultz. Multimodal recognition of cognitive workload for multitasking in the car. In *Proc. 20th Int Pattern Recognition (ICPR) Conf*, pages 3748–3751, 2010.

Study of Different Interactive Editing Operations in an Assisted Transcription System

Verónica Romero, Alejandro H. Toselli and Enrique Vidal
Instituto Tecnológico de Informática, Universitat Politècnica de València, Spain
{vromero,ahector,evidal}@iti.upv.es

ABSTRACT

To date, automatic handwriting recognition systems are far from being perfect. Therefore, once the full recognition process of a handwritten text image has finished, heavy human intervention is required in order to correct the results of such systems. As an alternative, an interactive system has been proposed in previous works. This alternative follows an Interactive Predictive paradigm and the results show that significant amounts of human effort can be saved. So far only word substitutions and pointer actions have been considered in this interactive system. In this work, we study different interactive editing operations that can allow for more effective, ergonomic and friendly interfaces.

Categories and Subject Descriptors

H.4 [**Information Systems Applications**]: Interaction styles; I.5.5 [**Pattern Recognition**]: Interactive systems

General Terms

Interaction, Design

Keywords

Computer assisted transcription, Handwritten Text Recognition, Editing Operations

1. INTRODUCTION

Many documents used every day include handwritten text and, in many cases, it would be interesting to recognize these text images automatically. To date, automatic off-line handwriting recognition systems (HTR) have proven to be suitable for restricted applications with limited vocabulary, achieving in these kinds of tasks relatively high accuracy. However, in the case of unconstrained transcription applications, such as old handwritten documents, the current HTR technology typically achieves results which do not meet the quality requirements of practical applications. Therefore, when transcribing a document image, usually a post-edition process is needed, which is far from being an ideal solution.

An interactive on-line scenario has been presented in [8, 9] as an alternative to post-editing. This scenario is called "Computer Assisted Transcription of Handwritten Text Images" (CATTI). Rather than full automation, it aims at assisting the human in the proper recognition-transcription process; that is, at easing and at speeding up the task of handwritten text transcription. In this scenario, the system uses the text image and a previously validated part (prefix) of its transcription to propose a suitable continuation. Then the user finds and corrects the next system error, thereby providing a longer prefix which the system uses to suggest a new hopefully better continuation. According to experiments and real field tests [4], the approach saves significant amounts of estimated user effort.

In CATTI applications the user is repeatedly interacting with the system. Hence, making the interaction process easy is crucial for the success of the system. In previous works only substitutions [8] of the erroneous words have been considered. In this paper, we consider a new set of editing operations and study their effect on the CATTI performance and whether the interaction process might be friendlier to the user.

2. CATTI FRAMEWORK

In the CATTI framework, the user is involved in the transcription process since she is responsible for validating and/or correcting the HTR output [8]. The protocol that rules this process can be formulated in the following steps, which are iterated until a correct transcription is obtained (see Fig. 1):

(a) The HTR system proposes a full transcription ($\hat{s}$) of an input handwritten text line image. (b) The user validates the longest prefix which is error-free and enters some keystrokes (word v) to correct the first error in the suffix. (c) An extended correct prefix (p) is produced based on the previously validated prefix and the corrections made by the user. (d) Using this new prefix, the system suggests a suitable continuation ($\hat{s}$) and the process iterates (b)–(d) until a satisfactory result is achieved.

At each step of this process, both the image representation, x, and a correct transcription prefix p are available and the HTR system should try to complete this prefix by searching for the most likely suffix $\hat{s}$ according to [8]:

$$\hat{s} = \arg\max_s P(s \mid x, p) = \arg\max_s P(x \mid p, s) \cdot P(s \mid p) \quad (1)$$

Since the concatenation of p and s constitutes a full transcription hypothesis, $P(x \mid p, s)$ can be approximated by

	x	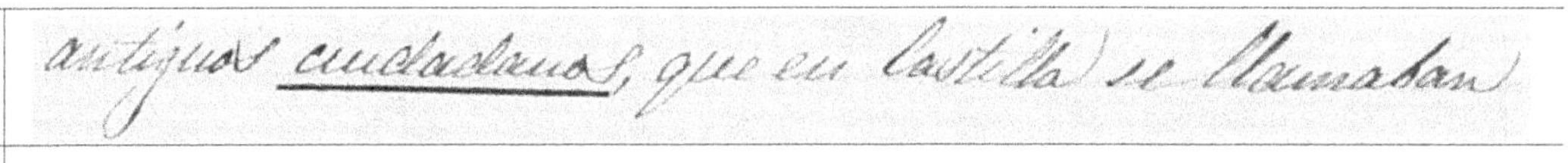							
INTER-0	p								
INTER-1	$\hat{s} \equiv \hat{w}$	antiguos	cuidadores	que	en	el Castillo	sus	llamadas	
	p'	antiguos							
	v		ciudadanos						
	p	antiguos	ciudadanos						
INTER-2	$\hat{s}$			que	en	el Castillo	sus	llamadas	
	p'	antiguos	ciudadanos	que	en				
	v					Castilla			
	p	antiguos	ciudadanos	que	en	Castilla			
FINAL	$\hat{s}$						se	llamaban	
	v								#
	$p \equiv T$	antiguos	***ciudadanos***	que	en	***Castilla***	se	llamaban	

Figure 1: Example of CATTI interaction. Initially the prefix p is empty, and the system proposes a complete transcription $\hat{s} \equiv \hat{w}$ of the input image x. In each interaction step the user validates its longest well-recognized prefix p' and corrects the following erroneous word v generating a new prefix p (p' plus the word v). At this point, the system suggests a suitable continuation $\hat{s}$ of this prefix p and this process is repeated until a complete and correct transcription of the input signal is reached. In the final transcription, T, the underlined boldface words are the words typed by the user. In this example the estimated post-editing effort is 5/7 (71%), while the corresponding interactive estimate is 2/7 (29%). This results in an estimated effort reduction of 59%.

concatenated character Hidden Markov Models (HMMs) [2] as in conventional HTR. On the other hand, $P(s \mid p)$ is approximated by dynamically modifying a n-gram model in order to cope with the increasingly consolidated prefixes [8]:

$$P(s \mid p) \simeq \prod_{j=1}^{n-1} P(s_j \mid p_{k-n+1+j}^{k}, s_1^{j-1}) \cdot \prod_{j=n}^{l} P(s_j \mid s_{j-n+1}^{j-1}) \tag{2}$$

where $p = p_1^k$ is a consolidated prefix and $s = s_1^l$ a possible suffix.

In order to improve human transcriber productivity and to make the previous defined protocol friendlier for the user, in addition to allowing the user to write the full correct word [8], "pure" *pointer action feedback* was studied in [6].

Furthering the goal of making the interaction process friendlier to the user, in this work, we carry out a study of additional interactive editing operations. Note that each interactive editing operation generates a different prefix. Therefore, the suffix proposed by the system in each user interaction depends on the editing operation carried out. In the next subsection a detailed description of the different interactive editing operations is given.

2.1 Interactive editing operations in CATTI

We consider here that user interaction is not limited to writing fully correct words or make pointer actions. Now the different editing operations that can be carried out (using pen-strokes and/or keystrokes) and the corresponding validated prefix are:

- *Substitution:* This is the conventional editing operation. Here the first erroneous word is replaced with the correct word. The accepted prefix consists of all the words preceding the wrong word plus the correct word. This kind of interaction has been studied in [9, 8] using a keyboard and/or an e-pen or a touchscreen.
- *Insertion:* A new word is inserted between two correct words. The validated prefix is composed of all the words preceding the inserted word, the inserted word and the word that follows the inserted word.
- *Deletion:* An incorrect word between two correct words is deleted. The accepted prefix consists of all the words preceding the deleted word plus the word that follows the deleted word.
- *Swap:* The order of two consecutive words is exchanged. The accepted prefix contains all the words until the swapped words plus the swapped words in the new order.
- *Join:* Two consecutive (incorrect) words are joined to generate a new correct word. The validated prefix is composed of all the words that precede the joined words plus the new generated word.
- *Split:* An (incorrect) word is divided into two different words. The validated prefix consists of all the words until the splitted word followed by the new two words.

In this study we will focus mainly on the new editing operations; that is, insertion, deletion, swap, join and split. The aim of these additional editing operations is to make the transcription process friendlier to the user and to reduce the human effort required to obtain a perfect transcription. For example, if the recognizer made a joining mistake, it will take less effort from the user to make a "splitting" operation, rather than two substitutions.

3. HTR SYSTEM OVERVIEW

The off-line HTR system used here follows a classical architecture composed of three modules: preprocessing, feature extraction and recognition.

The following steps take place in the preprocessing module: first, the skew of each page is corrected. Then, conventional noise reduction methods are applied on the whole document image, whose output is then fed to the line extraction process which divides it into separate text lines images. Finally, slant and slope correction and size normalization are applied to each separate line. A detailed description can be found in [7].

Each preprocessed line image is represented as a sequence of feature vectors. The feature extraction module applies a grid to divide a text line image into squared cells and three smoothed features are calculated from each of them: normalized gray level, horizontal gray level derivative and vertical gray level derivative. The way these three features are determined is described in [7]. Columns of cells or *frames* are processed from left to right and a feature vector is constructed for each *frame* by stacking the three features computed in its constituent cells.

Each character is modelled by a continuous density left-to-right HMM with a Gaussian mixture per state. In turn, each lexical entry (word) is modelled by a stochastic finite-state automaton, which represents all possible concatenations of individual characters to compose the word. On the other hand, text lines or sentences are modelled using bi-gram models, with Kneser-Ney back-off smoothing [3], estimated from the training transcriptions of the text images.

All these (character, word and lines) models can be easily *integrated* into a single *global* finite-state model with which a search process is performed for decoding the input feature vectors sequence x into a (huge) set of most probable word sequence hypotheses, represented as a *word graph*. This search is efficiently carried out using the Viterbi algorithm. The resulting word graph can then be used to efficiently solve Eq. (1) at each interactive-predictive step.

4. EXPERIMENTAL FRAMEWORK

In order to test the effectiveness of using these interactive editing operations in a CATTI system, different experiments were carried out. The corpus, the different measures and the obtained experimental results are explained below.

4.1 CS Corpus

This corpus was compiled from a legacy handwritten document from the XIX century identified as "Cristo-Salvador" (CS), which was provided by the *Biblioteca Valenciana*[1].

It is composed of 53 text page images, written by only one writer and scanned at 300dpi. This corpus is a legacy document and it suffers the typical degradation problems of this kind of documents [1]. Among these are the presence of smear, significant background variations and marks resulting from the ink that goes through the paper. In addition, other kind of difficulties appear, such as different text sizes, underlined words, etc. The combination of these problems make the recognition of this document a difficult process. Figure 2 shows a portion of one of the CS pages.

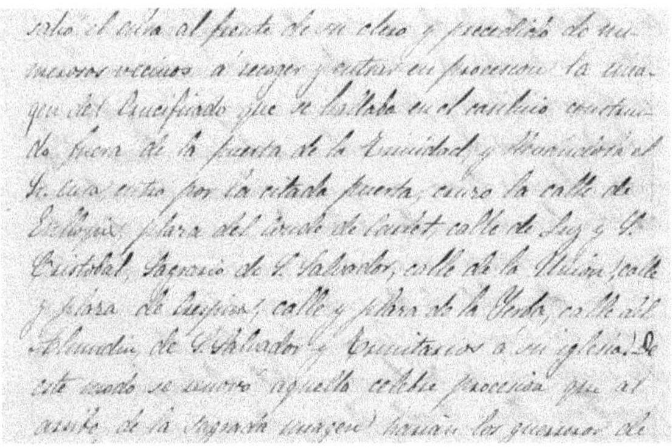

Figure 2: Detail of a page from the CS corpus.

[1]http://bv2.gva.es

The page images were preprocessed and automatically divided into line images. The results were visually inspected and the few line-split errors (around 4%) were manually corrected, resulting in a data-set of 1,172 text line images. The transcriptions corresponding to these images are also available, containing 10 918 running words with a vocabulary of 3,287 different words. These text line images where divided into training and test sets. The test set is composed of 497 line samples belonging to the last 20 document pages, whereas the remaining 675 lines (the 33 initial pages) were assigned to the training set. This partition is known as the "book" or "hard" partition in [5]. All the information related with this corpus is summarized in the Table 1.

Table 1: Basic statistics of the CS dataset.

Number of:	Training	Test	Total	Lexicon	Tr. Ratio
Pages	33	20	53	–	–
Text lines	675	497	1,172	–	–
Words	6,227	4,691	10,918	2,237	2.8
Characters	35,863	26,353	62,216	78	460

Only the text corresponding to the training partition has been used to train the n-gram and HMM models. However, test words not seen in training are added to the back-off 1-gram model (this is often called a "closed vocabulary" experiment). On the other hand, the last column shows the "*training ratio*", that is, the average number of times that one word/character has appeared in the training text. It is important to remark that this corpus has quite a small word training ratio (around 2.8 training running words per lexicon-entry). This is expected to result in undertrained (n-gram) language models, which will clearly increase the difficulty of the recognition task.

4.2 Evaluation metrics

Different objective evaluation measures based on labelled test corpora have been adopted. On the one hand, the post-editing human effort needed to fix the errors produced by (non-interactive) automatic transcription is estimated by the well known word error rate (WER). And, on the other hand, the effort needed by a human transcriptor to produce correct transcriptions using the CATTI system is assessed by the word stroke ratio (WSR). Both measures are defined as follow:

WER : Minimum number of words that need to be substituted, deleted or inserted to convert a sentence recognized by the system into the corresponding reference transcription, divided by the total number of words in this transcription.

WSR : Number of required interactive word corrections divided by the total number of reference words.

WSR is computed using a reference transcription of the text image considered. After a first CATTI hypothesis, the longest common prefix between this hypothesis and the reference is obtained and the first unmatching word from the hypothesis is replaced with the corresponding reference word. This process is iterated until a full match with the reference is achieved.

The relative difference between WER and WSR (called Estimated Effort-Reduction) gives us an estimation of the reduction in human effort that can be achieved, in terms of words to be corrected, by using CATTI with respect to using a conventional HTR system followed by human postediting.

4.3 Results

Table 2 shows the performance of the post-editing approach (WER), the performance of the conventional CATTI system (WSR) (only considering the word substitution operation) and the relative difference between these two results (EFR). It is important to note that the results in table 2 differ from those reported in [5]. The differences are because of recent preprocessing and modelling improvements and because here we are adopting a more detailed interaction protocol which assumes the user will disable CATTI predictions when there is just one error to amend in the remaining system-proposed transcription. Clearly, in these specific cases, this prevents possible new prediction errors, leading to better estimates of WSR and EFR.

Table 2: Performance of the HTR system (WER) and the CATTI system (WSR) and the corresponding estimated effort reduction (EFR).

WER	WSR	EFR
33.5 %	30.7 %	8.4 %

In table 3 we can see the WSR obtained for each of the new considered editing operations, applied in an isolation way, but in conjunction with the normal substitution operation to the interactive CATTI process. The WSR is calculated under the simplifying (but reasonable) assumption that the cost of the different editing operations is the same. Note that this assumption makes the results rather pessimistic, because they are obtained asssuming all the operations cost as much as in the worst case. In the last row, all the 5 different editing operations have been jointly applied in the CATTI process. Note, that the improvement obtained in this last case is not the sum of the improvements obtained for the separately application of each editing operation. This is because, the interactive transcriptions that the CATTI system proposes depend on the application order and type of editing operations that are taken into account. So, considering all the editing operations, the number of times each operation is applied in the CATTI process may be different.

Table 3: Performance of the CATTI system (WSR) when the different editing operations are added to the interactive process and the relative difference between them and the WER. Corresponding number of times that each editing operation is applied is also reported.

	#Occurrences	WSR(%)	EFR(%)
Insertion	94	30.3	9.6
Deletion	65	30.6	8.7
Swap	1	30.7	8.4
Join	2	30.7	8.7
Split	2	30.6	8.7
All	94, 64, 0, 2, 0	30.2	9.9

According to the results, the number of user interactions needed to obtain perfect transcriptions using the different editing operations seems to be slightly reduced with respect to using the conventional CATTI. In addition, the interaction process is more comfortable for the user. Insertion and deletion operations are by far the most frequently applied and consequently contribute with the most significant improvement with respect to the baseline. However, it is worth noting that the join and split operations have achieved similar improvement level, mainly due to their inherent high degree of correction, in spite of their small appearance frequency.

5. CONCLUSIONS

In this paper we have tested a new set of interactive editing operations for CATTI system. The interaction in conventional CATTI was in the form of substitution interactions. In this work insertion, deletion, swap, join and split have been also considered. The results reported should be considered preliminary. While these results are certainly encouraging, it should be taken into account that the small amount of data used in the experiments does not allow for a reasonable statistical sgnificance of the results. Future works with larger corpora are therefore needed.

6. ACKNOWLEDGMENTS

Work supported by the EC (FEDER/FSE) and the Spanish MEC/MICINN under the MIPRCV "Consolider Ingenio 2010" program (CSD2007-00018) and MITTRAL (TIN2009-14633-C03-01) projects. Also supported by the Generalitat Valenciana under grant Prometeo/2009/014.

7. REFERENCES

[1] F. Drida. Towards restoring historic documents degraded over time. In *Proceedings of the DIAL'06*, IEEE Computer Society, pages 350–357. 2006.

[2] F. Jelinek. *Statistical Methods for Speech Recognition.* MIT Press, 1998.

[3] R. Kneser and H. Ney. Improved backing-off for m-gram language modeling. volume 1, pages 181–184, Los Alamitos, CA, USA, 1995. IEEE Computer Society.

[4] L. A. Leiva, V. Romero, A. H. Toselli, and E. Vidal. Evaluating an interactive-predictive paradigm on handwriting transcription: A case study and lessons learned. In *Proceedings of the COMPSAC 2011*, pages 610–617, Jul.

[5] V. Romero, A. H. Toselli, L. Rodríguez, and E. Vidal. Computer Assisted Transcription for Ancient Text Images. In *ICIAR 2007*, volume 4633 of *LNCS*, pages 1182–1193. Springer-Verlag, Montreal (Canada).

[6] V. Romero, A. H. Toselli, and E. Vidal. Using mouse feedback in computer assisted transcription of handwritten text images. In *Proceedings of the ICDAR 2009*, IEEE Computer Society. Barcelona, Spain, July.

[7] A. H. Toselli, A. Juan, D. Keysers, J. González, I. Salvador, H. Ney, E. Vidal, and F. Casacuberta. Integrated Handwriting Recognition and Interpretation using Finite-State Models. *IJPRAI'04*, 18(4):519–539.

[8] A. H. Toselli, V. Romero, M. Pastor, and E. Vidal. Multimodal interactive transcription of text images. *Pattern Recognition*, 43(5):1814–1825, 2010.

[9] A. H. Toselli, V. Romero, L. Rodríguez, and E. Vidal. Computer Assisted Transcription of Handwritten Text. In *ICDAR 2007*, pages 944–948. IEEE Computer Society, Curitiba, Paraná (Brazil), September 2007.

Dynamic Perception-Production Oscillation Model in Human-Machine Communication

Igor Jauk
Artificial Intelligence Group
Faculty of Technology
Bielefeld University, Germany
ijauk@techfak.uni-bielefeld.de

Ipke Wachsmuth
Artificial Intelligence Group
Faculty of Technology
Bielefeld University, Germany
ipke@techfak.uni-bielefeld.de

Petra Wagner
Faculty of Linguistics and Literature
Bielefeld University, Germany
petra.wagner@uni-bielefeld.de

ABSTRACT

The goal of the present article is to introduce a new concept of a perception-production timing model in human-machine communication. The model implements a low-level cognitive timing and coordination mechanism. The basic element of the model is a dynamic oscillator capable of tracking *re-occurring* events in time. The organization of the oscillators in a network is being referred to as the *Dynamic Perception-Production Oscillation Model (DPPOM)*. The DPPOM is largely based on findings in psychological and phonetic experiments on timing in speech perception and production. It consists of two sub-systems, a *perception sub-system* and a *production sub-system*. The perception sub-system accounts for information clustering in an input sequence of events. The production sub-system accounts for speech production *rhythmically entrained* to the input sequence. We propose a system architecture integrating both sub-systems, providing a flexible mechanism for perception-production timing in dialogues. The model's functionality was evaluated in two experiments.

Categories and Subject Descriptors

I.2.11 [**Artificial Intelligence**]: Distributed Artificial Intelligence—*intelligent agents, languages and structures*

General Terms

Languages

Keywords

Oscillation, Timing, Rhythm, Dynamic systems, Perception, Production, Dialogue Technology

1. INTRODUCTION

Modern real-time dialogue systems, such as embodied conversational agents (e.g Max [2]), have to deal with timing and coordination issues. Some of them need *only* to time turn-taking. Some of them also integrate gestures which have to be timed with their own speech. One way is to explicitly specify the synchronization points of speech and gestures (e.g. [2]). Difficulties arise when the demand is to create a system which is capable of *natural* real-time conversation and behavior. Such a system should integrate all possible aspects of timing in dialogues, as the gestures accompanying speech (or vice-versa), but also the adequate and coordinated interaction of the conversational agent with the human speaker. This interaction could be expressed in terms of *turn-taking* and *back channels*. Wilson & Wilson [6] proposed an oscillator model for timing phenomena in conversations and showed how their oscillator model can explain various phenomena in speech and dialogues, such as syllable timing and turn-taking.

Turn-taking has also been discussed by Bonaiuto and Thórisson [1]. They implemented a hybrid model composed of the *Ymir Turn-Taking Model (YTTM)* and the *Augmented Competitive Queuing (ACQ)*. Using it, they implemented a conversation between two agents. For their experiments they used a restricted set of only few possible non-verbal and speaking actions. However, real natural-language conversation is much more complex. Turn-taking signals have to be filtered from a set of complex acoustic cues and gestures. Another inflexible aspect in their model is that it only achieves successful turn-taking after a training session. In addition, trained neural networks might not be flexible enough to adapt to the high variance of timing in natural-speech conversations.

2. DYNAMIC PERCEPTION-PRODUCTION OSCILLATION MODEL (DPPOM)

We propose a model which implements cognitive low-level timing processes, the *Dynamic Perception-Production Oscillation Model (DPPOM)*. The DPPOM is based on findings in psychological and phonetic experiments on timing in dialogues, speech perception and production. The general task of the model is to produce reaction signals to a rhythmic input. There are several requirements imposed on such a model. First, it has to be able to adapt to different timing situations in real-time dialogues *dynamically*. Second, it has to be able to filter out the necessary signals in order to time the feedback.

2.1 Basic terms

The incoming speech is being referred to as *system input*.

The system input is composed of *re-occurring events*. A cue or a set of cues indicating a certain marked event in a conversation will probably indicate the same event at the next point of time of its occurrence (consider a stressed syllable, a pitch rise at the end of an echo question or a final lengthen at the end of a phrase). The re-occurrence of certain events in speech is being referred to as *speech rhythm*. Each rhythmic event in speech can be described in two ways: (1) *when* does it occur (the *timing* of the event), and (2) *what* does characterize the event (the *form* of the event). Since we consider acoustic events only, we can express the form in terms of *amplitude*. Amplitude mirrors the relative *prominence* of the events and thus represents the cues which indicate individual events.

A timing model should be able to filter out important events, predict their occurrence in the future, and coordinate an entrained response, regardless of the complexity. With this we identify two tasks. The first task is a *perceptual* task. The model has to perceive the input signal and filter the important events. The second task is a *coordination task*. The model has to coordinate production with perception. The challenge in this demand is the flexibility of the model.

2.2 General architecture

Fig. 1 shows a system overview of the *Dynamic Perception-Production Oscillation Model (DPPOM)*.

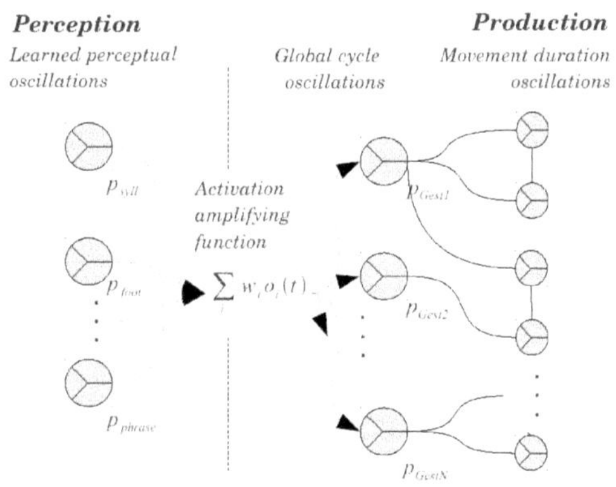

Figure 1: *DPPOM overview.*

The DPPOM is composed of two sub-systems, the *perception* and the *production* sub-system. The system split is motivated by findings which reveal at least two timing components, a perceptual and a motor control component (e.g. Steinbüchel et al [5]). The basic component is an oscillator model. In our implementation we use the oscillator model proposed by Large [3].

Each sub-system implements distinct layers of oscillators organized in a special way. The communication between layers is considered to be a matter of activation. A single oscillator in each layer produces a periodic pulse with a period p and an activation c. The activation is implemented as oscillator *confidence* (Large [3]). Let c_{max} and c_{min} define the confidence range, then the confidence is defined as:

$$c = c_{min} + 0.5(c_{max} - c_{min})(1 + tanh\Omega) \quad (1)$$

where Ω is a control parameter. It is being adjusted during entrainment and translates the confidence value in the defined range. The output confidence of an oscillator can be limited in order to limit its activation capabilities. On the other hand we introduce a threshold level of activation, such that the oscillators might need summed activation in order to be driven. Summed activation results from simultaneous firing in a real-time network. It can be approximated as:

$$\vec{o'} = \sum_i w_i \vec{o_i} \quad (2)$$

where $\vec{o_i}$ is the oscillator output of the oscillator i and w_i the individual oscillator weight. Weighting would provide different coupling strength between oscillators.

We can define the oscillator model in terms of system theory:

$$o(t') = S\{s(t)\} \quad (3)$$

Since t' is not necessary equal to t, both, the input signal, and the system are time variant. Thus, the oscillator output $o(t')$ considers the modification of time t with respect to the input sequence. Considering equations 2 and 3 we can define our system as:

$$\vec{y}(t'') = S\{\sum_i w_i o_i(t')\} \quad (4)$$

where $\vec{y}$ is the output of a vector of oscillators in the output layer. Let γ be a reverse term of the receptive window width of the oscillator, then according to the output definition proposed by Large [3] we define the DPPOM output as:

$$\vec{y}(t'') = S\{\sum_i w_i[1 + tanh(\gamma(cos(2\pi\Phi(t)) - 1)]_i\} \quad (5)$$

It might be a conceptual question, whether the task of the system is to keep the point of time t'' close to the point of time t, or to insert some irregularity. In the next sections we take a closer look at the individual sub-systems.

2.3 Perception sub–system

The perception sub-system processes the input stimuli. It identifies the important events in the input train. The important events in some way are more prominent than others. They indicate places where a reaction or feedback is more probable. We assume, that the important events are organized in a *metrical* structure. The meter defines the re-occurrence of such events. In the Fig. 1 the oscillators, which track the important events, are organized in the perception sub-system layer. They have different periods, according to the periods of the events they track. In the figure we give exemplary oscillators for syllables, feet, and phrases. In this case these oscillators are motivated phonetically. Their periods can be considered as learned during language acquisition.

2.4 Production sub–system

The production sub-system coordinates any kind of DPPOM's output. The output is defined as entrained reaction to the input. In general, the output is given by motor coordination. We can sub-divide motor coordination in two groups, articulatory gestures, and all the other gestures.

Each motor oscillator controls a distinct motor task. We have to configure the motor oscillators concerning the demands of the individual motor tasks, e.g. if we want to time arm movements it might be significantly distinct from timing of head nodding. Another crucial point in the configuration is concerning the events which activate the reaction of oscillators. Such an important event can be a phrase boundary. Now, we can wish to react to every important occurring event, or only to few of them. This can be controlled by distinct coupling ratios of the motor oscillators and the perceptual system response. We also can construct complex response timing patches by introducing an intermediate motor layer and calculating complex coupling ratios.

If we consider a simple arm movement we can figure out at least two oscillation processes. The first process defines the duration of the actual movement, reflecting the inertia of the arm. This process is important since other motor tasks eventually have to be coordinated with the arm movement (consider simultaneous movement and speech). The second oscillation process is the one which coordinates the global movement cycle, i.e. it defines the re-occurrence of the movements. If we define a motor event to occur at each important input event, then maybe we do not need the global cycle coordination. It will be done intrinsically by the perceptual layer and can be controlled via the activation. However, if we define more complex ratios, then we also have to define the global cycle coordination.

3. PERCEPTION SUB-SYSTEM TEST

In the first experiment we used a German rap song, the first minute annotated on the syllable level. We believe that rap music is rhythmically highly structured and thus could be a good first approach to test our model. Since we model a perceptual system it is reasonable to implement perceptually motivated tracking. Thus we calculated *perceptual centers (P-centers)* of syllables, according to Marcus [4].

We ran a set of three oscillators organized in a parallel fashion, on a syllable, "foot" and "phrase" level, respectively. A "foot" as defined to be the distance between two stressed syllables, thus effectively we tracked *stressed* syllables on this level. A "phrase" is defined to be the distance between two *accentuated* syllables due to the rhythm of the song. We assigned an amplitude of 1 to all unstressed syllables, of 2 to all stressed syllables, of 3 to all accentuated syllables and of 0.5 to all non-speech units (like breathing pauses). We initiated the oscillator periods with mean duration values of 174 ms, 458 ms, and 1868 ms, on the syllable, "foot", and "phrase" levels respectively. The oscillators started firing and entraining when they received the first pulse on their level. We also configured oscillator's adaptation thresholds according to the amplitude of the input syllables, thus the oscillators only entrained to pulses of their own levels. Since there is no second layer, the oscillator weigths can be disregarded.

Derived from the period values, the oscillators coupled with ratios of *1:1* for the syllable level to the input sequence, *2:5* for the "foot" to the syllable/input level, and *1:10* for the "phrase" to the syllable/input levels. We can observe these ratios on Arnold's tongue coupling diagram [3]. The *1:1* ratio is the most stable one, *2:5* and *1:10* are rather unstable. According to the Arnold's tongue diagrams we can adjust the maximal τ values (maximal receptive window size) in order to provide more stability for certain coupling ratios. We should choose a high τ_{max} value for the *1:1* ratio and rather low or middle τ_{max} values for the *2:5* and *1:10* ratios. We ran the oscillators with τ_{max} values of 0.05, 0.1, 0.2 and 0.5 in order to figure out the best configuration.

For the evaluation we calculated Euclidean distances (in ms) of tracked pulse times to the pulse times in the input sequence. The values describe the temporal deviation of individual events. Thus they represent the error which commits the oscillator. We calculated root mean square errors (RMSE) of the Euclidean distances for all τ_{max} values comparing them with the original sequence on each level. We also calculated correlation with time for all Euclidean distances using Pearson coefficients. Successful entrainment should cause smaller distances. Thus, small or negative correlations indicate better accuracy. Close-to-zero correlations would occur in the case of a perfect match if $RMSE = 0$ or in the case of a constant mismatch if $RMSE \neq 0$.

Table 1: RMSE and correlation values for Euclidean distances in Experiment 1.

τ_{max}	Syllable		"Foot"		"Phrase"	
	RMSE	CORR	RMSE	CORR	RMSE	CORR
0.05	33.67	0.87	34.14	0.13	28.22	-0.34
0.1	38.56	0.86	47.65	0.88	28.02	-0.33
0.2	44.58	0.73	29.62	-0.43	27.24	-0.41
0.5	24.49	0.36	67.30	0.99	42.20	0.50

3.1 Results & Discussion

Table 1 shows the RMSE and correlation results for all levels and all τ_{max} values. The best accuracy on the syllable level, as expected, shows the oscillator with the largest τ_{max} value. For the "Foot" level the best accuracy shows the oscillator with $\tau = 0.2$; and for the "Phrase" level the oscillators with low and middle τ_{max} values.

The results show the general capability of the oscillators to track rhythmic speech input on distinct levels. To assure best accuracy it is crucial to adapt the maximal receptive window size τ_{max} to the expected oscillator coupling ratio.

4. DPPOM IN MAX

For the second experiment we combined both sub-systems to the DPPOM. We used the same rap input as in Experiment 1. We also conserved the same configuration for the perception layer. For the production layer, we defined two gestural actions, head nodding and arm movement. The actions were timed to certain important events in the input sequence. Head nodding is a faster and smaller movement, thus we timed it with certain stressed syllables. Arm movement was timed to certain accentuated syllables.

Figure 2: *Conversational agent Max.*

The movements were performed by the conversational agent Max [2], see Fig. 2. The DPPOM values were translated to *MURML*, an XML representation language for speech and gesture generation in conversational agents [2].

We used a global cycle coordination layer. The movement duration was kept stable for both movements in order to simplify the evaluation of DPPOM, so were kept the oscillator weights. The head nodding needed 1 second to be

Table 2: RMSE, RMSD (Root Mean Standard Deviation) and correlation values in Experiment 2.

	Head nodding	Arm movement
RMSE (EUCL)	9.84	23.22
RMSD (EUCL)	9.54	18.67
CORR (EUCL)	-0.25	0.05
RMSE (PERIOD ORIG)	40.26	62.23
RMSD (PERIOD ORIG)	15.83	33.57
RMSE (PERIOD SYS)	40.28	62.35
RMSD (PERIOD SYS)	11.65	10.40

completed, the arm movement 2 seconds. The head oscillator was initiated with the period of 1500 ms, coupling ratio of approx. *1:10*. The arm oscillator was initiated with the period of 4000 ms, coupling ratio of approx. *1:20*. Both ratios are rather unstable. Thus we chose small τ_{max} values: 0.2 for the head oscillator and 0.05 for the arm oscillator. The activation (confidence) output of the oscillators ranged between 0 and 1. We defined activation thresholds for both motor oscillators to be 0.5.

4.1 Results

Table 2 shows the statistical results of the second experiment. The first three lines show the RMSE, RMSD and correlation values for the Euclidean distances between the original pulses and the corresponding system answer. For head nodding the values are relatively low. The correlation indicates improvement in accuracy throughout tracking activity. The values for the arm oscillator show higher accuracy errors. The correlation value is very low, thus the error is produced consistently.

The lower four lines show the RMSE and RMSD (Root Mean Standard Deviation) values for the intrinsic period development for the sequence of original pulses and the system answer, respectively. We see that the head oscillator was able to reproduce the mean period and also the period variance of the input sequence. The arm oscillator reproduced well the mean period, but failed in the variance. Thus the arm oscillator averaged the input.

4.2 Discussion

The system was able to create adequate rhythmic response in order to produce feedback signals at special events in a rap input sequence. The head oscillator showed better accuracy than the arm oscillator. However, the actual arm movement takes longer time. So we can define a temporal tolerance range to control the actual movements. So we can adapt movement periods (= the time in which a movement has to be completed), accelerating or decelerating the movement speed, in order to compensate temporal deviations. The information of deviation can be encoded in the activation level.

5. CONCLUSIONS

In the present study we introduced a new model for coordination of motor tasks as a response to rhythmic input (DPPOM). We introduced two sub-systems of the model, the perceptual and the production sub-systems. We evaluated the perceptual sub-system on a rap input. In this evaluation we introduced a simple use of input amplitude. We used it to entrain the oscillators only when an activation threshold was reached. Afterwards we used a complete DPPOM system in order to coordinate gestural response to the rap input in the conversational agent Max. The results showed realistic timed reactions to the rap input.

We also have revealed important lines of future investigation. First, it is important to study a flexible integration of amplitude in the entrainment and maybe in the activation of the oscillators. The amplitude provides an important source of information about the *form* of the events received. Especially the phonetic source information has to be investigated in order to identify the most effective clues for important events in the input speech. Second, it is important to investigate the relationships between the perceptual and the production layers. It is also important to study the interaction between the global cycle coordination and the coordination of the individual movements in the motor planning. Machine learning techniques could be used to combine both lines of investigation using statistical training approaches.

6. ACKNOWLEDGEMENTS

This work is partially supported by the Deutsche Forschungsgemeinschaft (DFG) in the Collaborative Research Center SFB 673.

7. REFERENCES

[1] J. Bonaiuto and K. Thórisson. Towards a neurocognitive model of turn taking in multimodal dialog. In M. L. I. Wachsmuth and G. Knoblich, editors, *Embodied communication in humans and machines*, pages 451–483, New York, 2008. Oxford University Press.

[2] S. Kopp and I. Wachsmuth. Synthesizing multimodal utterances for conversational agents. *Journal of Computer Animation and Virtual Worlds*, 15:39–52, 2004.

[3] E. W. Large. *Dynamic representation of musical structure*. The Ohio State University, Ohio, 1994.

[4] S. M. Marcus. Acoustic determinants of perceptual center (p-center) location. *Perception & Psychophysics*, 30(3):247–256, 1981.

[5] N. von Steinbüchel, M. Wittmann, and E. Pöppel. Timing in perceptual and motor tasks after disturbances of the brain. In M. Pastor and J. Artieda, editors, *Time, internal clocks and movement*, pages 281–304. Elsevier Science B.V., 1996.

[6] M. Wilson and T. Wilson. An oscillator model of the timing of turn-taking. *Psychonomic Bulletin and Review*, 12(6):957–968, 2005.

The Effect of Clothing on Thermal Feedback Perception

[1]Martin Halvey, [1]Graham Wilson, [1]Yolanda Vazquez-Alvarez, [1]Stephen A. Brewster and [2]Stephen A. Hughes

[1]School of Computing Science, University of Glasgow, Glasgow, United Kingdom G12 8QQ

[2]SAMH Engineering, 1 Leopardstown Drive, Blackrock, Dublin Ireland

martin.halvey@glasgow.ac.uk, gawilson@dcs.gla.ac.uk, yolanda@dcs.gla.ac.uk, stephen.brewster@glasgow.ac.uk, stephenahughes@gmail.com

ABSTRACT

Thermal feedback is a new area of research in HCI. To date, studies investigating thermal feedback for interaction have focused on virtual reality, abstract uses of thermal output or on use in highly controlled lab settings. This paper is one of the first to look at how environmental factors, in our case clothing, might affect user perception of thermal feedback and therefore usability of thermal feedback. We present a study into how well users perceive hot and cold stimuli on the hand, thigh and waist. Evaluations were carried out with cotton and nylon between the thermal stimulators and the skin. Results showed that the presence of clothing requires higher intensity thermal changes for detection but that these changes are more comfortable than direct stimulation on skin.

Categories and Subject Descriptors

H5.2. User Interfaces: Haptic IO.

General Terms

Design, Human Factors.

Keywords

Thermal, haptic, touch, non-visual.

1. INTRODUCTION

Thermal feedback has a number of potential uses in HCI and mobile interaction. It can act as a non-visual notification channel for situations that are too bumpy or noisy for vibrotactile or audio feedback. It can enhance both visual and non-visual feedback by adding extra depth to the interaction experience, e.g. thermal feedback could be used to add affect that is not provided by other modalities [3, 8]. Thermal output is also entirely private; audio may be heard by others, vibrotactile may be heard and felt by others and visual may be seen by others. A great deal of research has looked at the underlying characteristics of human thermal perception [1, 4, 10]; however thermal feedback and interaction is a relatively new area of research [2-3, 8, 11-12]. The majority of this previous work does not take environmental factors, such as ambient temperature, humidity or clothing into account. In addition, many systems that investigate thermal perception assume direct contact with the skin. In an attempt to overcome some of these shortcomings, we investigate one particular environmental factor, namely the presence of clothing. We investigate thermal perception at body locations normally associated with mobile devices, i.e. waist (where the phone might be clipped to a belt) and upper thigh (phone in a trouser pocket) and look at the effect of materials with different thermal properties (nylon and cotton) on perception of thermal cues. The results will help us understand how to construct thermal feedback for a user interface that is usable in a wider range of usage contexts.

ICMI'11, November 14–18, 2011, Alicante, Spain.

2. RELATED WORK

Jones and Berris [5] summarise the "desired features" of a thermal display based on both VR research and psychophysical evidence. They recommend using stimulus temperatures of 22-42°C and using higher rates of change to maximize detection of stimuli. They also suggest a thermal interface should be capable of heating and cooling resolutions of 0.001°C and 0.002°C. Wettach et al. [11] designed a Peltier heat pump-based thermal device for mobile interaction and tested users' ability to differentiate three different stimulus temperatures (32°C, 37°C and 42°C). Initial error rates were approximately 65%, although this figure was reduced to 25% after long-term user training. None of these temperatures would be considered "cool" and so this study suggests that individuals can identify varying degrees of warmth, not simply a change from one temperature to another. Also using Peltier-based thermal feedback, Wilson et al. [12] present two studies looking into how well users could detect different warm and cool stimuli presented to the fingertips, palm, dorsal surface of the forearm and the upper arm. Evaluations were carried out in static and mobile settings. Results showed that the palm is most sensitive, cool is more perceivable and comfortable than warm and that stronger and faster-changing stimuli are more detectable but less comfortable. In this paper we extend the work conducted by both Wettach et al. and Wilson et al. by looking at different body locations and by investigating the effects of clothing on perception.

Other related research investigating thermal feedback has looked at more abstract issues. Gooch [2] found that adding thermal feedback to remote, mediated communication could lead to increased feelings of 'social presence'. Nakashige et al. [8] accompanied photographs of warm and cold scenes with either warm or cold feedback. A small study indicated that the foods appeared more appealing when accompanied by the appropriate temperature. Iwasaki et al. [3] suggest a system that could be used to convey emotional information to another user through augmentation of an existing mobile phone. When investigating preconceptions of meaning/significance associated with thermal sensations, Lee and Lim [7] found that users treat sensations as a continuum and that sensations were almost meaningless without context. They also found that cold stimuli were generally less preferred than warm. Kushiyama et al. [6] developed 'Thermo-pict', using Peltiers it provides patterns of thermal stimulation, including thermal tactile 'pictures' and visible displays. Narumi et al. [9] developed a contextual/ambient thermal display for more mobile scenarios. Although not tested experimentally the latter two examples show some interesting potential uses of thermal interfaces.

3. EVALUATION

Fifteen participants (10 male, 5 female) aged 22 to 39 (mean=28.87, median=26) took part in this experiment. Most were studying or working at the University. All were right-handed and paid £12 for participation, which lasted just over an hour. We used a custom microcontroller board that could independently drive four Peltier heat pumps [12]. These permit a high level of control over temperature output and also allow for both warming and cooling. Each Peltier device could be independently controlled over USB, with the temperature set anywhere within the temperatures of -20°C to +45°C, accurate to 0.1°C. The Peltiers were bonded to circuit boards with a heatsink bonded to the other side. Safety mechanisms on the board prevented them from becoming hotter than 45°C and cut off all power and input if a thermistor detecting the Peltier output became electrically or physically disconnected. For our study we used two Peltiers; two instead of one gave a larger stimulus area and meant that we would need lower intensity output to produce detectable sensations [10]. No more than two were used as this would have required too large an area of skin for mobile use.

3.1 Stimuli

The thermal stimuli used in this evaluation were the same as those used by Wilson *et al.* [12]. A neutral starting temperature of 32°C was chosen as this is within the defined 'neutral zone' of thermal sensation [5, 10, 12] and has been used in other studies [12]. The skin was adapted to this temperature before each trial session and was returned to it between each stimulus presentation. Two different rates of stimulus change (ROC) were used: 1°C/sec and 3°C/sec. Three different stimulus intensities were used: 1°C, 3°C and 6°C. As thermal perception is bipolar, both warming and cooling stimuli were used. Therefore a single stimulus consisted of warming or cooling at a set intensity (1°C, 3°C or 6°C) at one ROC (1°C/sec or 3°C/sec), for example, warming 3°C at 1°C/sec. These temperatures are well removed from cold and hot pain thresholds. Each stimulus was delivered twice, giving a total of 24 stimuli per session (3 intensities x 2 directions x 2 ROC x 2 presentations).

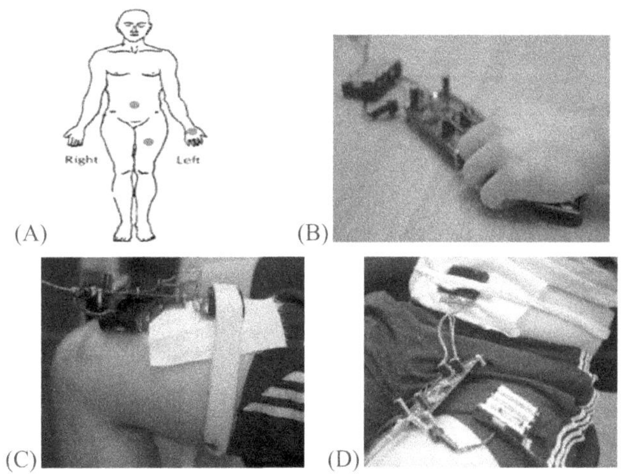

Figure 1: Stimulator sites on the body (A), the thenar with no material (B), the thigh with cotton (C) and waist with nylon (D).

As our interest is in using thermal feedback for mobile interaction and also to investigate the impact of clothing, we selected three body locations that are used to either hold, transport or interact with a mobile device, or locations that a mobile device might be located where clothing would also be present. The thenar eminence (the bulbous region of the palm adjoining the thumb) of the non-dominant hand was chosen as a mobile device would press against it when held in the hand. The upper thigh of the left leg was chosen as this is akin to having a device in a trouser pocket. Finally, the waist was chosen as this would simulate having a device on a belt. Both the waist and the thigh are commonly covered by clothing. Although the thenar is not normally covered by clothes (only when wearing gloves), Wilson et al. [12] found it had the best sensitivity in their study and as such the thenar provided us with a best case to compare against.

To simulate clothing, two different materials were chosen: cotton and nylon. These two materials are both commonly used in clothing and have different thermal properties. Swatches of these materials were placed between the Peltier stimulators and the skin of the participants during experimental sessions. The thermal properties of the materials can be dependent on the thickness of material used, weave, surface area etc. Efforts were taken to make sure that material samples were approximately the same thickness and were the same surface area, just covering the peltiers and heat sinks. To ameliorate some of the potential problems caused by differences in the materials, the two materials have very different thermal properties, cotton[1] has a thermal conductivity of 0.04 W·m−1·K−1 approximately and nylon[2] has a thermal conductivity of 0.25 W·m−1·K−1 approximately.

3.2 Design and Procedure

The design was based on that of Wilson et al. [12]. The task was split into 3 conditions, with participants receiving stimulations at all locations (thenar, waist, thigh) and with all materials (none, cotton, nylon). The order of the location and the material was rotated using a Latin square. The participant was sat at a desk upon which there was a computer monitor and mouse. For the thenar conditions, the Peltier stimulator lay on the desk in front of the seated participant, facing up so that the users could lay their thenar on the stimulator. For the waist and thigh conditions, the stimulator was held against the body with an elastic fabric strip (Figure 1). At the start of each condition the stimulators were set to a neutral starting temperature of 32°C for 2 minutes so as to adapt the skin to this temperature. After the adaptation period, all 24 stimuli were presented in random order. A stimulus presentation comprised of 10 sec. of stimulus followed by a return to the neutral temperature and 30 sec. of adaptation. There were no visual or auditory cues as to when stimuli were presented. Participants were instructed to click the mouse button as soon as they felt a change in thermal stimulation, in any direction and at any intensity. Once this occurred, the time elapsed since the initiation of the stimulus was taken as the time-to-detection. At this point, two 7-point Likert scales appeared on screen asking the participants to rate the stimulus in terms of *intensity* (from "very cold" to "very hot") and *comfort* (from "very uncomfortable" to "very comfortable"), similar to others used before [1, 12]. They then clicked on a submit button and another stimulus was presented after the 30 seconds of adaptation. If the participant clicked the mouse button before the full 10 seconds of stimulation had passed, the Peltiers were immediately returned to neutral and the rating scales were presented. In total a user would receive 72 (24 stimuli * 3 sessions) stimulations over an entire experimental session. As we had 15 participants this resulted in 1080 total potential stimulations. The independent variables were: *Rate of change (ROC), Stimulus intensity, Direc-*

---

[1] http://physics.info/conduction/

[2] http://www.engineeringtoolbox.com/thermal-conductivity-d_429.html

tion of change (warm or cool), *Body location* and *Material Present*. The dependent variables were: *Stimulus detection* (if one was perceived), *Detection time* (how long after the initiation of a stimulus that it was detected), *subjective intensity of stimulus* and *subjective comfort of stimulus*.

4. RESULTS

Due to some technical issues with the hardware not all conditions being completed, as a result 932 of the possible 1080 stimulations were submitted to the participants. This was taken into account when calculating all of the results and statistics. For all variables Friedmans analysis of variance of ranks was used to analyse the effect of intensity of change, body location and material on the number of stimuli detected. Wilcoxon T comparisons were used to analyse the effect of direction of change and ROC. Non parametric statistics were utilized as our data did not fit a normal distribution. Environmental temperature can influence skin temperature [5], in particular particularly high (>25°C) or low (<=15°C) environmental temperatures can cause the skin temperature to shift from the neutral zone. As such we recorded room temperature and humidity during each trial and the ambient temperature did not fall outside the range that would cause a shift in skin temperature.

4.1 Number of Detections

Intensity of change was found to have a significant effect on the number of thresholds produced ($\chi 2$ (2) =185.009, p<.001). Post hoc Wilcoxon T comparisons showed significant differences between stimulus intensities: 1°C vs. 3°C (T =9842 x p<0.001), 1°C vs. 6°C (T=15910 p<0.001) and 3°C vs. 6°C (T=2242 p<0.001). The number of stimuli detected increased as the intensity increased with means of 19.42%, 58.06% and 70.93% for 1°C, 3°C and 6°C intensities respectively. Location was also found to have a significant effect on the number of changes detected ($\chi 2$ (2) =47.03, p<.001). Post hoc Wilcoxon T comparisons showed that the thenar (64.04%) produced more detections that both the waist (T=6930 p<0.001) and the thigh (T=2256 p<0.001), although the number of detections for the waist (45.33%) was high than that of the thigh (38.81%) the difference was not significant. The presence of different materials was also significant ($\chi 2$ (2) =52.81, p<.001). Post hoc Wilcoxon T comparisons showed significant differences between all materials: none vs. cotton (T = 1716 p<0.001), none vs. nylon (T=2275.5 p<0.001) and cotton vs. nylon (T=2436 p<0.001). The number of stimuli detected decreased as the thermal conductivity decreased with means of 65.42%, 46.83% and 36.39% for none, nylon and cotton materials respectively. ROC was shown to be significant (T=9576.5 p=0.007) with the higher ROC producing more detections. There was no significant effect of direction.

As well as looking at the number of stimuli detected we also investigated the false detections that were made. There are two types of error; the first is when a participant believed they had felt a change when no change had been submitted and the second is when a user has missed a stimulus but detects the change back to neutral. The thenar as the most sensitive area has the most errors per location (Average 3.6 errors for thenar, average 3.23 errors for waist and average 2.83 errors for thigh). It was also seen that the presence of material increases the number of both types of error made (Average 2.43 errors for none, average 3.3 errors for cotton and average 3.93 errors for nylon). In the majority of cases nylon causes more errors than cotton. Some participants noted that sometimes they felt the device or the material retained some heat, this would explain why nylon with a higher thermal conductivity would cause more errors. If it is the case that some materials retained more heat this could also potentially lead to errors in identifying if a stimulus is warm or cool, this will be investigated in more detail in Section 4.3.

4.2 Time to Detection

Location was found to have a significant effect on the time to detection ($\chi 2$ (2) =25.034, p<.001). Post hoc Wilcoxon T comparisons showed that the thigh (median = 4.04sec) produced significantly slower detection times than both the waist (3.4sec) (T=2575 p=0.012) and the thenar (3.29sec) (T=1621 p<0.001), with no significant difference between the thenar and waist. The presence of different materials was also significant ($\chi 2$ (2) =46.908, p<.001). Post hoc Wilcoxon T comparisons showed significant differences cotton and the other conditions: none vs. cotton (T=5772 p<0.001) and cotton vs. nylon (T=5884 p<0.001). The time to detection increased as the thermal conductivity decreased with medians of 3.06 sec, 3.3 sec and 4.71 sec for no material, nylon and cotton materials respectively. Direction significantly affected time to detection (T=17263 p<0.001) with cool stimuli (median=3.27sec) being detected more quickly than warm (median=3.84sec). ROC also significantly affected time to detection (T=7050.5 p<0.001) with higher ROC (3°C/sec) producing a significantly lower time to detection (median=3.36) than the lower ROC (1°C/sec; median=3.36sec). Intensity did not have an effect.

4.3 Subjective Stimulus Intensity

As was noted in Section 4.1 some users noted that they felt it difficult to distinguish between warm and cold stimuli when materials were placed between the skin and the Peltier stimulator. Users were asked to rate stimuli on a seven point scale from very hot (0) to very cold (6). These ratings were used to measure errors e.g. warm being perceived as cold. In total 26 errors were made, of those more were for hot (17) than cold (9) and more of these occurred with no material being present (12) than with cotton (6) or nylon (8) being present. As it did not appear that the participants made as many errors as they believed, the 0-6 scales were mapped to intensity scales of 0 – 3, with 0 being neutral and 3 being very intense. Intensity had a significant effect on perceived intensity ($\chi 2$ (2) =28.826, p<.001). Post hoc Wilcoxon T comparisons showed the higher intensity changes to be different from the other two stimulus intensities: 1°C vs. 6°C (T=533 p<0.001) and 3°C vs. 6°C (T=1037.5 p<0.001). The perceived intensity increased as the intensity increased 1°C (mean=1.071 median=1), 3°C (mean=1.295 median=1) and 6°C (mean=1.716 median=1) intensities respectively. Direction significantly affected perceived intensity (T=2410 p=0.015) with cool stimuli (mean=1.549 median=1) being more intense than warm (mean=1.392 median=1). ROC also significantly affected intensity (T=4693.5 p<0.001) with the lower ROC (1°C/sec) being less intense (mean=1.253 median=1) than the higher ROC (3°C/sec; mean=1.646 median=1). Location and the presence of material were found to not have an effect.

4.4 Subjective Stimulus Comfort

Subjective stimulus comfort was measured on a seven point scale from very comfortable (0) to very uncomfortable (6). Intensity of change was found to have a significant effect on the perceived comfort of stimuli ($\chi 2$ (2) =14.385, p<.001). Post hoc Wilcoxon T comparisons showed the higher intensity changes to be different from the other two stimulus intensities: 1°C vs. 6°C (T=1063 p<0.001) and 3°C vs. 6°C (T=3287 p<0.001). The perceived comfort decreased as the intensity increased 1°C (mean=1.649 median=1), 3°C (mean=2 median=2) and 6°C (mean=2.425 median=2) intensities respectively. The presence of different materials was also significant ($\chi 2$ (2) =11.164, p=.004). Post hoc Wilcoxon T comparisons showed that the presence of cotton (mean=1 median=1.769) resulted in participants feeling significantly more comfortable than with no material (mean=2.522 median=2). While nylon was found to be more comfortable than no material (mean=1.946 median=1) there was no significant difference between it and either no material or cotton. However it can be seen that comfort increases as thermal conductivity decreases. Direction significantly affected perceived comfort ($T=6001$ $p<0.035$) with warm stimuli (mean=2.013 median=2) being more comfortable than cool (mean=2.311 median=2). ROC also significantly affected comfort ($T=6707$ $p=0.021$) with the lower ROC (1°C/sec) being more comfortable (mean=1.995 median=2) than the higher ROC (3°C/sec; mean=2.296 median=2). Location was found to not have an effect. It should be noted that the mean and medians of all variables were in the comfortable range.

5. DISCUSSION AND CONCLUSIONS

Based on the results in this paper there are several new, interesting and important factors that should be considered when designing thermal feedback both in general and for mobile devices.

While the thenar eminence is the optimal location for feedback, the waist is suitable. In measures of 'number of stimuli detected' and 'time-to-detection' the thenar eminence was shown to be the most sensitive area. Although the waist suffered lower overall detection rates, it had similar time to detection. All three locations had similar perceived comfort and intensity ratings.

Different materials result in different design recommendations for thermal feedback. Materials with lower thermal conductivity require more intense changes; the required changes in intensity are lower for materials with higher thermal conductivity, although materials with higher thermal conductivity do not affect time to detection significantly. Materials with higher thermal conductivity can also result in more errors than those with lower thermal conductivity.

Materials mean that it should be possible to use higher intensity changes. While participants perceived stimuli delivered when materials were present to be as intense as direct contact with the skin, they perceived higher intensity changes to be more comfortable than when the stimulators are directly in contact with the skin. This may allow more intense changes to be used, and indeed if lower intensity changes cannot be detected then these are necessary. It should also be noted that although not supported in the results that some users stated that they found it difficult to identify changes as sometimes the material appeared to retain heat, this may mean that care should be taken to not present stimuli in rapid succession.

It is not clear if warm or cold changes are "better". Wilson et al. [12] put forward that cold changes were "better", in contrast in the study by Lee and Lim [7] warms changes were perceived to be "better". Our study used similar apparatus to Wilson et al, and in contrast to their findings we found that with the presence of material that cool changes were perceived as more intense, warm changes were more comfortable. However both studies did find that cool stimuli were detected more quickly than hot. It may be a case that the "dulling" effect of material on intensity makes warms changes more acceptable to users, but more research is required to investigate which, if any, direction is more useable and acceptable.

In conclusion, this paper has presented a user study which investigated how well users were able to detect warm and cold stimuli presented to three body locations and the effect of different clothing material on user's ability to detect those changes. Simple guidelines for design of feedback based on our results are outlined, with a view to identifying features of stimulus presentation that are impacted by the presence of clothing.

6. ACKNOWLEDGEMENTS

This research has been funded by the Industrial Members of MobileVCE (www.mobilevce.com), with additional financial support from EPSRC grant EP/G063427/1.

7. REFERENCES

[1] Cherycroze, S. Painful Sensation Induced by a Thermal Cutaneous Stimulus. Pain, 17(2), (Jan 1 1983), 109-137.

[2] Gooch, D. An Investigation into Communicating Social Presence With Thermal Devices. MSc Dissertation(Oct 17 2009), 1-390.

[3] Iwasaki, K., Miyaki, T. and Rakimoto, J. AffectPhone: A Handset Device to Present User's Emotional State with Warmth/Coolness. BIOSTEC2010, 2010, B-Interface Workshop (Apr 16 2010), 1-6.

[4] Johnson, K., Darian-Smith, I. and LaMotte, C. Peripheral neural determinants of temperature discrimination in man: a correlative study of responses to cooling skin. Journal of Neurophysiology, 36(1), (1973), 24.

[5] Jones, L. A. and Berris, M. The Psychophysics of Temperature Perception and Thermal-Interface Design. 10th Symposium on Haptic Interfaces for Virtual Environment and Teleoperator Systems (Sep 29 2002), 1-6.

[6] Kushiyama, K., Baba, T., Doi, K. and Sasada, S. Thermo-Pict neo. In Proccedings of SIGGRAPH 10 (Feb 18 2010), 1-1.

[7] Lee, W. and Lim, Y. K. Thermo-Message: Exploring the Potential of Heat as a Modality of peripheral Expression. In Proceedings of ACM CHI 2010: Extended Abstracts (Atlanta, GA, 2010) .

[8] Nakashige, M., Kobayashi, M. and Suzuki, Y. "Hiya-Atsu" media: augmenting digital media with temperature. In Proceedings of ACM CHI 2009 (Boston, MA, 2009).

[9] Narumi, T., Akagawa, T., Seong, Y. A. and Hirose, M. Thermotaxis. SIGGRAPH 2009 (Feb 16 2009), 1-1.

[10] Stevens, J. C. Thermal Sensibility. Lawrence Erlbaum, City, 1991.

[11] Wettach, R., Behrens, C., Danielsson, A. and Ness, T. A thermal information display for mobile applications. In proceedings of MobileHCI 2007, (Sep 1 2007).

[12] Wilson, G., Halvey, M., Brewster, S. A. and Hughes, S., A. Some Like it Hot? Thermal Feedback for Mobile Devices. In Proceedings of ACM CHI 2011 (Vancouver, Canada, 2011).

Comparing Multi-Touch Interaction Techniques for Manipulation of an Abstract Parameter Space

Sashikanth Damaraju
Interface Ecology Lab,
Texas A&M University

Andruid Kerne
Interface Ecology Lab,
Texas A&M University

ABSTRACT

The adjustment of multidimensional abstract parameter spaces, used in human-in-the-loop systems such as simulations and visualizations, plays an important role for multi-touch interaction. We investigate new natural forms of interaction to manipulate such parameter spaces. We develop separable multi-touch interaction techniques for abstract parameter space manipulation. We investigate using the index and thumb to perform the often-repeated sub-task of switching between parameters. A user study compares these multi-touch techniques with mouse-based interaction, for the task of color selection, measuring performance and efficiency. Our findings indicate that multi-touch interaction techniques are faster than mouse based interaction.

ACM Classification: H5.2 [Information interfaces and presentation]: User Interfaces. - Graphical user interfaces.

General terms: Design, Human Factors, Measurement, Performance, Experimentation.

Keywords: input separability, multi-touch, multi-touch, abstract parameter spaces

INTRODUCTION

We investigate multi-touch techniques to develop new natural forms of interaction for the multidimensional abstract parameter spaces that affect human-in-the-loop systems such as simulations and visualizations. While many current generation devices come equipped with multi-touch input sensing, utilization of this medium of interaction is still limited. Multi-touch researchers have developed techniques for manipulating objects in literal 2- and 3-D spaces, such as maps. For direct spatial manipulation, mappings for actions such as rotate, translate and scale to finger movements are easily understood. The dexterous operations we regularly perform with our fingers in the real world are used to manipulate virtual objects.

In contrast to manipulations in physical spaces, we consider manipulations in multidimensional abstract parameter spaces that lack a literal spatial representation. A range of significant interaction tasks require users to work with multidimensional abstract parameter spaces. Application areas include visual analytics, data mining, aircraft flight operations, power station and manufacturing system operations, and image, video and audio editing. Multi-touch manipulation of abstract parameter spaces will enable continuous adjustment of multiple values, for example replacing banks of sliders, each with separate mouse activations. For example, the Photoshop "film grain" filter has 3 numerical parameters: grain, highlight area, and intensity. The user must separately click each slider. To isolate the effect of interaction technique, in the present research, we use a simple task, color matching. The dimensions of this abstract parameter space are hue, saturation and value.

This research studies the ability of people to manipulate an abstract parametric space through fine motor control of multi-finger movement, as represented by the functional usability of a set of multi-touch interaction techniques that were designed in consideration of physical properties of the hand and problems that people have separating and coordinating movements of individual fingers.

With embodied interaction media, such as multi-touch and haptics, relevant physical properties expand to emphasize the tactile and corporeal. We hypothesize that operative aspects of good affordance design include minimizing physical effort and efficient adjustment of parameters.

In this paper, we develop a user study comparing multi-finger and mouse-based interaction for selecting a color. Our principal hypothesis is that multi-dimensional manipulations through movements of fingers of a single hand are faster than mouse-based interaction.

RELATED WORK

Multi-touch interaction use cases have focused on literal spatial manipulations of rotation, scaling and translation of elements in two [10, 12] or three dimensions [15]. Literal spatial multi-touch direct manipulation has also been applied to deformable shapes for animation [8], and physics for natural interaction [18]. Nacenta et al [17] have developed techniques to improve the separability of multi-finger input for literal spatial manipulations.

The notion of input separability for interactive systems was introduced by Jacobs et al for analysis of the perceptual structures of multidimensional parameter spaces and input devices [9]. They describe two ways of perceiving parameter spaces: *integral* (e.g.: x, y and z to define position) and *separable* (such as size and color) that can prescribe design decisions regarding the choice of input device or widget.

Malik designed widgets that use bi-digit input, using the thumb and the index finger, for cursor control and single parameter adjustment [13]. Recent research shows multi-finger chords can be used for discrete selection of mode or menu items [1, 11]. The present complementary research investigates the use of multi-finger input to adjust multiple parameters in continuous multi-dimensional abstract spaces, instead of discrete item selection.

There has been considerable research detailing the benefits of bimanual over single-handed interaction, with various input modalities [1, 3, 7]. For the purpose of this study, we do not aim to build the ideal interaction for color selection, but are using the dimensions of color as an example abstract parameter space in which to investigate the level of control exhibited by fingers of the same hand across interaction techniques.

Moscovich et al studied differences in performance while using (a) the index and thumb of one hand, and (b) the index fingers of the left and right hands [13]. They articulated a notion of direct manipulation dependent on the fingers directly touching the object they manipulate. Forlines et al [5] recommend the mouse over single finger interaction due to a lack of accuracy and occlusion problems while using the finger. The present research investigates the design space of indirect interaction, wherein the fingers do not touch the object of interest. Wu and Balakrishnan took a similar approach, but with the usual operation of scaling [19]. Indirection helps reduce issues for touch-based direct manipulation, such as occlusion of the target by the hand, and the target being out of reach.

Experiment design

We conduct a within-subjects study to compare the efficacy of techniques that map movement of fingers of a single hand to the adjustment of multiple parametric dimensions. The independent variable is the interaction technique used. The dependent variable measured is the time taken to complete the task. We focus our attention primarily on the index finger and thumb, because they are motorically characterized by highly independent degrees of freedom. The independent variable has five conditions, described below. The participant performs multiple trials (a trial is selection of a single color) with each condition.

APPARATUS

We fabricated an FTIR based configurable multi-touch device [6]. The screen has a diagonal of 35" (88.9cm) with a rear projected display at 1920×1080 resolution, with an input rate of 60Hz (latency of 17ms). The surface of interaction is a Rosco Grey projection screen.

Figure 1: The interface widget for color selection.

The multi-touch device enables configuration of height and tilt of the interactive surface, from a vertical wall, through an inclined easel, to a horizontal tabletop. For this study, the inclination of the surface was fixed at an angle of 23° from the horizontal, with the closest edge of the screen at a height of 28" (a standard work desk is 30" high). The inclined surface enables participants to maintain a comfortable upright posture, without having to strain their neck to lean forward during use, as they would with a horizontal tabletop configuration. A support was provided for participants to rest an elbow on during interaction.

INTERFACE DESIGN

The interface widget for color selection is shown in Figure 1. In a square at the center of the widget, we represent the saturation-value varying subset of the HSV color space for a given hue. A ring around this square visualizes the range of hue. The thumb is differentiated from the index finger by being closer to the user (lower on the screen). The motor space for the hue is the same as that of saturation and value, i.e., to move from one end of the range to the other, the participant moves the same distance for each of the HSV dimensions of color. The multi-finger conditions described below (**C1, C2**) have a common mapping for hue variation – the horizontal movement of the index finger is mapped to change in hue, while the thumb is used as a pivot.

PARTICIPANTS

There were 18 participants between the ages of 21 to 26. Each participant received a $5 gift card. All of the participants were right handed, except one.

STUDY TASK

For our study, participants are asked to select a target color, starting from a given initial color, each characterized by the three parametric dimensions of hue, saturation, and value. They are asked to perform a set of 12 trials for each of three interaction technique conditions. Each trial requires adjusting all three dimensions. Of the three conditions, 2 involve multi-finger interaction with different mappings. The remaining condition is mouse-based interaction. The study lasted half an hour.

INTERACTION TECHNIQUE CONDITIONS

The multi-touch technique conditions develop variations on the mappings of finger/thumb movement to color dimension. We design interaction techniques to enable the user to effectively manipulate the abstract parameter space of color. The interface widget in Figure 1 helps reinforce the mappings from the movements of the fingers to the adjustment of a specific parameter – hue, saturation or value.

In each multi-touch technique, interaction begins when the user places two fingers anywhere on the screen, without depending on touching a widget in a certain place, and ends at the last adjustment made by the user before touching the 'done' button.

C1. Constrained Manipulation: The mappings are as follows: as follows: horizontal movement of the index finger, with the thumb as pivot, is mapped to change in hue. Horizontal and vertical movements of the thumb, with the index finger as pivot, are mapped to changes in saturation and value, respectively; however only one of saturation or value can be manipulated at a given time. The components of the velocity vector of the thumb movement select the parameter to be manipulated.

C2. Index+Middle: Again, horizontal movement of the index finger pivoting from the thumb controls hue. But in this condition, the index and middle finger together are dragged horizontally to adjust saturation, and vertically for value. We hypothesize that by shifting the fingers in contact with the screen, the effort for selection of parameters will be reduced.

C3. Mouse Interaction: This is a control condition that enables practical comparison with the multi-touch conditions. The circular marker in the saturation-value swatch moves by clicking at a specific point on the square. Participants click directly on the desired value, either on the 2 dimensional saturation-value color square or on the hue ring, which is not possible with the previous conditions. We hypothesize that users will be slower in this one parameter at a time manipulation condition than in the multi-finger conditions. We use the mouse condition as a baseline to compare the effects of the multi-touch interaction techniques on task performance time.

STUDY PROCEDURE

The participant is presented with the initial and final colors as two squares above the color picker widget, with numerical values shown below each square. For each trial, the participant uses one of the interaction techniques to manipulate the initial color to match the target color. The current color is continuously updated to match the values adjusted by the user. The participant is asked to click the 'done' button to signify the end of each trial.

Each set of trials is constructed by selecting 12 initial and target color tuples. They are held constant across all

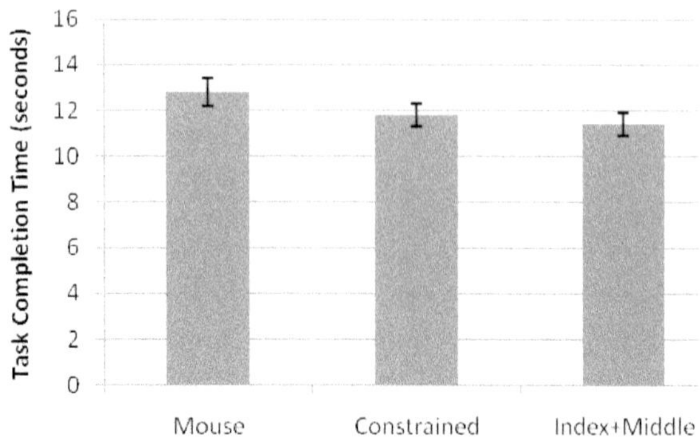

Figure 2: Time for multi-touch interaction technique conditions; error bars show 95% confidence.

conditions and participants. The order of the trials is randomized for each condition. The order of conditions is randomized for each participant by selection from a Latin square.

Each new interaction technique condition begins, for each participant, with a tutorial screen. The experimenter accompanies this with a short demonstration of the interaction technique. The participant is allowed to practice with each interaction technique at the start of each trial set until s/he is ready to begin the set. The participant is encouraged to rest between trial sets.

We log the movement of each finger for each trial for all of the study conditions. Color matching is a cognitively demanding task, with considerable variation across users and trials. To avoid errors resulting from the user's perceived level of accuracy, a fixed accuracy measure is used for all trials. When the participant sets a parameter within range of the target value, a mark is shown next to it. Once all the parameters are within range, the next trial begins.

HypothesES

H1. Multi-finger manipulations will be faster than the mouse condition for color selection.

H2. The efficiency of the multi-finger conditions (**C1-C2**) will be comparable to that of the mouse (**C3**).

We will verify **H1** by comparing completion times for trials against the mouse condition. Since we use a fixed accuracy measure for all trials, the traditional metric of error is not applicable. Instead, to test **H2**, we use Zhai and Milgram's measure of *inefficiency* [21]. Inefficiency is defined as $(d - s) / s$ where d is the distance traversed by the user through the parameter space, and s is the shortest path from initial position in the parameter space to the target. This measures the level of control the user exhibits during the task.

Results

Each trial is performed by all participants in all 3 conditions. Figure 2 graphs task completion times across conditions. In the following analysis, we normalize the time taken for each trial, with the equivalent time taken to perform the same trial by that participant with the mouse.

The following results are produced using a Welch two sample t-test. Participants performed 9.25% faster with the constrained multi-finger condition (**C1**) than with the mouse condition. The result was statistically significant ($t = 2.951$, $df = 17$, $p < 0.005$). They performed even faster (11.12%) with the index+middle finger condition (**C2**) than with mouse, and again this was significant ($t = 2.71$, $df = 17$, $p < 0.008$). The results validate our first hypothesis **H1**.

We also found from the results that the efficiencies of the multi-finger conditions (**C1, C2**) as good as the mouse condition ($p = 0.48$, 0.43 respectively), proving our second hypothesis (**H2**).

Conclusion

We began addressing the crucial problem of how-to use multi-touch as an input modality for users working with abstract parameter spaces. We developed multi-touch interaction techniques for manipulation of values in these spaces. A user study compared performance of the constrained manipulation and index+middle techniques with mouse-based interaction. Our results show that multi-touch manipulation is faster than with the mouse, and no less efficient. Constraining manipulation along a single dimension contributes to the efficiency of manipulation by increasing the separability between parameters. Future research will work to combine the techniques, letting users select among ensembles of affordances to accomplish different parts of a task. Operation selection techniques, such as multi-finger chorded marking menus [11], can be used in conjunction with abstract parameter space manipulation techniques, to fluidly connect menu operation with dexterous parameterization of selected operations.

To extend the utility of multi-touch beyond literal parameter spaces, such as maps, is a key problem for natural user interaction. The value of multidimensional visualizations and simulations will be synergized with new interaction techniques that facilitate exploration of high dimensional data spaces. We have begun to explore this design space with multi-touch interaction techniques that employ separability. We find evidence that participants quickly learn to adjust multiple parameters of an abstract parameter space through single-handed, multi-finger movement, outperforming mouse based interaction. Future research will investigate the impact of multi-touch interaction techniques for manipulation of abstract parameter spaces in contexts such as design and information-based ideation.

REFERENCES

1. Bailly, G., Lecolinet, E., & Guiard, Y. Finger-count & radial-stroke shortcuts: techniques for augmenting linear menus on multi-touch surfaces. *Proc. CHI '10*, 591-594.
2. Balakrishnan, R., Hinckley, K., The role of kinesthetic reference frames in two-handed input performance. *Proc. UIST '99*, 171-178.
3. Buxton, W., Myers, B. A study in two-handed input. *SIGCHI Bull.* 17, 4, 1986, 321-326.
4. Esenther, A. & Ryall, K. Fluid DTMouse: better mouse support for touch-based interactions. *Proc. AVI '06*. 112-115.
5. Forlines, C., Wigdor, D., Shen, C., Balakrishnan, R., Direct-Touch vs. Mouse Input for Tabletop Displays. *Proc. CHI '07*, 647 - 656.
6. Han, J., Low-cost multi-touch sensing through frustrated total internal reflection. *Proc. UIST '05*, 115-118.
7. Hinckley, K., Czerwinski, M., Sinclair, M., Interaction and modeling techniques for desktop two-handed input. *Proc. UIST '98*, 49-58.
8. Igarashi, T., Moscovich, T., Hughes, J. F., As-rigid-as-possible shape manipulation. *ACM Trans. Graph.*, 24, 3, 2005, 1134-1141.
9. Jacob, R. J., Sibert, L. E., McFarlane, D. C., Mullen, M. P., Integrality and separability of input devices. *ACM Trans. CHI* 1, 1, 1994, 3-26.
10. Kruger, R., Carpendale, S., Scott, S. D., Tang, A., Fluid integration of rotation and translation. *Proc. CHI '05*, 601-610.
11. Lepinski, G. J., Grossman, T., and Fitzmaurice, G. The design and evaluation of multi-touch marking menus. *Proc. CHI '10*, 2233-2242.
12. Liu, J., Pinelle, D., Sallam, S., Subramanian, S., Gutwin, C., TNT: improved rotation and translation on digital tables. *Proc. GI '06*, 25-32.
13. Malik, S. An Exploration of Multi-finger Interaction on Multi-touch Surfaces. *Ph.D. Thesis*. University of Toronto, September 2007.
14. Moscovich, T., Hughes, J. F., Multi-finger cursor techniques. *Proc. GI '06*, 1-7.
15. Reisman, J. L., Davidson, P. L., Han, J. Y., A screen-space formulation for 2D and 3D direct manipulation. *Proc. UIST '09*, 69-78.
16. Matejka, J., Grossman, T., Lo, J., and Fitzmaurice, G. The design and evaluation of multi-finger mouse emulation techniques. *Proc. CHI '09*, 1073-1082.
17. Nacenta, M. A., Baudisch, P., Benko, H., Wilson, A., Separability of spatial manipulations in multi-touch interfaces. *Proc. GI '09*, 175-182.
18. Wilson, A. D., Izadi, S., Hilliges, O., Garcia-Mendoza, A., Kirk, D., Bringing physics to the surface. *Proc. UIST '08*, 67-76.
19. Wu, M. and Balakrishnan, R. Multi-finger and whole hand gestural interaction techniques for multi-user tabletop displays. *Proc. UIST '03*, 193-202.
20. Wu, M., Shen, C., Ryall, K., Forlines, C., and Balakrishnan, R. Gesture Registration, Relaxation, and Reuse for Multi-Point Direct-Touch Surfaces. *Proc Tabletop '06*, 185-192.
21. Zhai, S., Milgram, P., Quantifying coordination in multiple DOF movement and its application to evaluating 6 DOF input devices. *Proc. CHI '98*, 320-327.

A General Framework for Incremental Processing of Multimodal Inputs

Afshin Ameri E., Batu Akan, Baran Çürüklü, Lars Asplund
Mälardalens Högskola, Box 883, 721 23
Västeras, Sweden
afshin.ameri@mdh.se, batu.akan@mdh.se, baran.curuklu@mdh.se, lars.asplund@mdh.se
*

ABSTRACT

Humans employ different information channels (modalities) such as speech, pictures and gestures in their communication. It is believed that some of these modalities are more error-prone to some specific type of data and therefore multimodality can help to reduce ambiguities in the interaction. There have been numerous efforts in implementing multimodal interfaces for computers and robots. Yet, there is no general standard framework for developing them. In this paper we propose a general framework for implementing multimodal interfaces. It is designed to perform natural language understanding, multimodal integration and semantic analysis with an incremental pipeline and includes a multimodal grammar language, which is used for multimodal presentation and semantic meaning generation.

Categories and Subject Descriptors: I.2.7

General Terms: Design, Languages

Keywords: Multimodal Interaction, Multimodal Framework

1. INTRODUCTION

In-person communications between humans is a multimodal and incremental process [1]. These two features benefit the interaction between humans in several ways:

First, some modalities are more error-prone to some special types of information and can transfer other data types more precisely [8]. In a multimodal communication, humans can use the modality that is more reliable for the information to be transferred.

Second, in a multimodal interaction, different modalities are complementary to each other. This helps to reduce the ambiguity in perceived information and removal of vague data [8].

*This project is funded by Robotdalen, VINNOVA, Sparbanksstiftelsen Nya, EU European Regional Development Fund.

ICMI'11, November 14–18, 2011, Alicante, Spain.

Third, the incremental nature of communication in humans helps to start processing of perceived inputs from different modalities as they are being received and build up the semantic meaning of them [7]. It means that humans build up their response or reaction as they perceive the inputs [7, 1]. In HCI/HRI domain, incremental processing helps to improve response times of computer systems. Multimodal systems should be very responsive, because (if not) they may lead to repetition of commands from the user, more ambiguity in the recognition process and user annoyance [2].

In this paper we propose a framework for rapid development of multimodal interfaces. The framework is designed to perform modality fusion and semantic analysis through an incremental pipeline. The framework also employs a new grammar definition language, which is called COactive Language Definition (COLD). COLD is responsible for multimodal grammar definition and semantic analysis representation.

2. BACKGROUND

Multimodal grammars were proposed in [6, 4] for definition of mixed inputs from different modalities. They have used unification-based approaches and later, finite-state transducers (FST) to parse and fuse different modality inputs [4, 5].

A more dynamic approach compared to FST model is presented in [10]. The model uses a graph with terminal and non-terminal nodes for grammar representation. This approach allows for on-the-fly expansion of graph during the recognition [10].

A framework that uses spatial ontologies and user context for multimodal integration is described in [3]. The grammar is defined as a part of Microsoft Speech API, which means that object and other modalities' anchors are defined as part of the speech grammar. In other words, non-speech modalities need a specific speech anchor in order to be integrated into the multimodal interaction.

A framework for rapid development of multimodal applications is presented in [2]. Although authors accept the fact that system responsiveness is an important factor in such systems, they refuse to perform the fusion during the speech and discuss that such an approach may lead to constraints on user interaction.

An interesting multimodal system with an incremental pipeline is presented in [1]. Their system, which is called RISE, can process syntactic and semantic information from audio/visual inputs incrementally and generates the feedback on-the-fly. RISE's architecture is based on incremental parsing of speech input with different sub-systems that try to resolve the references in the speech through visual data or the context of dialogue.

An abstract model for implementing an incremental dialogue manager is proposed in [9]. Although the model is not designed for multimodal interactions, but it can easily be modified for that.

Like [3] and [1], we also use object references during fusion. In order to dismiss the problem of using speech as the main modality, we have defined a multimodal language (which we call it COLD) that allows us to define any mixture of different modalities. Pure non-speech communications are easily achievable through COLD. We also take a similar approach as [10] for grammar representation and parsing. We have expanded this model to a more general one that represents several modalities in the same graph.

3. ARCHITECTURE

An important part of the framework is COLD language. COLD definitions are used to (1) generate separate grammars for each modality, (2) define the fusion pattern, (3) define the semantic variables and calculations and (4) define dialogue patterns and dialogue turns.

3.1 COLD Language

In a similar approach to [4]; COLD language is capable of defining the grammar of multimodal sentences and their respective semantic representation. We have expanded Johnston's grammar to (1) include optional phrases and (2) support semantic variable handling.

3.1.1 COLD Syntax

A sample of COLD code is shown in Figure 1. COLD's syntax can be divided into two subcategories: (1) grammar definition and (2) semantic representation. Semantic representation code is always inside curly braces. It can be any Prolog code that is syntactically correct. The rest of the code defines the grammar with the following syntax:

```
predicate (variable list) --> atom/predicate list
```

The "-->" sign, separates a predicate from its definition. Predicates can define variables that will be used in semantic analysis. Predicate definition is a space-separated list of atoms or reference to other predicates. In order to separate atoms for different modalities a colon ':' is used. For example the first definition of "pickup" in Figure 1 means that `pickup` is the atom for first modality and `singleObjectSelect` is an atom for the second modality.

References to other predicates must be enclosed within "<>" with all the variables that should be passed to them. For example the second definition of `pickup` in the sample image refers to `object` predicate and passes `TargetObj` and `Props` variables to it.

Finally, optional phrases are enclosed in "[]". They are atoms or predicates that can be omitted from the interaction. For example the first definition of `putin` in figure 1 contains "`[here]`". It means that the user can omit the word "here" and still get the same response.

3.2 Incremental Multimodal Parsing

To make integration of new modalities easier, COLD performs parsing of inputs through dedicated parsers for each modality (unimodal parsers). All of them have access to a shared copy of the multimodal grammar graph and a pool of different hypothesis.

```
command(ObjetAnchor, Retval) --> <pickup(ObjetAnchor, Retval)>
{call(Retval)}.
command(ObjetAnchor, Retval) --> <putin(ObjetAnchor, Retval)>
{call(Retval)}.
command(ObjetAnchor, Retval) --> <execute>.

pickup(TragObj, Retval) --> pickup:singleObjectSelect
{TargObj=mouseReturnValue, Retval=pickup(TargObj)}.
pickup(TragObj, Retval) --> pickup <object(TargObj,Props)>
{Retval = (Props,pickup(TargObj))}.

object(TargObj, Retval) -->a wooden block {Retval = property
(TargObj,name,woodenblock)}.

putin(TargLoc, Retval) --> put it [here]:singleObjectSelect
{TargLoc=mouseReturnValue, Retval = (holding(CurObj), putin
(CurObj, TargLoc))}.
putin(TargLoc, Retval) --> put it in <object(TargLoc,Props)>
{Retval = (holding(CurObj), Props, putin(TargLoc, CurObj))}.

execute --> execute {execute}.
```

Figure 1: Some Sample code of COLD

3.2.1 Multimodal Grammar Graph

Multimodal grammar graph contains all of the data defined in COLD code. It includes three different types of nodes: rules, rule references and phrases. Rules contain a list of all the phrases and rule references that define its grammar. Rule references are references to other rules and phrases are atoms that can be matched and parsed by parsers.

Each phrase or rule reference node contains a Prolog code block object. The Prolog object stores related semantic code. This allows for incremental semantic analysis through incremental execution of the code.

Optional phrases are marked with a boolean property. All the nodes also include a list of variables that they can access. Since variable values may be different for different competing hypotheses, the values are not defined at graph level.

3.2.2 Hypothesis

Hypotheses are objects that include parse related data. Their most important job is to store values for different semantic variables during a parse. Each hypothesis also contains a list of references to graph nodes that build up that hypothesis. Hypothesis objects have the ability to expand rule references when needed. This means that if a rule reference is to be parsed, its representation in the hypothesis is replaced by the complete representation of referred rule. In such cases, it may be possible that a rule expands into several different lists. Therefore, new copies of the hypothesis object and its related semantic variables are created and added to the pool.

3.2.3 Incremental Parser

Different components involved in parsing and their relations are shown in figure 2. Each modality needs an input registrar. Its job is to capture the data, pack it and send it to the central parser. The central parser receives data from registrars and sends it to its respective parser. It also detects completely parsed hypotheses and fires events in such cases. Unimodal parsers are only responsible for parsing inputs that are related to them.

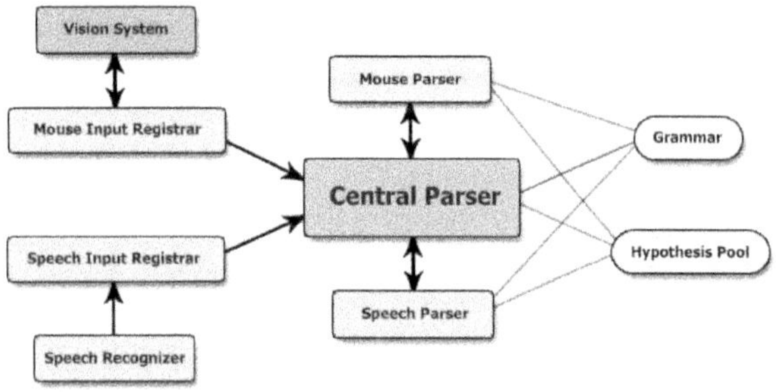

Figure 2: Different components involved in parsing.

Figure 2 shows the components as they are in our test setup, but there may be more input registrars and unimodal parsers for other scenarios.

3.3 Modality Fusion

A direct result of using multimodal grammar graph is that parsers will also contribute to fusion during their parse. Because different modalities are already represented in a unified format in the graph; as the incremental parsing goes forward, the results from different parsers, will be fused together consequently.

An important factor in modality fusion is synchronization of different modalities. For example the `putin` command (Figure 1) is defined as `put it [here]:singleObjectSelect` but it should not mean that the object selection can only be accepted after saying the word "here". Related inputs from different modalities have a relation in time. This time relation is reported to be 1000 ms in [10] and between 1000 ms to 2000 ms in [5]. We use a 2000 ms time difference.

In order to account for time relations, parsers are allowed to postpone a parse request if the next node in the graph does not have the same modality as the new input. In such cases, parsers store the information locally and return a value to the central parser indicating a postponed parse. Upon arrival of a new input, the central parser first sends the new input to the respective parser then asks the postponed parser to check for a new parse. The parser then decides to (1) accept the data (2) remove the data if the two seconds time difference does not approve; or (3) request for another postpone, if the two seconds difference still stands.

3.4 Semantic Analysis

Semantic analysis can be referred to as a search on the set of possible target objects and actions. In this sense each phrase of each modality can affect the final outcome of semantic analysis. An easy way of performing this search is to define different variables and narrow down their values based on the inputs from different modalities. Prolog language has proven to be the language of choice in such cases for many researchers, mostly due to its ease of use.

The COLD framework supports Prolog predicates and variables within COLD language. Each phrase or rule reference can have its related Prolog code and variables. When they are successfully parsed, the respective Prolog code is executed and variables are updated. We use SWI-Prolog as the core Prolog engine in the framework.

Because rule references act like a function call to a rule, all the variables that are defined within the rule reference should be passed to the rule. This happens as a call-by-reference function call. This design helps us to define semantic variables in the highest level of the grammar and allow lower parts of it to manipulate them. The final value of the variable is the semantic representation of that rule.

```

SpeechRegisterer:
New Input > Input: put , Time
    :634412439907006250

Central Parser : Hypothesis Pool Change
cputin(@putin putin(put . it here
    singleObjectSelect))
cputin(@putin putin(put . it in @object))
(_G17561,_G17562)
(_G17564,_G17565)

SpeechRegisterer:
New Input > Input: put it , Time
    :634412439909506250

Central Parser : Hypothesis Pool Change
cputin(@putin putin(put it . here
    singleObjectSelect))
cputin(@putin putin(put it . in @object))
(_G17573,_G17574)
(_G17576,_G17577)

MouseRegisterer:
New Input > Type: singleObjectSelect ,
    Target:object119 ,
      Time:634412439909662500

Central Parser : Hypothesis Pool Change
cputin(@putin putin(put it . in @object))
cputin(@putin putin(put it . here
    singleObjectSelect))
(_G17588,_G17589)
(object119, (holding(_G17602),putin(_G17602
    ,object119)))

SpeechRegisterer:
New Input > Input: put it here , Time
    :634412439914818750

Central Parser : Hypothesis Pool Change
cputin(@putin putin( put it in . @object))
cputin(@putin putin( put it here .
    singleObjectSelect))
(_G17768,_G17769)
(object119, (holding(_G17782),putin(_G17782
    ,object119)))

Central Parser : Input Recognized
(object119, (holding(_G17743),putin(_G17743
    ,object119)))
```

Figure 3: output of the system while parsing the sentence "put it here" and a click.

Prolog statements in COLD language are not used for semantic analysis only, but are also useful for real-time feedback to the user. For example, the `pickup` phrase can contain a predicate that highlights all pickable objects after receiving the word "pickup" from audio channel. This happens during the speech by the user and helps the user to develop a better interaction with the system.

Figure 3 shows system's output during a parse. In order

to fit the output in the paper, it has been edited. At lines 2 and 3, SpeechRegistrar reports the input: "put". Central parser creates two hypothesis based on it (lines 6,7) and reports their respective semantic representation (lines 8,9). Note that at this point the semantic representation only includes empty Prolog variables. After arrival of word "it", both hypothesis stand and since the word has no semantic code assigned to it, nothing changes (lines 11-18). At line 20, a mouse input arrives and it carries the selected object (object119) with it. Now the parser can parse the "singleObjectSelect" node, which belongs to mouse modality and this leads to a more meaningful semantic representation (lines 20-28). In this case, the parser did not wait for the word "here", because it is defined as an optional phrase in grammar. After arrival of the word "here", the parser fires a recognition event and reports its semantic meaning. The changes that are made in variable names during different steps of parse are due to variable copying that was described before.

4. RESULTS

To demonstrate the use of the proposed framework, we are presenting a test case. Our setup consists of an ABB IRB140 industrial robot with a gripper and a camera attached to the 6th joint, therefore the user can view the world through the robots eyes. The images from the camera are overlaid with the transparent virtual objects creating an augmented reality (AR) user interface. Using the mouse, the user can select objects and give voice commands to pick them up and to put them in a location. The semantically analyzed voice and mouse commands are converted to simple Prolog commands such as `pickup(ObjectName)`, which are later expanded to approach, and grasping patterns and finally converted to RAPID language (programming language for ABB robots), and sent to the robot controller for execution.

We used a kitting theme including a palette with empty places. Red, blue and green colored objects in 3 different stacks are placed on the workbench. The task is to create a robot program for re-arranging the colored objects on the palette. The Prolog statements generated at the end of the semantic analysis can be saved to a file, and recalled later on to recreate the robot program.

To assist the user, we highlight possible objects that are applicable to the given command. For example in the pickup case, when the user says the words "pickup" all pickable objects are highlighted. As the user continues to describe which object he wants the robot to pickup, irrelevant highlights are removed. In Figure 4 samples of this highlighting can be seen. The incremental nature of our system can be used to generate early feedback and assistance to the user even before the voice commands end. It is also useful in conditions when user commands are ambiguous; the feedback can help the user to recognize the ambiguity before finishing the sentence.

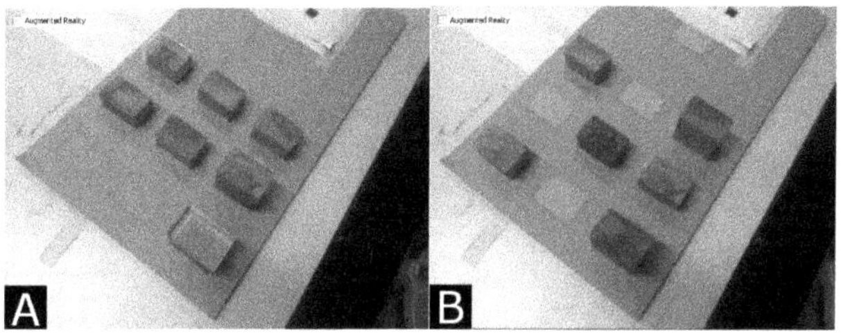

Figure 4: AR UI. (a) Blue objects are highlighted after user says "pickup a blue object". (b) While the robot is holding an object, the user says "put", and all empty locations are highlighted.

5. CONCLUSION

We have designed and implemented an incremental framework for development of multimodal interactions and tested it in a kitting scenario. Incremental processing of inputs allows for in-time interaction between the robot and its human colleague. As a part of this framework we introduced COLD language, which we use to define the multimodal grammar and semantic analysis procedures. Semantic analysis code is directly written in COLD with a Prolog-like syntax, making development easier.

We plan to add context-manager and dialogue manager to the pipeline in the next steps. The context-manager will try to resolve inter-dialogue relations. Dialogue manager will get the outputs of the semantic analysis routines and builds up a dialogue response for the user.

6. REFERENCES

[1] T. Brick and M. Scheutz. *Incremental natural language processing for HRI.* ACM Press, New York, New York, USA, 2007.

[2] F. Flippo, A. Krebs, and I. Marsic. A framework for rapid development of multimodal interfaces. *Proceedings of the 5th international conference on Multimodal interfaces - ICMI '03*, page 109, 2003.

[3] S. Irawati, D. Calderón, and H. Ko. Spatial ontology for semantic integration in 3D multimodal interaction framework. In *Proc. ACM VRCAI2006*, volume 1, pages 129–135, New York, New York, USA, 2006.

[4] M. Johnston. Unification-based multimodal parsing. *Proceedings of the 36th annual meeting on Association for Computational Linguistics -*, page 624, 1998.

[5] M. Johnston and S. Bangalore. Finite-state multimodal integration and understanding. *Natural Language Engineering*, 11(02):159–187, 2005.

[6] M. Johnston, P. R. Cohen, D. McGee, S. L. Oviatt, J. a. Pittman, and I. Smith. Unification-based multimodal integration. *Proc. ACL 35th meeting*, pages 281–288, 1997.

[7] Y. Kamide, G. T. M. Altmann, and S. L. Haywood. The time-course of prediction in incremental sentence processing: Evidence from anticipatory eye movements. *Journal of Memory and Language*, 49(1):133–156, 2003.

[8] S. L. Oviatt. Ten myths of multimodal interaction. *In CACM*, 42(11):74–81, 1999.

[9] D. Schlangen and G. Skantze. A general, abstract model of incremental dialogue processing. *Proc. EACL '09*, (April):710–718, 2009.

[10] R. Stiefelhagen, C. Fogen, P. Gieselmann, H. Holzapfel, K. Nickel, and a. Waibel. Natural human-robot interaction using speech, head pose and gestures. *IROS 2004*, pages 2422–2427, 2004.

Learning In and From Humans: Recalibration Makes (the) Perfect Sense

Marc O. Ernst
Department of Cognitive Neuroscience & CITEC Cluster of Excellence, Bielefeld University
33615 Bielefeld, Germany
marc.ernst@uni-bielefeld.de

Abstract

The brain receives information about the environment from all the sensory modalities, including vision, touch and audition. To efficiently interact with the environment, this information must eventually converge in the brain in order to form a reliable and accurate multimodal percept. This process is often complicated by the existence of noise at every level of signal processing, which makes the sensory information derived from the world imprecise and potentially inaccurate. There are several ways in which the nervous system may minimize the negative consequences of noise in terms of precision and accuracy. Two key strategies are to combine redundant sensory estimates and to utilize acquired knowledge about the statistical regularities of different sensory signals. In this talk, I elaborate on how these strategies may be used by the nervous system in order to obtain the best possible estimates from noisy sensory signals, such that we are able of efficiently interact with the environment. Particularly, I will focus on the learning aspects and how our perceptions are tuned to the statistical regularities of an ever-changing environment.

Categories & Subject Descriptors: A. General Literature, A.1 Introductory and Survey, Human Multisensory Perception, Perception and Action, Perceptual Learning

General Terms: Experimentation, Theory.

Bio

Marc Ernst is chair of the Cognitive Neuroscience Department and member of the CITEC cluster of Excellence at Bielefeld University, Germany. He received his Ph.D. from the Max Planck Institute for Biological Cybernetics for investigations on human visuomotor behavior. For this work he was awarded the Attempto-Prize (2000) from the University of Tübingen and the Otto-Hahn-Medaille (2001) from the Max Planck Society. After his Ph.D., he spent 2 years as a research associate at the University of California, Berkeley, USA working with Prof. Martin Banks on psychophysical experiments and computational models investigating the integration of visual-haptic information. In 2001, Marc Ernst returned to the Max Planck Institute and became principle investigator of the Sensorimotor Lab in the Department of Prof. Heinrich Bülthoff. In 2007 Marc Ernst then became leader of the Max Planck Research Group on Human Multisenory Perception and Action. In 2011 he then moved to Bielefeld.

The scientific interest of Marc Ernst is in human multisensory perception, sensorimotor integration and men-machine interaction. Marc Ernst has published over 50 papers and conference proceedings in high profile journals including Nature, Science and Nature Neuroscience. He was involved in several international collaborative grants, including several European Projects. Furthermore, Marc Ernst was coordinating the FP6 IST European Project CyberWalk, which developed an omnidirectional treadmill in order to enable natural free walking in Virtual Environments.

ICMI'11, November 14–18, 2011, Alicante, Spain.
ACM 978-1-4503-0641-6/11/11.

Detecting F-formations as Dominant Sets

Hayley Hung
Intelligent Systems Lab
University of Amsterdam
H.Hung@uva.nl

Ben Kröse
University of Amsterdam and
Hogeschool van Amsterdam
b.j.a.krose@hva.nl

ABSTRACT

The first step towards analysing social interactive behaviour in crowded environments is to identify who is interacting with whom. This paper presents a new method for detecting focused encounters or F-formations in a crowded, real-life social environment. An F-formation is a specific instance of a group of people who are congregated together with the intent of conversing and exchanging information with each other. We propose a new method of estimating F-formations using a graph clustering algorithm by formulating the problem in terms of identifying dominant sets. A dominant set is a form of maximal clique which occurs in edge weighted graphs. As well as using the proximity between people, body orientation information is used; we propose a socially motivated estimate of focus orientation (SMEFO), which is calculated with location information only. Our experiments show significant improvements in performance over the existing modularity cut algorithm and indicates the effectiveness of using a local social context for detecting F-formations.

Categories and Subject Descriptors

H.3.1 [**Information Storage and Retrieval**]: Content Analysis and Indexing indexing methods

General Terms

Algorithms, Human Factors

Keywords

social surveillance, dominant sets, modularity cut

1. INTRODUCTION

Automatically estimating relationships between humans is a challenging problem, being a highly varied and subjective phenomenon which is difficult to categorise and capture. By relationships, we refer to behavioural phenomena such as dominance, interest, or attraction which can be perceived during prolonged conversation. Typically, such behaviours have been recorded and tested in restricted environments where the number of participants is relatively small (2 people: [19], 4 people: [2, 14]), though some studies have started

ICMI'11, November 14–18, 2011, Alicante, Spain.

Figure 1: Screen-shot from our data (best seen in colour). Some example F-formations are circled. The associate on the right side of an F-formation is indicated by an arrow.

to consider scenarios where more people (7-12) are involved [22, 13]. In most studies, the participants are seated or remain seated for most of the time, which inhibits the natural inclination of people to adjust their proximity and body orientation towards each other when they converse. In addition to the visual and and auditory senses, the ability to adjust one's inter-personal proximity has a significant influence on the perception of smells, touch or body temperature of the other person [11] and can indicate significant differences in the relationships between people. By addressing natural social behaviour in cases where people are standing we are able to capture a wider range of body language. This provides important cues about a person such as their personality, [22], and also their relationship with other people e.g. if they are in an intimate relationship [7].

In this work we focus on freely formed and congregated groups of individuals who are meeting purely to exchange information or foster existing relationships (see Fig. 1). The gathering is such that most of the approximately 50 participants are acquainted with about half of the people at the event, This differs from the scenarios usually used to detect people who are walking together as the scenes are more likely to be filled by mostly unacquainted groups [23, 9, 1]. Unacquainted groups will interact with each other through avoidance strategies but this is clearly a different form of communication than actually having a conversation.

As the number of people in a scene increases, the likelihood of conversations being restricted to a single floor reduces significantly [6] and people tend to split off into separate groups to converse more directly with one another. Under such circumstances, the first challenge in understanding the relationship between group members is to be able to identify them. An initial step towards this, which has received relatively little attention and is the focus of this paper, is the detection of *focused encounters*. By approaching the task of detecting focused encounters, we provide a solid framework for measuring more qualitative behaviour such as aggression [21], or dominance [14]. Focused encounters were first defined by Goffman [10] as a collection of people who are gathered together such that a shared space is maintained between them within which a conversational exchange can occur. They differ from *unfocused encounters* [10] which refer to the way people move to ensure they do not bump into each other, or greeting someone when walking past them, for example. An *F-formation* is considered as a specific instance of a focused encounter [5], which we will describe in more detail in the next section. Unfocused encounters and focused encounters can appear very similar since proximity and orientation cues can be used in both cases. However, clearly interactions during focused encounters can have a much more substantive meaning as all the participants co-operate to sustain a continued period of information exchange. Distinguishing between them allows us to identify differing levels of potential influence.

Detecting F-formations automatically may appear to be a relatively simple task which can be easily extracted from who is 'standing with whom' (as suggested by Yu et al. [20]), but one quickly finds that in more crowded situations where perhaps, the more interesting behavioural phenomena are to be found, proximity can be significantly affected by the layout of a room (e.g. position of furniture) or how crowded it is [5]. Body orientation also plays a role as it provides a prior on the direction of attention of a person but can again be influenced by the same external factors. One can also observe frequent situations at social gatherings where someone tries to join a group but is left standing on the periphery, trying to listen or join in on the conversation. If no one in the group lets him, he clearly has a different status to the full participants in the conversation. Therefore, there are different aspects to being involved in a focused encounter, which goes beyond a person's willingness (through their body behaviour) to be part of it.

The contributions of this paper are twofold. First, we address the new problem of identifying F-formations in crowded social scenes. The classification task is informed by prior work in psychology and social sciences and provides a principled framework from which more complex social behaviours can be identified. Second, we make improvements over the baseline method proposed by Yu et al. [20] by formulating the problem as one of identifying dominant sets [17]. A dominant set is a form of maximal clique that can be applied to edge weighted graphs so that the affinity between all nodes within it is higher than that between the internal nodes and those that are external to it. This differs from *modularity cut* [16] which is a global optimisation method where partitions of the graph are made according to the difference between the affinity of two nodes and the expected degrees of the vertices. Since participants of an F-formation require equal access to a shared space, clustering people within them can be considered more of a local rather than global optimisation task. Finally, we suggest a modification to Pavan and Pelillo's peeling off strategy, which is used to identify all the dominant sets in a graph, by introducing a stopping criterion which enables better detection of singletons.

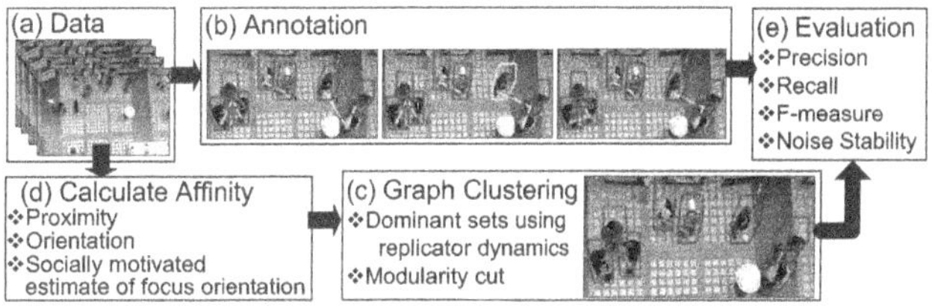

Figure 2: Flow diagram summarising our approach. Green lines:annotated F-formations, Yellow box: associate, Red lines: detections.

For the remainder of this paper, we will discuss related work. Then we motivate the need to consider F-formations as dominant sets (Sec. 3). We describe the data and annotation process used to evaluate our methods in Sec. 4. In Sec. 5, we provide a brief description of the modularity cut algorithm to highlight the differences between it and our proposed clustering method (Sec. 6). In Sec. 7, we provide a description of how the affinity matrix was calculated using proximity and orientation information as well as our socially motivated estimate of visual focus, which is calculated from location information only. We present our experimental results in Sec. 8 and conclude in the final section. Our approach is summarised in Fig. 2.

2. RELATED WORK

Goffman [10] defined focused interaction as being "concerned with clusters of individuals who extend one another a special communication license and sustain a special type of mutual activity that can exclude others who are present in the situation"(p. 83). He went on to say that such a spatial and orientational arrangement "tends to be carefully maintained, maximizing the opportunity for participants to monitor one another's mutual perceivings"(p. 95). Ciolek and Kendon [5] took this idea further by defining a focused interaction more precisely as an F-formation

> "whenever two or more individuals in close proximity orient their bodies in such a way that each of them has an easy, direct and equal access to every other participant's transactional segment, and when they maintain such an arrangement, they can be said to create an F-formation" (p.243).

The transactional segment is the region in front of the body where limbs can reach easily, and hearing and sight is most effective. They defined the *F-formation system* to be the system of spatial and postural behaviours by which people create and sustain the shared interaction space between them. *Associates* of an F-formation were defined as people who may adjust their position relative to the F-formation system but are not included in its boundaries; they can come and go from an F-formation without the usual rituals that full participants of an F-formation would undergo. Examples of F-formations and associates are shown in Fig. 1.

In the computer science community, work on detecting groups has tended to focus more on finding people who are 'together' based on the persistence of their proximity and direction of motion [9, 23, 1, 18] during walking, which are readily measurable from the extracted trajectories. In these scenes, individuals walk with people they know and it is unlikely that they will be acquainted with other walking groups. Unfocused encounters, are therefore much more prominent. Focused encounters on the other hand, give a far richer semantic meaning to the interactions between people. To our knowledge, little work has tried to identify the key factors involved in being in a focused encounter.

Zen et al. have addressed some of the issues involved in approaching people to interact with them, within the framework of estimating personality traits from proxemic behaviour [22]. However, the identification of F-formations was not explicitly addressed.

The closest work to ours was done by Yu et al. [20], who proposed a system that could track and discover groups of interacting people. The *modularity cut* algorithm [16] was applied to identify these groups from automatically extracted trajectories. A problem with this work is the choice of data and experimental design. The 30 minute test data set was rather artificial as 23 people were asked to "mingle in a 3-group configuration" [20] (p.1468). Three groups were indeed identified but given the average number of people per group, it is unlikely that such large F-formations could be sustained [6]; typically, large gatherings tend to split or merge into smaller F-formations over time as the conversation changes. It is difficult to conclude what the 3 groups represented semantically, other than spatially separated locations. The same authors have subsequently used modularity cut to identify groups for classifying group activities in a prison scenario [3] where collective aggressive behaviour from people acting as 'gangs of inmates' are analysed. Also, they used only proximity information and not body orientation, when computing the affinity between detected people. Other work which is close to ours is that of Brdiczka et al.[2] who analysed speech activity to identify who was interacting with whom among 4 subjects. Their algorithm could automatically identify pre-scripted periods when different combinations of pairs of people were speaking or the whole group was speaking together. It is not clear if their algorithm could scale to larger group sizes and also whether using more realistic conversational data would have provided similar results.

3. GRAPH-THEORETIC DEFINITION OF F-FORMATIONS

The people in a scene can be represented as a graph $G = (V, E, w)$ with a set of vertices V, edges E, and a positive edge weight function w. In this case, the vertices or nodes are the people, E correspond to the set of connections between the people and w represents the affinity measured using some extracted features between each pair in the scene. We can express the relationship between all the nodes or people in the scene by a weighted affinity matrix $\mathbf{A}$ such that each of its elements $a_{ij} = w(i, j)$.

3.1 F-formations as High Modularity

Yu et al. [20] defined the task of identifying groups of people in terms of the recursive global partitioning of the graph by maximising the remaining modularity of the uncut edges. Modularity was proposed by Newman [16] as a metric for clustering social networks. The modularity between two nodes in a graph is represented in the corresponding element of *modularity matrix* $\mathbf{B}$ where each of its elements is defined

$$b_{ij} = a_{ij} - \frac{k_i k_j}{2m}. \quad (1)$$

a_{ij} is the affinity between node i and j, k_i and k_j are defined as the expected degrees of the vertices, indicating how 'connected' that particular node is to the rest of the network; $k_i = \sum_j a_{ij}$, and $2m$ is a normalisation term; $m = \frac{1}{2}\sum_{ij} a_{ij}$.

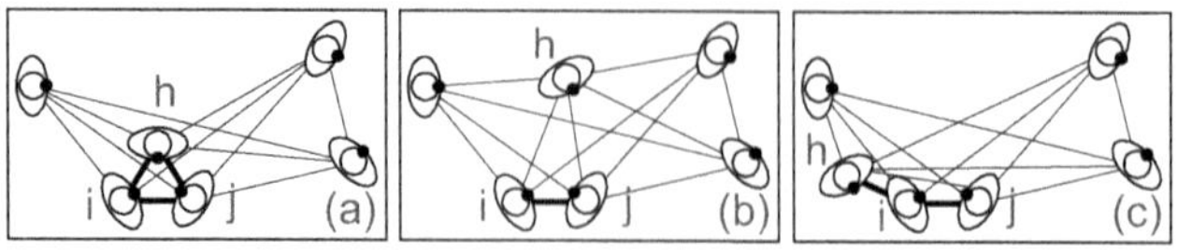

Figure 3: Example of how modularity would differ counter-intuitively. Thick lines represent high affinity while thin lines show low affinity. (a): h, i, and j are in an F-formation. (b): i and j are in an F-formation while h is far away from them. (c): i and j are in an F-formation while h is very close to i.

For a network with n nodes, which is divided into two groups by the indicator vector $\mathbf{s}$, each of its n elements are either labelled as $s_i = 1$ for all vertices in group 1 and $s_i = -1$ for those in group 2. The modularity of the entire network

$$Q = \frac{1}{4m}\sum_{ij} b_{ij} s_i s_j, \quad (2)$$

defines how well connected it is when cuts are made according to $\mathbf{s}$. The main assumption of modularity is that the affiliation between any pair of nodes is only significant if its value is greater than the expected affiliation of those two nodes with the rest of the network.

The modularity is well adapted to finding two-node maximal cliques but is not specifically designed for larger clique sizes, as can be demonstrated by the following example. Let us suppose that we have a network where nodes i, j and h are in an F-formation (Fig. 3(a)). In this case, b_{ij} would be smaller given the proximity of node h compared to if node h was not part of the F-formation (Fig. 3(b)). If h was standing closer to i than j (Fig. 3(c)), thus breaking the triadic F-formation, b_{ij} would be higher than if h was standing equally close to i and j. So in (Fig. 3(a)), b_{ij} is penalised because of the proximity of h to i and j whereas it makes more sense that the proximity of h should *support* the affinity of i and j.

3.2 F-formations as Dominant Sets

As already mentioned, an F-formation is defined as a group of people who have easy and equal access to the same shared space, around which they can communicate for a prolonged time. By its definition, therefore, mutual affinity between all of its members should be higher than the affinity between any of its members and those outside of it. In the case of an associate of an F-formation (e.g. someone who wishes to, but is unsuccessful at joining the group), they are clearly close to one or two members of the F-formation but may not have access to all of them. Based on these definitions, it seems clear that using modularity to identify F-formations is not precise enough for our task.

Pavan and Pelillo [17] proposed a different way of thinking about a cluster as a dominant set, which is a generalisation of maximal cliques to edge-weighted graphs. If we consider a subset S of the set of nodes V in graph G, the average weighted degree of a vertex $i \in S$ with respect to set S is

$$k_S(i) = \frac{1}{|S|}\sum_{j \in S} a_{ij}. \quad (3)$$

Note that in this definition of the degree of i, the value is strictly related to only a subset of the graph V. Ideally, S defines a semantically meaningful local context such as the F-formation consisting of persons i, j, and h in Fig. 3 (a).

The relative affinity between node $j \notin S$ and i is

$$\phi_S(i,j) = a_{ij} - k_S(i), \quad (4)$$

and the weight of each i with respect to a set $S = R \cup \{i\}$ is defined recursively as

$$w_S(i) = \begin{cases} 1 & \text{if} |S| = 1 \\ \sum_{j \in R} \phi_R(j,i)\, w_R(j) & \text{otherwise} \end{cases} \quad (5)$$

and $\phi_{\{i\}}(i,j) = a_{ij}$. $w_S(i)$ measures the overall relative affinity between i and the rest of the vertices in S, weighted by the overall affinity of the vertices in R. Therefore $w_{\{ij\}}(i)$ and $w_{\{ij\}}(j)$ would not vary for any of the conditions in Fig. 3, while $w_{\{ijh\}}(h)$ would be highest for (a), lower for (c), and lowest for (b). This relationship between internal and external nodes of a dominant set S is defined formally using the following conditions;

$$w_S(i) > 0, \forall i \in S \quad (6)$$

$$w_{S \cup \{i\}}(i) < 0, \forall i \notin S. \quad (7)$$

Therefore, dominant sets describe very compact structures, which is ideally suited to represent F-formations of any size.

4. OUR DATA

The data we used (see Fig. 1) consists of real footage of over 50 people who met to present scientific work during a poster session. The focused encounters that are formed were all natural and unscripted, motivated only by each individual's real relationships with other people at the event. The data captures interactive behaviour between people who are closely acquainted (e.g. work colleagues or friends), as well as strangers. The event lasted for approximately 3 hours and was captured by video from a camera that was mounted approximately 15 m overhead. The distance and orientation of the camera helps to conserve the privacy of the participants while enabling the analysis of a crowded scene. To our knowledge, this is currently the largest data set which captures naturally formed focused encounters.

4.1 Annotating the Data

Images from the data were selected so that each one contained different F-formations. In total, 82 images were selected for annotation, containing $\sim$ 1700 people. Selection was made based on leaving at least 10s between images and that no consecutively selected images contained the same formations of people. We also tried to maximise on the crowdedness and ambiguity of associates in the scenes. The positions of all the people in the scene were pre-labelled so that the annotators could concentrate on identifying the F-formations. Software was written to allow easy labelling of the data. 24 annotators from different international cultural backgrounds volunteered to label the data. The annotators were grouped into 3-person subgroups to label the same data so that variability in the labelling could be taken into account during evaluation. After being given appropriate definitions, annotators were asked to identify F-formations and their associates from static images. Asking for explicit labels for associates ensured that annotators would consciously decide how involved they thought each person was in the corresponding F-formation. The annotators labelled 10 - 11 images each, with on average $\sim$ 170 instances of people to label. After the annotation task, the annotators were asked to provide free comments about what they found difficult or easy about the task. Cues that they reported to use for determining who was a member or associate of an F-formation included gaze direction, proximity and body orientation.

F-formation Size	1	2	3	4	5	6	Total *
Full Agreement	340	378	69	2	1	0	450
Union	340	452	136	8	1	2	599

Table 1: Distribution of labelled F-formation sizes using full agreement or the union of labelled members. *Not including singletons.

4.2 Annotation Analysis

We analysed the annotations to see how many sizes of F-formation there were and how frequently each size occurred based on whether there was full agreement between the annotators about all members of an F-formation, or when the union of all overlapping groups was considered. The frequency of occurrence of each F-formation size is shown in Table 1. 340 singletons were labelled, with 450 full agreement F-formations and 599 when the union was used. Using both cases, dyads occurred most frequently. The form of the distribution aligns with those found by Ciolek who studied how people gathered in public areas [4]. The level of annotator agreement was calculated using the F-measure per F-formation (or singleton) for each pairwise combination of annotators who labelled the same data. The mean of these values was taken for each triad of annotators and then finally the average for all groups of annotators was calculated. The mean average F-measure was 94.74% so the annotator agreement was high.

5. MODULARITY CUT

To highlight the difference between our proposed method and modularity cut, we will provide a brief introduction here. Further details can be found in Newman's original paper [16]. Modularity cut was originally developed for social network analysis and discovers groups in social networks, where the size of the communities being tested on are large and consequently, the discovered communities are also of quite large. Given this application domain, maximal cliques or dominant sets are less likely to occur and for discovering social groups based on people with common hobbies or interests, the density of connections between community members is not as important as how connected each person is to everyone else in the network. For the task of identifying spatially separated groups, Yu et al. [20, 3] have shown the effectiveness of using modularity cut. However, as we have demonstrated in Sec. 3, modularity may not be the best representation of F-formations.

From Eq. 2 in Sec. 3, we can see that by carefully selecting $\mathbf{s}$, it is possible to maximise the modularity Q by summing over the higher-valued elements of the modularity matrix $\mathbf{B}$. Since Eq. 2 can be conveniently arranged so that

$$Q = \frac{1}{4m}\mathbf{s}^T\mathbf{B}\mathbf{s}, \quad (8)$$

performing Eigen decomposition on $\mathbf{B}$ and choosing appropriate values for the elements of $\mathbf{s}$ such that the largest or most positive eigenvalues are given the most weight, will lead to a maximisation of Q. In our case, however, the elements of $\mathbf{s}$ are restricted to be either ± 1 and finding the optimal solution for $\mathbf{s}$ is likely to be NP-hard. In practice, a good approximate solution can be found by taking the principal eigenvector of $\mathbf{B}$, $\mathbf{u}_1$, and setting the sign of each element of $\mathbf{s}$ to match those of $\mathbf{u}_1$. Note that the degrees, k_i, are always calculated relative to all the other vertices in the network so the graph is partitioned using a global context. In practice, this can have negative consequences for F-formation estimation, particularly when we consider how people typically arrange themselves spatially in a room. This can be influenced by both the furniture and function of the occasion. In our case, people typically tend to cluster around the edges of the space either to watch others passing through, or to present a poster. This means that the people tend to distribute in clusters of rings around the space. Under such circumstances, a partition can occur that splits apart an F-formation near the centre of the scene just because the scene is equally crowded on both sides. The modularity is still maximised as the people in this central F-formation are, on average, the furthest away from the rest of the nodes in the graph so that cutting most of the edges still leads to a small reduction in modularity. This particular example indicates well the problem of treating F-formation detection as a purely global optimisation task.

Kernighan-Lin (KL) Refinement.

Since the principal eigenvector can only provide an approximation for the division, a step inspired by the Kernighan-Lin algorithm [16] can be applied to try to maximise Q further. This involves taking each node in turn, moving it to the other group and then recalculating Q. The node change which results in the highest Q (even if this leads to a negative change in modularity) is kept and then the process is repeated until all nodes have been swapped. If the final modularity leads to an overall improvement, then the partitioned refinement is kept. This step has been used widely for network analysis with significant improvements [16].

Further Subdivisions of the Network.

Recursive division of the network is carried out by considering an $n_G \times c$ matrix $\mathbf{S}$ which serves to indicate with a one when a node n belongs in community c and zero otherwise. G is the sub-community of the network (with n_G nodes), that is being considered for further subdivision. By measuring the change in modularity before and after the subdivision of the network, we can decide to keep the split based if it leads to a decrease in modularity.

$$\begin{aligned}\Delta Q &= \tfrac{1}{2m}\sum_{i,j\in G}\sum_{k=1}^{c} B_{ij}S_{ik}S_{jk} - \sum_{i,j\in G} B_{ij} \\ &= \tfrac{1}{2m}\mathrm{Tr}(\mathbf{S}^T\mathbf{B}^{(G)}\mathbf{S}).\end{aligned} \quad (9)$$

$\mathbf{B}^{(G)}$ can be considered as the sub-matrix of $\mathbf{B}$ for the subgraph G. By re-arranging ΔQ to have the same form as Eq. 8, we can conveniently re-apply the same eigenvector-based selection process to subdivide the communities. To achieve this form however $\mathbf{B}^{(G)}$ is defined differently to $\mathbf{B}$:

$$B_{ij}^{G} = B_{ij} - \delta_{ij}\sum_{l\in G} B_{il}. \quad (10)$$

6. IDENTIFYING DOMINANT SETS WITH REPLICATOR DYNAMICS

As described in Sec. 5, one way of clustering the graph is to recursively partition it using spectral techniques such as eigen decomposition. However, finding dominant sets could be considered better suited to a local optimisation problem. In doing so, we also ensure that the resolution of the clique sizes are not affected by the number of positive links and the cardinality of the graph [8]. Pavan and Pelillo [17] showed that the notion of a cluster and its relationship to dominant sets were mathematically equivalent by formulating the optimisation problem as a standard quadratic programme where

$$f(x) = \mathbf{x}^T\mathbf{A}\mathbf{x} \quad (11)$$

is maximised subject to the constraint that $\mathbf{x}$ lies on the standard simplex $\Delta = \{x \in \mathbb{R}^n : \mathbf{x} \geq 0 \text{ and } \sum_n x_n = 1\}$. $\mathbf{A}$ in this case is still defined as the affinity matrix of the graph. However, $\mathbf{x}$ is slightly different from the indicator vector $\mathbf{s}$ that was used to maximise the modularity in Eq. 8. Here, $\mathbf{x}$ is defined as the weighted characteristic vector and when defined in terms of the subset of vertices S,

$$x_i^S = \begin{cases} \frac{w_S(i)}{W(S)} & \text{, if } i \in S \\ 0 & \text{, otherwise} \end{cases}, \quad (12)$$

where $W(S) = \sum_{i\in S} w_S(i)$ is the total weight, which must be greater than 0. Pavan and Pelillo [17] proved that by using this definition of $\mathbf{x}$, the maximisation of the objective function is the same as finding dominant sets. Further details of this proof can be found in [17].

To find a local solution of the objective function f, a method taken from evolutionary game theory, called replicator dynamics was used. The first-order replicator equations are defined as

$$x_i(t+1) = x_i(t)\frac{(\mathbf{A}\mathbf{x}(t))_i}{\mathbf{x}(t)^T\mathbf{A}\mathbf{x}(t)} \quad (13)$$

and are applied to all nodes in the network in turn. Since $\mathbf{A}$ is symmetric, the replicator equations provide a strictly increasing update to the characteristic vector $\mathbf{x}$, which converges upon the local solution of f. By taking the support or non-zero indices of the final $\mathbf{x}$, we identify the elements of the graph that are a dominant set. That is, the solution of the replicator equations converges exactly on a characteristic vector that conforms exactly to conditions 6 and 7. In practice, $\mathbf{x}$ is initialised with uniform weights, which corresponds to the centroid of the standard simplex.

Further Subdivisions of the Network.

Since the replicator equations only converges on the most dominant set of a particular graph, an effective way of identifying further clusters in the network is to apply a peeling strategy [17]. This involves identifying a dominant set using Eq. 13, removing the corresponding nodes, and then re-applying the replicator equations to the remaining subgraph. In practice, the elements of the characteristic vector rarely converged to exactly 0 so a threshold was used to identify numbers that were extremely close. The same threshold was also used to ensure that if the value of the maximised objective function was too small, we considered that all the remaining nodes in the graph were singletons.

Local vs Global Context.

There is one disadvantage of using a peeling off strategy to determine dominant sets. As more dominant sets are removed from the original graph, fewer and fewer nodes remain until it is likely that those that are not clustered yet are more likely to be singletons than in an F-formation. We modify the peeling strategy suggested by Pavan and Pelillo [17] by introducing a more principled stopping criterion, which takes into account the global context of the complete graph. Given the nature of dominant sets, we know that conditions 6 and 7 must hold. Using the peeling off strategy, this is certainly the case for the dominant set that has been identified within the sub-graph. However, if we compare $w_{S\cup\{i\}}(i)$, for all $i \notin V$, where V is the set of all nodes in the entire graph, we also ensure that the clustering makes sense within the global context and the need for assigning a slightly arbitrary threshold as a stopping criterion is removed.

7. BUILDING THE AFFINITY MATRIX

Proximity.

Perhaps the most obvious way of measuring the affinity between people is to use their relative proximity, as proposed by Yu et al.[20]. The symmetric distance function between person i and j is defined as

$$A_{ij}^{prox} = -e^{\frac{d_{ij}}{2\sigma^2}} \tag{14}$$

where d_{ij} is the Euclidean distance in the ground plane between person i and j and σ is the variance of the function. Given the nature of our data, σ was set to approximately 2 metres; the commonly accepted distance at which focused encounters occur [12]. Note that unlike Yu et al., our affinity matrix is generated from a single static image.

Proximity and Orientation.

Using proximity alone can lead to errors in the F-formation estimates as the space becomes more crowded. Fortunately, the body orientation can help to identify the shared space between all the F-formation members. This is particularly relevant for cases where associates exist as they may be oriented towards an F-formation but those closest to the associate may have their backs to them. To address this case, A_{ij} is defined by taking the worst case in both directions;

$$A_{ij}^{ori} = \underset{\mathbf{q}}{\operatorname{argmin}}(\begin{cases} e^{-\frac{d_{\mathbf{q}}}{2\sigma^2}} & -\frac{\pi}{2} \geq \theta_{\mathbf{q_1}} - \alpha_{\mathbf{q}} \geq \frac{\pi}{2} \\ 0 & \text{otherwise} \end{cases}, \tag{15}$$

$\forall \mathbf{q} \in \{(i,j),(j,i)\}$, where θ_i is the angle of body orientation of person i, $\mathbf{q_1}$ is the first element of q, and α_{ij} is the angle of the vector from i to j. An asymmetric or directed version of A_{ij} can be considered by taking the actual values of the affinity rather than the minimum in both directions and using an extension of modularity that can deal with a directed affinity matrix[15]. Though our experiments with a directed graph performed better than the basic modularity cut, using the undirected graph led to better performance.

Socially Motivated Estimate of Focus Orientation.

Compared to person position, body orientation can be particularly difficult to extract robustly in crowded environments. To bypass the need to extract body orientation information as well, we propose a *socially motivated estimate of focus orientation* (SMEFO) γ based on the relative distance between participants in the scene. Given a person in the scene, we expect that they are most likely to be oriented towards the people they are motivated to converse with. If the motivation to talk to others is correlated with proximity, people will tend to be much closer to those that they wish to talk to. The SMEFO is defined as

$$\gamma_i = \arccos(\alpha(p_i, f_i)), \tag{16}$$

where p_i is the location of person i and $\alpha(p_i, f_i)$ is the angle of the vector from person i to their estimated centre of focus

$$f_i = \frac{1}{k_i} \sum_j p_j A_{ij}^{prox}. \tag{17}$$

θ in Eq. 15 can then be replaced by γ. Note that k_i here is the degree of i for the entire graph.

8. EXPERIMENTS

To evaluate our methods, the precision, recall and f-measures were calculated for each F-formation and singleton, labelled by the annotators. An F-formation in the annotations was considered to be the union of all labelled groups that overlapped. The groupings were scored for each labelled F-formation by comparing each person in it to the corresponding detected group. Any overlapping nodes between the labelled and detected groups was given a score of $\frac{1}{3}$ per annotation, depending on whether the detection was a true positive, false positive, or false negative. As there were three annotators per image frame, given a labelled group, each person in it could be scored from 0 up to 1, depending on how many annotators agreed that the person was in the F-formation. Then, the set of annotations was compared against the detected F-formation and accumulated to get the precision, recall and f-measure of that particular group. We report the average of each of these measures over all the groups. For the purposes of evaluation the set of all possible groups consisted of all the F-formations and also the singletons. The position and orientation of people were manually labelled in the images, which were then used for building the affinity matrices in Sec. 7. The positions were projected onto the ground plane using orthogonal projection.

First, we present our results using a factorial combination of the different features and methods that were described earlier, shown in Table 2. The features used were proximity (**P**: Eq. 14), proximity and the manually labelled orientation (**P+O** : Eq. 14, 15), and proximity and the SMEFO feature (**P+F**: Eq. 14–16). The methods we used were the dominant set identification using replicator dynamics (**DS**: Eq. 13) with local context where a threshold on the value of the objective function was used (**LC**), and the global context where a stopping criterion was defined based on when $w_S(i) > 0$ for any i not in the identified dominant set S (**GC**), as described in Sec. 6. We compare our results with the method of Yu et al. [20], that used modularity cut and proximity to create the affinity matrix (**MC**: Sec. 5).

For space reasons, we only show the best most automated method of extracting features in combination with modularity cut, which used the proximity and SMEFO features with modularity cut and Kernighan-Lin refinement (**MC+KL**), though the performance in all cases was improved over [20]. In addition to the performance of different methods, we also provide a baseline based on if all people in the data were labelled as singletons. Note that the performance of this baseline is quite high because most of the high performance is distributed in the set of annotated singletons. Note also the high precision is biased towards the naturally high precision of detecting singletons in the data.

Table 2 shows that all our proposed methods out-performs that the baseline [20]. Both fully manual methods with our proposed dominant set technique (**P+O, DS**) performed the best but was comparable to using **(P+O,MC)**. If we examine the performance of the methods when not using the manually labelled body orientation, a clearer picture emerges about the effectiveness of both methods. It is particularly interesting to note that using the position information only (**P, DS+GC**), the dominant set method outperforms all methods that use the SMEFO feature. When considering proximity features only, both **DS** methods outperform the corresponding modularity cut method by over 8.2% in absolute terms. Compared to (**P+F,MC +KL**),

Cues	Methods	Prec	Recall	F-Meas
P	DS+LC	80.24	95.72	84.85
P	DS+GC	87.29	91.79	**86.83**
P	MC	68.72	97.43	76.57*
P+O	DS+LC	90.36	96.63	91.87
P+O	DS+GC	91.94	95.57	**92.24**
P+O	MC	89.50	98.40	92.02
P+F	DS+LC	83.08	94.25	85.85
P+F	DS+GC	85.40	93.26	**86.50**
P+F	MC+KL	77.06	96.28	82.32
All Singletons		95.63	66.27	75.57

Table 2: Results summary in terms of the mean precision, recall and F-measure per F-formation. The boldened values show the highest average F-measure per F-formation for each feature combination. The last row shows the performance if everyone was labelled as singletons. *Baseline from Yu et al. [20].

the absolute improvement of (**P, DS+GC**) is 4.5%, despite not taking into account any orientation information.

The SMEFO feature was proposed as another way of addressing the problem of associates of F-formations who are often close to full participants but may not have equal access to all of them. Using SMEFO, it was possible to identify some cases where someone clearly would not be able to converse with the other person because there would be someone else in between. When using dominant sets to identify the F-formations, this idea of equal mutual access between all the participants is represented more explicitly, which may explain why the performance is better.

The similar performance of both dominant sets and modularity cut, when using both manually annotated location and orientation information, suggests that body orientation is a strong cue for detecting F-formations. However, while the increase in performance when using fully labelled data compared to location information only with modularity cut is 15.5%, using **DS**, the performance improvement is much less, at 5.41%. This suggests that the importance of body orientation may be less important than ensuring equal and high affinity between all members of the F-formation. It also questions whether using more direct estimates of body orientation (i.e. from the imagery data) would necessarily provide a significant improvement for F-formation estimation compared to using position information alone. When comparing the singleton baseline to all other methods, we see that using the basic modularity cut algorithm proposed by Yu et al. [20] only just out performs it, indicating how poor modularity cut is for detecting F-formations. We also found that for the dominant set method, the **GC** method consistently out-performed the corresponding **LC** method, which demonstrate the effectiveness of our improvement to the stopping criterion of the peeling back strategy.

Simulating Tracking Errors.

So far, our experiments have shown F-formation detection using manual annotations of the position and body orientation information. Using the SMEFO feature, while the body orientation becomes an estimate, the positions are still manually extracted. To test the stability of our method compared to the baseline methods, we applied increasing levels of Gaussian noise to the manually labelled positions. For cases where we tested the clustering methods using manually annotated body orientation information, we did not add noise to the orientations as adding noise to the positions, given the body angle, would already affect the affinity sufficiently. It also provided a more consistent framework from which to compare the different features and methods. The results are summarised in Figure 4.

We noticed when analysing the breakdown of the performance across different group sizes, that a significant increase in the performance of the dominant set method over modularity cut was due to significantly better estimation of singletons. Since these are not really considered to be F-formations, we provide the performance based on all F-formations that contain at least 2 people. This is indicated as a thin black line in Figure 4, while the thick black line shows the overall performance for all cluster sizes. We also noticed when applying noise to the positions, that the F-formation performance tended to saturate as the noise level increased. On closer inspection we found that there was a tendency for all nodes to be labelled as singletons as they became more spread out. To illustrate this, we also show a dashed line in Figure 4, which represents the performance when all nodes are labelled as singletons, and a dot-dashed line which shows the performance for the same method evaluated without the singletons. As expected, when the labelled singletons are excluded from the calculation, the performance drops significantly from 75% to 62%.

Note that using modularity cut, the performance increases significantly when singleton detection is not evaluated, which suggests that modularity cut is better at detecting larger group sizes. In almost all cases when singletons are not evaluated, the dominant set method performs worse. In terms of noise stability, the deterioration in performance occurs much sooner for modularity cut, compared to the dominant set methods. For the SMEFO feature, it provides more stability during noisy conditions for the modularity cut method, while improvements for the dominant set method is less significant. Using the manual body orientation labels, however, appear to provide much more stability for the **DS** method, suggesting that estimates of body orientation may still be useful when the tracking estimates are very noisy.

9. CONCLUSIONS AND FUTURE WORK

In this paper, a new approach for detecting F-formations was presented by formulating the problem as one of finding dominant sets. Compared to modularity cut [20], significant and more stable performance improvements were observed. Our SMEFO feature also provided better performance, showing that some estimate of body orientation can help to improve the F-formation estimation performance but having accurate position information is more likely to provide better estimates. Since the method currently does not use automated person detection or body orientation, further investigations are needed to see the effect on F-formation estimation. Our test data is currently limited to scenarios where everyone is standing. In public spaces, a variety of sitting and standing behaviours occur depending on possible seating areas or other furniture. This was represented to some extent in our current data with high circular coffee tables but could be extended to more extreme cases. Increased furniture in the space can lead to spatial deformations of the F-formations that occur more in standing scenarios. So dominant sets constructed from instantaneous spatial cues alone will have limited success. Examining co-ordinated conversational movement in video may help to mitigate this problem.

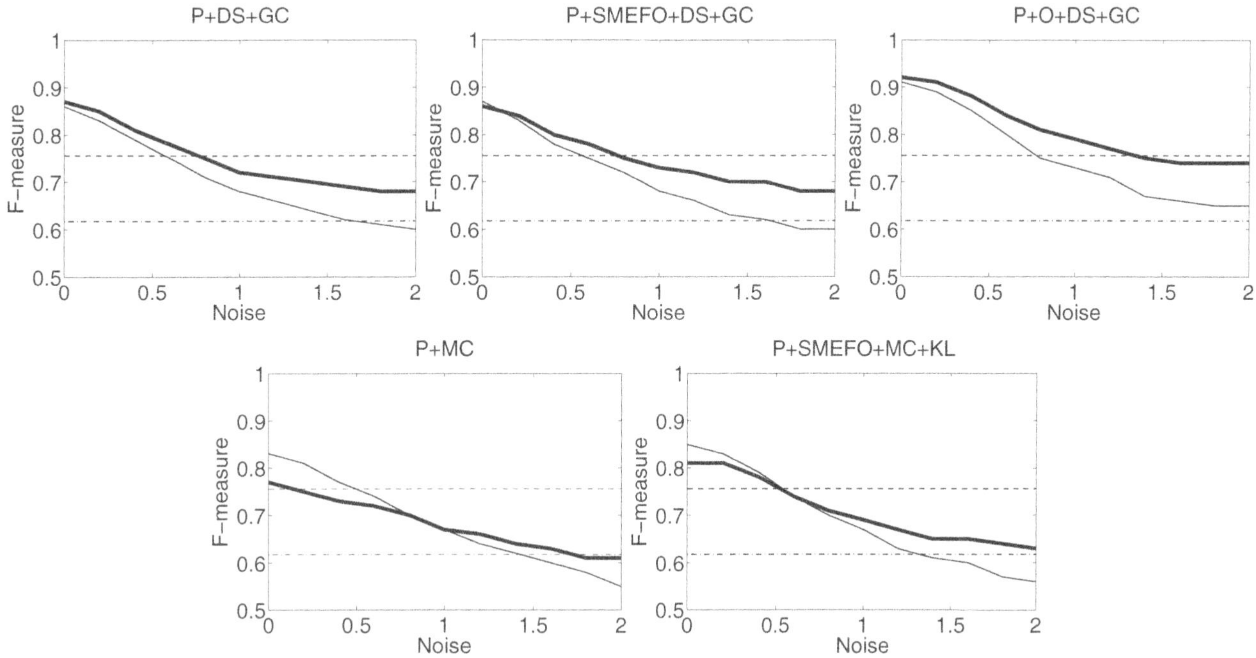

Figure 4: Comparison of results when Gaussian noise was added to the people's positions. The noise is expressed in terms of the proportion of the approximate width of a person. Thick black line shows the mean f-measure evaluating over all F-formation sizes while the thin black line indicates the performance when labelled singletons were excluded from the evaluation. Horizontal lines indicate the f-measure if every node was labelled as a singleton (dashed lines) and when labelled singletons were not evaluated (dot-dashed lines).

Acknowledgements

This research was supported by a Marie Curie Research Training Network fellowship in the project "AnaSID" (PIEF-GA-2009-255609). We thank Jagan Varadarajan, Bastien Crettol, and Valérie Devanthéry for their help during the capture and processing of the data, and Gwenn Englebienne for his template-based orthogonal projection code.

10. REFERENCES

[1] A.French, A. Naeem, E. Dryden, and T. Pridmore. Using social effects to guide tracking in complex scenes. In *AVSS*, pages 212–217, 2007.

[2] O. Brdiczka, J. Maisonnasse, and P. Reignier. Automatic detection of interaction groups. In *ICMI*, pages 32–36, 2005.

[3] M.-C. Chang, N. Krahnstoever, S. Lim, and T. Yu. Group level activity recognition in crowded environments across multiple cameras. *AVSS*, pages 56–63, 2010.

[4] T. M. Ciolek. Location of static gatherings in pedestrian areas: an exploratory study. *Man-Environment Systems*, 7:41–54, 1977.

[5] T. M. Ciolek and A. Kendon. Environment and the spatial arrangement of conversational encounters. *Sociological Inquiry*, 50(3-4):237–271, 1980.

[6] R. Dunbar, N. Duncan, and D. Nettle. Size and structure of freely forming conversational groups. *Human Nature*, 6(1):67–78, 1995.

[7] J. J. Edney and N. L. Jordan-Edney. Territorial spacing on a beach. *Sociometry*, 37(1):92–104, March 1974.

[8] S. Fortunato and M. Barthélemy. Resolution limit in community detection. *Proceedings of the National Academy of Sciences*, 104(1):36, 2007.

[9] W. Ge, R. Collins, and B. Ruback. Automatically detecting the small group structure of a crowd. In *Workshop on Applications of Computer Vision*, pages 1–8, 2009.

[10] E. Goffman. *Behavior in Public Places: Notes on the Social Organization of Gatherings.* Free Press, 1966.

[11] E. T. Hall. *The silent language.* Doubleday, Garden City, N. Y., 1959.

[12] E. T. Hall. *The Hidden Dimension.* Doubleday, Garden City, N.Y. :, [1st ed.] edition, 1966.

[13] H. Hung and G. Chittaranjan. The wolf corpus: Exploring group behaviour in a competitive role-playing game. In *ACM Multimedia*, 10 2010.

[14] D. B. Jayagopi, H. Hung, C. Yeo, and D. Gatica-Perez. Modeling dominance in group conversations using nonverbal activity cues. *IEEE Transactions on Audio, Speech and Language Processing*, 17(3):501–513, 2009.

[15] E. A. Leicht and M. E. J. Newman. Community structure in directed networks. *Phys. Rev. Lett.*, 100:118703, 2008.

[16] M. E. J. Newman. Modularity and community structure in networks. *Proceedings of the National Academy of Sciences*, 103(23):8577–8582, June 2006.

[17] M. Pavan and M. Pelillo. Dominant sets and pairwise clustering. *IEEE Transactions on PAMI*, 29, 2007.

[18] S. Pellegrini, A. Ess, K. Schindler, and L. J. V. Gool. You'll never walk alone: Modeling social behavior for multi-target tracking. In *ICCV'09*, pages 261–268, 2009.

[19] R. Ranganath, D. Jurafsky, and D. McFarland. It's not you, it's me: Detecting flirting and its misperception in speed-dates. In *EMNLP'09*, pages 334–342, 2009.

[20] T. Yu, S. Lim, K. A. Patwardhan, and N. Krahnstoever. Monitoring, recognizing and discovering social networks. In *CVPR*, 2009.

[21] W. Zajdel, J. Krijnders, T. Andringa, and D. Gavrila. Cassandra: audio-video sensor fusion for aggression detection. *AVSS*, 0:200–205, 2007.

[22] G. Zen, B. Lepri, E. Ricci, and O. Lanz. Space speaks: towards socially and personality aware visual surveillance. In *1st ACM international workshop on Multimodal pervasive video analysis*, pages 37–42, 2010.

[23] W. Zheng, S. Gong, and T. Xiang. Associating groups of people. In *BMVC*, September 2009.

Toward Multimodal Situated Analysis

Chreston Miller
Center for HCI, Virginia Tech
2202 Kraft Drive, Blacksburg,Va. 24060, USA
chmille3@vt.edu

Francis Quek
Center for HCI, Virginia Tech
2202 Kraft Drive, Blacksburg,Va. 24060, USA
quek@vt.edu

ABSTRACT

Multimodal analysis of human behavior is ultimately situated. The situated context of an instance of a behavior phenomenon informs its analysis. Starting with some initial (user-supplied) descriptive model of a phenomenon, accessing and studying instances in the data that are matches or near matches to the model is essential to refine the model to account for variations in the phenomenon. This inquiry requires viewing the instances within-context to judge their relevance. In this paper, we propose an automatic processing approach that supports this need for situated analysis in multimodal data. We process events on a semi-interval level to provide detailed temporal ordering of events with respect to instances of a phenomenon. We demonstrate the results of our approach and how it facilitates and allows for situated multimodal analysis.

Categories and Subject Descriptors

I.2.4 [**Artificial Intelligence**]: Knowledge Representation Formalisms and Methods—*relation systems, temporal logic*

General Terms

Algorithms, Design

Keywords

Situated Analysis, Multimodal Analysis, Temporal Relations

1. INTRODUCTION

Multimodal analysis of human behavior is ultimately situated. Consider an analysis of several students solving a math problem together with a focus on how the students 'co-construct' space together in the course of their discussion. This co-construction is done through pointing (where spatial reference may be initiated or referenced), gaze (as students co-attend to the shared space that now has meaning), and other gestural forms (that shape the space). The students' gaze, speech, and gesture channels are recorded into a database. During their session, a door slams outside their workspace, at which point all the students turn around. The question is: "Is this very strong, temporally coherent alignment of gaze important?". Looking at the gaze data alone, the strong temporal and spatial alignment may suggest an important event has occurred, but for co-construction of space, it is probably unimportant. The only way to judge relevance is to look at the specific instance.

However, what if the analysis is focused on how an external attention-synchronizing event may alter shared decision making, e.g., clearing out irrelevant distractor concepts when the group returns and picks up where they left off. In this case, the door-slam incident and gaze alignment phenomenon is very relevant. One analyst's data is another analyst's noise. The tension is that we want to have machine help to filter events and focus analysis.

The question is how to solve the problem of filtering and focusing analysis. Such detailed analysis is characterized by focused attention on particular instances of behavior within-context where inter-relations (temporal order) among events in the channels for a particular instance are analyzed. This process is time consuming and very tedious as some form of manual inspection referencing the original media context (e.g., video) is necessary. The situated contexts of individual instances are very important - an instance being a particular occurrence of a phenomenon within the data. We propose a situated analysis approach that supports viewing instances of a phenomenon within-context and automates processing of temporal ordered relationships across channels. Our approach is to allow the analyst to define a model of a phenomenon, guided by what is in the data, then, to identify and locate instances of the model (and sub-structures) within the data and show the context(s) of the occurrence(s). Typically, the data consists of time intervals describing observed events, e.g. "Student 1 begins a gaze event at Student 2 at time t_i and ends at time t_j", for $i \geq 0$ and $j > i$. Flexible representation of events (and the model) are provided through semi-interval processing [9] where a time interval of an event is viewed as comprising of beginning and end atomic units (semi-intervals). The semi-intervals are viewed as base representative units as opposed to a complete interval. We process these time intervals to extract the necessary information that supports our approach.

Multimodal analysis integrates multiple data channels (e.g., gaze, gesture, and speech) where incorporation of such information provides more accurate analysis results [35]. These data channels are conduits of data streams that contain events describing actions in the data-set. We extract "within-context temporal relations" with respect to the model from these data streams. We abstract away from the data streams and focus on the situated events that describe the observed actions. Then for each instance found, the situated events can be viewed, providing the analyst the opportunity to judge the relevance of the instance with respect to their analysis goal and to further investigate other identified instances.

In §2 we provide an overview of our approach. We then review related work in §3. §4 describes multimodal data streams in terms of the events they contain and how we abstract away from streams and focus on viewing the events they contain. Afterwards, §5 describes how our approach extracts temporally ordered relations between events in all data streams and the process of identifying specific instances of a phenomenon. §6 details how we support situated analysis through automated means by combining the components described. §7 follows with a discussion of example analyses using our approach on multimodal human behavioral corpus. Lastly, §8 provides conclusions and discussion of future work.

2. APPROACH OVERVIEW

Here we describe an overview to our approach that will serve as the foundation to the rest of the paper.

Our approach specifically seeks to incorporate the knowledge and guidance of the domain expert (such as a psycholinguist, or other behavioral expert) in human behavior analysis tasks. Conversely, we want automatic processing to support domain experts as they apply their knowledge in exploring multimodal data. Other attempts at providing automation support for analysis include [40] and [5]. As models of phenomena are created and discovered (through exploration and refinement), the identification of other instances of the models is needed. Our approach is to provide automatic processing of temporal relations between data stream events and view such relations situated (within-context) within instances of a phenomenon.

We provide support in three ways. *First*, we view the analysis process as beginning with the domain expert advancing a hypothesis (model) of a behavior phenomenon and proceeding to explore instance(s) of the phenomenon (point of focused attention). How the phenomenon is present in the data may be unknown at the start of analysis, hence, the expert starts to explore the data with an initial idea. This initial idea is likely to be an incomplete model but a general structure of the phenomenon. *Second*, our approach can identify instances of this model in the data and present *related* events to each specific instance. *Related* events refer to events found in context to a specific instance and their respective temporal relations to the instance. The *related* events presented are from all data streams enabling situated analysis as we extract within-context information of a domain expert's model. *Third*, all instances of the model are identified, allowing a comparison of relations across contexts which may help in formulating new insights. With these three components, our approach allows a situated view of cross-stream relations with respect to a phenomenon.

3. BACKGROUND AND RELATED WORK

Temporal Event Data: The ordered relations that are inherent to temporal event data is an active area of research. Allen in [1] formulated thirteen relationship principles that express all the possible orderings between two event intervals. These orderings describe how events between data streams relate. Research, such as [11, 13, 26, 27, 38], has focused on processing numerical or descriptive univariate, multivariate, or symbolic temporal data with the goal of discovering events and temporal relationships from temporal data. Others have explored the discovery of temporal knowledge and associated patterns, such as [12, 19, 28].

The stream data of multimodal data-sets is a mixture of ordinal and nominal data. As per the temporal data models reported in [28], gesture traces are a collection of univariate numerical time series (ordinal) while speech and gaze target fixations are multivariate symbolic interval series in which their meaning is categorically descriptive (nominal). Explorations into the relational structures of nominal data can be seen in [6, 20, 43, 44]. More specifically, our prior research [25] explores how to structure nominal event data based on semi-interval processing using n-gram techniques from speech processing. Other research [9, 29] has explored the concept of breaking temporal events into core units of beginnings and endings through semi-interval temporal ordered processing. Previously mentioned research ([1, 13, 27, 38]) has investigated patterns and relations among interval data irrespective of the data being ordinal or nominal.

Multimodal Analysis: Multimodal analysis of human behavior typically involves multiple time-synchronized data streams which consist of different observable human behavior signals (e.g. different gesture types, gaze fixations, and speech). The streams are then annotated either by hand, automatically, or a mixture of both. Then manual analysis, normally with some machine automated help, of the streams is performed. Example application and results of this process can be seen in [5, 4, 16, 18, 23, 31, 34, 42].

There has been much work in automatically detecting and recognizing certain behavior, a few examples being [10, 30, 41]. However, it is the more detailed analysis prominently exemplified by the math students example that is much more difficult to automate and is the kind of analysis where human guidance is needed. The goal of this detailed process is to explore the data and to identify and understand instances of phenomena. This is done through inspection of the temporal relations of the events within the streams. However, several challenges surface in this process. The identification of instances of a phenomenon that are relevant to the analysis being conducted can be difficult. Plus, coordination between the multiple streams requires careful attention as seen in [5, 35]. Both of these challenges were exemplified in the previously described analysis scenario of math students.

In terms of the analysis focus, we have observed two viewpoints employed for multimodal analysis of human behavior. The first focuses on identifying behavior instances within sections of recorded data (e.g. recorded video/audio sessions). This is a useful and powerful means as it shows the context in which the behavior occurs. However, what if an expert is interested in identifying instances of a particular behavior (e.g., co-construction of space) and viewing all the contexts in which they are situated. The second viewpoint is the reverse of the first by showing the behavior within-context. This is a plausible approach since the focus of some analyses is instances of a specific behavior. Examples of this can be seen in [5] where cues were identified within a group meeting setting that could signal floor

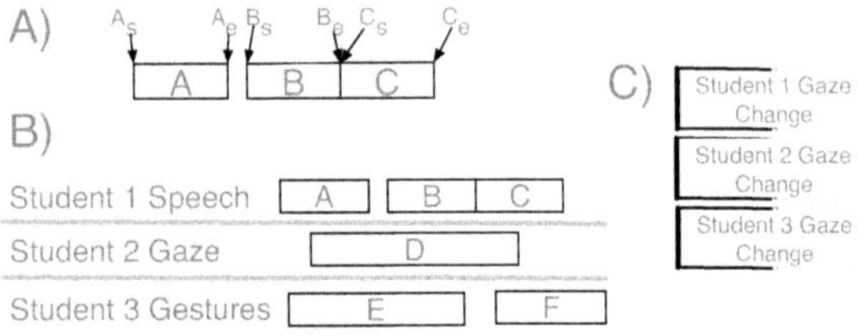

Figure 1: A) Example of a sequence of events with their labeled start and end times, respectively. B) Example of event overlap between streams. C) Example of an attention-synchronizing model with concurrent change of student's gaze.

control events. Other research [34] has found cues in gaze and gestures that aid in discourse analysis. These cues can be flags in the identification of specific behavior of interest for which the expert would want to view the different instances within their respected situated contexts. This prior research exemplifies that the difficulty is in identifying how phenomena are manifested within the corpus. By taking the viewpoint of behavior within-context, we can begin with a general structure (model), or sub-structure, that describes the phenomenon and see how events within the corpus are *related* to the structure.

4. MULTIMODAL DATA TO EVENTS

The first component of our approach has the expert start with a hypothesis with which to identify instances. Hence, we need a way to describe the multimodal data to allow for defining a model of the hypothesis. We want to abstract away from data streams and view the descriptive events. In this section we define data streams and the events they produce and how this desired abstraction can be obtained.

Multimodal data typically exist in the form of data streams (time series of data points and signals) and music score data. Music score data are multivariate time series data that describe event intervals in time that possibly overlap. A number of multimodal analysis tools (e.g., [17, 36]) employ this form of multimodal data representation. Our first step is to convert these data streams into a homogeneous stream of events. An event is an interval in time representing when an action begins and ends. It comprises of a beginning, end, and description. Figure 1A shows three examples of events, A, B, and C, with their respective beginning (start) and end times. Viewing events with respect to their beginning and end is known as semi-interval processing [9] where a beginning or end is a semi-interval. Sometimes it is difficult to determine what is an event within a data stream (e.g., deciding exactly when an event begins and ends) however, we assume such detection occurs prior to our processing. Our focus in this paper is not on how to extract events from data, but on how to interpret these events after they are extracted.

Multimodal analysis comprises multiple data streams by definition. Hence, there will be overlaps between the multiple streams and cross-modal relations supportive of multimodal analysis. In Figure 1B, we see three data streams, Student 1's speech, Student 2's gaze, and Student 3's gestures, with respective events. It can easily be observed how these represented events occur in overlap.

We abstract away from various specific representations in the separate data streams and focus on the events they contain while keeping the context (data stream) from which they originate. The strict notion of data streams fades into the background as the events become a prevalent part of the analysis. It is the events and what they represent that aid in the analysis. This approach allows the flexibility of processing that is mode independent where the kind and number of modes used does not matter.

Figure 1C shows an example model of a hypothesis an expert might use to find instances of attention-synchronizing events during the math student session described earlier. Assuming three students are involved, the expert specifies a model where the student's gaze change at the same time. This involves specifying the temporal order of start gaze change semi-intervals for each student. In this case, the order represents concurrent action (equality). This will identify instances where the students have a synchronized gaze change. This example shows how we abstract away from the idea of three gaze data streams and focus on the gaze events of the students.

5. MODEL ASPECTS

Following from our first component, temporal relations between the model and *related* events is needed. The coordination between events within multiple data streams is necessary to understand a specific model instance. The temporal order in which events occur is key in describing a specific phenomenon, e.g., the coordinated gaze in response to a door-slam describes an attention-synchronizing phenomenon. This leads to the need of our second component which is identifying an instance of a model and extracting within-context temporal information between the model and *related* events. First we will address extracting the temporal information, after which, we will describe the process for identifying a model instance.

5.1 Event Temporal Relations

The challenge is temporal relations describing phenomena are structural in nature and not a set of parameters. Such a structure must be learned. Consider the scenario where a group of four History students use a horizontal, high-resolution, interactive tabletop display [24] to perform analysis of information snippets on virtual notecards (displayed on the table) [2]. The students were not given any instructions for making sense of the data, however, over time their actions around the shared space evolved into a ratification process in which changes to the notecard placement and utilization of the display space could be made. This process begins with the wielder of the interaction device announcing a statement or question around a piece of data (*announcement*) which lead to the coordinated gaze of the other three students (*co-gaze*). The wielder and other student(s) then proceeded to discuss a piece of data and decide (*ratify*) what to do with it.

The students' interaction resulted in a sequence of proposal, echo, and act with enunciation that produced a ratification process which advanced the joint project and common ground. This temporal sequence exemplifies the structural nature of temporal relations in multimodal data. Other approaches, such as HMMs [37] and n-grams [3, 39], can be viewed as piece-wise parametric models that get some sense of overall structural relations. The problem is that approaches such as these 'linearize' behavior structure of these piece-wise models and do not address how to combine these linearized pieces structurally. Research in the numerical domain has also investigated structural means to numerical model modification, for example [8, 14, 21].

We approach representing temporal relations structurally by viewing events from the semi-interval level and how such atomic units of events relate temporally. Other research has investigated the use of semi-intervals for its representational flexibility with respect to incomplete or partial knowledge in identifying event interval sequences of interest [29]. Our prior work [25] investigated the use of n-gram processing of semi-intervals for providing comparison means for events in event sequences in which the processing takes advantage of the structure of the events.

With this structural approach, we provide automatically extracted temporally ordered relations within and between streams. This extracted information includes how semi-intervals relate with respect to order (e.g., "<", and "=") and their likelihood with respect to a model. Given a model consisting of semi-intervals, *related* events to each semi-interval are classified occurring either *before*, *current* (concurrent), or *after*. This is the same classification as used in [25] with the addition of *current*.

To obtain this information we first segment all interval events into semi-intervals. Next, all the events from all data streams are serialized into one linear encoding with temporal ordering preserved through the use of ordered relations. An example of this can be seen in Figure 2 where the events from 1A and B are linearlized. Due to this serialization process, results will contain temporal ordered relations within and between data streams as seen in Figure 2B. Here, the semi-interval events from multiple data streams are integrated into one sequence allowing comparison across streams and handling of overlap. Hence, given a focal point (model) in the data, one is able to view events across streams that *relate* to the focal point within-context. Semi-intervals that co-occur are set to be equal ('=') preserving their co-occurrence (e.g. B_e and C_s in Figure 2).

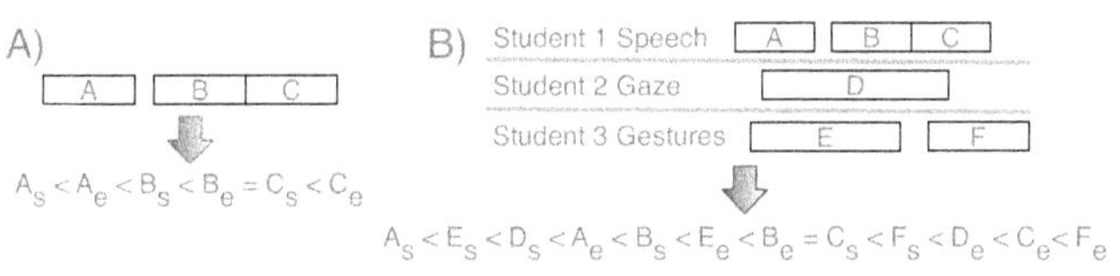

Figure 2: A) Example of linearizing events and preserving their temporally ordered relations. B) Example of how serialization of multiple streams allows for comparison across them.

5.2 Model Instance Identification

The process of how we identify an instance of a model and subsequently provide *related* event semi-intervals to the model can be seen in Figure 3. To identify an instance given a model (in terms of semi-intervals), we search the data-set for matches to the semi-intervals (1). In this step, multiple matches may be found as can be seen from the two potential models. This occurs because events may repeat. A first approximation may be to assume that the closer of two events of the same type is the better candidate. Hence, we search for the match where all the semi-intervals are temporally closest. This mainly applies to semi-intervals of a different event type, e.g., A_e and B_s or a gaze event versus a speech event. Hence, Potential Model 2 is chosen. We also process sub-structures (sections) of the model to detect overlap, e.g., D_s overlaps with A. Note that identified instances may have semi-intervals that "interrupt" the instance, e.g. event H occurs between A and B. After identification is complete, the *related* semi-intervals to the model are extracted using n-gram processing at the semi-interval level (2). The set of *related* semi-intervals are then presented as relating to the model (3). This set also includes events that may only relate to a substructure of the phenomenon but are part of the same instance. This allows for identification of overlap and semi-intervals not seen by viewing the whole model solely, as seen in Figure 3 step (2).

6. ASSISTED SITUATED ANALYSIS

The identification of an instance of the hypothesis (model) allows a within-context view of *related* events. However, the expert is interested in all instances of the hypothesis, leading to a need to view the multiple instances of the hypothesis within context and, potentially, to compare them. In this section, we address our third component through initial discussion of identifying all instances of a phenomenon, how an expert can toggle between them, and the resulting aggregate view of all the results. After which, we discuss how our approach facilitates comparison across contexts.

To identify all instances of a phenomenon, the process described in Figure 3 is repeated until all instances have been identified. The expert can then step through all unique instances, observing the *related* events and the differences and similarities. Through this process we can support analysis of the interrelationships among events with respect to the model wherever it occurs in situ, hence providing relations within-context and across data streams. We call this assisted situated analysis as we use automation to identify instances and the associated temporal relations for each instance and provide support to the expert in viewing and exploring this information.

We also allow the expert to view the *related* events from all contexts at once. An example of this can been seen in Figure 4 where a model and sub-structures are identified in three contexts and the *related* events within each context are aggregated to allow a view of all *related* events. With the aggregation of all results, the likelihood that the events occurred given all the contexts is provided when comparing the *related* events. The likelihood calculation is with respect to the whole model and its sub-structures and follows the same procedure of our prior work [25]. This aids in comparison among the instances extracted and also provides information on the event frequency with respect to the model. The number of semi-intervals used in calculating the likelihood is given as a confidence level as it is a measure of the amount of information used in the calculation. We are more confident in a result that incorporated more information.

An interesting artifact of this process can be seen in Figure 4 where the frequency of G may suggest an event of interest. However, the frequency is only seen through comparing multiple contexts. The aggregation of the results from all instances of the model and sub-structures allows for the opportunity to discover new temporal relations between events and the model. Alternatively, H occurs only once but may hold equally or more important value than G's frequency (frequent vs. infrequent). Presenting the results from all contexts provides the opportunities for the researcher to investigate variations of the model (through inspection of their

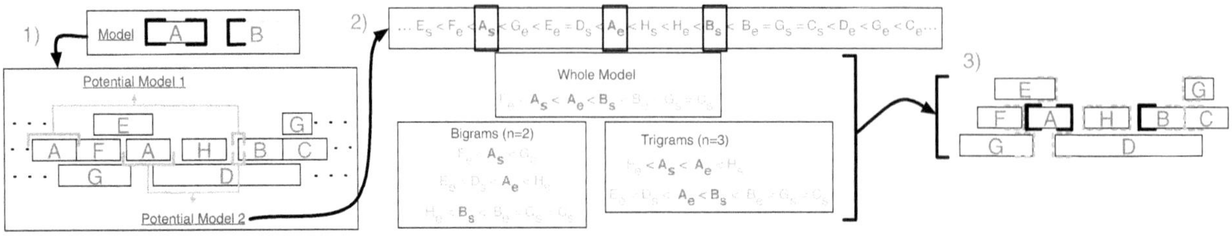

Figure 3: Localization of model instances and subsequence processing of temporal relations: 1) Begin with a model and identify where potential instance(s) reside at the semi-interval level. 2) Choose instance and perform processing on the whole model and select values of N. 3) Present *related* semi-intervals.

original context) and decide their relevance to the current analysis. Hence, given the above procedure, we are able to provide assisted support to multimodal situated analysis.

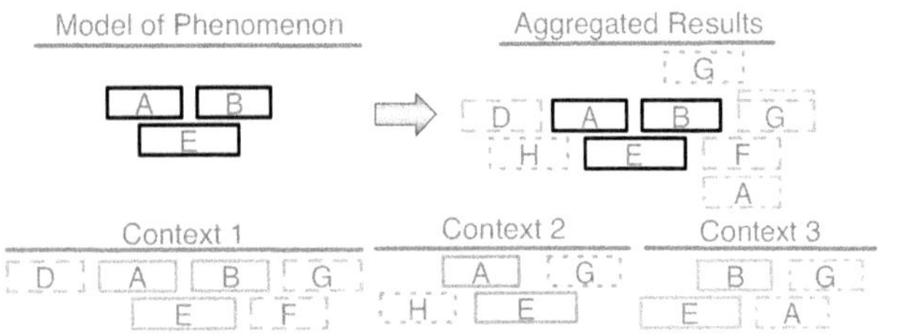

Figure 4: Identification of a model and substructures in several contexts and the aggregation of *related* events across contexts. Overlap of G after model event B represents its multiple occurrence.

7. IMPLEMENTATION AND USE

Here we present example analyses that illustrate how our approach is able to provide support for multimodal situated analysis. A real data-set was chosen to exemplify our approach. The data-set consists of meetings of U.S. Air Force officers from the Air Force Institute of Technology (AFIT) engaging in military wargaming scenarios [4]. In this section we discuss the implementation of our approach, the data-set used, and example analyses.

7.1 Implementation

The core algorithm of our approach is based on the system described in [25] with a number of updates and enhancements. An interactive layer was added to allow user interaction and viewing of the context of any specific model instance and its respective *related* events. Implementation is in Python using QT 4.5 [33] for the user interface, and the Pymunk physics engine [32] (a Python wrapper of the C library Chipmunk [7]) is used as a means of collision detection for creating the spatial layout of the graphical semi-interval instances. Although it is necessary to show our user interface to explain our results, the interface is not the focus of the current paper. Our focus is on the event processing.

7.2 Demonstration Domain

We demonstrate key aspects of our approach with a comparison of an original manual analysis of the AFIT data. There are multiple days of data recordings that have been carefully hand annotated by behavior domain experts. We discuss a study focused on exploring one session in which the officers (labeled C, D, E, F, and G) are discussing potential candidates for a scholarship. The scenario is that C, D, F, and G are department heads meeting with the institute commandant E to select three scholarship award recipients. It was discovered that in such meetings, the social interaction among the participants have as much to do with the outcome of the meeting as the specific merits of the scholarship candidates being discussed. The participants dynamically formed coalitions to support each-other's candidates through a process of mutual gaze fixations and back-channel expressions of support during discussions [23].

This session is approximately 45 minutes long. A coalition to support a proposed idea is initialized when the proposer of the idea seeks to make eye-contact with other participants while he is presenting the idea. Participants who supported the idea would return the eye-contact, while those who disagreed with the idea would avert gaze. When a return gaze is attained, the presenter's gaze moves to another member. This phenomena was recorded within this scholarship session and we want to compare the results of our extraction methods against this real world recorded scenario. This scenario describes C's sequence of gaze events starting with one to G, then D, then E. During this sequence, D and E's gaze is fixated on C.

There are three key areas we want to demonstrate. The first is our ability to automate the processing of cross-modal relations. Given a snapshot of a real analysis scenario, we want to compare our automatically extracted relation information with the relation information employed in the original analysis. Second, closely tied to the first, we would like to show how our approach is able to report *related* events that are within-context to a respective model. Then, switch between the different identified contexts to view different *related* events. Lastly, we will show how we can view the *related* events of all contexts at the same time allowing an aggregate view. Through this we will show how we can discover variations not seen in the original analysis.

7.3 Analyses Examples

Single Context Cross-modal Relations: First, we demonstrate the ability to automate processing of cross-modal relations. The emphasis in the original analysis was observing the gaze behavior. However, there are many other data channels available of which our approach also handles. One of the difficulties for this detailed data-set is there are many channels of information (approximately 37). Viewing the relevant information across all the streams within these channels is a challenge of wading through visual clutter. For this example (and subsequent ones) we use 22 channels consisting of F-formations, gaze fixations, nodding gestures, and gesture phrases. F-Formations, or focus formations, were first identified by Adam Kendon to be units of topical cohesion marked by gaze cohesion of participants to common

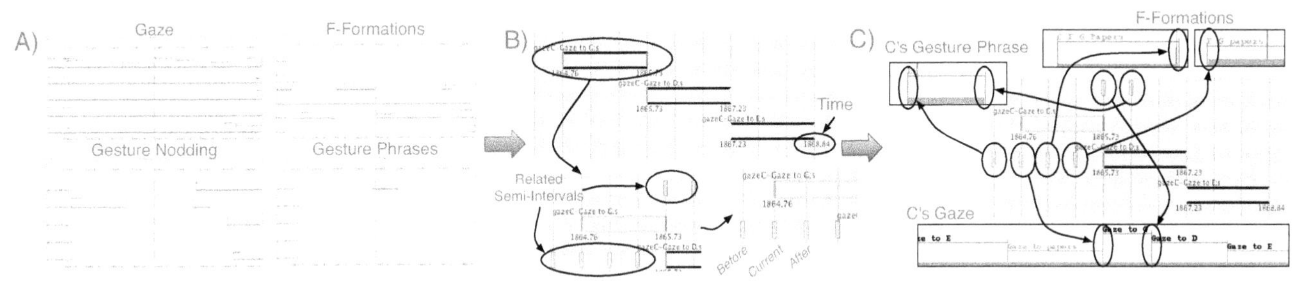

Figure 5: A) Music score event information for AFIT session. Vertical line is the current time. B) Model constructed of C's gaze sequence. C's gaze to G is highlighted showing all the *related* semi-intervals to the instance. C) Highlight of semi-intervals in the original data that are reported as *related* to the instance.

objects or spaces [15]. Gesture phrases are atomic gestural motions marking a single motion trajectory that typically coincide with atomic speech phrases [22]. The data streams used numbered 6,500+ semi-intervals.

Table 1: Results for start of AFIT gaze model

Context #	Model semi-interval: C gaze to G:s		
	Before	Current	After
1	C's ges phrase LH:s	C gaze to paper:e	F-Formation C F G to papers:e
2	C gaze to papers:e C gaze to E:s	C gaze to E:e	E gaze to papers:e E gaze to D:s
3	E gaze to G:e E gaze to papers:s	C gaze to E:e	C ges phrase LH:s
4	G gaze to D:e G gaze to papers:s	C gaze to F:e	F gaze to papers:e F gaze to D:s
5	F Gaze to C:e F gaze to papers:s	C gaze to papers:e	E gaze to C:e E gaze to papers:s

The model for this example details the order of C's gaze events to G, then D, and then E where each event has a start and end semi-interval. For our demonstration, we use the same situated instance from the original analysis. Figure 5 illustrates the connection between the annotation data and the results of our approach. In (A) is a visualization of the event data in the multimodal analysis tool MacVisSTA [36] (used for the original analysis). (B) graphically shows the model constructed using semi-intervals: [C gaze to G:s < C gaze to G:e = C gaze to D:s < C gaze to D:e = C gaze to E:s < C gaze to E:e], where ':s' or ':e' represents the start or end semi-interval, respectively. The first event, C's gaze to G, is highlighted showing three sets of *related* events for each semi-interval, each set corresponding to events that occurred *before*, *current* to, or *after* the semi-interval. (C) highlights how the *related* events link back to the multimodal data from (A). A detailed sub-set of results can be seen in Table 1, context 1. The table shows the results for one of the six semi-intervals of the model and exemplifies the information provided to the analyst. The reported events are the *related* event semi-intervals seen amongst the 22 data streams, allowing a quick view of these events with respect to the instance. These reported events are indeed events seen holding relation to the instance used (context 1) for the original analysis. With this information, an analyst can judge if the instance is deemed interesting enough to jump to the video and view the instance further. Also, identifying semi-intervals that adhere to equality ('=') seen in the model is not strictly upheld to allow for more flexibility in instance identification.

Multiple Context Cross-modal Relations: Our second example is motivated by judging the relevance of an instance. Here we show the viewing of and switching between results for multiple contexts. There were approximately 14 instances of C's gaze sequence model. To exemplify the varying contexts, we list results from five of these in Table 1. By switching between contexts, it can be seen that the *related* events vary providing interesting variations of context. Each context can be used to query the video content and allow a more detailed look. Switching between the contexts can show the differing events that occur and may aid the analyst in judging the relevance between multiple instances. Some results contain more than one *related* semi-interval, e.g. context 2, *Before*. This shows when either multiple events started and/or ended at the same time marking a transition between events. For the case of context 2, *Before*, C's gaze to the papers ends then C's gaze changes to E.

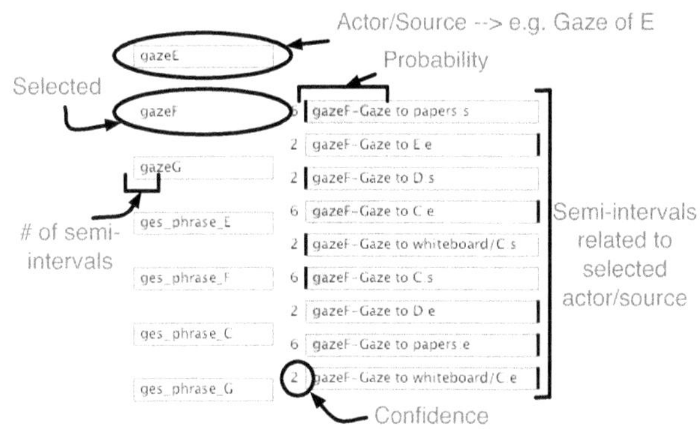

Figure 6: Example of *before* aggregated *related* results for the C gaze to G:s semi-interval.

Aggregated Results: Our third and last example takes the results from all contexts and aggregates them into one view to allow statistical comparison among the contexts and identification of variations. Here, instead of viewing one set of results at a time (e.g. one row of Table 1), we can view all sets (e.g. all rows) together. This combines the results into one view where the likelihood of each *related* event is presented as a comparison metric allowing a statistical comparison view of all *related* events across all contexts. One powerful aspect of this approach is that results from both complete and partial matches to the model are presented together. This allows the analyst to view instances that have some commonality to that of the model of interest and may prove informative in the analysis as illustrated in Figure 4 and related discussion.

An example of this aggregation can be seen in Figure 6 where the presented results correlate to a sub-set of the *before* results for C gaze to G:s. The first column (left) represents the actor/source of an event with the percentage fill of the representative graphical rectangle being the total number of semi-intervals associated with the respective actor/source. When one actor/source is selected, a second column is displayed which illustrates all the semi-intervals *related* to the actor/source that occur *before* C's gaze to G:s. This second column displays each semi-interval's description and associated conditional probability and confidence. The probability is mapped to the percentage fill of the graphical rectangle where more fill equals a greater probability. A bold bar is displayed on either end of the graphical rectangle depicting whether the semi-interval is a start (left side) or end (right side).

Given this aggregated view of *related* events, we can identify variations of *related* events to the model. A variation is described as a sequence of semi-intervals not recorded in the original analysis or that differs from the original model of interest. The reasoning for these variations was exemplified in Figure 4 and related discussion. In this example, three variations were identified that were of interest. The first stemmed from the question of if G returns C's gaze at some point. This is a valid point of interest as such gaze exchange is an important indicator for coalition building, as mentioned earlier. Upon inspection of *related* events in the aggregate view of C's gaze sequence detailed earlier, we see a gaze return from G during C's gaze to G and ending while C's gaze was on D. The resulting model of this variation (variation in bold) is: [C gaze to G:s < **G gaze to C:s** < C gaze to G:e = C gaze to D:s < **G gaze to C:e** < C gaze to D:e = C gaze to E:s < C gaze to E:e]. Using this modified model, we performed another query of the data-set and found two instances of this model. At this point the analyst can view the *related* events of those instances and jump to their situated context in the video data.

Next, we looked to see if D returned C's gaze. Similar to the prior case, D's return gaze begins during C's gaze to D and ends afterwards. This is in contrast to the original analysis where D's gaze was already fixated on C prior to the start of C's gaze sequence. Using this new model, we performed a query and found partial matches to the variation. No instances of this model variation were seen in the data-set. The only "instance" seen was matches found through identifying sub-structures of the model within the data (as seen in Figure 4). The resulting matches were very close to that of the desired variation leading to the identification of a variation not originally conceived in the data. This variation represents a new structure of how a coalition can be constructed with which such knowledge can be applied to other data-sets (e.g. the other AFIT sessions).

The detection of a coalition can be strengthened through using other data streams of interaction such as acknowledgement gestures in response to gaze. Hence, we identified another variation where G responds to C's gaze with a gesture nod (absent of G's gaze fixation). However, no instances of this model variation were seen in the data-set. The only "instance" seen was found through identifying sub-structures (same as the previous variation). Hence, this variation represents another model structure of a potential coalition that can be used in searching other data-sets.

7.4 Discussion

Given a set of events describing multimodal behavior of multiple individuals, we were able to identify events that were potentially relevant to particular instances of a phenomenon model. In doing so, we support expert exploration of large corpora of multimodal behavior to understand and extend behavioral models. Our approach is situated in that the expert works with particular instances of the behavior in the data and is able to inspect the original video/audio record of the behavior. However, our approach transcends the confines of the current instance in that it reveals other occurrences of the behavior being studied in the data. It allows the user to explore these occurrences within their contexts to determine if recurring event patterns are indeed relevant to the behavior being studied. Hence, this situated analysis also allows the comparison of phenomenon instances across different contexts.

The aggregated view of results adds an extra level to situated analysis as it provides a means to view all the results to all instances at once. This allowed identification of variations not originally conceived, providing opportunities for new thought constructions of models to be used in future analyses.

8. CONCLUSION AND FUTURE WORK

We were able to facilitate the situated analysis of multimodal corpus of human behavior. The expert is able to view *related* events of different instances of a phenomenon, view the cross-stream relations, compare across instances, and be assisted in the discovery of variations of phenomenon. We were able to illustrate how our approach is a beneficial aid in analysis through application to a data-set with known ground truth.

Through this investigation of situated analysis, we see areas where our processing can be improved to provide advantageous benefits to the analyst. The first is expanding the processing of our results to include more than boundary relations to events. Currently, our processing reports *related* semi-intervals with respect to the boundary (start/end) of events. Other equally important information is events occurring during a model but their start or end semi-interval is not temporally close. These events are on-going during instance(s) of the model. We are also interested in allowing more flexibility in identifying instances of a model with respect to how the order of model semi-intervals are realized in the data-set. For example, the hypothesis representation in Figure 1B may not surface in the data as all the gaze semi-intervals occurring at the exact same time, but very close to each other. This exemplifies the idea of temporal constraints, an area of research for this kind of processing and analysis discussed in [25]. Also, semi-intervals occurring in a slightly different order could pose a beneficial instance match, hence flexibility for this would be beneficial.

9. ACKNOWLEDGMENTS

This research was partially funded by FODAVA grant CCF-0937133, and by NSF IIS-1053039 "Multimodal Corpus for Vision-Based Meeting Analysis".

10. REFERENCES

[1] J. F. Allen. Maintaining knowledge about temporal intervals. *Commun. ACM*, 26(11):832–843, 1983.

[2] C. Andrews et al. Cardtable: An embodied tool for analysis of historical information. In *Tabletop 2007*.

[3] P. Brown et al. Class-based n-gram models of natural language. *Comp. Linguist.*, 18(4):467–479, 1992.

[4] L. Chen et al. Vace multimodal meeting corpus. *MLMI '06*, pages 40–51.
[5] L. Chen et al. A multimodal analysis of floor control in meetings. In S. Renals, S. Bengio, and J. Fiscus, editors, *MLMI*, volume 4299 of *LNCS*, pages 36–49. Springer Berlin / Heidelberg, 2006.
[6] V. Cheng et al. Dissimilarity learning for nominal data. *Pattern Recognition*, 37(7):1471 – 1477, 2004.
[7] Chipmunk. *http://code.google.com/p/chipmunk-physics/*, Last Checked: Aug., 2010.
[8] C.-P. Chou and P. M. Bentler. Model modification in structural equation modeling by imposing constraints. *Comput. Stat. Data Anal.*, 41(2):271–287, 2002.
[9] C. Freksa. Temporal reasoning based on semi-intervals. *Artificial Intelligence*, 54(1-2):199 – 227, 1992.
[10] S. Gorga and K. Otsuka. Conversation scene analysis based on dynamic bayesian network and image-based gaze detection. In *ICMI-MLMI '10*, pages 54:1–54:8.
[11] G. Guimarães and A. Ultsch. A method for temporal knowledge conversion. *AIDA*, pages 369–380, 1999.
[12] F. Höppner. *Knowledge Discovery from Sequential Data.* PhD thesis, Technischen Universität Braunschweig Genehmigte, 2003.
[13] P. Kam and A. Fu. Discovering temporal patterns for interval-based events. *Data Warehousing and Knowledge Discovery*, pages 317–326, 2000.
[14] D. Kaplan. Evaluating and modifying covariance structure models: A review and recommendation. In *Multivariate Behavioral Research*, volume 25, pages 137–155. Psychology Press, 1990.
[15] A. Kendon. *Conducting Interaction: Patterns of Behavior in Focused Encounters.* Cambridge: Cambridge University Press, 1990.
[16] M. Kipp. *(to appear) Multimedia Annotation, Querying and Analysis in ANVIL*, chapter 19. Multimedia Info. Extraction. IEEE Comp. Soc. Press.
[17] M. Kipp. Anvil - a generic annotation tool for multimodal dialogue. In *Eurospeech*, 2001.
[18] M. Kipp. Spatiotemporal coding in anvil. In *LREC*, 2008.
[19] S. Laxman and P. Sastry. A survey of temporal data mining. *Sadhana*, 31(2):173–198, 04 2006.
[20] C. Li and G. Biswas. Unsupervised learning with mixed numeric and nominal data. *IEEE Trans. on Knowl. and Data Eng.*, 14(4):673–690, 2002.
[21] V. Y. Lunin and A. G. Urzhumtsev. Improvement of protein phases by coarse model modification. *Acta Crystallographica Section A*, 40(3):269–277, May 1984.
[22] D. McNeill. *Hand and Mind: What gestures reveal about thought.* Chicago: U. of Chicago Press, 1992.
[23] D. McNeill et al. Mind-merging. In *Expressing oneself / expressing one's self: Communication, language, cognition, and identity*, 2007.
[24] C. Miller et al. Interaction techniques for the analysis of complex data on high-resolution displays. In *ICMI '08*, pages 21–28.
[25] C. Miller, F. Quek, and N. Ramakrishnan. Structuring ordered nominal data for event sequence discovery. In *ACM MM '10.*
[26] C. Mooney and J. Roddick. Mining relationships between interacting episodes. In *SDM'04.*
[27] F. Mörchen. Algorithms for time series knowledge mining. In *KDD '06*, pages 668–673.
[28] F. Mörchen. Unsupervised pattern mining from symbolic temporal data. *SIGKDD Explor. Newsl.*, 9(1):41–55, 2007.
[29] F. Mörchen and D. Fradkin. Robust mining of time intervals with semi-interval partial order patterns. In *SIAM Conference on Data Mining (SDM)*, 2010.
[30] L.-P. Morency, C. M. Christoudias, and T. Darrell. Recognizing gaze aversion gestures in embodied conversational discourse. In *ICMI '06*, pages 287–294.
[31] F. Oliveira et al. Fun to develop embodied skill: how games help the blind to understand pointing. In *PETRA '10*, pages 16:1–16:8. ACM, 2010.
[32] Pymunk. *http://code.google.com/p/pymunk/*, Last Checked: Feb., 2011.
[33] QT. *http://qt.nokia.com/*, Last Checked: Nov., 2009.
[34] F. Quek et al. Gesture, speech, and gaze cues for discourse segmentation. In *CVPR '00*, pages 247–254 vol.2.
[35] F. Quek, T. Rose, and D. McNeill. Multimodal meeting analysis. In *IA*, 2005.
[36] R. T. Rose, F. Quek, and Y. Shi. Macvissta: a system for multimodal analysis. In *ICMI '04*, pages 259–264.
[37] S. Russell and P. Norvig. *Artificial Intelligence A Modern Approach.* Prentice Hall, 2003.
[38] E. Schwalb and L. Vila. Temporal constraints: A survey. *Constraints*, 3(2/3):129–149, 1998.
[39] M. Siu and M. Ostendorf. Variable n-grams and extensions for conversational speech language modeling. *Speech and Audio Processing, IEEE Transactions on*, 8(1):63 –75, Jan. 2000.
[40] I. Spiro, G. Taylor, G. Williams, and C. Bregler. Hands by hand: Crowd-sourced motion tracking for gesture annotation. In *CVPRW*, pages 17 –24, 2010.
[41] M. Voit and R. Stiefelhagen. 3d user-perspective, voxel-based estimation of visual focus of attention in dynamic meeting scenarios. In *ICMI-MLMI '10*, pages 51:1–51:8.
[42] R. Yang et al. Efficient generation of large amounts of training data for sign language recognition: A semi-automatic tool. In *Computers Helping People with Special Needs*, volume 4061 of *LNCS*, pages 635–642. Springer Berlin / Heidelberg, 2006.
[43] L. Zadeh. Soft computing and fuzzy logic. *Software, IEEE*, 11(6):48–56, Nov 1994.
[44] L. Zadeh. Fuzzy logic = computing with words. *IEEE TFS*, 4(2):103–111, May 1996.

Finding Audio-Visual Events in Informal Social Gatherings*

Xavier Alameda-Pineda
INRIA Grenoble Rhône-Alpes
655, Av. Europe
38334 Montbonnot, France
xavier.alameda-pineda@inria.fr

Vasil Khalidov
IDIAP Research Institute
Rue Marconi 19
1920 Martigny, Switzerland
vasil.khalidov@idiap.ch

Radu Horaud
INRIA Grenoble Rhône-Alpes
655, Av. Europe
38334 Montbonnot, France
radu.horaud@inria.fr

Florence Forbes
INRIA Grenoble Rhône-Alpes
655, Av. Europe
38334 Montbonnot, France
florence.forbes@inria.fr

ABSTRACT

In this paper we address the problem of detecting and localizing objects that can be both seen and heard, e.g., people. This may be solved within the framework of data clustering. We propose a new multimodal clustering algorithm based on a Gaussian mixture model, where one of the modalities (visual data) is used to supervise the clustering process. This is made possible by mapping both modalities into the same metric space. To this end, we fully exploit the geometric and physical properties of an audio-visual sensor based on *binocular vision* and *binaural hearing*. We propose an EM algorithm that is theoretically well justified, intuitive, and extremely efficient from a computational point of view. This efficiency makes the method implementable on advanced platforms such as humanoid robots. We describe in detail tests and experiments performed with publicly available data sets that yield very interesting results.

Categories and Subject Descriptors

G.3 [**Mathematics of Computing**]: Probability and Statistics—*Multivariate statistics, Probabilistic algorithms*; I.4.8 [**Image Processing and Computer Vision**]: Scene analysis

General Terms

Algorithms, Theory, Experimentation

Keywords

audio-visual fusion, scene analysis, 3D localization, event detection

*This work was supported by the European project HUMAVIPS FP7-ICT-2009-247525, `http://humavips.eu/`

ICMI'11, November 14–18, 2011, Alicante, Spain.

1. INTRODUCTION

The ability to describe the semantic content of a complex environment is important for a wide variety of applications such as human-robot interaction, communication and cooperation. Providing information associated with audio-visual (AV) events is an intermediate step for further processing towards a higher-level understanding of various situations such as informal meetings and social gatherings. Note that people are faced with the problem of interpreting complex auditory and visual input in everyday life, and that they have no difficulties in focusing their attention onto a dialog between two speakers in an extremely noisy environment, i.e., in the presence of a multitude of other auditory and visual events. Therefore, one challenge is to develop a methodological framework that is able to detect and localize multiple AV events from unrestricted multimodal sensory input. In particular, our long-term goal is to implement robust AV capabilities using an agent-centered architecture such as a humanoid robot.

More generally, we address the problem of detecting and localizing objects that can be both seen and heard, e.g., people emitting sounds such as speech, sounds produced by foot steps and clothe chafing, etc. This immediately raises the interesting question of how to optimally associate, fuse, and cluster observations that are gathered with physically different sensors, e.g., cameras and microphones, and that live in semantically different spaces, e.g., how to associate *spatiotemporal visual features* with *temporal auditory signals*.

The task of simultaneous detection and localization of multiple AV events can be cast into a probabilistic framework. In this paper we propose to use a Gaussian Mixture Model (GMM) for multimodal data and we derive an Expectation-Maximization (EM) algorithm. This algorithm is able to deal with multiple AV events whose number varies over time. Moreover, it incorporates a mechanism that gives more strength to one of the modalities in order to semi-supervise the bi-modal clustering process. This is made possible by mapping both modalities into the same metric space. To this end, we fully exploit the geometric and physical properties of an AV sensor composed of *binocular vision*, i.e., a stereoscopic camera pair and *binaural hearing*, i.e., a microphone pair. The proposed algorithm is theoretically sound, efficient, intuitive, and yields very interesting and promising results. Indeed, it performs clustering in the one-dimensional Interaural Time Difference (ITD) space associated with two microphones and it takes full advantage

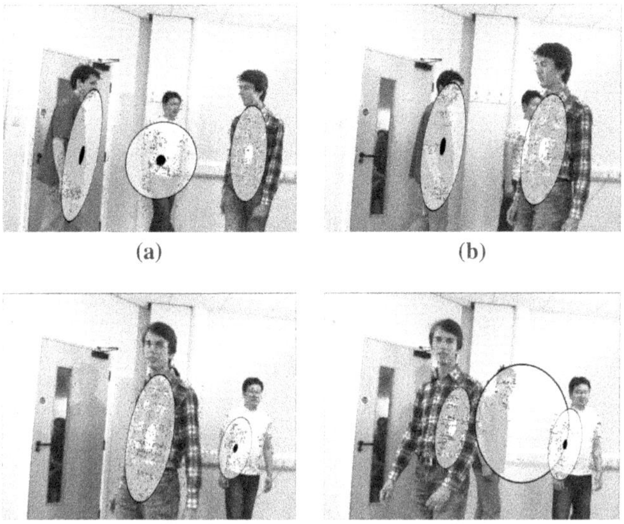

Figure 1: This figure illustrates the results obtained with the method described in this paper. The proposed algorithm is able to deal with a varying number of people, appearing and disappearing from the field of view of the cameras or being occluded; some of these people emit sounds such as *speech*, or non-speech, e.g., *clothe chafing*, *foot steps*, etc. The ellipses correspond to 2D projections of the 3D covariance matrices centered at 3D AV events. A white dot indicates an auditory activity.

of a generative model that allows, first to *project* visual observations onto this space and second to *back-project* the detected 1D clusters into the 3D physical space without any additional computational effort. We describe a complete EM algorithm, including algorithm initialization and model selection in order to estimate the number of clusters, each cluster being associated with an AV event. We show experiments performed with publicly available data sets.

Figure 1 illustrates one result obtained with the method described in this paper. The plotted ellipses correspond to 2D projections of the 3D covariance matrices centered at the 3D locations of the AV events. A white dot indicates an auditory activity and a black dot indicates a silent object.

1.1 Related Work

A method based on an information theoretic framework is proposed in [12] in order to identify the speaker among a group of people. The authors propose to learn maximally informative projections in order to map the observations space onto the feature space by maximizing the mutual information. The main drawback of this approach is the assumption that the visual data are correctly segmented prior to learning the projections just mentioned. The *factorization test* method in [17] builds on the work of [12] to determine the statistical dependency among a set of variables. The main problem is to discover the dependency structure inside the set. In [6], the authors propose to design certain optimal auditory features which are then used in [5]. This work exploits the framework introduced in [12, 17] to determine which one of the people in the visual scene is actually speaking, in order to solve the task of speaker detection.

The approaches just described have a number of disadvantages. In such a task as understanding the AV configuration of a scene, it is important to be able to estimate the number of AV objects as well as the physical location of each one of these objects. None of the above approaches deals with these issues. One can formalize the first problem, e.g., "how many AV objects are out there?", as a *model selection* problem. The second problem, e.g., "where are they located in the 3D scene?" can be formulated as a parameter estimation problem.

Audiovisual scene analysis has also been addressed within the framework of developing smart-room environments [8, 23, 27] making use of several camera and microphone arrays: One can perform *separate* auditory and visual localization in the 3D space. Multimodal alignment is straightforward and consists in finding spatial relationship between the auditory and the visual features. This requires auditory and visual reconstruction which in turn needs careful AV calibration. Alternatively, one can learn the relation between the AV object positions in the 2D image space and in the 1D auditory space directly, through *mapping* sounds onto images [4, 13, 16]. Nevertheless, these approaches make certain restrictive assumptions on the observed environment: They are only suitable for scenarios where the environment is predefined and if the sensors are stationary, e.g. meeting rooms and smart kiosks with a near-field interaction.

The task of simultaneous detection and 3D localization using multimodal data has also been addressed in [20, 21]. The authors propose a probabilistic framework based on a *conjugate* GMM. Two GMMs are estimated, one for each modality (vision and auditory) while these two mixture parameters are constrained through a common set of *tying parameters*, namely the 3D locations of the AV events being sought. This leads to the conjugate EM algorithm described in detail in [21]. The M-step of this algorithm involves a non-linear optimization procedure because of the presence of the tying parameters. The authors propose a stochastic optimization technique that is computationally intensive. Moreover, the model selection (the number of AV events) must be carefully studied in the particular context of the conjugate mixture model since the standard selection procedure based on the Bayesian information criterion (BIC) [26] is not straightforward.

1.2 Paper Contributions and Organization

The main contributions of this paper are the following: (i) we propose a method that fully exploits the geometrical and physical properties of the AV sensor, i.e., mapping of 3D visual features into the 1D auditory space and 3D localization performed by projecting 1D clusters back into the 3D space, (ii) we combine spatio-temporal visual features with temporal auditory signals, (iii) we propose a semi-supervised clustering method that puts more trust in one of the two modalities and (iv) we propose both initialization and model selection mechanisms to account for dynamic changes in the number of AV events that are actually present in the scene. Unlike the vast majority of existing approaches, our method is able to find *multiple* AV events and not just the most prominent one.

The remainder of the paper is organized as follows. Section 2 introduces the mathematical notation, specifies the generative model and outlines the general probabilistic formulation. Section 3 develops in detail the steps of the proposed algorithm. Implementation details and results obtained with both synthetic and real data are described in section 4. Finally, section 5 draws some conclusions and suggests directions for future work.

2. PROBLEM FORMULATION

The input data consists of M visual observations $\boldsymbol{f}$ and K auditory observations $\boldsymbol{g}$ (see [21] for a more detailed account of the audiovisual mixture model and the associated notation):

$$\begin{aligned} \boldsymbol{f} &= \{\boldsymbol{f}_1, \dots, \boldsymbol{f}_m, \dots, \boldsymbol{f}_M\}, \quad \boldsymbol{f}_m \in \mathbb{S} \subseteq \mathbb{R}^3 \\ \boldsymbol{g} &= \{g_1, \dots, g_k, \dots, g_K\}, \quad g_k \in \mathbb{G} \subset \mathbb{R} \end{aligned}$$

acquired within the same time interval ΔT. We assume that ΔT is short enough so that the AV objects remain at approximately the same 3D location, while small motions, e.g., head and hand movements, are supposed to occur within this time interval.

A visual observation $\boldsymbol{f}_m$ is extracted using a stereo-motion reconstruction method that we briefly outline. First, we detect interest points, e.g. [14], in the left and right images gathered at the beginning of the time interval ΔT. Second, we only consider a subset of theses points, namely those points where motion occurs. For each interest-point image location (u, v) we consider the image intensities at the same location (u, v) in the subsequent images within ΔT and we compute a temporal intensity standard deviation $\sigma_{\Delta T}$ for each interest point. Assuming stable lighting condition over ΔT, we simply classify the interest points into static ($\sigma_{\Delta T} \leq \tau$) and dynamic ($\sigma_{\Delta T} > \tau$) where τ is a user-defined threshold. Third, we apply a standard stereo matching algorithm and a stereo reconstruction algorithm to yield a set of 3D features $\mathbf{f}$ associated with ΔT.

An auditory observation g_k corresponds to an ITD between the left and right microphones. There are many methods to extract ITD values from the left and right microphone signals. We found that the method proposed in [9] yields very good results that are stable over time. The relationship between an auditory source located at $\boldsymbol{s} \in \mathbb{R}^3$ and an ITD observation g depends on the relative position of the acoustic source with respect to the locations of the two microphones, $\boldsymbol{s}_{\mathrm{M}_1}$ and $\boldsymbol{s}_{\mathrm{M}_2}$. If we assume linear sound propagation and constant sound velocity c, this relationship is given by the $\mathbb{R}^3 \rightarrow \mathbb{R}$ mapping:

$$g = \mathrm{ITD}(\boldsymbol{s}) = \frac{\|\boldsymbol{s} - \boldsymbol{s}_{\mathrm{M}_1}\| - \|\boldsymbol{s} - \boldsymbol{s}_{\mathrm{M}_2}\|}{c} \qquad (1)$$

It will be assumed that the audio-visual sensor (two cameras and two microphones) is calibrated, namely that the 3D locations of the two microphones, $\boldsymbol{s}_{\mathrm{M}_1}$ and $\boldsymbol{s}_{\mathrm{M}_2}$ are expressed in the coordinate system associated with the stereo camera pair [19].

We consider an arbitrary number N of AV objects:

$$\mathbf{S} = \{\boldsymbol{s}_1, \ldots, \boldsymbol{s}_n, \ldots, \boldsymbol{s}_N\}, \quad \boldsymbol{s}_n \in \mathbb{R}^3$$

as well as an *auditory status* associated with each one of these objects

$$\mathbf{e} = \{e_1, \ldots, e_n, \ldots, e_N\}, \quad e_n \in \{0, 1\},$$

where $e_n = 1$ if the object n emits a sound and $e_n = 0$ if it does not.

There are several issues that need to be addressed in order to localize an arbitrary number N of AV objects and to estimate their auditory status: (i) the visual and auditory observations lie in physically different spaces with different dimensionality, (ii) the object-to-observation assignments are not known in advance and hence one has to define additional hidden variables to account for this *multimodal* object-to-data association problem, (iii) both visual and auditory observations are contaminated with noise and outliers, (iv) the relative importance of the two types of data is difficult to be accounted for and hence the task of reliably combining the two modalities is not a trivial one and (v) since we want to be able to deal with a variable number of AV objects over a long period of time, the number of AV object that are effectively present in the scene must be estimated; this is a difficult model selection problem.

We formulate the task of AV fusion within the framework of maximum likelihood with hidden variables. Therefore we introduce two sets of assignment variables $\boldsymbol{A}$ and $\boldsymbol{B}$:

$$\boldsymbol{A} = \{A_1, \ldots, A_m, \ldots, A_M\}$$
$$\boldsymbol{B} = \{B_1, \ldots, B_k, \ldots, B_K\}$$

The notation $A_m = n$, where $m \in [1 \ldots M]$ and $n \in [1 \ldots N+1]$ means that the observation $\boldsymbol{f}_m$ was either generated by a 3D object $n, 1 \leq n \leq N$ or it is an outlier, i.e., it belongs to class $N+1$. Similarly, variable B_k is associated with the auditory observation g_k.

An important contribution of this paper is the multimodal fusion strategy based on mapping the visual observations $\{\boldsymbol{f}_m\}_{m=1}^{M}$ into the ITD space $\mathbb{G}$. For this purpose we apply (1) and obtain the set

$$\tilde{\boldsymbol{f}} = \left\{\tilde{f}_1, \ldots, \tilde{f}_m, \ldots, \tilde{f}_M\right\}, \quad \tilde{f}_m \in \mathbb{G} \subseteq \mathbb{R},$$

where

$$\tilde{f}_m = \frac{\|\boldsymbol{f}_m - \boldsymbol{s}_{\mathrm{M}_1}\| - \|\boldsymbol{f}_m - \boldsymbol{s}_{\mathrm{M}_2}\|}{c} \qquad (2)$$

This means that 3D audio-visual event detection and localization can be achieved by grouping together 1D visual features and 1D auditory features. The 3D layout of these events can be easily retrieved from the one-to-one 1D-to-3D known associations $\tilde{f}_m \leftrightarrow \boldsymbol{f}_m$. This fusion strategy combines several benefits: (i) complexity reduction since the computations are performed in 1D; (ii) complementarity between the two modalities since relatively dense visual features compensate for the relative sparsity of the auditory features. We refer to the latter as audiovisual enhancement [2].

We formulate the multimodal probabilistic fusion model under the assumption that all observations g_k and $\tilde{f}_m$ are independent and identically distributed, i.e, an AV event n generates both visual and auditory features normally distributed around $\mathrm{ITD}(\boldsymbol{s}_n)$ and both the visual and auditory outliers are uniformly distributed in the ITD space. Thus we can define a generative model for the observations $x \in \mathcal{X}$ where $\mathcal{X} = \{\tilde{f}_m\}_{m=1}^{M} \cup \{g_k\}_{k=1}^{K}$:

$$\mathrm{p}(x; \Theta) = \sum_{n=1}^{N} \pi_n \mathcal{N}(x; \mu_n, \sigma_n) + \pi_{N+1} \mathcal{U}(\mathbb{G}; V), \qquad (3)$$

where $\mu_n = \mathrm{ITD}(\boldsymbol{s}_n)$ and σ_n are the mean and the standard deviation of the Gaussian component $\mathcal{N}(x; \mu_n, \sigma_n)$, $\mathcal{U}(\mathbb{G}; V)$ is the uniform distribution on the ITD set $\mathbb{G}$ and π_n are the prior probabilities of the mixture's components. The prior probabilities satisfy $\sum_{n=1}^{N+1} \pi_n = 1$. The model parameters are denoted with:

$$\Theta = \{\pi_1, \ldots, \pi_{N+1}, \mu_1, \ldots, \mu_N, \sigma_1, \ldots, \sigma_N\}$$

The ultimate goal is to determine the number N of AV events, their 3D locations $\mathbf{s} = \{\boldsymbol{s}_1, \ldots, \boldsymbol{s}_n, \ldots, \boldsymbol{s}_N\}$ as well as their auditory activity $\boldsymbol{e} = \{e_1, \ldots, e_n, \ldots, e_N\}$. However, the 3D location parameters can be computed only indirectly, once the multimodal mixture's parameters Θ have been estimated. Hence, the task of "finding AV objects" is twofold: (i) estimate the mixture's parameters Θ via maximum likelihood with hidden variables and (ii) use the known $\tilde{f}_m \leftrightarrow \boldsymbol{f}_m$ correspondences to infer their locations, auditory status, and associated statistics. The observed-data log-likelihood function is given by:

$$\mathcal{L}\left(\tilde{\boldsymbol{f}}, \boldsymbol{g}; \Theta\right) = \sum_{m=1}^{M} \log \mathrm{p}\left(\tilde{f}_m; \Theta\right) + \sum_{k=1}^{K} \log \mathrm{p}\left(g_k; \Theta\right), \qquad (4)$$

where p is the probability distribution described in (3). This will be solved by maximizing the expected complete-data log likelihood conditioned by the observed data [11].

3. THE PROPOSED METHOD

Algorithm 1 below summarizes the proposed method. Algorithm 1 takes as input the visual ($\mathbf{f}$) and auditory ($\boldsymbol{g}$) observations gathered during a time interval ΔT. The algorithm's output is the estimated number of clusters $\hat{N}$, the estimated 3D positions of the AV events $\{\hat{\boldsymbol{s}}_n\}_{n=1}^{\hat{N}}$ as well as their estimated auditory activity $\{\hat{e}_n\}_{n=1}^{\hat{N}}$.

At each time interval the algorithm starts by mapping the visual observations onto the ITD space by means of the ITD generative model (2). Then, for $N \in [1, \ldots, N_{\max}]$ it iterates through the following steps: (a) Initialize a model with N components using the output of the previous time interval (section 3.1), (b) apply EM using the selected N to model the 1D projections of the visual data (section 3.2), (c) apply the visually supervised EM (*ViSEM*) algorithm to both the auditory and projected visual data (section 3.3) in order to perform audiovisual clustering, and (d) compute the BIC score associated with the current model, i.e., (9). This allows the algorithm to select the model with the highest BIC score, i.e., (10). The post-processing step is then applied to the selected model (section 3.5) prior to computing the final output (section 3.6).

3.1 Algorithm Initialization

EM is a constrained local optimization technique that requires proper parameter initialization to avoid local maxima. In our case the model is a mixture of Gaussian distributions with an outlier component. Although the AV objects can appear, move and disappear, we assume that the dynamics are constrained in such a way that the positions of the AV objects in a time interval are close to the ones in the previous interval. Hence, it is reasonable to take into account the model computed in the previous time interval in order to initialize the EM algorithm. The implementation details are given in section 4.

3.2 Fitting the Visual Data

Because of the higher density and better temporal continuity of the visual information, we start by fitting a 1D GMM to the projected visual features $\{\tilde{f}_m\}_{m=1}^{M}$. This is done with the standard EM algorithm [7]. In the E step of the algorithm the posterior probabilities $\alpha_{mn} = P(A_m = n|\tilde{f}_m)$ are updated via the following formula (see [21] for details):

$$\alpha_{mn} = \frac{\pi_n P(\tilde{f}_m|A_m = n)}{\sum_{i=1}^{N+1} \pi_i P(\tilde{f}_m|A_m = i)} \quad (5)$$

The M step is devoted to maximize the expected complete data log-likelihood with respect to the parameters, leading to the standard formulas (with $\bar{\alpha}_n = \sum_{m=1}^{M} \alpha_{mn}$):

$$\pi_n = \frac{\bar{\alpha}_n}{M}$$

$$\mu_n = \frac{1}{\bar{\alpha}_n} \sum_{m=1}^{M} \alpha_{mn} \tilde{f}_m$$

$$\sigma_n^2 = \frac{1}{\bar{\alpha}_n} \sum_{m=1}^{M} \alpha_{mn} (\tilde{f}_m - \mu_n)^2$$

3.3 Visually Supervised EM

Once the model is initialized and fitted to the projected visual data, the clustering process proceeds by including the auditory under the supervision of the visual information which has already probabilistically been assigned to N clusters. Hence, we are faced with a constrained maximum-likelihood estimation problem: maximize (4) subject to the constraint that the posterior probabilities α_{mn} were previously computed. This leads to *visually supervised* EM (*ViSEM*) in which the E-step only updates the posterior probabilities associated with the auditory observations while those associated with the visual observations remain unchanged. This semi-supervision strategy was introduced in the context of text classification [24, 22], but to the best of our knowledge, it has not been applied to enforce the quality and reliability of one of the sensing modalities within a multimodal clustering algorithm. To summarize, the E-step of the *ViSEM* algorithm updates only the posterior probabilities of the auditory observations $\beta_{kn} = P(B_k = n \mid g_k)$:

$$\beta_{kn} = \frac{\pi_n P(g_k \mid B_k = n)}{\sum_{i=1}^{N+1} \pi_i P(g_k \mid B_k = i)} \quad (6)$$

while keeping the visual posterior probabilities, α_{mn}, constant. The M-step of the *ViSEM* algorithm has a closed-form solution. The prior probabilities are updated with:

$$\pi_n = \frac{\gamma_n}{M + K}, \quad n = 1, \ldots, N + 1,$$

with $\gamma_n = \sum_{m=1}^{M} \alpha_{mn} + \sum_{k=1}^{K} \beta_{kn} = \bar{\alpha}_n + \bar{\beta}_n$. The means and variances of the current model are estimated by combining the two modalities:

$$\mu_n = \frac{1}{\gamma_n} \left(\sum_{m=1}^{M} \alpha_{mn} \tilde{f}_m + \sum_{k=1}^{K} \beta_{kn} g_k \right) \quad (7)$$

$$\sigma_n^2 = \frac{\sum_{m=1}^{M} \alpha_{mn} (\tilde{f}_m - \mu_n)^2 + \sum_{k=1}^{K} \beta_{kn} (g_k - \mu_n)^2}{\gamma_n} \quad (8)$$

3.4 Model Selection

Once we estimated the maximum likelihood parameters for models with different number of AV objects, we need a criterion to choose which is the best one. This is estimating the number of AV objects (clusters) in the scene; which is not known a priory. BIC [26] is a well known criterion to choose among several maximum likelihood statistical models. BIC is often chosen for this type of tasks due to its attractive consistency properties [18]. It is appropriate to use this criterion in our framework, due to the fact that the statistical models after the ViSEM step, fit the AV data in an ML

Algorithm 1 Audio-visual EM

- **Input:** Visual $\{\boldsymbol{f}_m\}_{m=1}^{M}$ and auditory $\{g_k\}_{k=1}^{K}$ features.
- **Output:** Number of AV events $\hat{N}$, 3D localization $\{\hat{\boldsymbol{s}}_n\}_{n=1}^{\hat{N}}$ and auditory status $\{\hat{e}_n\}_{n=1}^{\hat{N}}$.
- Map the visual features onto the ITD space, $\tilde{f}_m = \text{ITD}(\boldsymbol{f}_m)$ (eq. (2)).
- **for** $N = 1 \to N_{\max}$ **do**
  - **(a)** Initialize the model with N clusters (section 3.1).
  - **(b)** Apply EM clustering to $\{\tilde{f}_m\}_{m=1}^{M}$ (section 3.2).
  - **(c)** Apply the *ViSEM* algorithm to cluster the audio-visual data (section 3.3).
  - **(d)** Compute the BIC score (eq. (9)).
- **end for**
- Estimate the number of clusters based on the BIC score (eq. (10)).
- Post-processing (section 3.5).
- Compute the final outputs $\{\hat{\boldsymbol{s}}_n\}_{n=1}^{\hat{N}}$ and $\{\hat{e}_n\}_{n=1}^{\hat{N}}$ (section 3.6).

sense. In our case, choosing among these models is equivalent to estimate the number of AV events $\tilde{N}$. The formula to compute the BIC score is:

$$\text{BIC}(\tilde{\boldsymbol{f}}, \boldsymbol{g}, \Theta_N) = \mathcal{L}\left(\tilde{\boldsymbol{f}}, \boldsymbol{g}; \Theta_N\right) - \frac{D_N \log(M+K)}{2}, \quad (9)$$

where $D_N = 3N$ is the number of free parameters of the model. The number of AV events is estimated by selecting the statistical model corresponding to the maximum score:

$$\hat{N} = \arg\max_N \text{BIC}(\tilde{\boldsymbol{f}}, \boldsymbol{g}, \Theta_N), \quad (10)$$

3.5 Post-processing

Post-processing is needed to transform the model chosen by BIC into a meaningful model regarding our application. We need to deal with two problems: (i) the visual outliers are not exactly uniform, and (ii) in some time intervals there is a shortage of observations.

The first problem leads to spurious clusters. Although the 3D visual observations associated with these clusters may be uniformly spread, their ITD projections may form a spurious cluster. Hence these clusters are characterized by having their points distributed near some hyperboloid in the 3D space (hyperboloids are the level surfaces associated with the inverse of the ITD mapping (1)). As a consequence, the volume of the back-projected 3D cluster is small. We discard those clusters whose covariance matrices have a small determinant (estimated via (12), see section 3.6).

The second problem leads to clusters whose interactions may describe an overall pattern, instead of different components. We solve this problem by merging some of the mixture's components. There are several techniques to merge clusters within a mixture model (see [15]). Since the components to be merged lie around the same position and have similar spread, the *ridgeline* method [25] best solves our problem.

3.6 3D Localization

The 3D positions are estimated using the probabilistic assignments of the projected visual features ($\tilde{f}_m$) to the 1D clusters, namely α_{mn}, through the formula:

$$\hat{\boldsymbol{s}}_n = \frac{1}{\bar{\alpha}_n} \sum_{m=1}^{M} \alpha_{mn} \boldsymbol{f}_m. \quad (11)$$

The covariance matrices in the 3D space are also estimated using:

$$\hat{\boldsymbol{\Sigma}}_n = \frac{1}{\bar{\alpha}_n} \sum_{m=1}^{M} \alpha_{mn} \left(\boldsymbol{f}_m - \hat{\boldsymbol{s}}_n\right)\left(\boldsymbol{f}_m - \hat{\boldsymbol{s}}_n\right)^{\top}. \quad (12)$$

In order to determine whether the clusters emit sound or not, the auditory activity associated with each cluster is estimated as follows (τ_A is a threshold defined in section 4 below):

$$\hat{e}_n = \begin{cases} 1 & \text{if } \bar{\beta}_n > \tau_A \\ 0 & \text{otherwise} \end{cases} \quad (13)$$

4. IMPLEMENTATION AND RESULTS

We validated the proposed algorithm using both synthetic and real data. In section 4.1 we describe the different synthetic sequences as well as how they were generated. We also describe how we quantitatively evaluate our method. Results with publicly available real data are described in section 4.2. Before presenting the results, some implementation details are given.

As already explained, the *ViSEM* algorithm is initialized using the mixture model computed in the previous time interval. The intuition behind this approach is that the AV objects' dynamics are constrained such that from one time interval to the next one, their positions do not vary a lot. We now describe how to initialize the current model based on the previous model such that the number of clusters between previous and current models is allowed to vary.

We denote by $N^{(p)}$ the number of AV objects found in the previous model. The aim is to generate a new 1D GMM with N clusters, $N \in \{0, \ldots, N_{\max}\}$. In the case $N \leq N^{(p)}$, we take the N clusters with the highest weight. For $N > N^{(p)}$, we incrementally split a cluster at its mean into two clusters. The cluster to be split is selected on the basis of a high Davies-Bouldin index [10]:

$$DB_i = \max_{j \neq i} \frac{\sigma_i + \sigma_j}{\|\mu_i - \mu_j\|},$$

We chose to split the cluster into two clusters in order to detect AV objects that have recently appeared in the scene, either because they were outside the field of view, or because they were occluded by another AV object. This provides us with a good initialization for the *ViSEM* algorithm. In our case the maximum number of AV objects is $N_{\max} = 10$.

In order to detect auditory activity, our method thresholds the expected amount of audio samples for each AV object (13). The threshold τ_A has to take into account how many audio observations (K) are gathered during the current time interval ΔT as well as the number of potential audible AV objects (N). For instance, if there is just one potential AV object, most of the audio observations should be assigned to it, whereas if there are three of them the audio observations may be distributed among them (in case all of them emit sounds). The threshold τ_A was experimentally set to $\tau_A = K/(N+2)$.

4.1 Synthetic Data

In order to precisely evaluate the proposed method, several synthetic sequences were generated. Four sequences containing one to three AV objects were generated. These objects can move and they are not necessarily visible/audible along the entire sequence. At each time interval, 300 visual features per visible object and seven auditory features were generated. This choice has been made to be as close as possible to the real data (see section 4.2).

Table 1: Visual evaluation of results obtained with synthetic sequences. *Sta/Dyn* states for static or dynamic scene; the AV objects move or do not move. *Var/Con* states for varying or constant number of AV objects. FP stands for false positives, MD for missing detections, TP for true positives and ALE for average localization error (expressed in meters).

Seq.	FP	MD	TP	ALE [m]
StaCon	12	16 (3.9%)	392 (96.1%)	0.03
DynCon	43	139 (34.1%)	269 (65.9%)	0.10
StaVar	46	69 (30.1%)	160 (69.9%)	0.03
DynVar	40	82 (35.9%)	147 (64.1%)	0.11

To evaluate the results, we compute a distance matrix between the detected clusters and the ground-truth clusters. The cluster-to-cluster distance corresponds to the Euclidean distance between cluster means. Let $\mathbf{D}$ be the distance matrix, then entry $D_{ij} = \|\mu_i - \hat{\mu}_j\|$ is the distance from the i-th ground-truth cluster to the j-th detected cluster. Next, we associate at most one ground-truth cluster to each detected cluster. The assignment procedure is as follows. For each detected cluster we compute its ground-truth associated cluster. If it is not closer than a threshold τ_{loc} we mark it as a *false positive*, otherwise we assign the detected cluster to the ground-truth cluster. Then, for each ground-truth cluster we determine how many detected clusters are assigned to it. If there is none, we mark the ground-truth cluster as *missing detection*. Finally, for each ground-truth cluster, we select the closest (*true positive*) detected cluster among the ones assigned to the ground-truth cluster and we mark the remaining ones as *false positives*.

Table 2: Audio evaluation of the results obtained with synthetic sequences. *Sta*/*Dyn* states for static or dynamic scene; the AV objects move or do not move. *Var*/*Con* states for varying or constant number of AV objects.

Seq.	FP	MD	TP
StaCon	161	33 (13.4%)	214 (86.6%)
DynCon	144	56 (21.2%)	208 (78.8%)
StaVar	53	33 (18.8%)	143 (81.2%)
DynVar	56	34 (19.7%)	139 (80.3%)

We can evaluate the localization error and the auditory state for those clusters that have been detected correctly. The localization error corresponds to the Euclidean distance between the means. Notice that by choosing τ_{loc}, we fix the maximum localization error being allowed. The auditory state is counted as *false positive* if detected audible when silent, *missing detection* if detected silent when audible and *true positive* otherwise. τ_{loc} was set to 0.35 m in all the experiments. Table 1 shows the visual evaluation of the method when tested with synthetic sequences. The sequence code name describes the dynamic character of the sequence (*Sta* means static and *Dyn* means dynamic) and the varying number of AV objects in the scene (*Con* means constant number of AV objects and *Var* means varying number of AV objects). The columns show different evaluation quantities: FP (*false positives*), i.e., AV objects found that do not really exist, MD (*missing detections*), i.e., present AV objects that were not found, TP (*true positives*) and ALE (average localization error). Recall that we can compute the localization error just for the true positives.

First, we observe that the right detection rate is always above 65%, increasing to 96% in the case where there are 3 visible static clusters. We also observe that the fact that the number of AV objects in the scene varies does not impact the localization error. The effect on the localization error is due, hence, to the dynamic character of the scene; if the AV objects move or not. The third observation is that both the dynamic character of the scene and the varying number of clusters have a lot of impact on the detection rate.

Table 2 shows the auditory evaluation of the method when tested with synthetic sequences. The remarkable achievement is the high number of right detections, around 80%, in all cases. This means that neither the dynamic character of the scene nor the fact that the number of AV objects varies have an impact on sound detection. It is also true that the number of false positives is large in all the cases.

4.2 Real Data

The proposed method was tested on the CTMS3 sequence from the CAVA data set [3] and on the CPP sequence from the RAVEL data set [1]. In both cases the audio-visual acquisition device was calibrated as follows. First we calibrated the stereo camera pair using the OpenCV calibration software package. This provides both intrinsic parameters for the two cameras as well as extrinsic stereo calibration. To estimate the 3D positions of the microphones, we used the procedure described in [19] which yields accurate values for the microphone positions s_{M_1} and s_{M_2} in (1).

These data were processed as briefly outlined below. 3D visual observations were obtained as described in section 2. In all our experiments we used a time interval of 3 visual frames, $\Delta T = 0.2s$; we found that this value is short enough such that the AV objects

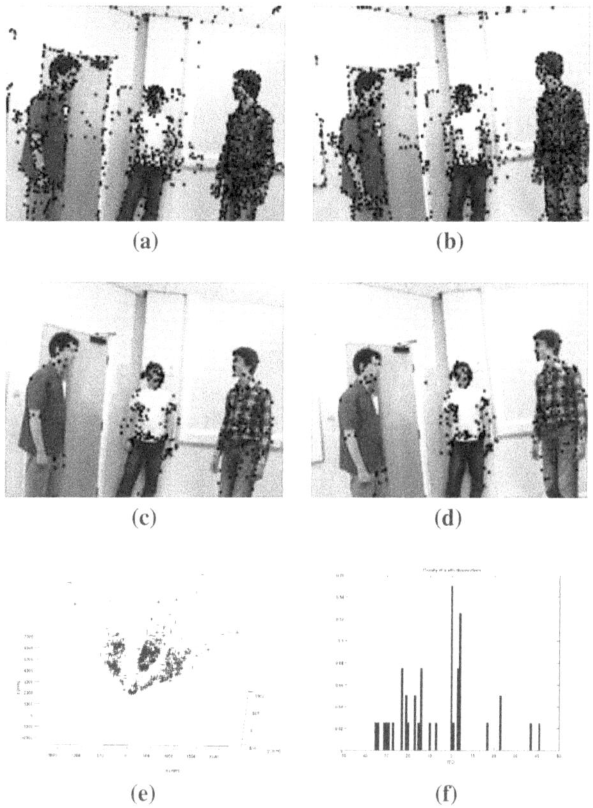

Figure 2: Interest points as detected in the left (a) and right (b) images. Dynamic interest points detected in the left (c) and the right (d) images.3D visual observations within a time interval of $\Delta T = 0.2s$. (f) 1D auditory observations (ITD values) detected in the same time interval.

remain at approximately the same 3D location, and is long enough to detect small motions, e.g., head motions. In practice there are approximately 2,000 visual observations and 20 auditory observations within each such time interval. A typical set of visual and auditory observations are shown in Figure 2. how Notice that both auditory and visual data are corrupted by noise and by outliers. Visual data suffer from reconstruction errors either from wrong matches or from noisy detection. Auditory data suffer from reverberations, which enlarge the pics' variances, or from sensor noise which is sparse along the ITD space.

4.2.1 Results with the CAVA data set

The CAVA (*computational audio-visual analysis*) data set was specifically recorded to test various real-world audio-visual scenarios. The data acquisition setup is described in detail in [3].

The audio-visual fusion method presented in the previous sections was tested and validated with the CTMS3 sequence[1]. This sequence consists on three people freely moving in a room and taking speaking turns. Two of them count in English (one, two, three, ...) while the third one counts in Chinese. The recorded signals, both auditory and visual, enclose the difficulties found in natural situations. Hence, this is a very challenging sequence: People come in and out the visual field of the two cameras, hide each other, etc. Aside from the speech sounds, there are acoustic reverberations and

[1] http://perception.inrialpes.fr/CAVA_Dataset/Site/data.html#CTMS3

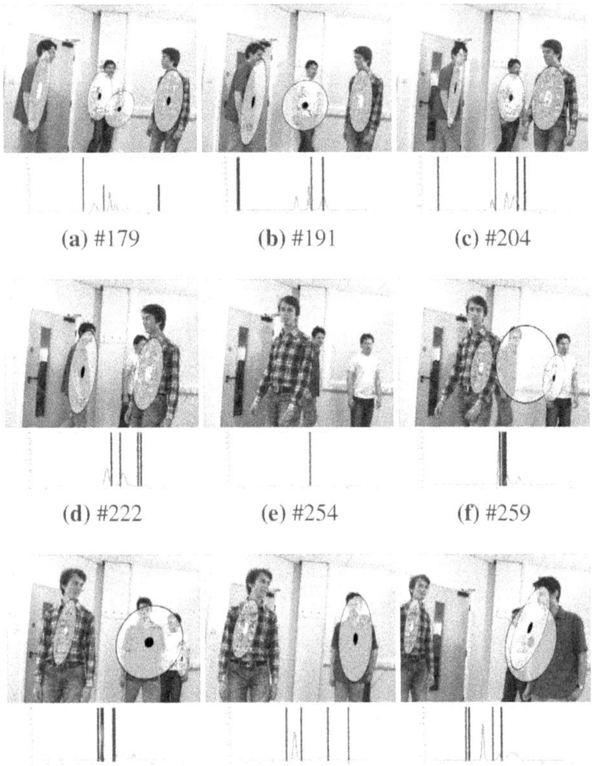

Figure 3: Results obtained with the CTMS3 sequence from the CAVA data set: Time intervals #179, ... #349. The ellipses correspond to the 3D covariance matrices projected onto the image. The circle at each ellipse center illustrates the auditory activity: speaker emitting a sound (white) or being silent (black) during each time interval. The plot associated with each image shows the auditory observations as well as the fitted 1D mixture model.

non-speech sounds such as those emitted by foot steps and clothe chafing. Occasionally, two people speak simultaneously.

We consider time intervals of length $\Delta T = 0.2s$. At 25 frames per second, there are 5 image-pairs in each time interval. A time-interval is indexed by the first image-pair namely #178, #179, #180, etc. Figure 3 shows the results obtained with nine time intervals chosen to show both successes and failures of our method and to allow to qualitatively evaluate it. Table 3 summarizes the results obtained with this sequence. The method correctly detected 22 out of 25 objects (people). The auditory activity correctly detected speech in 9 cases out of 15.

Table 3: This tables compares the detected auditory activity with the ground-truth for the examples shown in Figure 3. The figures correspond to the number of AV objects having an auditory activity in each time interval.

Time Interval	#179	#191	#204	#222	#254
Ground truth	1	2	2	2	1
Detected	1	1	1	1	0
Time Interval	#259	#297	#307	#349	Total
Ground truth	2	2	1	2	15
Detected	2	1	1	1	9 (60%)

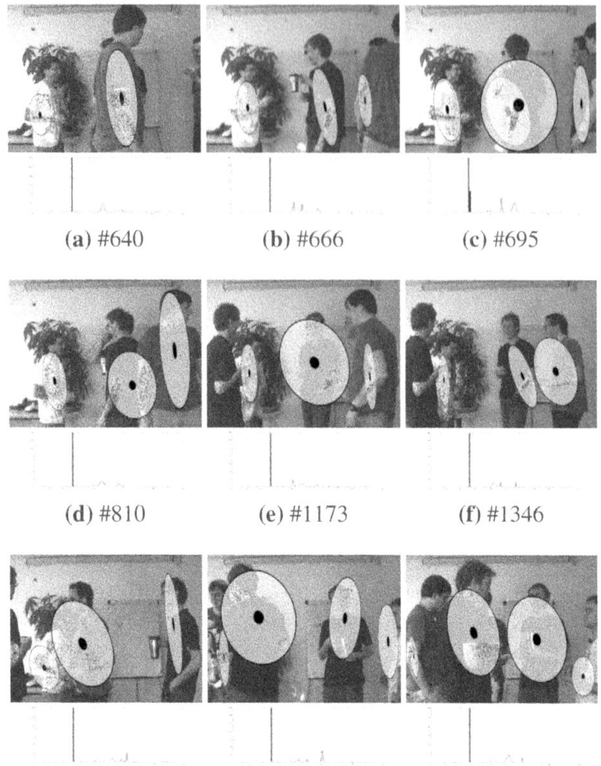

Figure 4: Results obtained with the CPP sequence from the RAVEL data set.

4.2.2 *Results with the RAVEL data set*

The RAVEL (*Robots with audio-visual interaction abilities*) data set was specifically recorded to test various real-world audio-visual scenarios, see [1] for more details. These scenarios involve up to three actors at a time. The recorded scenarios contain natural interaction between actors and between actors and the robot observer (whose actions are simulated by a person). The data consist of binocular video sequences and binaural audio tracks.

The method was validated using the CPP sequence[2] from the RAVEL data set. In this scenario there are up to five actors simulating a cocktail party. The actors come in and out of the field of view, they move and talk together or by groups. There are visual occlusions and two or more people speak simultaneously several times along the sequence. Background outdoor noise as well as background music were present and the lighting conditions of the environment also changed along the recording of the scene. Figure 4 shows the results of our method over nine frames of this sequence. It correctly detected and localized 26 objects out of 33 (78.8%) and there were 4 false positives at time intervals #695, #1573, #1715 and #2257. In this example the ITD observations correspond to the background music that is continuously present through the sequence. For this reason, it has not been possible to associate an auditory activity with an object in any of the time intervals.

[2] `http://ravel.humavips.eu/interaction.html#CPP`

5. CONCLUSIONS

In this paper we proposed a method that simultaneously localizes AV objects and detects their auditory activity. This is cast into a probabilistic framework. More precisely, we propose a new multimodal clustering algorithm based on a 1D Gaussian mixture model, an initialization procedure, and a model selection procedure based on the BIC score. We show how to take advantage of the geometric and physical properties associated with the visual and auditory sensors: these properties allow us to transform the visual features from the 3D space to an 1D auditory space. We also show how one of the two modalities can be used to weakly supervise the clustering process. We propose an EM algorithm that is theoretically well justified, intuitive, and extremely efficient from a computational point of view. This efficiency makes the method implementable in advanced platforms such as humanoid robots.

The presented method solves several technical issues: (i) it fuses and clusters visual and auditory observations that lie in physically different spaces with different dimensionality, (ii) it models and estimates the object-to-observation assignments that are not known, (iii) it handles noise and outliers mixed with both visual and auditory observations whose statistical properties change across modalities, (iv) it weights the relative importance of the two types of data, and (v) it estimates the number of AV objects that are effectively present in the scene during a short time interval.

One prominent feature of our algorithm is its robustness. It can deal with various kinds of perturbations, such as the ones encountered in unrestricted physical spaces. We illustrated the effectiveness and robustness of our algorithm using challenging audiovisual sequences from publicly available data sets.

There are several possible ways to improve and to extend our method. Our current implementation relies more on the visual data than on the auditory data, although there are many situations where the auditory data are more reliable. The problem of how to weight the relative importance of the two modalities is under investigation. Our algorithm can also accommodate other types of visual cues, such as 2D or 3D optical flow, face detectors, etc., or auditory cues, such as time-difference of arrival (TDOA). In this paper we used one pair of microphones. The method can be easily extended to several microphone pairs. Each microphone pair yields one ITD space and combining these 1D spaces would provide a much more robust algorithm. Finally, another interesting direction of research is to design a dynamic model that would allow to initialize the parameters in one time interval based on the information extracted in several previous time intervals. Such a model would necessarily involve dynamic model selection, and would certainly help to guess the right number of AV objects, particularly in situations where a cluster is occluded but still in the visual scene, or a speaker is occluded by another speaker/sound source.

6. REFERENCES

[1] X. Alameda-Pineda, J. Sanchez-Riera, V. Franch, J. Wienke, J. Cech, K. Kulkarni, A. Deleforge, and R. Horaud. The Ravel data set. Technical Report RR-7709, INRIA, Aug. 2011.

[2] T. J. Anastasio, P. E. Patton, and K. E. Belkacem-Boussaid. Using Bayes' rule to model multisensory enhancement in the superior colliculus. *Neural Computation*, 12(5):1165–1187, 2000.

[3] E. Arnaud, H. Christensen, Y.-C. Lu, J. Barker, V. Khalidov, M. Hansard, B. Holveck, H. Mathieu, R. Narasimha, E. Taillant, F. Forbes, and R. Horaud. The cava corpus: synchronised stereoscopic and binaural datasets with head movements. In *ICMI'08*, pages 109–116, New York, NY, USA, 2008. ACM.

[4] M. Beal, N. Jojic, and H. Attias. A graphical model for audiovisual object tracking. *IEEE Transactions on Pattern Analysis and Machine Intelligence*, 25(7):828–836, 2003.

[5] P. Besson and M. Kunt. Hypothesis testing for evaluating a multimodal pattern recognition framework applied to speaker detection. *Journal of NeuroEngineering and Rehabilitation*, 5(1):11, 2008.

[6] P. Besson, V. Popovici, J. Vesin, J. Thiran, and M. Kunt. Extraction of audio features specific to speech production for multimodal speaker detection. *Multimedia, IEEE Transactions on*, 10(1):63 –73, jan. 2008.

[7] C. Bishop. *Pattern Recognition and Machine Learning*. Springer, 2006.

[8] N. Checka, K. Wilson, M. Siracusa, and T. Darrell. Multiple person and speaker activity tracking with a particle filter. In *Proc. of IEEE Conference on Acoustics, Speech, and Signal Processing*, pages 881–884. IEEE, 2004.

[9] H. Christensen, N. Ma, S. Wrigley, and J. Barker. Integrating pitch and localisation cues at a speech fragment level. In *Proc. of Interspeech*, pages 2769–2772, 2007.

[10] D. Davies and D. Bouldin. A cluster separation measure. *Pattern Analysis and Machine Intelligence, IEEE Transactions on*, PAMI-1(2):224–227, January 1979.

[11] A. Dempster, N. Laird, and D. Rubin. Maximum likelihood from incomplete data via the EM algorithm. *Journal of the Royal Statistical Society. Series B (Methodological)*, 39(1):1–38, 1977.

[12] J. Fisher III and T. Darrell. Speaker association with signal-level audiovisual fusion. *IEEE Transactions on Multimedia*, 6(3):406–413, June 2004.

[13] D. Gatica-Perez, G. Lathoud, J.-M. Odobez, and I. McCowan. Audiovisual probabilistic tracking of multiple speakers in meetings. *IEEE Transactions on Audio, Speech, and Language Processing*, 15(2):601–616, 2007.

[14] C. Harris and M. Stephens. A combined corner and edge detector. In *Proc. of Fourth Alvey Vision Conference*, pages 147–151, 1988.

[15] C. Hennig. Methods for merging Gaussian mixture components. *Advances in Data Analysis and Classification*, 4:3–34, 2010. 10.1007/s11634-010-0058-3.

[16] T. Hospedales and S. Vijayakumar. Structure inference for Bayesian multisensory scene understanding. *IEEE Transactions on Pattern Analysis and Machine Intelligence*, 30(12):2140–2157, 2008.

[17] A. Ihler, J. Fisher III, and A. Willsky. Nonparametric hypothesis tests for statistical dependency. *IEEE Transactions on Signal Processing*, 52(8):2234–2249, August 2004.

[18] C. Keribin. Consistent estimation of the order of mixture models. *Sankhya Series A*, 62(1):49–66, 2000.

[19] V. Khalidov. *Conjugate Mixture Models for the Modeling of Visual and Auditory Perception*. PhD thesis, University of Grenoble, Grenoble, France, October 2010.

[20] V. Khalidov, F. Forbes, M. Hansard, E. Arnaud, and R. Horaud. Detection and localization of 3D audio-visual objects using unsupervised clustering. In *ICMI '08*, pages 217–224, New York, NY, USA, 2008. ACM.

[21] V. Khalidov, F. Forbes, and R. Horaud. Conjugate mixture models for clustering multimodal data. *Neural Computation*, 23(2):517–557, February 2011.

[22] D. Miller and J. Browning. A mixture model and em-based algorithm for class discovery, robust classification, and outlier rejection in mixed labeled/unlabeled data sets. *IEEE Transactions on Pattern Analysis and Machine Intelligence*, 25(11):1468 – 1483, nov. 2003.

[23] K. Nickel, T. Gehrig, R. Stiefelhagen, and J. McDonough. A joint particle filter for audio-visual speaker tracking. In *Proc. of ICMI*, pages 61–68, New York, NY, USA, 2005. ACM.

[24] K. Nigam, A. McCallum, S. Thrun, and T. Mitchell. Text classification from labeled and unlabeled documents using EM. *Machine Learning*, 39(2-3):103–134, 2000.

[25] S. Ray and B. G. Lindsay. The topography of multivariate normal mixtures. *The Annals of Statistics*, 33(5):2042–2065, 2005.

[26] G. Schwarz. Estimating the dimension of a model. *The Annals of Statistics*, 6:461–464, 1978.

[27] D. N. Zotkin, R. Duraiswami, and L. S. Davis. Joint audio-visual tracking using particle filters. *EURASIP Journal on Applied Signal Processing*, 11:1154–1164, 2002.

Please, Tell Me About Yourself: Automatic Personality Assessment Using Short Self-Presentations

Ligia Maria Batrinca
CIMec, Univ. of Trento and FBK-irst
Corso Bettini, 38068 Rovereto, Italy
batrinca@fbk.eu

Nadia Mana
FBK-irst
via Sommarive 18, 38123 Povo, Italy
mana@fbk.eu

Bruno Lepri
FBK-irst and MIT Media Lab
via Sommarive 18, 38123 Povo, Italy
lepri@fbk.eu

Fabio Pianesi
FBK-irst
via Sommarive 18, 38123 Povo, Italy
pianesi@fbk.eu

Nicu Sebe
DISI, University of Trento
via Sommarive 14, 38123 Povo, Italy
sebe@disi.unitn.it

ABSTRACT

Personality plays an important role in the way people manage the images they convey in self-presentations and employment interviews, trying to affect the other's first impressions and increase effectiveness. This paper addresses the automatically detection of the Big Five personality traits from short (30-120 seconds) self-presentations, by investigating the effectiveness of 29 simple acoustic and visual non-verbal features. Our results show that Conscientiousness and Emotional Stability/Neuroticism are the best recognizable traits. The lower accuracy levels for Extraversion and Agreeableness are explained through the interaction between situational characteristics and the differential activation of the behavioral dispositions underlying those traits.

Categories and Subject Descriptors

H.1.2 [**User/Machine Systems**]: Human Information Processing; I.5.4 [**Pattern Recognition Applications**]: Computer Vision, Signal Processing;
J.4 [**Computer Applications**]: Social and Behavioral Sciences – *Psychology, Sociology, Economics.*

General Terms

Algorithms, Measurement, Experimentation, Human Factors.

Keywords

Personality trait detection, Big Five, Self-Presentation.

1. INTRODUCTION

Social psychology research showed that personality plays an important role in the way people manage the images they convey in self-presentations and employment interviews, trying to affect the audience first impressions and increase effectiveness [21].

At the same time, other studies provided evidence that interviewers perform personality inferences during personnel selection interviews: for instance, Huffcut et al. [17] found that personality traits and social skills were the most frequently measured constructs.

ICMI'11, November 14–18, 2011, Alicante, Spain.

Moreover, the type and degree of interview structure seem to moderate this correspondence. Roth et al. [36] found that the extent to which interviews inadvertently measure an applicant's personality seems to depend on the extent to which interpersonal skills are allowed to play a role throughout the interview process.

Nonverbal cues play a major role in this complex process ([15], [34]). DeGroot and Gooty [11] examined the mutual influences between personality attributions, performance ratings and interviewees' non-verbal behaviors. Using a structured behavioral interview setting, they found that raters can make personality attributions even using only one channel of information (e.g., acoustic, visual, etc.) and that these attributions mediate the relationships between the interviewee's nonverbal cues and performance ratings. More in detail, Conscientiousness attributions explain the relationship between visual cues and interview ratings. Extraversion attributions mediate the relationship between vocal cues and interview ratings, and Neuroticism attributions had a suppressing effect for both visual and vocal cues. Regarding Extraversion, the results show that the interviewers infer this trait only from the speaker's voice characteristics.

Our goal is to build machines able to automatically detect personality traits from simple acoustic and visual non-verbal signals, extracted from short (30-120 seconds) self-presentations. Following much psychosocial work on first impressions formation, we exploit the concept of *thin slices* [1] to refer to the short amount of expressive behaviors that we, humans, rely on to produce impressively precise judgments on an individual's or group's properties, such as personality, teaching capabilities, negotiation outcomes, etc.

To our knowledge, this is the first time that the self-presentation scenario is addressed. Given the mediating role of personality in the assessment of interviewees' performance, systems capable of understanding personality traits during short self-presentations would be very helpful to interviewers in their personnel and student selection job. At the same time, they could be the core of coaching systems that support people in their preparation for job interviews or, more generally, that help people manage the first impressions they convey, helping them in defining and achieving personal goals. The rest of the paper is organized as follows: the next section reports some previous works addressing automatic recognition of personality traits. Section 3 describes the corpus used in this work. Section 4.1 and 4.2 present the acoustic and visual features extracted from the collected data, while Section 4.2

and Section 4.4 present the analysis and selection of these features. The automatic machine learning approaches used to automatically predict personality traits are described in Section 5 and the achieved results are discussed in Section 5.1. Finally, Section 6 draws the conclusions.

2. RELATED WORK

Previous work on automatic recognition of personality is relatively recent. Pioneering work addressing this task was carried out by Argamon et al. [2] in 2005. They used word categories based on systemic functional grammar (SMG) and relative frequency of function words to train support vector machines (SVMs) for the recognition of two (Extraversion and Emotional Stability) of the five Big Five traits, measured by means of self-reports. Similarly, in 2006 Oberlander and Nowson [29] trained Naïve Bayes classifiers and SVMs, using n-gram features, to isolate four (Agreeableness, Conscientiousness, Extraversion and Neuroticism) of the Big Five traits on a corpus of personal weblogs. Also Mairesse et al. ([24], [25]) worked on recognition of the Big Five personality traits, while systematically investigating the usefulness of different sets of acoustic and textual features, as suggested by psycholinguistic and psychosocial literature. They separately trained their automatic recognition algorithms on personality data coming from self-reports and observed data. The results showed that: (a) Extraversion is the easiest personality trait to model from spoken language; (b) prosodic features play a major role, and (c) the automatic recognition was closer to observed personality than to self-reports.

Olguin et al. [30] collected various behavioral measures, extracted from daily activities of 67 professional nurses in a hospital. The data were collected by means of a socio-meter badge, a wearable device integrating a number of sensors (accelerometer, infrared sensor and microphone) measuring aspects such as physical and speech activity, level of proximity to relevant objects (people, but also beds, etc.), number of face-to-face interactions with others, and social networks parameters. Although the data collection was not targeting prediction of personality traits, a lot of information about personality came out from the correlation analysis conducted by the authors.

More recently, Pianesi et al. [33] and Lepri et al. [22] showed the feasibility of automatically recognizing the Extraversion and Locus of Control personality traits, using simple non-verbal features. This approach was based on the assumption that: a) personality shows up in the course of social interaction and b) thin slices of social behavior are enough to classify personality traits. The first assumption was realized by exploiting classes of acoustic features encoding specific aspects of social interaction (*Activity*, *Emphasis*, *Mimicry*, and *Influence*) and three visual features (head, body, and hands fidgeting). For the second, they demonstrated personality assessment based on inferences from 1-minute-long behavioral sequences.

Kalimeri et al. [19] studied the classification performance of two models incorporating theoretically motivated hypotheses about personality trait relationships and their behavioral manifestations. In the first model, the classification task exploits the relationship between people's personality traits and their behavior to infer traits from observed behaviors. The second model includes the context, meant as an additional causal factor beside personality traits.

Zen et al. [39] used proxemic features (e.g., number of intimate, personal, and social relationships; minimum distance between two subjects, etc.), extracted from video tracking and head pose estimation, to investigate the automatic recognition of two personality traits (Extraversion and Neuroticism). Mohammadi et al. [28] showed how prosodic features can be used to predict the personality assessments of human experts on a collection of 640 speech samples.

Recently, de Oliveira et al. [31] showed that variables derived from the users' mobile phone call behavior as captured by call detail records and social network analysis of the call graph can be used to automatically infer the users' personality traits defined by the Big Five. On the same line, Chittaranjan et al. [10] analyzed the relationship between smartphone usage and self-assessed personality. Their study is based on a large-scale dataset of 8 months of real usage of smartphones by 83 people and personality surveys that are suitable for large mobile or online studies Applications usage, call and SMS logs contained several meaningful relationships to the Big-Five personality framework.

3. SELF-PRESENTATIONS CORPUS

3.1 Participants

The 89 participants of our study were recruited among employees of a research centre (9 subjects from the administration and 14 subjects from the various research areas), university students (43 subjects) and other external people (23 subjects).

The distribution of the participants was quite balanced in terms of gender (46 male and 43 female) and age (47 young people, i.e. under 25, and 42 adults, i.e. over 25).

Due to the large participation of students, the average age was quite low (29 years) but in any case falling within the adult range (over 25).

3.2 Technical Setup and Recording Procedure

The subjects, involved in individual sessions, were invited to sit in front of a monitor with a webcam on its top (see Figure 1-a). They used the computer mouse just to fill in an online questionnaire (see Section 3.4) and to accept the Skype call from the experimenter at the beginning of the experimental session. A clip-on microphone, worn close to the shirt or sweater collar, was used to communicate with the experimenter.

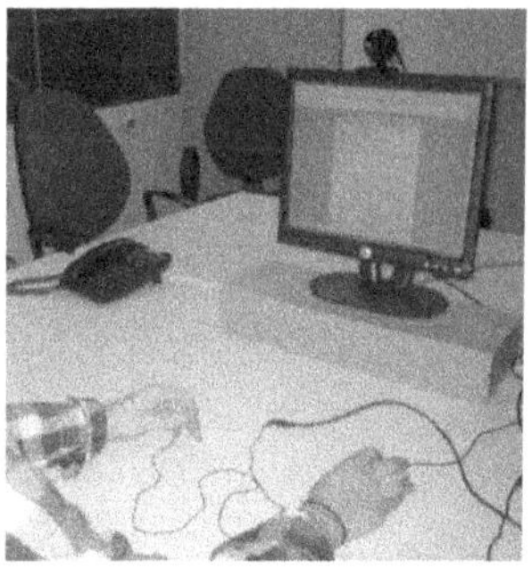

(a)

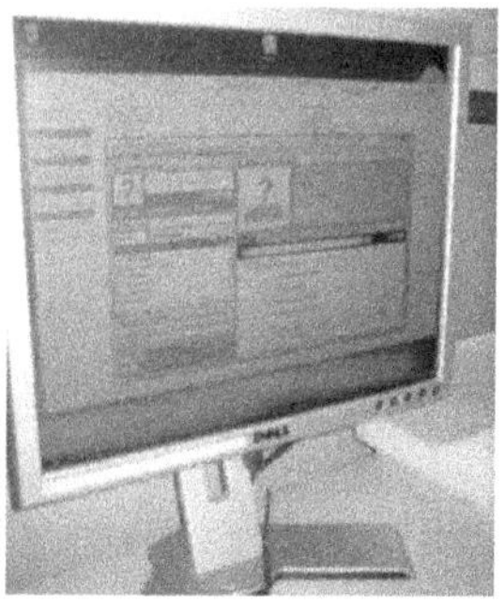

(b)

Figure 1. A view of the experimental setting on the subject's side (a) and on the experimenter side (b)

At the beginning of the session, the experimenter provided each subject with the necessary details. Then she asked the subject to sign the informed consent form and to fill in an online personality questionnaire (see section 3.4.1). After checking that the subjects properly wore the clip-on microphone and securing that the webcam was properly placed for frontal and central shots, the experimenter left for the recording room. Afterwards, she called the subject via Skype, informing him/her that he/she could start the self-introduction session.

3.3 Task Description

The subjects were asked to introduce themselves in front of a camera. Possible topics (e.g. talking about their job, last read book, last holiday, preferred food, preferred sport, etc.) were suggested. However, they were left absolutely free to choose any of them or any other topics they liked.

In order to obtain a good quality frontal image of the subject to be later used for initialization purposes, the participant was initially asked to look into the camera for a few seconds without moving.

The length of resulting self-presentations ranged from 30 up to 120 seconds.

3.4 Personality

We used the Big Five model, asking to the subjects to fill in the Italian version of the questionnaire [18], presented online.

3.4.1 Big Five Questionnaire

The Big Five questionnaire owes its name to the five traits that it takes as constitutive of people's personality:

1. Extraversion vs. Introversion (sociable, assertive, playful vs. aloof, reserved, shy)
2. Agreeableness vs. Disagreeable (friendly, cooperative vs. antagonistic, faultfinding)
3. Conscientiousness vs. Un-conscientiousness (self-disciplined, organized vs. inefficient, careless)
4. Emotional stability vs. Neuroticism (calm, unemotional vs. insecure, anxious)
5. Creativity or Openness to experience (intellectual, insightful vs. shallow, unimaginative)

In the standard questionnaire, validated on the Italian language [32], each trait is investigated through ten items, each of them assessed by means of 1 to 7 points scale.

3.4.2 Questionnaire Scores

The Big Five scores were calculated summing single raw scores, properly inverted, per each personality trait. The results (average and standard deviation values) are reproduced in Table 1.

Table 1. Averages and standard deviations of Big Five scores

	Women		Men	
	<25	≥25	<25	≥25
Agree	49.05 (6.383)	50.68 (5.867)	47.65 (7.985)	51.45 (7.564)
Consc	41.76 (9.643)	46.36 (8.693)	39.45 (9.944)	48.25 (9.124)
EmSt	36.57 (7.047)	36.59 (5.518)	40.50 (7.458)	44.65 (6.968)
Creat	45.43 (6.896)	46.55 (7.482)	48.69 (6.279)	47.00 (7.861)
Extra	47.00 (7.791)	45.50 (8.245)	42.04 (9.075)	42.55 (8.370)

In order to investigate the dependence of traits' scores on gender and age, the latter was split in two classes: people younger than 25 and people 25 or more years old. The analysis was conducted by means of a series of ANOVA with dependent variables, the factorial scores for Extraversion, Agreeableness, Conscientiousness, Emotional Stability and Creativity, and Age and Gender as predictors. The results are reported in Table 2.

As evident from the table, no effects were found for Agreeableness and Creativity. Conscientiousness exhibited an Age effect ($F=11.387$, $p<.05$) and Emotional Stability and Extraversion a Gender effect ($F=17.054$ and $F= 4.859$ respectively, $p<.05$). According to our data, therefore, people tend to become more conscientious with age (47.26 vs. 40.43) and independently of their gender; on the other hand, men are more emotionally stable than women (42.30 vs. 36.58), whereas women are more extravert (46.23 vs. 42.26).

Table 2. Dependence of personality traits' scores on subjects' gender and age. F-statistics values for main and interaction effects from ANOVA analyses. *, p<.05; **, p<.01; ***p<.001; n.s., not significant.

	Gender	Age	Gender*Age
Agree	n.s.	n.s.	n.s.
Consc	n.s	11.387***	n.s.
EmSt	17.054***	n.s.	n.s.
Creat	n.s.	n.s.	n.s.
Extra	4.859*	n.s.	n.s.

4. NON-VERBAL CUES AND FEATURES

4.1 Acoustic and Visual Cues

Many acoustic and visual cues have been shown to be related to personality traits. In particular, the importance of acoustic features, such as pitch and intensity, for personality has often been pointed out ([12], [37]). Furnham [14] discussed how extraverted people are characterized by a particular speaking style: they talk more, louder, faster and have fewer hesitations. Others pointed out that frequency of hand movements/gestures was positively correlated with Extraversion [9]. Riggio [35] suggested that extraverts have a higher head movement frequency than introverts and they change their posture more often. Moreover, they maintain eye-contact for longer [26], have higher speaking and gestural fluency. Laughing was associated with high scores in Openness to Experience/Creativity [27]. Many visual cues have been correlated to Agreeableness ([13], [8]). Conscientiousness was correlated with gaze, speaking fluency, speech rate and hand movements ([13], [8], [3]).

Drawing on this and related literature, we derived a set of audio and visual cues, extending their usage also to traits for which less evidence was available, e.g., Creativity. Pitch and acoustic intensity were automatically extracted using Praat [6]. The pitch algorithm is based on the autocorrelation method. Setting the default values for the time step and pitch ceiling (600 Hz) parameters, but lowering the pitch floor from 70 Hz to 50 Hz, the algorithm, uses a time step of 0.015 seconds and a window length of 0.06 seconds. It computes 67 pitch values per second. Intensity is calculated taking into consideration the minimum periodicity frequency in the signal [7]. Visual cues (see in Table 3) were hand-annotated by means of the ANVIL annotation tool [20].

Table 3. Visual cues, manually annotated

Cue	Label	Notes
Eye-Gaze	Up down right left closedEyeLid desktopCtc camCtc	a) upward directed -gaze; b) downward directed-gaze; c) rightward directed gaze; d) leftward directed gaze; e) lids closed for longer than 2 sec; f) -gaze directed toward the desktop; g) -gaze directed toward the webcam.
Frowning	Yes, no	
Hand Movement	MovFace MovAir MovBody Stillface StillAir StillBody	a) hand(s) on the face; b) hand(s) moving in the air; c) hand(s) on parts of the body, except on the face.
Head orientation	Left right down up front rightSide leftSide rightIncl leftIncl	a) head oriented left; b) head oriented right; c) head oriented down; d) head oriented up; e) head oriented frontal; f) head tilted right; g) head tilted left; h) head half oriented right; i) head half oriented left
Mouth Fidgeting	Smile tongueLips biteLips tightLips retractLips	a) smiles; b) subject passing her tongue over her lips; c) subject biting her lips; d) subject pressing her lips; e) subject moving her lips by lowering both mouth corners.
Posture	Back straight forward	a) subject leaning back; b) straight posture; c) subject leaning forward.

4.2 Extracted Features

From the acoustic and visual cues of the previous section we extracted the 29 features of Table 4, to be used in our classification experiments: 17 visual features, 9 acoustic features and 3 features concerning the total speech time, the average duration of voiced segments and the length of the self-presentation.

4.3 Feature Analysis

The (linear) relationships between our features and the Big Five personality traits were analyzed by means of number of backward linear regression analyses, one per each trait, with all our features as predictors.

Table 5 reports for each of the final models the retained predictors and the portion of dependent variable variance explained. As can be seen, the linear models account only for a small portion of variance.

Table 6 reports the partial correlations between the retained predictors and the various traits. Agreeable people tend to gain more often the straight posture, to have a lower maximum pitch and produce longer presentations. More conscientious people smile more frequently and use a longer portion of their presentation for speaking than less conscientious ones; but they move their head around less, tend to exhibit a lower average pitch and lower minimal vocal energy, and produce shorter (on average) voiced segments. More creative people lean towards the camera more often than less creative ones but gesticulates less. Higher emotional stability is associated with a greater number of rather short leaning forward events, lower amount of gesticulation and lower vocal intensity.

Table 4. Feature list

	Ref	Label	Description
Visual Features	1	avDurationBack	Average duration of leaning back episode
	2	avDurationCam	Average duration of looking into the webcam episodes
	3	avDurationDow n	Average duration of looking down episodes
	4	avDurationFrow	Average duration of frownings
	5	avDurationFwd	Average duration of leaning forward episodes
	6	avDurationStr	Average duration of straight posture episodes
	7	freqBack	Rate of leaning backward postures
	8	freqCam	Rate of looking into the webcam events
	9	freqDown	Rate of looking down events
	10	freqForward	Rate of leaning forward postures
	11	freqFrowning	Rate of frownings
	12	freqHandMovin g	Rate of hand-movement events.
	13	freqHandStill	Rate of hand-still events
	14	freqMouth	Rate of lip moving or biting events
	15	freqSmile	Rate of smiles
	16	freqStraight	Rate of straight postures
	17	NrHeadOrient	Rate of head orientation change
Acoustic Features	18	pitch_mean	Mean of Pitch
	19	pitch_min	Minimum of Pitch
	20	pitch_max	Maximum of Pitch
	21	pitch_med	Median of Pitch
	22	pitch_sdev	SD of Pitch
	23	i_mean	Mean of Intensity
	24	i_min	Minimum of Intensity
	25	i_max	Maximum of Intensity
	26	i_sdev	SD of Intensity
Additional Features	27	avTimeVoiced	Av. duration of voiced segments
	28	TimeVoiced	Portion of self-presentation taken by speech
	29	videoLength	Total length of self-presentation

Finally, extraverts produce longer voiced segments, but smile and frown less frequently and maintain for shorter time the straight posture in front of the camera.

Table 5. Retained predictors and portion of dependent variable variance explained

	Retained predictors	R^2
Agree	16, 20, 29	.127
Consc	15, 17, 18, 23, 27, 28	.188
Creat	10, 12	.107
EmSt	5, 10, 12, 13, 23	.148
Extra	6, 11, 15, 27	.172

Table 6. Partial correlations between the retained predictors and the various traits; see Table 4 for features' reference numbers.

Feat	16	20	29
Agree	.303	-.216	.217

Feat	15	17	18	23	27	28
Consc	.203	.208	-.337	-.207	-.183	.274

Feat	10	12
Creat	.321	-.195

Feat	5	10	12	13	23
EmSt	-.280	.290	-.258	.287	-.195

Feat	6	11	15	27
Extra	-.259	-.184	-.265	.240

4.4 Feature Ranking

A known problem in classification tasks is to find strategies to reduce the dimensionality of the feature space in order to avoid over-fitting. In our experiment, we applied the Weka implementation of the Support Vector Machine Recursive Feature Elimination (SVM-RFE) algorithm (called Support Vector Machine attribute evaluation method in Weka) in order to evaluate the importance of a feature. This algorithm was introduced by Guyon et al. [16] in a cancer classification problem with the goal of finding a subset of features which maximize the performance of the classifier. Roughly speaking, a linear SVM is a hyper-plane that separates two classes of examples (positive and negative) maximizing the separation margin. The SVM creates a weight vector, where a weight is assigned to each feature. The weight vector is used to determine the least important feature, defined as the one with the *smallest* weight. At each iteration, the least important feature is removed and the procedure is repeated on the reduced feature set. This method is used with a Ranker search method and the features are ranked according to the square of the weights assigned to them. Hence, the first feature is the most relevant for the classification task at hand and the last feature of the least relevant one.

For reasons of space, we do not report here the feature rankings produced; see the next section for more on this topic.

5. AUTOMATIC PREDICTION OF PERSONALITY TRAITS

For the sake of our classification experiments, all personality traits' scores were quantized (Low/High) along their median values (Agreeableness = 50, Consciousness = 44, Creativity = 46, Emotional Stability = 39, and Extraversion = 45).

Three machine learning algorithms, namely Naïve Bayes, SVM with linear kernel and SVM with RBF one, were used in 5 binary classification tasks, one per personality trait. The bound-constrained SVM classification algorithm was used for the two SVM classifiers. The cost parameter C and the RBF kernel parameter γ were estimated trough an inner leave-one- out cross validation on the training set of the first fold using the first 88 subjects for the parameter estimation. The best performing values of the parameters were then kept fixed for the outer-cross validation.

Naïve Bayes is a simple probabilistic classifier that applies the Bayes theorem and assumes that the presence/absence of a particular feature of a given class (e.g. a personality state) is unrelated to the presence/absence of any other feature. The main advantage of using Naïve Bayes is that it only requires a small amount of training data to estimate the parameters (means and variances of the variables) necessary for classification.

For each classifier and for each trait, we executed 29 classification runs, each exploiting a subset of the features aggregated according to the ranking provided by the SVM-RFE algorithm. We started from the single feature experiment using the first ranked feature, then executed the 2-feature experiment with the first two ranked features, and so on.

The leave-one-out cross-validation strategy was employed. Hence, 89 models for each personality trait were trained on 88-subject subsets, evaluating them against the remaining ones and finally averaging the results.

5.1 Results and Discussion

Table 7 reports, for each classifier and for each trait, the feature combination producing the highest accuracy value. All the accuracy values reported are statistically significant, according to binomial tests that compared the observed accuracy to that of the baseline classifier that exploits the observed frequencies of the two classes. The significance was set at $p \leq 0.01$ and the resulting threshold values for accuracy where 0.618 for Agreeableness, Conscientiousness and Emotional Stability, and 0.629 for Creativity and Extraversion. The highest accuracy values, greater or equal to 70%, were obtained on Conscientiousness (SVM-RBF), Emotional Stability (SVM-RBF and SVM-Lin) and Extraversion (SVM-RBF and Bayes). To further characterize the predictive power of our features and the behavior of the classifiers, we investigated how they worked on the two classes each trait was split into. We started from the confusion matrix of the conditions in Table 7 and compared the hits for the High and Low classes with those expected from the baseline classifier. The comparison was conducted by means of Pearson residuals, standardized scores - they are $N(0, 1)$ - that measure the difference between observed and expected outcomes. On hits, the absolute value of a Pearson residual measures how much the classifier performs better (positive sign) or worse (negative sign) than the baseline in terms of recall. For errors, the reverse is true. Here we focus on hits.

Table 7. Accuracy (Acc), recall on the Low class (Rec1) and on the High class (Rec2) for the best conditions per each personality trait. The features used are also reported; see Table 4 for the reference number.

		SVM-RBF	SVM-Lin	Bayes
Agree	Acc, Rec1, Rec2	65.16, 50, 80	65.16, 50.00, 80.00	64.04, 34.09, 93.33
	Features	8, 22, 6, 15, 29, 10	8, 22, 6, 15, 29, 10	8, 22, 6, 15, 29, 10, 16
Consc	Acc, Rec1, Rec2	73.03, 73.91, 72.09	68.53, 76.09, 60.47	
	Features	19, 22, 27,6, 14, 24, 20, 17, 25	19, 22, 27,6, 14, 24, 20, 17, 25, 12, 9, 16	
Creat	Acc, Rec1, Rec2	64.04, 72.00, 53.85	66.29, 76.00, 53.85,	64.04, 68.00, 58.97
	Features	16, 8, 15, 26, 12, 7, 6, 4, 24, 20, 14, 13, 2, 5, 1, 17, 9, 11, 21, 3, 22	16, 8, 15, 26	16, 8, 15, 26, 12, 7, 6, 4, 24, 20, 14, 13, 2, 5, 1, 17, 9, 11
EmSt	Acc, Rec1, Rec2	76.40, 80.44, 72.09	75.28, 82.61, 67.44	64.04, 45.65, 83.72
	Features	25, 22, 20, 13, 12, 10, 16, 9, 2, 19, 8	25, 22, 20, 13, 12, 10, 16, 9, 2, 19	25, 22, 20, 13, 12, 10, 16, 9, 2
Extra	Acc, Rec1, Rec2	70.78, 76.60, 64.29		69.66, 74.47, 64.29
	Features	24		24

Finally, we took advantage of the $N(0, 1)$ distribution of Pearson residual and fixed a threshold of ±3sd for the statistical significance of the difference between observed and expected hits. Table 8 reports the results.

Table 8. Pearson residual for the condition of Table 4. Only residuals greater or equal in absolute value than 3 are reported.

	SVM-RBF		SVM-Lin		Bayes	
	Low	**High**	**Low**	**High**	**Low**	**High**
Agree		4.25		3.95		5.74
Consc	3.02	3.12	3.31			
Creat						
EmSt	3.90	3.12	4.20			4.65
Extra	3.27				2.97	

SVM-RBF was the only classifier yielding balanced performances on at least two traits: Conscientiousness and Emotional Stability. In all the other cases, good performances arose only from either the Low or the High class. For instance, with Agreeableness good performances are limited to the High class whereas with Extraversion they are limited to the Low class. For Creativity, no classifier yielded significant performances on any class.

We think it is by no chance that Conscientiousness and Emotional Stability are the traits that yielded the best results, both in terms of accuracy values and of the level of balance between the recall values for the Low and High classes. Conscientiousness, in fact, relates to the individual's capacities for behavioral and cognitive control. Conscientious individuals are described as responsible, attentive, careful, persistent, orderly, and planful; those low on this trait are irresponsible, unreliable, careless, and distractible. High conscientiousness has been connected to positive engagement within task-related behavior [4]. Apparently, the request of introducing themselves in front of a monitor, with camera and microphone on, activated our subjects' Conscientiousness dispositions, doing so for both those high and those low in this trait. Those dispositions, in turn, affected some of the considered behaviors, including: the dynamics of pitch (minimal and maximal pitch, and pitch range as captured by pitch_sdev) and of voice energy (minimal and maximal intensity) on the acoustic side; posture (average duration of episodes of sitting straight in front of the monitor) and head movements and lip-related events on the visual one.

Emotional stability and its counterpart, neuroticism, concern the susceptibility to negative emotions, which we one might think are elicited by the task of introducing oneself in front of a computer screen while being audio-video recorded. Emotional Stability/Neuroticism includes both anxious and irritable distress. The former is inner-focused and includes dispositions to anxiety, sadness and insecurity. Irritable distress, in turn, involves outer-directed hostility, anger, frustration and irritation. We can easily figure out that the self-introduction task activates one of those two sets of dispositions, depending of the person's internal constitution. The behavioral signs that proved effective concerned pitch dynamics (maximum and minimum pitch, and pitch standard deviation), maximum voice intensity, and several visual features: dynamic of hand movements, posture dynamics (straight and forward position), camera fixation and camera aversion, hand fidgeting.

According to this line of explanation, both the request of executing a task and the nature of the task (introducing oneself) activated dispositions connected to Conscientiousness and Emotional Stability. We think that a similar rationale can be given to account for the performances with other traits.

A good accuracy level was obtained with Extraversion too, but this result was basically due to the performance with introverts. One might suggest that the unbalance might be (at least partially) due to the fact that the situation/task was not appropriate for fully activating Extraversion-related dispositions, especially with extraverts. It has been argued, in fact, that the core of Extraversion lies in the tendency to behave in a way so as to engage, attract and enjoy social attention, *i.e.*, extraverts invest time and energy in activities that attract the attention of others ([5],[23]). One possible consequence of this view is that Extraversion-related disposition are activated to a lesser extent in situation like the one we are considering here where there are no others whom to attract attention from, and that this should affect especially extraverts' behavior. Notice, finally, that only one feature (minimal vocal intensity) is used in the best case.

Agreeableness does not reach the same levels of accuracy as Conscientiousness and Emotional Stability. However, the recall for the High class, both measured in absolute term (see Table 7) and through Pearson residuals (see Table 8) is very high: in absolute terms, it reaches 80% with SVM-RBF and SVM-Lin and 93% with Naïve Bayes. This trait includes a number of dispositions that foster congenial social behavior: generosity, consideration, cooperation, willingness to accommodate others wishes, etc. Agreeable people do not aim to attract social attention like extraverts, but to please others. We believe that, again, the key to understanding the performance of our features and classifiers with this trait is in the nature of the situation: it activates a pleasing attitude that somehow masks non-agreeable dispositions (being aggressive, rude, manipulative, etc.).

Finally, the dispositions linked to Creativity seem to be uniformly activated to much a lesser extent by the task of introducing oneself.

6. CONCLUSION

The aim of this paper was to contribute to advance the state of the art in the automatic analysis of people personality. In particular, we investigated the feasibility of detecting the Big Five in short videos of self-presentation. In doing so, we adopted a thin-slice perspective and we investigated the contribution of a large set of different acoustic and visual non-verbal cues.

The main findings of our paper are the following:

a) Conscientiousness and Emotional Stability are the easiest traits to automatically detect during self-presentation. The reason could be that the first trait is connected to engagement within task-related behavior and that the second one is connected to the emotional reactions (e.g. distress) it elicits.

b) Our task does not seem to activate the full range of dispositions of Agreeableness and Extraversion. For the latter, the reasons can be that introducing oneself in front of a computer screen does not provide enough social audience to let the social attention dispositions of extraverts fully activate. As to Agreeableness, we have invoked the masking effect of the necessity of pleasing the experimenter, implicit in the nature of the situation.

On the practical side, our results are a first important step towards automatic systems assisting either interviewers or interviewees in improving their performance in job interviews. On a more theoretical side, they emphasize the influence of the situation for a full unfolding of the behavioral dispositions tied to personality traits.

Of course, more work is needed to fully explore the automatic analysis of personality traits in self-introduction, e.g., by considering even larger sets of non-verbal feature, as well as verbal ones (e.g., lexical choice, presence of emotion-related words; topic dynamics, etc.); using larger samples and/or exploiting regression or ordinal techniques. Finally, we also consider the possibility of extending the work to interviewer/interviewee interactions by collecting new data to model this scenario too, where the system can work with the mediation of an interviewer.

7. ACKNOWLEDGMENTS

The data collection and research presented in this paper have been supported by the EU NETCARITY Project - Integrated Project of the Sixth Framework Programme (IST-2006-045508). Bruno Lepri's research is funded by PERSI project inside the Marie Curie COFUND – 7th Framework.

8. REFERENCES

[1] Ambady, N. and R. Rosenthal. 1992. 'Thin slices' of expressive behaviors as predictors of interpersonal consequences. A meta analysis. Psychological Bulletin. 111, 156-274.

[2] Argamon, S., Dhawle, S., Koppel, M., and Pennbaker, J. 2005. Lexical predictors of personality type. In Proceedings of Interface and the Classification Society of North America.

[3] Aronovitch, C. D. 1976. The voice of personality: Stereotyped judgments and their relation to voice quality and sex of speaker. *The Journal of Social Psyhcology*, 99, 207-220.

[4] Ashton MC, Lee K. 2001. A theoretical basis for the major dimensions of personality. *European Journal of Personality*. 15:327–53.

[5] Ashton, M. C., Lee, K., and Paunonen, S. V. 2002. What is the Central Feature of Extraversion? Social Attention Versus Reward Sensitivity. *Journal of Personality and Social Psychology*, 83, 245-252.

[6] Boersma, P., Weenik, D. – Praat: doing phonetics by computer. Computer Program, Version 5.2.05. www.praat.org

[7] Boersma, P., Weenik, D. – Praat: doing phonetics by computer. User Manual, Version 5.2.05. www.praat.org

[8] Borkenau, P. and Liebler, A. 1992. Trait inferences: Sources of validity at zero acquaintance. *Journal of Personality and Social Psychology*, 62, 645-657.

[9] Brebner, J. 1985. Personality theory and movement. In B. D. Kirkcaldy (Ed.), Individual differences in movement (pp. 27-41). Lancaster, England: MTP Press Limited.

[10] Chittaranjan, C., Blom, J., and Gatica Perez, D. 2011. Who's Who with Big Five: Analyzing and Classifying Personality Traits with Smartphones. In Proceedings of IEEE International Symposium on Wearable Computers (ISWC), San Francisco.

[11] DeGroot, T., and Gooty, J. 2002. Can Nonverbal Cues be Used to Make Meaningful Personality Attributions in Employment Interviews. In Journal of Business Psychology, 24, pp. 179-192.

[12] Dewaele, J. M., Furnham, A. 2000. Personality and speech production: a pilot study of second language learners. In *Personality and Individual Difference*.

[13] Funder, D. C. and Sneed, C. D. 1993. Behavioral manifestations of personality: An ecological approach to judgmental accuracy. *Journal of Personality and Social Psychology*, 64, 470-490.

[14] Furnham, A. 1990. Language and personality. In K. R. Scherer and H. Giles and W. Robinson (Eds). *Handbook of Language and Social Psychology,* Winley.

[15] Gifford, R., Ng, C., & Wilkinson, M. 1985. Nonverbal cues in the employment interview: Links between applicant qualities and interviewer judgments. The Journal of Applied Psychology, 70.

[16] Guyon I, Weston J., and Barnhill S. 2002. Gene Selection for Cancer Classification using Support Vector Machines. In Machine Learning, volume: 46, Issue: 1, Publisher: Springer, Pages: 389-422.

[17] Huffcutt, A. I., Conway, J. M., Roth, P. L., & Stone, N. J. 2001. Identification and meta-analytic assessment of psychological constructs measured in employment interviews. Journal of Applied Psychology, 86, 897–913.

[18] John, O. P., Srivastava, S. 1999. The Big five trait taxonomy: History, measurement and theoretical perspectives. In Pervian, L. A. & John, O. P., (Eds.) Handbook of personality theory and research. Guilford Press. New York.

[19] Kalimeri, K., Lepri, B., and Pianesi, F. 2010. Causal Modelling of Personality Traits: Extraversion and Locus of Control. Proceedings of the Second International Workshop on Social Signal Processing (SSPW 2010)

[20] Kipp, M. 2001. Anvil – A generic Annotation Tool for Multimodal Dialogue. In Proceedings of the 7th European Conference on Speech Communication and Technology, Eurospeech, pp. 1367-1370.

[21] Leary, M.R. and Allen, A.B. (in press). Personality and Persona: Personality Processes in Self-Presentation. In Journal of Personality.

[22] Lepri, B., Mana, N., Cappelletti, A., Pianesi, F., Zancanaro, M. 2009. Modeling Personality of Participants during Group Interaction. In Proceedings UMAP – User Modeling, Adaptation and Personalization. Trento, Italy.

[23] Lepri, B., Subramanian, R., Kalimeri, K., Staiano, J., Pianesi, F., and Sebe, N. 2010. Employing Social Gaze and Speaking Activity for Automatic Determination of the Extraversion Trait. In *Proceedings of the ACM International Conference on Multimodal Interfaces, ICMI 2010*. Beijing, China, 2010.

[24] Mairesse, F., and Walker, M. 2006. Automatic recognition of personality in conversation. In Proceedings of HLT-NAACL.

[25] Mairesse, F., and Walker, M. 2006. Words mark the nerds: Computational models of personality recognition through language. In Proceedings of the 28th Annual Conference of the Cognitive Science Society, pp. 543–548.

[26] Mehrabian, A. 1969. Significance of posture and position in the communication of attitude and status relationships. In *Psychological Bulletin* 71(5), 359-372.

[27] Mergl, R., Vogel, M., Prässl, A., Graf, B., Karner, M., Mavrogiorgou, P., Hegerl, U.,, Juckel, G. 2006. Facial Expressions and Personality: *A Kinematical Investigation during an Emotion Induction Experiment.* Neuropsychobiology, 54, 114-119.

[28] Mohammadi, G., Vinciarelli, A., and Mortillaro, M. 2010. The Voice of Personality: Mapping Nonverbal Vocal Behavior into Trait Attributions Proceedings of the Second International Workshop on Social Signal Processing (SSPW 2010).

[29] Oberlander, J. and Nowson, S. 1992. Whose thumb is it anyway? Classifying author personality from weblog text. In Proceedings of the Annual Meeting of the ACL. Association for Computational Linguistics, 627-634.

[30] Olguin, D., Gloor, P.A., and Pentland, A. 2009. Wearable Sensors for Pervasive Healthcare Management. Proceedings of 3rd International Conference on Pervasive Computing Technologies for Healthcare, London, UK.

[31] Oliveira, R.; Karatzoglou, A.; Concejero, P.; Armenta, A.; Oliver, N. 2011. Towards a psychographic user model from mobile phone usage. *Proc. of 29th ACM conference on human factors in computing systems, Works-in-Progress session (ACM CHI).* Vancouver, Canada.

[32] Perugini, M. and Di Blas, L. (2002). Analyzing Personality related Adjectives from an Eticemic Perspective: The Big Five marker Scales (BFMS) and the Italian AB5C Taxonomy. In B. De Raad and M. Perugini (eds.) Big Five Assessment, Hogrefe und Huber Publishers, Göttingen, 281-304.

[33] Pianesi, F., Mana, N., Cappelletti, A., Lepri, B., and Zancanaro 2008. Multimodal Recognition of Personality Traits in Social Interactions. In Proceedings of International Conference on Multimodal Interfaces, Chania, Crete, Greece.

[34] Raza, S. M., & Carpenter, B. N. 1987. A model of living decisions in real employment interviews. The Journal of Applied Psychology, 72, 596–603.

[35] Riggio, R., Friedman, H. 1986. Impression formation: The role of expressive behavior. In *Journal of Personality and Social Psychology* 50(2), 421-427.

[36] Roth, P. L., Van Iddekinge, C. H., Huffcutt, A. I., Eidson, C. E., Jr., & Schmit, M. J. 2005. Personality saturation in structured interviews. International Journal of Selection and Assessment, 13, 261−273.

[37] Scherer, K. R. 1979. Personality markers in speech. In K. R. Scherer and H. Giles (Eds)., *Social Markers in Speech.* Cambridge University Press.

[38] van Dam, K. 2003. Trait perception in the employment interview: A five-factor model perspective. International Journal of Selection and Assessment, 11, 43−55

[39] Zen G., Lepri B., Ricci E., Lanz O. 2010. Space Speaks - Towards Socially and Personality Aware Visual Surveillance. Multimodal Pervasive Video Analysis Workshop - MPVA 2010 - workshop in conjunction with ACM MM 2010, Firenze, Italy, October 29th, 2010.

Gesture-Aware Remote Controls: Guidelines and Interaction Techniques

[1,2]Gilles Bailly [2]Dong-Bach Vo [2]Eric Lecolinet [2]Yves Guiard

[1] Deutsche Telekom Laboratories, TU Berlin, Ernst-Reuter-Platz 7, D-10587, Berlin, Germany

[2] Telecom-ParisTech, CNRS LTCI UMR 5141, 46 rue Barrault, 75013 Paris, France

Gilles.Bailly@ telekom.de {dong-bach.vo, eric.lecolinet, yves.guiard}@telecom-paristech.fr

ABSTRACT

Interaction with TV sets, set-top boxes or media centers strongly differs from interaction with personal computers: not only does a typical remote control suffer strong form factor limitations but the user may well be slouching in a sofa. In the face of more and more data, features, and services made available on interactive televisions, we propose to exploit the new capabilities provided by gesture-aware remote controls. We report the data of three user studies that suggest some guidelines for the design of a gestural vocabulary and we propose five novel interaction techniques. Study 1 reports that users spontaneously perform pitch and yaw gestures as the first modality when interacting with a remote control. Study 2 indicates that users can accurately select up to 5 items with eyes-free roll gestures. Capitalizing on our findings, we designed five interaction techniques that use either device motion, or button-based interaction, or both. They all favor the transition from novice to expert usage for selecting favorites. Study 3 experimentally compares these techniques. It reveals that motion of the device in 3D space, associated with finger presses at the surface of the device, is achievable, fast and accurate. Finally, we discuss the integration of these techniques into a coherent multimedia menu system.

Categories and Subject Descriptors

H5.2. **[Information interfaces and presentation]**: User Interfaces-Evaluation/methodology, Interaction styles.

General Terms: Human Factors

Keywords:

Mid-air gestures, remote control, 10-foot interaction, menu, ITV.

1. INTRODUCTION

Interaction with TV sets, set-top boxes or media centers strongly differs from interaction with personal computers. This context of use, which we believe has received too limited attention so far in HCI, is quite challenging [3] [6]. The number of available features and services has been uninterruptedly increasing. Not only hundreds of channels are now available through cable TV but also Web services provide various kinds of digital media (podcasts, video on demand, digital stores...). Moreover, set-top-boxes can also provide access to personal data such as photos, music, etc.

The WIMP model, that relies on efficient devices such as a mouse and a keyboard makes it reasonably easy to interact with numerous sources of data on the PC. However, this model is not adapted to the context of TV and "sofa interaction" [3][6]. They must usually deal with much more limited devices, such as remote controls and must thus navigate long lists or deep hierarchical menus by making repetitive presses on a directional pad or to cope with remote controls that are overcrowded with buttons. Moreover, users can be leaning back on a sofa. In either case we face an usability problem [8][15][37]. This is especially true for favorite commands that users perform frequently (e.g. for displaying their favorite TV channels or accessing their favorite Web services, personal data, etc.).

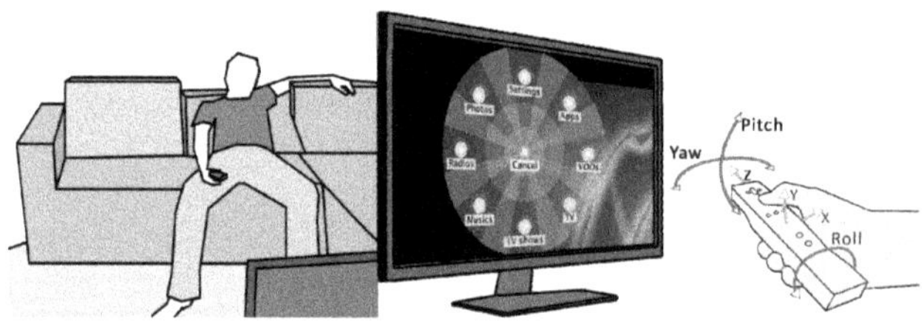

Fig. 1. Left: Sofa interaction. Right: Augmenting a remote control with mid-air gestures allowing 6 degrees of freedom.

One solution for augmenting the interaction bandwidth consists in transforming the traditional remote control into a sophisticated device including a touchscreen [22] or even in using a smartphone or a tablet as a replacement [21][38]. We focus on another approach that exploits the new capabilities provided by gesture-aware remote controls [13][33]. A few prototypes and even some commercial products [11][16] have been recently introduced, but to date little HCI research has been done on interaction techniques with remote-controls [3] and gesture-augmented devices.

Mid-air gestures are known to be well accepted by users in the domestic context [14][30] and they offer several notable advantages. Unlike buttons and other physical interactors, they consume no real estate on the remote control and so the input vocabulary can be enriched at no cost with regard to device size. They do not confiscate visual attention—the users' gaze need not alternate between the TV screen, their only source of interest, and the remote control. Previous research on 2D gestures, especially on Marking menus [1][20], suggest that certain gestures are easy to remember, a property that makes them good candidates for acting as shortcuts for performing favorite commands. Finally, mid-air gestures only require low-cost sensors such as accelerometers or gyroscopes.

We thus investigated how mid-air gestures can augment interaction with remote controls in the context of interactive television (Fig. 1). Study 1 shows that the optimal mapping between mid-air gestures and directional actions depends on context and that pitch & yaw rotations should be preferred for remote control interaction. We then focused on eyes-free roll gestures. Study 2 indicates that users can accurately select up to 5 items, up to 7 items if the system takes into account the identity of the user. The data we gathered helped us to design a vocabulary of simple mid-air gestures combinations. We proposed five different techniques using either device motion, button-based interaction, or both. Study 3 experimentally compares them. It reveals that motion of the device in 3D space, associated with finger presses at the surface of the device, is achievable, fast and accurate. Finally, these techniques were implemented in the context of interactive television for navigating in multimedia data and quickly selecting favorite elements. They make gestures visible and easy discoverable [25] and favor the fluid transition from novice to expert usage [18].

2. RELATED WORK

2D or 3D gestures can be conveniently classified as symbolic, physical, metaphorical or abstract [37]. An example of *symbolic* gestures is provided by users who enter numbers by drawing their shape in the air using the MagicWand [7]. *Physical* gestures work as their counterpart in the real world as in [2], where users manipulate virtual 3D objects. *Metaphorical gestures* transpose physical gestures in the digital world, as the swipe gesture in 3D space to go to the next chapter as if browsing a real book [4] or to go to the next slide with the Gyration mouse [11]. For these three gesture categories, however, there is little coherence among users [14]. With *abstract gestures*, on which we will focus below, the mapping is arbitrary between the gesture and its semantics. A well-known 2D-space instance is the Marking menu [18] which maps gestures onto an arbitrary arrangement of actions. Although proved to be remarkably efficient [1] [18] [39], the Marking menu has received limited attention in the field of 3D interaction where techniques generally rely on the other three categories.

Mid-air gestures on mobile devices. Motion Marking menus [27] are an adaptation of Marking menus for mobile devices where users perform pitch rotations to select commands in a 3x3 hierarchical menu system. Mid-air gestures have also been used to enter text on mobile devices [28] [31] [34] [35]. Unigesture [31] uses pitch and roll rotations for choosing a group of characters and an inference engine to overcome ambiguities. TiltType [28], TiltText [35], and Shrimp [34] combine button clicks for choosing a group of characters and pitch and roll rotations for further choosing the desired character within the selected group.

Mid-air gestures on remote controls. Text entry using a gesture-sensitive remote control has also been investigated. In GesText [13] users combine pitch and roll gestures, without the help of any buttons. With Cube Key [32], each letter (placed in a 3x3x3 matrix) can be accessed from translations in 3D space. Gesture-sensitive remote controls are well known in the video game industry, following the example of Nintendo Wii remote control (Wiimote). XWand [36], which works in an intelligent environment, is used to select elements by pointing and to execute a small set of commands using roll gestures. A likely reason why most of the above-described techniques use pitch and roll rotations is that they rely on accelerometers, which cannot detect yaw rotations. We will see below that this technological constraint may appreciably impact usability in the case of remote-control interaction.

Vision-based remote controls. Various vision-based solutions, exploiting a video camera, have been proposed for remote control systems [5] [10] [16], most relying on hand-gesture interaction. These techniques do not provide tactile feedback and they can introduce mode-switching problems due to the lack of buttons as delimiters. Typically, they offer a limited set of commands, although the domain is evolving at a fast pace [10] [16]. Besides, if our study considers interaction with a hand-held device, our results are relevant to gestural interaction in general, our focus being the set of gestures rather than the hardware technology.

3. STUDY 1: MAPPING PREFERENCES FOR MID-AIR MOTION

Six geometrical degrees of freedom (DoF) are available for the motion of a remote control (Fig. 1), but the question whether it is possible to base interaction on a distinction between rotations and translations is open, and the sort of motion users actually produce may be context dependent (e.g. when they use a remote control vs. a smartphone). This exploratory investigation considered an eight-choice selection to be made by means of gestures. Items appeared at 8 possible locations on a 3x3 matrix whose central cell was empty. With such an arrangement each item could be identified just as well by its cartesian (*x-y*) or polar (directional) coordinates. So the task, selecting items in menu systems, did not bias participants toward performing translations (x, y or z) or rotations (pitch, yaw, roll).

Methods. For each trial, one matrix cell was highlighted at chance. Following the approach proposed in [37], "first portray the effect of a gesture, and then ask users to perform its cause", we asked our participants to perform the mid-air gesture that, in their opinion, should have caused this effect. We also explained them that the central cell corresponded to the resting position (i.e., when the device was roughly parallel to the floor) and that they had to start from this position to perform the gesture. They had to come back to the resting position before performing the next trial. The sessions were videotaped with participant's informed consent.

While previous studies dealing with this sort of tasks were run with handheld devices, we tested our participants with a smartphone (an iPhone, S condition) vs. a remote control (a basic model with no screen, RC condition). In the S condition, the stimuli appeared on the device they were manipulating. In the RC condition the stimuli appeared on a 3m-distant (10 feet) TV screen and so the participants never had to look at the remote control.

We used a between-participant design. For each condition (S and RC), we recruited 9 participants (18 in total) aged 24-30. Each participant performed 8 gestures, one for selecting each matrix cell.

Gestures were classified from videos in one of the 6 following categories: X, Y, Z translations and yaw, pitch, roll rotations. This classification was performed separately by two different people and the same results were obtained in both cases. As this classification was done from naked-eye observations it only accounts for the main tendencies (visually indiscernable small auxiliary movements may have also been produced).

Results. While 7 of the 9 participants of the Smartphone group demonstrated conspicuous pitch and roll rotations, the pattern was opposite in the Remote-control group, in which 7 of the 9 participants showed no less conspicuous pitch and yaw rotations ($p<.001$ by the Fisher exact probability test). Two participants showed translations in each of the two groups.

Implications for HCI. This exploratory study delivered three suggestions of potential relevance to the design of a mid-air gesture vocabulary:

(1) The participants made gestures that were unambiguously of either the rotational or translational category. The behaviors were consistent, no participant switched from one category to the other during the experiment.

(2) Fourteen or our 18 participants spontaneously demonstrated rotations and only four demonstrated translations (p<.04 by the binomial probability test, two-tailed). This outcome, perhaps simply a reflection of the fact that rotations are easier to perform for a multi-joint arm [12], encouraged us to investigate rotations in the rest of the present study.

(3) Different sets of rotations were performed by participants in the S vs. RC conditions: while all the rotations observed in the S group combined the pitch and the roll (in keeping with previous interaction techniques on smartphones [28][31][35]), all those observed in the RC group combined the pitch and the yaw. If this result suggests that accelerometers, which capture pitch&roll, are sufficient for smartphones, it points to the utility of gyroscopes, which can also detect yaw gestures, for directional tasks with remote controls.

None of our participants demonstrated translations along the z axis or roll rotation in the RC condition. This means that these two components remain free for performing other tasks while combined with pitch and yaw movement. As z-translations require the combined motion of both the elbow and shoulder joints, they are likely to be cumbersome for seated users. This is why we decided to focus on roll gestures in the rest of the study.

4. STUDY 2: USING ROLL GESTURES

Device rotations about the roll axis (Fig. 1), which result from wrist pronation and supination, have been considered in a number of papers. While Rahman et. al.'s users were able to select 16 items by rolling a smartphone with visual feedback [29], only three levels of roll movements were used in [26], which proposed an eyes-free menu technique. This rather large difference is easily explained by the absence of visual feedback in the latter case, but we suspected that users should be able to select a larger number of commands eyes-free with a reasonable level of accuracy. This led us to design two user studies to explore the potential of roll gestures for eyes-free selection. We used a TV screen to deliver stimuli, our participants being asked to perform the required roll movements with a Wiimote.

4.1 Study 2A

This user study aimed to evaluate the impact of two factors, *number of items* and *user posture*, on the feasibility of eyes-free roll selection.

Number of items. We considered four different set sizes with 5, 7, 9, and 11 items, leaving aside the easy three-item condition tested in [26]. We expected our participants to be able to accurately discriminate up to 7 or 9 different eyes-free roll movements.

Posture. Roll movements may imply several joints, the wrist, the elbow and even possibly the shoulder for very large amplitudes. In the context of 'sofa interaction' with a remote control, motion about these joints must be more or less constrained by the user's posture. We asked participants to perform the rolls in three different postural conditions:

- Posture 1: only the wrist is free, the forearm resting on the thigh.
- Posture 2: the upper arm is kept in contact with the body so that only the elbow and the wrist can freely move.
- Posture 3: all three joints are free to move.

Roll movement. We used a *press-tilt-release* strategy for measuring the roll movement [29]: the captured value was the amount of angular change recorded with the Wiimote from an initial angular position marked by a trigger press to a final angular position marked by trigger release (Figure 2-right). This strategy has two main advantages. One is that the input value is relative, meaning one need not care about the absolute vertical, unlikely to be correctly perceived by slouching users. The other is a considerable increase of the range of available angular values. For example, to produce a large-amplitude roll in the clockwise direction the gesture begins with a preparatory counter-clockwise roll at the end of which the trigger is pressed, setting an angular zero, say, at -45° (Figure 2-left); if, the trigger being kept pressed, the device is then rolled clockwise up to +75° and the trigger is released at that new position, the obtained angular delta will be 120°. With this technique the possible range can then reach 200° and even more (depending on the user and the posture).

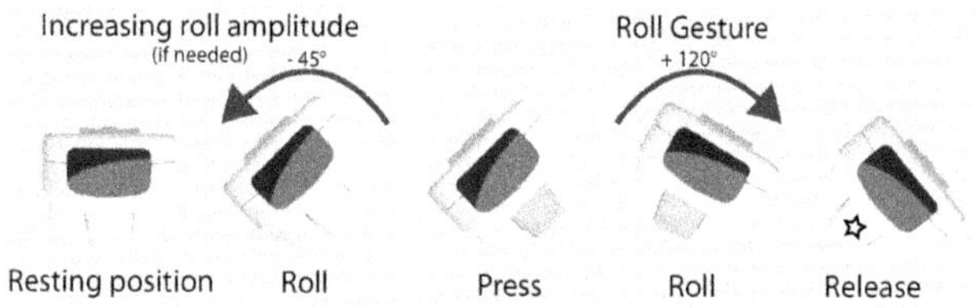

Figure 2: Example of a roll gesture. Left: a preparatory back-roll for increasing the total roll movement. Right: Execution of the roll gesture (the trigger being kept pressed).

Stimulus and Feedback. We used a TV screen to display a horizontal array of constant-sized boxes. A variable number of boxes served to vary the number of items that had to be discriminated using roll movements. An example with seven items (7 boxes) is shown in Fig. 3. The stimulus consisted of one square being highlighted. If the central square was highlighted, no roll was needed, the participant having just to press and release the trigger. The position of the highlighted box served to specify the direction and the relative amplitude of the required roll movement without providing any cue about where in the absolute range of positions the angular variation was to be produced. In practice, the more to the right (resp. left) the stimulus, the larger the roll amplitude the participants had to cover in the clockwise (resp. counter-clockwise) direction from their initial trigger press to their final trigger release. Apart from proprioception no feedback was provided in this experiment. Indeed, we wished to determine which angular changes users would spontaneously perform, and which patterns the distribution would exhibit.

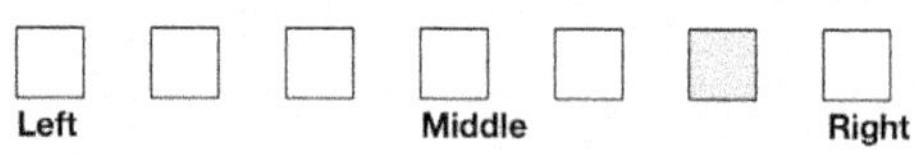

Fig. 3. The stimulus for 7-item selection. The highlighted box indicated which item of the set had to be selected (left = counter-clockwise, right = clockwise).

Task. In response to each new stimulus the participant could prepare his/her gesture by changing the starting position if necessary and then perform a *press-tilt-release* roll (Figure 2) as fast and accurately as possible. An inter-trial interval of 1.5 seconds was used to give time to the participant to return to their rest position before the next trial.

Participants and Apparatus. Nine volunteers (aged 22-28, 8 men) were recruited from our institution. The experiment was performed using a MacBook Pro and a 40" LCD HD TV set.

Participants were seated in a couch, about 3m (10 feet) away from the TV set. The remote control was a Nintendo Wiimote. The experimental software (C++/Qt) used an adaptation of the DarwiinRemote framework [9] to communicate with the Wiimote.

Procedure. The experimental session started with a few warm-up trials using a three-item set. Each participant completed 5 blocks for each combination of item set size and posture. Within a block each item appeared once in a randomized succession. The four set sizes (5, 7, 9, and 11 items) were presented in increasing order, task difficulty thus increasing with familiarity. The posture was counterbalanced across participants using a Latin Square design. In summary, the experiment involved:

9 participants x 4 item-set sizes x 3 postures x 5 blocks x 5, 7, 9 or 11 items (depending on item-set size) = 4320 gestures. The total duration of the experiment was about 45min.

4.1.1 Results

Angular ranges. The participants having received no indication about the angular amplitudes they had to cover with their rolls, considerable differences were observed among them. For instance, the angular max-min range varied from 162° to 326° in the 7-items condition (the max-min range could reach 326° because we used a *press-tilt-release* strategy, as explained above). We normalized the angular variation by dividing it by the observed max-min range for each participant and each item-set size. Unsurprisingly, the max-min angular range was strongly dependent on item-set size ($F_{3,24}$=97.47, p<.0001) and increases with the *number of items* (5: 159°, 7: 306°, 9: 343°, 11: 371°). The max-min angular range depended slightly but significantly on *posture* ($F_{3,24}$=9.8, p<.001), with on average 273° for posture 1, 290° for posture 2, and 321° for posture 3.

Table 1: mean angular variations (in degrees) for each item.

Nb of items	Item identity										
	-5	-4	-3	-2	-1	0	1	2	3	4	5
5				-81.2	-43.6	-0.3	42.8	78			
7			-155	-90.3	-49.6	-0.9	52.9	88.6	150.2		
9		-173	-116	-83.1	-51.3	-0.6	50.9	81.9	118.5	171	
11	-188	-136	-101	-77.5	-46.8	-0.6	46.4	70.6	99.3	138.8	184.4

Angular Variations. Table 1 shows the average angular variation for each item and for each item set size. Participants adjusted the angular amplitude of their rolls proportionally to the number of items. A nearly perfect linear relationship was found for each of the four item-set sizes (all r^2>.995), with a virtually zero *y*-intercept (all four intercepts being less than 1° and non-significant). Moreover, the angular change between two contiguous items was fairly constant, about 45° (especially in the 5 and 7 item conditions).

Recognition rates. We used a KNN algorithm [17] with *k*=5 and the Euclidian distance on the angular variation to calculate the recognition rate. KNN is useful to reduce the effect of noise on the classification [17] and is fast and effective [1]. The testing and learning bases were separated by using a leave-one-out cross-validation technique [23]. There was a strong effect of item-set size on accuracy ($F_{3,24}$=53.52, p<.0001). Accuracy decreases with the *number of items* (5: 96.3%; 7: 87.7%; 9: 77.1%; 11: 63.1%). No significant effect of posture was detected.

4.1.2 Implications for HCI

This user study led to four informative findings.

(1) Whether or not users are provided with feedback impacts the relationship between angular variation and item-set size. While Rahman [29] found a *quadratic* relationship with a continuous visual feedback, our results reveal a *linear* relationship when gestures are performed eyes-free.

(2) The angular change between two contiguous items was fairly constant, about 45° (especially in the 5 and 7 item conditions).

(3) Surprisingly, the posture did not impact the recognition rate while it had an effect on maximal angular variation. As noted, participants divided the available amplitude in about equal sectors, whose size depended on posture. This is encouraging as it suggests good robustness.

(4) Users were able to easily select five items by performing eyes-free roll gestures with recognition rates above 95%. The conditions with 9 and 11 items turned out to be quite difficult without visual feedback. The seven-item case (87.7%) seemed inconclusive. This led us to the next study.

4.2 STUDY 2B: FOCUS ON 7-ITEM

Participants were now presented with numeric values on the TV screen (-135°, -90°, -45°, 0°, 45°, 90°, 135°). These values were chosen in light of the results of the previous experiment, the step values being simply rounded up to 45° to facilitate mental representation. We no longer inquired into the posture issue.

A sample of 20 fresh volunteers (aged 25-31 years, all right-handed) participated. The experiment comprised a learning and a testing phase. During the 5min learning phase, the value of the angular variation actually covered by the participant was displayed on the screen (this feedback was no longer delivered during the testing phase). Each participant ran 15 blocks in each of which the 7 items appeared once in a randomized order. In summary, the experiment involved 20 participants x 15 blocks x 7 items = 2,100 selections.

4.2.1 Results

Accuracy. As previously, we used the KNN algorithm with *k*=5 and a leave-one-out cross-validation technique [23]. Recognition rate ranged from 88 to 95%, with an average of 90.9%. We also analyzed the data by participant, that option corresponding to the case where the recognizer already has information about user identity (e.g., if a user profile has been selected or thanks to an automatic face recognition system). We then obtained an accuracy rate of 96% (from 91.4 to 98.1%).

Selection Time. Measured from stimulus appearance to button release, selection time was, as expected, strongly dependent on item position ($F_{6,114}$=32.4, p<.0001). On average, the central item (1.40s) was significantly faster than items -1 (2.44s) and +1 (2.60s), both significantly faster than items -3 (3.53s) and +3 (3.27s). The central item was also significantly faster than items -2 (2.67s) and +2 (2.98s).

Angular variation. Table 2 shows the mean angular variations, which will serve to parameterize the roll-based techniques.

Table 2. Mean, 5th percentile, and 95th percentile of angular change (in degrees) for each item

Item	-3	-2	-1	0	1	2	3
delta angle (mean)	-134	-85	-51	0	49	86	127
delta angle (p05)	-164	-106	-70	-4	31	61	100
delta angle (p95)	-109	-66	-32	4	70	111	166

4.2.2 Summary

Our investigation of eyes-free roll selections revealed that this approach is fairly robust, as the posture does not impact the recognition rate. It turned out that all users could easily perform five-item selections and even seven-item selections if the database is adapted to the user (i.e the system takes into account the identify of the user). Seven items appeared to be an upper limit for eyes-free roll gestures.

5. DESIGN SPACE & TECHNIQUES

Building on the results obtained in previous sections, we now propose several multimodal techniques for interacting with a remote control. All of them aim at selecting items in a two-level hierarchical menu and can work both in novice mode (with the menu shown on the TV) and in expert mode (eyes-free). We will describe some novice-mode visual representations, but let us start with eyes-free selection. Even though visual feedback is needed for some commands in a complex interactive multimedia system, open-loop selection without the burden of TV menu navigation is especially desirable for frequent actions like selecting a *favorite* channel.

Table 3: Design space for a two-level menu. Techniques that appear over a white background are evaluated in the next section.

2nd. level ⇒ ⇓ 1st. level	*Pitch & Yaw*	*Roll*	*Pad*
Pitch & Yaw	P&Y/P&Y	P&Y/Roll	P&Y/Pad
Roll	Roll/P&Y	Roll/Roll	Roll/Pad
Pad	Pad/P&Y	Pad/Roll	Pad/Pad

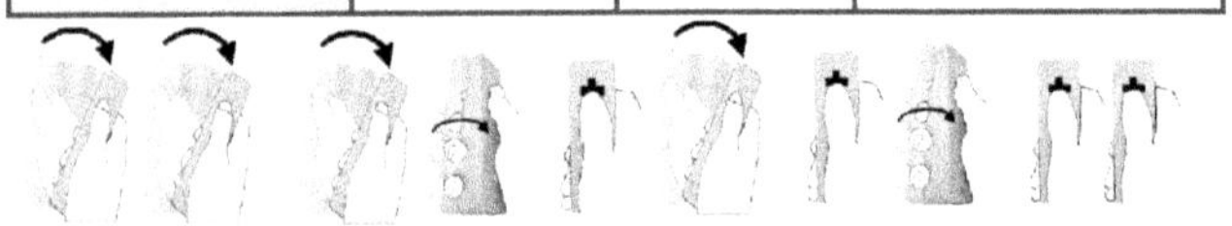

Figure 4: The gestures of the five two-level menus

The foregoing suggests that three gestural modalities, pitch&yaw, roll, and button interaction, are of special interest. Table 3 combines them. As each menu level can be controlled by one of three modalities, nine combinations are theoretically possible. Below we describe each modality and then explore the design space.

Pitch and yaw gestures *(P&Y)* involve two rotational DoF. Yet we will consider them here as a single input modality because they combine in an integral way for the task under consideration (a 2D directional task performed relatively to the TV screen). Any combination of pitch and yaw rotations specifies a movement in a certain direction as in Marking menus [18]. Marking menus have been shown to be very efficient in 2D space, especially for eyes-free interaction, and so expanding them to mid-air interaction looked especially promising. Note incidentally that our transposition of Marking menus to 3D space is quite different from Motion Marking menus [27] and closer to the original.

Roll gestures (*Rolls*) correspond to the second modality and will be used as explained in the previous section.

The third modality, Pad gestures *(Pad),* consists in pressing the buttons of a directional pad (d-pad). D-pads are quite common in remote controls and are well suited for directional tasks. This latter property is interesting because it will allow direct comparison with pitch and yaw gestures, thus making it possible to answer the question whether gestural interaction is competitive compared with button-based interfaces. Moreover, pad gestures can easily be combined with gestural modalities.

5.1 Interaction Techniques for 2-Level Menus

P&Y / P&Y. This technique is reminiscent of Multi-Stroke menus [39] in the sense that user makes two successive gestures, but these are pitch and yaw gestures. Each gesture, as already described, consists of pressing the trigger button at the beginning of the gesture and releasing it at the end.

P&Y / Roll. Different gestures are then used for the first (P&Y) and second (Roll) level of the menu system. A theoretical advantage is that these gestures do not need to be performed sequentially as they imply different modalities.

Roll / P&Y. This technique was discarded because pretests showed the difficulty of performing roll *then* pitch&yaw gestures. The case of performing roll and pitch&yaw gestures simultaneously is already covered by the previous technique.

Roll / Roll. This technique was discarded based on poor pre-test results. Both steps require angular variations that theoretically do no depend on each other, but many participants were confused, failing to perform the second gesture. Often, they felt the need to perform the second gesture according to an absolute vertical position, thus wasting time. And the users that did not follow this pattern made many mistakes.

Pad / Pad. This technique acts as a baseline and we expected it to be especially efficient, as the user just needs to click two times on the appropriate buttons of the d-pad.

Pad / P&Y. The promise of this technique is that it combines d-pad and mid-air gestures. It also saves one action because the d-pad also serves as an on/off control.

Pad / Roll. This technique is similar to *Pad / P&Y* except that the second gesture is a roll.

P&Y / Pad. Although this technique looks similar to *Pad/P&Y*, it worked poorly in our tests and we discarded it. In Pad/P&Y, the d-pad press and release actions serve as start- and end-delimiters for the mid-air gesture. But P&Y/Pad does not allow that. Another button (such as the trigger) is then needed to delimitate the gesture (this being needed to improve the precision and avoid accidental detections whenever the device is moved). Asked to press several buttons in the correct order while performing mid-air gestures, participants made too many errors for this technique to deserve further consideration.

Roll / Pad was discarded for the same reason as *P&Y / Pad.*

In sum, we retained the *five* interaction techniques of Figure 4, combining the 3 above-described modalities: *P&Y/P&Y, P&Y/Roll, Pad/Pad, Pad/P&Y and Pad/Roll.*

5.2 Experiment 3

The goal of this experiment was to compare the efficiency of the five above-described techniques in expert, eyes-free mode. As noted above, the Pad/Pad technique may be seen as a nearly ideal case serving as a baseline.

Participants and Apparatus. 13 adult volunteers (all right-handed, seven male) participated in a single 45mn session. The same equipment and software was used as in the previous experiment except that to capture yaw gestures we used the MotionPlus expansion of the Wiimote, which carries a gyroscope.

Number of items. Because the Wiimote d-pad, like most common d-pads, has only four directions, all menus were limited to 4 items. Cardinal directions on the main axes were used for the *P&Y* modality, and 90° and 45° items on each side of the neutral position for the *Roll* modality. All menus thus contained 4x4 = 16 items.

Task. We used the symbolic stimuli in Fig. 5. For each trial, two symbols were displayed on the center of the screen. The first symbol corresponded to the first modality, the second symbol to the second modality (for instance, we used the stimuli Fig. 5-a and Fig. 5-b for the Pad-Roll technique). We used different symbol for each modality to increase the mapping between symbol and the required gesture and to avoid possible biases. The participant then performed the corresponding gesture. The gestures actually recognized by the system were then displayed on the TV screen for 3 seconds. This visual feedback was provided in order to help the user to improve the gestures and to better represent real usage, as some sort of a feedback is always obtained in real conditions. The 3s delay also ensured that the participant had time to come back to the rest position.

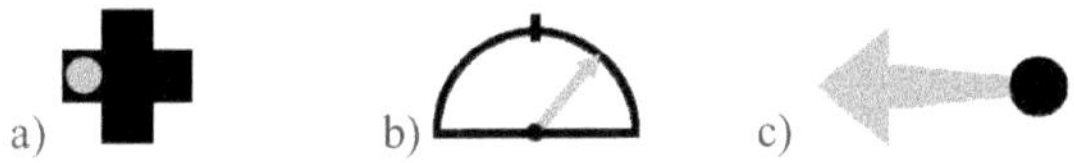

Fig. 5: Stimuli for: a) pad; b) roll; c) pitch&yaw modalities.

Design. Following instructions, participants were offered the possibility of performing up to three warm-up blocks per technique. The experiment was organized in five blocks. For each block, the 16 items appeared one time in randomized order. The order of technique was counter-balanced across participants using a Latin Square design. In summary, the experiment involved:

13 users x 5 techniques x 5 blocks x 16 items = 5200 selections.

At the end of the experiment, participants were given a questionnaire to investigate subjective preferences, which covers speed, complexity and fun about the technique.

5.3 Results

Speed (Fig.6). An ANOVA revealed a significant effect of technique ($F_{4,48}$= 25.34, p<.0001). Post-hoc Tukey tests showed that Pad/P&Y (1.39s) and Pad/Pad (1.40s) were significantly faster than Pad/Roll (1.65s) and P&Y/P&Y (1.68s), both significantly faster than P&Y/Roll (2.02s).

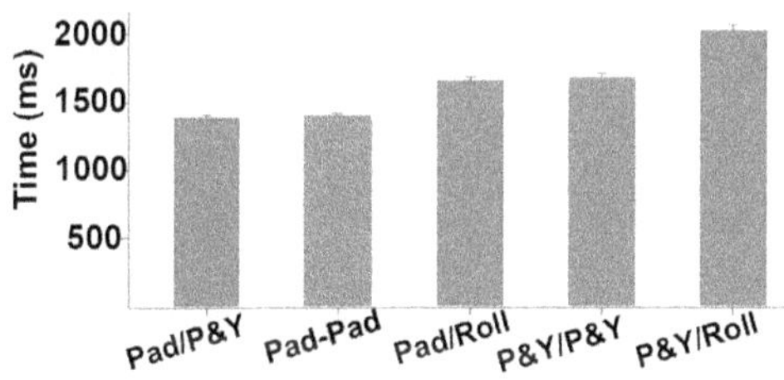

Fig. 6: Mean selection time for each technique with 95% confidence interval marked.

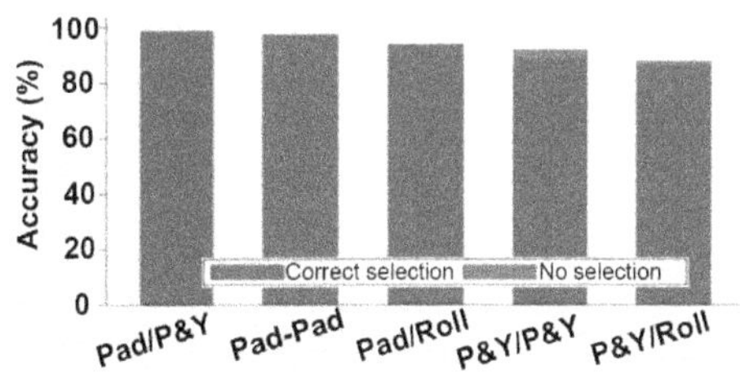

Fig. 7: Mean accuracy rate (% correct) for each technique.

Accuracy (Fig.7). There was a significant effect of technique ($F_{4,48}$= 17.52, p<.0001). Post-hoc Tukey tests showed that Pad/P&Y (98.4%) and Pad/Pad (97.4%) were significantly more accurate than P&Y/P&Y (89.5%) and P&Y/Roll (86.8%). Pad/Roll (94.2%) was also significantly more accurate than P&Y/Roll. Inaccuracy reflected not only erroneous selections but also, in some instances, failure to make any selection. This was especially true of P&Y/P&R (2.5% of total selections; 24.5% of inaccuracies) and P&Y/Roll (1.3% and 10.2%).

Subjective preferences. In the post-study questionnaire the participants ranked the five techniques as follows: Pad/Pad (mean rank=1.5), Pad/P&Y (2.4), P&Y/P&Y (2.8), Pad/Roll (3.5) and P&Y/Roll (4.8). We also recorded subjective evaluations of the 5 techniques using a 7-point Likert scale (Table 4) and analyzed them with a Kruskal-Wallis test. The results showed that Pad/Pad was significantly perceived faster, more accurate, simpler and less tiring than Pad/Roll and P&Y/Roll. They also showed that Pad/P&Y was perceived faster than P&Y/Roll and P&Y/P&Y, and simpler than P&Y/Roll. No technique was judged significantly more 'fun'.

Table 4: Subjective preference

	Pad/Pad	Pad/P&Y	Pad/Roll	P&Y/P&Y	P&Y/Roll
Speed	6.4	5.5	4.5	4.8	3.1
Accuracy	6.8	5.4	4.5	4.9	3.8
Pleasant	6.5	5.5	4.1	5.5	3.3
Tiring	1.2	2.6	4.5	3.2	5.4
Easy To Learn	6.9	5.9	4.8	5.8	3.6
Fun	4.1	5.1	4.3	5.2	4.1

5.4 Discussion

Button-based techniques. The strategy of merging button and gestural interactions was remarkably successful for activating commands. Besides Pad/Pad, Pad/P&Y and, to a lesser extent, Pad/Roll were the fastest techniques (resp. 1.40s, 1.39s and 1.65s) and demonstrated high accuracy rates (resp. 97.4%, 98.4% and 94.2%). This result is worth noting since Pad/Pad was expected to be especially efficient as the user just needs to click two times on the appropriate buttons of the d-pad. We expected mid-air gestures to take more time and be more error prone than purely button-based interactions but we obtained similar results for Pad/Pad and Pad/P&Y, this showing the effectiveness of combining modalities. While slightly inferior Pad/Roll performance was also pretty good.

An important advantage of these three techniques is that they are compatible together: all of them can coexist without interference, thus increasing the number of possible commands. Besides, d-pads are commonly used for other features such as channel or system navigation. This makes the Pad/Pad technique hardy usable: either an additional d-pad would be needed or a button mode that would make the interaction unnecessarily complex. However, this problem does not affect hybrid strategies combining button and gestural interactions. Clicking a button without moving would then produce the usual action when the button is released, while pressing a button then performing a pitch&yaw or a roll gesture would activate a command. Gestural interaction would then provide a mean to augment remote controls while allowing usual interactions.

Purely gestural techniques. P&Y/P&Y gave good results (1.68s, 89.5%) but P&Y/Roll performance (2.02s, 86.8%) was a bit deceiving. A possible explanation is that combining pitch&yaw and roll gestures requires more attention than other gestures. Biomechanically constraints may be another reason, making it hard for users to perform pitch&yaw then roll gestures. For instance, one participant said: "P&Y/Roll would be my favorite technique if there were only three different angular variations" (one of them being the central position, not used in this experiment). Besides, an analysis of the video record revealed that a noticeable number of errors corresponded to correct gestures that were wrongly recognized by the system (about 50% for P&Y/P&Y and 17% for P&Y/Roll). Better signal processing algorithm, such as those developed by Movea/Gyration [11] would certainly improve results. The problem is that gyroscopes accumulate drift over time and produce errors with motion, even for relatively small movements. As a consequence, the raw data generated by a gyroscope cannot be directly processed by a recognition algorithm. Not only the gyroscope must be recalibrated as often as possible (using an accelerometer) but the data must be constantly corrected (typically by means of Kalman filters). Unfortunately, the algorithm we used, based on trigonometry functions, was not as sophisticated. Hence our accuracy figures should be seen as a lower baseline.

5.4.1 Further Improvements

Besides better gyroscope signal processing, another improvement would be to associate translations and rotations. Study 1 showed that most users naturally perform rotations. Yet, some users preferred translations. Taking both translations and rotations into account would allow more flexibility and would probably improve accuracy. Other specific aspects, such as the fact that users sometimes start the second gesture while the device is already in movement should also be taken into account to finely tune the recognition algorithm and increase its robustness.

We only considered four item menus, mainly because of technical constraints (the Wiimote d-pad provides only four directions) but also to avoid making the experiment too long. Difficulties were reported in GesText [13] for performing diagonal gestures, but contrary to the recommendations that emerged from Study 1 this technique was using pitch&roll rather than pitch&yaw gestures. More work is anyway needed to evaluate the efficiency of pitch&yaw gestures with eight items.

The expert mode involves gesture recall from user memory. Full expert mode evaluation thus requires a memorization and recall phase [20][1]. This means long-lasting experiments out of reach in the present study with many techniques to evaluate. We thus used a simpler experiment where the stimulus indicates which gestures must be performed. However, given the proximity between Marking menus and the techniques based on pitch&yaw or pad gestures, there are likely to share similar properties with respect to memory coding. The case is different with Roll gestures, which requires further research (but this is debatable as they also rely on a circular representations).

6. NOVICE MODE

The proposed techniques are inspired by Marking menus [1][18] [39] and thus provide both an expert and novice mode. The expert mode consists of one of the five above-described techniques and can be performed without visual feedback. The novice mode consists in navigating in a two-level menu which graphical design. It depends on the technique used in expert mode, as explained below. The items of the first level are either activated by Pad or P&Y gestures (depending of the expert mode) and the items of the second level by Pad, P&Y or Roll gestures. Interestingly, hybrid techniques combining button interaction and mid-air gestures allow parallelism as item selection and rely on different modalities for each level.

The novice mode is activated by pressing a button without performing gestures during 300ms. The first-level menu, which is always circular, then appears (Fig. 8, left). Each item corresponds to a submenu, which is also circular except for Roll gestures, in which case it is half-circular (Fig. 8, right). Circular menus can contain up to 8 items. Half of them (on-axis items) will be used in case of a 4 directional d-pad or if diagonal P&Y gestures are disabled. Items are selected in the same way in expert and novice modes. Half-circular menus work according to the same principle but only contains 5 items.

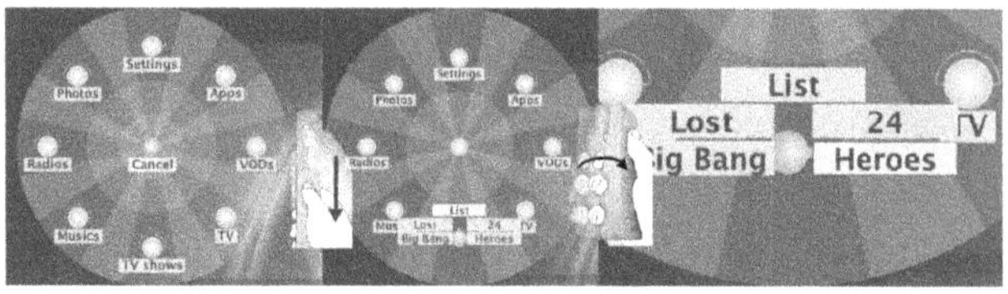

Fig. 8: Novice-mode for P&Y and Pad gestures (left) and Roll gestures (right).

As for regular Marking menus, users can easily understand how the technique works as there is a direct mapping between the orientation of the displayed items and the gestures users have to perform with the thumb or the wrist. A key point of the technique is that it favors a fluid transition from novice to expert usage [18]: as users perform the same gesture in both modes, the user can implicitly learn the expert mode just by repeating the same gesture in novice mode. Finally, our technique not only makes it possible gestural interaction with a remote control, but makes actions visible, easily discoverable and easy to learn, thus answering the concerns expressed in [25] about purely gestural interfaces.

Fig. 9: Yaw gestures for navigating in a table.

Finally, as circular menus can only contain a limited number of items, we also considered the case when activating an item of the first-level menu does not open a submenu but a tabular representation containing as many elements as needed. For instance, selecting the "TV Shows" item in the first-level menu would display the table illustrated in Fig. 9. Roll gestures or d-pad navigation are then used for selecting an item in the table that is currently displayed. Yaw gestures allow making the previous or following table to appear.

7. CONCLUSION

In this article, we investigated the new possibilities offered by mid-air gestures for augmenting and improving remote control interaction. Remote controls tend to be cluttered with buttons, a consequence of an overwhelming number of functions. Mid-air gestures seem appropriate for alleviating this problem while offering the ability to perform favorite actions eyes-free.

The first study revealed that the optimal mapping between mid-air gestures and directional actions strongly depends on context and that pitch & yaw rotations should be preferred for remote control interaction. The second study, focused on the ability of users to perform roll gestures eyes-free, suggested that users can accurately select up to 5 items, up to 7 items with an adaptive algorithm. We then proposed and experimentally compared five different techniques using either mid-air gestures, directional-pad manipulation, or a combination of both.

The results showed that mid-air gestures have promise as an additional input resource. Hybrid techniques combining mid-air gestures and buttons were especially efficient, with the further advantage of compatibility with pure button-based techniques. Techniques using the d-pad or pitch and yaw for transposing 2D Marking menus to the mid-air space proved especially well suited for eyes-free interaction. Finally, purely gestural techniques yielded slightly lower performance but more careful analysis pointed to a possible bias due to technical limitations.

In this article, we focused on an interesting and little studied context: remote control interaction for controlling interactive television or media-center. We plan to generalize these results to different technologies such as free-hand interaction or different contexts such as large-screen displays.

8. ACKNOWLEDGMENTS

This work was partly achieved as part of the Quaero Programme, funded by OSEO, French State agency for innovation and by the Alexander von Humboldt Fellowship.

9. REFERENCES

[1] Bailly, G., Lecolinet, E., Nigay, L. 2008. Flower menus: a new type of marking menu with large menu breadth, within groups and efficient expert mode memorization. ACM AVI'08, p. 15-22.

[2] Balakrishnan, R., Baudel, T., Kurtenbach, G., Fitzmau-rice, G. 1997. The Rockin'Mouse: integral 3D manipu-lation on a plane. ACM CHI '97, p. 311-318.

[3] Barkhuus, L. and Brown, B. 2009. Unpacking the television: User practices around a changing technology. ACM TOCHI. 16, 3, p. 1-22.

[4] Baudel, T. and Beaudouin-Lafon, M. 1993. Charade: remote control of objects using free-hand gestures. Commun. ACM 36, 7 (Jul. 1993), 28-35.

[5] Cao, X. and Balakrishnan, R. 2003. VisionWand: interaction techniques for large displays using a passive wand tracked in 3D. ACM UIST '03, p.173-182.

[6] Cesar, P., and Chorianopoulos, K. 2009. The evolution of TV systems, content and users toward interactivity. New Foundation and Trends in HCI, vol.2: n°4, p.373-95.

[7] Cho S-J., Oh J. K., Bang W.-C., Chang W., Choi E., Jing Y., Cho J., Kim D. Y. 2004. Magic wand: a hand-drawn gesture input device in 3-D space with inertial sensors. *Frontiers in Handwriting Recognition. IWFHR-9 2004*. p. 106- 111.

[8] Cooper W. 2008. The interactive television user experience so far. Proc. ACM UXTV '08, p. 133-142.

[9] http://sourceforge.net/projects/darwiin-remote/

[10] Freeman, W. T., and Weissman, C. 1995. Television control by hand gestures. Int. Workshop IEEE FG'95, p. 179-183.

[11] Gyration. http://www.gyration.com/

[12] Hogan, N., 1985, The mechanics of multi-joint posture and movement control, Biol. Cybern., 52:315-331.

[13] Jones, E., Alexander, J., Andreou, A., Irani, P., Subra-manian, S. 2010. GesText: accelerometer-based gestural text-entry systems. ACM CHI'10, p. 2173-82.

[14] Kela, J., Korpipää, P., Mäntyjärvi, J., Kallio, S., Savino, G., Jozzo, L., and Marca, D. 2006. Accelerometer-based gesture control for a design environment. Personal Ubiquitous Comput. 10, 5 (Jul. 2006), 285-299.

[15] Kiger. J. I. 1984. The depth/breadth trade-off in the design of menu-driven user interfaces. Int. J. Man-Mach. Stud. 20, 2 (March 1984), 201-213.

[16] Kinect: http://www.xbox.com/kinect

[17] http://en.wikipedia.org/wiki/K_nearest_neighbor_algorithm

[18] Kurtenbach, G. and Buxton, W. 1991. Issues in combining marking and direct manipulation techniques. ACM UIST '91, 137-144.

[19] Kurtenbach, G. and Buxton, W. 1993. The limits of expert performance using hierarchic marking menus. IFIP INTERACT '93 and ACM CHI '93, p. 482-487.

[20] Kurtenbach, G. P., Sellen, A. J., and Buxton, W. A. 1993. An empirical evaluation of some articulatory and cognitive aspect of marking menus. Hum.-Comp. Int.. 8, 1 (Mar. 93), 1-23.

[21] http://www.l5remote.com/

[22] http://www.logitech.com/en-us/remotes/universal-remotes

[23] http://en.wikipedia.org/wiki/Cross-validation_(statistics)

[24] Nelson, M. 1999. Remote controls. The Digital Knowledge Handbook, 3(4).

[25] Norman D. A. 2010 Natural User Interfaces are Not Natural. ACM magazine Interactions 17,3, p. 6-10.

[26] Oakley, I. and Park, J. 2007. Designing eyes-free interaction. Springer HAID'07, p. 121-132.

[27] Oakley, I. and Park, J. 2009. Motion marking menus: An eyes-free approach to motion input for handheld devices. *Int. J. Hum.-Comput. Stud.* 67, 6, p. 515-532.

[28] Partridge, K., Chatterjee, Sazawal, V., Borrielo, G. 2002. TiltType: Accelerometer-Supported Text Entry for Very Small Devices. ACM UIST'02, p. 201-204.

[29] Rahman, M., Gustafson, S., Irani, P., and Subramanian, S. 2009. Tilt techniques: investigating the dexterity of wrist-based input. ACM CHI '09, p. 1943-1952.

[30] Rico, J. and Brewster, S. 2010. Usable gestures for mobile interfaces: evaluating social acceptability. ACM CHI, p. 887-896.

[31] Sazawal, V., Want, R., and Borriello, G. 2002. The Unigesture Approach. Springer Mobile HCI '02, p. 256-270.

[32] Shoemaker, G., Findlater, L., Dawson, J. Q., and Booth, K. S. 2009. Mid-air text input techniques for very large wall displays. ACM GI'09, p. 231-238.

[33] http://www.uwand.com/

[34] Wang, J., Zhai, S., and Canny, J. 2010. SHRIMP: solving collision and out of vocabulary problems in mobile predictive input with motion gesture. ACM CHI '10, p. 15-24.

[35] Wigdor, D. and Balakrishnan, R. 2003. TiltText: using tilt for text input to mobile phones. ACM UIST '03, p. 81-90.

[36] Wilson, A. and Shafer, S. 2003. XWand: UI for intelligent spaces. ACM CHI '03, p. 545-552.

[37] Wobbrock J. O., Morris M. R., Wilson A. D. 2009. User-defined gestures for surface computing. ACM CHI'09, p. 1083-1092.

[38] http://www.voomote.tv/

[39] Zhao, S. and Balakrishnan, R. 2004. Simple vs. compound mark hierarchical marking menus. ACM UIST '04, p. 33-42.

The Effect of Sampling Rate on the Performance of Template-based Gesture Recognizers

Radu-Daniel Vatavu
University Stefan cel Mare of Suceava
13 Universitatii
Suceava, Romania
vatavu@eed.usv.ro

ABSTRACT

We investigate in this work the effect of motion sampling rate over recognition accuracy and execution time for current template-based gesture recognizers in order to provide performance guidelines to practitioners and designers of gesture-based interfaces. We show that as few as 6 sampling points are sufficient for Euclidean and angular recognizers to attain high recognition rates and that a linear relationship exists between sampling rate and number of gestures for the dynamic time warping technique. We report execution times obtained with our controlled downsampling which are 10–20 times faster than shown by existing work at the same high recognition rates. The results of this work will benefit practitioners by providing important performance aspects to consider when using template-based gesture recognizers.

Categories and Subject Descriptors

H.5.2 [[**Information Interfaces and Presentation**]]: User Interfaces; I.5.2 [[**Pattern Recognition**]]: Design Methodology—*Classifier design and evaluation*

General Terms

Algorithms, Experimentation, Performance

Keywords

gesture recognition, recognition rate, classifier performance, execution time, comparing classifiers, sampling resolution, experimentation

1. INTRODUCTION

Gesture-based commands have become increasingly accessible for user interfaces in the measure that sensing and recognition technologies developed to allow reliable acquisition and robust classification of users' input motions. Although under the appanage of pattern recognition experts, several recognizers have been proposed for or by the human-computer interaction (HCI) community in order to enable practitioners and designers to rapidly prototype and experiment gesture-based interfaces [8, 10, 11, 14, 23].

Most of these recognizers use the principle of nearest neighbor classification (NN) which works by comparing the gesture candidate to a set of examples (referred to as the training set). A metric is used to compute the dissimilarity between two gesture executions describing *how far* they are positioned one from another in some feature space. The candidate is recognized as belonging to the class of its *closest* or *nearest* example.

Nearest-neighbor classifiers provide several advantages over other recognition techniques such as ease of implementation and clear understanding of the inner workings even for non-experts. Also, there is no need for complex parametric modeling that most pattern recognition techniques demand such as weights computation for neural networks [20, 22] or probabilities estimation for hidden markov models [1, 16]. Still, probably the most important advantages of the NN approach for HCI are its flexibility and adaptability: new or user-specific gestures can be added by simply providing training examples without the need of rethinking the structure or retraining the classifier. Such advantages have been remarked before [3, 11] and many nearest-neighbor classifiers have been proposed with high reported recognition rates [10, 11, 23]. While the search algorithm for the closest neighbor is always the same, the proposed classifiers differ in the metric they employ which decides their performance in practice.

The performance of a recognizer is primarily measured by its *recognition rate* which represents the estimate of the percentage of gestures which are expected to be correctly recognized. While the recognition rate represents the most important criterion, there are other factors that determine system performance such as the *execution time* required for classification and the amount of *system memory* employed for storing the training set. Their importance is especially revealed for mobile computing for which resources are restrictive.

The metrics that proved successful for NN gesture recognizers are the Euclidean distance [2, 8, 10, 23], dynamic time warping [15, 18], and the angular inverse cosine distance [9, 11]. They all work directly on the motion input that is normalized and resampled into the same number of n equally-distanced points [5, 10, 11, 23]. Although not needed for dynamic time warping (DTW), resampling the raw input gestures at the same rate is mandatory for computing the Euclidean and angular metrics that require point-to-point computations. Table 1 briefly describes the metrics and shows their time complexities. Note that these are met-

ICMI'11, November 14–18, 2011, Alicante, Spain.

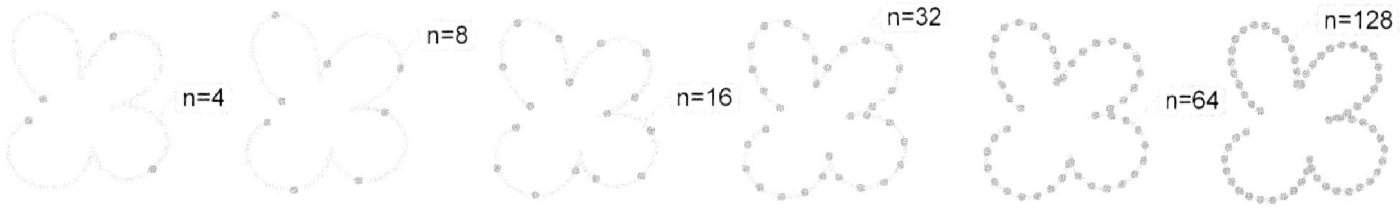

Figure 1: Sampling resolution rates n ranging from under- to over-sampling for the same gesture motion.

Metric	Definition	Time
Euclidean (d_1)	$d_1(p,q) = \sum_{i=0}^{n-1} \lVert p_i - q_i \rVert = \sum_{i=0}^{n-1} \sqrt{(p_{ix}-q_{ix})^2 + (p_{iy}-q_{iy})^2}$	$O(n)$
Dynamic time warping (d_2)	$d_2(p,q) = c_{n-1,n-1}$ $c_{i,j} = \lVert p_i - q_j \rVert + \min \begin{cases} c_{i-1,j-1} \\ c_{i-1,j} \\ c_{i,j-1} \end{cases}$ $i,j \in \{0..n-1\}$	$O(n^2)$
Angular inverse cosine (d_3)	$d_3(p,q) = \arccos \frac{p \cdot q}{\lVert p \rVert \cdot \lVert q \rVert}$ $p \cdot q = \sum_{i=0}^{n-1} (p_{ix}q_{ix} + p_{iy}q_{iy})$ $\lVert p \rVert = \sum_{i=0}^{n-1} \sqrt{p_{ix}^2 + p_{iy}^2}$	$O(n)$

Table 1: Gesture metrics commonly used with nearest-neighbor recognizers working directly on the motion inputs $p = \{p_i = (p_{ix}, p_{iy}) \in \mathbb{R}^2 | i = 0, n-1\}$ and $q = \{q_i = (q_{ix}, q_{iy}) \in \mathbb{R}^2 | i = 0, n-1\}$. Note: $\lVert a - b \rVert$ denotes the regular Euclidean distance between points a and b from $\mathbb{R}^2$.

rics defined over the gesture space not to be confounded with local metrics between points (such as the regular Euclidean distance between two points in $\mathbb{R}^2$ or $\mathbb{R}^n$). Also, we will use the notions of *metric* and *distance* interchangeably along the paper as they represent the same concept in the pattern recognition community.

The choice of the metric together with the size of the training set determine directly both *recognition rate* and *execution time*. The total execution time needed for performing a classification with T samples available in the training set and using a sampling resolution of n points will be $O(n \cdot T)$ for Euclidean and angular metrics and $O(n^2 \cdot T)$ for DTW.

As the number of training samples T increases, the recognition rate of a NN classifier should improve (as the feature space is more accurately represented). All the 3 metrics have been found to report rates above 99% with 3 or more samples loaded per gesture type [11, 23]. This is a definite advantage of NN over other classification techniques such as Rubine's [14] for which 15+ samples are needed[1].

With respect to the other factor that determines performance directly (the sampling rate n - see Figure 1) there seems to be little agreement between the existing works and thus little information for designers on what rate to use. Wobbrock et al. [23] propose $n = 64$ for the \$1 recognizer (which makes use of the Euclidean metric) while they also state that any value between 32 and 128 will work as fine. Li [11] reports a speed-up by using only 16 points with Protractor (the inverse cosine metric). Cao and Zhai [5] use $n = 25$ with the Euclidean metric of ShapeWriter [10] and Kratz and Rohs [8] report a value of $n = 150$ for their extension of the \$1 recognizer to 3D data. Although all these works report performance results using the same metrics, the multiple and different choices for the sampling resolution seem arbitrary and left at the intuition and experimentation of the practitioner. However, as the sampling rate influences execution time directly in a linear or quadratic manner (see Table 1), it is important to investigate its effect in practice. The goal of this work is therefore to understand the effect of sampling rate on recognizer performance in order to inform practitioners on the rates to use for pre-processing gesture input motions so that *execution time* is lowest while *recognition rate* highest. In order to achieve this goal, an analysis is conducted for the metrics commonly used with NN gesture recognizers.

1.1 Contributions

We contribute important design aspects for template-based gesture recognizers that work directly on the motion input:

1. An investigation is conducted on the sampling rate n in order to understand its effect on the recognition rate of commonly used metrics. The goal is to inform practitioners on the sampling rate to use motivated by the fact that current research report various results [5, 8, 11, 23] while n directly determines execution time;

2. We show that a linear relationship exists between the number of gestures r used by the interface and the minimum sampling rate n needed to achieve a high recognition rate. We found 6 sampling points sufficient for Euclidean and angular metrics and reasonably-sized gesture sets ($r < 30$ gestures) while a ratio of $n : r = 2 : 5$ was derived for DTW. We highlight the impact on execution time by reporting classifications that run $10 - 20$ times faster than reported by existing works;

3. A theoretical argument is proposed in order to explain the experimental results and a validation test is performed on a different set of gestures. An application tool for assisting practitioners when designing their gesture recognizers is also provided as a companion for the paper.

[1]The Rubine recognizer does not employ a metric nor does it use the nearest-neighbor approach. Instead, it divides the feature space using linear boundaries that isolate gestures of the same type - therefore, it needs many samples to achieve a good space partitioning.

2. EXPERIMENT 1: THE EFFECT OF SAMPLING ON RECOGNITION RATE

Low sampling rates will make recognizers execute faster but it is likely for a trade-off to be observed with respect to recognition accuracy as fewer points are used to represent each gesture. We start by exploring the effect of sampling on recognition accuracy on the \$1 gesture set of Wobbrock et al.[2] [23] in order to correlate our recognition rates with those reported by previous works on the same data [11, 23]. The set is composed of 16 gesture types (Figure 2). As we progress, we will extend our analysis on more gestures.

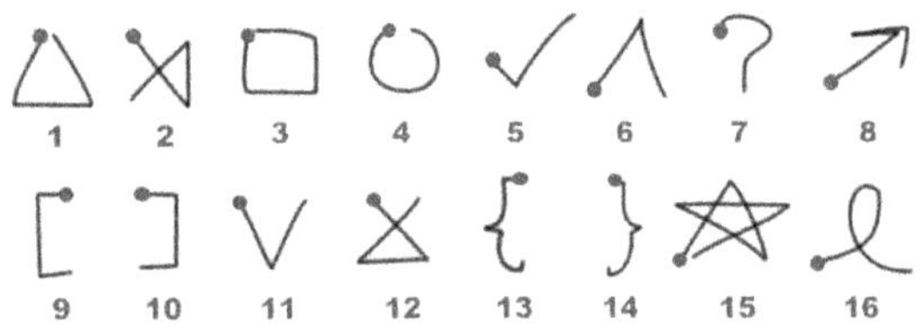

Figure 2: Gestures used for the 1st experiment [23]. 100 executions are available at normal speed for each gesture = 10 participants × 10 repetitions.

In order to test the effect of sampling over recognition rate, we consider for our analysis:

- 7 different sampling rates, $n = 4, 8, 16, 32, 64, 128, 256$. They include Wobbrock's et al. $n = 64$ [23]; Li's $n = 16$ [11]; but also intermediate, higher and lower resolutions;
- the 3 most commonly used metrics with NN recognizers: Euclidean [5, 10, 23], angular inverse cosine [11], and dynamic time warping [18];
- 4 progressive values for the number of training samples available for each gesture type, $T = 1, 2, 4$, and 8 (out of the total 10 executions available for each gesture in the \$1 set).

Recognition rates were computed similarly to previous work [23] for user-dependent training scenarios: T samples were randomly chosen for training and one candidate was selected as the test for each gesture type. The process was repeated 100 times in order to compute the rate for a given metric, using a given sampling rate n, and T training samples. We report recognition rates averaged from 3 (metrics) $\times$ 7 (n) $\times$ 4 (T) $\times$ 100 (repetitions) $\times$ 16 (gestures) $\times$ 10 (participants) $\approx 1.4 \cdot 10^6$ recognition tests.

Figure 3 illustrates the mean recognition rate for each metric versus the sampling rate. In order to compare the effect on the metric alone, we only applied elementary preprocessing to the input gestures leaving out specific operations such as the golden rule search of Euclidean \$1 [23] or the optimum rotation of angular Protractor [11] which would favor one recognizer but not the others[3]. All gestures were therefore normalized with form factor preservation and centered to origin. As we expect from previous literature, recognition

[2] Available at http://depts.washington.edu/aimgroup/proj/dollar/

[3] Actually, Wobbrock et al. [23] specify that their optimum alignment adds only 0.23% to recognition accuracy. Li's Protractor [11] does the same rotation but faster. We skip these operations in order to analyze the effect on the metrics alone.

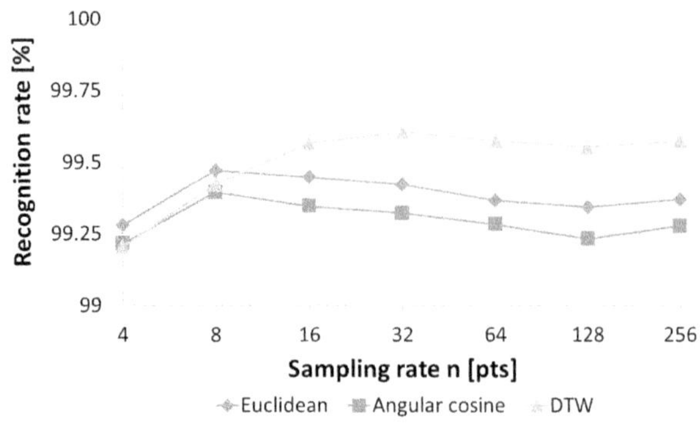

Figure 3: Recognition rate [%] versus sampling rate n [points] (the x axis shown on logaritmic scale). Note: 95% CI bars not shown on the graphic for clarity purposes but they are discussed in the text.

rates are high with a mean of 99.39%, $CI_{.95}: 99.34-99.45\%$. It is interesting to note that the accuracy is above 99% for all metrics and all rates including the lowest one, $n = 4$. The mean recognition rate for the lowest resolution ($n = 4$) is 99.23% which is just 0.18% smaller than the highest rate obtained (for $n = 64$) but the average gain in execution time is between 1 : 10 and 1 : 20 as showed later in the paper.

The effect of sampling rate was found significant overall, $\chi^2(6) = 46.93, p < .001$. When performing the analysis separately on each metric, the effect was significant for angular and DTW but was not significant for the Euclidean distance, $\chi^2(6) = 10.58, n.s.$ This shows that, at least for the \$1 set, the Euclidean distance performing with $n = 4$ points is just as discriminative as if 32, 64, or 128 points had been used which represents a considerable reduction in execution time (given that the time complexity of the Euclidean distance is linear in n). The recognition rates did not differ significantly for $n \geq 8$ for the angular distance and $n \geq 16$ for DTW. Also, the differences between $n \in \{4, 8\}$ for angular and $n \in \{4, 8, 16\}$ for DTW were below 0.3% and showed small Cohen effects, $r < .3$.

The number of training samples T had a significant effect on recognition rate for each metric and for each sampling rate n (at $p < .001$). As expected, recognition improved from using 1 to 8 samples (with approximately 1%). No interaction effect was observed between T and n.

The results obtained on this particular set of 16 gestures show that a low sampling rate can achieve the same high recognition accuracy as much finer resolutions (specifically, $n = 4$ for Euclidean, $n = 8$ for angular, and $n = 16$ for DTW). The immediate gain is that of execution time: for linear metrics, using $n = 8$ instead of $n = 64$ would lead to a 1 : 8 reduction ratio while for DTW a reduction of 1 : 64 can be envisaged. Also, the gestures included in the \$1 set are common shapes likely to be also included by other designers in their gesture-based interfaces (such as *circle*, *rectangle*, *question-mark*, or *check*). This first experiment not only suggests that few points are feasible for the gesture metrics investigated but it also shows that such an aggressive downsampling works very well for shapes likely to be encountered in gesture-based interfaces. However, in order not be biased by the specific gestures of the \$1 set or its size ($r = 16$), we continue our analysis by adding more gestures and investigating multiple sets and multiple sizes.

3. EXPERIMENT 2: SAMPLING RATE VS. THE SIZE OF THE GESTURE SET

The results from the previous section were obtained on a set composed of $r = 16$ gestures. It is natural to hypothesize that a relation exists between the size of the gesture set r and the minimum sampling rate n that attains the same high recognition accuracy as much finer rates. When few gestures are present in the set (e.g. $r \leq 8$), low n rates could suffice for discrimination: even if the resolution is poor for representation, it may be enough for attaining a high recognition rate. However, when the set is large ($r \approx 30$), few sampling points may not be discriminative enough so a finer resolution should be used. Therefore, it is important to continue our investigation on which rate to use for a given size of the gesture set. For this second experiment we used additional 16 gestures acquired in similar conditions with Wobbrock et al. [23] which were selected from the set of Vatavu et al. [19] (Figure 4). Therefore, we report results from a larger set of 32 gestures. It is important to note that we are only interested in performance results for reasonably-sized gesture sets (e.g. $r \approx 30$ which represents a more than enough upper limit for the number of gestures to be included in an interface cause of human limits on learnability and memorability). These results may not apply to specific applications that need larger gesture sets such is the case of the SHARK vocabulary [10].

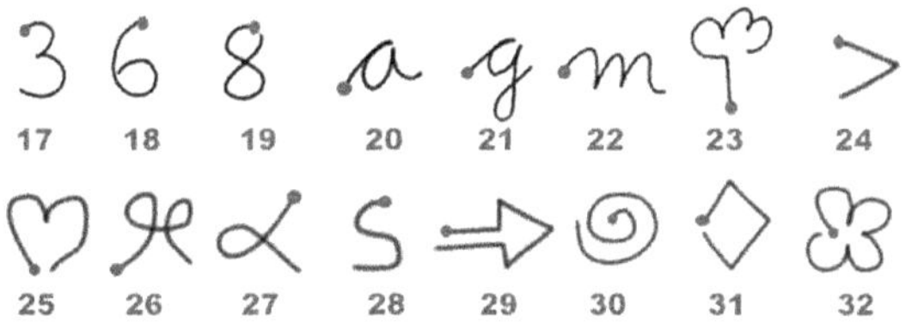

Figure 4: Additional gestures used for the 2nd experiment. Gestures are selected from [19]. Numbers continue from Figure 2.

In order to assemble data for analyzing the relation between sampling rate and set size, we used the 32 gestures as basis for generating sets with different sizes. We report results for 8 different values for $r = 4, 8, 12, 16, 20, 24, 28$, and 30. For each size, r gestures were chosen at random from the available 32. We considered the 3 metrics and the 4 different values for T for each set. We repeated the process 100 times for each value of r or for 100 different gesture sets or combinations out of $\frac{32!}{(32-r)! \cdot r!}$. The number of test cases was therefore 8 (r) $\times$ 100 (r-sets) $\times$ 3 (metrics) $\times$ 4 (T) = 9600 tests. For each test, we started with $n = 4$ sampling points and incremented the value of n until the recognition rate did not differ significantly from the recognition rate of $n = 64$ used as benchmark [23] (the Wilcoxon signed-rank test was used to test for significance at $p < .05$). The value of n for which the difference was not significant was stored.

Figure 5 illustrates the mean sampling rates n that achieve the same recognition accuracy as the benchmark of 64 points [23]. Linear regression models were found for each metric ($R^2 > .86$) with a slope of 0.06 for Euclidean and angular distances and 0.42 for DTW. The same intercept of 4 points was found for all metrics.

The mean rate was $n = 5.2$ points (SD=1.0) for the Euclidean distance and $n = 5.5$ (SD=1.1) for the angular cosine. As the slope value was small (0.06), we can consider that $n = 0.06 \cdot 30 + 4 = 6$ points are sufficient for the two metrics in order to attain the same recognition rates of $n = 64$ for sets up to 30 gestures. DTW had a larger mean of $n = 11.4$ points (SD=5.1) while the regression gives $n = \lceil 0.4 \cdot r \rceil + 4$. The stronger linear dependence showed by the DTW metric could be explained by its flexibility in the way the points of the two motions are being aligned in the search of an optimum alignment. This feature exactly makes DTW report very high recognition rates but has also made researchers find it *too elastic* for recognizing gestures. For example, Kristensson and Zhai considered the metric as a first choice for their SHARK recognizer but found in early testing that elasticity was undesirable when there were many similarly competing samples available [10]. Similar observations were noted by Wobbrock et al. [23] when reporting comparison results between DTW and \$1. Again, the same flexibility could explain the stronger linear dependence for the metric trying to achieve an optimal alignment.

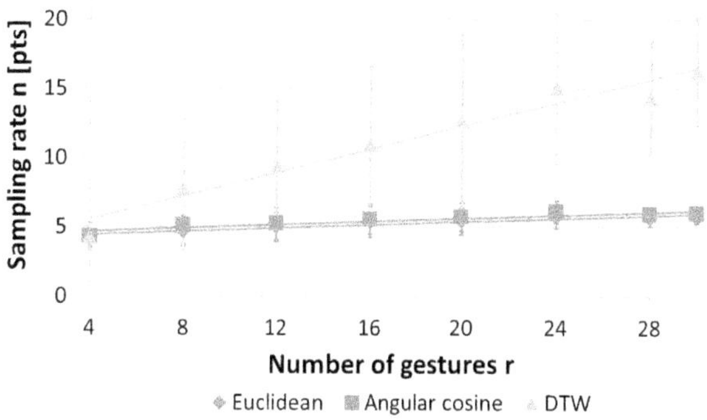

Figure 5: Sampling rate vs. the size of the gesture set. Note: error bars represent ±1 SD.

The recognition rates and execution times for $n = 64$ and regression n values are illustrated in Figure 6 for each metric. The differences in accuracy are 0.01% for Euclidean (n.s.), 0.01% for angular (n.s.), and 0.08% for DTW while the gains in execution time are $1 : 12$, $1 : 10$, and $1 : 20$ respectively[4]. There was a significant effect on recognition rate for DTW at $p < .001$ but the 0.08% difference is small with medium Cohen effect, $r < .5$. This can be explained by the much higher SD for DTW which makes regression n underestimate the optimum rate but by a very small difference.

In addition to these findings, we investigated whether gesture length could affect individual recognition rates. The hypothesis was that long gestures could have lower recognition rates than short ones as the n points are more scattered. We correlated individual rates with normalized lengths for all the 32 gestures. No significant Pearson correlations were found for the Euclidean metric. We found significant correlations for angular ($n \in \{4, 8, 16\}$) but their effect was too small, $R^2 < .16, p = .05$, as well as for DTW ($n \geq 16$) with also small effects, $R^2 < .27, p = .01$. Actually, the longest

[4] \$1 actually takes far more time than our reported value for the Euclidean distance as it also searches for the optimum rotation for aligning two gestures. This extra operation scales the execution time by a factor of 10 ([23], p.163) which makes the overal gain to be 1:120! The gain with respect to Protractor [11], which uses $n = 16$, is smaller $6 : 16 = 1 : 2.5$.

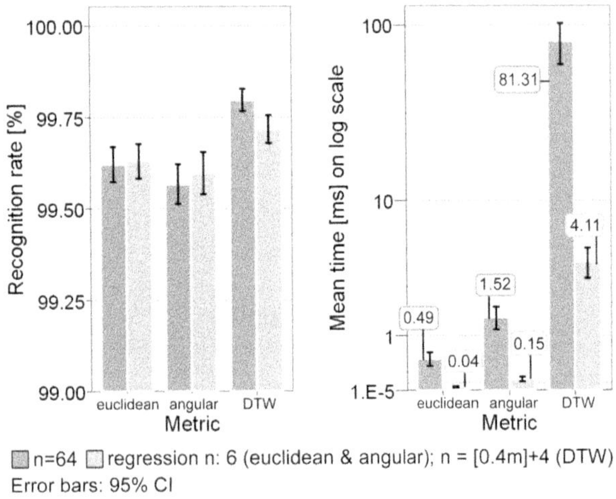

Figure 6: Recognition rates and execution times for $n = 64$ vs. regression n. Rates are averaged for all r. Execution times are computed on a 2.6 GHz P4 processor for the maximum value of $r = 32$ gestures.

gestures 15-*star* and 30-*spiral* attained rates of 99.9% while 14-*right curly brace* (2.5 times shorter) had 97.9%. The length effects were either non significant or very small compared to the strong significant influence of the set size r.

4. A THEORETICAL ARGUMENT

The results of the reported experiments are very intriguing as they show that recognition rates above 99% can be obtained by using just a few sampled points only. Also, low sampling rates translate into low execution times for the recognizer that is able to compute the classification result more quickly.

We try to explain in the following these experimental results by proposing a theoretical argument built on the probability that two gestures are still being perceived different even when they are heavily downsampled. To this end, we introduce the notion of *probability of equivalence* for two gestures and analyze it as a function of the sampling rate. As the rate becomes lower it is more likely (more probable) that two different gestures will look similar just because the recognizer does not dispose of enough data points to discriminate on. Calculating the probability values for low sampling rates will explain the experimental results if these values are small enough for the event to occur extremely rarely in practice.

Therefore, we are set to prove that the probability of two or more gestures to be perceived similar when they are subjected to heavy downsampling (e.g. the chance of their remaining points to be located very close together) is actually very small. Although this may feel counterintuitive, we need to stress the difference between the sampling rate needed for representing a shape (for humans) and that for recognizing it (by machines). These two don't need to be (and are not) the same. While humans need more points for representation, this is not the case for the machine that matches shapes. We start our argumentation by introducing the concept of equivalence for points and curves on which we base our calculation of the probability of equivalence of gestures.

4.1 The notion of equivalence for points and curves

For all further discussion, we assume that gestures have been normalized so that they would fit in the $\mathcal{D} = [0..1] \times [0..1] \subset \mathbb{R}^2$ unit square. This is a common preprocessing step [18, 23] also being used in our two experiments.

DEFINITION Points $p, q \in \mathcal{D}$ are *equivalent* with respect to $\epsilon \in \mathbb{R}$ (and we denote $p \equiv q$) if their Euclidean distance is less than ϵ:

$$p \equiv q \Leftrightarrow \|p - q\| \leq \epsilon \quad (1)$$

Due to the fact that gestures represent continuous motions generated by the moving hand which are being artificially sampled by the acquisition device, we use in the following the formalism of plane curves.

Let $\mathcal{A}$ be the set of all plane curves α parametrized by arc-length and taking values in $\mathcal{D}$:

$$\mathcal{A} = \{\alpha : [0, L(\alpha)] \to \mathcal{D} \mid \alpha(s) = (x(s), y(s)) \in \mathcal{D}\}$$

where $L(\alpha)$ is the length of α.

Let $\alpha \in \mathcal{A}$. We can sample α into n points and obtain a finite set $\alpha[n]$ by choosing n arc-lengths s_i from $[0, L(\alpha)]$:

$$\alpha[n] = \{\alpha_i = \alpha(s_i), i = 0, n - 1\}$$

We refer to $\alpha[n]$ as an $n-$sampling of α.

Given $\alpha \in \mathcal{A}$ and $\alpha[n]$ an $n-$sampling of α, we can further sample $\alpha[n]$ into $m < n$ points by selecting m points out of n and obtain the subset $\alpha[m] \subset \alpha[n]$.

DEFINITION The $n-$samplings $\alpha[n]$ and $\beta[n]$ corresponding to curves $\alpha, \beta \in \mathcal{A}$ are *equivalent* ($\alpha[n] \equiv \beta[n]$) if all their corresponding points are equivalent:

$$\alpha[n] \equiv \beta[n] \Leftrightarrow \alpha_i \equiv \beta_i \; \forall i \in \{0, n - 1\}$$

Figure 7 illustrates the concept of equivalence for points and gesture samplings. The constant ϵ can be chosen as fine as required. We will provide a reasonable practical estimation for ϵ later in the article.

We denote by $e(n)$ the number of pairs of equivalent points of $\alpha[n]$ and $\beta[n]$ and by $\lambda(n)$ the proportion of equivalent pairs, $\lambda(n) = e(n)/n$. Obviously, $\lambda(n) \in [0..1]$.

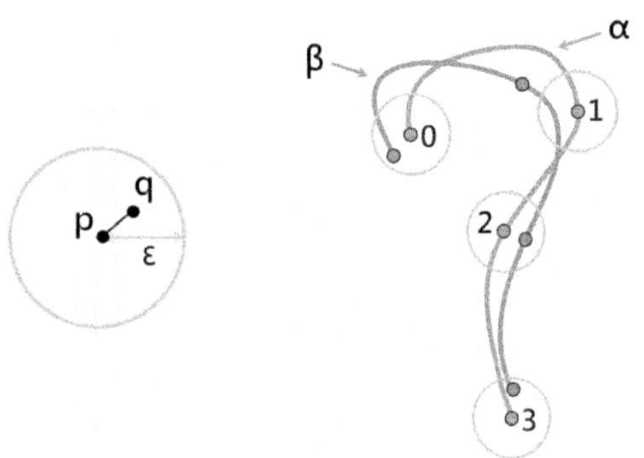

Figure 7: The concept of equivalence. Left: points p and q are equivalent with respect to ϵ if their Euclidean distance is $\leq \epsilon$. Right: gestures α and β sampled in $n = 4$ points are equivalent if all their pairs of points are equivalent.

4.2 Probability of equivalence (2 gestures)

Let $\alpha, \beta \in \mathcal{A}$ and let $\alpha[n]$ and $\beta[n]$ be their samplings into n points. The probability that $\alpha[m] \equiv \beta[m]$ for $m < n$ is given by:

$$\frac{e(n)}{n} \cdot \frac{e(n)-1}{n-1} \cdots \frac{e(n)-(m-1)}{n-(m-1)} \leq (\lambda(n))^m \tag{2}$$

4.3 Probability of equivalence (r gestures)

We extend the probability of equivalence for $r > 2$ gestures by considering the probability that at least 2 gestures out of r are equivalent when sampled into m points.

Let $\lambda_{i,j}(n)$ be the proportion of equivalent pairs for gestures i and j with $i, j = 1, r, i \neq j$. The probability that the $m-$samplings of the two gestures are equivalent was found before as being $\leq (\lambda_{i,j}(n))^m$. Therefore, the probability for at least one pair of gestures to be equivalent has the upper bound:

$$\leq \sum_{i=1}^{r} \sum_{j=i+1}^{r} (\lambda_{i,j}(n))^m \tag{3}$$

4.4 Upper bounds for the probability of equivalence

We are interested in estimating the values of $\lambda(n)$ in order to calculate upper bounds for equations 2 and 3.

THEOREM The probability that two points $p, q \in \mathcal{D}$ are equivalent can be approximated as follows:

$$P(p \equiv q) \approx \pi\epsilon^2 \tag{4}$$

Proof. The probability function of the Euclidean distance between two points picked at random in the unit square is $P(t) = 2t\left(t^2 - 4t + \pi\right)$ [21]. Therefore, the probability that the distance between p and q is at most ϵ will be:

$$P(t \leq \epsilon) = \int_0^{\epsilon} P(t)dt = \frac{1}{2}\epsilon^4 - \frac{8}{3}\epsilon^3 + \pi\epsilon^2$$

which can be approximated by $\pi\epsilon^2$ for small $\epsilon \leq 1$. □

If the n pairs of points are chosen independently from α and β then the random variable $e(n)$ follows the Binomial distribution with the probability of success $p = \pi\epsilon^2$. Therefore, the expected value for $e(n)$ is $E[e(n)] = np$ [7](p.181) which makes the expected value for $\lambda(n)$ to be p. However, we are interested in the expected value of $(\lambda(n))^m$ that appears in equations 2 and 3:

$$\begin{aligned} E\left[(\lambda(n))^m\right] &= E\left[\left(\frac{e(n)}{n}\right)^m\right] \\ &= \frac{1}{n^m} E\left[e^m(n)\right] \\ &= \frac{1}{n^m} \sum_{k=0}^{n} k^m \binom{n}{k} p^k (1-p)^{n-k} \end{aligned} \tag{5}$$

THEOREM The sum $S(n, m)$ of equation 5 is a polynomial in n of order m with the coefficient of n^m being p^m.

Proof. By using $\binom{n}{k} = \frac{n}{k}\binom{n-1}{k-1}$, putting $k - 1 = t$ and expanding $(1+t)^{m-1}$ in (5), it can be easily showed that:

$$S(n, m) = np \sum_{i=0}^{m-1} \binom{m-1}{i} \cdot S(n-1, i)$$

with $S(n, 0) = S(n-1, 0) = 1$.

Next, the principle of induction can be used. For $m = 1$, $S(n, 1) = np$ and for $m = 2$, $S(n, 2) = n^2p^2 + n(p - p^2)$. We assume that $S(n, m) = n^m p^m + O(n^{m-1})$ where by $O(n^{m-1})$ we denote a polynomial in n of order $m - 1$.

$$S(n, m+1) = np \sum_{i=0}^{m} \binom{m}{i} \cdot (p^i(n-1)^i + O(n^{i-1}))$$

in which n^m appears once for $i = m$ with the coefficient $\binom{m}{m}p^m$. Therefore, $S(n, m+1) = n^{m+1}p^{m+1} + O(n^m)$. □

Using these findings, we can write:

$$E\left[\left(\frac{e(n)}{n}\right)^m\right] = \frac{S(n,m)}{n^m} = \frac{p^m n^m + O(n^{m-1})}{n^m}$$

If we consider n to be large enough[5] then we can approximate the expected value of $(\lambda(n))^m$ to p^m. We can further use Markov's inequality [7](p.437) in order to obtain an upper bound value λ for $(\lambda(n))^m$ for which the probability $P((\lambda(n))^m \geq \lambda)$ can be neglected (e.g. the probability is less than ≤ 0.01):

$$P((\lambda(n))^m \geq \lambda) \leq \frac{E[(\lambda(n))^m]}{\lambda} \approx \frac{p^m}{\lambda} = 0.01$$

Therefore, by choosing $\lambda = 100 \cdot p^m$, we are 99% confident that $(\lambda(n))^m \leq \lambda$. By using this upper bound in equation 3, we obtain an upper bound for the probability of equivalence of the $m-$samplings of r gestures:

$$P(m, r) \leq 50 \cdot r(r-1) \cdot p^m = 50 \cdot r(r-1) \cdot \left(\pi\epsilon^2\right)^m \tag{6}$$

The only unknown factor so far is the constant ϵ that actually defines the equivalence of two points (see equation 1) for which we still need to choose a suitable value. A simple method to estimate ϵ is to look at the data sets from experiments 1 and 2 and average the Euclidean distances for all pairs of points that *should be equivalent*, i.e. for all the points that occupy the same index locations on gestures of the same class. After performing the computation, an average value of $\epsilon = .08$ (SD=.02) was obtained. We can therefore safely choose an upper bound value of $\epsilon = .1$ for all our further calculations. Equation 6 becomes:

$$P(m, r) \leq 50 \cdot r(r-1) \cdot 0.0314^m \tag{7}$$

In practice, template-based recognizers work with several samples T stored for each gesture class. Therefore, we need to consider T for each of the r gesture classes which makes the upper bound of equation 7 become:

$$P(m, r) \leq 50 \cdot r \cdot T \cdot (r-1) \cdot T \cdot 0.0314^m \tag{8}$$

Figure 8 illustrates the values for the probability of equivalence $P(m, r)$ for different sampling rates m and set sizes r. Values were computed for $T = 8$ which is a more than reasonable value (Wobbrock et al. [23] showed that recognition rates above 99% can be obtained for $T \geq 3$ samples per class). For $m = 5$, the upper bound of the probability is $\approx 8\%$ for sets of $r = 30$ gestures, drops down to 2% for $r = 20$, and stays under 1% for smaller sizes. For $m \geq 6$, the probability stays under 0.3% for all $r \leq 30$ and becomes $\leq 0.01\%$ for $m \geq 7$. These values support our experimental results by showing that the probability for any two gestures

[5]we can safely make this assumption as n can be viewed as a very fine sampling of a continuous curve from $\mathcal{A}$.

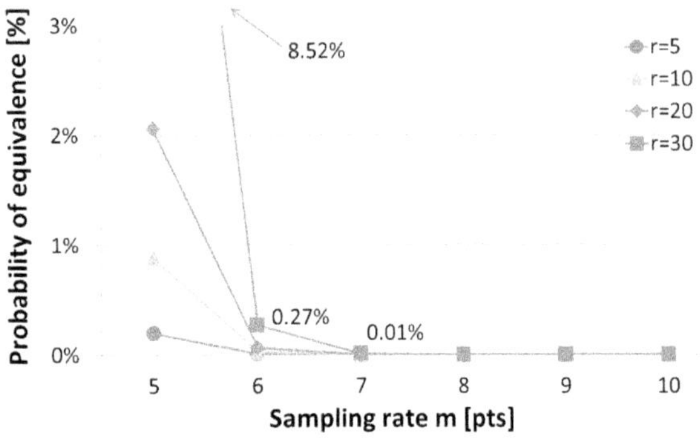

Figure 8: Upper bounds for the probability of equivalence for sets of size r, sampling rates m, and $T = 8$ training samples (see equation 8).

to be perceived similar cause of downsampling is very small. Although there might exist differences with respect to these theoretical values caused by constraints related to gesture production (e.g. we made the assumption that points are drawn randomly from the unit square), our theoretical calculations provide at least some evidence that the probability of equivalence is very small even for low sampling rates.

5. EXPERIMENT 3: VALIDATION

In order to validate our results, we performed a new recognition experiment using the UJIPenchars2 pen strokes set [12] available from the UCI Machine Learning Repository[6] [6]. The set consists in 97 gestures including 10 digits, 52 English letters (lower and upper case), 14 Spanish characters and other 21 strokes including various punctuation marks. The total number of available samples is 11,640 = 60 participants × 97 gestures × 2 repetitions.

The purpose of this experiment was to validate the sampling rates suggested by the regression models of Figure 5 for other gestures. We used the same experimental plan as before with 4 sizes $r = 10, 20, 30, 40$; 100 repetitions for each r (for each repetition r gestures were randomly chosen out of the 97 available); 1 training and 1 testing sample (limited by the set); 2 repetitions (one for each training sample). Therefore, we had 3 (metrics) × 4 (r) × 100 (r-sets) × 2 = 2400 tests. The sampling rate n was automatically computed from the regression models (to which we refer to as model n) and the recognition rate was tested for significance against that of the benchmark of 64 points.

Results showed a very good fit of the linear model for the Euclidean and angular metrics. For the Euclidean, the recognition rate of model n was not significantly different from $n = 64$ in 98% of the tests (at $p < .05$). Similarly, no significant difference was observed for the angular metric in 99% of the tests. The average rates were 6 points (SD=.71) for Euclidean and 6.5 points (SD=.50) for angular cosine.

For the DTW however, only 68% of the tests showed n.s. differences between the recognition rates. As discussed in experiment 2, the larger SD for DTW could account for this result. The difference however was of just 0.5%. Nevertheless, another model could better fit the behaviour of the DTW metric in the sense that larger values should be suggested for the sampling resolution n. For this purpose, we analyzed the frequency distribution of n for DTW using data from experiment 2 and, instead of computing the mean rate for each size r (as in Figure 5), we computed an upper threshold for n so that the probability of n falling beyond the threshold becomes non significant (.05) which we denoted $n_{.95}$. In other words, there are 95% chances that n will fall $\leq n_{.95}$. Using these rates we derived a more tight model for DTW for which a logarithmic regression showed the strongest fit ($R^2 = .86$):

$$n_{.95} = 8.47 \cdot ln(r) - 3.79 \tag{9}$$

When using the $n_{.95}$ threshold for the cases in which a significant difference was noticed between the recognition rates of DTW, the total percentage of n.s. tests increased to 96%. We also tried the $n_{.95}$ approach for the Euclidean and angular metrics as well but we found a non-interesting value of 7 points in both cases (vs. 6 obtained with the linear model). Interestingly, the experiment showed that the linear relationship works and extrapolates very well for these two metrics (note that a set of size $r = 40$ was also used).

[6]http://archive.ics.uci.edu/ml

6. CONCLUSIONS

An investigation was conducted on the effect of motion sampling rate on the performance of recognizers that HCI practitioners will likely use in order to develop gesture-based interfaces. We found that 6 points are sufficient for attaining high recognition rates for Euclidean and angular distances while both a linear and logarithmic relationship with the size of the gesture set were derived for DTW. Our findings relate to the *peaking phenomenon* encountered in pattern recognition [17] that describes the situation in which adding more features up from one point does not improve but actually increases the classification error.

We must stress that this work does not address the recognition of very large gesture sets (e.g. the 10k set of [10] for which special techniques were developed). Instead, we focus on the practical needs of designers that would likely choose between \$1 or DTW as recognizers and design reasonably sized sets of 10-20 gestures for their interfaces. Although our observations were derived for sets up to 30 gestures, this upper limit is usually enough for common gesture-based interfaces (as limited by the number of gesture commands users can learn and recall).

6.1 A note on extreme under-sampling

The recognition rates above 99% obtained using just few sampling points are very intriguing. As a more intriguing note, we also investigated $n = 2$ (first and last points of each gesture) and $n = 3$ (first, middle, and last) which simplify gestures at the most extreme levels. Recognition rates of 87.8% and 95.5% were obtained on the set of 32 gestures from Figures 2 and 4 using $n = 2$ and $n = 3$ points respectively. This confirms the preprocessing operation of Kristensson and Zhai [10] (p.45) that pruned their massive 10k database of strokes using a filter on the first and last points of each gesture (which equivalates to using the Euclidean distance with $n = 2$ sampling points) but they do not give numeric data on how good this pruning actually is. However, there is distinction between sampling for recognition (which is the goal of this work) and sampling for filtering [10]. Although such extremely aggresive downsampling showed high recognition rates for our gestures, it appears too extreme to be used for other purposes than filtering.

6.2 Sampling Rate Analysis Tool

Our analysis showed that the sampling rate can significantly reduce the processing time of gesture recognizers. Small rates of 6 points were found sufficient for attaining high recognition rates. However, in practice and with different gestures, 6 points may not always prove the best minimum choice. Therefore, the appropriate sampling rate for a given gesture set and metric will need to be determined by the practitioner. In order to assist this process, a simple tool was developed for helping practitioners working out the sampling resolution that would attain the highest recognition rate as well as the lowest execution time. This follows the tradition of providing assisting tools for designers of gesture-based interfaces in the line of the gesture development toolkit *gdt* of Long et al. [13] or the MAGIC application of Ashbrook and Starner [4]. The application includes the regression models derived in the paper but also computes recognition rates and execution times for other sampling rates. At the end of the analysis, it will provide the C# class representing the already implemented NN recognizer with the provided metric and sampling rate. The application can be downloaded from the author's web page[7].

6.3 Future work

Future work could investigate the effect of non-uniform vs. uniform samplings (such as samplings resulted from polyline simplification algorithms or from identifying corners or high curvature points on the motion input). Also, it remains to investigate whether the same small rates still apply for 3D gestures.

It is important to consider this work as the first exploration of sampling rate and its effects on recognizer performance. We hope that the results will prove useful to practitioners concerned with performance issues when implementing gesture-based recognizers.

7. ACKNOWLEDGMENTS

This paper was supported by the project "Progress and development through post-doctoral research and innovation in engineering and applied sciences- PRiDE - Contract no. POSDRU/89/1.5/S/57083", project co-funded from European Social Fund through Sectorial Operational Program Human Resources 2007-2013.

The author would also like to thank mathematician Bianca Satco for verifying a first draft of the theoretical argument described in Section 4.

8. REFERENCES

[1] D. Anderson, D. Bailey, and M. Skubic. Hidden markov model symbol recognition for sketch-based interfaces. In *AAAI Fall Symp.: Making Pen-Based Interacttion Intelligent and Natural*, pages 15–21, 2004.

[2] L. Anthony and J. O. Wobbrock. A lightweight multistroke recognizer for user interface prototypes. In *GI '10*, pages 245–252, 2010.

[3] C. Appert and S. Zhai. Using strokes as command shortcuts: cognitive benefits and toolkit support. In *CHI '09*, pages 2289–2298, 2009.

[4] D. Ashbrook and T. Starner. Magic: a motion gesture design tool. In *CHI '10*, pages 2159–2168, New York, NY, USA, 2010. ACM.

[5] X. Cao and S. Zhai. Modeling human performance of pen stroke gestures. In *CHI '07*, pages 1495–1504, 2007.

[6] A. Frank and A. Asuncion. UCI machine learning repository, 2010.

[7] S. Ghahramani. *Fundamentals of Probability, 2nd Ed.* Prentice Hall, 2000.

[8] S. Kratz and M. Rohs. A $3 gesture recognizer: simple gesture recognition for devices equipped with 3d acceleration sensors. In *IUI '10*, pages 341–344, 2010.

[9] S. Kratz and M. Rohs. Protractor3d: a closed-form solution to rotation-invariant 3d gestures. In *IUI'11*, pages 371–374, New York, NY, USA, 2011. ACM.

[10] P.-O. Kristensson and S. Zhai. Shark2: a large vocabulary shorthand writing system for pen-based computers. In *UIST '04*, pages 43–52, 2004.

[11] Y. Li. Protractor: a fast and accurate gesture recognizer. In *CHI '10*, pages 2169–2172, 2010.

[12] D. Llorens and et al. The UJIpenchars database: A pen-based database of isolated handwritten characters. In *Proc. 6th Int. Conf. on Language Resources and Evaluation*, 2008.

[13] A. C. Long, Jr., J. A. Landay, and L. A. Rowe. Implications for a gesture design tool. In *CHI '99*, pages 40–47, New York, NY, USA, 1999. ACM.

[14] D. Rubine. Specifying gestures by example. In *SIGGRAPH '91*, pages 329–337, 1991.

[15] T. Sebastian, P. Klein, and B. Kimia. On aligning curves. *IEEE Transactions on Pattern Analysis and Machine Intelligence*, 25(1):116–125, 2003.

[16] T. M. Sezgin and R. Davis. Hmm-based efficient sketch recognition. In *IUI '05*, pages 281–283, New York, NY, USA, 2005. ACM.

[17] C. Sima and E. Dougherty. The peaking phenomenon in the presence of feature-selection. *Pattern Recognition Letters*, 29:1667–1674, 2008.

[18] R.-D. Vatavu, L. Grisoni, and S.-G. Pentiuc. Gesture recognition based on elastic deformation energies. In *LNCS 5085*, pages 1–12. Springer Berlin / Heidelberg, 2009.

[19] R.-D. Vatavu, D. Vogel, G. Casiez, and L. Grisoni. Estimating the perceived difficulty of pen gestures. In *INTERACT'2011, Part II, LNCS 6947*, pages 89–106. Springer, 2011.

[20] A. Webb. *Statistical Pattern Recognition*. John Wiley & Sons, Inc., 2002.

[21] E. W. Weisstein. Square line picking. from mathworld–a wolfram web resource. http://mathworld.wolfram.com/squarelinepicking.html.

[22] D. Willems, R. Niels, M. v. Gerven, and L. Vuurpijl. Iconic and multi-stroke gesture recognition. *Pattern Recognition*, 42(12):3303–3312.

[23] J. O. Wobbrock, A. D. Wilson, and Y. Li. Gestures without libraries, toolkits or training: a $1 recognizer for user interface prototypes. In *UIST '07*, pages 159–168, 2007.

[7] http://www.eed.usv.ro/~vatavu

American Sign Language Recognition with the Kinect

Zahoor Zafrulla
Sch. of Interactive Computing
Georgia Inst. of Technology
Atlanta, GA 30332-0760
zahoor@gatech.edu

Helene Brashear
Tin Man Labs, LLC
Austin, Texas
helene@tinmanlabs.com

Thad Starner
Sch. of Interactive Computing
Georgia Inst. of Technology
Atlanta, GA 30332-0760
thad@cc.gatech.edu

Harley Hamilton
Sch. of Interactive Computing
Georgia Inst. of Technology
Atlanta, GA 30332-0760
hhamilton@cc.gatech.edu

Peter Presti
Interactive Media Tech. Center
Georgia Inst. of Technology
Atlanta, GA 30332-0760
peter.presti@imtc.gatech.edu

ABSTRACT

We investigate the potential of the Kinect depth-mapping camera for sign language recognition and verification for educational games for deaf children. We compare a prototype Kinect-based system to our current CopyCat system which uses colored gloves and embedded accelerometers to track children's hand movements. If successful, a Kinect-based approach could improve interactivity, user comfort, system robustness, system sustainability, cost, and ease of deployment. We collected a total of 1000 American Sign Language (ASL) phrases across both systems. On adult data, the Kinect system resulted in 51.5% and 76.12% sentence verification rates when the users were seated and standing respectively. These rates are comparable to the 74.82% verification rate when using the current (seated) CopyCat system. While the Kinect computer vision system requires more tuning for seated use, the results suggest that the Kinect may be a viable option for sign verification.

Categories and Subject Descriptors

H.5.2 [**Information interfaces and presentation (e.g., HCI)**]: User Interfaces (D.2.2, H.1.2, I.3.6); K.3.1 [**Computers and Educations**]: Computer Uses in Education

General Terms

Experimentation, Performance

Keywords

Educational Games, Sign language Verification, Microsoft Kinect

1. INTRODUCTION

The CopyCat project was designed to develop an interactive educational adventure game to help deaf children acquire language skills. The main goals of the project are to improve the language and memory abilities of deaf signing children, advance basic research in computer-based sign language recognition, and design an efficient language interaction model in order to assist in the language learning of deaf children.

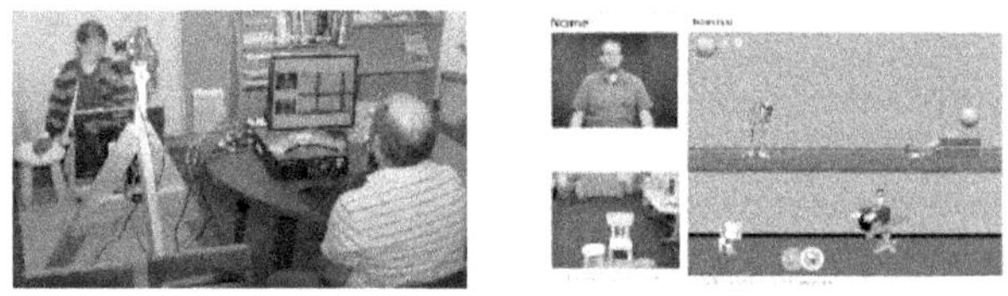

(a) (b)

Figure 1: (a) CopyCat system kiosk deployed at a partner school. (b) CopyCat game screen with tutorial video (top-left) and the raw video (bottom-left).

Table 1: CopyCat game vocabulary

subject	object	prepositions	adjectives
alligator, cat, snake, spider	bed, box, chair, flowers, wagon, wall	behind, in, on, under	black, blue, green, orange, white

As part of the CopyCat project, several computer-assisted language learning games have been designed [ ]. In each game, children interact with the hero via sign language. After a child signs a phrase to the hero, the child's signing is classified as correct or incorrect. The phrases consist of a subject, preposition and an object with one or two optional adjectives. See Table 1 for a complete list of signs in the game vocabulary. If the child signs game phrases correctly, he or she will progress through the game and gain points.

The CopyCat systems have included research towards both automatic sign language recognition [,] and sign language phrase verification [,]. Both approaches have used hidden Markov models (HMMs) to model signs used during game play. User studies suggest that the CopyCat system provides educational benefits to deaf children of hearing parents in as little as three weeks [ ]. Figure 1a shows the CopyCat system as deployed at a partner school.

The previous CopyCat sensor framework consisted of two types of sensors, a camera for eye and hand tracking and a pair of accelerometers that were strapped on the wrists over colored gloves.

Although the gloves and accelerometers enhance the performance of the system, there are other significant drawbacks with their use. They increase the complexity of the system making it harder for teachers to setup the system in the classroom. They require constant maintenance; the batteries need to be charged frequently; and the gloves need to be washed regularly. Additionally, the wearable sensors add a possible point of failure.

In this paper, we propose a new multimodal system that uses the Microsoft Kinect sensor. The depth information is used for ASL phrase verification, whereas the RGB image stream is used to provide live signing feedback to the signer. The CopyCat game itself remains unchanged [ ] (see Figure 1b) . We present experimental results that show that the Kinect system can yield performance comparable to the CopyCat sensor platform but may require a change in user interaction. With the Kinect, we are focusing on improving user comfort, robustness, user interaction, cost, system sustainability and ease of system deployment.

1.1 Related Work

Sign language recognition is a growing research area in the field of gesture recognition. Research on sign language recognition has been performed around the world using many sign languages, including American Sign Language [,], Korean Sign Language [ ], Taiwanese Sign Language [ ], Chinese Sign Language [,], Japanese Sign Language [ ], and German Sign Language [ ]. Many sign language recognition systems use HMMs for their ability to train useful models from limited and potentially noisy sensor data [, ,]. Sensor choices vary from data gloves [ ] and other tracker systems to computer vision techniques using a single camera [ ], multiple cameras, and motion capture systems [ ] to hand-crafted sensor networks [ ].

A variety of computer vision features are used in ASLR. Ong lists the following categories in his survey paper [ ]: two dimensional segmentation, two dimensional moment-based, motion vectors, three dimensional hand positions and three dimensional hand orientations. In addition to these common features we would add: two dimensional head tracking [,], three dimensional head orientation [ ], and motion templates [,].

Researchers differ greatly in their approach to modeling basic units of signed languages. The simultaneous nature of meaningful left hand, right hand, and head gesture in sign languages poses a challenge to many of the sequential techniques used in speech recognition [ ]. Many researchers choose to use the sign as a base unit of modeling [,], while others attempt to use a structure similar to phonemes to create models [,].

Vogler and Metaxus have proposed several techniques for handling simultaneous phonemes using the Movement-Hold linguistics model and parallel HMMs [ ]. Bowden et. al. use a two-tiered approach which classifies the TAB-SIG-DEZ features from Stokoe's phonology [ ] and passes the results to a Markov chain. Bowden's approach is designed to learn from small amounts of data; he achieved results of 84% on a dataset of 49 signs performed in isolation by a single user. When the set was pruned for signs that require non-manual markers or context for meaning, Bowden's technique achieved an accuracy of 97.67% on 43 signs [ ].

1.2 Depth Mapping

Depth maps can be generated by a number of algorithms and varying special camera configurations. RADAR, LIDAR, structured light techniques and sonar have all been used to generate depth maps [ ]. Time-of-flight cameras are popularly used in computer vision and robotics to generate depth maps at a high frame rate [ ]. Until now commercially available depth camera systems were expensive, and only a few researchers have used depth information to determine 3D hand pose [ ]. Most previous works either use appearance based methods [ ] or use some form of nearest neighbor matching in a database of poses [ ] to determine the hand pose.

The release of the Microsoft Kinect sensor has provided a cheap ($150), off-the-shelf option for depth sensors. The Kinect consists of an infra-red (IR) light projector, standard CMOS camera (for the IR), color camera, and two microphones in a single housing. It uses a standard USB interface [ ]. The distortion of the IR pattern is used to calculate depth maps, which have a per-pixel depth resolution of 1cm when the camera is 2 meters away [ ]. The images are 640x480 and are transferred at 30 frames per second [ ]. The Kinect will enable researchers to develop novel algorithms for 3D pose estimation using depth data.

2. DATA COLLECTION

We collected data using the CopyCat sensor framework and the Microsoft Kinect in order to compare the performance of the two sensor platforms. The data contains phrases from the CopyCat task but was collected from adult participants for preliminary testing. The three datasets used for comparison are

- **CopyCat Adult- seated** contains data collected from adult users playing the CopyCat game using colored gloves, wrist-mounted accelerometers and a camcorder.
- **Kinect - seated** contains data which mimics the CopyCat game interactions using the phrase repetition task (discussed in the next section) in a seated position. The seated position matches the configuration used in previous CopyCat studies.
- **Kinect - standing** contains data which mimics the CopyCat game interactions using the phrase repetition task (discussed in the next section) in a standing position. The standing position differs from the original CopyCat task but is more compatible with Kinect skeleton tracking algorithms (which were optimized for standing, not sitting).

2.1 Kinect Data Collection

We recruited seven participants, all of whom were hearing adults with varying levels of ASL expertise, ranging from beginner to expert. All seven users participated in data collection for the seated data, and three users participated in data collection for the standing set. During each session, users had 60 minutes to perform as many phrases from a 60 phrase set as comfortably possible. The dataset contains between one and two sessions per user. One user was unable to complete a standing session due to an interruption, so that user has fewer standing examples. A total of 555 phrase samples were collected in the seated pose and 155 phrase samples were collected in the standing pose.

2.1.1 Phrase Repetition Task

The phrase repetition task required participants to view videos of ASL phrases from the CopyCat game and sign them back to the camera. A front end application was developed in Java which allowed the users to view the ASL videos and view real time information from the Kinect camera consisting of the depth map image with skeleton tracking superimposed and the two-dimensional RGB image. The Java interface is shown in Figure 2.

Once the participant viewed a video, he or she would click the "Start Signing button" to begin signing and then clicked the "Stop Signing" button to indicate the termination of the ASL phrase. Since the purpose of this task was to collect data to examine the feasibility

Figure 2: User interface for the phrase repetition task: The left video shows a tutorial for the phrase. The right side shows the raw video (bottom) and the video annotated with the skeleton tracking (top). The bottom buttons allow the user to navigate the system.

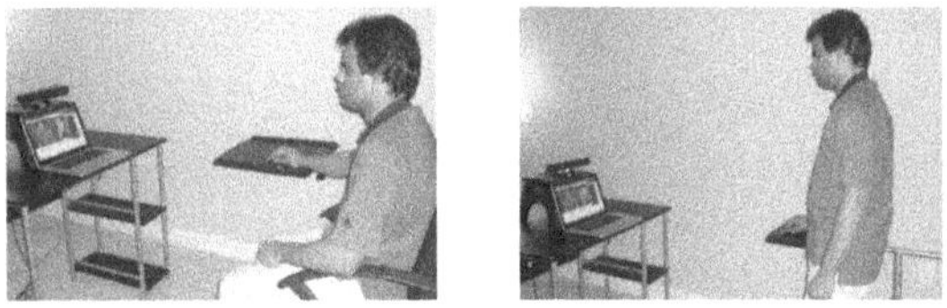

(a) (b)

Figure 3: Participant pose: (a) Seated (b) Standing.

of the Kinect camera as a sensor for doing sign language recognition, we encouraged the participants to repeat signing the phrase until they signed it correctly. Each participant was asked to complete signing all the 60 phrases of the CopyCat game at least once. Figure 3a shows the physical setup where the participant is seated facing the Kinect camera and watching ASL videos on a laptop computer. The user controls the interface via a mouse placed on a table next to the chair.

2.1.2 User Pose: Seated vs. Standing (Kinect data)

We observed that the skeleton tracker suffered from performance issues in the seated position, losing track of the participant's body pose several times accompanied by jitter in the limb positions. Since we did not anticipate this problem to be a major issue, we did not gather statistics on the frame-level accuracy of the tracker. In many cases the researchers allowed a participant to ignore tracking errors and move forward once the phrase was signed correctly. Two signs that caused most of the failures were BED and ALLIGATOR, with BED being the most unfavorable of the two (see Figure 4).

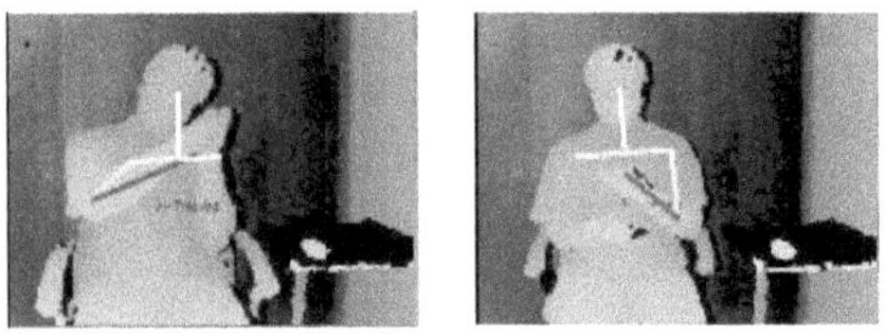

Figure 4: Tracking failure with BED and ALLIGATOR, respectively (Kinect data). Note that the lines should correspond with the user's arm positions but do not.

The experiment in the seated position represents the ideal case for a straightforward comparison since it correctly mimics user interaction used in previous work for the CopyCat project. Once we realized the high occurrence of tracking failures in the seated condition, we collected Kinect phrase repetition data for three users in the standing position. The standing position setup is shown in Figure 3b. The configuration difference for the standing position is that the camera is angled to capture the body knee up, and the mouse is place on a platform that can be easily reached in a standing position. We hypothesized that the skeleton tracking library that we used (OpenNI Framework) may yield better tracking performance in the standing position.

2.1.3 Data Pruning

We collected a total of 555 samples in the seated position and 155 in the standing position. The standing position suffers significantly less amount of tracking errors as compared to the seated position. However, we have not confirmed that all the available skeleton tracking implementations for Kinect depth data suffer from the same problem. The resulting dataset, after removing the samples with tracking errors, contained 146 signed phrases in the standing pose and 348 signed phrases in the seated pose.

2.2 CopyCat Adult Data Collection

For the CopyCat adult dataset we recruited eight participants, all of whom were hearing adults with varying levels of ASL expertise, ranging from beginner to expert. Of the eight participants recruited for this data set, three also participated in the Kinect data collection. The dataset contains two sessions per participant. Each session contains 20 phrases, for a total of 320 phrases in the dataset. Users sat at the CopyCat kiosk (Figure 1a) and played the CopyCat game.

2.2.1 Sensor Configuration

The CopyCat platform data collection used the CopyCat system as described in previous work [, , ,]. CopyCat uses computer vision and in-house designed three-axis accelerometers to collect data for use in sign language recognition [,]. Video is collected on a single IEEE 1394 DV camcorder that faces the signer. The signer wears colored gloves, which contain small accelerometers mounted on the outside of the wrist (shown in Figure 5). These accelerometers provide information on movement: acceleration, direction, and rotation of the hand. The distinct color of the gloves helps distinguish the hands from the skin color of the face and cluttered backgrounds.

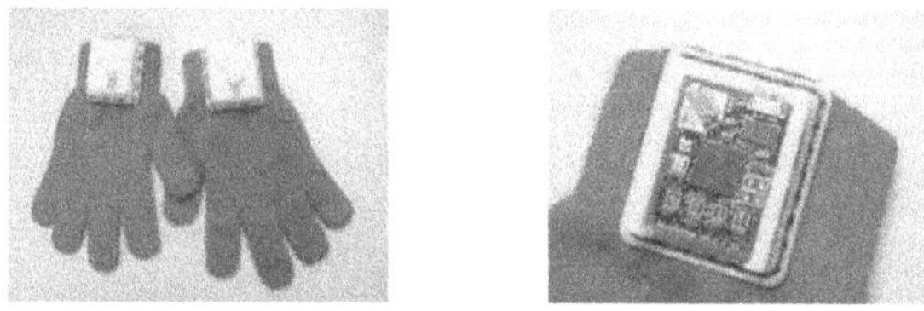

Figure 5: Left: Gloves with accelerometer. Right: Detail of wrist-mounted accelerometers (CopyCat sensor platform).

2.2.2 Data Pruning

A total of 320 phrase samples were collected for the CopyCat adult dataset. In order to choose samples compatible with the phrase repetition task, we selected samples that contained only correct signing. Five samples were excluded due to incorrect signing, and 26 samples were excluded because they contained variations in the signing such as sign repetition or other disfluencies. One of the signs excluded for language variation also contained machine errors. The resulting dataset contained 290 signed phrases of which 33 samples were removed due to data corruption (hand tracking errors or loss of accelerometer samples).

2.3 Data Collection Summary

Table 2 summarizes the number of samples collected in each dataset, sans all human anomalies, and the percentage of the dataset that was unusable due to data collection errors (machine errors). A total of 1000 ASL phrases were collected and the least amount of data collection errors were observed in the Kinect standing dataset.

Table 2: Samples collected versus sensor failures for all data

Configuration	#Samples	Corrupt Samples%
Kinect Seated	555	37.3%
Kinect Standing	155	5.8%
CopyCat Adult	290	14.8%

3. EXPERIMENTAL DESIGN

We follow a three step process. The first step is feature extraction where salient information that will enable us to perform automatic recognition is obtained. The second step is to train Hidden Markov Models (HMMs) for each sign in the game vocabulary. In the final step, the generalization performance of these models is measured by testing on independent data.

3.1 Features

The details of the feature extraction process for the Kinect sensor and the CopyCat sensor platform are given below.

3.1.1 Kinect

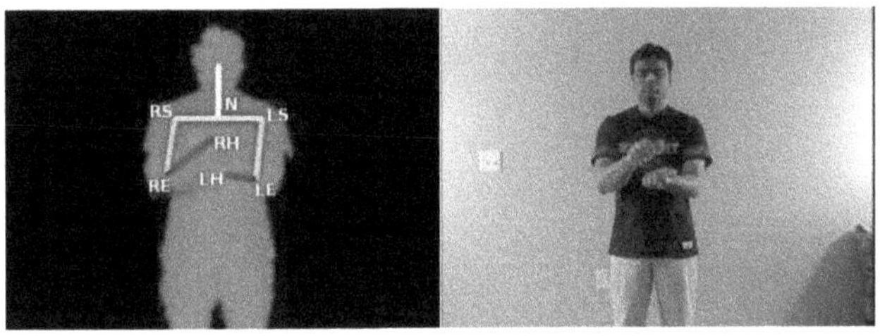

Figure 6: Visualization of upper body skeletal joints generated using OpenNI Framework (Kinect data).

Table 3: The 20 body pose features generated using OpenNI framework (Kinect data)

Unit 3D Vectors	Angles	distances
$RS \rightarrow RE$ (3)	$\angle N - RS - RE$ (1)	$(RH \rightarrow LH)$ (1)
$RE \rightarrow RH$ (3)	$\angle RS - RE - RH$ (1)	
$LS \rightarrow LE$ (3)	$\angle N - LS - LE$ (1)	
$LE \rightarrow LH$ (3)	$\angle LS - LE - LH$ (1)	
$RH \rightarrow LH$ (3)		

The Kinect features are a combination of body pose and hand shape features.The pose features are extracted using the skeletonization capability provided by the the OpenNI framework. OpenNI stands for "Open Natural Interaction" and provides a set of APIs that allows developers to write applications that utilize natural interaction. The OpenNI framework interfaces with NITE middleware provided by PrimeSense, the company that developed the Kinect hardware [ ]. The skeleton tracker is configured to return only the joints in the upper body. We obtain the shoulder, elbow and hand positions for the right and the left side of the body. We build the body pose feature from the joint angles of the shoulders and the elbows, the unit vectors of the elbows with respect to the shoulder, the hands with respect to the elbows and finally the left hand with respect to the right hand. See Figure 6 and Table 3 for details of the body pose feature. The body pose feature has 20 dimensions.

For generating the hand shape feature we collect all the 3D points in the neighborhood of each of the hand positions (RH and LH in Figure 6). We cluster the points corresponding to each hand separately to obtain a mixture of six Gaussians (MoG). We use six Gaussians because the human hand with the palm open has 6 distinct regions, five for the fingers and one for the palm. For simplicity we use diagonal covariance matrices while learning the mixture using Expectation Maximization (EM). The parameters of the Gaussians serve as the initial features. Each gaussian has six parameters, three for the mean and three for the diagonal of the covariance matrix. This results in a combined feature of 72 dimensions. We then perform Principal Component Analysis (PCA) on the entire dataset of MoG hand features to reduce the dimensionality of the hand shape feature from 72 to 20.

3.1.2 CopyCat

Features for data collected with the CopyCat kiosk are a combination of vision and accelerometer data. Video frames are captured at 20 fps, and the accelerometers, which have a range of +2g to -2g, are sampled at 40 Hz. Vision features are obtained by tracking the eyes and the colored gloves while playing the game [ ]. The corresponding accelerometer features are obtained by matching the accelerometer sample that is nearest in time to the video frame and computing the Fast Fourier Transform (FFT) within a window of samples. For a complete list of features generated for each hand, see Table 4.

Table 4: Feature types generated from the CopyCat sensor platform

Type	Description
Blob (hand Shape)	second moment shape descriptors (length of major and minor axes, eccentricity, orientation of major axis)
2D Image Motion	d_x and d_y of the blob center
Acceleration	x, y & z acceleration values and frequency domain representation of each axis.
Pose (2D geometry)	angle formed between the blob center and the horizontal passing through the midpoint between the eyes

3.2 Training and Testing

Once the features are collected, we train 4-state Hidden Markov Models (HMMs) for each of the 19 signs in the vocabulary shown in Table 1. Training and testing was done using the Georgia Tech Gesture Toolkit GT^2K [ ]. To evaluate the performance of the system, we perform two types of tasks: *recognition* and *verification*. We encourage the reader to understand the difference between the two in this context. In **automatic sign language recognition** the most probable transcription, based on models, is chosen that fits the input. We use the part of speech grammar shown below for our automatic recognition:

[adjective] subject preposition [adjective] object

This phrase structure supports three to five sign phrases using the optional adjectives. From a fixed dictionary of signs shown in Table 1 the *Recognizer* fills in one sign for each slot. If the right sign has been filled into all the slots then the phrase is recognized as correct, otherwise it is incorrect.

In **automatic sign language verification**, prior knowledge of the expected ASL phrase is used to determine if the input data matches the sentence. To perform the matching, the *Verifier* aligns the input data with the signs that constitute the expected phrase and filters based on the likelihood values [ ]. If all tokens pass the likelihood threshold test, then the phrase is verified. Since the current real time CopyCat system, with the gloves and accelerometers, uses the thresholding approach, we use the same method which allows a comparison between the CopyCat system and the Kinect.

For both *recognition* and *verification* the generalization performance of trained models is assessed using leave one out cross validation (LOOCV). However, the procedure is different in each case. For *recognition*, the approach is straightforward. We set aside one participant's data for testing and train on data from the remaining participants. In *verification*, since a likelihood threshold is applied, we first need to determine the appropriate threshold to use. The procedure to learn a threshold for each sign is outlined in Figure 7. It is a two-level LOOCV procedure where the inner LOOCV step is used to determine the log likelihood threshold to be used for each sign and the thresholds thus computed are then used in the outer LOOCV step. The results from each LOOCV run, the outer runs in the case of verification, are combined to obtain the overall recognition and verification accuracy.

for all participants (**p**) **do**
  $V_p \leftarrow set\ aside\ participant\ \mathbf{p}'s\ data\ for\ validation$
  for all remaining participants (**r**) **do**
    1. $V_r \leftarrow set\ aside\ participant\ \mathbf{r}'s\ data\ for\ validation$
    2. $Train\ on\ remaining\ N-2\ participants\ and\ test\ on\ V_r$
    3. $For\ each\ instance\ of\ a\ sign\ in\ V_r\ note\ the\ log\ likelihood\ value\ obtained\ via\ Viterbi\ alignment$
  end for
  $For\ each\ sign\ calculate\ the\ mean(\mu)\ and\ standard\ deviation(\sigma)\ of\ the\ log\ likelihood\ values\ collected$
  $Set\ a\ log\ likelihood\ threshold\ for\ each\ sign$
  $(\mu - \kappa * \sigma, \kappa > 0)$
  $Train\ on\ remaining\ N-1\ participants\ and\ test\ on\ V_p\ using\ the\ computed\ thresholds$
end for

Figure 7: Procedure for computing log likelihood thresholds to perform verification.

4. RESULTS

We evaluate performance based on both recognition and verification accuracies.

4.1 Baseline from Previous Work

Previous work, which compared phrase recognition and verification rates for data from deaf children playing the game, resulted in a maximum phrase recognition accuracy of 67.0% and a maximum phrase level verification rate of 82.0% (see Table 5) [ ]. Training data for the experiments was collected using a Wizard of Oz version of the game in which an external observer played the role of the ASL verifier. A total of 1204 phrase examples were collected from 11 deaf children playing the game during the phase two deployment of CopyCat. This set included 894 correctly signed phrases and 310 phrases that were incorrectly signed.

Table 5: Phrase-level cross validation accuracies from previous work that show a maximum phrase recognition accuracy of 67.0% and a maximum phrase level verification rate of 82.0% [ ].

	Verification (%)			Recognition (%)		
	TP	FP	Acc.	TP	FP	Acc.
M=1	86.0	38.0	79.8	54.0	3.0	64.9
M=2	88.6	37.2	**82.0**	56.8	3.3	**67.0**

Hidden Markov Models were trained with the correctly signed phrases using the Georgia Tech Gesture Recognition Toolkit GT^2K [ ]. Cross validation was performed by using 90% of the data for training and 10% for testing. The trained models were then evaluated on the incorrectly signed data to determine the false positive rate. This process was repeated 50 times and the results were averaged. Additionally, up to two Gaussian mixtures components were used for the training process (M=1 and M=2). For verification, a common rejection threshold was applied to the normalized log likelihood score, obtained using forced alignment, for all classes.

4.2 Kinect Data

Table 6 and Table 7 show the recognition and verification results of leave-one-out cross validation in the seated and standing poses, respectively. For the seated dataset the threshold selection for verification was done using the procedure shown in Figure 7.

Table 6: Recognition and Verification results - Kinect seated

Kinect Seated				
	Recognition		Verification	
Subj	Word Acc	SENT Acc	Word Acc	SENT Acc
1	51.79	26.67	89.29	60.00
2	77.19	43.90	96.56	87.80
3	73.1	35.00	95.17	82.50
4	69.11	25.00	92.68	71.88
5	75.53	32.2	96.38	85.59
6	80.00	43.48	92.78	76.09
7	70.00	40.00	96.00	86.67
Overall	74.48	36.2	95.16	82.18

Table 7: Recognition and Verification results - Kinect standing

Kinect Standing				
	Recognition		Verification	
Subj	Word Acc	SENT Acc	Word Acc	SENT Acc
1	65.04	26.79	87.61	58.93
2	75.00	38.33	98.33	93.33
3	85.71	50	99.25	96.67
Overall	73.62	36.3	94.49	80.82

The value of κ was varied from 1 to 10. At $\kappa = 6$ the increase in verification accuracy begins to flatten. The results for $\kappa = 6$ are shown in Table 6. See the discussion section for the average verifcation accuracies for all values of κ. Since there were only three participants in the standing dataset the threshold selection procedure could not be applied. Instead we choose a common threshold for all signs, which was obtained by averaging the threshold values from the seated dataset, with $\kappa = 6$, across all signs (s) and all the participants (p) (see Equation 1).

$$\frac{1}{|p| * |s|} \sum_{p} \sum_{s} \mu - \kappa * \sigma \qquad (1)$$

Based on the overall recognition and verification accuracies, there appears to be no significant difference in performance between seated and standing positions. This result demonstrates that the recognition/verification framework is robust to the jitter that occurs in the seated position. When tracking errors are ignored, the seated pose does slightly better in terms of verification acheiving 82.18% accuracy compared to 80.82% in the case of the standing pose.

4.3 CopyCat Adult Data

Table 8 shows the recognition and verification results of leave-one-out cross validation on the CopyCat Adult dataset. The threshold selection to perform verification was done using the procedure outlined in Figure 7, which is the same approach used for the Kinect seated dataset. The value of κ was varied from 1 to 10 but only results for $\kappa = 6$, the point at which the verification accuracy begins to flatten, are shown in Table 8.

Table 8: Recognition and Verification results - CopyCat Adult

CopyCat Adult dataset				
	Recognition		Verification	
Subj	Word Acc	SENT Acc	Word Acc	SENT Acc
1	80.43	42.42	99.34	97.22
2	63.64	21.05	92.05	63.16
3	79.01	43.24	97.10	87.88
4	91.23	61.54	94.44	78.33
5	86.18	52.78	91.30	70.00
6	93.21	72.97	100.00	100.00
7	80.43	40.00	95.80	84.62
8	84.03	53.85	100.00	100.00
Overall	85.42	51.01	96.86	87.85

4.4 Discussion

Table 9 provides a comparison between the three datasets based on the following factors: Recognition/Verification accuracy, Robustness, Aesthetics & Comfort and User Interaction.

Table 9: Comparison chart between the three datasets (ratings: *good*, *fair*, *poor*, X - further investigation required)

	CopyCat Adult dataset	Kinect Seated	Kinect Standing
Recognition / Verification Acc.	good	fair	fair
Robustness	fair	X	good
Aesthetics & Confort	fair	X	X
User Interaction	good	X	X

4.4.1 *Recognition/Verification accuracy*

Our experiments showed that the exisiting CopyCat sensor platform performs significantly better than the Kinect in terms of recognition rates and also yields higher verification rates. Table 10 gives a summary of the overall recognition and verification rates for the three datasets. The baseline results on the CopyCat children dataset from previous work is also included for reference.

Table 10: Summary of recognition and verification results

	Recognition		Verification	
	Word Acc	SENT Acc	Word Acc	SENT Acc
Kinect Seated	74.48	36.2	95.16	82.18
Kinect Standing	73.62	36.3	94.49	80.82
CopyCat Adult	85.42	51.01	96.86	87.85
CopyCat children	-	67.0	-	82.0

Based on previous work, the features obtained from the CopyCat sensor platform have gone through several improvements. The Kinect features have been introduced for the first time for the CopyCat task. There definitely is scope for improving the Kinect features, especially with respect to the hand shape. Our current hand shape feature for the Kinect is still primitive and was selected keeping in mind that real-time performance is desired. In the future we will explore more sophisticated hand shape features derived from depth information.

4.4.2 *Robustness*

The CopyCat sensor platform involves more than one sensor resulting in more failure points. Moreover, since conventional computer vision algorithms are used for eye tracking and hand tracking, environmental factors such as lighting conditions can have a negative impact on the robustness of tracking. Accelerometer sampling errors can also occur. If a video frame could not be paired with a matching accelerometer sample, and this problem occurred consecutively for two or more frames, then it was considered as a accelerometer sampling error.

Since the Kinect estimates depth by projecting an infrared light pattern, it is unaffected by environmental factors, resulting in a very reliable depth map output. However, the skeleton tracking facility provided by the OpenNI framework is robust only in the standing pose and fails more than one third of the time when the user is seated. Once we factor in the tracking errors, considering them as recognition and verification failures, the standing pose emerges as the more favorable of the two configurations. A detailed comparison between the CopyCat sensor platform dataset and the Kinect seated dataset is shown in Figure 8. There is a significant drop in the overall verification accuracy for the seated dataset due to the large amount of corrupt data as identified in Table 2.

Further investigation is clearly warranted on the standing vs seated problem, and other frameworks for skeleton tracking also need to be thoroughly explored in order to determine if they may be able to overcome the tracking problem in the seated position.

Table 11 lists the updated recognition and verification rates once we factor in the errors that occur in data collection for all three datasets. The CopyCat sensor platform still performs better at recognition, but the effective verification accuracy for the Kinect standing dataset is better than the CopyCat Adult dataset once all sources of error are included.

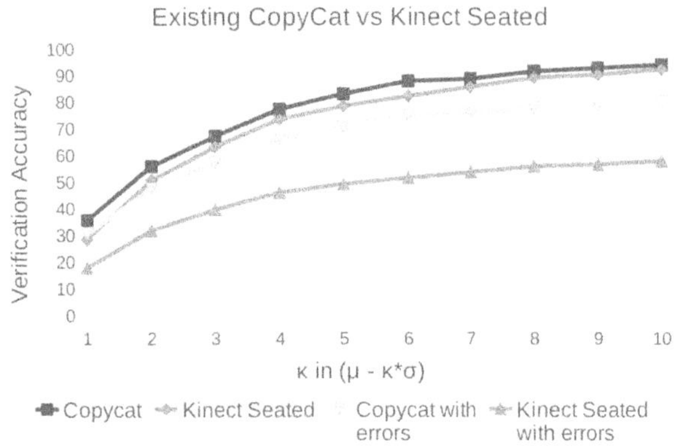

Figure 8: Comparison of verification accuracy between CopyCat Adult dataset and Kinect seated dataset, with and without data collection errors, for different values of the threshold.

Table 11: Results after factoring in tracking errors

	Recognition		Verification	
	Word Acc	SENT Acc	Word Acc	SENT Acc
Kinect Seated	47.74	22.7	58.86	51.5
Kinect Standing	70.45	34.19	88.02	76.12
CopyCat Adult	73.72	43.44	83.59	74.82

4.4.3 Aesthetics & Comfort

The Kinect is a clean and neat out-of-the-box solution for obtaining depth information. With minimal hardware, it provides a clutter-free environment to setup the CopyCat game.

The CopyCat sensor platform requires a kiosk-like setup. Additionally, accelerometer batteries may need to be regularly recharged, and circumstances may arise when controlled lighting is required. A researcher has to be present to run the CopyCat system during deployment, whereas the Kinect provides a plug-n-play interface that even individuals without a technical background will be able to operate with ease.

One of the major drawbacks of the CopyCat sensor platform is that it requires the user to wear gloves with accelerometers strapped to the wrist to enable the capture of gestural information. Although previous studies have shown that children did not have problems wearing the gloves, the comfort factor with Kinect and the facility to interact naturally without aids may have a greater appeal to the children for whom the game is designed.

4.4.4 User Interaction

The existing CopyCat setup, where the user is seated in a chair and interacts with the game using a mouse placed at a convenient location next to the chair (see Figure 1a), has been deployed several times in schools with deaf children. This interaction model was designed iteratively over several usability studies conducted in partnership with local deaf schools with the involvement of deaf children and their teachers. One of the concerns when deciding upon the seated pose for the user/child was that fatigue that may occur if the children have to stand continuously for a period of 30-45 minutes to play the game (approximately the time it takes to finish one session). That the Kinect skeleton tracking performs poorly in the seated position, but very well in the standing position, suggests an open area for research. We have yet to ascertain the effect that standing may have on user experience and to what extent fatigue may factor.

One critical aspect of CopyCat involves set-up and tear down of the system. With the current CopyCat sensor platform, the teacher would be required to manage the hardware extensively (e.g., charge the batteries regularly and maintain the gloves in good usable condition). In contrast, the Kinect provides a convenient, out-of-the-box solution. Moreover, the Kinect is easy and inexpensive to replace.

5. CONCLUSION

We have presented an alternative approach to the automatic sign language verification task suitable for the CopyCat game using the Kinect camera. This approach mitigates the need for users to wear gloves and strap sensors on their wrists, which is the most significant drawback of the current CopyCat system. The experimental results show that verification results with the Kinect are comparable to the existing system. However, we discovered that when the users are seated the skeleton tracking system tends to make a significant number of tracking errors, which could have a negative impact on the overall user experience while playing the CopyCat game. One alternative is to change the way users interact with system, having them stand rather than being seated. Experiments have shown that standing results in fewer tracking errors and may have suitable verification accuracies. Changing the user's pose from a seated to standing position involves a shift in the interaction model for the game. We are only beginning to explore the effects that this may have on the user experience.

Our future plan is to develop a real time version of the CopyCat game that uses the Kinect sensor and is suitable for deaf children. Our past experience has shown that recognizing children's signing is an extremely challenging task. Our goal is to exploit the potential of the Kinect depth information to its fullest, especially with regards to spotting hand shapes.

6. REFERENCES

[1] V. Athitsos and S. Sclaroff. 3d hand pose estimation by finding appearance-based matches in a large database of training views. In *In IEEE Workshop on Cues in Communication*, 2001.

[2] B. Bauer, H. Hienz, and K. Kraiss. Video-based continuous sign language recognition using statistical methods. In *Proceedings of the 15th International Conference on Pattern Recognition*, volume 2, pages 463–466, September 2000.

[3] H. Brashear. *Improving the Efficacy of Automated Sign Language Practice Tools.* PhD thesis, Georgia Institute of Technology, College of Computing, 2010.

[4] H. Brashear, K.-H. Park, S. Lee, V. Henderson, H. Hamilton, and T. Starner. American Sign Language Recognition in Game Development for Deaf Children. In *Assets '06: Proceedings of the 8th International ACM SIGACCESS Conference on Computers and Accessibility*, Portland, Oregon, 2006. ACM Press.

[5] H. Brashear, T. Starner, P. Lukowicz, and H. Junker. Using Multiple Sensors for Mobile Sign Language Recognition. In *Proceedings of the Seventh IEEE International Symposium on Wearable Computers*, pages 45–52, 2003.

[6] H. Brashear, Z. Zafrulla, T. Starner, H. Hamilton, P. Presti, and S. Lee. CopyCat: A Corpus for Verifying American Sign Language During Game Play by Deaf Children. In *4th Workshop on the Representation and Processing of Sign*

Languages: Corpora and Sign Language Technologies, Proceedings of the 7th Annual International Language Resources and Evaluation Conference, Valetta, Malta, 2010.

[7] Cooper and Bowden. Sign Language Recognition: Working with Limited Corpora. In *Universal Access in Human-Computer Interaction. Applications and Services 5th International Conference, UAHCI 2009, Held as Part of HCI International 2009*, pages 472–481, 2009.

[8] O. Eng-Jon and R. Bowden. A boosted classifier tree for hand shape detection. In *Proceedings of the Sixth IEEE International Conference on Automatic Face and Gesture Recognition*, pages 889–894, May 2004.

[9] G. Fang, W. Gao, and D. Zhao. Large Vocabulary Sign Language Recognition Based on Hierarchical Decision Trees. In *International Conference on Multimodal Interfaces*, pages 125–131, 2003.

[10] W. Gao, G. Fang, D. Zhao, and Y. Chen. Transition Movement Models for Large Vocabulary Continuous Sign Language Recognition (CSL). In *Sixth IEEE International Conference on Automatic Face and Gesture Recognition*, pages 553–558, 2004.

[11] J. L. Hernandez-Rebollar, N. Kyriakopoulos, and R. W. Lindeman. A New Instrumented Approach for Translating American Sign Language into Sound and Text. In *Proceedings of the Sixth IEEE International Conference on Automatic Face and Gesture Recognition*, pages 547–552, 2004.

[12] J. S. Kim, W. Jang, and Z. Bien. A Dynamic Gesture Recognition System for the Korean Sign Language KSL. *IEEE Transactions on Systems, Man and Cybernetics*, 26(2):354–359, 1996.

[13] R. Liang and M. Ouhyoung. A Real-Time Continuous Gesture Recognition System for Sign Language. In *Third International Conference on Automatic Face and Gesture Recognition*, pages 558–565, 1998.

[14] Z. Mo and U. Neumann. Real-time hand pose recognition using low-resolution depth images. In *Proceedings of the 2006 IEEE Computer Society Conference on Computer Vision and Pattern Recognition - Volume 2*, CVPR '06, pages 1499–1505, Washington, DC, USA, 2006. IEEE Computer Society.

[15] S. Ong and S. Ranganath. Automatic sign language analysis: a survey and the future beyond lexical meaning. *Pattern Analysis and Machine Intelligence, IEEE Transactions on*, 27(6):873 – 891, jun 2005.

[16] Prime Sense. *The PrimeSensor^{TM}Reference Design 1.08*. April 2011.

[17] H. Sagawa and M. Takeuchi. A method for recognizing a sequence of sign language words represented in a Japanese Sign Language sentence. In *Proceedings of the 4th IEEE International Conf. on Automatic Face and Gesture Recognition*, pages 434–439, Grenoble, France, Mar 2000.

[18] J. Shotton, A. Fitzgibbon, M. Cook, T. Sharp, M. Finocchio, R. Moore, A. Kipman, and A. Blake. Real-Time Human Pose Recognition in Parts from Single Depth Images. *Proceedings of IEEE Conference on Computer Vision and Pattern Recognition*, 2011.

[19] M. Sonka, V. Hlavac, and R. Boyle. *Image Processing, Analysis, and Machine Vision*. Thomspon Learning, Toronto, Ontario, Canada, third edition, 2008.

[20] T. Starner and A. Pentland. Visual Recognition of American Sign Language Using Hidden Markov Models. In *Proceedings of the International Workshop on Automatic Face and Gesture Recognition*, 1995.

[21] W. Stokoe. Sign Language Structure: An Outline of the Visual Communication Systems of the American Deaf. *Studies in Linguistics, Occasional Papers 8*, 1960.

[22] J. Stuckler and S. Behnke. Combining depth and color cues for scale- and viewpoint-invariant object segmentation and recognition using random forests. In *Intelligent Robots and Systems (IROS), 2010 IEEE/RSJ International Conference on*, pages 4566 –4571, October 2010.

[23] G. Ten Holt, P. Hendriks, and T. Andringa. Why Don't You See What I Mean? Prospects and Limitations of Current Automatic Sign Recognition Research. *Sign Language Studies*, 6(4), Summer 2006.

[24] C. Vogler and D. Metaxas. Adapting Hidden Markov Models for ASL recognition by using three-dimensional computer vision methods. In *Proceedings of the IEEE International Conference on Systems, Man and Cybernetics*, pages 156–161, Orlando, FL, October 1997.

[25] C. Vogler and D. Metaxas. ASL Recognition Based on a Coupling Between HMMs and 3D Motion Analysis. In *Proceedings of the IEEE International Conference on Computer Vision*, pages 363–369, 1998.

[26] C. Vogler and D. Metaxas. Handshapes and Movements: Multiple-Channel American Sign Language Recognition. In *Gesture-Based Communication in Human-Computer Interaction*, volume 2915, pages 247–258. Springer-Verlag, January 2004. Lecture notes in Artificial Intelligence.

[27] C. Vogler, H. Sun, and D. Metaxas. A framework for motion recognition with applications to American sign language and gait recognition. In *Proceedings of Workshop on Human Motion*, pages 33–38, 2000.

[28] R. Y. Wang and J. Popović. Real-time hand-tracking with a color glove. *ACM Trans. Graph.*, 28:63:1–63:8, July 2009.

[29] K. A. Weaver, H. Hamilton, Z. Zafrulla, H. Brashear, T. Starner, P. Presti, , and A. Bruckman. Improving the Language Ability of Deaf Signing Children through an Interactive American Sign Language-Based Video Game. In *Proceedings of 9th International Conference of the Learning Sciences*, June 2010.

[30] T. Westeyn, H. Brashear, A. Atrash, and T. Starner. Georgia Tech Gesture Toolkit: Supporting Experiments in Gesture Recognition. In *ICMI '03: Proceedings of the 5th International Conference on Multimodal Interfaces*, New York, NY, USA, 2003. ACM Press.

[31] A. Wilson. Using a Depth Camera as a Touch Sensor. *The ACM International Conference on Interactive Tabletops and Surfaces*, November 2010.

[32] R. Yang, S. Sarkar, and B. Loeding. Handling movement epenthesis and hand segmentation ambiguities in continuous sign language recognition using nested dynamic programming. *The IEEE Transactions on Pattern Analysis and Machine Intelligence*, 32(3):462–477, March 2010.

[33] Z. Zafrulla, H. Brashear, H. Hamilton, and T. Starner. A novel approach to American Sign Language (ASL) Phrase Verification using Reversed Signing. In *Proceedings of IEEE Conference on Computer Vision and Pattern Recognition*, 2010.

[34] Z. Zafrulla, H. Brashear, H. Hamilton, and T. Starner. Towards an American Sign Langauge Verifier for Educational Game for Deaf Children. In *Proceedings of International Conference on Pattern Recognition*, 2010.

Perceived Physicality in Audio-Enhanced Force Input

Chi-Hsia Lai
Matti Niinimäki
Department of Media
Aalto University
School of Art and Design
PO Box 31000 00076 Aalto, Finland
chi-hsia.lai@aalto.fi
matti.niinimaki@aalto.fi

Koray Tahiroğlu
Department of Media
Aalto University
School of Art and Design
PO Box 31000 00076 Aalto, Finland
koray.tahiroglu@aalto.fi

Johan Kildal
Teemu Ahmaniemi
Nokia Research Center
PO Box 407, FI-00045
Nokia Group, Finland
johan.kildal@nokia.com
teemu.ahmaniemi@nokia.com

ABSTRACT
This paper investigates how the perceived physicality of the action of applying force with a finger on a rigid surface (such as on a force-sensing touch screen) can be enhanced using real-time synthesized audio feedback. A selection of rich and evocative audio designs was used. Additionally, audio-tactile cross-modal integration was encouraged, by observing that the main rules of multisensory integration were supported. The study conducted showed that richness of perceived physicality increased considerably, mostly in its auditory expression (what pressing sounded like). In addition, in many instances it was observed that the haptic expression of physicality also increased (what pressing felt like), including some perception of compliance. This last result was particularly interesting as it showed that audio-tactile cross-modal integration might be present.

Categories and Subject Descriptors
H.5.2 [**Information Interfaces and Presentation**]: User Interfaces - *auditory (non-speech) feedback, user-centered design; evaluation/methodology.*

General Terms: Design, Experimentation, Human Factors.

Keywords: Force Input Device, Audio Feedback, Physicality, Multimodal.

1. INTRODUCTION
Interaction with touch displays is currently enjoying its height in popularity. However, it is still used almost exclusively as a binary form of input, in which the only two possible states are *touch* and *no touch*. Ahead of this binary-touch metaphor, there is a long way for touch interaction to get to benefit from the richness that human touch, interacting with the physical world, can offer. In reaching that goal, force sensing stands out as an essential element to expand the potential of touch interaction [1-4]. From the user's perspective, varying the force applied on an interaction surface is a natural effort to transcend the surface and interact in the depth dimension or its Z axis [5]. This opens up possibilities for tangible three-dimensional interaction [6].

ICMI'11, November 14–18, 2011, Alicante, Spain.

One important element missing in most, if not all, force-sensing touch interaction systems is *haptic physicality*. Perceived by a combination of the sensory channels, physicality informs about the physical properties of an object [7]. It is the way in which matter gets expressed when interacting with it, and it is therefore a function of the type of interaction [8]. Haptic physicality, therefore, is the expression of the matter that is captured by a person's skin and proprioceptive system in the act of interaction.

If the material is a rigid touch surface and the interaction is to simply press on it, the features of perceived haptic physicality are very plain. The skin mechanoreceptors sense the reaction force that the touch surface is exerting on the finger. The skin deformation, as a function of the force, indicates that the surface does not deform. Finally, proprioception indicates that the force applied caused no displacement [9].

From the perspective of the touch interaction designer, however, the system will respond to active force input in a variety of ways. The response output will typically be through visual rendering and change in the system's behavior. Such cases would clearly benefit from changes in the haptic physicality that is perceived. It is clear that, if the touch surface remains physically rigid and unaltered throughout the interaction cycle, the richness of haptic physicality will have to be achieved by some alternative stimulation of the user's senses.

In [5], Kildal studied the augmentation of force input in the scenario just described making use vibrotactile output. With the technique employed (3D-Press), the force applied was closely monitored by the system. Vibrotactile responses where synthesized in real time to respond to the variations in the force. This close coupling was designed to reproduce a displacement friction model. As a result, the haptic illusion of physical displacement of the point of contact emerged spontaneously and reliably, as an example of tactile-proprioceptive cross-modal interaction. Thus, this technique allowed increasing the richness of tangible physicality by manipulating the perceived mechanical properties of the touch surface through software (rigid or compliant, deep or shallow, smooth or rough, etc.). It should be remembered, though, that every force interaction with the physical environment is multimodal in nature. Thus, it might be possible to further enrich the physicality –even the haptic physicality itself– by including additional congruent stimuli from other sensory channels, as discussed in [10].

In the study presented in this paper, attention was given to the role of hearing in augmenting the physicality of active force input. Before combining sound with the vibrotactile stimuli, which was left for future work, the current study considered audio-only augmentation of the force input experience. The research question investigated was twofold: *how does audio enrich the physicality of active force input on a rigid surface?* And *how does, if to any extent, audio enrich haptic physicality in particular, in the same input action?* In this study, it was expected to observe that audio augmentation increased in some way the richness of auditory physicality for the action of pressing. The second question, however, would require that audio-haptic cross-modal integration took place to some extent. Thus, the study was also expected to reveal if such sensory integration took place or not.

1.1 Modeling User Experience with Sound

The very idea of sound design carries an implication of the aesthetic brand identity and the refinement of feedback channels of the designed product. Most notably, a similar design process may conceptually include reducing the role of audio to audio messages (eg. Earcons and icons) in order to provide discrete information in interactive context [11]. While it is tempting to infer that sound design is inevitably employed to enhance usability, it must still be stressed that audio in itself can play a more significant role in interaction design. The auditory modality can provide alternative opportunities in interaction design and make interaction continuous and dynamic [12].

Techniques and strategies for multimodal audio-haptic integration to enhance user interfaces have been introduced in various projects [13-17], including touch surfaces [18,19]. The study presented in this paper introduces a different direction. As stated in the introduction, we aimed to investigate which qualities of audio create the illusion of enhancing the haptic physicality of a flat surface. It is quite apparent that audio is a fundamental and significant source for musical creation, which brings forth its role as conveyor of emotions. Thus, besides the physical characteristics of audio modules, this medium may also have the potential to model the action of applying force by enriching it with emotional charge. Our main motivation in the current phase of our research is to explore the vocabulary of sound-action coupling. We aimed to investigate what forms of our design decisions meet the expectations of enriched physicality in sound-action experiments as well as whether audio is able to enrich haptic physicality. The goal of this user study is to identify the main qualities of physicality created through audio augmentation rather than to quantify this effect in any accurate way. Consequently, the outcome of this study is expected to serve as audio design criteria for similar touch input scenarios, such as touch-screen-based mobile interfaces.

In the following sections, a user test is described in detail. We then discuss further elements that we found in the experiment. The paper concludes with a presentation of the outcomes and indicates the future directions of our research.

2. USER STUDY

Ten different audio synthesis modules were created to test what kind of audio quality could increase the richness of the perceived haptic physicality in the action of pressing on a flat rigid surface. For that purpose, a simple interface with a force sensitive resistor was built, and the force value from the sensor was used to control different parameters of the audio synthesis modules.

2.1 Participants

A group of 14 participants was recruited for this study (5 female, 9 male, aged 21-45, originally from 6 different countries). The participants were students or employees from various departments at University, and they were all naïve to the research questions and goals of the study. All the participants were directly or indirectly connected to the creative field (designers, artists, engineers working with designers, design researchers). Two of the participants worked specifically with audio creation, and at least seven of them had backgrounds in interactive design. Therefore, some of the participants were well aware of the implication of such term as *haptics*, and used them to describe their experience during the user study. It is possible that this segmentation of participants from creative disciplines (as opposed to a group of participants picked randomly from the general public) influenced the results of the study to some extent. If the participants were selected from the general public, less technical terms in the descriptions could be expected. However, this study was conducted with explicit questions plus a think-aloud process that aimed to let the participants speak freely.

2.2 Environment and Procedure

The user study was conducted in a quiet room, where each participant sat in front of a desk. On the desk there was a clear acrylic box with a force sensitive resistor attached to its top. The sensing area of the sensor was hidden under a square-shaped piece of green tape and the rest of the sensor was hidden under a strip of white tape. A similar-looking setup with a strip of white tape and square-shaped piece of red tape - without the sensor under it - was placed to the left of the actual sensor. The two squares were intended to feel identical to touch, but there was a slight difference due to the fact that the green square was slightly more elevated than the red one. The function of this red tape is described in more detail below. The audio synthesis was played through a speaker placed on the table behind the acrylic box. This location was chosen for the speaker so as to facilitate sensory integration between touch and audio through the spatial collocation cue [20]. The interviewer sat on the opposite side of the desk, and other research assistant sat behind another table next to the interviewer controlling the technical setup (see Figure 1).

(a) (b)

Figure 1. Technical setup.

In the beginning, it was stated that the test was not an accuracy test and that there were no right or wrong answers. As there was no time limit for each session, the participants were asked to spend as much time as they liked applying varying levels of pressure with the tip of a finger on the hard surface (not a button) where the green piece of tape was. The time each session took varied between 20 to 40 minutes. If it was noted during the first audio module that the participants were not using enough force to reach the maximum value, they were instructed to try pressing even harder. This action triggered and modeled the synthesis of audio as a response, which followed the actions (variations in force) of the user in near-real time; this synchrony was also intended to encourage sensory integration through the temporal cue [20]. It is worth to note that, since the actual haptic physicality of pressing on a rigid surface was so plain, the inverse effectiveness rule of sensory integration was most likely also supported [20].

Each participant went through all 10 different audio modules. The order of the modules was randomized for each user in such a way that each module would still be before or after its corresponding pair. After each audio synthesis module, the participants were initially asked explicitly the three following questions:

"Could you describe what is happening here?"

"What is the thing you are pressing?"

"How does it feel when you are pressing this?"

These questions were purposely designed to be open and exploratory, as the aim of this study was to encourage the participants to express their impressions freely without forcing them to think in one way or another. For this reason, closed questions were avoided at all times. However, additional clarifying questions (e.g. "what kind of a button?") were asked if the answer (e.g. “a button”) was vague or ambiguous.

After this first set of questions, the participants were also asked to apply pressure in a similar way on the red square with their eyes closed and then alternate pressing between the red and green squares. The interviewer would then ask the participant to compare and describe if there were any differences in how both squares felt or if the comparison invoked any new ideas or comments. The red square was just a piece of tape, so naturally it did not give any audio feedback, but it was included in the user test to gain additional comments about the physicality of the pressing action.

2.3 Technical Details

The pressure sensor used was a Tekscan FlexiForce force sensor (model A201-1). The sensor was connected to an Arduino[1] UNO microcontroller through a voltage divider circuit. The microcontroller was programmed to send the level of pressure through a serial port connection (57600 baud) at a refresh rate of 100 Hz. This setup provided the force values with a 10 bit resolution.

Table 1. Audio synthesis modules sorted in categories.

Categories	Pairs	Audio Module	Name
Event Based	Pair 1	Module 1	Elastic 1
		Module 2	Elastic 2
	Pair 2	Module 3	Sand 1
		Module 4	Sand 2
Event Based With Climax	Pair 3	Module 5	Bubble Wrap 1
		Module 6	Bubble Wrap 2
	Pair 4	Module 7	Mechanical Button 1
		Module 8	Mechanical Button 2
Continuous	Pair 5	Module 9	Motor
		Module 10	Wind

The Arduino microcontroller was connected to a laptop computer, where the serial data was read and parsed with Pure Data[2] (Pd-extended 0.42.5) environment. The force sensor was calibrated in a way that the force range of the pressure was measured to be 0.0 to 5.0 N when the force was applied evenly to the sensing area of the sensor. The force value from the sensor was normalized in Pure Data to a value between 0.0 and 1.0, which was then used to control different parameters of the audio synthesis. The latency of Pure Data audio synthesis was configured to 20 ms and the Arduino board was set to send sensor readings every 10 milliseconds. Therefore, the overall latency of the system was estimated to be between 30-45 ms.

The diameter of the sensing area of the sensor was only 9 mm and the sensor was pressed directly by the participants with their index finger. Therefore, it has to be noted that the sensitivity of the setup would be affected by the size and position of the user's finger. If the user applied pressure over a larger surface area than the actual sensing area of the sensor, the sensitivity decreased and more force had to be applied to explore the full range. In practice, this meant that forces up to 10 N might be required to reach the maximum value. This inaccuracy was considered to be acceptable, because even though there would be differences between users, each user would operate the sensor in a similar way throughout the experiment. Therefore, the subjective experience would be similar enough for each module given the objectives of the study.

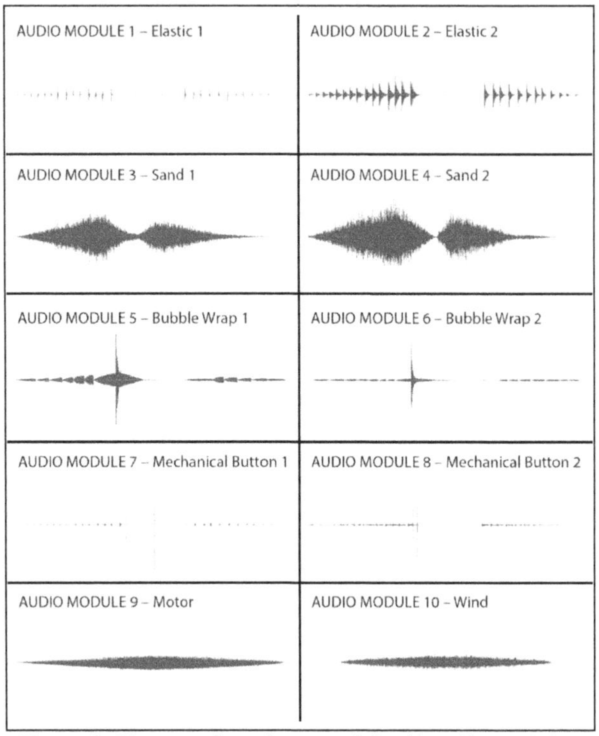

Figure 2. The waveform images of the 10 audio modules.

2.4 Audio Synthesis Modules

10 different audio synthesis modules were developed to be tested in the user study. The design of each audio module was based on some real-world material, object or phenomenon. The design principles were to include a variety of sound qualities that either imitated the sound of pressing on an actual material, or embraced

[1] http://www.arduino.cc/

[2] http://www.puredata.info/

an abstract relationship between action and responding sound, in which both aimed to find out what kind of sound quality could enrich the force input experience. The modules were divided into three categories: *event-based sounds*, *event-based sounds with a climax*, and *continuous sounds*. The first two categories had four audio modules each and the last category had two modules. The categories were then further divided into pairs. The two modules of each pair behaved similarly to each other with some changes in the audio characteristics. The following table illustrates the division of the modules.

In both event-based categories sound would be produced only while the level of force was being changed, thus constant force resulting in silence (or in the decay of the so-far-produced sound in some cases). In the Continuous case, instead, a constant force would result in a constant but audible sound rendering.

Figure 2 illustrates the audio waveforms of all of the audio modules. All of the waveform images were recorded by simulating a linear change in the pressure level: Increasing the pressure from 0 to 1 over a period of one second, pausing for 0.5 seconds, and finally releasing the pressure from 1 to 0 over a period of one second. The recordings vary in length because some modules have a much longer decay time and it takes more time for the sound to die out completely.

2.4.1 Event-Based

Modules 1 and 2 (Elastic 1 and Elastic 2) were designed to correspond to the real-world action of pressing on elastic material, which displaces when force is applied to it and goes back to its original shape when the force is released. This module resembles the friction grain model developed by Kildal in his 3D-Press experiment [5]. In Kildal's model, a number of small grains were overcome, mimicking the friction that displacement along the Z axis, if the material was compliant, would produce, as the force applied on the surface changed. Thus, the user would feel the friction as a pattern of discrete grains [5].

The audio synthesis had discreet steps, which were triggered when the pressure level increased or decreased by a set amount. If the pressure level was kept constant, there would be no audio feedback and the next grain of audio would be produced only after more or less pressure was applied. The pressure level also controlled the amplitude of the grains. The more pressure applied, the louder the sound was. The discreet steps or grains of audio were synthesized with a white noise generator that was split into three signals and each signal was filtered through a different bandpass filter. Finally, each of the signals was triggered with varying attack and decay times when the pressure level reached the next step or grain.

The attack time of Module 1 was 1 millisecond and the decay time was 30 ms, which produced very short discreet ticks or grains of sound. On Module 2, the attack time was the same, but the decay time was 240 ms. The frequencies of the bandpass filters of Module 2 were also higher, resulting in a sound with a higher pitch. These changes introduced a clear difference in the sound quality between the two modules.

The other two audio modules of the first category (Sand 1 and Sand 2) were designed to resemble the displacement of sand or other finely grained material. During the design process, this module was modeled to be the sound of pushing a finger into a pile of sand. When force is applied, the grains of sand start to fall over creating a sound of countless grains of sand moving at the same time. Similarly to the Elastic sounds, the sound synthesis would stop when you stop applying pressure. However, the decay of the sound was much longer, so the sound would continue playing for a small amount of time, much like the grains of sand would continue to roll until they lose their momentum. This model is of course a greatly simplified attempt to imitate the complexity of the movements of real sand, but was deemed to be interesting enough to be worth testing with users.

Modules 3 and 4 (Sand 1 and Sand 2) differ from each other by their filter and reverb parameters. The filtering frequency ranges of module 5 produce a lower-pitched sound compared to module 4 and the reverb effect is not as prominent. During the sound design process, this was thought to change the sound characteristics in a way that it resembled gravel or some other coarser type of sand.

2.4.2 Event-based with climax

Modules 5 and 6 (Bubble Wrap 1 and Bubble Wrap 2) were created to emulate the sound of popping bubble wrap. The event-based sound in the beginning of the pressure range was modeled to sound like the shuffling of a piece of light plastic. The sound increased in pitch and amplitude according to the pressure. Once the force increased over the threshold level (0.95), a synthesized sound of popping one bubble of a bubble wrap sheet was triggered. The differences between Modules 5 and 6 were mainly in the way the plastic shuffling noise behaved. The range of pitch change in the shuffling of Module 5 was larger and more consistent, while the pitch of Module 6 changed in a smaller scale.

Modules 7 and 8 (Mechanical Button 1 and Mechanical Button 2) were designed to resemble the way a mechanical button, such as the push-button of a ballpoint pen, would sound. These modules had two distinct sounds. The first part of the synthesis was the event-based part that was intended to resemble the sound of the friction from loading the spring of the button. The second part, or the climax part, was the button locking into place with a click. The friction or spring synthesis was created in an identical way to modules 1 and 2. Only the filtering and attack/decay parameters were changed so that the sound characteristic would be different from the first two modules. These settings also differed between modules 7 and 8. Additionally, the climax sounds were also different. Module 7 had a two-part click and Module 8 had a one-part click.

2.4.3 Continuous

Modules 9 and 10 (Motor and Wind) were designed to be distinctly different from the other audio modules for comparison purposes. They were intended to be controllers or triggers for creating sound without any strict connection to a real-world material that could be pushed with a finger. They provided continuous audio feedback as long as force was being applied to the sensor, and various parameters of the synthesis were affected by the force sensor value.

Module 9 was based on the Motor component from Andy Farnell's Delux Machine-o-Matic synthesizer [21]. This module has two distinct layers of sound that can be heard simultaneously: main motor sound and quieter brushing sound. The motor sound is synthesized by combining pulse width modulated bursts of noise with a frequency-modulated oscillator. The width of the pulses decreased and the pitch of the FM synth increased depending on the amount of force applied on the sensor making the motor sound like it was accelerating based on the pressure. The brushing sound is a combination of six white noise signals, each filtered through different bandpass filters. The amplitude of the brushing sound increased slightly when more force was applied. Both layers of sound also used inertia simulation, for imitating the sound of starting-up or shutting-down the motor.

The brushing noise from Module 9 was the basis for Audio Module 10. However, the inertia simulation was removed and the force sensor value was connected to control the bandpass filter frequency of each noise signal separately. This design created a sound that the sound designers described to resemble wind. The pitch of the wind would increase when more pressure was applied to the sensor.

3. RESULTS

As explained in the introduction, this qualitative user study was conducted to investigate how the audio synthesis modules enhanced the perceived physicality during force input on a rigid surface. Additionally, the question about possible audio-haptic cross modal integration was formulated, which would be assessed by observing if the haptic part of physicality was enhanced.

3.1 Analysis Method

Each interview was videotaped and the collected verbal descriptions of the 14 participants' experiences and feelings were transcribed with time code, and sorted. A thematic analysis [22] methodology was used to categorize and organize the body of terms and expressions collected. Following this method, we first read and familiarized with the transcribed descriptions. A list of ideas of interesting features, such as sonic properties, feelings, materials felt, metaphors, judgments, understanding comparisons and so on was generated for the coding process, which was done line by line. Once the data was coded and collated, we looked at the broader level of recurrent themes and patterns, and followed by grouping the codes and data into potential categories, which were reviewed and named. Section 3.2 details the five finalized categories.

The evaluative questions posed to the participants were deliberately open and exploratory, in order to identify which perceived features arose spontaneously and when. Thus, the descriptions provided were not initially expected to fit into any specific theme. Instead, the thematic categories were identified from analyzing the whole set of collected data.

3.2 Description Categories

With 14 participants and 10 audio synthesis modules each, a total of 140 descriptions were collected and grouped under 5 categories: (1) Characteristics of Sound, (2) Tactile Illusion, (3) Analytic Process, (4) Similarity, and (5) Personal Feelings. Figure 3 illustrates the summary of the results of these five categories with three sub-categorized types in Characteristics of Sound.

The description of each audio module provided by each participant might contain words and expressions associated with multiple categories. For example, one user provided the following description for audio module 9:

> "*Some mechanic machine I am controlling. I am kind of accelerating, not directly controlling the speed. There's this lag here. Giving it more force, then it starts rotating faster.*"

This description was counted as one description in this study analysis and it belonged to both category 1 (Characteristics of Sound) and category 3 (Analytic Process). The comment of "*some mechanic machine I am controlling*", described the perceived sound with a scenario, was grouped under category 1, and the rest of the comments showed that the participant was aware of the relationship between the amount of pressure level applied and the variation of sound, thus this description was also grouped under category 3.

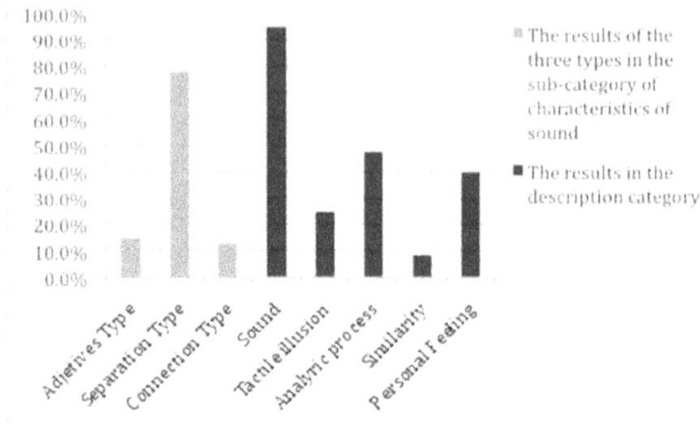

Figure 3. An overview of the results in five thematic categories.

3.2.1 Characteristics of Sound

As this study involved presenting audio feedback to the action of pressing, almost all participants provided detailed descriptions for each perceived sound. The analysis of transcriptions showed that 133 of the 140 (95%) descriptions contain words associated with description of sounds. Therefore, this category was sub-categorized into three types: adjective, separation and connection. Figure 4 illustrates the relationship between the Characteristics of Sound category and its sub-categories.

Some participants described the sound using adjectives. The participants used words such as artificial, organic, harsh and realistic, and these were grouped under the *adjective* type. Of the 133 sound descriptions, 21 contained adjectives. It can be noticed that 4 of the 14 participants provided two thirds of the adjectives, while the rest of the participants used them only occasionally or never. This may suggest that the sound nature of the experience was more prevalent for some participants than for others. It should be mentioned also that all sound modules received at some point adjectives describing the sound.

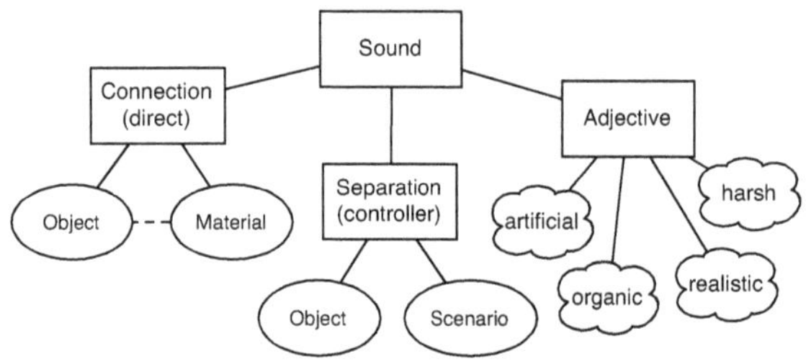

Figure 4. One of the main category from thematic analysis: Characteristics of Sound and its sub-categories.

The *separation* type referred to descriptions containing sonic metaphors that associated the pressing action with the sound produced. Many audio modules were described as a controller, such as a trigger of a drill, or as a sound event that occurred in a metaphorical scenario. For example, scratching a turntable, opening a window with strong wind blowing outside, and rewinding or fast-forwarding an old cassette tape. The scenario-based descriptions provided were often associated to participants' personal experiences and memories, described in the session as "it reminds me of the sound of sand", or "it sounds like water sprinkles on the stove in sauna". This type of description was the most frequent of all, and all participants used it when describing sound characteristics. It was accounted for 109 of the 133 sound descriptions recorded. This indicated that most participants focused on the direct relationship between the sound they hear and the source of the sound. Many of the descriptions in this type were perhaps slightly less interesting, however it was a consequence of the open methodology applied in this study, and it was discussed as being normal, an expected finding.

The *connection* type contained the descriptions that indicated direct link between the action of pressing and the sounds perceived. Participants often described the sound in relation to a kind of material (metal, plastic) or more specifically an object (metal spring, plastic box) that they were pressing. 18 of the 133 sonic characteristics descriptions referred to this connection type. Figure 5b illustrates that these 18 descriptions were distributed to 4 audio modules, which were module 1, 2, 7, and 8.

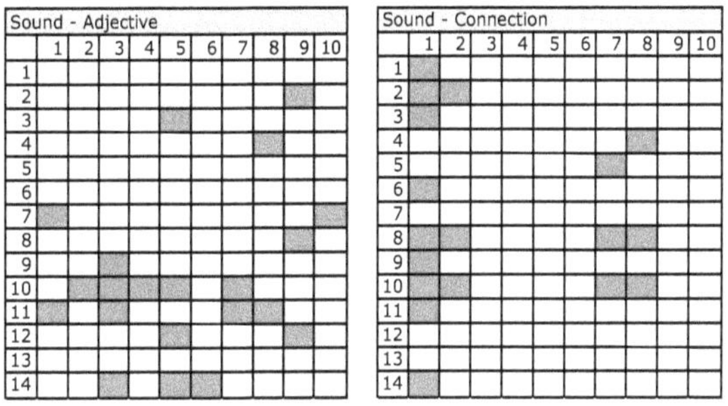

(a) (b)

Figure 5. Summary of results in the Characteristics of Sound category; (a) the occurrence of the adjective type; (b) the occurrence of connection type (columns are audio synthesis module 1-10 and rows are participants 1-14)

3.2.2 Tactile Illusion

25% of all descriptions were accounted in this category. The participants were able to associate certain audio modules with the tactile feel of pressing the 'user interface'. 7.9% of all descriptions, as shown in Figure 6a, revealed the experience of some physical sensation or tactile-related feelings when pressing on the green square. Some examples include:

1. [Module 8] "It fools me that there is a haptic feedback (that's what I think, but it's not really). It's a bit strange, because I hear haptic feedback but there is none."
2. [Module 1] "It feels like my finger is moving much more than in any other situation."

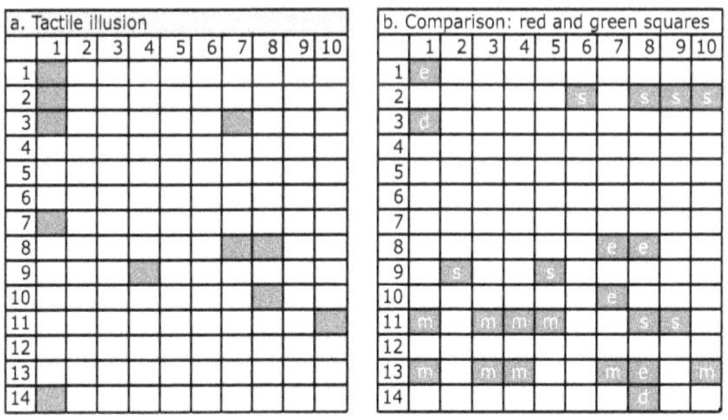

(a) (b)

Figure 6. Summary of results that descriptions containing tactile feel before or after posing a comparative question; (a) before; (b) after (columns are audio synthesis module 1-10 and rows are participants 1-14)

An addition of 24 comments (17.1%) regarding Tactile Illusion feelings were provided when the participants were asked to compare the feel of the red square (without audio feedback) and the green square (with audio feedback). These are shown in Figure 6b, where the letters indicate the type of tactile feeling reported by the participants (e: elasticity, d: depth, h: hardness, m: movement, s: softness).

3.2.3 Analytic Process

There were 67 of 140 descriptions (47.9%) accounted for this *Analytic Process* category. The participants expressed their awareness and understanding of the relationship between the amount of force applied and the sound variation. For example:

1. [Module 4] "This one works in a continuous mode more, so I can press it, and I hear a feedback about how much I press, but I don't get the separation of the steps anymore."
2. [Module 10] "The harder I press, the windier it gets."
3. [Module 6] "It's not continuous it kind of jumps also. There is some kind of threshold, if I press hard enough; I get this "tack", and sound stops there."

3.2.4 Similarity

8.6% of all descriptions were explained with reference to module comparison. As the order of presenting the modules of a family was randomized for each of the 14 participants, the term "previous" in the descriptions referred the module a participant had tried immediately previously, which could be any within a family of modules. Similarity comparisons were frequently mentioned in the pair of bubble wrap modules (module 5 & 6) - in total of 8 times by 8 participants. The following descriptions are examples of similarity references given by the participants.

1 [Module 5] "I think it's more or less the same as the previous one (#6). It's almost sound like the same. But this one there is something more fast going on."

2 [Module 6] "I can't tell the difference between this one and the previous one (#5)."

3 [Module 7] "Basically the same as previous (#8), but it sounds not more like metal, more like plastic. It's lighter, the steps in between are smaller."

3.2.5 Personal Feelings

Of all descriptions recorded, 40% included participants' expression of their personal and subjective judgments, desires and emotional feelings. These descriptions contrast with other descriptions provided with the clear intention to offer objective descriptions. Examples in this category include**:**

1. [Module 10] "I feel it's a very sensitive car, I like it."
2. [Module 2] "I feel like I am 5 years old again, it's nice."
3. [Module 7] "I wanted to hear the last bit. I wanted to end it at some point, because I thought it's too much time spending on this task, but I really wanted to hear the thing (climax sound), so I pressed it 2 times more."
4. [Module 9] "I can feel the happiness of a dentist."
5. [Module 4] "It's a disturbing one, somehow uncomfortable."

3.3 Participants' First Reactions

Collecting the first reaction from each participant exploring a module might inform particularly well about the most dominant nature of the aspects of physicality that were being conveyed. For this purpose, the first sentence of each description was analyzed separately. In every case, the first question after exploring a module was "*could you describe what is happening here*". The interpretation of this question varied from participant to participant, and so did the beginning of their responses. Once the participants were familiar with the experiment procedure, some descriptions were spontaneously volunteered before the experimenter asking any question. These initial descriptions provided, before and after first question was asked were considered as the participants' first reactions. It was interesting to notice that some participants' initial focus was on providing the overall experience of the pressing action and the sound heard, whereas others focused on explaining sonic characteristics. 83.6% of these initial descriptions included references to sound. For example:

1. [Module 1] "It has this dry sound when I press harder. Something like dry plastic."
2. [Module 4] "I think that might be the sound of wind, or somebody blowing into the microphone."
3. [Module 1] "Kind of matches with the plastic (box) I am pressing. Somehow dry."

In addition, 41.4% of the initial descriptions contained aspects of Analytic Process, 7.9% contained Similarity comparison, and tactile-related descriptions as well as personal feelings were both accounted for 6.4% of all initial descriptions.

4. DISCUSSION

The results of this user study showed that audio, as an interaction channel, can indeed enrich the perceived physicality of pressing on a rigid surface. As it was expected from the nature of the feedback, it was mostly the auditory expression of physicality that grew in richness. The variety of results in this category, as presented above, are prove of the range of characteristics that sound was able to evoke in the action of pressing. It is possible that some of the sound descriptions were intended for the sound itself and not as descriptions of qualities of the action of pressing. There is, however, evidence from the descriptions that these referred to the action of pressing as a whole and not to the sound that came out of the speaker only, such as with all the *connection* and *separation* descriptions. The sub-categories of sound descriptions, as summarized in section 3.2.1, answer the first research question (the way in which audio augmentation enriches physicality in the action of pressing).

With regard to the second research question, which referred to the particular case of enriched haptic physicality, the findings were significant and even surprising. One quarter of the descriptions referred to haptic aspects of the action that went beyond describing the rigid surface that the users could feel. The spectrum of richness in haptic physicality was narrower than the spectrum of auditory physicality. The evidence obtained referring the evoked haptic experience was striking but limited. Thus we were careful not to generalize these results. Still, it is of much interest to notice that the enrichment in haptic physicality was conveyed cross-modally. Users experienced the action of pressing with richer physical properties by combining the action of pressing with a variety of audio designs. Many of these properties were specifically tactile. Some of the properties described when comparing pressing on the green (augmented) and the red (not augmented) squares implied perceived displacement of the contact point with the surface. Thus, the green square was described as feeling softer, more elastic, and references to depth and sense of movement were collected. These characteristics are similar to some of the features in the haptic illusion of elasticity achieved with 3D-Press in [5]. However, the two studies are different in nature as in Kildal's [5] study, the feedback was tactile and the evoked experiences were haptic; where as in our study, the feedback was audio only and the evoked experiences were mostly about audio metaphors and emotional responses, but interestingly also haptic physicality, to a limited extent.

Explanations for such cross-modal integration can be found in the literature. Both sound and the mechanical vibration sensed with touch are similar in their rich temporal structures. At a neural basis, the brain processes both sound and vibration on the skin as transduction of movement into neural activation [23], so much so that vibrotactile input gets processed in the auditory cortex [24].

From a sound design perspective, the illusion of physical sensation was mostly mentioned for audio synthesis modules 1, 7 and 8, which were all created based on similar event-based synthesis techniques. The *Elastic* pair (Module 1 & 2) was designed with a real-world action of pressing elastic material in mind, and the nature of discrete steps in the he *Mechanical Button* pair (Module 7 & 8) was created similarly, with additional sound triggered when the pressure applied was over a threshold (climax point). These modules were also identified in the *Connection* type of the *Sound* category. This further suggests that discrete steps in sound associated to increments in the force level applied are an important element to achieve cross-modal integration.

Finally, it is worth highlighting the 40% of all descriptions that referred to subjective feelings This fact showed that, as expected, audio is a good vehicle to convey affective and emotional content to an otherwise neutral action, as is to press with a finger on a rigid surface.

5. CONCLUSIONS AND FUTURE WORK

Actively pressing with a finger on a rigid surface is the basis for force input in touch interaction, as we know it today. This paper has presented a study in which the authors investigate how the very plain physicality of this action could be enhanced using audio. Through a qualitative think-aloud method and later thematic analysis, determined the main characteristics of the enrichment in perceived physicality that the participants reported.

The results of the experiments confirmed that sound could increase the illusion of physicality beyond the perceptual baseline of pressing on a rigid surface. As expected, audio augmentation made the auditory part of perceived physicality richer, being this the main effect. This effect was stronger when participants perceived and recognized some form of real-world action. Thus, the feedback acted upon the types of physicality it was associated with. In addition, it was observed that audio augmentation invoked emotional responses in the users, also confirming this hypothesis brought from the sound design discipline.

One of the more interesting findings in the study was to observe clear indications of audio-tactile cross-modal integration. The experimental setup and stimuli had been designed to fulfill the rules of sensory integration so as to encourage that haptic physicality was enriched through cross-modal integration with sound. It was found that one quarter of the descriptions contained references to haptic experiences (both tactile and proprioceptive), which clearly transcended the actual haptic experience that the participants could perceive. In relation to earlier work with vibrotactile augmentation of similar actions, it was interesting to observe that in both cases the rigid surface was perceived to be compliant, with varying other mechanical properties. The study of the physical sensation can be centered upon any or all of the different interaction channels or modalities. The similarities found in both studies and the strengths of each approach, suggest that the next step in this line of research could be to combine both types of augmentation. This multimodal approach might render a realistic illusion of compliance refined by a rich gamut of perceived properties modeled through audio augmentation.

To conclude, multimodal augmentation of the action of pressing on a rigid surface is showing to be an effective way of increasing physicality of the action and even perceptually making the depth dimension tangible. Immediate applications for this approach can be found in improving the user experience, and possibly the performance, of interacting with force sensing touch surfaces.

6. ACKNOWLEDGMENTS

This research was a part of Human Emotional Interaction project funded by the Finnish Funding Agency for Technology and Innovation TEKES and steered by Nokia Research Center and the Academy of Finland (project 137646). We would also like to thank the volunteers who took part in the experiment.

7. REFERENCES

[1] Brewster, S.A. and Hughes, M. 2009. Pressure-based text entry for mobile devices. In *Proceedings of the 11th International Conference on Human-Computer Interaction with Mobile Devices and Services* ACM.

[2] Mccallum, D.C., Mak, E., Irani, P. and Subramanian, S. 2009. PressureText: pressure input for mobile phone text entry. In *Proceedings of the 27th international conference extended abstracts on Human factors in computing systems* ACM, 4519-4524.

[3] Wilson, G. and Brewster, S.A. 2010. Pressure-Based Menu Selection for Mobile Devices. In *Proc. MobileHCI 2010* ACM Press.

[4] Ramos, G., Boulos, M. and Balakrishnan, R. 2004. Pressure widgets. In *Proceedings of the SIGCHI conference on Human factors in computing systems* ACM.

[5] Kildal, J. 2010. 3D-Press: Haptic Illusion of Compliance when Pressing on a Rigid Surface. In *Proc. International Conference on Multimodal Interfaces (ICMI)* ACM.

[6] Bowman, D.A., Coquillart, S., Froehlich, B., Hirose, M., Kitamura, Y., Kiyokawa, K. and Stuerzlinger, W. 2008. 3D User Interfaces: New Directions and Perspectives. *IEEE Comput. Graph. Appl. 28*, 6, 20-36.

[7] Reeves, S. 2006. Physicality, spatial configuration and computational objects. In *Proc. First International Workshop on Physicality*.

[8] Büscher, M. 2006. Making the Digital Palpable. In *Proc. First International Workshop on Physicality*.

[9] Srinivasan, M.A. and Lamotte, R.H. 1995. Tactual discrimination of softness. *J Neurophysiol 73*, 1, 88-101.

[10] Kildal, J. 2011. Tangible 3D Haptics on Touch Surfaces: Virtual Compliance. In *ACM CHI* ACM Press, Vancouver, Canada.

[11] Blattner, M. M., Sumikawa, D. A. and Greenberg R. M. 1989. Earcons and icons: their structure and common design principles. *Human-Computer Interaction 4*, 11-44.

[12] Tahiroğlu, K. and Ahmaniemi, T. 2010. Vocal Sketching: a Prototype Tool for Designing Multimodal Interaction. In *Proceedings of the 4th International Conference on Multimodal Interfaces and Workshop on Machine Learning for Multimodal Interaction ICMI-MLMI '10*. Beijing, China.

[13] Chang, A. and O'Sullivan, C. 2005. Audio-Haptic Feedback in Mobile Phones. *In Proceedings of CHI 2005*. Portland, Oregon, USA.

[14] M.T. Marshall, M.T. and Wanderley, M.M. 2006. Vibrotactile Feedback in Digital Musical Instruments. *In Proceedings of Conference New Interfaces for Musical Expression*. Paris, France.

[15] Andresen, M. B. and Kristian R. K. 2010. The LapSlapper - Feel the Beat. In Proceedings of the 4th International Conference on Haptic and Audio Interaction Design, HAID '10. Copenhagen, Denmark.

[16] Havryliv, M., Geiger, F. Guertler, M., Naghdy, F., Schiemer, G. 2009. The Carillon and Its Haptic Signature: Modeling the Changing Force-Feedback Constraints of a Musical Instrument for Haptic Display. *In Proceedings of the 4th International Conference on Haptic and Audio Interaction Design, HAID '09*. Dresden, Germany.

[17] Hoggan, E, Crossan, A, Brewster, S.A. and Kaaresoja, T. Audio or Tactile Feedback: Which Modality When? *In Proceedings of ACM CHI2009* ACM Press, Boston, USA.

[18] Lee, J., Poliakoff, E., Spence, C. 2009. The Effect of Multimodal Feedback Presented via a Touch Screen on the Performance of Older Adults. *In Proceedings of the 4th International Conference on Haptic and Audio Interaction Design, HAID '09*. Dresden, Germany.

[19] Altinsoy, E. M. and Merchel, S. 2009. Audiotactile Feedback Design for Touch Screens. *In Proceedings of the 4th International Conference on Haptic and Audio Interaction Design, HAID '09*. Dresden, Germany.

[20] Holmes, N.P. and Spence, C. 2005. Multisensory Integration: Space, Time and Superadditivity. *Current Biology 15*, 18, R762-R764.

[21] Farnell, A. (N.D.). Machine-o-Matic. Retrieved 6 May 2011. http://obiwannabe.co.uk/html/toys/machineomatic/machine-o-matic.html

[22] Braun, V. and Clarke, V. 2006. Using thematic analysis in psychology. *Qualitative Research in Psychology 3*, 2, 77-101.

[23] Schürmann, M. 2010. Multimodal Interactions: Tactile-Auditory. In *Encyclopedia of Perception*, E.B. Goldstein Ed. SAGE, 592-593

[24] Caetano, G. and Jousmäki, V. 2006. Evidence of vibrotactile input to human auditory cortex. *NeuroImage 29*, 1, 15-28

BeeParking: An Ambient Display to Induce Cooperative Parking Behavior

Silvia Gabrielli, Rosa Maimone, Michele Marchesoni, Jesús Muñoz
Ubiquitous Interaction Group, CREATE-NET
Via Alla Cascata 56/D – 38123 Trento - Italy
Phone: +39 0461 408400 ext.703
name.surname@create-net.org

ABSTRACT
Interactive ambient systems offer a great potential for attracting user attention, raising awareness and supporting the acquisition of more desirable behaviors in the shared use of limited resources, like physical or digital spaces, energy, water and so on. In this paper we describe the iterative design of BeeParking, an ambient display and automatic notification system aimed to induce more cooperative use of a parking facility within a work environment. We also report main findings from a longitudinal in-situ evaluation showing how the system was adopted and how it affected users' parking behavior over time.

Categories and Subject Descriptors
H5.m. Information interfaces and presentation (e.g., HCI): User Interfaces, Prototyping.

General Terms
Design, Experimentation.

Keywords
Ubiquitous Computing, Feedback Interfaces, Ambient Displays, Persuasive Computing, Behavior Change.

1. INTRODUCTION
Ubiquitous Computing technology has opened up several possibilities for improving human-human and human-computer interaction in daily living and working practices. Also, novel ambient systems and feedback interfaces have been designed with the aim of inducing more desirable human behaviors, both at individual and collective level, as in the area of sustainable consumption [2, 3, 4]. More work is needed in order to understand how to induce more cooperative behaviors when people are using common resources like public goods, spaces, facilities in the physical or digital world [5, 7], since this could bring important benefits to collectivity. However, as it is difficult to find clear design standards that can guide the development of effective interventions for complex, real-life situations, a possible solution is to conduct precise design cases and learn from these experiences how to cope with the challenges presented [6].

ICMI 2011, November 14–18, 2011, Alicante, Spain.

In this paper, we present as a case study the iterative design of BeeParking, a physical ambient display and notification system aimed to encourage more effective and cooperative use of limited parking spaces in a work environment. We first introduce the main motivation of our study; then we describe the design of the BeeParking prototype and some main results of its deployment in the field over several weeks of usage. Finally, we conclude the paper by summarizing the main contribution provided by this design experience and our future steps.

2. BEEPARKING STUDY
We designed the BeeParking feedback interface as part of an exploratory study whose main goals were to: 1) better understand which role a feedback display could play to improve the daily car parking routines of a group of employees, sharing a same but undersized parking area, 2) identify key requirements and features of the tool designed to best inducing an evolution of cooperation processes among participants, across the typical behavior change phases of raising awareness, inducing more desirable behaviours and sustaining them in the long term.

In the early stages of this study we conducted qualitative in-situ observations to better understand the daily parking routines of employees working in three different departments of a research centre (about 60 people in total). From anedoctal interviews with employees and direct observations in the parking area it was clear that there was a peak of car arrivals in the garage each morning from 9.30 to noon. Due to the limited space available and the particular parking slots configuration, each day at least 10 cars had to be parked irregularly in the central corridor, often obstructing emergency exits or other regularly parked cars. Most of the interviewees reported to find the current parking situation very stressful; some had come up with the solution of arriving at work earlier in the morning and to avoid moving their car over lunch break for the fear of not finding any parking space available then. The building receptionists had pinned up on walls several warnings, inviting drivers who had parked irregularly to leave a note on their car with contacts details. Very few people did so, and this was causing further inconvenience in the shared use of the parking facility.

2.1 The BeeParking Ambient Display
We conducted brainstorming sessions to come up with ideas for the design of a new feedback technology solution able to promote more cooperative behavior among colleagues in the use of the parking area. We were aware of the importance of finding a solution that would be well accepted by users from both a functional and an aesthetic point of view.

The concept eventually chosen was based on the zoomorphic metaphor [1] of bees-beehive, since bees communities are generally held in high regard for their social nature and reputation for diligence (their organization has often been proposed as an ideal model for human society). Beelike plastic keys, each enhanced with an iButton chip[1], were planned to be assigned to the users of the parking facility as identification devices. A beehive-like feedback interface, located at the building entrance, was meant to enable a user who had been compelled to park irregularly and block someone else car, to automatically notify the driver of the obstructed car (Figure 1).

Employees passing by the interface on their way to coffee breaks or other transfers might have the chance of getting a cue on the current situation in the parking area.

Figure 1: A participant notifying a car block through the Beeparking display

2.2 The BeeParking HW/SW Architecture

To meet the technical requirements, we considered the opportunity of using different identification devices, such as RFID, magnetic strips, bar codes or smart cards. Finally, we decided to use iButtons technology (Figure 2) because it allows to connect multiple probes, and to potentially scale up the system components in order to meet future needs.

iButton is a small and portable identification device. The information stored can be read by a host system (a computer or embedded system) simply by touching a probe with the iButton. For our application we have used an iButton with a factory-lasered number of 64bits on a Read Only Memory (ROM), which works like as an electronic serial number that is never duplicated. In previous studies this type of identification technology has been deployed to develop novel tangible surface concepts [6, 8, 10].

In BeeParking the beehive-like display consists of 24 iButton probes, each probe placed at the center of a beehive cell, representing the number assigned to a colleague's car (Figure 3). Each iButton identifies a user, whilst a beehive's cell identifies a car. Each probe contains a led in order to provide a clear visual feedback when it is activated. If the led is on, it means that the car identified by this cell has been blocked by another car, otherwise its led is off.

[1] http://www.maxim-ic.com/products/ibutton/

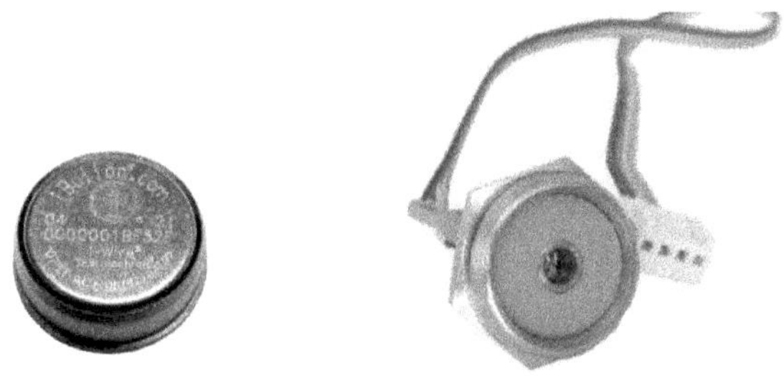

Figure 2: The iButton identification device (left), and a probe with led (right)

A dedicated beehive cell (labeled "Exit") is used to notify the end of a block, as when the author of the block leaves the office and removes his car from the irregular position in the garage.

The BeeParking back-end consists of a server and a database which track the situation in the parking area, notifying all persons affected by car obstructions or end of obstructions. When somebody slides his iButton into a probe, the system reads this information and sends it to the server (Figure 4). The database is updated and an email notification is delivered to both the author and recipient of an obstruction, informing about its occurrence and exchanging relevant contact details among the interested parties. Furthermore, the server sends a command for switching on or off the cell led. A similar process occurs when a user leaves the parking facility, unblocking a car.

In brief, the embedded system communicates with the server for updating the database, and the server communicates with the embedded system for updating the led(s) status.

We used the Arduino microcontroller board, to quickly set up a running BeeParking prototype. To easily install the BeeParking ambient display on a visible position at the building entrance, a Bluetooth connection has been deployed, by simply connecting a Bluetooth radio module to the Arduino board.

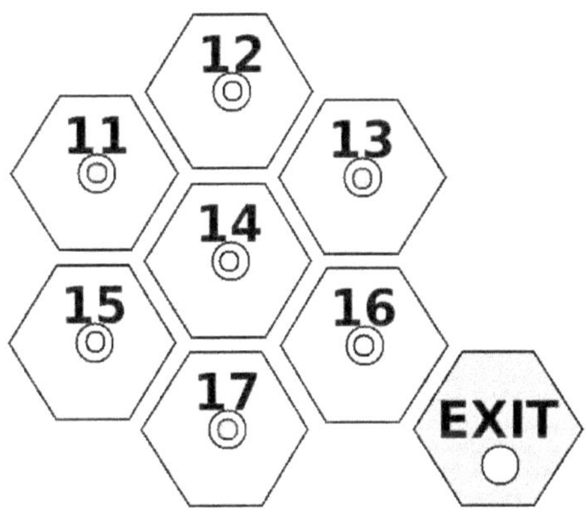

Figure 3: The beehive-like ambient display diagram

The BeeParking experimentation has involved 24 colleagues at the research centre. To set up all the 24 probes required on the display we designed a printed circuit board (PCB), by expanding the input/output ports of the Arduino. Each PCB allows to connect 8 iButtons probes with their correspondent leds. For the experimentation we used 3 PCB, but in the future we can potentially add new ones to expand the number of users. Each PCB board has 2 integrated circuits: an 8-bit register to individually control the probes led and a 3:8 decoder to manage the probes. The decoder selects only one probe at a time (connecting the probe's ground pin to LOW level) if an iButton is put in contact with that specific probe. The Arduino will read the 64-bit registration number set on the decoder.

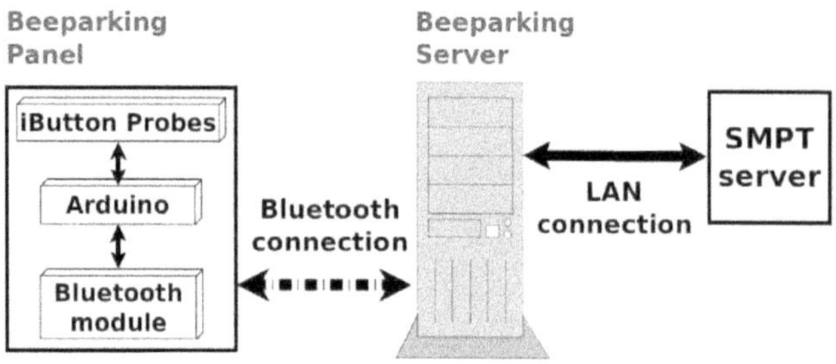

Figure 4: The BeeParking system diagram

We decided to proceed with a rapid prototyping of this concept and quickly start deploying and testing it in situ with an initial group of 24 colleagues who had promptly answered to our invitation.

The main objective of deploying this mid-tech prototype in the field was to start collecting longitudinal feedback from users, through observations, weekly interviews and log data, on the way this ambient display was able to support a change in the daily parking routines of participants, and the evolution of cooperation mechanisms over time.

The longitudinal evaluation set up was also meant to provide insights on how to extend the BeeParking features, increase their efficacy and derive further design implications for feedback technology to support behavior change. BeeParking has been in usage for evaluation purposes for about 15 weeks. Below we provide a brief report of the main findings derived from our analysis of the log data (amount and type of blocks notified), from weekly interviews and participant observations collected over the system usage, which were useful to understand how the system was adopted and to uncover possible directions for its further development.

2.3 Initial Adoption Challenges

Of the 172 blocks found in the system logs we analyzed which pairs of participants were involved and day/time of each block/unblock to derive typical variations in BeeParking usage patterns over the 15 weeks.

In the first two weeks of the study, four participants stood out for behaving like early adopters, showing full trust and enthusiasm for the features offered by the new system. They used to park their car in such a way to leave some space available for possible irregular parking by colleagues, placing the number assigned to their car in highly visible positions on the car's window (so as to facilitate possible obstructions). By contrast, the remaining participants adopted a strategy that could be described as an attempt to take advantage of the potential benefits offered by BeeParking, while trying to reduce as far as possible any eventuality of paying a cost. They were happy to use the system in case of need (irregular parking), but in the other cases preferred to keep somehow hidden their car number (thus discouraging any potential block by other drivers). When interviewed for explanation of this behavior some participants mentioned concerns regarding the possible need of leaving the building in a hurry and having troubles in resolving a block situation. As expected, over the first two weeks most of the blocks notified occurred between the same pairs of colleagues, mainly participants sharing the same office or office floor. Reciprocity was a main motivator of system use at this stage, with pairs of colleagues arranging to swap parking space in the garage (e.g., after lunch break) by using the BeeParking notification mails. Also, the early adopters played an important role in stimulating the other participants to act more cooperatively (e.g., by inviting them to stick their car number in a more visible position in the car window).

2.4 Long Term Effects of System's Deployment

In the later weeks of the experimentation the system logs showed a larger number of participants using BeeParking, with a wider mix of people involved in the daily obstructions notified through the system. We also observed an increase of gossiping activity around the system (e.g., by means of jokes, comments made by participants and other colleagues at lunch break, near the BeeParking display or in their offices) mostly centered on reporting novel effects of the system introduction on parking habits of the facility's users. Attention was paid on learning who was using the system in a proper and altruistic way, as well as who was not. Several participants put some effort on trying to learn/guess the correct matching between BeeParking car numbers and their correspondent owners (some said to better inform their choices on who to block once more alternatives were available in the garage). During the inteviews some participants said there was an amusing aspect in using BeeParking: it offered a further excuse for having some chats with colleagues working in different building areas with whom they rarely had the opportunity to interact (e.g., newcomers). More generally, there was a main emotional benefit provided by the system to users. It had contributed to turn the blocking behavior, mostly experienced as individually stressful and unfair to others (e.g., associated to negative feelings such as wasting of time for parking, late arrival, sense of guilt, etc.) into a more socially acceptable and shared behavior, now regulated by the BeeParking system/community rules.

Qualitative findings from our study interviews showed that BeeParking had a behavior change effect also on some colleagues not involved in the experimentation: once they blocked a car with the BeeParking number, instead of leaving their business card with contacts on the car window, as was usual before, they preferred to look for the car driver's name (e.g., by asking to participants or system support guys) reach his office and notify the block in person. Early notification of obstructions by blockers (through any available means) is becoming the standard rule followed by colleagues of the research centre, thanks to the BeeParking intervention and the way it raised discussions (including gossiping) around parking behavior in the facility.

As observed in previous studies [9], we realized that the aesthetics and methaphorical qualities of our feedback interface were effective means for attracting interest and further participation in the system usage.

Some participants developed a strong commitment towards BeeParking, showing signs of personalized use and appropriation of the materials delivered (e.g., attaching original neck strings to bee-keys and car numbers), as well as creative thinking and reflection over its features refinement (e.g., by asking to make the system accessible also from smarphone applications, through QR Code technology).

3. CONCLUSION AND FUTURE WORK

Ubiquitous Interaction systems and ambient displays can provide valuable solutions to support more sustainable behaviors and improve the collective use of shared resources in our society.

This paper has provided insights on how to approach the empirical design of these solutions and build on results of their direct experimentation in the field.

The iterative design of BeeParking and analysis presented has shown how knowledge about the evolution of user adoption and cooperation mechanisms, can inform the design of ambient displays from a functional and form factor perspective, as well as support longitudinal analyses of behavior change at individual and group level.

As current work, we are extending multimodal access to the BeeParking system by providing users with alternative versions of the interactive board made available on mobile and web interfaces (Figure 5), that will be demonstrated at the conference.

This additional work will also be integrated into our longitudinal evaluation, by analyzing any user preference and effects of interacting with BeeParking system through different modalities and interfaces.

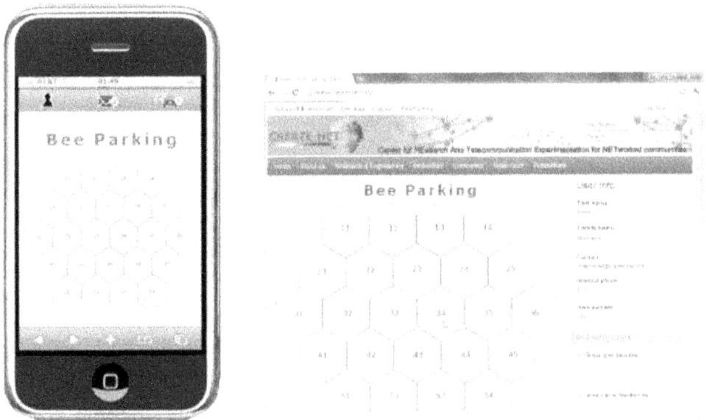

Figure 5: Screenshots of BeeParking mobile and web interface

4. ACKNOWLEDGMENTS

We are grateful to Cristina Costa and Alessandra Sabatino for the support provided during the BeeParking development and experimentation.

5. REFERENCES

[1]. Bush, D.J. Body Icons and Product Semantics. In Vihma, Susann (Ed.) *Semantic Visions in Design.* Helsinki, Finland: University of Art and Design Helsinki Press. 1990.

[2]. Fogg, B.J. *Persuasive Technology: Using Computers to Change What We Think and Do.* Morgan Kaufmann Publishers, San Francisco, CA, 2003.

[3]. Froehlich, J., Findlater, L., Landay, J..The Design of Eco-Feedback Technology. *Proc. CHI'10*, 2010, 1999-2008.

[4]. Goldstein, N., Cialdini, R., Griskevicius, R. A Room with a Viewpoint: Using Social Norms to Motivate Environmental Conservation in Hotels. *J. of Consumer Research 35*, 2008, 472-482.

[5]. Lakhani, K. R., & von Hippel, E. How open source software works: "Free" user-to-user assistance. *Research Policy*, *32*(6), 2003, 923-943.

[6]. Ljungblad, S., Hakansson, M., and Holmquist, L.E., Ubicomp challenges in collaborative scheduling: Pin & Play at the Gothenberg Film Festival. *Personal and Ubiquitous Computing*, 11 (7), (2007), 563--575.

[7]. Mankoff, J., Matthews, D., Fussell, Susan, R. Johnson, M. Leveraging social networks to motivate individuals to reduce their ecological footprints. *Proc. HICSS'07*, 2007, 87-96.

[8]. Pedersen, E., Sokoler , T., Nelson, L. PaperButtons: expanding a tangible user interface. *Proceedings of the conference on Designing interactive systems: processes, practices, methods, and techniques*, 216-223, August 17-19, 2000, New York City, New York, United States DOI=http://doi.acm.org/10.1145/347642.347723

[9]. Riche, Y., Dodge, J., Metoyer, R.A. Studying Always-On Electricity Feedback in the Home. *Proc. CHI'10*, 2010, 1995-1998.

[10]. Svanaes, D., Verplank, W. In search of metaphors for tangible user intefaces, *Proceedings of DARE 2000 on Designing augmented reality environments*, 121-129, April 2000, Elsinore, Denmark DOI=http//dx.doi.org/10.1145/354666.354679

Speech Interaction in a Multimodal Tool for Handwritten Text Transcription

María José Castro-Bleda and Salvador España-Boquera
Dep. de Sistemas Informáticos y Computación, Universitat Politècnica de València
Valencia, Spain
mcastro@dsic.upv.es, sespana@dsic.upv.es

David Llorens and Andrés Marzal
Institute of New Imaging Technologies, Universitat Jaume I
Castelló, Spain
dllorens@lsi.uji.es, amarzal@lsi.uji.es

Federico Prat
Dep. de Lenguajes y Sistemas Informáticos, Universitat Jaume I
Castelló, Spain
fprat@lsi.uji.es

Juan Miguel Vilar
Institute of New Imaging Technologies, Universitat Jaume I
Castelló, Spain
jvilar@lsi.uji.es

Francisco Zamora-Martínez
Dep. de Ciencias Físicas, Matemáticas y de la Computación, Universidad CEU-Cardenal Herrera
Alfara del Patriarca, Valencia, Spain
fzamora@dsic.upv.es

ABSTRACT

STATE is a multimodal tool for document processing and text transcription. Its graphical front-end can be easily connected to different text recognition back-ends. New features and improvements are presented in this work: the interactive correction of one word in the transcribed line has been improved to reestimate the entire transcription line using the user feedback and speech input has been integrated in the multimodal interface enabling the user to also utter the word to be corrected, giving the user the possibility to use the interface according to her preferences or the task at hand. Thus, at the current version of STATE, the user can type, write on the screen with a stylus, or utter the incorrectly recognized word, and then, the system uses the user feedback in any of the proposed modalities to reestimate the transcribed line so as to hopefully correct other errors which could be caused by the mistaken word the user has corrected.

Categories and Subject Descriptors

H.5.2 [**User Interfaces**]: Input devices and strategies; I.7.5 [**Document Capture**]: Optical character recognition (OCR); J.5 [**Arts and Humanities**]: Literature-Ancient document transcription

General Terms

Documentation, Human factors

ICMI'11, November 14–18, 2011, Alicante, Spain.

Keywords

Multimodality, Interactive pattern recognition, Computer assisted transcription, Handwriting text recognition, Ancient documents, Speech recognition

1. INTRODUCTION

The main libraries and document archives are digitizing their collections. Most of them are scanning the documents and publishing the resulting images without their corresponding transcriptions. This seriously limits the usefulness of this digitizing efforts as tasks as simple as textual searches are impossible using only the images. Although the performance of conventional Optical Character Recognition (OCR) systems is sufficient for modern printed documents, it is very poor on ancient or handwritten documents. Thus, when a high quality transcription is required, it has to be manually obtained or at least validated and corrected by experts, resulting in a very expensive, time consuming, and error-prone task. The use of assisted transcription tools, which integrate specialized OCR or handwritten text recognition (HTR) engines able to take into account the user feedback, is very helpful to reduce the human effort.

The STATE system [2, 4, 8] has been designed from the perspective that automatic recognition cannot be perfect on handwritten or ancient printed documents and human help will be required in order to transcribe them accurately. It has been designed as a multimodal tool for assisted document processing and text transcription, which intends to improve the existing printed and HTR systems by enabling the adaptation to particularities of each book or period style in a very flexible way: it is very easy to learn new glyphs, new lexicons, new language models and so on. Moreover, in the current version of STATE, the recognition systems for online handwritten characters and continuous offline handwritten text are leaders in performance at international level [6, 9, 1].

In previous versions of the STATE system, the user could introduce text in the STATE system by typing it or by writing it directly

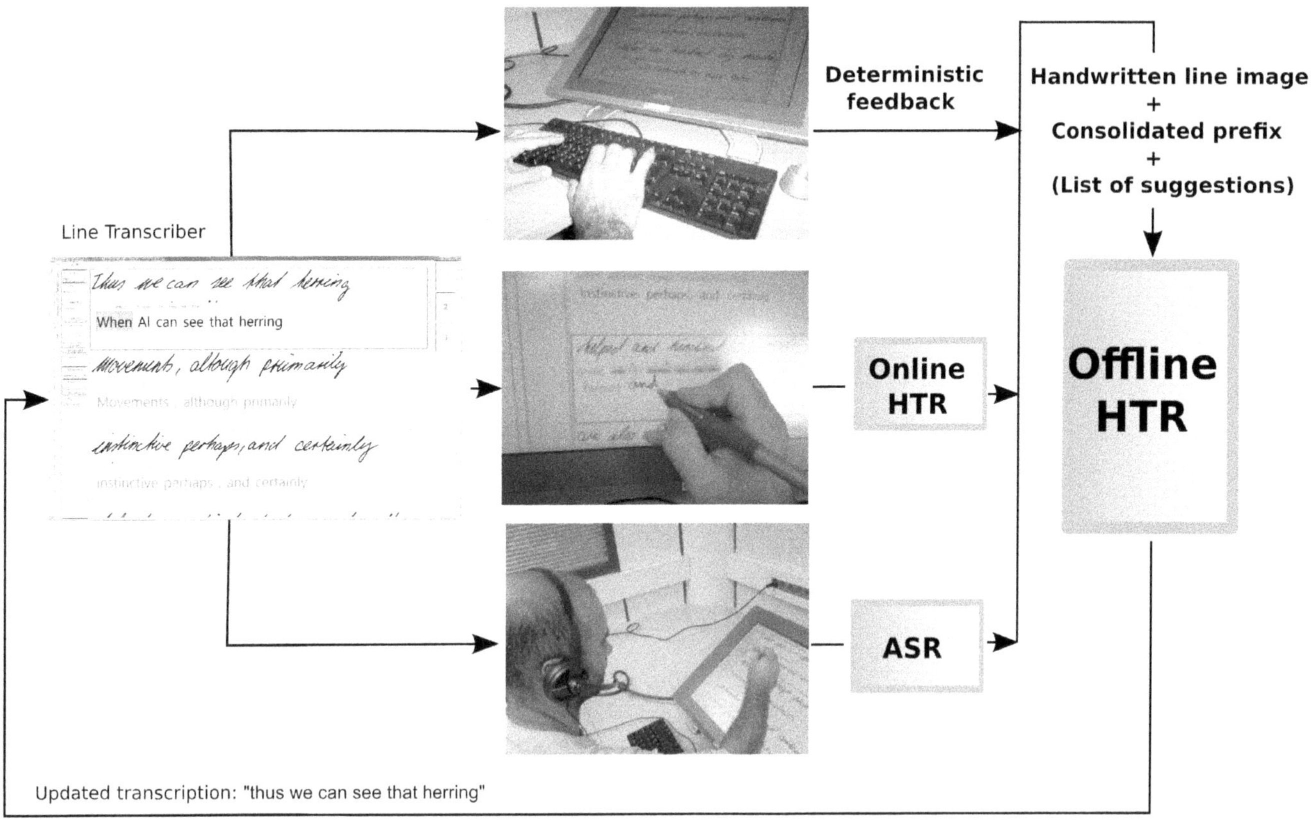

Figure 1: User-interaction cycle with STATE via keyboard, stylus, or voice.

on the screen using a stylus. The version presented in this work allows the use of speech to correct a word (as is done in other platforms [3]) in addition to the keyboard and the stylus.

An interactive feedback has also been added into the current version of STATE: when the user finds a mistake, the incorrectly transcribed word is corrected. Usually, the presence of a transcription mistake is followed by more transcription errors since the search has been guided by a wrong word history thereafter. This is the reason why reruning the HTR system with the updated information might also recover these mistakes and, hopefully, reduce the number of errors in the same line. To do so, the HTR system is fed with the consolidated prefix (the part of the transcribed line just before the wrong word), the suggested correction candidate(s), and the task language model. The cycle starts again when the user marks another error at the same line, page or document. Figure 1 outlines a user-interaction cycle with STATE via keyboard, stylus, or voice.

We have developed the platform in close collaboration with historians and document archive institutions, paying special attention to their suggestions and having in mind the possibility of using multimodal interfaces which can reduce the effort necessary to interactively correct transcription errors. The freedom of the user to change the input entry methods (typing, writing with a stylus, or speaking) may help to adapt to different user preferences, to reduce the fatigue and to increment the productivity.

2. SYSTEM OVERVIEW

STATE is a flexible system that comprises a graphical front-end that can be easily connected to different text recognition back-ends. This flexibility arises from the way the connection is achieved: the front-end and the back-end are separate processes, possibly in different machines, that communicate via web services.

The front-end of STATE is designed to work with projects. The user selects one project and can open simultaneously as many different pages as desired. For each page, a pipeline of three stages is built: the Image Conditioner, the Layout Manager, and the Line Transcriber (see some screenshots in Figure 2). These stages are accessible through the tabs on the left of the window. The tabs on the top correspond to the pages currently open. On right, a series of thumbnails gives access to all the pages of the document. The tab named "Main" is used to control the overall aspects of the project and the application. The order of the stage tabs is designed after the order of usual workflow on a page: first, the page is conditioned (a set of image processing tools are applied to it); then, its layout is detected; finally, each line in the page is transcribed.

The Image Conditioner and the Layout Manager offer a similar interaction behavior: both show a view of the page and let the user act on it by executing commands. The Image Conditioner offers commands to remove noise and to enhance the text in the image. The Layout Manager offers commands to automatically detect and to interactively edit the layout (lines, columns, and text flows). Finally, the Line Transcriber allows the user to obtain transcriptions of the lines using a recognition engine and to interactively correct these transcriptions. A detailed description of each part can be found in previous communications [2, 4, 8].

3. MULTIMODAL TRANSCRIPTION

The Line Transcriber handles pen, keyboard, mouse, and speech input. It can be comfortably used with a Tablet PC, digitizing tablet, pen-sensitive screen, or microphone. Figure 2 shows the GUI of

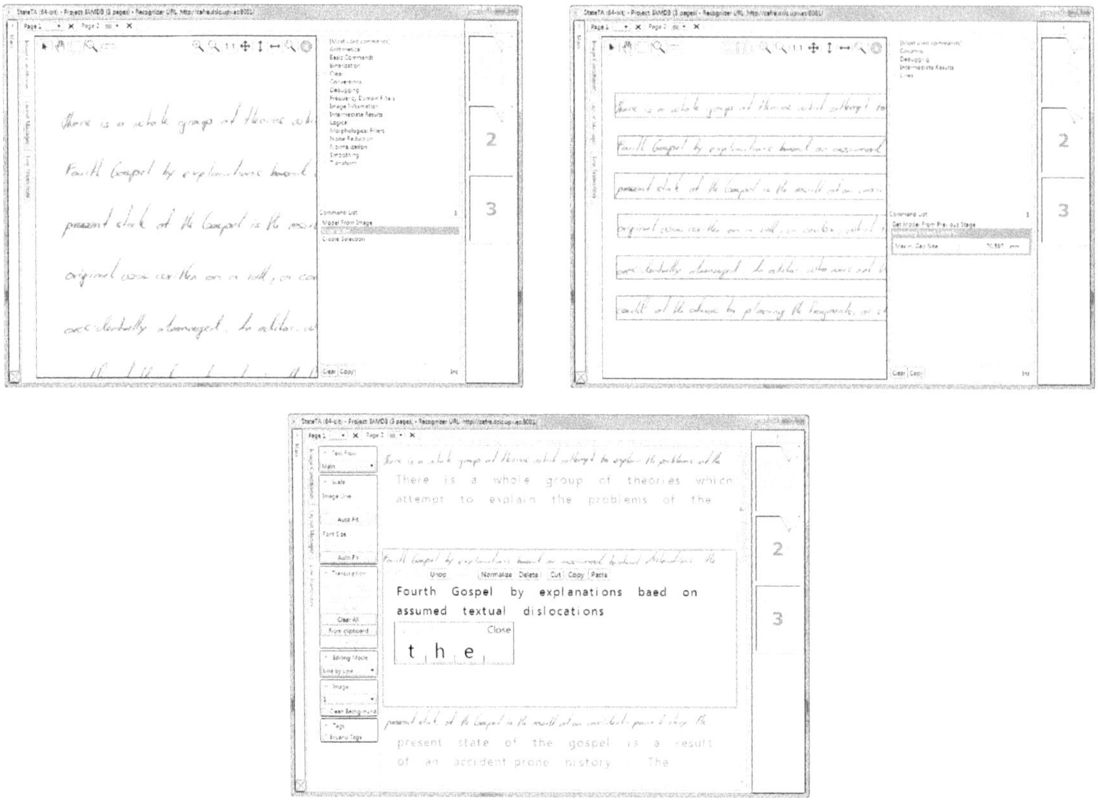

Figure 2: An overview of STATE. Top row: Image Conditioner and Layout Manager; bottom row: Line Transcriber.

the Line Transcriber. It gives access to the transcription of the lines corresponding to a text flow. The lines can be presented isolated as seen on the figure or in the context of the image of the page. In either case, an initial version of the transcriptions can be obtained from the recognition engine. When corrections are needed, the user can directly type them, write them with a stylus, or utter the correct word (see Figure 1). Moreover, the samples (line images and their corresponding transcriptions) that have been validated can be used by the system to adaptively improve the recognition engine.

Checking the transcriptions is quick and easy when the Line Transcriber shows the text transcriptions under the graphical view of each line (Figure 2). The user has at her disposal different ways of correcting the transcription:

1. Direct writing over the transcription is handled by capturing electronic ink and feeding it to the recognition engine[1]. The text or gestures so recognized are integrated in the transcription.

2. For single character corrections, the user can employ our own pen input panel which handles gestures and ink. The Microsoft Ink Input panel from the .NET 3.5 platform could have been used, but we decided to build our own online isolated character recognition engine and input widget for the sake of flexibility and extensibility. Some fonts, like those in ancient documents, include glyphs which are not recognized by standard online handwritten text recognizers. Our pen-input panel can be adaptively trained enriching its training set with these new symbols. A detailed description of this recognition engine can be found in [6].

3. To add the speech correction feature, we have used the standard Automatic Speech Recognition (ASR) provided by Microsoft. Using a stylus or a mouse, the user can mark the incorrect transcribed word. After that, using a microphone, the user utters the correct transcription and the ASR system recognizes it, returning an N-best list of the best candidates, along with a confidence value. The HTR system receives via web service the whole text line image and optionally the user feedback information which comprises the consolidated prefix and the information relating the corrected word (which, in case of being corrected by speech or by stylus may also include scores or confidence measures about the recognition hypotheses) so the HTR system will propose an improved transcription as described later in more detail.

4. Pen-based input is appropriate when the user is checking a transcription and must correct a few errors, but it can be tiresome if the user must provide a full transcription or there are many errors in the automatic transcription. To help in these cases, the user can use the keyboard or the mouse to move a cursor, navigate from line to line, and also type, copy or paste text, etc.

4. INTERACTIVE HTR

In this work, a particular case of multimodal interaction is proposed where only one word is corrected by means of keyboard, stylus, or speech at each user-interaction, and where that correction influences on the rest of the line.

[1]Standard recognition engine provided by Windows has been used in this part.

The front-end communicates with a back-end recognition engine in order to find the transcription of a line image. This communication is performed by means of a web service described in [8]. The current version of STATE has two recognition systems: one based on Nearest Neighbor Search that has proven useful for ancient printed fonts [2] and another recognition system based on Hidden Markov Models hybridized with Artificial Neural Networks (HMM/ANN) or conventional Hidden Markov Models (HMMs) for unconstrained offline handwritten text [1, 9].

The HMM decoder has been adapted in order to deal with the assisted transcription paradigm and the web service message to communicate with it has been extended. After a sentence has been corrected, there is a prefix (we call it the *consolidated prefix*), that is considered correct. The idea is that the message sent to the decoder includes the image of the line together with this consolidated prefix. How do we decide which is this prefix? In general, we assume that the cursor position indicates that the words up to and including the cursor position are correct. This way, the user can validate a prefix of any length. For the case of speech input we have introduced a slight variation: the consolidated prefix extends to the word prior to the corrected word and the decoder receives the prefix together with information from the ASR engine. This information comprises the most probable word together with a list of alternatives and their confidences. This approach allows the synergistic use of two input modalities, audio and image.

The integration of these feedback features into our HTR decoder is done in a *language model agnostic* way, that is, there is no adaptation of an n-gram language model so as to cope with the consolidated prefix as proposed in [7]. Instead, the consolidated prefix is used by the decoder to force the system to transitate by this prefix path during the first stage of recognition, but the language model probabilities are computed as usual. When available, the confidence measures provided by the ASR are combined with the probability corresponding to the image. In this way, any type of language model such as a combination of several NNLMs as done in [9] can also be transparently used with this method.

5. OUTLINE OF THE DEMONSTRATION

In order to show the proposed speech interactive feature, we have recorded a video (which can be found in the Videos page of the HI-TITA project official website `http://hitita.uji.es`) showing the STATE system when working in an unrestricted handwritten task from the IAM database [5]. In the demonstration, the user loads and prepares a project to be transcribed, and it can be seen some examples of how to interactively correct the transcription by keyboard, stylus, or speech.

6. CONCLUSIONS

We have presented the current version of the STATE system for assisted transcription of handwritten documents which incorporates an interactive interface for correcting errors in transcriptions. A lot of effort has been put in usability aspects and the application can be controled with mouse, keyboard, stylus, and speech.

The design of the interface and its adaptability to new fonts and writing styles allow a great reduction of the transcription effort. Moreover, STATE is currently in use by different institutions and companies and the feedback from real users (historians and document archive institutions) is very positive and valuable to improve the current version of the STATE system, taking special attention to the ergonomics of the final system, incorporating multimodal interfaces that can reduce the effort necessary to correct transcription errors and can allow to change the interface (typing, writing with a stylus, or speaking) to reduce fatigue or to follow the preference of the human transcriber, incrementing productivity.

7. ACKNOWLEDGMENTS

Work partially supported by the Spanish Government (TIN2010-18958 and *Consolider Ingenio 2010* CSD2007-00018), the Generalitat Valenciana (*Prometeo*/2010/028), and *Fundació Caixa Castelló-Bancaixa* (P11B2009-48).

8. REFERENCES

[1] S. España-Boquera, M. J. Castro-Bleda, J. Gorbe-Moya, and F. Zamora-Martínez. Improving Offline Handwritten Text Recognition with Hybrid HMM/ANN Models. *IEEE Trans. Pattern Anal. Mach. Intell.*, 33(4):767–779, Apr. 2011.

[2] A. Gordo, D. Llorens, A. Marzal, F. Prat, and J. M. Vilar. State: A multimodal assisted text-transcription system for ancient documents. In *8th IAPR Workshop on Document Analysis Systems*, pages 135–142, Nara (Japan), 2008.

[3] A. L. Lagarda, V. Alabau, C. D. Martínez-Hinarejos, A. H. Toselli, V. Romero, J. R. Navarro-Cerdan, and E. Vidal. Computer-assisted handwritten text transcription using speech recognition. In *V Jornadas en Tecnología del Habla (VJTH'2008)*, pages 229–232, Bilbao (Spain), Nov 2008.

[4] D. Llorens, A. Marzal, F. Prat, and J. M. Vilar. State, an assisted document transcription system. In *Proc. ICMI-MLMI*, pages 233–234, 2009.

[5] U. V. Marti and H. Bunke. The IAM-database: an English sentence adatabase for offline handwriting recognition. *International Journal on Document Analysis and Recognition*, 5:39–46, 2002.

[6] F. Prat, A. Marzal, S. Martín, R. Ramos-Garijo, and M. J. Castro. A Template-based Recognition System for On-line Handwritten Characters. *Journal of Information Science and Engineering*, 25(3):779–791, 2009.

[7] A. H. Toselli, V. Romero, M. Pastor, and E. Vidal. Multimodal interactive transcription of text images. *Pattern Recognition*, 43(5):1814 – 1825, 2010.

[8] J. M. Vilar et al. A Flexible System for Document Processing and Text Transcription. In *8th Conf. on Technology Transfer (TTIA 2009)*, pages 467–476, Sevilla (Spain), 2009.

[9] F. Zamora-Martínez, M. J. Castro-Bleda, S. España-Boquera, and J. Gorbe-Moya. Unconstrained Offline Handwriting Recognition using Connectionist Character N-grams. In *IEEE WCCI IJCNN*, pages 4136–4142, Barcelona, Spain, July 2010.

Digital Pen in Mammography Patient Forms

Daniel Sonntag
German Research Center for AI
Saarbrücken, Germany
sonntag@dfki.de

Marcus Liwicki
German Research Center for AI
Kaiserslautern, Germany
liwicki@dfki.uni-kl.de

Markus Weber
German Research Center for AI
Kaiserslautern, Germany
Markus.Weber@dfki.de

ABSTRACT

We present a digital pen based interface for clinical radiology reports in the field of mammography. It is of utmost importance in future radiology practices that the radiology reports be uniform, comprehensive, and easily managed. This means that reports must be "readable" to humans and machines alike. In order to improve reporting practices in mammography, we allow the radiologist to write structured reports with a special pen on paper with an invisible dot pattern. A handwriting software takes care of the interpretation of the written report which is transferred into an ontological representation. In addition, a gesture recogniser allows radiologists to encircle predefined annotation suggestions which turns out to be the most beneficial feature. The radiologist can (1) provide the image and image region annotations mapped to a FMA, RadLex, or ICD10 code, (2) provide free text entries, and (3) correct/select annotations while using multiple gestures on the forms and sketch regions. The resulting, automatically generated PDF report is then stored in a semantic backend system for further use and contains all transcribed annotations as well as all free form sketches.

Categories and Subject Descriptors

H.5.2 [**User Interfaces**]: Input Devices and Strategies, Natural Language, Graphical HCIs, Prototyping

Keywords

Design, Pen/Ink Interface, Medical Healthcare

General Terms

Reliability

1. INTRODUCTION

The current practice in hospitals is that a radiologist's dictated or written patient report is transcribed by hospital staff and sent back to the radiologist for approval. The turnaround time is 2-30 hours and the process inefficient. In order to improve the general medical scenario, we implemented a prototype for radiology findings [8]. In our improved scenario presented in this paper, we use a pen-based interface and a new "interactive" paper writing modality. We extend the interactive paper for the patient reporting approach with an even more specific approach for mammography (the examination of the human brest). The goal of mammography is the early detection of breast cancer and involves computer tomography (CT), magnetic resonance imaging (MRI), as well as a physical examination. Our goal is to provide one computer-based user interface that can be used for all three scenarios: the CT images are examined at a desktop station, the physical examination is done in a separate room, and the MRI is only assessed for ambiguous cases a few days later at the imaging centre. In all three examinations, a written report with specific manually written annotation is compulsory. In this situation, we are developing intelligent user interfaces that eliminate the proofing of transcriptions and generate more accurate and complete finding reports without interrupting the compulsory annotation process on a physical finding form. A digital pen based interface should enable radiologists to create high-quality mammography reports more efficiently. In addition, in the current mammography practice the results are often inaccurate because pre-specified standardised terminologies for anatomy, disease, or special image characteristics are seldom used. That's why we base our development on a special mammography form where radiologists can encircle special characteristics and add free text commands which can only be filled in with medical terms of a prespecified medical vocabulary or free form sketches.

In this paper, we present a new interaction method that shows how a radiologist can use our special mammography paper writing system to conduct a full mammography patient finding process. Thereby, he or she uses a digital pen-based interface where the user can write on normal paper which is printed with a light-grey dot pattern in order to allow for the recognition of the writing. A special feature is the possibility to mark regions (circles, checkmarks, or arrows) of interest on the predefined sketches and refer to them in the prespecified and free-form annotations. The results of the writing process on normal paper can then be inspected on the computer screen in this multimodal setting. The radiologist's signature triggers the PDF generation process. We will focus on the new pen-based interface and new interaction possibilities with gestures in this multimodal scenario.

2. DIGITAL PEN TECHNOLOGY

We developed a digital pen interface which recognises and interprets the semantics of handwritten annotations on printed paper sheets. A variety of approaches have been investigated to enable these kinds of paper-driven digital services: cameras, pen tablets (www.wacom.com), ultrasonic positioning, RFID antennas, bar code readers, or Anoto's technology (www.anoto.com). The Anoto technology, which we use, is particularly interesting because it is based on regular paper and the recording is precise and reliable. In order to become interactive, documents are Anoto-enabled at print time by augmenting the paper with a special Anoto dot pattern. We use *iGesture* to recognise any pen-based gestures and to translate them into the corresponding digital operations. These gestures turn out to be of utmost importance, because in the current practice, prespecified finding terms on the physical paper are encircled by the radiologists. In addition, when the user uses the tree text areas, he or she can encircle, underline, or cross out his or her own writing to trigger external search functionalities or corrections. For the recognition of the contents of the form's text fields, either the MyScript Builder from Vision Objects [7] or the Microsoft handwriting recognition engine [6] can be used. Our framework interprets the paper-based user actions and activates the corresponding digital actions.

Many digital writing solutions that specialise in healthcare with Anoto (http://anoto.com/healthcare-cases-3.aspx) are available, but these systems are "one-way" and do not use a special terminology for the terms to be recognised or support any gestures. In our scenario, we developed a prototype with these extensions. The user (radiologist) is in the patient finding process, namely the extended mammography part.) The complete interactive system is based on a generic framework for implementing multimodal dialogue systems, see [9, 10].) More modalities, such as the new digital pen modality, allow for more natural communication, which normally employs multiple channels of expression. In particular, while using the interactive paper, we address the knowledge acquisition bottleneck problem for image contents in the context of medical findings/structured reporting. A *structured report* [2] is a report generation technique that permits the use of pre-determined data elements or formats for semantic-based indexing of image report elements (figure 1). (The Radiological Society of North America (RSNA) provides textual templates for us.) With the RSNA templates (and similar ones), we are able to pre-specify annotation vocabulary fields. This means "more natural communication" applies not only for a potential casual user of the digital pen technology, but to radiology experts who fill in physical document forms with prespecified fields as part of a complex, educated patient management and medication process. The written documents with signatures are an important part of the patient management process which cannot be replaced by purely digital forms according to treatment responsibility laws (in the German public health sector.) These requirements are quite unique in the research literature. In other related work, [1] for example, the input modality of choice is a tablet PC. While a tablet PC supports handwritten strokes, writing on it does not feel the same as writing on normal paper. Likewise, the physical paper serves as a certificate.

The form filling process of CT image reporting elements (as shown in figure 1, bottom) has been extended by the mammography form which, essentially, differs from the CT image forms in the input fields by providing freeform sketch areas and the predefined annotation vocabulary fields (see figure 2). The "operational" interactive paper form for structured mammography reports spans over two full pages and is a bit more complicated as illustrated in this paper. However, the important new development concerns the interplay between the free-form sketches and the annotation vocabulary fields. This will be presented in detail in the next section.

3. SCENARIO IMPLEMENTATION

Figure 3 shows the mammography scenario. The digital pen annotation framework is available at the patient finding workstation and the examination room. The radiologists finish their mammography reports at the patient finding station where they can inspect the results of the digital pen process. With the radiologist's signature, a formal report is generated according to the mammographgy annotations. The sketches the expert has drawn are also included in the final digital report. Anoto's digital pen was originally designed to digitise handwritten text on normal paper and uses a patented dot pattern on a very fine grid that is printed with carbon ink on conventional paper forms. We use the highest resolution dot pattern (to be printed with at least 600 dpi) to guarantee that the sketches in the freeform sketches can be digitised with the correct boundaries. To use the high resolution dot pattern, the Bluetooth receiver is installed at the finding station; this ensures an almost perfect wireless connection. Please note that we use the digital pen in the streaming mode to ensure that the radiologist can inspect the results on screen at any time; our special Anoto pen version accommodates a Bluetooth sender to transmit pen positions and stroke information in real-time to the nearby host computer at the finding station.

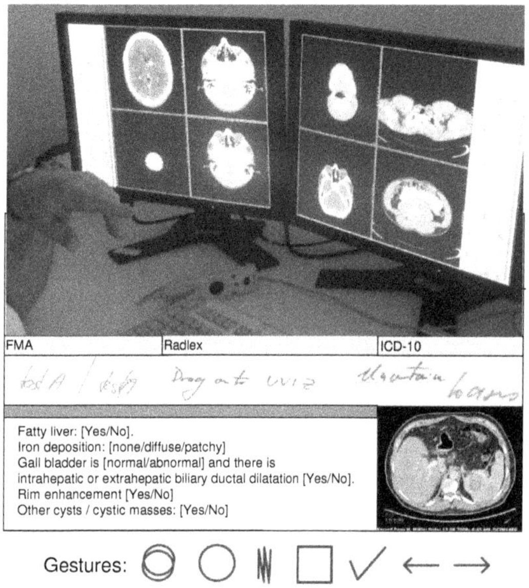

Figure 1: Radiology environment, paper and gesture set

Freeform Text Area.

In the medical finding process, standards play a major role. In complex medical database systems, a common ground of terms and structures is absolutely necessary. For annotations, we reuse existing reference ontologies and terminologies. For anatomical annotations, we use the Foundational Model of Anatomy (FMA) ontology [4]. To express features of the visual manifestation of a particular anatomical entity or disease of the current image, we use fragments of RadLex [3]. Diseases are formalised using the International Classification of Diseases (ICD-10). In any case, the system maps the handwriting recognition (HWR) output to one ontological instance (similar to [5]). Images can be segmented into *regions of interest* (ROI). Each of these regions can be annotated independently with anatomical concepts (e.g., "lymph node"), with information about the visual manifestation of the anatomical concept (e.g., "enlarged"), and with a disease category using ICD-10 classes (e.g., "Nodular lymphoma" or "Lymphoblastic"). However, any combination of anatomical, visual, and disease annotations is allowed and multiple annotations of the same region are possible.

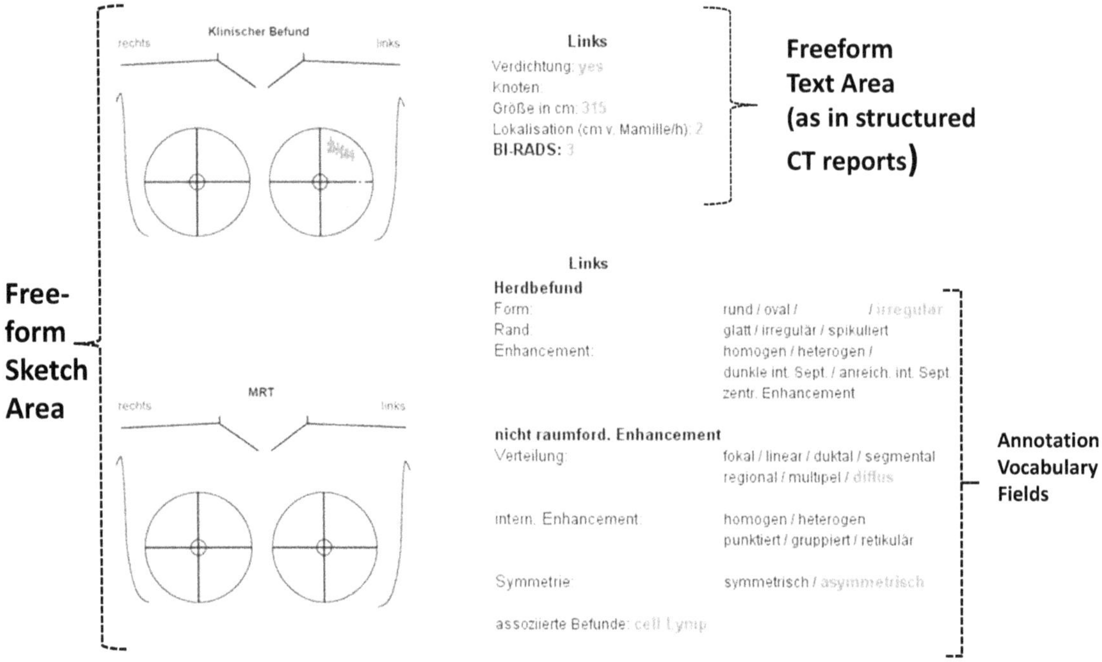

Figure 2: Interactive paper for structured mammography reports

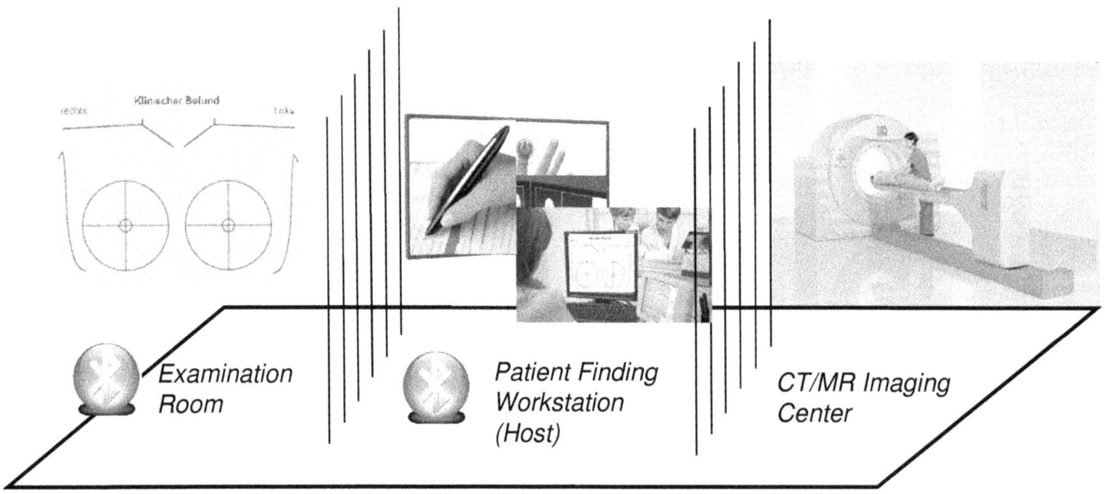

Figure 3: Complete mammography scenario

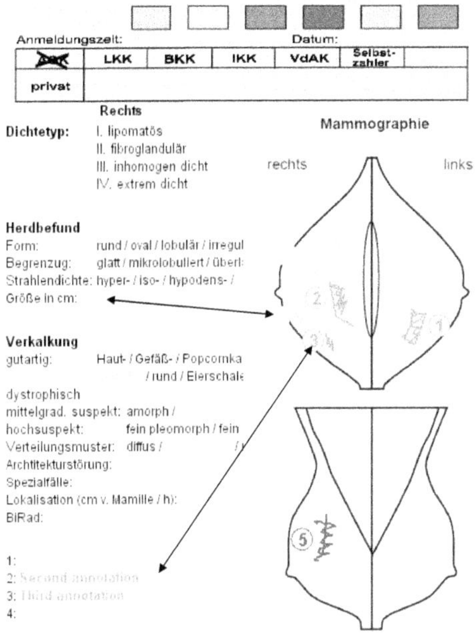

Figure 4: Multiple annotions with automatic numbering

Multiple Sketch Annotations.
The structured form eases the task of finding appropriate annotations (from FMA, ICD-10, or RadLex); some yes/no or multiple choice questions complete the finding process. As can be seen in figure 2, multiple colours can be selected for multiple tissue manifestations. A specific feature is the automatic numbering mode. A new manifestation (i.e., a new sketch) is recognised automatically after a delay time of 500ms without any stroke and numbered automatically. As preliminary user tests show, this feature can be learned easily, and the automatic numbering delegates the user to fill out a free text field. When this process is properly applied, the resulting annotations (figure 4) are much less ambiguous and less prone to error as the annotations gained from a pure physical form filling pcocess.

Annotation Selection and Correction.
The user is able to use multiple gestures, e.g., underline or scratch out a concept in the free text fields. Then he has the possibility to select a more specific term (displayed on the computer screen) or refine/correct a potential recognition error. This makes the paper interaction really interactive and multimodal. We also use the iGesture framework to select the colours on a virtual colour palette printed on the physical forms (in colour); the user can circle a new paint-pot to get this colour's ink (figure 4, bottom) to sketch and annotate in a specific colour.

4. CONCLUSION AND DISCUSSION

We presented a digital pen based interface for mammography forms. The radiologist can (1) provide the image and image region annotations mapped to a FMA, RadLex, or ICD10 code, (2) provide free text entries, and (3) correct/select annotations while using multiple gestures on the forms and sketch regions. Finally, after controlling the results on screen, a signature triggers a PDF report generation process. This improves the quality and consistency of mammography reports. It can be shown with our first demo systems that the time required to release a digital report is within seconds instead of several hours (when assuming a manual transcription phase). The common annotation and querying framework for pen-based structured reporting will now be tested at the University Hospital in Erlangen as a part of a clinical evaluation study. Educators may find these interactive papers for mammography can help trainees learn the important elements of reports and encourage the proper use of special radiology terms.

Our system does not target to recognise the meaning of the handwritten strokes in the sketch areas. [1] try to recognise sketches, but their system does not support unconstrained sketches and handwritten text. Although they're very fancy and interesting, these and similar sketch recognition features are not needed in the mammography scenario; rather, the uninterpreted and digitised sketches serve as supportive material in the resulting PDF document.

Acknowledgements.
This research has been supported in part by the THESEUS Program in the MEDICO Project, which is funded by the German Federal Ministry of Economics and Technology under the grant number 01MQ07016.

5. REFERENCES

[1] G. Feng, C. Viard-Gaudin, and Z. Sun. On-line hand-drawn electric circuit diagram recognition using 2d dynamic programming. *Pattern Recognition*, 42(12):3215 – 3223, 2009. New Frontiers in Handwriting Recognition.

[2] F. M. Hall. The radiology report of the future. *Radiology*, 251(2):313–316, 2009.

[3] C. P. Langlotz. Radlex: A new method for indexing online educational materials. *RadioGraphics*, 26:1595–1597, 2006.

[4] J. L. Mejino, D. L. Rubin, and J. F. Brinkley. FMA-RadLex: An application ontology of radiological anatomy derived from the foundational model of anatomy reference ontology. In *Proc. of AMIA Symposium*, pages 465–469, 2008.

[5] M. Möller, S. Regel, and M. Sintek. Radsem: Semantic annotation and retrieval for medical images. In *Proc. of The 6th Annual European Semantic Web Conference (ESWC2009)*, June 2009.

[6] J. A. Pittman. Handwriting recognition: Tablet pc text input. *Computer*, 40(9):49–54, 2007.

[7] S.Knerr and E.Augustin. A neural network-hidden Markov model hybrid for cursive word recognition. In *Int. Conf. on Pattern Recognition*, volume 2, pages 1518–1520, 1998.

[8] D. Sonntag, M. Liwicki, and M. Weber. Interactive paper for radiology findings. In *Proceedings of the 16th international conference on Intelligent user interfaces*, IUI '11, pages 459–460, New York, NY, USA, 2011. ACM.

[9] D. Sonntag and M. Möller. Unifying semantic annotation and querying in biomedical image repositories. In *Proceedings of International Conference on Knowledge Management and Information Sharing (KMIS)*, 2009.

[10] D. Sonntag, N. Reithinger, G. Herzog, and T. Becker. *Proceedings of IWSDS2010—Spoken Dialogue Systems for Ambient Environment*, chapter A Discourse and Dialogue Infrastructure for Industrial Dissemination, pages 132–143. Springer, LNAI, 2010.

MozArt: A Multimodal Interface for Conceptual 3D Modeling

Anirudh Sharma, Sriganesh Madhvanath, Ankit Shekhawat, Mark Billinghurst*
Hewlett-Packard Labs, Bangalore, India
*HIT Lab NZ, University of Canterbury, NZ
{anirudh.sharma, srig, ankit.shekhawat}@hp.com, mark.billinghurst@hitlabnz.org

ABSTRACT
There is a need for computer aided design tools that support rapid conceptual level design. In this paper we explore and evaluate how intuitive speech and multitouch input can be combined in a multimodal interface for conceptual 3D modeling. Our system, MozArt, is based on a user's innate abilities - speaking and touching, and has a toolbar/button-less interface for creating and interacting with computer graphics models. We briefly cover the hardware and software technology behind MozArt, and present a pilot study comparing our multimodal system with a conventional multitouch modeling interface with first time CAD users. While a larger study is required to obtain statistically significant comparison regarding efficiency and accuracy of the two interfaces, a majority of the participants preferred the multimodal interface over the multitouch. We summarize lessons learned and discuss directions for future research.

Categories and Subject Descriptors
H.5.2 **[Information Interfaces and Presentation]:** User Interfaces – *Input devices and strategies*

General Terms
Design, Human Factors

Keywords
Multimodal interfaces, CAD, 3D modeling, Speech input

1. INTRODUCTION
Computers have become more affordable and accessible, but 3D modeling remains a complex task involving a steep learning curve and extensive training. There are several reasons for this, such as the need to learn a dense toolbar and menu based WIMP interface, and use of effectively only one I/O device (either the keyboard, or the mouse)[10]. This increases the application learning time.

In our research we are interested in the problem of designing a 3D modeling application for conceptual modeling. During early stage concept design the user's attention is focused on overall appearance of the model, and exact dimensions, positions and tolerances are dealt with during the later design phase. Unfortunately, most CAD interfaces force the designer to define the model precisely through a large number of icons and menu options even at the concept modeling stage. Another key issue is the extensive use of keyboard and mouse input to operate a complex GUI. It takes a substantial effort to attain design proficiency with these tools, and it is commonly observed that designers prefer pen and paper for early stages of design.

In this paper, we present *MozArt*, a prototype interface that explores how multimodal input and appropriate hardware may be applied to simplify conceptual 3D modeling for first-time CAD users. MozArt features a minimalist UI, and uses a touch table with tiltable orientation. Generally speaking, a drafting table is a preferred means of drawing, commonly used by artists and architects during drawing and modeling tasks. Studies show that a tiltable touchscreen is more efficient than its vertical counterpart since it allows resting of elbows upon the bezel of the screen [3].

This paper is organized as follows. We first cover related work in multimodal interfaces for computer modeling. Next, we describe the MozArt hardware prototype - a tilt-able drafting-table style interactive touch surface. In Section 4, we describe the MozArt user interface, and the touch and speech interactions we have enabled for 3D modeling. Next, we present results from an initial user study of user performance using multimodal and pure multitouch interfaces. We conclude the paper with a discussion of lessons learned and directions for future research.

2. RELATED WORK
Beginning with Bolt's *"Put that there"* [15], there have been many interfaces that show the value of combining speech and gesture input for graphical applications. Boeing's *"Talk and Draw"* [16] application allowed users to draw with a mouse and use speech input to change UI modes, and was one of the first multimodal drawing applications. In [9], speech and glove based gesture input were integrated with a stand-alone CAD package. Multimodal interaction has also been used in 3D graphic environments and compared to traditional interfaces; e.g. Hauptmann [1] investigated the use of multimodal interaction for a simple 3D cube manipulation task and found that people strongly preferred using combined gesture and speech for the graphics manipulation, instead of either modality alone.

These systems typically used pen or glove based input devices, but recently multitouch table-top displays have made it possible to directly manipulate 3D graphics. For example, SpaceClaim demonstrated a prototype CAD tool with a multitouch screen [17]. However this application does not easily support task-switching and continues to use the same toolbars and buttons as used with a keyboard and mouse metaphor. The work of Arangarasan and Gadh [2] makes use of multimodal input and output for working with 3D models, however, it requires the use of a Head-Mounted Displays (HMDs) that can be obtrusive to beginners due to ergonomic issues. ILoveSketch [4] combines stylus input with automation to allow users to create accurate 3D models primarily by sketching using an electronic stylus. SenStylus [11] demonstrates a stylus based 6DOF input system for 3-D modeling. While well suited for the creation of curved and organic shapes, these interfaces may be more complex than necessary for simple

3D design. Computer modeling has traditionally been viewed as the domain of experts, and these systems are in general targeted towards their needs.

In contrast to these efforts, our emphasis is on supporting 3D modeling by novice users using a minimalist multimodal interface on appropriate hardware, and attempting to ensure that the user's focus is on the design task rather than the UI elements.

3. MOZART TABLE

In this section, we describe the MozArt table, the hardware prototype that we have built. The prototype draws inspiration from the architect's drafting table. It is a common observation that designers often work on their sketches and design drafts on a table that allows them to change orientation of the base plate, while resting their hands and elbows on the bezel. This affords idea sharing by virtue of the table's size, visibility, and provides a platform that enables discussion about designs [5]. The MozArt table involves a fabricated tilt mount with a multi-touch display with which the user can interact using voice and touch (Figure 1).

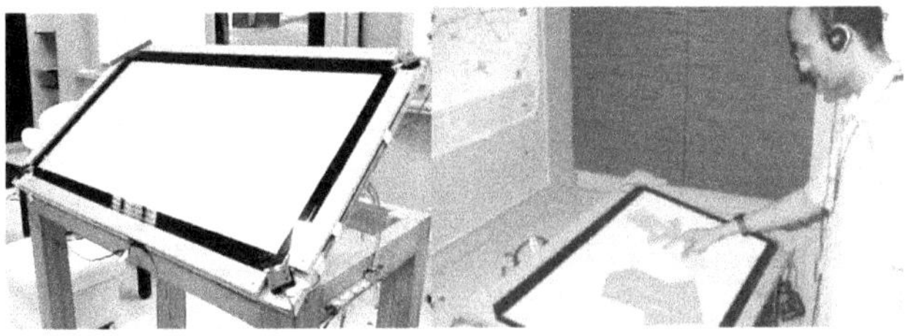

Figure 1: MozArt Table hardware prototype

Multi-touch detection is implemented using the optical Laser Line Plane technique [14]. The surface is illuminated with 850nm Infrared lasers. Scattered light generated upon touching the surface is captured by a modified infrared camera below the table surface, and is processed using Community Core Vision libraries [8] to detect and track touchpoints. The system is capable of tracking up to 255 touch-points with an accuracy of 3mm.

4. MOZART USER INTERFACE

Our chief goal was to explore a natural and minimalist multimodal interface for 3D modeling allowing the user to focus on the design process rather than the user interface components. To create a multimodal design tool, we decided to add support for speech and gesture input to an existing modeling tool, SketchUp [12]. It is worth noting that by default, the SketchUp UI is designed for keyboard and mouse interaction, and features extensive use of menus for selecting modes, views and shapes. For our prototype, we designed a custom interface, which replaced the use of toolbars and buttons for a subset of common tasks, with touch and speech commands.

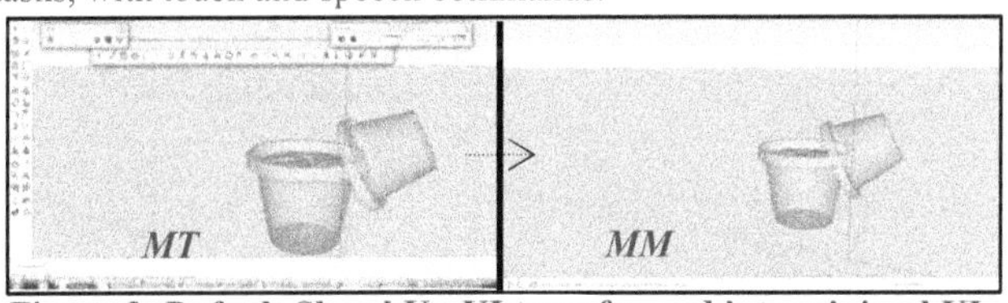

Figure 2: Default SketchUp UI transformed into minimal UI

The vocabulary of Touch and Speech commands is shown in Table 1 and Table 2 respectively.

Table 1: Touch Gestures

Touch Gesture	Outcome
Two finger pinch	Zoom in/ Zoom out
Single touch drag	Specify extent of M and O

Table2: Speech Commands

Speech input	Category	Mode
"Circle"	Activate (circle)	Modify (M)
"Rectangle"	Activate(Rectangle)	Modify (M)
"Line"	Active(Line)	Modify (M)
"Pull it up"	Activate(Push/Pull)	Operate (O)
"Show Isometric"	Show isometric model view	Change viewport(V)
"Top View"	Show top view	Change viewport(V)
"Show me around"	Activate 3D orbiting	Change viewport manually (V)
"Undo"	Undo last step	Modify (M)

Figure 3 shows the drawing of a square, extruding it into a cube, and zooming in and out using speech and multitouch gestures.

Figure 3: Draw/Extrude/Zoom modes of the multimodal UI

4.1 System Design

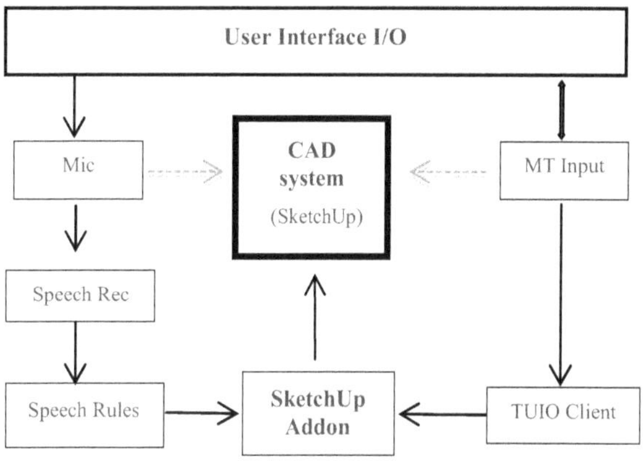

Figure 4: System Design

The multitouch data from the table is captured in TUIO[13] format, parsed using a client written in C++ and loaded into SketchUp using a Ruby script. The multitouch gestures are then mapped to events such as dragging, zooming, and panning. CMUSphinx [7] is used to process speech from a microphone. The commands are forwarded to SketchUp to initiate keyboard shortcuts for switching between tasks (Figure 4).

4.2 User Evaluation

MozArt is intended to simplify the design process for users familiar with computers but not expert at 3D CAD modeling. In order to evaluate MozArt, we conducted a user study with 8 male and 4 female participants from an office environment. The participants were 20-29 years old. The user evaluation consisted of a training phase followed by a testing phase.

Training Phase

Each subject was shown a 5-minute introductory video about face and line modeling concepts using SketchUp's conventional mouse/keyboard interface. They were then allowed to try the multitouch gestures and menus for 5 minutes. Being first time CAD users, most of the subjects tried drawing, and extruding objects, similar to what was shown in the introductory video.

Testing Phase

The testing phase consisted of subjects completing two modeling tasks of different complexity. For each task, subjects were shown one model on-screen and were asked to make a copy of it. The models were designed to test basic modeling skills such as drawing polygon faces, extrusion, navigating the UI, and so on. Each modeling task was completed by the user using two interface conditions, Multitouch and Multimodal.

Multitouch only (MT)

For this interface condition, a conventional Toolbar/Button based touch interface was enabled. The interaction tools had to be selected from the interface menu. The size of the buttons was increased to reduce touch-based selection errors. The user was constrained to use only multitouch gestures.

Multimodal (MM)

For this condition, the Toolbars/Buttons were disabled and hidden. Only the blank modeling canvas was presented to the user and speech and touch based interaction was enabled. The user was constrained to use speech commands together with multitouch gestures. A printed sheet listing the available speech commands was provided to the user.

One half of the participants used MT followed by MM, while the other half used MM first. As participants completed each modeling task the following experimental measures were collected:

- Task completion times
- X-Y coordinates of touch-points on the screen
- User errors measured as the number of "undo" commands
- NASA Task Load Index surveying user workload

At the conclusion of both tasks using both techniques, participants were asked to state and discuss their personal preference of technique.

Average Task Completion Times

The average task completion times (in minutes) for different tasks and techniques are shown in Figure 5.

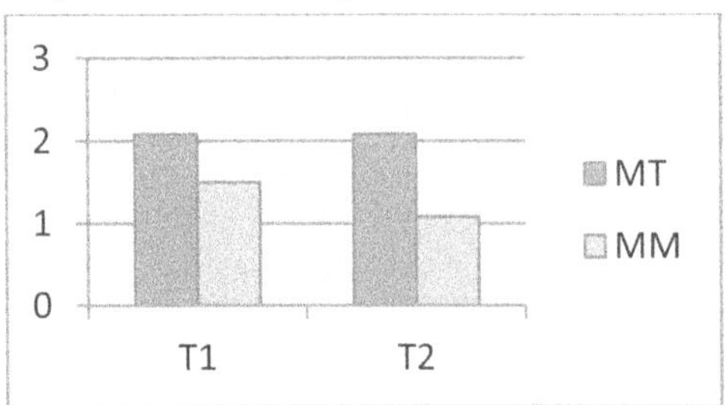

Figure 5: Average task completion times (in minutes)

We compared task completion times using a two factor ANOVA test with replication alpha=0.05, which yielded F= 0.468 < $F_{critical}$= 4.062, p>0.05. This shows that the influence of the technique on the task completion time is not significant. However, we did observe that some of the task completion times were unusually large. For example, one of the participants with unusually large hands had issues selecting the correct menu buttons in the MT condition. Another user had an accent that was not recognized well by the speech recognizer.

Errors

The number of errors was defined as the number of times a user mis-selected a tool and used Undo. This was measured for each condition. Figure 6 shows the average number of errors per user for each task and condition. We used a one-tailed t-test to test whether the MM condition produced fewer errors for Task 1 than the MT condition, and found (t(11) = 1.02, p = 0.164). For Task2 a one t-tailed t-test found (t(11) = 3.07, p = 0.005). Thus for Task 2 the MM condition produced significantly fewer errors than the MT condition, whereas for Task1 there was no significant difference in average number of errors.

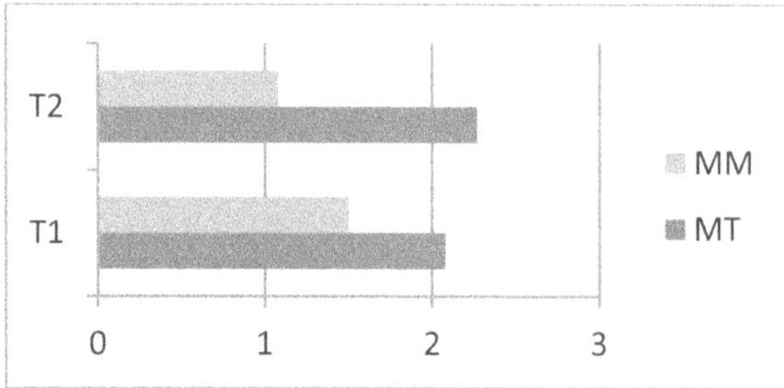

Figure 6: Average number of errors per user

The decrease in number of errors in the MM method for Task 2 compared to Task 1 is potentially due to the user's increased familiarity with speech commands. Despite designing a more complex model during Task 2 participants committed fewer errors since they had become familiar with the simple speech commands and hence did not have to refer to the printed sheet of commands as frequently.

On the contrary, in the MT method we noticed that as the complexity of the model increased from Task 1 to Task 2, the participants had to move their hands, resulting in a greater number of touch based false positives.

Heat maps

A visual comparison between multitouch and multimodal conditions was enabled using heatmaps plotted from the complete set of logged touch coordinates (Figure 7). Based on these heatmaps and our discussion with the participants, it was evident that the MT condition required participants to shift their visual attention more often between model and toolbars/menus at the top and sides of the screen. It was observed that every time the user changed a tool, their hand and focus of attention needed to shift to the top and sides of the screen and back to the center. However, for the MM condition, touch interaction took place primarily on the model itself.

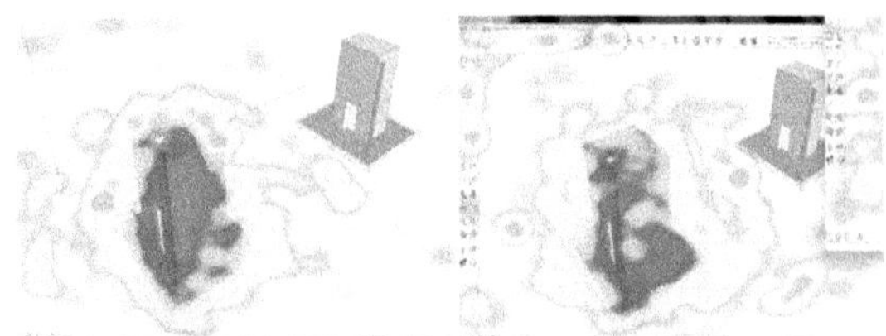

Figure 7: Heatmap generated from touch coordinates for MM (left) and MT (right) . Darker color implies more points.

Task Load Index

We used the NASA TLX method to collect subjective task load data after each modeling task. Upon analysis we found a general trend towards increased frustration and physical demand for the MT condition (Figures 8 and 9).

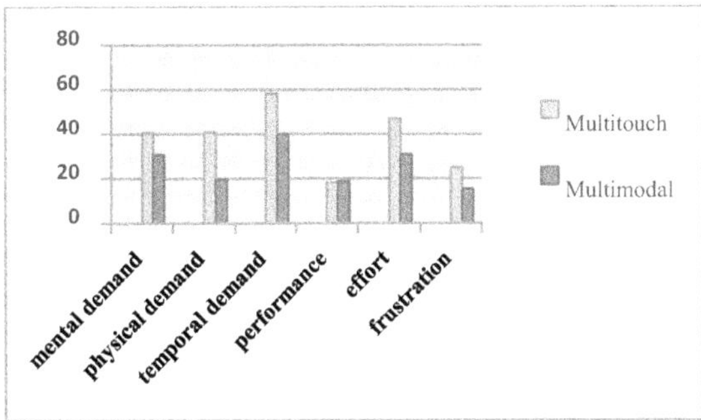

Figure 8:Task Load Index for Task1

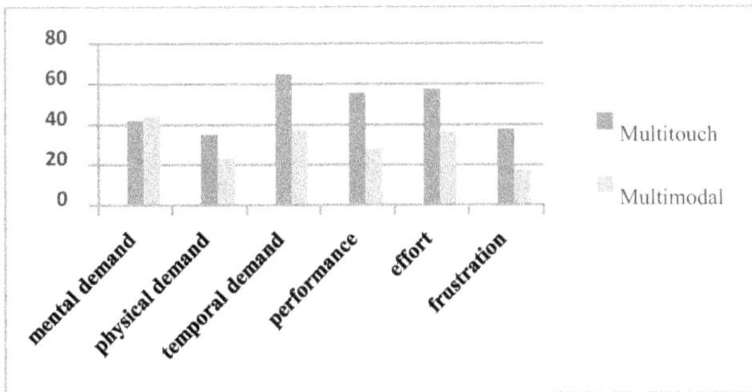

Figure 9: Task Load Index for Task2

The higher frustration may be attributed to the higher frequency of errors, and increased physical demand to the fact that considerable hand movement was required every time a tool had to be changed.

Subjective Preference

On completion of both tasks, all participants were given an opportunity to select one of the two interfaces and build a model of their own choice; 9 out of 12 participants chose the MM interface while 3 chose the MT interface. Participants also reported on difficulties faced with the MT interface, e.g. ones with sweaty and/or large fingers reported problems selecting the exact buttons from the toolbar, leading to larger task completion times.

6. SUMMARY AND FUTURE WORK

We have described our prototype MozArt system, a tiltable multi-touch table with a multimodal interface that attempts to present an easier way to create 3D models. The form factor chosen provides a greater sense of directness because participants put their fingers directly onto the item of interest and manipulate it. The tilt enhances collaboration and prevents fatigue over prolonged working sessions [3]. MozArt allows the use of speech commands to perform actions that would ordinarily require the manipulation of menus and icons. By so doing, we believe the interface allows the user to focus on the task rather than the interface itself.

We evaluated the system with a user study. We conducted a Two Factor ANOVA with replication and found the results to be statistically insignificant, primarily due to the small number of participants taken for the study. Other factors were the presence of outliers in some of the methods. Our next step is to repeat the study with a larger number of participants so that any differences in task efficiency and accuracy between the use of multitouch only and multimodal techniques may be brought out. We would also like to include a Likert test to study subjective preference for the two techniques.

In the future we will work on further expanding the multimodal vocabulary. For many modeling tasks, precision of extents becomes a key issue. To address this, we intend to support spoken commands that allow precise dimensions to be specified.

Finally, speech input using an open microphone suffers from the problem of false positives (spurious input) due to ambient sounds, especially in multi-user environments. This could be solved by adding lip movement detection based on image processing to detect when the user is speaking.

5. ACKNOWLEDGMENTS

The authors would like to thank Prasenjit Dey for his valuable inputs and help with the statistical analysis of the results.

6. REFERENCES

[1] Alexander. G. Hauptmann: "Speech and Gestures for Graphic Image Manipulation." CHI 1989 241-245.

[2] Arangarasan, R., and Gadh, R., "Geometric Modeling and Collaborative Design in a Multi-modal Multi-sensory Virtual Environment." ASME DETC'00

[3] A. Sears. "Improving touchscreen keyboards: design issues and a comparison with other devices." Interacting with Computers, 3(3), 1991.

[4] Bae, S.-H., Balakrishnan, R., And Singh, K.. "ILoveSketch: As-Natural-As-Possible Sketching System for Creating 3D Curve Models." UIST, 2008.

[5] Buxton W., Fitzmaurice G., Balakrishnan R., Kurtenbach G., 2000, "Large Displays in Automotive Design", IEEE Computer Society 20 (4), 68–7.

[6] C. Muller-Tomfelde, A. Wessels, and C. Schremmer, "Tilted Tabletops: In Between Horizontal and Vertical Workspaces". TABLETOP '08.

[7] CMUSphinx Libray http://cmusphinx.sourceforge.net/

[8] Community Core Vision http://nuicode.com/projects/tbeta

[9] D. Weimer and S. K. Ganapathy, "A synthetic visual environment with hand gesturing and voice input," CHI 1989, pp. 235–240.

[10] Darren A., Yaser G., Frank Maurer 2010 "Adapting existing applications to support new interaction technologies: technical and usability issues". ACM SIGCHI symposium on Engineering Interactive Computing Systems.

[11] Fiorentino, M., G. Monno And A. Uva . "The Senstylus: a Novel Rumble-Feedback Pen Device for CAD Application in Virtual Reality", WSCG 2005.

[12] Google SketchUp http://sketchup.google.com/

[13] M. Kaltenbrunner, et. al, "TUIO - A Protocol for Table Based Tangible User Interfaces," in GW '05: Proc. of the 6th International Workshop on Gesture in HCI and Simulation, 2005.

[14] Park, J. and Han T.: LLP+: multi-touch sensing using cross plane infrared laser light for interactive based displays, SIGGRAPH Posters, 2010.

[15] Richard A. Bolt. 1980. "Put-that-there: Voice and gesture at the graphics interface", SIGGRAPH 1980, 262-270.

[16] M. Salisbury , J. Hendrickson , T. Lammers , C. Fu , S. Moody, Talk and Draw: Bundling Speech and Graphics, IEEE Computer, v.23 n.8, p.59-65, August 1990.

[17] SpaceClaim CAD http://www.spaceclaim.com/en

Query Refinement Suggestion in Multimodal Image Retrieval with Relevance Feedback

Luis A. Leiva, Mauricio Villegas, Roberto Paredes
ITI – Institut Tecnològic d'Informàtica
Universitat Politècnica de València
Camí de Vera, s/n - 46022 (Spain)
{luileito,mvillegas,rparedes}@iti.upv.es

ABSTRACT

In the literature, it has been shown that relevance feedback is a good strategy for the system to interact with the user and provide better results in a content-based image retrieval (CBIR) system. On the other hand, there are many retrieval systems which suggest a refinement of the query as the user types, which effectively helps the user to obtain better results with less effort. Based on these observations, in this work we propose to add a suggested query refinement as a complement in an image retrieval system with relevance feedback. Taking advantage of the nature of the relevance feedback, in which the user selects relevant images, the query suggestions are derived using this relevance information. From the results of an evaluation performed, it can be said that this type of query suggestion is a very good enhancement to the relevance feedback scheme, and can potentially lead to better retrieval performance and less effort from the user.

Keywords

Image Retrieval, Relevance Feedback, Query Suggestion

Categories and Subject Descriptors

H.3.3 [**Information Search and Retrieval**]: Relevance feedback, Query formulation; I.5.5 [**Pattern Recognition**]: Interactive systems

General Terms

Experimentation, Performance, Human Factors

1. INTRODUCTION

Most of the current approaches to retrieve images from online and offline databases are focused on the content-based image retrieval (CBIR) paradigm. However, CBIR systems have not yet gained widespread acceptance, even after more than a decade of research [8]. The main reason for this is what is known as *the semantic gap* [7], which refers to the discrepancy there exists between the low-level content (i.e., the features extracted from the image) and the higher-level concepts (i.e., the interpretation that a person gives to the image in a particular context).

A popular approach for improving the retrieval performance of CBIR systems is by means of relevance feedback. In this approach, the system presents an initial set of images and the user selects which of these are relevant and possibly which are non-relevant. Then, taking into account this new information, the system presents a new set of images, and again the user can select more images. In this way, the user iteratively helps the system to retrieve the desired images. In the literature it has been shown that relevance feedback improves considerably the retrieval performance of a system [3, 4, 5, 9]. Unfortunately, though, if for a given query the image features are unable to represent the relevant images, e.g., when the semantic gap is very wide, then many relevance feedback iterations will be required and few relevant images will be retrieved. A possible way to overcome this problem, is to provide alternative ways of interaction with the user which can give better results when the relevance feedback fails.

Another popular type of user interaction that can improve the retrieval performance is by the system suggesting a refinement of the initial textual query. In contrast to relevance feedback, query suggestion has the benefit that it is optional for the user. If the suggested query is not adequate, then it is unlikely that users will use it, however it is more likely that they will use the good suggestions.

In the literature there is a lot of work on textual query suggestion, although most of them are targeted at document retrieval [10]. Even though most of these can be used in an image retrieval system, they do not consider the way most CBIR with relevance feedback work. Related to image retrieval, Zha and co-authors [10] present what they call the Visual Query Suggestion (VQS) scheme, in which, as the user types, the system shows a drop-down list of suggested queries including some examples of images related to that query. In the work of Cui et al. [2], by using a single query image the system suggests a category among a predefined set, such as object, portrait, etc. which is then used to improve the performance of the relevance feedback.

In this work, we propose to integrate a query suggestion scheme into an image retrieval system based on relevance feedback. By providing these two types of user interaction we aim at reducing the effort from the user and obtain better results for queries which are more text driven. The query suggestion is derived by taking advantage of the selection of the relevant images. Each time the user selects an image, the indexed terms associated to the images are analyzed to determine which ones are more characteristic for the selected images in comparison to the rest of the presented images. At the moment, we are not aware of any paper on query suggestion in this manner.

The remainder of the paper is organized as follows. The next section briefly describes our system, the Relevant Image Search Engine (RISE), including the database, how the relevance feedback is performed, and the proposed query suggestion method. Section 3 presents the results of an evaluation performed, followed by a Discussion section. The final section draws the conclusions and directions for future research.

2. RISE SYSTEM OVERVIEW

2.1 Web Crawling and Image Indexing

The image database of the RISE system is composed of images found in the Internet. Thus, the RISE system includes a web crawler which is constantly downloading new images and adding them to the database. Currently the database has over 24 million images. In order to guaranty a wide variety of images, without having to crawl a large portion of the Internet, the crawling has been started using a list of image URLs obtained from popular image search engines (namely Google, Bing and Yahoo) when searching for words in the English dictionary. For each image the crawler stores a thumbnail and a snapshot of the web page that contains that image. Then such web page is analyzed and to each term in the page a relevance score is derived, which depends on: *1)* the number of appearances, *2)* the document object model (DOM) attributes, and *3)* the distance to the image. Finally, the image is indexed using the terms with the highest relevance scores.

2.2 Retrieval Engine and Relevance Feedback

The retrieval engine of the RISE system starts by receiving a textual query given by the user. Then the images in the database associated with the terms in the query are ranked according to the relevance scores derived during the indexing, and the thumbnails of the first N ranked images are presented to the user. At this stage the relevance feedback starts, by letting the user select some of the images as being relevant (the unmarked images are considered as being non-relevant). Using the selected relevant and non-relevant images, the system presents a new set of images which (hopefully) is closer to what the user is searching for. Again, the user can select more relevant images to refine further the results, and this iterative procedure continues until the user is satisfied. The ranking of the images according to the selected relevant images is based on the probabilistic framework proposed by Paredes et al. [5]. For the relevance feedback, we use a multimodal approach, using both the text annotation extracted from web pages, and features extracted from the image [6]. As image features we are using quantized color histograms and as a similarity measure, the Jensen-Shanon divergence.

2.3 Query Refinement Suggestion

In order to suggest a new query to the user we propose an approach that essentially accounts for the (weighted) words that appear in the text associated to the relevant images but do not appear in the text associated to the non-relevant images. This selection of words can be accomplished in different ways but here we show the selection that gave us the most promising results.

Let be $\{w_1, \cdots, w_n\}$ the n words of the vocabulary. We denote the set of relevant images as R and the set on non-relevant images as N. Let be W the set of words w_i that appear in *all* the relevant images. If this set is empty then no suggestion is produced. If this set is not empty we compute a score for each one of these words:

$$\mathrm{sc}(w_i) = \frac{\sum_{j \in R} t_{ij}}{\sum_{j \in R} t_{ij} + \sum_{k \in N} t_{ik}}, \quad \forall w_i \in W \qquad (1)$$

where t_{ij} is the relevance score of the word w_i in the relevant image j and t_{ik} is the relevance score of the word w_i in the non-relevant image k. In order to avoid ties in the image rank for the cases in which $\mathrm{sc}(w_i) = 1.0$, the value of $\sum_{j \in R} t_{ij}$ is added to the score.

Then if the scores of the words $w_i \in W$ are higher than a certain threshold and using at most the top 2 of them, these are suggested to the user as a new query. For the evaluation described in the next section, the threshold was not applied, since the objective was to assess the quality of the suggestions using this approach.

A version of the RISE system which includes this proposal for query refinement suggestion is temporarily available at `http://risenet.iti.upv.es/qs/`.

3. EVALUATION

Note that our image database is built from real data gathered from the Internet with completely unsupervised annotations, so we have no ground truth, i.e, labeled samples. Thus, in order to evaluate our approach, we conducted an informal field study. The procedure was simple: to measure the user's subjectivity towards our query suggestion technique.

For the evaluation, we selected 81 of the 99 concepts from the ImageCLEF 2011 dataset[1], and used these as the initial text search query. The reason to remove 18 concepts was because they were related to specific image properties rather than high-level concepts, e.g., "Neutral Illumination", "No Blur", etc.

The task consisted of two stages. First, the user was presented with the first 10 ranked images for the given text query, e.g., "cat". Then the user would select a subset of the images which had a common concept or relation among them, e.g., "all are black cats". If the system was able to derive a query refinement, the user interface (UI) would show it and let the user rate if the suggestion was either good, bad, or neutral. The number of times there was no query (NQ) suggested was also recorded (Table 1). In the second stage of the evaluation, users were presented with the images after following the query suggestion, and they had to mark all of the images considered relevant to the concept they had in mind when selecting the images in the first stage of the evaluation. This two-stage process was repeated for all of the subsets of related images the user could identify. Three people from our department took part in the evaluation.

The results of the study are presented in Figure 1 and Tables 1 and 2.

Table 1: Results for stage 1 of the evaluation, showing ratings for the suggested queries.

# selected	# samples	Bad	Neutral	Good	NQ
1	194	35	42	106	11
2	74	11	13	29	21
3	24	2	4	6	12
>3	30	0	0	3	27
Overall	322	48	59	144	71

Table 2: Results for stage 2 of the evaluation, showing mean (and SD) values of the number of retrieved relevant images after following the suggested queries.

# selected	# ratings	Bad	Neutral	Good
1	183	1.5 (1.5)	4 (3)	4.3 (3)
2	53	0.9 (1.4)	4.8 (3.2)	5.1 (3.3)
3	12	0 (0)	4.8 (4.8)	5.8 (2.8)
>3	3	0 (0)	0 (0)	9.6 (0.5)
Overall	226	1.3 (1.5)	4.3 (3.2)	4.7 (3.2)

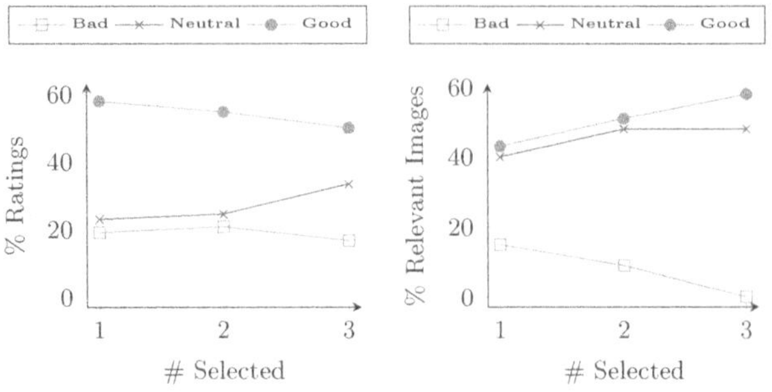

(a) (b)

Figure 1: Evaluation results. 1a: Average rating of the suggested queries in relation to the number of initially selected images. 1b: Percentage of images considered as relevant after following the query suggestions in relation to the number of initially selected images.

4. DISCUSSION

Regarding the first stage of the evaluation, the first thing to note is that as more images are selected, it is less probable that the system will suggest a query (see Table 1). This is understandable since it is less likely that there will be common terms to all selected images. Moreover, the terms associated to each image depends totally on the Web pages in which the image appears, thus not all of the images will be well annotated. Nonetheless, most of the suggested queries were rated as being good, which indicates that this approach of deriving the suggestions based on the selected relevants can be quite useful.

Regarding the second stage of the evaluation, as expected, the query suggestions which were rated as good or neutral, retrieved more relevant images than the bad query suggestions (see Figure 1b). This is convenient since it is unlikely that a user will use a suggestion considered to be bad. A peculiar behavior that is also observed is that the performance tends to be better for suggestions that were derived using more selected relevant images. Then, overall, as more images are selected, it is less likely that the system will suggest a query, however if there is a suggestion it tends to be a better one.

Another observation from the evaluation was that the quality of the query suggestions depends highly on the particular query. There are some queries where the images presented to the user clearly belong to different subgroups, which, if selected, most of the time a query will be suggested that relates to that subgroup. An example of a query that gives good suggestions is shown in Figure 2. In such figure it can be observed that when only one image is selected, the suggested queries tend to be very specific to that image. This is another possible factor why when fewer images were selected, the percentage of retrieved relevant images was lower: a very specific query might be very good, however this also means that there will be less images available of this type.

5. CONCLUSION AND FUTURE WORK

In this paper we have presented a simple method to derive a query refinement suggestion by taking advantage of the selection of relevant images commonly used in image retrieval with relevance feedback. This proposal has been implemented in a real-world image search prototype which can be accessed at http://risenet.iti.upv.es/qs/. An evaluation was performed and from which it has been observed that the proposed method most of the time is effective and may reduce user workload while improving user experience. The perceived (subjective) satisfaction towards the system was positive, although several enhancements remain to be implemented in order to consolidate our approach.

Firstly, even though it is unlikely that a user will use a query suggested which is not considered adequate, it would be ideal to find a way to avoid showing these low-quality suggestions. A simple threshold can partially deal with this, however a more advanced method would be desired. For example, we could analyze what would happen when the images are re-ranked after following the suggested query. If the new top-ranked images are not clearly similar to selected relevant images and dissimilar to the non-relevants, it is an indication that the suggested query is not adequate.

Another problem of the proposed approach is that it is limited by the annotations that were obtained from the Web pages containing the images. A better performance would be expected if, for instance, we would use a thesaurus such as Wordnet[2] to somewhat clean up the annotations and use hypernyms [1] to find the common terms to the selected relevant images. Also there are images on the Web with few text around it, text that does not give any clue regarding the content of the image, or even with no text at all. For these cases it would be required to have a technique which automatically assigns them proper annotations.

Finally, we are considering to incorporate natural language processing techniques, not only to build query suggestions, but also to constrain initial user queries. While the latter falls under the relatively well-covered natural language understanding domain (that is, convert text into easy-to-manipulate structures for computers), the former case is related to natural language generation (convert information from computers into readable human language), and we feel it is more challenging. In this way, for instance, following Figure 2d, instead of suggesting "marathon people", a more appropriate query would be "marathon with people"; and

(a) Initial set of images for the query "marathon".

(b) Number of selected images: 1. Suggested query: "marathon brandenburg gate".

(c) Number of selected images: 1. Suggested query: "marathon belfast city".

(d) Number of selected images: 4. Suggested query: "marathon people".

Figure 2: Example of query refinement suggestions when searching for "marathon". The suggestions tend to be very specific when only one image is selected (2b,2c). Conversely, when several images are selected the suggestions tend to be a common characteristic among them (2d).

searching for "marathon with people" and "marathon without people" indeed should produce slightly different results — although many image search engines today would generally treat both queries the same way.

Notes

[1] http://imageclef.org/system/files/concepts_2011.txt

[2] http://wordnet.princeton.edu/

Acknowledgements

This work is supported by the Spanish MICINN under the MIPRCV Consolider Ingenio 2010 (CSD2007-00018) and RISE (TIN2008-04571) projects, and by the Generalitat Valenciana under grant Prometeo/2009/014.

REFERENCES

[1] K. Chandramouli, T. Kliegr, J. Nemrava, V. Svatek, and E. Izquierdo. Query refinement and user relevance feedback for contextualized image retrieval. In *Proc. of VIE*, pp. 453–458, 2008.

[2] J. Cui, F. Wen, and X. Tang. User intention modeling for interactive image retrieval. In *Proc. ICME*, pp. 1517–1522, 2010.

[3] R. Datta, D. Joshi, J. Li, and J. Z. Wang. Image retrieval: Ideas, influences, and trends of the new age. *ACM Computing Surveys*, 40(2):1–60, 2008.

[4] E. Hörster, R. Lienhart, and M. Slaney. Image retrieval on large-scale image databases. In *Proc. CIVR*, pp. 17–24, 2007.

[5] R. Paredes, T. Deselaers, and E. Vidal. A probabilistic model for user relevance feedback on image retrieval. In *Proc. MLMI*, pp. 260–271, 2008.

[6] F. M. Segarra, L. A. Leiva, and R. Paredes. A relevant image search engine with late fusion: Mixing the roles of textual and visual descriptors. In *Proc. IUI*, pp. 455–456, 2011.

[7] A. W. M. Smeulders, M. Worring, S. Santini, A. Gupta, and R. Jain. Content-based image retrieval at the end of the early years. *IEEE Trans. PAMI*, 22(12):1349–1380, 2000.

[8] J. Urban and J. M. Jose. Can a workspace help to overcome the query formulation problem in image retrieval? In *Proc. ECIR*, pp. 385–396, 2006.

[9] J. Urban, J. M. Jose, and C. J. van Rijsbergen. An adaptive technique for content-based image retrieval. *Multimedia Tools Appl.*, 31(1):1–28, 2006.

[10] Z.-J. Zha, L. Yang, T. Mei, M. Wang, Z. Wang, T.-S. Chua, and X.-S. Hua. Visual query suggestion: Towards capturing user intent in internet image search. *ACM Trans. Multimedia Comput. Commun. Appl.*, 6(3):13:1–13:19, 2010.

A Multimodal Music Transcription Prototype

First steps in an interactive prototype development

Tomás Pérez-García, José M. Iñesta, Pedro J. Ponce de León, Antonio Pertusa
Departamento de Lenguajes y Sistemas Informáticos
Universidad de Alicante
{tperez, inesta, pierre, pertusa}@dlsi.ua.es

ABSTRACT

Music transcription consists of transforming an audio signal encoding a music performance in a symbolic representation such as a music score. In this paper, a multimodal and interactive prototype to perform music transcription is presented. The system is oriented to monotimbral transcription, its working domain is music played by a single instrument. This prototype uses three different sources of information to detect notes in a musical audio excerpt. It has been developed to allow a human expert to interact with the system to improve its results. In its current implementation, it offers a limited range of interaction and multimodality. Further development aimed at full interactivity and multimodal interactions is discussed.

Categories and Subject Descriptors

I.5.4 [**Pattern Recognition**]: Aplications; J.5 [**Arts and Humanities**]: Music

General Terms

Demo, music transcription, onset detection, interactive music application.

Keywords

Multimodal, Pattern Recognition, Transcription, Music

1. INTRODUCTION

The goal of automatic music transcription is to extract a human readable representation, like a musical score, from an audio signal containing a music performance. This process requires to estimate the pitches, onset times, and durations of the notes, the tempo, meter, and tonality of a musical piece.

A multiple fundamental frequency (f_0) estimation method is the core component of a music transcription system. It analyses the input signal and infers the pitches of the harmonic sounds evolving along time. This is a challenging task that has been studied in the literature using different strategies, like supervised and unsupervised learning, statistical inference, deterministic methods, and matching pursuit, among others. Previous reviews on this topic can be found in [3, 8, 9].

These methods can implicitly infer the note onsets (note beginnings) from the harmonic content of the audio signal, as consecutive pitch detections can be associated to the same note. However, onsets can also be directly estimated from the input signal using strategies independent from the former [2], which typically tries to find strong energy variations. Onsets provide a temporal segmentation of the audio that can help transcription in such a way that new pitches can not appear in the frames contained in each segment. Like onsets, beats[1] are another sourcce of information for transcription, and their positions can also be detected from the audio, providing the meter of the piece and musical meaning to the note durations [5].

Currently, the success rate expected for monotimbral polyphonic music transcription [1] is not particularly satisfactory due to the complexity of this task. Therefore, human post-processing is still necessary to correct the results obtained from unattended transcription systems.

In this work, informations like onsets and beats are used to complement the pitch estimation in a multimodal interactive scheme. The proposed system aims to interact with a user to get a correct music score from a possibly imperfect transcription, trying to minimize the number of user interactions.

Some of the user informations provided can be considered deterministic, like pitch or note duration corrections when they are provided with a qwerty or music keyboard, but other should be considered noisy, like note or other event positions that are input with the mouse.

The next section brings a system overview, including descriptions of its core transcription engine and auxiliary modules. Next, its current interaction capabilities are discussed, and finally, some conclusions and further development lines are presented.

A screencast of this prototype can be found currently at `http://miprcv.iti.upv.es/index.php?option=com_content&task=view&id=234&Itemid=205`

2. SYSTEM DESIGN

A flowchart of the interactive transcription system prototype at its current development stage is shown in Figure 1.

ICMI'11, November 14–18, 2011, Alicante, Spain.

[1]Beats can be defined as a sense of equally spaced temporal units related to perceived rhythm [6].

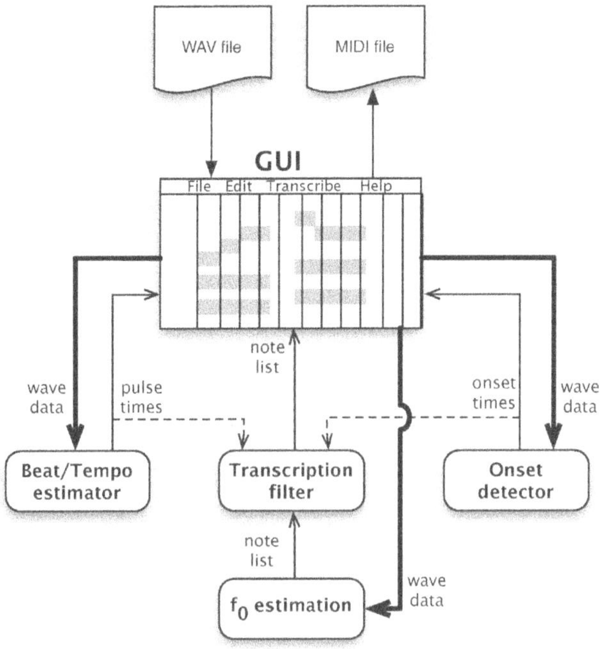

Figure 1: System design schema.

It consists of a GUI that communicates with the core transcription engine and the other information providing modules. This core engine is capable of transcribing polyphonic WAV files into single track MIDI files that contains a symbolic representation (a piano roll, i.e., a kind of music score) of the music piece. This transcription is frame-based and contains all the notes active at each frame.

The frame-based transcription can be enhanced in two ways: using beat and tempo information, provided by the *beat estimator*, or using onset (note beginning) times provided by a specialized *onset detector*. The GUI controls the flow of information between the different core modules, while being able to visualize transcribed notes, beat, tempo, and onset information. It also allows the user to tune up the different module parameters.

The multiple f_0 estimation is based on the joint estimation method described in [9, 10], which obtained a high success rate with a low computational cost in an independent evaluation contest [1].

Next, the core modules, as well as the GUI, are briefly described.

2.1 Multiple fundamental frequency estimation

The method described in [9] selects a set of pitch candidates from the input signal, and all possible combinations of these candidates are generated at each frame limited by a maximum polyphony value. Each combination is independently evaluated considering source interactions, and the one with the highest score is selected at each frame.

The details of the f_0 estimation method are out of the scope of this paper. Essentially, the output at each audio frame consists of a set of pitch combinations with an associated score. For instance, at a given frame t, a combination $\mathcal{C}(t) = \{C_3, G_3\}$ with score $\mathcal{S}(\mathcal{C}(t))$ can be yielded. This scores are important. They permit to select that with the highest one a the first stage (will be denoted as $\mathcal{C}_0(t)$), but they are also utilized for offering the user other possibilities when an error is reported and the system is asked for a new combination. For that, all the available combinations for frame t, $\mathcal{C}_i(t)$, are sorted in terms of their scores, $\mathcal{S}(\mathcal{C}_i(t))$.

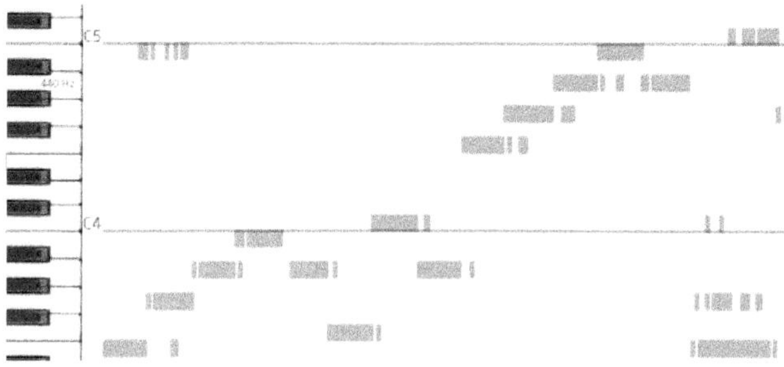

Figure 2: Example of pitch evolution along time using transcription by frame analysis.

In order to get a robust detection considering short context, K, the scores of combinations with the same pitches within the $2K+1$ neighbouring frames are added, obtaining a new score $\tilde{\mathcal{S}}$ for each combination:

$$\tilde{\mathcal{S}}(\mathcal{C}_i(t)) = \sum_{j=t-K}^{t+K} \mathcal{S}(\mathcal{C}_i(j)) \quad (1)$$

and finally the combination with highest $\tilde{\mathcal{S}}$ is selected at the central frame t.

This methodology shows an interesting property. The possibility of merging combinations across frames also allows us to merge similar information between two consecutive onsets and within a given tempo grid. Consecutive frame estimations of the same pitch are associated to the same note, unless a new onset event associated to it is detected, which effectively will last a number of frames.

Some arguments of f_0 estimation can be tuned up through the user interface, like the maximum polyphony (the maximum number of simultaneous pitches that can be combined) the minimum pitch (the lowest f_0 that can be estimated) and the maximum pitch (the highest f_0 that can be estimated).

In Figure 2 a portion of a frame-based transcription analysis is shown using $K = 2$ neighboring frames. Note the presence of some very short notes. Most of these are actually fragments of a note with the same pitch preceding or following them. Some of these situations can be filtered out by merging or deleting too short notes by parameters that can be controlled by the user through the GUI. There are also false positive notes that have been fired due to local energy fluctuations in the spectrogram.

2.2 Multimodal transcription

This type of transcription combines the a frame-based multiple f_0 estimation with other information sources, like onsets and beats, to improve the results. The main idea is to segment the audio signal either in terms of pitched energy variation local maxima (provided as onset times) or music pulses (fractions of the estimated beats). After sound segmentation, note sets with the same pitches are merged in a wider, more meaningful, segment.

Therefore, the system offers three alternatives to perform

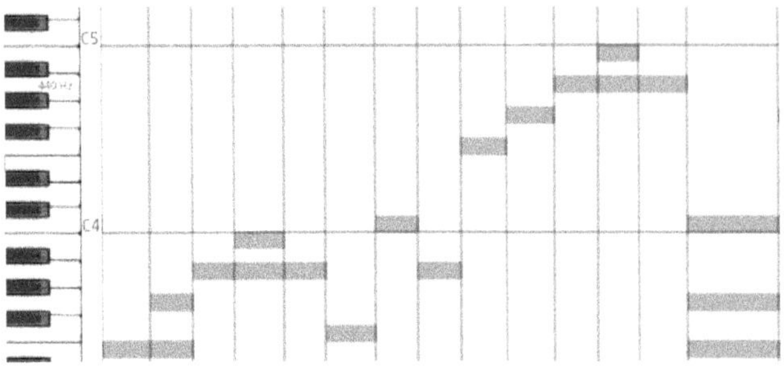

Figure 3: Transcription of the same sound sample in Fig. 2, but assisted by onsets (vertical lines).

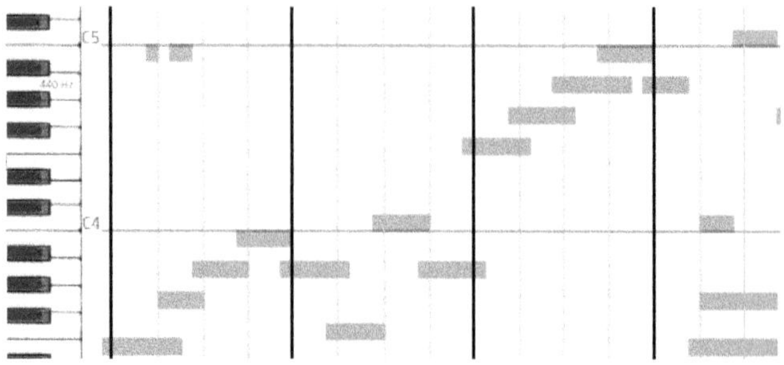

Figure 4: Example of transcription based on pulses using $q = 2$ (quantization to a eighth note)

the transcription task: raw frame by frame estimation, transcription assisted by onset segmentation or transcription assisted by pulses.

2.2.1 Transcription based on onsets

An onset time is an instant where one or more notes begin. The f_0 estimator module can use this information to improve the transcription. A method described in [11] is used to get the onset times in the audio file. Energy variations between consecutive frames are detected using one semitone band-pass filterbank in the frequency domain. The algorithm outputs a list of time frames (in seconds) where onsets were detected. Two parameters are used to calculate the onset times: onset detection threshold (the minimum value to consider an energy burst as an onset) and silence threshold (the minimum energy value to perform the onset detection).

The onset information partitions the musical piece in a number of sound segments, where each segment is the time interval between two consecutive onsets. No new notes can appear within these time segments, so the yielded combination $C_i(t)$ is valid for all the frames in that segment. The combinations selected by the multiple f_0 estimation method for all the frames in each segment are merged, combining their scores, yielding a set of pitches within the segment duration.

In Figure 3 a portion of the same sound transcription example in Fig. 2 is shown, now based on onsets. Each vertical line marks the instant where an onset was detected. Note that in this kind of transcription the detected notes have a more continuous aspect and very short notes that appeared in the frame-based transcription are removed.

2.2.2 Transcription based on pulses

For tempo estimation and beat tracking, BeatRoot [4] was used. This tool tries to detect the implicit (or audible) tempo of the piece by infering a list of more or less steady pulse times, that in the ideal case would correspond to beats of the music piece time signature.

Similarly to onsets, the transcription module can use this pulse information and combine it with the raw f_0 estimation data to compute note candidates within each region. The beats are also used to predict and track the tempo.

The time gap between two pulses can be considered as a segment for merging pitch sets detected within that region. In this case, a divisor number q (for *quantization*) can also be used to consider pulse fractions (a quarter note, a half note, etc.). Therefore, although the beats are detected, the actual segments where the note combination must be kept are the $1/q$ division of the beat.

In Figure 4 a transcription based on pulses is shown using a quantization grid of $q = 2$. Each vertical line marks the instant where a pulse has been detected. The darker lines mark the beginning of bars whereas lighter lines mark the beats inside bars. This means that the time signature for this particular example is 4/4. Note that all the detected notes last, at least 1/2 of the detected beats.

One additional advantage of performing pulse-based transcription is that, with pulses, the note durations acquire musical meaning. Without beats, note positions and durations are conditioned by the frame duration, which is subjected to mathematical aspects of the short-tiem Fourier transform. Therefore, pulse detection is required if the user aims to get a music score as the final output, otherwise only a piano roll can be obtained.

3. USER INTERACTION

The nature of the music transcription task is clearly interactive. Interaction with a human expert is needed to validate the initial transcription performed by state of the art automatic transcription systems. This interaction should be done from left to right in the time line and in some cases it should be possible to automatically propagate certain proposed changes to the rest of the transcription. Currently, two different type of interactions are developed in this prototype, interaction with onsets and interaction with pulses. The goal is to minimize the number of interactions that a human expert should perform to obtain a reliable transcription.

3.1 Interaction with onsets

When a human expert works with the transcription system, he can hear/see the transcribed notes and the sound source in order to decide whether the onsets are detected correctly. Each onset can be added, moved, or removed by the user. When an interaction is done on an onset o_i, the system recalculates the transcription between o_{i-1} and o_{i+1}. The five sets of notes $C_i(t)$, $i = 1..5$, with the highest score in this new scenario are presented to the human expert in order to decide which is the best transcription for the new inter-onset interval.

3.2 Interaction with pulses

The user can interact with the pulses for visualization purposes, validating pulses as beats or indicating a different relationship between them (for example, 2 pulses can be 1 beat). Also, the initial time signature, initially set to the most frequent one (4/4), and the first bar pulse (upbeat situations) can be set up. Time signature changes can also be set up at any bar. This has no impact in the transcription, which still uses q division pulse times to improve the result of the frame-based transcription.

4. CONCLUSIONS AND FURTHER DEVELOPMENT

The current development state of a multimodal interactive music transcription prototype has been presented in this paper. The system is capable of transcribing monotimbral polyphonic music audio signals in WAV format, and export the transcription as a single track MIDI file. It can use several sources of information extracted from the audio signal, such as multipitch estimates, beat times, and onset times. Currently, the system allows the user to interact with onset times and subsequently modify the transcription. Also, manipulation of beat and meter is available for visualization purposes.

One of the ongoing tasks is the quantitative evaluation of the improvements achieved by onset and pulse assisted transcription, compared to the raw frame-based output. This need of accurately timed databases and the definition of a metric that can assess the goodness of the performance. This is not a trivial task. For example, from a qualitative point of view, the onset-based transcription is perceived as clearly better than frame-based when one hears the result, but the beat-based one seems much better when one sees the transcribed scores, so the evaluation seems to be objective-dependent and, what is worse, subjective.

This interactive transcription prototype is still in an early stage of development. It is conceived as a platform for interactive multimodal research in the context of sound and symbolic music data, but is also aims at providing a tool to help musicians and music educators and students to transcribe a music piece with a minimum number of interactions, so many new features are planned for the near future, including:

- Full graphical interaction with the transcribed notes (add, delete, move, split, merge, etc.) using both mouse, qwerty, and MIDI keyboards.
- Textual interaction (change note pitch by name, note duration by value, etc.) by typing the modified values.
- Propagation of user editions from the current edit point to the end of the piece, in order to eliminate the need for further similar modifications (adaptive learning).
- Addition of a module like [7] for harmonic segmentation, and implementation of user interaction based on the chords detected.
- Improved interface usability capabilities.
- Addition of new user input modalitites, such as MIDI instrument live input.

5. ACKNOWLEDGMENTS

This work was supported by the project DRIMS (code TIN2009-14247-C02), the Consolider Ingenio 2010 research programme (project MIPRCV, CSD2007-00018), and the PASCAL2 Network of Excellence, IST-2007-216886.

6. REFERENCES

[1] M. Bay, A. F. Ehmann, and J. S. Downie. Evaluation of multiple-f0 estimation and tracking systems. In *Proc. of the 10th International Conference on Music Information Retrieval (ISMIR)*, pages 315–320, 2009.

[2] J. P. Bello, L. Daudet, S. Abdallah, C. Duxbury, M. Davies, and M. B. Sandler. A tutorial on onset detection in music signals. *IEEE Trans. on Speech and Audio Processing*, 13(5):1035–1047, September 2005.

[3] A. de Cheveigné. Multiple F0 estimation. In D. Wand and G. J. Brown, editors, *Computationaly Auditory Scene Analysis: Principles, algorithms and applications*. Wiley-IEEE Press, 2006.

[4] S. Dixon. Evaluation of the Audio Beat Tracking System BeatRoot. *Journal of New Music Research*, 36:39–50, 2007.

[5] M. Goto. An audio-based real-time beat tracking system for music with or without drum-sounds. *Journal of New Music Research*, 30:159–171, 2001.

[6] S. Handel. *Listening: An introduction to the perception of auditory events*. Bradford Books / MIT Press, 1989.

[7] C. Harte and M. Sandler. Automatic chord identifcation using a quantised chromagram. In *Audio Engineering Society Convention 118*, 5 2005.

[8] A. Klapuri and M. Davy. *Signal processing methods for music transcription*. Springer, 2006.

[9] A. Pertusa. *Computationally efficient methods for polyphonic music transcription*. PhD thesis, University of Alicante, 2010.

[10] A. Pertusa and J. M. Iñesta. Multiple fundamental frequency estimation using Gaussian smoothness. In *Proc. of the IEEE Int. Conf. on Acoustics, Speech, and Signal Processing (ICASSP)*, pages 105–108, Las Vegas, NV, 2008.

[11] A. Pertusa, A. Klapuri, and J. M. Iñesta. Recognition of note onsets in digital music using semitone bands. *Lecture Notes in Computer Science*, 3773:869–879, 2005.

Socially assisted Multi-view Video Viewer

Kenji Mase Kosuke Niwa* Takafumi Marutani
Graduate School of Information Science,
Nagoya University, Nagoya 464-8601 Japan
mase@nagoya-u.jp, niwa@arch.itc.nagoya-u.ac.jp,
marutani@cmc.ss.is.nagoya-u.ac.jp

ABSTRACT

We have developed a novel viewer for multi-point video with a socially accumulated viewing log for viewing assistance. The viewer uses annotations of objects in the scene and stabilizes the viewpoint to the user-selected object(s) along with the viewing-point selections. Starting from discussion on two viewing interfaces, i.e. camera-centered and target-centered, we propose a novel socially assisted viewing interface as a director-agent assisted target-centered system. A histogram of the viewing log in terms of time, camera and target of many people's viewing experiences, which we call a *viewgram*, is used as the source of the director agent, which exploits the viewgram as the visualized popular viewing behavior for particular content. The system can compose the most preferred viewing sequence by referring to the viewgram, for example. The viewgram can also be used as a map of preferences useful in choosing the viewing point.

Categories and Subject Descriptors

H.5.1 [**Multimedia Information Systems**]: Augmented realities

General Terms

Design, Human Factors

Keywords

Multi-view Video, Social Viewing, Recommendation, Annotation

1. INTRODUCTION

As they become cheaper and more ubiquitous, video cameras are increasingly being used for recording sporting events, artistic performances and sightseeing, and in daily life for entertainment, education, health and security. Recorded videos are used to share exciting experiences, aid memory, and increase knowledge. An event may be recorded by official cameras set up systematically, by private cameras brought independently or a mixture of the two. As the number of cameras increases, the depiction of an event is expected to become richer with the freedom to choose among various viewpoints. Computer vision and image coding techniques can produce more viewing points by interpolating scenes or modeling three-dimensional scenes. In the near future, an enormous amount of captured and generated video data will be available for a single event. One hundred channels of television programs will be multiplied by hundreds of viewing-point alternatives very soon. We eagerly anticipate the freedom of controlling video viewpoints.

We can explore various viewpoints and angles to obtain the best views to learn more about an event with multiple recorded footage. Additional modality can be incorporated by using other sensors such as GPS, LPS, and accelerometers, for more detailed description. The viewing exploration of an event will aid learning and training in manufacturing, sports, and live performances as well as increasing admiration for the performance. Such ability, however, will simultaneously usher in the chaos of dynamic scene selection. A subscriber will struggle in choosing the desired view rather than enjoying the content. One solution is to offer a personalized video director agent for private recommendations.

A video director of filming and broadcasting edits content by choosing the best camera position and framing, cutting the duration and arranging the presentation order. The computerized director agent is expected to perform such roles. A function to cut and edit was achieved by Mase et al. [1], in which wearable/mobile event-logging technology was applied to digitize interactive events collaboratively. All participants had a wearable computer with a head-mounted video camera and an infrared identification (IrID) sensor to capture events by video and interaction annotations. The same sensor systems were installed on the room ceiling and walls. Thus, the events in the room were captured collaboratively by multiple cameras. The IrID sensors were used to annotate the interaction with the help of Ir tags attached to the people and the room. Hence the *social interests* of a small group were extracted. The interaction duration and the social interests were used to produce a compact visit summary video.

In this paper, we discuss the viewpoint and framing selection function from multi-viewpoint video content to create director agents. We have already proposed a target-centered viewing interface for such content, i.e. the PegScope Viewer

*Currently working for DENSO Corporation, JAPAN

ICMI'11, November 14–18, 2011, Alicante, Spain.

(PSV) [2]. We newly propose to construct a director agent that collects the social use logs of the PSV since it gives people's preference of viewing points for each target object. The histogram of the viewing log in terms of time, camera and target of many people's viewing experiences, which we call the *viewgram*, is used as the source of the director agent that exploits the viewgram as the visualized popular viewing behavior for particular content. The temperate agent provides the viewing log as a suggestion map and automatically constructs the most appreciated sequence.

In the following sections, we discuss related works and introduce the PegScope Viewer interface. Then we propose the socially assisted viewing method followed by future directions for research.

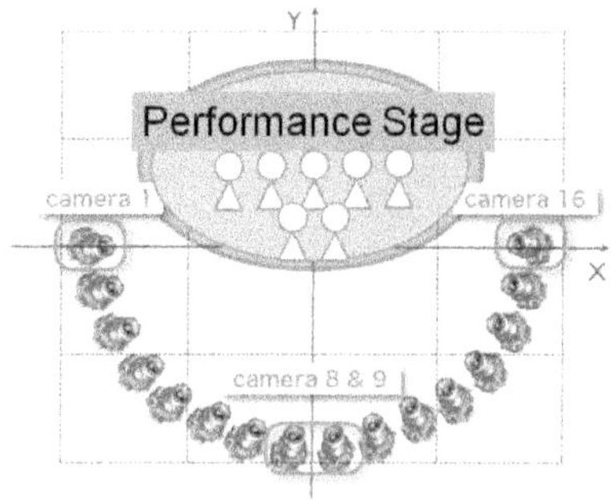

Figure 1: Multi-view video filming setup

2. RELATED WORKS

There have been many studies on multi- (or free-) viewpoint video content generation. The Immersive Video project used multiple cameras to build a 3-D model of targets for arbitrary point viewing by the silhouette volume intersection modeling method [3]. The appearance-based algorithm, e.g. the ray-space interpolation method [4] and light field rendering [5], are other approaches to free-viewpoint video.

Once cameras are set in the location and calibrated, data acquisition is fairly smooth. Moreover, the obtained data are ready for interpolation for arbitrary viewpoints with the above technologies. The next issue is the viewing interface for such multi-point-view video content. We will discuss the viewing interface by contrasting the viewpoint-specifying methods: camera-centered versus target-centered.

2.1 Camera-centered viewing

We first address the *camera-centered viewing method*. There are at least seven degrees of freedom for a virtual camera in 3D: camera position (x, y, z), camera angle $(yaw, pitch, roll)$, and field-of-view angle θ (zoom factor). Controlling these parameters simultaneously is not easy for casual viewers. There are a few research directions on the issue of the camera-centered viewpoint direct manipulation interface: eye-coupled and eye-decoupled interfaces.

2.1.1 Eye-coupled interface

The free-viewpoint viewing system generally uses a head-mounted display (HMD) for the *eye-coupled viewing interface* with head position and an orientation-sensing system. HMD is an ideal solution for direct free-viewpoint viewing for personal use. However, the technology remains immature; HMD is too heavy and low-quality for long-time viewing. Recent display technology has enabled a glass-free 3-D monitor; Integral Photography provides the user a motion parallax sensation with micro lenses[6]. A combination of a hand-held display and Augmented Reality (AR) annotation is another solution for eye-coupled viewing.

2.1.2 Eye-decoupled interface

Even though eye-coupled viewing is intuitive and immersive, it suffers from the above problems. Alternatively, a simple *eye-decoupled viewing interface* can be constructed by conventional GUI, although controlling seven parameters at a time is not easy. A few useful interactions have been proposed. One provides a pilot/driver-style interface that resembles a flight/driving simulator. A trained camera person could control such a camera very smoothly. However, if the target in the event is moving, for example, soccer players, tracking the target will be as difficult as a similar manipulation in an air-combat action.

Another solution is to control the tangible camera by hand. If a miniature scenery site is given and the camera position is measured, the camera view can be displayed on any kind of screen[7] . This kind of interface is more valuable for applications where the viewing position control is critical, including medical operations. Hand-controlling without any support in the open air is inadequate for a longer subscription. Viewers may soon get tired, and the manipulation could become unstable.

2.2 Target-centered viewing

An alternative to camera-centered viewing is *target-centered viewing*. If we have a target of interest in the scene, specifying it is more natural than specifying the camera direction. While camera-centered viewing is effective for cases where we don't have a particular interest or we don't know the target's location, if we have identified our target of interest and its location, we don't want to control the camera by ourselves to lock-on to the target. Rather, we want to spend effort watching it closely and from various viewpoints. Shen et al. [8] introduced a new confidence measure to automatically evaluate the camera view performance and applied it to suspect targeting in criminal surveillance video viewing.

2.2.1 Peg-to-the-point interface

Peg-to-the-point viewing (*Peg-SCOPE*) has been proposed for easy operation of multi-camera video viewing as a target-centered viewing [2]. The user is expected to choose explicitly any viewing target, i.e., a peg-point, that is virtually attached to a specific target in the video collection, such as a player, his/her face, the center of a team formation, or a ball in play while viewing. The peg-points are given with state-of-the-art computer vision object tracking or manual annotations.

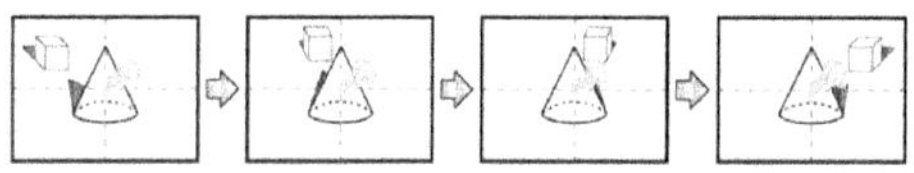

Figure 2: Example of Peg-SCOPE viewing: tagged target (cone) is located at center of frames of each camera, regardless of original target object (e.g., cube).

Figure 3: Peg-SCOPE viewer: target-centered viewing tool

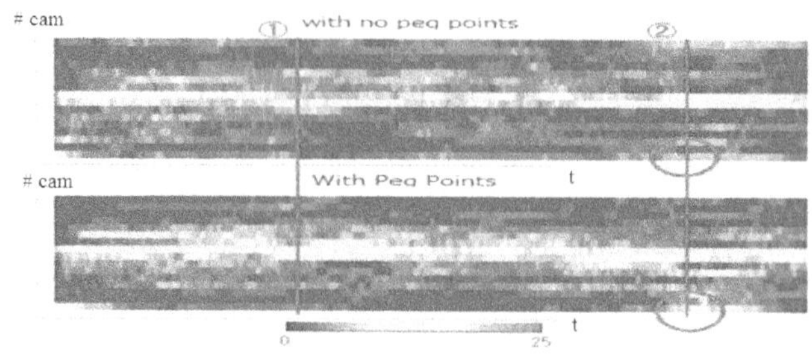

Figure 4: Viewgram: A video frame visit frequency by many viewers being visualized through time (horizontal) and camera (vertical).

Figure 5: Viewgram for girl E: $histogram(t, i, girl\_E)$: Example of viewgram for a cheerleading performance with 16 cameras.

Peg-scope viewing can provide stabilized targeting to a new object even if the original camera arrangement at the filming did not place the object in the center of the frame of each camera (fig 1). Figure 2 illustrates such a viewing result, where the cube was the original target at the time of the video shooting by four cameras, and the new target is the cone. The cube would have been located at the center of the original video frames of all cameras, but not the cone. We may often want to change the target to a different object (e.g., cone in the figure) in the scene when viewing the video.

Peg-SCOPE viewing expects the viewer to specify the viewing target first. It reduces the degrees of freedom from seven to four. How do we control the remaining parameters? One way is to provide a control clue to viewers, as shown in Fig. 3. This is a snapshot of a GUI-based Peg-SCOPE viewer. It contains the standard video play buttons, camera selector, zoom, peg-point list selector, etc. Peg-points, which are given as a list, are manually collected or given by image-processing object tracking. The camera selector chooses the camera position. Camera selection can be performed while the video is playing.

3. SOCIALLY ASSISTED VIEWING

The use of the target-centered interface will concentrate the interest of people to the content on various levels. We can collect the view logs of many users of PSV and construct a *viewgram* that illustrates the view visit frequencies for each camera-frame of a group of people. The log is, for example, expressed in a histogram format $histogram(t, i, O)$, where t is time (video frame), i is camera number (view position), and O is tagged target. This result is considered a visualization of the people's interest.

3.1 Preliminary experiment

Figure 4 illustrates a viewgram of cheerleading performance (110 seconds, 300 fps, 16 cameras). We performed a preliminary experiment, where subjects were instructed to view the content freely, with a peg-choosable PSV interface one time, and a no-peg PSV interface the other time. Only a few pegs are assigned to the object (performing cheer leaders). As shown in the figure, a peg-choosable interface has influenced the viewer's behavior resulting in more diverse camera (viewpoint) selections.

3.2 Target dependency

We performed a simple experiment with the same content. Sixteen subjects (13 males, 3 females, 20s to 30s) were recruited and instructed to watch the content with the PSV for 15 minutes freely in any direction. All viewing logs were recorded. Nine target tags were provided; image center, stage center and each of 7 performers.

Figure 5 shows the viewgram for the logs with the girl E selections: $histogram(t, i, girlE)$. In the beginning of the play (left side), the right-side views (upper rows) are more numerous. The position is good for watching girl E. In the middle of the scene, the high score moves to the center cameras (middle rows). This is the part when the cheerleaders form letters with their arms, where girl E is easy to watch from the center camera and the letter formation is very comprehensible.

The white polygonal line shows a trace of the best, i.e. most popular, camera for each time frame connected smoothly by a Viterbi algorithm. The sequence can be recommended to the users who are fond of girl E. Likewise, the director agent will make use of the histogram to compose a video sequence by tracing high-score frames to produce a most-popular edition in terms of view frequencies. The camera agent exploits the annotation of each frame segment to seek the best view. Figure 6 is a snapshot of a modified Peg-SCOPE viewer. A viewgram is added. Users can access the arbitrary temporal-viewpoint by clicking a point on the viewgram.

Figure 6: Viewgram-added Peg-SCOPE viewer: users can access the arbitrary temporal-viewpoint by clicking a point on the viewgram (bottom left).

4. FUTURE DIRECTION

Since the source of the viewgram is social viewing, we need to deploy the PegSCOPE viewer for a wider range of users to collect the viewing log on a large scale. We plan to extend the viewer system to a Web-based video streaming system. It will be a multi-channel streaming service that sends a main video channel of full-screen resolution along with the peg-point sequence and a few adjacent channel videos in a lower resolution. All of them must be transmitted in a synchronized manner. If a user chooses another channel, the lower resolution video will be switched to become the new main channel. The peg-based stabilization is performed locally on the peg-point sequence data.

A good video director agent should be available to casual users in the future, being personalized to support individual viewing preferences. This becomes possible by combining the camera-centered, target-centered and socially assisted viewings and is called *hybrid agent-assisted viewing*. It consists of two kinds of computer-based autonomous agents: camera and director. The autonomous camera agent (for example, [9]) seeks the local-best camera-centered views, and the director agent chooses one of the camera agent's suggestions. The camera agent also reflects the socially accumulated interests of various viewers. Each agent may track different players or take a perspective view from the main stand.

5. CONCLUSION

We introduced a socially assisted multi-point video viewer that is a modified version of the Peg-SCOPE Viewer, a target-centered viewing interface. The idea was to exploit the use (view) log of PSV of many users for each content selection. It showed a fairly good trend of users' preference and interest. In particular, it is more useful when the log is divided into target-oriented subgroups. Thus far, the accumulated log is not large enough to discuss the effect of a society-wide log. The modality of the viewgram is simple for the time being, but it can be extended, for example, to camera control parameters such as a zoom factor, and to composition levels such as cut transitions.

Sensing technology for rich content continues to expand. Wider free viewpoints, while desirable, are difficult to generate due to the immaturity of technology advancement of a large number of cameras and the limitation of camera locations due to event contexts. Weak camera calibration and non-wired system configuration are the next steps. Innovations in camera manufacturing technology will scale down the module and scale up the density of cameras. The dense configuration brings up another interesting issue. Other sensors such as accelerometers, gyros, direction, pressure and other biometrics will be integrated for sensing and annotating. Multi-modal sensing and pattern recognition will produce more accurate and robust contexts for richer annotation. Finally, hierarchical pattern mining and recognition are indispensable for higher levels of abstraction and event descriptions. They will increase the user's value and attention sensing. Meaning is added to the event, and knowledge brings the realm of true experience sharing and a virtually collaborative working society.

Acknowledgments

The authors would like to thank Tetsuya Kawamoto, Hideo Saito, Toshiaki Fujii, and Shogo Tokai for their collaborations on the multi-viewpoint video research, which is supported by the National Institute of Information and Communications Technology and the SCOPE program (111706003).

6. REFERENCES

[1] Mase, K., Sumi, Y., Toriyama, T., Tsuchikawa, M., Ito, S., Iwasawa, S., Kogure, K., and Hagita, N.: Ubiquitous experience media. IEEE Multimedia, Vol. 13, pp. 20–29 (2006).

[2] Tokai, S., Kawamoto, T., Fujii, T. and Mase, K.: Pegged to Point Browsing: An Approach to Browse Multi-view Video with View-Switching, and its Applications, ICPR 2008 workshop on Sensing Web. Dec. (2008).

[3] Moezzi, S., Katkere, A., Kuramura, D.Y., and Jain, R.: Immersive video. In: IEEE Virtual Reality Annual International Symposium, pp. 17–24. CA, USA (1996).

[4] Fujii T., Kimoto, T., and Tanimoto, M.: Ray space coding for 3d visual communication. In: Picture Coding Symposium '96, pp. 447–451 (1996).

[5] Levoy, M. and Hanrahan, P.: Light field rendering. SIGGRAPH '96, pp. 31–42. ACM, New York, NY, USA (1996).

[6] Okano F. et al.: Real-time three-dimensional pickup and display system based on Integral Photography, Proc. SPIE, Conference on Novel Optical Systems Design and Optimization II, Vol. 3430, pp.70-79 (1998).

[7] Inamoto, N. and Saito, H.: Intermediate View Generation of Soccer Scene from Multiple Videos., *ICPR (2)'02*, pp. 713–716 (2002).

[8] Shen, C., Zhang, C. and Fels, S.: A Multi-Camera Surveillance System that Estimates Quality-of-View Measurement, *Image Processing, 2007. IEEE ICIP 2007*, pp. III-193 – III-196 (online) (2007).

[9] He, L.-w., Cohen, M. F. and Salesin, D. H.: The virtual cinematographer: a paradigm for automatic real-time camera control and directing, SIGGRAPH '96, New York, NY, USA, ACM, pp. 217–224 (1996).

Long-term Socially Perceptive and Interactive Robot Companions: Challenges and Future Perspectives

Ruth Aylett
MACS, Heriot-Watt University
Riccarton
Edinburgh EH14 4AS, UK
r.s.aylett@hw.ac.uk

Ginevra Castellano
Schl of EECE
University of Birmingham
Birmingham, B15 2TT, UK
g.castellano@bham.ac.uk

Bogdan Raducanu
Computer Vision Centre
Edifici "O" – Campus UAB
08193 Bellaterra (Barcelona), Spain
bogdan@cvc.uab.es

Ana Paiva
INESC-ID and Instituto Superior Técnico,
Universidade Técnica de Lisboa, Portugal
ana.paiva@inesc-id.pt

Marc Hanheide
School of Computer Science
University of Birmingham
Birmingham, B15 2TT, UK
m.hanheide@cs.bham.ac.uk

ABSTRACT
This paper gives a brief overview of the challenges for multi-model perception and generation applied to robot companions located in human social environments. It reviews the current position in both perception and generation and the immediate technical challenges and goes on to consider the extra issues raised by embodiment and social context. Finally, it briefly discusses the impact of systems that must function continually over months rather than just for a few hours.

Categories and Subject Descriptors
I.2 ARTIFICIAL INTELLIGENCE: **I.2.9** Robotics: Operator interfaces; Sensors

General Terms: Human Factors

Keywords: Social robotics, human-robot interaction, multi-modal interaction

1. SOCIAL ROBOTICS
In the last fifteen years or so, there has been a perceptible shift away from a narrow task-oriented view of the relationship between human users and computer-based technologies. Thus in HCI, the focus has moved from usability to the user experience [Law]; graphical Embodied Conversational Agents (ECAs) have been developed in which multi-modal interaction to support expressive behaviour and affective engagement has become a research area [7], and a whole new field known as Human-Robot Interaction, or HRI, has developed [12]. Here robots are no longer merely machines for achieving tasks but become social actors in real-world human environments. The special session "Long-term socially perceptive and interactive robot companions: Challenges and future perspectives" at the International Conference on Multimodal Interaction 2011 was a further illustration of this trend.

2. MULTI-MODAL INTERACTION
An early result with respect to graphical characters was that users would often treat them as if they were human interaction partners, even though they knew that they were not [29]. Work with early social robots such as Kismet [5] substantiated this for robots too. Users act as if these technological artefacts had their own inner life: motives, goals, beliefs, and feelings; thus applying the Intentional Stance [13] to them. We argue that the term *believability* [2], often used as an evaluation metric for such interactions, is closely related to how far a user feels able to take this intentional stance and suspend their disbelief in the actual status of the interaction partner as machine or collection of graphical pixels.

A significant factor in believability, and thus user engagement, is the extent to which the interaction partner displays appropriate affective behaviour, thus allowing the user to track their putative inner state, and the extent to which it responds appropriately to the user's affective behaviour. This is sometimes called the *affective loop* [31] and has implications for multimodal interaction both on the side of perception and the side of generation.

2.1 Multimodal perception
The socially perceptive abilities that are a key requirement for a robot to be able to interact socially with human users [9] include: recognising people's social affective expressions and states, understanding their intentions, and accounting for the context of the situation.

These cannot be reduced to issues of speech recognition or natural language understanding, important though these modalities are. It is known that in the human-human case, a substantial proportion of the overall interaction may be carried by body language [26] and that this is at its greatest for affective aspects of communication. Overall, face and body appear to be the most important channels for communicating behavioural information, including affective states [1].

Recent work in affective computing is making progress towards the design of systems capable of perceiving social affective cues and using them to infer a person's affective state or intention [34, 37]. In addition to these natural modalities, work is also being carried out into the use of biological and physiological signal modalities. Thus the advent of sports monitoring equipment for heart-rate and pulse also facilitates the detection of states of raised arousal known to be associated with some affective states.

Brain-computer interfaces make use of external sensors registering the activation of particular areas of the brain and particular patterns of brain electrical activity [19].

However a limitation of much work so far on the automatic detection of user behaviour and states is that it is usually specialised for handling specific situations and is often much less successful under the natural and unanticipated conditions that occur in a real environment. This is why the design of socially perceptive robots requires the research community to address more comprehensively a specific set of key technical challenges [8]

1) **Spontaneous and non-prototypical affective expressions and states.** Research on automatic affect recognition needs to move towards systems sensitive to spontaneous, non-prototypical affective expressions and states. A typical issue in real environments is that the affect being expressed is likely to be fleeting and of low magnitude. Furious rage or ecstatic happiness are rare in HRI, and if they do occur – usually as the result of a deliberate experimental design – they are unlikely to last for very long. An alternative is to give a user explicit modalities with which to express their state, whether using devices such as the WiiMote to carry out specific gestures [25], or specifically designed interfaces [30].

2) **Multimodal nature of affective expressions**. Humans usually rely on several different channels of information to understand the affective messages communicated by others. Similarly, an automatic affect recognition system should also be able to analyse different types of affective expressions. Moreover, all of the modalities involved in natural human-robot interaction are difficult to process, especially outside of laboratory-based protocols or the use of actors to exaggerate the affective body language. Thus a multimodal approach, often one tailored to the specific interaction domain, is currently required to achieve acceptable results.

3) **Robustness to affect dynamics and real-world environments.** Social robots employed in real world applications require systems for the detection and interpretation of social affective cues that are robust to dynamic and noisy real world environments. This implies the ability to, in real-time, account for affective states and expressions with variable initialisation times, as well as for their temporal dynamics.

4) **Sensitivity to context**. The detection of the most subtle and complex states and intentions can only be achieved through a comprehensive analysis, not only of their effects, but also of their causes and context. An affect recognition system for a social robot should take into account the events that triggered the generation of an affective state and be context sensitive. Thus it should be able to capture, elaborate and integrate contextual information such as individual differences in affect expression, personality, preferences, goals, task, environment, etc..

2.2 Multimodal generation

Multimodal generation of social signals has been extensively investigated in the area of intelligent graphical characters, notably in those known as Embodied Conversational Agents, or ECAs [7]. Here, back-channel behaviour during conversations focused researchers on the generation of appropriate contextual use of facial expression, glance, and gesture [7], in systems that often had a pseudo-human appearance. Facial animation typically used the Facial Action Coding System (FACS) [16] which was derived from the analysis of human faces.

However, what counts as an appropriate social signal cannot be divorced from the way an interaction partner is embodied. This issue becomes far more significant in the case of robots, where embodiment must to a greater or lesser extent be physically implemented and thus is not easy to vary. While some work, typically in Japan, is based on robots intended to look as human as possible – robots sometimes referred to as *androids* [27] - this is only a small segment of the robot field. A 2003 survey [18] identifies *anthropomorphic* as only one approach to embodiment, with *zoomorphic*, *caricatured* and *functional* as other possibilities.

Human-like embodiments are seen as having advantages, for example in supporting imitation-based learning. On the other hand, the by-now well-known concept of the Uncanny Valley [28], in which close-to-human robots may provoke very negative feelings in interacting humans, has led to work studying social signals in other types of robots. There is evidence that a perceived consistency between the social role suggested by the embodiment and the range and type of social signals is a desirable aim [36]. It is clear that some researchers seek naturalism in expressive behaviour whether inspired by human or by animal behaviour. Others are more influenced by dramatic inventions, or by a more functional view of robot expressive behaviour.

Certainly there are feasibility as well as consistency issues. A functional-type robot without a face cannot generate facial expression. Here, modalities such as flashing lights may be required, or the use of movement dynamics (for example surprise could be conveyed by a short rapid movement backwards by a mobile robot). Movement dynamics are an area in which animated film offers design inspiration since these are techniques long-used there.

A robot that looks like a dog (Aibo) or a seal (Paro) cannot generate standard FACS-based facial expressions. Even in the case of caricatured robots with elements of humanoid embodiment, it is not always clear that naturalistic FACS-based facial expressions should be the aim as distinct from the exaggerated and simplified expressions of animated cartoon characters. Kismet [6], which had controllable eyebrows, ears, eyeballs, eyelids lips, and neck, had this type of expressive behaviour.

Apart from embodiment and consistency issues, research in multi-modal generation also covers the models used to determine in context what is an appropriate expressive behaviour. In intelligent graphical characters, the use of cognitive appraisal-based architectures [14] is one approach to linking perceived events to an appropriate affective state to be expressed. In robots, such symbolic-level architectures are much more complex to implement since they must depend on deriving symbolic information from sensor data that may be noisy and ambiguous. Lower level architectures have tried to produce more direct mappings [33] between sensor data and expressive behaviour and this facilitates the use of imitation learning as a way of developing such behaviours [4]. However these approaches do not integrate well with the use of natural language where expressive behaviour should relate to semantic content and are thus more appropriate in robots playing a more animal- or machine-like role.

3. FROM LAB TO REAL WORLD

The test of multi-modal interaction is the extent to which it can be embedded in real-world artefacts that can function successfully in human social environments.

3.1 Applications - Companions

Once the issue of a social environment is raised, then the social role that a robot companion is being asked to play becomes a key factor in defining its desired interactive capabilities. The very term *companion* is ambiguous in this context and may be given quite different interpretations by different groups [11]: for example a pet; a butler; a care assistant; a lab team member; a playmate; a pseudo-child. Some work suggests that more functional robots that do not attempt to masquerade as objects of affective attachment are preferred [11]; on the other hand work in graphical characters has shown that the development of a perceived personality may also improve interaction outcomes [3].

Some work focuses on developmental robotics, in which the pseudo-child role is the context for the development of learning capabilities [17] but there are also significant projects looking at specific companion applications [22, 10, 15 , 20]. As an example, the LIREC project [22] has studied the scientific issues relating to robot companions in the home, as assistants in maintaining independence for the elderly; in the work environment, as assistants to a lab-based research team or visitors to a new building; and as playmates for children in the context of a game such as chess.

The most successful companion project in terms of real-world deployment is Paro [35], a seal robot intended to provide extra interactive stimulation for elderly sufferers from dementia. In picking an animal-like embodiment , moreover an animal that few humans actually interact with, it avoids heightened expectations as well as over-demanding multi-model interaction requirements.

Where conventional robotics focused on health and safety, and often solved such issues with straightforward engineering approaches such enclosures and bumper-bars for an automatic stop, the embedding of robot companions into social environments both makes those issues much more demanding and adds concerns relating to privacy, data security, and ethical standards [32]. Multi-modal interaction must then not only deal with the demands of the specific interaction, but also with these constraints on the nature and content of the interaction in the given interaction context and with the given interaction history. Much further research is needed in this area.

3.2 From days to months

The ability to perform a social role successfully in most cases also implies the ability to do so for open-ended periods of time. Yet interaction over the long-term, past the period in which a novelty effect operates, raises serious research issues that are only beginning to be explored.

Some of these issues relate to basic competence, robustness and autonomy. Thus a robot that claims human attention for recharging every couple of hours lacks a basic capability for long-term social interaction. Similarly, a robot that perpetually collides with furniture or people, or is forever asking a human interaction partner to repeat itself due to inaccurate speech recognition is not able to play any long-term social role other than that of intolerable irritant. In domestic settings, we know how to deal with a washing machine that has broken down, but not with a robot in a like case.

While these are not trivial problems to solve or to engineer around, there are also issues relating specifically to interaction. What may be engaging and pleasurable when it is a novelty, may be boring or irritating as a long-term behavioural pattern. Over-emphatic multi-modal output may perform badly over the long-term just as failures in multi-modal perception may become more obtrusive. The mutual adaptation of long-term human-human interaction remains largely to be studied in human-robot interaction, though existing studies do already demonstrate its necessity if human engagement in the interaction is to be maintained [23].

In long-term interaction, the detection of subtle differences between users, so as to adapt in a personalized way, becomes essential. This requires not only the ability to change the interaction repertoire, but also to detect and act upon the preferences of the user as well as the specific history of interaction with them. Longer periods of interaction do help with the detection problem, but work in adaptive interfaces suggests that a disconcerting inconsistency may be perceived by human interaction partners if adaptation is carried out automatically, without explicit communication. This has implications for the mix of declarative and procedural components of a long and short-term companion memory: what cannot be explicitly recalled cannot be explicitly discussed either. Thus the development of acceptable human-like memory capabilities may be a central research issue for successful long-term interaction [24].

4. CONCLUSIONS

In a new field there are always many challenges. All the more so when long-term integration into human social environments is the overall aim. We have argued that both multi-model perception and generation face many as yet unsolved research issues. However, perhaps more important is the impossibility of separating the multi-modal interaction challenges from issues of embodiment on the one hand, and social context on the other. As an example, consider a simple affective loop in which a robot companion recognizes a smile and smiles back.

Certainly there are technical challenges in recognizing a smile in the first place, especially if the recognizing system is mounted on a mobile robot in a variably-lit human environment, and the user can be standing at variable distances and angles, with skin, facial and head hair of different colours, and variable height and clothing.

However, even when these are overcome, a companion still needs to know what the significance of the smile is before automatically assuming it reflects a happy interaction partner. Here contextual information, from other modalities, from a memory of previous interactions with this user, as well as the generic information about the relationship between events and emotions supplied by a cognitive appraisal system, can all help. Knowing whether the user has just entered the lab and is greeting the robot or whether they have just dropped a whole pile of paper and might be embarrassed would also help.

Once the relevant expressive behaviour is determined, the robot companion still has to respond. And with: a mouth? Some lights? Happy movement? A purring noise? Raising ears? Something else? Some combination? Here in miniature are some of the challenges of a fascinating research field.

5. REFERENCES

[1] Ambady, N. and Rosenthal, R. (1992). Thin Slices of Expressive Behavior as Predictors of Interpersonal Consequences: A Meta-Analysis. Psychological Bulletin, 111(2), 256-274.

[2] Bates, J. (1994) The role of emotion in believable agents. Communications of the ACM: Special Issue on Agents 37(7) (Jul 1994) 122–125

[3] Bickmore,T.W; Shulman, D. & Yin, Langxuan (2009) Engagement vs. Deceit: Virtual Humans with Human Autobiographies. IVA 2009: 6-19

[4] Boucenna, S.; Gaussier, P.; Andry, P.; Hafemeister, L.; (2010) Imitation as a communication tool for online facial expression learning and recognition. IROS 2010 pp 5323-28

[5] Brezeal, C. (2002) Designing Sociable Robots. MIT Press.

[6] Breazeal, C. (2009) Role of expressive behaviour for robots that learn from people. Philosophical Transactions of the Royal Society B, 364:3527–3538, 2009.

[7] Cassell J. 2000. Embodied conversational interface agents. *Communications of the ACM*, 4 (April), 70–78.

[8] Castellano, G., Leite, I., Pereira, A., Martinho, C., Paiva, A, & McOwan, P. W. (2010). Affect Recognition for Interactive Companions: Challenges and Design in Real World Scenarios. *Journal on Multimodal User Interfaces*, 3(1), 89-98, Springer.

[9] Castellano, G., & Peters, C. (2010). Socially Perceptive Robots: Challenges and Concerns. *Interaction Studies*, 11(2), John Benjamins Publishing Company.

[10] CompanionAble: http://www.companionable.net/ Accessed 5/9/11

[11] Dautenhahn, K., Woods, S., Kaouri, C., Walters, M., Koay, K. L. & Werry, I. (2005) What is a robot companion—friend, assistant or butler? In Proc. IEEE IRS/RSJ IROS 2005

[12] Dautenhahn, K. (2007) Socially intelligent robots: Dimensions of human-robot interaction. Philosophical Transactions of the Royal Society B: Biological Sciences, 362(1480):679–704, 2007.

[13] Dennett, D.C. (1989) The Intentional Stance. MIT Press

[14] Dias, J., Paiva, A.: Feeling and reasoning: A computational model for emotional agents. In: 12th Portuguese Conference on Artificial Intelligence (EPIA 2005), Portugal, Springer (2005) 127–140

[15] DOMEO: http://www.aal-domeo.org/ Accessed 5/9/11

[16] Ekman, P. & Friesen, W. (1982) Measuring facial movement with the facial action coding system. In: Emotion in the Human Face, Cambridge University Press 1982

[17] FEELIX Growing: http://www.feelix-growing.org/ Accessed 5/9/11

[18] Fong, T; Nourbaakhhsh, I. & Dautenhahn, K. (2003) A survey of socially-interactive robots. Robotics and Autonomous Systems, v42, pp143-166

[19] Gunes, H., and Pantic, M. (2010). Automatic, Dimensional and Continuous Emotion Recognition, International Journal of Synthetic Emotions, Vol. 1, No. 1, pp. 68-99, 2010.

[20] KSERA: http://ksera.ieis.tue.nl/ Accessed 5/9/11

[21] Law, E., Roto, V., Hassenzahl, M., Vermeeren, A., Kort, J.(2009) Understanding, Scoping and Defining User Experience: A Survey Approach. CHI'09. April 4-9, 2009

[22] LIREC: http://lirec.eu Accessed 5/9/11

[23] Leite, Y; Pereira.A; Castellano,G; Mascarenhas,S; Martinho.C & Paiva,A. (2010) Social Robots in Learning Environments: a Case study of an Empathic Chess Companion. Personalization Approaches in Learning Environments (PALE), CEUR Workshop Proceedings

[24] Mei Yii Lim, Ruth Aylett, Wan Ching Ho, Patricia Vargas and Sibylle Enz, (2009) *A Socially-Aware Memory for Companion Agents,* IVA2009 pp20-26, Springer

[25] Lim, M.Y; Aylett, R.S; Enz,S; Kriegel,M; Vannini,N; Hall, L. and Jones, S. (2009), Towards Intelligent Computer Assisted Educational Role-Play, 4th Int. Conf on E-Learning and Games, Banff, Canada, August 9-11, 2009, Springer

[26] Mehrabian, Albert (1972). *Nonverbal Communication.* Chicago, IL: Aldine-Atherton

[27] Minato, T., Shimada, M., Ishiguro, H., & Itakura, S. (2004). Development of an Android Robot for Studying Human-Robot Interaction. Innovations in Applied Artificial Intelligence, (pp. 424-434).

[28] Mori, M. (1970) Bukimi no tani [the uncanny valley]. Energy, 7:33–35

[29] Reeves,B. & Nass,C.I. (1996) The media equation: How people treat computers, television, and new media like real people and places. Univ Chicago Press

[30] Ståhl A., Höök K., Svensson M., Taylor A., Combetto M. (2008). Experiencing the affective diary. J. Pers. Ubiquit. Computing

[31] Sundström, P. (2005). *Exploring the affective loop,* Stockholm: Stockholm University.

[32] Vargas, P. A., Fernaeus, Y., Lim, M. Y., Enz, S., Ho, W. C., Jacobsson, M. and Aylett, R. (2011): Advocating an ethical memory model for artificial companions from a human-centred perspective , *Artificial Intelligence & Society*

[33] Velasquez, J.D. (1997) Modeling Emotions and Other Motivations in Synthetic Agents. Proceedings, 14th National Conference on AI, AAAI Press, pp10-16

[34] Vinciarelli, A., Pantic, M., & Bourlard, H. (2009). Social signal processing: Survey of an emerging domain. Image and Vision Computing Journal, 27(12), 1743-1759.

[35] Wada,K. and Shibata,T. (2007) 'Living with seal robotsits sociopsychological and physiological influences on the elderly at a care house', IEEE Transactions on Robotics, 23(5), 972–980

[36] Walters ML;,Syrdal DS; Dautenhaun K; te Boekhorst R. & Koay KL (2008) Avoiding the uncanny valley: Robot appearance, personality and consistency of behavior in a an attention-seeking home scenario for a robot companion. Auton Robot 24:159–178

[37] Zeng, Z., Pantic, M., Roisman, G. I., & Huang, T. S. (2009). A survey of affect recognition methods: Audio, visual, and spontaneous expressions. IEEE Transactions on Pattern Analysis and Machine Intelligence, 31(1), 39-58.

Living with a Robot Companion – Empirical Study on the Interaction with an Artificial Health Advisor

Astrid M. von der Pütten
University of Duisburg-Essen
Forsthausweg 2
47048 Duisburg, Germany
astrid.von-der-puetten@uni-due.de

Nicole C. Krämer
University of Duisburg-Essen
Forsthausweg 2
47048 Duisburg, Germany
nicole.kraemer@uni-due.de

Sabrina C. Eimler
University of Duisburg-Essen
Forsthausweg 2
47048 Duisburg, Germany
sabrina.eimler@uni-due.de

ABSTRACT

The EU project SERA (Social Engagement with Robots and Agents) provided the unique opportunity to collect real field data of people interacting with a robot companion in their homes. In the course of three iterations, altogether six elderly participants took part. Following a multi-methodological approach, the continuous quantitative and qualitative description of user behavior on a very fine-grained level gave us insights into when and how people interacted with the robot companion. Post-trial semi-structured interviews explored how the users perceived the companion and revealed their attitudes. Based on this large data set, conclusions can be drawn on whether people show signs of bonding and how their relation to the robot develops over time. Results indicate large inter-individual differences with regard to interaction behavior and attitudes. Implications for research on companions are discussed.

Categories and Subject Descriptors

K.4.m, H.5.2 user interfaces (D.2.2, H.1.2., I.2.6) subjects: natural language; J.4. subject psychology

General Terms

Measurement, Design, Reliability, Experimentation, Human Factors, Theory

Keywords

Artificial companions, socially assistive robots, field study, long-term evaluation, health advisor, elderly people, multimodal interaction

1. INTRODUCTION

Against the background of population aging -a problem which has to be faced by most industrial countries- and the thereby emerging societal problems, especially within the health care sector, a lot of research focuses on so called artificial companions and explores how they can help to solve upcoming deficits in our health care systems. For instance, in 2006 the World Health Organization [20] reported about an estimated shortage of almost 4.3 million doctors, midwives, nurses and support workers worldwide. This is one of the reasons why RTD aims to support maintaining health, functional capability and mobility of elderly individuals to extend the time people can live in their homes. Companions shall assist the elderly individuals, increase their autonomy and help them to gain and maintain a better and healthier lifestyle. Moreover, companions shall prevent social isolation, and support families and care organizations. Therefore, an increasing amount of research projects aim at assisting elderly to live independently at home as long as possible by using companion systems. However, a frequently occurring phenomenon in the interaction of humans with machines is that people are initially interested in interacting with an artificial entity; but are, however, quickly bored or annoyed with it, refuse to use it again and even show aggression towards the system [1,7,19]. While it is easy to attract people´s attention to a new technology in the short term, it is harder to keep them engaged in the long run. Nevertheless, particularly for health related systems it is highly important that people interact with the assistive technology over a long period of time. To achieve this, the central challenge is to further refine the sociability of artifacts that is considered to facilitate human-robot interaction [15].

The EU project SERA (Social Engagement with Robots and Agents) accepted this challenge and addressed (among others) the following questions: How do users interact with companions? What does it mean for a companion to be sociable? Do people show signs of bonding with a companion? The primary goal in SERA was not system development, but rather basic research in the field of social robotics. Moreover, the SERA project followed a new multi-methodological approach: We installed a robot companion within the homes of elderly participants and observed their interactions with the robot in three iterations. The collected video-data was analyzed using quantitative and qualitative research methods. In contrast to many other studies on the social effects of robots, the existence of this long-term data is a resource that will help research to consider the users' needs and the specific requirements for home robotics in the future.

So far, only few long-term studies with virtual and robotic companions have been conducted; most of them relying mainly on subjective data (interviews, questionnaires) or very simple performance measures. For instance, Koay, Walters and Dautenhahn [14] set up a longitudinal study that ran over a period of five weeks. This comprised eight interaction sessions in which they investigated proximity in the context of human-robot-interaction. Participants used a comfort-level-device to stop the approaching robot when they began to feel uncomfortable. However, the participants were not continuously confronted with a robot over a long period, but rather met the robot at eight

ICMI'11, November 14–18, 2011, Alicante, Spain.

separated sessions in the laboratory. Other studies are also just snapshots of sequences of short, reoccurring interactions between humans and artifacts although the systems were installed for a longer period of time. One of these examples is Carnegie Mellon´s Roboceptionist "Valerie" which was permanently located in the entranceway to Newell-Simon Hall in a reception booth [8]. Gockley and colleagues report their observations over a period of 180 days with a daily average of 88 interactions with Valerie. Unfortunately, they only automatically assessed the interaction time people spent with the robot via motion sensors, but did not analyze in more detail how people interacted with the robot (e.g. whether or not they talked to the robot, their nonverbal behavior, etc.). Similar to this, Hayashi et al. [9] reported results of a field study which took place in a train station for eight days. In this study, the researchers also assessed how many passersby stopped and interacted with the robot. In a more fine-grained analysis of the 900 videos of interacting people, the experimenters observed varying behaviors. Some people changed their course to stop and watch the robot; some touched the robot or took pictures. However, these were on-off interactions. Similarly, Kanda et al. [10] reported about interaction times in their 18-day field trial held at a Japanese elementary school where they introduced two English-speaking "Robovie" [11] robots to first- and sixth-grade pupils. They collected data on the interaction time, the interaction situation (i.e. whether pupils interacted alone with the robot or in groups with other children) as well as an English test as performance measure. Although there has been a large amount of video data, the researchers did not analyze the material more profound regarding e.g. relationship-building. Sung et al. [18] reported about a long-term study investigating the novelty effect. They introduced the Roomba vacuum robot to 30 households and conducted a series of five interviews. The results showed that after two months at the latest people had integrated Roomba into their daily routines. The authors discussed that they had balanced interventions with a natural adoption experience and therefore resigned to log, audio- or video-record interactions. Thus, although a number of participants reported about a relationship to their Roomba or about Roomba being integrated into their lives it remained unclear how the individuals actually interacted with the robot and how these relationships were established. With regard to virtual agents, studies by Bickmore and colleagues on relational agents [3,4] invited users to continuously use the PC-based FitTrack system to keep track of their physical exercise for several weeks. Results relied on e.g. log-in times, the willingness to read information material or amount of physical exercise. However, due to the web-based setting, Bickmore and colleagues were not able to investigate how people behaved while interacting with the agent or whether and how they built a relationship.

All the above mentioned studies share certain restrictedness in the measures used. Some simply do not exhaustively use the material they collected [10] - which is admittedly very time-consuming. However, merely assessing the interaction times does not allow for conclusions on what actually happened during the interaction and how people perceived the situation. Other studies are conducted in a way which simply does not provide insights into the nature of people's interactions with these artifacts, because they are for instance web-based [3,4].

2. RESEARCH QUESTIONS

The three iterations in the SERA project offered the unique opportunity to analyze real field data and explore how people interact with a robot in their homes. To answer our *guiding questions*, we followed a multi-methodological approach. *How do users interact with companions?* The continuous quantitative and qualitative description of user behavior on a very fine-grained level gave us insights into when and how people interacted with our companion. *What would it mean for a companion to be sociable?* Post-trial semi-structured interviews investigated how the users perceived the companion and reveal their attitudes. *Do people show signs of bonding with a companion?* Altogether, we were able to draw conclusions on whether people show signs of bonding and how this develops over time.

In this paper, we will illustrate our analysis of the behavioral data. We decided to annotate the participants´ behavior using categories as the result of a first overview of the material in the sense of a bottom-up approach. Since we did not have high resolution material due to the employment of small, unobtrusive cameras, we stuck to categories of verbal and nonverbal behavior that are audible and/or observable in the material. Besides smiling as a (mostly) positive social reaction we included as well eye contact as a sign of attention as categories.

3. SCENARIO AND SETUP

3.1 Scenario

The designated long-term aim for the scenario was to provide care for people recovering from a heart-attack. The British Heart Foundation provides brochures for patients with heart failure in order to encourage, maintain, and increase physical activity while at the same time avoiding the "over activity-rest-cycle" [5]. This cycle explains older people's tendency to physically overstrain and then take a longer rest period which results in a general downward trend toward being less fit. The companion had access to the participants´ diary with scheduled activities as well as other information resources which will be described in more detail in the following chapter. By keeping track of exercise and reminding participants not to do too much, the companion used in the SERA project monitored people's activity and secured that people avoided the "over activity-rest-cycle".

3.2 Initial Setup

The system installed in the participants´ homes comprised a wooden column and a hidden desktop computer with broad-band internet connection (cf. figure 1). As a visible core piece, the system featured the robot Nabaztag (now called Karotz, see: http://www.karotz.com). The Nabaztag was shaped like a small, stylized white rabbit. It was about 30 cm high, had movable ears and LEDs in its "belly" which could blink in different colors. Furthermore, the system´s peripheries included an infrared motion sensor (PIR), a micro switch on a key hook that tracked whether the keys were taken away or were hung back, an array microphone and a webcam which recorded the interactions on a voluntary basis. Participants agreed on being videotaped by pressing the video button. The dialog system covered the following topics: good morning dialog (including a weather report, advice on activity level, and weighing; initiated by first appearance in the morning), going out and coming home dialog (initiated by the key hook switch), evaluation of the day´s activity (initiated by PIR sensor after the last scheduled activity), information about the system (initiated by user) and read out messages from the researchers (e.g. "Sarah and Peter hope that you enjoyed your lunch at the Park Hotel."). The system was designed to initiate at least three interactions per day: the good morning dialog, the evaluation dialog and the researchers´ message. In iteration 1, the participants navigated through the dialogs using two buttons (yes and no). Based on our data analysis' results we changed the setup in each iteration. The changes are described in chapter 4.1 and 5.1.

Figure 1: The setup in a participant´s hallway

3.2.1 Participants

Participants were recruited via the Sheffield 50+ targeted mailing list. They received an initial visit to provide detailed information on the study [http://showcase.project-sera.eu/_downloads/SERA informationsheet090615.pdf], get consent and to receive their activity plan. Participants were not financially compensated for their participation. At the second visit, the setup was installed. Participants received an introduction to the robot´s functions (or new features in the following iterations, respectively). In iteration 1 three female users participated; two of them had a full trial of 10 to 12 days while one user´s setup was also implemented for 10 days, but did not function correctly. Therefore, this participant (P3) was not able to use the system to its full extent. The three female users also participated in iteration 2 and 3 (referred to as P1, P2, and P3). In iteration 2, we were able to recruit one more female user (P4) and a male user (P5) – both were subsequently included in iteration 3. Furthermore, we had one more new male user (P6) in this last iteration. Participants were all in the age segment of 50+ with the oldest being 76 years old. P1 was living alone in her house, but received frequent visits by her son. The Nabaztag was located in her kitchen. P2 was living alone, and the rabbit was located in her hallway. She was frequently visited by friends in the same age. P3, P5 and P6 were each living together with their spouse. The Nabaztags of P5 and P6 were installed in the hallway; the one of P3 in her living room. P5 and his wife received frequent visits of their children and grandchildren. P4 was living alone. The Nabaztag was located in her living room. All participants completed a 44-item version of the Big-Five inventory [2]. All participants are relatively extraverted, agreeable and open to new experiences. P2 and P6 scored relatively high in neuroticism indicating that these participants get nervous easily (see table 1).

3.2.2 Data Collection

Data collection took place in participants´ homes where video data was stored only when participants gave consent by pressing a video button. Each participant had the system at home for about ten days. During this time, we collected 22 videos per person on average, ranging from two to 51. The data collection resulted in 13 sets of video data (3*P1, 3*P2, 2*P3, 2*P4, 2*P5, 1*P6) which equals a total of over 300 video sequences, with an average length between one and two minutes, hence an overall duration of over five hours. The coding of all three iterations was done by four coders in total. Ten percent of all videos were coded twice. The codings were compared on a basis of 1-second pieces. The percentage of agreement is reported.

Table 1. Participants´ personality trait scores

No.	Extra-version (8 items, max 40)	Agree-ableness (9 items, max 45)	Conscien-tiousness (9 items, max 45)	Neuro-ticism (8 items, max 40)	Openness (10 items, max 50)
1	28,00	34,00	30,00	18,00	40,00
2	29,00	30,00	20,00	28,00	27,00
3	25,00	27,00	27,00	23,00	39,00
4	36,00	37,00	31,00	18,00	42,00
5	26,00	37,00	36,00	13,00	43,00
6	29,00	31,00	26,00	31,00	43,00

4. ITERATION 1

4.1 Method Iteration 1

Analysis of behavior. In iteration 1 we used the system "mediatags" for the annotation process. As mentioned above, resulting from a first overview of the material, we chose categories to describe the material in the sense of a bottom-up approach. The category system consisted of four categories:

- *Smiling* (no smile, smile without showing teeth, smile with showing teeth, laughter, not observable)
- *Verbal behavior* (speaks with system, speaks about system with a third person, soliloquizing, does not speak, speaks to the system instead of performing an action e.g. say yes instead of pressing yes-button), speaks to the system while performing an action, e.g. say yes while pressing yes-button), not observable
- *Eye Contact* (eye contact with camera, eye contact with Nabaztag, looks down to buttons, no eye contact = attention directed to the system but looks away from the system, e.g. to hear better, no attention = is still in the room, but e.g. does dishes and is not paying attention to system, not observable)

The annotation values and times were exported and then analyzed in Microsoft Excel. We indicate percentages of the total *interaction time*, which is not the actual length of the video, so for instance, for smiling and verbal behavior we subtracted the times for "not observable" from the total length of the video and for eye contact we subtracted the times for "not observable" and "no attention", respectively. The coded behavior is then denoted as percentage of the remaining interaction time.

Post-trial Interviews. After the 10 days field trial with the Nabaztag a semi-structured interview was conducted to evaluate people´s perception of their interaction with the Nabaztag (for a detailed description of the interviews see [13]). Questions were asked about the following topics: utilitarian factors (usefulness, usage, ease of use), social factors (self-identity), hedonic factors (e.g. perceived playfulness), general use, personal interest in technology and relationship development with the Nabaztag. After the interviews, the audio recordings of the interviews were transcribed verbatim. After analyzing the interviews, using simple serial indexing and cross-sectional analysis, the results of the interviews were used to verify/disconfirm the results of the video data and vice versa. In this paper we will only occasionally refer to corresponding interview results (for an extensive report see [13]).

4.2 Results Iteration 1

For the coding of the participants behavior inter-rater reliability was as follows: over all three participants the reliability for smiling was 89% and for verbal behavior 92%. For the category eye contact we found that "eye contact with buttons" was generally not reliably codable. Therefore, we skipped this category and coded it as "no eye contact". After this eye contact reliability was acceptable for P1 (69%) and P3 (63%), but not for P2 (53%).

Eye contact. During the phase of setup development we were concerned that the webcam might distract the participants from the Nabaztag. According to our analyses, we could resolve these concerns. P1 and P3 had more eye contact with the Nabaztag compared to the camera. Unfortunately, the eye contact for P2 was not reliably codable. However, anecdotally we can say that this participant looked down to the buttons a lot because these did not work properly (see table 2).

Smiling. With regard to smiling, we observed differences in the participants´ smiling behavior (see table 2): P1 smiled 22% of the interaction time, P2 smiled 15% of the interaction time, and P3 did not smile at all during the interactions

Verbal behavior. Furthermore, the verbal behavior of the participants was annotated. We observed that P1 not only talks a lot with the system (telling the system about her day, or about what she is going to do next), she also talked to it instead of performing an action (e.g. saying yes instead of pressing the yes button). From the transcripts we also know that P1 tried to teach the rabbit when she had the impression that the system did not understand what she is going to do. Participant 2 hardly spoke with the system and only sometimes verbally accompanied her actions (e.g. saying yes while pressing the yes button). She sometimes spoke in front of the system, but this was unrelated to the system (e.g. reminding herself not to forget something before going out). Over 54% of speech was conversations with a third person about the Nabaztag. The specific linguistic behavior was analyzed in more detail in [17]. Payr showed that P2 showed different behavior and speech patterns when interacting alone with the Nabaztag versus interacting with the rabbit in the presence of another person. P3 spoke a lot with the system and also accompanied her actions verbally.

Interviews. The results showed that with regard to the utilitarian factors, the participants did not find the Nabaztag useful. However, they found the Nabaztag easy to use, except for the conversation buttons. Still, all participants would like to continue using the Nabaztag in the second and third iteration. The hedonic factors, enjoyment and playfulness, did not seem to be of importance for the acceptance of robots. However, results indicate that hedonic factors are of importance in building a relationship with the Nabaztag. Social factors seemed to be of importance for the acceptance of the Nabaztag. However, they did not seem to be of importance with regard to relationship-building with the Nabaztag. Name-calling also appears to be related to relationship building with the Nabaztag. P1 reported with regard to relationship building: "of course we did, he asked questions and I answered them." However, she also stated that "I just got used to this, he was a presence. He's a man-made presence or even a women-made presence, in my kitchen, who was doing a job of research. I always knew that that's what it was." (see [13] for an extensive description of the interview results).

Summary. In sum, we could observe that the participants showed very different behavior. P1 somehow integrated the Nabaztag into her daily life and treated it like a companion. She made the effort to speak to the rabbit, correct its obviously wrong assumptions about her actions, she smiled a lot and also stated in the interviews that she formed a kind of relationship with the Nabaztag whom she gave the name Harvey (see [13]). Participant 2 also smiled in front of the rabbit. However, looking at the data more closely the smiling only takes place when a third person is present. The same tendency could be observed with regard to the verbal behavior. She talks about the system rather than with the system. The setup in Participant 3´s home had a lot of technical problems. This participant did not smile at all and when she was talking, she mostly complained that the system did not work.

5. ITERATION 2

5.1 Setup Changes in Iteration 2

Based on the results from data analysis on iteration 1 the setup was modified like described in the following. The interaction mode was altered. Instead of the yes and no buttons the participants were provided with so called flash cards with RFID stickers on it which could be recognized by the rabbit. The flash cards offered more possibilities to answer questions asked by the system and by this allowed a richer dialog. Furthermore, the dialog itself was changed. With regard to the underlying "Transtheoretical Model of Behavior Change" [16] data analysis showed that the assumption that people are in the "preparation" or "action" phase (according to the model) was wrong and that they were rather in the "maintenance" phase, meaning that they are not preparing to take an action, but rather already integrated physical exercise in their daily routine. Thus, the dialog contents were changed and aligned with the "maintenance" phase. The voice of the rabbit was changed into a more comic-like high pitch voice. This design decision was based on results from a user study which focused on the question whether the female voice used in iteration 1 caused an impression of inconsistency (see [6]). Furthermore, the system was supplemented by the SALT(E) (Sleeping, Alert, Listening, Talking, Engaged) interaction manager which distinguishes between three states at the top level. The system is either:

- Sleeping: not seeing or hearing anything (indicated by horizontal ear position)
- Alert: 'attending to' the person (indicated by vertical ear position)
- Engaged: it is committed to a conversation, either Listening or Talking (indicated by vertical ear position, with the right ear slightly further forward than the left)

5.2 Method Iteration 2

For iteration 2 we changed the annotation system and used "ANVIL" [12]; a system which allows to integrate the new automatically generated logfiles. Furthermore, we refined the verbal behavior category as it was hard to distinguish between "talking to the system" and "talking to system without expecting a reaction". Also "talking while pressing a button" may be also "talking to the system". We decided to join these three categories into "talking to the system". Because participants did not laugh in iteration 1, we skipped this value in the smile-category. With regard to eye contact, we included the category "eye contact with cards". However, the following inter-rater reliability analysis showed that raters could not reliably distinguish between "no eye contact" and "eye contact with cards", because if participants look down this causes confusion whether they broke eye contact or are looking for the next card. We therefore decided to skip this category which improved the eye contact reliability.

5.3 Results Iteration 2

Overall inter-rater reliability was as follows: verbal: 86%, Smiling: 82%. For eye contact inter-rater reliability was inacceptable for P1 and P5, but acceptable for P2 (81%), P3 (82%), and P4 (75%).

Eye contact. Unfortunately eye contact was not reliably codable for P1, as well as for P5. For P2 and P3 results show that people establish eye contact with the Nabaztag rather than with the camera. Because P3´s eye contact was also reliably codable in iteration 1, we can compare the percentages of eye contact (of the total interaction time) which showed to be smaller than in iteration 1. However, when she established eye contact, she only concentrated on the Nabaztag. In general, participants only briefly look to the camera after agreeing that they will be videotaped in order to check whether the camera works. All three participants established eye contact with the system for 22% to 45 % of the attention time, which is definitely a decrease of total eye contact compared to iteration 1. The answering buttons in iteration 1 were easier to handle than the flash cards, because it offered less interaction possibilities (just yes and no). In the second iteration participants took longer to choose their answer, because they had more options (for instance indicate their well-being on a scale from 1-10) and hence also concentrated on the cards in their hands (see table 2).

Smiling. With regard to smiling we observed changes in the participants´ smiling behavior compared to iteration 1 (note: only P1, P2, P3): Compared to iteration 1 P1 smiled less, namely only 2% of the interaction time. The same counts for P2 who also smiled only 2% of the interaction time. P3 did not smile at all like in the first iteration.

The two new participants (P4 and P5) smiled a lot more. P4 smiled 22% of the interaction time and P5 smiled 19% of the interaction time. This might indicate that we observe a novelty effect and participants smile less when they get used to the system (see table 2).

Verbal behavior. Furthermore, the verbal behavior of the participants was annotated. Again we can compare the behavior of P1, P2 and P3 with their behavior in iteration 1. P1 showed the same tendencies of verbal behavior. She talked a lot with the system (42% of total interaction). P2 changed her verbal behavior in iteration 2. She talked more to the Nabaztag and hardly talked about it with others. Participant 3 surprisingly did not talk at all in front of the rabbit. The new Participant 4 did not talk much, but when she did this it was mostly directed to the rabbit (29% of interaction time). Participant 5 spoke to the rabbit (32%) as well as talked about the rabbit with others (50% of interaction time). He often explained the rabbit´s capabilities to his visiting family.

Interviews. Three participants seem to have incorporated the system into their everyday lives and routines (P1, P2, P4). Important indicators for incorporation into everyday life seem to be utilitarian-, hedonic- and social factors. Two participants (P3, P5) stopped using the system due to privacy issues (rabbit was in hallway between bed and bathroom and participant did not want to be recorded in the morning) and not having enough control over it. This indicates that normative issues are very important to consider in future domestic studies. When looking at personal interest in technology, all participants were fairly interested in new technology. However, not every participant managed to use the system very well. It seems that experience is a more important factor for the usage and acceptance of the system. When looking at relationship building with the social robot, the term 'relationship' didn't seem to be appropriate at this moment (e.g. participants stated that they would not call their bond to the robot a relationship), but there were definitely signs that some participants started to form a relationship, for instance, P1 and P5 stated both that they did not build a relationship with the rabbit, but missed the rabbit when it left their homes. (see [6] for an extensive overview about results).

Summary. Again, also in iteration 2 we could observe that the participants showed very different behavior. Interestingly, the smiling behavior of the participants who took part for the second time decreased. Results also show changes in the participants´ verbal behavior. However, all these changes are still on an individual basis. There does not seem to be a general trend in the behavior for all participants. Behavior as well as behavior change seems to be idiosyncratic. This is also true for the interview results.

6. ITERATION 3

6.1 Setup Changes for Iteration 3

Based on the data analysis results from the second iteration the setup was amended again. Changes to the dialogue content introduced a new flash card for the robot to recommend social events while simultaneously emphasizing its autonomy from the researchers. This means that the researchers were not sending messages anymore (like in the previous two iterations, see chapter 3.2), but the rabbit would read out a recommendation for an event (e.g. "I've found a good exhibition which is on at the moment in the Millennium galleries and is all about drinking tea! It's called Teatopia and has collected together exhibits on tea including historic ceramics and tea-related textiles."). An additional flash card was introduced to allow more control for the user in a conversation. The user could use this "shut-up"-card to interrupt the Nabaztag and go back to the main dialog. This iteration uses non-verbal cues to display empathy through the movement of the rabbit's ears (based on results of [6]). Because of the negative evaluation in the interviews the voice of the companion was also changed to the original voice used for iteration 1.

6.2 Method Iteration 3

For iteration 3 "ELAN" was used for the annotation, which offers easy annotation, cross-coding and checking of inter-rater reliability. Upon request we also included "Speaks instead of using a card" in the verbal behavior category.

6.3 Results Iteration 3

Unfortunately, Participant 3 did not agree to be videotaped at all. The overall inter-rater reliability for the remaining participants´ verbal behavior was 77%. With regard to smiling P2 was not reliably codable (49%), the reliability for the remaining participants was 86%. Regarding eye contact the reliability was inacceptable for P2 (5%) and P4 (27%), but acceptable for P1 (88%), P5 (86%), and P6 (65%).

Eye contact. In this third iteration P1 totally ignored the camera and only established eye contact with the Nabaztag (63% of interaction time). P5 concentrated a lot on the flash cards and in addition, he had health problems with his eyes. He blinked a lot, and looked up in order to wet his eye. Subsequently he established less eye contact with the system (26%). The new P6 also only established little eye contact (19% of interaction time). P2 and P4 were not reliably codable (see table 2).

Smiling. With regard to smiling we observed changes in the participants´ smiling behavior compared to iteration 2. Compared to iteration 2 P1 smiled more again (13%). P2 and P3 were not codable. P4 smiled less than in iteration 2 (only 2,5% of the interaction time). The same tendency is observable for P5 who smiled 2% of the interaction time. The new P6 smiled 33% of the interaction time.

In sum, we see the same tendency of decreasing smiling for P4 and P5 in their second field trial which was also observable for P1, P2 and P3 in their second field trial (see table 1).

Verbal behavior. With regard to the verbal behavior we see almost no changes in the verbal behavior of P1. She still talks a lot to the system. P2 almost did not talk at all in front of the rabbit. But when she did she talked to the rabbit rather than about it. P4 also talked a lot with the system (31% of interaction time) and occasionally spoke instead of using a card. P5 is most of the time quiet while interacting with the rabbit. He hardly spoke to the rabbit or about it (it seems that the visiting family now knows how the rabbit works) and when he is talking in front of the Nabaztag it is mostly unrelated to the system. P6 talked to (17%) and about (11%) the Nabaztag. He also occasionally spoke instead of using a card.

Interviews. With regard to utilitarian factors and general usage, P1 and P4 reported that the rabbit fulfilled its purpose and they observed a change in their own behavior; e.g. P1 stated "The rabbit stopped me from over-exercising. Because I was used to thinking I am so tired, and go upstairs and watch television in the attic and fall asleep on the bed. And the rabbit kept asking me: Am I over-exercising? And it suddenly clicked one day that yes I was. I was doing it all wrong." and P4 mentioned "So what this whole experiment has done is introduced an idea of recording that and bringing in a notion of "do I do what I think I am doing?" With regard to relationship-building we observe mixed results like in the previous iterations. For instance, when asked why she is talking to the rabbit so much P1 answered "Yes, because that is what he is there for. I am not such a daft mapped person. On Wednesday morning, the day after you picked him up, you would actually miss him. I should not say it really, because I know it is all computerized. But you are such a sweet little thing." P6 also built quite a relationship: "My wife and I became very fond of it. We liked the idea of personalizing it. And the rabbit is as good as a person as anything else. And we were charmed by it. (…) Very interesting the way that you are half recognizing it as a person, and the rational part of you is recognizing it not as a person. (…) We missed her. Oh yes. Missed her physically, because we got used to her there." P4 reported that she had mixed experiences: "It disappointed me a lot. And I think that when it did something that I perceived to be right, I would effusive with praise and be really pleased. So it was a relationship with extremes. (…) So I don't think I really missed it. But I missed the process of thinking about my exercise." However, the other participants denied to have a relationship at all and treated the Nabaztag more like a tool; e.g. P3: "The rabbit was only here for a few days, so I did not have the time to create an emotional bond with it.", P5: "I treated it like a tool." These participants also mentioned that they would like to change the outer appearance and have the tool more alike their other decoration (e.g. abstract piece of art).

Table 2. Participants´ behavior in percentage of total interaction

		Iteration		
		1	2	3
Participant 1	*Eye contact percentage of total int.*	*78,21*	-	*36,69*
	• camera	10.97	-	0,00
	• buttons/RFID cards	27.51	-	-
	• Nabaztag	61.52	-	100,00
	smiling percentage of total int.	*22,33*	*2,25*	*12,69*
	• With teeth	22.88	67.40	13,05
	• Without teeth	77.12	32.60	86,95
	• laughter	0.00	0,00	0,00
Participant 2	*Eye contact percentage of total int.*	-	*32,59*	-
	• camera	-	4.52	-
	• buttons/RFID cards	-	-	-
	• Nabaztag	-	95.48	-
	smiling percentage of total int.	*15,51*	*2,25*	-
	• With teeth	66.37	67,40	-
	• Without teeth	33.63	32,60	-
	• laughter	0.00	0,00	-
Participant 3	*Eye contact percentage of total int.*	*74,66*	*23,41*	-
	• camera	30.63	3,64	-
	• buttons	22.01	-	-
	• Nabaztag	47.36	96,36	-
	smiling percentage of total int.	*0*	*0*	-
	• With teeth	0	0	-
	• Without teeth	0	0	-
	• laughter	0	0	-
Participant 4	*Eye contact percentage of total int.*		*45,09*	-
	• camera	-	19,82	-
	• buttons	-	-	-
	• Nabaztag	-	80,12	-
	smiling percentage of total int.		*32,32*	*3,32*
	• With teeth	-	61,87	24,59
	• Without teeth	-	38,13	52,07
	• laughter	-	0,00	23,34
Participant 5	*Eye contact percentage of total int.*		-	*35,99*
	• camera	-	-	26,73
	• buttons	-	-	-
	• Nabaztag	-	-	73,27
	smiling percentage of total int.		*19,35*	*2,70*
	• With teeth	-	19,76	57,32
	• Without teeth	-	80,24	12,44
	• laughter	-	0,00	30,24
Participant 6	*Eye contact percentage of total int.*			*24,02*
	• camera	-	-	19,36
	• buttons	-	-	-
	• Nabaztag	-	-	80,64
	smiling percentage of total int.			*33,55*
	• With teeth	-	-	19,96
	• Without teeth	-	-	79,41
	• laughter	-	-	0,63

P4 mentioned that she got especially annoyed when the Nabaztag did not recognize a card and then proceeded to another dialog forcing her to wait with what she wanted to do: "Not only is it refusing my request, it is asking me to remember to remind it to do that later. It is giving me a burden, and I do not want to do that." Another general comment was that sometimes users were in a rush and did not want to proceed through the dialogs when leaving the house. The system here showed not enough flexibility. Again normative issues where mentioned in the interviews. P5 for instance did not want to be videotaped in the morning and "would ignore it because I was not properly dressed to put the video on or anything." P3 did not like the idea that she has no control over the videos taken by the Nabaztag: "then I could not check what it have recorded and I could not go and say I am going to delete that. So I did not have control. So I did not want to do the videos." However, P5 was willing to be videotaped at any other daytime and P3 agreed on being videotaped for the first two iterations.

Summary. Also, in iteration three it becomes obvious that there are massive inter-individual differences with regard to all categories of behavior. However, we observed the same tendency of decreasing smiling for Participants 4 and 5 in their second trial like for P1, P2 and P3 in their second trial. We also see that verbal behavior is stable in some participants while others change over time. From the interviews we see, that some participants are able and willing to establish a relationship with the Nabaztag although some state that they now that this is not comparable to human relationships.

7. GENERAL DISCUSSION

This paper presents results of the analysis of a set of video data, collected in the course of three consecutive iterations, showing older people interacting with a companion in their own homes for ten days (per iteration). We coded the participants' verbal behavior as well as their nonverbal behavior, especially smiling and eye contact. Based on our data, it seems people only show facial expressions under specific circumstances. The system should work properly, with no delays and no interruptions; e.g. P3 faced technical problems in the first two iterations which hindered successful interaction and this seemed to be reflected in the nonverbal behavior: she did not smile at all in the first two iterations and in the third iteration, she refused to be videotaped at all. However, we observed huge inter-individual differences in behavior. This also seemed to be connected to relationship building. P1 and P6 initially decided to integrate the rabbit into their lives. They talked a lot to the rabbit and enjoyed its presence. These two participants also reported about emotional bonding and that they missed the rabbit after it was gone. Furthermore, they gave the Nabaztag a name (Harvey, Bunnycans). P4 and P5 treated the rabbit as a tool. Both participants had very precise expectations what the Nabaztag should be capable of resulting from their backgrounds and experiences with health-related systems. They found the functionality very limited and the conversations more annoying or distracting than helpful. P2 and P3 had varying opinions on the rabbit. For instance, P2 showed off the rabbit to visitors while quietly interacting with it when alone. She once said that she somehow liked the rabbit, but later on, she stated that she would prefer a more abstract piece of art that better fits in her hallway, but fulfills the same tasks. Although we found all these differences in behavior and attitude towards the robot, they do not seem to be resulting from their individual personality – which overall are not particularly peculiar.

With regard to the participants' nonverbal behavior we cannot observe a general trend for all participants. However, on aspect is similar across participants: the smiling behavior of the participants who took part for the second time decreased. We observed the same tendency of decreasing smiling for P1, P2 and P3 in iteration 2 and for P4 and P5 in their second trial in iteration 3. However, we were not able to resolve the question whether participants' decrease in smiling behavior in iteration 2 was due to the novelty effect, because we had no material for P2 and P3 in iteration 3 to compare with. Eye contact behavior seemed to be very stable over time. Participants were more focused on the Nabaztag than on the webcam in all iterations. They just quickly checked whether the webcam is recording and then concentrated on their interactions. However, the interaction mode with the RFID-cards distracted from the Nabaztag, because participants looked down to find the right card. In addition, the interaction with the cards was not intuitive enough for the participants as P3 stated "Putting cards in front of somebody's nose is not a very easy thing, it is not very obvious." Also, some other participants reported to prefer another interaction mode and mentioned for instance touch screen, keyboard or voice input.

The verbal behavior of the participants seemed to be a relatively stable variable as well. Participants tended to talk more about the rabbit with others in the beginning, which is decreasing over time as their peers know about the system's functions. Participants who talked a lot with the rabbit continued with this behavior during all iterations. Whereas others kept interacting with the system merely only based on the given interaction mode; they did not talk to the rabbit but stuck to pressing the buttons or showing the RFID cards to the Nabaztag, respectively.

In sum, we can say that users are willing to start interactions and even conversation with a robot even though its perceptive and expressive capabilities are limited. Although they are aware of interacting with an artificial being, some of the users built relationships with the robot, while others treated the robot like a tool. In general, keeping control over the companion seemed to be of great importance for almost all users. Those who treated the Nabaztag more like a tool and regarded the conversations as distracting were especially frustrated when they were in a rush and the dialogs took too long. The system was taking over control over their time plan. P4 reported that she wanted to be in control over the topic of conversation and the rabbit was "giving her a burden" when it jumped to another dialog and she could not proceed with her task. Therefore, being in control seemed to be of high relevance when interacting with the companion. The interaction was perceived as pleasant as long as the Nabaztag did what the user wants it to do. Usually, humans would allow their counterparts to have their own way of doing things and accept this as a humanlike feature. The artificial companion, however, is expected to follow the user's preferred interaction path. The system itself and the dialogs where designed not to be patronizing and the Nabaztag's contributions in the dialogs were very submissive. However, the participants still felt patronized, because they could not control for the dialog topic. Thus, contrary to assumptions made in the project's contexts, the previously outlined results allow the conclusion that users tended to be more pragmatic in their relationship toward companions. Some people tended to like it as long as it helps and they have a feeling of being in control. Others seemed to integrate the companion into their live, although it did not always work properly and was perceived as being of limited use. For instance, P1 took part in all iterations and although the system did not always work as expected she integrated the robot into her daily routines and moreover she did not seem to be subject to the novelty effect.

Most importantly, our long-term field study demonstrated that the all-time presence of a robot in people's homes raises challenges to research that are unlikely to be discovered in a single laboratory interaction or several sessions of on-off interactions between human and robot. This is true for the previously discussed issues of floor management (who is in control for the dialog topic), for example. In addition, laboratory experiments which rely on mean values would not reveal such massive inter-individual differences for specific behaviors as those found in our study. Moreover, results demonstrated that having a robot in the kitchen is different from having it in the hall or in the living room. In addition, also the circumstances the participants are living in influenced how people treat the robot. Some behaved differently in the presence of friends and family than interacting with the robot alone. Some used the robot as a topic for conversation with others. Thus, we can finally conclude that the behavior of the robot has to be adapted to the specific environmental situation and location in the user's home as well as to the social situation.

Limitations. As the main goal of SERA was to see how people react to a robot in their house with increasing interaction capabilities, we did not design an instantly perfectly usable system, but implemented an incremental research design which included changes of the robot interface (e.g. voice) and its behavior (e.g. ear positions) as well as changes in dialog. This, however, makes it impossible to disentangle habituation and long-term acclimatization effects from those effects elicited by the changes in interface and dialog. Also, due to the qualitative approach and thus the huge amount of data which had to be coded, we were limited to a small sample size. This small sample size does not allow identifying any generally statistically significant trends in the data. All trends reported in this study are limited to the study´s participants. Additionally we can derive from the videos that more interactions took place than were videotaped which is unfortunate but results from our ethically correct procedure to have participants agree to the recording of every single interaction

Conclusion. Altogether, our approach shows that – despite a number of problems - it is possible to study companion-human relationships in real-life settings and that useful insights are yielded although the robot´s functions are still limited. Furthermore, it is possible to include real, that is naïve, users and real application environments into research. This should encourage other researchers to extend the research in this area as it will give more valid and generalizable insights compared to commonly conducted laboratory studies that rely on short term interactions and self-report questionnaires.

8. ACKNOWLEDGMENTS

The research leading to these results has received funding from the European Community's Seventh Framework Programme [FP7/2007-2013] under grant agreement no. 231868. We thank our cooperation partners: University of Sheffield, University of Twente, and Austrian Research Institute for Artificial Intelligence.

9. REFERENCES

[1] Angeli, A. de, Brahnam, S., Wallis, P., and Dix, A. 2006. Misuse and abuse of interactive technologies. In *CHI´06. Proceedings of the Conference on Computer-Human Interaction*, Montréal, Québec, Canada, 1647–1650.

[2] Benet-Martinez, V., & John, O. P. 1998. *Los Cinco Grandes* across cultures and ethnic groups: Multitrait multimethod analyses of the Big Five in Spanish and English. *Journal of Personality and Social Psychology*, 75, 729-750.

[3] Bickmore, T., Gruber, A., and Picard, R. 2005. Establishing the computer–patient working alliance in automated health behavior change interventions. *Patient Education and Counseling* 59, 1, 21–30.

[4] Bickmore, T.W., and Picard, R.W. 2005. Establishing and Maintaining Long-Term Human-Computer Relationships. *ACM Transactions on Computer-Human Interaction,* 12, 2, 293–327.

[5] British Heart Foundation. *The Heart Failure Plan*. London (2005). http://bhf.org.uk/.

[6] Creer, S., Eimler, S., Krämer, N., Payr, S., von der Pütten, A., Wallis, P. 2011. *D1.3b Data Analysis Results. Technical Report*. EU Project SERA. http://showcase.project-sera.eu/doc/dataanalysis.html

[7] De Angeli, A., Brahnam, S., and Wallis, P. 2005. ABUSE: the dark side of human-computer interaction. In *Proceedings of the Interact 2005 Workshop on Abuse*, Rome, Italy.

[8] Gockley, R., Bruce, A., Forlizzi, J., Michalowski, M., and Mundell, A. 2005. Designing Robots for Long-Term Social Interaction. In *Proceedings of the IEEE/RSJ International Conference on Intelligent Robots and Systems (IROS 05)*, 2199–2204.

[9] Hayashi, K., Sakamoto, D., Kanda, T., Shiomi, M., Koizumi, S., Ishiguro, H., Ogasawara, T., and Hagita, N. 2007. Humanoid robots as a passive-social medium. In *HRI '07. Proceedings of the ACM/IEEE international conference on Human-robot interaction*. Washington DC, USA.

[10] Kanda, T., Hirano, T., Eaton, D., and Ishiguro, H. 2004. Interactive Robots as Social Partners and Peer Tutors for Children: A Field Trial. *Human-Comp. Interaction,* 19, 1, 61–84.

[11] Kanda, T., Ishiguro, H., Ono, T., Imai, M., and Nakatsu, R. 2002. Development and evaluation of an interactive humanoid robot "Robovie". *Proceedings of IEEE International Conference on Robotics and Automation (ICRA '02)*, 1848–1855.

[12] Kipp, M. 2001. Anvil - A Generic Annotation Tool for Multimodal Dialogue. In *Proceedings of the 7th European Conference on Speech Communication and Technology (Eurospeech)*, 1367-1370.

[13] Klamer, T. and Ben Allouch, S. 2010. Acceptance and Use of a Zoomorphic Robot in a Domestic Setting. In *European Meetings on Cybernetics and Systems Research (EMCSR) 2010*, Vienna, Austria.

[14] Koay M.L., S. a. W. and Dautenhahn, K. 2007. Living with Robots: Investigating the Habituation Effect in Participants' Preferences During a Longitudinal Human-Robot Interaction Study. In *Proceedings of the 16th IEEE International Workshop on Robot and Human Interactive Communication (RO-MAN 2007)*, 564–569.

[15] Krämer, N.C.; Eimler, S.C.; von der Pütten, A.M. & Payr, S. 2011. "Theory of companions" What can theoretical models contribute to applications and understanding of human-robot interaction? *Applied Artificial Intelligence*, 25, 6, 474-502.

[16] Prochaska, J., & Velicer, W. 1997. The transtheoretical model of behavior change. *American journal of health promotion,* 12, 38-48.

[17] Payr, S. 2010. Ritual or Routine: Communication in Long-Term Relationships with Companions. In Trappl R. (ed.): *Cybernetics and Systems 2010*, Austrian Society for Cybernetic Studies, Vienna.

[18] Sung, J., Christensen, H.I., and Grinter, R.E. (2009). Robots in the Wild: Understanding Long-Term Use. In *Proceedings of 4th ACM/IEEE international conference on Human robot interaction (HRI '09)*.

[19] Walker, M. A., Langkilde-geary, I., Hastie, H., Wright, J., and Gorin, A. 2002. Automatically Training a Problematic Dialogue Predictor for a Spoken Dialogue System. *Journal of Artificial Intelligence Research*, 293–319.

[20] World Health Organization. 2006. The world health report 2006 - working together for health, Geneva.

Child-Robot Interaction in The Wild: Advice to the Aspiring Experimenter

Raquel Ros
Imperial College London
r.ros-espinoza@imperial.ac.uk

Marco Nalin
Hospital San Raffaele
nalin.marco@hsr.it

Rachel Wood
University of Plymouth
rachel.wood@plymouth.ac.uk

Paul Baxter
University of Plymouth
paul.baxter@plymouth.ac.uk

Rosemarijn Looije
TNO
rosemarijn.looije@tno.nl

Yiannis Demiris
Imperial College London
y.demiris@imperial.ac.uk

ABSTRACT

We present insights gleaned from a series of child-robot interaction experiments carried out in a hospital paediatric department. Our aim here is to share good practice in experimental design and lessons learned about the implementation of systems for social HRI with child users towards application in "the wild", rather than in tightly controlled and constrained laboratory environments: a trade-off between the structures imposed by experimental design and the desire for removal of such constraints that inhibit interaction depth, and hence engagement, requires a careful balance.

Categories and Subject Descriptors

H.1.2 [**Models and Principles**]: User/Machine Systems—*software psychology*; I.2.9 [**Artificial Intelligence**]: Robotics—*commercial robotics and applications*; J.3 [**Computer Applications**]: Life and Medical Sciences—*health*

General Terms

Design, Experimentation, Human Factors, Theory.

Keywords

Child-robot interaction, experimental practice, human-robot interaction, interaction design, social robotics.

1. THE CHALLENGES OF LONG-TERM HUMAN-ROBOT INTERACTION

Over the last few decades electromechanical progress in robotics has outpaced developments in artificial cognition. This has been noticeable across the various sub-fields of robotics, but never more so than in social robotics. Robots embedded in a social environment not only need to deal with the challenges encountered by field robots, but in addition need capabilities for coping with highly dynamic and stochastic elements inherent in the social milieu. As such, social robots have to face a number of challenges which are to a large extent still beyond the current state of the art in science and technology. The three main challenges yet to be surmounted by social robotics are:

1. *Contingent responding in dynamic social environments:* In field robotics, an action by the robot does not necessarily induce a significant reaction from the environment: an unmanned vehicle driving around a rock, does not precipitate a response from the rock. In a social environment however, an action by a robot will almost always prompts some reaction from the user or users. Endowing robots with capabilities for contingent and appropriate handling of user responses, plus some capacity for the prediction of responses to their subsequent actions, is one of the main challenges in HRI.

2. *Interpretation of social sensory information:* in contrast to robots which do not engage in interaction over natural communication channels, social robots are required to make sense of social signals. For interactions that go beyond proto-social responses, this has proven to be a tremendous challenge. The multi-modal aspect of social interaction thus continues to elude us, but even the interpretation of single modalities, such as gesture or language, has proven to be extremely challenging. The early promise of multi-modal communication channels constraining the interpretation of social information has delivered limited progress.

3. *Designing sociable robots:* while progress in the electromechanical design of robots has been impressive and we seem to have a fairly clear understanding of which elements of the physical embodiment of a robot engage the user, the biggest challenge remains the creation believable, contingent behaviour. Arguably, this largely stems from our inability to endow robots with the capacity to correctly interpret the social world,

ICMI'11, November 14–18, Alicante, Spain.

thus hampering their ability to construct appropriate responses (i.e. linking points 1 and 2, above).

As such, the study of multi-modal human-robot interaction has been largely performed through using Wizard of Oz (WoZ) techniques, whereby an operator stands in for the socially cognitive capacities of the robot. Clearly, WoZ does not necessarily in itself form a problem: for some applications of human-robot interaction remote control suffices. The use of robots to interact with children with Autistic Spectrum Disorders, for example, seems promising and does not necessarily require the robot to be autonomous [11]. However there are application domains in which WoZ control is simply not sufficient or practicable for real-world applications.

We wish to use this paper to share good practice and insights gained from a series of human-robot interaction experiments executed in the paediatric department of a hospital. Too often, valuable practical information is glossed over in publications and is only accessible through word of mouth, the *practice* of experimentation being almost seen as trivial compared to the empirical data gathered from studies. We aim to redress this imbalance and in the next sections will give an overview of evaluation methods which we have successfully and less successfully used in child-robot interaction studies, hoping to provide some hard-won insights into the design of child-robot evaluation studies.

1.1 Child-robot interaction

It is clear that social interaction with robots is challenging, but there is a point of entry to human-robot interaction which is, in some respects at least, easier. Children, for reasons not fully understood, respond much more readily and strongly to social robots. As such, human-robot engagement is significantly more easily attained with younger children than it is with adolescent or or adult users. Short-term human-robot interaction is the low hanging fruit of the field, toddlers and young children respond very well to robots with a very basic social repertoire. Several studies have even shown how such social interaction with robots can be temporally extended.

Tanaka et al, for example, showed how a small humanoid robot was perceived as social agent by toddlers (1.5 to 2 years of age) and how the quality of the interaction improved as the robot spent more time in the day care centre [17]. The robot had a wide repertoire of behaviours, but it appeared that simple reactive routines (for example, touching the head resulted in the robot playing a pre-recorded giggle) were surprisingly effective at engaging the young children.

Tanaka et al. concluded that for this particular age-group haptic interaction is highly salient, an interpretation supported by the finding that participants often touched and hugged the robot. Higher-level behaviour, such as linguistic interaction, was not implemented and seemed unnecessary to engage children in this age range. Kanda et al. introduced a humanoid robot in a primary school setting, with children aged between 10 and 11 years. The robot was able to identify children using RFID tags and used a gradual "unlocking" of new behaviours and sharing of "secrets" as children interacted with it as a means to maintain their engagement over an extended period of time. While some of the children stayed engaged over the full duration of the experiment (2 months), about 2/3 of the children gradually lost interest. It was unclear if this was due to the robot's behaviour, or due to other external factors [6].

These findings serve to demonstrate two fundamental issues in the design and implementation of robots intended to engage socially with human users. Firstly, the problem of age, young children are very willing endow the behaviour of artificial agents with social meaning and to interact with them accordingly. This finding may well reflect the predominance of imaginative play as a means for exploring and learning about the world in early childhood. Older children appear to be less likely to view a robot as a social actor and maintaining their engagement is more challenging.

The second issue concerns the interactive complexity of the system. Tanaka [17] found a simple, reactive giggle behaviour to be highly effective in engaging young children. It is reasonable to expect that in order to engage with older users a robot would require more complex behaviours and a richer repertoire of social responses. Yet Kanda's findings provide evidence for a phenomena which is easily observed in HRI, the more sophisticated the robot, the greater a user's expectations of it and thus the greater the risk of their disengaging on discovering the system's limitations.

2. THE ALIZ-E PROJECT AND INTERACTION SCENARIOS

The ALIZ-E project[1] seeks to address the challenges in human-robot interaction described above by emphasising the principle of coordinated multi-modal, any-depth, interaction. The aim is to develop the state-of-the-art in human-robot interaction through the application of this principle to the development of companion robots for children engaged in residential treatment programmes in a hospital environment, lasting on the order of four to five days. It is thus necessary to provide the companion robot with the capacity for extended interaction, and over multiple, separate interaction episodes. The maintenance of engagement with the child over this time is of central importance: the multi-modal approach must support an engaging, naturalistic interaction. There is an additional emphasis on robust interactions, where the robot should be capable of sustaining an interaction (albeit in a more limited fashion) in the face of partial disruption to some of its capabilities (i.e. any-depth).

Despite the particular application domain for this project being child-robot interaction in a hospital setting, the issues involved are general to the wider concerns of HRI. The question of how engagement should be maintained is brought into sharper focus with the emphasis on extended interactions, for two reasons. Firstly, and almost trivially, there is more time/scope for errors to occur, leading to a breakdown in engagement. Secondly, with multiple interaction episodes, with a potentially variable amount of time between them, comes increase variability in the context of interaction, requiring differing social behaviours, all of which must be handled. Indeed, the emphasis on robustness is important for a similar reason: since engagement over multiple interaction episodes is likely, for children in particular (see above, section 1.1), to be linked to the naturalistic, adaptive nature of the robot. Given that the goal is multi-modal interaction, should one of the interaction modalities fail (either through technical failure, or environmental constraints), then the interaction should not stop, but should gracefully degrade,

[1] http://www.aliz-e.org/

and rely on the remaining modalities. This must therefore be a general goal of human-robot interaction: if a robot in a noisy room cannot maintain even a rudimentary social interaction because the speech recognition system is impaired by transient environmental conditions, the robustness requirement is not addressed (with similar scenarios for other modalities).

The ALIZ-E project approaches these problems in an iteratively defined interaction scenario methodology, where a companion robot is designed to interact with a child in different social contexts, using a variety of multi-modal competencies [2]. The following section describes a number of these. In so doing, valuable lessons can be learned regarding the use of social techniques and of multiple modalities in the maintenance of engagement with real children: problems that may be glossed over in simulation studies are, in this context, brutally exposed.

The target group for the ALIZ-E project are diabetic children in the 8-10 years age range. The project aims to develop companion robots able to engage child users and support them in learning about and managing their metabolic condition. Thus a set of interaction scenarios were designed to provide structure for the implementation and evaluation of encounters between robot and child. The following scenarios were developed as a means to assess our progress towards this aim.

2.1 The Dance scenario

One of the desirable outcomes of interaction with the robot is that child users should be encouraged to be physically active as a means to manage weight (an important issue in diabetes care) and to support general health. Physical education also supports the acquisition and development of motor skills. The development of such skills may be influential in fostering a child's interest in a broader range physical activities, thus and more importantly, in a healthy lifestyle [1, 10]. For these reasons, it is fundamental to ensure adequate motor skill development during childhood.

Dance is a physical activity that not only promotes the development of motor skills, but also allows the acquisition of other important attainments such as social compentence (cooperation, leadership, communication, awareness of others, sense of belonging), emotional expression and creativity [14]. Current state-of-the-art humanoid robots, such as the NAO robot used in this project, are physically embodied agents capable of relatively complex patterns of movement such as dancing. These behaviours have the capacity to engage human users, particularly children: a dancing game was thus chosen as an interaction scenario [13].

Social components of the Dance scenario.

The scenario was constructed around the use of social-cues to encourage the child to participate and foster the formation of a temporally extensible social bond between child and robot. Robot dancers have been proposed previously (eg. [16, 18, 8]). However these approaches have focused on individual aspects of dance, such as rhythm, entertainment or the level of interaction. The main motivation here is to advance the study of child-robot social interaction, however we also aim at promoting the development of physical skills based on each individual child's capabilities.

To increase familiarity with the user during the overall interaction the robot refers to the user by her name from time to time. This information is given *a priori* to the robot. Regarding the user's feedback, it is manually typed in through the WoZ. Both positive (e.g. "*Nice!*") and negative (though positively valenced, e.g. "*That was close! Can you repeat it?*", with a maximum of three failures before another move is proposed) verbal feedback is provided to the child throughout the interaction session.

The dance activity was designed to involve three consecutive stages, each with a specific functional and social component: introduction, exploration, and dance. The child had the opportunity to halt the interaction at any point in this scheme.

1. Introduction: the robot greets the child and shows a sample dance. From the task performance perspective the goal is to exhibit the robot's motor capabilities to the user and to draw her attention to the task. From the social perspective the primary aim is to enjoin the child to participate in the activity (i.e. to dance together with the robot). This is achieved through three steps: initiate interaction (greeting), motivate (showing dance) and establish engagement (dancing together until the user elects to stop).

2. Exploration: at this point the child has agreed to begin the activity. The robot shows various different moves, one a time, to assess the child's capability to perform the various movements. As the robot executes a motion, it asks the child to execute it as well. This process is repeated, for each movement until an evaluation of the child's performance is obtained. Currently a WoZ is in charge of the evaluation. Based on this assessment the robot either proposes a new motion, if the evaluation was positive, or repeats the same motion, if the evaluation was negative. Three consecutive failures for a given motion are allowed before a new movement is automatically introduced.

The child is encouraged and supported in continuing to dance through the robot's adaptation of the game to suit her abilities, thus fulfilling the general aim of encouraging physical activity in the user. From the social perspective the challenge here is to maintain the user's engagement with the robot and hence the task. The social aspect requires careful handling of the evaluation process so as not to discourage the user with negative feedback. Thus, all evaluation feedback is designed to be positively valenced. Three main sources of feedback are given: move description (a brief description of the motion being performed), evaluation outcome and motivational feedback ("Go ahead", "You can do it!") to encourage the user to keep trying the moves.

Because we are interested in long-term interactions, the set of moves performed are stored after each session. In terms of task performance this affects the selection of moves: thus subsequent sessions are based on the outcomes of previous interactions in order to gradually increase the complexity of the moves proposed to the user while still taking account of her individual abilities. The feedback given to the user also varies based on the history of interaction. Hence, if a movement demonstrated previously is proposed again, the robot can address the user making reference to that earlier experience (e.g. "Remember this move? Let's try it again!").

3. Dance: the robot creates a sequence of moves for the dance using only those successfully performed in the previous stage. The sequence is performed along with music as

Figure 1: Child performing a motion with the robot during a dance session.

many times as the user desires (figure 1). Once the user decides to end the interaction, the robot thanks the user and the dance session ends. This stage of the session was found to be the most rewarding for the user and this was reflected in the greater levels of child-robot engagement.

2.2 'Simon Says' scenario

The Simon Game scenario is based on the "Simon Says" game in which players must do what 'Simon' tells them to do whenever asked with a phrase beginning with "Simon says". Thus the the player designated as Simon gives the directive "Simon says jump", the players must jump (those that do not that do not are eliminated). For the purposes of this interaction scenario the game was adapted to be played by two players (robot and child) and only arm movements were used, to ensure that the robot could perform all the moves adequately [4]. The game was further modified to include a memory component for the child such that the robot would demonstrate a move with one of its arms (left/right up, left-/right down) and the child had to copy this move and add another one. Next the robot repeated the moves from the child and added another one, up to a maximum of 5 movements. After this a new series began where the child started with the first move. In the case of an error a new series started.

When the robot moved its right arm up it was expected that the child should mirror the action. This was supported by the robot giving verbal descriptions of the moves that the child should make to mirror its actions (e.g. when putting its right arm up the robot would say "left up" to indicate the movement required from the child). The game was subsequently further adapted to incorporate simple mathematical exercises as a means to support the acquisition of competence in arithmetic which is a key skill for children with diabetes (e.g. for counting carbohydrates and measuring insulin).

Social components of the 'Simon Says' scenario.

The main focus of the Simon Game was to create an entertaining structure for interaction and to enhance companionship through shared activity, through the coordinated use of multiple modalities. The speech output of the robot was designed to support this. For instance the robot would explain that she and the child were secret agents that needed to learn a sign language and that after finishing a level they would be closer this shared goal. The complexity of the movements was incrementally increased, i.e. making it more challenging based on child performance, was envisaged to aid in the maintenance of engagement and motivation, which are proposed to be essential elements in making an activity enjoyable for the user. The general theme of the dialogue was motivational: the child was encouraged to go on and when she made an error the robot encouraged her to try again. In one experiment we included an additional manipulation providing different dialogues to children rated as extrovert and introvert in a pre-test evaluation. Previous research has shown that different forms of verbal encouragement are effective (e.g. "you can do better" vs. "I really believe you can do this") [12]. No significant difference between groups was observed in this experiment, however in future implementations we plan to adapt the dialogue component further to reflect the speech style of the child, as a additional means to foster feelings of companionship [7].

2.3 Quiz scenario

In this interaction scenario the robot played quiz master with the child answering the questions. The questions were all multiple choice and related to health, with the goal of supporting the educational goal of the child in the hospital [7]. In the case that the child answered incorrectly she was given another turn, if the question was answered incorrectly a second time the robot provided the correct answer and a new question. After each correct answer the child received a point.

Social components of the Quiz.

The main focus of the quiz was educational but again using a game format to motivate the child and foster feelings of social engagement with the robot thus supporting sustained interaction. This scenario was primarily aimed at testing the capacity of a companion robot to provide support to a child in learning about their medical condition. The feedback given to the child after an incorrect answer was designed to have a positive valance and verbal feedback was provided after each answer provided by the child, regardless of whether its was correct or incorrect in order to facilitate the individual learning process. In future implementations we would like to increase the element of joint activity by changing the arrangement from robot as quiz master to a trivial pursuit setup in which both child and robot alternate in the quiz master role and they compete for the best score.

3. LESSONS LEARNED

Testing human-robot interaction in a hospital setting with young patients is certainly no trivial undertaking. There are several obstacles to be overcome and a number of issues that must be carefully considered, both during the design and the execution of possible experiments. In this section we try to provide a comprehensive summary of these aspects, based on experience gained in the ALIZ-E project, during testing of first year prototypes in the paediatric department of the San Raffaele Hospital, in Milan.

3.1 Legal and administrative issues

One important consideration for HRI experimentation is the regulation of new technologies in institutional settings such as hospitals. These regulations vary between settings and across Europe but certain constraints apply almost universally. One such relates to CE[2] marking of devices. Problems arise for the experimenter when prototypes are used with modifications of the original hardware or software which effectively invalidate any CE mark the product may have. Introducing non-certified devices that can come in contact with end-users (patients) in an hospital environment (for example) is a major issue and in this case the prototype must be exhaustively documented and additional electromagnetic and mechanical tests may be required before local ethical approval can be obtained.

Another issue concerns *confidentiality*. When experimenting with participants drawn from this population two issue arise 1)participants are minors and 2) participants are patients. It is thus crucial that data are collected in compliance with existing confidentiality procedures, and that data collection is limited to the information strictly necessary for the experimental hypothesis under test. Particular issues can arise with the collection of audio/video data, but also in case of collection of sensitive patient information which the experimenters may wish to share with other research institutes, for example in multi-centre studies. An additional issue can arise through the use of sub-symbolic network architectures for instance as used in ALIZ-E for implementation of memory system functionality [3]. Clearly there is a requirement for experimenters to be fully cognisant of the confidentiality requirements of the all the institutions involved plus any relevant legislation and to have robust procedures for anonymising their data.

3.2 The experimental environment

The studies described here were carried out in a hospital setting which presents some additional challenges to the experimenter, while the majority of these problems are present to some extent in all institutional settings (e.g. schools and day-care facilities). There are some aspects of the hospital environment which are more or less unique, for example the fact that hospitalization is very often unavoidably traumatic, and the patient may have to undergo intrusive or painful procedures administered by unfamiliar adults. For diabetic children (the focus group for ALIZ-E), hospital also means an intensive regime of dietary control, blood sugar monitoring and insulin administration. All of these factors render the hospital environment a particularly challenging one in which to implement and test social engagement. On the other hand, if the particularly stringent requirements for setting up non-trivial levels of social interaction between child and robot can be met in a hospital setting then this provides a very strong indication of the efficacy and robustness of the approach taken.

One important issue in designing studies with children and robots concerns the setting for the experiment, finding a neutral space (i.e. in hospital avoiding areas associated with treatment or other potentially traumatic events). The appearance of the room, of the robot and even the experimenters needs careful control in order to avoid biasing the child's initial impressions and expectations of the interaction. Clearly the ideal is to create a friendly environment in which the child can feel comfortable, however these effort must necessarily be balanced against technical requirements of the interaction (e.g. neutral background colours to support the functioning of vision systems on the robot, minimising extraneous noise to support speech processing and so on) It is certainly valuable for experimenters to distinguish themselves as far as possible from medical staff adopting a *casual* style of dress to avoid possibly stressful associations with medical staff.

Another key aspect of experimentation which is particularly emphasised in the hospital setting is the *recruitment* of participants for the experiments. In-patients have a schedule of procedures during the day which is very dynamic and dependent on factors which are hard to predict (e.g., availability of X-Ray machines, magnetic resonance, surgery theatres, etc.). In addition, medical personnel will discharge patients as soon as they are deemed fit enough to return home, these decisions often cannot be predicted in advance and this cannot easily be predicted in advance. Thus suitable participants who have agreed to take part may be discharged from hospital before testing can take place and this is another factor which experimenters must take into account when scheduling periods of experimentation with clinical populations.

A further, important factor, is the requirement for experimenters to liaise with the persons responsible for a child's care in order to fully assess their suitability for the study, in a hospital this may entail discussions with not just doctors and nurses but also psychologists and other therapists. In the experiments at San Raffaele Hospital, many apparently eligible children had to be excluded from the study for reasons other than their primary medical condition. This factor can introduce significant delays into the running of experiments and while a particular issue in hospital based studies can also be relevant in schools and other institutional settings.

3.3 Working with children

Conducting studies involving child participants places significant constraints on the experimenter. In the context of HRI, younger children are generally very willing to view the robot as more than a simple mechanical object (readily anthropomorphising artefacts [19]). As has been previously demonstrated [9], children have the tendency to attribute *human characteristics and behaviors* to robots (at least to anthropomorphic robots). For this reason, where the aim of the experiment is to foster *social* interaction between robot and child, it is important that the procedure for introducing the robot to the child should take this into account. For example, the naming of the robot and the way in which it is first presented to the child can have a profound impact on the way in which it subsequently perceived and the 'believability' of the interactions. Older children may attribute social capacities less readily to a robot, making it all the more important that the initial encounter between robot and participant is carefully managed. Of particular importance are behavioural expectations such as contingent responding and behavioural robustness (e.g. not falling when walking) which if violated tend to significantly diminish the quality of subsequent interaction.

The *briefing* of the child plays an important role and should if possible prepare the child for potential problems in the robot's behaviour, for instance if it stops moving or runs out of battery power. Ideally these issues should be dealt with with an explanation from the robot itself but it

[2] *Conformitè Europèenne*: declaration of product conformity to the relevant European directives

is also helpful if the child is given some indication of such possibilities in advance so as to avoid leaving the participant unsure as to what they should do in such a situation. In the current series of experiments an adult was present ion the room throughout and was able to mediate the interaction in the case of mechanical and or software problems. This person did not interact with the child or the robot during the experiment, but was present solely to intervene in the event of a technical problem, The adult chaperone was instructed to pretend not to be following the interaction (being seated at a desk out of the child's sight-line and apparently doing some paperwork) so as to allow the child to respond as spontaneously as possible. The number of times the participant referred to the adult in the room (with speech, or with glances, etc.) for clarification during the scenario was also taken as an additional metric for assessing the quality of interaction with a greater number of clarification gestures from the child taken as an indicator of reduced engagement. As a further means to support the child in feeling comfortable in the experimental set up she was invited to participate, briefed and accompanied in the experiment by the same person. Clearly there is a risk that the presence of this 'known' adult might introduce some unspecified bias in the child's response to interaction with the robot. However, in this context, with a specific aim of fostering *social* interaction, we considered it more important to ensure that the child was at ease than to adhere to the strictest tenets of empirical protocol. This is another area where a trade-off must be devised between the requirements for setting up and maintaining an interaction and the necessity for experimental rigour.

The *debriefing* is also an important aspect of the protocol. It is very likely that experimenters will need children to fill in questionnaires as a means to assess their experience of an interaction. In a our hospital based experiments this did not prove to be a major issue as patients are well used to filling forms and answering questions. In some cases this was even taken by participants as an enjoyable extension, somehow, of their experience with the robot. these effect might be explained by the fact that very often in hospital children are quite bored and welcome any variation of the usual daily routine.

Clearly, a simple "Thanks and goodbye" is not appropriate for terminating an experiment with child participants. It is important, if possible, provide some follow-up activity to remind the child of the experience and allow them to express any subsequent reactions to it. One example of this follow-up procedure, that was used in conjunction with the experiments described here, is the creation of comics with the robot as subject, that can be left with the children and used as a basis for talking about the experience subsequently. Simple certificates showing an image of the robot and some expression of official thanks were also found to be a useful way to demonstrate appreciation for the child's contribution in taking part. Interestingly, some children asked if there is a website where they can follow the development of the robot.

3.4 Planning the interaction

The design of the interaction itself requires additional care if the experiment involves children. We noticed that, while with an adult if the robot suddenly stops participating in the interaction (e.g., through a technical failure, falling over, or some other error), is not a major issue, child participants are quite disappointed by such 'breaks' in the flow of their joint activity. This implies that it is very important, when dealing with children, to have very robust code, that the robot must be mechanically reliable, and that the interaction scenario must be *tested exhaustively*. Furthermore the experimenter, should be aware mind that children are relatively *unpredictable* in their reactions, so it is important to stress test the robot with unexpected actions as much as possible in the lab environment, before going on with field experiments.

Another implication is that the robot (or the experimenter, especially in interactions using the Wizard of Oz) should have a *backup strategy* to finish the experiment earlier than planned in case of a technical failure. Often in these cases the data for that trial is automatically invalidated. However the backup strategy can still form a useful part of the protocol, permitting a degree of graceful degradation which might still generate some qualitative data from observation of the participant's response to the back-up strategy for mechanical or software failure. Strategies can even be varied for different experimental groups. For example when studying child-robot engagement, in the case of low battery participants in the experimental group might hear the robot say:

```
R: 'I'm sorry, I was really having
fun, but now my battery is too
low and I should rest'
```

while participants in the control group might hear:

```
R: 'Out of battery'
```

Clearly it is also important that the interaction should be as natural as possible, and that the robot should at least follow *basic social conventions*. Greetings, a personal introduction and a request for some basic details of the other person (e.g., "Hello, my name is R2D2, what's your name?") are minimal requirements for initiating an interaction. Furthermore, even though the experimenter has already explained what will happen beforehand to the child, it is still important that the robot is very clear in guiding the interaction, telling to the child what to do and when. Also the closing dialogue should be carefully designed, thanking the child for the fun they had together and hoping to meet again soon, etc. Of these requirements must also be adapted to suit the particular characteristics of the experimental protocol under evaluation. The robot should also have a routine available for situations where the child chooses to end the interaction sooner than expected, the child has the option to stop the interaction at any time, and if he decides to do so, the robot should respond appropriately to the situation (or the WoZ provide it) and have a "gentle stop" strategy, again thanking the child, so as to ensure the participant does not feel she has done something wrong in choosing to withdraw.

Another element we found to be useful in making the interaction happen more naturally is the use of additional behaviors, not directly related to the experiment or interaction itself (and that of course will not influence its result), but that can be useful to support the *credibility* of the robot as something which is "living". An example is to implement a fake "breathing" behavior, which is constantly executed by the robot in parallel with other routines. Another example is to avoid the "statue" effect, making the robot move, continuously, albeit very slightly. Additional behaviors can also be inserted into verbal interaction, for example providing variability in the possible answers, or commenting now and then on what's been said, and asking specific questions related to what's happening and so on).

A final remark for experimenters, when dealing with children, regards the understandable desire to *make the child happy*. When an experimenter notices that a participant appears to be bored, especially during Wizarded interactions, there is strong temptation to somehow "fix the situation" (e.g., making the robot say something, etc.). While it is clearly appropriate in some cases to interrupt the actual experiment (e.g., if the child is becoming particularly anxious, or unhappy), it is important to maintain the designed protocols, as additional interventions will adversely influence the study by introducing biases that will invalidate the results.

4. PLAYFUL DESIGN

The observations drawn from our experiences with implementing and child-robot interaction in a hospital setting centre on common themes reflecting the necessity for taking account of the special requirements of the participant group and the setting in which the encounter takes place. While some of the lessons learned reflect more or less standard considerations for experimental design some less obvious requirements become apparent through such experimentation "in the wild". One issue concerns the trade off between efforts to foster naturalistic interaction and the need for robust experimental paradigms for testing the efficacy of an approach to implementation.

When we set out to create scenarios for believable robot-child interaction most often we envisage some notion of play as the basis for the encounter. Thus the robot is endowed with routines which allow it to initiate or participate in games which provide a structure for interaction with a child. There is a difficulty with this approach in that play, is in itself ill-defined, there is a clear common-sense notion of what it is to engage in play but the characteristics that define playful activity as such, are less well-specified. Huizinga characterises play as being distinct from the constraints of 'normal' behaviour and of reality [5]. In this view, the fundamental essence of play is its freedom to subvert norms for action and interaction. Thus in play, a child can designate a banana to stand-in for a telephone and can take the role of parent giving her mother the role of child.

However, when we set out to design and experiment with child-robot interactions we construct scenarios which afford the application of metrics for measuring quality of engagement between interactants and to test the effects of various manipulations. In the ALIZ-E project we have used games (such as "Simon Says") as the basis for evaluation scenarios. However, it has become clear from these experiments that the highly structured format of such scenarios can easily inhibit engagement on the part of the child participant. In this sense we found that less really can be more in child robot interaction.

As an illustrative example, we found that during the dance game, due to the mechanical requirements of the dance steps sometimes led to the robot being oriented away from the child part-way through the interaction. As a stop-gap measure, during the piloting phase, the robot was given a routine in which it would call on the experimenter to 'help' it turn back to face the child. If the child was no longer in view the robot's speech generation system would output an utterance of the form "Hey [experimenter's name], could you help me turn around so that I can see [child's name] properly".

This utterance was found to be at least as effective in fostering engagement with the child as the games themselves. Like Tanaka's giggling robot [17], a spontaneous request for help showed the robot as behaving in a socially contingent fashion (acting to regain a shared gaze space with an interaction partner) and as having some capacity to go beyond the constraints of the game scenario i.e. to take some action not directly involved in gameplay. Indeed, a similar effect is seen with children who interact with a spontaneously malfunctioning robotic artefact: engagement levels rise as the children are drawn into an interaction [15].

The 'request for help' example, though a seemingly trivial implementation detail which would never have come to our attention if the robot had been programmed to correct its own position from the outset, illustrates a more subtle point. In play based interactions, externally imposed structure, whether to ease the process of implementation or as a requirement of an experimental protocol can have the counterintuitive effect of inhibiting interaction depth. Simple reactive behaviours which allow a robot to behave in a socially contingent fashion and afford imaginative engagement on the part of the child participant can be considerably more effective in supporting engagement and long-term interaction than structured games and complex behavioural routines.

These observations serve to demonstrate that experimenting with children and robots requires careful thought, regardless of the setting. In the experiments described here a selection of interaction types are implemented with the robot taking varied roles (such as instructor, companion, and playmate) this allows more general observations to be drawn which are of relevance to a broad range of HRI applications.

5. ACKNOWLEDGMENTS

This work is supported by the EU Integrated Project ALIZ-E (FP7-ICT-248116).

6. ADDITIONAL AUTHORS

Tony Belpaeme (University of Plymouth, tony.belpaeme @plymouth.ac.uk); Alessio Giusti (Hospital San Raffaele, giusti.alessio@hsr.it); Clara Pozzi (Hospital San Raffaele, clara.pozzi@fastwebnet.it)

7. REFERENCES

[1] Physical Education, The National Curriculum for England. http://curriculum.qcda.gov.uk.

[2] P. Baxter, T. Belpaeme, L. Canamero, P. Cosi, Y. Demiris, V. Enescu, A. Hiolle, I. Kruijff-Korbayova, R. Looije, M. Nalin, M. Neerincx, G. Sommavilla, F. Tesser, and R. Wood. Long-Term Human-Robot Interaction with Young Users. In *IEEE/ACM Human-Robot Interaction 2011 Conference (Robots with Children Workshop)*, 2011.

[3] P. Baxter, R. Wood, T. Belpaeme, and M. Nalin. On memory systems for companion robots: Implementation methodologies and legal implications. In *AISB Symposium on Human Memory for Artificial Agents*. AISB, 2011.

[4] H. Cuayahuitl and I. Kruijff-Korbayova. Towards Learning Human-Robot Dialogue Policies Combining Speech and Visual Beliefs. In *To appear in proceedings of the Workshop on Paralinguistic Information and its Integration in Spoken Dialogue Systems, Granada, Spain, Sep 2011.*, 2011.

[5] J. Huizinga. *Homo Ludens*. Beacon Press, 1971.

[6] T. Kanda, R. Sato, N. Saiwaki, and H. Ishiguro. A two-month field trial in an elementary school for long-term human-robot interaction. *IEEE Transactions on Robotics (Special Issue on Human-Robot Interaction)*, 23(5):962–971, 2007.

[7] R. Looije, M. Neerincx, and V. de Lange. Children's responses and opinion on three bots that motivate, educate and play. *Journal of Physical Agents*, 2(2):13–20, 2008.

[8] M. P. Michalowski, R. Simmons, and H. Kozima. Rhythmic attention in child-robot dance play. In *18th IEEE International Symposium on Robot and Human Interactive Communication*, pages 816–821, 2009.

[9] M. Nalin, L. Bergamini, A. Giusti, I. Baroni, and A. Sanna. Children's perception of a robotic companion in a mildly constrained setting. In *IEEE/ACM Human-Robot Interaction 2011 Conference (Robots with Children Workshop) Proceedings*, 2011.

[10] A. Okely and J. Wright. The gender bias in fundamental motor skills tests - a new agenda needed! In *Proceeding of AARE International Education Research Conference*, 1997.

[11] B. Robins, K. Dautenhahn, R. T. Boekhorst, and A. Billard. Robotic assistants in therapy and education of children with autism: can a small humanoid robot help encourage social interaction skills? *Universal Access in the Information Society*, 4(2):105–120, 2005.

[12] S. Rollnick, W. Miller, and C. Butler. *Motivational interviewing in health care: helping patients change behavior*. The Guilford Press, 2007.

[13] R. Ros, Y. Demiris, I. Baroni, and M. Nalin. Adapting Robot Behavior to User's Capabilities: a Dance Instruction Study. In *HRI (Human-Robot Interaction) Conference 2011*, 2011.

[14] I. E. V. Rossberg-Gempton, J. Dickinson, and G. Poole. Creative dance: Potentiality for enhancing social functioning in frail seniors and young children. *The Arts in Psychotherapy*, 26:313–327, 1999.

[15] T. Salter, I. Werry, and F. Michaud. Going into the wild with child-robot interaction studies. *Intelligent Service Robots*, 1(2):93–108, 2007.

[16] K. Shinozaki, Y. Oda, S. Tsuda, R. Nakatsu, and A. Iwatani. Study of dance entertainment using robots. In Z. P. et al. et al., editor, *Edutainment*, volume 3942 of *Lecture Notes in Computer Science*, pages 473–483. Springer-Verlag Berlin Heidelberg, 2006.

[17] F. Tanaka, A. Cicourel, and J. Movellan. Socialization between toddlers and robots at an early childhood education center. *PNAS*, 104(46):17954–17958, 2007.

[18] F. Tanaka, J. R. Movellan, B. Fortenberry, and K. Aisaka. Daily hri evaluation at a classroom environment: reports from dance interaction experiments. In *Proceedings of the 1st ACM SIGCHI/SIGART conference on Human-robot interaction*, pages 3–9. ACM, 2006.

[19] S. Turkle, C. Breazeal, O. Dasté, and B. Scassellati. Encounters with Kismet and Cog : Children Respond to Relational Artifacts. In P. Messaris and L. Humphreys, editors, *Digital Media: Transformations in Human Communication*, pages 1–20. Peter Lang Publishing, New York, 2006.

Characterization of Coordination in an Imitation Task : Human Evaluation and Automatically Computable Cues

Emilie Delaherche
Institut des Systèmes Intelligents et de Robotique
CNRS UMR 7222
Université Pierre et Marie Curie - Paris 6
4 Place Jussieu
Paris, France
emilie.delaherche@isir.upmc.fr

Mohamed Chetouani
Institut des Systèmes Intelligents et de Robotique
CNRS UMR 7222
Université Pierre et Marie Curie - Paris 6
4 Place Jussieu
Paris, France
mohamed.chetouani@upmc.fr

ABSTRACT

Understanding the ability to coordinate with a partner constitutes a great challenge in social signal processing and social robotics. In this paper, we designed a child-adult imitation task to investigate how automatically computable cues on turn-taking and movements can give insight into high-level perception of coordination. First we collected a human questionnaire to evaluate the perceived coordination of the dyads. Then, we extracted automatically computable cues and information on dialog acts from the video clips. The automatic cues characterized speech and gestural turn-takings and coordinated movements of the dyad. We finally confronted human scores with automatic cues to search which cues could be informative on the perception of coordination during the task. We found that the adult adjusted his behavior according to the child need and that a disruption of the gestural turn-taking rhythm was badly perceived by the judges. We also found, that judges rated negatively the dyads that talked more as speech intervenes when the child had difficulties to imitate. Finally, coherence measures between the partners' movement features seemed more adequate than correlation to characterize their coordination.

Categories and Subject Descriptors

J.4 [**Social And Behavioral Sciences**]: Psychology; I.5.4 [**Pattern Recognition**]: Applications—*Signal Processing*; I.2.10 [**Artificial Intelligence**]: Vision and Scene Understanding—*Video Analysis*

General Terms

Measurement, Algorithms, Experimentation

Keywords

Social signal processing, coordination, imitation

1. INTRODUCTION

Building robots capable of fluent interactions is a persistent goal of social robotics. The understanding of social and cognitive abilities at stake during interactions represents a puzzling but necessary question for social robotics. Multiple attempts have been made to provide human abilities to robots, like showing expressivity [5], decoding emotion [6], giving appropriate feedback [19] or sharing attention [20, 4] with a human peer. The development of such robots able to devise with oneself in a friendly manner surely represents a long-term objective at the cross-over of multiple disciplines ranging from psychology, to engineering, through signal processing and machine learning. A short-term question could be what human abilities are strictly require to fulfill naturalistic interaction with a peer. Or are there unbreakable rules, that once broken, ruins every attempt to carry on the interaction.

Psychologists commonly refer to coordination as one of those rules. Bernieri et al. define interactional synchrony as "the degree to which the behaviors in an interaction are non-random, patterned, or synchronized in both timing and form" [1]. According to [1], coordination is related to the "interrelatedness" of individuals behavior. It is not necessarily linked with positive affect; two persons fighting are in fact very well-coordinated. Moreover, several psychologists have highlighted that human are efficient and reliable judges of human-human coordination [12, ?]. Even in degraded conditions, without vocal cues or without the details of facial expressions, this trend remains. Thus the great challenge is to define what perceptual cues help us, human, to consider an interaction as smooth and coordinated...

Several successful attempts have been made in the field of social signal processing to characterize high level nuances of interaction with simple and automatically extracted cues. For instance, cohesion in small group meetings was characterized with audio and visual cues like pauses between individual turns, pauses between floor exchanges, motion turn lengths or synchrony [8]... Dominance was characterized with para-linguistic features [18], speaking length [9] or motion [16]. To identify group conversational behavior, [10] proposed an unsupervised approach based on low-level non verbal cues (speaking length, interruptions, speaking distribution across participants, overlaps...).

In this paper, we investigate the notion of coordination between dyadic partners. We take the example of an imitation task fulfilled by a child and a therapist. We propose to measure the correlation between : (1) automatic and semi-automatic audio-visual cues extracted on the different dyads and (2) the perceived degree of coordination of the dyads, rated by external judges. Our goal, in this paper, is to identify which automatic cues are related with the perceived coordination of the dyads (Fig 1). The following step will be to identify the most appropriate cues to predict low or highly coordinated dyads during the task.

We present the experimental setup and the task in section 2. In section 3, we describe the human evaluation procedure and the results we obtained. Then, we present the automatically and semi-automatically extracted cues to characterize the dyads based on turn-taking, gestures and dialog acts in section 4. At last, in section 5, we present the correlations we found between the coordination scores and the cues we extracted from the video clips.

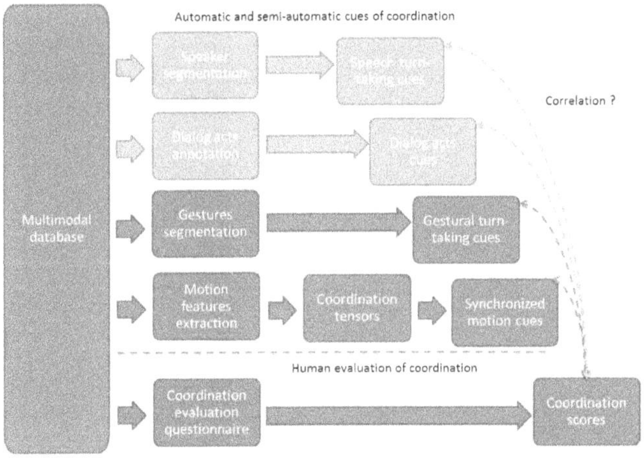

Figure 1: Synopsis

2. EXPERIMENTAL SETUP

We designed an imitation task to evaluate the ability of young children to imitate a partner.

2.1 Participants

21 children participated to the study (developmental ages = 4-9 years) : 14 typically developing children and 7 children followed in the day-care hospital la Pitié-Salpétrière for Pervasive Developmental Disorders. Those children suffered from various social impairments : language disabilities, poor communicative skills, gesture impairments... The current work focuses on the perception of coordination regardless of the children population group. The comparison between groups will be treated in future work.

2.2 Procedure

The task consisted in building a clown with 7 polystyrene elements (2 hands, 2 legs, body, head and hat). The child sat across from the therapist. The same polystyrene elements were arranged on a table in front of them. Therapist led the task and showed to the child each step of the construction task. Speech interventions from the therapist were limited to the times the child encounters difficulties. The children were asked to "do as the therapist" in order to encourage the imitation.

Figure 2: Experimental setup

2.3 Material

The interactions were recorded using a single camera, put up above the participants. The audio recordings were collected at 48 kHz and the video recordings at 25 fps. The participants were equipped with color bracelets to easily track their hands. Audio data were annotated with Anvil annotation tool [11] by two language therapist interns in order to segment the speakers' speech turns and label the utterances according to their dialog acts category (see section 4.2). The total duration was approximately 40min with a mean duration of 1min53s and a standard deviation of 1min09s.

3. EVALUATION OF PERCEIVED COORDINATION

3.1 Evaluation procedure

A questionnaire was built to evaluate the perceived coordination and smoothness of the interactions. The grid was previously used to assess coordination [1]. 17 judges rated the video recordings from the puzzle task. The questionnaire consisted in a 4-item grid :

- Item1 The partners engaged in simultaneous movement
- Item2 The partners had similar tempos of activity
- Item3 The partners' interaction was coordinated and smooth
- Item4 The child matched the adult behavior

The video clips were rated on a six-point Likert scale ranging from 1 (Strongly Disagree) to 6 (Strongly Agree).

3.2 Results

We chose the weighted kappa with quadratic weights to measure the agreement among judges. The weighted kappa was calculated between each pair of annotators for each video and each item of the questionnaire. The mean weighted kappa corresponds to the averaged kappa across all possible pairs of judges. Mean weighted kappa was in average lower for the first item (k = 0.23) and higher for the 4th item (k = 0.34). The lowest kappa value was obtained on item1 (k = 0.13) : this value is usually considered as a slight agreement among raters. We may explain the low agreement by the liberty given to the raters in the interpretation of the 4 items ; no further information was given on the behaviors to rate or the modalities to observe. Considering the small size of our database, we nevertheless decided to keep the 21 video clips in the study.

Fig. 3 represents the evaluation scores versus the mean weighted kappa for the 4 items and the 21 videos. We can see that the plot has a C-shape, similar with the one obtained on a study on cohesion [8] : the agreement tends to be higher at the extreme points of the scale, for the video clips rated as "poorly coordinated" or "highly coordinated".

Finally, the average scores on the 4 items ranged from 1.5 to 5.15, with an average value of 3.54 and a standard deviation of 1.19. The dispersion of the scores showed that our database contains data representative of various degrees of coordination. Moreover, it promotes the idea that coordination is not a all-or-none phenomenon but a continuous notion and that a dyadic interaction can approach or move away from synchrony.

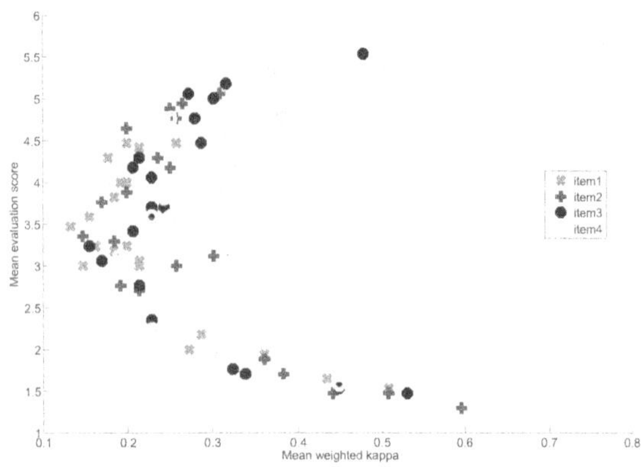

Figure 3: This figure shows the degree of coordination perceived by the raters (mean evaluation score) versus the strength of their agreement (mean weighted kappa), for each dyad and each item of the questionnaire. Agreement tends to be higher for the dyads whose coordination is very low or very high.

4. EXTRACTION OF SEMI-AUTOMATIC AND AUTOMATIC CUES OF COORDINATION

In the following sections, we adopted the abbreviation *Chi* for the Child and *The* for the Therapist. We present in this section the extracted audio and visual features that we assumed were linked with the perceived coordination between the child and therapist.

4.1 Speech turn-taking cues

Raw characteristics on turn-taking have shown to predict efficiently high level characteristics of interaction (cohesion [8], dominance [9]...).

Based on the manual segmentation of the speakers' turns with Anvil, we extracted several features to describe the alternance of speech turns during the task:

- Pause durations (Pause_dur_statname). A time-segment was considered as a pause if none of the participants was talking. We extracted all the pause segments from the task and calculated standard statistics on the duration of the segments (mean, median, standard deviation, range, minimum and maximum).
- Pause ratio (Pause_ratio). We measured the percentage of interaction time that was silent.
- Speech turn durations (Speech_dur_statname). A speech turn is a continuous time segment when one participant is speaking. We extracted all speech turns for each participant and calculated standard statistics on the duration of the segments.
- Speech ratio (Speech_The_ratio and Speech_Chi_ratio). We measured the percentage of interactional time when each of the participant was talking.
- Overlap ratio (Ovlp_ratio). We measured the percentage of interactional time when both participants were talking at the same time.

4.2 Dialog acts cues

Therapists and children utterances were labeled in Anvil according to the following categorization : initiative assertions, questions, retorts, answers, orders/requests. Moreover, the children answers were labeled according to their adequacy. Conventional head gestures (head nods or head shakes) were also annotated and accounted for adequate answers. We selected the categories that were predominant in the database and related to coordination. We describe in the following paragraphs the cues we chose for the child and the therapist.

4.2.1 Therapist dialog act cues

For the therapist, we focused on the number of questions and orders/requests which were the predominant categories in the database. Moreover, we believed the presence of questions and requests could be linked with a need to engage the child more and thus to a lack of coordination in the dyad. Therapist' questions were more precisely labeled as :

- closed (yes/no) : the answer is yes or no (e.g. "Are you okay?"),
- closed (alternative) : the question holds the answer (e.g. "Is it the blue one or the red one?"),
- categorial : who, what, when, where ... questions (e.g. "Where is the hat?"),
- open : the form of the answer is free (e.g. "What shall I do next?"),
- reopening : repetition of a previously enounced question.

4.2.2 Children dialog act cues

For the children, we focused on the presence and the adequacy of their answers. We hypothesized that an absence of answer or an inadequate answer would be perceived as disruptive for the interaction by the judges. We counted the number of answers according to their adequacy :

- adequate,
- unexpected. The form of the answer if correct but the content is unexpected (e.g. "Q:Where may I put the hands?...A:*In* the arms" instead of "*At the tip of* the arms").
- inadequate. Inadequacy is in both form and context of the answer (e.g. using a spatial deixis (here, there) while not sharing the same visual information with your partner).

Moreover, we counted the number of unanswered questions. An answer was linked to a question if it came after the beginning of the question, in a 10 seconds delay and before a new utterance from the therapist. This way, we took into account a possible overlap between the therapist question and the child answer. The 10 seconds delay may seem outsize but took into account observed time responses from disabled children.

4.3 Gestural turn-taking cues

Turn-taking is a pre-requisite of imitation. In the task we proposed, the child needs to look at the demonstrator and then reproduce the same actions. While the child is imitating, the demonstrator waits that he has finished to show him the next stage of the assembly. So we would expect to find an alternation of sections when the demonstrator is gesturing and the child stays still and sections when the demonstrator observes and the child assembles the pieces : a gestural turn-taking. We assumed the respect of this balance would be a positive predictor of perceived coordination.

We tracked the participants hands trajectory with the coupled Camshift algorithm [3]. The participants were equipped with salient color bracelets to easily follow their gestures. We then compressed x and y Cartesian coordinates to the polar coordinate $r = \sqrt{x^2 + y^2}$ and derived r to obtain the hands velocity.

Based on the hands velocity, we extracted a binary feature that was set to 1 if hands velocity was above a threshold (participant assembling) and 0 otherwise (participant still). We operated morphological post-processing to remove isolated 1 (cleaning) and to connect continuous gestures (dilatation).

From the binary features of the child and the therapist, we extracted four features to depict the gestural turn-taking:

- The_off_Chi_on_ratio. Percentage of time when the child is gesturing and the therapist stays still,
- The_on_Chi_off_ratio. Percentage of time when the therapist is gesturing and the child stays still,
- The_on_Chi_on_ratio. Percentage of time when therapist and child are gesturing at the same time,
- The_off_Chi_off_ratio. Percentage of time when therapist and child are staying still at the same time.

Moreover, the task is particularly repetitive (succession of assembling and observing phases); so we can assume that a rhythm is established during the task. All pause segments should last approximately the same duration, so as the gesturing segments. A deviation of the duration of the segments could be perceived as a disruption of the fluency of the interaction. Thus we extracted several statistics on the duration of the gestural and pause segments :

- Gestural Pause Durations (Pause_dur_statname). From the pause segments, we calculated standard statistics on the duration of the segments (mean, median, standard deviation, range, minimum and maximum).
- Gestural Segments Durations (Gest_dur_statname). We extracted the same statistics on the duration of the segments when the participant was moving.
- Pause ratio (Pause_The_ratio or Pause_Chi_ratio). We measured the percentage of interaction time that the participant stayed still.

Lastly, we simply counted the number of continuous sequences of movements for each participant (Seq_The_nb and Seq_Chi_nb) and the ratio between the number of sequences of each participant (Seq_The_Chi_ratio).

4.4 Synchronized motion cues

We also propose to measure the coordination between the child and the therapist as the degree of similarity between their motion features. Thus, we extracted various motion features from the database, computed similarity measures on windows of interaction. We then applied a bootstrap method to classify the windows as "coordinated" or "not coordinated" and deduced a measure of coordination from the percentage of windows classified as "coordinated". The method was previously described to study multimodal coordination in a similar task [7].

4.4.1 *Video features*

We extracted the following features at 25Hz for each participant. First, Motion energy (ME) is defined as the number of pixels in movement between the current video frame and a reference image in a region of interest. Preciously studied to assess interactional synchrony [13], motion energy informs about a shared dynamics between the two partners movement. For each speaker, we defined three regions of interest in the video : one centered on the head and torso of the participants, to capture postural movement, one centered on the hands to capture manipulative gestures and a last region that covered all the participant. We also extracted Hands velocity as described in section 4.3.

4.4.2 *Coordination tensors*

Various measures have been proposed to evaluate the similarity between two time series on the time or the frequency domain : cross-correlation [13], phase synchronization [17], mutual information [15], cross-spectral coherence [14] ...

We opted for cross-correlation and cross-spectral coherence for the simplicity of their estimation, opposed to mutual information or phase estimation and the fastness of their computation. We selected cross-correlation to capture the similarity of the time series in the time domain.

Cross-spectral coherence measures the similarity of the participants in the frequency domain, comparing the similarity of the power spectral densities of the time series in each band of frequency. Thus it may be useful to identify variations that share the same spectral properties, the same rhythm, regardless of an eventual time-lag between the processes occurring in the time series.

We performed the two measures across all possible pairs of features on 1s, 2s and 5s frames delayed of 0s, 1s or 2s lags. Thus large 3D coordination tensors (feature x x feature y x duration of the video) were obtained where each coefficient represents the similarity between a pair of features for a given time window (see Fig 1).

4.4.3 *Ruling out random coordination*

A critical question when we try to detect dependence relationships between features is beyond which score should we consider the measure as significant. Consequently, we needed a reference to compare our score and conclude about the significance of our measure.

[2] originally proposed a rating method ("the pseudo synchrony experimental paradigm") to evaluate the interactional synchrony that occurred in a dyadic interaction. The method consisted in synthesizing pseudo interactions : video images of dyadic partners were isolated and re-combined in a random order. After judges rated original videos and pseudo interactions videos. Pseudo interactions scores constituted

a baseline to judge the scores obtained on the original interaction.

We used an extension of this method to automatic computation to classify each window of interaction as "coordinated" or "not coordinated" [13]. First, features were extracted for each dyadic partner on the original video. The features extracted for first partner were time-shuffled and re-associated with the second partner original features. With this bootstrap method, 100 pseudo interactions were generated. Genuine coordination measures were assessed on original features and 100 pseudo interactions coordination measures were computed on the time-shuffled features. Then, to replace human judges from the Bernieri method, a one-sided z-test ($p = 0.05$) was performed to compare genuine interaction measures and pseudo interactions measures. We concluded that a given window was "coordinated" if genuine coordination measure was two standard deviations above the pseudo coordination measures.

We finally characterized the degree of synchronized movements between partners with the percentage of frames for which the measure was significant.

5. RESULTS

In section 3, we obtained a human evaluation of coordination for each video clip in our database. In section 4, we extracted semi-automatic and automatic cues that we assumed were related with the coordination of the dyads. In this section, we finally measure the Pearson correlation coefficient between the scores from the evaluation and the cues extracted on the video clips. Only the cues that presented significant relations with the coordination scores are provided in the tables below.

5.1 Speech turn-taking cues

First, judges rated better interaction with longer speech pauses: pauses duration (mean, median and minimum) was positively correlated with coordination scores from all items (see Table 1). Also, when silence covered a larger part of the interaction, the coordination scores were higher. Therapist shorter speech turns corresponded to the interaction rated as less coordinated and the amount of therapists speech turns was negatively correlated with coordination scores. The duration of children speech turns (mean, median, minimum and maximum) were significantly higher in interaction poorly coordinated. Then, children turns durations varied more in interactions poorly coordinated (range and standard deviation). And the greater was the proportion of the child speech turns the worst the raters perceived the dyad. At last, the amount of speech overlaps were not significantly linked with perceived coordination.

5.2 Therapist and children dialog acts cues

Although we did not find a significant correlation, we observed a negative trend that linked the number of yes/no questions with the perceived coordination (see Table 2). The number of categorial and open questions, as well as the overall number of questions from the therapist was negatively linked with the evaluation scores. The number of requests was also negatively correlated with the first item of the questionnaire.

There was no significant relation between the adequacy of the answers and the coordination scores (see Table 3). On the other hand the number of not answered questions was

Table 1: This table presents the correlation between speech turn-taking cues and coordination scores. The less the therapist and the child needed to speak the better coordinated the dyad was perceived.

Features	Item1	Item2	Item3	Item4
Pauses				
Pause_dur_mean	0.59^{**}	0.61^{**}	0.65^{**}	0.64^{**}
Pause_dur_min	0.42^{1}	0.48^{*}	0.48^{*}	0.46^{*}
Pause_dur_med	0.57^{**}	0.61^{**}	0.63^{**}	0.61^{**}
Therapist				
Speech_dur_min	0.53^{*}	0.5^{*}	0.5^{*}	0.44^{*}
Child				
Speech_dur_mean	-0.63^{**}	-0.59^{**}	-0.64^{**}	-0.62^{**}
Speech_dur_std	-0.5^{*}	-0.43^{1}	-0.47^{*}	-0.38^{1}
Speech_dur_min	-0.35	-0.31	-0.37^{1}	-0.39^{1}
Speech_dur_max	-0.71^{***}	-0.67^{***}	-0.7^{***}	-0.67^{***}
Speech_dur_range	-0.74^{***}	-0.7^{***}	-0.72^{***}	-0.68^{***}
Speech_dur_med	-0.59^{**}	-0.56^{**}	-0.61^{**}	-0.6^{**}
Ratios				
Pause_ratio	0.62^{**}	0.64^{**}	0.66^{**}	0.65^{**}
Speech_The_ratio	-0.35	-0.37	-0.38^{1}	-0.38^{1}
Speech_Chi_ratio	-0.64^{**}	-0.65^{**}	-0.65^{**}	-0.66^{**}

^{1} $p<0.1$ * $p<0.05$ ** $p<0.01$ *** $p<0.001$

Table 2: This table presents the correlation between therapist dialog acts cues and coordination scores. Questions and requests occurred when the child needed more support to accomplish the task.

Features	Item1	Item2	Item3	Item4
Closed (yes/no)	-0.37^{1}	-0.38^{1}	-0.38^{1}	-0.41^{1}
Categorial	-0.45^{*}	-0.49^{*}	-0.48^{*}	-0.46^{*}
Open	-0.52^{*}	-0.47^{*}	-0.44^{*}	-0.45^{*}
Total questions	-0.5^{*}	-0.52^{*}	-0.51^{*}	-0.54^{*}
Order/Request	-0.45^{*}	-0.35	-0.41^{1}	-0.36

^{1} $p<0.1$ * $p<0.05$ ** $p<0.01$ *** $p<0.001$

directly linked with a negative perception of the coordination.

5.3 Gestural turn-taking cues

Large variations of the gestural pause durations of the therapist (range and standard deviation) were negatively linked with coordination, as larger maximal duration of gestural pause during the interaction (see Table 4). Therapist's maximum and range of gestural segments duration were lower for highly coordinated video clips (significant correlation for item 4 and trend for item 1 and 3).

The child's gestural pauses (minimum, mean and median duration) tended to last longer for well-coordinated dyads. Several items showed this significant relationship.

The proportion of time when the therapist was gesturing and the children was not, was higher in interaction perceived as highly coordinated. Finally, there was significantly more movement sequences from both child and adult on poorly coordinated dyads whereas the number of puzzle elements stayed constant. And there were proportionally more movement sequences from the child than from the therapist on those dyads. In fact, the interactions were more fragmented, the child had to start again several times before adjusting

Table 3: This table presents the correlation between children answers and coordination scores. More adequate answers and less unanswered questions characterized the well coordinated children.

Features	Item1	Item2	Item3	Item4
Adequate	-0.3	-0.38^{1}	-0.34	-0.32
Not answered	-0.41^{1}	-0.39^{1}	-0.39^{1}	-0.45*

^{1} p<0.1 * p<0.05 ** p<0.01 *** p<0.001

Table 4: This table presents the correlation between gestural turn-taking cues and coordination scores. In the well coordinated dyads, the duration of the therapists gestural pauses were more homogeneous and the child spent less time gesturing while the therapist was demonstrating

Features	Item1	Item2	Item3	Item4
Therapist' gestures pauses				
Pause_dur_mean	-0.35	-0.43^{1}	-0.33	-0.3
Pause_dur_std	-0.43^{1}	-0.52*	-0.45*	-0.45*
Pause_dur_max	-0.58**	-0.64**	-0.61**	-0.62**
Pause_dur_range	-0.58**	-0.64**	-0.61**	-0.62**
Therapist' gestures				
Gest_dur_max	-0.41^{1}	-0.36	-0.37^{1}	-0.49*
Gest_dur_range	-0.41^{1}	-0.36	-0.37^{1}	-0.49*
Child' gestures pauses				
Pause_dur_mean	0.3	0.32	0.35	0.37^{1}
Pause_dur_min	0.44*	0.46*	0.4^{1}	0.4^{1}
Pause_dur_med	0.41^{1}	0.44*	0.48*	0.48*
Ratios				
Pause_The_ratio	-0.3	-0.37^{1}	-0.3	-0.21
The_on_Chi_off_ratio	0.42^{1}	0.48*	0.44*	0.38^{1}
The_off_Chi_off_ratio	-0.35	-0.42^{1}	-0.35	-0.31
Number of sequences				
Seq_The_nb	-0,83***	-0,8***	-0,84***	-0,86***
Seq_Chi_nb	-0,88***	-0,89***	-0,89***	-0,91***
Seq_The_Chi_ratio	-0,54*	-0,62**	-0,55**	-0,54*

^{1} p<0.1 * p<0.05 ** p<0.01 *** p<0.001

two elements together. The therapist needed to demonstrate several times the same stage of the assembly. We did not find significant relations between the movement features extracted on the children movements duration statistics and the coordination scores.

5.4 Synchronized motion cues

5.4.1 Measures based on correlation

We measured a significant negative relation between synchronized motion cues and coordination scores for Global Motion (ME) on windows of 2s and 5s with a delay of 1s between the therapist and the child (see Table 5). We also observed this negative trend for Posture Motion (ME) on windows of 1s with 1s delay and on windows of 2s with 0s or 1s delay.

For Hands Motion (ME), we measured a negative relation with raters evaluation for windows of 5s with no delay but the relation was positive for windows of 1s and 5s with 2s delay. For Left Hand (Tracking), there seems to be a negative trend for windows delayed of 1s but the tendency seems to be inverse for windows delayed of 2s. Nevertheless, those relations did not reach significance.

Table 5: This figure presents the correlation between synchronized motion cues (measures based on correlation) and coordination scores.

Features	Item1	Item2	Item3	Item4
Global (ME)				
Win=2s_delay=1s	-0,39^{1}	-0,38^{1}	-0,36	-0,32
Win=5s_delay=1s	-0,41^{1}	-0,37^{1}	-0,43^{1}	-0,28
Posture (ME)				
Win=1s_delay=1s	-0,42^{1}	-0,39^{1}	-0,4^{1}	-0,32
Win=2s_delay=0s	-0,37	-0,44*	-0,31	-0,28
Win=2s_delay=1s	-0,55**	-0,54*	-0,57**	-0,49*
Hands (ME)				
Win=1s_delay=2s	0,39^{1}	0,37	0,31	0,37^{1}
Win=5s_delay=0s	-0,42^{1}	-0,41^{1}	-0,44*	-0,46*
Win=5s_delay=2s	0,47*	0,5*	0,42^{1}	0,41^{1}
Left hand (Tracking)				
Win=5s_delay=1s	-0,39^{1}	-0,36	-0,32	-0,24
Win=5s_delay=2s	0,29	0,27	0,31	0,38^{1}

^{1} p<0.1 * p<0.05 ** p<0.01 *** p<0.001

5.4.2 Measures based on coherence

For Global Motion (ME), we measured a positive relation between coordination parameters and scores (trend on windows of 2s with 2s delay on item3 and significant relation on windows of 5s with 2s delay)(see Table 6). We also observed a significant positive link between Posture Motion (ME) of the participants measured on 1s windows with 2s delay. For Hands Motion (ME), we assessed a positive significant link on windows of 2s and 5s with 2s delay. But the relation was negative for Right Hand (Tracking) on 2s windows with 1s delay. For Left Hand (Tracking), there were some positive and negative trends for windows of 1s without delay, windows of 2s with 2s delay and windows of 5s with 1s delay. The only relation that reached significance was between Left Hand (Tracking) measured on 5s windows with 2s delay and scores from item2.

6. DISCUSSION

6.1 Speech as a last resort

First, the raters tended to judge negatively the dyads where the therapist was more talkative. In fact, there is no clear necessity to speak to fulfill the task ; the clinician tended to use speech when the visual demonstration was not sufficient. Consequently, the longer the speech pauses lasted the more coordinated the dyad was perceived. No words were needed.

We also observed that the length of the therapist utterances tended to be shorter for "low coordination" interactions. We can hypothesize that the therapist adapted the length of his speech according to the child need. She used shorter utterances for children with poor abilities. Therapist intervenes more on "low coordination" videos trying

Table 6: **This figure presents the correlation between synchronized motion cues (measures based on coherence) and coordination scores. Global Motion (ME) and Hands Motion (ME) with 2s delay were more synchronized for well coordinated dyads. For shorter delays, we observed opposite relations for hands motions.**

Features	Item1	Item2	Item3	Item4
Global (ME)				
Win=2s_delay=2s	0,27	0,35	0,37^{1}	0,33
Win=5s_delay=2s	0,44*	0,48*	0,42^{1}	0,4^{1}
Posture (ME)				
Win=1s_delay=2s	0,6**	0,66**	0,6**	0,54*
Mains (ME)				
Win=2s_delay=2s	0,46*	0,48*	0,47*	0,44*
Win=5s_delay=2s	0,44*	0,41^{1}	0,39^{1}	0,36
Right hand (Track.)				
Win=2s_delay=1s	-0,48*	-0,43*	-0,42^{1}	-0,36
Left hand (Track.)				
Win=1s_delay=0s	0,4^{1}	0,36	0,37	0,37
Win=2s_delay=2s	0,41^{1}	0,41^{1}	0,38^{1}	0,38^{1}
Win=5s_delay=1s	-0,43^{1}	-0,39^{1}	-0,4^{1}	-0,33
Win=5s_delay=2s	0,38^{1}	0,44*	0,42^{1}	0,42^{1}

^{1} p<0.1 * p<0.05 ** p<0.01 *** p<0.001

to engage or help children with semantic informations. We tended to have more categorial questions and open questions for those videos. There were also more orders and requests : "look", "go", "do just like me"...

For the children, we observed that the utterances mean duration and standard deviation were lower for highly coordinated dyads. In fact, children who performed the task without difficulty only used speech for short utterances. They gave back-channels to the clinician for example. Some of them even did not speak at all. On the contrary, when the interactions were less smooth, children asked more questions... We also observed digressions and echolalia for some of them. Standard deviation of child turn duration represents the alternation of short turns with long turns. Children who showed high coordination produced only short utterances (back channels). Absence of answer to the therapist questions was also typical of interactions judged with low coordination.

6.2 Fluency of gestural turn-taking

Therapist gestural pauses represent the time that therapist waits for the child to fulfill next step of the assembly. The interactions in which the therapist had to wait for the children where perceived as poorly coordinated. The variation of the pause durations of the therapist (range and standard deviation) is related to rhythm : when pause durations were stable, the interactions were perceived as well coordinated. There was a comparative trend for the range duration of gestural sequences of the therapist, which was smaller for highly coordinated dyads.

On the contrary when there was a large range between short and long pauses durations, it means that some steps of the assembly took longer than the others. Those interactions were perceived as less fluent by the annotators. We also observed that the movement maximal durations were higher in low coordinated tasks. We can assume that sometimes the therapists repeated the movement several times or did it more slowly to help the child decompose the steps. This was confirmed by a smaller number of movement sequences of the therapist in the well-coordinated dyads.

Lastly we noted that the percentage of time that the child was moving while the therapist was demonstrating was correlated with the perception of coordination. We can assume a link between these features and the attention of the child towards the therapist. Children who gestured a lot while the therapist was demonstrating were perceived less attentive and concentrated on the task. We also observed that the gestural pauses were longer for children who appeared well-coordinated.

6.3 Similar rhythm more than synchronized movements

When we designed our automatic cues, we hypothesized that coordination parameters would be positively linked with evaluation scores. But surprisingly, we found several coordination parameters, for measures based on correlation, that were negatively linked with the evaluation scores. Thus, we can make several assumptions to explain these results.

First, the features we used might be too global to discriminate between the actual gestures required to perform the task and interfering gestures that we implicitly filter when we watch the video clips. Also, our features are not capable of discriminating between two people moving the same piece of the puzzle and two persons moving two different elements at the same time. Despite the bootstrap stage, there are certainly windows of interaction that are classified as synchronous whereas they are not.

Then, we can remark that the tendency tends to reverse when we increase the time-lag between the windows on which the correlation is calculated (negative relation for 5s windows with no delay, but positive relation for 5s windows with 2s delay). Thus, we may not deal properly with the time-lag between the partners. In our model, we measure the percentage of windows that are "coordinated" for arbitrarily fixed time-lags of 0s, 1s and 2s. But this lag certainly vary in a dyad from one puzzle element to another and from one dyad to another. A related question is how do we humans perceive and tolerate the lag between the partners. For instance, the first item of the coordination questionnaire ("the partners engaged in simultaneous movement) was the most puzzling for the annotators as illustrates the low kappa coefficient. In fact, there are no perfectly simultaneous movements during the task as the child imitates the therapist. There is always a certain lag between the demonstration from the therapist and the imitation from the child. And the judges according to their tolerance to the time-lag rated more or less harshly the dyads.

At last, the task is very complex to analyze automatically; there are plenty of manners to assemble two elements together. If the two participants don't follow the same strategy, the model won't find them coordinated while extern judges may find they are. To circumvent the features issues, to rule out the interfering gestures and to limit the degree of freedom of the participants, we are setting up a computerized jigsaw task. The principle will be similar to the clown task but the assembly will be completed on a computer. This way, we may only record gestures related to the task (mouse trajectories) and know which element of the jigsaw is actually moved.

Finally, coordination parameters based on coherence gave more interesting results for global motion, posture and hand motion. As it is independent of the lag between partners, coherence captured a shared rhythm of the dyadic partners. This measure appears to be more adapted to our task and to the perception of the judges to characterize the coordination of the dyad.

7. CONCLUSION

We presented in this work several automatically computable cues that are related with the perception of coordination in an imitation task. The population we chose to work with is special as it involves children, including several ones with social impairments. The task we propose also bears special features. Imitation is a certainly a special type of interaction but it was originally suggested by psychologists as it requires multiple abilities to coordinate and cooperate with the partner : turn-taking, joint attention or planning. So, even if the task is specific, it can give a good insight on general abilities required in everyday life. And the evaluation questionnaire rates general characteristics of coordination : smoothness, behavior matching, similar tempos. Then, identifying low level cues to evaluate and compare children interactive abilities is particularly relevant for psychologists. Imitation is also a simple framework for human-robot interaction. Our work could give insight on how to evaluate or adapt robots to fulfill such tasks. We observed for example that the similarity of gestures was not particularly relevant. On the contrary, demonstrator's variations of rhythm and difference of rhythm between the partners were badly perceived by the judges.

Acknowledgments

The authors would like to thank F. Bigouret, A.L. Cornuault and C. Debray for their assistance in gathering and annotating the data. The authors also wish to thank L. Chaby, M. Plaza and D. Cohen for providing useful comments and advices. This work was supported by the UPMC "Emergence 2009" program.

8. REFERENCES

[1] F. Bernieri, J. Reznick, and R. Rosenthal. Synchrony, pseudo synchrony, and dissynchrony: Measuring the entrainment process in mother-infant interactions. *Journal of Personality and Social Psychology*, 54(2):243–253, 1988.

[2] F. Bernieri and R. Rosenthal. *Interpersonal coordination: Behavior matching and interactional synchrony. Fundamentals of nonverbal behavior.* Cambridge University Press, 1991.

[3] G. R. Bradski. Computer vision face tracking for use in a perceptual user interface. *Intel Technology Journal*, (Q2), 1998.

[4] C. Breazeal and B. Scassellati. A context-dependent attention system for a social robot. In *Proceedings of the Sixteenth International Joint Conference on Artificial Intelligence*, pages 1146–1153, 1999.

[5] C. L. Breazeal. *Sociable machines: expressive social exchange between humans and robots.* PhD thesis, 2000.

[6] A. Delaborde and L. Devillers. Use of nonverbal speech cues in social interaction between human and robot: emotional and interactional markers. In *Proceedings of the 3rd international workshop on Affective interaction in natural environments*, pages 75–80, 2010.

[7] E. Delaherche and M. Chetouani. Multimodal coordination: exploring relevant features and measures. In *Second International Workshop on Social Signal Processing, ACM Multimedia 2010*, 2010.

[8] H. Hung and D. Gatica-Perez. Estimating cohesion in small groups using audio-visual nonverbal behavior. *IEEE Transactions on Multimedia*, 12(6):563–575, 2010.

[9] H. Hung, Y. Huang, G. Friedland, and D. Gatica-Perez. Estimating dominance in multi-party meetings using speaker diarization. *IEEE Transactions on Audio, Speech & Language Processing*, 19(4):847–860, 2011.

[10] D. B. Jayagopi and D. Gatica-Perez. Mining group nonverbal conversational patterns using probabilistic topic models. *IEEE Transactions on Multimedia*, 12(8):790–802, 2010.

[11] M. Kipp. Spatiotemporal coding in anvil. In *LREC*, 2008.

[12] D. Lakens. Movement synchrony and perceived entitativity. *Journal of Experimental Social Psychology*, 46(5):701 – 708, 2010.

[13] F. Ramseyer and W. Tschacher. Nonverbal synchrony or random coincidence? how to tell the difference. In A. Esposito et al., editors, *Development of Multimodal Interfaces: Active Listening and Synchrony*, volume 5967, pages 182–196. Springer Berlin / Heidelberg, 2010.

[14] M. J. Richardson, K. L. Marsh, R. W. Isenhower, J. R. Goodman, and R. Schmidt. Rocking together: Dynamics of intentional and unintentional interpersonal coordination. *Human Movement Science*, 26(6):867 – 891, 2007.

[15] M. Rolf, M. Hanheide, and K. Rohlfing. Attention via synchrony : Making use of multimodal cues in social learning. *IEEE Trans. Auton. Mental Develop.*, 1(1):55–67, 2009.

[16] G. Varni, A. Camurri, P. Coletta, and G. Volpe. Toward a real-time automated measure of empathy and dominance. In *CSE (4)*, pages 843–848, 2009.

[17] G. Varni, M. Mancini, G. Volpe, and A. Camurri. Sync'n'move: social interaction based on music and gesture. *Proceedings of the 1st International ICST Conference on User Centric Media*, 2009.

[18] S. F. Worgan and R. K. Moore. Towards the detection of social dominance in dialogue. *Speech Communication*, In Press:–, 2011.

[19] B. Wrede, S. Kopp, K. Rohlfing, M. Lohse, and C. Muhl. Appropriate feedback in asymmetric interactions. *Journal of Pragmatics*, 42(9):2369 – 2384, 2010. How people talk to Robots and Computers.

[20] Z. Yucel, A. A. Salah, C. Merici, and T. Merici. Joint visual attention modeling for naturally interacting robotic agents. In *ISCIS*, pages 242–247, 2009.

The Sounds of Social Life: Observing Humans in their Natural Habitat

Matthias Mehl
University of Arizona
P.O. Box 210068,
Tucson, AZ 85721-0068
520-626-2374
mehl@email.arizona.edu

ABSTRACT

This talk presents a novel methodology called the Electronically Activated Recorder or EAR. The EAR is a portable audio recorder that periodically records snippets of ambient sounds from participants' momentary environments. In tracking moment-to-moment ambient sounds, it yields acoustic logs of people's days as they naturally unfold. In sampling only a fraction of the time, it protects participants' privacy. As a naturalistic observation method, it provides an observer's account of daily life and is optimized for the assessment of audible aspects of social environments, behaviors, and interactions. The talk discusses the EAR method conceptually and methodologically and identifies three ways in which it can enrich research in the social and behavioral sciences. Specifically, it can (1) provide ecological, behavioral criteria that are independent of self-report, (2) calibrate psychological effects against frequencies of real-world behavior, and (3) help with the assessment of subtle and habitual behaviors that evade self-report.

Categories and Subject Descriptors: J.4 [**Social and Behavioral Sciences**]: Psychology

General Terms: Experimentation.

Keywords: Electronically Activated Recorder, Ecological Momentary Assessment, Social Interaction, Social Environment

SPEAKER BIOGRAPHY

Matthias Mehl is Associate Professor of Psychology and an Adjunct Associated Professor of Communication at the University of Arizona. He received his doctorate in social and personality psychology from the University of Texas at Austin. Over the last decade, he developed the Electronically Activated Recorder (EAR) as a novel methodology for the unobtrusive naturalistic observation of daily life. He has given workshops and published numerous articles on novel methods for studying daily life. Dr. Mehl is a founding member and the current Vice President of the Society for Ambulatory Assessment and co-editor of the Handbook of Research Methods for Studying Daily Life. His research has been published in various high impact journals (incl. *Science, Psychological Science, Journal of Personality and Social Psychology, Psychological Assessment, and Health Psychology*) and has been funded, among other sources, by the American Cancer Society and the NIH (NCI, NCCAM).

ICMI'11, November 14–18, 2011, Alicante, Spain.
ACM 978-1-4503-0641-6/11/11.

Smartphone Usage in the Wild: a Large-Scale Analysis of Applications and Context

Trinh Minh Tri Do
Idiap Research Institute
Switzerland
do@idiap.ch

Jan Blom
Nokia Research Center
Switzerland
jan.blom@nokia.com

Daniel Gatica-Perez
Idiap Research Institute
EPF Lausanne, Switzerland
gatica@idiap.ch

ABSTRACT

This paper presents a large-scale analysis of contextualized smartphone usage in real life. We introduce two contextual variables that condition the use of smartphone applications, namely places and social context. Our study shows strong dependencies between phone usage and the two contextual cues, which are automatically extracted based on multiple built-in sensors available on the phone. By analyzing continuous data collected on a set of 77 participants from a European country over 9 months of actual usage, our framework automatically reveals key patterns of phone application usage that would traditionally be obtained through manual logging or questionnaire. Our findings contribute to the large-scale understanding of applications and context, bringing out design implications for interfaces on smartphones.

Categories and Subject Descriptors

H.5.m [**Information Interfaces and Presentation (e.g., HCI)**]: Miscellaneous

General Terms

Human Factors

1. INTRODUCTION

The short history of mobile phones has witnessed several stages, as phone adoption has increased rapidly across the globe. Today, several billion individuals carry these devices, becoming reachable almost anytime, anywhere. Mobile technology adoption has widespread social implications, ranging from western teenagers using mobile phones to exchange gifts [21], to economically challenged users leveraging the mobile phone to improve their livelihood [7].

A recent trend is associated with the rise of the smartphone - computationally powerful computing devices available to users across an increasingly wide range of prices [14]. Such devices have increased the functionalities available to users partly due to their large number of built-in sensors (GPS, Bluetooth, accelerometer, microphone, camera, etc). It is now commonplace to talk about an ecosystem of functions, applications, and services enabled by smartphones. End users are at the center of such an ecosystem, creating content with their devices, accessing content available through the mobile Internet, sharing it with their social networks.

The issues of multimodal interaction through mobile phones and context-aware mobile services are growing in importance. It has become key to understand how such devices are used, especially with the emergence of the App culture, where a multitude of mobile services and applications can be downloaded from the web and used on smartphones. Is it the case that smartphone usage is uniformly distributed across application types, or is there still a bias toward traditional communication means like voice calls and SMS? Given the multiple facets of these devices, it is also increasingly important to investigate how usage unfolds with respect to different types of contexts. In other words, to what extent does the selection of a given application depend on the physical or social context? Are certain applications independent of the type of environment where the phone is used? Addressing these questions is key for the design of successful mobile user experiences for smartphone users. In industry, the understanding of how these platforms are appropriated as part of everyday life could be leveraged across several layers of product design. From the user interface viewpoint, knowing which applications are relevant where and when could facilitate access to different functionalities. From the viewpoint of service discovery, it could be useful to know when a user is likely to be in need of specific information so that it can be offered at the right time. From the viewpoint of facilitating human communication, contextual insights could be used to modify specific phone features to make them more suitable to the given social and spatial situation.

When aiming to understand the impact of context on usage of mobile phones, traditional research techniques have focused on ethnographic observation [4] or quasi experiments on the field [18]. This paper, on the other hand, follows recent practices in mobile sensing [14] and adopts a large-scale approach, by analyzing rich data collected by the smartphones of a set of 77 participants from a European city over 9 months, where phones are carried around and used in a natural, unobtrusive manner in everyday life. Furthermore, we go beyond recent analyses of application usage patterns from automatically recorded logs [3, 6, 10] by introducing two contextual variables that condition the use of smartphone applications, namely semantic places and physical proximity. In our work, these two contextual cues are automatically extracted by exploiting multiple sensors available on the phones (GPS, GSM, Wifi, Bluetooth, and accelerometer). Our work examines the effects of individual as well as joint contextual cues on the use of communication, web, and media applications. Our study reveals a number of key patterns and shows that phone usage depends significantly on both location

ICMI'11, November 14–18, 2011, Alicante, Spain.

and social context. Furthermore, our findings directly suggest several smartphone design implications related to user needs.

The paper is organized as follows. Section 2 discusses related research. Sections 3, 4, 5 and 6 describe the data collection procedure, the resulting dataset, and the specific variables used in our study. Section 7 discusses the findings of the analysis. Section 8 discusses the implications of the results on features that could better address the contextual needs of smartphone users. Section 9 draws conclusions.

2. RELATED WORK

The existing works related to the understanding of mobile phone usage can be broadly categorized into those that have analyzed usage behavior through standard ethnographic and user studies (based on questionnaires, self-reports, diaries, and often conducted on small numbers of subjects), and recent studies that exploit the automatic recording and subsequent analysis of phone activity logs for larger populations and periods of time.

In the first category, early works on patterns of SMS usage include [12] and [11], in which users where asked to manually log their texting activity. Reid and Reid [20] studied differences of SMS and call usage preferences using questionnaire data. In a more recent example, Butt and Phillips presented a study on the relation between mobile phone usage and personality traits from the popular Big-Five model, using self-reports of weekly usage levels of calls, SMS, and a few applications including games and ringtones [5]. Recently, Barkhuus and Polichar [2] investigated how users adapt and adopt the different functions in smartphones based on interviews and daily diaries over 3 weeks from 21 users. Other studies have focused on other phone applications and mobility [4, 24].

Self-reported data can be prone to errors, due to personal biases, recall limitations, etc., and therefore the feasibility of automatically capturing logs of mobile phone usage at large scale has generated a second, more recent body of work, where longitudinal analyses of phone application logs is collected by combining automatic collection of smartphone data and human-centric data analysis [14, 1]. This practice is becoming increasingly relevant for mobile phone manufacturers, operators, and service providers. Nokia has released brief findings related to phone usage patterns in the context of the Smartphone 360 effort [17]. One study involved over 500 users in three countries over three months, and reported that both the time spent on the phone and the frequency of usage of certain applications increased with respect to previous years. Nielsen Mobile has also disclosed summaries of their analysis on operator-based data from thousands of users, in particular about mobile web usage given basic demographics (age, gender, income level, country, and phone type) [16]. Zokem, whose work originated in academia [22], also analyzes mobile phone application logs, and has recently made some initial findings public [25]. Anderson et al. have applied "ethno-mining" techniques to understand use practices of a number of mobile devices, including laptops, netbooks, and phones [1]. A large-scale study of patterns of phone application usage using the time of the day as contextual anchor was recently presented [6]. In [10], a study on 255 users of Android and Windows Mobile smartphones, characterized usage in terms of energy consumption, traffic, time spend with the device, and applications. Statistics of popular apps, relations to basic demographics, and basic day/night patterns were reported. In all these cases, however, no usage analysis grounded on location and social proximity automatically estimated from sensor data has been presented, as we do here. Battestini et al. [3] presented a large-scale study of SMS usage, based on a population of 70 university students over four months who used a loggging software that also recorded the location where the SMS were received or sent, using a GSM cell positioning method. Unlike this work, our paper analyzes multiple phone applications (SMS included), with location anchors automatically estimated from multiple sensor data types (GPS, GSM, Wifi, motion), which results in higher accuracy in location estimation. In addition, we present an analysis of usage with a proxy for social context derived from Bluetooth.

3. DATA COLLECTION FRAMEWORK

Our data collection framework was based on a server-client architecture built around the Nokia N95 8GB smartphone. Phone usage was continuously collected using non-intrusive client software. Information pertaining to usage of apps and contextual information such as location and proximity was recorded. The client was programmed to start automatically at startup of the phone, run in the background and collect data on a 24/7 basis with the only restriction of having to recharge the phone once a day. In order to achieve sensing over a full day, the client was designed using a state-machine approach similar to [23], which results in a power-efficient adaptive sensing procedure. The client changes the sensors that are activated and the corresponding sampling rate at any given time according to the status of the state machine. This is key to be able to maintain all phone sensors active without draining the phone battery in a few hours (specially GPS sensing is power consumming). States are defined by the current readings of many of the phone sensors (GPS, GSM, WiFi, accelerometer, etc.). We omit the implementation details for space reasons. The recorded data is first stored in the phone local memory and then uploaded daily to a server via a user-defined WiFi connection. We used the following sources of usage data:

App logs. App logs consist of the usage events of all applications, including system apps, pre-installed apps like Camera or Calendar, and other user downloaded apps. Note that in the rest of the paper, we use the term "app" to denote all phone applications, and not only Ovi Store-like applications. Each time the user accesses an app, the client software captures the event and stores it together with the timestamp. Due to technical difficulties on capturing accurately the timestamp of close/switch events for some apps, we did not consider the usage duration and our analysis was focused on usage frequency.

Location data. The outdoor location information is obtained from the phone built-in GPS. For common visited places in a person's daily life, it is also possible to locate the user based on WiFi access points (APs). The software client periodically scans for WiFi APs and maintains a list of known-location APs (based on the simultaneous availability of GPS). Each time the client observes a AP in the list of known-location WiFi APs, the GPS sensor is turned off and the client uses the recorded location of the AP. This technique helps saving phone battery and allows having location information in many indoor environments.

Bluetooth data. The smartphone scans nearby Bluetooth devices every 1-3 minutes, depending on the state of the client. The number of discovered nearby devices can be used as an approximate measure of the human density and the type of environment, and provides to some degree the social context of the user. Bluetooth has been used as a noisy, yet reasonable proxy for social context in ubiquitous computing [19, 9], although it clearly does not imply actual face-to-face interaction (e.g. a person can be detected as being proximate while being in a contiguous room).

4. FROM GEOGRAPHIC LOCATIONS TO SEMANTIC PLACES

While our client provides instantaneous physical location information, access to the semantic meaning of any given location would be useful in order to understand how people use the phone in different contexts. Semantic information would allow elaborate analyses to be performed on the behavioral differences between different kinds of places. For this purpose, we transformed the geographic location into a semantic place by following a two-step procedure: 1) automatic discovery of visited places and 2) human annotation of most visited places. Each step is summarized below.

Automatic place discovering. The data collection client on the phone recorded the location of the user in a continuous fashion. From these traces, we first extracted stay points which are timestamped, small circular regions in which user stays for at least 10 minutes. These stay points were then clustered into meaningful places (or location anchors) with the maximum size of a cluster being limited to 250m, using a grid clustering algorithm recently proposed [15]. The output of the algorithm produces a personalized list of places for each user that are visited over the whole sensing period along with the timestamps when they were visited (see Section 5). Note that location sensing sometimes fails and thus not all locations can be detected, and also that many initially detected user locations do not give rise to the discovery of a place, either because users were on the move (e.g. on a train), or because they did not stay long enough in those regions.

Semi-automatic place labeling. The algorithm produces a diary of visited places that make geographic, but not semantic, sense. To provide semantics for places, the participants were required to fill in an online survey at the end of the experiment. Each participant was presented with a set of eight automatically chosen places. Five of the eight places were the most frequently visited locations of the user, across the entire experiment period. Places such as user's home and office typically ended up on the top five list. In order to also illuminate the semantics of less frequently used places, three of them were randomly chosen from the lowest tenth percentile (in terms of time spent) of the place list of the given individual. These eight places were then presented to the respondent in a random order, one by one. Each place represented by a rectangle whose size was determined by the grid clustering algorithm. For each place, a separate web page was generated, displaying the location on a map as a rectangle. The respondent then had to label the place by using a set of 22 mutually exclusive predefined labels. These labels were subsequently mapped to the following 11 labels: *Home, Work, Friend-Home, Friend-Work, Restaurant, Sport, Transport, Holiday, Shopping, Relaxing and Other*. The set of locations consists of 10 explicit categories and a special category called "Other" which includes both unlabeled places and labeled places that does not belong to any of the ten mentioned categories. "Friend" denotes both relatives or friends of the participant. All discovered places are static by construction, and the "Transport" category corresponds to transportation-related places such as train or metro station, bus stop, etc.

5. LARGE-SCALE DATA

Our analysis was conducted on the data from the Lausanne data collection campaign [13]. We use a subset of data consisting of 77 volunteer users who were given the smartphone and the cost for the mobile phone plan during the data collection period. The phone plan used by the volunteers includes the data plan (1GB/month) so that people are expected to use the web. The population is mainly composed of middle class individuals who are university students or professionals. Of them, 63% used public transportation, 27% used a car, and 7% used both. Figure 1 shows the composition of the studied population in terms of age and gender. All participants previously owned a mobile phone, although most of them were not familiar with the N95 before the study. Users used their smartphone as their only mobile phone. The data was collected between October 2009 and June 2010. All users filled out consent forms to have their data recorded and agreed to participate in the place labeling survey. There were roughly 8.6 million location entries and about 6.2 million of non-empty Bluetooth readings during the recording period. Among 7156 discovered places, 616 of them were annotated by participants, covering 95% of the total time people spent in detected places.

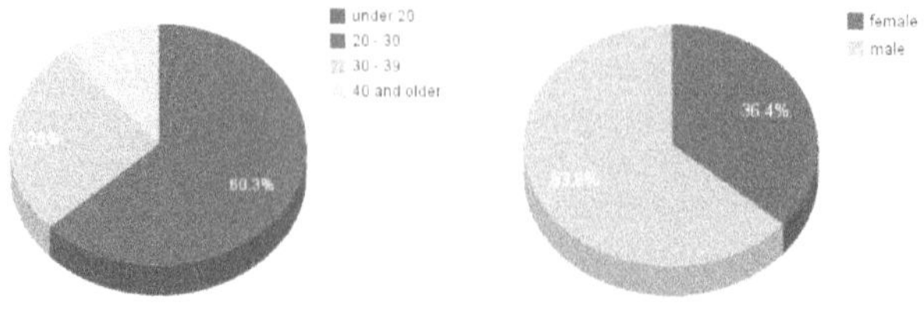

Figure 1: Age and gender of the studied population.

SMS and Voice Call	The two primary applications of mobile phone.
Web	Available web browsers. We consider both native the smartphone browser and user-installed browsers (e.g. Opera Mobile).
Multimedia	A group of multimedia applications including music players, video players, and image viewer.
Clock	The native application for setting the alarm and adjusting time.
Camera	The native application for taking photos and recording video.
Email	We consider both native the e-mail client and mobile Gmail.
Calendar	The native calendar app.
Voice chat	A set of messenger clients including Fring, Skype, and "Internet tel."
Maps	Apps access GPS and get user location. Both native map and Google map are studied.
Sport Tracker	Nokia app to track user route, speed and timings while engaging in sports.
Visual Radio	Interactive radio with FM radio over a data connection for graphics and text.

Table 1: Selected apps.

6. SELECTED APPS FOR THE STUDY

As stated earlier, we investigate the use of both native and installed apps during the data collection period. Among hundreds of applications found in the data, we selected a subset of the most popular ones for this study, listed in Table 1.

Figure 2 shows the total number of uses of each app in decreasing order. As can be seen, Voice Call and SMS are the most used applications followed by Web and Multimedia. On average, people accessed SMS 11.2 times per day and had 5.7 phone calls per day. For other applications, the usage frequency was relatively low, suggesting that relatively few participants used these apps actively. To clarify this, in Figure 3, we show the percentage of people who are interested in these applications (trying them at least once) and the percentage of people who accept them (using the app more than 10 times). As can be seen, the first six applications are used at least 10 times by almost all users which reflects the need for these apps and their acceptance. Calendar and Maps are also interesting for most users, but the percentage of actual users is slightly lower (around 70-75%). For other apps, the percentage of people who use them

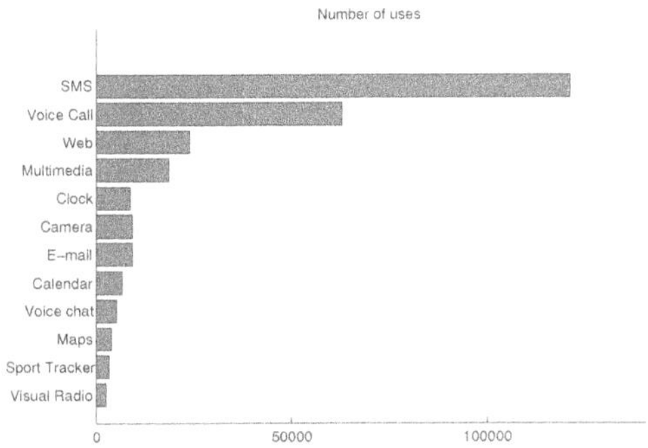

Figure 2: Number of events for each application.

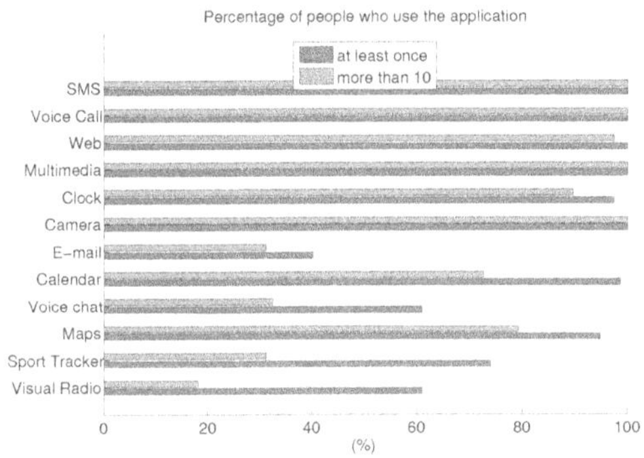

Figure 3: Percentage of active users for each apps.

more than 10 times is relatively low (less than 30%) and there are big differences between the number of users who try them and the number of users who actually use them. An interesting exception is the case of E-mail, where people who tried it once are likely to continue using it. Note that, while having less than half of number of users of Calendar or Maps, the number of uses of E-mail is high, which reflects the fact that E-mail is frequently used.

7. FINDINGS

7.1 App usage vs location

In this section, we study phone usage patterns with respect to user location. Figure 4 reports the aggregated time of stay in each semantic location for all users without counting night time (0-6am). Note that the stay time is plotted in log-scale since it varies significantly depending on the location category. For instance, the total time people stay at home (without night time) is twice the time people spend at work. Among labeled locations, places for Relaxing (e.g. Park) has the lowest staying time with about 14 hours (accumulated from 25 visits). Note also that the 'Other' catch-all category does correspond to the third most used label.

Table 2 reports the number of usage events occurring in each place. Notice that the number of events is strongly correlated with the total time people spent in each place (Pearson correlation $r = 0.44, p < 0.001$). The top 4 most popular places (Home,Work,Friend-Home,Other) cover 96.7% of all location-detected usage events. In order to study how people use the phone in each context, we introduce the notion of *hourly usage frequency* (huf), defined as follows for application i and location j:

$$huf(i,j) = \frac{number\ of\ events\ for\ application\ i}{total\ staying\ time\ in\ hours\ in\ location\ j}$$

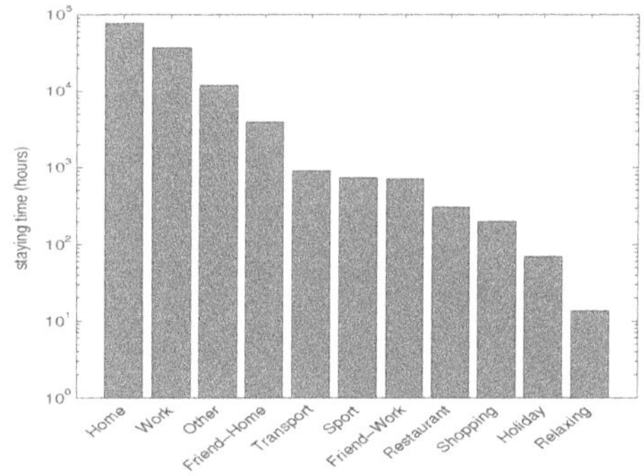

Figure 4: Staying time in each place category (in hours) and plotted in log scale.

	Home	Work	Friend-Home	Friend-Work	Restaurant	Sport	Transport	Holiday	Shopping	Relaxing	Other
SMS	31696	18706	2427	516	159	685	301	6	42	2	8756
Voice Call	13701	10708	1295	217	83	189	515	10	64	7	4721
Web	3783	3041	1157	12	58	57	460	30	39	4	1850
Multimedia	4808	2451	242	38	6	19	157	15	16	4	1043
Clock	4473	319	203	11	4	10	57	1	2	0	182
Camera	1532	759	113	34	9	19	67	56	17	0	1091
E-mail	2171	1481	393	0	13	137	7	3	0	0	729
Calendar	1177	961	121	9	12	36	123	0	4	0	1093
Voice chat	1390	475	133	3	0	68	7	24	1	0	208
Maps	560	283	53	2	12	16	10	5	1	1	423
Sport Tracker	706	423	86	0	0	32	3	0	0	0	175
Visual Radio	700	496	2	0	0	4	1	0	0	0	91

Table 2: Number of events occured in each place during the data collection period.

	Home	Work	Friend-Home	Friend-Work	Restaurant	Sport	Transport	Holiday	Shopping	Relaxing	Other	Avg.
SMS	0.41	**0.51**	0.63	0.72	0.52	0.93	**0.33**	**0.09**	0.21	0.15	**0.75**	0.48
Voice Call	0.18	**0.29**	0.34	0.30	0.27	0.26	**0.57**	**0.14**	**0.33**	0.51	**0.40**	0.24
Web	0.05	**0.09**	0.30	0.02	0.19	0.09	**0.52**	0.43	0.22	0.29	**0.16**	0.08
Multimedia	0.06	0.07	0.06	0.05	0.02	**0.03**	0.17	0.22	0.08	0.29	**0.09**	0.07
Clock	**0.07**	**0.01**	0.06	**0.02**	**0.01**	**0.01**	0.07	**0.01**	**0.04**	0.00	**0.02**	0.05
Camera	0.02	0.02	0.03	0.05	0.03	0.03	0.07	0.81	0.09	0.00	**0.09**	0.03
E-mail	0.09	0.11	0.17	0.00	0.10	0.32	**0.07**	0.06	0.00	0.00	**0.20**	0.11
Calendar	0.02	0.04	**0.04**	0.04	0.05	0.07	0.15	0.00	**0.03**	0.00	0.11	0.04
Voice chat	0.06	0.05	0.05	0.04	0.00	0.23	**0.05**	0.35	0.06	0.00	0.05	0.06
Maps	0.01	**0.01**	0.01	**0.01**	0.06	0.03	0.04	0.07	0.01	0.07	**0.05**	0.01
Sport Tracker	0.03	0.04	0.04	0.00	0.00	0.10	0.04	0.00	0.00	0.00	0.05	0.03
Visual Radio	0.06	0.05	**0.00**	0.00	0.00	**0.04**	0.01	0.00	0.00	0.00	0.05	0.05

Table 3: Hourly usage frequency (huf) for each app in each semantic place.

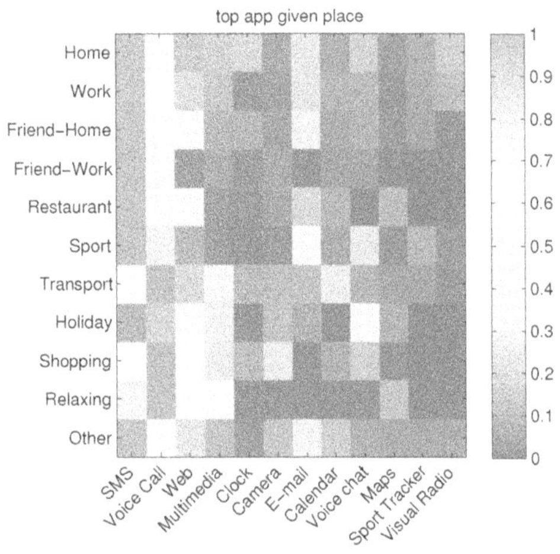

Figure 5: Top apps at a given place are highlighted in each row. A unity value (red) corresponds to the most frequently used app given a place.

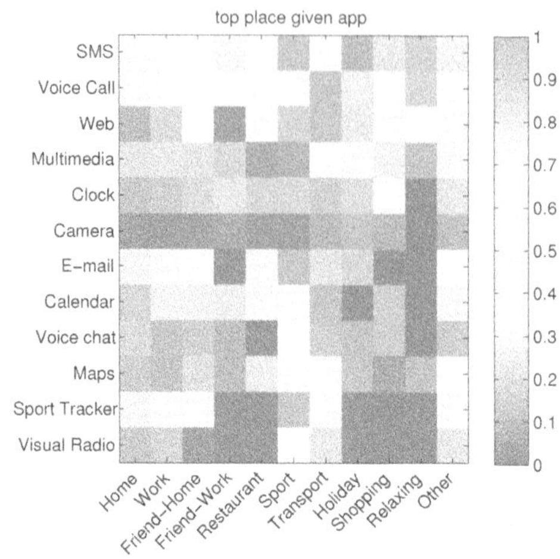

Figure 6: Top places for a given application are highlighted in each row. A unity value (red) corresponds to the place where the app is used the most.

which characterizes how frequently people use an application in a specific context. To have a practical meaning, for each app we only consider data from the set of active users of that app (i.e. those using the app more than 10 times). Table 3 reports the hourly usage frequency for each app at each place. For reference purposes, we also report the hourly usage frequency for each app averaged over all place (Avg.). For instance, we can see that the use of Voice Call at Work (0.29) is above average (0.24) but Clock usage at Work (0.01) is below average (0.05).

It is important to look at the generalization of the observations in Table 3 and to verify whether the observations have occurred by chance. For instance, if there are only a few people going to a sport center and they happened to be very active SMS users, then one can not draw the conclusion that all people use SMS a lot at the sport center. We conducted a statistical significance test by splitting data by user, and performed T-tests for the 2 hypotheses that the usage frequency of an app at a given location is above (respectively, below) the global average. Statistically significant cases ($p < 0.05$) are highlighted in bold in Table 3. As can be seen, having very low support in terms of active users and labeled locations, we do not have statistically significant results for Relaxing place and for Sport Tracker.

Visualizing apps that are used the most at a given place. Figure 5 highlights the top applications at each place by showing the app usage frequencies normalized by the maximum value over applications. The top applications are highlighted in each row with value close to 1. It is not surprising to notice that SMS and Voice Call are the top applications in most locations. However, while SMS is highly used in many indoor locations, people seem to prefer the use of Voice Call in moving contexts such as waiting at train or metro station (Transport category), or while shopping or relaxing in the park. This is a very interesting pattern of place-based communication preferences. At Friend-Home, Web and E-mail join SMS and Voice Call in the list of top apps. Finally, when on holidays people have a preference for the camera.

Visualizing places where apps are used the most. We continue the analysis by investigating frequency of use of the applications across different locations. Figure 6 illustrates the top places for an app by showing the usage frequency normalized by the maximum value in each row. First very interestingly, besides the Clock and Radio, none of the apps get used the most at Home or at Work (in terms of usage frequency). This indicates that mobile usage is directed towards other place than Home or Work. The use of Web is highest at transportation-related places such as bus stop or train station. In such contexts, the Internet is likely to be used for reading news, looking for information or killing time. People also surf the Web a lot during Holiday time, at a Friend's Home, and at Relaxing places like the park, which reflects the fact that for these places, smartphones replace computers as the primary web access device. A related app to Web is Email, which is similar to the Web in that it is frequently used in locations Friend-Home and Holiday. The main difference is that people are not likely to check email at transportation-related places, but they use email at frequently visited places such as the sport center. Calendar, in contrast, gets used the most in Transport places, and much less so at Work. This might be due to the fact that people rely on other devices at Work (desktop or laptops) to see their calendar in office hours. For other apps, the highlighted places are also meaningful. For instance, Multimedia is highly used at outdoor places such as Relaxing, Holiday, and Transport places. The Clock gets used at Home, Friend-Home and Transport. Maps is highly used during Holidays, at Restaurants and Relaxing places, which are often "first time visit" places. Sport Tracker, unsuprisingly, is used the most at Sport places.

Correlation between common places and app usage. The amount of time that people spend in different locations can tell us about the user's lifestyle [8]. In this section, we examine the relation between user lifestyle and app usage by studying the correlation between the proportion of time that people spend in each place and the app usage frequency. Table 4 reports Pearson correlation between these two types of variables for cases that are statistically significant ($p < 0.05$ or less). We can see that people who spent more time at Friend-Home also used Voice Call and Web more. This might correspond to people who are in a relationship, who called their significant other frequently, and used the phone to surf the net from their friend's place.

The second finding is related to people who spent more time waiting at transportation related locations. Given that these users travel often, they might use Web and Multimedia both while waiting and during the trip. Note however that in our study we do not infer what happens when people are actually moving, as we only consider (static) places. Clock and Camera usage also have significant correlation values with the time spent at transport-related

Location	App	Correlation
Friend-Home	Voice Call	0.26*
Friend-Home	Web	0.26*
Transportation	Web	0.26*
Transportation	Multimedia	0.27*
Transportation	Clock	0.52***
Transportation	Camera	0.51***
Holiday	Multimedia	0.24*
Holiday	Camera	0.28*
Holiday	Voice chat	0.36**
Holiday	Visual Radio	0.23*
Other	Calendar	0.42***

* $p < 0.05$, ** $p < 0.01$, *** $p < 0.001$

Table 4: Correlation between the percentage of time people spent in each location and the app usage frequency.

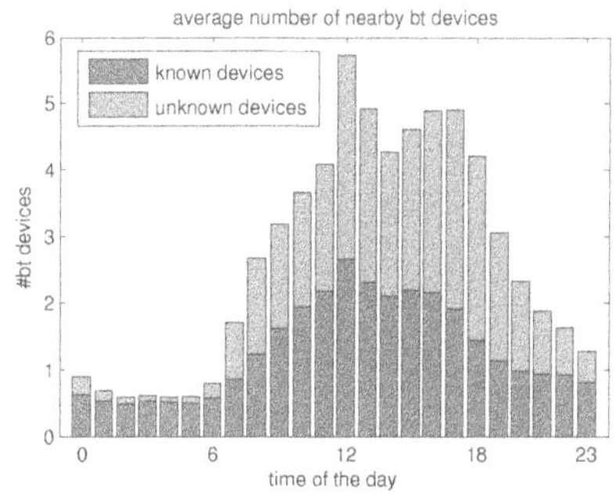

Figure 7: Number of nearby Bluetooth devices during the day.

locations. The use of the camera could be explained by people passing time while waiting. The use of clock id also intuitive, as users might consult the clock while waiting, e.g. in case of delays, etc. As a third finding, people who spent long time on holidays are likely to use Multimedia, Camera, and Voice Chat, which matches the analysis of phone usage wrt. location shown in Figure 5. Last but not least, there is a strong correlation between people who spent a lot of time in other location categories and the use of Calendar. As Other corresponds to a multitude of places corresponding to short or infrequent visits, one can think of these users as dynamic people for whom Calendar is a useful app when on the move.

7.2 App usage vs Bluetooth density

Using the Bluetooth sensor, one can make a coarse estimate of human density around the user. While some BT devices correspond to devices other than phones (e.g. laptops, netbooks), these devices themselves are mobile and carried by people. A high number of nearby Bluetooth devices likely means that there are many people around the user, such as a public place, a working place, or a large meeting. We refer to Bluetooth density as a rough proxy for social context (e.g. being alone or in a small or large group).

Figure 7 shows the average number of nearby Bluetooth devices to our population's phones on different times of the day, separating them into known (i.e., devices that have been previously observed at least on 5 different days) and unknown devices. Not surprisingly, there are few nearby Bluetooth devices during sleeping time (0-6am), and they are known Bluetooth devices in most cases. Office hours are the most active times, and the number of known devices seems to be somewhat proportional to the number of unknown devices. In the evening, the number of known devices tends to stabilize while the number of unknown devices gradually decreases. An explanation is that users are likely to be nearby the same people (relative or friend in proximity or neighbors across walls) in the evening, and the probability that they go out depends on the time.

We also study the usage frequency of the set of selected apps with respect to the social context proxy given by Bluetooth. Figure 8 shows different trends for usage frequency when the number of nearby Bluetooth devices increases. Again, we performed T-tests on the data splitted by user for the hypotheses that the usage frequency of a given app at high Bluetooth density places is above (or below) the usage frequency at low Bluetooth density places. Interestingly, we observe an statistically significant increase in app usage frequency when the Bluetooth density is high for SMS ($p = 0.03$), VoiceCall ($p = 0.0004$), and Web ($p = 0.008$). For instance, the use of Voice Call and Web at high Bluetooth density places is 50% higher than when people's phones do not detect any nearby Bluetooth device. In contrast, Clock has generally low use in high density Bluetooth environments, which matches our location analysis where people were found to use Clock highly at home and friends' home. Finally, a different pattern is observed in E-mail usage, where people are more likely to check email at either low Bluetooth density places or very high Bluetooth density places, which could resemble the "being alone" (no nearby BT devices) and "being in a class" (many nearby BT devices) situations. For the other investigated apps, there are no significant dependencies between app usage frequency and Bluetooth density.

7.3 App usage vs joint location and BT density

The analysis showed relevant patterns of phone app usage based on location information or based on Bluetooth density. We now consider a richer context by combining both of them. In order to have large enough support for each joint location-Bluetooth density category, we use a more compact set of 5 place labels: {*Home*, *Work*, *Friend Home* , *Other Indoor* and *Other Outdoor*} by merging the place categories previously used. Figure 9 shows the stay time in each joint location-Bluetooth context, where the most popular joint context is at Home without nearby BT device and the least one (184 hours in total) is the case of observing at least 8 nearby Bluetooth devices at home of a friend or a relative. As can be seen, people observe relatively few Bluetooth nearby devices in all places other than work. On the contrary, phones are likely to observe many nearby Bluetooth devices at work. This obviously is often a result not only of people carrying phones, but also laptops, netbooks, etc.

The app usage frequency in each location-Bluetooth density context is shown in Figure 10. Note that unlike Figure 5 and Figure 6, we do not need any normalization here because each app is plotted separately, and the raw hourly usage frequencies are shown. Note that to stress the differences in usage frequency in different contexts, we use different scales in these plots. For Voice and SMS, we see that people are likely to communicate with others when they are outdoors, especially when there are high number of nearby Bluetooth devices. This can be as high as 1 SMS per hour and 1 phone call every two hours on average. This is an interesting result, that could relate both to the high density of European cities and the associated lifestyle of people (spending time at coffee shops and bars, commuting or public transport). Some apps are highly used when the Bluetooth density is low in outdoor environments, including Multimedia, Camera and Map. This is likely to correspond to the case when people are in natural environment (e.g. mountains). Web has the highest frequency when people are at a friend's home and some nearby devices are detected. This is a somewhat puzzling finding.

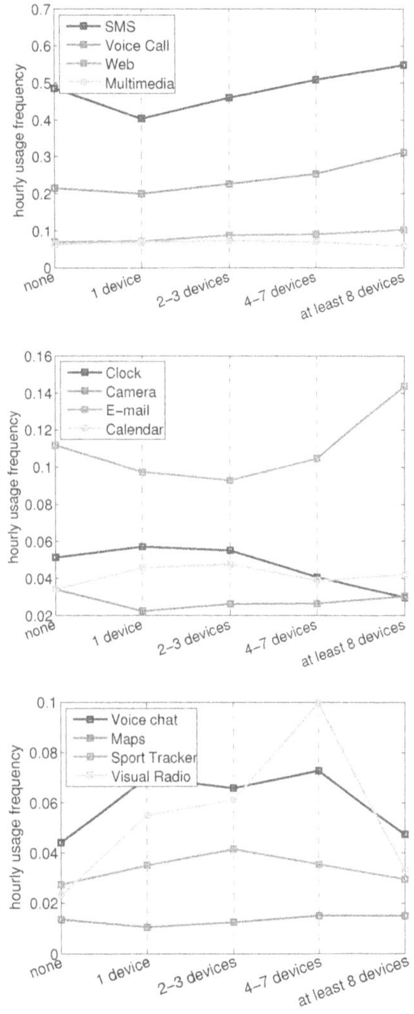

Figure 8: Usage vs Bluetooth density.

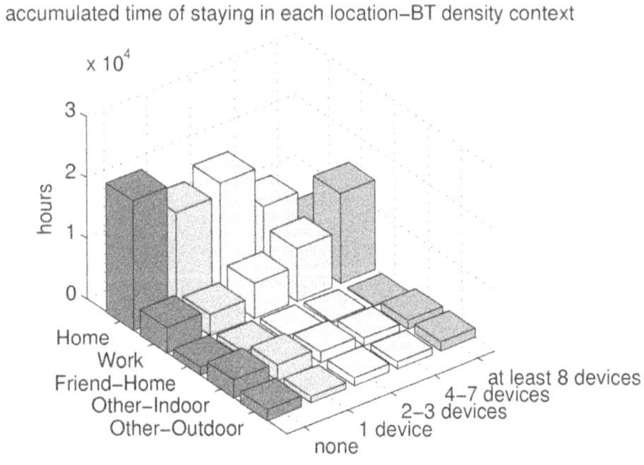

Figure 9: Accumulated time of each context (in hour unit).

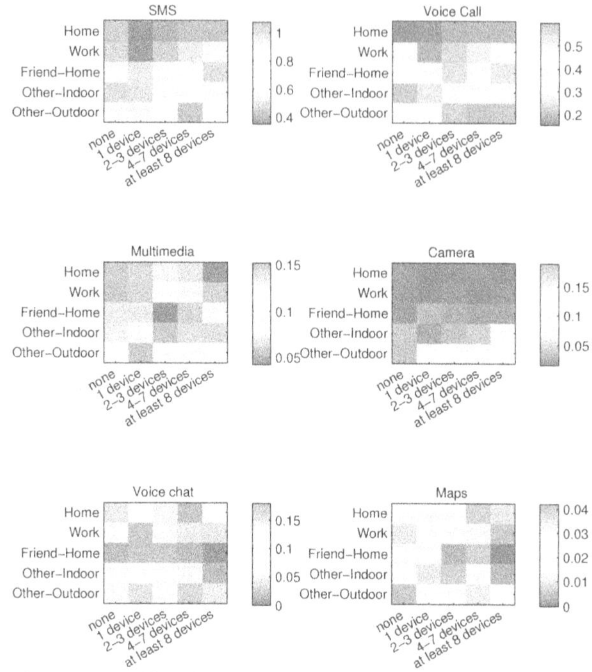

Figure 10: Hourly usage frequency for each app in each location-BT context.

8. DESIGN IMPLICATIONS OF CONTEXTUAL PHONE USAGE

The data-driven analysis revealed that the smartphone was used in a differential manner across various types of spatial and proximity contexts. Two design implications of this context-dependent behavior are highlighted in this section: supporting synchronous communication and context-dependent offering of functionality.

Supporting synchronous communication. Differences were observed between SMS and voice call usage. The former was associated with stable and stationary locations, such as one's home, the home of friends, and work. The latter stood out in nomadic contexts such as the park, bus stop, or shopping center. Such locations are likely to be associated with a certain degree of user movement and a relatively short duration of stay. The nomadic contexts may hence be associated with a need to exercise micro-coordination, i.e., fixing meetings and coordinating actions with members of one's social network. The fact that the calendar was used the most at places related to transportation also points in this direction. Choosing a voice call over SMS in these types of situations can be indicative of a preference for synchronous communication to handle coordination related activities. To satisfy this kind of preference, a design requirement emerges, namely ensuring that the device supports coordination and synchronous communication. Examples of such features could include communicating the current location of members of the social network to the user, prompting for a fast response from the recipient of a message, and providing a shared digital space for parties in need of coordinating with one another.

Context-dependent offering of functionality. Some locations were associated with using the phone in a multitasking way. Moreover, different patterns of multitasking emerged. Being at a friend's home or a restaurant triggered the use of voice call, SMS as well as browser. Being in a park was associated with making voice calls, browsing the web, and viewing images. Holiday-related location was the most distinctive context with respect to the use of browser, maps, camera, and voice chat. How can such differences in the preferred phone functionality be taken into account in the design of mobile interfaces and devices? A differential set of applications and functionality could be brought forth in the phone UI based on the context the user is in at any given time. This could be achieved through adaptive UI techniques. However, further research is needed across a range of topics. First, the generality of the effects reported here should be investigated using a larger, and more geographically diverse population. Given our current mobile sensing techniques, as demonstrated here, this goal seems feasible within certain scales. Second, motivational factors behind the contextual usage should be studied in order to reliably understand what makes users disposed to using the phone in certain ways given particular contexts. This is an area where our data-driven work would be complemented by ethnographic methods. Third, the ability to generate adaptive features that are user-friendly and intuitive is a design challenge requiring significant future research.

9. CONCLUSIONS

We presented a large-scale study of smartphone usage conditioned on two key contextual cues (location and proximity) automatically estimated from phone sensors. We found intuitive patterns of usage that help understanding how people use their phone. On a general level, the overarching conclusion is that recognizing aspects related to physical and social context could be an important ability in a device, so as to facilitate the extent to which relevant content is provided to the user in any given situation. The area touched by the paper, is complex, however, necessitating further research to be done. The current study was implemented with a relatively outdated phone (given the fast pace of smartphone technology), in terms of both the user interface and the applications available to the users, and with a population sample which is not generalizable to the general population. These aspects point to the importance of replicating the method using a larger sample, ideally spanning multiple cultures. The degree to which the user interface affects the usage, beyond the contexts themselves, seems to play a key role but remains to be quantified at large-scale. Furthermore, the study of phone usage while people are actually moving (e.g. on public transport) was not addressed here. Despite the limitations, the fact that contextual factors were indeed found to affect the use of the phone is a relevant finding and shows that the method chosen for the study is promising.

Several of the findings are non-surprising given the regularity of daily life, and the fact that we explicitly set out to study the main trends of our population, rather than the existence of any anomalies of deviations from the trend. As future work, we plan to examine the issue of anomalies. In terms of design, creating relevant contextual adaptations to user interfaces, without increasing their complexity, remains a significant challenge to study.

Acknowledgments

We thank Raul Montoliu (University of Castellon) for code for place extraction and Juha K. Laurila (NRC) for valuable discussions. This work was funded by Nokia Research Center Lausanne (NRC) through the LS-CONTEXT project.

10. REFERENCES

[1] K. Anderson, D. Nafus, T. Rattenbury, and R. Aipperspach. Numbers have qualities too: Experiences with ethno-mining. *Ethnographic Praxis in Industry Conference Proceedings*, 2009(1):123–140, 2009.

[2] L. Barkhuus and V. Polichar. Empowerment through seamfulness: smart phones in everyday life. *Personal and Ubiquitous Computing*, pages 1–11, Dec. 2010.

[3] A. Battestini, V. Setlur, and T. Sohn. A large scale study of text-messaging use. In *Proc. MobileHCI*, pages 229–238, Lisbon, Portugal, 2010.

[4] J. Blom, J. Chipchase, and J. Lehikoinen. Contextual and cultural challenges for user mobility research. *Commun. ACM*, 48:37–41, July 2005.

[5] S. Butt and J. G. Phillips. Personality and self reported mobile phone use. *Computers in Human Behavior*, 24:346–360, March 2008.

[6] T. M. T. Do and D. Gatica-Perez. By their apps you shall understand them: mining large-scale patterns of mobile phone usage. In *Proc. MUM*, pages 27:1–27:10, Limassol, Cyprus, 2010.

[7] J. Donner. Microentrepreneurs and mobiles: An exploration of the uses of mobile phones by small business owners in Rwanda. *Inf. Technol. Int. Dev.*, 2:1–22, September 2004.

[8] N. Eagle and A. Pentland. Eigenbehaviors: identifying structure in routine. *Behavioral Ecology and Sociobiology*, 63(7):1057–1066, May 2009.

[9] N. Eagle, A. S. Pentland, and D. Lazer. Inferring social network structure using mobile phone data. *PNAS*, 106(36):15274–15278, 2009.

[10] H. Falaki, R. Mahajan, S. Kandula, D. Lymberopoulos, R. Govindan, and D. Estrin. Diversity in smartphone usage. In *Proc. MobiSys*, pages 179–194, San Francisco, California, USA, 2010.

[11] R. Grinter and M. Eldridge. Wan2tlk?: everyday text messaging. In *Proc. CHI*, pages 441–448, Ft. Lauderdale, Florida, USA, 2003.

[12] R. E. Grinter and M. A. Eldridge. y do tngrs luv 2 txt msg? In *Proc. ECSCW*, pages 219–238, Bonn, Germany, 2001.

[13] N. Kiukkonen, J. Blom, O. Dousse, D. Gatica-Perez, and J. Laurila. Towards rich mobile phone datasets: Lausanne data collection campaign. In *Proc. ICPS*, Berlin, 2010.

[14] A. O. Mika Raento and N. Eagle. Smartphone: An emerging tool for social scientists. *Sociological Methods and Research*, pages 426–454, 2009.

[15] R. Montoliu and D. Gatica-Perez. Discovering human places of interest from multimodal mobile phone data. In *Proc. MUM*, pages 12:1–12:10, Limassol, Cyprus, 2010.

[16] Nielsen. Critical mass: The worldwide state of the mobile web. Available at `http://www.nielsenmobile.com/documents/CriticalMass.pdf`, July 2008.

[17] Nokia. Smartphone 360 study: Responding to what the user wants and needs. Press Release, Oct. 2007 available at `http://www.nokia.com/NOKIA_COM_1/Press/twwln/press_kit/Nokia_Smartphone360_study_Press_Backgrounder_October_2007.pdf`.

[18] A. Oulasvirta, R. Petit, M. Raento, and S. Tiitta. Interpreting and acting on mobile awareness cues. *Human-Computer Interaction*, 22:97–135, May 2007.

[19] M. Raento, A. Oulasvirta, R. Petit, and H. Toivonen. Contextphone: A prototyping platform for context-aware mobile applications. *IEEE Pervasive Computing*, 4(2):51–59, 2005.

[20] D. Reid and F. Reid. Insights into the social and psychological effects of sms text messaging. Available at `http://www.160characters.org/documents/SocialEffectsOfTextMessaging.pdf`, 2004.

[21] A. S. Taylor and R. H. R. Harper. The gift of the *ab?*: A design oriented sociology of young people's use of mobiles. *Computer Supported Cooperative Work*, 12(3):267–296, 2003.

[22] H. Verkasalo. Handset-based analysis of mobile service usage. Doctoral dissertation, Helsinki University of Technology, 2009.

[23] Y. Wang, J. Lin, M. Annavaram, Q. A. Jacobson, J. Hong, B. Krishnamachari, and N. Sadeh. A framework of energy efficient mobile sensing for automatic user state recognition. In *Proc. MobiSys*, pages 179–192, Krakow, Poland, 2009.

[24] C. Y. Wei. Capturing mobile phone usage: Research methods for mobile studies. In *Proc. IPCC*, Seattle, 2007.

[25] Zokem. Mobile web and app. usage goes up in the evenings,but communication services fall. Available at http://www.zokem.com/2010/12/mobile-web-and-application-usage-goes-up-in-the-evenings-but-communication-services-fall, Dec 2010.

Multimodal Mobile Interactions: Usability Studies in Real World Settings

Julie R. Williamson, Andrew Crossan, and Stephen Brewster
Glasgow Interactive Systems Group
University of Glasgow, Glasgow G12 8QQ
{julie, ac, stephen}@dcs.gla.ac.uk

ABSTRACT
This paper presents a study that explores the issues of mobile multimodal interactions while on the move in the real world. Because multimodal interfaces allow new kinds of eyes and hands free interactions, usability issues while moving through different public spaces becomes an important issue in user experience and acceptance of multimodal interaction. This study focuses on these issues by deploying an RSS reader that participants used during their daily commute every day for one week. The system allows participants on the move to access news feeds eyes free through headphones playing audio and speech and hands free through wearable sensors attached to the wrists. The results showed participants were able to interact with the system on the move and became more comfortable performing these interactions as the study progressed. However, participants were far more comfortable gesturing on the street than on public transport, which was reflected in the number of interactions and the perceived social acceptability of the gestures in different contexts.

Categories and Subject Descriptors
H5.2 **[User Interfaces]**: *Input devices and strategies.*

General Terms
Human Factors.

Keywords
Whole body interaction, mobile interaction, inertial sensing, user studies in the wild, wrist rotation.

1. INTRODUCTION
Multimodal mobile systems allow for improved interaction while on the go by allowing users to access functionality in new ways, giving users new methods of presenting themselves with technology, and bringing interaction out beyond the device to the whole body. However, usability in mobile settings suffers both practically and socially due to the fluid environments where these interfaces might be used. This paper presents a study that examines a multimodal mobile interface used while commuting where users can interact with and receive information eyes and hands free.

ICMI'11, November 14–18, 2011, Alicante, Spain.

Previous work in this area has looked at many aspects of multimodal interaction without tackling the issues of usability and experience in the wild. There is a large body of work looking at how gestures might be recognized and how usability can be improved through the use of multimodal feedback. This also includes work that examines the feasibility of using different parts of the body for interaction and control. Other work has looked at the user experience of interacting with multimodal interfaces in public spaces, focusing on the social acceptability of adopting new interactions. There has been a large push to bring multimodal user studies out of the lab and into the wild, with advocates highlighting the importance of creating real world experiences.

In this paper, we present an in the wild study of a multimodal mobile system used during participants' everyday commutes. The Gesture RSS Reader is a multimodal system employing gesture controls with speech and non-speech audio feedback designed to be used while on the move. Seven participants used this system during their daily commutes over 5 days with a total of 21.9 participant hours included in our analysis. The results of this study describe the practical technical challenges of making the system robust when users are walking, how context of use affected frequency of interaction, and how user experience and social acceptability developed for system adoption in the wild.

2. RELATED WORK
The current generation of mobile phones offers interaction through traditional menus and buttons as well interaction using sensors such as touch sensitive screens, accelerometers, or GPS that allow the user to interact in a variety of new ways. Research in gesture-based interaction explores a wide variety of issues, from improving sensing technology by disambiguating user intention [27], incorporating multiple modalities to improve usability [8], to designing continuous feedback to enhance interaction [26]. However, we will focus here on previous work that looks at enabling eyes and hands free interactions that can be used while on the go in real world settings. This focuses on two styles of interacting; using the hands and using the body. We will then go on to discuss previous work in user experience, social acceptability, and evaluating multimodal interfaces in real world settings.

2.1 Gesturing Using the Hands
Interfaces that make use of the hands allow users to perform a wide variety of gestures, from simple actions like taps and shakes to complex actions such as drawing and writing. Interactions that involve gesturing with the fingers on a touch sensitive screen do not always require visual attention. One early example of this is described by Pirhonen *et al.* [16]. They demonstrate the success of a mobile music player controlled eyes free through touch alone. They use a touchscreen PDA as the player, and allow users to change track or control the volume by drawing gestures with a finger on the touchscreen using the physical form of the device to

guide the gesture. While screen-based gestures can be designed for eyes free use they restrict users in that touch sensitive surfaces must be in contact with fingertips for interaction. Outside of the touchscreens, there is a growing body of work incorporating inertial sensing into hand-based gestures using accelerometers within the interaction device. Oakley and O'Modhrain [14] describe an eyes-free device tilt system that uses tactile feedback to allow a user to maintain position in the system. The goal of their work was to provide a system that allowed users to interact with menus non-visually. Linjama and Kaaresoja [11] describe tapping the device in different places to gesture, allowing low effort, discreet interactions ideal for discrete action events with tactile feedback to alert the user to the completion of an action. These systems might allow for eyes free interactions but still require users to touch [27], shake [26], or tilt their device [7] using their hands.

Recently, the idea of touchless gestures is becoming more prevalent. The Magiwrite system uses a hand-mounted magnet to interact with a magnetometer in a mobile device [9]. Here, the user can perform three dimensional gestures in the air around the magnetic sensor without directly touching the device. Gustafson et al. [6] describe a mobile camera-based hand tracking system to entirely remove the device from interaction, again with the goal of interaction without the need to remove the device from the pocket. These examples describe a selection of the work that examines how users might interact using hand-based gestures for eyes free interaction. However, they still require that the users' hands are free to hold the device or perform gestures around the device. This may not be possible if the user is carrying shopping bags, holding on to children or operating machinery as part of a job.

2.2 Body-Based Gesturing

The use of body-based gesturing, or those gestures that involve moving part of the body such as an arm or one's head, allows for hands and eyes free interactions in a variety of styles. Work in this area has focused on allowing for subtle interaction, keeping hands free, and determining the usability of different body-based gestures for menu selection. Costanza *et al.* [2] describe an interface designed for subtlety using electromyogram (EMG) based interactions, where the system can detect muscle flexing on a user's upper arm. Other work in body-based gesturing has focused on keeping hands free without compromising control. For example, Rekimoto [20] designed GestureWrist, a system that recognises user gestures without encumbering the user's hands. Also very relevant is Oakley & Park's motion-based marking menu system [15], which relies on wrist rotation (roll) to allow menu selection in a hands-free manner. Other work includes a study of mobile head pointing using ego-centric nod gestures to select items spatialised around the user with 3D audio [12]. These studies show that using different body locations for input is possible, but have not yet looked systematically at interaction across the body. One notable exception is Rahman et al. [17] who extensively investigated wrist tilt input techniques showing the potential of the technique using either flexion/extension or pronation/supination if appropriate care is taken with the design. They did not, however, consider the social issues of using body-based interaction while mobile in public spaces.

The work described in this paper builds from of a series of studies examining body-based gesturing for mobile interaction. Previous work has examined wrist rotation [4] as a position control mechanism for moving a cursor on a phone. Participants rotated their wrist within a 90° workspace to move a cursor the length of the screen and click a button when over a target to select. Results showed that an accelerometer could successfully be used to target in this manner in static conditions but was less successful when used while walking. A similar study demonstrated that head tilting sensed using a head mounted accelerometer was a viable technique for a mobile targeting task [5]. Results showed mobile performance could be improved with the use of velocity control and a deadzone. Foot tapping was also investigated for a menu navigation task [6] using discrete tap events to navigate a hierarchical menu. This work demonstrated an entirely hands and eyes free menu navigation system that achieved high rates of accuracy in a seated laboratory-based study. These previous studies provide important design recommendations for body-based gesturing, including the use of a dead zone, discrete selections, and providing a guide to the limits of control using these gestures while on the move. Here we build on these laboratory results by evaluating the techniques in 'the wild,' with an application designed from the ground up to be used hands and eyes free.

2.3 User Experience and Social Acceptability

As hand and body-based gestures become a part of mainstream mobile interaction, the experience of using these gestures and the social acceptability of performing gestures in public places becomes an important issue. Although gesture-based interface can be designed for discreet use, many gestures still have a high level of visibility. Previous work on the social acceptability of using gestures input has explored the issues of visibility and perceived meaning as important factors of acceptance. Rico and Brewster completed an on-the-street study where participants were asked to perform gestures in public settings and discuss their experiences [22]. Montero *et al.* ran a focus group study that looked at how the social acceptability of gestures is evaluated based on the visibility of the gesture with relation to the visibility of its effects [13]. These studies have focused on two important aspects of the user experience of performing gestures: the comfort and personal experience of the performer and the perceived opinions of spectators. Previous studies have also highlighted the importance of extended use and experience when making decisions about social acceptability [22]. This is an important aspect of acceptability because only during a longer deployment can users have the opportunity to explore the interaction technique in a variety of settings, experience the responses of divergent spectators, and appropriate the performance in their own way.

Much of the previous work in social acceptability has focused on user experience as a way of exploring how users make decisions about acceptability. Although the exact definition of user experience is still debateable, there are some aspects of user experience research that are widely agreed on. Firstly, that user experience is fluid and dynamic since the personal moods, social context, and past experiences are ever changing and clearly have and significant effect on the current experience [25]. Secondly, the user experience is inherently an individual and personal experience, albeit at times heavily influenced by others and social groups [10]. Because an individual user is the one creating the perceptions and responses that user experience is so interested in, this is where the experience exists. This study focuses on user experience by building on previous usability studies. Although user experience and usability are intertwined, this study looks first at qualitative experience and perceived success and accuracy, and secondly at quantitative usability metrics.

2.4 Mobile Evaluation in Real World Settings

Although the need for user studies while mobile or in the wild [23][22] has been indentified, there are still very few longitudinal deployments of multimodal mobile interfaces. However, there is significant work addressing how to deal with the issues of extended deployment and discussion of the benefits of longitudinal studies versus traditional lab based ones. When evaluating a mobile interface there are conflicting factors that we must consider. First of all, it is important to maintain control over the study to allow clear measurements to be taken to allow appropriate conclusions to be drawn. This is most easily done in the laboratory, where the different factors that influence the interaction can be measured and controlled. However, lab based studies do not give users a real world experience, which is key for understanding social acceptability. Sherwood *et al.* [24] address the issue of mobile usability advocating real world evaluation with instrumentation, monitoring and questionnaires for feedback. The advantage of real world evaluation is to improve the validity of the findings. Experimental participants will be facing the same challenges as the real target user group and will experience the same issues with the interactions. The concept of instrumented usability described by Crossan *et al.* [4] is a powerful tool to gather data for studies in the wild where constant observations or experimenter interventions are not practical. For our study, we instrument the participants with sensors that are later used to gain insight into the context of use of the mobile device when analyzing the interactions. This could be used for high level classification of location or current mode of transport, or low level classification of moment-to moment actions such as the current phase of gait [[1], [3]] for interactions while walking. The study we present in this paper combined instrumented usability techniques with qualitative interviews to identify context of use to better understand when and where and why users choose to interact in public spaces.

3. The Gesture RSS Reader Study

The study we present here used instrumented usability techniques to identify context of use to better understand when and where users choose to interact in public spaces. The study was designed to take place during our participants' daily commutes to provide a real world experience of interacting with a multimodal interface while moving through different public spaces. In designing the system and our user study, we were guided by three goals;

- Support hands and eyes free interaction while mobile;
- Create a usable gesture experience;
- Study usability and experience in the wild.

The Gesture RSS Reader application was designed to allow users to browse and listen to news feeds while on the move. We chose to create an RSS reader because reading news stories or social feeds is a common activity for commuters who walk, drive or take public transport to work. Additionally, this application requires continuous browsing and interaction unlike other applications areas that we explored, such as a music player, that only require initial or sparse interaction.

To support hands and eyes free interaction while mobile, this system utilized body-based gestures combined with audio feedback. The system used a hierarchical menu system where users could browse through news sources, such as the BBC, select a news category, such as Sport, and browse through a list of available news items to choose one to listen to. Each menu item was read out as speech and navigation was completed using wrist gestures. These gestures could be done even if the hands were holding bags or other items that might be carried when our participants we commuting to or from work.

For audio feedback, we used the Microsoft Speech API to read out menu items and news feed text through standard earphones. Each user could choose both the voice and the rate of playback. There was also non-speech audio played for confirmation of each 'Selection' or 'Back Up' action. The user was alerted to the state of the system through a low volume ambient background sound played when gesture interaction was active with silence when gesture interaction was not active. This was controlled by the user with a gesture to initiate or end interaction, known as a gating gesture.

Command	*Action*	*Hand and sensor*	*Gesture*
Next	Move to the next item	Dominant / Accelerometer	Rotate right wrist clockwise
Previous	Move to the previous item	Dominant / Accelerometer.	Rotate right wrist anti-clockwise
Select	Move down hierarchy or select node	Dominant / Accelerometer.	Shake right wrist
Back Up	Move up hierarchy	Non-dominant / Accelerometer	Shake left wrist
Gate	Turn on/off gesture recognition	Non -dominant / Magnetometer.	Rotate left wrist palm up

Table 1. The available commands in the system, their meaning within the program, how they are sensed, and the gesture required to perform them.

Browsing the hierarchical menu and selecting menu items could all be completed non-visually using wrist gestures. The system was activated using a gating gesture (turning the left wrist palm up), such that interactions would only occur when the user performed the gating gesture simultaneously to one of the action gestures. This simple gating motion meant that the system did not respond to the regular movements of walking or riding on public transport as inputs to the application. Table 1 shows the name of each interaction technique, the action associated, the sensing technique, and a description of the gesture.

In order to interact with the system, the user must first perform the gating gesture to begin. Then, a user may browse the hierarchical menu by rotating the dominant wrist clock-wise or anti-clockwise respectively to move down or up a menu. Menu selections can be made by performing a short rapid shake with the dominant wrist. Once a new item is selected, it is read as speech output. Figure 1 shows a user interacting with the system.

3.1 Creating a Usable Gesture Experience

To create a usable gesture experience, we had to consider both the user experience of performing gestures as well as the accuracy of our gesture recognition. We drew from previous work to choose which gestures to use, to design the actions the gestures would correspond to, and how the gestures would be recognized.

Because we designed our system to be used in public spaces, the user experience and acceptance of the system would depend heavily on selecting socially acceptable interactions. In previous work [22], both wrist rotation and foot tapping have been identified as socially acceptable body-based interactions. Because foot tapping would be impractical when walking, we chose to use wrist rotation and wrist shaking for hands-free interaction. Because this system would be used mainly while walking or in transit, previous work indicated this would be relatively acceptable, although different personalities can often produce outliers.

In selecting how gestures mapped to actions in the RSS Reader, previous work [6] suggested that discrete actions, rather than continuous ones, would be more usable in a mobile setting. Therefore, all menu browsing actions used discrete up/down commands where one action corresponded to moving a cursor one item up or down on the menu. Other gestures where mapped to actions such that the most frequent actions would be easiest to perform with the dominant hand and less frequent actions would be more difficult or be performed with the non-dominant hand. For example, "Back Up" was mapped to a non-dominant hand shake gesture since this was likely to be a less frequent interaction.

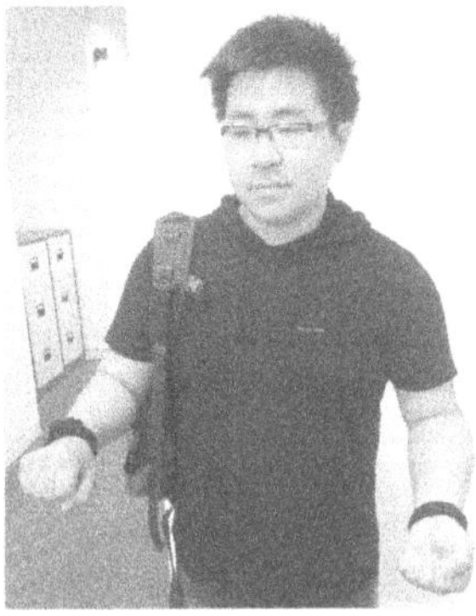

Figure 1. One participant using the system. A UMPC is in a backpack while two wrist bands contain sensors used for input. An additional sensor is worn on the back of the collar.

Previous work has also identified anxieties users have when interacting with a multimodal system in public [21], with false positive recognition being one of the top concerns. This is also a technical issue, known as the segmentation problem [24], where there is difficulty identifying the difference between everyday movements and actions directed towards the system. A common solution to this is incorporating an on/off switch that controls when interaction can occur. Although this is often done using a button or similar technique, we incorporated a gating gesture to keep our system hands-free. An ideal gating gesture would be one that is simple, quick and comfortable to perform and hold, unobtrusive but happens rarely in everyday life. It must be robust at filtering out general body movements, be discreet enough that a user will feel happy performing the gesture in public, and be physically comfortable enough to sustain during short periods of interaction. For our gating gesture, we exploit the sensor attached to the user's non-dominant wrist. No fine grain control is required as a gating gesture will simply return a binary on/off response. The 'gating on' command was to hold the wrist with the palm facing upwards. There are a number of discreet ways this gesture can be performed and it is not uncomfortable if held for short periods of time.

3.2 Equipment

The equipment used to run the Gesture RSS application is shown in Figure 2. The logging, processing of sensor data and gesture recognition was done on a Samsung Q1 Ultra, an ultra mobile tablet PC (UMPC). For interaction and context sensing, three JAKE sensor packs were used (code.google.com/p/jake-drivers). The JAKE, shown in Figure 2, is a very small, lightweight sensor pack (10x18x10mm, weight approx 7g) that connects through Bluetooth to the UMPC. It contains a three axis linear accelerometer and a three axis magnetometer that allow us to sense movement and heading information in three dimensions. The two interaction JAKEs were placed inside wrist bands, shown in Figure 3, and worn around each of the users wrists. The third JAKE, used for context sensing, was worn on the collar.

The UMPC is slightly larger than a phone and too large to fit in a pocket, so not ideal for a truly mobile interaction as it had to be carried in a rucksack. We chose it as it offered several advantages over a smartphone. Firstly, it runs a standard version of Windows XP. Critical to the success of this application was speech synthesis of the news stories as the user must be able to interpret the news feeds non-visually. The Microsoft Speech API is mature, works with many different voices and the UMPC allowed us access to this API. Secondly, the UMPC allows a reliable simultaneous connection for the three Bluetooth sensor packs at a sampling rate of 100HZ without processor overload or issues with dropped packets.

Figure 2. All the equipment used to interact with the Gesture RSS system. At the top, three JAKE sensor packs with two wristbands and one clip to attach the device to a user's wrists and back of the collar. The sensors connected to the UMPC (carried in a rucksack) via Bluetooth.

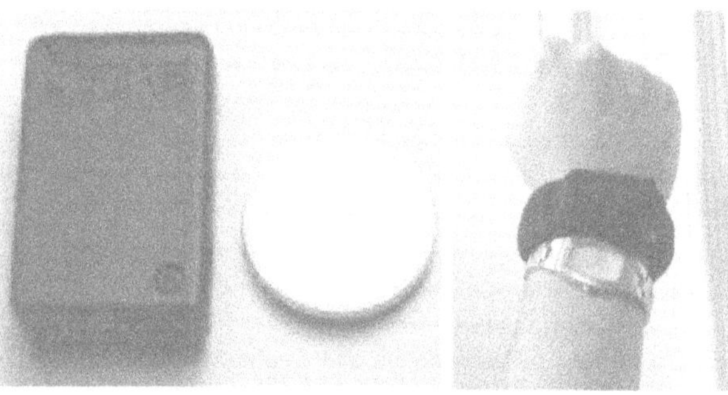

Figure 3. The JAKE sensor pack (left). A user shown wearing the JAKE (right) as used during the study.

3.3 Gesture Recognition

To recognize gestures in the Gesture RSS Reader, we use three basic inertial sensing techniques: orientation estimation using a magnetometer, orientation estimation using an accelerometer, and shake detection using an accelerometer.

For the gating gesture, our main goal was to make this system robust to the noise of general walking or transportation movements. This is not a trivial task since, unlike the discrete actions of back/next, the gating gesture must be maintained while walking and interacting. Here we use the magnetometer in a JAKE sensor pack (see Figure 3) to determine whether the device is upside down. The magnetometer signals are generally exocentric so less suited to mobile interaction where a change in the user's heading will affect the signal from the sensor. Here though, only the vertical component of the magnetic field is used. This is relatively robust to changes in heading and is not affected by lateral motion of the sensors. By using a simple thresholding algorithm we define a range of values that correspond to the sensor on the non-dominant wrist being upside down. Gestures with the dominant hand are only recognised when they are gated in this manner.

The accelerometer in the JAKE was used for orientation estimation with a low-pass filter allowing frequencies up to 2Hz used to remove noise from the signal. The tilt is then estimated using the sensed acceleration with respect to the fixed gravitational acceleration. Based on previous work [5], we designed our gesture recognition with a dead zone of control defined between -40 and +40 degrees where no interaction events occur. Once the orientation angle crosses the 40 degree threshold, a 'Next' menu item event occurs. When crossing the -40 degree threshold, a move to 'Previous' menu item event occurs.

For shake detection, we first approximate the rate of change of acceleration by taking the difference between successive sensor values. We then calculate the magnitude of this signal and high pass filter it using a Butterworth filter to remove the low frequencies in the signal that correspond mostly to non-shake movements. The remaining high frequencies correspond to fast movements, collisions or rapid changes in direction that would be characteristics of tapping or shaking. Shakes are then detected using a thresholding algorithm. Evaluation of this system led to a minimum length of shake set to 0.4 seconds before a second shake is detected. This was to avoid the potential problem of a single shake event being recognized twice. Because the "Back Up" interaction had to be completed while maintaining the gating gesture, the gesture recognizer included flexibility in recognizing a non-dominant hand shake in case performing this command interfered momentarily with gating. The system was designed to respond to gesture events that happened a fraction of a second after gating was turned off. This meant that if the shaking interfered with the gating, the back up gesture was still recognized.

3.4 Usability and Experience in the Wild

The goal for this study was to run the application in real world settings over an extended period of time. To give users a chance to interact with the system while on the move, we deployed the system during users' everyday commute over at least 5 days.

This style of study presents significant experimental challenges that need to be addressed to run the study successfully as well as collect appropriate data to analyze the results. Therefore, we gathered a variety of quantitative and qualitative data from usage logs, sensors, interviews, and questionnaires. In previous laboratory studies, researchers were able to use pointing accuracy and time to target metrics to give a measure of performance of each technique. Here, we have no set task and the users were free to customize their news feeds. Allowing users to browse and locate stories of interest is far more appropriate and engaging in the real world than specifying a regimented task to. We therefore decided not to have a set task for the participants to perform.

Participants were given instructions to use the system as much or as little as they wanted during their standard commute over the span of at least 5 days. No information was collected on any of the topics accessed by participants for privacy reasons. However, quantitative usage data were collected through usage logs and a collar mounted accelerometer that was used for context sensing. This method of determining context based on gait phase [3] has been a successful metric in previous work. The quantitative data was combined with quantitative interview and questionnaire data to make the context data more complete and provide insight into user experience.

As this task was likely to lead to a different experience from the users' normal commute, it was important that the equipment was used for an extended period of time. Previous studies have shown that two or more experiences [22] represent the point where users make decisions about social acceptability and user experience, so we extended this to five experiences to capture additional usage data and confirm these earlier results. An important concern for any system employing unusual techniques or technologies is how comfortable people feel using the system in public. This is difficult to measure in a purely quantitative way. For this reason, we use a combination of techniques to measure user acceptance. *Post hoc* interviews and questionnaires were presented to the users to gain insight into the social implications of using the system in public. As well as these measures, prior to the first session and after the third session and the final session, participants were asked to rate their experiences on a series of Likert scales and answer questions on perceived social acceptability.

3.5 Challenges

There were a number of challenges to be met for this study to succeed. First, there were four different pieces of technology (the UMPC and 3 sensor packs) that each needed to be charged at least every second day. The sensor packs needed to be placed in the correct wristbands and attached at the appropriate locations for the application to function correctly. Each sensor pack was labeled with a function and arrows demonstrating the correct orientation such that the participants could easily place the sensors themselves. Short daily meetings with the participants were used to ensure that the sensors remained charged and there were no issues with the technology. A decision was taken at the start of the study that the daily meetings with participants would also be used to resolve any interface issues they had. Much of the system was customizable, but features such as thresholds for rotation and shake recognition were initially standard for all users. These thresholds were adjusted if requested by the user. Although this obviously means that each participant had a slightly different experience, this also ensured that the user was not frustrated by interaction difficulties and allowed us to see the kinds and ranges of customizations needed to create a system usable by a wider audience in the real world.

4. RESULTS

A total of seven participants all took part in either five or six sessions (37 sessions in total), generating in total 11,544 interaction events for a total of 21.9 hours of commuting data. During this time 1536 stories were read and 6632 headlines were browsed. Figure 4 shows the interactions per minute during each session. Participants were recruited through email from the University mailing lists. Participants were limited to those whose normal daily commute was at least 30 minutes and who travelled either by walking or public transport. We discounted cyclists and drivers due to potential safety concerns. They were asked to use the interface for at least five sessions, although two participants completed a total of 6 sessions.

4.1 Where am I? Context and Interaction

When comparing different contexts of use, we group the data into walking or public transport. This was done through data gathered from the context sensing JAKE clipped to the users' collars combined with self-reported data from the participants collected during interviews. The data was categorised using a mixture of automated sensing techniques to identify features in the data and manual tagging completed by the experimenter using the self reported data for disambiguation of automatically derived contexts. There were 39 occasions where a user was walking, and 17 occasions where a user was on public transport. Walking was a more common context since only 3 of the 7 participants used public transport during their daily commute. The mean rates of interaction events were 10.0 interactions per minute (std. dev. = 6.8) while walking compared to 4.9 interactions per minute while on public transport (std. dev. = 2.7). A two tailed t-test was used to that interaction rates were significantly higher while walking (T_{54}=2.91, $P < 0.01$).

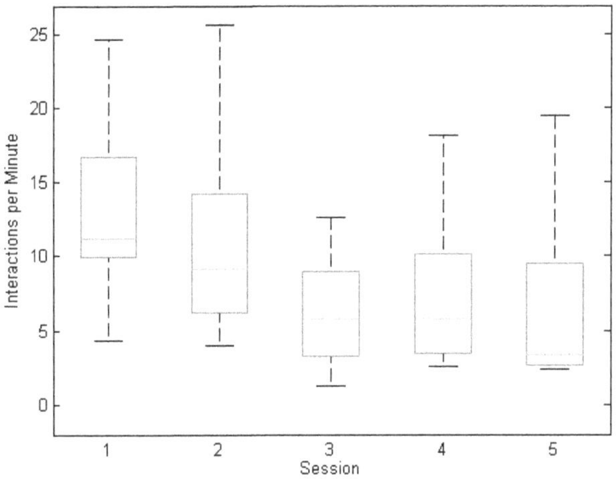

Figure 4. Mean number of overall interactions per minute over the five sessions.

The main reason for this significant difference between interactions on public transport and while walking is that spectators may be able to watch your actions while on public transport as opposed to only catching momentary glimpses when passing by on the street. This is discussed in more detail in the next section.

4.2 I'm Not Doing That: Social Acceptability

Even though the system included a very small gesture vocabulary, users experienced both positive and negative aspects of using the gestures on their daily commutes. The gestures were originally designed to be as discreet as possible to encourage acceptance [22] and it was therefore surprising when some of the gestures were deemed unacceptable in certain settings. However, participants developed different methods of performing gestures throughout the course of the study to improve their experience.

4.2.1 Strange Behaviour and Strangers

Although previous work in social acceptability has identified that strangers create situations with the lowest levels of acceptability, participants described two kinds of strangers with differing effects on social acceptability. Participants described their experiences of using this system on public transport as being significantly different from experiences walking on the street because the strangers around them could watch them for the duration of a bus or train ride, as opposed to momentarily passing them while walking. In both situations, participants became aware that observers might be noticing them but this was not an issue when the participant could simply continue walking and any unwanted attention quickly passed by. In comparison, users riding on a bus or train were aware that others might be watching them and the unwanted attention could extend for as long as the entire trip. One participant pointed out the people in places like underground or train stations are often very watchful and even suspicious of others. This participant felt extremely uncomfortable with this negative attention while on public transport, even doing something as simple as a wrist rotation. Another participant mentioned that the underground was the least comfortable setting because the gestures were particularly noticeable there due to constrained space.

The other interesting aspect was that participants were unable to predict their experiences in settings where spectators were sustained rather than transitory, where spectators might act in unexpected ways. The kind of interaction that one experiences with strangers and passersby seemed difficult for users to predict not only because those situations are often fluid and changeable but also because the appearance of the user and their attitudes towards the strangers' opinions varied widely. Several participants felt that spectators were becoming suspicious of their interactions of the system and were much more worried about attracting this kind of attention than others. On the other hand, one participant stated that "people look strange at you but you get used to and I didn't mind in the end". These differences in personality and appearance played a role in social acceptability, although more work would need to be done to look at this in greater depth.

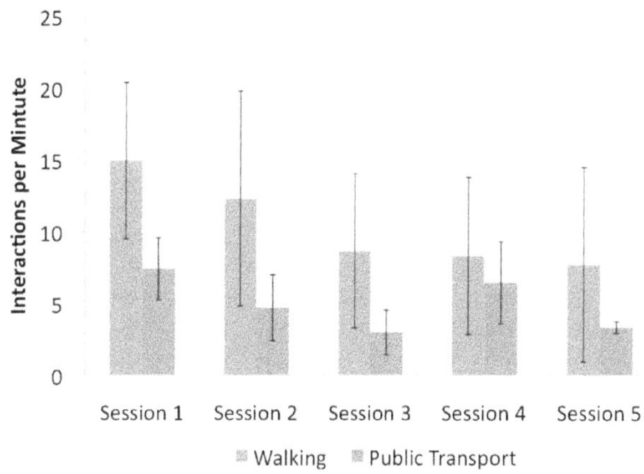

Figure 5. Interactions per minute grouped by context for all users across 5 sessions.

4.2.2 Appropriating Gestures: Usage Over Time

The gating gesture was in general well received by participants, and was the easiest gesture to appropriate into everyday movements by, for example, resting a hand at the appropriate rotation on a leg while seated in a bus, or holding a backpack strap with the non-dominant hand in a particular manner that looked natural but also turned the gating on. There were however some issues in specific situations that a laboratory-based study would not have detected. One user had issues on a rainy day when carrying an umbrella and carrying a bottle of water. In each instance rotation of the wrist has undesirable results that meant that for some forms of this technique cannot be considered truly hands free.

4.3 Mobility: Ease of Use While Walking

When moving between next and previous menu items, the data suggest a strong preference for moving in one direction. There were 7475 'Next' events compared with 1161 'Previous' events. This may be expected in a visual menu system where the user is conditioned to move down the menu due the visual layout of the system. As this system was used non-visually, there was no layout to guide the user. One possible reason for this is that the 'Next' event was more physically comfortable and natural to perform (users were required to rotate their right wrist clockwise). The right wrist has a larger range of rotation clockwise than anti-clockwise, so "Next" gestures would be physically easier to perform than "Previous" gestures that utilized anti-clockwise rotation. In this system, the mapping of "Next" and "Previous" to clock-wise and anti-clockwise respectively meant that users strongly favoured "Next" events, which would typically be the most common action when browsing through a list of menu items. The fact that the system mapping matched existing practices is an important factor in creating an enjoyable gestural experience.

4.3.1 Thresholding Techniques and Mobility

Issues with gesture thresholds being set too high or low were a common complaint after the first session. During subsequent meetings with participants, it became clear that thresholds must be adjusted on an individual basis to provide comfortable and robust interactions. For example, no universally appropriate shaking threshold seemed to exist for all users, highlighting the importance of calibration and customization when using thresholds for gesture recognition.

Another unsolved issue involved the shake gestures being combined with rotation gestures. The menu browse and selection gestures were performed by rotating and shaking the right wrist respectively. In the initial training session, the users were instructed to shake with the palm facing down such that the sensor pack was on top of the wrist. When the user's wrist was rotated during a selection event, this could cause both a rotation and selection event to occur almost simultaneously. This was a common issue for participants particularly during the early sessions and resulted in the selection of an unexpected menu item. Clearly a danger with overloading multiple gestures on the same sensor is interference between the gestures. Due to the technology chosen for orientation estimation, it is impossible to separate out rotational and translational motions. By using additional sensors, it would be possible to improve recognition and solve this issue. For example, by combining the accelerometer signal with gyroscope and magnetometer data only shake actions that occur downwards, rather than to the side, could be recognized as a "shake" and rotations could still be successfully recognized using angle estimation.

5. DISCUSSION

The goal of this study was to complete a longitudinal deployment of a multimodal system in the wild that was usable both technically and socially while moving through a variety of public places. We deployed this system during users' daily commutes, with usage logs covering 21.9 hours of usage while walking and using public transport. During the course of the study, frequent meetings with participants meant we were able to identify and correct issues with usability and technical problems with the system as they arose. Most commonly, adjustments to gesture recognition thresholds had to be changed on an individual basis to create an algorithm accurate enough for each user. Users with an energetic style of walking reported more false positives and required higher thresholds to feel satisfied with the accuracy of the gesture recognizer. On the other hand, some users found it difficult to maintain the gating position or reliably complete a gesture and required thresholds to be lowered. These differences were partially due to physical attributes such as walking style or flexibility, but also heavily dependent on the user's willingness to perform larger or more performative gestures in public. Users who were less comfortable using the system in public would also have trouble successfully performing gestures if their movements did not produce enough acceleration to be recognized. Here, there is a clear tradeoff between successful recognition and an enjoyable user experience. However, designing interactions such that the technology supports both extravagant and subtle behaviour presents and interesting solution to this issue.

An important aspect of this study was that participants had the opportunity to perform gestures and interact with the system in a variety of real world settings. Previous work in the area of social acceptability and user experience has primarily focused on imagined or semi-controlled situations [13], [21], [22], whereas this study provides data about social acceptability and user experience of multimodal deployments in the wild. During interviews, participants described two kinds of strangers, sustained and transitory, creating two very different experiences. Montero *et al.* [13] describe how the visibility of actions and the resulting effects changes social acceptability based on the work of Reeves *et al.* [18]. Although this work identifies perceptions decreased social acceptability when actions are visible but the results are not, this is only an issue when you have sustained spectators. The discomfort caused in performing otherwise unexplainable actions in front of transitory strangers did not affect user acceptance and enjoyment of gesture interaction. This can be seen in the significant difference in the number of interactions per minute while walking as compared to while on public transport. While walking, users performed significantly more interactions than while on public transport. This is especially surprising when you consider that users typically have more idle time and fewer distractions while on public transport than while navigating a safe route while walking. During interviews, participants explained this by describing how uncomfortable it was to interact with the system knowing others might be watching you and could continue to watch you for the duration of the ride. This highlights the need for systems to provide ways of demonstrating interaction and expressing intent to spectators, an issue that has been identified in previous work and remains unsolved.

5.1 Design Recommendations

Based on these results, we present design recommendations with respect to the technical changes in recognition that came out of this study and the qualitative feedback from the user experience aspects of this study.

Recognition Flexibility – Users in this study often changed their performance of these gestures in order to increase their comfort and flexibility. One way of increasing the flexibility of gesture performance is to correct the relative angle of inertial sensing using a gyroscope. This allows users to perform the same actions in different ways. For example, wrist rotations can be performed with the wrist held parallel or perpendicular to the ground if the accelerometer values are normalized using the gyroscope.

Designing for Strangers – Users often described how sustained spectatorship was significantly less comfortable than transitory spectatorship. Users did not consider this before the study, showing that they found it difficult to imagine how different spectators might affect their experience. This shows the benefits of usability studies in the wild, and demonstrates an important aspect of context that must be considered for systems that will be deployed in public places where sustained or transitory spectatorship is likely.

Evaluation in the Wild – There are many examples here of results that would be difficult to discover in a lab setting. Despite the difficulties of evaluating in the wild, this work argues that these evaluations are important for systems that are likely to be used in a social context. To run such a study however, researchers should consider being flexible in their approach such that small issues resulting from unexpected situations can be resolved as the study progresses. For example, this study required that recognition thresholds be adjusted throughout the study for individual participants.

6. CONCLUSIONS

The results of this study demonstrate the successful use of body-based gestures for eyes and hands free interaction on the move. Much of the difficulty in deploying such a system is in creating gesture recognition that is robust enough for use while walking where sensor noise is high while also creating a socially acceptable and enjoyable experience. If gesture recognition requires extravagant movements, this will limit the acceptability of those interactions in daily life. This is due as much to context of use and personal comfort as to practical attributes such as flexibility and style of walking. However, these issues can be considered and designed for when selecting gestures and appropriately mapping these to actions in the interface.

Previous work has identified that the presence of strangers influences acceptability, but this work identifies the difference in comfort when interacting in front of sustained versus transitory strangers. In situations where strangers have the opportunity to watch an interaction occurring over a sustained period of time, such a during a train ride, participants were much less comfortable interacting through gesture. This is clearly shown in the significantly lower level of interactions per minute while on public transport versus while walking.

This study also puts to the test some recognition techniques in the wild that have been previously evaluated in lab settings. The use of a dead zone of control, discrete interactions, and sensing that combines accelerometers and magnetometers was successful while walking but required individual changes and adjustments for each participant. These changes improved usability and experience, and this kind of flexibility would be necessary for future deployments of real world systems.

7. ACKNOWLEDGEMENTS

This work was supported by a National Science Foundation Graduate Research Fellowship and the EPSRC funded GAIME Project (EP/F023405). Equipment was provided by Nokia.

8. REFERENCES

[1] Byrne, R., Eslambolchilar, P., Crossan, A., Health Monitoring using Gait Phase Effects, in PETRA'10: PErvasive Technologies Related to Assistive Environment, June 2010.

[2] Costanza, E., Inverso, S.A., and Allen, R., Toward subtle intimate interfaces for mobile devices using an EMG controller, in *Proc. of the ACM CHI*. 2005. 481 - 489.

[3] Crossan, A. Murray-Smith, R. Brewster, S. Kelly, J. Musizza, B. Gait Phase Effects in Mobile Interaction, *In Proc CHI 2005*.

[4] Crossan, A., Williamson, J., Brewster, S., and Murray-Smith, R., Wrist Rotation for Interaction in Mobile Contexts, in the *Proc. of Mobile HCI*. 2008, ACM Press.

[5] Crossan, A., McGill, M., Brewster, S., and Murray-Smith, R. Head Tilting for Interaction in Mobile Contexts. in *Proc. of MobileHCI*, 2009, ACM Press, (Bonn, Germany).

[6] Crossan, A., Brewster, S., and Ng, A. Foot Tapping for Mobile Interaction. in *Proc. of BCS HCI*, 2010, (Dundee, UK).

[7] Harrison, B., Fishkin, K., Gujar, A., Mochon, C., and Want, R. Squeeze me, hold me, tilt me! An exploration of manipulative user interfaces. In *Proc. of* CHI '98, ACM, New York, NY, USA, 17-24.

[8] Kajastila, R. A. and Lokki, T. 2009. A gesture-based and eyes-free control method for mobile devices. In *Extended Abstracts CHI '09*. ACM, New York, NY, 3559-3564.

[9] Ketabdar, H., Roshandel, M., and Yüksel, K. A. 2010. MagiWrite: towards touchless digit entry using 3D space around mobile devices. *In Proc. of MobileHCI'*10.

[10] Law, E., Roto, V., Hassenzahl, M., Vermeeren, A., and Kort, J. Understanding, scoping and defining user experience: a survey approach. In *Proc. of CHI 2009*. ACM, New York, NY, USA, 719-728.

[11] Linjama, J. and Kaaresoja, T. Novel, minimalist haptic gesture interaction for mobile devices. in *Proc. of NordiCHI*. 2004. Tampere, Finland: ACM Press, 457-458.

[12] Marentakis, G.N. and Brewster, S.A. Effects of Feedback, Mobility and Index of Difficulty on Deictic Spatial Audio Target Acquisition in the Horizontal Plane. *In Proc. of ACM CHI* '06. ACM Press Addison-Wesley, 359-368.

[13] Montero, C. S., Alexander, J., Subramanion, S., Marshall, M. Would you do that? – Understanding Social Acceptance of Gestural Interfaces. *in Proc. of ACM MobileHCI*. 2010 (Lisbon, PR) ACM Press.

[14] Oakley, I. and O'Modhrain, M. Tilt to scroll: evaluating a motion based vibrotactile mobile interface. in *Proc. of World Haptics*. 2005: IEEE, 40-49.

[15] Oakley, I. and Park, J. A motion-based marking menu system. in *Extended Abstracts of ACM CHI*. 2007. San Jose, CA: ACM.

[16] Pirhonen, A., Brewster, S.A., and Holguin, C. Gestural and Audio Metaphors as a Means of Control for Mobile Devices. In *Proc. of ACM CHI*. 2002. Minneapolis: ACM Press Addison-Wesley, 291-198.

[17] Rahman, M., Gustafson, S., Irani, P. and Subramanian, S. Tilt Techniques: Investigating the Dexterity of Wrist-based Input. In *Proc. of ACM CHI*, 2009, 1943-1952.

[18] Reeves, S., Benford, S., O'Malley, C., and Fraser, M. Designing the spectator experience. *In Proc. of CHI*, ACM Press (2005), 741-750.

[19] Rekimoto, J. Tilting Operations for Small Screen Interfaces. In *Proc. of UIST*. 1996, 167-168.

[20] Rekimoto, J. Gesturewrist and gesturepad: Unobtrusive wearable interaction devices. In *Proc. of ISWC '01*. 2001.

[21] Rico, J., and Brewster, S.A. Gesture and Voice Prototyping for Early Evaluations of Social Acceptability in Multimodal Interfaces. In *Proc. of ICMI 2010*. ACM Press.

[22] Rico, J. and Brewster, S.A. Usable Gestures for Mobile Interfaces: Evaluating Social Acceptability. In Proc. of A*CM CHI*, 2010, ACM Press Addison-Wesley, pp 887-896.

[23] Sherwood, S., Reeves, S., Maitland, J., Morrison, A. and Chalmers, M. Adapting Evaluation to Study Behaviour in Context. *International Journal of Mobile Human Computer Interaction. 1(2)*. 2009. 37-55.

[24] Strachan, S., Murray-Smith, R. and O'Modhrain, S. *BodySpace: inferring body pose for natural control of a music player*. In: CHI '07 Extended Abstracts. ACM.

[25] Vermeeren, A., Law, E., Roto, V., Obrist, M., Hoonhout, J., and Väänänen-Vainio-Mattila, K. 2010. User experience evaluation methods: current state and development needs. In *Proc. of NordiCHI '10*. ACM, New York, NY, USA.

[26] Williamson, J., Murray-Smith, R., and Hughes, S. Shoogle: Multimodal Excitatory Interaction on Mobile Devices. in *Proc. of ACM CHI*. 2007. San Jose.

[27] Zhai, S. and Kristensson, P. Shorthand writing on stylus keyboard. in *Proc. of CHI* '03. Florida, USA: ACM, 97 - 104.

Service-Oriented Autonomic Multimodal Interaction in a Pervasive Environment

Pierre-Alain Avouac, Philippe Lalanda and Laurence Nigay
Université Joseph Fourier Grenoble 1
Laboratoire d'Informatique de Grenoble LIG UMR 5217, Grenoble, F-38041, France
{Pierre-Alain.Avouac, Philippe.Lalanda, Laurence.Nigay}@imag.fr

ABSTRACT

Heterogeneity and dynamicity of pervasive environments require the construction of flexible multimodal interfaces at run time. In this paper, we present how we use an autonomic approach to build and maintain adaptable input multimodal interfaces in smart building environments. We have developed an autonomic solution relying on partial interaction models specified by interaction designers and developers. The role of the autonomic manager is to build complete interaction techniques based on runtime conditions and in conformity with the predicted models. The sole purpose here is to combine and complete partial models in order to obtain an appropriate multimodal interface. We illustrate our autonomic solution by considering a running example based on an existing application and several input devices.

Categories and Subject Descriptors

D.2.2 **[Software Engineering]**: Design Tools and Techniques – User interfaces

General Terms

Algorithms

Keywords

Multimodal interaction, service-oriented components, autonomic computing, model-based engineering.

1. INTRODUCTION

The pervasive computing area has recently gained major importance from both industry and academia and is changing the way we interact with our environment [20, 16]. This computing domain emphasizes the use of small, intelligent and communicating everyday life objects to interact with the computing infrastructure. These devices tend to blend in their environment. This is especially true in homes and buildings where new electronic devices such as photo frames aim to be decorative as well as powerful in terms of interaction. This new equipment has the ability to communicate with other devices, to configure itself, and perform context-based cognitive and physical actions. The vision of coordinated or cooperating devices teaming up transparently to provide human beings with services of all sorts is actually getting closer and closer. However, the main part of the research effort has focused so far on providing hardware that can actually enable such interactions and on developing ad-hoc software solutions for predefined devices (e.g., controlling the home's lighting or the TV with a mobile phone). Consequently, plenty of electronic devices providing these kinds of features are already commercialized, whereas very few interesting applications take full advantage of this new infrastructure. Indeed, the complexity of building software that can actually benefit from these devices is often underestimated. Usual software engineering techniques and tools are not suitable. Indeed several software engineering challenges remain to be solved before fulfilling the vision of a true pervasive world. Notably the high degree of dynamism, distribution, heterogeneity and autonomy of the electronic devices involved raises important challenges. The envisioned environment is open to dynamic connections: devices may enter and leave the network spontaneously, providing context-dependent features (e.g. according to user's activity). It is also open to heterogeneous devices: protocols and devices' types differ according to application domains and service providers.

It is envisioned that, in the mid-term, devices and applications will disappear from the users' awareness. Users will then reason in terms of services and no longer in terms of concrete computing elements. At the same time, it is foreseeable that unimodal, well-identified interfaces will also disappear. Users will simply express their needs or desires with any available interaction modalities and the environment and its objects/devices will react accordingly. As defined by Oviatt [13]:

> "Multimodal interfaces process two or more combined user input modes in a coordinated manner with multimedia system output. They are a new class of interfaces that aim to recognize naturally occurring forms of human language and behavior, ..."

Multimodal interfaces fit well in the pervasive landscape. They offer a more natural/efficient way for users to interact with device-stuffed environments by means of speech, gestures or other interaction modalities. They also leave the ability for humans to use a variety of modalities to interact with an application, depending on the context (e.g. availability and reliability of interaction devices, user's mood, etc.). Moreover multimodal interfaces have been demonstrated to offer better flexibility and reliability than WIMP interfaces (interfaces based on Windows, Icons, Menus, Pointing device) [14].

The dark side of multimodal interfaces in pervasive environments is their management complexity. Recent work has proposed component-based or agent-based frameworks to support the development of such interfaces [3, 17]. These approaches are based on the definition of an interaction modality as the coupling of an interaction device with an interaction language (i.e., a set of transformations of raw data from input devices). These approaches allowed a better separation of concerns, clearly distinguishing functional aspects like data fusion and non-functional aspects like communication and synchronization. Most of these approaches are however not flexible enough to deal with highly dynamic environments where interaction devices, applications, and the way multimodal interactions take place, are rapidly evolving. We thus believe that, one of the great challenges

ICMI'11, November 14–18, 2011, Alicante, Spain.

of multimodal interfaces in pervasive environments, is to build reliable and autonomic processing systems able to analyze and understand multiple communication means and reconfigure itself in real-time.

In this paper we present an autonomic framework for the development and runtime management of input multimodal interfaces in pervasive environments. Our discussion will concentrate on input (i.e., from the user to the system) although our model holds for output as well. Nevertheless we did not test our approach for output so far. This framework leverages recent advances in service-oriented components [15, 17] and in model-based engineering. The paper is organized as follows. First we recall the key characteristics of pervasive multimodal interfaces. We then present our framework by describing the execution machine, the multimodal process and the autonomic manager. The autonomic manager is driven by partial models to manage multimodal processes: we present the two types of models that we defined and in particular the interaction model. We conclude with a simple example that illustrates how the autonomic manager works.

2. PERVASIVE MULTIMODALITY

Pervasive computing systems typically consist of multiple devices and software entities that are capable of interacting with one another. Various types of software-equipped devices may be available for various purposes, such as for interaction with the real environment (i.e., interaction output/input device), providing display and control services to users, or for exposing data and application interfaces to other devices. The main challenge of the pervasive computing domain is to provide coherent pervasive environments, offering useful applications and services, based on an entanglement of heterogeneous, distributed and dynamic devices and software services, communicating via various technologies and protocols. In this context, several characteristics specific to pervasive devices make this domain appealing from a business and customer perspective, while raising difficult problems for system development, runtime interactions and management practices. Such device properties include:

• **Distribution**. Devices are typically scattered across the physical environment and are accessible via various communication protocols, generally over a wireless communication support.

• **Heterogeneity**. A vast range of devices, software technologies and communication protocols are currently available for the pervasive computing domain. A common consensus on uniform and compatible implementations is not presently foreseen: today, more than fifty candidate protocols, working groups and standard specifications for home networking already exist for providing communication and interoperation between access and indoor networks (e.g., ZigBee, HomePlug).

• **Plural authority**. Devices present in a pervasive environment generally belong to different vendors. In addition, applications deployed and run on such devices may be provided by yet different vendors and may require cooperation with other services and/or devices. In this context, it is foreseeable that equipment vendors and service providers will prefer to maintain a certain control over their devices and software and may consequently limit access requests from external entities.

• **Dynamism**. Availability of devices is by far the most volatile in pervasive systems with respect to other computing system types. This is due to several facts, including: i) users may freely and frequently change their locations and hence the locations of the devices they carry; ii) users may voluntarily activate and deactivate devices, or devices may unexpectedly run out of battery; iii) users and providers may periodically update deployed software services.

In addition to device and software dynamism, pervasive systems are constantly confronted with the evolution of their execution contexts. This may include modifications in the user's current behavior, location, mood, or general routine, as well as changes in other software applications' availability and behaviors. Another important characteristic of pervasive environments is the generally limited resource availability on the physical execution platforms involved. Typically, in the home context, software applications will run on a small gateway, with little memory space and low processing capabilities. Finally, an essential requirement for any successful pervasive system is the simplicity of operating and managing the system, by users not necessarily knowledgeable in the computer science domain. Furthermore, privacy, security and safety concerns represent major challenges for the pervasive computing community.

Technically speaking, pervasive computing is today much influenced by recent advances in service-oriented computing. Service-oriented Computing (SOC) has recently appeared in the software engineering landscape. The very purpose of this reuse-based approach is to build applications through the late composition of independent software elements, called services. Many smart devices are today exposed as services. More precisely, their capabilities are described and dynamically published by service providers; at runtime they are chosen and invoked by service consumers. This is achieved within a service-oriented architecture (SOA), providing the supporting mechanisms. Service orientation brings major software qualities. It promotes weak coupling between consumers and providers, reducing dependencies among composition units. Late binding and substitutability improve adaptability. Since a service can be chosen or replaced at runtime, it is possible to optimize the way requirements are met. A number of implementations have been proposed in the last years. Web Services (www.w3c.org), for instance, represent a solution of choice to expose software applications on the Web. UPnP (www.upnp.org) and DPWS (Devices Profile for Web Services) are heavily used in order to implement volatile devices. OSGI (www.osgi.org) and iPOJO (www.ipojo.org) provide advanced dynamic features that are exploited to build component-based pervasive applications.

Service orientation brings in solutions to deal with environment dynamicity. It also allows the development of more flexible software, regarding the core functions (the functional core component of the Arch software architectural model [1]) or the interaction functions (the interaction components of the Arch model [1]). However, these solutions are still complex, hard to manage and heterogeneous. Devices and applications still belong to different authorities and there is no real hope to see reifying standards in the short term.

The presented characteristics and desired properties of pervasive environments and applications must be taken into consideration when building and administering pervasive multimodal interfaces. Most importantly, the dynamicity property and requirement must be constantly dealt with by adapting pervasive systems to internal and external modifications. Such modifications may include changes in a system's constituent services and execution platform, or into its constantly evolving physical and social context (e.g. availability of resources, or user's location, habits and preferences). In the pervasive computing context, system adaptation should remain largely transparent to users, while seamlessly coping with resource heterogeneity, distribution and plural authority. As such, necessary management operations should require minimum human intervention, while meeting specific performance and dependability constraints.

Multimodal interfaces should then be designed to adapt easily to different contexts, user's profiles and application needs. Adaptability is always a challenging requirement. It requires first to prepare adaptation points in the code, which can be at different levels of abstraction (parameter, function, object, component, etc.). It also requires the definition of a language to specify the possible runtime adaptations. Finally, it requires some intelligence to decide when, how and where in the code to adapt multimodal interfaces. In pervasive multimodal interfaces, this intelligence cannot be entirely provided by end-users who are not supposed to play a heavy administrative role. Adaptations have to be undertaken by the system itself, in conformance with the users' current goals. As a consequence, the system has to be able to deal with a great range of computing elements, being input interaction devices or applications, with little help from users.

3. APPROACH: DYNAMO

The autonomic computing initiative [9] aims to limit the need for human intervention in computer management processes by enriching software applications with self-management capabilities, such as self-building, self-optimization, self-configuration, self-repair and self-protection. Conforming to this approach, autonomic management abilities would enable software applications to seamlessly and transparently self-adapt to their changing environments and evolving business goals. Therefore, autonomic computing seems to provide a viable solution to the difficult concerns and constraints specific to the pervasive multimodal interfaces.

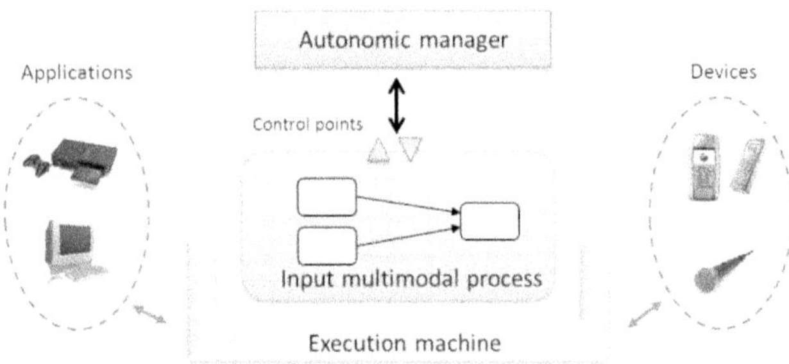

Figure 1. Overall approach

In that spirit, we have developed a complete suite for the development, execution and management of multimodal processing, called "*DynaMo*" (*Dynamic multimodality*). The management is autonomic in the sense that the whole multimodal processing system is generated and maintained at runtime by an autonomous manager. The processing system is modular. It is made of service-oriented components in interaction.

As illustrated by figure 1, our purpose is to clearly separate the multimodal processes, the volatile input interaction devices joining and leaving the environment, and the applications that may also appear or disappear dynamically. The schema highlights the main architectural elements of DynaMo, which are:

- The execution machine supporting multimodal processes. The purpose of this machine is to provide a flexible, context aware runtime environment. It is based on iPOJO, a dynamic service-oriented component framework built on top of OSGi. The goal of this machine is also to monitor the environment in order to trace any computing evolution.

- The multimodal process itself. Input interaction modalities are developed and executed with a dedicated component model. The purpose of this domain-specific component model is to provide the right level of abstraction for developers and maintainers of multimodal interfaces. Low-level technical aspects like synchronization are hidden away by the model.

- An autonomic manager whose purpose is to build and manage the multimodal interfaces. To make its decisions, it uses contextual information provided by the execution machine. It builds multimodal interfaces through the composition of pre-defined components conforming to the component model presented above.

These three architectural elements of DynaMo are presented in detail in the next subsections.

3.1 Execution machine

The purpose of the execution platform is twofold. First, it is a supporting infrastructure for the execution of dynamic, component based applications. Then, it also monitors the environment and integrates the discovered entities seamlessly within the running applications. In particular, the execution machine captures services arrival and departure. Services expose both input interaction devices and applications.

As illustrated by figure 2, the execution machine is built on top of OSGi and iPOJO, the Apache service-oriented component model, and ROSE, available on ObjectWeb [2]. ROSE is an OSGi-based open source middleware dealing with distribution. It includes communication drivers for different technologies (Web Service, DPWS, UPnP) and is able to trace the availability of services. ROSE builds and maintains an advanced service registry. Service registries play an important role in service-oriented architectures, allowing late-binding and weak-coupling. It is a means for providers to publish their services and consumers to be aware of available services and, possibly, select one of them for execution. Each service technology has a particular standard for the registry. Web Services, for instance, are described on WSDL files and published in UDDI compliant registries. In our architecture, we have introduced an advanced registry, which supports many service technologies and a detailed description of services including functional and non-functional properties. The very purpose of this advanced registry, of course, is to support the dynamic selection of services.

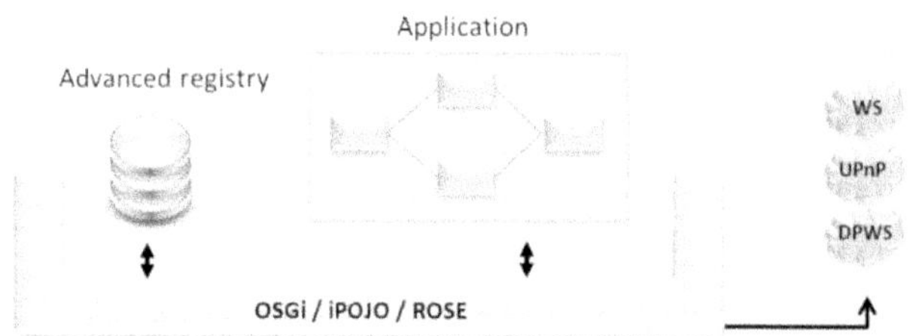

Figure 2. Execution machine

Finally, the principle of this advanced registry is to have a global view of the runtime environment. The registry is updated regularly by the work engine and ROSE according to the arrival and/or the departure of the services. More precisely, it is implemented by a set of registries enhanced with service runtime properties. A registry contains the information for a particular technology. This advanced registry is defined in the model-driven engineering articles as a runtime model [6]. The main advantages of using a runtime model are 1) to store only the relevant information required for selection 2) to hide the technological characteristics of concrete services and 3) to hide the dynamic context with arrival and departure of services. In addition, since the runtime model is modular, with a clear separation between functional and security concerns, it can be extended. In fact, we could support new non-functional properties such as quality of service with non-functional runtime extensions linked to the functional part of the global runtime model.

OSGI, iPOJO, and ROSE are all heavily used and validated in industrial applications. The execution machine integrating these technologies is very robust and used by our industrial partners (Schneider Electric and France Telecom in particular).

3.2 A domain-specific component model

The activity of integrating disparate information sources in a timely fashion is known under the name of mediation. Mediation has been historically used to integrate data stored in IT resources [12]. Recent work has been using mediation to allow interoperation between applications and services [7]. Service mediation implements all the operations that are necessary to enable the actual communication within service-based applications. The most common functions to be provided are:

- Communication. The primary purpose of mediation is to enable applications and devices using different communication protocols to interoperate. This is implemented by means of protocol transformations as in a network bridge. This function can also play the role of a broker, hiding for instance the applications network addresses.

- Synchronization. Time is a major aspect in mediation. Data shared by different elements have to be time-stamped, organized, synchronized.

- Syntactic alignment. The purpose of this function is to align data formats. This can be done between each application or through an intermediary format. In the latter case, the number of data transformations to be made is obviously reduced.

- Semantic alignment. The purpose of this function is to align data semantics. In the absence of recognized and used standards, applications develop different ontologies to represent (static and dynamic) knowledge.

- Non-functional properties. The purpose of this function is to ensure certain quality properties in the application exchanges, as for instance security or availability.

These functions are obviously at the heart of multimodal processes. As a matter of fact, developing a multimodal interface requires dealing with communication, synchronization, alignment and non-functional aspects.

Encapsulating mediation operations in dedicated software is clearly a good practice. Indeed mediation software provides a single point of interface to the different applications implied in the communication. This reduces the number of connections needed and facilitates change management. Mediation also provides an isolation layer from software details and, if appropriately configurable, permits the quick and cost-effective development of new applications. The mediator layer improves reusability and evolution of applications. It also permits the transparent addition of new QoS properties such as security and reliability.

Modern mediation frameworks are modular, mostly based on component-based engineering. They however lack flexibility. Adaptation in the mediation process generally requires stopping and restarting the process, which is hardly acceptable in pervasive environments. In order to deal with dynamic mediation as needed for multimodal processes, we have developed a domain-specific component model called Cilia. A mediation process in Cilia is a set of components interacting in a loosely coupled way through, but not limited to, event-based protocols. As with any component-based model, Cilia relies on two main models, the specification model and the composition model. The specification model is used to define components. The composition model defines the way components are combined. Components are specified at development time. They are made of three java classes and an XML-based specification. More precisely, a component includes the following Java classes (figure 3):

- A scheduler class. The purpose of this constituent is to synchronize data reception. It intercepts incoming data, store them and initiates their processing. The processing decision can be time-based, content-based or, any other condition in relation with the mediation context.

- A processor class. The processor performs the mediation algorithm per se. When notified by the scheduler, it processes the collected data and passes them to the dispatcher.

- A dispatcher class. The dispatcher receives the processed data from the processor. This constituent decides on the data destination and triggers their delivery. The dispatcher choice is a logical destination because of loosely coupled relations between mediators.

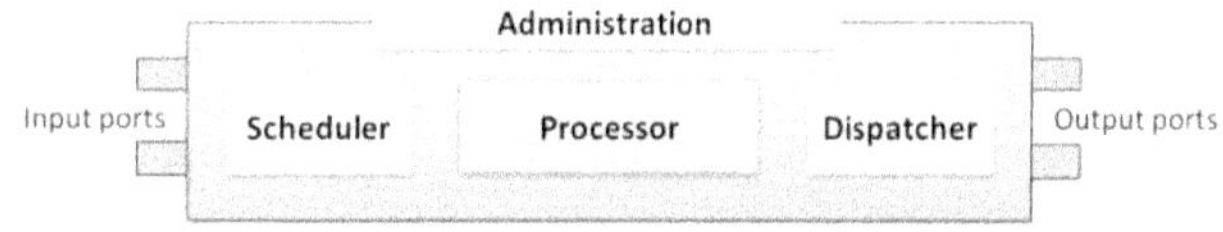

Figure 3. Component model

Developers of a mediation process concentrate on the processor class where they express the way data should be processed. The scheduler and dispatcher can also be entirely specified but are generally simply reused. Most frequent operations like periodic consumption are provided. Moreover we defined generic mediation processes that include fusion algorithms as defined in multimodal interfaces. Such mediation processes represent high-level reusable abstractions. They correspond to generic composition operations, defining elementary temporal fusion operations, independent from devices, modalities and application tasks. To define such mediation composition operations we draw on the CARE properties [19]. The CARE properties were proposed as a simple way of characterizing and assessing aspects of multimodal interaction: the Complementarity, Assignment, Redundancy, and Equivalence that may occur between the interaction modalities available in a multimodal interface. We define mediation operations related to Redundancy and Complementarity of CARE.

Mediation components are connected through typed ports. Bindings are also defined at development time. A binding specification describes how communication is established. Binding specifications are independent of mediators logic, thus mediators could use any binding specification, essentially event-based and RPC based. Figure 4 provides a simplified example where three mediation components are used to allow a multimodal interaction with an embedded application. Each mediation component is composed of three parts as defined in figure 3. The middle parts of the mediation components correspond to alignment and fusion code provided by the interface developers. Such an example could correspond to the combination of speech commands with gestures on a tactile surface to control a multimedia player: one complementary mediation component is used to combine speech and gesture events processed by two mediation components.

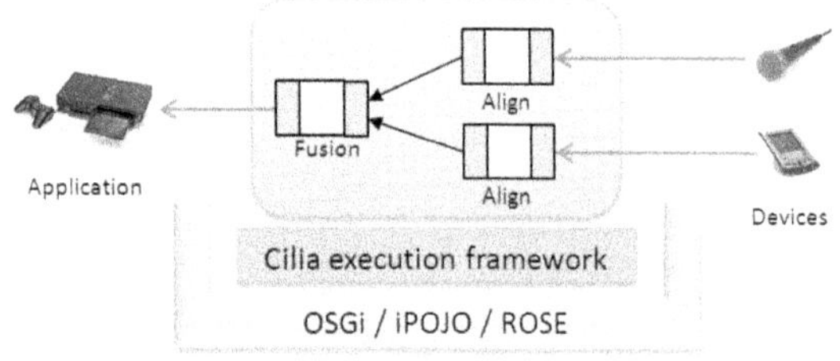

Figure 4. Example of mediation chain

Figure 5 presents the Cilia stack, detailing the computing responsibilities of each layer. Cilia has been developed in iPOJO (more precisely, a component specification is transformed into a set of iPOJO components). Cilia is fully adaptable: it provides interfaces allowing us to add, remove, replace, configure a mediation component at runtime. To do so, the Cilia execution framework maintains internal states and deals with components quiescence. This means that, when a component is replaced, the new component gets the state of the replaced one (i.e., the data to be processed).

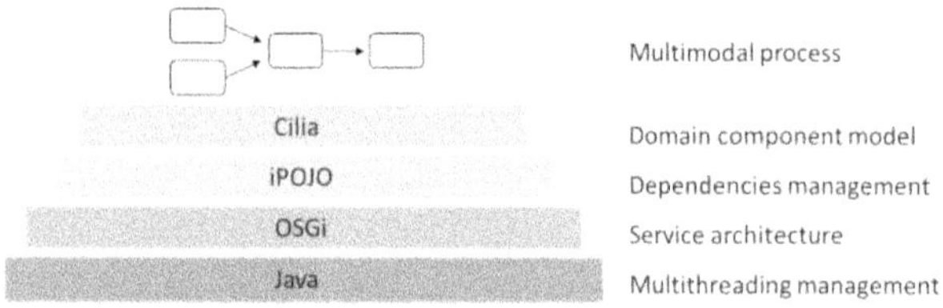

Figure 5. Cilia execution stack

Regarding quiescence, computing threads are controlled at a fine grain: a component can be changed or replaced only when there is no running client (proxies are used to intercept calls to a component to be replaced).

3.3 Autonomic manager

The runtime management of a pervasive application requires the use of some sort of autonomic capabilities. Obviously, an application cannot be dynamically updated by a user who is supposed to be unaware of the surrounding infrastructure.

Autonomic systems are usually structured according to a simple reference architectural model introduced by IBM [10]. This reference architecture clearly defines two distinct entities: the managed artifacts and an autonomic manager. Managed artifacts are the software entities that are automatically administered in an autonomic element. The autonomic manager is the module in charge with the run time administration of the managed artifacts. Managed artifacts provide specific interfaces, called control points or touch points, for monitoring and adaptation.

Here the managed artifacts are clearly the mediation chains realizing the multimodal interactions. The purpose of the autonomic manager is to create and adapt the multimodal interactions, using the dynamic capabilities of the underlying component model (Cilia). It is driven in its decisions by high level goals set by the users (or by an initial administrator). A user can choose an interaction policy at runtime. For now, a user can choose between two predefined interaction policies: *simple* and *bind-all*. If the *simple policy* is selected, the autonomic manager tries to connect each task of the application to sensors of the devices. With the *bind-all* policy, the autonomic manager tries to connect all available sensors to tasks of the application. This policy likely implies that different modalities are defined for a given task (i.e., equivalence of modalities for a given task as defined by the CARE properties). The selection of the interaction policies is made through the DynaMo-settings graphical interface.

The autonomic manager is reactive: when a modification occurs in the environment, it computes a new mediation chain or adapts the current one. Similarly, if the user changes the interaction policy, the mediation chain is changed or adapted. Adaptations can be done globally, that is at the mediation chain, or at the component level. Impacts of a modification are actually well delimited from an architectural point of view. On the one hand, the multimodal process is decoupled from the autonomic manager and, on the other hand, devices and applications are simply not aware of the mere existence of the multimodal processes.

From the users' point of view, the impacts of modification are obviously more important. First, the time needed to completely change an interaction is about 3 seconds (for up to 15 mediation components). It is less than 1 second when a single component is removed or replaced. The biggest impact is obviously due to the change in the way interactions are conducted. A new device is used or the same device is used differently. Of course, the adaptation is supposed to better serve the user and her/his interaction preferences.

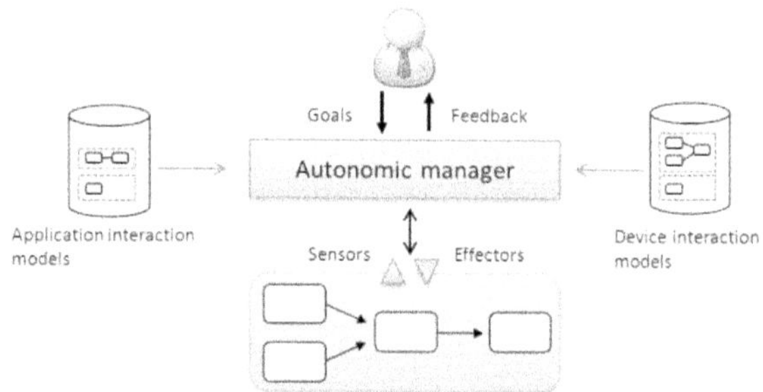

Figure 6. Model-driven autonomic management

The autonomic manager contains the domain-specific knowledge needed to appropriately create and update mediation chains. In most autonomic systems, this knowledge is encoded in rules and thus is not really explicit. Recently, several studies have used explicit models in order to specify the autonomic manager knowledge or constraints [8]. In particular, architectural models are used as a basis for system construction and update. The purpose of the autonomic manager is here to maintain consistency between a target architectural structure, generally made of collaborating components, and the actual structure of a running system. Models make explicit global and local properties. It is possible to use more generic autonomic managers that are easier to understand and maintain.

This latter approach is limited to domains where clear reference architecture can be defined. This is usually not the case for multimodal interfaces in very dynamic settings: we cannot define a reference architectural model of the mediation chain for multimodal process. Based on the architectural work in the Arch model [1], we have defined an alternative approach where the autonomic manager manipulates incomplete models, named interaction models. These interaction models are specific to devices and applications. The purpose of the autonomic manager is then, depending on the runtime context, to relate the interaction models of the devices and applications in order to define the architecture of the mediation chain. These interaction models are presented in detail in the following section.

We conclude the presentation of the autonomic manager by considering the users' involvement in the whole process. Users are involved at different stages. First, they select the high level goals (i.e., interaction policy) driving the autonomic manager. Users also decide on the applications to be controlled through multimodal interaction and, somehow, on the available devices (turning them on or off for instance). Moreover a major aspect of autonomic computing is the feedback provided by the system to the administrators or the users. In our case, appearance and disappearance of a service (i.e., an application or a device) are notified to the user by a pop-up window. Also, semantic alignment allows a device dedicated to a task to be bound to that task, if this task is present in the controlled application. The main limit so far concerns observability by the user of an interaction modality. We provide partial observability of the available modalities by graphically displaying which sensors of the devices are connected to the tasks of the current active application. Although this representation is updated each time a change occurs in the multimodal process, it is only useful for simple cases (e.g., a press button of a device to trigger a simple action of the application). For complex cases with complementary modalities and equivalent modalities for a given task, the representation is too partial to be useful. Information from the mediation chain is accessible and further work must be done to define the way to present the interaction modalities. We focused so far on designing and developing our DynaMo framework, but DynaMo clearly defines a good candidate platform for studying and experimenting this aspect of dynamic multimodal interfaces.

4. MODELS

As previously indicated, the autonomic manager is driven by partial models to manage multimodal processes. These models store and make explicit most of the information necessary to generate interactions. Two kinds of models are defined: proxy models and interaction models. This separation has been done in order to target the two different stakeholders: developers and interaction designers. Indeed for developing a multimodal application with DynaMo, developers first create proxies (in Java) for the applications and the interaction devices as well as their proxy models. Interaction designers can then define interaction models for these applications and devices. Interaction models are expressed in an xml language and we provide a graphical editor to define such interaction models.

Proxy models defined by developers are attached to applications and devices. A proxy model contains information about the process that is used by the discovery manager in the execution machine (see section 3.1). From this information, the discovery manager is able to track the corresponding applications or devices and start its corresponding proxy. The model also contains information about the protocols and ports to be used to communicate with other devices and about provided data types. Based on this information, the autonomic manager can connect the endpoints of a mediation chain to the proxies. If a data type is a number (float or integer), an interval has to be provided. An interval is composed of a lower bound and an upper bound. This information enables the autonomic manager to adapt intervals at runtime by inserting an adaptor between incompatible intervals. For example, if a device provides numbers in the interval [-180, +180], and a connected application task handles numbers in the interval [0, +100], the automatically inserted adaptor does a linear transformation for each value between these two intervals. Figure 7 shows the meta-model of the proxy models.

Interaction designers, now, specify one or several interaction models for each proxy. Such an interaction model defines the way an application or a device can be used from an interaction point of view. Because such a model relates to a single proxy, it only describes a partial interaction that has to be completed by the autonomic manager. Interaction models contain information about data semantics, data processing and data path. Semantics-related knowledge is important for the autonomic manager in order to go beyond type alignments. Through data processing, an interaction designer is able to enhance an interaction by adding tasks to an application, synchronizing data and so on. For example, if a media player application proposes a task to control sound volume through a number, then the interaction designer can add a task that mutes the volume. A data path is a series of functions that data will pass through. Figure 7 shows the meta-model of the interaction models.

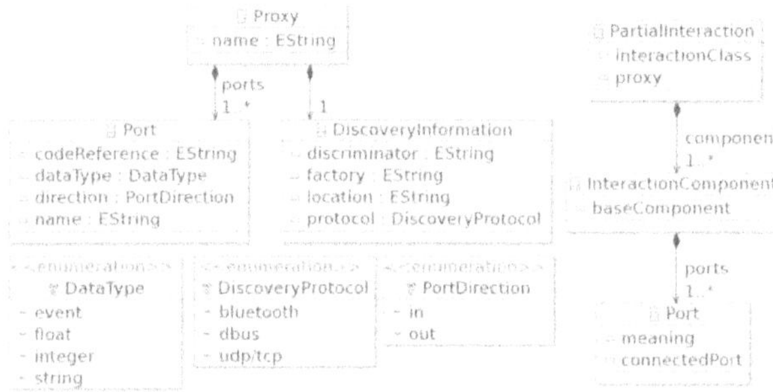

Figure 7. Proxy (left) and interaction (right) meta-models

It is to be noted that defining semantics without any guidance does not really make sense because the autonomic manager needs to match meanings defined in the different interaction models. Several interaction classes have been predefined. An interaction class defines several meanings that make sense together. An interaction model references one interaction class, so only the meanings of this class can be attached to data of this model. For instance in the example of the following section, we use the interaction class named MediaPlayer that defines meanings including *Pause* and *Mute* (figure 10) and the interaction class GamePad including the meanings *Up* and *Down*.

In order to ease data processing definition, a predefined library of processing functions is provided. The interaction designer declares which function has to be used and provides a configuration for the function. For example, a triggering function sends an event as soon as it receives a value greater than a configured maximum value. Moreover generic composition functions (e.g., temporal fusion) based on the CARE properties [19] are provided. These functions are specific to the interaction domain. They have been crafted with reuse concerns in mind. The functions are implemented by components. Thus, the interaction designer specifies a partial interaction by declaring which base components to use, configuring them and binding their ports together in the graphical editor. At this stage of the specification, data types can generally be ignored because the autonomic manager will be able at runtime to infer each port data type. This inference leads to a completion of the component configuration, and adds a data type converting component if necessary.

Specifying a partial interaction by assembling and configuring several domain-specific components facilitates the work of the interaction designer. This approach maximizes reusability by providing generic components, decreases technical difficulties by hiding implementation details. These models are conformed through instantiation to their corresponding meta-model. The autonomic manager relies on a general meta-model that integrates these two meta-models and notably includes relation between proxies, partial interactions and component library.

5. ILLUSTRATIVE EXAMPLE

The following example shows how the autonomic manager deals with two devices and two applications. The first application is a media player software, named *VLC* (www.videolan.org/vlc). The second application is a sudoku game (KSudoku, http://games.kde.org/game.php?game=ksudoku). *VLC* and *KSudoku* can receive commands through an inter-process communication system, named *D-Bus* (dbus.freedesktop.org). The first device is a Blu-ray remote control, namely *BD Remote Control* (or *BDRC*). The second device is a controller for a video game console, namely *Wii Remote* (or *Wiimote*). The two devices use the *Bluetooth* protocol to send data. Figure 8 shows an excerpt of the proxy models of *VLC* and the two devices.

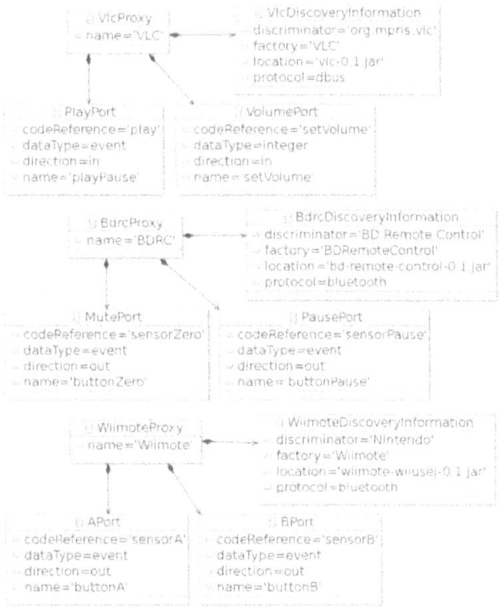

Figure 8. Excerpt of the proxy models

The example follows this scenario: "Alice has previously used DynaMo. She wants to watch a movie. She starts *VLC* and activates her *BDRC*. Bob comes and talks to Alice, so she pauses the movie. Later, when the *BDRC* runs out of power, she activates her *Wiimote*. Finally, she found the movie boring, so when Bob comes to ask something, she just mutes the sound volume to answer. She then finally decides to play Sudoku, with the *Wiimote* that she is holding".

From the autonomic manager point of view, it receives a discovery notification about *VLC*, hence it downloads the *VLC* binary proxy from the repository and starts it. Since no device is discovered, no mediation chain is generated. Then, it receives a discovery notification about the *BDRC*. It starts the *BDRC* proxy. Now, a mediation chain can be generated. Amongst the interaction models of *BDRC* and *VLC*, it selects the two that use the same interaction class, namely the *MediaPlayer* interaction class. It instantiates the components declared in the interaction models, and binds mediators of each interaction if their semantics match. When Alice pushes the pause button, a data is sent by the *BDRC*. The proxy gets the data and passes an event to a mediator. The event follows a path through the mediation chain and is received by the pause port of the *VLC* proxy. The proxy calls the pause task on *VLC*. As soon as the autonomic manager is notified of the *Wiimote* discovery, it starts the proxy. No interaction class of *VLC* and *Wiimote* interaction models matches each other. The autonomic manager generates the same mediation chain plus a part that connects the *Wimote* proxy to the *VLC* proxy. This new part is created only from information about data type, because it does not have any semantic information. Finally, when the *BDRC* runs out of energy, the autonomic manager is notified, and generates the same mediation chain without the *BDRC* part. Finally when Alice starts the *KSudoku* game, the corresponding binary proxy is started. Since both *KSudoku* and *Wiimote* have an interaction model of the same class, namely *GamePad*, the manager will instantiate the components declared in the interaction models of the *GamePad* class. For the Wiimote, the *GamePad* interaction model declares in particular that the accelerometer coupled with a gesture recognition has the meanings *up* and *down* of the *GamePad* class. Alice can then perfom vertical movements with the Wiimote to change the selected cell in the Sudoku.

Figure 9 presents excerpts of partial interaction models for *VLC* and *BDRC*. The matching interaction class is *MediaPlayer*. Its meaning set contains *pause* and *mute*. Since only components can be declared in the interaction models, attaching a meaning is done by declaring an *identity* component and by attaching a meaning to a port of the component. Since same meanings are employed in each model, the autonomic manager can directly bind these ports. The same approach is applied for *KSudoku* and *Wiimote*: the matching interaction class is *GamePad* and its meaning set contains *up* and *down*.

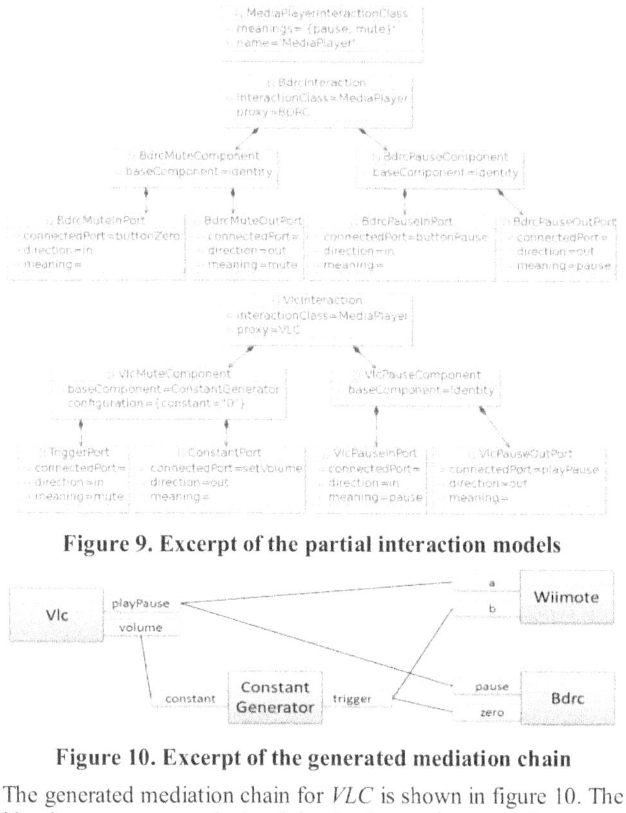

Figure 9. Excerpt of the partial interaction models

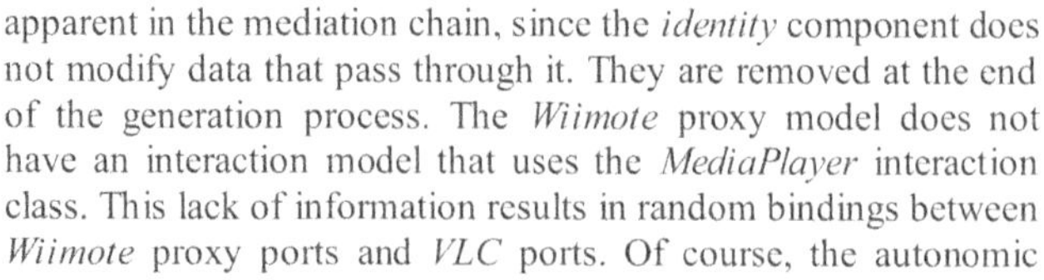

Figure 10. Excerpt of the generated mediation chain

The generated mediation chain for *VLC* is shown in figure 10. The identity components declared in the interaction models are not apparent in the mediation chain, since the *identity* component does not modify data that pass through it. They are removed at the end of the generation process. The *Wiimote* proxy model does not have an interaction model that uses the *MediaPlayer* interaction class. This lack of information results in random bindings between *Wiimote* proxy ports and *VLC* ports. Of course, the autonomic manager verifies the data type compatibility. Moreover, since the interaction policy is set to *simple,* it distributes the bindings between application tasks to prevent that a single task is bound to all sensors. With a policy set to *bind-all*, all the *Wiimote* sensors would be bound to the tasks: for instance two buttons could command the same task.

6. CONCLUSION

Pervasive computing implies dynamic and heterogeneous environments. Multimodal interfaces fit well in this pervasive landscape. In particular dynamic multimodality allows the users to use whatever devices to engage an interaction, depending on the context. In this paper we presented the autonomic DynaMo framework for the development and runtime management of pervasive multimodal interfaces. Our contribution is dedicated to software engineering of dynamic multimodal interfaces by providing a robust and extensible framework based on service-oriented and autonomic computing. Indeed the DynaMo architecture relies on three main parts: a domain-specific component model, an autonomic manager, and an execution machine. The component model enables developers and interaction designers to express their knowledge. The autonomic manager used these models to generate and maintain a multimodal interaction. The multimodal interaction data-flow from input devices to an interactive application is managed by a generated mediation chain. The execution machine is able to effectively realize the interaction provided by the autonomic manager.

DynaMo adopts a global approach for developing multimodal interfaces: On the one hand, DynaMo supports the cases where multimodal adaptable interaction is completely defined at design time as with the existing toolkits and platforms HephaisTK [4] ICARE [3], OpenInterface [17] and Squidy [11]. In these cases, the interaction models are complete and the autonomic manager does not have to complete partial interaction models. For instance using DynaMo we have developed the multimodal map navigator described in [18] for illustrating OpenInterface. On the other hand, DynaMo also defines an autonomic solution when partial models are defined and multimodal interaction is not fully defined at design time. The role of the autonomic manager is to build complete input multimodal interfaces based on runtime conditions and in conformance with the predicted partial interaction models.

The DynaMo framework being fully operational, as further work, we will first perform experimental evaluations with users. Such experiments will enable us to enrich the autonomic manager by identifying new policies. For example, the adaptation is currently realized without learning from the users' inputs. However, several cases would obviously leverage the learning. For example, if a button is never used by a user, DynaMo could propose to bind this button to another function. The usage of an autonomic architecture will ease the machine learning process because sensing and actuating are already done. Moreover based on our framework we will study an important aspect of dynamic multimodal interfaces that is how to make observable by the users the performed changes in multimodal interaction. Our general research direction is to make the autonomic manager observable and controllable by the users by defining different levels for tuning the autonomic capacity of the framework and therefore make the user in control of her/his pervasive environments.

7. REFERENCE

[1] 1992. A metamodel for the runtime architecture of an interactive system: the UIMS tool developers workshop. *SIGCHI Bull.* 24, 1 (Jan. 1992), 32-37.

[2] Bardin, J., Lalanda, P., Escoffier, C. 2010. Towards an Automatic Integration of Heterogeneous Services and Devices. *Proc.* of *APSCC'10*. IEEE, 171-178.

[3] Bouchet, J., Nigay, L., Ganille, T. 2004. ICARE software components for rapidly developing multimodal interfaces. *Proc. of ICMI'04*. ACM, 251-258.

[4] Dumas, B., Lalanne, D., Ingold R. 2009. HephaisTK: A Toolkit for Rapid Prototyping of Multimodal Interfaces. *Proc. of ICMI-MLMI 2009*. ACM 231-232.

[5] Escoffier, C., Hall, R. S., Lalanda, P. 2007. iPOJO: an Extensible Service-Oriented Component Framework. *Proc. of SCC'07*. IEEE, 474-481.

[6] France, R., Rumpe, B. 2007. Model-driven Development of Complex Software: A Research Roadmap. *Proc. of FOSE'07*. IEEE, 37-54.

[7] Garcia, I., Pedraza, G., Debbabi, B., Lalanda, P., Hamon, C. 2010. Towards a service mediation framework for dynamic applications. *Proc. of APSCC'10*. IEEE, 3-10.

[8] Garlan, D., Cheng, S. W., Huang, A. C., Schmerl, B., Steenkiste, P. 2004. Rainbow: Architecture-Based Self Adaptation with Reusable Infrastructure. *IEEE Computer* 37, 10 (Oct. 2004), 46-54.

[9] Huebscher, M. C., McCann, J. A. 2008. A survey of autonomic computing. *ACM Comput. Surv.* 40, 3, Article 7 (Aug. 2008).

[10] IBM Corporation. An Architectural Blueprint for Autonomic Computing. http://www-03.ibm.com/autonomic/pdfs/AC%20Blueprint%20White%20Paper%20V7.pdf

[11] König, W. A., Rädle, R., Reiterer, H. 2009. Squidy: a zoomable design environment for natural user interfaces. *Proc. of CHI EA'09*. ACM, 4561-4566.

[12] Lalanda, P., Bellissard, L., Balter, R. 2006. Asynchronous Mediation for Integrating Business and Operational Processes. *IEEE Internet Computing* 10, 1 (Jan. 2006), 56-64.

[13] Oviatt, S. 2003. Advances in Robust Multimodal Interface Design. *IEEE Comput. Graph. Appl.* 23, 5 (Sept. 2003), 62-68.

[14] Oviatt, S. 2007. Multimodal interfaces. *Human-Computer Interaction Handbook: Fundamentals, Evolving Technologies, and Emerging Applications*, 2nd edition. L. Erlbaum Assoc. Inc., Chap. 14, 286-304.

[15] Papazoglou, M. P., Georgakopoulos, D. 2003. Service-Oriented Computing: Introduction. *Commun. ACM* 46, 10 (Oct. 2003), 24-28.

[16] Satyanarayanan, M. 2001. Pervasive computing: vision and challenges. *IEEE Personal Communications*, 8, 4 (Aug. 2001), 10-17.

[17] Serrano, M., et al.. 2008. The openinterface framework: a tool for multimodal interaction. *Proc. of CHI EA'08*. ACM, 3501-3506. www.oi-project.org

[18] Serrano, M., Juras, D., Nigay, L. 2008. A three-dimensional characterization space of software components for rapidly developing multimodal interfaces. *Proc.of ICMI'08*. ACM, 149-156.

[19] Serrano, M., Nigay, L. 2009. Temporal aspects of CARE-based multimodal fusion. *Proc. of ICMI-MLMI'09*. ACM, 177-184.

[20] Weiser, M. 1991. The computer for the 21st century. *Scientific American*, 265, 3 (Sept. 1991), 66-75.

Evaluation of Graphical User-Interfaces for Order Picking Using Head-Mounted Displays

Hannes Baumann
TZI
University of Bremen
Am Fallturm 1
28359 Bremen, Germany
hannes@tzi.de

Thad Starner
GVU Center and School of Interactive Computing
Georgia Tech
Atlanta, GA 30332
thad@gatech.edu

Hendrik Iben
TZI
University of Bremen
Am Fallturm 1
28359 Bremen, Germany
hiben@tzi.de

Anna Lewandowski
SAP Research Center Darmstadt
64283 Darmstadt, Germany
anna.lewandowski@sap.com

Patrick Zschaler
Daimler AG, Plant Mannheim
68305 Mannheim, Germany
patrick.zschaler@daimler.com

ABSTRACT

Order picking is the process of collecting items from an assortment in inventory. It represents one of the main activities performed in warehouses and accounts for about 60% of the total operational costs of a warehouse. In previous work, we demonstrated the advantages of a head-mounted display (HMD) based picking chart over a traditional text-based pick list, a paper-based graphical pick chart, and a mobile pick-by-voice system. Here we perform two user studies that suggest that adding color cues and context sensing via a laser rangefinder improves picking accuracy with the HMD system. We also examine other variants of the pick chart, such as adding symbols, textual identifiers, images, and descriptions and their effect on accuracy, speed, and subjective usability.

Categories and Subject Descriptors

H.5.2 [**Information interfaces and presentation**]: User Interfaces—*Evaluation/methodology*

General Terms

Design, Experimentation, Human Factors, Performance

Keywords

user interface, evaluation, user study, order picking, wearable computers, head-mounted display

1. INTRODUCTION

Order picking accounts for 55% [1] to 65% [2] of the total operational costs of a warehouse. According to an estimate by de Koster et al. [5], 80% of the warehouses in Western Europe are picked manually from storage racks or bins (low-level picking), where the picker moves among the parts (picker-to-parts) and picks multiple objects based on a particular order. In many cases, workers use a computer generated text-based *pick list* which simply lists the parts to pick and their locations for a given order. Common optimizations on this process include *pick-by-light* where a computer controls lights mounted on shelves to indicate from which part bin to pick and *pick-by-voice* where the worker wears a computer that announces which parts to pick.

Seeking to improve the picking process, Schwerdtfeger et al. [7] compared three options which used a HMD: a graphical 2D representation of the shelf, an augmented reality (AR) solution and a textual pick list. In this study neither the graphical 2D representation nor the AR solution showed a significant improvement over the textual pick list.

Reif et al. [6] created an AR *pick-by-vision* system to guide the picker to each item using arrows and *attention tunnels*. These tunnels are overlaid on the user's visual field as they traverse the pick area. Pick speed increased by 3.7% over a paper list, but pick accuracy did not show a statistically significant improvement.

In contrast, our HMD based picking chart does not rely on AR. As a result, we do not require additional hardware to track the current position and head orientation. Furthermore, independent of the current position and head orientation, we can simultaneously visualize all locations of the parts to be picked for the current shelving unit, allowing the user to optimize his movements. While these advantages do not imply that our system is superior, it at least justifies further investigation.

In our previous work [8], a pick list presented graphically on a wearable computer with head mounted display (HMD) enabled faster picking than the same graphical representation on a paper pick list, a pick-by-voice system, and a standard text-based pick list. For convenience, we define the graphical representation of where to pick parts from a shelving unit as a **pick chart**. Subjectively, the HMD system was preferred overall to the other methods, and it resulted in fewer errors and less overall task load (as measured by the NASA Task Load Index) than the text pick list.

ICMI'11, November 14–18, 2011, Alicante, Spain.

All comparisons mentioned above showed statistical significance, and the HMD system trended toward less errors than all the other systems.

In interviewing managers in large assembly plants, errors were the most important concern. Pick errors can stop an assembly line, creating large losses. In these plants, pick by light systems had *virtually eliminated* errors and improved pick speed for some of their pick lines. However, due to the wiring and custom work involved, these systems can be expensive, costing more than 1000 € to upgrade one meter of a pick line. In contrast, a HMD system could be significantly less expensive and easily re-purposed as pick lines change.

A logical next step is to test our HMD system in a real picking environment, comparing it to a pick-by-light system and determining its suitability in an industrial environment. However, we first wish to optimize the system to decrease the error rate based on extensions suggested by subjects and interaction principles in the literature. The goal of the work presented here is to identify which user interface variations might most effect the upcoming industrial study, as opposed to variations that may cause insignificant improvements or actually have negative effects. The goal of the presented study is therefore to identify the user interface variations which suit the upcoming industrial study. To avoid multiple hypothesis statistical testing issues inherent in testing all combinations of the extensions, we have focused our attention on two hypotheses:

Color The use of colors that match the rows of the shelves with the rows of the HMD pick chart will reduce errors (as color is perceived easily and helps the picker to identify the correct row).

Context Highlighting detected picks (both correct and incorrect) in the HMD pick chart will reduce errors.

2. COLOR EXPERIMENT

The goal of this experiment was to test the color hypothesis and gain an intuition on the amount of improvement that might be expected. Monochrome HMDs are often brighter, lighter, less bulky, less expensive, and/or use less power than color HMDs. Thus, if the improvement is negligible, we would feel free to specify different equipment for industrial settings. In addition, we wish to explore several variations of the interface to see if there are positive or negative trends in accuracy, workload, or pick speed that suggest the need for future experimentation.

2.1 Picking Environment

We constructed three shelving units in a laboratory. Each row houses three part bins, and each shelving unit has five rows (Figure 1). The participants wear a vest made by teXXmo with a TX-1000 Wearable PC using a 1.6GHz Intel Atom Z530 and 1GB of RAM. An opaque monocular HMD device (MicroOptical SV-6) provides visual instructions. The HMD connects to safety glasses and is worn over the picker's right eye (Figure 2). The participants use a rugged mouse from Vuzix with two large buttons to navigate through the tasks. The mouse is carried vertically near the left hip.

Figure 1: Three Shelving Units

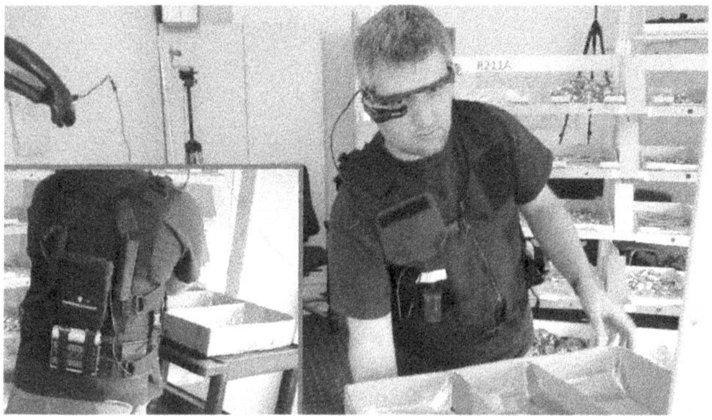

Figure 2: Wearable and HMD

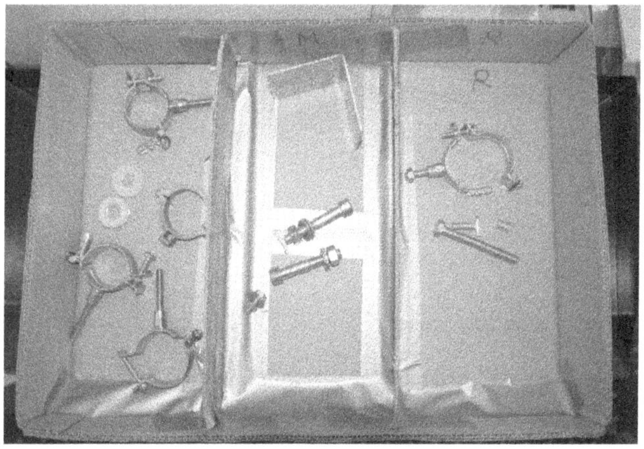

Figure 3: Order bins

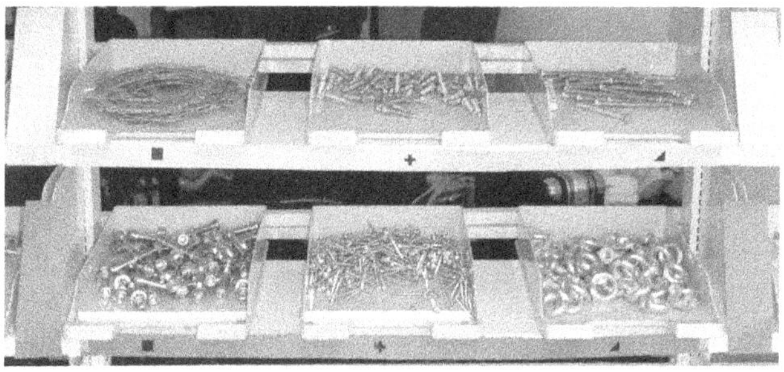

Figure 4: Part bins (colored modalites)

2.2 Task Description

As in our previous work [8], the picking task consists of picking the required parts for three orders at the same time. This process mimics what we observed in industrial environments. The participants use a pick cart with three order bins called *LINKS* (left), *MITTE* (center) and *RECHTS* (right) (Figure 3). We define a pick as reaching into a part bin and removing one or more parts from the bin. A place is defined as putting all of the items currently being carried into an order bin.

A pick task starts by scanning a bar code with a bar code scanner. The first screen of the task is displayed in the HMD showing the first parts to pick. Each screen shows a pick chart of the parts to pick from one shelving unit for one order (see Figure 5a as an example). Every part bin in the pick chart is represented as a rectangle, and the size and position of this rectangle correlates with the size and position of the real part bin in the shelf. Part bins scheduled for picking are highlighted in the pick chart, and the number in the center of that rectangle defines the number of items to pick from it. The shelving unit identifier is shown on top of the pick chart; the order bin in which to place the picked parts is shown on the top right side of the screen.

Using Figure 5a as an example, the participant should make two picks from shelf R211B – taking three items per pick – and put them into the *LINKS* order bin. After the first screen is completed the participant presses the lower mouse-button (*forward-button*) to see the next pick screen. The participant can navigate through all the screens of the current pick task using the mouse-buttons. One task always consists of three screens (one screen for each order bin). After the third screen is completed and the participant presses the *forward-button*, the system confirms the completion of the task and waits for the participant to scan the next task. The number of part bins from which to pick within a screen varies from one to six. The number of items to pick from a bin ranges from one to five. The number of picks per task ranges from 7 to 13 (11.4 in average).

2.3 User Interface Variations

We want to compare the pick chart variations shown in Figure 5:

Monochrome (M) This variant is similar to the pick chart in our previous work [8].

Monochrome, Ids (MId) This variant adds identifiers to the lower right side of the part bins in the pick chart. The first digit of an identifier indicates the row of the part bin; the second digit indicates the position in that particular row. Whenever a monochrome modality is used, the identifiers are displayed under each part bin on the physical shelf, allowing participants to verify the correct bin.

Colored (C) Each row on the pick chart and on the physical shelves are marked with corresponding colors to help identify the correct row for each pick.

Colored, Symbols (CS) Symbols are added to the part bins and on the pick chart to help identify the correct column for each pick. Whenever a colored modality was used these symbols where also shown under each part bin in the shelves (Figure 4).

Colored, Symbols, Descriptions (CSD) Descriptions of the items are added to the right side of the pick chart.

Colored, Symbols, Images (CSI) Images of the items are added to the right side of the pick chart.

These conditions are grouped into three classes: the **Monochrome modalities (MM)** (Figures 5a and 5b), the **Colored modalities (CM)** (Figures 5c and 5d) and the **Colored modalities with descriptions or images (CM+)** (Figures 5e and 5f). Since our hypothesis concerns the effect of color on accuracy, our primary analysis will concentrate on the *MM* and *CM* classes. Post-hoc analysis on the additional classes will provide guidance for future experiments.

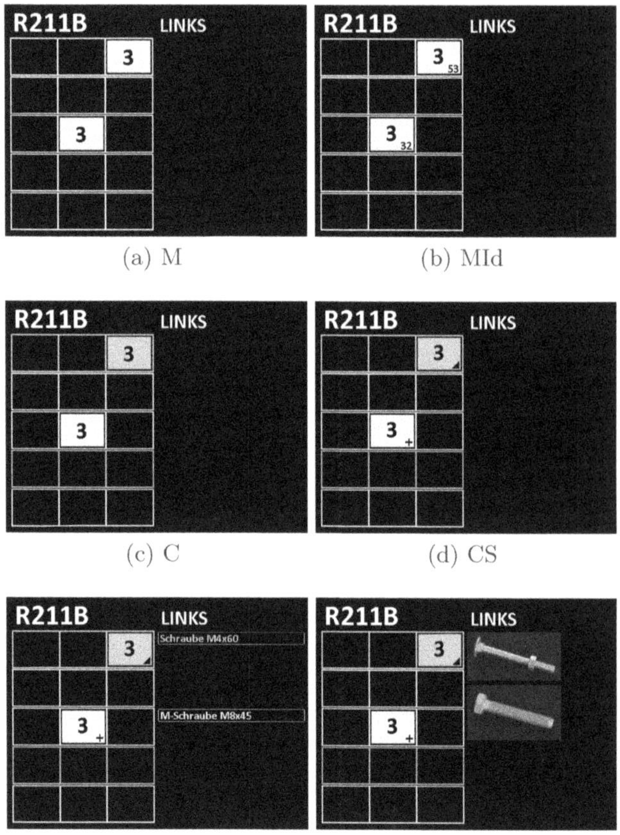

(a) M (b) MId (c) C (d) CS (e) CSD (f) CSI

Figure 5: Modalities tested in the Color experiment

2.4 Method

Six participants were recruited; five were right-handed. All participants were right-eye dominant, and one participant wore glasses. Four subjects had some picking experience from previous employment in a logistics company. All subjects were native German speakers from a German university, and all instructions, interactions with the picking methods, and survey instruments were provided to the participants in German during the study. Participants were instructed to work as if they were in a real occupation and that it is more important to avoid errors than to work extremely fast. The study took about two hours per participant, and participants were paid 20 €.

All participants completed a training phase. During this phase, the experimenters explained each method in the order shown in Figure 5, and the participant performed two tasks using each method. The participants could pose questions to the experimenters, and the experimenters provided feedback in case of mistakes during the training phase. After completing the training sessions, the participants began the testing phase of the study. During the testing phase, the order in which the participant used each picking method was determined by a balanced Latin Square. Picking tasks were randomly generated in advance of the study, and the same sequence was used for each subject. Each participant performed seven tasks with each picking method during the testing session, resulting in 42 tasks (485 picks) for each participant.

Times were recorded for each interaction with the interface. The task time was defined as the time from the scan of the task to the last interaction through the navigation buttons before the next picking task was read. After each modality the participant completed surveys containing subjective measures, including the NASA Task Load Index (TLX) [3]. At the end of the testing phase, participants were asked to rank the methods from best (1) to worst (6) based on overall preference, learnability, comfort, speed and accuracy. A free response space was provided as well. Picking accuracy was determined from pictures of the order bins after each task. Three cameras recorded the experiment from different views. When an error was detected in the pictures, it was confirmed through review of the video from the corresponding pick task. This analysis also helped to determine the cause of an error.

2.5 Accuracy

We use the following ontology when considering errors. **Errors** are composed of *Item mistakes* and *Wrong numbers*. **Item mistakes**, in turn, are divided into *Substitutions*, *Missing part* and *Additional part*. Finally, **Substitutions** are divided into *Wrong shelf*, *Wrong row*, and *Wrong column*. The classes which are not further divided are defined as follows:

Wrong number The participant picked from the correct part bin but took the wrong number of items. (The difference in number of items is not considered.)

Missing part; Additional part The participant missed a pick completely or picked from a part bin not requested. (Note that *Substitutions* take precedence where applicable. The number of items requested/picked was not taken into consideration.)

Wrong shelf; Wrong row; Wrong column The participant picked from the wrong shelf, row or column.

Figure 6 shows the mistakes in the *Color experiment*. One mistake within a modality (over all subjects) is equal to 0.0344% mistakes per pick.

As we formulated just one hypothesis per study, a correction for multiple comparisons is not needed for the hypothesis itself. There is a statistically significant difference between the average errors made in the monochrome (*MM*) conditions versus the color (*CM*) conditions (0.206% vs. 0.086% errors on average; $p = 0.0063$; one-tailed, paired t-test). Looking at the errors of the type *Wrong row*, on average there was one mistake of this type per 28 tasks for

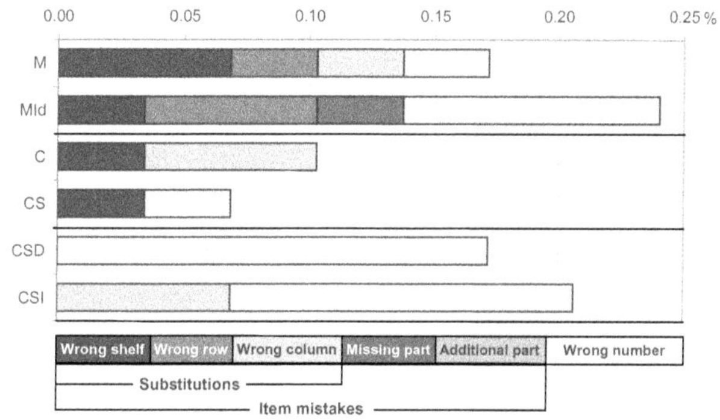

Figure 6: Mistakes/pick in Color experiment

the *MM* conditions while there were no mistakes of this type made during the 168 picking tasks in the four colored conditions (*CM* and *CM+*). These findings support our hypothesis, which was that the usage of color would improve accuracy.

2.5.1 Post-Hoc Analysis

We report p-values without correction for multiple comparisons (e.g., Bonferonni correction). Observations reported are intended as possible areas for future exploration.

The *CS* condition shows less errors than the *M* condition ($p = 0.038$) and the *MId* condition ($p = 0.021$). The average number of errors is less than twice as low for the *CM* conditions than the *CM+* conditions, which adds descriptions or images. Examining the errors in the *CM+* conditions more carefully, we can see that more than 80% of the mistakes are of the type *Wrong number*. Considering only this type of mistake and comparing the *CM* conditions against the *CM+* conditions, the *CM* conditions show only one error of this type (over the whole experiment) while there are 9 errors of this type for the *CM+* condition. A paired t-test for this comparison shows a p-value of 0.08 (two-tailed).

Examining the mistakes of the type *Item mistakes* within the *CM+* conditions, only two mistakes occurred in total, while within the *CM* conditions four mistakes occurred in total. Not a single mistake of the type *Wrong shelf* occurred in the *CM+* while in all other modalities at least one mistake of this type occurred. Although not significant, this effect might be caused by the additional information in the image, which helps the participants to recognize that they were picking from the wrong shelf. However, *CM+* conditions had more *Wrong number* mistakes. *Item mistakes* for *CM+* were the same or less than in the other conditions.

2.6 Speed

Comparing picking speeds between different modalities requires normalization of the recorded times. Each participant has an individual picking speed; in addition, the complexity of the tasks varies.

The first step in normalizing is to calculate the average picking time per task for each participant and then to divide each specific task's time by this average. This procedure results in normalized task times that allow comparing picking times for individual tasks between all participants.

In a second step, the normalized individual task times from step one are used to calculate the average normalized value for each individual task. The final normalization step divides the normalized values from step one by the corresponding normalized average task time. This second normalization allows the comparison of task times regardless of the individual task's complexity.

Comparing the normalized times of the *MM* and *CM* conditions, we get an average value of 0.988 (dimensionless value) for the *Monochrome modalities* and an average value of 0.987 for the *Colored modalities*. As these values are nearly the same, we think there is no relevant difference in speed between the *CM* and *MM* conditions.

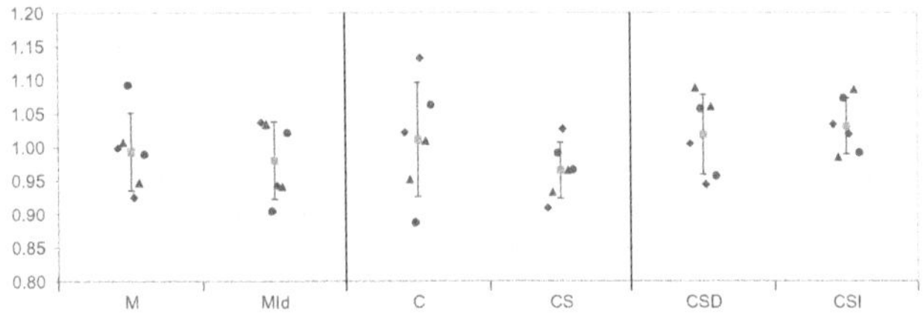

Figure 7: Pick speeds of the different conditions relative to the average (1.00); lower is faster

The fastest condition with a normalized average task time of 0.965 is *CS*. The slowest modality with an average of 1.031 is *CSI*, 6.9% slower than *CS*. A two-tailed paired t-test returns a p-value of $p = 0.028$. Also, the modality *CSD* is 5.6% slower than the modality *CS*. These modalities are probably slower because of the amount of time the worker refers to the additional information provided.

2.7 Subjective measures

We asked the participants to rank the six different conditions from first to last (6th) place. The median ranks are shown in Table 1. Comparing the rankings of the *CM* conditions against the *MM* conditions, all five categories show a p-value of $p < 0.05$ (using a Wilcoxon-Test with the hypothesis that the *CM* have a better ranking than the *MM*). Looking at the table, no single condition seems best. However, the two *CM* conditions stand out. Only in the category *Accuracy* does the *CSD* condition trend a little better.

	M	MId	C	CS	CSD	CSI
Overall	6	4.5	2	2	4.5	3.5
Learnability	4.5	4	2	2	6	2.5
Comfort	6	4.5	2	2.5	4	2.5
Speed	5.5	4.5	1.5	2	4.5	2.5
Accuracy	5.5	5	3.5	2.5	2	2.5

Table 1: Ranking of conditions (lower values are better)

We also asked participants to rate their experience with the different conditions as *very good*, *good*, *neutral*, *bad* or *very bad*. The participants gave only positive feedback on the *colored modalities* and rated the use of color for the row as *very good* (3 persons) or *good* (3 persons). The question *Did you like the use of images for the items to pick?* resulted in *neutral* (4 persons) or *good* (2 persons) responses. The inclusion of descriptions of the item was not as well received: *very bad* (2 persons), *bad* (1 person), *neutral* (1 person), and *good* (2 persons). The NASA TLX results did not show any significant difference between conditions.

During the open response section of the survey, participants judged the navigation as good. In particular, they liked the smooth navigation between screens. People with picking experience said that it required time to adapt to the new concept, but that they liked it. Many participants pointed out that additional information like the images helps to pick the correct part, but that the number of items to be picked seems to be less emphasized by the interface.

3. CONTEXT EXPERIMENT

In a preliminary study [4], we used a *Wizard of Oz* approach to display completed and inaccurate picks on a HMD. Adding this context information reduced mistakes as compared to a text-based paper pick list. However, the standard text-based pick list is a relatively easy system to outperform. Can a context system improve upon our current graphical HMD pick chart, and will an automatic context monitoring system be sufficient (in terms of accuracy and detection time) to provide those advantages (and outweigh the cost of the automatic context monitoring system)? In industry, laser rangefinders are currently used for monitoring picks. In comparison to infrared sensors, a laser rangefinder is more attractive in regards of price (per part bin) and flexibility, which are two important arguments of our approach; thus, we use the same equipment for our study.

3.1 Task Description

We use the same picking environment and procedures from our first experiment to explore the effect of adding context to the HMD pick chart. Specifically, whenever a pick is detected by the laser rangefinder (LRF) from a requested part bin, this bin is highlighted (using a white background) in the pick chart for the duration of the pick (and, in the case where an image of the part is displayed, that image is inverted). Figure 8 demonstrates how the LRF detects picks and Figure 9a shows the corresponding user interface. After the pick is completed the corresponding part bin (and image) is marked as cleared as shown in Figure 9b. In case of a wrong pick – or a wrongly detected pick – the corresponding part bin is marked as a mistake as shown in Figure 10. When the participant reaches again into that part bin, the mistake is assumed to be rectified and the marking is removed. Since picking detection with the LRF does not work perfectly, we allow the participants to ignore wrong or undetected picks when they believe they have picked all the requested parts correctly.

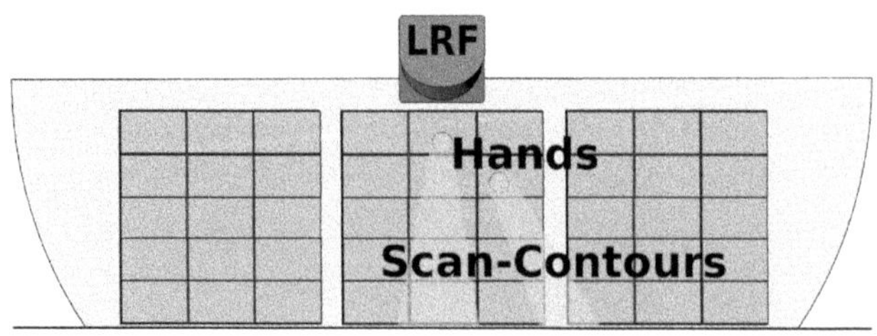

Figure 8: A laser rangefinder detects the worker's hands as they pass the front plane of the shelving units

Based on the reduction in errors in the last experiment, we decided to use colored pick charts only. We also removed the pick chart condition with additional descriptions (*CSD*)

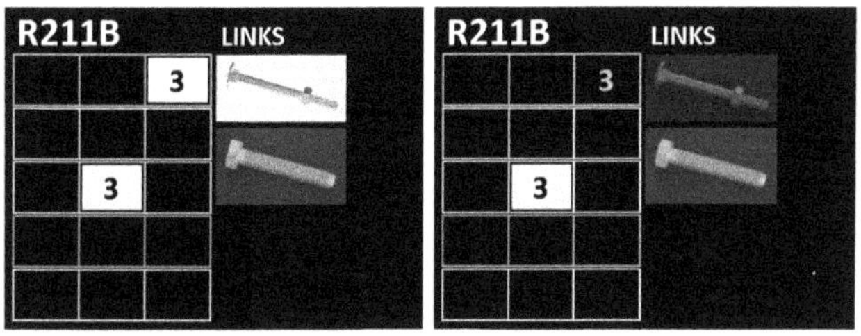

(a) During the pick (b) After the pick

Figure 9: Interface showing pick (CI+LRF)

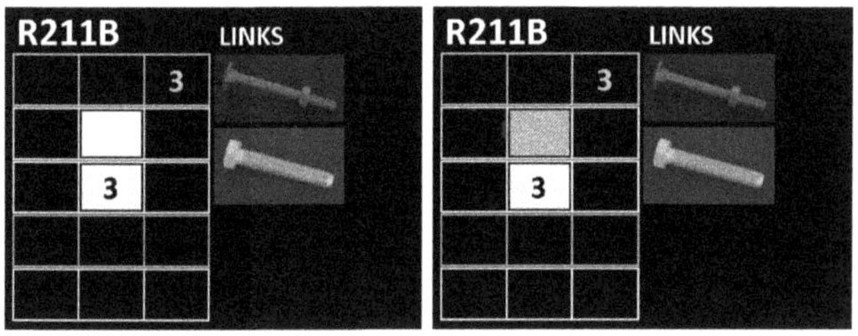

(a) During the pick (b) After the pick

Figure 10: Interface showing wrong pick (CI+LRF)

since it received the worst feedback from the users. Based on feedback from users in the first experiment indicating that the symbols combined with the images provided "too much information", we removed the symbols from the *CSI* condition. Thus, we have three picking chart variations (*C* for color, *CS* for color and symbols, and *CI* for color and images). Since our main concern is whether the context provided by the laser rangefinder further reduces errors, we will test six variants: *C*, *CS*, *CI*, *C+LRF*, *CS+LRF*, and *CI+LRF*.

3.2 Method

Twelve participants were recruited; eleven participants were right-handed, and ten were right-eye dominant. Four participants wore glasses. One subject had some picking experience from previous employment in a logistic company. Each participant performed eight tasks with each picking method during the testing session resulting in 48 tasks (543 picks) for each participant. As in the first experiment, we told the participants to work as if they were in a real occupation and that it is more important to avoid errors than to work extremely fast. In contrast to the first experiment, we also told the participants that they need to fulfill all tasks of a modality within a fixed time.

3.3 Accuracy

Figure 11 shows the errors made for each condition. One mistake within a modality (over all subjects) is equal to 0.0153% mistakes per pick.

Our hypothesis was that the use of context feedback would improve pick accuracy. Comparing the modalities *With LRF* against the modalities *Without LRF* shows about one third fewer errors for the former. However, a paired, one-tailed t-test results in p-value of 0.13. By its nature, the LRF can not directly help reduce *Wrong number* errors as it only can sense when the worker's hand reaches for a bin. In addition, the worker can accidentally trigger the LRF with his head by leaning toward the shelving units or brushing past them while moving, causing false feedback on missing or additional parts. However, the LRF is especially useful in providing feedback for picks that happened on wrong shelving units, wrong rows, or wrong columns. These errors are immediately recognizeable on the HMD as the mistake is often adjacent to the correct bin. Comparing these *Substitution* errors in the conditions *Without LRF* context to those *With LRF* context shows a statistically significant improvement ($p = 0.019$; one-tailed, paired t-test). However, the absolute numbers of errors are small: ten errors and six errors, respectively.

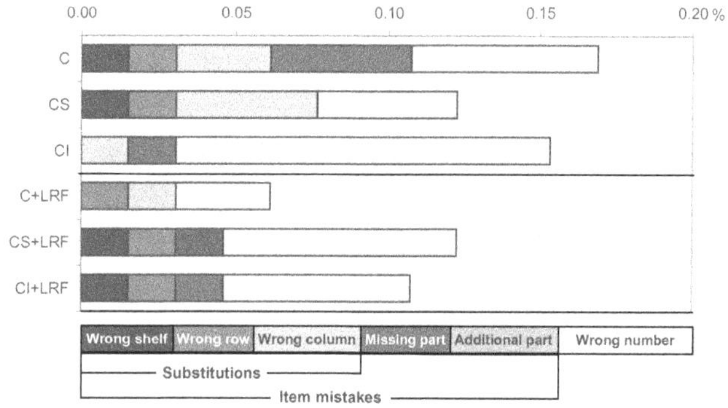

Figure 11: Mistakes/Pick in Context experiment

3.3.1 Post-Hoc Analysis

Examining the results post-hoc, it is noteworthy that the *CI* condition had only one *Substitution* error. Interestingly, the *CI* condition has twice as many errors of the type *Wrong number* than the *CI+LRF* condition (8 vs. 4) and also about twice as many errors of that type than the *CS* (3 errors) and *C* (4 errors) conditions.

3.4 Speed

Normalization is performed as in the *Color experiment* but using the average pick speed from the *Color experiment* for convenience. The reader is warned that detailed comparisons across the two experiments is unwise due to the different instructions given and the different participants involved. In fact, participants picked on average 23% faster in the *Context experiment* than in the *Color experiment*. However, the *C* and *CS* conditions are the same across experiments, which allows comparison relative to them and may suggest trends to investigate in future studies.

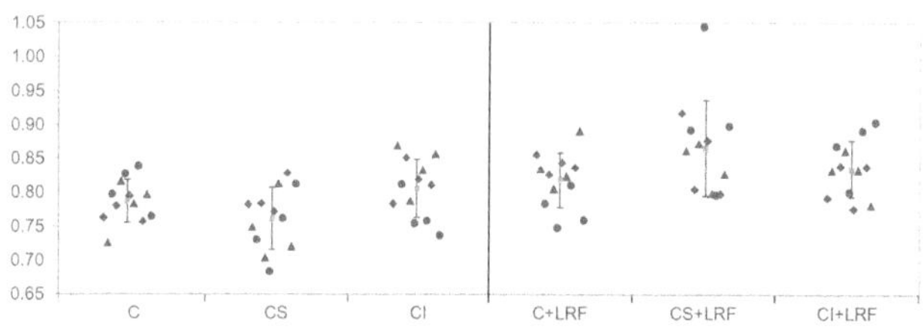

Figure 12: Pick speeds relative to the average (1.00) and normalized to the Color experiment (lower is faster)

The modalities *With LRF* are in average about 7% slower than the modalities *Without LRF* ($p < 0.0001$; two-tailed, paired t-test). When comparing *CI* with *CS* the modality with images is 5.8% slower than the modality with symbols ($p = 0.029$; two-tailed, paired t-test), showing a similar trend as in the previous experiment. Between the modalities *With LRF* there is no significant difference in speed.

3.5 Subjective Measures

The *CI+LRF* condition was rated first in all five categories of rankings (see Table 2). Conditions *With LRF* are ranked better than those *Without LRF* across all five categories ($p < 0.05$; Wilcoxon test).

	Without LRF			With LRF		
	C	CS	CI	C	CS	CI
Overall	4.5	5	4	3	3	1
Learnability	5	5	3	3	3	1
Comfort	5	5	4	3	3	1
Speed	3.5	5.5	4	3	3.5	1.5
Accuracy	5	5	4	2.5	3	1

Table 2: Ranking of context conditions (lower values are better)

When asked *Did you like the use of images for the items to pick?* participants answered more positive for the conditions *With LRF* than for the conditions *Without LRF*. *With LRF*: *very good* (7 persons), *good* (4 persons), *neutral* (1 person). *Without LRF*: *very good* (1 person), *good* (7 persons), *neutral* (3 persons), *bad* (1 person). Asking the participants *How well they could find the items to pick?* the condition *CI+LRF* received the best results: *very good* (8 persons), *good* (4 persons). The modality *CI* however, was nearly as good: *very good* (7 persons), *good* (5 persons).

During the open response section of our survey, some participants noted that the picking detection produces too many errors, which confuses them. Apart from that, the users agreed that working with picking detection facilitates the process of picking. The highlighting to provide feedback on correct or incorrect picks was very appreciated and favored.

Mod.	Workload
C	42.9±08.8
CS	45.3±11.9
CI	41.7±11.7
C+LRF	41.2±11.0
CS+LRF	40.8±12.1
CI+LRF	39.1±10.0

(a) Workloads

Fac.[1]	Score	Weight
PD	28.5±14.4	(13.9±7.5)%
MD	40.6±24.6	(19.7±7.8)%
TD	43.7±23.0	(22.8±8.9)%
Pe	71.8±18.0	(23.5±9.2)%
Ef	36.0±19.0	(19.8±9.1)%
Fr	6.7±10.8	(0.3±1.3)%

(b) Factors

Table 3: TLX-Results (lower is better)

Workloads as measured by the NASA TLX (see Table 3a) did not differ much for the conditions tested (range 0-100, lower is better). Table 3b shows average scores (range 0-100) for individual stress factors across all tested systems and their weighting in the workload. No significant difference for these factors was found between conditions. Note, however, the low scores for frustration and physical demand. These values indicate that all systems are suitable for the task and do not burden the user. The highest factor (in value and weight) is performance. This result suggests that the users had the impression of being able to work very effectively with all systems.

[1]Factors are: Physical Demand (PD), Mental Demand (MD), Temporal Demand (TD), Performance (Pe), Effort (Ef) and Frustration (Fr)

4. DISCUSSION

Our hypothesis that color labeling the rows would reduce error rates is supported by the data. The error rate with the color conditions (*CM*) is less than half as high as the error rate with the monochrome (*MM*) conditions without any negative effect on speed. The color conditions were also ranked more favorable than the monochrome conditions. These results suggest that color HMDs are worth the expense for inventory picking.

The hypothesis that adding context via the LRF would reduce errors is supported by a reduction of *Substitution* errors. There is also a trend of less errors in total, but the result was not significant statistically. Subjects preferred conditions with LRF context but were confused on occasion when picking detection did not work properly. Conditions that used LRF context were slower than ones that did not. The results may have been better if the picking detection would have worked better.

As higher costs are involved with such a system and speed and accuracy of context detection systems might improve, a final recommendation for or against such a system can not be given here. Further studies should review the benefits and disadvantages of a picking detection system. Also, a warehouse manager must weigh whether or not such a system is worthwhile in his specific environment. Errors may be so few with the HMD system that the improvement added using a LRF could be considered negligible. On the other hand, in some environments any pick errors may be considered unacceptable. Using the observations and experimental techniques described in this paper, pick line owners can perform experiments for their specific situation and balance errors and pick speed versus costs.

Interestingly, for conditions without the use of a LRF, the use of symbols (*CS*) resulted in the lowest error rates and fastest speeds. More investigation is needed to determine what role such symbolic cues might play in inventory picking.

Wrong number errors have not been addressed by the extensions introduced in this paper, yet they are clearly a major contributor to the overall error rate. One option is to place load sensors in the order bins to measure the number of objects placed and signal when errors occur on the worker's HMD. A simpler option comes from observing the trends from the experiments. In both experiments there have been more errors of this type in the conditions with images or description (within the conditions *Without LRF*). These conditions also trended to be slower. Perhaps interpreting the additional information reduces the user's concentration on the correct amount of items, and placing the number of items that need to be picked above the part's image would help reduce this effect. If such a modification could reduce these errors for the conditions with color and images (*CI*), it might become the best modality to use when picking detection is not available.

With picking detection available, the simultaneous highlighting of the box (with the number of items to pick) and the image may help the user to keep track of the number of items to pick. This assumption is supported by the feedback of the users and reduction of errors between the *CI* and *CI+LRF* condition. However, within the modalities *With LRF* the condition *C+LRF* showed the fewest errors. Assuming a perfectly working context detection system, this result becomes obvious, as people should then be able to concentrate more on the feedback from the context detection system. Still, the participants liked to be supported by images in an unknown domain.

The navigation of the picking client was found to be good. The animation showing a shelving unit change was mostly liked and was perceived to be helpful. However, there have been still some mistakes of the type *Wrong shelf*. Therefore, it might be useful to prompt the user explicitly for a change of the shelving unit (especially for modalities without the use of picking detection and images).

In general, the low number of errors in the study makes comparisons difficult. We had to add more variety to the pick tasks than in our previous studies in order to elicit even the few errors seen here. In many senses, this situation is encouraging. From industrial environments, we know that pick-by-light systems are very successful in speeding up picking and eliminating errors but are expensive. HMD-based systems could offer a lower cost alternative, and our previous studies have shown they can be fast and accurate. The obvious next step is a direct comparison between the two techniques.

5. FUTURE WORK

The presented wearable system shows much potential for use in an industrial picking environment. We now plan to compare this system against a commercial pick-by-light system and a traditional paper based pick list for reference. Pick-by-light systems are growing in use in warehouses and show many benefits over traditional paper based picking and pick-by-voice systems. We plan our first study for laboratory-controlled conditions. A second study will compare the systems in a real industrial warehouse. During an extended period, skilled pickers will evaluate the usability of our system in a real picking environment. The planned studies will compare these systems with and without the use of context feedback. Also the use of images (as proposed in the discussion) will be further evaluated. Error rates, speed, investment costs, and the flexibility of these systems will be compared to create a series of guidelines as to which system is best for a given environment.

6. CONCLUSION

Extending previous work on the use of a head-mounted display for order picking, we have improved our picking charts by coordinating colors and symbols between the chart and the physical part bins. These extensions show a reduction in errors of more than 50%. Adding picking feedback information showed an additional reduction in the already low error rate. In general, users preferred colored modalities, feedback, and the inclusion of images, though the last two improvements trended slower in pick speeds.

7. ACKNOWLEDGMENTS

This work is part of the project SiWear[2]. The project is funded with reference number 01MB07029A by the German Federal Ministry of Economics and Technology within the program SimoBIT [3].

8. REFERENCES

[1] J. Bartholdi and S. Hackmann. Warehouse and distribution science. Technical report, Supply Chain & Logistics Institute, Georgia Institute of Technology, 2011.

[2] J. Coyle, E. Bardi, and J. Langley. *The Management of Business Logistics: A Supply Chain Perspective.* South-Western College, Cincinnati, 7th revised edition, 2002.

[3] S. G. Hart and L. E. Staveland. *Development of NASA-TLX (Task Load Index): Results of empirical and theoretical research.* Amsterdam: North Holland, 1988.

[4] H. Iben, H. Baumann, T. Starner, C. Ruthenbeck, and T. Klug. Visual based picking supported by context awareness: comparing picking performance using paper-based lists versus lists presented on a head mounted display with contextual support. In *ACM ICMI-MLMI '09: Proceedings of the 2009 International Conference on Multimodal interfaces*, pages 281–288, New York, NY, USA, 2009.

[5] M. d. Koster, T. Le-Duc, and K. Roodbergen. Design and control of warehouse order picking: a literature review. Technical report, Erasmus Research Institute of Management (ERIM), Erasmus University, 2006.

[6] R. Reif and W. Günthner. Pick-by-vision: augmented reality supported order picking. *The Visual Computer*, 25:461–467, 2009.

[7] B. Schwerdtfeger, T. Frimor, D. Pustka, and G. Klinker. Mobile information presentation schemes for supra-adaptive logistics applications. In Z. Pan, A. Cheok, M. Haller, R. Lau, H. Saito, and R. Liang, editors, *Advances in Artificial Reality and Tele-Existence*, volume 4282 of *Lecture Notes in Computer Science*, pages 998–1007. Springer Berlin / Heidelberg, 2006.

[8] K. A. Weaver, H. Baumann, T. Starner, H. Iben, and M. Lawo. An empirical task analysis of warehouse order picking using head-mounted displays. In *ACM CHI '10: Proceedings of the 28th International Conference on Human Factors in Computing Systems*, pages 1695–1704, New York, NY, USA, 2010.

[2] http://www.siwear.de

[3] http://www.simobit.de

Modeling Parallel State Charts for Multithreaded Multimodal Dialogues

Gregor Mehlmann
Human Centered Multimedia
Augsburg University
Universitätsstrasse 6a
Augsburg, Germany
mehlmann@hcm-lab.de

Birgit Endrass
Human Centered Multimedia
Augsburg University
Universitätsstrasse 6a
Augsburg, Germany
endrass@hcm-lab.de

Elisabeth André
Human Centered Multimedia
Augsburg University
Universitätsstrasse 6a
Augsburg, Germany
andre@hcm-lab.de

ABSTRACT

In this paper, we present a modeling approach for the management of highly interactive, multithreaded and multimodal dialogues. Our approach enforces the separation of dialogue content and dialogue structure and is based on a statechart language enfolding concepts for hierarchy, concurrency, variable scoping and a detailed runtime history. These concepts facilitate the modeling of interactive dialogues with multiple virtual characters, autonomous and parallel behaviors, flexible interruption policies, context-sensitive interpretation of the user's discourse acts and coherent resumptions of dialogues. An interpreter allows the realtime visualization and modification of the model to allow a rapid prototyping and easy debugging. Our approach has successfully been used in applications and research projects as well as evaluated in field tests with non-expert authors. We present a demonstrator illustrating our concepts in a social game scenario.

Categories and Subject Descriptors

D.1.7 [**Visual Programming**]

General Terms

Algorithms, Languages, Theory

Keywords

Dialogue Modeling, Multimodality, Multithreading

1. INTRODUCTION

Virtual characters in interactive applications can enrich the user's experience by showing engaging and consistent behavior. To what extent virtual characters contribute to measurable benefits is still fiercely discussed [11, 25]. Therefore, virtual characters need to be carefully crafted in cooperation with users, artists and programmers. The creation of interactive virtual characters with a consistent and believable dialogue behavior poses challenges such as modeling personality and emotion [19], creating believable facial expressions, gestures and body movements [16], expressive speech synthesis [31] and natural language recognition as well as dialogue and interaction management [35]. In this work, we address the tasks of modeling consistent, highly interactive multithreaded and multimodal dialogue behavior and realizing effective interaction management for dialogue situations with embodied conversational characters.

During the last years, several approaches for modeling interactive dialogue behavior of virtual characters have been researched. A variety of systems such as, frame-, plan-, rule- and finite state-based systems were presented. Most of these systems required a substantial degree of expert knowledge and programming skills, thus, being unserviceable for non-computer experts, such as artists and screenwriters that wanted to craft interactive applications with virtual characters. Therefore, as a next step, authoring systems were developed to exploit related expert knowledge in the area of games, film or theater screenplay.

These systems are created to facilitate the modeling process and to allow non-computer experts to model believable natural behavior for virtual characters. They can be categorized by their conceptual and methodological approaches. On the one hand, *character-centric* approaches aim on creating autonomous agents for multi-agent systems. These approaches usually generate parallel behavior of several agents, however they do not explicitly include support for scripting the behavior of multiple agents and their synchronization in a simple and intuitive way for an author. Examples for character-centric systems are *Improv* [27] or *Scream* [28], where an author defines an agents' initial goals, beliefs and attitudes. These mental states determine the agents' behavioral responses to received communicative acts. In *author-centric* approaches, on the other hand, a human author can communicate an artistic vision with the primary focus of scripting at the plot level. The user can contribute to the plot within the narrative boundaries defined by the author. Examples for author-centric systems include the CSLU toolkit [23], *Cyranus* [12], *Scenejo* [33], *Deal* [1] and *Creactor* [13]. *Hybrid* approaches, as described in [7] or [8], try to bridge the gap between the author-centric and character-centric approach by combining the advantages of both.

So far, none of the mentioned systems supports easily handled concepts for both, a dialogue and interaction his-

ICMI'11, November 14–18, 2011, Alicante, Spain.

tory and the modeling of concurrent processes for creating and synchronizing parallel behavior on an intuitive authoring level. However, this would facilitate the modeling task and reduce the complexity of the model. It would allow to follow a modular and compositional modeling paradigm, thus increasing clarity and reusability of the model. This would help to handle typical challenges in the creation of applications with interactive virtual characters, such as the modeling of reactive and deliberate behavior, the use of multiple virtual characters and their synchronization and the handling of user interaction. In this paper, we face these challenges by presenting a hybrid approach to contribute on the user modeling level for the creation of multithreaded and multimodal interactive virtual character applications in a rapid-prototyping style.

2. DIALOGUE MANAGEMENT

Central concept of our modeling approach is the seperation of dialogue content and structure. Multimodal dialogue content is specified in a set of *scenes* that are organized in a *scenescript*. The narrative structure of an interactive performance and the interactive behavior of the virtual characters is controlled by a *sceneflow*, which is a statechart variant specifying the logic according to which scenes are played back and commands are executed. Sceneflows have concepts for the *hierarchical refinement* and the *parallel decomposition* of the model as well as an exhaustive *runtime history* and multiple *interaction policies*. Thus, sceneflows adopt and extend concepts that can be found in similar statechart variants [10, 37].

Sceneflows and scenescripts are created using a graphical modeling tool and executed by an *interpreter* software. This allows the realtime extension and modification of the model and the direct observation of the effects without the need for an intermediate translation step or even the need to pause the execution of a sceneflow. The realtime visualization of a sceneflow's execution and active scenes within the graphical user interface allows to test, simulate and debug the model. These features facilitate and accelerate the modeling process and, thus, allow the creation of interactive virtual character performances in a rapid-prototyping style.

2.1 Creating Multimodal Dialogue Content

As shown in Fig. 1, a scene resembles the part of a movie script consisting of the virtual characters' utterances containing stage directions for controlling gestures, postures, gaze and facial expressions as well as control commands for arbitrary actions realizable by the respective character animation engine or by other external modules. Scenescript content can be created both manually by an author and automatically by external generation modules. The possibility to parameterize scenes may be exploited to create scenes in a hybrid way between fixed authored scene content and variable content (Fig. 1 ①), such as retrieved information from user interactions, sensor input or generated content from knowledge bases.

A scenescript may provide a number of variations for each scene that are subsumed in a *scenegroup*, consisting of the scenes sharing the same name or signature (Fig. 1 ②,③). Different *blacklisting strategies* are used to choose one of the scenes from a scenegroup for execution. This mechanism increases dialogue variety and helps to avoid repetitive be-

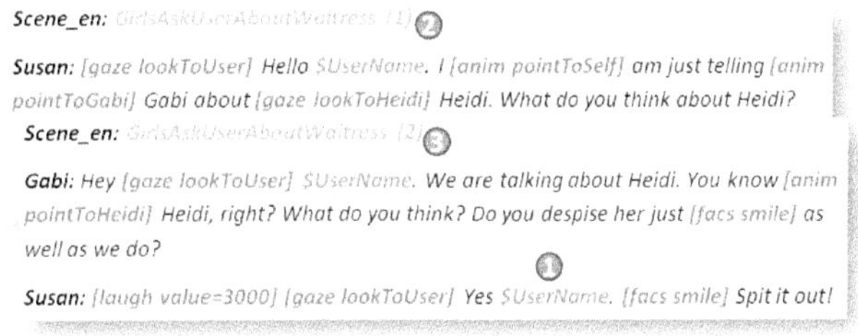

Figure 1: Parameterizable scenes of a scenegroup.

havior of virtual characters, which would certainly impact the agents' believability.

2.2 Modeling Dialogue Logic and Context

A sceneflow is a hierarchical and concurrent statechart that consists of different types of *nodes* and *edges*. A *scenenode* can be linked to one or more scenegroup playback- or system commands and can be annotated with statements and expressions from a simple scripting language, such as type- and variable definitions as well as variable assignments and function calls to predefined functions of the underlying implementation language (Fig. 2 ①). A *supernode* extends the functionality of scenenodes by creating a hierarchical structure. A supernode may contain scenenodes and supernodes that constitute its subautomata. One of these subnodes has to be declared the *startnode* of that supernode (Fig. 2 ②). The supernode hierarchy can be used for type- and variable *scoping*. Type definitions and variable definitions are inherited to all subnodes of a supernode. The supernode hierarchy and the variable scoping mechanism imply a hierarchy of *local contexts* that can be used for context-sensitive reaction to user interactions, external events or the change of environmental conditions.

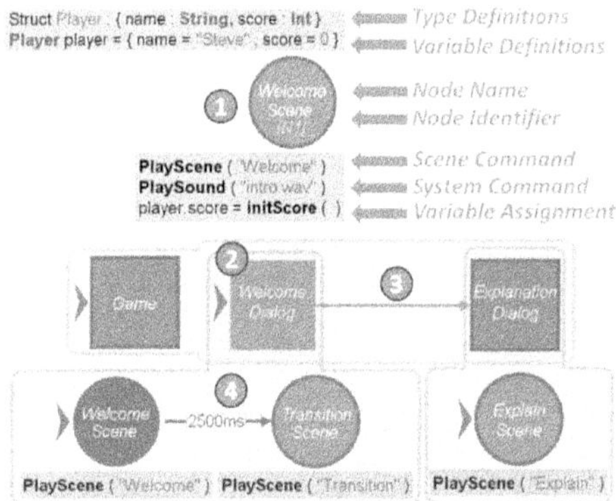

Figure 2: Node statements and supernode hierarchy.

Different *branching strategies* within the sceneflow, such as logical and temporal conditions or randomization, as well as different *interaction policies*, can be modeled by connecting nodes with different types of edges. An *epsilon edge* represents an unconditional transition (Fig. 2 ③). They are used for the specification of the order in which computation steps are performed and scenes are played back. A *timeout edge* represents a timed or scheduled transition and is labeled with a *timeout value* (Fig. 2 ④). Timeout edges are used to regulate the temporal flow of a sceneflow's execution and to schedule the playback of scenes and computation steps. A *probabilistic edge* represents a transition that is taken with a certain probability and is labeled with a *probability value* (Fig. 5 ②). Probabilistic edges are used to create some degree of randomness and desired non-determinism during the execution of a sceneflow. A *conditional edge* represents a conditional transition and is labeled with a *conditional expression*, as shown in Fig. 3. Conditional edges are used to create a branching structure in the sceneflow which describes different reactions to changes of environmental conditions, external events or user interactions.

2.3 Interaction Handling Policies

User interactions as well as other internally or externally triggered events within the application environment can rise at any time during the execution of a model. Some of these events need to be processed as fast as possible to assert certain realtime requirements. There may, for example, be the need to contemporarily interrupt a currently running dialogue during a scene playback in order to give the user the impression of presence or impact. However, there can also exist events that may be processed at some later point in time allowing currently executed scenes or commands to be regularly terminated before reacting to the event. These two different interaction paradigms imply two different *interaction handling policies* that find their syntactical realization in two different types of *interruptibility* or inheritance of conditional edges:

- *Interruptive conditional edges* (Fig. 3 ①,③) are inherited with an interruptive policy and are used for handling of events and user interactions requiring a fast reaction. Whenever an interruptive conditional edge of a node can be taken, this node and all descendant nodes may not take any other edges or execute any further command. These semantics imply, that interruptive edges that are closer to the root have priority over interruptive edges farther from the root.

- *Non-interruptive conditional edges* (Fig. 3 ②,④) are inherited with a non-interruptive policy, which means that a non-interruptive conditional edge of a certain node or supernode can be taken after the execution of the node's program and after all descendant nodes have terminated. This policy is implicitly giving higher priority to any conditional edge of nodes that are farther from the root.

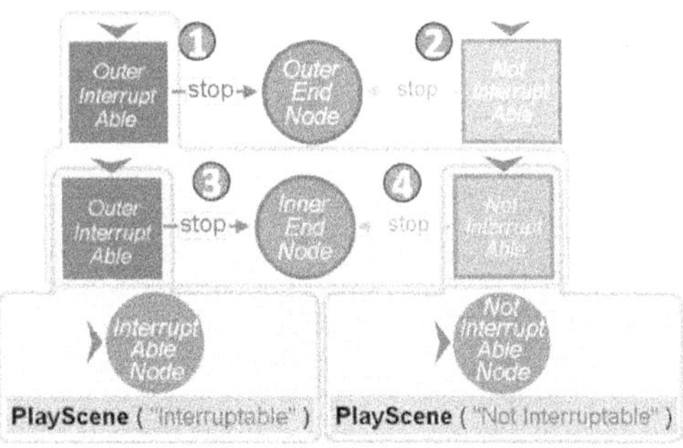

Figure 3: ①,③ Interruptive conditional edges and ②,④ simple non-interruptive conditional edges.

Fig. 3 shows a supernode hierarchy with different conditional edges. If the condition `stop` becomes true during the execution of the two innermost scene playback commands, then the scene within the supernodes with the non-interruptive conditions (Fig. 3 ②,④) will be executed to its end. However, the scene within the supernodes with the interruptive conditions (Fig. 3 ①,③) will be interrupted as fast as possible. In the non-interruptive case the execution of the sceneflow continues with the inner end node (Fig. 3 ④) before the outer end node is executed (Fig. 3 ②). In the interruptive case the execution of the sceneflow immediately continues with the outer end node (Fig. 3 ①) because the outer interruptive edge has priority over the inner interruptive edge (Fig. 3 ③).

2.4 Modeling Multihreaded Dialogue

Sceneflows exploit the modeling principles of *modularity* and *compositionality* in the sense of a hierarchical and *parallel decomposition*. Multiple virtual characters and their behavior, as well as multiple control processes for event detection or interaction management, can be modeled as concurrent processes in parallel automata. For this purpose, sceneflows allow two syntactical instruments for the creation of concurrent processes. By defining multiple startnodes for a supernode (Fig. 4), each subautomaton which consists of all nodes reachable by a startnode, is executed by a separate process. By defining *fork edges* (Fig. 5 ①), an author can create multiple concurrent processes without the need for changing the level of the node hierarchy.

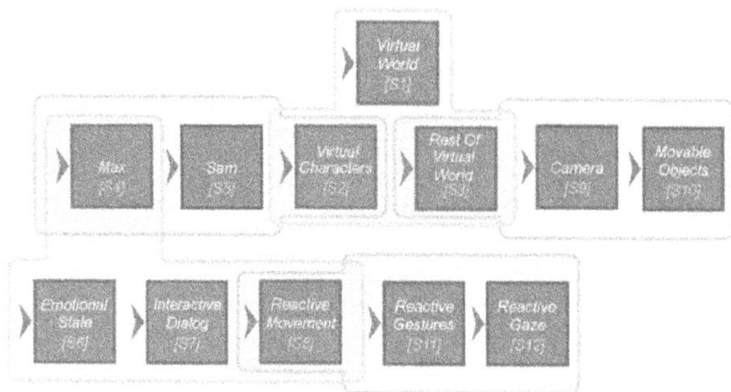

Figure 4: Hierarchical and parallel decomposition.

Following this modular approach, an author is able to separate the task of modeling the overall behavior of a virtual character into multiple tasks of modeling individual behavioral aspects, functions and modalities. Behavioral aspects can be modified in isolation without knowing details of the other aspects. In addition, previously modeled behavioral patterns can easily be reused and adopted. Furthermore, premodeled automata that are controlling the communication with external devices or interfaces can be added as plugin modules that are executed in a parallel process.

Individual behavioral functions and modalities that contribute to the behavior of a virtual character are usually not completely independent, but have to be synchronized with each other. For example, speech is usually highly synchronized with non-verbal behavioral modalities such as gestures and body postures. When modeling individual behavioral functions and modalities in seperate parallel automata, the processes that concurrently execute these automata have to be synchronized by the author in order to coordinate all be-

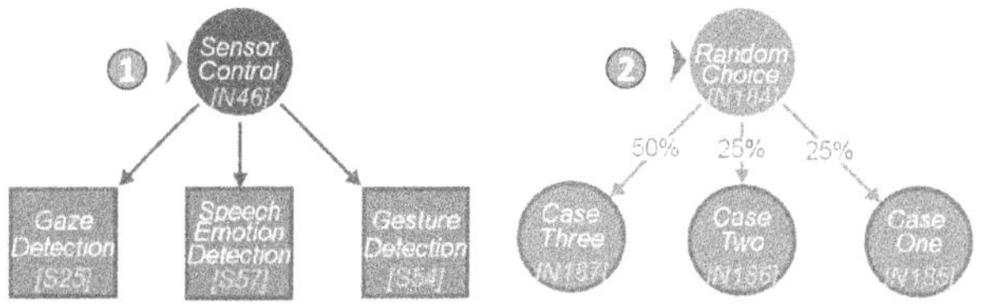

Figure 5: ① Concurrent processes with fork edges and ② randomization with three probability edges.

havioral aspects. This communication is realized by a *shared memory model* which allows an asynchronous non-blocking synchronization of concurrent processes.

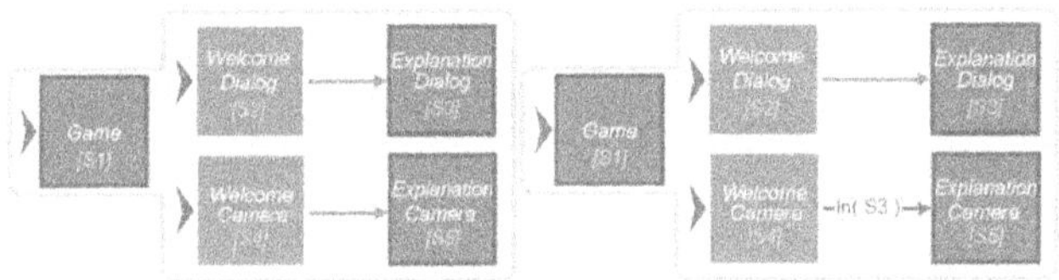

Figure 6: Synchronization over configuration states.

Thereby, sceneflows enfold two different syntactic features for the synchronization of concurrent processes. First, they allow the synchronization over common *shared variables* defined in some supernode. The interleaving semantics of sceneflows prescribe a mutually exclusive access to those variables to avoid inconsistencies. Second, they enfold a *state query condition* (Fig. 6) which represents a more intuitive mechanism for process synchronization. This condition allows to request weather a certain parallel automaton's state is currently executed by the sceneflow interpreter.

2.5 Consistent Resumption of Dialogue

Our concept of an exhaustive *runtime history* facilitates modeling reopening strategies and recapitulation phases of dialogues by falling back on automatically gathered information on past states of an interaction. During the execution of a sceneflow, the system automatically maintains a *history memory* to record the runtimes of nodes, the values of local variables, executed system commands and scenes that were played back. It additionally records the last executed substates of a supernode at the time of its termination or interruption. The automatical maintainance of this history memory releases the author of the manual collection of such runtime data, thus efficiently reducing the modeling effort while increasing the clarity of the model and providing the author with rich information about previous interactions and states of execution.

The scripting language of sceneflows provides a variety of built-in *history expressions* and conditions to request the information deposited in the history memory or to delete it. The history concept is syntactically represented in form of a special *history node* which is an implicit child node of each supernode. When reexecuting a supernode, the supernode starts at the history node instead of its default startnodes. Thus, the history node serves as a starting point for the author to model reopening strategies or recapitulation phases.

Fig. 7 shows a simple exemplary use of a supernode's history node and a history condition. At the first execution of the supernode `Parent`, the supernode starts at its startnode

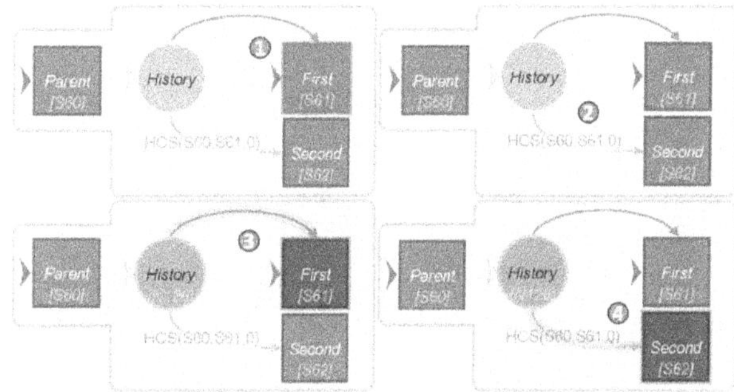

Figure 7: History node and condition.

`First` (Fig. 7 ①). If the supernode `Parent` is interrupted or terminated at some time and reexecuted afterwards, it starts at the history node `History`. The history memory is requested (Fig. 7 ②) to find out if the supernode had been interrupted or terminated in the node `First` or the node `Second`. As the snaphot of the visualized execution shows, depending on the result, the either the node `First` (Fig. 7 ③) is executed or the node `Second` (Fig. 7 ④) is started over the history node.

3. *SOAP:* MULTI-PARTY DIALOGUES IN INTERACTIVE STORYTELLING

The development of *interactive digital storytelling* systems has been a growing topic of research over the past years. They have been applied for applications in education and training [20, 32, 34] as well as in entertainment and art [21, 30, 3]. While some of these systems explore user interaction by putting the user into the role of an observer that can change the world as the story progresses, the majority of them pursues a *dialogue-based* interaction approach. Such systems focus on creating a dramatic experience by offering a selection of dialogue situations in which the user is able to influence the progress and the outcome of the story through interactions.

For the development of interactive storytelling applications it is indispensable to provide authoring software that can be used by non-experts such as artists and screenwriters in order to create highly interactive and consistent multi-party dialogues with the virtual actors. Thereby, there arise challenges such as the continuous realtime processing and context-sensitive interpretation of user interactions, an adequate contemporary reactions to the user's discourse acts and the resumption and revision of dialogue content after unexpected interruptions. We address these challenges in the social game scenario *Soap* by using the concepts of our approach presented in Section 2. We realized our ideas of dialogue-based interactive entertainment in a demonstrator, which is explained in the following.

3.1 Concept Overview

To this end, we choose a social game located in our *Virtual Beergarden* scenario (Fig. 8). In the soap-like story, the user and the virtual characters are involved in a romantic conflict. The user, who is represented by an avatar (Fig. 8 ①), meets a group of girls (Fig. 8 ②) and a group of guys (Fig. 8 ③) as well as a waitress (Fig. 8 ④). The user can approach the focus groups, listen to their conversations or contribute to the story. In case the user does not focus a certain group, the characters show idle dialogue behavior and talk gibberish. Through dialogue interactions, the user can advise the characters and, thus, influence the progress and outcome of the story.

Figure 8: The setting in the virtual beergarden.

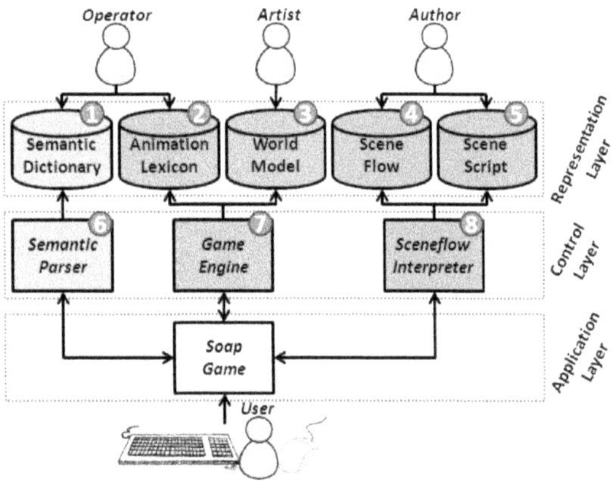

Figure 9: Component-based system architecture.

The different components of the system architecture are embedded in three independent layers: The representation layer contains knowledge bases and models specifying the scenario content (Fig. 9 ①-⑤). The control layer manages the processing of user input and the computation of system output (Fig. 9 ⑦-⑧). Finally, the application layer enfolds the user interface. Vertically, the components can be categorized into dialogue and interaction management (Fig. 9 ④,⑤,⑧), natural language interpretation (Fig. 9 ①,⑥) and autonomous behavior control (Fig. 9 ②,③,⑦).

3.2 Dialogue and Interaction Management

The behavior modeling as well as the dialogue and interaction management of the virtual characters is realized with our modeling tool. An author can specify dialogue- and behavior content in a *scenescript* (Fig. 9 ⑤) and model the logic of behavior and dialogue with a *sceneflow* (Fig. 9 ④). An interpreter software executes the model and is, thus, controlling the virtual characters in the game (Fig. 9 ⑧).

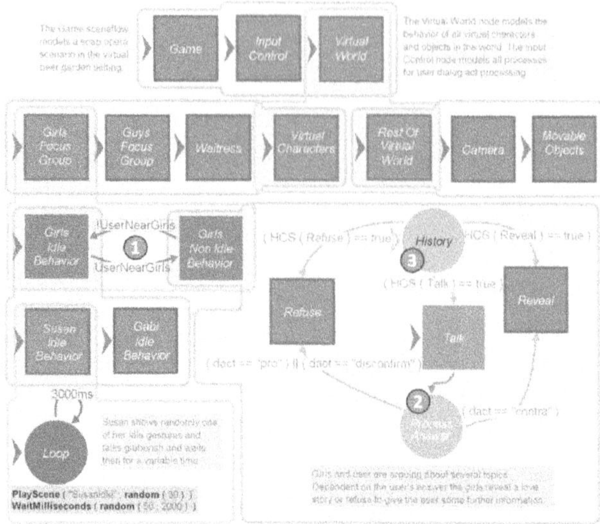

Figure 10: Part of the sceneflow from Soap.

Fig. 10 shows a part of the modeled sceneflow. Each focus group, the user avatar and other game objects are modeled in separate concurrent automata. We also recursively make use of parallel automata in order to model the behavior of individual characters and their behavioral aspects. This procedure reduces the modeling effort and increases the clarity of the model because it prevents the state explosion of the model, which could be observed if we modeled the whole scenario with a simple flat statechart. Furthermore, it allows us to change the behavior of individual focus groups or characters in isolation.

A major requirement in this application was to allow the user to change the focus group, or initiate and terminate a conversation respectively, at any time. Therefore, each dialogue situation had to be contemporarily interruptible. To create a coherent storytelling experience, an interrupted dialogue situation had to be consistently resumed after reentering the target group. For these reasons, a highly interactive dialogue structure was modeled and the runtime history was used in order to keep track of previous interactions and the progress of the dialogue. Ongoing dialogues are interrupted whenever the user leaves a focus group and resumed whenever the user reenters the focus group (Fig. 10 ①). Consistent resumption or reopening of a previous dialogue is guaranteed by a recursive use of the runtime interaction history (Fig. 10 ③). Context-sensitive reaction to the user's interaction is modeled by branching the dialogue structure dependent on the current state of the dialogue and the user's dialogue act provided by the NLU pipeline (Fig. 10 ②).

To factor out the logic for the detection and the processing of user interactions, we modeled a separate parallel automaton, as shown in Fig. 11. This reduces the effort of modeling such logics within the automata for the individual dialogue situations to a minimal amount, again effectively increasing the clarity of the model.

3.3 Natural Language Interpretation

This component allows the natural language communication between the user and the focus groups. Our natural language recognition and interpretation pipeline relies the

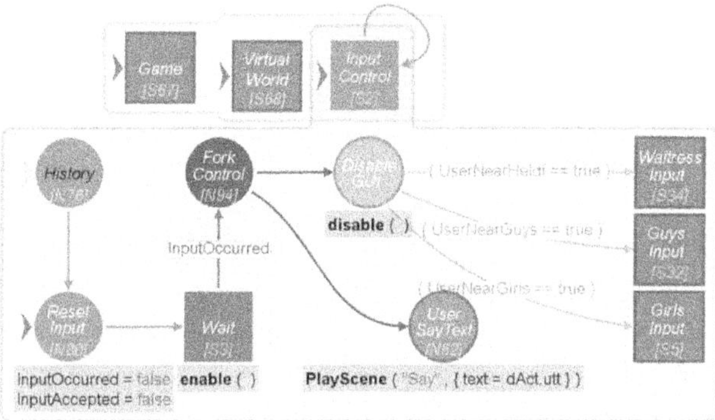

Figure 11: User input processing and control.

semantic parser Spin [6] (Fig. 9 ⑥), allowing text input to be processed by semantic rules mapping the users utterances into abstract *dialogue acts* based on the *DAMSL* coding scheme [4]. These rules are specified in a set of dictionaries that are created by an operator or the author (Fig. 9 ①). The dialogue acts are processed by the sceneflow interpreter according to the rules defined by the sceneflow model to ensure a contemporary, adequate and context-sensitive reaction to the user's utterances.

Fig. 12 exemplifies a set of rules, syntactic and semantic categories as well as preprocessing steps. The example rule (Fig. 12 ③) states that if the user's input contains one of the words "how", "do" or "what" in correlation with the word "you" and any word belonging to the semantic category *location*, the abstract speech act *ask-location* is triggered. The semantic category *location* (Fig. 12 ④) contains the words "location", "place", "beergarden", "here" and "party". Thus, different user utterances (Fig. 12 ⑤) are parsed into the same dialogue-act. In addition, word stems (Fig. 12 ②) and other pre-processing steps can be defined (Fig. 12 ①) such as summarizing negations. In addition, we integrated a *spell checker* into our language recognition component to be able to cope with faulty or incomplete text input. In interactive entertainment applications this is of special interest, since typos or incomplete sentences occur rather often.

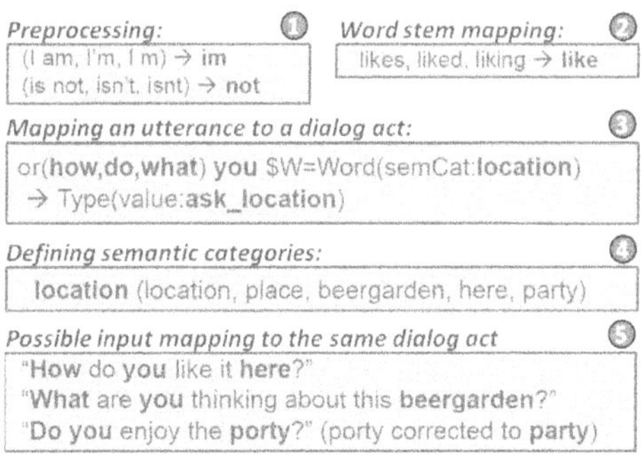

Figure 12: Knowledge for the semantic parser.

The language recognition engine also allows the dynamic exchange of dictionaries from the sceneflow model. In that manner, authors can adapt the dictionary rules to the local dialogue context. User interactions could, for example, be interpreted differently in different contexts. With a set of dictionaries, these are less complex, clearly arranged and exchangeable. In addition, the parsing of sentences can be a lot easier in limited domains. Dictionaries that do not deliver interpretable results in a certain context, can be dynamically substituted with more general dictionaries.

3.4 Autonomous Behavior Control

The game component is responsible for the graphical representation of our scenario. The scene displayed in the Virtual Beergarden is described by a world model created by an artist (Fig. 9 ③). Core concept of this component is the automatic animation selection for autonomous low-level behaviors. While high-level behaviors of the virtual characters such as speech and gestures are specified using the modeling tool, low-level behaviors such as positioning, agent orientation and proximity or inter-agent gazing can be handled automatically by the application. They are triggered by the system automatically, accompanying the behavior specified by the author, so that the author does not need to take care of them. If, for example an author specifies that an agent should move through the scenario and approach another agent, the virtual characters will automatically detect each other when entering their social distance zones and react by e.g. turning their bodies in a way that they are facing each other or turning their gaze towards the other characters face.

As shown in Fig. 9, animations are specified in a nonverbal knowledge base, an *animation lexicon* (Fig. 9 ②). In the current version of the system, each agent can perform over 40 different gestures and postures. Following [22], we divide every animation into the following phases: preparation, stroke and retraction. In the preparation phase, the hands are brought into the gesture space, the stroke phase carries the content of the gesture, while in the retraction phase, the hands are finally brought back into a resting position. These phases are used as a basis for gesture customization, e.g. to match the agent's social or personal background. In particular, the stroke phase of a gesture can be varied in order to show different gestural expressivities (see [26]), such as speed or repetition. In the Virtual Beergarden application the parameter repetition, can be varied by playing the stroke phase several times, while it can be played faster or slower to customize the speed parameter. A Bayesisian network can be set for the agents in order to define aspects such as personality or emotional state that influence the manner in which nonverbal behaviors are executed. This has been exemplified for the phenomena of culture-related differences in behavior [29]. In order to create different characters in an interactive story, the Bayesisian network can easily be replaced, e.g. to focus on other aspects such as personality or emotional state. Depending on the values set for a virtual character, animations are customized accordingly. In that manner, the author of a story needs to define a character only once, e.g. as being extroverted. In case the author wants to change the gestural style for a characters, e.g. because of a different emotion, this can easily be done at runtime.

4. FIELD TESTS AND DISCUSSION

Success in building different interactive applications with virtual characters for entertainment [9], education [24, 14] and commerce [18] permits very promising conclusions with respect to the suitability of our approach. However, mainly computer-experts have been involved in the development of these applications. For this reason, we conducted several field tests and practical workshops with students of different age groups and genders to determine in how far the approach is suited for non-experts [5]. The participating students from various educational levels brought no specific background skills or previous knowledge. Nevertheless, they were able to quickly pick up most of our concepts for modeling interactive narrative with statecharts and writing scenescripts was promptly and completely understood. This comprehension was directly transfered into the creation of vivid interactive scenarios with virtual characters. During the field tests, it has been noticeable that the students, in contrast to the computer experts, occasionally had difficulties to apply the more complex concepts of our approach. While the concept of hierarchical and parallel decomposition was fully understood, the students mostly used concurrent processes to model completely independent parallel behaviors while they rarely utilised the synchronization measures of our language. Furthermore, the history concept was rarely used, because the dialogue structure modelled by the students was mostly linear or a tree-like branching structure. They only occasionally had the idea to model dialogue situations that could be resumed or reopened after an interruption by using the history concept of our approach. These observations could be be explained with the short amount of practice time for the students. The field tests all had the same schedule. After a short introduction (20 mins) into the concepts of the modeling approach and the handling of the graphical user interface, the students had some time for brainstorming and sketching the dialogue (40 mins). Afterwards, they modelled the sceneflow with minimal assistance (40 mins). We believe that the more complex modeling concepts of our approach will also be fully understood by non-experts after more intensive practice. In the future we plan to do more field test over a longer period of time in order to prove our assumption. This would also allow us to evaluate the quality of the stories and dialogues modeled by the students.

5. CONCLUSION AND FUTURE WORK

In this paper, we described a modeling approach for multithreaded and multimodal dialogues with virtual characters. Our approach allows an author to model complex dialogue behavior and interaction management for multiple virtual characters in a rapid-prototyping style. The statechart language provides different interaction handling policies for an author to handle continuous real-time interaction. An interaction history allows an author to model reopening strategies for dialogues so that they can consistently be resumed and previous dialogue topics can be revised. Hierarchical and parallel decomposition allows to model different behavioral aspects, functions and modalities in isolation. This modular approach reduces the complexity of the model while improving extensibility and reusability. Dialogue content can be authored manually or generated automatically. Autonomous behavior can be specified without the need for an author to explicitly model it. We realized our ideas of dialogue-based interactive entertainment in a demonstrator application.

Our future work refers on the one hand to technical improvements of the modeling tool based on the user feedback we received so far and refinements of our modeling approach, on the other hand to additional user studies that explore further issues, such as the quality of the scenarios generated with our approach. For the future we plan to integrate our system with other components, as for example emotion simulation and emotional speech synthesis, nonverbal behavior generation as well as speech recognition. This implies the use of standard languages such as FML, BML and EmotionML [36, 15, 17]. Furthermore, we want to integrate a dialogue domain knowledge component to the authoring framework, which allows authors to easily define domain knowledge and rules that can map utterances to abstract dialogue acts dependent on the dialogue domain. This implies the use of an ISO standard for dialogue act annotation [2]. Feedback from users in different field tests and projects has shown that one strength of the presented modeling approach is the reusability of already modeled behavioral patterns in the form of sub-models, because this can drastically reduce the modeling effort and complexity. We plan to factor a library of reactive behavior patterns that can be reused for an easy creation of different behavioral aspects for multiple virtual characters. Therefore, one of our main purposes is to identify abstract universal behavioral patterns that appear in multi-party dialogues with multiple virtual characters. We want to provide the author with a library of predefined and parameterizable statechart models, implementing behavioral patterns that can be reused in several projects and can easily be adjusted to the respective context.

Regarding the experiences with the presented approach in many applications and the feedback from several field tests, we conclude that our approach is suitable for modeling complex multithreaded and multimodal dialogue behavior and interaction management for multiple virtual characters in a rapid-prototyping style and that our modeling tool can be used as an educational device.

6. ACKNOWLEDGMENTS

The work described in this paper was supported by the European Commission within the 7th Framework Programme in the project IRIS (project no. 231824).

7. REFERENCES

[1] J. Brusk, T. Lager, A. Hjalmarsson, and P. Wik. Deal: Dialogue management in scxml for believable game characters. In *ACM Future Play*, pages 137–144. ACM, 2007.

[2] H. Bunt, J. Alexandersson, J. Carletta, J.-W. Choe, A. C. Fang, K. Hasida, K. Lee, V. Petukhova, A. Popescu-Belis, L. Romary, C. Soria, and D. R. Traum. Towards an ISO standard for dialogue act annotation. In *7th International Conference on Language Resources and Evaluation (LREC)*, Valletta, Malta, May 19-21, 2010 2010.

[3] M. Cavazza, F. Charles, and S.-J. Mead. Agents' Interaction in Virtual Storytelling. In *IVA 2001*, pages 156–170, 2001.

[4] M. Core and J. Allen. Coding Dialogs with the DAMSL Annotation Scheme. In *Working Notes of AAAI Fall Symposium on Communicative Action in Humans and Machines*, 1997.

[5] B. Endrass, M. Wissner, G. Mehlmann, R. Buehling, M. Haering, and E. André. Teenage Girls as Authors for Digital Storytelling - A Practical Experience Report. In *Workshop on Education in Interactive Digital Storytelling on ICIDS*, 2010.

[6] R. Engel. Robust and efficient semantic parsing of freeword order languages in spoken dialogue systems. In *Interspeech 2005*, 2005.

[7] S. Gandhe, N. Whitman, D. Traum, and R. Artstein. An integrated authoring tool for tactical questioning dialogue systems, 2008.

[8] P. Gebhard, M. Kipp, M. Klesen, and T. Rist. Authoring scenes for adaptive, interactive performances. In *AAMAS 2003*, pages 725–732. ACM, 2003.

[9] P. Gebhard, M. Schröder, M. Charfuelan, C. Endres, M. Kipp, S. Pammi, M. Rumpler, and O. Türk. IDEAS4Games: Building Expressive Virtual Characters for Computer Games. In *IVA 2008*, pages 426–440, 2008.

[10] D. Harel. Statecharts: A visual formalism for complex systems. In *Science of Computer Programming*, volume 8, pages 231–274. Elsevier, 1987.

[11] S. Heidig and G. Clarebout. Do pedagogical agents make a difference to student motivation and learning? A review of empirical research. *Educational Research Review*, 2010.

[12] I. Iurgel. Cyranus : An authoring tool for interactive edutainment applications. In *Technologies for E-Learning and Digital Entertainment*, Hangzhou, China, April 16-19 2006. Springer, Berlin.

[13] I. A. Iurgel, R. E. da Silva, P. R. Ribeiro, A. B. Soares, and M. F. dos Santos. CREACTOR - An Authoring Framework for Virtual Actors. In *IVA 2009*, pages 562–563. Springer, 2009.

[14] M. Kipp and P. Gebhard. IGaze: Studying reactive gaze behavior in semi-immersive human-avatar interactions. In *IVA 2008*, pages 191–199, 2008.

[15] M. Kipp, A. Heloir, P. Gebhard, and M. Schröder. Realizing multimodal behavior: Closing the gap between behavior planning and embodied agent presentation. In *IVA 2010*. Springer, 2010.

[16] M. Kipp, M. Neff, K. H. Kipp, and I. Albrecht. Toward natural gesture synthesis: Evaluating gesture units in a data-driven approach. In *IVA 2007*, LNAI 4722, pages 15–28, 2007.

[17] S. Kopp, B. Krenn, S. Marsella, A.-N. Marshall, C. Pelachaud, H. Pirker, K.-R. Thórisson, and H. Vilhjálmsson. Towards a common framework for multimodal generation: The behavior markup language. In *IVA 2006*, 2006.

[18] A. Kröner, P. Gebhard, L. Spassova, G. Kahl, and M. Schmitz. Informing customers by means of digital product memories. In *1st international Workshop on Digital Object Memories*, 2009.

[19] S. Marsella and J. Gratch. Ema: A computational model of appraisal dynamics. In *Agent Construction and Emotions*, 2006.

[20] S. Marsella, W.-L. Johnson, and C.-M. Labore. Interactive pedagogical drama for health interventions. In *Artificial Intelligence in Education*, pages 341–348. IOS Press, 2003.

[21] M. Mateas and A. Stern. Facade: An experiment in building a fully-realized interactive drama. In *Game Developer's Conference: Game Design Track*, 2003.

[22] D. McNeill. *Hand and Mind: What Gestures Reveal about Thought*. University of Chicago Press, 1992.

[23] M. F. Mctear. Using the cslu toolkit for practicals in spoken dialogue technology. In *University College London*, pages 1–7, 1999.

[24] G. Mehlmann, M. Häring, R. Bühling, M. Wissner, and E. André. Multiple agent roles in an adaptive virtual classroom environment. In J. Albeck, N. Badler, T. Bickmore, C. Pelachaud, and A. Safonova, editors, *IVA 2010*, pages 250–256. Springer, 2010.

[25] J. Miksatko, K.-H. Kipp, and M. Kipp. The persona zero-effect: Evaluating virtual character benefits ona learning task. In *IVA 2010*. Springer, 2010.

[26] C. Pelachaud. Multimodal expressive embodied conversational agents. In *ACM international conference on Multimedia*, pages 683–689, 2005.

[27] K. Perlin and A. Goldberg. Improv: A system for scripting interactive actors in virtual worlds. In *Computer Graphics (SIGGRAPH)*, pages 205–216. ACM, 1996.

[28] H. Prendinger, S. Saeyor, and M. Ishizuk. MPML and SCREAM: Scripting the Bodies and Minds of Life-like Characters. In *Life-like Characters – Tools, Affective Functions, and Applications*, pages 213–242. Springer, 2004.

[29] M. Rehm, N. Bee, B. Endrass, M. Wissner, and E. André. Too close for comfort? Adapting to the user's cultural background. In *Workshop on Human-Centered Multimedia*, 2007.

[30] M. Riedl, C.-J. Saretto, and R.-M. Young. Managing interaction between users and agents in a multi-agent storytelling environment. In *AAMAS 2003*, pages 741–748. ACM, 2003.

[31] M. Schröder. *Emotions in the Human Voice, Culture and Perception*, volume 3, chapter Approaches to emotional expressivity in synthetic speech, pages 307–321. Pural, 2008.

[32] M. Si, S. Marsella, and D. Pynadath. Thespian: An architecture for interactive pedagogical drama. In *AIED 2005*, 2005.

[33] U. Spierling, S.-A. Weiss, and W. Mueller. Towards accessible authoring tools for interactive storytelling. In *Technologies for Interactive Digital Storytelling and Entertainment*. Springer, 2006.

[34] W. Swartout, J. Gratch, R. Hill, E. Hovy, S. Marsella, J. Rickel, and D. Traum. Toward virtual humans. *AI Magazine*, 27(2):96–108, 2006.

[35] D. Traum, A. Leuski, A. Roque, S. Gandhe, D. DeVault, J. Gerten, S. Robinson, and B. Martinovski. Natural language dialogue architectures for tactical questioning characters. In *Army Science Conference*, 2008.

[36] H. Vilhjalmsson, N. Cantelmo, J. Cassell, N.-E. Chafai, M. Kipp, S. Kopp, M. Mancini, S. Marsella, A.-N. Marshall, C. Pelachaud, Z. Ruttkay, K.-R. Thórisson, H. van Welbergen, and R.-J. van der Werf. The behavior markup language: Recent developments and challenges. In *IVA 2007*, 2007.

[37] M. von der Beeck. A comparison of statecharts variants. In *ProCoS 1994*, pages 128–148. Springer, 1994.

Virtual Worlds and Active Learning for Human Detection

David Vázquez
Computer Vision Center and
Computer Science Dpt. UAB,
Campus UAB, Spain
david.vazquez@cvc.uab.es

Antonio M. López
Computer Vision Center and
Computer Science Dpt. UAB,
Campus UAB, Spain
antonio@cvc.uab.es

Daniel Ponsa
Computer Vision Center and
Computer Science Dpt. UAB,
Campus UAB, Spain
daniel@cvc.uab.es

Javier Marín
Computer Vision Center,
Campus UAB, Spain
jmarin@cvc.uab.es

ABSTRACT

Image based human detection is of paramount interest due to its potential applications in fields such as advanced driving assistance, surveillance and media analysis. However, even detecting non-occluded standing humans remains a challenge of intensive research. The most promising human detectors rely on classifiers developed in the discriminative paradigm, *i.e.*, trained with labelled samples. However, labelling is a manual intensive step, especially in cases like human detection where it is necessary to provide at least bounding boxes framing the humans for training. To overcome such problem, some authors have proposed the use of a *virtual world* where the labels of the different objects are obtained automatically. This means that the human models (classifiers) are learnt using the appearance of rendered images, *i.e.*, using realistic computer graphics. Later, these models are used for human detection in images of the *real world*. The results of this technique are surprisingly good. However, these are not always as good as the classical approach of training and testing with data coming from the same camera, or similar ones. Accordingly, in this paper we address the challenge of using a virtual world for gathering (while *playing a videogame*) a large amount of automatically labelled samples (virtual humans and background) and then training a classifier that performs equal, in real-world images, than the one obtained by equally training from manually labelled real-world samples. For doing that, we cast the problem as one of *domain adaptation*. In doing so, we assume that a small amount of manually labelled samples from real-world images is required. To collect these labelled samples we propose a non-standard *active learning* technique. Therefore, ultimately our human model is learnt by the combination of virtual and real world labelled samples (Fig. 1), which has not been done before. We present quantitative results showing that this approach is valid.

ICMI'11, November 14–18, 2011, Alicante, Spain.

Categories and Subject Descriptors

I.4.8 [**Image Processing and Computer Vision**]: Scene Analysis—*Object recognition*

General Terms

Experimentation, Performance

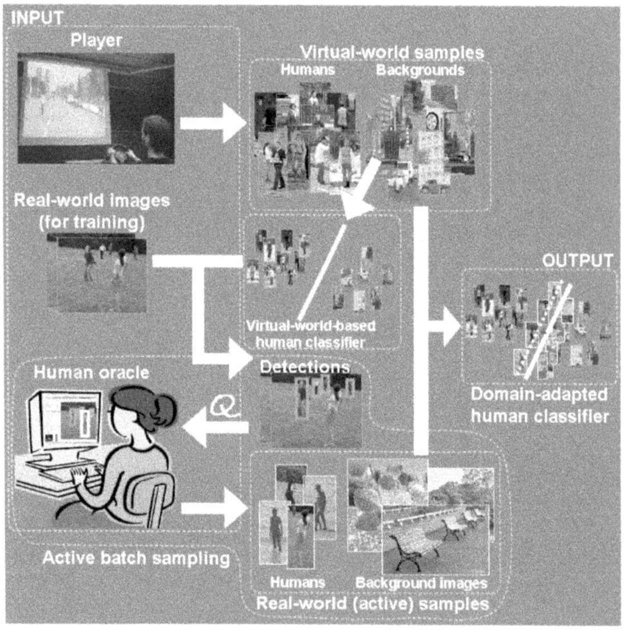

Figure 1: By playing a videogame we automatically gather labelled samples of virtual humans and backgrounds, which are used to learn a human classifier. This classifier is applied to real-world images, collecting all detections. Then, for each real-word image, we ask a human oracle if it is a human-free image; if not, non-detected humans must be labelled by him/her. Finally, a new classifier is learnt by using the original virtual-world samples and the actively collected real-world ones. Thus, virtual world is adapted to real world by active learning, highly reducing the human-based labelling effort.

1. INTRODUCTION

Image based human detection is of paramount interest due to its potential applications in fields such as advanced driving assistance, video surveillance and media analysis. However, in reading some recent surveys of the field [10, 13] we see that even detecting non-occluded standing humans remains challenging. This is not surprising due to the great variety of backgrounds (scenarios, illumination) in which humans are present, as well as their intra-class variability (pose, clothe, occlusion). Nowadays, the most relevant baseline human detector relies on a (holistic) human classifier that uses the so-called histograms of oriented gradients (HOG) as features, and the support vector machines (SVMs) as learning method [7, 6]. New methods have been developed on top of this baseline in order to take into account relative pose of human parts [12], to handle occlusions [20], to take advantage of color [19], etc.

One can deduce, from the state-of-the-art proposals in this field, that the most promising human detectors rely on classifiers developed by following the discriminative paradigm, *i.e.*, trained with labelled samples. Being, HOG and SVM key ingredients. However, labelling is an intensive manual step, especially, in cases of human detection where labelling objects (humans) means to provide at least bounding boxes. Note that this is more costly for a *human labeller* than just answering *yes/no*-questions like *is there any human in this image?* (*i.e.*, without specifying *where* in the affirmative cases). In addition, it is well accepted that having sufficient variability in the labelled samples is decisive to train classifiers able to generalize properly [4]. However, traditional (passive) manual labelling do not evaluate the degree of variability achieved by the labelled samples. A common approach is assuming that the larger the set of labelled samples the higher the variability. However, subjectively adding more examples only does not guarantee higher variability, *e.g.*, it can happen that we are just adding human samples too similar to the ones we already collected. Accordingly, different authors have worked in the problem of reducing the labelling burden.

In [5] a hierarchy of synthesized (non-realistic) *pedestrian*[1] templates are used for pedestrian detection in far infrared images, *i.e.*, images capturing relative temperature. However, the authors admit poor performance and high computational cost.

In [9] a set of pedestrians is first manually segmented, and then different types of transformations (jittering, mirroring, shape deformations, texture variations, etc.) are applied to obtain joint pedestrian and background variability. A classifier is then learned following the discriminative paradigm. Local receptive fields with neural networks, and so-called Haar filters with SVM are tested. Since the mentioned transformations encode a generative model, the overall approach is seen as a generative-discriminative learning paradigm. The generative-discriminative cycle is iterated several times in a way that new synthesized samples are added in each iteration by following a probabilistic *selective sampling* to avoid redundancy in the training set. The reported results show that this procedure provides classifiers of the same performance than when increasing the number of training samples with new manually labelled ones. However, the authors show that much of the improvement comes from enlarging the training set by applying jittering to the pedestrian samples as well as by introducing more background ones. Note that jittering does not involve synthesizing pedestrians since it only requires shifting their framing bounding box (assuming a little background frame around the pedestrian), *i.e.*, it is introduced to gain a certain degree of shift invariance in the learnt classifiers. Besides, to apply the different proposed transformations the overall pedestrian silhouette must be traced, which requires a manual labelling may times more labor intensive than standard bounding box framing of pedestrians.

In [1] a pure *active learning* technique is used. In particular, starting 215 passively (arbitrary) labelled pedestrians and sufficient background samples, a pedestrian classifier is constructed using an AdaBoost cascade, where the weak rules are single-feature decision stumps, and the features are referred as YEF (yet even faster). This classifier is applied to unseen videos and detections are presented to a *human oracle* that has to report if they correspond to actual pedestrians or to background (false positives). In fact, not all detections are presented to the oracle. First, only image windows that intersect a predefined horizon line are examined. This reduces the application of the current classifier to around 170,000 windows. Then, from these windows, just those classified with a score falling into the ambiguity region of the current classifier are passed to the oracle. Once a full video is processed, the new collected (labelled) samples together with the previous ones are used to retrain a new classifier, *i.e.*, the active learning follows a *batch* scheme. The process is iterated with new videos until a desired performance is achieved (determined by hold-out validation in the labelled data, 2/3 for training and 1/3 for testing).

Finally, in [14] it is proposed the use of a realistic videogame in order to capture labelled samples of pedestrians and background by *playing*. More specifically, a *driver* moves a virtual car equipped with a forward facing virtual camera along the road of a virtual city, and all the pedestrians appearing in the image are automatically extracted up to a precise pixel-level segmentation (from which it is trivial to obtain a bounding box). The pixels of the image not labelled as pedestrian pixels are considered background. The challenge then is to see if the appearance of the virtual pedestrians and background is sufficiently realistic to lead to a pedestrian model that can be successfully applied in real images. For that, again, a discriminative paradigm is followed. In particular, HOG features and linear SVM are used. The presented results show that, when using HOG/linear-SVM, the pedestrian classifier trained with only virtual data is totally equivalent, in terms of performance, to its counterpart trained using real images.

In this paper, we are not interested only in pedestrian detection as in [5, 9, 1, 14], but in detecting humans out of cities as well. On the other hand, with these works we share the interest of reducing manual labelling. In fact, collecting good data at low cost for training appearance-based classifiers is a new research area as reviewed in [3]. Roughly speaking, we establish three levels of labelling from the point of view of object detection: (1) LIL: image level (*is there an object inside this image? yes/no*); (2) LBBL: bounding-box level (*e.g., framing objects inside the images with rectangles*); (3) LPL: pixel level (*e.g., delineating the silhouette of the objects present in the images*). In [3]several tech-

[1]In this paper we use the term *pedestrian* to refer to a human as a traffic participant of an urban area.

Figure 2: Our framework for acquiring virtual images with pixel-level groundtruth of pedestrians.

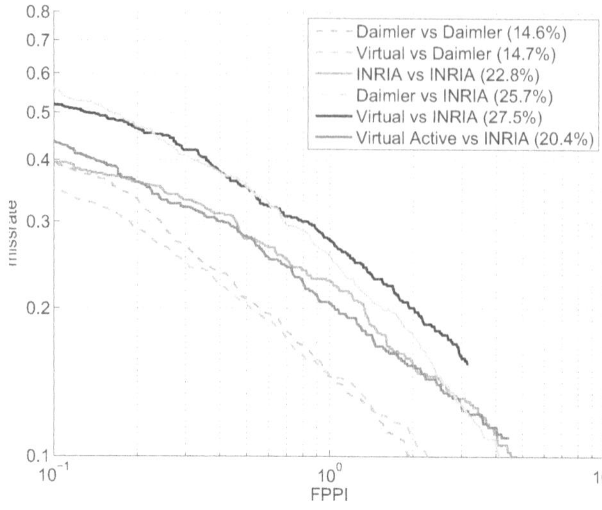

Figure 3: Per-image evaluation of different pedestrian detectors. The notation *DB1 vs DB2*, means that the corresponding classifier was learnt using *DB1* training data, and evaluated in *DB2* testing data. Daimler refers to the data sets used in [10, 14] for pedestrian detection (videos taken from a car inside a city). INRIA refers to a widely used data set for human detection first introduced in [7, 6] (it contains photographic images). Virtual refers to the data sets we have collected in our virtual city (with automatic labelling of pedestrians). In all cases the percentage inside the parenthesis indicates the missrate for one false positive per image. Virtual active refers to the approach in this paper (Fig. 1).

niques are reviewed to automatically collect labelled samples from the internet using context (*e.g.*, the captions of the figures). This is not trivial and it is focused only on LIL, which is useful for applications like image retrieval. However, for applications that require locating objects inside an image only manual-based labelling of type LBBL and LPL is reported (*e.g.*, using the web-based Amazon's Mechanical Turk[2]). Note, that LBBL is far more costly than LIL, and LPL much more expensive than LBBP. In fact, in order to reduce such a tedious tasks, some approaches [18] try to transform it into a web-based interactive game.

According to the exposition done so far, we choose the approach proposed in [14]. There are several reasons for that, which we summarize in the following. Videogames are reaching very high degrees of realism, not only at the objects level but even at reproducing the characteristic spectral slope of natural images [15]. Besides, the videogame industry is one of the most powerful worldwide, so players are abundant. In addition, in the near future realistic videogames will be an internet-based experience, allowing the possibility for collecting labelled data from many virtual scenes in centralized special sites (game servers). In fact, computers on their own could be playing games, thus not needing human players. Note, that videogames have generative models behind (scene formation, character design, physic laws, artificial intelligence, etc.). Thus, precise contextual information can be obtained, not only noisy context like when using the internet for collecting data [3].

Currently, like in [14], we have a software that can obtain a continuous labelling of pedestrian pixels by driving through a virtual city (Fig. 2), *i.e.*, groundtruth of type LPL, the most difficult to collect manually. This is done frame by frame, thus not only appearance-based features can be used, but also temporal features as well as temporal processes (*e.g.*, tracking as in [16]). Note, that such temporal information can not be obtained by approaches like [5, 9, 1] because it is totally prohibitive in practice. In the future we will use more than one virtual camera, so that even stereo data acquisition can be simulated (similar to [17]).

In order to address our problem of human detection, we followed the approach in [14], *i.e.*, we developed a pedestrian detector as follows. We collected a data set of images acquired at urban scenarios with labelled pedestrians. Then we learnt a HOG/linear-SVM classifier with such virtual labelled samples. For building the whole pedestrian detector, the pedestrian classifier must be completed with a previous stage that selects windows to be classified from the image (pyramidal windows search) and with a posterior stage that eliminates redundant detections due to shift-invariance of the classifier (non-maximum-suppression) [13]. For such pre- and post-classifier stages we also followed the suggestions in [14]. Finally, we tested the learnt pedestrian model in the video sequences of Daimler A.G. [10] as done in [14]. The obtained *per-image*[3] performance can be seen in Fig. 3 compared to the one obtained by learning the pedestrian classifier using manually labelled pedestrians of Daimler real-world images. In both types of training, virtual and real, we used the same amounts of samples. Basically, the conclusion is the same than in [14], namely, both pedestrian models lead to pedestrian detectors of analogous performance.

For the more general problem of human detection we followed the same scheme than before. In this case our experiments were based on the widespread INRIA dataset for human detection [7, 6]. The differences between Daimler and INRIA datasets are that while the former is composed of video sequences of urban scenarios, the latter is composed

[2]www.mturk.com

[3]In the so-called *per-image* evaluation it is usually plotted the number of false positives (pedestrians) per image vs the missrate (ratio of undetected pedestrians). The overlapping measure between detections and groundtruth, required for such evaluation, is the proposed in PASCAL VOC challenge [11]. It is worth mentioning that one false positive per image is an interesting point of such performance curve for pedestrian detection in the driving assistance context, since, if such noise is not correlated from frame to frame, then it could be easily removed by temporal coherence analysis.

Figure 4: Top: virtual pedestrians and city scenarios. Bottom: INRIA photographs with humans and diversified scenarios as city, countryside, beach, etc. Humans appear also in such scenarios.

of photographic pictures of people in different environments (city, countryside, beach, etc.). Besides, humans in INRIA were captured with more resolution than pedestrians in Daimler. Thus, using our virtual samples, we trained a new pedestrian classifier for INRIA using a canonical pedestrian window of higher resolution than for Daimler. Then, we applied the corresponding pedestrian detector to the testing set of INRIA dataset. Again, we compared the obtained results with the counterpart human classifier learnt from the training data of INRIA dataset, *i.e.*, using images of the real world. As can be appreciated in Fig. 3, the performance provided by the virtual-based classifier is significatively worse than that provided by the real-based one (the real-based one is giving the performance reported in [7, 6]). There is a doubt here of whether the difference comes from the virtual-vs-real training style, or that the human detection is different from pedestrian detection in the sense that the former must deal with more types of environments (not only cities) and with more pose variability than the pedestrians one (most can be catalogued as side/frontal/rear-views while walking). In other words, doubts remain if the HOG/linear-SVM scheme fails to be robust to world changes or if we have a problem of *domain adaptation* [2], or both. In order to assess this question, we also learnt a pedestrian classifier adapted to INRIA resolution by using Daimler training data (up-scaling the images was required). The results of applying the corresponding detector in the INRIA training set are plotted in Fig. 3 too. Note that they are analogous to those obtained with the virtual-based pedestrian detector. It is worth mentioning that the number of pedestrians/humans used for training was the same independently of the training data (virtual, INRIA and Daimler), and the same for background examples (Fig. 4 shows samples from virtual and INRIA datasets). Thus, we argue that, in fact, we are facing a problem of domain adaptation.

Accordingly, in the context of virtual worlds we have the option of developing other environments out of cities in which to capture virtual humans with corresponding labelling. However, if the HOG/linear-SVM scheme is not totally world invariant we still could have troubles reaching the performance of classifiers based on real-world images for training. The same can happen with other features, since HOG/linear-SVM scheme still remains as a state-of-the-art baseline [8, 19]. Thus, we propose to face the domain adaptation problem. Therefore, we assume that a small amount of manual annotations from real-world images is required. In particular, in order to transform virtual-world learnt pedestrian classifiers into real-world human classifiers, we explore an *active learning* scheme (summarized in Fig. 1) that brings together virtual-world automatically labelled data and difficult-to-classify real-world data actively labelled by a human oracle. As far as we know, such across-world training has not been done before in the field of human detection.

Comparing our approach to previously mentioned works we observe the following. In [9] the major benefit came from jittering, as we have mentioned, including jittering and mirroring is always easy (in fact, training done for obtaining Fig. 3 already incorporate such operations). Besides, further work using temporal features is not possible, while with virtual data it is. In addition, in [9] the state-of-the-art HOG/linear-SVM baseline it is not tested. Moreover, [9] requires LPL for a set of pedestrians in order to initialize the proposed generative model, while virtual-world-based approach does not require initial manual labelling. In [1] such baseline is not tested either. Besides, neither the used video sequences nor the code are publicly available. In addition, the proposed active learning scheme can lead to a high number of *yes/no*-questions. Moreover, some *yes*-answers can be given to pedestrians just roughly aligned in the detected window (extrem jitter) which can significantly drop further training based on densely computed features as widespread HOG and Haar, *i.e.*, the most promising ones [8, 19]. As we will see, our proposal does not suffer from that. We share with [1] the use of a batch approach during active learning, for computation efficiency. However, as we will see, our selective sampling scheme is different since in [1] the training and testing domains are the same, *i.e.*, images captured from the same camera, which is not our case. Again, [1] requires LBBL for a set of pedestrians in order to learn the initial pedestrian classifier, while virtual-world-based approach does not require initial manual labelling. With respect to [14], the approach we present here incorporates domain adaptation by batch active learning in order to transform pedestrian detectors in human detectors by jointly considering virtual-world labelled data and a small amount of real-world manually labelled data. In fact, we will demonstrate how just by simply using the 25% of the labelled data of the INRIA training set, together with the virtual training set, we achieve the same or better performance than by using the whole INRIA training set alone (Fig. 3). Additionally, note that in our proposal, the input of the human users (those contributing in the process of training classifiers) is of multimodal nature: player/driver and oracle roles.

The rest of the paper is organized as follows. In Sect. 2 we provide more details of our proposal. In Sect. 3 we draw our experiments, discussing the corresponding results. Finally, Sect. 4 summarizes the main conclusions of our work.

2. FROM PEDESTRIAN TO HUMAN CLASSIFIERS USING ACTIVE LEARNING

Let us start by introducing some notation and concepts. We denote by $\mathcal{D}_s$ and $\mathcal{D}_t$ two domains from which we observe samples. We refer to $\mathcal{D}_s$ as the *source* domain, while $\mathcal{D}_t$ is the *target* domain. Our problem is that given a sample $x_t \in \mathcal{D}_t$, we want to know if $x_t \in w_t$, using w_t to denote the samples in $\mathcal{D}_t$ with a particular property in which we are interested in. We want to face this problem by learning a classifier $\mathcal{C}$ able to answer if $x_t \in w_t$. To learn $\mathcal{C}$ we want to follow a discriminative paradigm, *i.e.*, learning from labelled samples. If $x_t \in \mathcal{D}_t$, its corresponding label ℓ_{x_t} equals $+1$ if $x_t \in w_t$ and -1 otherwise. It turns out that we have very few labelled samples drawn from $\mathcal{D}_t$ as to learn a reliable classifier. However, we have sufficient labelled samples drawn from $\mathcal{D}_s$. If the distributions of the samples in $\mathcal{D}_s$ and $\mathcal{D}_t$ are uncorrelated, then we have nothing to do. However, if they have a sufficient correlation, then we are facing a problem of *domain adaptation* [2]. More specifically, we can use the large amount of labelled data from $\mathcal{D}_s$ and a low amount of labelled data from $\mathcal{D}_t$ to learn a $\mathcal{C}$ with chances of succeeding in the task of classifying unseen samples from $\mathcal{D}_t$. Roughly speaking, our $\mathcal{D}_s$ is the set of image windows cropped from virtual images, and our $\mathcal{D}_t$ the set of image windows cropped from the real-world images in which we want to detect humans. A sample x_t is just an image window, w_t is the property of imaging a human (*human* class), and $\mathcal{C}$ a human classifier.

Since we can collect in a cheap way as many examples as we need from our virtual cities, the setting for $\mathcal{D}_s$ holds. However, we assume that we start with no labelled samples from $\mathcal{D}_t$. As we have seen in Sect. 1 (Fig. 3), a pedestrian classifier trained on virtual samples works quite well when applied to real-world video sequences of city driving. Then we can assume that there is sufficient correlation between $\mathcal{D}_s$ and $\mathcal{D}_t$, at least to the *eyes* of the features and base learning machine we use, *i.e.*, as we have already mentioned in Sect. 1, HOG features and linear SVM. Of course, as we deduce also from results in Fig. 3, $\mathcal{D}_s$ and $\mathcal{D}_t$ are not equal at all. In our case, $\mathcal{D}_t$ is more general (*i.e.*, human detection is more general than pedestrian detection) because more types of scenarios are faced ($\mathcal{D}_s$ is urban like).

Therefore, our problem reduces to obtain some labelled samples from $\mathcal{D}_t$, in an inexpensive way. For that, our proposal consists in following an *active learning* procedure using a *human oracle* to label *difficult samples* from $\mathcal{D}_t$. Usually, the difficult samples are defined as those falling in the ambiguity region of the base classifier at hand. For instance, in the case of a SVM this may correspond to the area inside the margins. However, in these cases, $\mathcal{D}_s$ and $\mathcal{D}_t$ are, in fact, the same distribution and the aim is to label as few samples as possibles but being meaningful. Our case, however, is different. Let us say that $\mathcal{C}_s$ has been learnt from $\mathcal{D}_s$ (using HOG and linear SVM) and that $x_t \in \mathcal{D}_t \wedge x_t \in w_t$. If $\mathcal{C}_s(x_t)$ is a negative value, large in magnitude, it turns out that from the viewpoint of $\mathcal{D}_s$, x_t is far from being in w_t, from imaging a human in our case. In our domain adaptation proposal, we do not consider such x_t as an outlier. On the contrary, these are the informative samples for adapting the domains, *i.e.*, the samples that must label the human oracle.

Accordingly, given a collection of real-world images it is processed using $\mathcal{C}_s$ to detect pedestrians. Detections are kept. By detections we consider those image windows x_t for which $\mathcal{C}_s(x_t) > th$. For our SVM, $|\mathcal{C}_s(x_t)| \geq 1$ means to be out of the learnt margins. Then, a working session is started in which such images and detections are presented to the human oracle. The responsibility of the oracle is to say if a given image contains no humans (*yes/no*-question) and to label missed humans with a rectangular bounding box (Fig. 5). Once the whole sequence is processed by the oracle, a new classifier is trained using the labelled samples that were used to build $\mathcal{C}_s$ (virtual-world ones) as well as the new collected difficult samples (real-world ones). This type of active learning is termed as *batch mode*, because a set of images is processed before re-training. The overall approach is summarized in Fig. 1. We think that a noticeable fact is to use virtual- and real-world samples to train a human classifier, something not done before, to the best of our knowledge. This kind of process can be iterated in order to incrementally obtain better classifiers.

Some additional details are that: (1) each real-world sample labelled by the oracle is mirrored to duplicate the number of positives; (2) for each new positive we collect ten negative ones (because everything not being a human is background) from the images labelled as *human-free*, we call this 1:10 ratio and it is pretty common in human detection [7, 10, 14]. If our system must sample N negatives, it selects the N closest to th (and larger) according to the classification score. The initial $\mathcal{C}_s$ is learnt following such ratio as well.

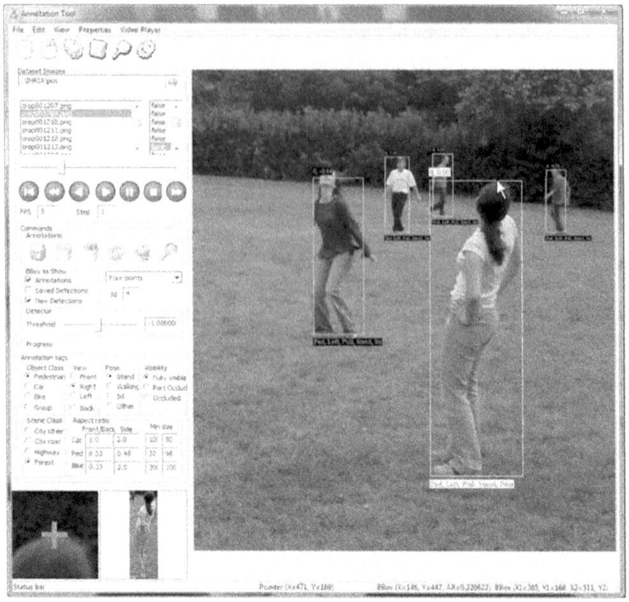

Figure 5: Snapshot of our labelling tool. For each displayed image, the human oracle (see Fig. 1) does the following tasks: (1) if there are not humans in the image, he/she marks this image as *human-free*; (2) if there are humans, some of them have been detected by the previous classifier (green bounding boxes), but others may not (not framed). The undetected humans must be manually framed by the human oracle (yellow bounding boxes).

3. EXPERIMENTAL RESULTS

Datasets.

In this section we conduct a series of experiments for assessing the goodness of the proposal sketched in Sect. 2. However, instead of actually having a human oracle *working actively*, we will use a dataset passively labelled beforehand by a human oracle. In this way we can compare fully passive labelling with *simulated* active one. In particular, as we pointed out in Sect. 1, we will use the widespread INRIA dataset for human detection [7, 6].

INRIA dataset is divided in separated sets of null intersection for training and testing, say $\mathcal{I}^{\text{train}}$ and $\mathcal{I}^{\text{test}}$, resp. The training set contains 2,416 *positive* samples consisting in image windows (original plus vertical mirror, *i.e.*, 1,208 manually labelled samples), each one containing a human framed by a certain amount of background. We term this set of windows as $\mathcal{I}_+^{\text{train}}$. For collecting *negative* samples, *i.e.*, image windows that do not contain humans, there are 1,218 human-free available images. We term this set of images as $\mathcal{I}_-^{\text{i,train}}$. Windows are randomly collected from $\mathcal{I}_-^{\text{i,train}}$ to fulfil a ratio of ten negatives per one positive sample (1:10 ratio), we term $\mathcal{I}_-^{\text{train}}$ the collected negative windows. All positive and negative windows are down-scaled to a canonical window size. After this, we define $\mathcal{I}^{\text{train}} = \mathcal{I}_+^{\text{train}} \cup \mathcal{I}_-^{\text{train}}$. The testing set consists of: (1) $\mathcal{I}_-^{\text{i,test}}$: 453 human-free images; (2) $\mathcal{I}_+^{\text{i,test}}$: 288 images containing 563 labelled humans (ground truth). Therefore, we define $\mathcal{I}^{\text{test}} = \mathcal{I}_-^{\text{i,test}} \cup \mathcal{I}_+^{\text{i,test}}$.

Passive learning.

As we mentioned in Sect. 2 we use HOG features and Linear SVM learning machine for training human/pedestrian classifiers. We follow the implementation proposed in [7, 6] as well as the parameter settings identified as the best ones in these works. We also apply the mirroring technique to double the number of training samples. Accordingly, we train the human classifier using $\mathcal{I}^{\text{train}}$ and the pedestrian one using $\mathcal{V}^{\text{train}} = \mathcal{V}_+^{\text{train}} \cup \mathcal{V}_-^{\text{train}}$. The cardinality of $\mathcal{I}_+^{\text{train}}$ and $\mathcal{I}_-^{\text{train}}$ equals the one of $\mathcal{V}_+^{\text{train}}$ and $\mathcal{V}_-^{\text{train}}$, resp. During training, *bootstrapping* is used, *i.e.*, appending the respective negative training sets with hard negative samples and re-training. Hard negatives are collected from the corresponding negative training images by applying the initially learnt classifier. The process is iterated until very few new negatives are incorporated. In practice, these training sets saturate with a single step. Let us refer by $\mathcal{C}_{\mathcal{I}}^{\text{pas}}$ to the passively learnt classifier based on $\mathcal{I}^{\text{train}}$, and by $\mathcal{C}_{\mathcal{V}}^{\text{pas}}$ to the equivalent one based on $\mathcal{V}^{\text{train}}$.

Active learning.

Given $\mathcal{C}_{\mathcal{V}}^{\text{pas}}$, we have conducted several experiments following our proposal (Sect. 2), where $\mathcal{I}^{\text{train}}$ is used as real data set for performing the (simulated) active learning. We denote by $\mathcal{C}_{\mathcal{V}}^{\text{act}}$ any classifier learnt by using $\mathcal{V}^{\text{train}}$ and samples actively collected from $\mathcal{I}^{\text{train}}$.

Discussion.

Experiments have been conducted to give different insights about our proposal (*e.g.*, dependence of the results on th, on the p:n ratio, etc.), always using $\mathcal{I}^{\text{test}}$ for testing. Performance curves of Fig. 6 summarize the results obtained in our experiments, and draw us to the following observations:

- According to Fig. 6-(1), even introducing a 2% ($th = -2$, 27 new manually labelled humans) of samples from $\mathcal{I}^{\text{train}}$ (1:10 ratio, *i.e.*, one from $\mathcal{I}_+^{\text{train}}$ and ten from $\mathcal{I}_-^{\text{train}}$) provides a $\mathcal{C}_{\mathcal{V}}^{\text{act}}$ of better performance than $\mathcal{C}_{\mathcal{V}}^{\text{pas}}$. Using $th \leq -1$ (*i.e.*, negative score out of the uncertainty area of $\mathcal{C}_{\mathcal{V}}^{\text{pas}}$) implies to improve performance (the best is at the margin border (*i.e.*, in $th = -1$), which implies to consider the 20% of samples from $\mathcal{I}^{\text{train}}$ (manually labelling 246 new humans[4]).

- It is also worth mentioning that we trained a classifier using only the actively collected real-world samples from $\mathcal{I}^{\text{train}}$ ($th = -1$, 1:10 ratio). The performance was quite poor (100% missrate at one FPPI), thus, denoting that such real samples are a complement of the virtual ones, but they are not useful on their own.

- According to Fig. 6-(2,3), introducing either only positive or only negative samples from $\mathcal{I}^{\text{train}}$ (*i.e.*, from $\mathcal{I}_+^{\text{train}}$ and $\mathcal{I}_-^{\text{train}}$, resp.) can improve slightly the performance of $\mathcal{C}_{\mathcal{V}}^{\text{pas}}$, again if $th \leq -1$, but still remaining far from $\mathcal{C}_{\mathcal{I}}^{\text{pas}}$.

- According to Fig. 6-(4), it seems that the ratio 1:10 for introducing actively obtained samples from $\mathcal{I}_+^{\text{train}}$ and $\mathcal{I}_-^{\text{train}}$, is a good compromise. The ratio 1:1 already offers significative performance improvements with respect to $\mathcal{C}_{\mathcal{V}}^{\text{pas}}$.

- According to Fig. 6-(1,5), it seems that by randomly sampling $\mathcal{I}^{\text{train}}$ in equivalent amounts to the considered active selection of samples (*i.e.*, for $th \in \{-2.0, -1.5, -1.0, -0.5, 0.0\}$), we obtain similar performance improvements. In fact, the active method is slightly better. In this context, such a random sampling would correspond to the human oracle labelling humans from $\mathcal{I}^{\text{train}}$ on his own. However, it is unclear if by doing so the human oracle would actually provide random samples; it may be the case that he/she is biased to cases that he/she likes more. Thus, all these above observations have led us to recommend the active paradigm, after all, the labelling effort is the same.

- Finally, Fig. 6-(6) simulates the case in which the human oracle only labels a certain percentage of the undetected humans. We see that even only labelling a 25% (61 new labelled humans) of the cases already provides a $\mathcal{C}_{\mathcal{V}}^{\text{act}}$ clearly better than $\mathcal{C}_{\mathcal{V}}^{\text{pas}}$. Missing the 25% of the labelling suggested by the active procedure is unnoticeable (185 humans would be labelled).

After this analysis there is still a remaining question: *what type of humans need manual labelling?*. In order to answer, we classified all the humans in $\mathcal{I}^{\text{train}}$ according to the scenario where they are. The defined scenarios are: city, beach, countryside, indoor, and snow. There are, resp., 916, 50, 138, 87, and 17 humans. Thus, 292 humans are not from the city. Therefore, most of the humans are of the type used for training $\mathcal{C}_{\mathcal{V}}^{\text{pas}}$ (*i.e.*, pedestrians) but the 32% are not.

[4]Manual labelling of 250 human bounding boxes takes around 25 minutes using the program shown in Fig. 5.

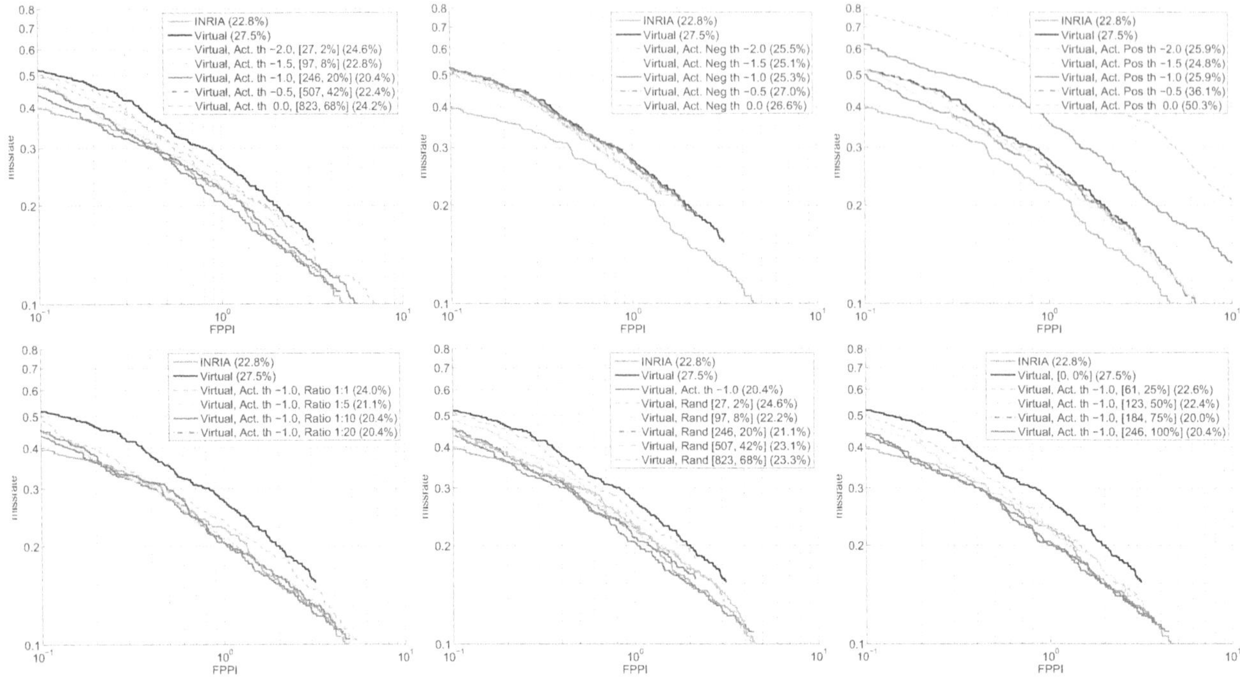

Figure 6: The percentage inside the parenthesis is the missrate at FPPI=10^0. In all cases the testing set is $\mathcal{I}^{\text{test}}$. Label 'Virtual' refers to using $\mathcal{V}^{\text{train}}$ as training set. The different 'Active' curves correspond to different ways of complementing $\mathcal{V}^{\text{train}}$ by actively taking examples from $\mathcal{I}^{\text{train}}$. *Top, from left to right*: (1) Results for different th, $[N, P]$ refer to the number of samples (N) chosen from $\mathcal{I}_{+}^{\text{train}}$ given th, and P is the corresponding percentage. From $\mathcal{I}_{-}^{\text{train}}$ we take $10N$, *i.e.* 1:10 ratio. (2) Analogous to '(1)' but only considering the samples taken from $\mathcal{I}_{-}^{\text{train}}$. (3) Only considering the samples from $\mathcal{I}_{+}^{\text{train}}$. *Bottom, from left to right*: (4) Analogous to '(1)' but changing the ratio of positive vs negative samples actively taken from $\mathcal{I}_{+}^{\text{train}}$ and $\mathcal{I}_{-}^{\text{train}}$, resp., running from 1:1 to 1:20. (5) Analogous to '(1)' but instead of using the th rule we just sample randomly $\mathcal{I}_{+}^{\text{train}}$ and $\mathcal{I}_{-}^{\text{train}}$, taking the same percentage of samples than for the considered th in '(1)'. (6) Results for $th = -1.0$ but rather than to take all the samples of $\mathcal{I}_{+}^{\text{train}}$ fulfilling such threshold condition, we only take the percentage in brackets. Of course, we take also the number of samples from $\mathcal{I}_{-}^{\text{train}}$ that keeps the 1:10 ratio.

Accordingly, $\mathcal{C}_{\mathcal{V}}^{\text{pas}}$ should not be far away from $\mathcal{C}_{\mathcal{I}}^{\text{pas}}$ in performance, as it happens, but $\mathcal{C}_{\mathcal{I}}^{\text{pas}}$ is also expected to be $\mathcal{C}_{\mathcal{I}}^{\text{pas}}$ better. Of course, we are assuming that the data distributions of $\mathcal{I}^{\text{train}}$ and $\mathcal{I}^{\text{test}}$ are correlated as is to be expected too. We have checked that the active learning procedure suggests to label the following distribution of humans, according to the same scenarios: 156, 14, 24, 46, and 6. These numbers correspond to the 17.03%, 28.00%, 17.39%, 52.87%, and 35.29% of each scenario, resp. Note that 90 humans to be labelled are not from the city (30% of the ones to be labelled). This confirms that some pedestrians where not well represented by the $\mathcal{C}_{\mathcal{V}}^{\text{pas}}$ model, however, most of the badly represented in percentage correspond to indoor, snow, beach, countryside and, finally, city. We think that these results reinforce our approach of casting the performance gap between $\mathcal{C}_{\mathcal{I}}^{\text{pas}}$ and $\mathcal{C}_{\mathcal{V}}^{\text{pas}}$ as a domain adaptation problem, and that batch active learning can be effective to address it.

As summary Fig. 7 plots the performance of $\mathcal{C}_{\mathcal{I}}^{\text{pas}}$, $\mathcal{C}_{\mathcal{V}}^{\text{pas}}$ and the best $\mathcal{C}_{\mathcal{V}}^{\text{act}}$ ($th = -1$, 1:10 ratio). Additionally, we include the performance of a classifier obtained by passive learning using all the examples in $\mathcal{I}^{\text{train}}$ and $\mathcal{V}^{\text{train}}$. Note that, in this case, just mixing samples from different worlds in a blind way just harms the performance of both $\mathcal{C}_{\mathcal{I}}^{\text{pas}}$ and $\mathcal{C}_{\mathcal{V}}^{\text{pas}}$.

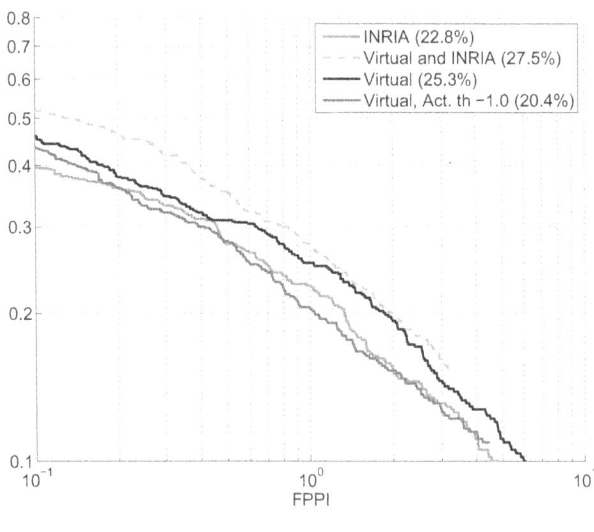

Figure 7: Final comparative results.

4. CONCLUSION

In this paper we have addressed a core problem in the field of human detection, namely, the acquisition at low cost of good samples to train. In order to collect most of the human and background samples we rely on players/drivers of a videogame, *i.e.*, we automatically collect labelled samples while enjoying a game. With them we learn a virtual-world based pedestrian classifier that must work as a human classifier in images depicting the real world. In city scenarios, those where the pedestrian classifier is initially trained, the exhibited performance is equivalent to the one obtained by a counterpart real-world based classifier, *i.e.*, requiring costly manual labelling. However, in scenarios out of the city, both types of classifiers can not reach the performance of a classifier learnt using data manually labelled for training in such new scenarios. In order to keep the advantage of the cost-free labelling in virtual-worlds, we have cast the problem of transforming the virtual-world based pedestrian classifier into a human classifier for real world images of general scenarios, as a domain adaptation problem. To perform the adaptation, we have proposed a batch active learning technique that, with just a few manually labelled humans from the real images, is able to reach the same performance than a human classifier entirely trained from a much large amount of manually labelled data. Ultimately, or human classifier has been trained by using samples from virtual and real worlds, which is totally new in the field of appearance based human detection, to the best of our knowledge. We observe that, in a way, we have adopted a multimodal approach from two view points: (1) using two different types of raw data (virtual and real), and (2) collecting the data by playing in the one hand and by working on the other. Finally, we would like to mention that our proposal can be extended in the future in several ways, *e.g.*, detecting other targets and incorporating spatio-temporal features, just to mention a few. Using incremental learning machines, *e.g.* incremental SVM, will be also assessed with the aim of eliminating the batch mode from the active learning to see if the manual labelling can even be more reduced.

Acknowledgments

This work was supported by the Spanish MICINN, in particular by projects TRA2010-21371-C03-01 and Consolider Ingenio 2010: MIPRCV (CSD200700018).

5. REFERENCES

[1] Y. Abramson and Y. Freund. SEmi-automatic VIsuaL LEarning (SEVILLE): a tutorial on active learning for visual object recognition. In *IEEE Conf. on Computer Vision and Pattern Recognition*, San Diego, CA, USA, 2005.

[2] S. Ben-David, J. Blitzer, K. Crammer, A. Kulesza, F. Pereira, and J. Vaughan. A theory of learning from different domains. *Machine Learning* , 79(1):151–175, 2009.

[3] T. Berg, A. Sorokin, G. Wang, D. Forsyth, D. Hoeiem, I. Endres, and A. Farhadi. It's all about the data. *Proceedings of the IEEE* , 98(8):1434–1452, 2010.

[4] C. Bishop. *Pattern Recognition and Machine Learning.* Springer, 2006.

[5] A. Broggi, A. Fascioli, P. Grisleri, T. Graf, and M. Meinecke. Model–based validation approaches and matching techniques for automotive vision based pedestrian detection. In *IEEE Conf. on Computer Vision and Pattern Recognition*, San Diego, CA, USA, 2005.

[6] N. Dalal. *Finding people in images and videos.* PhD Thesis, Institut National Polytechnique de Grenoble / INRIA Rhône-Alpes, 2006.

[7] N. Dalal and B. Triggs. Histograms of oriented gradients for human detection. In *IEEE Conf. on Computer Vision and Pattern Recognition*, San Diego, CA, USA, 2005.

[8] P. Dollár, C. Wojek, B. Schiele, and P. Perona. Pedestrian detection: a benchmark. In *IEEE Conf. on Computer Vision and Pattern Recognition*, Miami Beach, FL, USA, 2009.

[9] M. Enzweiler and D. Gavrila. A mixed generative-discriminative framework for pedestrian classification. In *IEEE Conf. on Computer Vision and Pattern Recognition*, Anchorage, AK, USA, 2008.

[10] M. Enzweiler and D. Gavrila. Monocular pedestrian detection: survey and experiments. *IEEE Trans. on Pattern Analysis and Machine Intelligence* , 31(12):2179–2195, 2009.

[11] M. Everingham, L. V. Gool, C. Williams, J. Winn, and A. Zisserman. The PASCAL visual object classes (VOC) challenge. *Int. Journal on Computer Vision* , 88(2):303–338, 2010.

[12] P. Felzenszwalb, D. McAllester, and D. Ramanan. A discriminatively trained, multiscale, deformable part model. In *IEEE Conf. on Computer Vision and Pattern Recognition*, Anchorage, AK, USA, 2008.

[13] D. Gerónimo, A.M. López, A.D. Sappa, and T. Graf. Survey of pedestrian detection for advanced driver assistance systems. *IEEE Trans. on Pattern Analysis and Machine Intelligence* , 32(7):1239–1258, 2010.

[14] J. Marín, D. Vázquez, D. Gerónimo, and A.M. López. Learning appearance in virtual scenarios for pedestrian detection. In *IEEE Conf. on Computer Vision and Pattern Recognition*, San Francisco, CA, USA, 2010.

[15] T. Pouli, D. Cunningham, and E. Reinhard. Image statistics and their applications in computer graphics. In *European Computer Graphics Conference and Exhibition*, Norrköping, Sweden, 2010.

[16] G. Taylor, A. Chosak, and P. Brewer. OVVV: Using virtual worlds to design and evaluate surveillance systems. In *IEEE Conf. on Computer Vision and Pattern Recognition*, Minneapolis, MN, USA, 2007.

[17] W. van der Mark and D. M. Gavrila. Real-time dense stereo for intelligent vehicles. *IEEE Trans. on Intelligent Transportation Systems* , 7(1):38–50, 2009.

[18] L. von Ahn, R. Liu, and M. Blum. Peekaboom: a game for locating objects in images. In *ACM SIGCHI Conf. on Human Factors in Computing Systems*, Montréal, Québec, Canada, 2006.

[19] S. Walk, N. Majer, K. Schindler, and B. Schiele. New features and insights for pedestrian detection. In *IEEE Conf. on Computer Vision and Pattern Recognition*, San Francisco, CA, USA, 2010.

[20] X. Wang, T.X. Han, and S. Yan. An HOG-LBP human detector with partial occlusion handling. In *Int. Conf. on Computer Vision*, Kyoto, Japan, 2009.

Making Virtual Conversational Agent Aware of the Addressee of Users' Utterances in Multi-user Conversation using Nonverbal Information

Hung-Hsuan Huang
Department of Information & Communication Science,
Ritsumeikan University, Japan
hhhuang@acm.org

Naoya Baba
Graduate School of Science and Technology,
Seikei University, Japan
dm116233@cc.seikei.ac.jp

Yukiko Nakano
Department of Computer and Information Science,
Seikei University, Japan
y.nakano@st.seikei.ac.jp

ABSTRACT

In multi-user human-agent interaction, the agent should respond to the user when an utterance is addressed to it. To do this, the agent needs to be able to judge whether the utterance is addressed to the agent or to another user. This study proposes a method for estimating the addressee based on the prosodic features of the user's speech and head direction (approximate gaze direction). First, a WOZ experiment is conducted to collect a corpus of human-human-agent triadic conversations. Then, analysis is performed to find out whether the prosodic features as well as head direction information are correlated with the addressee-hood. Based on this analysis, a SVM classifier is trained to estimate the addressee by integrating both the prosodic features and head movement information. Finally, a prototype agent equipped with this real-time addressee estimation mechanism is developed and evaluated.

Categories and Subject Descriptors

H.1.2 [**User/Machine Systems**]: Human factors; H.5.2 [**User Interfaces**]: Evaluation/methodology; I.2.1 [**Applications and Expert Systems**]: Games, Natural language interfaces

General Terms

Design, Experimentation, Human Factors

Keywords

Virtual agent applications and empirical studies, Multimodal interaction, Verbal and nonverbal expressiveness, Agents in games and virtual environments

1. INTRODUCTION

Various kinds of kiosk information systems are used in public places, such as shopping malls, museums, and visitor centers. The typical situation in which such systems are used is that a group of people stand in front of the kiosk and operate it in order to retrieve the information they request while talking with one another. Therefore, in order to implement conversational agents that can serve as an information kiosk in public places, multi-party conversation functionality for simultaneous interaction with multiple users is indispensable. In dyadic dialogues where only two participants are involved, it can be assumed that in most cases, one participant is the addressee when the other one participant is speaking. In multi-party dialogues, however, distinctions must be made among the roles of the participants, such as speaker, addressee, and listeners standing by. When a person is involved in a human-human-agent triadic conversation, he/she may speak to the agent or may talk to the other person (his/her partner). When the person speaks to the agent, the agent needs to respond to that utterance. However, when the person speaks to the partner, the agent should not mistakenly respond to that utterance. Therefore, one of the basic functionalities a conversational agent needs in order to engage in multi-party conversation is the ability to identify the addressee of each user utterance.

Based on this need, this paper presents a work that aims to determine the addressee of user utterances in triadic conversations among two users and an agent. In the literature, [10, 3, 20], it has been reported that in addition to their explicit verbal utterances, humans use nonverbal signals such as their gaze, nods, and postures to regulate their conversation, e.g., to show their intention to yield or willingness to take turns in speaking. If there are specific patterns in the user's gaze behavior that depend upon whom he/she is talking to, it would be possible for the kiosk agent to automatically identify the addressee. Thus, as regards eye-gaze approximation, this study will exploit head direction information obtained from a face-tracking system. It has also been found that in human multi-party conversations and human-robot communication, not just visual cues such as eye gaze and head direction are useful in predicting the addressee, but prosodic cues of the voice as well [22, 9]. In this study, both visual and prosodic cues are exploited. To establish an addressee estimation model based on such multimodal information, first, a corpus of human-human-agent triadic conversations is collected in a Wizard-of-Oz (WOZ) experiment. Second, an analysis is performed regarding how visual and prosodic cues correlate with the addressee-hood, and the labeled data is then used to train a support vector machine (SVM) classifier that has an up to 80% degree of accuracy. A real-time addressee estimation subsystem for embodied conversational agents is then developed and evaluated.

This paper is organized as follows. The next section discusses previous studies related to analyses of addressee-hood as well as addressee estimation. Then, in Section 3, the WOZ experiment that was conducted for corpus collection is introduced. Section 4 presents an analysis of how visual and prosodic cues correlate

ICMI'11, November 14–18, 2011, Alicante, Spain.

with addressee-hood. Section 5 proposes an addressee estimation method based on visual or/and prosodic cues, and Section 6 presents a real-time addressee estimation system and an evaluation of that system. The paper concludes with a discussion of the results and future directions for research.

2. RELATED WORKS

Many studies on the processes of recognition and interpretation in multi-party meetings have been done in the AMI and AMIDA projects [18] and in projects by DARPA [25, 26]. By applying speech and natural language processing technologies, a number of useful components were developed in these projects, such as speech transcription, speaker diarization, and meeting summarization. Identifying the addressee is also an important issue in meeting interpretation. In addition to linguistic and contextual information, it was found that eye gaze provides useful information in identifying the addressee in multi-party human conversations [16, 15, 4]. Moreover, research on human communication showed that the eye gaze is an important communication signal in face-to-face conversations. The speaker looks at the addressee to monitor her/his understanding or attitude, and, the addressee looks at the speaker in order to be able to offer positive feedback in return [10, 1]. Eye gaze also plays an important role in turn taking. When yielding his/her turns to speak, the speaker looks at the next speaker at the end of his/her utterances [3]. Vertegaal [24] reported that the gaze is a reliable predictor of addressee-hood. Likewise, Takemae [21] provided evidence that the speaker's gaze indicates addressee-hood and plays a regulatory role in turn management.

Similar results were found in mixed human-human and human-computer conversations in [22, 14, 2]. In these works, perception experiments were conducted in which subjects guessed who the addressee of a given utterance was. It was found that prosodic and visual cues were about equally effective, and that the combination of auditory and visual cues resulted in better performance. Moreover, the motivation of [9] was quite similar to that of this study, in that researchers proposed a method of identifying the addressee in a human-human-robot interaction by combining prosodic and visual cues. As a visual cue, they used the horizontal head orientation to distinguish addressees. They reported that in 35% of the cases, a person talked to the other human while looking at the robot. They then addressed the fact that visual cues alone might not be sufficient, and proposed the further incorporation of prosodic cues. As prosodic cues, they identified a number of linguistic features obtained from the speech recognition system, such as sentence length, typical phrases, and language models, and used them to distinguish the addressee from the other human. They reported that the speech addressed to the robot was detected with an F-measure of 0.72.

In this study, we share a similar motive but tackle the problem using a different approach. First, to estimate the head direction, we add more parameters, namely the position and rotation of the head. We also focus on shifts in head direction during an utterance. As for the prosodic cues, while [9]focused on linguistic features, we assume that the user's tone of voice may be different depending on whether he/she is speaking to the agent or to the partner. Thus, to measure the user's tone of voice, this study focuses on pitch, intensity (volume), and the rate of speech as the most important prosodic features [19]. It has already been found that prosodic features are useful in the recognition of emotion, and can thus be expected to be useful in characterizing the tone of voice. Considering all these aspects discussed in previous studies, this study employs machine learning techniques to create an automatic classifier for estimating the addressee via the integration of visual and prosodic information.

3. INTERACTION CORPUS COLLECTING WOZ EXPERIMENT

To collect the video corpus for an analysis of addressee-hood in human-agent multi-party conversation, a WOZ experiment on two information-retrieval tasks was conducted.

3.1 Experiment setting

Pairs of subjects were instructed to interact with a life-size virtual agent on a screen, and to retrieve information in order to make a joint decision regarding given tasks. As shown in Figure 1, the subjects stood about 1.5 m away from the screen and interacted with a female virtual character. Each pair was instructed to complete two decision-making sessions as follows:

Lecture registration task: the subjects were instructed to request help in choosing 3 out of 12 lectures to attend together the next semester. The information about the lecturer, textbook, course difficulty, prerequisites, etc. for each lecture was defined in advance. The lectures were divided into four categories: information science, engineering, languages and communication, and social science. The subjects could freely ask the agent "mentor"for any information about the lectures or the agent itself, and then discuss this on their own in order to make a final decision. To increase the likelihood of inter-subject negotiation, each subject was asked to set up a "busy" half-day in which their schedules were in conflict so they could not attend class together.

Travel planning task: the subjects were instructed to enact a situation in which they had a coupon from a travel agency that allows them to visit 3 of 14 sightseeing spots in Kyoto for free. The information, which includes a brief history, highlights, nearby restaurants, for each location was defined in advance. The sightseeing spots were divided into the northern, western, eastern and central areas of Kyoto. The participants were instructed to complete their task by freely retrieving information from the "travel agent" agent, and to discuss their decisions on their own.

Half of the subject pairs performed the lecture registration task first, and the other half performed the travel planning task first. In addition to the subject pairs who acted as kiosk users, four students who major in computer science were recruited to operate the WOZ agent. They were chosen due to their familiarity with operating a GUI-based WOZ application, which ensured that there would be smooth interaction. The operators were asked to practice on the WOZ user interface for one hour prior to the experiment to further ensure that the agent's response time was quick enough. All the sentences that the agent could speak during the experiment were listed in a menu where relevant sentences were grouped for the WOZ operator to select from. There was also a text field that allowed them to type arbitrary utterances, in case these were needed. The WOZ operators were instructed to try to limit the interaction sections to 10 minutes, if possible. They were also instructed to try to actively help the subjects who participated the experiment in user role, that is, to provide useful information on their own even if the users did request that information.

3.2 The subjects

A total of 21 pairs of university students were recruited as subjects for the experiment, all of whom were native Japanese speakers. The students came from various departments ranging from literature to engineering, and their average age was 20.1 years. Of the 21 pairs, 14 were male pairs and seven were female pairs. In this study, only 17 pairs (10 male and 7 female pairs, or 34 subjects) were analyzed. Not all of the collected data were used, due to insufficient quality. Some subjects nearly always laughed loudly, so their voice data could not be used. Others nearly always faced each

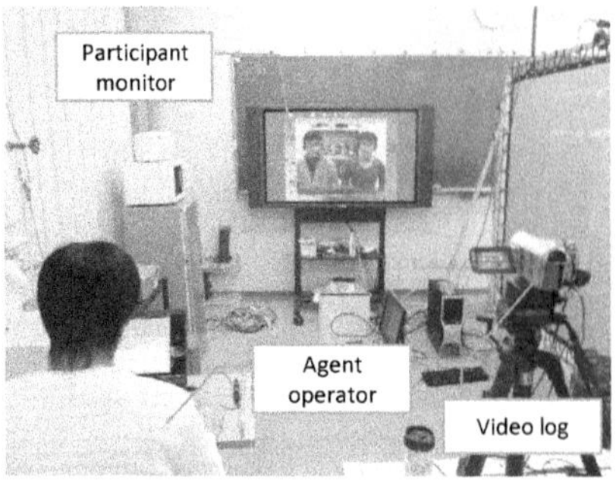

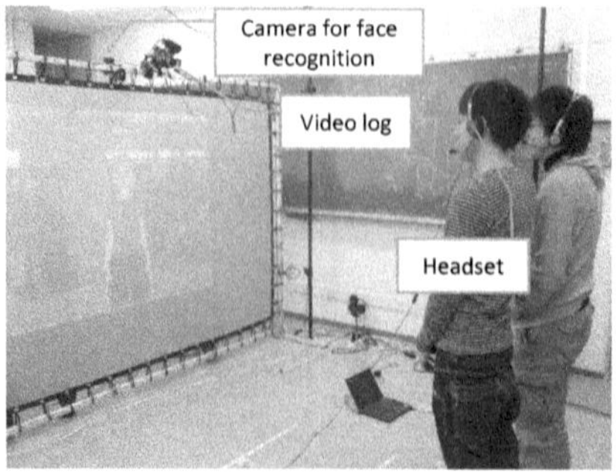

Figure 1: Setup of WOZ experiment to collect data for the interaction corpus: (a) WOZ operating booth, (b) information providing agent and participants. The booth is hidden behind a curtain so the subjects cannot see the operator

other, so their head movements could not be recorded correctly. All of the participants' interactions with the agents were recorded by two video cameras (in front of and behind them). In addition to these regular video cameras, a USB webcam (960 x 720 pixels, 30 fps) was set on the top of the screen (Figure 1). Each subject was equipped with a wireless Bluetooth headset to transmit their voice.

4. CORPUS ANALYSIS

4.1 Data preparation

Because of the fact that the interactions between the participants and the agent (or the WOZ operator) appeared to be smoother in the second session, only the data recorded in the second sessions was analyzed, which resulted in the analysis of 6 lecture registration conversations and 11 travel planning conversations. The average length of a conversation in each session was 629 seconds. Because the longer sessions could have a stronger influence on the machine learning results, we only used the first 10 minutes of each conversation. This resulted in an average corpus length of 524 seconds. The corpus was prepared for further analysis in the following two steps.

1. Identification of individual utterances from raw audio track: first, the speech audio was divided into utterances as a unit of analysis. The speech was automatically separated using a Julius adintool [12]. When more than 200 ms of silence was observed, it was automatically identified as the end of the current utterance, and the subsequent speech was regarded as a new utterance. Through this process, 1,830 utterances were identified and saved as speech audio.

2. Manual labeling on the addressee of each utterance: using the video annotation tool Anvil 4.7.7 [11], two coders annotated the speaker and the addressee for each utterance identified by the process in Step 1, and used these labels as the ground truth. The results of labeling are shown in Table 1. Because the face tracking software sometimes did not capture the face of the user being tracked, head tracking data was available for only 1,237 utterances (67.6% of the corpus).

4.2 Analysis of prosodic features

The characteristics of pitch, intensity, and rate of speech of each user utterance were selected as prosodic features. In previous studies in the field of affective computing, it was found that voice pitch and intensity are useful indicators for identifying a user's emotion. In the corpus collection experiment introduced in Section 3, it could also be observed that the subjects' tone of voice seemed to differ, depending on whether they were speaking to the agent or to their partners. Moreover, the subjects seemed to speak more slowly when they were speaking with the agent. This may be because they had low expectations of the agent's capacity to understand them.

Table 1: Labeled results of collected corpus regarding gender of speaker and available information of the utterances

	Voice		Head Tracking		Corpus
	Agent	Partner	Agent	Partner	Size
Male	509	522	415	410	1,031
Female	354	445	207	205	799
Total	863	967	622	615	1,830

4.2.1 *Prosodic feature extraction*

The prosodic features of each utterance were extracted using a speech analysis tool, Praat [1]. Two separate Praat scripts were used to calculate the pitch (fundamental frequency or F_0) and intensity at 0.01-second intervals. The rate of speech was calculated using another Praat script by measuring the number of phonemes in each utterance, and the value was further divided by the utterance length (second). Thus, the number of phonemes per second was used as the speech rate feature.

4.2.2 *Correlation between prosodic information and addressee-hood*

Figure 2 shows an example of how prosodic and visual information are correlated with addressee-hood. The transcription of each utterance is shown at the top of the figure. F_0 and the intensity of these utterances are shown below the transcription. Utterance (a) is addressed to the agent, and utterance (b) is addressed to the partner. As shown in the graphs, F_0 in utterance (a) is higher than it is in (b) (the average F_0 for each kind of utterance was 167 Hz and 120 Hz, respectively). Likewise, comparing the intensity of these utterances, the peaks in utterance (b) are higher than those in utterance (b) (which had an average intensity of 64 dB and 61 dB, respectively).

Based on the above observations, we calculated the averages of the F_0 and intensity for each utterance. We also computed the speech rate per utterance. These results are shown in Table 2. As can be seen in the table, there were obvious differences in how the subjects talked to the agent and one another. The F_0 and intensity are higher when the person was speaking to the agent than when speaking to the partner. In addition, the speech rate was slower when the person was speaking to the agent. These results suggest that people speak to the agent with a higher tone of voice and also

[1] http://www.fon.hum.uva.nl/praat/

Table 2: Results of prosodic analysis. All these features showed a statistically significant difference by t-test between the utterances addressed to the agent and those addressed to the other subject (partner), except for the F_0 of female subjects

	F_0 (Hz)		Intensity (dB)			Speech Rate (phoneme/s)			Duration (s)		
	Male	Female	Male	Female	Combined	Male	Female	Combined	Male	Female	Combined
Agent	131.6	241.3	63.8	63.6	63.7	4.59	4.65	4.61	1.99	2.22	2.08
Partner	124.3	233.0	60.2	60.7	60.4	4.91	5.10	4.99	0.96	1.06	1.00
p	<.01	.08	<.01	<.01	<.01	<.01	<.01	<.01	<.01	<.01	<.01

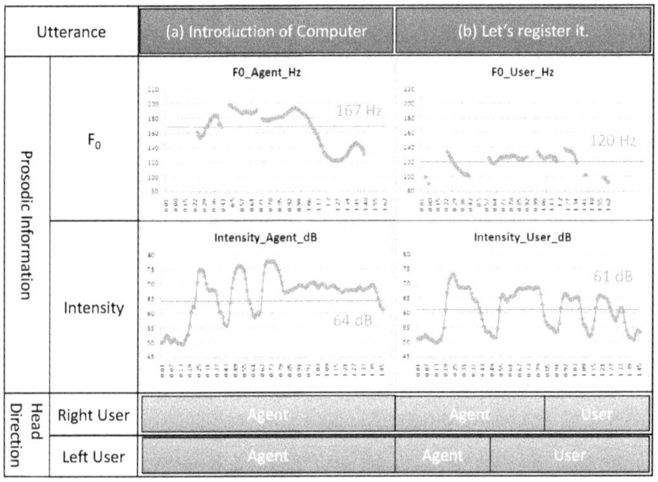

Figure 2: Example of prosodic information and head direction. Utterance (a) and (b) are spoken to the agent and the partner, respectively

speak more loudly and slowly. We consider that these prosodic cues are useful in estimating the addressee.

4.3 Analysis of head direction

4.3.1 Automatic identification of head direction

The video data collected in the experiment were analyzed using the face tracking software FaceAPI [2], which can measure the head position and rotation in terms of the x, y, and z axes. In order to eliminate the influence of different users (their distance from the screen, habits when speaking, etc.) and to prevent overfitting to slight head movements, for the purpose of estimating the addressee, only three conditions of the users' head directions were considered relevant to the final result: facing the agent, facing the partner, or facing elsewhere. The head directions of four randomly chosen pairs (or eight subjects) were manually labeled as target values (forward, left, and right for each subject). For example, in the case of the subject who is standing on the left side, he/she is evaluated as looking at the agent if he/she faces forward, as looking at his/her partner if he/she faces to the right, or as facing elsewhere if he/she faces to left. All of the six head-pose data and their measurement confidence scores were used as input teaching data. A C4.5 [17] decision tree was then trained with the Weka [5] data mining tool. The results of the decision tree learning are shown in Table 3. As a result of 10-fold cross-validation, the classification accuracy of the learned model was 97.2%. Since this is a good enough degree of accuracy, this model was used to automatically label the head direction of the entire corpus (the four manually labeled groups were relabeled with the decision tree).

[2]http://www.seeingmachines.com/product/faceapi/

Table 3: Results of learning for head direction evaluation

	Precision	Recall	F-measure
Agent	0.982	0.984	0.983
Left	0.935	0.940	0.937
Right	0.929	0.900	0.914
Accuracy	97.20 %		

4.3.2 Correlation between head direction and addressee-hood

It was assumed that the subjects were looking at the agent when speaking to the agent, and looking at the partner when speaking to the partner. To measure the correlation between head direction and addressee-hood, the degree of agreement between head direction and the addressee label that was manually annotated in Section 4.1 was computed. By looking at the 30fps video data frame by frame (30fps), 49,129 samples of head direction data were obtained. These frames were then used for analyzing the time ratio the addressee looked at by the speaker. The subjects looked at the agent for 93.2% of time when they were talking to it. On the other hand, the speaker only looked at his/her partner for 33.5% of time when talking one another (65.0% for the agent). This result suggests that there would be difficulty to identify the other user as the addressee using time ratio of head direction alone. However, there should be some patterns of head direction that can contribute to the estimation. Further improvement of accuracy can be expected with additional prosodic information.

5. ADDRESSEE ESTIMATION METHOD

Previous sections reported that prosodic information regarding the voice and head direction were expected to be useful in predicting the addressee in triadic human-agent conversations. In this section, we propose a method for estimating the addressee that utilizes a machine learning technique.

5.1 Definition of feature set

To consider both prosodic and visual cues in judging the addresseehood, the following features were selected based on the empirical results reported in Section 4. As the prosodic cues, the average pitch (F_0), intensity, rate of speech, and duration for each utterance (feature f_{p1}, f_{p2}, f_{p3}, f_{p4}) were used. In addition, as a parameter for measuring the difference from regular values, the F_0 and differences in intensity from the average of all the subjects were used.

- f_{p1}: average F_0 of the utterance
- f_{p2}: average intensity of the utterance
- f_{p3}: speech rate of the utterance

- f_{p4}: duration of the utterance
- f_{p5}: difference between f_{p1} and the average of F_0 for all the subjects
- f_{p6}: difference between f_{p2} and the average intensity for all the subjects

As head direction features, we used the ratio of the time looking at the agent/partner/elsewhere to the duration of the utterance, and bigrams of the head direction transitions. We defined four types of bigrams. For example, parameter f_{h4} is a head direction shift from the agent to the partner. All the combinations were defined as features, except for partner->elsewhere and elsewhere->partner, because these combinations needed to be divided into two shifts: partner->agent and agent->elsewhere, and vice versa. These seven features were also applied to the other subject who was not speaking, as the status of the partner's head direction. Thus, the following 14 features were used as head direction information.

- f_{h1}: ratio of the time the speaker spends looking at the agent to the duration of the current utterance.
- f_{h2}: ratio of the time the speaker spends looking at the partner to the duration of the current utterance.
- f_{h3}: ratio of the time the speaker spends looking elsewhere to the duration of the current utterance.
- f_{h4}: the number of shifts in head direction from the agent to the partner in the current utterance (agent->partner).
- f_{h5}: the number of shifts in head direction from the agent to elsewhere in the current utterance (agent->elsewhere).
- f_{h6}: the number of shifts in head direction from the partner to the agent in the current utterance (partner->agent).
- f_{h7}: the number of shifts in head direction from elsewhere to the agent in the current utterance (elsewhere->agent).

5.2 Results of automatic classification

A feature set composed of 20 features (6 prosodic features and 7 x 2 = 14 head direction features for the speaker and the partner) was used to extract training data from the corpus for SVM classifier training (called SMO in the Weka implementation, with a polynomial kernel value of C=1). Three classifiers were trained by using prosodic features only, head direction features only, and the full set of 20 features. Since the prosodic characteristics differ, depending on the gender of the speaker, the classifiers for male speakers and female speakers were trained separately. The utterances for which head tracking data were absent were not used for the head direction classifier training. The classification results are shown in Table 4.

To sum up the results, in terms of accuracy, the performance of the classifiers slightly exceeds 80%. The F-measure values ranges from 0.5 to 0.8. The data for male and female subjects was then integrated by adding a gender feature to the original feature set. The performance was then slightly worse than that of the male model talking to the agent. No notable decline in performance could be observed for the combined classifier, which demonstrated a 80.3% degree of accuracy, as compared to 80.0% for the male and 80.1% for the female classifier. This same observation was also the case for the F-measure values.

The classifier with the full set of features always performed better than the prosodic or head-direction-only classifiers in all metrics. This means that there are a number of coincidences between the visual (head direction) and prosodic cues, and they do not contradict one another.

The head direction features distinguish utterances that are addressed to the agent better than prosodic features do. This confirms the observations made during the experiment. When the subjects were talking to the agent, they had a strong tendency to keep looking at the agent and seldom looked at their partners. On the other hand, when they were talking to their partner, they did not always turn to face their partners but remained facing the agent. This may be due to the social relationship of the participants in the triadic dialogue. The two subjects know each other well and are friends in most cases, while the agent is not part of their group and is unfamiliar to them.

On the other hand, the prosodic cues performed better in distinguishing the utterances addressed to the partner. This implies that the subjects had a strong tendency toward shorter, faster, and lower toned speech when talking with their partners, and used a more varied speaking style with the agent. This was particularly true for female subjects, who seemed to enjoy their conversation with the agent more than male subjects. Some of the female subjects were excited throughout the session and spoke loudly, even with their partners. This difference in gender behaviors may be due to the influence of the female agent. Female subjects may feel empathy more easily, while male subjects maintained a greater social distance from the agent. Such differences in speaking may make it difficult for the training algorithm to distinguish the prosodic characteristics of utterances that are addressed to the agent.

6. PROTOTYPE VIRTUAL AGENT SYSTEM

Based on the SVM classifier obtained in the previous section, a real-time addressee identifying subsystem was implemented. This subsystem is being integrated into a prototype virtual agent system which currently consists of automatic speech recognition, prosodic analysis, head-direction evaluation, addressee estimation, dialogue management, and character animation components.

6.1 System architecture

The system components are run simultaneously on the GECA [6] platform; the overall system architecture is shown in Figure 3. The functionalities of each component are described below.

Automatic Speech Recognition (ASR) component: each user is equipped with a headset that takes his/her voice and transmits it to a speech recognizer that is connected to the headset. The speech recognizer is a wrapped Julius Japanese ASR engine. The Julius ASR engine generates the five best hypotheses of spoken Japanese sentences using the words in its dictionary, or the phonemes if no matching words can be found. Practical experience with this engine shows that it has a high degree of precision but a low recall capacity. That is, the word outputs can be considered quite precise (higher than 95%) if they are successfully recognized. In most cases, however, only hypothetical phonemes can be obtained. In order to improve the precision of speech recognition, we therefore used the recognized words if they were available, and measured the Levenshtein distance [13] between the hypothesized phoneme strings and the keywords as defined in an application-dependent keyword table. As a result, only predefined keywords and short phrases with acceptable confidence factors are sent out from the component. This component also generates the events, indicating whether there are voice inputs. These events are used in the Head Direction Evaluation component, which is discussed later.

Prosodic Analysis component: this component receives a speech audio file from the Julius adintool, which intersperses intervals of silence in the speech audio. The prosodic information extraction

Table 4: **Evaluation of addressee classification for male subjects, female subjects, and combined results for collected corpus. The accuracy of each classifier is calculated by 10-fold cross-validation**

			Prosody	Head Direction	Prosody + Head Direction
Male	F-measure	Agent	0.729	0.782	0.807
		Partner	0.759	0.691	0.792
	Accuracy		74.9%	74.4%	80.0%
Female	F-measure	Agent	0.693	0.709	0.793
		Partner	0.802	0.571	0.808
	Accuracy		76.0%	65.3%	80.1%
Combined	F-measure	Agent	0.717	0.759	0.799
		Partner	0.781	0.656	0.806
	Accuracy		75.3%	71.6%	80.3%

component reads the audio file of the utterance, and calls three Praat scripts which then calculate the average of the F_0, intensity, and rate of speech for the utterance. The calculated parameters are then sent to the Addressee Estimation component.

Head Direction Evaluation component: this component receives head pose data from FaceAPI, which can process the data captured from a webcam. Because a single FaceAPI tracking engine cannot track multiple faces simultaneously, the video images from the webcam are duplicated and fed to two FaceAPI tracking engine instances in real time . One engine processes the user standing on the left side (a 60% area on the right-hand side of the original image), and the other one processes the user standing on the right side (a 60% area on the left-hand side of the original image). By applying the head position and rotation data to the decision tree that was created, as discussed in Section 4.3, this component evaluates the speaker's and the partner's head direction and determines whether the speaker is looking at the agent, at the partner, or elsewhere. Since it receives the speaking period events from the ASR component, it can then calculate the feature values for each utterance, such as the time ratio of a given head direction to the utterance, and the frequency of occurrence for each head direction bigram. A set of these feature values is then sent to the Addressee Estimation component.

Addressee Estimation component: this component receives the prosodic and head direction information of one specified user, constructs a set of feature values for the current utterance, and feeds these data to the combined SVM classifier (Section 5.2). The result of the addressee prediction is then sent to the Dialogue Management component.

Dialogue Management component: the speech recognition results and addressee are sent as input for interpretation by the front-end of the Dialogue Management component. The front-end synchronizes the various inputs, identifies their relationships, and interprets them into user intentions (or dialogue moves) as a predefined lexicon. The interpreted results are then stored in an input buffer that is read by the dialogue manager during its update cycles. The dialogue manager is a dialogue move engine based on information state theory [23], and is being implemented on a JAM [8] planning engine. It manages the agent's private knowledge and the shared knowledge with the users. It reads the interpreted dialogue moves from the input buffer of the input interpreter, updates the agent's internal state, and selects the applicable plan that has the highest utility under the current condition. The plan is a list of the agent's own intentions (dialogue moves). While the plan is being executed, the agent's dialogue moves are converted into actual utterances to be spoken and gesture animation commands by the behavior generator component. If the estimated addressee is the agent, the component selects the agent's response. If the estimated addressee is the partner, the component does not choose any verbal response for the agent and the agent behaves like a side-participant. This process is currently being done by template matching. The utterances are then spoken and the animation commands are rendered as character animations by the Character Animator component.

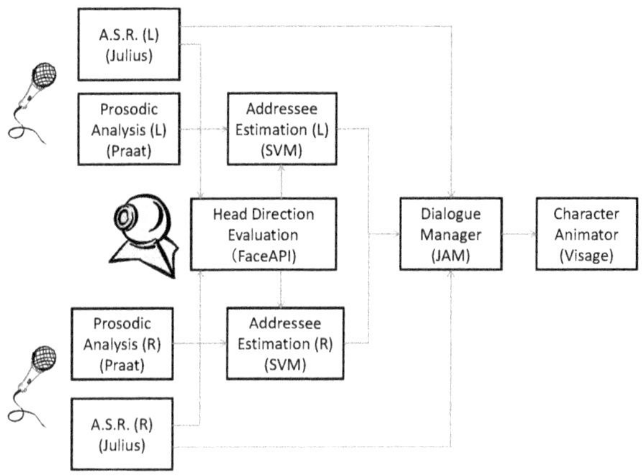

Figure 3: Architecture of prototype agent system

Character Animator component: this component is implemented using the visage|SDK [3] character animation library. The character is projected onto the screen at life-size and is animated with lip-synchronized speech in real time. The status of the animation that is being played is fed back to the related components.

6.2 Evaluation of Addressee Estimation Subsystem

The analysis performed in Sections 4 and 5 was done off-line with manual labeling. It would be interesting to see how the addressee estimation mechanism works when handling unseen data in life. Since the dialogue management component works on the hypothesis wherein the addressees of all input utterances are correctly identified 100% of the time, the dialogue will crash whenever any estimation fails. This prototype agent, then, is simply not ready for practical use. The evaluation was therefore performed by another WOZ experiment in real-time addressee estimation, though the results were not actually used.

6.2.1 Experiment setting and the subjects

The experiment setting is basically the same as the one presented in Section 3, but with some rearrangement. This time the experiment was conducted at Ritsumeikan University, which is close to

[3] http://www.visagetechnologies.com/products.html

Table 5: Summary of evaluation experiment results. The "Annotation" column shows the number of utterances addressed to the agent or the partner, as realized by manual labeling. The "System" column shows the number of system outputs while the "Coincided" column shows the ones which coincide with the manual annotation. The "Accuracy" column indicates the ratio of correctly estimated utterances over the entire corpus

Result	Addressee	Annotation	System	Coincided	F-measure	Accuracy
Error Included	Agent	173	164	125	0.742	68.1%
	Partner	321	438	285	0.751	
Error Excluded	Agent	173	161	125	0.749	83.0%
	Partner	321	333	285	0.872	

Kyoto, so the recruited subjects were considered to be familiar with the sightseeing spots in Kyoto. In order to prevent the possible bias, all subject pairs performed the travel planning task first, to get used to the virtual agent, and only the data of the second task (lecture registration) were used in the analysis. Also, there was only one WOZ operator this time, and he operated the agent from a different room where he was connected with Skype. The data of the six pairs (or 12 subjects) was collected in the evaluation experiment. All the participants were students recruited from Ritsumeikan University. There were four male pairs and two female pairs, with an average age of 22.7 years.

The system was installed in six ordinary PCs with MS Windows: one for the character animator component (Intel Core 2 Duo), one for the head direction evaluation component (Intel Core i7), two sets for prosodic analysis and the addressee estimation components (Intel Core 2 Duo), one for the GECA integration platform and logging (AMD Athlon 64 x2), and one for the WOZ interface (Intel Core 2 Duo) instead of the dialog management component. All of these PCs were connected in the same gigabit LAN. The processing time of each utterance was measured as ranging from 400ms to 530ms. From the observation of preliminary tests, the threshold at which the input sound is divided into utterances was set at 1,000ms, which clearly distinguishes two utterances from one another. Therefore, the total period of latency following the end of one utterance is about 1,500ms. This may not be good enough to create smooth human-human interactions, but should not be too long for a human-agent dialogue.

6.2.2 Evaluation results

Table 5 shows the results of the evaluation experiment. A total of 602 outputs (or utterances) were identified by the system. However, 108 (three are addressed to the agent and 105 are addressed to the partner) of these were triggered by a microphone that mistakenly received sound that did not come from the subject who was wearing it. Most of the outputs came from the other subject, because the two subjects stood close to each other (the system does not accept sound input when the agent is speaking). The results were not satisfying. However, if those errors are removed (the same condition as the learning data which are manually labeled). the results were very encouraging. The level of performance was even slightly better than it was with the learning data (83.0% versus 80.3% in accuracy). The improvements on voice input such as the use of bone-conduction microphone or speaker detection via the difference of intensity from multiple microphones remained as a future work.

7. CONCLUSION AND FUTURE WORK

This paper has proposed a method for estimating the addressee based on prosodic and visual information. First, a WOZ experiment was conducted to assemble a corpus of human-agent triadic conversation. The results of an analysis performed on this corpus showed that the prosodic information such as F_0, intensity, and rate of speech rate were correlated with the addressee-hood. Second, in an analysis of the subjects' head movements, a decision tree was constructed to automatically label the subjects' head direction. In analyzing the correlation between the head direction and the addressee-hood, it was found that head direction is definitely a useful predictor of the addressee, but this information by itself is not robust. Based on these results, a SVM classifier for addressee estimation was trained by integrating both the prosodic and head direction information. A second evaluation experiment was then conducted to evaluate the real-time addressee estimation system based on the SVM classifier. Both the training data and the data from the evaluation experiment could be estimated with approximately an 80% degree of accuracy.

Compared to the method in a previous study by [9], the proposed method performs better when the subject is talking to the agent (F-measures of 0.72 and 0.8, respectively). When the subject is talking to the partner, [9] reported that when a person looked at the partner while speaking, he/she was really addressing the partner in 99.5% of the cases. However, in the data collected for this study, estimating the addressee during conversation with the partner was not so simple, and the task of prediction was much more difficult than it was with their data. To compare the two methods, it would be necessary to consider the situation of the task. The addressee can be identified because a number of different patterns govern how subjects speak to the agent, as opposed to their partners. It can be argued that these patterns exist because of the low quality of the agent (both in outlook and conversational capability) Our previous study [7], however, showed that when a human agent is compared with a virtual agent in a human-human-agent triadic dialogue, the subjects displayed similar reactions to both the human and the virtual character. The patterns in the ways people speak can also be considered to reflect the social relationship between the participants.

As regards future work related to this study, we would first note that this project is still in an early stage and the estimation is not yet very precise. Both the voice and head direction inputs are not reliable enough. More robust face tracking and clearer voice input are required. There is some latency (about 500 ms, as shown in Section 6.2.1) in conducting the output. This can be improved, and if possible, we would like to realize the addressee prediction before the utterance ends, just as humans do. We have not yet analyzed the behaviors of the WOZ operators. The timing and contexts in which the operators decided to intervene in the inter-user conversation is an interesting variable in this experiment. By exploring this in more depth, it should become possible to create virtual agents that are more active and more helpful. The current system cannot actually estimate whether the agent's utterances are grounded with the users. Therefore, only a naive grounding evaluation (i.e., no matter what the agent says, it is understood by the users) can be implemented in the dialogue manager. We would also like to explore the corpus further to see whether there are cues that can be integrated to facilitate the evaluation of grounding. The conversation context estimation is not yet very precise, which means that there will be errors from time to time; such errors cannot be ignored. Presently, every time the agent makes a wrong prediction, and thus, produces a wrong utterance, the dialogue among the users crashes. A mechanism to detect this error automatically and repair the dialogue is an important future work. Both WOZ experiments were conducted in conversations in Japanese, and all the subjects were college students and native Japanese speakers. It is obvious, then, that their learned conversation patterns are culture-, gender-, and age-dependent. It would be interesting to make a deeper investigation of the influences that a human subject's background has upon a partially virtual conversation.

8. ACKNOWLEDGMENTS

Special thanks to Prof. Toyoaki Nishida of Kyoto University and Prof. Igor Pandzic of the University of Zagreb for their useful advice. This work is partially funded by JSPS under a Grant-in-Aid for Young Scientists (B) (23700183) and a Grant-in-Aid for Scientific Research (S) (19100001).

9. REFERENCES

[1] M. Argyle and M. Cook. *Gaze and Mutual Gaze*. Cambridge University Press, 1976.

[2] J. Dowding, R. Alena, W. J. Clancey, M. Sierhuis, and J. Graham. Are you talking to me? dialogue systems supporting mixed teams of humans and robots. In *AAAI Fall Symposium*, 2006.

[3] S. Duncan. Some signals and rules for taking speaking turns in conversations. *Journal of Personality and Psychology*, 23(2):283–292, 1972.

[4] M. Frampton, R. Fernandez, P. Ehlen, M. Christoudias, T. Darrell, and S. Peters. Who is "you"? combining linguistic and gaze features to resolve second-person references in dialogue. In *12th Conference of the European Chapter of the Association for Computational Linguistics*, 2009.

[5] M. Hall, E. Frank, G. Holmes, B. Pfahringer, P. Reutemann, and I. H. Witten. The weka data mining software: An update. *ACM SIGKDD Explorations*, 11(1):11–18, 2009.

[6] H.-H. Huang, A. Cerekovic, Y. Nakano, I. S. Pandzic, and T. Nishida. The design of a generic framework for integrating eca components. In L. Padgham, D. Parkes, and J. P. Muller, editors, *The 7th International Conference of Autonomous Agents and Multiagent Systems (AAMAS'08)*, pages 128–135, Estorial, Portugal, May 2008. Inesc-Id.

[7] H.-H. Huang, S. Takeda, M. Ono, Y. Nakano, I. Pandzic, and T. Nishida. Toward a proactive information providing agent in multi-user collaborative decision-making conversation. In *International Workshop on Interacting with ECAs as Virtual Characters, 9th International Conference on Autonomous Agents and Multiagent Systems (AAMAS'10)*, pages 46–52, Toronto, Canada, May 2010.

[8] M. J. Huber. Jam: a bdi-theoretic mobile agent architecture. In *Proceedings of the third annual international conference on Autonomous Agents (Agents'99)*, pages 236–243, 1999.

[9] M. Katzenmaier, R. Stiefelhagen, and T. Schultz. Identifying the addressee in human-human-robot interactions based on head pose and speech. In *Proceedings of the 6th international conference on Multimodal interfaces (ICM 2004)*, 2004.

[10] A. Kendon. some functions of gaze direction in social interaction. *Acta Psychologica*, 26:22–63, 1967.

[11] M. Kipp. Spatiotemporal coding in anvil. In *Proceedings of the 6th international conference on Language Resources and Evaluation (LREC-08)*, 2008.

[12] A. Lee and T. Kawahara. Recent development of open-source speech recognition engine julius. In *Asia-Pacific Signal and Information Processing Association Annual Summit and Conference (APSIPA ASC)*, 2009.

[13] V. Levenshtein. Binary codes capable of correcting deletions, insertions, and reversals. *Soviet Physics-Doklady*, 10(8):707–710, February 1966.

[14] R. Lunsford and S. Oviatt. Human perception of intended addressee during computer-assisted meetings. In *Proceedings of the 8th international conference on Multimodal interfaces*, ICMI '06, pages 20–27, New York, NY, USA, 2006. ACM.

[15] H. op den Akker and R. op den Akker. Are you being addressed? - real-time addressee detection to support remote participants in hybrid meeting. In *The 10th Annual SIGDIAL Meeting on Discourse and Dialogue (SIGDIAL'09)*, 2009.

[16] R. op den Akker and D. Traum. A comparison of addressee detection methods for multiparty conversations. In *DiaHolmia : 2009 Workshop on the Semantics and Pragmatics of Dialogue*, pages 99–106, Sockhom, Sweden, 24-26 June 2009. KTH Stockholm.

[17] J. R. Quinlan. *C4.5: Programs for Machine Learning*. Machine Learning Representation and Reasoning Series. Morgan Kaufmann, 1993.

[18] S. Renals, T. Hain, and H. Bourlard. Recognition and understanding of meetings the ami and amida projects. In *IEEE Workhshop on Automatic Speech Recognition and Understanding (ASRU'07)*, 2007.

[19] H. Rodriguez, D. Beck, D. Lind, and B. Lok. Audio analysis of human/virtual-human interaction. In *Proceedings of the 8th International Conference on Intelligent Virtual Agents (IVA'08)*, pages 154–161, 2008.

[20] H. Sacks, E. A. Schegloff, and G. Jefferson. a simplest systematics for the organization of turn-taking for conversation. *language*, 50(4):696–735, 1974.

[21] Y. Takemae, K. Otsuka, and N. Mukawa. Video cut editing rule based on participants' gaze in multiparty conversation. In *11th ACM International Conference on Multimedia*, 2003.

[22] J. Terken, I. Joris, and L. D. Valk. Multimodalcues for addressee-hood in triadic communication with a human information retrieval agent. In *Proceedings of the 9th international conference on Multimodal interfaces (ICMI 2007)*, 2007.

[23] D. R. Traum and S. Larsson. *Current and New Directions in Dscourse and Dialogue*, chapter The information state approach to dialogue management, pages 325–353. Kluwer, Dordrecht, 2003.

[24] R. Vertegaal, R. Slagter, G. van der Veer, and A. Nijholt. Eye gaze patterns in conversations: there is more to conversational agents than meets the eyes. In *Proceedings of the SIGCHI conference on Human factors in computing systems*, pages 301–308, 2001.

[25] A. Waibel, M. Bett, M. Finke, and R. Stiefelhagen. Meeting browser: Tracking and summarizing meetings. In *DARPA Broadcast News Transcription and Understanding Workshop*, pages 281–286, 1998.

[26] A. Waibel, M. Bett, F. Metze, K. Ries, T. Schaaf, T. Schultz, H. Soltau, H. Yu, and K. Zechner. Advances in automatic meeting record creation and access. In *Proceedings of the International Conference on Acoustics, Speech, and Signal Processing 2001 (ICASSP'01)*, Seattle, USA, May 2001.

Temporal Binding of Multimodal Controls for Dynamic Map Displays: A Systems Approach

Ellen Haas Krishna Pillalamarri Chris Stachowiak
U.S. Army Research Laboratory
Human Research and Engineering Directorate
Aberdeen Proving Ground, Maryland, USA 21005
01 410 278-5825 01 410 278-5932 01 410 278-4397
Ellen.c.haas.civ@mail.mil Ramakrishna.s.pillalamarri.civ@mail.mil
Christopher.c.stachowiak.civ@mail.mil

Gardner McCullough
University of Maryland Baltimore County
Department of Psychology
Baltimore, Maryland, USA 21250
01 443-417-7463
gar2@umbc.edu

ABSTRACT

Dynamic map displays are visual interfaces that show the spatial positions of objects of interest (e.g., people, robots, vehicles), and can be updated with user commands as well as world changes, often in real time. Multimodal (speech and touch) controls were designed for a U.S. Army Research Laboratory dynamic map display to allow users to provide supervisory control of a simulated robotic swarm. This study characterized the effects of user performance (input difficulty, modality preference, and response to different levels of workload) on multimodal intercommand time (i.e., temporal binding), and explored how this might relate to the system's ability to bind or fuse user multimodal inputs into a unitary response. User performance was tested in a laboratory study using 6 male and 6 female volunteers with a mean age of 26 years. Results showed that 64% of all participants used speech commands first 100% of the time, while the remaining used touch commands first 100% of the time. Temporal binding between touch and voice commands was significantly shorter for touch-first than for speech-first commands, no matter what the level of workload. For both speech and touch commands, temporal binding was significantly shorter for both roads and swarm edges than for intersections. Results indicated that all of these factors can be significant in relating to a system's ability to bind multimodal inputs into a unitary response. Suggestions for future research are described.

Categories and Subject Descriptors

H.1.2. [**User/Machine systems**]: *Human factors, Human information systems, Software psychology.*

General Terms

Human Factors.

Keywords

Multimodal controls, speech, touch.

ICMI'11 November 14-18, 2011, Alicante, Spain.

1. INTRODUCTION

Dynamic map displays can be used for tasks such as delineating the spatial position of different map entities such as vehicles, people, or landmarks [1]. Changes in location or characteristics of dynamic map entities can be made by user control, such as when the user changes the spatial position or characteristics of map objects. Oviatt [1] found that interacting with dynamic map interfaces with multimodal controls as inputs (in her case, pen-based and speech controls) was more advantageous for the user than speech input alone, because unimodal speech control can lead to more user errors, longer task completion times, and greater user frustration. Other researchers [2] found that multimodal controls for dynamic maps allows users to choose which input modality they want to use, in which order, when inputting information. Haas, Fields, Stachowiak, Hill and Pillalamarri [3] explored the use of multimodal touch and speech controls in a dynamic map display to allow U. S. Army Soldiers to maintain supervisory control of a simulated robotic swarm (a large number of small, relatively simple robots capable of autonomous travel and operation) to provide sentry protection to a simulated convoy of four vehicles. These researchers found that multimodal speech and touch control allowed efficient Soldier supervisory control of a dynamic map display showing swarm and convoy spatial information.

The research described in the previous paragraph [1-3] has a "human-centered" viewpoint, which explores the efficiency of human performance in a human-computer interface. However, few researchers have explored a system-centered viewpoint, which examines the effects of human output on enabling the computer system to be more adaptable to multimodal user command [4]. In a human-computer interface dealing with multimodal user input, it is necessary for the system to identify and bind multiple user commands into a unitary response (i.e., to define multiple user control actions as being related to each other as part of the same command) in order to create an interface that is useful to the human operator. In this study, we take a systems approach by characterizing user factors that relate to the system's ability to bind multimodal inputs into a unitary response.

Several researchers [5, 6, 7] found that changes in timing of multimodal commands provide the effective system organizational cues for binding multimodal input. The time between the onset of a first control action (e.g., a speech command) relative to the onset of a second, dependent control action (e.g., a consequent touch command) can be defined operationally as temporal binding, and is critical for the system to correctly interpret the operator's intent. Additionally, as recommended by human factors guidelines, the onset of the touch command should be defined as being that point in time when the participant removed his or her finger from the touchscreen [8]. However, no one has researcher actually measured inter-command temporal binding using this operational definition, or with speech and touch controls. In addition, few researchers have explored user input characteristics that might affect temporal binding. These characteristics include user touch input difficulty when touching different types of screen targets (map locations), user preference in order of commands, and user performance under different levels of workload. These issues are described below.

The first issue is the need to define input difficulty. In considering motor actions with touch screen displays, neither Oviatt [1, 5], Oviatt, Lunsford, and Coulston [9], nor any other researcher, explored human performance using touch commands to identify map locations with different levels of difficulty, such as static (nonmoving) versus dynamic (moving) touch screen locations such as roads, intersections, and the swarm itself. In the above research, all map locations were static and none were differentiated by size. However, emphasis on participant response time and accuracy can have an effect on these factors. If response accuracy was held constant (i.e., by emphasizing accurate responses), the time taken to touch a relatively small location (e.g., an intersection) should be longer than that involved in touching a relatively larger location (e.g., anywhere on a road) [6]. Similarly, the time taken to touch a moving entity should be longer than that required to touch a static entity of the same size. If response time were held relatively constant (i.e., by emphasizing fast response time), accuracy of touch response for moving locations and smaller stationary locations should be less than that for larger stationary locations. Because swarm displays can include moving elements, research should explore the effects of locations of increasing level of difficulty (large static locations, small static locations, and small moving locations) on temporal binding of speech and touch commands, with special care given to emphasis on response time and accuracy.

The second issue is user preference in order of presenting commands. Oviatt, Coulston and Lunsford [9] noted that user preference in the order of which modality is used in commands (henceforth known as preferred modality) is important, because multimodal systems usually have fixed, predefined temporal thresholds between commands. Oviatt et al. noted that a system with a fixed temporal threshold that is too short might not integrate speech and touch signals correctly, causing the system to miss and/or eliminate the second part of a multimodal command, thus increasing system error. Oviatt, Coulston, Tomko, Xiao, Lunsford, Wesson and Carmichel [7] and Raisamo [4] examined user preference in presenting speech and pen commands, or speech and touch commands, but in both experiments, but the speech commands consisted of unconstrained natural language. There has been no study examining user preference using speech and touch commands, where speech commands consisted of short, constrained, speech commands such as those used in military environments.

The third issue concerns the effect of different levels of workload on temporal binding. The Army battlefield is a complex, dynamic environment, involving different levels of operator mental effort (workload) for different tasks, at different points in time. There have been several different theories on the effect of secondary task workload on temporal binding. Naumann et al. [2] noted that different input modalities may interfere with each other in multimodal commands. Jokinen and Raike [10] found that multimodality requires more effort for combination and coordination, and may even increase cognitive load, because the selection of the appropriate modality requires additional cognitive resources. Although no specific research has been found on the effect of different modalities on temporal binding, Reeves, Fuller and Fine [11] found that competing secondary tasks have negative effects on perceptual binding, finding that the addition of a demanding secondary fovea task caused lower levels of perceptual binding than conditions without a secondary task. Thus, higher levels of workload might be a detriment to temporal binding. In this study, we conducted simultaneous primary and secondary tasks, and used the decrement in primary task performance as an operational definition of workload [12], to study the effect of different levels of workload on temporal binding.

The purpose of this study was to characterize the effects of input difficulty, user modality preference, and different levels of workload, on temporal binding time relative to the system's ability to fuse the multimodal user output into a unitary response, in a dynamic map display. The dynamic map used in this study was a human-robot interface providing spatial information regarding a simulated robotic swarm. For map location, we conjectured that small static objects such as intersections would produce longer and more variable temporal binding times, especially when combined with a moderately demanding secondary task. For user preference, we hypothesized that touch-first commands would have a show faster temporal binding than speech-first commands. We hypothesized that the addition of a secondary task would have a detrimental effect on temporal binding of speech and touch.

2. METHOD

2.1 Participants

Participants were 6 male and 6 female employees of the U.S. Army Research Laboratory, with a mean age of 26 years. The voluntary, fully-informed consent of the persons used in this research was obtained by US Army human use regulations [13, 14]. All had normal hearing level (HL) and had normal color vision, as determined by self-report.

2.2. Apparatus

2.2.1. Software.

The swarm software was developed on an Unreal Tournament 2004® (Epic Games Inc.) platform. The software simulated the travel of a 40-member airborne robotic swarm as it protected a 4-member truck convoy, as both traveled across a terrain containing roads, intersections, and buildings. A simulated swarm and convoy were used because limitations of technology, dollar, and time resources would not allow us to use actual robots. SoundForge® software was used for visual measurement of command onset and offset during data analysis. The secondary task was the visual monitoring task from the SynWin multiple task battery from Activity Research Services, Inc. [15].

2.2.2. Hardware.

Audio apparatus included Sennheiser HMD 280 headphones with boom microphone. Visual apparatus included three Intel-based PC computers. Two computers had LCD monitors, and one had a touchscreen monitor. The touchscreen monitor was located directly in front of the participant. A second computer (located to the left of the participant, out the participant's field-of-view) controlled the movement of the swarm and the convoy across the touchscreen monitor used in the primary task. The participant provided touch commands by touching the touchscreen with the index finger of their right hand. A third computer monitor located 45 degrees to the right of the participant was used for the SynWin secondary task, in which the participant gave input by manipulating a computer mouse affixed to the table, below the center of the SynWin task screen.

2.2.3 Stimuli.

The dynamic map display is shown in Figure 1. Intersections were 3 mm x 3 mm (length and width), and roads were approximately 7-10 cm long and 3 mm wide. The swarm had a 10 mm diameter circle, with edges approximately 4 mm in length. The user's eyes were approximately 52 cm away from the screen. Additional visual and audio stimuli played simultaneously, acting as messages from headquarters to signal the start of each interactive map task. An example of a visual stimulus, which appeared as a text message "from headquarters" at the bottom of the touschscreen, defined each map task, is shown in Table 1. The audio stimulus was a pre-recorded binaural audio tone signal (the same sound was heard in both ears), which was played simultaneously over the participant's headphones when a new visual message appeared at the bottom of the screen. The audio signal was a digitally prerecorded sound file which consisted of three simultaneous tones of 1000, 2000 and 3000 Hz, played at 65 dBA. The audio signal had a total duration of approximately 1.0 sec., and sounded once at the beginning of each task. The visual text message remained for the duration of the task.

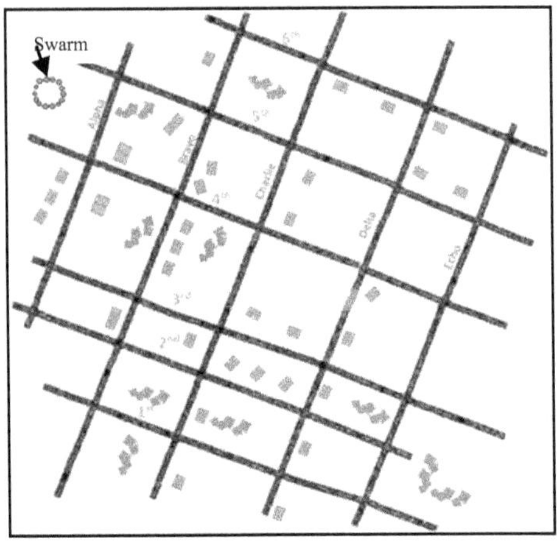

Figure. 1. Dynamic Map Display. Roads are black, buildings and trees are green. Robotic swarm is shown as the circle at upper left-hand corner.

2.2.4 Questionnaires.

Questionnaires included a demographic questionnaire to record the participant's age, gender, and other personal characteristics including number of hours spent using a computer per day. A final questionnaire was administered after the experiment ended to allow the participant to give comments on the ease of use of the multimodal controls.

2.3 Procedure

Each participant was taken to a temperature-controlled trailer near the ARL Ground Vehicle Experimentation Course at Aberdeen Proving Ground, where they filled out the Volunteer Agreement Affidavit. Each was given an audiogram, and asked about their vision to determine whether or not their hearing and vision fit the experimental criteria. Participants who fit the criteria then filled out the demographic questionnaire. Only one participant took part in the experiment at a time.

After a short break, each participant was seated at a workstation and trained to perform the experimental task and the workload task. For the experimental task, each was told that as swarm supervisors, they would hear an audio tone, and see a simultaneous visual message from Headquarters at the bottom of the touchscreen. The text message would specify one specific map object and map location that they must communicate to the swarm in real-time by means of both touch and speech commands. An example of messages from headquarters, and resulting participant touch and speech commands, are seen in Table 1.

Table 1. Examples of map tasks and participant responses

Message from Headquarters (Map Task)	Participant Response
"Put a hot spot anywhere on 1st Street."	In any order, **Say** "hot spot." **Touch** screen anywhere on 1st Street.
"Put a waypoint at the intersection of 2nd Street and Bravo Street."	In any order, **Say** "waypoint," **Touch** screen at the intersection of 2nd Street and Bravo Street.
"Put a target anywhere at the lagging edge of the swarm."	In any order, **Say** "target." **Touch** screen anywhere at the lagging edge of the swarm.

Before the task, the participant placed his or her right hand on the computer mouse located below the center of the SynWin screen to the right of the participant. To give touchscreen commands, participants were told that they must lift their right hand from the computer mouse, and then use the index finger of their right hand to touch the touchscreen at the desired location to emplace an object (target, hotspot, or waypoint) at the specified map location (road, intersection or swarm edge) on the touchscreen. They were to do this as quickly and accurately as possible, and then move their hand back and rest it on the computer mouse after each touch command. To give speech commands, participants were told to speak the name of the map object that they were emplacing (target, hotspot, or waypoint) into the boom microphone connected to their headphones, as quickly and accurately as possible. In order to ensure that the participant used and maintained their natural speech/touch response pattern, participants were told to use touch and speech commands in whatever order they were most comfortable. Participants then received a total of 32 training trials in which they were given feedback by the experimenter (feedback was given during practice trials, but not during experimental trials).

Before trials involving the workload condition, the participant was also trained to perform the SynWin workload task. The participant was told that they were to monitor a gauge labeled "Fuel" that was presented on the computer screen to their right. On this gauge, a pointer slowly moved horizontally from the right to the left of the display, through adjoining blocks colored green (implying a full fuel tank), yellow, and red (implying an empty fuel tank). The participant was to click the left mouse button below the secondary task screen to "refill" the fuel tank before it reached the extreme left of the red area of the display. The participant's mouse click caused the pointer to jump back to the far right on the green area of the display, after which the secondary task was repeated (the pointer began to move to the left again). The participant was told that the closer to the far left in the display the pointer was located when they clicked the mouse button, the greater number of points awarded to the participant for performing this task. The experimenter also informed the participant that the primary task was the most important, and that they should perform this task as quickly and accurately as possible, even to the detriment of the secondary task. The experimenter then practiced performing 10 workload trials, in which the experimenter gave feedback to the participant. After this, the participant performed 36 trials in which they performed the primary and secondary task simultaneously. The experimenter gave feedback to the participant. When this was completed, the participant had a short break.

The participant then performed 72 experimental trials for that particular experimental condition (emplacing map objects and map locations, under one level of workload). After the experimental trials ended, the participant had a 30-minute break, then performed 72 additional experimental trials (emplacing different combinations of map objects and map locations, under a different level of workload). After the last experimental condition, the participant filled out a final questionnaire.

2.4 Experimental Design

The experimental design used for data collection and to structure the data analysis was a 3 (map object) x 3 (map location) x 2 (level of workload) x 2 (preferred order of command modality) full factorial, mixed design. Map object, map location, and workload level were within-subject variables and were manipulated by the experimenter. The preferred order of modality for each command was recorded during the experiment, and was a between-subject variable.

To provide task validity, as well as words with the same number of syllables and duration, the three types of map objects consisted of the words "waypoint," "hotspot," and "target." The three types of map locations were (1) swarm leading or lagging edges (one-dimensional moving points), (2) map intersections (two-dimensional stationary points); and (3) map roads (one-dimensional stationary points). Participant preferred modality (speech or touch command first) was recorded for each command.

Dependent variables for the primary task included the proportion of correct speech and touch commands, the proportion of commands with speech-first and touch-first preferred modality, and inter-command temporal binding time (the difference in time between the onset of the participant's first audio or touch command, and the onset of the second command). As recommended by human factors guidelines, the onset of the touch command was defined as being that point in time when the participant removed his or her finger from the touchscreen [8]. Participant workload ratings and comments were also recorded.

3. RESULTS

3.1 Data Analyses

Data analyses were performed after the conclusion of the experiment. Data for one participant (participant #11) were eliminated because the data indicated that the participant did not fully understand the experimental task. Data analyses included the proportion of accurate speech and touch commands, and the proportion of speech or touch commands used first in each command, for each subject. For temporal binding times, a natural log transformation was performed to give the data a normal distribution [16]. An SPSS Mixed Linear Model was performed on the transformed temporal binding time data, and effects showing a p value greater than 0.05 were not considered statistically significant. A Bonferroni post-hoc test was performed on significant effects, and effects showing a p value greater than 0.05 were not considered statistically significant.

3.2 Accuracy

Results indicated that participant use of speech and touch commands were very accurate. Only a very small proportion (less than 2%) of the total speech commands were incorrectly uttered (i.e., the participant saying "target" instead of "waypoint"). Less than 3% of touch commands were incorrectly placed on the touchscreen (i.e., touching the incorrect intersection).

3.3 Preferred Order of Command Modality

Figure 2 shows the number of touch and speech responses presented first for each participant. A total of 64% (7 out of 11) participants used speech first exclusively (100% of the time) when issuing commands, while the remaining four used touch commands first exclusively (100% of the time).

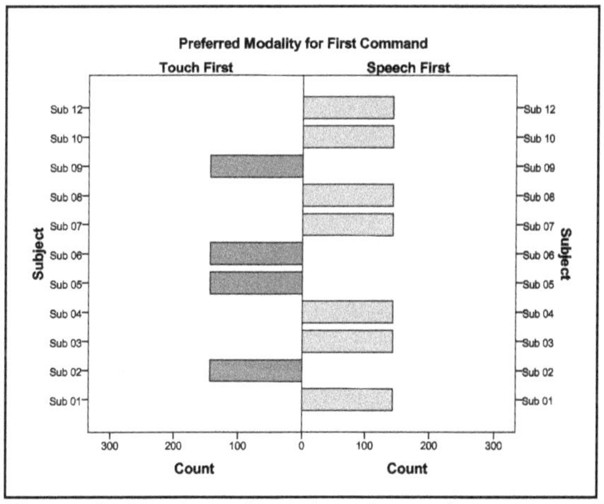

Figure. 2. Number of touch and speech responses for each participant.

3.4 Temporal Binding Time

An SPSS Mixed Linear Model performed on the transformed data indicated a significant main effect for map location ($F = 25.741$, $p < 0.001$), and significant interactions for workload level x user modality preference ($F = 23.820$, $p < 0.001$), and for map location x user modality preference ($F = 8.2585$, $p < 0.001$). There were no other significant main effects or interactions.

A Bonferroni post-hoc test on the temporal binding time data for the workload condition x user modality preference indicated that response time between touch and voice (temporal binding) was significantly shorter ($p \leq 0.05$) for touch-first than for speech-first commands, no matter what the level of workload. As can be seen in Figure 3, temporal binding of touch-first commands were significantly shorter than speech-first commands by approximately 0.4 sec in conditions with no workload (no secondary task), and by approximately 1.0 sec in conditions with a secondary task. Temporal binding of speech-first commands were significantly shorter in no workload conditions than in workload conditions. There was no significant difference in temporal binding of touch-first commands in workload and no workload conditions. The difference between the shortest and longest temporal binding time in this interaction (speech first vs. touch first in workload conditions) was approximately 1.0 sec, which may make a practical difference in the system's ability to fuse multimodal cues. Further analysis showed that shorter temporal binding with touch-first commands may have occurred because participants who input speech first often waited until their command was completely uttered before touching the screen, while participants who touched first did not always wait until their input was complete before uttering their speech commands.

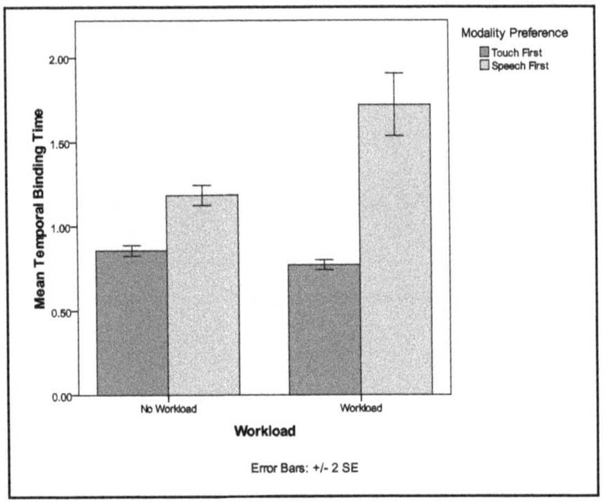

Figure. 3. Mean temporal binding time as a function of workload and modality preference

As seen in Figure 4, the Bonferroni post-hoc test on the temporal binding time data for the map location x modality preference indicated that the temporal binding of touch-first commands were significantly shorter than for speech-first commands for all map locations. For both speech and touch commands, temporal binding time was significantly shorter for both roads and swarm edges, than for intersections. For all commands, there were no significant differences between roads and swarm edges, and the same was true for speech-first commands. Between speech and touch-first modality preferences, the difference between speech-first and touch-first commands increases differentially from roads (approximately 0.50 sec) to swarms (approximately 0.60 sec), to intersections (approximately 0.9 sec). A difference of approximately 0.9 sec may make a practical difference in the system's ability to fuse multimodal cues. Again, further analysis showed that shorter temporal binding with touch-first commands most likely occurred because participants who input speech first often waited until their command was completely uttered before touching the screen, while participants who touched first did not always wait until their input was complete before uttering their speech commands.

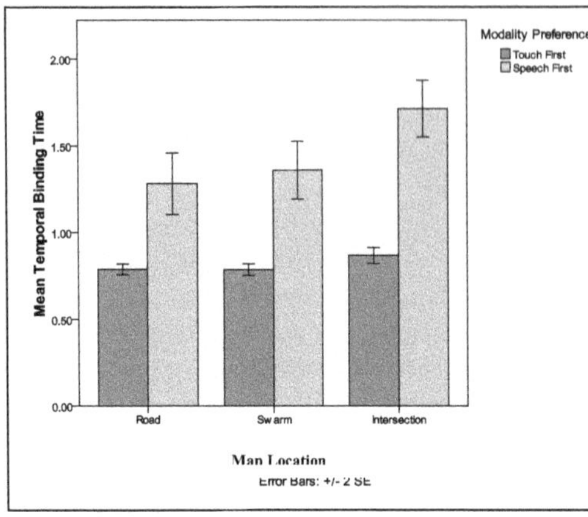

Figure 4. Mean temporal binding time as a function of map location and modality preference

As seen in Figure 5, the Bonferroni post-hoc test of the of the map location main effect indicated that temporal binding time for intersections was significantly longer (by approximately 0.2 sec) than for roads and swarm edges. There was no significant difference between roads and swarm edges. The comparatively short mean response times for moving swarm edges could have been due to the slow (one update/second) screen update rate, which may have resulted in rate of movement of the swarm being slow enough to reduce the level of task difficulty. Further research should involve faster swarm update rates, and an investigation of any potential time/accuracy tradeoffs involved in performing this task.

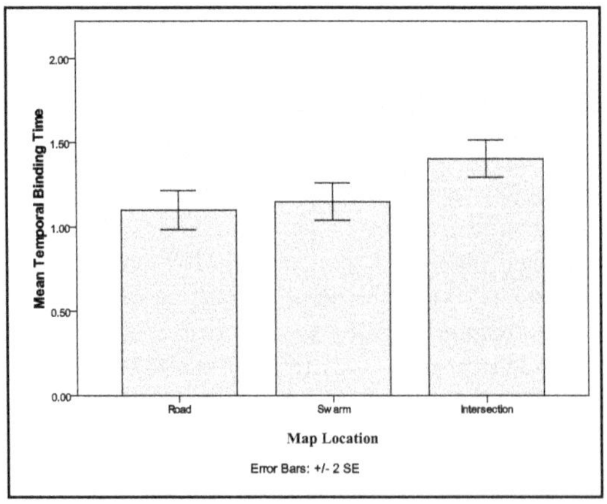

Figure 5. Mean temporal binding time as a function of map location and modality preference

3.5 Questionnaire Demographic Data

Questionnaire demographic data included inter-user variability data regarding participant age and gender. A Spearman *rho* test was performed to explore the correlation between participant gender and age, first with temporal binding, then with preferred modality. Results indicated only small correlations between age (0.29) and gender (0.09), with temporal binding, indicating that these factors had a very small correlation with temporal binding. Results also showed a weak correlation for age (0.43) and a small correlation for gender (0.07), with preferred modality. This data indicated little practical relationship between inter-user variability factors of age and gender, with either temporal binding or preferred modality.

3.6 User Comments

On their final questionnaires, participants commented that both touch and speech multimodal controls were fast, simple and intuitive to use, easy to remember, and very helpful. Participants liked using touch and speech controls together, and all agreed that touching the intersections was the most challenging part of the touchscreen task.

4. CONCLUSIONS

This study explored the effects of input difficulty, modality preference, and workload on temporal binding time relative to how this might affect the system's ability to fuse multimodal speech and touch cues into a unified response (i.e., define multimodal control actions as being related to each other as part of the same command). In this study, the dynamic map was a human-robot interface providing spatial information regarding a simulated robotic swarm. The results indicated that map location, level of task workload, and user preference in order of command modality, all had a significant effect on the temporal binding of user multimodal speech and touch commands. In general, results indicated that all of these factors could be significant in relating to a system's ability to bind multimodal inputs into a unitary response.

For map location, we hypothesized that small static targets such as intersections would produce longer and more variable temporal binding times, especially when combined with a moderately demanding secondary task. Our study showed that for both speech and touch commands, temporal binding time was significantly greater for intersections, with no significant differences between roads and swarm edges. The results also showed an interaction between target location and preferred modality; speech-first commands had longer mean temporal binding times than touch-first commands, for all map locations. However, because the update rate of the moving swarm was rather slow, future research is needed in the area of map location interaction with preferred modality, especially when using moving map entities.

We also hypothesized that higher levels of workload, created by the presence of a secondary task, would affect temporal binding time. As with Haas et al [3], we found that temporal binding time for touch-first commands was significantly shorter than for speech-first commands, no matter what the level of workload. However, temporal binding time for speech-first commands was perceived to be two times greater than touch-first commands in the presence of the secondary task, while this difference was less in conditions with no workload. Further research should be conducted to explore the effect of workload on temporal binding, perhaps with a greater number of levels of workload.

We conjectured that the majority of participants would use speech commands first exclusively, while the remaining would exclusively use touch. This proved true; results indicated that a majority of participants used speech commands first almost exclusively, while the remaining used touch commands first exclusively. The data indicate that there were individual differences in multimodal response patterns which were consistent and stable over time. This agrees with the results found by Oviatt, Coulston, Tomko, Xiao, Lunsford, Wesson and Carmichel [7], who also found consistent, stable individual differences in submitting commands in multimodal displays. However, Oviatt, Lunsford and Coulston [9], and Oviatt, Coulston and Lunsford [6], who worked with pen and natural language speech commands, found that timing of responses was a dominant trend in individual differences, but did not note a trend involving order of touch or speech output.

When describing the individual differences found in their studies, Oviatt [1] and Oviatt, Coulston, and Lunsford [6] noted that most individuals can be classified as having simultaneous (speech and pen at least partially overlapped in time) or sequential (speech or pen not overlapped in time) command input patterns, and that these differences are present from childhood, are thought to remain stable across user lifespan, and are highly resistant to change. Oviatt, Coulston, Tomko, Xiao, Lunsford, Wesson and Wesley [7] noted that 70% of participants in their study had a simultaneous output command style. However, observation of data in our study (visual waveforms of touch and speech responses) noted that none of the participants showed a simultaneous (overlapping over time) speech/touch response; all subjects used sequential commands (no overlapping over time). The differences in results shown between Oviatt, Coulston, Tomko, Xiao, Lunsford, Wesson and Wesley [7] and this study may have occurred because 1) Oviatt et al. [7] used pen rather than touch as an output modality; and 2) The commands used in this study were short one-word commands, while Oviatt et al. [7] used natural language commands which consisted of several words used in one or more sentences. The second difference implies that users who employ short commands (such as the commands used in this study) behave differently than those delivering natural language commands, which usually involve a larger number of words. Future research should explore this issue.

Data from indicated that some elements of inter-user variability (age and gender) had low correlations with either temporal binding or preferred modality. These results are not surprising; research shows that factors other than age and gender have been significant predictors in use of multimodal controls. Arning and Ziefle [17] found that factors such as that ease of use and user confidence are major factors in individual performance with multimodal controls. Confidence is closely related to computer experience, and Arning et al. found that people who do have a wide range of experience with technology do show superior performance with multimodal controls.

The results of this study are relevant to other research concerning the implementation of temporal binding in a human-system interface. Nigay and Coutaz [18] described a software architecture model (PAC-Amodeus) that could be used in conjunction with a generic mechanism for fusing (i.e., uniting or merging) user redundant or complementary multimodal inputs. In [18], the criteria for fusion information included input time and structural complementarity. In their evaluation of a multimodal route navigation system with speech and tactile/visual modes, Jokinen and Hurtig [19] noted the importance of interpretation accuracy for information encoded in redundant or complementary modalities. Jokinen et al. noted that building one single system to accommodate most users would not be reasonable; they suggested instead the use of an adaptive system to allow the users to use different modalities when interacting with the system, and tailor system responses according to preferences and expectations.

This study indicates that it is critical that research foster the understanding of the importance of temporal binding in multimodal systems, and uses a systems approach to explore how these factors might enable the ability of systems to fuse multimodal cues into a useful whole. Knowledge of factors that can cause individual command variability should be valuable in the design of future speech/touch systems such as dynamic map displays, to help support a smoother fusion of user commands and to reduce system error. These efforts are important because multimodal systems often have fixed, predefined temporal thresholds between commands [20], and a system with a fixed temporal threshold that is too short might not integrate speech and touch signals correctly, causing the system to miss and/or eliminate the second part of a multimodal command, thus increasing system error [6]. As noted by Oviatt, Lunsford and Coulston [9], knowledge of users' spoken and multimodal communication patterns will allow for the design of more powerful and reliable multimodal interfaces. Future research should be conducted to show how well this multimodal controls work with dynamic map displays in degraded environments, especially those of the Army battlefield, which may contain high levels of vibration, dust, and noise, as well as high-workload conditions.

5. REFERENCES

[1] Oviatt, S.L. 1996. Multimodal interfaces for dynamic interactive maps. In *Proceedings of the SIGCHI Conference on Human Factors in Computing Systems: Common Ground* (Vancouver, British Columbia, Canada) 13-18.

[2] Naumann, A.B., Wechsung, I., Hurtienne, J. 2010. Multimodal Interaction: A suitable strategy for including older users? *Interacting with Computers*. 465-474.

[3] Haas, E. C., Fields, M., Stachowiak, C., Hill, S., and Pillalamarri, K. 2010. *Extreme Scalability: Designing Interfaces and Algorithms for Soldier Robotic Swarm Interaction, Year 2*. Technical Report 5222. U. S. Army Research Laboratory, Aberdeen Proving Ground, Maryland.

[4] Raisamo, R. 1999. *Multimodal Human-Computer Interaction: A Constructive and Empirical Study*. Doctoral Dissertation. Report A-1999-13, Department of Computer Science, University of Tampere.

[5] Oviatt, S. L. 2000. Multimodal system processing in mobile environments. In *18th ACM Symposium on User Interface Software Technology (UIST)*, ACM Press, New York, NY, 21-30.

[6] Oviatt. S. L., Coulston, R., and Lunsford, R. 2004. When do we interact multimodally? Cognitive load and multimodal communications patterns. In *Proceedings of the Sixth International Conference on Multimodal Interfaces (ICMI'04)*, 129-136..

[7] Oviatt., S. L., Coulston., R., Tomko, S., Xiao, B., Lunsford, R., Wesson, M., and Carmichael, L. 2003. Toward a theory of organized multimodal integration patterns during human-computer interaction, In *Proceedings of the 5th IEEE International Conference on Multimodal Interfaces (ICMI'03)*, 44-47.

[8] Microsoft Touch Design Guidelines, *http://msdn.microsoft.com/en-us/library/cc872774.aspx*, accessed on December 12, 2009.

[9] Oviatt, S. L., Lunsford, R., and Coulston, R. 2005 . Individual differences in multimodal integration patterns: what are they and why do they exist. In *Proceedings of Computer-Human Interaction Papers, Eye Gaze and Multimodal Integration Patterns*, 241–249.

[10] Jokinen, K., and Raike, A., 2003. Multimodality – technology, visions and demands for the future. In *Proceedings of the The 1st Nordic Symposium on Multimodal Interfaces, Copenhagen, September.*

[11] Reeves, A., Fuller, H., and Fine, E. 2005. The role of attention in binding shape to color. *Vision Research*, 45, 3343-3355.

[12] Gawron, V.J. 2000. *Human Performance Measures Handbook*, Lawrence Erlbaum Associates, London, 54-55.

[13] U.S. Department of the Army, 1990. *Use of Volunteers as Subjects of Research*, Technical Report AR 70-25. Government Printing Office, Washington, DC. DOI =, http://www.army.mil/usapa/epubs/pdf/r70_25.pdf

[14] U.S. Department of Defense, Office of the Secretary of Defense. 1999. *Code of Federal Regulations, Protection of Human Subjects.* Government Report 32 CFR 219, Government Printing Office, Washington, D.C. DOI = http://www.dtic.mil/biosys/downloads/32cfr219.pdf

[15] SynWin (Version 1.2.28) [Computer Software.] Chula Vista, California: Activity Research Services.

[16] Cleveland, W. S. 1984. Graphical methods for data presentation: Full scale breaks, dot charts, and multibased logging. *The American Statistician,* 38(4), 270-280.

[17] Arning, K., and Ziefle, M. 2007. Understanding age differences in PDA and acceptance Performance. *Computers in Human Behavior*, 2904-2927.

[18] Nigay, L., and Coutaz, J. 1997. Multifeature systems: The CARE properties and their impact on software design. *Intelligence and Multimodality in Multimedia Interfaces*, AAAI Press.

[19] Jokinen, K., and Hurtig, T. 2006. User expectations and real experience on a multimodal interactive system. *Proceedings of Interspeech 2006.*

[20] Oviatt, S.L. 2006. Human-centered design meets cognitive load theory: designing interfaces that help people think.

Author Index

www.ingramcontent.com/pod-product-compliance
Ingram Content Group UK Ltd.
Pitfield, Milton Keynes, MK11 3LW, UK
UKHW051511290926
15471UKWH00008B/1551

9 781450 306409